International Handbook of Violence Research

VOLUME 2

International Handbook of Violence Research

Edited by

Wilhelm Heitmeyer

and

John Hagan

KLUWER ACADEMIC PUBLISHERS
DORDRECHT / BOSTON / LONDON

A C.I.P. Catalogue record for this book is available from the Library of Congress.

ISBN 1-4020-3980-8

Published by Kluwer Academic Publishers,
P.O. Box 17, 3300 AA Dordrecht, The Netherlands.

Sold and distributed in North, Central and South America
by Kluwer Academic Publishers,
101 Philip Drive, Norwell, MA 02061, U.S.A.

In all other countries, sold and distributed
by Kluwer Academic Publishers,
P.O. Box 322, 3300 AH Dordrecht, The Netherlands.

Printed on acid-free paper

All Rights Reserved
© 2003 Kluwer Academic Publishers

No part of this book may be reproduced, stored in a retrieval system, or transmitted
in any form or by any means, electronic, mechanical, photocopying, microfilming, recording or
otherwise, without written permission from the Publisher, with the exception of any material
supplied specifically for the purpose of being entered and executed on a computer system, for
exclusive use by the purchaser of the work.

Preface

An international manual is like a world cruise: a once-in-a-lifetime experience.

All the more reason to consider carefully whether it is necessary. This can hardly be the case if previous research in the selected field has already been the subject of an earlier review—or even several competing surveys. On the other hand, more thorough study is necessary if the intensity and scope of research are increasing without comprehensive assessments. That was the situation in Western societies when work began on this project in the summer of 1998. It was then, too, that the challenges emerged: any manual, especially an international one, is a very special type of text, which is anything but routine. It calls for a special effort: the "state of the art" has to be documented for selected subject areas, and its presentation made as compelling as possible. The editors were delighted, therefore, by the cooperation and commitment shown by the eighty-one contributors from ten countries who were recruited to write on the sixty-two different topics, by the constructive way in which any requests for changes were dealt with, and by the patient response to our many queries.

This volume is the result of a long process. It began with the first drafts outlining the structure of the work, which were submitted to various distinguished colleagues. Friedhelm Neidhardt of Berlin, Gertrud Nunner-Winkler of Munich, and Roland Eckert of Trier, to name only a few, supplied valuable comments at this stage.

A working group set up by the Interdisciplinary Institute for Conflict and Violence Research developed the draft into a form that was discussed in the spring of 1999 by Wilhelm Heitmeyer and John Hagan (who was then still working in Toronto). Invitations to contributors were then sent out—successfully, as this compilation demonstrates.

The complexity of this project was further increased by the fact that we had planned from the outset to publish as nearly simultaneously as possible in German and in English. This meant that, even while the chapters were still being written and revised, they also had to be translated, into German or English as the case might be. We recruited Ina Goertz of Tradukas, Berlin, as our translation coordinator: she and her team including Adelheid Baker did excellent work, and our working relationship was an exceptionally friendly one. But for her, this manual could never have arrived at its present form.

We received equally fruitful assistance when we found ourselves working outside the boundaries of the skills available to the Institute's editorial team and urgently needed additional expertise. In this context, we must especially mention Harald A. Euler of Kassel University, who provided invaluable assistance on, for example, the texts and problems relating to the evolutionary psychology of violence.

Editors can never achieve much without the support of a highly committed, enthusiastic team, able to draw upon a wide range of very different skills—academic, editorial, linguistic, organizational, communicative, and technical. That applies to the core editorial team: Heiner Bielefeldt and Johannes Vossen, in particular, were invaluable, and they were well supported at different times by other members of the Institute's staff, including some of the contributors to this manual.

For a long period, until she left the team to work in a different project, Julia Tölke was an outstanding coordinator, taking charge of communication with contributors and the technical revision of the text. She was replaced by Peter Sitzer, who worked closely with Stefanie Müller to maintain the same standards in this important task. Our secretaries, Mrs. Ward and Mrs. Passon, were persistent and efficient in dealing with our numerous and sometimes hectic communications needs and the collating of the translations. Finally—as was only to be expected—Monika Näther brought a perfectionist's dedication to the complex technical preparation of the print copy for the German version.

Last but not least, without financial support such project can not be brought to fruition—especially if it is to be published in two languages, with all the time and cost-intensive translation work involved. We are therefore deeply grateful to Dr. Wolf Jenkner of the Ministry of Science of the Land of North Rhine-Westphalia, without whose backing this project would never have been launched.

WILHELM HEITMEYER AND JOHN HAGAN
BIELEFELD AND CHICAGO

Contents

Preface v

I. THE FRAMEWORK OF THE HANDBOOK

1. Violence: The Difficulties of a Systematic International Review 3
   Wilhelm Heitmeyer and John Hagan

2. The Concept of Violence 13
   Peter Imbusch

3. The Long-Term Development of Violence: Empirical Findings
   and Theoretical Approaches to Interpretation 41
   Manuel Eisner

II. RESEARCH ON VIOLENCE: AN INTERDISCIPLINARY APPROACH WITH A FOCUS ON SOCIAL SCIENCES

1. Societal Structures and Institutions: Social Conditions and State Agents

1.1. *Social Structures and Inequalities*

1.1.1 Poverty and Violence 67
   Robert D. Crutchfield and Tim Wadsworth

1.1.2 Ethnic Segregation and Violence 83
   James F. Short, Jr.

1.1.3 A Comparative Examination of Gender Perspectives on Violence 97
   Carol Hagemann-White

1.2. *Violence in and by State Institutions*

1.2.1 Violence and the Rise of the State 121
   Michael Hanagan

1.2.2	Holocaust .... 139 *Peter Longerich*	
1.2.3	Violence within the Military .... 171 *Gerhard Kümmel and Paul Klein*	
1.2.4	Violence in Prisons/Torture .... 189 *Ronald D. Crelinsten*	
1.2.5	Violence and the Police .... 207 *Jean-Paul Brodeur*	

2. Groups and Collectivities: Political and Ideological Violence

2.1	Ethnopolitical Conflict and Separatist Violence .... 227 *Ted Robert Gurr and Anne Pitsch*	
2.2	Ethnic Violence .... 247 *Andreas Wimmer and Conrad Schetter*	
2.3	The Socio-Anthropological Interpretation of Violence .... 261 *Georg Elwert*	
2.4	Civil Wars .... 291 *Peter Waldmann*	
2.5	Terrorism .... 309 *Fernando Reinares*	
2.6	Violence from Religious Groups .... 323 *Jon Pahl*	
2.7	Vigilantism .... 339 *David Kowalewski*	
2.8	Pogroms .... 351 *Werner Bergmann*	
2.9	Violence and New Social Movements .... 369 *Dieter Rucht*	
2.10	Violence and the New Left .... 383 *Donatella della Porta*	
2.11	Right-Wing Extremist Violence .... 399 *Wilhelm Heitmeyer*	
2.12	Large-Scale Violence as Contentious Politics .... 437 *Charles Tilly*	

3. Violent Individuals: Perpetrators and Motives

3.1 Processes of Learning and Socialization

- 3.1.1 The Social Psychology of Aggression and Violence 459
  James T. Tedeschi
- 3.1.2 Emotions and Aggressiveness 479
  Roy F. Baumeister and Brad J. Bushman
- 3.1.3 Learning of Aggression in the Home and the Peer Group 495
  Ernest V.E. Hodges, Noel A. Card, and Jenny Isaacs
- 3.1.4 Violence and the Media 511
  Helmut Lukesch
- 3.1.5 Patterns and Explanations of Direct Physical and Indirect Nonphysical Aggression in Childhood 543
  Holly Foster and John Hagan

3.2. Evolutionary and Social Biological Approaches

- 3.2.1 Evolutionary Psychology of Lethal Interpersonal Violence 569
  Martin Daly and Margo Wilson
- 3.2.2 The Nature–Nurture Problem in Violence 589
  Laura Baker

3.3 Violent Individuals

- 3.3.1 Sociological Approaches to Individual Violence and Their Empirical Evaluation 611
  Günter Albrecht
- 3.3.2 Youth Violence and Guns 657
  Alfred Blumstein
- 3.3.3 Organized Crime and Violence 679
  Dick Hobbs
- 3.3.4 Understanding Cross-National Variation in Criminal Violence 701
  Steven Messner

4. Victims of Violence: Individuals and Groups

- 4.1 Violence against Children 719
  James Garbarino and Catherine P. Bradshaw
- 4.2 Violence in Intimate Relationships 737
  Russell P. Dobash and R. Emerson Dobash

	4.3	Suicide 753
		David Lester
	4.4	Violence against the Socially Expendable 767
		Ezzat A. Fattah
	4.5	Violence against Ethnic and Religious Minorities 785
		Tore Bjørgo
	4.6	Hate Crimes Directed at Gay, Lesbian, Bisexual and Transgendered Victims 801
		Jack McDevitt and Jennifer Williamson
	4.7	Trauma and Violence in Children and Adolescents: A Developmental Perspective 817
		Bessel A. van der Kolk and Annette Streeck-Fischer

5. Social Opportunity Structures: Institutions and Social Spaces

5.1 Violence in Social Institutions

	5.1.1	Violence in the Family 837
		Richard J. Gelles
	5.1.2	Violence in School 863
		Gabriele Klewin, Klaus-Jürgen Tillmann and Gail Weingart
	5.1.3	Work-Related Violence 885
		Vittorio di Martino
	5.1.4	Violence and Sport 903
		Eric Dunning

5.2 Violence in the Public Space

	5.2.1	Violence on the Roads 923
		Ralf Kölbel
	5.2.2	Juvenile and Urban Violence 937
		François Dubet

6. Violence Discourses: Ideologies and Justifications

6.1 Discourses and Ideologies

	6.1.1	Political Cultural Studies and Violence 957
		Thomas Meyer
	6.1.2	The Role of Elites in Legitimizing Violence 973
		Herfried Münkler and Marcus Llanque

CONTENTS

- 6.1.3 Violence in Contemporary Analytic Philosophy 989
  Keith Burgess-Jackson

- 6.1.4 Sacrifice and Holy War: A Study of Religion and Violence 1005
  Volkhard Krech

- 6.1.5 Violence and the Glorification of Violence in the Literature of the Twentieth Century 1023
  Jürgen Nieraad

6.2 Justification Strategies

- 6.2.1 The State Monopoly of Force 1043
  Dieter Grimm

- 6.2.2 The Monopoly of Legitimate Violence and Criminal Policy 1057
  Albrecht Funk

- 6.2.3 Freedom to Demonstrate and the Use of Force: Criminal Law as a Threat to Basic Political Rights 1079
  Otto Backes and Peter Reichenbach

- 6.2.4 The Right to Resist 1097
  Heiner Bielefeldt

- 6.2.5 Individual Violence Justification Strategies 1113
  Siegfried Lamnek

7. Processes and Dynamics: Escalation and De-Escalation

- 7.1 Fear of Violent Crime 1131
  Klaus Boers

- 7.2 Public Opinion and Violence 1151
  Hans Mathias Kepplinger

- 7.3 Groups, Gangs and Violence 1167
  Wolfgang Kühnel

- 7.4 Escalation and De-Escalation of Social Conflicts: The Road to Violence 1181
  Roland Eckert and Helmut Willems

III. THEORETICAL AND METHODOLOGICAL ISSUES IN RESEARCH ON VIOLENCE

1. Potentials and Limits of Qualitative Methods for Research on Violence 1203
   Andreas Böttger and Rainer Strobl

	2.	Strategies and Problems in Quantitative Research on Aggression and Violence 1219
		Rainer Dollase and Matthias Ulbrich-Herrmann

IV.	SUBJECT INDEX 1239
V.	NAME INDEX 1257
VI.	THE AUTHORS 1269

PART II-4

VICTIMS OF VIOLENCE: INDIVIDUALS AND GROUPS

CHAPTER II-4.1

Violence against Children

JAMES GARBARINO AND CATHERINE P. BRADSHAW

I. INTRODUCTION

The school shootings of the 1990s hit home for parents and adolescents across the United States. For decades, many Americans perceived that violence only occurred in inner-city neighborhoods; however, this wave of school shootings sent the message that violence could happen anywhere, even in "good schools." Other forms of violence against children, such as inner-city youth gang violence, also raised the public's concern and prompted several new programs and policies to protect our most vulnerable children. Fortunately, the rate of inner-city youth violence has been declining since its peak in the early 1990s. However, the problem of violence against children still exists, and is not experienced by Americans alone.

Child victimization is a global concern, and has even been characterized in the United States as a "public health epidemic" (Bell & Jenkins, 1993; Osofsky, 1997). The homicide rate in the United States for males aged fifteen to twenty-four far exceeds that of any other nonwarring nation (Osofsky, 1999). The rate of violent victimization of children age twelve to seventeen in the United States is nearly three times that for adults (Snyder & Sickmund, 1995). The risk of violent victimization among juveniles increased 17 percent between 1987 and 1991. Compared with other juveniles, Black American youths aged twelve to seventeen are more likely to be the victims of violent crimes than other youths (Snyder & Sickmund, 1995). Twenty-five percent of all reported juvenile murders in the United States in 1997 occurred in only five out of the approximately 3,000 U.S. counties. These five counties include the cities of Los Angeles, Chicago, New York, Philadelphia, and Detroit (Sickmund, Snyder, & Poe-Yamagata, 1997).

In 1997, approximately six juveniles were murdered each day in the United States, of which 70 percent were male and 47 percent were African-American (Snyder & Sickmund, 1999). The murder rate of juveniles in the United States increased 66 percent between 1985 and 1995 and the greatest increase was for older children (over fifteen). This increase is particularly troublesome considering the advances in emergency medicine during that decade. The number of juvenile murders peaked at 2,900 in 1993 and has since declined slightly to 2,600 in 1995 and to 2,100 in 1997 (Sickmund et al., 1997). There has also been an increase in the number of juvenile murders involving firearms. An estimated 56 percent of juvenile murders in 1997 involved the use of a firearm. Similarly, 77 percent of older juveniles murdered by other juveniles were killed with a firearm. The rate of firearm-related homicides for United States children is more than twice that of Finland, the nation with the second highest rate of child death by firearm (Sickmund et al., 1997). Clearly, easy access to guns is a factor contributing to the high rates of youth violence and death in the United States (Garbarino, 1999).

Of the estimated 2,600 children (under age eighteen) murdered in the United States in 1995, the murder rates were greatest for older adolescents and second greatest for infants. Nearly 30 percent of all children murdered in 1997 were less than six years old. The risk of being murdered is equal for boys and girls until the age of eleven, after which the risk for males increases dramatically (Snyder & Sickmund, 1995). Children over the age of twelve are more likely to be killed by someone other than a family member (95 percent), whereas younger children are more likely to be killed by family members (57 percent) (Sickmund et al., 1997). Overall, a family member perpetrates approximately 40 percent of all child murders whereas peers perpetrate approximately 45 percent.

An estimated 1,077 children died in the United States in 1996 as the result of maltreatment (Snyder & Sickmund, 1999) (0.16 per 10,000 children). Approximately one million cases of child maltreatment were substantiated in 1997 (14.7 per 1,000 children), however, the National Incidence Study of Child Abuse and Neglect estimated that nearly three million children were maltreated. Forty-seven percent of the substantiated cases were for incidence of physical neglect, 22 percent for physical abuse, 21 percent for emotional neglect, 19 percent for emotional abuse, 11 percent for sexual abuse, and 14 percent for educational neglect. The number of maltreatment reports increased 161 percent from 1980 to 1996. Increases in public awareness and availability of resources for high-risk families are likely factors affecting the increased willingness to report suspected maltreatment (Sickmund et al., 1997).

Despite the wave of lethal school shootings that occurred during the late 1990s, the occurrence of violent death in schools is rare. Violent victimization in American schools has been declining since 1993; however, the risk of violent assault is greater for urban students than for others (Snyder & Sickmund, 1999). Kachur and colleagues (1996) conducted a detailed review of news reports and obituaries in the Untied States for the 1992–1993 and 1993–1994 academic years, tallying the number of deaths occurring in schools. By their count, sixty-three students were murdered, thirteen students committed suicide, and twenty-nine nonstudents died at school or on school property during these two academic years (Kachur et al., 1996). Conversely, an estimated 7,294 school-aged juveniles were murdered outside of school during this same time frame (Snyder & Sickmund, 1999). School administrators and policy makers are quick to point out this disparity in victimization rates when questioned about school shootings and school safety.

One child died from suicide for every two children (under age nineteen) that were murdered in the United States in 1996 (Snyder & Sickmund, 1999). 7 percent of all people who committed suicide in 1996 in the United States were under the age of nineteen. The overall rate of suicide increased by 9 percent between 1980 and 1996, but increased by 113 percent for children under age fifteen. Most suicide victims are Caucasian males and most suicides involve firearms. The Center for Disease Control conducted a study on the international prevalence of firearm-related youth suicides in the early 1990's (Snyder &

Sickmund, 1999). They found that the most firearm-related suicides were committed by children in North Ireland, followed respectively by children in the United States, Norway, and Canada. The prevalence of youth suicide is of great concern; however, this issue receives little public attention. The reader should refer to the chapter of this book entitled "Suicide" for a detailed review of the research.

Data on violence against children in other countries that are comparable to U.S. data are difficult to find. The United States mandates that suspected child abuse and neglect be reported. Additionally, U.S. government agencies, such as the Office of Juvenile Justice and Delinquency Prevention and the Federal Bureau of Investigation, collect information on the prevalence of violence perpetrated both by and toward youth. The U.S. data collection system is by no means perfect, but it gives an estimate of the prevalence of several types of youth victimization. Not all countries, however, maintain records on the prevalence of child victimization on a national level (Gilbert, 1997). Some international comparisons are possible but one must bear in mind that data sources vary. Most published studies of international child violence rates include self-reported data collected in schools, in treatment centers, or over the telephone. While it is difficult to compare international data with U.S. data, two international studies are noted here to illustrate general trends in child violence rates.

In comparison with the United States, the rate of minor child physical abuse in Hong Kong is slightly less, whereas severe physical abuse toward children is slightly greater (Tang, 1998b). Other researchers have found low rates of child victimization in societies where children are valued for their potential financial contribution to the family. Children in Chinese cultures are typically viewed as the "property" of their parents; therefore, neighbors and other nonfamily members may be less likely to report abuse. These abuse trends, however, may be shifting somewhat in areas where there is less reliance on children for labor or financial gain (Tang, 1998a).

The rate of child abuse in Germany is estimated to be approximately 15 children per 1,000 when all data sources are included (Gilbert, 1997). Nearly half of all reported cases of maltreatment are for sexual abuse. Neglect is rarely reported or prosecuted because it is viewed more as a social problem than a crime. Approximately 133 children died in 1993 from abuse-related injuries in Germany (0.083 per 100,000 children), which is about half the rate in the United States (Gilbert, 1997; Snyder & Sickmund, 1999). Approximately 200,000 children are involved in the German child welfare system each year, although less than half of these children have been registered with the police for maltreatment. The child welfare system provides childcare, child and family health services, and counseling to children identified by their schools, medical care providers, or parents as having needs or "problems." These services are voluntary and free for most families. The focus in Germany is clearly on preventing or stemming several types of risks. In contrast, some countries focus more on investigating allegations of abuse and apprehending perpetrators than on supporting vulnerable children.

II. THEORETICAL APPROACHES TO DETERMINING RISK OF THE VIOLENT VICTIMIZATION OF CHILDREN

The risks associated with violent victimization are greater during certain developmental phases and transitions (Finkelhor, 1995). Additionally, the accumulation of risk factors (e.g., poverty, high-risk neighborhood, and single-parent families) may outweigh the protective factors (e.g., social support, education, and positive role models) (Rutter, 1989). The prevalence and associated risks of violence against children vary with the environment (Bronfenbrenner, 1979; Cicchetti & Toth, 1995; Lynch & Cicchetti, 1998). Both the child's development and exposure to violence on different environmental levels affect the accumulation of risks. Violence occurring against children on a microlevel (within the family, the school, or neighborhood) is proximal and can be quite detrimental. These proximal risks can either be mitigated by the presence of protective factors or exacerbated by distal risks within the exosystem (e.g., social isolation and high child care burden) and macrosystem (e.g., loose handgun policies and the exposure to violence in the media). The risks associated with violent victimization and violence exposure are presented in this chapter from both a human ecological and developmental perspective. These views emphasize the importance of accounting for developmental risks as well as risks present within the broader social context (Benson et al., 1998).

1. Child Factors Contributing to Violent Victimization

The risk of childhood violent victimization is greatest for older children and second greatest for infants (Finkelhor, 1995). Children under the age of two are more likely to be maltreated by their parents, whereas children over fifteen are more likely to be maltreated by strangers and peers. Additionally, these older children are more likely to be assaulted with a weapon, such as a handgun.

One-fourth of the victims of all sexual assaults committed in the United States are children under the age of twelve (Snyder & Sickmund, 1999). The risk for childhood sexual abuse is greatest between the ages of six and ten. Age not only affects the likelihood of being victimized but also the likelihood of reporting, as younger children are less likely to report sexual abuse than are older children.

The rate of sexual abuse of females is nearly three times that for males. This discrepancy may be due to the fact that as boys approach puberty, they are less willing to tell anyone that they have been sexually abused. This may be attributed to the boys' fear of being viewed as mentally and physically weak or as homosexual (Finkelhor, 1995; Hernandez, Lodico, & DiClemente, 1993; Powers, Eckenrode, & Jaklitsch, 1990).

School-aged children are at a greater risk for assault by peers when they begin school (Finkelhor, 1995). Since school-aged children begin to carry money, they are more likely to be mugged than are younger children. Similarly, physically mature adolescents are more likely to be sexually victimized by peers than by adults. Younger children, however, are more likely to be abducted by their parents because the parents may feel a stronger attachment to their younger children than to their adolescent children (Finkelhor, 1995).

Younger children are particularly dependent on adults for protection and thus are at greater risk for neglect and victimization (Finkelhor, 1995). Children with developmental disabilities are also at greater risk for being victimized, both physically and sexually (Kotch, Muller, & Blakely, 1999). Their ability to protect themselves is compromised, as they may be less assertive and have greater difficulty determining a potential assailant's trustworthiness. Many disabled children require more intensive supervision and care, and thus their caregivers may feel more stress. These children may also be targeted for sexual assault because they may be viewed as weak, ignorant, and less likely to report the incident (Hernandez et al., 1993).

Older children may be able to protect themselves from assault more easily than can younger children, as they can use verbal means of intervening and defending themselves in the face of physical assault. Additionally, older children can physically protect themselves or run away more easily than can younger children (Garbarino, Schellenbach, & Sebes, 1986). Abused girls are more likely to run away from home, whereas boys appear to deal with the abuse by dissociating until they are forced out of the home (Young et al., 1983). Boys are significantly more likely to be "pushed out" or forced out of their homes than are girls. There appears to be a protective bias toward females (Young et al., 1983); it is likely that girls are perceived as more vulnerable and are thus less likely to become "throw aways." Boys are often perceived as more self-reliant and able to defend themselves than are girls (Powers et al., 1990). This same gender disparity is observed in cases of neglect, such that boys are more likely to be neglected than girls (Sickmund et al., 1997; Snyder & Sickmund, 1999).

2. Family Factors Contributing to Violent Victimization of Children

Eighty-six percent of all child abusers had some relationship with their victim before the abuse and 32 percent abused their own child or stepchild. Single parents, especially mothers (Garbarino & Crouter, 1978), are vulnerable to maltreatment and report feeling alone, out of control, and overwhelmed by their household obligations (Bolton & MacEachron, 1986). Most perpetrators of child abuse in 1993 were women under the age of forty (Sickmund et al., 1997). Other family stressors, including poverty, parental unemployment, overcrowded housing, and concerns about money heighten the risk for maltreatment of children (Hampton & Gelles, 1991; Wilson & Saft, 1993). Family stress and conflict can limit the parents' time for caregiving and impair their use of effective parenting strategies. Ethnicity does not have a consistent effect on the prevalence of maltreatment when income and other demographic variables are statistically controlled (Wilson & Saft, 1993).

Most maltreating parents have interpersonal problems and poor social skills; therefore, they are likely to elicit negative responses from their neighbors and others in the community. Consequently, maltreating parents are typically viewed by their neighbors as less reliable, less social, and less neighborly than nonmaltreating neighbors (Wilson & Saft, 1993). Maltreating parents also report feeling socially isolated (Wilson & Saft, 1993) and that they lack social support from their community (Coulton, Korbin, & Su, 1999). Single maltreating mothers in particular report high levels of loneliness. From these data it appears that perceived social isolation has a stronger effect on child maltreatment than does socioeconomic status (Wilson & Saft, 1993).

These parents may even feel isolated before the onset of the abuse, but become more isolated after the maltreatment in order to keep the "family secret" (Salzinger et al., 1993). Dr. Brian Glaser, a colleague and professor of counseling psychology at the University of Georgia supports this notion of maltreating parents as the "protectors of the family secret" (B.A. Glaser, personal communication, April 23, 1999). In his twenty-five years of clinical work with high-risk and maltreating families, he has observed that not having residential telephone service is particularly indicative of pervasive family dysfunction; these families' problems are greater than just poverty or high residential mobility. He noticed that the lack of a telephone is often associated with child maltreatment and feelings of social isolation. Glaser believes this insulates the family and hinders communication with the outside world, and consequently, the child cannot call for help. This lack of a telephone also makes intervention by government agencies and/or counselors particularly difficult. Although this theory is based on clinical observation, the aforementioned factors of high residential mobility, poverty, and social isolation are also correlated with child maltreatment (Garbarino, Kostelny, & Grady, 1993; Wilson & Saft, 1993). This association, however, may not generalize to other societies where home telephones are less common or in situations where religious beliefs restrict the use of household telephones. Regardless, the issue of social isolation from the community, either perceived or self-imposed, warrants furthers empirical investigation.

Maltreating mothers report higher levels of depression and lower self-esteem than do nonabusing mothers (Culp et al., 1989). Maltreating parents are also less likely to consider the perspective and feelings of their children. Most maltreating parents have a difficult time selecting appropriate conflict resolution strategies (Newberger & Cook, 1983). Additionally, these compromised conflict resolution skills are particularly common among adolescent parents (Wilson & Saft, 1993). The risk for abuse is particularly high for children who live in single-parent households, more specifically, children of single parents are twice as likely to be maltreated than other children (Hernandez et al., 1993; Sickmund et al., 1997), and the risk of maltreatment increases with the number of children in the home (Sickmund et al., 1997). However, the presence of extended family or kinship members (i.e., grandmother) in single-parent homes can directly affect child-rearing practices by providing child care and helping with household chores (e.g., meal preparation and shopping) (Korbin, 1987; Wilson & Saft, 1993). Additionally, these family members can support the parent emotionally and thus help reduce the parent's stress and risk for maltreatment (Egeland, Jacobvitz, & Papatola, 1987).

3. Community Factors Contributing to Violent Victimization of Children

From an ecological perspective, neighborhoods can either mitigate or exacerbate the risk of violent victimization of children (Coulton et al., 1999). People living in neighborhoods with high rates of financial impoverishment, community instability, and high child-care burden describe their communities as disorganized, unstable, and lacking in positive qualities (Garbarino & Kostelny, 1992). Interviews with the leaders of high-risk neighborhoods reveal that they perceive their communities as having a weaker social fabric than do low-risk communities with similar economic disadvantages. However, access to social support and basic human services such as health care and childcare may moderate the risk of child victimization in these communities (Garbarino & Kostelny, 1992).

Raising children in unstable, impoverished, and isolated neighborhoods can be particularly challenging for parents. Due to the instability of high-risk environments, it may be difficult for parents and children to predict or control the outcome of certain social situations. Additionally, families living in poverty and unstable environments are at a greater risk for violent victimization of their children (Garbarino et al., 1993) and have limited access to safe housing, medical care, and childcare. Other individual risk factors such as limited social support, prior violence in the family, parental education level, access to childcare, and family income also contribute significantly to child maltreatment (Coulton et al., 1999). Thus, it is not surprising that child maltreatment rates in certain high-risk urban communities are nearly twice the national rate (Coulton et al., 1999).

Children who experience chronic exposure to violence typically live in socially impoverished communities (Garbarino et al., 1993). These neighborhoods lack social integration, have high concentrations of economically distressed families, have less positive neighboring experiences, have high rates of residential mobility, and are associated with increased stress levels for families in their daily activities (Wilson & Saft, 1993). These "toxic" environments place children at greater risk for violent victimization by their parents and others in the community (Garbarino, 1995). Furthermore, simply witnessing domestic and community violence has detrimental effects on the development of children of all ages.

4. Different Types of Violence Against Children

In 1991, 33 percent of violent crimes against juveniles were committed on the streets, 25 percent in their homes, and 23 percent in schools or on school property (Snyder & Sickmund, 1995). Violence occurring in the community is particularly harmful because it also puts bystanders at risk for physical injury and emotional problems (Bell & Jenkins, 1993). Children living in high-crime and low-income areas are exposed to particularly high levels of violence (Osofsky, 1999). In an informal sample of ten mothers from a public housing development in Chicago, all ten reported that their children had witnessed a shooting first-hand before the age of five (Dubrow & Garbarino, 1989). Children living in public housing developments are twice as likely to be exposed to violence than are other children (Garbarino & Kostelny, 1992).

Exposure to community violence can result in both internalized and externalized behavior problems. Younger children may exhibit dissociative and regressive reactions such as enuresis, reduced verbalization, and clinging behaviors. School-aged children may develop aggressive behaviors, psychosomatic problems, and learning difficulties in response to exposure to violence. Similarly, adolescents who have been exposed to community violence tend to exhibit more externalizing and self-destructive behaviors such as substance abuse, sexual promiscuity, delinquent behavior, and aggression (Garbarino et al., 1992).

5. Effects of Violent Victimization of Children

a. Sexual Assault. Depression is most commonly reported in both child and adult victims of childhood sexual abuse (Browne & Finkelhor, 1986). Initial effects of childhood sexual assault may include fear, anxiety, depression, anger and hostility, aggression, and sexually inappropriate behaviors. Long-term effects of sexual abuse may include self-destructive behaviors, anxiety, fear of isolation, poor self-esteem, difficulty trusting others, a tendency toward revictimization, substance abuse, and sexual maladjustment. Less than 20 percent of victims of childhood sexual abuse develop serious psychopathology, however, nearly all victims suffer some type of psychological distress (Browne & Finkelhor, 1986).

Acquaintances commit 49 percent of sexual assaults, followed by 47 percent by families and just 4 percent by strangers (Sickmund et al., 1997). Younger children are more likely to be victimized by a family member, whereas adolescents are more likely to be assaulted by someone outside the family. Children victimized by their father or stepfather typically experience the most severe psychological distress even when other factors have been statistically controlled. In cases of incest committed by the father, anger may also be directed at the mother because the child is likely to perceive that she "allowed" the abuse to happen. Low self-esteem is particularly common among children of incest.

Sexual abuse involving penetration of children younger than age eight has been found to have the most severe effects (Bouvier et al., 1999). The effects of sexual abuse are typically more severe when there was physical contact, the abuser was known to the child, and when the abuse is chronic (Bouvier et al., 1999). Similarly, feelings of betrayal and role confusion are likely to emerge when the perpetrator is a family friend or family member. The child may also have more contact with a family member or friend and thus may "reexperience" the trauma or be reminded of the event more often than if the perpetrator had been a stranger. Additionally, the psychological effects are typically more severe when the assault involves aggression, the child participates in (rather than physically resists) the experience, and when the parents are not supportive or do not believe the child upon disclosure (Bouvier et al., 1999).

Although most of the research on sexual abuse has been conducted with female victims, studies indicate that the effects of sexual abuse for males vary slightly from females and typically include substance abuse, running away from home, truancy, suicide attempts, forcing sexual acts on others, and committing violent acts (Hernandez et al., 1993). Additionally, boys may experience psychological problems including Posttraumatic Stress Disorder (PTSD), dissociation or affective numbing, low self-esteem, anxiety, depression, isolation, self-injurious behaviors, and difficulties with trust (Hernandez et al., 1993).

b. Physical Assault. Physical abuse during childhood can have negative effects on children's development of social competencies, autonomy, self-esteem, peer relationships, cognitive and intellectual abilities, and academic performance (Rowe & Eckenrode, 1999). Children who have been abused may also avoid certain people or situations that have the potential for evoking negative feelings. Other more pervasive effects can occur such as impairment in the formation of attachments, a compromised self-esteem, and psychological disassociation. Younger children may exhibit aggressive behaviors, but the symptoms may shift to a more internalized symptomatology as they develop into adolescents, a phenomena referred to as developmental symptom substitution (Shirk, 1988) or heterotypic continuity (Rutter, 1989).

The effects of physical abuse include adjustment problems, cognitive problems or delays, antisocial behavior, aggression, anger, and mistrust (Hernandez et al., 1993). Abused and maltreated children typically have lower IQ scores, lower self-esteem, insecure attachments and relationships, communication problems, behavior problems, and psychopathology. Some of these effects may be short-lived whereas other may last a lifetime (Wilson & Saft, 1993). The most severe effects of childhood violent victimization include Dissociative Identity Disorder (formally Multiple Personality Disorder) and PTSD (Berkowitz, 1998; Browne & Finkelhor, 1986).

Dissociative Identity Disorder (DID) may result from severe and chronic sexual or physical abuse most commonly experienced during childhood (American Psychiatric Association, Diagnostic and Statistical Manual of Mental Disorders (4th ed.). The essential feature if DID is the presence of two or more distinct personalities that alternately control the person's behavior. DID is not commonly observed outside the United States and therefore may be culture-specific (DSM-IV). There is some controversy over this diagnosis and its prevalence, as there has been an increase in the number of reported cases of DID over the past decade. This increase may be due in part to a heightened sensitivity and awareness of the disorder by clinicians (DSM-IV), or as some clinicians believe, certain clients may be particularly suggestible and thus are misdiagnosed. There have also been several authentic and fictitious cases of DID covered by the American media (e.g., movies and newspapers), which may contribute to awareness of, interest in, and misdiagnosis of this rare disorder.

A more common disorder associated with exposure to abuse is PTSD. Exposure to traumatic events before age eleven is three times as likely to result in PTSD than traumatic events experienced after age twelve (Davidson & Smith, 1990). PTSD in children is typically associated with hypervigilance, an exaggerated startle response, anxiety, and recurrent thoughts and dreams associated with the traumatic event (DSM-IV). Children's dreams may at first be re-enactments of the traumatic event but may then generalize to nightmares including other frightening stimuli (e.g., monsters). Children may attempt to avoid certain people, places, or objects that are reminiscent of the trauma. Similarly, "psychic stress" or psychological stress can be triggered when the child is exposed to aversive stimuli. "Psychic numbing" can also occur, which includes emotional detachment from others and decreased interests in activities previously enjoyed. Some victims may have difficulties expressing emotion and will respond to others with a shortened temper or outbursts of anger (DSM-IV). Childhood PTSD victims may also have a compromised outlook on life or fatalistic thoughts (Bell & Jenkins, 1993).

Severe trauma can have adverse effects on neurochemistry as well as brain structure and function (Perry et al., 1995; Pynoos et al., 1997). According to Bruce Perry and colleagues (1995), the brain has the ability to adapt to the environment, and consequently, traumatizing events can produce permanent changes in neurological response patterns. They specify that "the more frequently a certain pattern of neural activation occurs, the more indelible the internal representation [becomes]" (Perry et al., 1995:275). This may be one reason why children with histories of trauma are typically hypersensitive to relatively low levels of threat. This is likely an adaptive response to their experiences, one which helps to warn them that danger may be near (Kuperminc et al., 1997; Perry et al., 1995; Rieder & Cicchetti, 1989). Preschool-aged victims tend to respond to trauma by dissociating, with the development of DID being the most severe form of dissociation (Finkelhor, 1995). Conversely, adolescent males with histories of severe maltreatment typically respond to threats or stressful situations with aggressive posturing or defiant and/or violent behaviors. Consequently, placing youthful offenders with histories of maltreatment in programs that include the use of verbal or physical threats (e.g., boot camp or military model interventions) may exacerbate their aggressive behaviors. These threatening environments may actually elicit more violent and aggressive behaviors from the youth than do less confrontational interventions (Perry et al., 1995).

In addition to the aforementioned psychological effects of violent victimization, several studies have indicated that children who are victimized or exposed to violence often become perpetrators of violence themselves. Studies indicate that between 72 and 93 percent of adjudicated youth have experienced some form of physical abuse (Hernandez et al., 1993). The same is also true for nonidentified samples, such that youth who are exposed to high levels of domestic violence (i.e., spousal violence, child or sibling maltreatment, and a family climate of hostility) are twice as likely to report being violent themselves (Thornberry, 1994).

An American National Institute of Justice study compared 908 people who had a substantiated record of abuse or neglect before the age of twelve with a demographically matched sample of 667 people without an official record of abuse (Widom, 1992). Twenty-six percent of the abused or neglected children had juvenile arrest records, compared with only 17 percent of nonmaltreated children. Similarly, more of the maltreated children had adult arrest records (29 percent) than the nonmaltreated children (21 percent). Individuals who were maltreated as children were first arrested at a younger age, were arrested more frequently, and were charged with more offenses than those who were not maltreated.

In conclusion, victimization that is repetitive or chronic can have particularly severe effects on children's development, can add to other psychosocial stressors such as poverty and racial discrimination, and can exacerbate preexisting psychological disorders. The occurrence of victimization at developmentally sensitive times during childhood interrupts crucial transitions, such as attachment formation and puberty. When examining the risk associated with victimization, it is essential to consider developmental and environmental factors.

III. CURRENT CONTROVERSIES AND ASPECTS OF VICTIMIZATION NEEDING FURTHER EXPLORATION

There are numerous definitional problems inherent in determining the prevalence of violence against children. Certain types of child maltreatment may be viewed as violence against children, such as the obvious cases of physical and sexual abuse; however, labeling the emotional abuse and neglect of children as violent is more controversial. The emotional and behavioral effects of neglect and emotional abuse can be severe, (Thompson & Kaplan, 1999) and are likely to accompany other types of physical abuse.

The range of etiologies and effects of child assault complicates the issue of maltreatment, as the definition often varies with the type of inquiry. Social science researchers typically use psychological and environmental assessments to determine the level of risk, occurrence, or potential for assault. In the United States, the legal definitions of child victimization typically focus on determining culpability and appropriate intervention. These legal inquiries are less sensitive to psychological maltreatment or exposure to violence (e.g., community or domestic violence). Similarly, the statistics on prevalence generated by government agencies include only legally documented cases of victimization and thus are conservative estimates. It is widely acknowledged that only a fraction of the incidents of violence against children is legally documented. Similarly, it is often difficult to determine child victimization rates because many countries do not have formal documentation procedures or a national registry for such data.

These definitional concerns are further complicated by cultural factors affecting the labeling of behaviors as violent. Taking the child's culture and environment into consideration is important when assessing level of assault (Wilson & Saft, 1993); however, it can be problematic. For example, people from non-Western cultures may view the American practice of separate bedrooms for parents and newborns as neglectful. Most Americans, however, view this sleeping arrangement as a way to foster independence. Even more controversial is the practice of Female Genital Mutilation of young girls in some cultures (Gilbert, 1997). Similarly, circumcision of male infants in Western cultures may be viewed as a milder yet analogous form of genital mutilation.

Controversy over the issue of parental accountability for harm resulting from children's exposure to violence and access to weapons is growing. When examining this issue of accountability, it is often helpful to separate the types of assault into four broad categories. These four categories include acts involving random accidents, preventable accidents, negligence, and assaults, and can be viewed along a continuum indicating whether the acts were "random" or "purposefully inflicted" (Garbarino et al., 1992). For example, some communities in the United States hold the owner of the gun accountable when a child is injured after gaining access to the unsecured weapon. An incident in which a child is shot while playing with his/her father's handgun could be viewed as a preventable accident, or as a case of negligence. Similarly, the issue of parental accountability is unclear when a child is injured by violence in the community. The parents could be viewed as negligent because they failed to provide appropriate protection and supervision in high-risk neighborhoods, or the violence could be seen as a random accident.

Corporal punishment is particularly controversial because it is the most common form of violence perpetrated toward children. Child rearing practices such as discipline and socialization may all take different forms and have many diverse meanings and consequences depending on the culture (Wilson & Saft, 1993). Most of the research on European American children indicates that the use of authoritative parenting styles is associated with the most favorable outcomes in children. Research indicates, however, that the use of physical discipline and more authoritarian parenting is prevalent in high-risk communities, as this parenting style may buffer children from the risks associated with their environment (Bradley, 1998; Deater-Deckard et al., 1996; Portes, Dunham, & Williams, 1986).

The controversy over the use of corporal punishment is apparent from the movement to ban it in certain countries. Sweden was the first country to ban the use of corporal punishment of children by any caregiver. Since the enactment of this ban in 1979, changes have occurred in the public support for physical punishment. National poles conducted by the Swedish Opinion Research Institute indicate that 53 percent of Swedish parents were supportive of the use of corporal punishment in 1965, but that support dropped to 11 percent in 1994 (Durrant, 1999). Surprisingly, there has been a slight increase in the number of abuse related deaths since 1971 in Sweden (five deaths between 1971 and 1979 and nine deaths between 1980 and 1996), but child death by physical abuse is still extremely rare. Between 1982 and 1995, there was a significant reduction in the number of children placed in long and short-term out-of-home care, which likely indicates that both caregivers and the government are more receptive to in-home and community-based interventions (Durrant, 1999).

The number of physical abuse reports involving perpetrators under the age of fifteen peaked between 1984 and 1994. The authorities, however, were not able to act on these cases because an assailant must be at least fifteen years of age to be investigated or prosecuted for reports of abuse. It is unclear whether these data indicate that there are higher rates of youth violence, or if others are just more willing to report suspected cases. Durrant (1999) suggests that this increase in reports is more indicative of the changes in school policy and law enforcement rather than an actual increase in the number of abusive acts. These changes include a recent ban prohibiting bullying in schools, and thus most schools have forbidden all forms of aggressive behavior. Consequently, situations of mild or threatened violence that used to be handled internally by school administrators (e.g., bullying, verbal threats, and suspected assault) are now reported to the police (Durrant, 1999). As with cases of suspected abuse or corporal punishment, police must document all such reports, even if disciplinary action is not taken. One can only speculate about the increases in financial resources and personnel (e.g., police officers, caseworkers, and funding for interventions) needed to enforce this corporal punishment policy and the new ban on bullying.

The changes in attitude toward the usage of corporal punishment in Sweden have occurred on both a macro- and microlevel. The policy was initiated on a macrolevel, but most citizens appear to have internalized this nonphysical disciplinary style and it is now not acceptable to use corporal punishment within the Swedish culture. Despite the seemingly positive effects of this ban, one cannot infer causality. This society, like any other, is so complex that a direct relationship between the ban and change in social mores cannot be assumed (Durrant, 1999). These findings are encouraging, and policy makers in other countries would benefit from drafting similar creative policies.

The developmental risks associated with child victimization also warrant further empirical investigation. The effects of victimization vary depending on the type of assault, the age of onset, and the perpetrator, and much more research is needed to match appropriate tertiary interventions with children's needs (Browne & Finkelhor, 1986). Additionally, research on different types of child assault is often lumped together under the umbrella term "child maltreatment." More research should be conducted on the subtle differences in the effects of different types of abuse, such as the long-term effects of chronic exposure to community violence and the short-term effects of direct assault.

Most of the research conducted in the United States on child victimization includes primarily European and African-American samples. However, the effects of violent victimization are likely to vary across cultures and thus, more research on the differential effects is needed. Furthermore, intervention strategies need to be sensitive to the child and family's cultural background. For example, first generation Chinese parents living in the United States may feel a conflict between the parenting styles supported by their native culture and the social mores surrounding child maltreatment in America (Tang, 1998a).

Further research is needed on the prevalence of child victimization across cultures. The collection of more international data on child victimization would allow researchers to observe trends in victimization rates associated with public initiatives and macrolevel changes. Additionally, evaluation plans should be built into the interventions (Osofsky, 1999). The lack of rigorously evaluated programs underscores the need for more studies designed to evaluate the effects of different prevention methods.

IV. APPROACHES TO PREVENTION OF VIOLENT VICTIMIZATION

Eighty percent of young American children murdered by their parent had previously been abused by that parent (Snyder & Sickmund, 1995). This frightening statistic illustrates the need for immediate identification and protection of abused children. Provided below are three brief sketches of primary, secondary, and tertiary prevention programs for child victims and witnesses of violence. There are numerous other programs worthy of acknowledgment, however, these three were chosen because they include developmental and ecological approaches and their effectiveness is empirically supported.

1. Primary Prevention

The Prenatal and Early Infancy Project (PEIP) provided home visits by a nurse to young, low socioeconomic status women who were pregnant with their first child (Olds et al., 1997). During the first three years of the intervention, nurses visited the homes approximately thirty times to promote healthy behaviors during the pregnancy and first few years of the child's life. They also encouraged quality caregiving and maternal life-course development (e.g., family planning and work force participation). Olds and colleagues (1997) have continued to follow these youths and their mothers, and just recently collected the 19-year follow-up data. These randomized trials have shown PEIP to be effective at reducing overall rates of child abuse and neglect and producing other positive effects on the single mothers (e.g., significantly less reliance on welfare, fewer subsequent children), as well as reducing the youths' own aggressive behaviors. Other home visit programs such as the Healthy Start Program have demonstrated similar positive effects on both children and mothers, thereby illustrating that primary prevention can curb child assault (Buchanan, 1996).

2. Secondary Prevention

The Child Witness to Violence Project was founded by Boston City Hospital in the early 1990's to meet the needs of children exposed to community violence (Groves, 2002; Osofsky, 1997). The program initially provided therapeutic services to children and their caregivers but has since been expanded to include entire communities. The goal of this multisystemic intervention is to provide therapy for the children and to mobilize community support for these high-risk children. By including parents in the intervention, they learn more effective parenting skills appropriate for stressful environments, how to help their children cope more effectively, and ways of managing their own reactions to the stress. Additionally, teachers, court service workers, police officers, health workers, mental health counselors, and religious and community leaders participate in the intervention in an effort to support the child and to stabilize the community. Many communities in the United States are moving toward more community collaboration when targeting child victimization and other problems of great magnitude.

3. Tertiary Prevention

Unlike the broad primary and secondary programs, tertiary prevention programs are typically more individualized. These programs are essentially intervention programs, focusing on the needs of the child within her or his own context. Because these programs are tailored to meet the child's needs, they are typically implemented by a social worker or counselor in the child's home or counselor's office rather than in the community. There are few specific interventions for victimized children because the needs vary from child to child; therefore, it is difficult to conduct research on the effectiveness of therapeutic interventions with this population. Most treatment strategies, however, include a cognitive-behavioral approach that targets PTSD and other stress related symptoms (Melton & Barry, 1994; Saltzman et al., 2001). The use of more therapeutic foster-care placements for cases of severe victimization has also demonstrated some success, but more research in needed on its effectiveness. It is clear, however, that interventions which take ecological and developmental factors into consideration appear to be most promising for reducing the symptoms associated with violent victimization.

In addition to these specific prevention programs, there have been several movements toward increasing global awareness of children's rights. Claire Bedard, working in conjunction with the Childhope Foundation (United States) and Cornell University, has written a handbook for child protection professionals to use in their work with victimized children. Bedard describes the significance of the United Nations Convention on Children's Rights and provides a user-friendly "Twelve-Step Children's Rights" in a Child Protection Guide. Bedard draws clear connections between the articles of the Convention and their implications on global policy and practice. This resource is indicative of the move toward greater international collaboration to support children's rights.

V. WHAT HAVE WE LEARNED FROM THREE DECADES OF RESEARCH ON VIOLENCE AGAINST CHILDREN?

- Children are victimized at rates equal to or exceeding adults.
- The likelihood of victimization changes as the child develops.
- The effects of victimization are mediated and moderated by social and psychological protective factors.
- Children are vulnerable to risks in the family as well as in the community.
- Primary prevention programs that target high-risk children and their families can effectively reduce the violent victimization of children.

VI. CONCLUSION

Although severe forms of violence are actually relatively rare, social-ecological theory posits that *perceptions* rather than objective reality may be more important to understanding individuals' behavior and adaptation to their environment (Bronfenbrenner, 1979). Consequently, merely seeing violent images on the news or in the movies, or even hearing about incidents of serious violence can cause children great distress and concern about their personal safety (Groves, 2002). The shootings at Columbine High School, for example, affected the perceptions of safety for students across the nation (Garbarino & deLara, 2002). In conclusion, children's perceptions of their environment, including their home, school, and community, guide their behavior; if they perceive their environment to be unsafe, they are likely to expect violence and react aggressively. It is for these reasons that children's perceptions of safety in their environment are relevant to a discussion on violence against children.

REFERENCES

American Psychiatric Association. (1994). *Diagnostic and Statistical Manual of Mental Disorders (4th Edition)*. Washington: Author.

Bedard, Claire. (1996). *Children's Rights Handbook: An Introductory Guide for Child Protection Professionals and Agencies*. Cornell University and Childhope U.S.A.

Bell, Carl C., & Esther J. Jenkins. (1993). Community Violence and Children on Chicago's Southside. *Psychiatry, 56*, 46–54.

Benson, Peter L., Nancy Leffert, Peter C. Scales, & Dale A. Blyth. (1998). Beyond the Village' Rhetoric: Creating Healthy Communities for Children and Adolescents. *Applied Developmental Science, 2*, 138–159.

Berkowitz, Carol D. (1998). Medical Consequences of Child Sexual Abuse. *Child Abuse and Neglect, 22*, 541–550.

Bolton, F. G., & Ann MacEachron. (1986). Assessing Child Maltreatment Risk in Recently Divorced Parent–Child Relationships. *Journal of Family Violence, 1,* 259–275.

Bouvier, Paul, Daniel Halperin, Helene Rey, Philip D. Jaffe, Jerome Laederach, Roger-Luc Mounoud, & Claus Pawlak. (1999). Typology and Correlates of Sexual Abuse in Children and Youth: Multivariate Analyses in a Prevalence Study in Geneva. *Child Abuse and Neglect, 23,* 779–790.

Bradley, Carla R. (1998). Child Rearing in African-American Families: A Study of the Disciplinary Practices of African-American Parents. *Journal of Multicultural Counseling and Development, 26,* 273–281.

Bronfenbrenner, Urie. (1979). *The Ecology of Human Development: Experiments by Nature and Design.* Cambridge: Harvard University of Press.

Browne, Angela, & David Finkelhor. (1986). Impact of Child Sexual Abuse: A Review of the Research. *Psychological Bulletin, 99,* 66–77.

Buchanan, Ann. (1996). *Cycles of Child Maltreatment: Facts, Fallacies and Interventions.* New York: John Wiley & Sons.

Cicchetti, Dante, & Sheree L. Toth. (1995). A Developmental Psychopathology Perspective on Child Abuse and Neglect. *Journal of the American Academy of Adolescent Psychiatry, 34,* 541–565.

Coulton, Claudia J., Jill E. Korbin, Marilyn Su. (1999). Neighborhoods and Child Maltreatment: A Multi-Level Study. *Child Abuse and Neglect, 23,* 1019–1040.

Culp, Rex E., Anne M. Culp, Jeanne Soulis, & Dana Letts. (1989). Self-Esteem and Depression in Abusive, Neglecting, and Nonmaltreating Mothers. *Infant Mental Health Journal, 10,* 242–250.

Davidson, Johnathan, & Rebecca Smith. (1990). Traumatic Experiences in Psychiatric Outpatients. *Journal of Traumatic Stress Studies, 3,* 459–475.

Deater-Deckard, Kirby, Kenneth A. Dodge, John E. Bates, & Gregory Pettit. (1996). Physical Discipline among African-American and European-American Mothers: Links to Children's Externalizing Behaviors. *Developmental Psychology, 32,* 1065–1072.

Dubrow, Nancy F., & James Garbarino. (1989). Living in the War Zone: Mothers and Young Children in Public Housing Development. *Journal of Child Welfare, 68,* 3–20.

Durrant, Joan E. (1999). Evaluating the Success of Sweden's Corporal Punishment Ban. *Child Abuse and Neglect, 23,* 435–448.

Egeland, Byron, Deborah Jacobvitz, & Kathleen Papatola. (1987). Intergenerational Continuity of Abuse. In Richard J. Gelles & Jane B. Lancaster (Eds.), *Child Abuse and Neglect* (pp. 255–276). Hawthorne: Aldine DeGruyter.

Finkelhor, David. (1995). The Victimization of Children: A Developmental Perspective. *American Journal of Orthopsychiatry, 65,* 177–193.

Garbarino, James. (1995). *Raising Children in a Socially Toxic Environment.* San Francisco: Jossey-Bass.

Garbarino, James. (1999). *Lost Boys: Why Our Sons Turn Violent and How We Can Save Them.* New York: Free Press.

Garbarino, James, & Anne Crouter. (1978). Defining the Community Context of Parent–Child Relations: The Correlates of Child Maltreatment. *Child Development, 49,* 604–616.

Garbarino, James, & Ellen deLara. (2002). *And Words Can Hurt Forever.* New York: Free Press.

Garbarino, James, Nancy Dubrow, Kathleen Kostelny, & Carole Pardo. (1992). *Children in Danger: Coping with the Consequences of Community Violence.* San Francisco: Jossey-Bass.

Garbarino, James, & Kathleen Kostelny. (1992). Child Maltreatment as a Community Problem. *Child Abuse and Neglect, 16,* 455–464.

Garbarino, James, Kathleen Kostelny, & Jane Grady. (1993). Children in Dangerous Environments: Child Maltreatment in the Context of Community Violence. In Daate Cicchetti & Shree L Toth (Eds.), *Child Abuse, Child Development, and Social Policy* (pp. 167–189). Norwood: Ablex.

Garbarino, James, Cynthia Schellenbach, & Janet Sebes. (1986). *Troubled Youth, Troubled Families.* New York: Aldine.

Gilbert, Neil. (1997). *Combating Child Abuse: International Perspectives and Trends.* New York: Oxford University Press.

Groves, Betsy McAlister. (2002). *Children Who See too Much: Lessons from the Child Witness to Violence Project.* Boston: Becon Press.

Hampton, Robert L., & Richard J. Gelles. (1991). A Profile of Violence toward Black Children. In Robert L. Hampton (Ed.), *Black Family Violence* (pp. 21–34). Lexington: Lexington Books.

Hernandez, Jeanne T., Mark Lodico, & Ralph J. DiClemente. (1993). The Effects of Child Abuse and Race on Risk-Taking in Male Adolescents. *Journal of the National Medical Association, 85,* 593–597.

Kachur, S. Patrick, Gail M. Stennies, Kenneth E. Powell, William Modzeleski, Ronald Stephens, Rosemary Murphy, Marcie-jo Kresnow, David Sleet, & Richard Lowry. (1996). School-Associated Violent Deaths in the United States, 1992 to 1994. *Journal of the American Medical Association, 275*, 1729–1733.

Korbin, Jill E. (1987). Child Maltreatment in Cross-Cultural Perspectives: Vulnerable Children and Circumstances. In Richard J. Gelles & Jane B Lancaster (Eds.), *Child Abuse and Neglect* (pp. 31–57). Hawthorne: Aldine DeGruyter.

Kotch, Jonathan B., Greg O. Muller, & Craig H. Blakely. (1999). Understanding the Origins and Incidence of Child Maltreatment. In Thomas P. Gullotta & Sandra J. McElhaney (Eds.), *Violence in Homes and Communities: Prevention, Intervention, and Treatment* (pp. 1–38). London: Sage.

Kuperminc, Gabriel P. Bonnie J. Leadbeater, B. J., Christine Emmons, & Sidney J. Blatt. (1997). Perceived School Climate and Difficulties in the Social Adjustment of Middle School Students. *Applied Developmental Science, 1*(2), 76–88.

Lynch, Michael, & Dante Cicchetti. (1998). An Ecological-Transactional Analysis of Children and Contexts: The Longitudinal Interplay among Child Maltreatment, Community Violence, and Children's Symptomatology. *Development and Psychopathology, 10*, 235–257.

Melton, Gary B., & Frank D. Barry. (1994). *Protecting Children from Abuse and Neglect: Foundations for a New National Strategy.* New York: Guilford Press.

Newberger, Carolyn M., & Susan J. Cook. (1983). Parental Awareness and Child Abuse: A Cognitive-Developmental Analyses of Urban and Rural Samples. *American Journal of Orthopsychiatry, 53*, 512–524.

Olds, David L., John Eckenrode, Charles R. Henderson, Harriet Kitzman, Jane Powers, Robert Cole, Kimberly Sidora, Pamela Morris, Lisa M. Pettitt, & Dennis Luckey. (1997). Long-Term Effects of Home Visitation on Maternal Life Course and Child Abuse and Neglect: Fifteen-Year Follow-up of a Randomized Trial. *Journal of the American Medical Association, 278*, 637–643.

Osofsky, Joy D. (Ed.) (1997). *Children in a Violent Society.* New York: Guilford Press.

Osofsky, Joy D. (1999). The Impact of Violence on Children. *The Future of Children: Special Issue on Domestic Violence and Children, 9*, 33–49.

Perry, Bruce D., Ronnie A. Pollard, Toi L. Blakley, William L. Baker, & Domenico Vigilante. (1995). Childhood Trauma, the Neurobiology of Adaptation, and Use-Dependent' Development of the Brain: How States' Become Traits'. *Infant Mental Health Journal, 16*, 271–291.

Portes, Pedro R., Richard M. Dunham, & Shavon A. Williams. (1986). Assessing Child-Rearing Style in Ecological Settings: Its Relation to Culture, Social Class, Early Age Intervention and Scholastic Achievement. *Adolescence, 21*, 723–735.

Powers, Jane L., John Eckenrode, & Barbara Jaklitsch. (1990). Maltreatment among Runaway and Homeless Youth. *Child Abuse and Neglect, 14*, 87–98.

Pynoos, Robert S., Alan M. Steinberg, Edward M. Ornitz, & Armen K. Goenjian. (1997). Issues in the Developmental Neurobiology of Traumatic Stress In Rachel Yehuda & Alexander C. McFarlane (Eds.), *Psychobiology of Posttraumatic Stress Disorder, Vol. 821* (pp. 176–193). New York: New York Academy of Sciences.

Rieder, Carolyn, & Dante Cicchetti. (1989). Organizational Perspective on Cognitive Control Functioning and Cognitive-Affective Balance in Maltreated Children. *Developmental Psychology, 25*, 382–393.

Rowe, Elizabeth, & John Eckenrode. (1999). The Timing of Academic Difficulties among Maltreated and Nonmaltreated Children. *Child Abuse and Neglect, 23*, 813–832.

Rutter, Michael. (1989). Pathways from Childhood to Adult Life. *Journal of Psychology and Psychiatry, 30*, 23–51.

Saltzman, William R., Robert Pynoos, Christopher M. Layne, Alan Steinberg, & Eugene Aisenberg. (2001). Trauma and Grief-Focused Intervention for Adolescents Exposed to Community Violence: Results of a School-Based Screening and Group Treatment Protocol. *Group Dynamics: Theory, Research, and Practice, 5*, 291–303.

Salzinger, Suzanne, Richard S. Feldman, Muriel Hammer, & Margaret Rosario. (1993). The Effects of Physical Abuse on Children's Social Relationships. *Child Development, 64*, 109–187.

Shirk, Stephen R. (1988). The Interpersonal Legacy of Physical Abuse of Children. In Martha B. Straus (Ed.), *Abuse and Victimization across the Life Span* (pp. 57–81). Baltimore: Johns Hopkins University Press.

Sickmund, Melisa, Howard N. Snyder, & Eileen Poe-Yamagata. (1997). *Juvenile Offenders and Victims: 1997 Update on Violence.* Washington: Office of Juvenile Justice and Delinquency Prevention.

Snyder, Howard N., & Melissa Sickmund. (1995). *Juvenile Offenders and Victims: A National Report.* Washington: Office of Juvenile Justice and Delinquency Prevention.

Snyder, Howard N., & Melissa Sickmund. (1999). *Juvenile Offenders and Victims: 1999 National Report.* Washington: U.S. Department of Justice, Office of Justice Programs, Office of Juvenile Justice and Delinquency Prevention.

Tang, Catherine S. (1998a). Frequency of Parental Violence against Children in Chinese Families: Impact of Age and Gender. *Journal of Family Violence, 13,* 113–130.

Tang, Catherine S. (1998b). The Rate of Physical Child Abuse in Chinese Families: A Community Survey in Hong Kong. *Child Abuse and Neglect, 22,* 381–391.

Thompson, Anne E., & Carole A. Kaplan. (1999). Emotionally Abused Children Presenting to Child Psychiatry Clinics. *Child Abuse and Neglect, 23,* 191–196.

Thornberry, Terence P. (1994). *Violent Families and Youth Violence.* In OJJDP Fact Sheet. Washington: Office of Juvenile Justice and Delinquency Prevention.

Widom, Cathy S. (1992). The Cycle of Violence. *NIJ Research Brief* (pp. 1–6). Washington: National Institute of Justice, October.

Wilson, Melvin N., & Elizabeth W. Saft. (1993). Child Maltreatment in the African-American Community. In Dante Cicchetti & Sheree L. Toth (Eds.), *Child Abuse, Child Development, and Social Policy* (pp. 213–247). New Jersey: Ablex.

Young, Robert L., Wayne Godfrey, Barbara Mathews, & Gerald R. Adams. (1983). Runaways: A Review of Negative Consequences. *Family Relations, 32,* 275–281.

CHAPTER II-4.2

Violence in Intimate Relationships

RUSSELL P. DOBASH AND R. EMERSON DOBASH

I. INTRODUCTION

Research into the problem of violence between intimates in heterosexual relationships has been fraught with debate and controversy since it began in the 1970s.[1] Debates touch on almost all areas of the research process and have also characterized the areas of social and legal policies regarding appropriate and effective forms of intervention. Some of the more important issues concern the nature of adequate definitions and explanations of the violence itself, appropriate research methodologies for investigating violence, and establishing its extent and distribution within societies as well as the severity of its consequences for the individuals concerned and the nature of meaningful and effective responses to victims and perpetrators (involving criminal justice, social services, health care services, and/or informal, voluntary or community networks or support systems).

II. CONCEPTUALIZING VIOLENCE— SYMMETRY OR ASYMMETRY

In the last quarter of the twentieth century, violence between intimates has become a focus of concern for members of the general public, the media, policy makers, and academic researchers alike. Over time, various scientific and lay conceptions have driven debates, and various institutions from religion to criminal justice have at different times dominated policy debates and forms of intervention. Some theoretical accounts of the "genesis" of violence have come and gone while others have been more enduring. Some accounts conceptualize all forms of violence as outside of human rationality and comprehension; oth-

---

[1] We recognize that aggression and violence occurs in same sex relationships and that this is a problem worthy of serious attention, however, here we have not considered violence in same sex relationships which requires a separate analytical treatment.

W. Heitmeyer and J. Hagan (eds.), *International Handbook of Violence Research*, 737–752.
© 2003 Kluwer Academic Publishers. Printed in the Netherlands.

ers understand it as purposeful behavior occurring in a context of conflicts and aggression often between individuals or groups with conflicts of interest and with more or less to gain by its use.

In the area of violence between men and women in intimate relationships, the "source" of the violence has been differently located: within society and its institutional and ideological framework; within particular cultural subgroups whether defined by class, religion, or ethnicity; within individuals with different social or socio-demographic characters; within individuals with different personality traits; within individuals with different cognitions; and perhaps within the very biological makeup of men and women. While many researchers adhere to particular theoretical perspectives in preference to others, recently some scholars have embraced methods and explanations that cross over boundaries previously fixed by different academic domains and/or by various ideological perspectives. Much of the cross-fertilization of thinking in this domain has been about why this violence might occur with various social scientific perspectives (e.g., sociology, anthropology, and history) initially shaping explanations and approaches to research, but they are now being joined by theoretical thinking from the behavioral and biological sciences, with personality theory and evolutionary psychology firmly establishing themselves as additional explanatory approaches. Engagements and encounters across various disciplines have only just begun, but a lively cross-fertilization of ideas and evidence may be expected from the serious scholarship that engages across such areas. No doubt, there will be many future debates and disputes about ideas, evidence and methods, as researchers and scholars seriously engage with the issue of violence across ever-expanding disciplinary boundaries which offer the prospect of further important insights and/or more effective forms of intervention (Dobash & Dobash, 1998a). In this chapter, we will consider many of the conceptual, theoretical, empirical, and policy orientations emerging from the various research traditions in this domain and consider evidence regarding the usual direction, nature, and extent of violence in intimate relationships. We will also consider the predicament of victims and the nature of social and legal responses to the usual victims and perpetrators of such violence. We begin with an examination of the conflicting claims regarding the direction of violence between the genders and follow with a consideration of the related issues of measurement, context, and meaning.

Police, hospital accident and emergency services, social work and voluntary organizations struggle with questions about what to do with the victims who seek assistance as a consequence of violent episodes. Their focus is on injuries, homelessness, dislocation of children from their homes and schools, emotional stress, and a raft of other problems experienced by the women who seek assistance for themselves and their children. Across all of these organizations in countries throughout the world, the operating definition of the problem they confront is overwhelmingly one of male violence against a female partner. Almost all pragmatic interventions in the form of programs, emergency services, and other innovations are designed to respond to the serious problem of male violence against an intimate female partner and not the obverse. To those dealing with the issues, this is what is important, urgent, and pressing and is the problem in need of solution. It is here that one of the greatest disjunctures has occurred in definitions and research knowledge. The disjuncture of knowledge and findings centers on a puzzle about the nature of the phenomenon itself, which then leads into its explanation and various attempts to find effective solutions. The question of who is violent to whom and under what circumstances and with what consequences has led to research findings that present a puzzle about the very nature of this form of violence. While the research findings of most social scientists and the pragmatic experience of most professionals dealing with violence between intimates on a regular basis supports the proposition that this is overwhelmingly an issue of male violence against a female partner, findings from some social scientists, primarily from the U.S., appear to support the notion that the phenomenon is equally likely to involve women's violence against a male partner, and some claim that women are indeed even more likely to be violent than men.

In the U.S., some researchers claim symmetry in the perpetration of violence between men and women in intimate relationships. Other researchers claim that the perpetration of intimate violence is asymmetrical, pointing to the near monopoly of lethal and nonlethal violence by men in all settings whether intimate and domestic or impersonal and public. Claims of symmetry in violence between intimates arise almost exclusively from the results of a single measurement tool, the Conflict Tactics Scale or CTS, which has been used primarily in national and local surveys in the U.S. (Straus, 1979). In short, the finding of symmetry is primarily produced by one data collection instrument while other methods produce findings showing asymmetry between men and women in the perpetration of violence against an intimate partner. In the world of research, any single measurement tool which repeatedly yields findings at variance from those produced by all other forms of data collection must, at the very least, become a source of curiosity and warrant closer examination. A brief description of the CTS is therefore essential in order to consider the voracity of the claim of gender symmetry in the perpetration of violence between intimates.

The CTS is an index which includes a range of physical and nonphysical acts that men and women might use in settling conflicts in intimate relations. The items in the index include behaviors as diverse as pushing and shoving and throwing things at one's partner to "beating-up" and the use of a weapon. Using this index in different types of surveys, researchers have variously concluded near equivalence between men and women in the perpetration of violence against an intimate partner and/or that women are responsible for inflicting even "more serious violence" than men (based on the "assumed potential for inflicting injury" when committing a specific violent act rather than evidence of the actual injuries resulting from such acts). A corollary of the claim of symmetry is that theoretical explanations of violence between intimates are or should be gender neutral, with gender playing only a minimal role in the perpetration of this violence and in its explanation with social, personal, and cultural forces assumed to operate the same for men and for women (Dobash, Dobash, Cavanagh, & Lewis, 1998).

Critics of the notion of symmetry cite evidence from a broad base of studies including national crime surveys, victim surveys, crime statistics about violence and homicide, and studies from health and medicine which consistently show a pattern of asymmetry in violence between intimates. They are critical of a measurement of violence that is restricted almost solely to lists of acts (e.g., slap, punch, etc.) and are devoid of evidence regarding the context and consequences of such acts (Berk, Berk, Loseke, & Rauma, 1983; Dobash, Dobash, Wilson, & Daly, 1992; Dobash & Dobash, 1979, 1992; Kurz, 1993; Nazroo, 1995; Rokens, 1997). The CTS itself has been criticized for its inclusion of an extremely narrow range of violent acts which includes potentially trivial gestures alongside more serious acts such as punching. The problem of such a mixed list is compounded when CTS-derived results are translated into specific findings, wherein it is necessary to confirm the use of only one act of violence (as specified on the CTS list) to define a person as violent. With the CTS, both the woman who admits to "throwing something at her partner" (which might mean a pillow) and the man who admits "beating up" his partner would be defined as "violent." When examined more carefully in terms of content, this construction of the concept of "violence" would be unwarranted and the subsequent use of the concept in support of the notion of "symmetry" unjustified. Other limitations of purely "act"-based assessments of violence in intimate relationships include a failure to include sexual-violence as well as the sequel of acts preceding violence and the nature of responses to it. This makes it impossible to distinguish acts of self-defense and retaliation from purposefully malevolent acts intended to inflict pain and injury. Until relatively recently, research employing the CTS had generally failed to include a consideration of the consequences of violent acts, such as physical and emotional damage as well as broader effects, such as restrictions on the autonomy of the victim. Significantly, a failure to consider consequences has encompassed an inadequate consideration of the meanings and interpretations associated with the perpetration of violence and the experiences of victimization. Thus, there has been a failure to consider how men and women actually define their use and experiences of violence and its consequences (Dobash et al., 1998). As such, it is important to consider whether men and women are likely to be fearful of their partner and of his/her violent potential as a consequence of experiencing specific physical acts.

Those who claim asymmetry in violence between intimates propose that men are more likely than women to perpetrate serious violence against their partner and to inflict serious injuries and other damaging consequences. In supporting these claims, they point to evidence from a wide variety of sources. Records of divorce proceedings and criminal justice statistics in various countries persistently show that it is men and not women who are most likely to be cited in divorce petitions for violent and abusive behavior and to be arrested, prosecuted, and convicted for assaulting their female partners (Dobash & Dobash, 1992; Kurz, 1996). Crime victimization surveys conducted in several countries consistently find that it is women, not men, who are most likely to report being assaulted and to suffer serious injuries resulting from assaults from male partners (Bachman & Saltzman, 1995; Mirrlees-Black & Byron, 1999). Most research shows that women report a much higher lifetime prevalence rate of victimization from an intimate partner than do men (3–5 times as high) and are much more likely to experience injuries (13 times higher in one study), and to suffer other forms of emotional and psychological damage as a result of victimization from partners (Johnson, 1996; Schwartz, 1987; Tjaden & Thoennes, 1998). It should be noted that some survey findings suggest that women are only marginally more likely than men to report being the victims of a physical act of violence during a one-year period. Overall, however, most researchers and commentators now agree that the significant social problem regarding violence between intimate heterosexual partners is persistent violence against women which is serious and often has important physical, personal, and social consequences for them.

III. VIOLENCE AGAINST WOMEN

1. Empirical Results

Survey data from Canada, the United States, and Great Britain indicate that approximately one quarter of women report experiencing at least one act of violence while in an intimate relationship with a man, and about one in ten report several acts of violence during their lifetime (Bachman & Saltzman, 1995; Mirrlees-Black & Byron, 1999; Wilson, Johnson, & Daly, 1995; Greenfield, 1998; Tjaden & Thoennes, 1998). Although evidence indicates that this form of violence, unlike many other types of violence, occurs in all social classes, survey research from several countries suggests that younger women living in poverty and experiencing other forms of deprivation are more at risk than women from other classes, and those who are older. The type of intimate relationship is also implicated as a risk factor: women living in de facto, non-state sanctioned relationships are more at risk of nonlethal as well as lethal violence than are women living in state-sanctioned marriages. The risk of lethal and nonlethal violence is also elevated when women leave or attempt to leave a relationship (Wilson & Daly, 1993, 1998). Research also suggests that excessive alcohol consumption and substance abuse of male perpetrators may contribute to elevated risk, and recent research further suggests that a small proportion of violently abusive men may have personality traits not apparent in samples of non-abusive men (Holtzworth-Munroe & Stuart, 1994; Moffitt, Krueger, Caspi, & Fagan, 2000).

Historical and anthropological evidence confirms the asymmetrical pattern of nonlethal and lethal violence and its serious nature, and demonstrates how religious, social, and legal institutions have either condoned men's violence or failed to consider it a problem worthy of serious attention (Dobash & Dobash, 1979, 1981; Pleck, 1987; Gordon, 1988). For centuries, legal and religions institutions in Western societies granted a husband the right to physically chastise his wife for various "transgressions"; women had no equivalent rights. Anthropological and ethnographic evidence gathered in small kinship-based societies supports the accumulated historical and contemporary evidence from Western, industrial societies, suggesting that in many of these societies it is ubiquitous and highly consequential and occurs in a general context of male domination. Importantly, this evidence also suggests that violence against women is a rare event in a few kinship-based societies. There is no evidence of symmetry in these societies (Levinson, 1989; Campbell, 1992; Baumgartner, 1993; Descola, 1996).

Homicide statistics show that women are most at risk of lethal violence from an intimate male partner. Research in Great Britain, North America, and Australia reveal that every year between 40–60 percent of all women victims of homicide are killed by an intimate partner or ex-partner (Campbell, 1986; Browne, 1987; Daly & Wilson, 1988; Wilson & Daly, 1992; Polk, 1994). By contrast, men are much more likely to be killed by a male acquaintance or stranger, and only 5–10 percent of men are killed by an intimate partner. In addition, the context of homicides between intimates usually varies for men and women. Men often kill a woman partner after he has subjected her to a lengthy period of physical abuse (often years) and/or when in pursuit of her after she has left him (often because of his violence but also for other reasons). When women kill a male partner, it is more likely to be in a context of self-defense in response to his violence and/or in retaliation, usually in response to previous abuse by him.

Using a range of methodologies including historical research, in-depth interviews, survey research, secondary analysis of crime statistics and ethnographic methods, researchers have discovered that men's violence in intimate relationships, in contrast to that of women's violence, is likely to be serious and consequential and often includes sexual violence. Several studies have confirmed that between 10–15 percent of married women have been raped by an intimate male partner and that approximately one third of all rapes and sexual assaults against adult women involve an intimate male partner, and that they are much more likely to be raped or sexually assaulted by an intimate than by a stranger (Russell, 1990; Randall & Haskell, 1995; Ullman & Siegel, 1993). Interviews with abused women reveal that about one half of them have experienced at least one act of sexual assault from their intimate partners (Campbell, 1999). One British study showed that about one in ten abused women reported repeated sexual assaults during a typical year of their intimate relationship (Dobash, Dobash, Cavanagh, & Lewis, 2000). While the physical and sexual violence men perpetrate against women is usually experienced as coercive and intimidating, women's violence against an intimate male is very unlikely to include sexual assault, and their partners are not likely to feel intimidated and coerced by their physical violence (Browne, 1987; Dobash & Dobash, 1979; Dobash, et al., 1992; Saunders, 1986, 1988).

An important strand of research in this domain has involved intensive investigations of the contexts and situations associated with violence directed at women in intimate relationships. Survey research has identified the socio-demographic correlates of victimization; intensive investigations will enhance and extend this knowledge base and provide detailed information regarding the way specific contexts and the thinking and motivations of offenders lead to violent events (Toch, 1992; Athens, 1997). In-depth interviews with victims have played an important role in developing descriptions and explanations of violence and characterizing the predicament of victims, and recent studies of male perpetrators have added to this body of evidence (Dobash & Dobash, 1998b). Taken together, this research tells a common story. In contrast with conceptions of violence as expressions of a loss of control, research shows that men's violence is best seen as intentional, purposeful behavior undertaken to achieve specific ends.

Worldwide, conflict in intimate relationships revolves around a number of recurring issues: domestic labor, the allocation of economic and household resources, the care and correction of children, sexual access and practices, degrees of commitment to the relationship, and the fidelity and possessiveness of respective partners. Relationships characterized by recurring episodes of men's violence seem to be plagued by persistent conflicts regarding these issues, and such conflicts are invariably played out against a backdrop of power asymmetry between men and women. Men and women argue about women's labor including housework, preparation of meals, and childcare, and it is usually assumed that women are responsible for these tasks. They also argue about the use of family resources, with women trying to use them for rent, food, and children and men often seeking to retain them for their own interests and pursuits. Real and often imagined infidelities are a significant source of conflict in these relationships: men accuse women of having adulterous affairs, scrutinize their behavior, and restrict their mobility in order to control them and to restrict access to other men, even to the point of limiting contact with family, friends, and neighbors. While women are also concerned about the fidelity of their partners and their activities outside the home, they may complain but they are generally unable to exert such extreme control and/or physical punishment.

Intensive research provides details of the patterns uncovered in survey research, indicating that the violence is usually serious and suggesting that in many relationships men become habituated to using it to settle disputes and "solve" their problems. Survey and in-depth research has also established that violent acts are intrinsically linked to other forms of intimidation and coercion (Tolman, 1989; Pence & Paymar, 1993; Leibrich, Paulin, & Ransom, 1995; Johnson & Sacco, 1995; Yllo, 1993; Ptacek, 1999; Dobash et al., 2000). In North America these acts are often labeled "psychological abuse." In research conducted by the authors, these acts are defined as an integral element of a "constellation of violence" which includes a range of verbal and physical forms of abuse and restraint (Dobash et al., 2000). Many habitually violent men use a wide range of intimidating and coercive acts in their intimate relationships. The list is endless, but commonly includes: threatening to use violence; intimidating looks and gestures; destruction of personal property; threatening and using violence against pets; displaying and threatening with weapons; public belittlement; and continuous criticism of the woman and those close to her. Such coercive and/or intimidating acts constitute the wider context in which violence recurs.

Interviews with violent men suggest that they rarely accept responsibility for their violent and abusive behavior. Instead, they deny they are violent and/or attempt to deflect responsibility onto others, especially the women they abuse. Such men offer rationalizations and often suggest that women provoke their violence because of faults in their personalities and behavior: housekeeping and arguing or "nagging" are frequently mentioned (Dobash & Dobash, 1998b; Cavanagh, Dobash, Dobash, & Lewis, 2001). For these men, violence is "caused" by forces beyond their control, alcohol, drugs, unemployment, the woman's behavior, etc. Violence against their partner is seen as purely reactive and a direct result of anger and emotions. Yet when violent men are asked about what they hoped to achieve through the threats and violent acts they direct at their partners, their views reflect goal-oriented action aimed at achieving specific ends: to silence her; to intimate her from taking certain courses of action; to isolate her; to restrict her mobility; and to limit her social life. Violence is used as a means of obtaining an end, as an expression or product of men's power over women, and is deeply rooted in the historical legacy and contemporary manifestations of differential gender power.

Physical acts of violence by men against their partner are wide ranging, although evidence suggests that in any specific incident men are likely to slap, punch, and kick their partner; a common pattern is to punch a woman to the ground and then punch and kick her on the head and body (Dobash & Dobash, 1979, 1984; Dobash et al., 2000). Violence of this nature, often combined with acts of sexual violence, can have important physical and emotional consequences for women. Research from a wide variety of health and social science disciplines suggests that women are very likely to suffer severe bruising and abrasions to the face and body; as well as facial trauma, fractures and concussions, miscarriages and injuries to internal organs (Stark & Flitcraft, 1992; Campbell, 1998; Dobash et al., 2000). Sexual violence results in genital and urinary tract related health problems, and abuse during pregnancy threatens the health of the woman and the fetus (Campbell, 1998). Studies of physically abused women compared to women, who have not been subjected to such violence, show higher levels of poor health and chronic pain among those who have been abused (Campbell, 1998). Medical research indicates that permanent disfigurement, physical disability, and damage to hearing and vision are not uncommon among abused women. North American research suggests that domestic violence is a major reason for both injury and noninjury visits to emergency departments, and also shows that abused women are 6–8 times more likely to use health services than non-abused women (Campbell, 1998).

Evidence regarding the effects of such violence on psychological and emotional well-being, while somewhat mixed, suggests that women living in abusive relationships experience elevated levels of anxiety, depression, and stress compared to others (Jasinski, Williams, & Finkelhor, 1998; Dutton, 1992). They may also be more likely to contemplate or to commit suicide and other acts of self-harm. While some reports suggest that abused women may engage in substance abuse as a response to violence and suffer from low self-esteem, others show no difference on these factors between abused women and controls (Jasinski, et al., 1998; Hoff, 1990). More broadly, the physical and sexual violence and other coercive acts experienced by women may have significant negative effects on their employment history because abusive men may attempt to prevent them from seeking and maintaining employment (Lloyd & Taluc, 1999; Browne, Salomon, & Bassuk, 1999).

2. Theoretical Accounts

Explanatory accounts of violence between intimates have emerged from a number of disciplines and theoretical perspectives. Initial explanations built upon asymmetry in the perpetration of this form of violence and linked it to male domination and control. A breadth of historical, anthropological, and contemporary evidence was used to illustrate the nature of structures within the institution of the family and other institutions in society that supported the power of men over women in marital and familial relationships. These explanations are primarily sociocultural in nature. They stress the importance of "context" and of a multileveled analysis which includes the societal, cultural, situational, and interactional components as essential parts of an overall explanation of the problem (Dobash & Dobash, 1979, 1984; Edleson & Tolman, 1992; Dutton, 1996). Such accounts emphasize male power and point to evidence suggesting that violence between intimates occurs within a context of conflicts between men and women (often about domestic labor, allocation of resources, and sexual jealousy), wherein men use violence to attempt to silence, punish, and/or control women.

Evolutionary psychology also stresses the importance of power and of asymmetry in gender relations but locates the genesis of such social arrangement in the evolved psyche of men (Wilson & Daly, 1998). From this perspective, sexual proprietariness is an evolved feature particularly of the male psyche, which is related to men's attempts to control, dominate, and regulate the behavior of women. Evolutionary and feminist accounts have much in common: both stress the importance of asymmetry in violence, power and gender relations, and both identify sexual jealousy and male possessiveness as important features of violent relationships.

A third perspective also focuses on power but rests on a quite different assumption, i.e., that this form of violence is symmetrical in nature with women and men equally likely to be abusers. From this perspective, violence is viewed as a resource used equally by women and men in their attempts to maintain order and resolve conflicts within the family unit, and both genders justify its use for such purposes (Straus, 1989). Additionally, gender is deemed to be relatively unimportant within this account which focuses instead upon the "non-gendered" effect of background characteristics, personality disorders, and situational stresses.

As this field of study continues to develop and theoretical explanations and empirical evidence continues to expand, some of these accounts may begin to merge somewhat, and this is particularly likely if current evidence and thinking continue to stress the interrelationship between variables that are broadly "sociocultural" in nature and those that are more "biological." To date, evidence from the broadest base of sources covering the widest net of geographic, cultural, societal, anthropological, and historical evidence supports the view that violence in intimate relationships is most accurately conceptualized as asymmetrical (with men the usual perpetrators and women the usual victims), that it involves the use of power within hierarchical relationships, and that this form of violence is often "supported" or treated with indifference by numerous social/political institutions and finds a certain level of adherence within popular cultural beliefs and daily practices.

While the feminist and evolutionary explanations of violence resonate most closely with the breadth of available evidence, it is important to note that not all men use violence to dominate and control their women partners, and there is considerable variation in the rates of wife abuse between and within different countries. These variations provide a challenge not only to the understanding of "when," "why," and "how" some men use violence against a woman partner while others do not, they also challenge our understanding of variations that exist among those differently located within the same society as well as across the multitude of societies in the world and, of course, at different historical points in time. The challenge to provide a more fulsome explanation will, of necessity, incorporate sociocultural, individual, and situational factors rather than focus more narrowly upon a single aspect of this broad-based problem. It may be that men who use violence to try to control and dominate their partner live in a cultural milieu which promotes violence as a problem-solving technique in a wide range of circumstances. It may be a small proportion of abusers exhibit untoward personality characteristics or have some form of personality disorder that can be identified clinically and treated accordingly. Some commentators have recently suggested the puzzling notion that, while some abusers exhibit "untoward personality characteristics," they at the same time articulate motivations for the use of violence and inclinations regarding the control of women partners that parallel those of "normal" men without such personality problems. As new arenas of study and theoretical speculation continue to expand, each, in turn, must of necessity be critically examined in ways that combine a range of individual and sociocultural variables within a dynamic contextual framework if an adequate explanatory account is to be achieved. Adequate explanations contribute to the creation of sounder policies and practices that should, in turn, lead to more meaningful interventions focused on eliminating men's violence and providing greater safety for women (see, Dobash et al., 2000; Lewis, Dobash, Dobash, & Cavanagh, 2001).

IV. HELP SEEKING, INTERVENTIONS, AND EVALUATIONS

As well as considering the genesis of violence, scholars have also attempted to chart and explain the predicament of women victims and to understand their attempts to seek help in ending violence and/or leaving a violent relationship. The evidence suggests that women who experience systematic and often escalating levels of violence from their male partner often engage in a range of help-seeking efforts. Evidence from several countries indicates that this process generally begins early in a violent relationship when women seek advice and assistance from family and close friends (Dobash & Dobash, 1979; Hoff, 1990; Bowker, 1983). Family and friends generally offer emotional and material support, such as short-term accommodation for women and children seeking safety from violent men. In Western industrial societies, many women also seek assistance from institutions of the state, such as the social services, housing authorities, and the police. Beginning in the 1970s in Great Britain, the United States and Canada, women's groups established shelters/refuges, safe houses, help lines and a range of other systems to assist women and children. Throughout the 1970s and 1980s, evidence collected by women working on help lines and in shelters as well as the results of systematic research revealed that women were poorly served by the traditional agencies of the state (Pahl, 1985; Pagelow, 1984; Bowker, 1983; Schechter, 1982; Mullender, 1996; Hague & Malos, 1998; Dobash & Dobash, 1992). The social services and police failed to identify abusive relationships and either ignored the concerns of victimized women and failed to deal with perpetrators, or dealt with the violence in an ineffectual manner.

As a result of local, national, and international efforts many countries enacted new legislation, embarked on public education programs, instituted new institutional policies and procedures primarily aimed at assisting women and children but also oriented to dealing with violent men. The various social service developments are too numerous to list but include: financial support for a range of victim assistance programs such as help lines, shelters, support services, and counseling for women and children, and improved access to social housing and other temporary and long-term social benefits. Legal developments include: the strengthening of civil orders of protection (i.e., injunctions, interdicts, protection orders) through the inclusion of provisions for exclusion as well as arrest for breach of such orders; the strengthening and extending of powers of arrest; and, in some jurisdictions, the introduction of mandatory or pro-arrest policies; an emphasis on increasing the rates of successful prosecution that also may include support and assistance to victims in order to secure more effective witnesses; and the creation of court-mandated counseling for abusive men (Dobash & Dobash, 1992; Mullender, 1996).

A few of the initiatives created to assist victims and to deal with offenders have been the subject of research evaluations. Despite the existence of refuges throughout the world, there have been few research studies of their impact on repeat victimization, the general pattern of abuse, and on the women and men concerned. However, such studies do reveal that shelters provide invaluable, safe, albeit temporary, accommodation for women and children, and can provide some women with a stepping-stone to permanent housing and an escape from a violent partner (Binney, Harknell, & Nixon, 1981; Berk, Newton, & Berk, 1986). Abused women report that leaving a violent man and staying in a refuge sometimes provides a context for negotiating a nonviolent relationship, although these reconstituted relationships do not necessarily remain violence free. In a few countries, social, health, and medical services have created innovative responses to battered women. Information gathered from these projects suggest that they have been successful in identifying victims of violence and providing services where once the problem was invisible and thus no services were delivered (Mullender, 1996; Campbell, 1998).

The most sophisticated research evaluations of new interventions have been in the areas of civil and criminal justice. Civil injunctions are now widely used in cases of violence against women in the home, and a number of critical evaluations have attempted to assess their impact. Evidence from North America suggests that orders of protection can be useful in providing a temporary respite for women when men are excluded from the shared residence and required to restrict their contact with their partners (Harrell and Smith, 1996; Ptacek, 1999; Fagan, Friedman, Wexler, & Lewis, 1984.). Although reports from Great Britain are more equivocal, a recent study of orders of protection suggests that a majority of abused women reported that they felt safer during the period when injunctions were in force and rated them as useful in their efforts to deal with violent partners (Lewis, Dobash, Dobash, & Cavanagh, 2000).

In North America, the most intensively evaluated intervention has been arrest. In the U.S., several studies using randomized designs have attempted to compare the impact of arrest to other types of intervention such as requiring the offender to leave the residence for a short period of time. The results of these studies have been equivocal and difficult to interpret; some suggest that arrest deters violent men while others find no effect, and while a few indicate that arrest may exacerbate the problem (Sherman and Berk, 1984; Berk, Campbell, Klap, & Western, 1992; Sherman, 1992; Garner, Maxwell & Fagan, 1995). On the basis of such results, commentators have suggested policies which emphasize arrest while others have rejected the use of arrest in cases of violence between intimates (Sherman, 1992; Stark, 1993; Hart, 1993). Other research on the impact of arrest reveals that it results in greater victim satisfaction with police response and reductions in violence (Langan &

Innes, 1986; Jaffe, Wolfe, Telford, & Austin, 1986). One of the most important conclusions to emerge from the various investigations of the impact of arrest is that arrest alone may not deter men who are persistently violent, and that more rather than less intervention may be needed in order to significantly reduce or bring about a cessation in the violence of such men (Fagan, 1989, 1992; Berk, et al., 1992). In this respect, investigations of prosecution have led to conclusions suggesting that it may be an important resource in dealing with violent men (Fagan, 1989, 1992; Ford, 1991; Ford & Regoli, 1992). The use of the justice system in cases of domestic violence is still a controversial issue, with some commentators arguing that violence against women should be dealt with through various forms of mediation and diversion away from the justice system, while others propose that a cessation of violence and changes in the attitudes of violent men will only be achieved through interventions which bring about greater costs to the offender for the use of violence and incorporate systems of control and surveillance as embodied in certain responses of the justice system (Fagan, 1992; Dobash et al., 2000).

Treatment programs for men who abuse their intimate partner are also proposed as a significant element of a more effective institutional response to violent men. These programs have been operating in the U.S. and Canada for a least two decades and are now operating in several other countries (Pence and Paymar, 1993; Edleson & Syers, 1991; Morran & Wilson, 1997). While some programs only deal with men who volunteer to participate, in North America most deal with court-mandated men who participate as a result of diversion from a legal sanction or as a requirement of a probation order. The philosophy and style of these programs are diverse; some adopt traditional psychodynamic or insight approaches while others are based on feminist knowledge and scholarship and combine these insights with those of cognitive-behavioral and educational approaches in dealing with violent men. Whatever the philosophy and practice, the aims are generally the same: to break down rationalizations and deflections of responsibility and to alter behaviors and attitudes in order to enhance the possibility of intimate relationships that are free of violence. Pro-feminist approaches usually seek to extend these lessons by attempting to change violent men's sense of rightful domination and control over women (Ptacek, 1988; Adams, 1988).

The majority of the research evaluations of the treatment programs for abusers have been conducted in the U.S. although a few have been carried out in other countries (Dutton, 1995; Edleson & Tolman, 1992; Gondolf, 1991; Saunders, 1996; Dobash et al., 2000). Until relatively recently, these studies have suffered from a number of methodological and procedural problems which make it difficult to interpret the results (Eisikovits & Edleson, 1989; Tolman & Bennett, 1990; Gondolf, 1997). In the last ten years, randomized and quasi-experimental designs have been used to assess program effectiveness, and they have shown that abuser programs can have important effects on the behavior and orientations of violent men and increase abused women's sense of safety and quality of life (Bersani, Chen, & Denton, 1988; Hamm & Kite, 1991; Dutton, 1995; Gondolf, 1999). Research on British court-mandated abuser programs reveals that twelve months after arrest and prosecution, men participating in such programs were more likely than men sanctioned in other ways to have stopped using violence, to have reduced their controlling and coercive acts, and to have improved their relationships with their partners (Dobash et al., 2000). While abuser programs have been judged effective by some evaluators, the differential effects are often small, and some commentators are not convinced by the results. In this arena, as in many others, additional research is necessary before definitive conclusions can be reached (Gondolf, 1997). Subsequent research will need to be attuned to the issues and evidence considered in this chapter including the differential patterns and levels of violence as well as differences in personality which may affect the effectiveness of various forms of intervention.

V. CONCLUSION

Violence against women in intimate heterosexual relationships has now been recognized as a social problem affecting the health and well-being of women throughout the world. It has been placed on the agenda of local, national, and international organizations, and in many countries social, health, and legal services have altered policies and practices in order to provide more effective interventions for victims and perpetrators. Research into violence in intimate heterosexual relationships has played an important role in advancing recognition and knowledge of this significant problem. In recent years, the enhanced and refined nature of the research questions, along with an increasing concern to evaluate the effectiveness of new innovations designed to end the violence, has shifted the arenas of theoretical questions of importance in this area. Consequently, the research area is now characterized by ever more sophisticated approaches to the creation of knowledge that will enhance knowledge of the problem as well as the effectiveness of interventions. While much of the earliest research was shaped within the disciplines of sociology, criminology, women's studies, law, and allied disciplines, the global expansion of interest in the problem of violence against women in intimate relationships has been mirrored by an equal expansion of disciplines contributing to the study of this problem which now includes medicine, education, conventional psychology, and evolutionary psychology. In order to advance the existing knowledge base, these disparate disciplines should come together in order to develop more fulsome interdisciplinary efforts. These explanations can then contribute to the creation of sounder and more precise policies and practices that might provide greater safety for women and a platform for enhancing their possibilities of living violence-free lives. Such investigations should also contribute to the development of sounder policies and practices directed at deterring men and offering them opportunities for altering their violent and coercive acts and ways of thinking. Evidence from around the world suggests that efforts to reduce violence in intimate relationships should incorporate interventions aimed at assisting victims and challenging perpetrators. It is also clear that these interventions must involve a range of social and legal institutions that have been mobilized within a wider community context of condemnation of and positive reactions to violence against women.

REFERENCES

Adams, David. (1988). Treatment Models for Men who Batter: A Profeminist Analysis. In Kersti Yllo & Michele Bogard (Eds.), *Feminist Perspectives on Wife Abuse* (pp. 176–199). Beverly Hills: Sage.

Athens, Lonnie. (1997). *Violent Criminal Acts and Actors Revisited*. Chicago: University of Illinois Press.

Bachman, Ronet & Saltzman, Linda E. (1995). *Violence against Women: Estimates from the Redesigned Survey. Special Report of the Bureau of Justice Statistics.* Washington, D.C.: U.S. Department of Justice.

Baumgartner, Mary Pat. (1993). Violent Networks: The Origins and Management of Domestic Conflict. In Richard B. Felson & James T. Tedeschi (Eds.), *Aggression and Violence: Social Interactionist Perspectives* (pp. 209–231). Washington: American Psychological Association.

Berk, Richard A., Alec Campbell, Ruth Klap, & Bruce Western. (1992). The Deterrent Effect of Arrest in Incidents of Domestic Violence: A Bayesian Analysis of Four Field Experiments. *American Sociological Review, 57,* 698–708.

Berk, Richard, Phyllis J. Newton, & Sarah G. Berk. (1986). What a Difference a Day Makes: An Empirical Study of the Impact of Shelters for Battered Women. *Journal of Marriage and the Family, 48*, 481–490.

Berk, Richard, Sarah Berk, Donileen R. Loseke, & David Rauma. (1983). Mutual Combat and Other Family Myths. In David Finkelhor, Richard J. Gelles, Gerald T. Hotaling & Murray A. Straus (Eds.), *The Dark Side of Families: Current Family Violence Research* (pp. 197–212). Sage: Newbury Park.

Bersani, Carl, Huey T.Chen, & Robert Denton. (1988). Spouse Abusers and Court-mandated Treatment. *Crime and Justice, 11*, 43–59.

Binney, Val, Gina Harkell, & Judy Nixon. (1981). *Leaving Violent Men: A Study of Refuges and Housing for Battered Women.* London: Women's Aid Federation England.

Bowker, Lee Harrington. (1983). *Beating Wife-Beating.* Lexington: Lexington Books.

Browne, Angela. (1987). *When Battered Women Kill.* New York: Free Press.

Browne, Angela, Amy Salomon, & Shari S. Bassuk. (1999). The Impact of Recent Partner Violence on Poor Women's Capacity to Maintain Work. *Violence Against Women, 5*(4), 393–426.

Campbell, Jacquelyn C. (1986). Nursing Assessment for Risk of Homicide with Battered Women. *Advances in Nursing Science, 8*, 36–51.

Campbell, Jacquelyn C. (1992). Wife-battering: Cultural Contexts Versus Western Social Sciences. In Dorothy A. Counts, Judith K. Brown & Jacquelyn C. Campbell (Eds.), *Sanctions and Sanctuary: Cultural Perspectives on the Beating of Wives* (pp. 229–249). Boulder: Westview Press.

Campbell, Jacquelyn C. (1998). Making the Health Care System an Empowerment Zone for Battered Women. In Jacquelyn C. Campbell (Ed.), *Empowering Survivors of Abuse: Health Care for Battered Women and Their Children* (pp. 3–22). Thousand Oaks: Sage.

Campbell, Jacquelyn C. (1999). Forced Sex and Intimate Partner Violence. *Violence Against Women, 5*, 1017–1035.

Cavanagh, Kate, Rebecca E. Dobash, Russell P. Dobash, & Ruth Lewis. (2001). 'Remedial Work': Men's Strategic Responses to Their Violence Against Intimate Female Partners. *Sociology, 35*, 695–714.

Daly, Martin, & Margo Wilson. (1988). *Homicide.* New York: Aldine De Gruyter.

Descola, Philippe. (1996). *The Spears of Twilight: Life and Death in the Amazon Jungle.* [Trans. J. Lloyd] New York: Harper-Collins.

Dobash, Rebecca E., & Russell P. Dobash. (1979). *Violence Against Wives.* New York: The Free Press.

Dobash, Rebecca E., & Russell P. Dobash. (1981). Community Response to Violence Against Wives: Charivari, Abstract Justice and Patriarchy. *Social Problems, 28*, 563–581.

Dobash, Rebecca E., & Russell P. Dobash. (1984). The Nature and Antecedents of Violent Events. *British Journal of Criminology, 24*, 269–288.

Dobash, Rebecca E., & Russell P. Dobash. (1992). *Women, Violence and Social Change.* London, New York: Routledge.

Dobash, Rebecca E., & Russell P. Dobash. (1998a). Cross-border Encounters: Challenges and Opportunities. In Rebecca E. Dobash & Russell P. Dobash (Eds.), *Rethinking Violence Against Women* (pp. 1–21). Thousand Oaks: Sage.

Dobash, Rebecca E., & Russell P. Dobash. (1998b). Violent Men and Violent Contexts. In Rebecca E. Dobash & Russell P. Dobash (Eds.), *Rethinking Violence Against Women* (pp. 141–168). Thousand Oaks: Sage.

Dobash, Russell P., Rebecca E. Dobash, Kate Cavanagh, & Ruth Lewis. (1998). Separate and Intersecting Realities: A Comparison of Men's and Women's Accounts of Violence Against Women. *Violence Against Women, 4*, 382–414.

Dobash, Russell P., Rebecca E. Dobash, Kate Cavanagh, & Ruth Lewis. (2000). *Changing Violent Men.* Thousand Oaks: Sage.

Dobash, Russell P., Rebecca E. Dobash, Margo Wilson, & Martin Daly. (1992). The Myth of Sexual Symmetry in Marital Violence. *Social Problems, 39*, 71–91.

Dutton, Donald G. (1995). *The Domestic Assault of Women: Psychological and Criminal Justice Perspectives.* Vancouver: UBC Press.

Dutton, Mary Ann. (1992). *Empowering and Healing the Battered Woman.* New York: Springer.

Dutton, Mary Ann. (1996). Battered Women's Strategic Responses to Violence: The Role of Context. In Jeffrey L. Edleson & Zvi C. Eisikovits (Eds.), *Future Interventions with Battered Women and Their Families* (pp. 105–124). Thousand Oaks, London, New Delhi: Sage.

Edleson, Jeffrey L., & Maryann Syers. (1991). The Effects of Group Treatment for Men who Batter: An 18-month Follow-up Study. *Research in Social Work Practice, 1*, 227–243.

Edleson, Jeffrey L., & Richard M. Tolman. (1992). *Intervention for Men who Batter: An Ecological Approach.* Newbury Park: Sage.

Eisikovits, Zvi C., & Jeffrey Edleson. (1989). Intervening with Men who Batter: A Critical Review of the Literature. *Social Science Review, 37*, 385–414.

Fagan, Jeffrey. (1989). Cessation of Family Violence: Deterrence and Dissuasion. In Lloyd Ohlin & Michael Tonry (Eds.), *Family Violence, Vol. 11, Crime and Justice: A Review of Research* (pp. 377–425). Chicago: University of Chicago Press.

Fagan, Jeffrey. (1992). The Social Control of Spouse Assault. In Freda Adler & William S. Laufer (Eds.), *New Directions in Crimininological Theory: Advances in Criminological Theory, Vol. 4* (pp. 187–235). New Brunswick, London: Transaction.

Fagan, Jeffrey, Elizabeth Friedman, Sandra Wexler, & Virginia O. Lewis. (1984). *National Family Violence Evaluation: Final Report, Vol. 1, Analytic Findings*. San Francisco: URSA Institute.

Ford, David A., & Mary Jean Regoli. (1992). The Preventive Impact of Policies for Prosecuting Wife Batterers. In Eve S. Buzawa & Carl G. Buzawa (Eds.), *Domestic Violence: The Changing Criminal Justice Response* (pp. 181–208). Westport: Greenwood.

Ford, David A. (1991). Prosecution as a Victim Power Resource: A Note on Empowering Women in Violent Conjugal Relationships. *Law and Society Review, 25*, 313–334.

Garner, Joel, Jeffrey Fagan, & Christopher Maxwell. (1995). Published Findings from the Spouse Abuse Replication Project: A Critical Review. *Journal of Quantitative Criminology, 11*, 3–28.

Gondolf, Edward W. (1991). A Victim-based Assessment of Court-mandated Counseling for Batterers. *Criminal Justice Review, 16*, 214–226.

Gondolf, Edward W. (1997). Batterer Programs: What We Know and What We Need to Know. *Journal of Interpersonal Violence, 12*(1), 83–98.

Gondolf, Edward W. (1999). A Comparison of Four Batterer Intervention Systems: Do Court Referral, Program Length, and Services Matter? *Journal of Interpersonal Violence, 14*, 41–61.

Gordon, Linda. (1988). *Heroes of Their Own Lives: The Politics and History of Family Violence. Boston 1880–1960*. New York: Viking.

Greenfield, Lawrence. (Ed.) (1998). *Violence by Intimates. Analysis of Data on Crimes by Current or Former Spouses, Boyfriends and Girlfriends*. Washington: U.S. Department of Justice.

Hague, Gill, & Ellen Malos. (1998). *Domestic Violence: Action for Change*. Cheltenham: New Clarion.

Hamm, Mark S., & John C. Kite. (1991). The Role of Offender Rehabilitation in Family Violence Policy: The Batterers Anonymous Experiment. *Criminal Justice Review, 16*, 227–248.

Harrell, Adele, & Barbara E. Smith. (1996). Effects of Restraining Orders on Domestic Violence Victims. In Eve S. Buzawa & Carl G. Buzawa (Eds.), *Do Arrests and Restraining Orders Work?* (pp. 214–242). Thousand Oaks: Sage.

Hart, Barbara. (1993). Battered Women and the Criminal Justice System. *American Behavioral Scientist, 36*, 624–638.

Hoff, Lee Ann. (1990). *Battered Women as Survivors*. London: Routledge.

Holtzworth-Munroe, Amy, & Gregory L. Stuart. (1994). Typologies of Male Batterers: Three Subtypes and the Differences Among Them. *Psychological Bulletin, 11*, 476–497.

Jaffe, Peter, David A. Wolfe, Anne Telford, & Gary Austin. (1986). The Impact of Police Charges in Incidents of Wife Abuse. *Journal of Family Violence, 1*(1), 37–49.

Jasinski, Jana L., Linda Meyer Williams, & David Finkelhor. (1998). *Partner Violence: A Comprehensive Review of 20 Years of Research*. Thousand Oaks: Sage.

Johnson, Holly, & Vincent F. Sacco. (1995). Researching Violence Against Women: Statistics Canada's National Survey. *Canadian Journal of Criminology, 37*, 281–304.

Johnson, Holly. (1996). *Dangerous Domains: Violence Against Women in Canada*. Scarborough, Ontario: Nelson Canada.

Kurz, Demie. (1993). Physical Assaults by Husbands: A Major Social Problem. In Richard J. Gelles & Donileen R. Loseke (Eds.), *Current Controversies on Family Violence* (pp. 88–103). Newbury Park: Sage.

Kurz, Demie. (1996). Separation, Divorce and Woman Abuse. *Violence Against Women, 2*, 63–81.

Langan, Patrick A., & Christopher A. Inness. (1986). *Preventing Domestic Violence Against Women. Bureau of Justice Statistics Special Report*. Washington, D.C.: U.S. Department of Justice.

Leibrich, Julie, Judy Paulin, & Robin Ransom. (1995). *Hitting Home: Men Speak about Abuse of Women Partners*. Wellington: Department of Justice and AGB McNair Associates.

Levinson, David. (1989). *Family Violence in Cross-Cultural Perspectives*. Newbury Park: Sage.

Lewis, Ruth, Russell P. Dobash, Rebecca E. Dobash, & Kate Cavanagh. (2000). Protection, Prevention, Rehabilitation or Justice? Women's Use of the Law to Challenge Domestic Violence. *International Review of Victimology, XX*, 179–205.

Lewis, Ruth, Rebecca E. Dobash, Russell P. Dobash, & Kate Cavanagh. (2001). Law's Progressive Potential: The Value of Engagement with the Law for Domestic Violence. *Social and Legal Studies, 10*, 105–130.

Lloyd, Susan, & Nina Taluc. (1999). The Effects of Male Violence on Female Employment. *Violence Against Women, 5*(4), 370–392.

Mirrlees-Black, Catriona, & Carole Byron. (1999). *Domestic Violence: Findings from a New British Crime Survey Self-Completion Questionnaire. A Research, Development and Statistics Directorate Report.* London: Home Office.

Moffitt, Terrie E., Robert F. Krueger, Avshalom Caspi, & Jeffrey Fagan. (2000). Partner Abuse and General Crime: How Are They the Same? How Are They Different? *Criminology, 38*, 199–232.

Morran, David, & Monica Wilson. (1997). *Men Who Are Violent to Women: A Groupwork Practice Manual.* Lyme Regis, Dorset: Russell House.

Mullender, Audrey. (1996). *Rethinking Domestic Violence.* London: Routledge.

Nazroo, James. (1995). Uncovering Gender Differences in the Use of Marital Violence: The Effect of Methodology. *Sociology, 29*(3), 475–494.

Pagelow, Mildred. (1984). *Family Violence.* New York: Prager.

Pahl, Jan. (1985). *Private Violence and Public Policy: The Needs of Battered Women and the Response of the Public Services.* London: Routledge & Paul.

Pence, Ellen, & Michael Paymar. (1993). *Education Groups for Men Who Batter.* New York: Springer.

Pleck, Elizabeth. (1987). *Domestic Tyranny.* Oxford: Oxford University Press.

Polk, Kenneth. (1994). *When Men Kill: Scenarios of Masculine Violence.* New York: Cambridge University Press.

Ptacek, James. (1988). Why Do Men Batter Their Wives? In Kersti Yllo & Michele Bogard (Eds.), *Feminist Perspectives on Wife Abuse* (pp. 133–157). Beverly Hills: Sage.

Ptacek, James. (1999). *Battered Women in the Courtroom: The Power of Judicial Responses.* Boston: Northwestern University Press.

Randall, Melanie, & Lori Haskell. (1995). Sexual Violence in Women's Lives. *Violence Against Women, 1*(1), 6–31.

Rokens, Renee. (1997). Prevalence of Wife Abuse in the Netherlands: Combining Quantitative and Qualitative Methods in Survey Research. *Journal of Interpersonal Violence, 12*(1), 99–125.

Russell, Diana E. H. (1990). *Rape in Marriage.* Bloomington: Indiana University Press.

Saunders, Daniel G. (1986). When Battered Women Use Violence: Husband-Abuse or Self-Defense. *Violence and Victims, 1*(1), 47–60.

Saunders, Daniel G. (1988). Wife Abuse, Husband Abuse, or Mutual Combat? In Kersti Yllo & Michele Bogard (Eds.), *Feminist Perspectives on Wife Abuse* (pp. 90–113). Beverly Hills: Sage.

Saunders, Daniel G. (1996). Feminist Cognitive-Behavioral and Process-Psychodynamic Treatments for Men who Batter: Interaction of Abuser Traits and Treatment Models. *Violence and Victims, 11*(4), 393–413.

Schechter, Susan. (1982). *Women and Male Violence: The Visions and Struggles of the Battered Women's Movement.* Boston: South End Press.

Schwartz, Martin D. (1987). Gender and Injury in Marital Assault. *Sociological Focus, 20*, 61–75.

Sherman, Lawrence W. (1992). *Policing Domestic Violence: Experiments and Dilemmas.* New York: Free Press.

Sherman, Lawrence W., & Richard A. Berk. (1984). The Specific Deterrent Effects of Arrest for Domestic Assault. *American Sociological Review, 49*(2), 261–272.

Stark, Evan. (1993). Mandatory Arrest of Batterers. A Reply to Its Critics. *American Behavioral Scientist, 36*, 651–680.

Stark, Evan, & Anne Flitcraft. (1992). Spouse Abuse. In John M. Last & Robert B. Wallace (Eds.), *Public Health and Preventive Medicine, 13th ed* (pp. 1040–1062). Norwalk: Appleton and Lange.

Straus, Murray A. (1979). Measuring Intrafamily Conflict and Violence: The Conflict Tactics Scale. *Journal of Marriage and the Family, 41*(1), 75–88.

Straus, Murray A. (1989). *The Social Causes of Husband-Wife Violence.* Minneapolis: University of Minnesota Press.

Tjaden, Patricia, & Nancy Thoennes. (1998). *Prevalence, Incidence, and Consequences of Violence Against Women: Findings from the National Violence Against Women Survey. Research in Brief. National Institute of Justice, Centers for Disease Control Prevention.* Washington, D.C.: U.S. Department of Justice.

Toch, Hans. (1992). *Violent Men: An Inquiry Into the Psychology of Violence, 2nd ed.* Chicago: Aldine.

Tolman, Richard M. (1989). The Development of a Measure of Psychological Maltreatment of Women by Their Male Partners. *Violence and Victims, 4*(3). pp.159–177.

Tolman, Richard M., & Larry W. Bennett. (1990). A Review of Quantitative Research on Men who Batter. *Journal of Interpersonal Violence*, 5(1), 87–118.

Ullman, Sarah E., & Judith M. Siegel. (1993). Victim–Offender Relationship and Sexual Assault. *Violence and Victims*, 8(2), 121–134.

Wilson, Margo, & Martin Daly. (1992). Who Kills Whom in Spouse Killings? On the Exceptional Sex Ratio of Spousal Homicides in the United States. *Criminology*, 30, 189–215.

Wilson, Margo, & Martin Daly. (1993). Spousal Homicide Risk and Estrangement. *Violence and Victims*, 8, 3–16.

Wilson, Margo, & Martin Daly. (1998). Lethal and Nonlethal Violence Against Wives and the Evolutionary Psychology of Male Sexual Proprietariness. In Rebecca E. Dobash & Russell P. Dobash, *Rethinking Violence Against Women* (pp. 199–230). Thousand Oaks: Sage.

Wilson, Margo, Holly Johnson, & Martin Daly. (1995). Lethal and Non-lethal Violence Against Wives. *Canadian Journal of Criminology*, 37, 331–362.

Yllo, Kersti. (1993). Through a Feminist Lens: Gender, Power and Violence. In Richard J. Gelles & Richard A. Berk (Eds.), *Current Controversies on Family Violence* (pp. 47–62). Newbury Park: Sage.

CHAPTER II-4.3

Suicide

DAVID LESTER

I. INTRODUCTION

Suicidal behavior includes a range of behaviors, ranging from suicidal ideation (thinking about suicide) through attempted suicide of varying levels of medical seriousness which the individual survives, to completed suicide where the individual dies. Recent scholarly writing on attempted suicide has questioned whether many of those attempting suicide have any intent to die. Because suicidal intent is often difficult to determine, the terms "parasuicide" and "deliberate self-harm" have become common terms for attempted suicide.

Psychoanalysts who accept Freud's proposal of a death instinct (thanatos) also see self-destructive desires as motivating many behaviors besides suicide *per se*. Menninger (1938) saw lifestyles such as alcoholism and drug addiction as ways of shortening one's life, and he labeled them as *chronic suicide*. Menninger also viewed acts that destroyed part of one's body, such as losing a limb in an accident and blinding or castrating oneself, as motivated in part by self-destructive impulses, and he labeled such acts as *focal suicide*.

Most psychological and psychiatric studies on attempted and completed suicides choose depressed psychiatric patients as a control or comparison group. By making this choice, suicidologists are construing suicide as a form of depression and as a product of affective disorders, which consist of unipolar and bipolar disorders, more commonly known as major depressive disorders and manic-depressive disorders, respectively.

In contrast, sociological research focuses on completed suicide (rather than nonfatal suicidal behavior) and a fair proportion of the research compares suicide with homicide, thereby construing suicide as an aggressive behavior like murder, differing only in the direction in which the aggression is released (inwardly versus outwardly).

The psychoanalytic view of suicide and depression (which, of course, is only one of many possible psychological views) sees suicidal behavior as a result of anger felt toward a (possibly lost) significant other, toward whom it is not possible to express the aggression (because the person is lost, perhaps deceased, or because aggression is not permitted toward the person, such as a beloved parent). The anger is therefore suppressed and may be repressed (become unconscious), and then turned inward upon the self. The depressed and suicidal individual may not, however, be conscious that the depression and suicidal desires are a result of this suppressed/repressed anger. Edwin Shneidman has called suicide "murder in the one hundred and eightieth degree" (Shneidman, 1985), a phrase which captures this idea.

II. THE CAUSES OF INDIVIDUAL SUICIDAL BEHAVIOR

1. The Motives for Suicide

Karl Menninger (1938) has described three major motives for committing suicide.

a. *To die* indicates that the individuals are in great psychological and/or physical pain and simply want to escape from the suffering. Percy Bridgman, a Nobel Prize winner in physics, was dying in severe pain from Paget's disease when he killed himself. His suicide note read:

> It isn't decent for Society to make a man do this thing himself. Probably this is the last day I will be able to do it myself. P. W. B. (Kemble, Birch, & Holton, 1970).

b. *To be killed* indicates that the individuals are depressed and feeling guilty over past misdeeds, perhaps viewing suicide as a way of expiating their guilt.

> Mary darling, it's all my fault. I've thought this over a million times and this seems to be the only way I can settle all the troubles I have caused you and others. This is only a sample of how sorry I am. This should cancel all (Shneidman & Farberow, 1957:206).

c. *To kill* indicates that the suicidal individuals are angry at others and are motivated in part by this anger. For example, shooting oneself in the head at home so that a significant other will discover the body is a particularly hostile act directed toward that significant other.

> Bill, I do hope you'll suffer more than I have done. I wish you'll die in beer joint (Wagner, 1960:63).

Many suicides, of course, show more than one of these motives in their suicidal act.

2. Physiological Factors

Many studies of the brain, cerebrospinal fluid, blood and urine of suicidal individuals have implicated the neurotransmitter serotonin in suicidal behavior. Suicides appear to have lower concentrations of serotonin in some regions of the brain and lower levels of the breakdown products of serotonin in the cerebrospinal fluid and urine (Lester, 2000).

For some time, therefore, serotonin was thought to be the neurotransmitter system involved in the causation of depression and suicidal behavior. However, it has been found that the current antidepressants (such as fluoxetine, a serotonin re-uptake inhibitor) which increase the level of serotonin in the brain also help patients with eating disorders and obsessive-compulsive disorders. Furthermore, other psychiatric patients and deviant individuals have been found to have depressed levels of serotonin, groups such as impulsive violent offenders and those who murder significant others. Thus, more recent speculation is that low levels of serotonin may lead to more impulsive action, perhaps increasing the risk that depressed individuals will engage in suicidal behavior and that they will use violent (and thus more lethal) methods for their suicidal acts.

3. Psychological Factors

Aaron Beck and his colleagues (e.g., Beck et al., 1990) have focused on the role that the cognitive component of depression plays in causing suicidal behavior, a component which Beck has called hopelessness and for which he has devised a simple self-report questionnaire. Most (but not all) studies find that hopelessness is a stronger predictor of current and future suicidal behavior than more general measures of the syndrome of depression.

Research has also shown the association of such variables as low self-esteem, poor problem-solving skills, rigid and dichotomous thinking, and impulsivity with suicidal behavior.

4. Psychiatric Factors

In general, the presence of any psychiatric disorder increases the risk of suicide. In particular, affective disorders and substance abuse disorders are found to increase the risk of suicidal behavior substantially, and recent research has indicated that comorbidity (the presence of two or more disorders in the same individual) also greatly increases the risk of suicide, particularly if one of the comorbid disorders is an affective disorder.

5. Stressors

Suicidal individuals are generally found to have experienced more stressors in the months prior to their suicidal actions than normal individuals or psychiatric patients, and a greater increase in stressors in the weeks and days prior to the suicide. The particular nature of the stressors is affected by such personal characteristics as the sex, age and psychiatric diagnosis of the suicide. For example, older suicides are found to have more medical and intrapsychic stressors while younger suicides are found to have more interpersonal conflict and work-related stressors.

6. The Suicidal Act

Suicidal individuals have a wide choice of ways to kill themselves, and one way in which suicidologists distinguish the methods is using the dichotomy *violent* versus *nonviolent*, a distinction which was formerly called active versus passive. Violent methods include those which damage the body seriously, such as firearms and jumping from a height. Nonviolent methods leave the body superficially intact, such as an overdose of medications or car exhaust.

Table II-4-3.1. Suicide rates by nation, 1990, per 100,000 per year

	Total	Male	Female
Hungary	39.9	59.9	21.4
Sri Lanka	33.2[1]	46.9	18.9
Finland	30.3	49.3	12.4
Slovenia	27.6	43.6	12.6
Estonia	27.1	41.8	14.1
Russian Federation	26.5	43.9	11.1
Lithuania	26.1	44.3	9.7
Latvia	26.0	43.5	10.8
Denmark	24.1	32.2	16.3
Croatia	23.9	35.0	13.5
Austria	23.6	34.8	13.4
Belarus	23.6[2]	40.4	8.6
Switzerland	21.9	31.5	12.7
Cuba	21.3[2]	24.6	18.0
Ukraine	20.7	34.6	8.7
France	20.1	29.6	11.1
Belgium	19.0	26.8	11.6
Czech Republic	19.3	28.5	10.6
Kazakhstan	19.1	29.7	9.1
Luxembourg	17.8	25.2	10.8
Germany	17.5[3]	25.0	10.5
Sweden	17.2	24.1	10.4
Japan	16.4	20.4	12.4
China	16.0[4]	14.4	17.8
Iceland	15.7	27.4	3.9
Norway	15.5	23.3	8.0
Moldova	14.8	24.1	6.3
Bulgaria	14.7	20.7	8.8
Mauritius	14.2	17.6	10.8
Trinidad & Tobago	13.7	20.4	7.2
New Zealand	13.5	21.7	5.4
Singapore	13.1	14.6	11.5
Poland	13.0	22.0	4.5
Australia	12.9	20.7	5.2
Slovakia	12.9	22.4	3.9
Canada	12.7	20.4	5.2
Kyrgyzstan	12.5	18.8	6.6
United States	12.4	20.4	4.8

Hong Kong	11.7	12.9	10.4
Puerto Rico	10.5	19.4	2.1
Uruguay	10.3	16.6	4.2
Netherlands	9.7	12.3	7.2
Ireland	9.5	14.4	4.7
Romania	9.0	13.3	4.7
Portugal	8.8	13.5	4.5
Turkmenistan	8.1	12.0	4.4
United Kingdom	8.1	12.6	3.8
Korea, South	9.4	12.8	5.8
Italy	7.6	11.4	4.1
Spain	7.5	11.2	4.1
Zimbabwe	7.4	—	—
Uzbekistan	7.2	10.0	4.4
Liechtenstein	6.7	—	—
Argentina	6.7	9.7	3.7
Surinam	6.7	11.6	2.0
Taiwan	6.7	8.1	5.2
Israel	6.5	9.5	3.6
Barbados	6.2	10.6	2.2
Chile	5.6	9.8	1.6
Costa Rica	5.2	9.2	1.2
Venezuela	5.0	8.0	2.0
Ecuador	4.7[3]	5.8	3.6
Tajikistan	4.4	5.4	3.4
Thailand	4.0[4]	5.6	2.4
Panama	3.8[5]	5.6	1.9
Georgia	3.6	5.4	2.0
Greece	3.5	5.5	1.5
Bahrain	3.1[6]	4.9	0.5
Columbia	3.1[5]	4.9	1.3
Armenia	2.8	3.9	1.7
Malta	2.3	4.6	0.0
Mexico	2.3	3.9	0.7
Albania	2.1[7]	3.2	1.0
Azerbaijan	1.6	2.6	0.7
Kuwait	0.8[1]	1.0	0.6

1) 1986 data; 2) 1992 data; 3) 1991 data; 4) 1994 data; 5) 1987 data; 6) 1988 data;
7) 1990 rates not available—1989 data

Source: Lester, 1997a (adapted).

Van Heeringen and his colleagues (1991) found that attempted suicides who used violent rather than nonviolent methods were more often male, older, and more likely to have a major depressive disorder (rather than a personality disorder).

Since males choose violent methods more often than females and since the violent methods are more lethal than the nonviolent methods (fewer people survive a gunshot wound than an overdose of barbiturates), this difference in choice of method explains in part why men are more likely to die as result of the suicidal act (and be labeled as completed suicides) whereas women are more likely to survive (and be labeled as attempted suicides). Indeed, in all nations of the world except China, males have a higher rate of completed suicide than do females (see Table II-4-3.1).

Lester (1993) suggested that the difference between the national suicide rates of men and women may be a result of the difference in the use of violent methods. He found that male and female suicide rates by nonviolent methods did not differ significantly in nations, whereas men had a much higher rate than did women of violent suicide. Lester speculated that this difference might be a result of the higher testosterone levels in men, which might lead them to engage in violent acts more often than women.

7. ARE SUICIDES MEEK AND UNAGGRESSIVE?

The classic psychoanalytic theory of suicide is that depression (and suicidal behavior) is the result of repressed (that is, unconscious) or suppressed anger felt toward others which, as a result of its inhibition, is turned inward upon the self. The theory is more complicated than this simple statement. The anger is hypothesized to be directed toward a significant other, such as a parent, child, or partner, and this close relationship is responsible in part for the anger being repressed because the individuals cannot deal with the knowledge that they feel anger toward their beloved parents or children. Psychoanalytic theory also assumes that the suicidal individuals have identified with this significant other toward whom they feel repressed anger, and thus they resemble the person toward whom they feel this anger. Therefore, aggressing against the self also satisfies symbolically the desire to aggress against the significant other.

This view suggests that suicidal individuals should be relatively meek and unaggressive individuals. Research indicates the opposite. Those with a history of violence have an increased risk of suicidal behavior, and those with a history of suicidal behavior have an increased risk of violence. For example, in an institution for the criminally insane, Hillbrand (1992) found that a history of prior violence and suicidality were associated with each other. Furthermore, the suicidal prisoners showed more verbal and physical aggression in the institution than the nonsuicidal prisoners. In a sample of Finnish twins, hostility predicted later fatal and nonfatal suicidal behavior (Romanov et al., 1994).

III. SOCIETAL SUICIDE RATES

Nations vary greatly in their suicide rates. Suicide rates have been highest in nations such as Hungary and Sri Lanka, reaching levels over fifty per 100,000 per year, and lowest in many Muslim nations, such as Kuwait and other Middle Eastern nations (Lester, 1997a) (see Table II-4-3.1). These rates are quite stable in the short term (over ten or twenty years), although some groups within the nation may show short-term changes, such as youths (aged fifteen to twenty-four) or the elderly.

Most nations have seen a rise in their suicide rates during the twentieth century, and those with good data going back further (such as Finland) show a steady rise over the last 250 years. In the latter part of the twentieth century, suicide rates have generally risen for males, but not for females. In the recent decade at the end of the century, nations with the highest suicide rates, such as Hungary, have witnessed a decline, while some developed nations which have traditionally had relatively low suicide rates (such as Ireland and Norway) have witnessed an increase.

Research has consistently shown that the suicide rates of immigrant groups to nations such as the United States and Australia are in roughly the same rank order as the suicide rates in the home nations. Hungarian immigrants to the United States have had the highest suicide rate of all immigrant groups, just as Hungarians in Hungary have had one of the highest suicide rates in the world. This suggests that national differences in suicide cannot be dismissed as a product of differences between nations in the certification of the cause of death, although a few nations do appear to have "undercounted" their suicides in the past.

1. Explanations of Differing National Suicide Rates

a. Physiological Theories. One possible explanation, of course, for differences in the suicide rates of nations could be that different nationalities differ in some relevant manner in their physiology. Perhaps, for example, there are differences in inherited psychiatric disorders, particularly affective disorders, or brain concentrations of serotonin. For example, in seventeen industrialized nations, Lester (1987) found that the lower the proportion of Type O people in a nation and the higher the proportion of Type AB people, the higher the suicide rate.

b. Psychological and Psychiatric Theories. The major psychological and psychiatric factors found to be associated with and predictive of suicidal behavior are depression (and in particular hopelessness) and psychological disturbance, labeled variously as neuroticism, anxiety, or emotional instability (Lester, 2000). Psychiatric disorder of any kind appears to increase the risk of suicide, with affective disorders and substance abuse leading the list. Perhaps nations differ in the proportions of the population afflicted with these disorders.

c. Composition Theories. Moksony (1990) has noted that one simple explanation of differences in suicide rates between nations is that the national populations differ in the proportion of those at risk for suicide. For example, typically in developed nations, suicide rates are highest in males and in the elderly. Therefore, nations with a higher proportion of men and the elderly will have a higher suicide rate.

d. Social Theories. The most popular explanations of social suicide rates focus on social variables. These social variables may be viewed in two ways: (1) as direct causal agents of the suicidal behavior, or (2) as indices of broader, more abstract, social characteristics in which nations differ.

The most important theory for choosing relevant variables has been that of Emile Durkheim (1897). Durkheim hypothesized that suicide rates were caused by the society's level of social integration (that is, the degree to which the people are bound together in social networks) and the level of social regulation (that is, the degree to which people's desires and emotions are regulated by societal norms and customs). Durkheim thought that this association was curvilinear—suicide was more common when the level of social integration was very high (resulting in altruistic suicide) or very low (resulting in egoistic suicide) and when the level of social regulation was very high (resulting in fatalistic suicide) or very low (resulting in anomic suicide).

Later sociologists have argued that altruistic and fatalistic suicide were rare in modern societies. For example, fatalistic suicide, a result of too high a level of social regulation, may have occurred in slaves and those subjected to high levels of oppression, but oppression has been greatly reduced in modern societies. Furthermore, sociologists have also found it difficult to operationally define social integration and social regulation in different ways. For example, a high divorce rate in a society is probably an index of relatively low levels of both social integration (since divorce disrupts social relationships) and social regulation (since divorce is frowned upon by most religions). Therefore, a linear association has been proposed for modern societies (Johnson, 1965), with suicide increasing as social integration/regulation decreases.

Studies of samples of nations have found that suicide rates are associated with such variables as the birth rate, female participation in the labor force, immigration, and the divorce rate (Stack, 1980). Some investigators see these associations as suggesting a direct link between divorce or immigration and suicidal behavior. For example, divorce may be associated with suicide at the aggregate level because divorced people have a higher suicide rate than those with other marital statuses. Other investigators see the associations as suggesting that divorce and immigration are measures of a broader and more basic social characteristic, perhaps social integration, which plays a causal role in suicide. In this latter case, nations with a higher rate of divorce may also have a higher rate of suicide for those in all marital statuses.

In a study of twenty-five nations in 1970, Lester (1994a) found that suicide rates were associated positively with the percentage of the elderly, the divorce rate and the gross domestic product, and negatively with the percentage of people under the age of fifteen, the unemployment rate and the birth rate. The association of suicide with birth and divorce rates is consistent with predictions from Durkheim's theory, the association with the percentage of elderly and young is consistent with a composition explanation of the suicide rate, and the association with unemployment and gross domestic product is consistent with previous empirical research findings (Platt, 1984).

IV. SUICIDE AND MURDER

1. Suicide as Murder and Murder as Suicide

Marvin Wolfgang (1958), in his classic study of murder in Philadelphia, found that, in about one quarter of the murder incidents, the victims played some role in precipitating their own murder. For example, in one case, a husband was beating his wife in the kitchen of their home. She picked up a knife and told him that, if he hit her one more time, she would stab him. He hit her, she stabbed him, and he died. Wolfgang called this behavior *victim-precipitated homicide*, and some have speculated that the victim is motivated, in part, by unconscious suicidal impulses. If suicide is seen as morally wrong, and if the suicidal impulses are unconscious, such victims may provoke others to murder them as a way of satisfying this unconscious desire. The phenomenon called in recent years "Suicide-by-Cop" is sometimes assumed to have the same dynamics. Individuals, often clearly suicidal, behave in such a way that they provoke the police officers called to the scene into killing them, often in self-defense after the victims threaten to assault and kill the police officers.

In contrast, Meerloo (1962) has described the phenomenon in which individuals provoke or encourage others to commit suicide as a way of satisfying their own murderous wishes directed against the victims. For example, Meerloo described the case of a man with a harsh and domineering alcoholic father. The man went away for a few days, making sure that the father had enough alcohol to drink and barbiturates on hand. His father committed suicide using the alcohol and sleeping pills. Meerloo called this phenomenon *psychic homicide*. Rosenbaum and Richman (1970) have documented that the murderous wishes that family members may feel toward the potential suicide may even be conscious. In one case, a mother told her son after he had tried to kill himself, "Next time, pick a higher bridge!"

2. Suicide after Murder

Some murderers kill themselves after committing their murder, about 5 to 10 percent in some nations. The higher the homicide rate in the nation, the smaller the percentage of murderers who commit suicide, perhaps because a high murder rate in a nation means that most murders are murders of strangers and those only marginally acquainted with the murderer rather than close intimates of the murderer.

The typical murder who commits suicide after murdering another is a man, murdering a spouse in the home. In the majority of cases, the suicide occurs within an hour of the murder. There is usually friction between the murderer and the victim—they are often separated or divorced. Other characteristics vary with the nation. For example, in the United States, Great Britain and Canada, murderers who commit suicide are more likely to use a firearm for the murder than murderers who do not commit suicide. Parents who murder children, especially mothers, are also at high risk for committing suicide. In the case of mothers murdering their children, sometimes the motive is "altruism"—the suicidal mothers think that the children will suffer after their mothers are dead and so they kill the children before committing suicide in order to spare them such suffering. In some cases, the child killed before the mother commits suicide is one whom the mother sees as most like herself.

It is becoming increasing common for the elderly to be involved in murder-suicides. Most commonly, these cases involved husbands and wives, one of whom is ill (perhaps terminally) or in great pain. Sometimes the husband is dying, and the wife does not wish to live alone after his death; in other cases, the wife is dying and the husband wants to end her suffering.

Several recent incidents involving mass deaths appear to have been a mix of suicide and murder, in which some of the individuals commit suicide while others appear to have been murdered first, such as that in Jonestown, Guyana, in November, 1978, where over 900 people died.

3. Suicidal Behavior in Murderers

Murderers are frequently found to have been suicidal in the past. For example, in Denmark, Gottlieb and Gabrielson (1990) found that 29 percent of murderers in their sample had attempted suicide in the past. After release (after serving their sentence), 10 percent completed suicide and 8 percent attempted suicide.

4. The Association between Suicide and Homicide Rates

Several investigators have explored whether suicide and homicide rates are associated. The rates are not associated over nations of the world and only weakly over the states of America. The associations over time depend upon the nation studied and the time period chosen. David Lester and Bijou Yang (1998) found a positive association for the period 1950 to 1985 for thirteen nations and a negative association for six nations. Andrew Henry and James Short (1954) hypothesized that the social conditions which increase the suicide rate should decrease the homicide rate, and *pari passu* the social conditions which decrease the suicide rate should increase the homicide rate. They based this hypothesis on the assumption that suicide and homicide are both a result of frustration produced by social stressors. If the outward expression of the anger resulting from this frustration is legitimized by the society, then assaultive (and, in the extreme, murderous) behavior will result. If the outward expression of anger is prohibited by the society, then the anger will be inhibited and turned inward on the self, resulting in depression (and, in the extreme, suicidal behavior). Thus, the more anger is expressed outwardly, the less depression and suicidal behavior there will be. As can be seen, a negative association between suicide and homicide rates is rarely found, either over regions or over time.

However, some research studies do support Henry and Short's theory. For example, over nations of the world, the higher the quality of life, the higher the suicide rate and the lower the homicide rate. The same associations are found over the states of America. Thus, some social conditions do appear to have opposite associations with the rates of suicide and homicide.

Furthermore, within some societies, some subcultures do appear to have higher suicide rates while other subcultures appear to have higher homicide rates. For example, in the United States, whites have higher rates of suicide while African-Americans have higher rates of murder. It has been suggested that these two subcultures react differently to social stressors, whites inhibiting aggression and becoming more depressed and suicidal whereas African-Americans do not inhibit their aggression and become more assaultive and murderous. For the United States, it has been argued that African-Americans can be legitimately angry at others when frustrated because of their history of oppression by the dominant subculture; in contrast, the anger of whites is not legitimized (since whites have been the oppressors), and so is inhibited and turned inward upon the self. However, although this explanation makes sense for the United States, the same ethnic difference in suicide and murder rates is found in Zimbabwe, where black Africans have been in control of the government for many years, and in South Africa.

5. Suicide and War

Suicide rates decline during war, and this decline has been observed in the victorious nations, the defeated nations and even in those which stay neutral (Lester, 1994b). Obviously, some potential suicides are able to get themselves killed in battle and so are classified as casualties of war rather than as suicides. Some who save others in death (for example, by throwing themselves on an enemy hand grenade) may be viewed as heroes. However, since the suicide rate declines in those not at the front and in neutral nations, this cannot be the sole explanation.

The decline in suicide rates during wartime is consistent with major sociological theories. In Durkheim's theory, war may serve to increase the level of social integration and regulation, thereby decreasing the incidence of egoistic and anomic suicide, respectively. In Henry and Short's theory, the presence of a clear enemy may serve to help people blame others for their misery, externalize their aggression, and become angry rather than depressed and suicidal.

V. PREVENTING SUICIDE

The major strategies for preventing suicide have included: psychiatric treatment, suicide prevention centers, education programs, and restricting access to lethal methods for suicide.

1. Psychiatric Treatment

In recent years, the efficacy of antidepressants has greatly increased, and the newer antidepressants for major depressive disorders (such as the serotonin re-uptake inhibitors) and lithium (for bipolar affective disorder) appear to be very effective in reducing the risk of suicide in patients taking these medications on the recommended schedule. In addition, new systems of psychotherapy, such as cognitive-behavior therapy (Beck et al., 1979) and dialectical behavior therapy (Linehan et al., 1991) appear to have potential for reducing the risk of suicide.

2. Suicide Prevention Centers

More than fifty nations of the world now have networks of telephone crisis intervention centers established so that a suicidal individual can obtain immediate crisis counseling twenty-four hours a day, seven days a week. Some of the centers also have walk-in clinics for face-to-face counseling, and a few have outreach services. These services not only provide immediate counseling for suicidal individuals, but they also have comprehensive information on resources available in their communities and can expedite access for callers who want to use these resources. A recent meta-analysis of the effect of suicide prevention centers on the suicide rates of the communities that they serve indicated a preventive effect (Lester, 1997b).

3. Education Programs

The majority of education programs have targeted school pupils, providing them with information on suicidal behavior and the detection of suicidal intent in their peers and with some basic crisis intervention skills. The usefulness of these program, however, has been disputed.

One program has been reported which educated general practitioners on the detection and treatment (using appropriate medication) of depression. This program, in Gotland (Sweden), appears to have had some success in reducing the number of suicides (Rutz, von Knorring, & Walinder, 1992). However, the results have been the subject of dispute, and no other program for general practitioners has been reported since the Gotland study.

4. Restricting Access to Lethal Methods

Clarke and Lester (1989) suggested that restricting access to lethal methods for suicide reduces the use of those methods for suicide and may reduce the overall suicide rate of the nation. They documented how the detoxification of domestic gas (as nations switched from coal gas which is highly toxic to natural gas which is less toxic) resulted in a decrease in the suicide rate in some nations (such as England). They also documented that emission controls on cars (which result in a lower level of carbon monoxide) also led to a decrease in the use of car exhaust for suicide and that gun control seems to reduce the use of guns for suicide and, in nations where guns are a popular method for suicide, the overall suicide rate.

The debate here has focused on the extent to which people who are deprived of easy access to one method for suicide will switch to alternative methods. Some of the studies suggest that switching does not occur to any great extent (as after the detoxification of domestic gas in England) while other studies show the presence of switching (as after tightened gun control in Canada).

REFERENCES

Beck, Aaron T., A. John Rush, Brian F. Shaw, & Gary Emery. (1979). *Cognitive Therapy of Depression.* New York: Guilford.

Beck, Aaron T., Gary Brown, Robert J. Berchick, Bonnie L. Stewart, & Robert A. Steer. (1990). Relationship between Hopelessness and Ultimate Suicide. *American Journal of Psychiatry, 147,* 190–195.

Clarke, Ronald V., & David Lester. (1989). *Suicide: Closing the Exits.* New York: Springer Verlag.

Durkheim, Emile. (1897). *Le Suicide.* Paris: Felix Alcan.

Gottlieb, Peter, & Gorm Gabrielson. (1990). The Future of Homicide Offenders. *International Journal of Law and Psychiatry, 13,* 191–205.

Henry, Andrew F., & James F. Short. (1954). *Suicide and Homicide.* New York: Free Press.

Hillbrand, Marc. (1992). Self-Directed and Other-Directed Aggressive Behavior in a Forensic Sample. *Suicide and Life-Threatening Behavior, 22,* 333–340.

Johnson, Barclay D. (1965). Durkheim's One Cause of Suicide. *American Sociological Review, 30,* 875–886.

Kemble, Edwin C., Francis Birch, & Gerald Holton. (1970). Bridgman, Percy Williams. In Charles C. Gillispie (Ed.), *Dictionary of Scientific Biography, 2,* 457–461.

Lester, David. (1987). National Distribution of Blood Groups, Personal Violence (Suicide and Homicide), and National Character. *Personality and Individual Differences, 8,* 575–576.

Lester, David. (1993). Testosterone and Suicide. *Personality and Individual Differences, 15,* 347–348.

Lester, David. (1994a). *Patterns of Suicide and Homicide around the World.* Commack: Nova Science.

Lester, David. (1994b). Suicide Rates before, during and after the World Wars. *European Psychiatry, 9,* 262–264.

Lester, David. (1997a). Suicide in an International Perspective. *Suicide and Life-Threatening Behavior*, 27, 104–111.

Lester, David. (1997b). The Effectiveness of Suicide Prevention Centers. *Suicide and Life-Threatening Behavior*, 27, 304–310.

Lester, David. (2000). *Why People Kill Themselves. 4th Edition*. Springfield: Charles Thomas.

Lester, David, & Bijou Yang. (1998). *Suicide and Homicide in the Twentieth Century*. Commack: Nova Science.

Linehan, Marsha M., Hubert E. Armstrong, Alejandra Suarez, Douglas Allmon, & Heidi L. Heard. (1991). Cognitive-Behavioral Treatment of Chronically Parasuicidal Borderline Patients. *Archives of General Psychiatry*, 48, 1060–1064.

Meerloo, Joost A. M. (1962). *Suicide and Mass Suicide*. New York: Grune and Stratton.

Menninger, Karl. (1938). *Man Against Himself*. New York: Harcourt, Brace and World.

Moksony, Ferenc. (1990). Ecological Analysis of Suicide. In David Lester (Ed.), *Current Concepts of Suicide* (pp. 121–138). Philadelphia: Charles Press.

Platt, Stephen. (1984). Unemployment and Suicidal Behavior. *Social Science and Medicine*, 19, 93–115.

Romanov, Kalle, Mika Hatakka, Esko Keskinen, Hannu Laaksonen, Jaakko Kaprio, Richard Rose, & Markku Koskenvuo. (1994). Self-Reported Hostility and Suicidal Acts, Accidents, and Accidental Deaths. *Psychosomatic Medicine*, 56, 328–336.

Rosenbaum, Milton, & Joseph R. Richman. (1970). Suicide. *American Journal of Psychiatry*, 126, 1652–1655.

Rutz, Wolfgang, L. von Knorring, & J. Walinder. (1992). Long-Term Effects of an Educational Program for General Practitioners Given by the Swedish Committee for Prevention and Treatment of Depression. *Acta Psychiatrica Scandinavica*, 84, 545–549.

Shneidman, Edwin S. (1985). *Definition of Suicide*. New York: Wiley.

Shneidman, Edwin S., & Norman L. Farberow. (1957). *Clues to Suicide*. New York: McGraw-Hill.

Stack, Steven. (1980). Domestic Integration and the Rate of Suicide. *Journal of Comparative Family Studies*, 11, 249–260.

Van Heeringen, C., C. Jannes, & L. Van Remoortel. (1991). Characteristics of Violent Attempted Suicides and Implications for Aftercare. *European Journal of Psychiatry*, 5, 152–160.

Wagner, Frederik. (1960). Suicide Notes. *Danish Medical Bulletin*, 7, 62–64.

Wolfgang, Marvin E. (1958). *Patterns of Criminal Homicide*. Philadelphia: University of Pennsylvania Press.

CHAPTER II-4.4

Violence against the Socially Expendable

EZZAT A. FATTAH

I. INTRODUCTION

Violent victimization is not evenly distributed within society. Victims of violence, therefore, do not constitute an unbiased cross-section of the general population. Violence, in fact, is clustered within certain groups. Those groups are much more prone to violence and run a far greater risk of being the recipients of violence than others. As other chapters in this volume deal with some of those vulnerable and highly victimized groups (children, ethnic and religious others, sexual minorities, prison inmates), and to avoid any potential overlap, this chapter will limit itself to violence against those who are often considered, culturally, socially and politically, to be expendable. Members of such groups could be rightly described as "culturally legitimate targets." Not infrequently, lethal violence against some of those who are socially burdensome, unneeded, or worthless, is welcomed as one way of ridding society of certain unwanted elements. Lesser forms of violence against the others are encouraged, condoned, or simply ignored. The outright relief or the startling indifference that quite often greets the violence against them is in sharp contrast to the outrage and demands for punishment that greets violent acts directed at the "valued" groups of society. The reaction of the authorities and the general public to the victimization of these "devalued" citizens is simply appalling. There is no outpour of sympathy. No one seems sorry for the victim. There is no outcry of indignation and little (if anything) is done to find, pursue, and bring to justice those who are responsible for the victimization. The few offenders who are occasionally caught are often treated with great leniency by the courts (Fattah, 1997:160). This attitude is exemplified in a story that recently appeared in the London newspaper, *The Independent* (May 29, 2000). The story is of a released pedophile that was killed. Neither the police nor the public seemed anxious to find the killer. The police, who in other murder cases usually get hundreds of tips and offers of assistance, did not receive a single call from the members of the public! Members of those expendable groups (and they are fairly numerous) may be described as "social junk" to use a term coined by Steven Spitzer (1975) to refer to those members of society who do not play an important role in the system of capitalist production. The proneness of those groups to violence is often the outcome of a complex interaction between their personal attributes and social attitudes. Certain attributes of those individuals (deviant lifestyle, old age, unproductivity, physical or mental handicap, etc.) render them easy prey to various forms of violence while the negative attitudes toward them invite or facilitate their victimization. This makes them popular and easy targets, not only for violence perpetrated by individuals and groups, but for institutional violence as well. A single example will suffice to illustrate the extreme vulnerability of those expendable groups. As unbelievable as it may seem, shocking eugenic practices persisted in some Canadian provinces (such as Alberta and British Columbia) way into the 1960s. Mentally handicapped persons (and those who were misdiagnosed as such) were institutionalized and involuntarily sterilized. These insidious practices came to light only some years ago when a number of victims filed civil suits against the government seeking compensation.

1. Social Expendability: The Concept

The idea that certain groups in society are expendable, and may (or should) therefore be disposed of, may seem both shocking and far-fetched. To designate groups of fellow citizens as "social trash" or "social refuse" may seem quite offensive. And yet this is precisely how certain individuals and certain groups are defined by the culture, by the economic and political systems, and how they are viewed by the general public or by the dominant groups in society. The death penalty is but one example of state violence against one of these expendable groups. The killing of newborn babies, particularly girls, in pre-industrialized societies is one of the oldest forms of violence against the socially unneeded. But the killing of the aged, the infirm, the deformed, the severely disabled, the mentally handicapped is still a common practice in some remote and tribal communities. The killing is sometimes motivated by egoistic considerations (ridding the community of unwanted, unneeded, unproductive, and burdensome members), and other times by altruistic motives where it is used as a form of euthanasia or mercy killing aimed at putting an end to the pain and suffering of the victims. Over the years, with social evolution, killing gave way in certain circumstances to lesser and more subtle forms of violence. The definition of the socially unwanted/unneeded also underwent certain changes though unproductivity remained an important criterion for determining who is socially expendable. The belief that certain groups are expendable is not limited to a given society, a specific culture, or a certain political or economic system. In totalitarian societies such attitude applies to dissidents, to troublemakers, to those perceived as a threat to the regime, and so forth. In capitalist societies it applies to those who live on the fringes of society and to those who are socially unproductive. Often, it makes little difference whether their lack of productivity is involuntary, due to advanced age, mental or physical handicap, or is believed to be voluntary as in the case of vagrants, hobos, beggars, tramps, drug addicts, alcoholics, etc. In a society dominated by the protestant work ethic, where the greatest emphasis is put on productivity, being unproductive, be it a personal choice or due to an unwanted condition, becomes a social handicap. Unproductive citizens are viewed not only as noncontributing members but also as a burden, as "parasites," or in the case of the elderly, as people living off the sweat and hard work of others. Not infrequently, the elderly, for example, regardless of whatever contribution they may have made in their younger years, are seen as not paying a fair share of taxes while placing enormous pressure on the health system and other social services. They have become too costly and the sooner they depart to the other world, the better it is for the younger members of society who are saddled with a heavy tax burden. And while individual violence against a helpless, sick elderly person, may raise people's ire and arouse their emotions, systemic victimization by the state and victimization in institutions for the elderly is often ignored or not given the same attention that is usually given to the victimization of children. The same is true of violence and abuse against those who are institutionalized, not because of old age but because of a physical or mental handicap, or for having committed a crime for which they were sent to a prison or a juvenile institution (MacNamara, 1983; Bartollas, Miller, & Dinitz, 1975, 1976). The same attitude prevails vis-à-vis other groups. Settlement of accounts by rival gangs or competing members of organized crime does not evoke sympathy or indignation, but a sigh of relief exemplified in the popular expression: good riddance! Social expendability is, therefore, a reality that contributes to, and helps explain, various acts of violence committed against those less fortunate members of society who, for one reason or another, are seen as dangerous, burdensome, troublesome, unproductive, worthless, unwanted and hence disposable.

II. EMPIRICAL RESEARCH

While empirical research on violence is rather abundant, specific studies on violence against the socially handicapped, the socially unneeded, and the socially expendable are conspicuous by their absence. The reasons for this penury of research are somewhat unclear. It seems, however, that the considerable conceptual and methodological problems that such research inevitably need to overcome may be partly responsible for the reluctance of researchers to tackle this largely unexplored subarea of violence. The same problems make it impossible to come up with an accurate (or even a reasonable) assessment of the extent, the scope, and the magnitude of violence against socially expendable groups. The hidden and insidious nature of many forms of violence perpetrated against members of those groups is such that there are no reliable statistics or even reasonable estimates of how widespread this violence is. There are, for example, no statistics available on violence against the physically or mentally handicapped. It is true, there is a great deal of anecdotal and case study evidence on violence against certain marginalized groups such as prostitutes, gays, drug addicts, homeless people, runaways, etc. But to my knowledge, there have been no epidemiological studies and no survey research aimed at measuring the incidence of violence against those groups. This is, of course, regrettable but understandable. For one thing, those groups are not highly visible and are therefore difficult to locate and more difficult to approach and to count. It is also very difficult to gain their confidence and secure their cooperation. For another thing, many members of those groups may be, because of their mental disabilities or the subtle nature of the violence directed against them, either unaware of, or unable to, report or to describe their victimization. The involuntary sterilization of the mentally handicapped and violence against the elderly in nursing homes are just a couple of examples. Members of other groups may be unwilling because of their deviant lifestyle or illegal activities to contact the authorities to report their victimization. Another reason for the glaring absence of empirical quantitative data on violence against the socially unneeded is the insidious and hidden nature of many forms of violence against them. Coupled with the unwillingness of many recipients of violence to report or to discuss it, this makes it extremely difficult to explore the phenomenological reality of this violence and to assess its frequency. How serious this research problem is becomes even more evident when one examines a single type of this violence, namely "elder abuse." Elder abuse became a popular research topic in the last two or three decades (Fattah & Sacco, 1989; Brillon, 1987; Phillips, 1986; Ahlf, 1994; Baurmann, 1981; Fattah, 1993; Kreuzer & Hürlimann, 1992; Sacco, 1993). Despite this, there is still no way of telling how prevalent or how widespread this abuse is. The reasons are not too difficult to comprehend. First, there is the thorny problem of formulating an objective standardized definition of both the study group, that is the elderly, and the behavior, that is the abuse. A satisfactory definition has to lend itself to adequate operationalization for empirical research purposes. This remains an unattained desideratum, mainly because abuse is a vague, ambiguous, highly subjective and elastic concept. The same is true of the concepts of "mistreatment" and of "neglect." Abuse is a generic or an umbrella term, a catchall category under which, for reasons of convenience, are grouped different behavioral patterns of the physical, emotional, sexual, and financial variety. The elasticity of the term "abuse" is such that it makes it possible for any researcher to downplay or blow up the incidence of abuse simply by adopting a narrow or a broad definition of the concept. Abuse is also culturally relative, and even within the same culture what may be considered abuse in a given social class may be a normal or standard practice in another. The elasticity of the term, the lack of a standardized definition, and the cultural and social relativity of abuse render both fruitless and frustrating any attempt to compare the findings of studies at a national or international level (Fattah, 1997:62). Sampling is yet another major obstacle in the way of measuring the incidence and prevalence of "elder abuse" as well as violence against socially unwanted and unneeded groups. Crime/victimization surveys, which have become the most popular instrument for gathering empirical data on violent victimization, data that are more reliable than official crime statistics, have not been of much use in determining the volume of victimization of socially expendable groups. None of those surveys, for example, includes variables such as physical or mental handicap. And although age of the respondents is a standard variable that allows a separate counting of certain acts of violence against the "elderly," the incidents reported by this age-group during the recall period (which is usually one year or less) are often much too small to allow any reliable extrapolation to the whole group in the general population.

III. THEORETICAL APPROACHES AND EXPLANATIONS

What differentiates violence against the socially expendable from other types of violence are the traits of the victims and the prevalent social attitudes toward them. It follows that a satisfactory explanation of this rather specific form of violence has to incorporate both victim characteristics and social attitudes in the explanatory theory or model. This, however, has never been done. An explanatory theory of violence against the socially unneeded thus remains to be developed. In the absence of such a theory, explanations for this seemingly widespread but hidden phenomenon have to be sought in some of the existing sociological, criminological, victimological and psychological theories. Unfortunately, there are very few theories that offer useful insights into this phenomenon or that may help understand and explain this neglected form of violence. To gain this understanding and to develop the much needed theory, it is imperative to analyze the mechanisms of social exclusion and the processes through which individuals and/or whole groups end up being perceived as unneeded, unwanted, and thus expendable. It is also necessary to identify the criteria that are used to define and label certain groups as such. Such criteria, needless to say, are bound to vary from society to society and from one culture to another. They are also dynamic and may change dramatically within a short period of time. And as with other types of human behavior, identifying and establishing the motive is a prerequisite to understanding and explaining the violence. Surely it is easy to label a certain act of violence as a "hate crime," (Academy of Criminal Justice Sciences, 1994; Herek & Berrill, 1992), thus indicating that the motive behind it is "hate." But such a term or label has very little explanatory value. It does not tell us why the targets of the violence are hated or why people hate others even when those others are totally unrelated to them. Nor does it explain why some individuals are consumed by their hatred, are more hateful than others, or why some are so carried away by their hatred that they are willing, despite the consequences, to commit serious acts of violence against the members of the hated groups. In an attempt to shed some light on violence against the socially unneeded, the paper will briefly examine a number of factors that may be loosely categorized as vulnerability factors, predisposing and risk factors.

1. Old Age as a Social Handicap

In our Western societies where "young is beautiful," where attractiveness is synonymous with youthfulness, the devaluation of the elderly is an unintended but inevitable consequence of those cultural values. To the younger members of society, the elderly are a painful reminder of what they will look and be like when they reach their age. This explains the deliberate and constant attempts in Western societies to keep them, whenever possible, out of sight. They are placed in institutions, they are confined to retirement communities, they are put in nursing homes where they are often easy prey to various forms of violence by unscrupulous caregivers that are in charge of their health and their well-being. But old age is a serious handicap for other reasons as well. In a society where a person's worth is measured not in terms of their humanity, but in terms of their present contribution and current productivity, retired individuals, who are no longer part of the work force, are often seen as having outlived their usefulness. Hence they are treated not as an asset but as a burden. And as with any burden, its removal is bound to bring a sigh of relief. Unproductivity and burdensomeness are probably the only traits that the elderly have in common with other unneeded groups. And yet their susceptibility to violent victimization is no lesser than that of those other groups. This is because certain conditions that accompany the aging process render the elderly easy or appropriate targets for certain types of violent and nonviolent victimization. The older people get, the more vulnerable they become. They become frail and many suffer from poor health, impaired hearing or eyesight, deteriorating mental faculties, and so forth. Add to this that a high percentage of them is socially isolated, that is living alone in their homes or apartments and lack the social protection that the presence of others provide. For all those reasons it is not surprising that they will be perceived by potential victimizers as easy targets who are unlikely to offer any meaningful resistance when attacked and who represent a lower risk of detection due to their reluctance to report their victimization or their inability to provide the police with reliable identifying information. As witnesses they are believed to be easy to intimidate and even easier to confuse on the witness stand. As a result they are bound to become the preferred choice for certain offenders like purse-snatchers (actually the elderly have the highest purse-snatching victimization rate among all age-groups), home invasions, and even robbery-motivated killings. In their study of criminal homicide in Canada, Kennedy and Silverman (1990) found that those in the elderly group (sixty-five years or over) were more than twice as likely to be victims of theft-based homicide than those in any other age-group. Forty-one percent of all homicides with elderly victims were theft-precipitated. It is noteworthy that this pattern is not unique to Canada (see Fattah, 1971). Another interesting finding of Kennedy and Silverman (1990) is that elderly victims of sixty-five and over were the least likely of all age-groups to be killed by someone they knew and the most likely to be killed by strangers, either during the course of another crime or not. Forty-five percent of the elderly victims fell into that group, which is almost twice as high as it is for any other age-group. The elderly, therefore, are extremely vulnerable and largely unprotected. The reason why their global victimization rates are lower than those of younger age-groups is that they are wise enough to reduce their exposure by changing their lifestyle, by taking certain precautions, by avoiding dangerous situations and high-crime places in order to shield themselves and to minimize their risks of victimization.

2. Social Exclusion as a Risk Factor

A national survey of attitudes toward violence in the United States found that excluding people from groups to which one feels related can serve as a rationalization that justifies violence toward them or that makes violence inflicted on such people more easily accepted (Blumenthal et al., 1972; Conklin, 1975). Once an individual or a group is believed to be unwanted, once they are considered expendable by their fellow members of society, they are at risk and become targeted for various types and forms of violence. Social unproductivity is but one factor. But while the elimination of those who are unproductive may not be regarded as a high priority, there are other groups whose elimination (or permanent segregation) could be seen as necessary for society's survival. An exhaustive list is practically impossible but a few examples of those groups will suffice to illustrate why social exclusion and social expendability are important risk factors:

- Those who are afflicted by serious illnesses, particularly infectious ones, for which there are no known cures. The lepers who were segregated in remote and isolated colonies are a good example. The same is true of those who are suffering from terminal diseases and are overburdening the health system. It is also true of those who suffer from serious physical and mental disabilities or handicaps.
- Those who are perceived as a serious threat to society. A good example in recent years is that of pedophiles and child molesters who, once released from prison, are hunted like wild animals and forced to go in hiding to avoid becoming the target of violence. Other categories of criminals (for example, the so-called merchants of death) may also be regarded as a social threat, as socially expendable, whose elimination (or perpetual segregation) is in the best interest of society. Moral panics (Cohen, 1972; Fattah, 1994) often lead to the relentless persecution and pursuit of certain groups who then suffer acts of violence, not only at the hands of their fellow citizens, but also at the hand of government systems who ironically have the duty to protect them.

- Social parasites: they are not considered a serious threat but are unneeded, unwanted. Getting rid of them is seen as a legitimate and desirable objective. Many groups fit the loose definition of "social parasites." Those are persons who have no legitimate means of subsistence, no means of support or livelihood. For survival they have to rely on the charity of others and when voluntary aid is not available, they often resort to harassment, tricks, cheating, theft, and violence. They include beggars, vagrants, alcoholics, and squeegees, to name but a few. The term also applies to "street kids" who commit a wide variety of petty offenses and pester tourists with their demands for money or other objects. In some Central and South American countries those kids are the preferred targets of death squads composed of current or former police officers, vigilantes, self-appointed or privately employed enforcers, and so forth (Campbell & Brenner, 2000; Sluka, 1999; Human Rights Watch Staff, Brazil, 1994; Huggins, 1991). Williams (1993) relates how an official radio station in an unnamed South American country openly urged private individuals to do away with street children physically. Quoting another author, Williams explains how in Rio de Janeiro "dead street children have been found trussed in barbed wire, with their eyes gouged out, and even decapitated with a chain-saw." Reportedly 1,397 of those kids were killed in a single year.
- Probably the most extreme form of social expendability is the one at the root of the most heinous form of violence, namely genocide, where the extermination of a whole ethnic or religious group is seen as imperative for society's survival. Genocide may be described as a form of "collective victimization" where the acts of violence are directed not just at individuals but at the group as a whole. Although the group may be diffuse and although its members may have little in common other than their group affiliation, the group is usually targeted as a specific entity. Members are victimized for the sole reason that they belong to an identifiable group that has been singled out for total or partial extermination. One of the most horrifying aspects of genocide is that the killing, the victimization, is not perpetrated by individual criminals or by groups of outlaws, but by government forces, militia, police, public officials, groups operating on behalf of the government, and so forth. Rummel (1994:36) estimates that in the twentieth century alone over a hundred million people were killed by political regimes in different parts of the world.

3. Social and Cultural Prejudices and Biases as Explanatory Variables

Social and cultural prejudices play an important role in violent victimization. Cultural biases and prejudices define certain groups and the members of those groups as "worthless," as "social trash," and thus shape others' attitudes toward them. The attitude to those expendable, disposable victims is one of hostility and antagonisms bordering on hate, and their victimization is often greeted with a sigh of relief. This is for example how witches were treated (and continue to be treated in communities that still believe in witchcraft) Marwick, 1964; Fritz, 1971; Midelfort, 1972). In many ways present day criminals are the modern equivalent to the old witches. They are disposable. They are readily sacrificed and used as scapegoats in a futile attempt to deter others or to simply show that society really means what it says when it threatens to punish those who commit crime. Whatever victimization they suffer, especially while they are behind bars, causes no uproar or even concern among the general public who couldn't care less what happens to them. They are seen as having got what they deserve. Their complaints, if ever heard, fall on deaf ears, as if they are not entitled to the same kind of protection other members of society enjoy (Fattah, 1991:100).

4. The Use of Victim Attributes as a Neutralization Technique

The marginalization of certain groups, by reason of their attributes or lifestyle, is a phenomenon that can be observed in every industrialized society. Members of those groups continue to live in society but are not really part of it. Having chosen a different lifestyle that the majority does not approve of, they live on the margin. They develop their own subcultures that neatly separate them from the rest of society. They are treated with contempt and their victimization is usually met with tacit approval (Fattah, 1997:161). Their attributes or lifestyle and the slang words that are used to describe them (faggot, queer, whore, narc, hobo, etc.) not only create motives for their victimization but also provide the necessary rationalizations and justifications that potential victimizers need in order to overcome whatever inhibitions they may have. Violence involves the deliberate infliction of pain and suffering upon a fellow human being. While a small minority of victimizers may fit the psychiatric label of the heartless, callous, unfeeling "psychopath," the majority are not completely insensitive, apathetic, or impassive, and are not totally devoid of the human feelings of pity and empathy. Thus, unless the victimizer becomes desensitized in advance, the victimization is bound to create moral tension and to elicit feelings of guilt, shame, remorse, and reproach in the perpetrator. Since the source of these negative feelings is the pain and suffering the victimization will cause to the victim, negating this pain and suffering can be an effective means of desensitization. To do so, the victimizer can use one or more of several techniques of desensitization. These include the denial of the victim, the reification, deindividuation, and depersonalization of the victim, the denial of injury to the victim, the blaming of the victim, and the devaluation, denigration, and derogation of the victim (Fattah, 1991:139).

5. Devaluation, Marginalization and Stigmatization as Predisposing Factors

The term "culturally legitimate victim" was coined by Weis and Borges (1973) to describe victims of rape. In reality it is a much broader concept that can be applied to all those members of society whose victimization is encouraged, condoned, tolerated, or even glorified by a given culture. This is so because cultural norms designate certain individuals or groups as appropriate targets for violent (and nonviolent) victimization. By demonizing certain groups, by attributing a host of negative qualities to them, by denouncing some of their traits or behaviors, by questioning their loyalty, by depreciating their worth, and by devaluing their status, their role and their contribution, by degrading, debasing and vilifying them, society designates them as appropriate or culturally legitimate targets for violence and other forms of victimization. Another way by which the culture encourages or promotes violence against members of those groups is to make them appear culpable, guilty, or blameworthy in some manner, and thus deserving to be victimized. It is noteworthy that hate crimes are directed almost exclusively against individuals and groups who have been devalued, marginalized, and stigmatized by the dominant groups in society. The roots of the negative attitudes that denigrate certain groups can be found in the normative system of society. By ostracizing those groups, by excluding them, and by making them outcasts (or outlaws), society does legitimize their victimization. It sends a signal that they are fair game, that they can be attacked, aggressed, or victimized, in different ways, with little fear of condemnation (or punishment). Thus by labeling certain groups as dangerous, as subversives, as troublesome and by casting them in the role of villains, society provides the necessary justifications and rationalization for their victimization. By so doing, the culture allows potential victimizers to attack and victimize others while avoiding any post-victimization cognitive dissonance. The labeling, and the stigmatization act as an invitation to use violence against those others without fear of moral culpability or even legal responsibility. To understand how the process works, one need only to look at what has been happening in a country like Zimbabwe in recent months where the white farm owners have been attacked, some killed, and others driven away from their property. The actions bear an uncanny resemblance to what happened in Nazi Germany where the hatred of Jews, promoted by the regime, culminated in the mayhem of "Kristallnacht." From that point on the message was clear, namely that violence against the Jewish community was endorsed and sanctioned by the German authorities.

6. Vulnerability and Proneness as Predisposing Factors

As mentioned in the introduction to this chapter, the risks of violent victimization are not evenly distributed within the general public, and the victims of violence do not constitute an unbiased cross-section of the population. This is because in the vast majority of cases victims are not chosen at random. The clustering of victimization in certain geographical areas and within certain groups suggests the presence of some sophisticated or crude selection processes. Although the selection criteria have not been the object of a great deal of empirical research, there are reasons to believe that victim traits and victim behavior play an important role in offenders' choices. The notions of proneness and vulnerability, which are not identical (Reiss, 1980:41; Fattah, 1991:260–262), have been frequently used to explain why some individuals/groups are more susceptible to violent victimization than others, and why they are more frequently victimized than others. And it is fair to say that such explanation enjoys a reasonable degree of popular and empirical support. It seems a truism to say that young children are more prone to victimization than older age-groups, or that the elderly are more vulnerable to victimization than younger age-groups. Although proneness and vulnerability are strong predisposing factors, they do not always lead to higher rates of victimization. This is because the sense of vulnerability may lead to more cautious attitudes, to avoidance behaviors, and to certain measures aimed at reducing vulnerability and minimizing the risks of victimization. The elderly (and women) are a good case in point (see above). It should also be evident by now that social exclusion and the negative social attitudes discussed earlier do enhance both the proneness and the vulnerability of the groups that are excluded, devalued, denigrated or ostracized. And it is also possible to identify various types of proneness, for example "structural proneness" (powerlessness; minority status; etc.), "deviance-related proneness" (delinquents; prostitutes; drug addicts; homosexuals; etc.). In addition to the negative social attitudes that designate those groups as "culturally legitimate targets" thus inviting or condoning their victimization, one important determinant of deviance-related proneness is the lack of adequate protection. Due to their deviant status and, often, the illegality of their deviant behavior, members of those groups lack the social resources necessary to protect them against victimization. They cannot rely on the official protective agencies to afford them the same kind of protection provided to conforming citizens. The fact that they cannot (or are not likely to) complain when victimized and the fact that if they complain they are not likely to be listened to, means that they can often be victimized with impunity. This is what Harry (1982:566) calls "derivative deviance." He defines it as "that subset of all victimizations which is perpetrated upon other presumed deviants who, because of their deviant status, are presumed unable to avail themselves of the protections of civil society without threat of discrediting." Kelly (1983:61–62) makes it abundantly clear that alcoholics and drug addicts occupy high-risk categories as potential victims. He points to two factors that greatly enhance the proneness of the heroin addict. First, the illegal status of heroin precludes conventional methods of recourse (the police, the courts) in the event of robberies and thefts of their drugs. Second, the subculture and environment that addicts inhabit are filled with criminals and others who are operating outside the bounds and controls of the law. Kelly concludes that together these two factors combine to create a lifestyle and a set of circumstances in which the risk of victimization is quite high. That drug addicts and drug traffickers are particularly vulnerable to criminal homicide has been empirically proven in some studies (Zahn & Bencivengo, 1974, 1975). Humphreys (1970) explains how the stigmatizing status of homosexuality and the difficulties of integrating it into an otherwise conventional lifestyle enhance the susceptibility of homosexuals to various types of victimization. Sagarin and MacNamara (1975:73) give various reasons why members of subsocial groups run a much higher risk of becoming victims of crime than other citizens. One of the reasons is that they live on the periphery of society and receive so little social support for their activities that the normal constraints of ordinary persons are neutralized, because the latter define the victims as worthless. In a subsequent paper, written with Jess Maghan (1983), Sagarin dwells further on the reasons for the vulnerability of the homosexual to criminal victimization, noting that this vulnerability derives from several sources so intertwined that they are hardly separable. Maghan and Sagarin (1983:153) explain the particular vulnerability of the homosexual in the following manner: There is, above all else, the cultural impact on impressionable heterosexuals of the almost incessant propaganda that derides and dehumanizes homosexuals. Taught to despise, many heterosexuals see the victim as deserving of his fate and themselves as performing an acceptable and just service. To this is added the secrecy and fragility of the homosexual lifestyle that can so easily be shattered, subjecting persons to blackmail, on the one hand, and to interaction with marginal people, on the other. Patterns of homosexual behavior, furthermore, may for many be inherently less than stable, and this instability can result in vulnerability to victimization.

7. Lifestyle and Routine Activities as Explanatory Concepts

Common sense tells us that a person's lifestyle or routine activities can greatly influence the probabilities of victimization by increasing or decreasing the chances of that person becoming a victim of certain types of violent and nonviolent offenses. In 1978, Hindelang, Gottfredson, and Garofalo used the lifestyle concept to explain the variations in risk and consequences of personal victimization. Their model posits that the likelihood an individual will suffer a personal victimization largely depends on their lifestyle. This occurs through the intervening variables of association and exposure. They point out that: "In our view, the centrality of lifestyle derives primarily from its close association with exposure to victimization risk situations ... Because different lifestyles imply different probabilities that individuals will be in particular places, at particular times, under particular circumstances, interacting with particular kinds of persons, lifestyle affects the probability of victimization" (1978:250–251).

A similar approach to explaining the differential risks of victimization was used by Cohen and Felson (1979) who labeled it "The routine activity approach." The focus of this approach is on "direct-contact predatory violations" including those involving direct physical contact between the offender and the victim. Cohen and Felson (1979) argue that the occurrence of such types of victimization is the outcome of the convergence in space and time of three minimal elements: motivated offenders, suitable targets, and absence of capable guardians. The central factors underlying the routine activity approach are opportunity, proximity/exposure, and facilitating factors. The lifestyle model and the routine activity approach offer plausible explanations for the high risk of violent victimization to which members of various marginalized and deviant groups are exposed. They are particularly useful in explaining the high victimization rates of those whose lifestyle forces them to spend a large amount of time in public places (e.g., on the street, in parks, etc.) especially at night. Empirical support for this theoretical premise of the lifestyle model can be found in various victimization surveys. The Canadian General Social Survey (Sacco & Johnson, 1990), for example, revealed that patterns of evening activity have profound implications for the risk of personal victimization, with the risk rising steadily as the number of evening activities increased. Street prostitution, whether male or female, is known to be one of the most dangerous and most hazardous occupations any person can engage in (Boyer & James, 1983; Edwards, 1984; Erbe, 1984; Perkins & Bennett, 1985; Hatty, 1989). The proneness associated with street prostitution shares several similarities with deviance-related proneness. The activities of those engaged in the sex trade on the street are high-risk activities that lend themselves to manipulation by predators of different kinds. Street sex workers are accessible and easy targets who cannot afford to be too selective about their customers. Their activities are characterized by the casualness and anonymity of the encounters and the privacy in which the sexual acts are usually performed. Potential victimizers can easily rationalize their victimization because of their marginal status and the negative label attached to the sex trade. In addition, they lack social protection and have little or no access to the protective agencies, notably the police. As a result they have to rely on pimps for protection, thus increasing their susceptibility to exploitation and abuse (Fattah, 1991). One factor in particular that adds to the extreme vulnerability of prostitutes is the prevalent negative attitude most members of society hold toward those involved in the sex trade on the street. Hatty (1989) contends that the discriminatory attitude toward violence against prostitutes is especially obvious in instances in which prostitutes are killed. In such cases, prostitutes are often portrayed as expendable objects, and their deaths are considered less worthy of attention than those of non-prostitutes. In support of her contention, Hatty quotes Sir Michael Havers, the Attorney-General of Britain, who, commenting on Peter Sutcliffe's (the Yorkshire Ripper) victims, said "some were prostitutes, but perhaps the saddest part of this case is that some were not."

8. Neutralization and Desensitization as Theoretical Explanations

In 1957 Sykes and Matza developed a theory of delinquency that has as its central focus the "techniques of neutralization" delinquents use to silence their conscience and to lessen the effectiveness of social controls. They argue that much delinquency is based on what is essentially an unrecognized extension of defenses to crimes in the form of justifications for deviance that are seen as valid by the delinquent, but not by the legal system or society at large. Sykes and Matza (1957) offer five major techniques of neutralization, two of which—the denial of injury and the denial of the victim—are particularly useful in explaining violence against the socially unwanted and the socially unneeded. Fattah (1991:136) analyzed the thought processes the victimizer engages in prior to the commission of the act. He identified three interrelated mental processes: neutralization, redefinition/auto-legitimization, and desensitization. Neutralization often has the victimizer as its focus and its main purpose is to enable him/her to remove the moral and cultural barriers that stand in the way of the victimizing act. The process neutralizes the mechanisms of formal and informal social control and makes it possible to overcome the moral inhibitions and inner restraints that he/she has internalized through the process of socialization. The second process, redefinition/auto-legitimization, has the victimization act as its focus. Here the main purpose is to mentally redefine, rationalize, and justify the behavior. Through this redefinition the act is stripped of its delinquent, illegal, and immoral character. The rationalization and justification make it possible to commit the act while avoiding self-condemnation and the condemnation of others and without tarnishing the victimizer's self-image. The third process, desensitization, has the prospective victim as its focus. Its aim is to desensitize the victimizer against the pain and suffering the act will inflict upon the victim, thus making it possible to commit the act without experiencing guilt feelings or cognitive dissonance. The first process renders the victimization possible by paving the way and removing the moral obstacles that could hinder its commission. The second allows the perpetrator to commit a horrendous act of violence while maintaining his self-image intact. The third enables the victimizer to kill, hurt, injure, or seriously harm the victim without suffering guilt feelings or experiencing bad conscience. It is easy to see how these three pre-victimization processes apply to violence against those who have been excluded, condemned, denigrated, marginalized, devalued, and stigmatized by society. Negative and disparaging social attitudes provide handy rationalizations and justifications that the delinquent cleverly uses to mentally prepare himself for the act. The techniques of neutralization, of auto-legitimization and of desensitization are learned. Either the global culture or the delinquent's subculture provides the rationalizations that are needed to overcome his antiviolence inhibitions. Goode (1969) points out that as part of the socialization toward degrees of violence we acquire a range of rationalizations that justify our own lapses into physical aggressiveness. He notes that few people are so deprived intellectually as to be unable to create a moral or ethical justification for their assault on another. He also insists that most of the rationalizations the delinquent uses are neither cynical nor morally obtuse. The redefinition/auto-legitimization relies almost entirely on social and cultural definitions of which acts of violence are justified and which ones are unacceptable, what forms of violence are tolerated and which are condemned, what groups are fair game, are culturally legitimate targets and which ones are taboo. Social exclusion and social stigmatization serve as powerful tools in the desensitization process. The condemnation and denigration of an ostracized group acts as an anesthetic on the victimizer's conscience. It has a strong desensitizing effect that allows potential victimizers to cast themselves in the role of the judge, or worse still in the role of executioner, and to perpetrate horrific acts of violence against powerless and helpless victims with the same aloofness and lack of emotion that characterize the hangman. By blaming the victim and by denying the injury, the victimizers are able to rid themselves entirely of any compassion for that victim and of any sense of personal culpability. As Sykes and Matza (1957:253) point out: "The injury, it may be claimed, is not really an injury; rather, it is a form of rightful retaliation or punishment. By a subtle Alchemy, the delinquent moves himself into the position of an avenger, and the victim is transformed into a wrongdoer."

IV. DESIDERATA

1. The Need for Research

As repeatedly mentioned throughout this chapter, research on violence against the socially unneeded and the socially unwanted is conspicuous by its absence. And while violence in general has been one of the most popular research topics in the social sciences, violence against expendable groups has been, for some reason, largely neglected, overlooked or ignored. Empirical research on the various aspects of this specific form of violence, along the lines highlighted in this chapter, is therefore badly and urgently needed. There is a great need for quantitative, and above all for qualitative, studies to gather the necessary empirical data and to provide the factual knowledge indispensable for developing theoretical explanations and models that would guide social and criminal justice policy in dealing with this highly troubling phenomenon. However, as also pointed out, there are several conceptual and methodological hurdles that need to be overcome before solid empirical research could be undertaken to tackle this thorny and complex area of violence research. The issues and the questions that need to be addressed by the desired research have already been highlighted throughout the text and there is no need, therefore, to repeat them here. Suffice to say that this particular area remains largely a virgin territory that offers great opportunities for original, exciting, and challenging research.

2. The Need for Theory

Traditional explanations of violence, whether using the perpetrator's biological make-up or his psychopathology as the major explanatory variables, are woefully inadequate in explaining violence against the socially expendable. As violence against the socially unneeded substantially differs in its basic nature and its dynamics from other conventional and common forms of violence, it needs its own specific theoretical explanations. But as mentioned earlier, a theory (or just a theoretical model) of violence against unwanted, unneeded, and expendable groups has yet to be formulated. This task, however, will have to await the findings of the research outlined above. Such a theory or an explanatory model will have to incorporate a large number of variables and borrow several insights from existing theories of victimization. It also has to include several important dimensions in addition to motives and social attitudes. It has to pay a great deal of attention to the processes through which groups are defined as unneeded and expendable, are ostracized and socially excluded, are debased and vilified, are labeled and stigmatized. It has to examine the proneness and vulnerability that inevitably result from social denigration and social condemnation, and analyze how certain groups end up being perceived as fair game and as culturally legitimate targets. Those are but some of the elements that need to form the basis of a successful explanatory theory.

3. The Need for Social and Attitudinal Change

If violence against socially expendable groups has its roots in the negative social attitudes and the prejudices held against those groups, and if violence is encouraged or promoted by the stigmatizing labeling and the social exclusion of those groups, then the only effective remedy is to change the attitudes and the processes that lead to this form of violence. And here lies the main difficulty. Changing entrenched and deeply anchored social attitudes, countering widely held cultural beliefs, fighting widespread biases and prejudices is a formidable challenge. The process is a very slow one and success is far from guaranteed. Attitudes such as anti-Semitism have been particularly resistant to change and have not been eradicated despite persistent and relentless efforts that started immediately after the end of the Second World War. Other attempts to promote tolerance of deviance, acceptance of ethnic and religious minorities, integration of dissenting and alienated groups have not been very successful. And although significant strides have been made in the fight against sexism, there has not been much progress in the way of eliminating racism, religious fanaticism, ageism, homophobia, to mention but a few.

V. PREVENTION

Although the popular saying maintains that "an ounce of prevention is better than a pound of cure," the major emphasis of criminal justice policy in most countries continues to be on punishment rather than prevention. Such a misplaced emphasis might have been understandable at a time when we did not know better, when it was naively thought that punishment, particularly harsh punishment, is essential for special and general prevention. But thanks to an abundance of research on deterrence, conducted in recent decades (Fattah, 1976), we now know that crime and violence rates, in a given society, increase or decrease for reasons that have nothing to do with the sentences meted out by the criminal courts or the general level of sanctions in that society. This realization should alert us to the need to rethink our obsession with punishment and to devote more attention and resources to the laudable and more positive goal of prevention. Prevention, however, is not an easy task. Violence is a complex and multifaceted phenomenon. Its roots can be traced to the structural and attitudinal make-up of society. Its reduction and its prevention usually require radical and sweeping social changes that may take quite a long time to materialize and to yield the desired results. Violence against the socially unwanted, the socially unneeded and the socially expendable is particularly difficult to prevent because it is often brought about by dominant social and cultural values, attitudes and stereotypes. Another reason is that the criminal justice system which is erroneously viewed by many as the protective shield against violence in society is totally ineffective when it comes to curbing the incidence of violence against the socially expendable. As mentioned above, quite often, members of those groups are victims of violence committed directly or indirectly by the government and its agents who perceive them as dangerous, threatening, or merely troublesome. In such instances, those in the criminal justice system are, most of the time, directly involved in the acts of repression and thus cannot be relied upon to protect the victims or the potential targets against the abuses of power by their political masters. This is not to say that nothing can be done to prevent violence against those powerless and helpless groups. Prevention may be difficult but not impossible. One of the major problems is the great diversity of the groups that fit the description of the socially unwanted, unneeded and expendable. Another problem, mentioned earlier, is the often hidden and insidious nature of the violence against those groups and the victimization they suffer. A policy of prevention will have to target the risk factors and the vulnerability factors that have been previously outlined. As violence against those groups finds its roots in the negative social attitudes, the prejudices, the biases that are held against them, it is essential to do everything possible to bring about a significant change in those attitudes. And as social exclusion is an extremely important risk factor, it is equally important to try to avoid at any cost the devaluation, the stigmatization, the marginalization, and ostracizing of social groups that inevitably lead to their exclusion and hence to their designation as "culturally legitimate victims" or "socially acceptable targets." Promoting social integration, accepting diversity, tolerating deviance, correcting erroneous stereotypes, using education from an early age to deal with the biases and the prejudices that are widely held, can go a long way toward the reduction of the incidence of violence against some of society's most powerless, most helpless, and most vulnerable members. But general and special prevention goes hand in hand. Thus, while these should be the basic elements of a general preventive policy targeting violence against the socially expendable, there are more concrete preventive measures that could be implemented without waiting for the long-term changes to take place. One of these immediate measures could be aimed at providing better protection to members of high-risk groups, thus reducing their vulnerability and discouraging their victimization. One example of such measures is to ensure careful and systematic monitoring of institutions, psychiatric hospitals, orphanages, nursing homes and other total institutions where members of vulnerable groups are frequently victimized. Legislative reforms are necessary and desirable. Neither their role nor their impact should however be overestimated. Their effect is more symbolic than real. It is the message that the law sends, rather than the actual impact it has, that may help in the long run to change social attitudes and thus reduce the chances of victimization against those who are devalued, degraded, vilified, and debased by the culture. Needless to say, national legislation is ineffective in preventing violence by the governments against their political opponents and those whom they define as subversive, dangerous, or merely troublesome. Legislation can also have little effect in curbing the motives for many forms of violence. Attempts to legislate against hate have not been, and are unlikely to be, very successful. It would be naïve to think or to expect criminal or social legislation to be effective in eliminating other negative emotions or in changing undesirable social attitudes. Violent victimization of deviants and criminals continues, not because of the lack of legislation prohibiting it, but despite such legislation. Racist attacks persist despite all the efforts to stem the tide of racism and to promote racial and religious tolerance. This is not to depreciate or belittle the role of legislation but simply to plead for realism and for a heightened awareness of the limitations of the law in the field of prevention. It is a call to seriously and critically examine what the law, particularly the criminal law, can and cannot achieve. It is also meant to raise consciousness about the complexity of the task and the strenuous efforts that are needed to achieve success in what is, without doubt, one of the most difficult areas of antiviolence research, policy and action.

REFERENCES

Academy of Criminal Justice Sciences (Mark S. Hamm). (1994). *Hate Crime: International Perspectives on Causes and Control*. Anderson Publications: Highlands Heights, Cincinnati.

Ahlf, Ernst-Heinrich. (1994). Alte Menschen als Opfer von Gewaltkriminalität. *Zeitschrift für Gerontologie*, 27, 289–298.

Altschiller, Donald. (1998). *Hate Crimes: A Reference Handbook.* Santa Barbara: ABC-Clio, Incorporated.

Bartollas, Clemens, Stuart J. Miller, & Simon Dinitz. (1975). Staff Exploitation of Inmates: The Paradox of Institutional Control. In Israel Drapkin & Emilio C. Viano (Eds.), *Victimology: A New Focus: Vol. V. Exploiters and Exploited.* Lexington: D. C. Heath.

Bartollas, Clemens, Stuart J. Miller, & Simon Dinitz. (1976). Organizational Processing and Inmate Victimization in a Juvenile Training School. In Emilio C. Viano (Ed.), *Victims and Society* (pp. 569–578). Washington: Visage Press.

Baurmann, Michael C. (1981). Alte Menschen als (Kriminalitäts-) Opfer. *Zeitschrift für Gerontologie, 14,* 245–258.

Boyer, Debra K., & Jennifer James. (1983). Prostitutes as Victims. In Donal E. J. MacNamara & Andrew Karmen (Eds.), *Deviants: Victims or Victimizers?* (pp. 109–146). Beverly Hills: Sage Publications.

Blumenthal, Monica D., Robert L. Kahn, Frank M. Andrews, & Kendra B. Head. (1972). *Justifying Violence: Attitudes of American Men.* Ann Arbor: Institute for Social Research.

Brillon, Yves. (1987). *Victimization and Fear of Crime among the Elderly.* Toronto: Butterworths.

Campbell, Bruce B., & Arthur Brenner. (2000). *Death Squads in Global Perspective: Murder with Deniability.* New York: St. Martin's Press.

Cohen, Stanley. (1972). *Folk Devils and Moral Panics—The Creation of the Mods and Rockers.* London: MacGibbon and Kee Ltd.

Cohen, Lawrence, & Felson, Marcus. (1979). Social Change and Crime Rates: A Routine Activity Approach. *American Sociological Review, 44,* 588–608.

Conklin, John. (1975). *The Impact of Crime.* New York: Collier-Macmillan.

Edwards, Susan S. M. (1984). *Women on Trial.* Manchester: Manchester University Press.

Erbe, Nancy. (1984). Prostitutes: Victims of Men's Exploitation and Abuse. *Law and Inequality: Journal of Theory and Practice, 2,* 607–623.

Fattah, Ezzat A. (1971). *La Victime Est-elle Coupable?* Montréal: Presses de l'Université de Montréal.

Fattah, Ezzat A. (1976). *Fear of Punishment. Report to the Law Reform Commission of Canada.* Ottawa: Ministry of Supply and Services.

Fattah, Ezzat A. (1991). *Understanding Criminal Victimization—An Introduction to Theoretical Victimology.* Scarborough: Prentice Hall.

Fattah, Ezzat A. (1993). *Internationaler Forschungsstand zum Problem Gewalt gegen alte Menschen und Folgen von Opfererfahrung.* Hannover: KFN Forschungsberichte.

Fattah, Ezzat A. (1994). The Criminalization of Social Problems: Child Abuse as a Case Study. In Simon Verdun-Jones & Monique Layton (Eds.), *Mental Health Law and Practice through the Life Cycle* (pp. 7–15). Burnaby: Simon Fraser University.

Fattah, Ezzat A. (1997). *Criminology: Past, Present and Future.* London: Macmillan, New York: St. Martin's Press.

Fattah, Ezzat A., & Vincent F. Sacco. (1989). *Crime and Victimization of the Elderly.* New York: Springer Verlag.

Fritz, Kathlyn. (1971). A Cross-Cultural Study of Witchcraft and Legal Control. *Yale Sociology Journal, 1,* 1–22.

Goode, William J. (1969). Violence between Intimates. In Donald J. Mulvihill, Melvin M. Tumin & Lynn Curtis (Eds.), *Crimes of Violence. A Staff Report to the National Commission on the Causes and Prevention of Violence* (pp. 941–977). Washington: Superintendent of Documents.

Harry, Joseph. (1982). Derivative Deviance: The Cases of Extortion, Fag-Bashing and Shakedown of Gay Men. *Criminology, 19,* 546–641.

Hatty, Suzanne E. (1989). Violence Against Prostitute Women. *Australian Journal of Social Issues, 24*(4), 235–248.

Herek, Gregory M., & Kevin T. Berrill. (Eds.) (1992). *Hate Crimes: Confronting Violence Against Lesbians and Gay Men.* Newburg Park: Sage.

Hindelang, Michael J., Michael R. Gottfredson, & James Garofalo. (1978). *Victims of Personal Crime: An Empirical Foundation for a Theory of Personal Victimization.* Cambridge: Balinger.

Huggins, Martha K. (1991). *Vigilantism and the State in Modern Latin America.* New York: Praeger.

Human Rights Watch Staff, Brazil. (1994). *Final Justice: Police and Death Squad Homicides of Adolescents in Brazil.* Human Rights Watch.

Humphreys, Laud. (1970). *Tearoom Trade.* Chicago: Aldine Publishing Company.

Kelly, Robert J. (1983). Addicts and Alcoholics as Victims. In Donal E. J. MacNamara & Andrew Karmen (Eds.), *Deviants: Victims or Victimizers?* (pp. 49–76). Beverly Hills: Sage Publications.

Kennedy, Leslie W., & Robert A. Silverman. (1990). The Elderly Victim of Homicide: An Application of the Routine Activities Approach. *The Sociological Quarterly, 31*(2), 307–319.

Kreuzer, Arthur, & Michael Hürlimann. (Eds.) (1992). *Alte Menschen als Täter und Opfer*. Freiburg: Lambertus.

MacNamara, Donal E. J. (1983). Prisoners as Victimizers and Victims. In Donal E. J. MacNamara & Andrew Karmen (Eds.), *Deviants: Victims or Victimizers?* (pp. 219–236). Beverly Hills: Sage Publications.

Maghan, Jess, & Edward Sagarin. (1983). The Homosexual as a Crime Victim. In Donal E. J. MacNamara & Andrew Karmen (Eds.), *Deviants: Victims or Victimizers?* (pp. 147–162). Beverly Hills: Sage Publications.

Marwick, Max. (1964). Witchcraft as a Social Strain Gauge. *Australian Journal of Science, 26*, 263–268.

Midelfort, H. C. Erik. (1972). *Witch-Hunting in Southwestern Germany, 1562–1684: The Social and Intellectual Foundations*. Stanford: Stanford University Press.

Perkins, Roberta, & Garry Bennett. (1985). *Being a Prostitute*. Sydney: George Allen and Unwin.

Phillips, L. Richard. (1986). Theoretical Explanations of Elder Abuse: Competing Hypotheses and Unresolved Issues. In Karl A. Pillemer & Rosalie S. Wolf (Eds.), *Elder Abuse: Conflict in the Family* (pp. 197–217). Dover: Auburn House.

Reiss, Albert, Jr. (1980). Victim Proneness in Repeat Victimization by Type of Crime. In Stephen E. Fienberg & Albert J. Reiss, Jr. (Eds.), *Indicators of Crime and Criminal Justice: Quantitative Studies*. Washington: U.S. Department of Justice, Bureau of Justice Statistics.

Rummel, Rudolph Joseph. (1994). *Death by Government: Genocide and Mass Murder since 1900*. New Brunswick: Transaction Publishers.

Sacco, Vincent F., & Holly Johnson. (1990). *Patterns of Criminal Victimization in Canada*, General Social Survey Analysis Series, No. 2. Ottawa: Statistics Canada.

Sacco, Vincent F. (1993). Conceptualizing Elder Abuse: Implications for Research and Theory. In Wolfgang Bilsky, Christian Pfeiffer & Peter Wetzels (Eds.), *Fear of Crime and Criminal Victimization* (pp. 71–82). Stuttgart: F. Enke Verlag.

Sagarin, Edward, & Donal E. J. MacNamara. (1975). The Homosexual as a Crime Victim. In Israel Drapkin & Emilio C. Viano (Eds.), *Victimology: A New Focus: Vol. V. Exploiters and Exploited: The Dynamics of Victimization*. Lexington: D.C. Heath & Co.

Sluka, Jeffrey A. (Ed.) (1999). *Death Squad: The Anthropology of State Terror*. Philadelphia: University of Pennsylvania Press.

Spitzer, Steven. (1975). Toward a Marxian Theory of Deviance. *Social Problems, 22*, 638–651.

Sykes, Gresham, & David Matza. (1957). Techniques of Neutralization: A Theory of Delinquency. *American Sociological Review, 22*, 664–670.

Weis, Kurt, & Sandra Borges. (1973). Victimology and Rape: The Case of the Legitimate Victim. *Issues in Criminology, 8*(2), 71–115.

Williams, Christopher. (1993). *Victims in Violence—Street Children and Abuse of Power*. Bristol: Norah Fry Research Center, University of Bristol (Manuscript, 23 pp.).

Zahn, Margaret A., & Mark Bencivengo. (1974). Violent Death: A Comparison between Drug-Users and Non Drug-Users? *Addictive Diseases: An International Journal, 1*(3), 283–296.

Zahn, Margaret A., & Mark Bencivengo. (1975). Murder in a Drug-Using Population. In Marc Riedel & Terry Thornberry (Eds.), *Crime and Delinquency: Dimensions of Deviance* (pp. 48–58). New York: Praeger.

CHAPTER II-4.5

Violence against Ethnic and Religious Minorities

Tore Bjørgo

I. INTRODUCTION

The present article will address acts of violence in which victims are selected because of their ethnic, racial, religious, cultural, or national origin. These victims are attacked not in their capacities as individuals, but as representatives of such minority groups. There is widespread consensus among researchers that this is the defining core of the phenomenon, but no agreement on how to delimit it or what label to use. This form of violence is described as racist violence, xenophobic violence, hate crime, or right-wing extremist violence.

Until the early 1990s, there was very little academic research published on racist violence or hate crimes. However, especially from 1993 onwards, a large number of substantial empirical studies were published, partly as a response to the worldwide attention to the problem caused by the wave of xenophobic violence in Germany and several other countries.

This study does not focus on racism, xenophobia, and right-wing extremism as such, but on the violent dimensions of these phenomena. However, all these notions are "essentially contested concepts," as they involve strong elements of moral and political evaluation. With regard to both ideological and violent dimensions, *racism, right-wing extremism, xenophobia,* and *hate crime* are to a large extent overlapping—but not completely interchangeable—categories. Different labels, covering different aspects, are used in academic and political discourse in various countries. "Racist violence" and "racial violence" (the latter often meaning "interracial violence") are predominant labels in British discourse. In Germany and the Scandinavian countries, a common label is *"fremdenfeindliche Gewalt"* / *"fremmedfiendtlig vold,"* which means xenophobic or, literally, "foreigner-hostile violence." In North America, "hate crime" is the predominant label in academic and legal

---

W. Heitmeyer and J. Hagan (eds.), *International Handbook of Violence Research*, 785–799.
© 2003 Kluwer Academic Publishers. Printed in the Netherlands.

discourse. These various labels are not synonymous, as they tend to restrict or expand the scope of the phenomenon in different ways and place the emphasis on different aspects, whether on the characteristics of the victims, or on the perpetrators with their motives and ideologies.

Racism, xenophobia, and hatred directed against specific categories of people are central elements in most forms of *right-wing extremism*, but there are also forms of right-wing extremism where racism or xenophobia does not necessarily play any role (cf. Sprinzak, 1995). Heitmeyer (1987:13–16) describes the basic elements of a right-wing extremist orientation as 1) an ideology of considering inequality between people as a nature-given principle and 2) an acceptance of violence as a legitimate form of political action. However, many researchers find it somewhat arbitrary to place this phenomenon on the one end of a right–left dichotomy, preferring other labels.

Racism is no less disputed as a concept and label. Some definitions of racism emphasize that it is an ideology of inequality based on certain phenotypical and/or genetic characteristics of human beings, in other words an ideology of superior and inferior races (cf. Miles, 1989:3). Others see racism as a practice of social exclusion that does not necessarily require a conscious or explicit ideology of racial differences or superiority (Barker, 1981).

Xenophobia (literally "fear of foreigners") does not require an ideological theory but is merely a reflection of people's negative "gut" feelings, prejudices, or aggression towards groups that appear strange and different. Thus, xenophobia is affective rather than cognitive. In its practical expressions, however, xenophobia can hardly be distinguished from other varieties of racism.

The notion of *hate crime* (McDevitt/Williamson in this volume) does not refer to any specific target group but rather to the more general tendency to give symbolic status to various categories of "others" that represent something or someone to hate. In American discourse, the label "hate crime" is therefore not restricted only to criminal acts against various ethnic minorities, but is also applied to violence against homosexuals, women, and others.

This general applicability of the concept represents both its theoretical attractiveness, but also its limitation. The heterogeneity of the concept of hate crime tends to widen the scope and soften its focus so much that specific features of the phenomenon may get lost, for example, by considering rape in general as a hate crime against women. There is a tendency that an increasing number of social categories invoke the concept of hate crime in order to enjoy special protection through hate crime legislation.

None of these labels are entirely satisfactory, as they may be too narrow and situational, or imply too much ideological consciousness from the offenders, or they may be too wide and unfocused. However, given different historical, demographic, and political contexts in different countries, it does not seem possible to find one unifying concept which would cover all the relevant aspects in the field we want to discuss in this chapter.

II. THEORETICAL APPROACHES AND EMPIRICAL RESULTS

Research on racist and xenophobic violence represents a variety of perspectives and methodologies. The present article will seek to sort out some general approaches by describing them according to their respective focus on agenda setting, victims, offenders, and incidents. It should be noted that these approaches are not mutually exclusive, in the sense that a specific study may incorporate several of these perspectives within a unified analytic framework.

1. Agenda Perspectives

One of the most fundamental questions to ask is how and why violence against ethnic and religious minorities becomes an issue on the agenda of research and policy-making. These processes have far-reaching consequences for the ways the issue is defined as a problem, how it is addressed by researchers, and for the kinds of solutions implemented in public policy. The mere fact that there is a considerable amount of violence directed against specific ethnic and religious minorities in a society does not necessarily mean that this is recognized as a problem that requires research or special intervention (cf. Lloyd, 1993; Witte, 1996; Bowling, 1998). Such violence may be considered as isolated incidents, as part of a general problem of law and order, as a youth problem, as a conflict between more or less equal parties or gangs, or even as understandable acts of frustration by locals who feel swamped by unwanted foreigners. It may also be recognized as a problem of racism and xenophobia, calling for more specific political responses. Research may serve a role in bringing the issue to the public agenda, and it may influence the ways in which the problem is conceptualized and understood. However, research may also simply reflect the fact that the issue has already been put on the political agenda and that the government demonstrates its will to address the problem by means of funding research.

In a comparative study of state responses to racist violence in Britain, France, and the Netherlands, Rob Witte (1996) has demonstrated that the issue typically goes through several stages on its way to the formal political agenda. It may at first be recognized as an individual problem. Later, it may be seen as a social problem when different groups in society perceive it as such and call for action. When racist violence has been recognized as a problem that needs to be dealt with by the state, it has entered the public agenda—although state responses may still be mainly of a symbolic nature. And finally, racist violence becomes a topic on the formal agenda only when it receives priority as an issue for active and serious state action.

However, at each of these stages of recognition, the responses from the state may take including or excluding forms in relation to the victimized groups. Including recognition means that the victimized groups are considered as an inextricable part of society, and offered protection by the state, for example through strengthened legislation against racially motivated violence, victim support, etc. Excluding recognition means that the state does not consider the victimized population groups as an integral part of society, and that the problem of violence against these groups of "foreigners" may be solved, for example by tightened immigration policies in order to reduce the presence of these groups (Witte, 1996).

It is also of importance for *whom* violence is considered a problem and who brings the issue to the political agenda. In Britain, it was first and foremost as a result of pressure from minority groups and allied antiracist activists that the issue of racist violence was gradually introduced to the public and formal agenda of the state. This political struggle served to emphasize the victim approach in what eventually became a state policy against racial violence and harassment. Studies of racial attacks in Britain also emerged from a broader concern about the position of the victim in the criminal justice system, and have remained almost entirely in that terrain until very recently (Bowling, 1998:303).

This contrasts remarkably with the situation in most other European countries where victimological perspectives were almost absent when the issue of racist or xenophobic violence entered the public agenda during the early 1990s. The waves of attacks against "foreigners" taking place in Germany from 1991 onwards scandalized Germany internationally because it was seen against the background of the country's historic legacy of National Socialism. The question was raised—are the Nazis back in Germany? The recent reunification of Germany and the frustrations among (in particular) large sections of East German youths with unfulfilled expectations also provided important aspects of the background when the issue hit the agenda. The targeted populations of asylum seekers and immigrants were hotly discussed, but largely in terms of representing a problem which to a degree caused or provoked the violence used against them. The serious scope of the problem of xenophobic violence and the strong responses to it (as well as allocated funding for research) resulted in a large output of academic studies in Germany on the phenomenon, in particular from 1993 onwards (e.g., Otto & Merten, 1993; Willems et al., 1993; Jäger & Link, 1993; Heitmeyer et al., 1995). Attention, however, was overwhelmingly focused on the youths involved on the perpetrator side, and on the responses from society. Victimological perspectives were almost entirely absent from the German studies.

The same has been the case in Scandinavian studies of racist or xenophobic violence. During the 1990s, Sweden has seen a number of serious violent incidents (including murders of immigrants and homosexuals), as well as a large output of Nazi and anti-Semitic propaganda from militant groups. However, what in particular brought the issue to the top of the formal agenda of the state in 1999 was a series of shootings, bombings, and serious threats directed against police officers, journalists, labor unionists, and politicians. Nazi activists were found guilty of several of these attacks and killings. For the first time, violent Nazi activities were considered a threat to national security and not only a problem for immigrant groups, gays, and antiracist activists. In addition to legal and police action, large emphasis was placed on information campaigns on the Holocaust directed towards youths in order to counter anti-Semitic and Nazi propaganda, and the "White Power" music industry in Sweden. Research in the field has focused mainly on the racist underground movement and its violent ideologies and practices (Lööw, 1993, 1995, 1998; Bjørgo, 1993, 1997), and on anti-Semitism and Holocaust denial (Bruchfeld, 1996; Lange et al., 1997).

In Norway, the Nazi dimensions of the problem were less predominant. In several local communities there were recurring incidents of violence against immigrants and asylum seekers committed mainly by xenophobic youth gangs. Usually, these gangs had little ideology and organization initially, but they often developed ties to more organized ultranationalist or Nazi groups and networks. Significantly, these recurring violent incidents in some cases badly stigmatized the local communities in which the events took place—in particular when local authorities were seen to be too passive. However, local action plans with participation from all relevant agencies, community organizations, and guidance from researchers, showed highly successful outcomes in several cases. This local community approach provided models for other communities with similar problems. The interaction between social scientists and local communities and agencies has also contributed to developing a tradition of applied research in the field of racist groups and violence, and community responses to such problems informed by research (Eidheim, 1993; Carlsson, 1995; Bjørgo, 1997; Bjørgo & Carlsson, 1999).

2. Victim-Oriented Perspectives

This approach focuses on the effects of violence and harassment on victims, and a number of related issues, such as the degree to which various ethnic groups are likely to become exposed to violence and harassment, and measures to support victims of racism. This victimological perspective is often linked with a critical analysis of government and police responses to racist violence.

Victimization may involve both physical injuries to the body and a mental violation of the person's integrity (Corbin, 1977). Frequently, the mental wounds are more lasting and serious to the victim than the physical ones. It is a characteristic of racist violence and harassment that the victim is attacked because of what he or she is and cannot change—color of skin, culture, and origin. To the victim, the purpose of the harassment and violence is often obvious—to humiliate, denigrate, frighten, and demonstrate "white supremacy" over inferior foreigners or minorities.

Britain is the country where the victim-oriented approach on racial violence has been most developed—in research agendas as well as in public statistics on violence, and in policies and responses from various agencies. In Britain, organizations and groups representing victims and their interests, such as Victim Support, local councils for racial equality, and minority organizations, are actively involved in assisting victims in reporting their complaints to the police. The government decision to start registering racial attacks was actually a result of pressure from organizations representing victim and minority interests, a fact which seems to have influenced both police practice and the statistics in significant ways.

Benjamin Bowling's (1998) study describes and analyzes how violent racism became an issue for policy, policing, and research in Britain. He shows how, during the last few decades, victimology and race relations have become the dominant paradigms for interpretation and response. Britain has experienced more than 1,000 years of immigration of ethnic and religious minorities. Antiforeigner riots and massacres, and policies of expulsion have been recurring themes through the centuries. A common response to the number of explicitly antiblack riots taking place in Britain from 1919 onwards was the claim that these black people were themselves the cause of the violence inflicted against them. Correspondingly, the solution to the problem that was advocated by the authorities was the removal and repatriation of the victims. Bowling shows how it took decades of political mobilization by immigrant and antiracist organizations in alliance with some mainstream politicians to redefine the problem and the solutions. The turning point came around 1980, when several reports (Bethnal Green and Stepney Trades Council, 1978; Institute of Race Relations, 1979; Home Office, 1981) documented that racial attacks were a genuine social problem, and that they should be interpreted within the framework of racism and racial relations (see also Gordon, 1993; Witte, 1996). Since then, the victimological perspective and the paradigm of race relations have dominated British academic and political discourse on the problem of violence against ethnic minorities. A large number of public and private institutions have been set up to document and respond to cases of racial violence and harassment.

One important aspect in British research on racist violence is a very strong critique of the ways the police have handled such incidents, and of the relationship of the police to minority populations in general. Bowling (1998:69–70) provides an overview of the various criticisms which have been made against the police and documented in a number of reports in Britain: failure to provide protection to minority communities; not preventing racist offences; refusing to recognize racial dimensions or motivation of violence; playing down attacks and not treating racial harassment seriously; redefining the problem; hostile treatment of victims; treating the victim as aggressor or as the problem; arresting the victim rather than the offender; unwillingness to investigate; unequal treatment and harassment of ethnic communities; racially discriminatory policing—just to mention some of the documented complaints. In fact, many of the British studies have concluded that racism within the police is very much part of the problem of violent racism (see also IRR, 1979; Gordon, 1983, 1993; Hesse et al., 1992).

One of the strengths of the British tradition of research on racist violence is its emphasis on not only spectacular incidents of violence but also on the less dramatic forms of harassment experienced on a more frequent basis by many minority members (Virdee, 1995; Bowling, 1998). Bowling argues that racist victimization should be seen as a process rather than as discrete incidents, as they are often understood to be by the police or in surveys. Even if each separate incident may not be very serious, the aggregate of many experiences of harassment may have an extra traumatizing effect on the victims. Attacks on other persons of the same ethnic category is often experienced in terms of "it could just as well have been myself," causing fear and trauma to others and not only to the direct victim. Racist violence and harassment is typically directed against particular persons and groups in a pattern of repeat victimization.

According to the British Crime Survey, four percent of the crime victims were victims of 44 per cent of the total crime. In recent years, British researchers have focused on the phenomenon of repeat victimization both as a problem and a key to more effective crime prevention (Farrell & Pease, 1993). Some minority groups and individuals are obviously victims of a disproportionate amount of violence, vandalism, and other forms of harassment—although different levels of victimization experienced by ethnic minorities are not necessarily primarily due to ethnicity. Racial motivation may rather be considered as an additional, compounding factor to other factors that make economically deprived minorities—statistically speaking—more exposed to violence (FitzGerald & Hale, 1996). Focusing research on the repeat character of such violence and harassment would in any case be worthwhile.

Violence against religious "others" is a recurring trait in human history. In modern Western societies, two particular religious minorities have frequently been singled out as targets of hatred and aggression: Jews and Muslims. In popular resentment against these groups, religious notions have often been mixed with more general racism and xenophobia. The anti-Jewish variety has produced series of small and large-scale pogroms (Klier & Lambrosa, 1992), culminating in Nazi Germany's industrial extermination of the Jews (Hilberg, 1985; Dawidowicz, 1987; Bauman, 1989; Longerich in this volume). To fuel and justify such hatred and violence, political regimes, religious bodies, and anti-Semitic groups have disseminated conspiracy theories claiming that the Jews were secretly plotting for world domination. The notorious "Protocols of the Elders of Zion" remains the prototype of such conspiracy theories. It was a forgery constructed by anti-Semitic circles in Tsarist Russia, and used by the Nazi movement in Germany to justify "the war against the Jews" (cf. Cohn, 1967). It is still being disseminated both in the Muslim world and by present-day neo-Nazis and other anti-Semitic movements. In several European countries, anti-Semitic propaganda and violence have clearly been on the rise during the 1990s.

With extensive Muslim immigration into western Europe over several decades, these minorities have become a main target of xenophobic violence. A great deal of resentment among the majority population focuses on immigrants competing with them over scarce resources. However, specific anti-Islamic arguments are also used to promote hatred and violence. Allegations of "a Muslim invasion to establish Islamic domination in Europe" show close parallels to anti-Jewish conspiracy theories (cf. Bjørgo, 1995b).

However, the most persecuted minority group in several southeastern European countries in particular is clearly the Roma (or Gypsies). Partly marginalized and discriminated against by the majority populations, and partly trying to live a lifestyle that does not fit easily into modern society, Roma individuals and communities have been victimized through attacks by Nazi skinheads as well as by virtual pogroms committed by seemingly ordinary neighbors (Reemtsma, 1993; Chabanov, 1998; Haller, 1998).

3. Offender-Oriented Perspectives

These perspectives generally focus on the violent actors and the factors that influence their violent or racist behavior. Obviously, when the issue is labeled "hate crime," "xenophobic," "racially motivated," or "right-wing extremist" violence, the motivations of the actors are by definition of particular relevance. There is an assumption that the act is guided by some kind of ideology, belief, prejudice, or bias that makes the offender disposed to direct his or her aggression against certain categories of people. Some studies take this for granted, others undertake empirical investigations of the explanations given by arrested offenders of their reasons and motives for carrying out their violent acts (Willems et al., 1993; Heitmeyer & Müller, 1995), or they make assumptions on motives based on circumstantial indicators. The latter is the case with most statistics on racist violence or hate crimes, which normally include large numbers of incidents where no suspects are apprehended (cf. Tegsten & Knutsson, 1996 for a discussion).

However, the relation between behavior and motivation is complex. One of the main empirical findings in the field of racist violence is that the offenders tend to have mixed motives (Willems et al., 1993; Bjørgo, 1993, 1997; Lööw, 1995). Although the violent acts may have elements of xenophobia or political considerations, such as opposition to current immigration policy, there are typically also distinct nonpolitical motives involved. Frequently, offenders explain that they carried out the violent act in order to show off to their friends, to prove their courage, toughness, or loyalty to the group, to avenge prior provocative acts committed by their victims, or just for the thrill of it. In many cases, these nonpolitical motives seemed to have been more decisive than the political ones, which often serve more as posterior justifications. However, if they are arrested, perpetrators are usually instructed by their lawyers to emphasize nonpolitical reasons and play down possible racist motives as these may be considered aggravating circumstances in the apportioning of the sentence. When researchers make use of police and court data, this should be taken into consideration.

One way to sort out these mixed motivations in racist violence is to make an analytic distinction between racism as expression and racism as motivation. Some acts that express racism—such as when a youth gang smashes the windows of an immigrant shop and paints swastikas—may have other driving forces or motivations than racism (achieving status in group, ego-publicity, etc.). As expression or behavior, this racism may be serious and real, and experienced as racism by the victims. It is obviously appropriate that society responds firmly and strongly against such racist expressions. However, to find methods for modifying and/or preventing the racist behavior of these offenders, one should also investigate the actual motivation behind such behavior. Only a minority among perpetrators of racist violence seem to be motivated primarily by racist convictions or ideologies (cf. Willems et al., 1993:190–207, 1995). For this minority, racism is both the motivation and the expression.

Heitmeyer's chapter in this volume describes in more detail the general characteristics of perpetrators of racist or xenophobic violence in terms of age, sex, class background, etc. However, xenophobic violence is a typical group crime. In the majority of cases (60–90 percent), there were two or more perpetrators (cf. Willems, 1995:168; Levin & McDevitt, 1993:16–18). In many of the remaining cases, there was a more or less approving audience of mates present when the violent act was carried out, or a lone perpetrator carried out the act in order to impress mates who were not *physically* present (cf. Bjørgo, 1997:114–121). Thus, group dynamic processes obviously play an important role in the developments leading up to the violent act. Understanding these processes is of great importance for developing measures for prevention and intervention.

Focusing on the motivations and backgrounds of individual violent offenders, and the groups and gangs to which they belong, is a micro-level approach, favored by many researchers in the field. Other research traditions focus more on macro-level explanations of xenophobic and racist behavior. Wilhelm Heitmeyer (1987) and Wilhelm Heitmeyer et al. (1995 and this volume) is an influential representative of this approach. However, one problem in such structure-oriented explanations is how to explain adequately why factors operating on the youth population as a whole (or at least large sections of it) only affect a few of them sufficiently to actually make them opt for violent xenophobia (Willems, 1995:174–177; Kühnel, 1998:151). This requires a more actor-oriented perspective, focusing on both groups and individuals, and their opportunity structures and motives for action.

A large body of research has focused on the ideological dimensions of groups and movements that promote and justify violence against ethnic and religious minorities. Such studies are often based on a combination of documentary research, interviews with activists, and, sometimes, participant observation in group settings. The analytical focus is often on how ideology influences group action and the behavior of individual group members. However, this influence may also work in the other direction: individual values and worldviews also change as a consequence of involvement with racist groups (Aho, 1994). Typically, young people, for example, do not join a racist skinhead group because they are racists; they gradually adopt racist views because they have become part of a racist group. In most cases, they join because the group fulfills some of their basic social and psychological needs (Bjørgo, 1997:193ff).

Racial ideologies promote violence to defend the white race against "foreign blood," whereas some nationalist ideologies endorse violence to defend the unity of the nation against cultural mixing. Common to most varieties of these ideologies is a tendency to develop a double set of enemy images—an external threat consisting of Jews, Muslims, or other ethnic or religious "aliens," and internal traitors who are seen as collaborators with the enemy (Sprinzak, 1995; Bjørgo, 1995a, b).

One striking difference between American and European racist movements is the much stronger role played by religious conceptions in some American versions of racist ideology (cf. Aho, 1990, 1994; Barkun, 1994; Kaplan, 1995, 1997). However, it is also a characteristic of globalization that such ideological ideas and violent role models travel between countries and continents and are adopted and modified by local movements (cf. Kaplan and Weinberg, 1999; Kaplan & Bjørgo, 1998). A prime example is how American racists adopted traditional anti-Semitic ideas from Europe and transformed them into a highly violence-oriented doctrine of the "Zionist Occupation Government" (ZOG) and "racial war", which was later taken up by European neo-Nazis. In this process, the ZOG ideology inherited from American racism an antigovernment hostility not previously common in European right-wing extremism, which traditionally was in favor of a strong state. This new version of anti-Semitism claims that the Jews now have a firm grip on the apparatus of power. Politicians, the police, and the media are seen as subservient tools of the Jews and therefore legitimate targets of violence (cf. Barkun, 1994; Bjørgo, 1993; Lööw, 1998; Fangen, 1998).

4. Incident-Oriented Perspectives

Both qualitative and quantitative methodologies may use incidents of violence as their starting point—although they then proceed in very different directions. Anthropologists and sociologists have applied the extended case method to describe and analyze the context in which a violent event took place. This includes the perspectives of the various actors involved and the social, historical, cultural, and economic circumstances that may provide insights into what happened. The responses to the violent event and the consequences and meanings it had to the individuals, groups and communities involved are also important issues. Eidheim (1993) provides a good example of this approach.

Most statistics on racist or xenophobic violence do not focus on one or a few key events, but rather try to quantify patterns in a large number of violent incidents. The immediate purpose is to describe the extent and seriousness of this violence, and whether it is increasing, decreasing, or changing in character. Some statistics also provide data on more specific patterns regarding the characteristics of perpetrators and victims/targets, methods of violence, which laws were violated, the time of day/week, type of location, etc. Obviously, such statistics are of direct practical value to policymakers, the police and other agencies, and to political activists. However, to researchers it is also of great interest to use such data to understand the factors and circumstances that cause increases and decreases in the level of racist and xenophobic violence. These may relate to macro factors such as modernization processes, changes in unemployment rates or immigration, or new legislation. Such data may also be used to evaluate the effects of interventions and changes in policy at the national or local levels.

During the 1990s, data on incidents of racist or xenophobic violence have become available from a number of European countries. The mere availability of such figures represents an irresistible temptation to researchers of comparative politics or violence. One example is a study by Ruud Koopmans (1996). He wanted to clarify the correlates and causes of the rise in extreme right-wing and racist violence and to examine its relation to electoral support for racist parties by comparing data from several western European countries. Although he duly notes the problems involved in comparing incident data sets based on different definitions and collection procedures, he nevertheless sets out to do this. The available figures showed high levels of recorded violent incidents per million inhabitants in England/Wales, Switzerland, and Germany (and when counting only serious forms of violence, Sweden), and relatively low levels in the Netherlands and France (as well as in Norway and Denmark for serious violence). The main finding was that "contrary to common wisdom, [...] the level of violence tends to be low where extreme right-wing and racist parties are strong and vice versa" (Koopmans, 1996:185).

However, the available data cannot in any way support such an interpretation, and are not suitable for cross-national comparative analysis. Different operational definitions and data collection procedures account for most of the enormous differences in the numbers of incidents of racist violence recorded in various countries. The extremes prove this: whereas the annual number of incidents of racial violence and harassment recorded in England and Wales from 1990 to 1996 has been in the range 6,000–12,000, official French statistics report only 10–76 cases annually of racist or anti-Semitic violence (Home Office, 1997; La Documentation Française, 1998). There is no reason to believe that these huge differences in any way reflect the real situations regarding racist violence on the English and French streets (cf. Lloyd, 1993).

In statistics covering England and Wales from 1991 onwards, a racially motivated incident is defined as "any incident in which it appears to the reporting or investigating officer that the complaint involves an element of racial motivation; or any incident which includes an allegation of racial motivation *made by any person*" (my emphasis, Home Office, 1997). This is an extremely inclusive definition by any standard. It is the result of political pressure from minority activists and antiracists to make official definitions and data collection procedures in England and Wales increasingly more victim-oriented, and geared towards reducing the well-known tendencies of underreporting and under-recording racist violence.

On the other hand, official French statistics of racist violence are extremely restrictive. Aggression against physical persons is only registered when it causes an absence from work for at least eight days, with the exception of acts of a particularly grave character (La Documentation Française, 1998:26). This probably also reflects the inability of minority populations in France to influence the political agenda and the official definitions that determine what constitutes a racist attack—quite unlike the situation in Britain. If the French definitions had been applied in Britain, and the British definition and data collection system had been used in France, the resulting figures would probably have shown an opposite pattern—low in Britain and high in France.

Statistics on incidents of racist or xenophobic violence are usually based on either police data or survey data. The first type, crimes reported to the police and recorded as having a (possible) racist or xenophobic dimension, involves several "filters" which tend to reduce the number of registered incidents and, as a result, lead to an underestimation of the problem. Immigrants and minority members are probably less likely than other citizens to report relevant cases to the police due to a lower level of confidence in the police. For a number of reasons (ranging from purely legal considerations to racist prejudices), police officers are also often reluctant to consider an incident as having a racist dimension or motivation—even when there would be good reasons to do so.

In studies from Great Britain and the Netherlands, the estimated level of underreporting of racist violence and harassment varies from 1:4 to 1:40—based on the discrepancy between the number of cases reported to and recorded by the police, and the estimated number of "experienced" cases in the minority population as a whole (Donselaar, 1995:211; Virdee, 1995:12–25; Maung & Mirrlees-Black, 1994:21). However, underreporting is likely to be much higher with regard to such incidents as threats, harassment, and less serious assaults than would be the case with arson, bombings, and/or grievous bodily harm. The level of underreporting of racist violence is also closely related to minority groups' degree of trust in the police. If the police itself is considered to be a perpetrator of racist violence and harassment, victims are less likely to go to the police with their complaint. The fact that most victims do not report cases of racist violence against them to the police is an essential aspect of the problem of racist victimization as such—just as for rape, domestic violence, and incest.

At present, only four European countries—Germany, Sweden, the Netherlands, and England/Wales— have established systems worth speaking of for monitoring racial or xenophobic violence. The European Union has also set up a monitoring center on racism and xenophobia in Vienna. One of its tasks is to promote better registration of violence. Canada and an increasing number of states in the USA have also established systems for monitoring hate crimes. However, it will still take a long time before any statistics suitable for meaningful cross-country comparison become available.

III. DESIDERATA

One main controversy regarding violence against ethnic and religious minorities concerns its interpretation. Various interest groups, institutions, and researchers dispute how these violent incidents are to be labeled, described, and counted. In turn, this leads to different understandings of the dimensions and political significance of the problem. Some maintain that it is the subjective experience of the victim that there was a racist dimension involved which in principle determines whether an incident should be considered as racial. Others emphasize that information about the circumstances surrounding the incident and the motives of the perpetrators often show that the violent act was caused by other factors and conflicts, and that the ethnic factor may be irrelevant to the perpetrators.

Although some minority groups are more exposed to violence than the general population, this is not necessarily due to racism or xenophobia. The difference may often be explained by other socioeconomic or situational factors. However, even in contexts where minority populations are *not* more exposed than others, those minority individuals who actually become victims tend to interpret the incident as an expression of racism (Junger, 1990). Whether this represents a tendency to overestimate the element of racism is not always obvious. Some cases of violence and harassment that include racial abuse may happen anyway, but the racial dimension may give the harassment an additional, humiliating dimension.

On the basis of studies from different countries, many researchers maintain that, in contrast to violence in general, racial violence is more likely to involve excessive brutality, multiple perpetrators, serial attacks, greater psychological trauma to victims, and a higher risk of retaliatory attacks (e.g., Bowling, 1998; B. Levin, 1999; J. Levin & McDevitt, 1993). On the other hand, Jacobs and Potter (1998) have analyzed statistical data on hate crime in the USA and find no evidence supporting the belief that hate-instigated violence is on the rise. They claim that the notion of hate crime and the development of hate crime legislation arises from the identity politics movements which have gained strength among various minority groups during the last decades. They argue that singling out particular social categories for special protection through hate crime legislation is counterproductive, and may even exacerbate perceived differences rather than create harmony.

New research in the field would in any case benefit from paying closer attention to the interpretive dimensions, and to the political and social circumstances and interests that influence these processes.

British activists and researchers, guided by victimological and racial relations principles, have successfully challenged the widespread tendency to explain violence against ethnic minorities by their mere presence—the view that they are themselves the cause of the violence against them. However, if this resistance to "blaming the victim" becomes a doctrine, it may represent a taboo against addressing some very real problems and issues. Serious crime and violence committed by individuals and groups within minority populations do often cause strong—and understandable—resentment and anger among the general population. This anger only acquires a racist dimension if it is generalized towards the entire minority population—blaming all of them for the wrongdoings committed by a few, and in particular if this is used as a justification for violence against arbitrary minority representatives.

However, if concerns for political correctness prevent researchers from addressing crime and violence by minority members and gangs as a factor in the processes of breeding resentment and xenophobia, this will limit knowledge and understanding. Racism between different ethnic minorities, or racially motivated hatred and violence against the white majority population are also issues that have largely been ignored by researchers in many countries due to the fear of being accused of racism, or that racist activists may exploit their findings. However, by tabooing such unpleasant issues, these problems are left to political demagogues alone, who may gain credibility for their biased interpretations.

IV. APPROACHES TO PREVENTION

As a response to the new concern about racist and xenophobic violence, a number of national and European action plans have been implemented during the 1990s. Most of these have focused on antiracist manifestations and declarations, and on changing attitudes towards racism and violence through various campaigns. It is hard to identify any effects from these efforts in terms of reducing xenophobic violence.

A more promising approach would be to focus on the social mechanisms and processes involved in generating and maintaining violence. Processes at the levels of individual, group, or community are more available for intervention than macro-level factors such as de-industrialization, globalization, and individuation processes. Research has shown that most perpetrators of such violence tend to have a mixture of political and nonpolitical motives (the latter often more decisive), that these acts are usually committed by youth groups, and that responses from peers and the social surroundings heavily influence whether such offences will be repeated or not. By addressing only the possible political dimensions, for example, through antiracist manifestations, one may inadvertently reinforce other undesirable processes, such as strengthening the group's image, status, and coherence. Thus, action that may make perfect sense from the perspective of a political struggle against racism may turn out to be counterproductive from a crime prevention point of view.

Preventive strategies should address several situational factors, such as reducing the social rewards for aggressive and xenophobic behavior, and increasing the social costs. Both traditional police work based on surveillance and investigation of violent crimes, and more inventive methods of preventive policing in close collaboration with other agencies have been effective in dissolving racist youth groups in Norway (Bjørgo & Carlsson, 1999:201–220).

At the local level, problems of racist and xenophobic violence are often associated with specific youth gangs or extremist groups. Promoting disengagement from violent groups and reinforcing inherent tendencies towards group disintegration are often effective strategies for reducing violence (cf. Bjørgo, 1997:193ff). General knowledge about group processes, combined with an adequate analysis of the local situation, will improve the probability of success. The characteristics of the groups in question, for example, age composition and employment situation, are highly relevant for the selection of prevention and intervention strategies.

Legislation against expressions of discrimination and racially motivated violence, and a more active implementation of such laws may have a deterring effect on potential offenders, and at least provide a legal framework for intervention and protection of victims. In general, measures to strengthen the position of (potential) victims and reducing their vulnerability are likely to have a positive effect in terms of reducing violence, harassment, and its negative impact. This may require training programs for the police and other relevant agencies. If the police and other public agencies take firm action against offenders and in support of victims, this is also likely to reduce the possibility that members of the victimized populations take violent revenge.

Since the problem of violence against minorities is so complex in terms of motivations, causes, and consequences, no single remedy or agency is likely to achieve substantial results alone. When several agencies, informed by a shared and adequate analysis of the problem, address the problem together combining their different approaches, the odds are much better for reducing such violence and harassment, rehabilitating offenders, and improving the lives of victimized groups.

REFERENCES

Aho, James A. (1990). *The Politics of Righteousness: Idaho Christian Patriotism*. Seattle: University of Washington Press.

Aho, James A. (1994). *This Thing of Darkness: A Sociology of the Enemy*. Seattle/London: University of Washington Press.

Barker, Martin. (1981). *The New Racism*. London: Junction Books.

Barkun, Michael. (1994). *Religion and the Racist Right: The Origins of the Christian Identity Movement*. Chapel Hill, London: The University of North Carolina Press.

Bauman, Zygmunt. (1989). *Modernity and the Holocaust*. London: Routledge.

Bethnal Green and Stepney Trades Council. (1978). *Blood on the Streets: A Report on Racial Attacks in East London*. London: The Council.

Bjørgo, Tore. (1993). Militant Neo-Nazism in Sweden. *Terrorism and Political Violence*, 5(3), 28–57.

Bjørgo, Tore (Ed.) (1995a). *Terror from the Extreme Right*. London: Frank Cass.

Bjørgo, Tore. (1995b). Extreme Nationalism and Violent Discourses in Scandinavia: 'The Resistance', 'Traitors', and 'Foreign Invaders'. In Tore Bjørgo (Ed.), *Terror from the Extreme Right* (pp. 182–220). London: Frank Cass.

Bjørgo, Tore. (1997). *Racist and Right-Wing Violence in Scandinavia: Patterns, Perpetrators, and Responses*. Oslo: Tano Aschehoug.

Bjørgo, Tore, & Yngve Carlsson. (1999). *Vold, rasisme og ungdomsgjenger: Forebygging og bekjempelse*. Oslo: Tano Aschehoug.

Bowling, Benjamin. (1998). *Violent Racism: Victimization, Policing and Social Context*. Oxford: Clarendon Press.

Bruchfeld, Stéphane. (1996). *Förnekandet av förintelsen: Nynazistiske historieförfalskning efter Auschwitz*. Stockholm: Svenska komittén mot antisemitism.

Carlsson, Yngve. (1995). *Aksjonsplan Brumunddal—ga den resultater? Bekjempelse av fremmedfiendtlig vold i lokalsamfunnet*. Oslo: NIBR-rapport 1995:13).

Chabanov, Serguei. (1998). *Skinhead Violence Targeting Roma in Yugoslavia*. Roma Rights, Spring. [http://errc.org/rr_spr1998/noteb1.shtml]

Cohn, Norman. (1967). *Warrant for Genocide: The Myth of the Jewish World Conspiracy and the Protocols of Zion*. London: Eyre & Spottiswoode.

Corbin, J. R. (1977). An Anthropological Perspective on Violence. *International Journal of Environmental Studies*, 10, 107–111.

Dawidowicz, Lucy S. (1987). *The War Against the Jews: 1933–1945*. Harmondsworth: Penguin.

Donselaar, Jaap van. (1995). *De staat paraat: De bestrijding van extreem-rechts in West-Europa*. Den Haag: Babylon-De Geus.

Eidheim, Frøydis. (1993). *Hva har skjedd i Brumunddal: Lokalsamfunnet i møte med de fremmede og seg selv.* Oslo: NIBR rapport, 1993:20

Fangen, Katrine. (1998). Living out our Ethnic Instincts: Ideological Beliefs Among Right-Wing Activists in Norway. In Jeffrey Kaplan & Tore Bjørgo, *Nation and Race: The Developing Euro-American Racist Subculture* (pp. 202–230). Boston: Northeastern University Press.

Farrell, Graham, & Ken Pease. (1993). *Once Bitten, Twice Bitten: Repeat Victimisation and Its Implications for Crime Prevention. Crime Prevention Unit Series Paper No. 46.* London: Home Office Police Department.

FitzGerald, Marian, & Chris Hale. (1996). *Ethnic Minorities, Victimisation and Racial Harassment. Home Office Research Study No. 154.* London: HMSO.

Gordon, Paul. (1983). *White Law: Racism in the Police, Courts, and Prisons.* London: Pluto Press.

Gordon, Paul. (1993). The Police and Racist Violence in Britain. In Tore Bjørgo & Rob Witte (Eds.), *Racist Violence in Europe* (pp. 167–178). Basingstoke: Macmillan.

Haller, István. (1998). *Lynching Is not a Crime: Mob Violence Against Roma in Post-Ceaușescu Romania.* Roma Rights, Spring. [http://errc.org/rr_spr1998/noteb2.shtml]

Heitmeyer, Wilhelm. (1987). *Rechtsextremistische Orientierungen bei Jugendlichen.* Weinheim, München: Juventa Verlag.

Heitmeyer, Wilhelm, Birgit Collmann, Jutta Conrads, Ingo Matuschek, Dietmar Kraul, Wolfgang Kühnel, Renate Möller, & Matthias Ulbrich-Herrmann. (1995). *Gewalt. Schattenseiten der Individualisierung bei Jugendlichen aus unterschiedlichen Milieus.* Weinheim, München: Juventa Verlag.

Heitmeyer, Wilhelm, & Joachim Müller. (1995). *Fremdenfeindliche Gewalt junger Menschen. Biographische Hintergründe, soziale Situationskontexte und die Bedeutung strafrechtlicher Sanktionen.* Bonn: Forum Verlag.

Hesse, Barnor, Dhanwant K. Rai, Christine Bennett, & Paul McGilchrist. (1992). *Beneath the Surface: Racial Harassment.* Aldershot: Avebury.

Hilberg, Raul. (1985). *The Destruction of the European Jews.* New York: Holmes & Meier Publishing.

Home Office. (1981). *Racial Attacks: Report of a Home Office Study.* London: Home Office.

Home Office. (1997). *Racial Violence and Harassment: A Consultation Document.* London: Home Office.

Institute of Race Relations. (1979). *Police Against Black People. Evidence Submitted to the Royal Commission on Criminal Procedure.* London: IRR.

Jacobs, James B., & Kimberly Potter. (1998). *Hate Crimes: Criminal Law & Identity Politics.* New York, Oxford: Oxford University Press.

Jäger, Sigfried, & Jürgen Link (Eds.) (1993). *Die Vierte Gewalt. Rassismus und die Medien.* Duisburg: DISS.

Junger, Marianne. (1990). Intergroup Bullying and Racial Harassment in the Netherlands. *Sociology and Social Research, 74*(2), 65–72.

Kaplan, Jeffrey. (1995). Right Wing Violence in North America. In Tore Bjørgo (Ed.), *Terror from the Extreme Right* (pp. 44–95). London: Frank Cass.

Kaplan, Jeffrey. (1997). *Radical Religion in America: Millenarian Movements from the Far Right to the Children of Noah.* Syracuse: Syracuse University Press.

Kaplan, Jeffrey, & Tore Bjørgo (Eds.) (1998). *Nation and Race: The Developing Euro-American Racist Subculture.* Boston: Northeastern University Press.

Kaplan, Jeffrey, & Leonard Weinberg. (1999). *The Emergence of a Euro-American Radical Right.* New Brunswick: Rutgers University Press.

Klier, John D., & Shlomo Lambrosa. (1992). *Pogroms: Anti-Jewish Violence in Modern Russian History.* Cambridge University Press.

Koopmans, Ruud. (1996). Explaining the Rise of Racist and Extreme Right Violence in Western Europe: Grievances or Opportunities? *European Journal of Political Research, 30,* 185–216.

Kühnel, Wolfgang. (1998). Hitler's Grandchildren? The Reemergence of a Right-Wing Social Movement in Germany. In Jeffrey Kaplan & Tore Bjørgo (Eds.), *Nation and Race: The Developing Euro-American Racist Subculture* (pp. 148–174). Boston: Northeastern University Press.

La Documentation Française. (1998). *La lutte ontre le racisme et la xénophobie: Exclusion et Droits de l'homme.* Paris: La Documentation Française.

Lange, Anders, Heléne Lööw, Stéphane Bruchfeld, & Ebba Hedlund. (1997). *Utsatthet för etniskt och politiskt relaterat hot mm, spridning av rasistisk och antirasistisk propaganda samt attityder till demokrati bland skolelever.* Stockholm: CEIFO/BRÅ rapport.

Levin, Brian. (1999). Hate Crimes: Worse by Definition. *Journal of Contemporary Criminal Justice, 15*(1), 6–21.

Levin, Jack, & Jack McDevitt. (1993). *Hate Crimes: The Rising Tide of Bigotry and Bloodshed.* New York and London: Plenum Press.

Lloyd, Cathie. (1993). Racist Violence and Anti-racist Reactions: A View of France. In Tore Bjørgo & Rob Witte (Eds.), *Racist Violence in Europe* (pp. 207–220). Basingstoke: Macmillan.

Lööw, Heléne. (1993). The Cult of Violence—The Swedish Racist Counter-Culture. In Tore Bjørgo & Rob Witte (Eds.), *Racist Violence in Europe* (pp. 62–79). Basingstoke: Macmillan.

Lööw, Heléne. (1995). Racist Violence and Criminal Behaviour in Sweden: Myths and Realities. *Terrorism and Political Violence*, 7(1), 119–161.

Lööw, Heléne. (1998). Nazismen i Sverige 1980–1997). *Den racistiske undergroundrörelsen: musiken, myterna, riterna.* Stockholm: Ordfront.

Maung, Natalie Aye, & Catriora Mirrlees-Black. (1994). *Racially Motivated Crime: A British Crime Survey Analysis.* London: Home Office Research and Planning Unit, Paper 82.

Miles, Robert. (1989). *Racism.* London, New York: Routledge.

Otto, Hans-Uwe, & Roland Merten (Eds.) (1993). *Rechtsradikale Gewalt im vereinigten Deutschland: Jugend im gesellschaftlichen Umbruch.* Opladen: Leske & Budrich.

Reemtsma, Katrin. (1993). Between Freedom and Persecution: Roma in Romania. In Tore Bjørgo & Rob Witte (Eds.), *Racist Violence in Europe* (pp. 194–206). Houndsmills, Basingstoke, London: Macmillan.

Sprinzak, Ehud. (1995). Right-Wing Terrorism in a Comparative Perspective: The Case of Split Delegitimization. In Tore Bjørgo (Ed.), *Terror from the Extreme Right* (pp. 17–43). London: Frank Cass.

Tegsten, Anders, & Johannes Knutsson. (1996). *Rutin för analys av brottsdata med främlingsfiendtliga och politiska inslag. Preliminary report.* Stockholm: SÄPO.

Virdee, Satnam. (1995). *Racial Violence and Harassment.* London: Policy Studies Institute.

Willems, Helmut, Roland Eckert, Stefanie Würtz, & Linda Steinmetz. (1993). *Fremdenfeindliche Gewalt: Eine Analyse von Täterstrukturen und Eskalationsprozessen.* Opladen: Leske & Budrich.

Willems, Helmut. (1995). Development, Patterns and Causes of Violence Against Foreigners in Germany: Social and Biographical Characteristics of Perpetrators and the Process of Escalation. In Tore Bjørgo (Ed.), *Terror from the Extreme Right* (pp. 162–181). London: Frank Cass.

Witte, Rob. (1996). *Racist Violence and the State: A Comparative Analysis of Britain, France, and the Netherlands.* Essex: Addison, Wesley and Longman.

CHAPTER II-4.6

Hate Crimes Directed at Gay, Lesbian, Bisexual and Transgendered Victims

JACK MCDEVITT[1] AND JENNIFER WILLIAMSON

I. INTRODUCTION

1. International Perspective

Globally, violent crimes committed against groups of people based on their "difference" have been occurring since biblical times. Perhaps the most egregious example to date has been the Holocaust, where six million Jews were killed by the Nazis and their collaborators. Other groups were also targeted by the Nazis, including 10,000 to 15,000 homosexual men who were arrested between 1933 and 1945 and deported to concentration camps (Hamm 1994; Comstock 1991). It is alarming to note that the voices of xenophobia and racism are once again reverberating throughout German society. "The resentment associated with hate crimes can be clearly seen in a sweeping new wave of violence—the largest spree of racial violence in Germany since the early days of Nazism" (Levin and McDevitt 1993a:149).

Much is being written about the surges of bias-motivated violence throughout Europe, and to some extent in South America and the Middle East. Most of this research is focusing on racial, ethnic and religious-based discrimination and violence. Little research or documentation on antigay/lesbian violence exists outside the United States. As recently as 1994, the United States was the only country in which crimes against persons based on

---

[1] The authors wish to thank Jennifer Balboni, Senior Research Associate, and Marion Sullivan for helpful comments and assistance on an earlier draft of this paper.

W. Heitmeyer and J. Hagan (eds.), *International Handbook of Violence Research*, 801–815.
© 2003 Kluwer Academic Publishers. Printed in the Netherlands.

sexual orientation (or perceived sexual orientation) was included in the definition of hate crimes (Hamm, 1994). This is not to say that antihomosexual crimes do not occur. In fact, Amnesty International (AI) has identified a growing need for the inclusion of lesbians and gay men in their protection of human rights world-wide. AI has documented cases of human rights abuses based on sexual orientation spanning the globe, including torture and ill-treatment, imprisonment, inadequate and unfair legal proceedings, and in some countries even the death penalty (Amnesty International, 1994). Examples include Columbian "death squads" routinely targeting gay men and transvestites in an effort to promote "social cleansing;" the death penalty as an available punishment for homosexual acts in Iran; and the decapitation and mutilation of a local politician in Brazil following the public announcement of his bisexuality (Amnesty International, 1994).

These examples make it very clear that inclusion in hate crime definitions are a long way off in many countries, and in fact may not be a particularly relevant social issue for those gays and lesbians living in countries where their very existence is considered illegal and immoral, and punishable by imprisonment, torture, or death.

2. Hate Crime Terminology

The term "hate crime" can be traced to a debate in the United States House of Representatives in 1985 on legislation sponsored by John Conyers, Barbara Kennelly and Mario Baiggi that eventually became the Hate Crime Statistics Act (Wang, 1999; Jacobs & Potter, 1998). This term has become the most common way to describe this behavior, widely used by most United States policy makers and human rights advocates. The term hate crime however does a rather poor job of characterizing the behavior in question. While hate is a characteristic of most of the crimes in question, hate is also a motivation for many other crimes that are not motivated by bias. For example, if a person kills his business partner over the ownership of the company, the offender may hate the victim but very few people would call that crime a hate crime. A better description for these crimes may be "bias" crimes because bias is one element that differentiates this crime from others. However, it seems that at least in the United States the term "hate crime" has become so widely used by the media and by policy makers that a change to bias crime may not be possible.

II. THEORETICAL APPROACHES

Comstock utilizes Sheila Collin's focus on patriarchy to analyze and predict antigay/lesbian violence. Patriarchy is the manifestation and institutionalization of male dominance over women and children. In Collin's model of patriarchy, the Father dominates the Wife, Brother and Daughter, as well as "aliens"—marginalized outsiders such as slaves or servants. Comstock ascribes the status of "alien" to lesbians and gay men. In this way, they are to be dominated due to their position in the social order, and subsequently do not have the protection others enjoy. Young males are the population most likely to commit hate crimes, which makes sense in their patriarchal role of "Brother." These young males are seen as lashing out at those they view as "aliens," in an effort to try to live up to the gender roles (dominant and controlling) that they perceive are appropriate, given their position in the social order. This behavior is seen as accepted by patriarchal society (Comstock, 1991). Given this view, we would expect to find less antigay/lesbian violence as we move further away from patriarchy.

Steven Onken (1998) has a similar theory to explain antigay/lesbian violence. His model interconnects oppression, power, moral exclusion, and stigmatization. He postulates that heterosexist oppression, in particular, should be explored. Oppression of sexual minority people is inherent throughout the levels, dimensions, and types of antigay violence. "Oppression is an institutionalized, unequal power relationship maintained by violence or the threat of violence" (Onken, 1998). Though not identified specifically as "patriarchal," this theory supports the idea that the heterosexual majority feels morally superior, and therefore appropriately justified in oppressing the homosexual minority. This oppression is then manifested in violence or the threat of violence.

Gregory Herek supports Onken's line of thinking in his article on cultural heterosexism (Herek, 1992). He argues that hate crimes against gays and lesbians must be understood in context—that antigay violence is a logical, albeit extreme, extension of the heterosexism that pervades American society. Heterosexism is the backdrop against which antigay violence occurs. Homosexuality is demonized, and gays and lesbians are seen as sick, deviant, and/or evil. This social stigma creates the social situation where gays and lesbians can be routinely victimized.

Finally, Karl Hamner offers a social identity theory of antigay violence. Hamner (1992) states that according to social identity theory, individuals desire positive self-esteem, and that their self-esteem is tied inextricably to the way their ingroup is evaluated relative to other groups. Therefore, they will seek to increase their own self-worth by increasing the worth of their group. A common way this is achieved is through the denigration of outgroups. The outgroup in this case is comprised of gays and lesbians—an easy target in our culture. While this theory has its weaknesses, most notably problems with identifying specific ingroups, it shows promise in explaining antigay/lesbian violence.

Patriarchy, oppression, cultural heterosexism, and social identity theory are certainly not mutually exclusive. These concepts are inextricably linked, and therefore none can offer a complete theory without the others. More research needs to be done in this area in order to determine the value of each in explaining antigay violence.

III. EMPIRICAL RESULTS

In American society today, GLBT citizens have come under increasing attack. The Federal Government and many States have proposed and a few have passed legislation such as the Defense of Marriage Act. This legislation states that relationships between gay men or lesbians are less deserving of government support and public acknowledgement than similar heterosexual relationships. In 1990, when the Hate Crime Statistics Act was passed, an amendment was included that stated that the Act was not intended to in any way indicate that the family was not the center of American society. This amendment, sponsored by U.S. Senator Jesse Helms, was specifically a reaction to the inclusion of gay men and lesbians in the list of hate crime victims for whom statistics would be collected. When agencies of the Government develop and pass legislation which explicitly limits the rights of one group of individuals, they send a message to members of society that this group is less equal than other groups. This kind of legislation only supports the feelings of those homophobic individuals in our society and leads them to believe that their bigoted thoughts are shared by public officials. It is not difficult to see how this kind of legislation could be seen as empowering some hate crime offenders to feel free to act on their bigoted beliefs.

1. Universal Substitute

Due in part to society's message that this is a group that it is "OK" to hate, gay men, lesbians, bisexuals and transgendered individuals have become frequent targets for hate-motivated violence. Prior research with hate crime offenders and police officials who have investigated hate crime incidents reveals that GLBT victims are often attacked (Levin & McDevitt, 1993b) as a substitute for offenders who cannot find a suitable member of a particular group. Interviews with offenders in prior research indicates that offenders may go out intending to attack a black man, but if they can't find a "suitable" target they can always go to a gay bar and wait for a man to leave alone (Levin & McDevitt, 1993b). Gay men seem to be the universal substitute for hate crime offenders in the United States. In addition, because of messages that are pervasive in American society, often hate crime offenders are surprised when the criminal justice system reacts to their attacks on members of the GLBT community. They are often expecting police officers, prosecutors, and judges to share their bias and to consequently minimize or ignore their violence.

2. Current Characteristics of Antigay Hate Crimes

In America most of what is known nationally about the characteristics of hate crime comes from the hate crime reporting system developed and maintained by the Federal Bureau of Investigation. In 1990, Congress passed the Hate Crime Statistics Act, the first piece of National legislation that authorized the collection of information on hate crime occurring across the country. The Act focused on police agencies as the primary collection point for hate crime information. This approach has both strengths and weaknesses. By using the police as the collection point, it was believed that there would be some level of standardization around which criminal acts were identified to be hate motivated since police agencies in most part act in ways that conform to their local criminal code. Also, by using the police, it was believed that the system would identify the most serious incidents and would document those incidents that could have some additional formal legal sanctions attached. These strengths must be balanced against the problems that using the police as the primary collection agency entails. Foremost among these problems is the fact that many crimes (including many hate crimes) are not reported to the police. The reasons for this lack of reporting will be discussed later; however, at the very least it is worth noting that not all hate crimes are counted in the national data. A second limitation of the official data involves differences in reporting by local police agencies. Since this Act did not require local police agencies to participate in the system, and in the United States all national crime reporting is voluntary, many agencies still do not report, or when they do they do so only nominally by filling in a "zero" for the number of incidents (Garcia et al, 1999). In 1998, 10,730 of the approximate 17,000 law enforcement agencies in the United States participated in the national hate crime reporting program (FBI, 1998).

An additional number of limitations of the data should be noted. As mentioned above, the information only includes crimes reported to the police. Since the local police agency are the collection agent for the FBI, if a victim decided not to report this crime to the local police agency, it will never be recorded in the national statistics. This is particularly a problem if different groups of hate crime victims report at different rates. If gay hate crime victims are less likely to report hate crimes than Jewish hate crime victims for example, the national data will present a distorted picture of the relative incidence of crime for each group. It is believed by many and supported by much anecdotal evidence that gay and lesbian victims of hate crimes are less likely to report to police than other bias victims. Thus, differential rates of hate crime reporting may, in fact, be a problem for America's hate crime statistics.

Other limitations exist with national hate crime statistics. One involves the differential legal landscape with regard to gay and lesbian hate crime victims. While the Federal government has included gay and lesbian victims of hate-motivated violence as part of the national hate crime data collection system since the beginning, many States do not include gay and lesbian victims under their State hate crime statutes. This will also make the national data less reliable, since not all States will investigate attacks on gay and lesbian victims as hate crimes.

Despite these limitations, the national hate crime data collected and maintained by the FBI remains the most comprehensive set of information on hate-motivated violence available.

3. Number of GLBT Victims

In 1998, the FBI recorded information on 7,755 hate-motivated criminal incidents involving 7,489 victims. The FBI records information on twenty-one different types of bias motivation (e.g., Anti-White, Anti-Black, Anti-male-homosexual, etc.). Of the total incidents in 1998, 1,260 incidents accounting for 16.3 percent of the total were directed at victims because of their sexual orientation (FBI, 1998). For the purpose of data collection the FBI has decided to collect information on five categories of hate crimes motivated by bias toward an individual's sexual orientation, these include: Anti-Male-Homosexual, Anti-Female-Homosexual, Anti-Homosexual, Anti-Heterosexual, Anti-Bisexual. A review of the 1998 data reveals that of all the reported hate crimes based on sexual orientation, the vast majority of these hate crimes were directed against gay men (Anti-Male-Homosexual) with fully 67.5 percent of all the sexual orientation hate crimes targeting this group. While the number of attacks targeted against bisexual victims is very small (less than one percent), it is probably true that most offenders do not differentiate between gay and bisexual victims—they attack victims who they perceive to be "gay." In addition, of those cases where the gender of the victims was known, 80 percent of the victims were male. One conclusion that may be drawn from this data is that gay men are the most common targets in hate crimes motivated by bias based on the victims sexual orientation.

4. Location of GLBT-Motivated Hate Crimes

Most anti-GLBT hate crimes occur either on a street (or road) or in a residence. One-half of all anti-GLBT hate crimes (50.2 percent) occur in these two locations. This is similar to the pattern for hate crimes targeted at other victims.[2] There is one difference in terms of the location of the attacks: antigay/lesbian attacks are more likely to occur around bars or nightclubs. While overall very few of the total hate crimes reported to the FBI occur at bars or nightclubs (only 1.9 percent), more than one-third of these (36.4 percent) involve attacks on individuals who are gay or lesbian. One reason for this concentration of attacks around bars

---

[2] The exception to this is incidents motivated against religion where in 1998 only 35.7 percent occurred in the street or resident. For these crimes, a greater percentage were at the place of worship.

and nightclubs involves the offender's ability to target potential victims. If an offender or group of offenders are looking to attack a black man they could drive around until they encounter a potential victim, however if these offenders are intending to attack a gay man, they have no way of identifying who on a street is gay. They can, however, wait outside a gay bar or nightclub and assume that all who enter of leave the establishment are gay.

IV. TYPOLOGY

Prior research based on a review of Boston Police Department hate crime investigative reports found that there were at least three separate motivations for offenders who commit hate crimes: 1) crimes committed for the "thrill" or excitement of it, 2) crimes committed to "defend" some perceived turf, and 3) crimes committed as part of a broader "mission" to rid the world of evil (Levin & McDevitt, 1993a).

1. Thrill Hate Crimes

This research obtained through police investigation interviews indicated that the most common type of hate crimes were those committed simply for the thrill or excitement of the experience. These "thrill hate crimes," were frequently committed by two or more offenders and often took place in the victim's neighborhood. Offenders were predominantly white teenage males, the vast majority of whom did not know the person they were attacking. These attacks often began with simple verbal harassment and ended with the victim being assaulted by the offenders.

For example, one winter evening five white males who were bored and looking for something to do, decided to go out and, as they later told police, "start some trouble." They drove to a gay bar in the South End of Boston and waited outside. When a man left the bar alone they attacked him, hitting him with a baseball bat and eventually stabbing him. After beating and stabbing the victim, while shouting antigay epitaphs, they quickly drove out of the area and back to their home. When arrested by the Boston Police, these youth told investigators they were just having some fun (McDevitt, 1989).

One surprising finding was the extent of the violence associated with these hate offenses. While people often describe these kinds of incidents as "just kids causing trouble," the analysis of the incidents reported to the Boston Police Department indicates instead that more than one-half of the crimes were assaults. This finding directly contradicts the notion that most hate crimes are merely childish pranks. When offenders got together and went out to "hassle" a gay man, their intention was most often to beat—not berate—their victim.

These thrill hate crimes constituted about two-thirds of the cases sampled in the Boston study and raise some serious concerns. When violence directed at innocent individuals because of their sexual orientation, race, religion, or ethnicity becomes something kids do for excitement the level of civility in American society is severely challenged.

2. Defensive Hate Crimes

Defensive (sometimes called "Reactive" hate crimes) involve those incidents where the offender perceives himself as defending his turf, be it their neighborhood, workplace or campus, from "outsiders." In these crimes the offenders want to send a message to an individual, and all those who share her/his characteristics, that they are not welcome in the offenders neighborhood, workplace, college campus, etc.

As with thrill hate crimes, most defensive hate crimes that came to the attention of the Boston Police were assaults. It is interesting to note that during the investigation by the Boston Police it became clear that there were two separate types of defensive hate crimes—the first being where the victim attempts to enter the offenders turf permanently (such as a lesbian couple moving into a "straight" neighborhood), and the second being where the victim simply crosses the offender's turf. For the first group, the permanent group, many of these assaults began with threats and acts of vandalism intended to "send the message" to the victim. The assaults frequently occurred when the victim failed to "get the message" (in most cases the offender is a neighbor or co-worker). In the second group where a victim simply crosses the turf of the offenders, the vast majority of the cases involved victims who were strangers to their attackers. In most of these cases, the victim was attacked by a group of offenders.

In one example, a gay couple moved into an apartment in a Boston apartment complex. Almost immediately the couple began receiving harassing phone calls and hate mail was left in their mailbox. After being in the apartment for three months and not having reported any of the harassment they had endured, they were awoken in the middle of the night to a Molotov cocktail being thrown through their window and their home being set ablaze.

An example of a defensive hate crime in Europe is the 1991 case of two Italian workers placing a high-powered air-compression hose into a Moroccan co-worker's anus, destroying his intestines and killing him. This was motivated by anti-immigrant sentiment, based on the view that immigrants were taking jobs from Italians. Immigrants represented a perceived threat to the offender's turf—in this case their jobs and economic well-being (Levin & McDevitt, 1993a).

When defensive hate crimes were compared to thrill hate crimes in the Boston data, it was noted that gay men and lesbians were more frequently targeted in thrill attacks. While only 8 percent of the reactive hate crimes were directed at gay men or lesbians almost three times as many (22 percent) of the thrill hate crimes were directed at these victims. This may be in part because of a "substitution effect." A number of the offenders told police that they had originally gone out looking for a black or Latino person to attack but not finding any, they went to a gay bar in order to attack an individual they believe to be gay or lesbian. In addition, many gay men and lesbians have not "come out" (revealed their homosexuality) to their co-workers and/or neighbors and therefore have not yet been seen as constituting a threat or a challenge to the job or the neighborhood.

3. Mission Hate Crimes

The least common hate crime type is the "mission" hate crime. These are incidents where the offender feels he is on a mission to "rid the world of evil" as he sees it, and thereby support the white race. Among all hate crimes, mission hate crimes are extremely rare, generally between 1–10 percent of all hate crimes, but are among the most violent. Mission offenders are generally fully committed to a white supremacist ideology, and this commitment plays a major role in their life. They will attempt to recruit new members who share their ideology, and they tend to view all events through their ideological lens. For example, if a friend loses her/his job, the reason is not the friend's poor job performance but the Government's policy of allowing immigrants into this country.

In the United States, these offenders have adopted a particularly troubling philosophy termed "leaderless resistance." This philosophy was adopted after Morris Dees and the Southern Poverty Law Center successfully sued the "White Aryan Resistance" organization for contributing to the death of an Ethiopian man in Portland, Oregon (Southern Poverty Law Center, 2000). The philosophy calls for organized hate groups to promote their philosophy with a preamble that says that they do not advocate violence, while hoping that individuals who hear their ideas will go out and act violent on their own. Because of this strategy, it is more difficult to hold the leaders of these supremacist organizations liable for the actions of those who hear their message.

Evidencing their infrequency, only one "mission hate crime" was uncovered in the prior analysis of Boston cases. However, this mission hate crime was among the most violent and most serious of the incidents in our sample. The case involved four white male skinheads from a suburb located west of Boston, who had previously painted swastikas on public structures in and around their town. They had not been arrested for any of these prior incidents. The group then began to escalate the violence until one night they drove to the South End in Boston looking for gay men to bash. They approached two white males they thought to be gay and began to verbally harass them. When the victims attempted to escape, the skinheads took baseball bats from their van and beat them. Upon arresting the four offenders, Boston Police Officers discovered that their van and their homes were full of hate literature. Two members of the group had white power tattoos on their bodies. A similar example of a mission hate crime was the 1991 case of East German neo-Nazi youth pushing a Mozambican man from a moving trolley in Dresden, killing him (Levin & McDevitt, 1993a).

V. VICTIMS AND OFFENDERS

1. Victims

While the national data on hate crime collected by the FBI offers the most broad based tabulation of hate crimes in America, the data suffers from a number of significant limitations as mentioned above. The only way to acquire systematic information on other characteristics of hate crime involves looking for alternative data sources. The most broad based and recent compilation of information on hate crimes targeted to the gay, lesbian, bisexual and transgendered (GLBT) community has been produced by the New York City Gay and Lesbian Anti-Violence project as part of the national Coalition of Anti-Violence Programs (AVP). The Report compiles data from thirteen geographic areas across the United States. These areas were chosen because they meet some limited data quality standards. To be included in the AVP Report an agency must utilize a standard Case Intake/Incident Tracking Form and must have submitted information to the national project for at least three consecutive years.

This report is still subject to a number of data limitations, most importantly, reports submitted to the local antiviolence project are not subjected to the same level of scrutiny and investigation as those incidents reported to the local police agencies. For example, the staff who take the reports in each agency are not all similar—while some offices utilize full-time staff to complete victim reports other smaller offices may use part-time volunteer staff to complete these reports. Other limitations include the fact that the Anti-Violence Project (AVP) Report collects information on incidents that may not rise to the level of a crime (such as some forms of harassment), and that the AVP Report only collects aggregate reports thus limiting the utility for analysis. Even with these data limitations, the data from the AVP present one of the most comprehensive statistical pictures of gay, lesbian, bisexual and transgendered (GLBT) violence available today in the Unites States. For 1999, the report identified 1,960 incidents of anti-GLBT violence, originating in the thirteen geographic areas submitting data. The report identified 29 murders and 704 assaults that program staff found to be motivated by anti-GLBT bias.

According to the AVP Report most victims of anti-GLBT violence were white (60 percent) males (64 percent) who self-identified as being gay (87 percent). These statistics correspond to the national data where at least two-thirds of the GLBT victims were white males. It does appear from the available data that most GLBT violence is directed at gay males. This does not mean that other groups (lesbians, bisexuals and transgender folks) are not also targeted but that most offenders seem to assault gay males. Prior research in Boston indicates that GLBT victims are also among the most unlikely to have done anything to cause the attack; most were victims of unprovoked attacks by strangers.

a) SEVERITY OF THE VIOLENCE. Some commentators have argued that hate crimes targeting gay and lesbian victims are among the most violent (Herek & Berrill, 1992; Comstock, 1991). The national data from the FBI seems to support this conclusion, at least for the most violent crimes. In 1998, the FBI reported that twenty-four hate-motivated homicides or rapes were reported to the FBI (thirteen Homicides/Non-Negligent Manslaughters and eleven Forcible Rapes), one-quarter of these (25 percent) were motivated by bias toward a person's sexual orientation. This rate, more than one-quarter of the most violence incidents, could be compared to the overall rate of bias crime victimization due to sexual orientation for the same year. Overall 15.5 percent of the hate-motivated offenses were directed at individuals due to their sexual orientation. This indicates that gay and lesbian victims were almost twice as likely to be involved in the most violent hate crimes when compared to their involvement in other hate crimes. When we look at assaults (both aggravated assaults and simple assaults) we see here also that gay and lesbian victims are more frequent targets. Again, in the entire sample, victims who are targeted because of their perceived sexual orientation constituted 15.5 percent of all the hate crimes reported to the police, and when we look just at the 2,790 assaults 20.4 percent of these crimes were directed at gay and lesbian victims. This indicates that, as is the case of the most violent crimes, a slightly higher ratio of assaults involve gay and lesbian victims than would be expected from their ratio in other hate crimes.

b. VICTIM IMPACT. As mentioned above, much of the legal debate focuses on the questions of differential impact of hate crimes on victims. Specifically, do hate crimes have a differential impact on victims when compared to other similar crimes? Few studies have looked at this question. It has been suggested that GLBT hate crime victims suffer in additional ways because the crime reflects the broad based anti-GLBT feelings in the society in general and thus cause the victim to develop a sense of hopelessness (Herek & Berrill, 1992).

The Garcia et al. (1999) study takes comparable groups of bias and nonbias victims of assault from the City of Boston and compares their responses to an "Impact of Events Scale" (developed by Horowitz, Wilner, & Alvarez, 1979) distributed via a mail survey. Although the response rate was low (n=136), several findings were striking in comparing these two groups. First, although not all of the differences were statistically significant, bias crime victims reported more intense and frequent adverse psychological sequelae in each of the nineteen categories. Of these reactions, five were statistically significant, including nervousness, depression, trouble concentrating, thinking about the incident when they did not mean to, and feeling as if they did not want to live any longer. This level of intrusiveness presented as more salient for the bias victims than for the nonbias victims of assault. Similarly, bias victims were much less likely to have a prior relationship with the offender; many more bias victims perceived the attack to be an unprovoked event.

Several reasons could explain the heightened posttraumatic effects for bias victims. First, bias victims are unable to "victim blame" in the same way that other victims of violence do. For instance, a nonbias assault victim may think (after the incident) "If I just don't go to that bar anymore" or "If I don't hang out with those people I will be safe." This line of reasoning allows the victim to feel that he or she has some control over future victimization. With bias victims, they are often painfully aware that the attribute which precipitated their victimization (for the offender) is not something they can change about themselves. A gay person can not suddenly become heterosexual, nor can an African-American change the color of his/her skin. Because of these immutable characteristics, bias victims may be left with fewer coping mechanisms after the victimization. The second reason posited for the heightened sense of post event stress is that the act may have been more violent than other assaults.

Such findings support the assertion that there are significant differences in bias-motivated assault. However, these data have some serious limitations. First, the response rate is low, causing questions about representativeness of the sample. Next, the sample size of this research constrains statistical analyses delineated by motivation type (i.e., race, sexual orientation, etc.) However, this research is another brick in the growing wall of literature, which argues that bias crimes have differential—and more intrusive—effects on their victims.

In a recent analysis of more than 2,000 GLBT individuals, Herek, Gillis and Cogan found "that lesbians and gay men who experienced an assault or other person crime based on their sexual orientation within the previous five years reported significantly more symptoms of depression, traumatic stress, anxiety, and anger than their counterparts who experienced non-bias person crimes in that period or no crimes at all" (Herek et al., 1998). The authors note that experiencing a hate crime for this group promotes feeling of powerlessness and vulnerability that makes it more difficult to overcome the feelings impact of the victimization.

While no research is definitive on this point, overall the extent research appears to indicate that GLBT victims of hate crimes are more likely to experience negative consequences than victims of other types of criminal victimization.

c. REPORTING BEHAVIOR. The AVP Report documented that the majority of hate crimes incidents reported to their offices were not reported to the police (61 percent). Hate crimes targeting GLBT victims are among the crimes least likely to be reported. These victims have a number of issues to consider when deciding to report a hate crime, issues that do not enter the decision-making process of most other hate crime victims. For example, in addition to the fear of reprisals that accompany most hate crimes, that is the threat that most offenders make "if you go to the police, it will be worse for you," GLBT victims fear that they will receive reprisals from co-workers or neighbors who also harbor homophobic attitudes (NCAVP, 2000). In addition, GLBT victims who are not out to the broader community fear that by going to the police their sexual orientation will become widely known and they will suffer discrimination in employment and housing as a result (Herek & Berrill, 1992; NCAVP, 2000). Also GLBT victims have had a long history of being victims of police harassment and abuse and as such do not trust that the police will take their reports seriously (Levin & McDevitt, 1993a). Also some GLBT victims have feelings of shame and feel (incorrectly) that some actions they took may have contributed to their victimization (NCAVP, 2000).

d. REPORTING TO THE POLICE. One fear for many GLBT victims is that the police will not take their allegations seriously. The AVP report seems to provide some support for this feeling. Again, it is important to note that this information is based on the victims perception and may reflect a lack of understanding of the criminal justice system or may be at odds with the way police might interpret the same events. In nearly 10 percent of the cases where the victim attempted to report an incident to the police, the police refused to take the complaint. There may be a number of legitimate explanations for the police refusal to take the complaint including the possibility the incident was not a crime (for example anti-GLBT slurs were directed at an individual). In the United States that behavior alone does not constitute a crime because in most instances the use of racial slurs, however offensive, is protected by the First Amendment guarantee of freedom of speech. However, if legitimate victims are being turned away when they come to the police for help, that will send a chilling message to the rest of the GLBT community. In Boston the police learned that the only way to build trust with the GLBT community that would result in increased reporting would be to go out to the community and offer assistance and support. Members of the Boston Police Departments hate crimes investigation unit asked to speak at GLBT functions, they attended GLBT events and attempted to send the message that if members of that community were victimized the BPD would take their allegations seriously, the victims would be treated with respect, and the Department would conduct a professional and thorough investigation. Only after an entire year of outreach did a few victims begin to come forward to report hate crimes to the Boston Police, and after three years the number of anti-GLBT hate crimes reported to the BPD seems to have stabilized and it appears that most members of the GLBT community believe that they will receive fair and professional treatment from the Police.

2. Offenders

The AVP Report paints a picture of the offenders in these anti-GLTB hate crimes. This information is based on those cases where some information on the offender is known. In many hate crime cases nothing is known about the offender. If, for example, a rock is thrown through a gay couple's window at night, the victims may not have any idea who committed the crime. As with other information on hate crime offenders (Levin & McDevitt,

1993a), the AVP reports that the majority of hate crime offenders are young males. According to AVP victim reports, 87 percent of the perpetrators were male and 67 percent were estimated to be under thirty years old, with 43 percent estimated twenty-two years old or younger. About one-half of the offenders were reported to be white (48 percent) and almost one-quarter of the offenders were reported to be African-American. About one-third of the incidents (34 percent) involved more than one offender with a few incidents (thirty-four) involving attacks by ten or more offenders. Finally, about one-half of the incidents involved attacks by individuals who were strangers to the victim. Also in a conclusion that supports much of the literature on hate offenders to date (Levin & McDevitt, 1993a), only a very small number of incidents, less than one percent (n=17) involved offenders who were members of organized hate groups. Realizing that this data involves victims reports and the hate group membership of some offenders may not be known to the victim, these numbers still indicate that the vast majority of hate crimes are committed by offenders who have no formal hate-group affiliation.

a. WEAPONS USED. The report noted that most of these assaults involved the offender using his hands and feet to beat the victim. In those cases where a weapon was used, the most common weapon used were bats, clubs, and blunt objects used in seventy-eight assaults. Other weapons used in assaults included knives or sharp objects used in sixty assaults, firearms in forty assaults, bottles, bricks, and rocks in thirty-seven assaults. The most troubling trend in this area involves the use of firearms. In the United States, where guns are a frequent weapon of choice in certain crimes, firearms are seldom used in hate crimes. The reason for this is unclear; some have suggested that the offenders in hate crimes want to demonstrate their perceived superiority to their victims in a face to face way. In the United States over the past two years we have seen an increase in the use of firearms in hate crimes. The most serious of which involved the Benjamin Nathaniel Smith rampage in Illinois and Indiana in 1999. Where Smith, a member of the white supremacist organization the Church of the Creator, shot nine persons and killed two (Dedham, 1999). The AVP has noted a similar trend with firearm assaults increasing from thirty-five to forty between 1998 and 1999 while the total number of Anti-GLBT incidents decreased slightly from 2,017 to 1,965. While this increase is relatively small, if it continued it could mark a very dangerous change in the character of hate-motivated violence. If firearms become more popular weapons in hate-motivated violence, it could signal a serious increase in the level of violence and subsequent injury to victims. If for example, the group of youths who now wait outside a gay bar to attack a vulnerable victim with baseball bats decided to use a gun and simply drive up to that same bar and begin to shoot into it (after all, in the opinion of the attackers, anyone in that bar must be gay and thus a suitable target), the level of injury and death would escalate dramatically. The use of weapons in hate crimes is a characteristic that must be monitored closely.

b. OFFENDER MOTIVATION. Prior research has indicated that hate crime offenders commit their crimes for many different reasons (Levin & McDevitt, 1993a; Wang, 1999; Comstock, 1991; Franklin, 1998). Comstock notes that many hate crime offenders act because of their perception that their behavior is socially acceptable rather than because of deeply held feelings of bigotry (Comstock, 1991). Wang notes that holding to a prototypical image that all offenders are acting with similar levels of "animus" is not supported by the prior research or our knowledge of the complexity of human behavior (Wang, 1999).

VI. APPROACHES TO PREVENTION

There are many approaches to prevention. Advocates believe that including gays and lesbians in state and federal hate crime statutes will offer protection to victims and produce a deterrent effect among offenders. Victims will feel more comfortable in coming forward to report incidents if they are covered under these statutes. Law enforcement will then be better equipped to investigate incidents and successfully prosecute offenders. Offenders will be deterred from committing offenses due to the increased likelihood of being apprehended and prosecuted, as well as the harsher sentences they will face.

Another approach being taken at the federal and local level is to improve the training being offered for police in identification and investigation of hate crimes. In 1990 the FBI developed a model hate crime training curriculum (this curriculum was updated in 1999) designed to equip state and local police officers with the specialized skills necessary for the identification, reporting, investigation, and prosecution of hate crimes. This curriculum was created with the goal of reaching an equitable balance of instruction in law enforcement, victim assistance, and community relations. In the past twelve months alone, over 4,000 law enforcement and other professionals have received this training (Wessler, 2000).

It is critical that police officers are properly trained to deal with victims of hate crime with sensitivity and an understanding of the devastating impact these incidents have on our community. Police officers are the gatekeepers of the criminal justice system. Victims need to feel confidence in police response, or these incidents will never be reported, and therefore offenders will never be brought to justice. Training is critical to improving police response.

Perhaps the most proactive approach to prevention is the development of school programs to increase awareness in both potential victims and offenders at an early age, thus preventing the development of prejudice attitudes and violent behavior that lead to hate crimes. Children are not born with these prejudice attitudes, they are learned. It is therefore possible for parents, teachers, and law enforcement to work together to make sure children learn attitudes of tolerance and appreciation for difference. School programs have been, and continue to be developed in schools throughout the country. These programs aim to instill in children an appreciation and respect for difference, by developing empathy, conflict resolution, and critical thinking skills (Safe and Drug Free Schools, Preventing Youth Hate Crime: A Manual for Schools and Communities, U.S. Department of Education, 1998).

In 1992, Congress acted for the first time to incorporate antiprejudice initiatives in The Elementary and Secondary Education Act, the principal funding mechanism for public schools. Title IV of the Act included a specific hate crimes prevention initiative promoting curriculum development and training for teachers and administration on the cause, effects, and resolutions of hate crimes or hate-based conflicts (Wessler, 2000). This was an important first step in institutionalizing prejudice reduction as a government concern.

Perhaps the most important and effective preventive tool we have is community condemnation. A society that does not tolerate prejudice and violence can change attitudes and curb behavior. Gay rights and civil rights advocacy groups have worked to increase public awareness and put hate crimes against gays and lesbians on the social policy agenda.

These groups have fought for equal protection under the law, lobbying for legislative action at the local, state, and federal level. They have worked with the gay and lesbian community to increase awareness and reporting, in addition to providing services for victims. They have worked to hold law enforcement agencies accountable for their necessary roles and responsibilities in dealing with hate crime incidents. And they have been a driving force behind the prioritization and development of school programs aimed at preventing prejudice attitudes and violent behavior.

The larger community has supported these efforts to a point. It is now time for the entire community to come together to send the message that prejudice, intolerance, and violence will not be tolerated. In the words of Attorney General Janet Reno, "pockets of bias-related violence and intimidation remain and threaten the progress we have made. Hate crime has no place in civilized society" (Reno, 1998).

VII. RECOMMENDATIONS FOR FURTHER RESEARCH

Though antigay/lesbian violence has begun to receive national attention in the past few years, there is much to be done in terms of research. To that end, we make six specific recommendations for further research.

- Research into antigay violence has been largely concentrated in America, therefore future research should examine cultural differences in the existence and dynamics of homophobia and antigay violence. This research should identify cross-cultural patterns in antigay violence and determine if certain cultural characteristics serve to inhibit this violence.
- Additional research should be developed examining the characteristics of antigay hate crime offenders. This research should examine the role of childhood abuse, homophobia, and other forms of violence in the development of these offenders. It should also identify what factors differentiate offenders who exhibit violence from those offenders who hold homophobic attitudes but do not act on their bigotry.
- Future research should examine the ways that homophobia is transmitted by the local culture. In many societies, antigay sentiments are transmitted in both direct and indirect ways throughout the culture. Research should identify the various messages being transmitted and suggest ways to counteract these antigay messages.
- Gay, lesbian, bisexual, and transgendered victims of hate crimes suffer trauma as a result of their victimization. Future research should increase our understanding of the impact of victimization on members of this community and identify effective strategies for reducing the impact of these crimes on their victims.
- Research should be conducted regarding the most effective ways of preventing antigay violence. This research should include legal impact analysis of the deterrent effects of various legal sanctions and studies assessing the effectiveness of specific anti-hate-crime training curricula.
- Finally, in many societies members of the GLBT community have little communication with the agencies of government, particularly agencies involved with the administration of justice. Research should identify culturally appropriate outreach strategies to increase communication between GLBT community and the agencies of government.

REFERENCES

Amnesty International USA. (1994). *Breaking the Silence: Human Rights Violations Based on Sexual Orientation.* New York: Amnesty International Publications.
Comstock, Gary David. (1991). *Violence against Lesbians and Gay Men.* New York, Oxford: Columbia University Press.
Dedham, Bill. (1999. July 6). Midwest Gunman Had Engaged in Racist Acts at Two Universities. *New York Times,* Section A, p. 1, Col. 4.
Federal Bureau of Investigations. (1998). *Crime in the United States.* Washington, D.C.: United States Department of Justice.
Federal Bureau of Investigations. (1999). *Uniform Crime Reports: Hate Crime Reporting Statistics.* Washington, DC: Federal Bureau of Investigation.
Franklin, Karen. (1998). *Psychological Motivations of Hate Crime Perpetrators: Implications for Educational Interventions.* Unpublished Paper. Annual Conference of American Psychological Association.
Garcia, Luis, Jack McDevitt, Joann Gu, & Jennifer Balboni. (1999). *The Psychological and Behavioral Effects of Bias and Non-Bias-Motivated Assault.* Washington, D.C.: Final Report submitted to The National Institute of Justice.
Hamm, Mark S. (Ed.) (1994). *Hate Crime: International Perspectives on Causes and Control.* Cleveland: Anderson Publishing Company.
Hamner, Karl M. (1992). Gay-Bashing: A Social Identity Analysis of Violence against Lesbians and Gay Men. In Gregory M. Herek & Kevin T. Berrill (Eds.), *Hate Crimes: Confronting Violence against Lesbians and Gay Men* (pp. 179–190). Newbury Park: Sage.
Herek, Gregory M. (1992). Psychological Heterosexism and Anti-Gay Violence: The Social Psychology of Bigotry and Bashing. In Gregory M. Herek & Kevin T. Berrill (Eds.), *Hate Crimes: Confronting Violence against Lesbians and Gay Men* (pp. 149–169). Newbury Park: Sage.
Herek, Gregory M., & Kevin T. Berrill (Eds.) (1992). *Hate Crimes: Confronting Violence against Lesbians and Gay Men.* Newbury Park: Sage.
Herek, Gregory M., Jeanine Cogan, J. Roy Gillis, & Erick Glunt. (1998). Correlates of Internalized Homophobia in a Community Sample of Lesbians and Gay Men. *Journal of Gay and Lesbian Medical Association, 2*(1), 17–25.
Horowitz, Mardi, Nancy Wilner, & William Alvarez. (1979). Impact of Events Scale: A Measure of Subjective Stress. *Psychosomatic Medicine, 41*(3), 209–218.
Jacobs, James, & Kimberley Potter. (1998). *Hate Crimes: Criminal Law and Identity Politics.* New York: Oxford University Press.
Levin, Jack, & Jack McDevitt. (1993a). *Hate Crimes: The Rising Tide of Bigotry and Bloodshed.* New York: Plenum Press.
Levin, Jack, & Jack McDevitt. (1993b). *Hate Crimes: The Study of Offender Motivation. Report Submitted to the Center for Criminal Justice Policy Research.* Boston: Northeastern University Boston Massachusetts.
McDevitt, Jack. (1989). *Characteristics of Bias-Motivated Incidents in Boston, 1983–1989. Report Submitted to the Boston Police Department.* Boston: Northeastern University Boston Massachusetts.
National Coalition of Anti-Violence Programs (NCAVP). (2000). *Anti-Lesbian, Gay, Transgender and Bisexual Violence in 1999. Preliminary Edition 2000.* New York. [URL: http://www.tri.org/99NCAVP.pdf]
Onken, Steven J. (1998). Conceptualizing Violence against Gay, Lesbian, Bisexual, Intersexual and Transgendered People. *Journal of Gay and Lesbian Social Services, 8*(3), 5–24.
Reno, Janet. (1998). *United States Attorney, Correspondence.* Washington, D.C.: Bureau of Justice. [URL: http://www.ojp.usdoj.gov/bja/html/reno.htm]
Sloan, Lacey M., & Nora S. Gustavsson (Eds.) (1998). *Violence and Social Injustice against Lesbian, Gay and Bisexual People.* New York: The Haworth Press.
Southern Poverty Law Center. (2000). *The Intelligence Report: The Decade in Review.* Montgomery, AL: Southern Poverty Law Center Montegomery Alabama.
United States Department of Education. (1998). *Safe and Drug Free Schools, Preventing Youth Hate Crime: A Manual for Schools and Communities.* Washington, D.C.: Department of Education, U.S. Government.
Wang, Lu-In. (1999). The Complexities of 'Hate'. *Ohio State Law Journal, 60*(3), 799–900.
Wessler, Stephen. (2000). *Addressing Hate Crimes: Six Initiatives that Are Enhancing the Efforts of Criminal Justice Practitioners.* Washington, DC: United States Department of Justice.

CHAPTER II-4.7

Trauma and Violence in Children and Adolescents: A Developmental Perspective

BESSEL A. VAN DER KOLK AND ANNETTE STREECK-FISCHER

I. INTRODUCTION

Interpersonal violence is a universal element of all human societies —violence is responsible for more years of life lost than any other single cause of death in the world. Even if it does not result in death, violence causes profound, and often lasting harm to its victims. In the United States, at least 15 percent of the population report having been molested, physically attacked or raped. In the United States, men are physically assaulted more than women (11,1 percent vs. 10,3 percent), while women report higher rates of sexual assault (7,3 percent vs. 1,3 percent) (van der Kolk, 2000a). Some societies are much more violent than others. Numerous factors, discussed elsewhere in this volume, are thought to contribute to the disparities in interpersonal violence between societies; these include poverty, sharp differentiation in sex roles, a large spread in income between the highest and lowest levels of society, tolerance of violence as a way of resolving differences, and strongly held ideological convictions that broach no deviation.

Most violence in the world is committed by young men—they make up the armies of the world, the violent street gangs, they are the perpetrators of organized and unorganized crime, they engage in most of the sexual violence and they are most prone to engage in partner violence. The role of women as facilitators and transmitters of violence is still poorly understood. Though interpersonal violence is one of the biggest problems facing humanity, there remains a scarcity of solid scientific literature on effective prevention and therapeutic interventions.

Any discussion about violence in young people must consider the role of prior exposure to violence, neglect, and deprivation while growing up, as well as their posttraumatic stress reactions that result from those experiences. Abused and neglected children are consistently found to be the most vulnerable to grow up to become the perpetrators and victims of aggression against self and others (Corvo, 1997; Elliot & Briere, 1994; Briere & Runtz, 1988). However in studies of violence the issue of childhood exposure to trauma has been largely ignored. Instead, troublesome boys tend to be labeled as "conduct disordered." Family factors usually are measured in such aseptic terms as "low cohesion," "family conflict," "management problems," etc., when, in fact, the real problem often is having a history of having been physical assaulted, sexually abused, having witnessed scenes of extreme horror and despair, or having been abandoned by caring adults.

II. TRAUMA AND VIOLENCE: DEFINITIONS AND SCOPE

1. Definition

A psychological trauma is an event that both overwhelms a person's psychological and biological coping mechanisms, and that is not responded to by outside help to compensate for the inability of the organism itself to cope. Thus, trauma is not an objective event that can be universally applied to all people, but an experience that overwhelms because of the personal interpretation of the victim. The DSM IV[1] committee struggled with the issue of a precise definition, and while the majority thought that objective criteria would violate the reality that every person has his or her own individual breaking point, the DSM IV committee decided that objective criteria (the person experiences extreme horror in the face of a threat to the integrity of the self and has an extreme physiological response) were necessary to prevent indiscriminate misuse of the diagnosis of PTSD (Post Traumatic Stress Disorder) in forensic settings. One immediate problem with the official definition is that those who are most vulnerable to eventually develop PTSD in response to a trauma are those who responded to an outside threat by dissociation, i.e., by not displaying autonomic arousal and possibly no objective signs of distress.

2. The Scope of the Problem

The National Center for Child Abuse and Neglect estimates that in the United States every year 2,7 million children are physically or sexually abused, or severely neglected by their caregivers (Sedlack & Broadhurst, 1996). In 1990 the German violence commission estimated that 10 percent of children in that country (1,6 million) are severely physically abused.

Numerous studies have demonstrated a strong correlation between child abuse and subsequent violence (Lewis et al., 1989; Lewis, 1992; Wetzels, 1997). For example, Levinson and Fonagy (1998, cited in Fonagy, 1998) found that 82 percent of criminal offenders, 36 percent of psychiatric controls and 4 percent of others had been abused as children. A large number of studies has found a relationship between childhood trauma

---

[1]DSM IV: Diagnostic and Statistic Manual of Mental Disorders of the American Association of Psychiatry.

and subsequent self-destructive behavior, such as substance use, committing suicide, and engaging in self-mutilation (van der Kolk, Perry, & Herman, 1991, van der Kolk et al., 1996). In the NIMH's[2] Epidemiologic Catchment Area Study, 15 percent of abused children, 21 percent of neglected children, and 6 percent of the control group became substance abusers (Chaffin, Kelleher, & Hollenberg, 1996). The culture surrounding the acquisition and distribution of drugs, in turn, is one of the major sources of intra- and extra-familial violence.

In the field trial study used to define "Post Traumatic Stress Disorder" (PTSD) for the Diagnostic and Statistical Manual (DSM-IV) of the American Psychiatric Association, van der Kolk et. al. (1996) found that 76 percent of a large sample of people with histories of early abuse reported experiencing frequent episodes of unmodulated anger, compared with 8 percent of an adult sample without early abuse. In another study, suicide attempts occurred sixteen times more often in adolescents who met criteria for PTSD than in adolescents without trauma histories (Gianconia et al., 1995). The Adverse Child Experiences (ACE) study of 10,000 visitors to medical clinics (Felitti et al., 1998) found that persons who had grown up with intensive exposure to intrafamilial violence had four- to twelve-fold increased risk for alcoholism, drug abuse, depression, and suicide attempts.

III. FACTORS AND CONSEQUENCES OF TRAUMA

1. Trauma Disrupts Basic Regulatory and Integrative Functions

After people have been traumatized they are prone to experience states of numbing and hyperarousal, and destructiveness against themselves and others, impulsive and dangerous behavior, alterations in consciousness, amnesias, hypermnesia, dissociation, depersonalization and derealization, flashbacks and nightmares (van der Kolk et al., 1996; Putnam, 1997). When reminded of their trauma, they are vulnerable to respond with simple Pavlovian conditioning: any situation, physical sensation, physiological state, image, or sound that is (unconsciously) associated with the trauma may elicit an automatic behavioral or physiological response that reflects a return of a traumatized state: they behave as if they were involved in a catastrophe. This often leads to extreme physiological reactions, that precipitate fight (violent) or flight (dissociative) responses, and causes them to live a life dominated by expectations of a return of the trauma, causing them to remain on constant alert for a return of traumatic experiences, which causes them to overreact even to minor stresses.

Lack or loss of capacity to modulate arousal causes secondary problems with maintaining appropriate boundaries between oneself and others, difficulties negotiating mutually satisfactory resolutions to conflict, lack of understanding of the other person's point of view, and a lack of trust that people with different needs can arrive at mutually satisfactory compromises. Many traumatized children have major deficits in the inhibitory and executive functions of planning, thinking, and imagining, that depend on the proper functioning of these brain areas.

[2] NIMH: National Institute of Mental Health.

Capacities are associated with the myelinization of various parts of the frontal lobe, particularly the cingulate gyrus, the orbitofrontal and the dorsolateral prefrontal cortex (Schore, 1997; Posner, 1998). However, Raines et al. (1998) describe another group of violent traumatized boys and men, the ones who engage in systematic and planned (instrumental) violence, who shows a good functioning frontal lobe. The critical issue here appears to be whether violent boys and men engage in *emotion-focused coping*, which is the result of impulsive, uninhibited emotionality, or of *problem-focused coping* where they are able to assess the situation for what it is, and can systematically plan for revenge or advantage. This, in turn, may be a function on how their physiology is affected by the disorganizing effects of trauma, i.e., whether they react predominantly with a sympathetic response, which is prone to lead to hyperarousal and impulsivity, or parasympathetic, which induces the decreased arousal typical of feeling shut down and may be associated with predatory aggression.

Lack of capacity for emotional self-regulation is probably the most striking feature of chronically traumatized children. One of the best established findings in the area of developmental psychopathology is the powerful relation between harsh and ineffective child rearing practices and subsequent aggressive behavior problems (Lyons-Ruth, 1991). The mediating factor here is the failure of caregivers to provide a safe environment in which a child can develop a sense of predictability, belonging, and efficacy. When a child lack secure attachment, it finds ways to soothe itself which to outsiders may appear bizarre and self-destructive including head banging, rocking, or withdrawing into states of extreme apathy (Cicchetti & Toth, 1994; van der Kolk & Fisler, 1994, 1995).

The security of attachment bonds (with caregivers, peers, and teachers) affects a range of critical issues: the particular responses to acute distress; the establishment of a scheme of the world. If children are traumatized, they construct a catastrophic map of the world, in which differences and problems are not resolved by negotiation, but by violence or surrender. Thus, the security of early relations shapes a child's adaptation to subsequent environmental challenges and profoundly shape future stress regulation.

2. Attachment, Abuse and Loss of Affect Modulation

Bowlby (1969, 1973, 1984) described secure attachment as the critical buffer against becoming overwhelmed by affective arousal. This is most noticeable in very young infants, but to some degree this need for affiliation to feel psychologically and physiologically secure persists throughout life. When a baby is distressed, it seeks proximity to familiar people in order to reduce physiological arousal. While this need for safety and predictability continues throughout development, lack of an emotionally available caregiver has particularly devastating effects on young children because it has such profound effects on the maturation of the brain itself, and on the development of perception of self and others.

In order to develop a good sense of causality and to learn one's place in the world, predictability and consistency are critical. A child needs to develop a coherent schema of the world in order to learn what behaviors will result in predictable outcomes. Learning to imagine a range of options when confronted with a difficult situation allows a child to learn to formulate playing an active role in its life. This is called the development of "problem-focused coping," a predictor of efficacy later in life, and a protection against.

3. The Genesis of Self-Regulation

Newborns are equipped with sensory and motor abilities that make it possible for them to attribute causal, as well as affective, meaning to incoming information (Sanders & Giolas, 1991; Ross et al., 1991). This helps them make rapid evaluations of how intense things are and how long they can be expected to last. As long as children are unable to grasp what is going on and formulate a range of possible outcomes, they tend to go immediately from (fearful) stimulus to (fight/flight) response (Fish-Murray et al., 1986).

When children are traumatized the flight/fight response often becomes an automatic reflex to threatening or ambiguous situations, including situations that are intrinsically benign, but that serve as reminders of early trauma or abandonment. Unless caregivers and teachers understand the nature of such reenactments they are liable to label the child as "oppositional," "rebellious," "unmotivated," and "antisocial." Many problems of chronically traumatized children can be understood as efforts to minimize the objective threat and to regulate their emotional distress (Pynoos et al., 1987, 1997; Streeck-Fischer, 2000a, 2000c).

If children are exposed to environmental extremes, and lack adults who provide continuity, they invariably have problems clearly understanding how people get their needs met. This fundamental problem with self-definition is expressed differently by children with different temperaments. Some become impulsive: overwhelmed by their affective arousal and unable to verbalize what is bothering them, they demonstrate that they are upset by their actions. Other children react by dissociating: they lose contact with their environment and avoid social interaction. Neither group is capable of using language to communicate how they feel. Both groups only know that they feel hurt, but have problems reflecting on what their own contribution is—they expect to be victimized. Dodge and Somberg (1987) call this "attribution bias": the perceptions of these children are determined by their traumatic experiences in which they view their aggressive behavior as a "legitimate" defensive response to an unbearable threat. While they incorporate and imitate other people's attitudes and behaviors, they literally are "out of touch" with their own reactions and tend to not only ascribe their own feelings to others, but manage to reinforce behaviors in others that conform with their expectations that the world is a dangerous place and people cannot be trusted (projective identification).

4. Family Problems and Violent Behavior

As they grow older, histories of exposure to violence and neglect in the family make boys, in particular, prone to adopt violent and aggressive behavior in their schools, neighborhoods or communities. Adequate family and community support clearly help boys avoid engaging in violence (Selner-O'Hagan et al., 1998). Lacking such external resources, they are prone to "be disruptive, acting aggressively towards objects and people, and throwing severe temper tantrums" (Wolfe, 1994). Carmen, Rieker, and Mills (1984) have suggested that boys are more likely to identify with the aggressor in abusive homes. Lisak (1993) found that most perpetrators of physical abuse (70 percent) had been victimized (physical or sexual abuse). However, the majority of abused boys do not grow up to become perpetrators.

Witnessing violence in the family is an important risk factor for intergenerational transmission of family violence: between 30 percent and 80 percent of women receiving treatment for battering report having witnessed violence between their parents as well as having been victims of physical abuse (Gayford, 1975). Patterson and Bank (1989) divided boys with adolescent conduct disorder into two groups: early starters and late starters. Early starters demonstrate early coercive parent–child interaction, characterized by explosive, irritable, and inconsistent discipline, leading to escalating aggressive behavior.

A survey of over 4,000 adults (Kalmuss, 1984) found that witnessing marital aggression between parents was the major risk factor predicting which adolescent girls would grow up to be victims of marital assault. In males, witnessing spouse abuse as children is associated with becoming perpetrators of marital violence: boys who witness their father's violence have a 1,000 percent greater likelihood of growing up to abuse their partners than boys not exposed to marital violence.

The notion of traumatic expectations (Pynoos et al., 1997; Streeck-Fischer & van der Kolk, 2000) provides a powerful explanatory concept for understanding the long-term consequences of trauma for the child's emerging personality. Trauma-related expectations transform traumatic stress into personality disorders that have multiple levels of expression: in thoughts, emotions, behavior, and biology. These expectations shape the child's inner plans of the world and their concepts of self, and shape the child's life trajectory.

Exposure to violence affects the way children process information and interpret future threats, and affects their ability to take effective action in response to future challenges, while maintaining an overarching sense of a "social contact" (Bell and Jenkins, 1993; Cicchetti & Carlson, 1989; Garbarino, Kostelny, & Dubrow, 1991; Macksoud, Dyregrov, & Raundalen, 1993; Richters & Martinez, 1993; Dodge, 1986; Dodge & Somberg, 1987). A traumatic experience involves intense moment-to-moment perceptual, kinesthetic, and somatic experiences that are accompanied by appraisals of external and internal threats. The ultimate imprint is determined by many actors: the intensity and duration of their physiological arousal, their emotional reactions, and the interpretation of what is happening. While exposed to violence, a child continuously tries to address the situation by changing its behavior, thoughts, and fantasies, in order to manage its physiological and emotional reactions. When the child is injured itself, or witnesses a caregiver being injured, he or she is likely to become preoccupied with concerns about the severity of injury, rescue, and repair (Pynoos et al., 1997).

5. Violence and Brain Development

In recent years there has been increasing evidence supporting the notion that maltreatment has profound psychobiological effects which may have a major impact on the capacity for affect regulation (Putnam & Trickett, 1997; DeBellis & Putnam, 1994). Maltreatment has been shown to have lasting effects on cognition, behavior, affect, and social interaction (Pynoos et al., 1997; Teicher et al., 1993; Perry & Pollard, 1998). Since the organizing brains of infants or young children are more malleable to experience than are mature brains, traumatization during childhood has more pervasive effects than similar events in people with well-organized brains.

When children are frequently threatened without being able to affect the situation, their biology is affected and sensitized by the continuous emergencies in which they find themselves. Their system becomes increasingly responsive to relatively minor stimuli by means of the processes of sensitization and kindling (Post et al., 1998). This may involve both decreased (impaired) frontal lobe functioning (maturation) and increased limbic system (amygdala) sensitivity.

Because of stimulus generalization maltreated children respond to minor triggers with a variety of full-blown catastrophic reactions: ordinary stresses become full-blown disasters. Impulsive reactions are modulated at various levels of the CNS: the brainstem modulates fixed action patterns and general level of arousal, the cerebellum plays a role in activating sensorimotor schemata, while the limbic loop precipitates contextually elicited fight, flight, or freeze responses. In recent years evidence is slowly mounting that all these systems, as well as various frontal areas of the brain, are affected by trauma, particularly early in the life cycle (for reviews, see Yehuda & McFarlane, 1995; van der Kolk, 2000b). Decreased frontal lobe functioning leads to defects in the ability to formulate the larger context of any particular event, and leads to decreased inhibition of subcortical systems. Hence, interventions that address the problems on any of these different levels may prove to be effective.

Early traumatic experiences also have been shown to have chronic effects on neurotransmitter, neuroendocrine, and immune systems (Putnam & Trickett, 1997). Hyper-aggressive boys, as well as sexually abused girls, have been shown to have significant dysregulation of the hypothalamic-pituitary axis (HPA) (Heim et al., 2000; Putnam, 1993). The major function of the HPA axis is to regulate the release of cortisol that regulates the body's biologic stress response by terminating the neutral defensive reactions that have been activated by stress. These data are compatible with the overall finding of HPA dysregulation in PTSD. DeBellis et al. (1994) have demonstrated a twofold increase of plasma antinuclear antibodies in abused subjects compared to controls. The presence of high antinuclear antibody levels is thought to reflect failure of the immune system to suppress auto-reactive lymphocytes, responses, which the environment is likely to perceive as acts of aggression.

6. Long-Term Effects of Loss of Self-Regulation

Adults with a history of child abuse trauma frequently report retraumatization (e.g., Briere & Runtz, 1988; Cloitre et al., 2000; Dutton & Painter, 1993). 65 percent of males and 72 percent of females with histories of sexual abuse were revictimized as adults, 51 percent of adults who were physically abused as children reported revictimization, while 77 percent of the adults who reported childhood physical and sexual abuse were revictimized as adults. Dissociation (van der Kolk & Ducey, 1989; Spiegel, 1988; Spiegel & Cardena, 1991) has a particular role in the pathogenesis of PTSD. Successful coping, i.e., formulating an appropriate reaction to a stressful event and doing something about it allows people to deal with extreme stress. Effective coping results in a relief of personal distress, maintains a sense of personal worth, and conserves one's ability to form rewarding social contacts. Effective coping may involve avoidance of becoming emotionally involved in traumatic situations and focusing on how to prevent the worst possible outcome. Recently, Noll et al. (2000) were able to show that emotional dissociation is the best predictor of good outcome after exposure to extreme stress. In contrast, children who dissociate ignore the reality of what is happening to them and do not take action to stay in control. As a result they are prone to become revictimized in response to subsequent stressors.

Borrowing Piaget's terminology (Piaget & Inhelder, 1968; Streeck-Fischer, 2000a), peritraumatic stress responses involve mainly *accommodation* (i.e., responding to external demand by using resources and structures that are already available), while post-exposure processes are, in essence, a matter of *assimilation* (i.e., changing internal structures in response to novelty (see Summit, 1983).

III. THE MANY FACES OF VIOLENCE

There are different subtypes of aggression that can be classified under a variety of psychiatric terminologies: adults who act impulsively in response to threatened abandonment or perceived slights usually meet criteria for borderline personality disorder or PTSD, while those who use violence to deliberately achieve their aims fall in the category of antisocial personality disorder, pathological narcissistic personality disorder or psychopathy. Child psychiatrists tend to classify most violent children as unsocialized aggressive reaction or conduct disorder.

These different types of violence can be otherwise dichotomized as overt versus covert, affective vs. predatory, hostile vs. instrumental. Many traumatized individuals display a superficially compliant behavior, which suggests that they have achieved a superficial adaptation to the environment that works as long as they are not emotionally aroused, but that disintegrates when they feel threatened. These distinctions are important when one studies group processes in schools, institutions, and among violent youth, such as juvenile gangs.

Parker and Gottman (1989), Jacobson and Richardson (1987), Jacobson and Herald (1990) measured physiological arousal in batterers *in vivo* during conflicts with their wives. They found two patterns of arousal in wife batterers; one with a flat, unemotional "cool" display in the course of conflict, accompanied by decreases in heart rate (Type 1), described by Jacobsen et al. (1994) as "vagal reactors." The other (Type 2) demonstrated heart rate increases during conflict. Both Saunders and Arnold (1993) and Dutton and Painter (1993) described a subgroup of batterers who scored high on impulsivity and who string emotional responses to physiological arousal. Dutton and Painter (1981) found that the majority of batterers reacted with increased arousal, anger and anxiety to videotaped "abandonment" scenarios of a woman asserting independence from a man, when compared to a normal control group. Adrian Raines showed similar findings using neuroimaging. Like PTSD subjects exposed to personalized trauma scripts (Rauch et al., 1996), affectively violent offenders have lower left and right prefrontal activity and higher right hemisphere subcortical functioning. In contrast, predatory violent offenders with instrumental behavior show relatively normal prefrontal functioning during increased right subcortical activity.

Similar to batterers, aggressive children of the impulsive reactive subtype are less capable of self-control and driven by poor frustration tolerance. Exposed to high levels of arousal (which impair cognition—Arnsten, 1998) they display as "attribution biases" (Dodge, 1986) in the direction of threat. While they stay in touch with their emotions, they are overwhelmed by hyperarousal, which precipitates state-dependent memory retrieval, during which they reexperience trauma-related feelings of helplessness, humiliation and annihilation fear, and react the way they did when the original trauma occurred: with fight reactions, or with flight.

1. Impulsive/Aggressive Violence

The case of an eleven year old boy illustrates the different levels of disorganization:

A. began inpatient treatment because of his brutal and bloody attacks against others. His behavior to his teachers was tough, disobedient, and disrespectful. His mother had separated early from his father, was preoccupied with her own concerns, neglectful, leaving him in the care of one stranger after another. A. appeared to be very threatened, has been very defiant, and either has been aggressive or withdraws in ordinary situations. His behavior has been perceived by others as arrogant. He used clichés to cover his inadequacies. His behavior raised the question whether he is of low intelligence though he showed over average possibilities. In tests of his sensorimotor integration, he showed problems with depth perception, abnormal postural reflexes, problems with his equilibrium, and disturbed hand–eye coordination. A child with such problems lacks a sense of physical mastery and has problems orienting himself in space. The most secure place for A. appeared to be his mother's computer. This machine supplied him with consistent reactions, as if it were a secure and predictable attachment figure.

Shortly after entering an inpatient unit because of his dangerously violent behavior, the following occurred: an aggressive dispute with two other children, in which another child had destroyed a game, escalated into punching and kicking. Finally, a counselor intervened and A. was "grounded," i.e., confined to his room. He felt like he'd been "hard done by", since he could not understand his contribution to this situation, only how he had been mistreated—first by the child and then by the counselor. Not long after, he left the room in a totally different mood: he seemed calm, but looked cold and detached. In this state he threatened another counselor. He attacked another counselor in the face and eyes with a weapon: a straw filled with tacks that he had made. Another boy intervened and when A. was frustrated in his aggressive attack, he climbed over a fence and threatened to throw himself down the cellar stairs, shouting that if he killed himself now, the counselor would go to prison.

A. alternates between different levels of disorganization:

1. through restless acting out behavior to avoid intrusive maltreating interactions which has been a way he most of the time interacts with others (he only feel calm in front of his computer)
2. self-aggrandizement, accompanied by shame about who he really was. This led to avoidance of relationships in which people might come to know him for who he is.
3. ice-cold revenge and fury with the loss of feeling for others.
4. reacting in a seemingly incomprehensible manner that could only be understood as relevant as a reaction to old, undigested traumatic experiences, without his having any sense of what is being reenacted.
5. In the next step he reacted with emotionless freezing. While shut down he was out of touch with what he feels, but remains goal-oriented. Confronted with his helplessness following his unsuccessful attack he went into a dissociated state, which he learned during prior episodes of being overwhelmed by trauma-related emotions. These adaptations, a continuation of reliving his traumatic past, kept him reacting to his environment with anger and violence and prevented him from engaging in the here-and-now in a way that would provide him with satisfaction and inspire confidence and a sense of belonging with those around him.

2. Covert/Instrumental Violence

Children and adolescents with covert instrumental violent behavior are less likely to present with affective instability—as they are capable of problem focused coping. The levels of physiological arousal usually are low and generally have a low heart rate and skin conductance (Vitello & Stoff, 1997). Some boys, called the "socialized type," display instrumental aggression that involves antisocial behavior in peer groups, while the "unsocialized type" is unable to form attachments in peer groups. They develop a superficial problem-focused coping in rather structured and predictable situations. The violent behavior of these pseudo-secure or unattached instrumental persons occasionally emerges under circumstances that are reminders of traumatic experiences. For pseudo-secure persons this might be exposure to a disorganized environment; for an unattached person it might be exposure to intimacy or authority.

Their tendency to violence is embedded in their dissociation. It usually is difficult to establish an emotional link with these children and adolescents. When stressed—such as being in a large group of children—their functioning disintegrates and they may become dangerous. Under ordinary conditions, these children and adolescents seem to have learned to accommodate by hiding or splitting off signs of anger, rage, hate, and disappointment. They are unaware of their feelings and are unable to articulate them (alexythymia). They superficially accommodate to the expectations of their early caregivers. Especially in early adolescence, when the regulations of parents are questioned, these children display violent behavior during which they seem to be involved in a reactivation of early experienced traumatic scenes.

Beginning during puberty D. displayed dangerous violent behavior such as tormenting other children. He came to his first interview with makeup in his face and smelled strongly of cheap perfume. His nonverbal behavior was armored. Though his face had traits of a deep frozen depression he was able to conform to the expectations of the interviewer. His behavior appeared superficially adjusted, while he simultaneously manifested a severe rigidity that permeated his body. His parents had adopted him at nine months of age.

Before the age of nine month he was terribly neglected by his young natural mother, who was not allowed to abort him, but made to bear the child as a punishment for her "mistake" with a foreigner. At the time of his adoption, he was clearly developmentally delayed, with extreme variation between different capacities. The skin on his buttocks was covered with scars from the sores from having been left to lie in dirty diapers. His capacity for sensory integration was clearly disturbed; he does not feel pain and shows marked problems with spatial orientation.

D liked to look at violent videos. When left unsupervised on the ward, he enjoyed torturing other children. When confronted by counselors he always denied having done anything. Before puberty he complied with the expectations of his parents, except that they occasionally caught him torturing animals. In structured situations he functioned quite well. In early adolescence he seems to lose his capacity to regulate himself and become disorganized in unstructured situations. As long as he spent his time in the structured ward milieu, he remained quite stabile. As soon as he started attending a public school, he became extremely disorganized and gravitated to other violent boys. In his regard he showed a different adaptation from the previous case. Boys like he often develop sadistically violent sexual acting out.

1. School Performance

Not knowing how people negotiate their needs, traumatized children tend to behave violently in school, in order to get what they want from their peers, to establish their position and acquire a sense of power and control. Children need to establish their territory via their social interactions. When people in general, but children in particular, lack the capacity to articulate what they need and want and are unable to communicate with words, violent behavior can serve a powerful communicative purpose.

Children with histories of insecure/disorganized attachment patterns are likely to feel unsafe anywhere and tend to experience school as threatening (unless they are fortunate enough to attend a school that taps their particular talents, in which case school may become a refuge). Most traumatized kids tend to be hyperactive, withdrawn and/or aggressive. Other children react to those behaviors by avoiding them, or by responding in kind: with violence.

Since school often is the first place outside the family where children are subject to outside scrutiny, school usually is the first place where violent behavior becomes a public problem (Oswald & Kappmann, 2000). Schools require children to explore new ways of doing things. This is difficult for children who are afraid of engaging in unfamiliar activities, common in abused and neglected children. Surrounded by unstructured groups of children who react unpredictably, and often confronted by the fact that they have more trouble learning than their peers, some abused and neglected children compensate by demonstrating their physical power, often modeled on their role models at home. As a result, they provoke and bully other children, join peer groups with similar problems, consisting of kids that also do not follow the rules, or understand why there are rules, since rules only seem to be made to brutalize people. They basically continue the violent interactions they are accustomed to.

Having problems focusing and paying attention (Noll et al., 2000), many of them derive little pleasure from learning. Being shunned as "weird" kids they are excluded from enjoyable contacts, cannot identify with their teachers are being labeled as intruders and outsiders: "rotten apples." Delinquent acts and involvement with deviant peer groups provides some of them an escape from their alienation and loneliness.

2. Learning problems

In recent years, the proportion of children who behave violently has increased (e.g., Meier & Tillmann, 2000). The connection between learning problems and aggressive behavior has been well established—it is a vicious cycle (Saigh, Mroueh, & Bremmer, 1997; Streeck-Fischer, 2000b). The attentional disorders in these children have several causes. Teicher et al. (2000) and Putnam (1999) have shown that maltreated children display an extraordinarily high degree of nongoal-directed motor activity. They have speculated that this disorganized motor behavior is a function of cerebellar vermis abnormalities. Traumatized individuals have trouble paying attention because they have problems distinguishing between relevant and irrelevant information (McFarlane et al., 1993). They tend to misinterpret innocuous stimuli as traumatic, and, if not interpreted as traumatic, they tend to ignore sensory input (van der Kolk & Ducey, 1989; Bower & Sivers, 1998). Since they have learned to focus on trauma-related stimuli, they often have difficulty learning from ordinary, day-to-day experiences.

Only if children feel secure can they engage a real sense of curiosity (Bion, 1962). Because the world is a terrifying place, they have little interest in exploring it. As a result, many of these children insist on a boring sameness in their environment. Hence, they miss out on the normal transmission of social skills (language, social graces, and cultural education). Instead, these children daydream, dissociate, or bully others.

Many abused and neglected children have acoustic and visual perceptual problems; their comprehension of complex patterns tends to be vague and undifferentiated. Their sensory shuts down (Bemporad, Smith, & Hanson, 1987; Cohen, Paul, & Volkmer, 1987; Towbin et al., 1993, Dopart, 1983; Mandler, 1984) and makes it difficult for them to integrate concepts and to comprehend information simultaneously at different levels of abstraction. Children that have difficulty with sensory processing have trouble making sense of incoming input. If they have speech problems, this interferes with understanding complex situations and with the narration of complex stories. Many have limited capacities to comprehend complex visual-spatial patterns. This, in turn, leads to problems with reading and writing. These children are likely to have difficulties learning that will impair both their academic and occupational performance throughout life.

IV. CONCLUSIONS

Violent behavior in children and adolescents usually is a behavioral expression of a subjective sense of threat. Uncontrollable exposure to previous violence is likely to be reenacted. This is especially true for people without other resources and with nervous systems that are hyperaroused and unmodulated. Gilligan (1996) describes the prevalence of feelings of overwhelming humiliation, shame and rejection as triggers for violent reactions. Similarly, Lempp (1977) has described a juvenile murderer who attacked another adolescent to eliminate an unbearably humiliating situation. Shaming, conceptualized as verbal or behavioral attacks on the global self, has been found to generate lifelong vulnerability to feel ashamed—a feeling that often leads to rage.

Since a) identification with a perpetrator, b) lack of self-regulatory capacities and c) lack of personal resources are the principal contributors to youth violence, prevention needs to address these three issues. Social services need to be offered that allow women to raise their children in homes in which they and their children can feel safe. Adequate daycare, sufficient financial resources for mothers to live in a home where they can raise their children safely, and a justice system that is responsive to family violence are the principal elements necessary to maximize the possibility that a child is raised in a home that is free of violence.

Self-regulatory problems are not *necessarily* the result of abuse and witnessing violence, and even if the child is uncontrolled, removing the offending stimulus does not reset its central nervous system. Talking, knowing and acknowledging what has happened, making mental schemes of options, being exposed to reparative experiences and medications all can greatly help children regain a sense of agency.

The treatment outcome literature suggests that traumatized children and adults need to be actively exposed to their traumatic memories in order for them to learn to process what has happened and integrate it in the totality of their experience. If that is not done, they are likely to mentally split off the experiences from consciousness and reenact their trauma when they feel scared and threatened. Traditionally, the treatment of choice has been long-term play therapy with which the child re-invents himself in the context of new opportunities and physically transforms the trauma by gradually expanding his repertoire of behavioral options. One particularly effective treatment of intrusive traumatic memories appears to be eye movement desensitization and reprocessing (EMDR).

The resources needed are not primarily financial, but the capacity to look after oneself and plan for a future in which children or adolescents views themselves as active participants in shaping their future. That means that traumatized children need to be helped to plan for themselves and the lives they wish to embark on. Given how many traumatized children also develop attention deficit problems and learning disabilities, helping them to maintain a clear head and the capacity to attend to matters not immediately related to survival or distractions from feeling horrible is a major therapeutic goal. Resources also may mean the availability of adequate medications to help master violent impulses.

Planning, thinking, and being able to put themselves in other people's shoes are essential skills to succeed. We use communal activities, such as theater groups, in which adolescents write plays that contain their own stories, which they then act out as one such means of resource installation. Learning to talk about oneself in groups, and learning to tolerate ambivalence and doubt are major skills that children and adolescents mainly learn form interaction with their peer group.

Any skill in which a child or adolescent can absorb him or herself is a protection against retraumatization: when one feels overwhelmed by interpersonal stress, few things can alleviate misery better than a finely honed skill. Playing a sport or a musical instrument gives even frustrated teenagers entrance to a peer group, and helps them organize their competencies and counteract anxiety and despair with absorption and activity. Convicted and incarcerated juvenile delinquents who manage to train for a job skill while in prison have a negligible recidivism rate. Learning to be part of the human race, by simultaneously keeping in mind one's own needs and that of others, and negotiating alliances with mutual understanding rather than force, are the most important skills needed to prevent resorting to violence. These skills are best learned in groups.

REFERENCES

Arnsten, Amy F. (1998). The Biology of Being Frazzled. *Science, 280,* 711–712.
Bell, Carl C., & Esther J. Jenkins. (1993). Community Violence and Children on Chicago's Southside. *Psychiatry, 56,* 46–54.
Bemporad, Jules R., Henry F. Smith, & Graeme Hanson. (1987). The Borderline Child. In Joseph Noshpitz (Ed.), *Basic Handbook of Child Psychiatry. Vol. 5* (pp. 305–311). New York: Basic Books.
Bion, Wilfried R. (1962). *Learning from Experience.* London: Heinemann.
Bower, Gordon H., & Heidi Sivers. (1998). The Cognitive Impact of Traumatic Events. *Development and Psychopathology, 10,* 625–653.
Bowlby, John. (1969). *Attachment and Loss. Vol. 1.* New York: Basic Books.
Bowlby, John. (1973). *Attachment and Loss. Vol. 2.* New York: Basic Books.
Bowlby, John. (1984). Violence in the Family as a Disorder of the Attachment and Caregiving Systems. *American Journal of Psychoanalysis, 44,* 9–27.
Briere, John, & Marsha Runtz. (1988). Symptomatology Associated with Childhood Sexual Victimization in a Nonlineal Adult Sample. *Child Abuse and Neglect, 12,* 51–59.
Carmen, Elaine H., Patricia P. Rieker, & Trudy Mills. (1984). Victims of Violence and Psychiatric Illness. *American Journal of Psychiatry, 141,* 378–379.
Chaffin, Marc, Kelly Kelleher, & Jan Hollenberg. (1996). Onset of Physical Abuse and Neglect: Psychiatric, Substance Abuse, and Social Risk Factors from Prospective Community Data. *Child Abuse and Neglect, 20,* 191–203.
Cicchetti, Dante, & Sheree Toth. (1994). *Disorders and Dysfunctions of the Self. Rochester Symposium on Developmental Psychopathology.* Rochester: University of Rochester Press.
Cicchetti, Dante, & Vicki Carlson. (1989). *Child Maltreatment: Theory and Research on the Causes and Consequences of Child Abuse and Neglect.* New York: Cambridge University Press.
Cloitre, Marylene, Karestan Koenan, L. Cohen, & Hyemee Han. (2000). *Skills Training in Affective and Interpersonal Regulation Followed by Exposure: A Phase-Based Treatment for PTSD Related to Childhood Abuse.* Paper Presented at the Meeting of the International Society for Traumatic Stress Studies, San Antonio, TX.
Cohen, Donald J., Rhea Paul, & Fred R. Volkmer. (1987). Issues in the Classification of Pervasive Develop-

mental Disorders and Associated Conditions. In Donald Cohen & Anne M. Donnelean (Eds.), *Handbook of Autism and Pervasive Developmental Disorders* (pp. 20–40). New York: John Wiley.

Corvo, Kenneth N. (1997). Community-Based Youth Violence Prevention: A Framework for Planners and Funders. *Youth and Society*, 28(3), 291–316.

DeBellis, Michael D., & Frank W. Putnam. (1994). The Psychobiology of Childhood Maltreatment. *Child and Adolescent Psychiatric Clinics of North America*, 3, 663–678.

DeBellis, Michael D., George P. Chrousos, Lorah D. Dorn, Lillian Burke, Karin Helmers, Mitchel A. Kling, Penelope K. Trickett, & Frank W. Putnam. (1994). Hypothalamic-Pituitary-Adrenal Axis Dysregulation in Sexually Abused Girls. *Journal of Clinical Endocrinological Metabolism*, 78, 249–255.

Dodge, Kenneth A. (1986). A Social Information Processing Model of Social Competence in Children. In Marion Perlmutter (Ed.), *Cognitive Perspectives on Children's Social and Behavioral Development: Minnesota Symposia on Child Psychology. Vol. 18* (pp. 77–125). Hillsdale, NI: Lawrence Erlbaum.

Dodge, Kenneth A., & Daniel R. Somberg. (1987). Hostile Attributional Biases Among Aggressive Boys Are Exacerbated Under Conditions of Threats of the Self. *Child development*, 58, 213–224.

Dopart, Theo. (1983). The Cognitive Arrest Hypothesis of Denial. *International Journal of Psychoanalysis*, 64, 47–58.

Dutton, Donald G., & Susan L. Painter. (1981). Traumatic Bonding: The Development of Emotional Attachments in Battered Women and other Relationships of Intermittent Abuse. *Victimology*, 6, 139–168.

Dutton, Donald G., & Susan L. Painter. (1993). Emotional Attachments in Abusive Relationships: A Test of Traumatic Bonding Theory. *Violence and Victims*, 8(2), 105–120.

Elliot, Diane, & Joane Briere. (1994). *Epidemiology of Memory and Trauma*. Paper presented at the International Society on Traumatic Stress Studies Meeting. Chicago, Illinois.

Felitti, Vincent J., Robert F. Anda, Dale Nordenberg, David F. Williamson, Alison M. Spitz, Valerie Edward, Mary P. Koss, & James S. Marks. (1998). Relationship of Childhood Abuse to Many of the Leading Causes of Death in Adults: The Adverse Childhood Experiences (ACE) Study. *American Journal of Preventive Medicine*, 14, 245–258.

Fish-Murray, Caroline C., Elisabeth L. Koby, & Bessel A. van der Kolk. (1986). How Children Think about Trauma. In Bessel A. van der Kolk, *Psychological Trauma* (pp. 89–100). Washington: American Psychiatric Press.

Fonagy, Peter. (1998). Frühe Bindung und die Bereitschaft zu Gewaltverhalten. In Annette Streeck-Fischer, *Adoleszenz und Trauma* (pp. 91–128). Göttingen: Vandenhoeck & Ruprecht.

Gayford, J. J. (1975). Wife-Battering: A Preliminary Survey of 100 Cases. *British Medical Journal*, 1, 194–197.

Gianconia, Rose M., Helen Z. Reiherz, Amy B. Silverman, Bilge Pakiz, Abbie K. Frost, & Elaine Cohen. (1995). Traumas and Posttraumatic Stress Disorder in a Community Population of Older Adolescents. *Journal of American Academy of Child and Adolescent Psychiatry*, 34, 1369–1380.

Garbarino, James, Kathleen Kostelny, & Nancy Dubrow. (1991). What Children Can Tell Us about Living in Danger. *American Psychologist*, 46(4), 376–383.

Gilligan, James. (1996). *Violence: Reflection on a National Epidemic*. New York: Vintage Books.

Heim, Christine, D. Jeffrey Newport, Stacey Heit, Yolanda P. Graham, Molly Wilcox, Robert Bonsall, Andrew H. Miller, & Charles B. Nemeroff. (2000). Pituitary-Adrenal and Autonomic Responses to Stress in Women after Sexual and Physical Abuse in Childhood. *Journal of the American Medical Association*, 284(5), 592–597.

Jacobson, Andrea, & Bonnie Richardson. (1987). Assault Experiences of 100 Psychiatric Inpatients: Evidence of the Need for Routine Inquiry. *American Journal of Psychiatry*, 144(7), 908–913.

Jacobson, Andrea, & Charaine Herald. (1990). The Relevance of Childhood Sexual Abuse to Adult Psychiatric Inpatient Care. *Hospital and Community Psychiatry*, 41(2), 154–158.

Jacobsen, Teresa, Wolfgang Edelstein, & Volker Hofmann. (1994). A Longitudinal Study of the Relation between Representations of Attachment in Childhood and Cognitive Functioning in Childhood and Adolescence. *Developmental Psychology*, 30(1), 112–124.

Kalmuss, Debra. (1984). The International Transmission of Martial Aggression. *Journal of Marriage and the Family*, 46(1), 11–19.

Lempp, Reinhard. (1977). *Jugendliche Mörder*. Bern: Huber.

Lewis, Dorothy O. (1992). From Abuse to Violence: Psychophysiological Consequences of Maltreatment. *Journal of the American Academy of Child and Adolescent Psychiatry*, 31(3), 383–391.

Lewis, Dorothy O., Richard Lovely, Catherine Yeager, & Donna Della Femina. (1989). Toward a Theory of the Genesis of Violence: A Follow-Up Study of Delinquents. *Journal of American Academy of Child Adolescent Psychiatry*, 28(3), 431–436.

Lisak, David. (1993). Men as Victims: Challenging Cultural Myths. *Journal of Traumatic Stress, 6*(4), 577–580.

Lyons-Ruth, Karlen. (1991). Rapprochment or Approchement: Mahler's Theory Reconsidered from the Vantage Point of Recent Research in Early Attachment Relationships. *Psychoanalytic Psychology, 8*(1), 1–23.

Macksoud, Mona S., Atle Dyregrov, & Magne Raundalen. (1993). Traumatic War Experiences and Their Effects on Children. In Beverly Raphael & John P. Wilson (Eds.), *The International Handbook of Traumatic Stress Syndromes* (pp. 625–633). New York: Plenum Press.

Mandler, George. (1984). *Mind and Body: Psychology of Emotion and Stress.* New York: Norton.

Mc Farlane, Alexander C., Darren L. Weber, & C. Richard Clark. (1993). Abnormal Stimulus Processing in Posttraumatic Stress Disorder. *Biological Psychiatry, 34,* 5, 311–320.

Meier, Ulrich, & Klaus-Jürgen Tillmann. (2000). Gewalt in der Schule. *Praxis der Kinderpsychologie und Kinderpsychiatrie, 49,* 36–51.

Noll, Jennie G, Penelope K. Trickett, & Frank W. Putnam. (2000). Social Network Constellation and Sexuality of Sexually Abused and Comparison Girls in Childhood and Adolescence. *Child Maltreatment, 5*(4), 323–337.

Oswald, Hans, & Lothar Kappmann. (2000). Phänomenologische und funktionale Vielfalt von Gewalt unter Kindern. *Praxis der Kinderpsychologie und Kinderpsychiatrie, 49*(1), 3–15.

Parker, Jeffrey G., & John M. Gottman. (1989). Social and Emotional Development in a Relational Context. In Thomas J. Berndt & Gary W. Ladd (Eds.), *Peer Relationships in Child Development* (pp. 95–131). New York: Wiley.

Patterson, G. R. & L. Bank. (1989). Some Amplifying Mechanisms for Pathologic Processes in Families. In Megan R. Gunnar & Esther Thelen (Eds.), *Systems and Development: The Minnesota Symposia on Child Psychology. Vol. 22.* Hillsdale, NJ: Erlbaum(pp. 167–209).

Perry, Bruce D., & Ronnie Pollard. (1998). Homeostasis, Stress, Trauma and Adaptation. *Child and Adolescent Psychiatric Clinic of North America, 7*(1), 33–51.

Piaget, Jean, & Baerbel Inhelder. (1968). *Die Entwicklung des inneren Bildes beim Kind.* Frankfurt a. M.: Suhrkamp.

Posner, Michael J. (1998). *Foundations of Cognitive Science.* Cambridge, MA: MIT Press.

Post, Robert M., S. R. B Weiss, He Li, M. A. Smith, L. X. Zhang, G. Xing, E. A. Osuch, & U. D. McCann. (1998). Neutral plasticity and emotional memory. *Development and Psychopathology, 10*(4), 829–855.

Putnam, Frank, W. (1993). Dissociative Disorders in Children: Behavioral Profiles and Problems. *Child Abuse and Neglect, 16,* 39–45.

Putnam, Frank, W. (1997). *Dissociation in Child and Adolescents.* New York: Guilford Press.

Putnam, Frank, W. (1999). *Childhood Maltreatment and Adverse Outcomes. A Prospective Developmental Approach.* The American Psychiatric Association 152, Annual Meeting, Washington D.C.

Putnam, Frank, W., & Penelope K. Trickett. (1997). The Psychobiological Effects of Sexual Abuse, a Longitudinal Study. *Annals of the New York Academy Science, 821,* 150–159.

Pynoos, Robert S., Calvin Frederick, Kathi Nader, William Arroyo, A. Steinberg, S. Eth, F. Nunez, & L. Fairbanks. (1987). Life Threat and Posttraumatic Stress in School Age Children. *Archiv of General Psychiatry, 44*(2), 1057–1063.

Pynoos, Robert S., Armen Goenjian, & Alan M. Steinberg. (1997). Strategies of Disaster Intervention for Children and Adolescents. In Stevan E. Hobfoll & Marten deVries (Eds.), *Extreme Stress and Communities: Impact and Intervention* (pp. 445–471). Dordrecht, The Netherlands: M. Kluwer Academic Publishers.

Raines, Adrian, J. Reid Meloy, Susan Bihrie, Jackie Stobbard, Lori LaCasse, & Monte S. Buchsbaum. (1998). Reduced Prefrontal and Increased Subcortical Brain Functioning. *Behaviour Sciences and the Law,* 319–332.

Rauch, Scott L., Bessel A. van der Kolk, Rita E. Fisler, & Nathaniel M. Alpert. (1996). A Symptom Provocation Study of Posttraumatic Stress Disorder Using Positron Emission Tomography and Script-Driven Imagery. *Archives of General Psychiatry, 53,* 380–387.

Richters, John, & Pedro Martinez. (1993). NIMH Community Violence Project: Children as Victims of and Witnesses to Violence. *Psychiatry, 56,* 7–21.

Ross, Colin A., Scott D. Miller, Lynda Bjornson, Pamela Reagor, G. A. Fraser, & G. Anderson. (1991). Abuse Histories in 102 Cases of Multiple Personality Disorder. *Canadian Journal of Psychiatry, 36*(2), 97–101.

Saigh, Philip A., Maria Mroueh, & J. Douglas Bremmer. (1997). Scholastic Impairments among Traumatized Adolescents. *Behavior Research and Therapy, 35*(5), 429–436.

Sanders, Barbara, & Marion H. Giolas. (1991). Dissociation and Childhood Trauma in Psychological Disturbed Adolescents. *American Journal of Psychiatry, 148*(1), 50–54.

Saunders, Eleanor, & Frances F. Arnold. (1993). A Critic of Conceptual and Treatment Approaches to Borderline-Psychopathology in Light of Findings about Childhood Abuse. *Psychiatry, 56*(2), 188–203.

Schore, Alan. (1997). *Affect Regulation and the Origin of the Self: The Neurobiology of Emotional Development*. Hillsdale, N.J.: Lawrence Erlbaum Associates.

Sedlack, Andrea J., & Diane D. Broadhurst. (1996). *Executive Summary of the Third National Incidence Study of Child Abuse and Neglect (NIS-3)*. U.S. Department of Health and Human Services, Administration for Children and Families, Administration on Children, Youth, and Families, National Center on Child Abuse and Neglect.

Selner-O'Hagan, Mary Beth, Daniel J. Kindlon, Stephen L. Buka, Stephen W. Raudenbush, & Felton J. Earls. (1998). Assessing Exposure to Violence in Urban Youth. *Journal of Child Psychology and Psychiatry and Allied Disciplines, 39*(2), 215–224.

Spiegel, David. (1988). Dissociation and Hypnosis in the Treatment of Victims of Sexual Abuse. *Psychiatric Clinics of North America, 12*, 295–305.

Spiegel, David, & Etzel Cardena. (1991). Disintegrated Experiences: The Dissociative Disorders Revisited. *Journal of Abnormal Psychology, 100*(3), 366–378.

Streeck-Fischer, Annette. (2000a). Impatient Psychoanalytically Oriented Treatment of Traumatised Children and Adolescents. In Kai von Klitzing & Dieter Bürgin (Eds.), *Psychoanalysis in Childhood and Adolescence* (pp. 87–99). Basel: Karger.

Streeck-Fischer, Annette. (2000b). Über Blockaden und Behinderungen im lebenslangen Lernen aus psychoanalytischer Sicht. In Wolfgang Lempert & Frank Achtenhagen (Eds), *Lebenslanges Lernen im Beruf—seine Grundlegung im Kindes- und Jugendalter* (pp. 133–146). Opladen: Leske & Budrich.

Streeck-Fischer, Annette. (2000c). Borderline-Störungen im Kindes- und Jugendalter—ein hilfreiches Konzept? Diagnostik und Therapie von neurotischen Entwicklungsstörungen. *Psychotherapeut, 45*(6), 356–365.

Streeck-Fischer, Annette, & Bessel van der Kolk. (2000). Down Come Baby Cradle and All: Diagnostic and Therapeutic Implications of Chronic Trauma in Development. *Australian and New Zealand Journal of Psychiatry*, 896–918.

Summit, Roland C. (1983). The Child Sexual Abuse Accommodation Syndrome. *Child Abuse and Neglect, 7*, 177–193.

Teicher, Martin H. et al. (2000). Personal communication, unpublished document.

Teicher, Martin H., Carol A. Glod, Janet Surrey, & Chester Swett. (1993). Early Childhood Abuse and Limbic System Ratings in Adult Psychiatric Outpatients. *Journal of Neuropsychiatry and Clinical Neuroscience, 5*(3), 301–306.

Towbin, Kenneth E., Elisabeth M. Dykens, Geraldine Pearson, & Donald J. Cohen. (1993). Conceptualising Borderline Syndrome of Childhood and Childhood Schizophrenia as a Developmental Disorder. *Journal American Academy of Child and Adolescent Psychiatry, 32*, 775–782.

van der Kolk, Bessel A. (2000a). Post Traumatic Stress Disorder and the Nature of Trauma. *Dialogues in Clinical Neuroscience, 2*, 7–22.

van der Kolk, Bessel A. (2000b). Trauma, Neuroscience and the Etiology of Hysteria: An Exploration of the Relevance of Breuer and Freud's 1893 Article in the Light of Modern Neuroscience. *Journal American Academy Psychoanalysis, 28*, 237–262.

van der Kolk, Bessel A., J. Christopher Perry, & Judith L. Herman. (1991). Childhood Origins of Self-Destructive Behavior. *American Journal of Psychiatry, 148*, 1665–1671.

van der Kolk, Bessel A., & Charles P. Ducey. (1989). The Psychological Processing of Traumatic Experience: Research Patterns in PTSD. *Journal of Traumatic Stress, 2*(3), 259–274.

van der Kolk, Bessel A., & Rita Fisler. (1994). Childhood Abuse and Neglect and Loss of Self-Regulation. *Bulletin of Menninger Clinic, 58*, 145–168.

van der Kolk, Bessel A., & Rita Fisler. (1995). Dissociation and the Fragmentary Nature of Traumatic Memories: Overview and Exploratory Study. *Journal of Traumatic Stress, 9*(4), 505–525.

van der Kolk, Bessel A., David Pelcovitz, Susan Roth, Francine Mandel, Alexander C. McFarlane, & Judith L. Herman. (1996). Dissociation, Somatization, and Affect Dysregulation: The Complexity of Adaptation to Trauma. *American Journal of Psychiatry, 153*, 83–93.

Vitello, Bernadetto, & David M. Stoff. (1997). Subtypes of Aggression and Their Relevance to Child Psychiatry. *Journal American Academy of Adolescent Psychiatry, 36*(3), 307–315.

Yehuda, Rachel, & Alexander C. McFarlane. (1995). The Conflict between Current Knowledge about PTSD and its Original Conceptual Basis. *American Journal of Psychiatry, 152*(12), 1705–1713.

Wetzels, Peter. (1997). *Gewalterfahrungen in der Kindheit*. Baden-Baden: Nomos.

Wolfe, David A. (1994). The Role of Intervention and Treatment Services in the Prevention of Child Abuse and Neglect. In Garry B. Melton & Frank D. Barry (Eds.), *Protecting Children from Abuse and Neglect* (pp. 224–303). New York: Guilford.

PART II-5

SOCIAL OPPORTUNITY STRUCTURES: INSTITUTIONS AND SOCIAL SPACES

PART II-5-1

VIOLENCE IN SOCIAL INSTITUTIONS

CHAPTER II-5-1.1

Violence in the Family

RICHARD J. GELLES

I. INTRODUCTION

During the last quarter of the twentieth century, violence in the family was transformed from a private trouble and an issue obscured by selective inattention to a social problem that receives increasing professional, public, and policy attention. We now know that violence in intimate relationships is extensive and is not limited to one socioeconomic group, one society, or one period in time. We recognize the social, emotional, economic, and societal costs of intimate violence. We are aware of the constraints on the victims that limit their ability to protect themselves and their dependents. Although there are numerous controversies among researchers, practitioners, and policy makers about how to best conceptualize and respond to the problem of violence in the family, one consensus has been reached—there is evidence that virtually every type and form of family and intimate relationship has the potential of being violent. Researchers and clinicians have found violence and abuse in every type of intimate relationship. Thus, although the title of this chapter is "Violence in the Family," the scope of chapter examines violence and abuse in intimate relationships.

II. THE NATURE AND SCOPE OF VIOLENCE IN THE FAMILY

Until the early 1960s, violence between family members and/or intimates was considered rare and committed mainly by mentally ill or otherwise disturbed individuals. Only the most sensational and lurid cases received public attention, and there was a general belief that even though family violence was a significant problem, it was not widespread.

The question of the extent of family violence has not been easy to answer and still leads to contentious debates over the scientific adequacy and rigor of incidence and prevalence estimates (see for example, Sommers, 1994).

The answer to the question, "How big is the problem?" depends on two factors: (1) What is the definition of "family violence"? and (2) How is the incidence and prevalence of family violence measured?

1. Defining "Family Violence"

The definitional question has been debated for more than three decades and has been contentious. On the one hand, one definition is that family violence is "*any* act that is harmful to the victim." This broad definition of family violence includes physical attacks, threatened physical attacks, psychological or emotional aggression and abuse, sexual assaults or threatened sexual assaults, neglectful behavior, or behaviors intended to control the other. On the other hand, there are narrower definitions of "violence" that are confined to only acts of physical violence.

There is no consensus as to how broad or narrow the definition of family violence should be, or as to how to define the specific components of any definition (e.g., violence, neglect, rape, psychological abuse, or even the terms "family" or "intimate"). The discussions about the appropriate definition of family violence are influenced by a variety of perspectives. First, there is the scientific or research perspective that seeks a clear nominal definition that is grounded in theory and can be reliably and validly operationalized. This perspective tends toward a narrow definition of violence, because violence is, at least theoretically, conceived to be conceptually distinct behavior from other methods of inflicting harm or pain on another person (Etzioni, 1971). A humanistic perspective takes a broader approach and conceptualizes a definition that captures the full range of harm that can be inflicted on individuals—harm being defined as acts of commission or omission that interferes with a human being achieving hers or his developmental potential. Finally, there is a political or advocacy dimension that defines the behavior in terms of advocacy or political goals. Thus feminists define the problem as one of "violence against women," rather than spouse abuse, domestic violence, or family violence.

A second consideration in the definition is the term "family." The U.S. Census Bureau defines "family" as a group of two or more persons related by birth, marriage, or adoption residing together in a household (U.S. Bureau of the Census, 1992). While such a definition is useful for enumerating the number of families, it limits the examination and analysis of violence to only those related individuals who share a residence. Violence in courtship, violence between couples that are divorced, and violence between gay and lesbian couples falls outside of this definition.

The National Academy of Sciences panel on "Assessing Family Violence Interventions" defined "family violence" as:

> Family violence includes child and adult abuse that occurs between family members or adult intimate partners. For children, this includes acts by others that are physically or emotionally harmful or that carry the potential to cause physical harm. Abuse of children may include sexual exploitation or molestation, threats to kill or abandon, or lack of emotional or physical support necessary for normal development. For adults, family or intimate violence may include acts that are physically and emotionally harmful or that carry the potential to cause physical harm. Abuse of adult partners may include sexual coercion or assaults, physical intimidation, threats to kill or harm, restraint of normal activities or freedom, and denial of access to resources. (National Research Council, 1998:19)

Here too the definition limited the scope of violence interactions.

One solution to the narrowness of the term "family violence" is to broaden the scope to consider violence in all intimate relationships.

2. Measuring Family Violence

Even if there were a consensus definition of "family or intimate violence," there would be various estimates of the scope of violence between intimates because there are various methods used to measure the incidence and prevalence of family violence.

There are three main sources of data on family violence: (1) clinical data; (2) official report data; and (3) social surveys. Clinical studies carried out by psychiatrists, psychologists, and counselors were traditionally a frequent source of data on family violence. This is primarily due to the fact that clinicians have the most direct access to cases of family violence.

The clinical or agency setting (including hospital emergency rooms and battered woman shelters) provides access to extensive in-depth information about particular cases of violence. Studies of violence toward women have relied heavily on samples of women who seek help at battered woman shelters (Dobash & Dobash, 1979; Giles-Sims, 1983; Pagelow, 1981). Such samples are important because they are often the only way of obtaining detailed data on the most severely battered women. Such data are also necessary to study the impact of intervention programs. However, such data, because they are based on small, nonrepresentative samples, cannot be used to estimate the incidence and prevalence of intimate violence.

Official reports constitute a second source of data on family violence. In the United States, there is an abundance of official report data on child maltreatment (because of mandatory reporting laws). On the other hand, few other countries have enacted mandatory reporting laws, and thus most nations rely on official data from hospitals or criminal justice agencies for their estimates on the extent of violence and abuse of children. There has not been a tradition of officially reporting spouse abuse in the United States or other countries, with the exception of a handful of states in the United States that collect data on spouse abuse.

In the United States, the U.S. Department of Justice, Federal Bureau of Investigation tabulates and publishes the *Uniform Crime Reports* (UCR). The UCR provide data on criminal family violence and family homicide, but these are limited to instances of family violence that are reported to the police, and only a small fraction of the instances of violence between marital partners are ever reported to the police (Gelles & Straus, 1988; U.S. Department of Justice, 1999). The Supplemental Homicide Report data from the UCR are available for analysis and yield detailed national data on the extent of partner homicide. As with all data from the Uniform Crime Reports, these data are limited by the accuracy and reliability of police reports. For instance, homicides that are unsolved in one year may be solved with an arrest and conviction in a subsequent year. Given the high proportion of homicides in which the perpetrator and victim are intimate partners, unless police departments update their data, the UCR homicide data will undercount domestic or intimate homicides. Other limitations of the Supplemental Homicide Report data are that some police departments do not file the Supplemental Homicide Reports or file only for portions of the year. In some years, entire states fail to file reports. The Supplemental Homicide Report data have missing data problems—a large portion of the reports lack information about the offender, including the relationship between the offender and victim. Finally, cases are misclassified.

The National Center for Health Statistics (NCHS) maintains mortality data that, theoretically, could be used to measure and track domestic homicides. The NCHS vital statistics data are victim-based—that is, they are based on death certificates completed by medical examiners or coroners. Health and medical data sources often rely on the *International Classification of Diseases* coding system, ICD-9 or ICD-10 (WHO, 1977, 1992). There is the likelihood of undercounting domestic homicides of women for two reasons when using health data sources: (1) ICD-9, the classification system used to code cause of death data from death certificates does not contain codes that could be used to identify offender-victim relationships; and (2) even if such codes were included, medical examiners would not necessarily be likely to identify a perpetrator because this is not their responsibility.

In both the UCR and NCHS data there is also the possibility of undercounting domestic homicides due to police or medical examiners categorizing a homicide as an unintentional event (accident) or of undetermined intent.

As noted above, the United States is one of the few nations (Canada is another) that requires suspected cases of child maltreatment to be reported to official agencies. Thus, official data on child abuse and neglect are collected in the United States and estimates of the extent of child maltreatment can be made from these data. The National Center on Child Abuse and Neglect, now named The Office of Child Abuse and Neglect, sponsors the collection of data on official reports of child abuse and neglect, dispositions, victims, services and perpetrators collected from states as part of the National Child Abuse and Neglect Data System (NCANDS). All fifty states and the District of Columbia submitted reports for the year 1998 (U.S. Department of Health and Human Services, Administration on Children, Youth and Families, 2000).

Social surveys are the third source of data. Such surveys are constrained by the low base rate of most forms of abuse and violence in families and the sensitive and taboo nature of the topic. Some investigators cope with the problem of the low base rate by employing purposive or nonrepresentative sampling techniques to identify cases. A second approach has been to use available large groups of subjects. Investigators of courtship violence have made extensive use of survey research techniques using college students as subjects (Cate et al., 1982; Henton et al., 1983; Laner, 1983; Makepeace, 1981, 1983). A third method is nationally representative surveys of violence between intimates such as the three National Family Violence Surveys (Straus, Gelles, & Steinmetz, 1980; Gelles & Straus, 1988; Straus & Kantor, 1994) and the National Survey of Violence Against Women (Tjaden & Thoennes, 1998). Another form of national survey is longitudinal surveys. Woffordt and her colleagues (1994) administered the Conflict Tactics Scales during one wave of the National Youth Survey—a longitudinal study of a birth cohort in the United States. A fourth type of survey data on violence between intimates are the victimization data collected in the National Crime Victimization Survey (NCVS). The U.S. Justice Department has published a number of reports on intimate violence based on the data collected by the NCVS (Bachman, 1994; Bachman & Saltzman, 1995; Greenfeld et al., 1998; Rennison & Welchans, 2000).

Each of the major data sources has its own validity problems. Clinical data are not representative, and few investigators gathering data from clinical samples employ comparison groups. Official records suffer from variations in definitions, differing reporting and recording practices, and biased samples of violent and abusive behaviors and persons (Finkelhor & Hotaling, 1984; Weis, 1989; Widom, 1988). The biases of social survey data on intimate violence include inaccurate recall, differential interpretation of questions, and intended and unintended response error (Weis, 1989).

This chapter does not use data from clinical studies, nor does it report data from studies using nonrepresentative samples. For the most part, the discussion of the scope of the problem of family violence draws on self-report survey data, and where self-report survey data are not available or do not examine a specific facet of family violence, from available official report data.

Because of the various definitions of abuse and neglect, and the differing methodologies used to examine incidence and frequency, there are inconsistencies in the data on extent of family violence. Various aspects of research design, including definitions, sampling, measurement, sources of data, and whether the information is collected prospectively or retrospectively generate varying findings. Even for the most extreme form of violence, homicide, where the data are thought to be the most reliable and valid (because there is a body that must be attended to) there are differing data depending on the source of the data. The FBI data on homicide are not identical with the National Center for Health Statistics data on murder—some homicides are reported in the FBI data set but not the NCHS data set and vise versa. Thus, where appropriate, this chapter either presents estimates of the range of the problem or provides data from different studies and/or data sources.

3. Child Maltreatment

Child abuse and neglect, or child maltreatment, are general terms that cover a wide range of acts of commission and omission, either carried out by a perpetrator or allowed to happen, which result in a range of injuries ranging from death, to serious disabling injury, to emotional distress, to malnutrition and illness.

There are six major types of child abuse and neglect (see National Center on Child Abuse, 1988):

- Physical abuse: acts of commission that result in physical harm, including death, to a child.
- Sexual abuse: acts of commission including intrusion or penetration, molestation with genital contact, or other forms of sexual acts in which children are used to provide sexual gratification for a perpetrator.
- Emotional abuse: acts of commission that include confinement, verbal or emotional abuse, or other types of abuse such as withholding sleep, food, or shelter.
- Physical neglect: acts of omission that involve refusal to provide health care, delay in providing health care, abandonment, expulsion of a child from a home, inadequate supervision, failure to meet food and clothing needs, and conspicuous failure to protect a child from hazards or danger.
- Educational neglect: acts of omission and commission that include permitting chronic truancy, failure to enroll a child in school, and inattention to specific education needs.
- Emotional neglect: acts of omission that involve failing to meet the nurturing and affection needs of a child, exposing a child to chronic or severe spouse abuse, allowing or permitting a child to use alcohol or controlled substances, encouraging the child to engage in maladaptive behavior, refusal to provide psychological care, delays in providing psychological care, and other inattention to the child's developmental needs.

The National Center on Child Abuse and Neglect has conducted three surveys designed to

TABLE II-5-1-1.1. Estimates of the total number of maltreated children, 1993

Maltreatment type	Total number of cases
Physical abuse	614,100
Sexual abuse	300,200
Emotional abuse	532,200
Neglect	1,961,300
Physical neglect	1,335,100
Emotional neglect	584,100
Educational neglect	397,300
Seriously injured children	565,000

Source: National Center on Child Abuse and Neglect. Third National Study of the Incidence of Child Abuse and Neglect, 1996.

measure the national incidence of reported and recognized child maltreatment (Burgdorf, 1980; NCCAN, 1988, 1996). A total of 2.9 million maltreated children were known by the agencies surveyed in 1993.

Table II-5-1-1.1 presents a summary of the incidence of the six major types of child maltreatment as well as data on the severity of the impairment caused by the maltreatment. Of the total number of maltreated children, an estimated 630,800 (9.2 per 1,000) were physically abused, 302,000 children (4.4 per 1,000) were sexually abused, 536,400 children (7.9 per 1,000) were emotionally abused, and 2,481,800 children (36.4 per 1,000) were neglected (1,368,200 physical neglect, 583,600 emotional neglect, and 530,000 educational neglect).

A second source of data on the extent of child maltreatment comes from the National Child Abuse and Neglect Data System (NCANDS). NCANDS is a national data collection and analysis project carried out by the Office of Child Abuse and Neglect (U.S. Department of Health and Human Services, 2000). The data are official report data collected from fifty states and the District of Columbia.

In 1998, more than 2.97 million children were reported to state agencies for investigation, based on data submitted by fifty states and the District of Columbia (U.S. Department of Health and Human Services, Administration on Children, Youth and Families, 2000). In terms of the actual number of confirmed child victims, the number increased from 790,526 in 1990 to 903,395 in 1998, an increase of 14.2 percent. (Note: forty-four states participated in the survey in 1990, and fifty-one states submitted data in 1998).

Although the number of victimized children increased between 1990 and 1998, the rate of confirmed child maltreatment increased from 13.4 per 1,000 in 1990 to a peak of 15.3 in 1993; thereafter, the rate of child abuse victimization declined (Fig. II-5-1-1.1).

A fourth source of data on violence toward children is self-report data. The National Family Violence Surveys interviewed two nationally representative samples of families— 2,146 family members in 1976 and 6,002 family members in 1985 (Straus, Gelles & Steinmetz, 1980; Gelles & Straus, 1987, 1988; Straus & Gelles, 1986). Violence and abuse were measured by asking respondents to report on their own behavior toward their children in the previous twelve months. Milder forms of violence, violence that most people think of as physical punishment, were the most common. However, even with the severe

VIOLENCE IN THE FAMILY

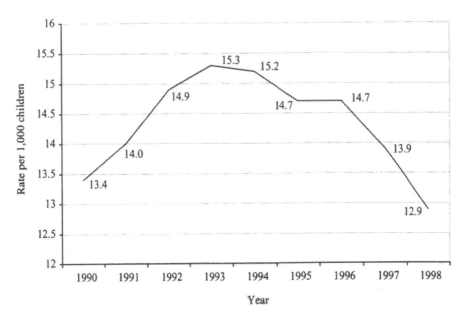

FIGURE II-5-1-1.1. Victimization rates, 1990–1998 (SDC).

forms of violence, the rates were surprisingly high. Abusive violence was defined as acts that had a high probability of injuring the child. These included kicking, biting, punching, hitting or trying to hit a child with an object, beating up a child, burning or scalding, and threatening or using a gun or a knife. Slightly more than twenty parents in 1,000 (2.3 percent) admitted to engaging in one act of abusive violence during the year prior to the 1985 survey. Seven children in 1,000 were hurt as a result of an act of violence directed at them by a parent in the previous year. Projecting the rate of abusive violence to all children under the age of eighteen years who live with one or both parents means that 1.5 million children experience acts of abusive physical violence each year and 450,000 children are injured each year as a result of parental violence.

a. SEXUAL ABUSE. The official report data cited above include the yearly incidence of cases of sexual abuse reported to state child welfare agencies. As with all forms of child maltreatment, reported cases are assumed to be underestimates of the true extent of sexual abuse. Unlike physical violence toward children, there has not yet been a self-report survey that attempts to measure the yearly incidence of sexual abuse. There have been a number of self-report prevalence studies. Peters, Wyatt, and Finkelhor (1986) report that estimates of prevalence range from 6 to 62 percent for females and 3 to 31 percent for males. A 1985 national survey of 2,626 adult men and women found a life prevalence of sexual abuse reported by 27 percent of the women and 16 percent of the men surveyed (Finkelhor et al., 1990).

b. PSYCHOLOGICAL ABUSE. Official report data are also assumed to underestimate the true extent of psychological abuse of children. There are few self-report surveys that attempt to assess the extent of psychological abuse or maltreatment. Using the "Psychological Aggression" scale from the Conflict Tactics Scales, Vissing and her colleagues (1991) report that 63.4 percent of a national sample of 3,346 parents stated that they used at least one form of psychological aggression at least once in the previous year. This operationalization of psychological aggression is a rather broad definition of psychological maltreatment (items included "insulted or swore at the child," and "did or said something to spite the child.").

c. CHILD HOMICIDE. The U.S. Advisory Board on Child Abuse and Neglect estimated that parents or caretakers kill 2,000 children under the age of eighteen each year (U.S. Advisory Board on Child Abuse and Neglect, 1995). The U.S. Advisory Board on Child Abuse and Neglect suggests that this estimate is low. McLain and his colleagues (McLain, Sacks, & Frohlke, 1993) report that abuse and neglect kill 5.4 out of every 100,000 children under four years of age, but this estimate is probably low as a result of misclassification of child deaths. A second estimate is that the rate of child death is 11.6 per 100,000 children under four years of age (U.S. Advisory Board on Child Abuse and Neglect, 1995). Prevent Child Abuse America projected that there were 1,238 child abuse fatalities nationwide in 1997[1], an increase from 1,143 in 1990 and a decrease from a high of 1,250 in 1994 (Fig. II-5-1-1.2). In terms of rate, the rate of child maltreatment fatalities was 1.78 per 100,000 children in the population in 1997[2] and 1.84 per 100,000 children in 1990 (Wang & Harding, 1999). There have been no changes in the rate of child maltreatment fatalities between 1995 and 1997 (Fig. II-5-1-1.3).

4. Violence in Adult Intimate Relationships

The initial definitions of domestic violence focused on acts of damaging physical violence directed toward women by their spouses or partners (Gelles, 1974; Martin, 1976). Further research broadened the definition to include sexual abuse, marital rape, and acts of emotional or psychological violence. Feminist scholars conceptualize the problem as one of coercive control of women by their partners (Yllo, 1993). The coercion can be physical, emotional, or sexual.

a. DATING AND COURTSHIP VIOLENCE. Studies that examine the possibility of violence in dating and courtship find that between 10 and 67 percent of dating relationships involve violence (Sugarman & Hotaling, 1989). Researchers have found that the rate of severe violence among dating couples ranged from about 1 percent each year to 27 percent (Arias, Samios, & OLeary, 1987; Lane & Gwartney-Gibbs, 1985; Makepeace, 1983).

b. Spouse Abuse. There are yet no national surveys of reported spouse abuse that collect state data in the same manner that child maltreatment report data have been collected and analyzed; thus, most of the data on the extent of violence toward women and between partners come from self-report surveys.

One source of self-report survey data is the data collected by the U.S. Department of Justice's National Crime Victimization Survey (NCVS). The NCVS collects data from a

---

[1] This projection is based on data from forty-three states. A total of 935 fatalities occurred in the forty-three states.
[2] No rate or projection is available for 1998 because too few states representing too small a percentage of the U.S. population of children reported data for 1998 to Prevent Child Abuse America.

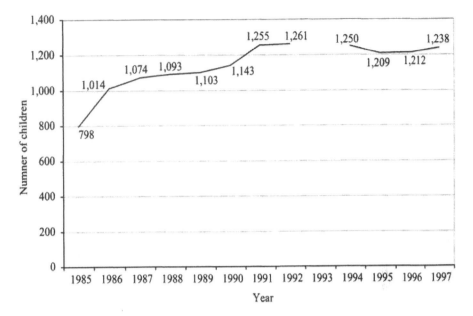

FIGURE II-5-1-1.2. Child fatalities. *Source*: [1]McCurdy & Daro, 1993; [2]National Committee to Prevent Child Abuse, www.childabuse.org, 2000.

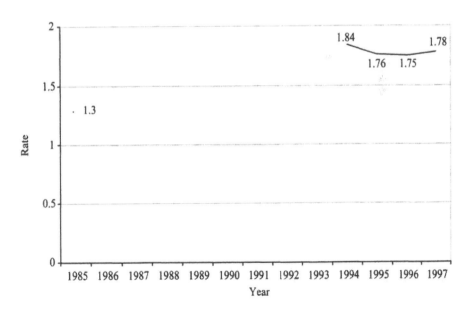

FIGURE II-5-1-1.3. Child fatality rates.

representative sample of some 60,000 households each year. Violent crimes included in the NCVS include rape, robbery, and assault (but not murder).

According to the NCVS, between 1987 and 1991, intimates committed an annual average of 621,015 rapes, robberies or assaults (U.S. Department of Justice, 1994). In 1992, 51 percent of the victims of intimate violence were attacked by boyfriends or girlfriends, 34 percent were attacked by spouses, and 15 percent were attacked by ex-spouses. Most of the violent acts were assaults. Females were ten times more likely to be the victims as were males. The annual rate of intimate violent victimizations was 5 per 1,000 for women and 0.5 per 1,000 for men. The highest rate of intimate victimization was for victims twenty to twenty-four years of age—a rate of 15.5 per 1,000. The lowest rate was for individuals fifty years of age and older (Bachman, 1994).

Prior to 1992 the NCVS studies of domestic violence did not specifically ask or cue respondents to the issue of violence between intimates. The Bureau of Justice Statistics redesigned the study and began administering the new survey in 1992. According to data from the redesigned survey, in 1992–1993, 9 women in 1,000, or one million women each year, experienced violence at the hands of an intimate (Bachman & Saltzman, 1995). The rate of violent victimization at the hands of a stranger was 7.4 per 1,000. The number of intimate victimizations and the rate dropped between 1993 and 1998—1998 survey data projected that 876,340 women were victims of intimate victimizations, or a rate of 7.7 per 1,000 (Rennison & Welchans, 2000).

Straus and Gelles and their colleagues have carried out three national surveys of domestic violence—in-person interviews with a nationally representative sample of 2,143 respondents in 1976 (Straus, Gelles & Steinmetz, 1980), telephone interviews with a nationally representative sample of 6,002 respondents in 1985 (Gelles & Straus, 1986; Straus & Gelles, 1986), and telephone interviews with a nationally representative sample of 1,970 respondents in 1992 (Straus and Kantor, 1994).

The rate of "minor violence" or violence that had a low probability of causing a physical injury declined from 100 per 1,000 women in 1975 to about 80 per 1,000 in 1985 and then rose to 91 per 1,000 in 1992. More serious or severe acts of violence toward women (acts labeled "severe assaults" or "wife beating" by the investigators) declined from 38 per 1,000 in 1975 to 19 per 1,000 in 1992.

The National Violence Against Women Survey (NVAW) involved telephone interviews with a nationally representative sample of 8,000 women and 8,000 men. The survey was conducted between November 1995 and May 1996 (Tjaden & Thoennes, 1998) The NVAW survey assessed lifetime prevalence and annual prevalence (violence experienced in the previous twelve months). The NVAW used a "modified" version of the Conflict Tactics Scales to measure violence victimization. Nearly 52 percent of women surveyed (519 per 1,000—52,261,743 women) reported experiencing a physical assault as a child or adult. Nearly 56 percent of women surveyed (559 per 1,000—56,289,623 women) reported experiencing any form of violence, including stalking, rape, or physical assault. The rate of lifetime assault at the hands of an intimate partner was 221 per 1,000 for physical violence and 254 per 1,000 for any form of violence-victimization. The rates of forms of violence less likely to cause any injury, such as pushing, grabbing, shoving, or slapping were the highest (between 160 and 181 per 1,000), while the rates of the most severe forms of violence (used a gun; used a knife, beat up) were the lowest (85 per 1,000 for "beat up;" 7 per 1,000 for used a gun).

The annual prevalence of violence was 19 per 1,000 for physical assault (1,913,243 women) and 30 per 1,000 for any form of violence victimization (3,020,910 women). The annual prevalence of women victimized by intimate partners was 13 per 1,000 for physical assault (1,309,061) and 18 per 1,000 (1,812,546 women) for all forms of victimization.

c. FEMALE TO MALE INTIMATE VIOLENCE. There has been quite a controversy in the field of family violence regarding the extent of male victimization (see for example, Wardell, Gillespie, & Leffler 1983; Dobash et al., 1992). Data from the earliest studies of spousal violence detected violence by women toward their husbands (see for example, Gelles, 1974). The two National Family Violence Surveys (Straus, Gelles, & Steinmetz, 1980; Straus & Gelles, 1986) also found a higher than expected incidence of violence toward men—the rate of violence was the same or even higher than that reported for male-to-female violence. In addition, women initiated violence about as often as men initiate violence (Straus, 1993). However, the researchers qualified their findings by noting that much of the female violence appeared to be in self-defense and that females, because of their size and strength, appeared to inflict less injury than male attackers. In addition, two national self-report surveys found that women reported victimization by partners or ex-partners ten times more often than men (Bachman, 1994; U.S. Department of Justice, 1994). These differences may be accounted for by the fact that the National Crime Victimization Surveys only included victimization serious enough to be considered a crime by the respondents. Studies have found that female partner victimization is more likely to be accompanied by sexual and emotional abuse (Saunders, 1988). Women victims of intimate violence also suffer more emotional and psychological consequences than do men (Stets & Straus, 1990). A final difference is the quality of male and female violence. Some researchers, such as Wilson and Daly (1992), use anecdotal and qualitative data to make the point that although the actual numbers may appear similar, the quality of female killings differs from male killings. Males, according to Wilson and Daly (1992), often stalk their victims and hunt down and kill spouses who have left them. Males often kill wives after lengthy periods of physical and emotional abuse. Males are much more likely to kill their wives and children in acts of familicide.

d. SEXUAL VIOLENCE/MARITAL RAPE. There have been a handful of studies that examine sexual violence, or what has been labeled "marital rape." Finkelhor and Yllo (1985) report that 10 percent of a sample of 323 women said they had been forced to have sex with their husbands. Of the 644 married women interviewed by Russell (1984), 14 percent reported one or more incidents of marital rape. Data from the Second National Family Violence Survey found that 1.2 percent of the 2,934 married women interviewed said they were victims of attempted or completed forced sexual intercourse with their husbands in the previous year (Gelles, 1992).

e. PSYCHOLOGICAL ABUSE. As with child maltreatment, there have been few attempts to assess the extent of psychological abuse among adult intimate partners. One key constraint to obtaining a measure of the extent of psychological abuse is developing an adequate nominal and operational definition of psychological maltreatment. Straus and Sweet (1992) using the "Psychological Aggression" scale from the Conflict Tactics Scales found that 74 percent of the men and 75 percent of the women surveyed for the Second National Family Violence Survey reported using at least one form of psychological aggression at least once in the previous year.

f. HOMICIDE OF INTIMATES. Researchers generally report that intrafamilial homicides account for between 20 and 40 percent of all murders (Curtis, 1974). Five hundred ten husbands and boyfriends were killed by their wives and girlfriends in 1998, whereas more than 1,320 wives and girlfriends were slain by their husbands or boyfriends (Rennison & Welchans, 2000).

5. Witnessing Domestic Violence

Children who witness domestic violence have recently been identified as a unique population warranting research and clinical attention (Rosenberg & Rossman, 1990). Witnessing is at the intersection of child abuse and neglect and domestic violence. Researchers and clinicians report that children who witness acts of domestic violence experience negative behavioral and developmental outcomes, independent of any direct abuse or neglect that they may also experience from their caretakers (Jaffe, Wolfe, & Wilson, 1990; Osofsky, 1995; Rosenberg & Rossman, 1990).

Estimates from the two National Family Violence Surveys are that between 1.5 and 3.3 million children from three to seventeen years of age are exposed to domestic violence each year (Gelles & Straus, 1988; Straus, Gelles, & Steinmetz, 1980).

6. Elder Abuse

As with child abuse and neglect, the abuse of the elderly includes a range of acts of commission and omission that has harmful consequences for the elderly victim. The types of elder abuse include physical abuse, psychological abuse, and material abuse (e.g., financial exploitation), or physical, psychological, or material neglect (Wolf, 1995). Some definitions of elder abuse include "self-abuse" or "self-neglect" as a form of elder mistreatment, although some researchers exclude this form of mistreatment and limit elder abuse to acts of omission and commission perpetrated by someone other than the elder victim.

The perpetrators of elder abuse can include children, spouses, or others who have a care-taking responsibility for the elder.

Measurement of the extent of elder abuse is even more elusive than the other forms of family violence. Researchers estimate that 5 percent of those sixty-five years or older are victims of physical abuse, psychological abuse, financial exploitation, and/or neglect in the previous year (Wolf, 1995). Pillemer and Finkelhor (1988) interviewed 2,020 community dwelling (noninstitutionalized) elderly persons in the Boston metropolitan area. Overall, 32 elderly persons per 1,000 reported experiencing physical violence, verbal aggression, and/or neglect in the past year. The rate of physical violence was 20 per 1,000. Although the conventional view of elder abuse is that of middle-aged children abusing and neglecting their elderly parents, Pillemer and Finkelhor found that spouses were the most frequent abusers of the elderly and that roughly equal numbers of men and women were victims. Women, however, were the victims of the most serious forms of abuse, such as punching, kicking, beating, and choking.

More recently, the National Elder Abuse Incidence Survey found that approximately 450,000 elderly persons living in domestic settings were abused and/or neglected in 1996 (National Center in Elder Abuse, 1998).

7. Other Forms of Intimate Violence

Although parent-to-child violence and violence toward women have received the most public attention, physical fights between brothers and sisters are by far the most common form of family violence. It is, however, rare that parents, physicians, or social workers consider sibling violence as problematic forms of family violence. Violence between siblings often goes far beyond so-called normal violence, for example, at least 109,000 children use guns or knives in fights with siblings each year (Straus, Gelles, & Steinmetz, 1980).

Child-to-parent violence is rarely mentioned in public discussions of family violence. Here the reason is less public acceptance for this type of violence and more the shame of the parent-victims who are reluctant to seek help or call attention to their plight for fear of being blamed for the violence. Each year, according to the National Family Violence Survey, between 750,000 to 1 million parents have violent acts committed against them by their teenage children (Cornell & Gelles, 1982).

Finally, researchers and clinicians have found significant levels of violence among gay and lesbian couples (Brand & Kidd, 1986; Lockhart et al., 1994; Renzetti, 1992).

III. RISK AND PROTECTIVE FACTORS

With regard to what are the risk and protective factors for family violence, there has also been heated debate. Some spokespersons argue that violence cuts across all social groups, while others agree that it cuts across social groups, but not evenly. Some researchers and practitioners place more emphasis on psychological factors, while others locate the key risk factors among social factors. Still a third group places the greatest emphasis on cultural factors, for example the patriarchal social organization of societies. In addition, the source of data has an impact not only on measures of incidence and prevalence of family violence, but also on what factors and variables are identified as risk and protective factors. When basing an analysis of risk and protective factors on clinical data or official report data, risk and protective factors are confounded with factors such as labeling bias or agency or clinical setting catchment area. Researchers have long noted that certain individuals and families are more likely to be correctly and incorrectly labeled as offenders or victims of family violence, and, similarly, some individuals and families are insulated from being correctly or incorrectly labeled or identified as offenders or victims (Gelles, 1975; Newberger et al., 1977; Hampton & Newberger, 1985). Social survey data are not immune to confounding problems either, as social or demographic factors may be related to willingness to participate in a self-report survey and a tendency toward providing socially desirable responses.

The definitional issue mentioned earlier in the chapter also constrains the fields ability to develop a comprehensive and coherent inventory of risk and protective factors. While this chapter uses a broad definition of "family violence," it is believed by many in this field that acts of physical violence are conceptually distinct from and arise from different generative causes than acts of nonphysical harm. Thus it is nearly impossible in the space allotted to this chapter, to enumerate, by type of violence, each set of risk and protective factors. Some factors will be more strongly related to one form of harm (e.g., injurious physical violence) and may be unrelated to others types of harm (neglect).

Because this chapter examines violence in all types of family and intimate relationships, the task of identifying risk and protective factors becomes even more complex because some factors are more strongly related to violence in one type of relationship (e.g., parent to child) and are not related to one or more of the other types of family violence (e.g., sibling violence or elder abuse).

The final caveat is that *any* listing of risk and protective factors may unintentionally convey or reinforce a notion of single factor explanations for family violence. Clearly, no phenomenon as complex as family violence could possibly be explained with a single factor model. Equally clear is the fact that almost all of the risk and protective factors discussed in this chapter and in the literature have relatively modest correlations with family violence. This chapter lists risk and protective factors for heuristic purposes, with the full knowledge that multiple factors are related to family violence and there is often an interaction between and among risk and protective factors.

With all these caveats in mind, this section reviews the most widely discussed risk and protective factors in the study of family violence and, where appropriate, identifies for which forms of violence and which types of relationships the factors are or are not relevant. By and large, risk and protective factors are discussed if they have been found to be related to family violence in self-report survey research *and* official report data. Because clinical research often does not employ appropriate comparison groups and because clinical research does not typically attempt to unpack risk and protective factors from the factors that brought cases to the specific clinical setting, this section does not review or cite clinical research.

1. Social and Demographic Risk Factors

The major social and demographic risk factors for family violence appear to be the following:

- *Age*: One of the most consistent risk factors is the age of the offender. As with violence between non-intimates, violence is most likely to be perpetrated by those between eighteen and thirty years of age. Young age is not a risk factor for elder abuse, although the rate of elder abuse is lower than the rate of the other forms of family violence.
- *Sex*: Similarly with non-intimate violence, men are the most likely offenders in acts of intimate violence as well. However, the differences in the rates of offending by men compared to women are much smaller for violence in the family compared to violence outside the home. Men and women have somewhat similar rates of child homicide, although women appear more likely to be offenders when the child victim is young (under three years of age) and males are the more likely offenders when the child victim is older.
- *Income*. Although most poor parents and partners do not use violence toward intimates, self-report surveys and official report data find that the rates of all forms of family violence, except sexual abuse, are higher for those whose family incomes are below the poverty line than for those whose income is above the poverty line.
- *Race*. Both official report data and self-report survey data often report that child abuse and violence toward women are overrepresented among minorities. Data from the NCVS indicate that the rate of intimate adult violence is slightly higher for blacks (5.8 per 1,000) compared to whites (5.4 per 1,000). The rate of intimate violence for Hispanics is 5.5. The Second Study of the National Incidence and Prevalence of Child Abuse and Neglect (National Center on Child Abuse and Neglect, 1988) found no significant relationships between the incidence of maltreatment and the child's race/ethnicity. There was no significant relationship for any of the subcategories of maltreatment.

The two National Family Violence Surveys, however, found stronger relationships between race/ethnicity and violence between partners and violence toward children. Although in the first National Family Violence Survey, the difference in rates between blacks and whites disappeared when income was controlled, an analysis of the larger data set from the Second National Family Violence Survey found that the differences persisted even when income was controlled.

2. Situational and Environmental Factors

a. Stress. Unemployment, financial problems, being a single parent, being a teenage mother, and sexual difficulties are all factors that are related to violence, as are a host of other stressor events (Gelles & Straus, 1988; Gelles, 1989; Parke & Collmer, 1975; Straus, Gelles, & Steinmetz, 1980).

b. Social Isolation and Social Support. The data on social isolation are somewhat less consistent than are the data for the previously listed correlates. First, because so much of the research on family violence is cross-sectional, it is not clear whether social isolation precedes violence or is a consequence of violence in the home. Second, social isolation has been crudely measured and the purported correlation may be more anecdotal than statistical. Nevertheless, researchers often agree that people who are socially isolated from neighbors and relatives are more likely to be violent in the home. Social support appears to be an important protective factor. One major source of social support is the availability of friends and family for help, aid, and assistance. The more a family is integrated into the community and the more groups and associations they belong to, the less likely they are to be violent (Straus et al., 1980).

c. The Intergenerational Transmission of Violence. The notion that abused children grow up to be abusing parents and violent adults has been widely expressed in the child abuse and family violence literature (Gelles, 1980). Kaufman and Zigler (1987) reviewed the literature that tested the intergenerational transmission of violence toward children hypothesis and concluded that the best estimate of the rate of intergenerational transmission appears to be 30 percent (plus or minus 5 percent). Although a rate of 30 percent is substantially less than the majority of abused children, the rate is considerably more than the between 2 and 4 percent rate of abuse found in the general population (Straus & Gelles, 1986; Widom, 1989). Egeland and his colleagues (Egeland, Jacobvitz, & Papatola, 1987) examined continuity and discontinuity of abuse in a longitudinal study of high-risk mothers and their children. They found that mothers who had been abused as children were less likely to abuse their own children if they had emotionally supportive parents, partners, or friends. In addition, the abused mothers who did not abuse their children were described as "middle class" and "upwardly mobile," suggesting that they were able to draw on economic resources that may not have been available to the abused mothers who did abuse their children.

Evidence from studies of parental and marital violence indicate that while experiencing violence in ones family of origin is often correlated with later violent behavior, such experience is not the sole determining factor. When the intergenerational transmission of violence occurs, it is likely the result of a complex set of social and psychological processes.

Although experiencing and witnessing violence is believed to be an important risk factor, the actual mechanism by which violence is transmitted from generation to generation is not well understood.

d. GENDER INEQUALITY. One of the important risk factors for violence against women is gender inequality. Individual, aggregate, and cross-cultural data find that the greater the degree of gender inequality in a relationship, community, and society, the higher are the rates of violence toward women (Browne & Williams, 1993; Coleman & Straus, 1986; Levinson, 1989; Morley, 1994; Straus, 1994b; Straus et al., 1980).

e. PRESENCE OF OTHER VIOLENCE. A final general risk factor is that the presence of violence in one family relationship increases the risk that there will be violence in other relationships. Thus children in homes where there is domestic violence are more likely to experience violence than are children who grow up in homes where there is no violence between their parents. Moreover, children who witness and experience violence are more likely to use violence toward their parents and siblings than are children who do not experience or see violence in their homes (Straus et al., 1980).

IV. RESEARCH ON VICTIMS

Compared to research on offenders, there has been somewhat less research on victims of family violence that focuses on factors that increase or reduce the risk of victimization. Most research on victims examines the consequences of victimization (e.g., depression, psychological distress, suicide attempts, symptoms of post traumatic stress syndrome, etc.) or the effectiveness of various intervention efforts.

1. Children

The very youngest children appear to be at the greatest risk of being abused, especially in regard to the most dangerous and potentially lethal forms of violence (Fergusson, Fleming, & ONeil, 1972; Gil, 1970; Johnson, 1974). Not only are young children physically more fragile and thus more susceptible to injury, but also their vulnerability makes them more likely to be reported and diagnosed as abused when injured. Older children are underreported as victims of abuse. Adolescent victims may be considered delinquent or ungovernable, and thus thought of as contributing to their own victimization.

Younger boys are more likely to be abused than older boys. The first National Family Violence Survey found that older girls were more likely to be victimized than younger girls (Straus et al., 1980).

Early research suggested that there were a number of factors that raise the risk of a child being abused. Low birth weight babies (Parke & Collmer, 1975), premature children (Elmer, 1967; Newberger et al., 1977; Parke & Collmer, 1975; Steele & Pollack, 1974), and handicapped, retarded, or developmentally disabled children (Friedrich and Boriskin, 1976; Gil, 1970; Steinmetz, 1978) were all described as being at greater risk of being abused by their parents or caretakers. However, a review of studies that examines the child's role in abuse calls into question many of these findings (Starr, 1988). One major problem is that few investigators used matched comparison groups. Secondly, newer studies fail to find premature or handicapped children being at higher risk for abuse (Egeland & Vaughan, 1981; Starr et al., 1984).

2. Marital Partners

Studies that examine the individual and social attributes of victims of marital violence are difficult to interpret. It is often not clear whether the factors found among victims were present *before* they were battered or are the result of the victimization. Such studies often use small samples, clinical samples, and fail to have comparison groups.

Battered women have been described as dependent, having low esteem, and feeling inadequate and helpless (Ball, 1977; Hilberman & Munson, 1977; Shainess, 1977; Walker, 1979). Descriptive and clinical accounts consistently report a high incidence of depression and anxiety among samples of battered women (Hilberman, 1980). Sometimes the personality profiles of battered women reported in the literature seem directly opposite. While some researchers describe battered women as unassertive, shy, and reserved (Weitzman & Dreen, 1982), other reports picture battered women as aggressive, masculine, frigid, and masochistic (Snell, Rosenwald, & Robey, 1964; Ball, 1977).

Hotaling and Sugarman (1990) reviewed the wife abuse literature and examined risk markers for abuse. They found few risk markers that identify women at risk of violence in intimate relations. High levels of marital conflict and low socioeconomic status emerged as the primary predictors of increased likelihood of wife assault.

3. Elder Victims

Research on elder abuse is divided on whether elder victims are more likely to be physically, socially, and emotionally dependent on their caretakers or whether it is the offenders dependence on the victim that increases the risk of elder abuse (see Pillemer, 1993; Steinmetz, 1993). Conventional wisdom suggests that it is the oldest, sickest, most debilitated and dependent elders who are prone to the full range of mistreatment by their caretakers. However, Pillemer (1993) has found that dependency of the victim is not as powerful a risk factor as perceived by clinicians, the public, and some researchers.

V. THEORETICAL MODELS OF FAMILY VIOLENCE

The first people to identify a problem often shape how others will perceive it (Nelson, 1984:13). Child abuse and neglect, the first form of family violence to receive scholarly and public attention, was identified by the medical profession in the early 1960s. The initial conceptualizations portrayed abuse and violence between intimates as a rare event, typically caused by the psychopathology of the offender. The perception of the abuser, or violent offender, as suffering from some form of psychopathology has persisted, in part because the first conceptualization of family violence was the guiding framework for the work that followed. The psychopathological or psychiatric conceptualization has also persisted because the tragic picture of a defenseless child, woman, or grandparent subjected to abuse and neglect arouses the strongest emotions in clinicians and others who see and/or treat the problem of intimate violence. There frequently seems to be no rational explanation for harming a loved one, especially one who appears to be helpless and defenseless.

Family violence has been approached from three general theoretical levels of analysis: (1) the intraindividual level of analysis, or the psychiatric model; (2) the social-psychological level of analysis, and (3) the sociological or sociocultural level of analysis.

1. The Psychiatric Model

The psychiatric model focuses on the offenders personality characteristics as the chief determinants of violence and abuse of intimates; although some applications focus on the individual personality characteristics of the victims (see for example, Snell, Rosenwald, & Robey, 1964; Shainess, 1979). The psychiatric model includes theoretical approaches that link personality disorders, character disorders, mental illness, alcohol and substance abuse, and other intraindividual processes to acts of family violence.

2. The Social-Psychological Model

The social-psychological model assumes that violence and abuse can best be understood by careful examination of the external environmental factors that impact on the family, on family organization and structure, and on the everyday interactions between intimates that are precursors to acts of violence. Theoretical approaches that examine family structure, learning, stress, the transmission of violence from one generation to the next, and family interaction patterns fit the social-psychological model.

3. The Sociocultural Model

The sociocultural model provides a macrolevel of analysis. Violence is examined in light of socially structured variables such as inequality, patriarchy, or cultural norms and attitudes about violence and family relations.

VI. THEORIES

A number of sociological and psychological theories have been developed to explain family violence. They include the following:

1. Social Learning Theory

Social learning theory proposes that individuals who experienced violence are more likely to use violence in the home than those who have experienced little or no violence. The theorys central proposition is that children who either experience violence themselves or who witness violence between their parents are more likely to use violence when they grow up. The family is the institution and social group where people learn the roles of husband and wife, parent and child. The home is the prime location where people learn how to deal with various stresses, crises, and frustrations. In many instances, the home is also the site where a person first experiences violence. Not only do people learn violent behavior, but also they learn how to justify being violent. For example, hearing a father say "this will hurt me more than it will hurt you," or a mother say, "you have been bad, so you deserve to be spanked," contribute to how children learn to justify violent behavior.

2. Social Situational/Stress and Coping Theory

Social situation/stress and coping theory explains why violence is used in some situations and not others. The theory proposes that abuse and violence occurs because of two main factors. The first is structural stress and the lack of coping resources in a family. For instance, the association between low income and family violence indicates that an important factor in violence is inadequate financial resources. The second factor is the cultural norm concerning the use of force and violence. In contemporary American society, as well as many societies, violence in general, and violence toward children in particular is normative (Straus, Gelles, & Steinmetz, 1980; Straus, 1994a). Thus individuals learn to use violence both expressively and instrumentally as a means of coping with a pile up of stressor events.

3. Resource Theory

Resource theory assumes that all social systems (including the family) rest to some degree on force or the threat of force. The more resources—social, personal, and economic—a person can command, the more force he or she can muster. However, the fewer resources a person has, the more he or she will actually use force in an open manner. Thus a husband who wants to be the dominant person in the family, but has little education, has a job low in prestige and income, and lacks interpersonal skills may choose to use violence to maintain the dominant position. In addition, family members (including children) may use violence to redress a grievance when they have few alternative resources available. Thus, wives who have few social resources or social contacts may use violence toward their husbands in order to protect themselves.

4. Exchange Theory

Exchange theory proposes that wife abuse and child abuse are governed by the principle of costs and benefits. Abuse is used when the rewards are greater than the costs (Gelles, 1983). The private nature of the family, the reluctance of social institutions and agencies to intervene—in spite of mandatory child abuse reporting laws or mandatory arrest laws for spouse abuse—and the low risk of other interventions reduce the costs of abuse and violence. The cultural approval of violence as both expressive and instrumental behavior raises the potential rewards for violence. The most significant reward is social control, or power.

5. Sociobiology Theory

A sociobiological, or evolutionary perspective of family violence, suggests that violence toward human or nonhuman primate offspring is the result of the reproductive success potential of children and parental investment. The theory's central assumption is that natural selection is the process of differential reproduction and reproductive success (Daly & Wilson, 1980). Males can be expected to invest in offspring when there is some degree of parental certainty (how confident the parent is that the child is their own genetic offspring), while females are also inclined to invest under conditions of parental certainty. Parents recognize their offspring and avoid squandering valuable reproductive effort on someone else's offspring. Children not genetically related to the parent (e.g., stepchildren, adopted, or foster children) or children with low reproductive potential (e.g., handicapped or retarded children) are at the highest risk for infanticide and abuse (Burgess & Garbarino, 1983; Daly & Wilson, 1980; Hrdy, 1979). Large families can dilute parental energy and lower attachment to children thus increasing the risk of child abuse and neglect (Burgess, 1979).

Smuts (1992) applied an evolutionary perspective to male aggression against females. Smuts (1992), Daly and Wilson (1988), and Burgess and Draper (1989) argue that male aggression against females often reflects male reproductive striving. Both human and nonhuman male primates are postulated to use aggression against females to intimidate females so that they will not resist future male efforts to mate with them and to reduce the likelihood that females will mate with other males. Thus males use aggression to control female sexuality to males' reproductive advantage. The frequency of male aggression varies across societies and situations depending on the strength of female alliances, the support women can receive from their families, the strength and importance of male alliances, the degree of equality in male–female relationships, and the degree to which males control the economic resources within a society. Male aggression toward females, both physical violence and rape, is high when female alliances are weak, when females lack kin support, when male alliances are strong, when male–female relationships are unbalanced, and when males control societal resources.

6. Feminist Theory

Feminist theorists (e.g., Dobash & Dobash, 1979; Pagelow, 1984; Yllo, 1983, 1988) see wife abuse as a unique phenomenon that has been obscured and overshadowed by what they refer to as a "narrow" focus on domestic or family violence. The central thesis of this theory is that economic and social processes operate directly and indirectly to support a patriarchal (male dominated) social order and family structure. Patriarchy is seen as leading to the subordination of women and causes the historical pattern of systematic violence directed against wives.

7. An Ecological Perspective

The "ecological perspective" is an attempt to integrate the three levels of theoretical analysis (individual, social psychological, and sociocultural) into a single theoretical model. James Garbarino (1977) and Jay Belsky (1980, 1993) have proposed an "ecological model" to explain the complex nature of child maltreatment. The model rests on three levels of analysis:

the relationship between the organism and environment, the interacting and overlapping systems in which human development occurs, and environmental quality. The ecological model proposes that violence and abuse arise out of a mismatch of parent to child and family to neighborhood and community. The risk of abuse and violence is greatest when the functioning of the children and parents is limited and constrained by developmental problems. Children with learning disabilities and social or emotional handicaps are at increased risk for abuse. Parents under considerable stress, or who have personality problems, are at increased risk for abusing their children. These conditions are worsened when social interaction between the spouses or the parents and children heighten the stress or make the personal problems worse. Finally, if there are few institutions and agencies in the community to support troubled families, then the risk of abuse is further raised. Garbarino (1977) identifies two necessary conditions for child maltreatment. First, there must be cultural justification for the use of force against children. Secondly, the maltreating family is isolated from potent family or community support systems. The ecological model has served as a perspective to examine other forms of family violence. However, the model has mostly served as a heuristic device to organize thinking and research about family violence. There has not yet been an actual empirical test of the integrated model, other than the research conducted by Garbarino in the 1970s.

8. A Model of Sexual Abuse

Finkelhor (1984) reviewed research on the factors that have been proposed as contributing to sexual abuse of children and has developed what he calls a "Four Precondition Model of Sexual Abuse." His review suggests that all the factors relating to sexual abuse can be grouped into one of four preconditions that need to be met before sexual abuse can occur. The preconditions are:

   a. A potential offender needs to have some motivation to abuse a child sexually.
   b. The potential offender has to overcome internal inhibitions against acting on that motivation.
   c. The potential offender has to overcome external impediments to committing sexual abuse.
   d. The potential offender or some other factor has to undermine or overcome a child's possible resistance to sexual abuse.

VII. SUMMARY

One overriding factor that influences the study and consideration of intimate and family violence is the emotional nature of both research and practice. Few other areas of inquiry in the field of criminal justice generate the strong feelings and reactions that child abuse, child sexual abuse, violence against women, elder abuse, and courtship violence generate. Even the most grotesque case examples fail to adequately capture the devastating physical and psychological consequences of physical abuse at the hands of a loved one or caretaker. Those in the field of criminal justice not only must face difficult and complex cases, but they often are frustrated by the inadequate conceptual and practical resources they can bring to bear on behalf of victims, offenders, and families.

There are no simple answers or "silver bullets." The relative recency of family and intimate violence as an area of study, and the fact that the first decade of research was dominated by a psychopathology model of causation, resulted in a limited level of theoretical development of the field. Moreover, the emotional nature of family and intimate violence has generated deep and heated controversies over estimates of extent, risk and protective factors, and causal models.

Yet, despite the controversies and limited theoretical development, one conclusion is inescapable. No one factor can explain the presence or absence of family and intimate violence. Characteristics of the child, parent, partners, family, social situation, community, and society are related to which family members are abused and under what conditions. Individual and emotional characteristics, psychological characteristics, and community factors, such as cultural attitudes regarding violence, are moderated and influenced by family structure and family situations. In addition, power and control are common features of nearly all forms of family and intimate violence. Thus, interventions and prevention efforts need to be aimed at the importance of power and control and the functions of the family system if family and intimate violence is to be effectively treated and prevented.

REFERENCES

Arias, Ileana, Mary Samios, & K. Daniel OLeary. (1987). Prevalence and Correlates of Physical Aggression during Courtship. *Journal of Interpersonal Violence, 2,* 82–90.
Bachman, Ronet. (1994). *Violence against Women: A National Crime Victimization Survey Report.* Washington: U.S. Department of Justice, Bureau of Justice Statistics.
Bachman, Ronet, & Linda Saltzman. (1995). *Violence against Women: Estimates from the Redesigned Survey.* Washington: U.S. Department of Justice, Bureau of Justice Statistics.
Ball, Margaret. (1977). Issues of Violence in Family Casework. *Social Casework, 58,* 3–12.
Belsky, Jay. (1980). Child Maltreatment: An Ecological Integration. *American Psychologist, 35,* 320–335.
Belsky, Jay. (1993). Etiology of Child Maltreatment: A Developmental-Ecological Approach. *Psychological Bulletin, 114,* 413–434.
Brand, Pamela A., & Aline H. Kidd. (1986). Frequency of Physical Aggression in Heterosexual and Female Homosexual Dyads. *Psychological Reports, 59,* 1307–1313.
Browne, Angela, & Kirk R. Williams. (1993). Gender, Intimacy, and Lethal Violence. *Gender and Society, 7,* 78–98.
Burgdorf, Kenneth. (1980). *Recognition and Reporting of Child Maltreatment.* Rockville: Westat.
Burgess, Robert L. (1979). *Family Violence: Some Implications from Evolutionary Biology.* Paper Presented at Annual Meetings of the American Society of Criminology, Philadelphia.
Burgess, Robert L., & Patricia Draper. (1989). The Explanation of Family Violence: The Role of Biological, Behavioral, and Cultural Selection. In Lloyd Ohlin & Michael Tonry (Eds.), *Family Violence: Crime and Justice: A Review of Research. Volume 11* (pp. 59–116). Chicago: University of Chicago Press.
Burgess, Robert L., & James Garbarino. (1983). Doing What Comes Naturally? An Evolutionary Perspective on Child Abuse. In David Finkelhor, Richard J. Gelles, Murray A. Straus & Gerald T. Hotaling (Eds.), *The Dark Side of the Families: Current Family Violence Research* (pp. 88–101). Beverly Hills: Sage.
Cate, Rodney M., June M. Henton, F. Scott Christopher, & Sally A. Lloyd. (1982). Premarital Abuse: A Social Psychological Perspective. *Journal of Family Issues, 3,* 79–90.
Coleman, Diane H., & Murray A. Straus. (1986). Marital Power, Conflict, and Violence in a Nationally Representative Sample of American Couples. *Violence and Victims, 1,* 141–157.
Cornell, Claire P., & Richard J. Gelles. (1982). Adolescent to Parent Violence. *Urban Social Change Review, 15,* 8–14.
Curtis, Lynn A. (1974). *Criminal Violence: National Patterns and Behavior.* Lexington: Lexington Books.
Daly, Martin, & Margo Wilson. (1980). Discriminative Parental Solicitude: A Biosocial Perspective. *Journal of Marriage and the Family, 42,* 277–288.

Daly, Martin, & Margo Wilson. (1988). *Homicide.* New York: Aldine DeGruyter.
Dobash, Rebecca E., & Russell P. Dobash. (1979). *Violence against Wives.* New York: Free Press.
Dobash, Russell P., Rebecca E. Dobash, Margo Wilson, & Martin Daly. (1992). The Myth of Sexual Symmetry in Marital Violence. *Social Problems, 39,* 71–91.
Elmer, Elizabeth. (1967). *Children in Jeopardy: A Study of Abused Minors and Their Families.* Pittsburgh: University of Pittsburgh Press.
Egeland, Byron, & Brian Vaughan. (1981). Failure of Bond Formation'as a Cause of Abuse, Neglect, and Maltreatment. *American Journal of Orthopsychiatry, 51,* 78–84.
Egeland, Byron, Deborah Jacobvitz, & Kathleen Papatola. (1987). Intergenerational Continuity of Abuse. In Richard Gelles & Jane B. Lancaster (Eds.), *Child Abuse and Neglect: Biosocial Dimensions* (pp. 255–276). New York: Aldine de Gruyter.
Etzioni, Amitai. (1971). Violence. In Robert K. Merton, & Robert Nisbet (Eds.), *Contemporary Social Problems* (pp. 709–741). New York: Harcourt Brace Jovanovich.
Fergusson, David M., Joan Fleming, & David P. ONeil. (1972). *Child Abuse in New Zealand.* Wellington, New Zealand: Research Division, Department of Social Work.
Finkelhor, David. (1984). *Child Sexual Abuse: New Theory and Research.* New York: Free Press.
Finkelhor, David, & Gerald T. Hotaling. (1984). Sexual Abuse in the National Incidence Study of Child Abuse and Neglect: An Appraisal. *Child Abuse and Neglect: The International Journal, 8,* 23–32.
Finkelhor, David, & Kersti Yllo. (1985). *License to Rape: Sexual Abuse of Wives.* New York: Holt, Rinehart and Winston.
Finkelhor, David, Gerald Hotaling, I. A. Lewis, & Christine Smith. (1990). Sexual Abuse in a National Sample of Adult Men and Women: Prevalence, Characteristics, and Risk Factors. *Child Abuse and Neglect: The International Journal, 14,* 19–28.
Friedrich, William N., & Jerry A. Boriskin. (1976). The Role of the Child in Abuse: A Review of Literature. *American Journal of Orthopsychiatry, 46,* 580–590.
Garbarino, James. (1977). The Human Ecology of Child Maltreatment. *Journal of Marriage and the Family, 39,* 721–735.
Gelles, Richard J. (1974). *The Violent Home.* Beverly Hills: Sage.
Gelles, Richard J. (1975). The Social Construction of Child Abuse. *American Journal of Orthopsychiatry, 45,* 363–371.
Gelles, Richard J. (1980). Violence in the Family: A Review of Research in the Seventies. *Journal of Marriage and the Family, 42,* 873–885.
Gelles, Richard J. (1983). An Exchange/Social Control Theory. In David Finkelhor, Richard J. Gelles, Murray A. Straus, & Gerald T. Hotaling (Eds.), *The Dark Side of Families: Current Family Violence Research* (pp. 151–165). Beverly Hills: Sage.
Gelles, Richard. J. (1989). Child Abuse and Violence in Single Parent Families: Parent Absence and Economic Deprivation. *American Journal of Orthopsychiatry, 59,* 492–501.
Gelles, Richard. (1992). *Marital Rape.* (mimeographed).
Gelles, Richard J., & Murray A. Straus. (1987). Is Violence towards Children Increasing? A Comparison of 1975 and 1985 National Survey Rates. *Journal of Interpersonal Violence, 2,* 212–222.
Gelles, Richard J., & Murray A. Straus. (1988). *Intimate Violence.* New York: Simon and Schuster.
Gil, David G. (1970). *Violence against Children: Physical Child Abuse in the United States.* Cambridge: Harvard University Press.
Giles-Sims, Jean. (1983). *Wife-Beating: A Systems Theory Approach.* New York: Guilford.
Greenfield, Lawrence A., Michael R. Rand, Diane Craven, Patsy A. Klaus, Craig A. Perkins, Cathy Ringel, Greg Warchol, Cathy Maston, & James A. Fox. (1998). *Violence by Intimates: Analysis of Data on Crimes by Current or Former Spouses, Boyfriends, and Girlfriends.* Washington: U.S. Department of Justice, Office of Justice Programs.
Hampton, Robert L., & Eli H. Newberger. (1985). Child Abuse Incidence and Reporting by Hospitals: Significance of Severity, Class and Race. *American Journal of Public Health, 75,* 56–60.
Henton, June M., Rodney M. Cate, James Koval, Sally Lloyd, & F. Scott Christopher. (1983). Romance and Violence in Dating Relationships. *Journal of Family Issues, 4,* 467–482.
Hilberman, Elaine. (1980). Overview: The Wife-Beaters Wife Reconsidered. *American Journal of Psychiatry, 137,* 1336–1346.
Hilberman, Elaine, & Kit Munson. (1977). Sixty Battered Women. *Victimology, 2,* 460–470.
Hotaling, Gerald T., & David B. Sugarman. (1990). A Risk Marker Analysis of Assaulted Wives. *Journal of Family Violence, 5,* 1–13.

Hrdy, Sarah B. (1979). Infanticide among Animals: A Review Classification, and Examination of the Implications for Reproductive Strategies of Females. *Ethology and Sociobiology, 1*, 13–40.

Jaffe, Peter G., David A. Wolfe, & Susan K. Wilson. (1990). *Children of Battered Women*. Newbury Park: Sage Publications.

Johnson, Clara L. (1974). *Child Abuse in the Southeast: An Analysis of 1172 Reported Cases*. Athens: Welfare Research.

Kaufman, Joan, & Edward F. Zigler. (1987). Do Abused Children Become Abusive Parents? *American Journal of Orthopsychiatry, 57*, 186–192.

Lane, Katherine E., & Patricia A. Gwartney-Gibbs. (1985). Violence in the Context of Dating and Sex. *Journal of Family Issues, 6*, 45–59.

Laner, Mary R. (1983). Courtship Abuse and Aggression: Contextual Aspects. *Sociological Spectrum, 3*, 69–83.

Levinson, David. (1989). *Family Violence in Cross-Cultural Perspective*. Newbury Park: Sage Publications.

Lockhart, Lettie L., Barbara W. White, Vicki Causby, & Alicia Isaac. (1994). Letting Out the Secret: Violence in Lesbian Relationships. *Journal of Interpersonal Violence, 9*, 469–492.

Makepeace, James M. (1981). Courtship Violence among College Students. *Family Relations, 30*, 97–102.

Makepeace, James. M. (1983). Life Events Stress and Courtship Violence. *Family Relations, 32*, 101–109.

Martin, Del. (1976). *Battered Wives*. San Francisco: Glide Publications.

McCurdy, Karen, & Beborah Daro. (1993). *Current Trends in Child Abuse Reporting and Fatalities: The Results of the 1992 Annual Fifty State Survey*. Chicago: National Center of Child Abuse Prevention Research, National Committee to Prevent Child Abuse.

McLain, Philip, Jeffrey Sacks, & Robert Frohlke. (1993). Estimates of Fatal Child Abuse and Neglect, United States, 1979–1988. *Pediatrics, 91*, 338–343.

Morley, Rebecca. (1994). Wife Beating and Modernization: The Case of Papau New Guinea. *Journal of Comparative Family Studies, 25*, 25–52.

National Center on Child Abuse and Neglect. (1988). *Study Findings: Study of National Incidence and Prevalence of Child Abuse and Neglect*. Washington: U.S. Department of Health and Human Services.

National Center of Child Abuse and Neglect. (1996). *Study Findings: Study of National Incidence and Prevalence of Child Abuse and Neglect: 1993*. Washington: U.S. Department of Health and Human Services.

National Center in Elder Abuse. (1998). *The National Elder Abuse Incidence Study*. Washington: American Public Human Services Association.

National Research Council. (1998). *Violence in Families: Assessing Prevention and Treatment Programs*. Washington: National Academy Press.

Nelson, Barbara J. (1984). *Making an Issue of Child Abuse: Political Agenda Setting for Social Problems*. Chicago: University Chicago Press.

Newberger, Eli, Robert Reed, Jessica H. Daniel, James Hyde, & Milton Kotelchuck. (1977). Pediatric Social Illness: Toward an Etiologic Classification. *Pediatrics, 60*, 178–185.

Osofsky, Joy D. (1995). The Effects of Exposure to Violence on Young Children. *American Psychologist, 50*, 782–788.

Pagelow, Mildred D. (1981). *Women Battering: Victims and Their Experiences*. Beverly Hills: Sage.

Pagelow, Mildred D. (1984). *Family Violence*. New York: Praeger.

Parke, Ross D., & Candace W. Collmer. (1975). Child Abuse: An Interdisciplinary Analysis. In E. Mavis Hetherington (Ed.), *Review of Child Development Research. Vol. 5* (pp. 1–102). Chicago: University of Chicago Press.

Peters, Stefanie D., Gail E. Wyatt, & David Finkelhor. (1986). Prevalence. In David Finkelhor (Ed.), *A Sourcebook on Child Sexual Abuse* (pp. 15–59). Beverly Hills: Sage.

Pillemer, Karl. (1993). The Abused Offspring Are Dependent: Abuse is Caused by the Deviance and Dependence of Abusive Caretakers. In Richard J. Gelles & Donileen R. Loseke (Eds.), *Current Controversies on Family Violence* (pp. 237–249). Newbury Park: Sage Publications.

Pillemer, Karl, & David Finkelhor. (1988). The Prevalence of Elder Abuse: A Random Sample Survey. *The Gerontologist, 28*, 51–57.

Rennison, Callie A., & Sarah Welchans. (2000). *Intimate Partner Violence*. Washington: U.S. Department of Justice, Office of Justice Programs, Bureau of Justice Statistics.

Renzetti, Claire M. (1992). *Intimate Betrayal: Partner Abuse in Lesbian Relationships*. Newbury Park: Sage Publications.

Rosenberg, Mindy S. and B. B. Robbie Rossman. (1990). The Child Witness to Marital Violence. In Robert T. Ammerman & Michel Hersen (Eds.), *Treatment of Family Violence. A Sourcebook* (pp.183–210). New York: John Wiley & Sons.

Russell, Diana E. (1984). *Sexual Exploitation: Rape, Child Sexual Abuse, and Workplace Harassment*. Newbury Park: Sage Publications.

Saunders, Daniel G. (1988). Wife Abuse, Husband Abuse, or Mutual Combat? In Kersti Yllo, & Michele Bograd (Eds.), *Feminist Perspectives on Wife Abuse* (pp. 90–113). Newbury Park: Sage Publications.

Shainess, Natalie. (1977). Psychological Aspects of Wifebeating. In Maria Roy (Ed.), *Battered Women: A Psychosocial Study of Domestic Violence* (pp. 111–119). New York: Van Nostrand Reinhold.

Shainess, Natalie. (1979). Vulnerability to Violence: Masochism as Process. *American Journal of Psychotherapy, 33*, 174–189.

Smuts, Barbara. (1992). Male Aggression against Women: An Evolutionary Perspective. *Human Nature, 3*, 1–44.

Snell, John, Richard Rosenwald, & Ames Robey. (1964). The Wifebeaters' Wife: A Study of Family Interaction. *Archives of General Psychiatry, 11*, 107–113.

Sommers, Christina H. (1994). *Who Stole Feminism? How Women Have Betrayed Women*. New York: Simon and Schuster.

Starr, Raymond H., Jr. (1988). Physical Abuse of Children. In Vincent B. van Hasselt, Randall L. Morrison, Alan S. Bellack & Michel Hersen (Eds.), *Handbook of Family Violence* (pp. 119–155). New York: Plenum.

Starr, Raymond H., Kim N. Dietrich, Joseph Fischhoff, Steven Ceresnie, & Debra Zweier. (1984). The Contribution of Handicapping Conditions to Child Abuse. *Topics in Early Childhood Special Education, 4*(1), 55–69.

Steele, Brandt F., & Carl B. Pollack. (1974). A Psychiatric Study of Parents who Abuse Infants and Small Children. In Ray E. Helfer & C. Henry Kempe (Eds.), *The Battered Child*. 2nd Edition (pp. 89–134). Chicago: University of Chicago Press.

Steinmetz, Suzanne K. (1978). Violence between Family Members. *Marriage and Family Review, 1*, 1–16.

Steinmetz, Suzanne K. (1993). The Abused Elderly Are Dependent: Abuse Is Caused by the Perception of Stress Associated with Providing Care. In Richard J. Gelles & Donileen R. Loseke (Eds.), *Current Controversies on Family Violence* (pp. 222–236). Newbury Park: Sage Publications.

Stets, Jan E., & Murray A. Straus. (1990). Gender Differences in Reporting Marital Violence and Its Medical and Psychological Consequences. In Murray A. Straus & Richard J. Gelles (Eds.), *Physical Violence in American Families* (pp. 151–166). New Brunswick: Transaction Publishers.

Straus, Murray A. (1993). Physical Assaults by Wives: A Major Social Problem. In Richard J. Gelles & Donileen R. Loseke (Eds.), *Current Controversies on Family Violence*. Newbury Park: Sage Publications(pp. 67–87).

Straus, Murray. A. (1994a). *Beating the Devil out of Them: Corporal Punishment in American Families*. New York: Lexington Books.

Straus, Murray A. (1994b). State-to-State Differences in Social Inequality and Social Bonds in Relation to Assaults on Wives in the United States. *Journal of Comparative Family Studies, 25*, 7–24.

Straus, Murray A., & Richard J. Gelles. (1986). Societal Change and Change in Family Violence from 1975 to 1985 as Revealed in Two National Surveys. *Journal of Marriage and the Family, 48*, 465–479.

Straus, Murray A., & Glenda Kantor. (1994). *Change in Spouse Assault Rates from 1975 to 1992: A Comparison of Three National Surveys in the United States*. Paper presented at the 13th World Congress of Sociology, Bielefeld, Germany.

Straus, Murray A., & Stephen Sweet. (1992). Verbal Aggression in Couples: Incidence Rates and Relationships to Personal Characteristics. *Journal of Marriage and the Family, 54*, 346–357.

Straus, Murray A., Richard J. Gelles, & Suzanne K. Steinmetz. (1980). *Behind Closed Doors: Violence in the American Family*. New York: Doubleday/Anchor.

Sugarman, David B., & Gerald T. Hotaling. (1989). Dating Violence: Prevalence, Context, and Risk Factors. In Maureen A. Pirog-Good & Jan E. Stets (Eds.), *Violence in Dating Relationships* (pp. 3–32). New York: Praeger.

Tjaden, Patricia, & Nancy Thoennes. (1998). *Prevalence, Incidence and Consequences of Violence against Women: Findings from the National Violence Against Women Survey*. Denver: Center for Policy: Research.

U.S. Advisory Board on Child Abuse and Neglect. (1995). *A Nation's Shame: Fatal Child Abuse and Neglect in the United States*. Washington: U.S. Department of Health and Human Services.

U.S. Bureau of the Census. (1992). *Statistical Abstracts of the United States*. Washington: Government Printing Office.

U.S. Department of Health and Human Services, Administration on Children, Youth and Families. (2000). *Child Maltreatment 1998: Reports from the States to the National Center on Child Abuse and Neglect*. Washington: U.S. Government Printing Office.

U.S. Department of Justice. (1994). *Uniform Crime Reports for the United States, 1993*. Washington: U.S. Department of Justice, Federal Bureau of Investigation.

U.S. Department of Justice. (1999). *Uniform Crime Reports for the United States, 1998*. Washington: U.S. Department of Justice, Federal Bureau of Investigation.

Vissing, Yvonne M., Murray A. Straus, Richard J. Gelles, & John W. Harrop. (1991). Verbal Aggression by Parents and Psychosocial Problems of Children. *Child Abuse and Neglect: The International Journal, 15*, 223–238.

Wang, Ching-Tung, & K. Harding. (1999). *Current Trends in Child Abuse Reporting and Fatalities: The Results of the 1998 Annual 50 State Survey*. Chicago: Prevent Child Abuse America.

Walker, Lenore E. (1979). *The Battered Woman*. New York: Harper & Row.

Wardell, Laurie, Dair L. Gillespie, & Ann Leffler. (1983). Science and Violence against Women. In David Finkelhor, Richard J. Gelles, Murray A. Straus & Gerald T. Hotaling (Eds.), *The Dark Side of Families: Current Family Violence Research* (pp. 69–84). Beverly Hills: Sage.

Weis, Joseph G. (1989). Family Violence Research Methodology and Design. In Lloyd Ohlin & Michael Tonry (Eds.), *Family Violence* (pp. 117–162). Chicago: University of Chicago Press.

Weitzman, Jack, & Karen Dreen. (1982). Wife-Beating: A View of the Marital Dyad. *Social Casework, 63*, 259–265.

Widom, Cathy S. (1988). Sampling Biases and Implications for Child Abuse Research. *American Journal of Orthopsychiatry, 58*, 260–270.

Widom, Cathy S. (1989). The Cycle of Violence. *Science, 244*, 160–166.

Wilson, Margo, & Martin Daly. (1992). Spousal Homicide Risk and Estrangement. *Violence and Victims, 8*, 3–16.

Woffordt, Sharon, Delbert Elliott Mihalic, & Scott Menard. (1994). Continuities in Marital Violence. *Journal of Family Violence, 9*, 195–215.

Wolf, Rosalie S. (1995). Abuse of the Elderly. In Richard J. Gelles (Ed.), *Families and Violence* (pp. 8–9, 36). Minneapolis: National Council of Family Relations.

World Health Organization. (1977). *Manual of the International Statistical Classification of Diseases, Injuries and Causes of Death, Based on the Recommendation of the Ninth Revision Conference, 1975*. Geneva: Author.

World Health Organization. (1992). *International Statistical Classification of Diseases and Related Health Problems. 10th Revision*. Geneva: Author.

Yllo, Kersti. (1983). Using a Feminist Approach in Quantitative Research. In David Finkelhor, Richard J. Gelles, Murray A. Straus & Gerald T. Hotaling (Eds.), *The Dark Side of Families: Current Family Violence Research* (pp. 277–288). Beverly Hills: Sage.

Yllo, Kersti. (1988). Political and Methodological Debates in Wife Abuse Research. In Kersti Yllo & Michele Bograd (Eds.), *Feminist Perspectives on Wife Abuse* (pp. 28–50). Newbury Park: Sage.

Yllo, Kersti. (1993). Through a Feminist Lens: Gender, Power, and Violence. In Richard J. Gelles & Donileen R. Loseke (Eds.), *Current Controversies on Family Violence* (pp. 47–62). Newbury Park: Sage.

CHAPTER II-5-1.2

Violence in School

GABRIELE KLEWIN, KLAUS-JÜRGEN TILLMANN AND
GAIL WEINGART

I. INTRODUCTION

The subject seems to be clear enough. The meaning of *school* is self-explanatory: a public institution which all young people between the ages of approximately five and sixteen are required by law to attend in any civilized society, and where teachers endeavor to train and educate the next generation of that society. In this article, we consider that institution from the angle of the *violence* to be found there. The first point to make here is that schools, historically and today, have a special, institutional relationship with violence: they practice it more or less continuously against the young people entrusted to them. Even in civilized countries, the manifestations of that violence have included, and still include, the directly physical form: in West German schools the teaching staff were still permitted to strike children until around 1970, and in many American states the practice is still permitted today (see Hyman 1996). In most schools, however, violence against pupils today is practiced in much less blatant forms, such as humiliation, discrimination, and abusive language (see Krumm & Weiss, 2000). Even today, though, there is still a significant "gray area," in which pupils are regularly the target of physical assault by teaching staff (see Wieviorka et al. 1999:148). The fact that this article does not pursue this aspect—the violence that emanates from the institution and its representatives—is in line with the current trend of current debate and research, because in many countries the focus has for some years been almost exclusively on violence by *pupils*. This covers primarily offenses such as damage to property, abusive language, threats, extortion, sexual harassment, fighting, and in some cases even murder. Research has been carried out in many countries into the extent to which such behavior is encountered in schools, its causes, and the appropriate moves to prevent it (see Smith et al. 1999). This academic debate on "violence in school" is to a very large extent concentrated on three clearly distinguishable categories of behavior by pupils.

W. Heitmeyer and J. Hagan (eds.), *International Handbook of Violence Research*, 863–884.
© 2003 Kluwer Academic Publishers. Printed in the Netherlands.

a. Physical compulsion and physical injury. This category always involves conflicts between two or more individuals in which at least one side uses physical means (bodily force or weapons) to cause intentional harm, or at least threaten such harm, to the other side. In these cases, the harm itself is also physical in nature: the spectrum ranges from a slap in the face or box on the ears through broken bones to life-threatening injuries and even killings. The use of physical force against property (vandalism) can also be included here.

b. Verbal aggression and mental cruelty. However, a definition of violence confined to its physical aspects alone would be too narrow. The fact is that the marginalization or degradation of an individual by the use of insults, humiliation, or emotional blackmail often causes much more severe "injury" than a kick on the shin. The harm caused to the victim here takes place on a different, mental level. Unlike a black eye, it is no longer clearly visible, but has to be interpreted in each case.

c. Bullying. This term refers to a *special variation* (subset) of violence, encompassing both physical and mental components. It involves a victim/perpetrator relationship, in which weaker individuals are regularly taunted and oppressed. Bullying takes many different forms: physical and verbal attacks play a part, as do indirect strategies (such as exclusion from the group, spreading of rumors). At the same time, however, this means that bullying by no means encompasses all acts of violence in school: an outburst of aggression by a pupil cannot be classified as bullying, any more than can a fight between two opponents of approximately equal strength.

A final point that should be added is that, especially in American research, the borderline between violence and deviant behavior in school (theft, drug abuse, truancy, cheating, etc.) is sometimes a fluid one. Research and theories on violence in schools deal, in the great majority of cases, with the forms of conduct among young people referred to here.

II. THEORETICAL APPROACHES AND EMPIRICAL RESULTS

1. Theoretical Approaches

Violence in school—like violence among young people as a whole—is a social phenomenon to which different academic disciplines adopt very different theoretical approaches. In addition to psychological explanatory models for aggression, sociological explanatory approaches to anomie and deviance play an important part here. In school, however, such general theories only become objectively significant if, at the same time, school as an institution is perceived as a social facility and as the theater of action for young people. Which are the social expectations within this theater, and which needs experienced by young people stand in the way of them? What potentials for aggression and what forms of dealing with it are typical of schools? To put it another way, theories acquire a special explanatory force if a subject perspective is associated with an examination of the structural elements of the school arena. In the next section of this article, we begin by outlining the structural features of school as an institution that are significant in the context of a discussion of violence, and then move on to look at a number of objectively relevant theoretical approaches.

a. SCHOOL AS A CONTEXT FOR ACTION. School attendance is compulsory for all young people, usually until they reach the age of sixteen. They are expected by the teaching body to concentrate, day by day and within a predetermined social setting (usually the class), on mastering an academic syllabus. Successes and failures are assessed individually and ultimately result in school-leaving certificates of different worth that, in due course, open the way to privileged or less privileged careers. That, briefly, is the institutional context within which children and young people spend at least nine years, a large proportion of their lives, in which they daily encounter large numbers of boys and girls of approximately their own age, in which they have to lead their social lives and, at the same time, be as successful as possible. At the same time, the schools require of their pupils that they behave "properly" in that context; in particular, this includes the expectation that they will learn to resolve conflicts without the use of violence. However, analyses of socialization in schools have repeatedly made the point that the fundamental expectations of obedience and good behavior laid down by the school and its staff are to some extent in conflict with the needs of the pupils themselves, which are geared to self-determination, enjoying themselves and "acting out" (see for example Willis, 1979). This is particularly likely to result in conflict when young people—especially during puberty—present identities that are remote from school and different from it, and at the same time display a tendency to violence.

School is initially regarded as a *venue* for acts of violence. The specific features of the institution (especially the large number of people of the same age and the teaching body's expectations of achievement and obedience) impose a certain framework on pupils' behavior. First, the high density of contact and reciprocal expectations of those involved offer sufficiently numerous points of friction where conflicts may flare up. Secondly, though, a school is an area of tight social control where gross violations of rules (including acts of violence) can easily be detected and can be punished accordingly (Tillmann, 2000:147ff.). To this extent, it is hardly surprising that the figures for violence and crime outside school are significantly higher than they are inside (Kaufman et al., 1999:2ff.).

School, though, is not only the venue of violence but, at the same time, a *habitat* that may contain *elements propitious to violence*. If we adopt that perspective, our critical eye is directed primarily at the conduct of the teaching body, the curriculum, and the expected standards of performance. Do teachers adopt patterns of behavior—such as a cold, authoritarian style—that build up aggression in pupils and encourage them to acts of violence? Do excessive expectations and radical selection processes result in a sense of failure for which, again, acts of violence then provide compensation? In brief, are there particular forms of school teaching practice that are likely to reinforce pupils' propensity to violence? This kind of approach is not only part of the tradition of research into the scholastic and educational climate (see for example Rutter et al., 1980; Fend, 1998) but also refers back to studies of deviant behavior in schools (see for example Hargreaves, Hester, & Mellor, 1981; Holtappels, 1987).

This is certainly not to say that all the "causes" of violent behavior by children and young people can be traced to the school itself. What a young person experiences at home, in front of the TV screen, and within his peer group is at least equally significant. Problems experienced in these areas—such as violent parents and aggressive cliques—have long been recognized as risk factors for violent conduct in school. But, in the search for risk factors, the school itself must not be excluded.

We have adopted the argument that theoretical approaches to aggression and violence in the school sector have a particularly strong explanatory force if the findings they produce can be related to the school arena outlined above and its structures. Schubarth

(2000:13–65) analyzed the theoretical arguments and found that a total of over twenty different individual concepts from six different lines of theory played a part in the academic debate on pupil violence. The spectrum here ranges from psychoanalytical aggression theories through sociological anomie concepts to more recent theories of modernization and individualization. We now move on to outline, by way of example, three concepts from different lines of theory. What they have in common is that they deal specifically with the school context.

b. THE PSYCHOANALYTICAL VIEW OF THE THREATENED SELF. In psychoanalytical theories that have taken up and developed the ideas of Freud (see for example Freud, 1972:113ff.), aggression is interpreted as the expression of a complex disorder of the entire personality. Such disorders are suggestive of severe trauma, especially in childhood (see for example Heinemann, 1996:27). They include, for example, violent parents, relational breakdowns, and humiliations. An excess of such damaging events prevents the development of a stable self, and it is very easy in such cases for the young or adult individual to perceive himself as personally threatened. From this angle, aggression can be interpreted as a desperate attempt to control feelings of danger and anxiety. In such cases, school is an institution where young people are constantly put to the test in the public arena of their contemporaries, and their own achievements and skills are constantly exposed to the scrutiny of others. But there are quite a number of children who, precisely because of their experiences in early childhood, find it hard to meet the behavioral and performance requirements imposed in school. Such children have "virtually no chance of achieving recognition and self-validation through confirming to norms at school. They are then all too likely to find other ways (for example, violence and deviant behavior) of attracting the necessary attention and interest" (Schubarth, 2000:24). This situation peaks during adolescence, because school provides far too little scope for the demands of self-esteem and social recognition (see Erikson, 1966) that are particularly important at that age. It is precisely those young people whose earlier experiences have in any case left them with an unstable self who are constantly exposed within the school institution to the kind of experience that damages their self-esteem (such as ridicule and underachievement). They then react with aggressive, rule-breaking forms of conduct as a way of defending the self against the unreasonable demands made by the school. Viewed in this light, violence is an attempt by the self to escape from an official school culture that constantly denies it recognition as a valuable individual (see Helsper, 1995:142ff.).

c. THE INTERACTIONIST VIEW OF THE LABELED INDIVIDUAL. Interactionist theories perceive acts of violence as subjectively meaningful but nevertheless socially unacceptable forms of self-identification. This dates back to the concept evolved by Mead (1968), according to which identities develop in communicative activity and the individual's "role-making" is always geared to the expectations of his opposite number in that communication ("role-taking"). On the basis of these assumptions, a theoretical concept has been evolved that deals with the origin and consolidation of "deviant behavior" and has become known as the "labeling approach" (see Goffman, 1967; Hargreaves, 1979). The central focus of this theory is the "deviant career"—the *process* which results in individuals slipping into the status of a deviant (a perpetrator of violence or a criminal). The institutions that make the rules—from school through social workers to the police—are subjected to critical questioning: are their own activities and attributions not themselves responsible to a significant extent for the production of "deviants"? There is a considerable body of empirical work that has analyzed the processes of socialization in schools against this theoretical background (see for example Brusten & Hurrelmann, 1973). These studies first point out that deviance in school is not the exception but the rule: the regulatory network is so dense that no pupil could be or would wish to be always be a conformist. The question, then, is how teachers react to breaches of rules by individual pupils. On this point, the "labeling approach" distinguishes between primary and secondary deviance. Primary deviance—for example, a first outbreak of violent fighting—may have a variety of causes; it becomes deviant only if it catches the eye of the controlling authorities—the teaching body, in this case—and is the subject of public discussion and punishment. In this process, the protagonist acquires a kind of official label: he becomes a "thug." From that point on, his opposite numbers in the process of interaction see all his acts from a new perspective; this involves a general redefinition of previous assumptions, evaluations, and ideas. The social environment expects people who have been labeled in this way to behave in accordance with that label; in the course of time, by accepting the definition attached to them by others, they develop a deviant self-image, and their behavior increasingly conforms to what is expected of a deviant. Research in schools has shown that such labeling processes take place constantly between teachers and pupils, though the teaching staff are frequently not conscious of this (see Brumlik & Holtappels, 1987). Social labels of this kind (for example, "thug") have far-reaching effects and may make a substantial contribution to forcing a child into the role of an aggressor. At the same time, however, it is true that such children can be led out of the role again by appropriate teaching measures (see Tillmann et al., 1999:253–73). From this theoretical angle, violence is a product of failed interactions within hierarchical relationships. Applied to school, it means that attention is drawn to the problem-creating effect of the institution and the educationally undesirable side effects of a regulatory, labeling approach by the teaching staff.

d. The Sociological View of the Individualized Subject. Recent sociological theories of modernization, taking their cue from "classical" concepts of anomie in Durkheim (1970) and Merton (1968), have been very frequently cited of late as explanatory models for youth violence. The macrosocial background to this explanatory model is provided, for example, in Germany by Beck's (1986) analysis of the "risk society." In most Western capitalist societies, the past thirty years have brought substantial changes not only in family structures but also in scholastic requirements and career opportunities. In many countries the scene is dominated by rising unemployment among the young, the increasing instability of the family as an institution, and tougher competition to achieve in school. Social scientists researching into the problems of young people have found that these processes of modernization in society as a whole produce upon young people the primary effect of pressure toward increasing individualization (see Heitmeyer & Olk, 1995). This means that children and young people find that security and certainties are becoming increasingly eroded in the various areas of their social lives. This applies to the family environment (with increasing divorce rates) just as much as it does to school (with high performance standards combined with uncertainty about future job prospects). By way of reaction, young people frequently look for security and stability among their peers, who thus become more influential. Heitmeyer (1994) makes it clear that this produces tendencies toward disintegration, which may also result in violent forms of behavior in a proportion of young people. These tendencies appeal to the "dark side of individualization" (Heitmeyer et al., 1995): the more uncertain and unstable living conditions become, the less clear the prospects for the future, the tougher the pressure of competition, and the less reliable the social relationships, then the more likely we are to encounter mentally and socially insecure young people, and the greater the probability becomes that they will attempt to solve their problems and come to terms with their lives through the use of violence. Böhnisch (1995) has analyzed this approach with specific reference to schools: he examines the contradictory situation within which pupils live inside the school, and finds tendencies toward disintegration here as well, for which he uses the term "anomie." Thus, he says, school has undergone a process of expansion to a point where it is synonymous with adolescence itself; as a result, school has become the comprehensive form of existence for young people but has not been able to provide an appropriate response to the associated needs of its subjects. To put it another way, the discrepancy between the functional system of school and the social environment—which the pupils themselves see mainly as the school—has become much more acute. Behind this, in turn, lie the processes of individualization described earlier: as adolescents are deprived of family support and environmental security, so school becomes "the (now unilateral) sphere of group dynamic/social environment stimulation, but without the structures or human resources to deal with that role" (Böhnisch, 1995:149). This and other school-based contradictions represent a "classically anomic configuration" (Böhnisch, 1995), to which pupils react with patterns of adaptation that may range from apathy to violence. "Violence as a means of coming to terms with anomic situations also represents, if there are no alternative means of proving oneself, an attempt to draw attention to oneself, to make the unclear and excessively demanding clear and—even if only briefly—understandable in a single act" (Böhnisch, 1995). From this standpoint, violence can be understood as a reaction by young people to disintegration and anomie in all social fields—school included.

2. Empirical Results

There is a comprehensive body of empirical research, including international research, into violence in schools, though its theoretical foundation often leaves something to be desired (see Krumm, 1997). Only a small number of studies can be explicitly assigned to one of the theoretical approaches mentioned above (or to another such approach). Instead, most studies create a fabric of variables and then analyze them using standardized methods, the researchers not being guided in their work by any specific theory of the origin of violence. Most of these studies are designed to describe frequencies and phenomena of violence in schools and to search for the factors conducive to violence (personality features, environmental factors, etc.). In most cases, the selection of variables is guided by existing findings on risk factors in the family, school, peer group, and neighborhood that are conducive to violence. Viewed in this light, the great majority of these studies are driven by ideas which—more implicitly than explicitly—come close to the concept of socioecological socialization research (see Bronfenbrenner, 1976).

In presenting these empirical results, we will now concentrate, by way of example, on three regions of the Western world—the United States, Scandinavia, and Germany.[1] In all three regions, there is an extensive body of research on violence in schools, which—as will become apparent—shows there is much in common between the three regions but also reflects distinct differences. Although all three regions comprise Western countries, the social context of their school systems differs considerably in each case. This applies, for example,

[1] Unfortunately, this means that we must refrain from describing the results of research in other countries, such as France (see Wieviorka et al., 1999), Britain (see Smith, 1999), and Japan (see Morita, 1997). However, such results will also be cited from time to time where interpretations overlap.

a. Violence in Schools in the United States

Public Debate, Manifestations and Extent. The forms of violent conduct to be found in present-day American schools can be depicted in the form of a continuum which begins with relatively moderate forms of violence (for example, verbal insults, sexual harassment, vandalism against school property) and extends to high-level "hard" violence (including threats, use of weapons, rape, robbery, and murder) (Goldstein & Conoley, 1997). A striking point here is that life-threatening offenses play a much more prominent part in American schools than in those of other Western countries. In view of this situation, it is surprising to find that violence among the young, both inside and outside school, was not seen as a major problem until the late 1950s (see Devine, 2000:45). In 1956, for example, a national survey of teachers revealed that fewer than 1 percent of their pupils were troublemakers (Goldstein & Conoley, 1997:6). But from the mid-1960s onward, violence escalated rapidly in American schools. A study commissioned by the United States government in 1975 (see Bayh, 1975) found that the sharpest increase was in fighting, followed by an increasing incidence of theft, vandalism, drug and alcohol abuse, and the carrying of weapons. Other studies during the 1970s confirmed this trend (Goldstein & Conoley, 1997:6). Since the early 1990s, the phenomenon of violence in schools has been the subject of such intensive media coverage as to create a high level of public alarm. During that period, violence by pupils has come to be regarded as the biggest problem confronting American schools. Whether this viewpoint is justified or must be regarded as a dramatization is also a subject of dispute in social sciences research (see Morrison, Furlong, & Morrison, 1997:237; Devine, 2000:44–47). Because of the high level of public interest, the American government has instructed various departments and higher federal authorities—for the first time in the 1970s, and increasingly during the 1990s—to gather precise statistical data on the extent and nature of violence by young people in the community and in school and develop preventive and interventionist programs on that basis (Coben et al., 1994:309).

Intensive research was undertaken during the 1980s and 1990s into the manifestations and frequency of violence by young people in school. Of the many existing studies on the subject, only a few can be mentioned here. The proportion of young people (ninth through twelfth grades) involved in fighting during the course of one year was about 15 percent in 1997, with significant differences between ages and sexes: almost twice as many ninth-graders as twelfth-graders, and more than twice as many boys as girls, were involved in such clashes (Kaufman et al., 1999:9). The most frequent offenses committed in school are theft and damage to property. Nearly 30 percent of pupils in 1997 reported articles stolen from them or intentionally damaged. Similar surveys carried out at various times during the 1990s showed that these figures remained very stable. Here again, the same differences between ages and sexes were apparent (Kaufman et al., 1999:12; Brener et al., 1999:443). Research into bullying among young people in the United States is not nearly as extensive as it is in Scandinavia (see below). In 1993, 8 percent of young people reported that they had been victims of bullying. Younger pupils in the sixth grade were more than four times as likely as twelfth graders to be bullied, and boys were targeted far more often than girls (Kaufman et al., 1999:11). Overall, however, bullying is not a primary focus of research or of public debate (see Harachi, Catalano, & Hawkins, 1999).

A particularly comprehensive source of information on violence in schools is the "Annual Report on School Safety," which has appeared each year since 1998 and summarizes data on safety and violence in schools drawn from a number of surveys and reports.[2] On the basis of these up-to date survey data, government departments have estimated that the actual frequency of acts of violence in American schools is much lower than media reports would suggest (U.S. Departments of Education and Justice, 1999:3). According to this view, the great majority of American schools are safe places, where pupils and teachers can learn and work in peace. It has also been pointed out that crime among young people has for years been much more widespread outside school than inside (Kaufman et al., 1999:2ff.). A particularly surprising result is that since 1993 the overall frequency of school violence among young people (aged twelve through eighteen) has actually declined. At the end of the 1990s, for example, significantly fewer pupils than previously carried weapons to school, and the percentage of pupils involved in fighting had also fallen significantly (U.S. Departments of Education and Justice, 1999:5ff.).

Of course, the reduction described here was a reduction from a strikingly high level, at least by the standards of Western European countries. This becomes particularly apparent if we focus on the ownership (and carrying) of firearms. There were many studies on this subject in the first half of the 1990s. A number of representative surveys independently present the finding that about 4–6 percent of high school pupils nationwide took firearms to school. A study confined only to inner-city schools concluded that the figure was significantly higher: 22 percent of pupils owned a firearm and 12 percent carried it regularly (Anderson, 1998:328ff.). When asked why, these young people usually stated that they needed the weapon for self-defense because "my enemies have handguns too" (Anderson, 1998:331). Here again, there are enormous differences between the sexes: boys are five to ten times as likely as girls to own firearms (Anderson, 1998). In a more recent study, Kaufman et al. (1999:26) admittedly come up with lower figures, interpreted by them as a decline over the course of time.

All these figures can only be understood against a background of largely unrestricted access to firearms, for which there is a long tradition in the United States. The studies quoted show that even children and young people take widespread advantage of this liberty. It is hardly surprising, then, that adolescents number among the victims of firearm use as well as the perpetrators. Devine (2000:43) reports that about 3,000 children and young people are shot dead every year in the United States, about fifty of them in school. This casualty rate is about sixteen times greater than the average for comparable industrialized countries (Center for Disease Control, 1998).[3] Various forms of careless handling of weapons, as well as deliberate attacks, play a part here. With regard to deaths attributable to acts of violence in schools, the U.S. Department of Education undertook a first comprehensive national survey in 1994. The authors of this study report that the number of deaths (including suicides) among children and young people had more than doubled in the previous ten years, but that such deaths in schools accounted for fewer than 1 percent of all documented cases among people of

---

[2] The 1999 *Annual Report on School Safety* (U.S. Departments of Education and Justice) refers *inter alia* to the following representative samples: the National Household Education Surveys (NHES), which have been carried out every two years since 1991 and extend to 12,000 pupils' parents and 6,000 children in the sixth through twelfth grades; the Schools and Staffing Survey (SASS) of 1993–1994, including 56,000 teachers in public schools and 11,500 teachers in private schools. In addition, the *Report* includes data from the Youth Risk Behavior Survey, a comprehensive study of ninth through twelfth graders carried out every two years.

[3] Another study arrives at the following figures for victims of shooting incidents in American schools during a five year period (1986–1991): 71 dead, 261 seriously injured, 242 taken hostage (Lane, 1991).

school age (Kachur et al., 1996:1732). In summary, the casualty rate is extremely high by international standards, but despite the absolute figures quoted the proportion accounted for by schools is relatively low (see Kachur et al., 1996:1731).

The explosion of violence that rocked the United States in April 1999 was also closely linked to the free access to firearms. At Columbine High School in Littleton, Colorado, two pupils attacked their own school and carried out a massacre in which thirteen people were shot dead and twenty-three severely wounded; the perpetrators then committed suicide (Devine, 2000:43–44).[4] The broad debate on this subject among the public and social scientists clearly indicates that events of this kind are almost impossible to interpret by applying conventional sociological and psychological theories. Devine (2000:48ff.), however, infers from this and other incidents that violence in schools and among the young is no longer a typical phenomenon of impoverished metropolitan areas but spread long ago to include the "nicer" residential areas inhabited by the middle class. The school massacres of the late 1990s re-ignited the controversy surrounding statutory control of weapons, which was made an issue in the 2000 presidential election campaign. At the same time, an increasing number of American schools are stepping up security technology, such as the use of metal detectors (see Devine, 2000:49).

Risk Factors. Since the 1970s, American researchers have been trying to identify risk factors responsible for violent conduct in schools. During the past ten years, these studies have also, increasingly, taken account of positive "protective factors," factors that promote mental security and resistance among school pupils and suppress the effect of stress factors. The two factors can frequently be reduced to one dimension, where one form can be seen as a risk but the other as protective. Both groups of factors include not only personality traits in the adolescents concerned but also their family, school, and neighborhood situations. The following main factors have been identified in existing research:

Personality Traits. Risk factors identified are: antisocial inclinations, impulsiveness, an individual history of aggressive behavior, lack of empathy, and a low frustration threshold. The main protective factors identified are: positive temperament, social skills.

Family Factors. Risk factors are regarded as: family poverty, weak emotional ties to parents, experience of violence in the home, high-level media consumption. Parents who provide social and emotional support, however, are regarded as a protective factor.

School Factors. Academic failure, lack of interest in school, and an unfavorable school climate have been identified as risk factors, while their precise opposites (academic success, favorable school climate, etc.) are protective factors.

Community Factors. Regional poverty, the existence of clans and gangs in the neighborhood, high crime rates, and the availability of drugs and weapons are the main risk factors. By contrast, positive standards in the community and involvement in community activities are designated as protective factors (see American Psychological Association, 1993; Walker, Colvin, & Ramsey, 1995; Hamburg, 1998).

---

[4]The school massacre at Littleton attracted worldwide attention because of the dramatic course of events and the high number of victims, but it is, sadly, not the only case of its kind in the United States. A compilation of newspaper reports between 1996 and 1999 identifies a total of seventeen cases in which young male perpetrators fired selectively or at random on groups of pupils; there were up to five deaths in each case (source: Internet http/www.abcnews.go.com /September 15, 2000).

In the United States, the features of young people's lifestyles mentioned above are often associated with membership of particular ethnic groups. Poverty and broken homes are much more frequent in "black" residential areas than in "white." Similarly, research indicates that black youths are far more likely to be involved in violence in schools (fighting, possession of weapons, etc.) than whites or Hispanics (see Brener et al., 1999:443–444). This is linked to the finding that neighborhood violence is a strong predictive indicator of school violence (see Gottfredson & Gottfredson, 1985). The existing studies indicate, however, that poor socioeconomic conditions in a neighborhood are far more closely associated with (school) violence than mere membership of an ethnic group. This means that race and ethnicity alone, without a corresponding socioeconomic association, hardly influence the level of violence (see Kingery, Biafora, & Zimmermann, 1996; Hamburg, 1998:44). Thus, while research as a whole shows that the frequency of violence in schools is closely linked to social deprivation (and its ethnic aspects) (see most recently Anderson, 1998), Devine (2000:51ff.) concludes, particularly from the recent school massacres, that violence in schools and among the young has now spread to the white middle class as well.

b. Violence in Scandinavian Schools

Public Debate, Manifestations and Frequency. Sweden, Norway, and Finland have a relatively long tradition of addressing the problem of violence in schools. As long ago as the late 1960s and early 1970s, violence—or more accurately bullying—was identified as a social problem (Björkqvist & Österman, 1999; Olweus, 1999a, 1999b). Apart from concerned parents and teachers, the subject attracted particular attention from the media. As a reaction to this, the Norwegian ministry of education launched a nationwide campaign in 1983 to prevent bullying in all schools up to the ninth grade (Olweus, 1999b). In Sweden, since 1994, action to prevent violence and bullying has been prescribed in the Education Act: academic personnel are required to prevent violence and notify any incidents to the school authorities (Olweus, 1999a:24). In Sweden, as in Norway, there is a children's ombudsman who addresses these problems. In Finland, too, the subject of bullying has been included in legislation; a case involving two fifteen-year-olds guilty of continuous bullying resulted in a fine (Björkqvist & Österman, 1999:64).

The first academic studies also date back to the 1970s. The academic debate has been greatly influenced by the work of Dan Olweus. The publication of his book "Hackkycklingar och översittare" (1973)[5] is regarded by Smith and Morita (1999:2) as the beginning of systematic research, while Björkqvist and Österman go so far as to describe it as a "milestone" (1999:57). Olweus's studies deal with a specific form of violence among pupils: bullying. He examines a wide range of factors: the extent and nature of the bullying, self-perception, sense of self-esteem, and the (family) conditions in which bullies and victims have grown up. This empirical approach is guided by theoretical concepts derived in the main from developmental psychology and aggression psychology, but oriented more toward social ecology in their analyses of conditions.

On the basis of a nationwide study in Norway, the proportion of pupils involved in bullying can be estimated at about 15 percent, with about 9 percent being victims of bullying, about 7 percent bullies, and 2 percent both victims and bullies (Olweus, 1995, 1997, 1999b). A national comparison between Sweden and Norway indicates a high degree of

---

[5] An English translation, *Aggression in the School: Bullies and Whipping Boys*, appeared in 1978.

coincidence between the basic findings (Olweus, 1995, 1999a; Laflamme, Menckel, & Aldenberg, 1998). While studies from Finland also confirm these results (Lagerspetz et al., 1982; Kumpulainen et al., 1998:708), there are virtually no studies on bullying in Denmark (Dueholm, 1999:52). Bullying is not a problem that affects all age-groups equally: if we consider the second through ninth grades (ages from eight to fifteen), it can be said that the percentage of victims decreases continuously with increasing age. By contrast, no such decline is apparent among the perpetrators, especially the male bullies (see Olweus, 1999b:33f.). Among both bullies and victims, the percentage of boys is higher than that of girls (see Olweus, 1999b; Kumpulainen et al., 1998). There are differences between the sexes, too, in the form that bullying takes: although nonphysical forms of bullying are more common in both sexes, acts of physical bullying as such are significantly more common among boys (see Olweus, 1999b; Österman et al., 1998).

There are virtually no studies on forms of violence other than bullying in Scandinavian schools. However, indications of the level of school violence can be inferred from a number of Swedish studies on physical injuries to pupils. Even so, the identifiable level of physical violence here can be classified as relatively low (Hammarström & Janlert, 1994:122).

Risk Factors. The extensive research carried out by Olweus has shown that four complexes of factors can adversely affect individual development during the course of growing up: lack of emotional involvement by parents, failure by reference persons to set limits in cases of aggressive behavior, physical and other "power-based forms of discipline," and a "hot-headed" temperament in the child (Olweus, 1995:48ff.). Furthermore, the influence of peer groups is important in young people especially (Olweus, 1995:50ff.). Contrary to widespread opinion, neither the size of the class or school nor competition for marks has any significant influence (Olweus, 1999b:36). Bullies generally have a high level of self-assurance, while their victims tend to suffer from somewhat low self-esteem (Olweus, 1999a:17).

A broader perspective on bullying can be found in the analysis by Salmivalli et al. (1996). Their opinion is that not only the bullies and their victims but also the other pupils in the class can influence the course of events by their action or lack of it. According to this theory, one of six different roles in the process of bullying could be ascribed to 87 percent of all pupils. Aligned with the bullies themselves are their supporters and assistants. On the side of the victim are pupils who defend the victim against attacks; finally, there are pupils who can be regarded as "bystanders." On the basis of these roles, it can be said that pupils have generally formed friendships with others of like mind, while victims frequently have very small or nonexistent circles of friends (see Salmivalli, Huttunen, & Lagerspetz, 1997). The roles of bullies, supporters, or assistants, especially among boys, and to a limited extent those of the victims as well, remained largely stable over the two-year period studied (see Salmivalli, Lappalainen, & Lagerspetz, 1998).

c. VIOLENCE IN GERMAN SCHOOLS

Public Debate, Manifestations and Frequency. Violence in schools was not an issue in Germany until the early 1990s, either in public debate or in educational sciences research. In West Germany during the 1970s and 1980s there were only isolated studies of "deviant behavior" in school (see Brusten and Hurrelmann, 1973; Holtappels, 1987), "disciplinary problems" (see Cloer, 1982), or "vandalism" (see Klockhaus & Habermann-Morbey, 1986). In East Germany (the GDR), deviant behavior among children and young people was treated as taboo for political reasons, and research into it was impossible (see Eckstein,

1996). A change set in at the beginning of the 1990s, with a substantial increase in outbreaks of far-right and xenophobic violence among the young, associated with the reunification of Germany (see Otto & Merten, 1993). This caused widespread alarm among the public; schools, too, became a focus of attention (see Schubarth, 1995). Against this background, extensive research efforts began in around 1993 and have dealt with the use of violence by pupils and with the experiences of perpetrators and victims. These studies have been mainly concerned with compiling descriptive data on the extent of violence in schools and its manifestations; at the same time, efforts have been made to identify factors in an individual's social environment that are conducive to violence. A fairly large number of studies were completed and published between 1995 and 1999. Most of these related to selected towns (see for example Dettenborn & Lautsch, 1993; Schwind et al., 1995; Greszik, Hering, & Euler, 1995; Funk, 1995; Lösel, Bliesener, & Averbeck, 1997). Some studies were more broadly based and examined representative samples for whole German states: Fuchs, Lamnek and Luedtke (1996) for Bavaria, Forschungsgruppe Schulevaluation (1998) for Saxony, and Tillmann et al. (1999) for Hesse. Most of these studies make a distinction between physical and psychological (verbal) violence and study the occurrence of both forms and the conditions under which they arise. However, explicit analyses of bullying are very rare (exception: Hanewinkel & Knaack, 1997). All the studies show broad agreement in their basic findings: they indicate, in particular, that the use of violence in German schools is far from having reached the dramatic extent that media reports might suggest (see Schubarth, 2000:73).

It becomes clear from these surveys of pupils and teachers that particularly serious and spectacular offenses, which in most cases come within the reach of the criminal law, are very unusual: severe physical injury, extortion, and gang warfare are still rare events in German schools. Possession of firearms by pupils is extremely uncommon, and killings were virtually unknown before 1999. Thus, more than 96 percent of secondary-school pupils questioned in Nuremberg said that they had never been threatened with a weapon by another pupil (see Lösel et al., 1997). Other studies, such as Greszik et al. (1995) and Fuchs et al. (1996), came to similar conclusions regarding acts of "hard" violence. At the same time, however, all studies agree that verbal aggression, abusive and insulting language between pupils, have become a much more frequent part of school routine. More than 50 percent of pupils in Hesse and Saxony (aged from six through ten) experience something of the kind several times a week or even daily (see Schubarth et al., 1997:158).

All studies indicate enormous differences between the sexes. Physical violence, especially, far more frequently involves boys—as both perpetrators and victims. As far as age-groups are concerned, violence appears to "peak" between the ages of thirteen and fifteen—in other words, approximately, in the eighth and ninth grades. After this stage, the frequency of physical violence declines again (see Forschungsgruppe Schulevaluation, 1998:69). No confirmation has been found for the frequently expressed view that there is more violence in urban schools than in rural ones, or large schools rather than small ones (see Fuchs et al., 1996:305ff.; Tillmann et al., 1999:200ff.).

Until 1999, unlawful killings committed by teenagers in school were unknown. Since then, however, there have been a number of high-profile murders committed in German schools, inevitably raising the question of whether this is another area in which Germany— despite its relatively strict laws on the carrying of weapons—is heading for the "American scenario." This series of crimes began in 1999, when a Gymnasium (pre-university school) student in the eastern German city of Meissen, motivated by revenge, stabbed a female teacher to death in class. During the years that followed, there were two more cases in which (former) pupils exacted revenge on their teachers in murderous attacks. This series of killings reached its apogee, to date, in a school massacre that claimed seventeen lives, committed by a nineteen-year-old at a Gymnasium in Erfurt (Saxony-Anhalt). This young man, who had been expelled from the school for disciplinary reasons a few weeks earlier and was barred from sitting his Abitur (graduation examination), forced his way into the school on the day of the examination and shot dead twelve teachers, the school secretary, and a police officer. Two female pupils also died in the shootings. The killer then took his own life (see Der Spiegel, 19/2000, pp. 118ff.). A shocked public has since been debating the reasons for this massacre, and the apportionment of blame: there have been demands for further tightening of weapons legislation and the banning of violent computer games. The rigid selection procedures at some German Gymnasien has also attracted renewed criticism.

Current theories on deviant behavior in school offer no academic explanations for such aggressive, life-destroying behavior. Initial, tentative interpretations have in some cases adopted the sociological approach, focusing on the subjective perception of "loss of recognition" by young people in a society driven by achievement and competition (see Heitmeyer, 2002); others have looked for a key to this frenzied behavior in individual psychological analyses of the perpetrators and in their previous histories (see Eisenberg, 2002). From the social sciences angle, however, it is striking that the perpetrators in all cases were males from "good" home backgrounds who felt that they had been treated unjustly by their teachers, and that their career prospects had been damaged as a result—which prompted them to resort to direct and murderous action against members of the teaching body.

Partly because of these high-profile murders, the German public has formed the impression that violence in school has increased dramatically in recent years or decades. Whether this also applies to "everyday" violence (beatings, vandalism, verbal abuse, etc.) is, however, highly contentious. The studies quoted above have almost without exception been cross-sectional, so that it is difficult to find any reliable scientific basis for this assertion (increase over the course of time). There are only three (regionally limited) studies that provide a longer-term perspective, and those studies arrive at very different results. Whereas Mansel and Hurrelmann (1998:95) find a very substantial increase in physical aggression in all types of school during the period from 1988 through 1996, Tillmann et al. (1999:141ff.), examining the period between 1972 and 1995, come to the conclusion that it is only in the lower-echelon *Hauptschule* (approximately equivalent to junior high school) that the proportion of offenders has increased significantly, whereas in the other types of school the level of violence has remained more or less constant. This view is corroborated by the study by Fuchs, Lamnek and Luedtke (2001), who were unable to verify any increase in school violence in Bavaria during the period from 1994 to 1999.

Risk Factors. Apart from the difference between the sexes, the type of school attended has proven particularly influential. This finding refers to the structure of the German secondary school system, which differs substantially from the comprehensive school systems in Scandinavia and the United States. Whereas in those countries all young people up to at least the age of sixteen attend the same school, Germany uses a system involving a hierarchical sequence of school types. At the age of about ten, children are assigned to one of these types of school in accordance with their previous academic records (which also reflect their social origins). The hierarchy of these types of school—*Sonderschule* (special schools for the educationally disadvantaged), *Hauptschule*, *Realschule* (preparing for vocational training), and *Gymnasium* (preparing for university)—and the social prestige associated with them are reflected very consistently in the statistics showing the frequency of violence: if all forms of physical aggression are considered, the special school for the educationally disadvantaged comes in first place (see Tillmann et al., 1999:103), generally followed by the *Hauptschule*—but the *Gymnasium* almost always shows the lowest frequencies (see for example Funk, 1995:48ff.; Fuchs, 1996:300ff.). It is consistent with this that certain family circumstances have been shown to be conducive to violence in schools: poorly educated parents, a rigidly authoritarian style of upbringing, lack of acceptance in the parental home, a father not in secure employment, and also personal experience of violence in the home—all these factors are significantly, though in most cases not really closely, associated with adolescent violence in schools (see for example Fuchs et al., 1996:201ff.; Funk, 1995:131ff.; Tillmann et al., 1999:155ff.). Factors originating in the peer group context and leisure activities prove particularly influential in the case of young people: the available studies unanimously agree here that involvement in aggressive gangs of young people and intensive viewing of horror, violent, and pornographic films vastly increase the probability of violence in school (see for example Funk, 1995:159ff., 223ff.; Forschungsgruppe Schulevaluation, 1998:171, 181ff.; Tillmann et al., 1999:177ff., 192ff.).

Some of these studies also look into the question of whether any conditions in the school itself are conducive to violence, and if so what conditions these are. From this standpoint, the school is regarded not only as a venue for violence but also as a contributory factor. There is evidence here that the social climate within the school is particularly likely to exert a significant influence: lack of recognition from fellow pupils, a restrictive attitude and tendency to attach labels on the part of the teaching staff, and keen competition between young people are closely related to their propensity for violence (see Forschungsgruppe Schulevaluation, 1998:211; Tillmann et al., 1999:232ff., 258ff.). In conclusion, then, it can be said that causative and exacerbating factors are to be found in every area of young people's lives, but that the school and peer-group contexts are particularly important.

d. INTERNATIONAL COMPARATIVE ASPECTS. If we undertake a cross-national comparison of the debate on violence in schools, and the associated research, both features in common and differences become apparent. Violence by pupils is a subject of great public and media interest in all the countries studied, as a result of which government departments too have in every case addressed the problem. Research has been stimulated or intensified by this public attention. Whereas academic consideration of the subject began in the United States and Scandinavia as long ago as the mid-1960s and early 1970s, respectively, violence among pupils is a relatively new topic for German researchers. Different aspects of the phenomenon are studied and discussed in each of the countries concerned. In Scandinavia, there is a clear focus on bullying; in Germany, great attention is paid to verbal as well as physical violence, although recently killings have become very much the central focus of public debate. In the United States, verbal violence is hardly mentioned in the reports, but extreme forms of physical violence and various manifestations of criminal behavior (theft, drug consumption, etc.) have long played a major part. On the one hand, these differences no doubt reflect the different social and scholastic realities in each case that make certain forms of behavior (such as extreme acts of violence in the United States) appear to be a particular problem and hence worthy of examination. On the other hand, however, different academic traditions have also grown up—such as research into bullying in Scandinavia—and these have then resulted in a specific violent situation in each country being constituted through research.

Despite these differences in emphasis, there are notable features in common between the various sets of findings. In every case, the great majority of pupils show no propensity to violence. The percentages involved in physical violence or bullying are indicated as being between about 10 percent and 15 percent in each case. This figure also depends upon whether a clear distinction is made between perpetrators and victims or whether all those involved in this kind of relationship are included. There is a high degree of correlation as far as differences between sexes and age-groups are concerned: in all the countries considered, boys are at least three or four times as likely as girls to be involved in physical conflicts; and the frequency of physical violence "peaks" among the thirteen through fifteen age-group in every case. Whereas there are significant differences in Germany between the levels of violence encountered in the various types of school within the hierarchy, similar differences within the American comprehensive system are primarily regional: the socioeconomic situation of a community, often associated with the ethnicity of its inhabitants, has a huge effect on the level of violence in schools. Both findings indicate how closely violence in school is linked to social inequality within society. As far as the Scandinavian comprehensive school systems are concerned, reports indicate almost no association between family socioeconomic circumstances and violence in school. This is attributed to the fact that the socioeconomic divide is far narrower here than in other countries (Olweus, 1995:50). In all the countries considered, the various areas of young people's lives (family, school, peer group, and community) have been analyzed to determine which factors cause problems and which reduce them. These results also show a large degree of coincidence as regards, for example, the influence of a deprived family background, academic failure, and aggressive peer groups. If features of the in-school environment are also included in the studies, particular reference is made to the significance of the social climate and the behavior of the teaching body.

III. DESIDERATA

In all the countries considered here, intensive research into violence in schools has been undertaken for years or even decades. The great majority of studies have been designed as cross-sectional ones, in which standardized questionnaires have been used. Other types of study (for example longitudinal surveys and observational studies) are extremely rare. These questionnaires are generally used to determine frequencies and manifestations of violence among pupils, and statistical methods are then applied to identify risk factors in the social environment. The fact that the dominance of this type of research involves limitations and "blind spots" has been pointedly criticized by some social scientists. These criticisms first focus on the thematic orientation of the studies concerned: "As if the authors had concluded an agreement among themselves, almost all of them consider only violence initiated by pupils. Other members of the school are hardly considered at all as *perpetrators*. If we assume that those responsible for violence tend to be those with power and resources, while their victims tend to be weak, then this is a striking point which in my view calls for explanation. I have not been able to find any. This is all the more remarkable when we note that teachers are mentioned as victims in quite a few of these studies" (Krumm, 1997:64). This criticism, in this case leveled at German researchers, can also be directed not only at research in Scandinavia and the United States but also, for example, at that undertaken in France and Britain. Evidently there was international agreement during the 1980s and 1990s that attention should be focused primarily, or even exclusively, on pupils as perpetrators. "Against the trend," as it were, Krumm himself undertook a study in which he asked former school pupils in Germany and Austria how often they had experienced abuse, injury, or even "mobbing" by the teaching body. The figures he arrived at were extraordinarily high (Krumm & Weiss, 2000). If we also take into consideration that some other studies have identified degrading, marginalizing, and labeling attitudes on the part of staff as a significant risk factor for pupil violence (see for example Forschungsgruppe Schulevaluation, 1998:211ff.), we find we are looking at a process for which the term "aggression spiral" seems appropriate. The two groups, pupils and staff, each perceive the other's behavior as provocative and insulting, react to it (within the context of their respective roles) aggressively, and so trigger a dynamic process which then results in increasingly conflictual and violent behavior. Yet, although a majority of research into violence in schools claims the existence of an interactive effect, these processes of "reciprocal inflammation" have hardly been analyzed at all to date. One reason for this is that, as a basic principle, no attention has been paid to the teaching staff as "perpetrators," but another is that there are virtually no studies in which interactive procedures have been analyzed truly systematically (longitudinally).

A second target of criticism is the fact that the methodological limitations of a cross-sectional study are often disregarded in interpreting the data. Thus, most of the quantitative studies referred to here draw their variables from the family, school, or peer group context and link them statistically to the frequency of violence at individual or class level. This results in correlative relationships which are then subjected to causal interpretation—admittedly a circumspect one in most cases (see for example Tillmann et al., 1999:299ff.). This kind of procedure is not without its methodological problems, and findings should at least refer to the uncertainties involved. That, however, is precisely what is not done in many cases (see Krumm, 1997:77). Consequently, there is a need for studies that make use of more complex designs. Within the quantitative paradigm, this would mean longitudinal studies using experimental or quasi-experimental designs to determine what causal relationships exist. Other researchers suggest here that more qualitative studies should be undertaken, in order to make it easier to trace the communicative and biographical process that results in acts of violence, providing a better understanding of the actions of young people within their various living environments (see Popp, 1997). At present, studies of this kind, using qualitative interviews or participatory observation, exist only in extremely isolated cases (see for example Krappmann & Oswald, 1995; Böttger, 1997; Oswald, 1999).

IV. APPROACHES TO PREVENTION

Research into violence in schools is nearly always undertaken in the hope of making a contribution to improving school practice—in other words, minimizing violence. To this extent, the formulation of the problem itself generally includes an interest in prevention. The identification of risk factors here is designed to determine the "right" starting points for teaching activity. Those responsible for such preventive activities are, generally, the schools themselves—or more accurately the teaching bodies, the school psychological services, the teacher further training facilities, and in some cases the school authorities too. But the link aimed at here between analytical research and preventive work, however reasonable it may be, also comes up against two fundamental problems. First, an empirical analysis is quite incapable, in itself, of suggesting what preventive action can be regarded as logical or promising. To this extent, preventive activities must be planned with an educational logic of their own; in that case, though, the same empirical analysis may very well result in different educational concepts (for example, greater control or greater trust). Secondly, *school-based* preventive activities cannot reach into every sphere of a young person's life. Even though many studies point out that a young person's family or neighborhood situation may provide the soil in which violence flourishes, the school is generally unable to provide any kind of family therapy or improve the socioeconomic situation of an urban district. However, a school can change its own forms of communication and working procedures, which is precisely what the majority of programs concentrate on (or restrict themselves to) doing. In all three regions studied here, there are extensive activities within the school system aimed at the prevention of violence in schools. These efforts have the longest history and have taken the most varied forms in the United States; in Germany they are of relatively recent origin (since about 1995). There is a significant association in all three regions between the focal points of research and those of prevention. This is most striking in the Scandinavian countries, where preventive activity is almost entirely focused on bullying.

An initial distinction that can be made between the various preventive programs concerns the social structure they target: individual behavior or the individual school. Many schools adopt an approach that begins with the conduct of individual pupils: they develop curricula which emphasize peaceful behavioral standards and are geared to the development of prosocial skills and capabilities; they provide behavioral training courses based on the theory of learning and focused especially on the control of rage and impulse and the reinforcement of empathy; or they employ role-playing methods designed to support the learning of nonviolent conflict resolution strategies. Early assessments of results, mainly from the United States, indicate that these programs encourage a pattern of change for the better in social behavior among pupils and are generally valued highly by the teaching staff (see Goldstein & Glick, 1994; Gottfredson, 1997; Dahlberg, 1998; Hawkins, Farrington, & Catalano, 1998; Petermann et al., 1997). The latter, too, however, are also involved in schemes designed to train them in appropriate behavior. The main focus here is on indicating a deescalating and less stigmatizing conflict approach in dealing with difficult pupils, reinforcing social diagnostic skills, and acquiring nondirective interview techniques. Especially in Germany, teacher retraining in many areas uses the "Konstanz training model" (see Dann, 1997) and Gordon's conflict training methods (1990).

Other preventive programs are directed at the individual school as a social unit. They include school variables such as teacher attitudes, pupil motivation, and the school climate, together with the structural features of the school facility (see Hamburg, 1998; Schubarth & Ackermann, 1998:85ff.). These concepts, especially in the United States, are driven by the growing understanding that school safety is primarily a problem for teachers rather than one that can be solved by the police or judiciary. In these school-based preventive concepts, it is generally assumed that violence by pupils can be prevented or reduced by schools encouraging the social ties and commitment of pupils, their parents, and the teaching staff. These methods include promoting standards of nonviolent conduct and refusing to tolerate the carrying of weapons in school (see Korte, 1993; Hawkins et al., 1998). At this point, there is a smooth transition between strategies of violence prevention and general approaches to improving school quality (school climate, learning culture, school life, etc.) (see Tillmann et al., 1999:302ff.). These school-based approaches very often involve mediation programs ("peer mediation"). They are widespread now, especially in Germany but also in Scandinavia, and are sometimes employed in conjunction with conflict resolution curricula (Hawkins et al., 1998:204; Jefferys-Duden, 1999).

Olweus's (1995) antiviolence program can be regarded as a particularly familiar strategy of this type. Its use has become widespread not only in Scandinavia but also in many other European countries (see Olweus, 1997:297). As a basic requirement for teaching staff, and to a limited extent for parents as well, Olweus calls for them to perceive the problem of bullying in schools and commit themselves to reducing the problem. The activities of the program encompass the whole school, with teachers, pupils, and parents as the main actors; external experts play only a marginal role. Activities take place on different levels. At school level, the first objective is to determine the extent of the problem in the school as a basis for planning further action. At class level, rules for the prevention of violence are introduced; at the same time, an agreement is reached on the penalties for noncompliance. In addition, regular classroom discussions with pupils take place, as do separate interviews with victims and perpetrators, and with their parents. Olweus himself has evaluated his program and found that these efforts have reduced the problem of violence in schools by half (or in some cases even more). Overall, the school climate has been demonstrably improved, and other forms of behavior deviating from school standards have been reduced in the context of these activities (Olweus, 1995:110f. 1997:291f. 1999b:38). The Olweus program has also been used in German schools, and an analysis of results here, too, is generally encouraging (see Hanewinkel & Knaack, 1997).

Mention should also be made of the fact that preventive programs exist in an ever-increasing number of American schools. These are not educationally based, but aim at technical forms of control and large-scale repression. They focus on the concept of the "safe school" and concentrate on forms of technology and human resources designed to improve safety (for example, the use of metal detectors to monitor the carrying of arms; surveillance cameras for buildings, schoolyards, and school buses; electromagnetic door-locking systems; campus policing). Other strategies for increasing school safety include building design, meticulous documentation of offenses, the formation of school crisis teams, and the preparation of crisis management plans (Stephens, 1998:270–289). In some cases, the possibility is even being debated at present of equipping school security staff with firearms (see Devine, 2000:49). It remains to be seen whether the recent cases of perpetrators running amok in German schools will prompt similar calls for security measures to be introduced there.

Overall, the large number of preventive programs and activities is somewhat disproportionate to the extent and quality of evaluation. Most evaluative studies have been produced in the United States; they are open to the criticism, however, that many of them have not conformed to minimum social science standards (see Dusenbury et al., 1997:414; Samples & Abers, 1998:242). In Scandinavia, although the antibullying program has been extensively evaluated, most of the evaluation has been undertaken by the inventor himself (see Olweus, 1997). And although preventive activities have evolved in Germany since the mid-1990s, there are virtually no evaluative studies of them to date (see Schubarth, 2000:139).

Translated by Richard Sharp

REFERENCES

American Psychological Association. (1993). *Violence and Youth. Psychology's Response. Vol. I: Summary Report of the American Psychological Association Commission on Violence and Youth.* Washington, D.C.: American Psychological Association.

Anderson, David C. (1998). Curriculum, Culture, and Community: The Challenge of School Violence. In Michael

Tonry & Mark H. Moore (Eds.), *Youth Violence* (pp. 317–363). Chicago/London: University of Chicago Press.

Bayh, Birch. (1975). *Our Nation's Schools—a Report Card: 'A' in School Violence and Vandalism. (Preliminary Report of the U.S. Senate Subcommittee to Investigate Juvenile Delinquency).* Washington, D.C.: U.S. Government Printing Office.

Beck, Ulrich. (1986). *Risikogesellschaft. Auf dem Weg in eine andere Moderne.* Frankfurt: Suhrkamp.

Björkqvist, Kaj, & Karin Österman. (1999). Finland. In Peter K. Smith, Yohji Morita, Josine Junger-Tas, Dan Olweus, Richard F. Catalano & Phillip T. Slee (Eds.), *The Nature of School Bullying. A Cross-National Perspective* (pp. 56–67). London: Routledge.

Böhnisch, Lothar. (1995). Schule als anomische Struktur. In Wilfried Schubarth & Wolfgang Melzer (Eds.), *Schule, Gewalt und Rechtsextremismus* (pp. 141–151). Opladen: Leske & Budrich.

Böttger, Andreas. (1997). Und dann ging so 'ne Rauferei los. In Heinz Günter Holtappels, Wilhelm Heitmeyer & Wolfgang Melzer (Eds.), *Forschung über Gewalt an Schulen* (pp. 119–136). Weinheim, München: Juventa.

Brener, Nancy B., Thomas Simon, Etienne Krug, & Richard Lowry (1999). Recent Trends in Violence-Related Behaviors Among High School Students in the United States. *Journal of the American Medical Association, 282*(5), 440–446.

Bronfenbrenner, Urie. (1976). *Ökologische Sozialisationsforschung.* Stuttgart: Klett.

Brumlik, Micha, & Heinz Günter Holtappels. (1987). Mead und die Handlungsperspektive schulischer Akteure—interaktionistische Beiträge zur Schultheorie. In Klaus-Jürgen Tillmann (Ed.), *Schultheorien* (pp. 88–103). Hamburg: Bergmann und Helbig.

Brusten, Manfred, & Klaus Hurrelmann. (1973). *Abweichendes Verhalten in der Schule.* München: Juventa.

Center for Disease Control. (1998). *Youth Risk Behavior Surveillance—United States 1997.* Morbidity and Mortality Weekly Report, August 14.

Cloer, Ernst (Eds.) (1982). *Disziplinkonflikte in Erziehung und Schule.* Bad Heilbrunn: Klinkhardt.

Coben, Jeffrey H., Harold B. Weiss, Edward P. Mulvey, Stephen R. Dearwater. (1994). A Primer on School Violence Prevention. *Journal of School Health, 64*(8), 309–313.

Dahlberg, Linda L. (1998). Youth Violence in the United States. Major Trends, Risk Factors, and Prevention Approaches. *American Journal of Preventive Medicine, 14*(4), 259–272.

Dann, Hanns-Dietrich. (1997). Aggressionsprävention im sozialen Kontext der Schule. In Heinz Günter Holtappels, Wilhelm Heitmeyer & Wolfgang Melzer (Eds.), *Forschung über Gewalt an Schulen* (pp. 351–360). Weinheim, München: Juventa.

Dettenborn, Harry, & Erwin Lautsch. (1993). Aggression in der Schule aus der Schülerperspektive. *Zeitschrift für Pädagogik, 39*(5), 745–774.

Devine, John. (2000). The School Massacres in the United States. *Journal für Konflikt- und Gewaltforschung, 2*(1), 43–53.

Dueholm, Niels. (1999). Denmark. In Peter K. Smith, Yohji Morita, Josine Junger-Tas, Dan Olweus, Richard F. Catalano & Phillip T. Slee (Eds.), *The Nature of School Bullying. A Cross-National Perspective* (pp. 49–55). London: Routledge.

Durkheim, Emile. (1970). *Die Regeln der soziologischen Methode.* Neuwied: Luchterhand.

Dusenbury, Linda, Mathea Falco, Antonia Lake, Rosalind Brannigan, & Kris Bosworth. (1997). Nine Critical Elements of Promising Violence Prevention Programs. *Journal of School Health, 67*(10), 409–414.

Eckstein, Andreas. (1996). Keine Republik der braven Pioniere—oder: Gewalt an Schulen der DDR. In Gaby Flösser, Hans-Uwe Otto & Klaus-Jürgen Tillmann (Eds.), *Schule und Jugendhilfe* (pp. 30–41). Opladen: Leske & Budrich.

Eisenberg, Götz (2002): Die menschlichen "Ungeheuer" entspringen unserer Normalität. Nach dem Amoklauf von Erfurt. *Frankfurter Rundschau,* May, 11, 2002, p. 7.

Erikson, Erik H. (1966). *Identität und Lebenszyklus.* Frankfurt a. M.: Suhrkamp.

Fend, Helmut. (1998). *Qualität im Bildungswesen. Schulforschung zu Systembedingungen, Schulprofilen und Lehrerleistungen.* Weinheim, München: Juventa.

Forschungsgruppe Schulevaluation. (1998). *Gewalt als soziales Problem in Schulen.* Opladen: Leske & Budrich.

Freud, Siegmund. (1972). *Abriß der Psychoanalyse/Das Unbehagen an der Kultur.* Frankfurt: Fischer.

Fuchs, Marek, Siegfried Lamnek, & Jens Luedtke. (1996). *Schule und Gewalt. Realität und Wahrnehmung eines sozialen Problems.* Opladen: Leske & Budrich.

Fuchs, Marek, Siegfried Lamnek, & Jens Luedtke. (2001). *Tatort Schule: Gewalt an Schulen 1994–1999.* Opladen: Leske und Budrich.

Funk, Walter. (Ed.) (1995). *Nürnberger Schüler-Studie 1994: Gewalt an Schulen.* Regensburg: Roderer.

Goffman, Erving. (1967). *Stigma. Über die Techniken der Bewältigung beschädigter Identität*. Frankfurt: Suhrkamp.
Goldstein, Arnold P., & Barry Glick. (1994). Aggression Replacement Training: Curriculum and Evaluation. *Simulation and Gaming, 25*(1), 9–26.
Goldstein, Arnold P., & Jane Close Conoley. (Eds.) (1997). *School Violence Intervention. A Practical Handbook*. New York: Guilford Press.
Gordon, Thomas. (1990). *Lehrer-Schüler-Konferenz: Wie man Konflikte in der Schule löst*. München: Heyne.
Gottfredson, Denise C. (1997). School Based Crime Prevention. In Lawrence W. Sherman, Denise C. Gottfredson, Doris MacKenzie, John Eck, Peter Reuter & Shawn Bushway (Eds.), *Presenting Crime. What Works, What Doesn't, What's Promising*. Washington D.C.: U.S. Department of Justice.
Gottfredson, Garry D., & Denise C. Gottfredson. (1985). *Victimization in Schools*. New York: Plenum.
Greszik, Bettina, Frank Hering, & Harald Euler. (1995). Gewalt in den Schulen: Ergebnisse einer Befragung in Kassel. *Zeitschrift für Pädagogik, 41*(2), 265–284.
Hamburg, Margaret A. (1998). Youth Violence is a Public Health Concern. In Delbert Elliott, Beatrix A. Hamburg & Kirk R. Williams (Eds.), *Violence in American Schools* (pp. 31–54). New York: Cambridge University Press.
Hammarströrm, Anne, & Urban Janlert. (1994). Epidemiology of School Injuries in the Northern Part of Sweden. *Scandinavian Journal of Social Medicine, 22*(2), 120–126.
Hanewinkel, Reiner, & Reimer Knaack. (1997). Prävention von Aggression und Gewalt an Schulen. Ergebnisse einer Interventionsstudie. In Heinz Günter Holtappels, Wilhelm Heitmeyer & Wolfgang Melzer (Eds.), *Forschung über Gewalt an Schulen* (pp. 299–313). Weinheim, München: Juventa.
Harachi, Tracy W., Richard F. Catalano, & David Hawkins. (1999). United States. In Peter K. Smith, Yohji Morita, Josine Junger-Tas, Dan Olweus, Richard F. Catalano & Phillip T. Slee (Eds.), *The Nature of School Bullying. A Cross-National Perspective* (pp. 279–295). London: Routledge.
Hargreaves, David H. (1979). Reaktionen auf soziale Etikettierungen. In Hans-Joachim Asmus & Rüdiger Peuckert (Eds.), *Abweichendes Schülerverhalten* (pp. 141–154). Heidelberg: Quelle und Meyer.
Hargreaves, David H., Stephen Hester, & Frank Mellor. (1981). *Abweichendes Verhalten im Unterricht*. Weinheim, Basel: Beltz.
Hawkins, J. David, David P. Farrington, & Richard F. Catalano. (1998). Reducing Violence through the Schools. In Delbert Elliott, Beatrix A. Hamburg & Kirk R. Williams (Eds.), *Violence in American Schools* (pp. 188–216). New York: Cambridge University Press.
Heinemann, Evelyn. (1996). *Aggression. Verstehen und Bewältigen*. Berlin/ Heidelberg/ New York: Springer.
Heitmeyer, Wilhelm. (1994). Entsicherungen. Desintegrationsprozesse und Gewalt. In Ulrich Beck & Elisabeth Beck-Gernsheim (Eds.), *Riskante Freiheiten: Individualisierung in modernen Gesellschaften* (pp. 376–401). Frankfurt a. M.: Suhrkamp.
Heitmeyer, Wilhelm. (2002). "Süchtig nach Anerkennung." *Die Zeit, 19*, 4.
Heitmeyer, Wilhelm, & Thomas Olk. (1995). The Role of Individualization Theory in Adolescent Socialization. In Georg Neubauer & Klaus Hurrelmann (Eds.), *Individualization in Childhood and Adolescence* (pp. 15–36). Berlin, New York: de Gruyter.
Heitmeyer, Wilhelm, Birgit Collmann, Jutta Conrads, Ingo Matuschek, Dietmar Kraul, Wolfgang Kühnel, Renate Möller, & Matthias Ulbrich-Herrmann. (1995). *Gewalt. Schattenseiten der Individualisierung bei Jugendlichen aus unterschiedlichen Milieus*. Weinheim, München: Juventa.
Helsper, Werner. (1995). Zur 'Normalität' jugendlicher Gewalt: Sozialisationstheoretische Reflexionen zum Verhältnis von Anerkennung und Gewalt. In Werner Helsper & Hartmut Wenzel (Eds.), *Pädagogik und Gewalt* (pp. 113–154). Opladen: Leske & Budrich.
Holtappels, Heinz Günter. (1987). *Schulprobleme und abweichendes Verhalten aus der Schülerperspektive*. Bochum: Schallwig.
Hyman, Irwin A. (1996). *The Enemy within: Tales of Punishment Politics and Prevention*. Philadelphia: National Center for the Study of Corporal Punishment and Alternatives in the Schools. [ERIC Document Reproduction Service No. ED397386]
Jefferys-Duden, Karin. (1999). *Das Streitschlichterprogramm. Mediatorenausbildung für Schülerinnen und Schüler der Klasse 3–6*. Weinheim, Basel: Beltz.
Kachur, S. Patrick, Gail M. Stennies, Kenneth E. Powell, William Modzeleski, William, Ronald Stephens, Rosemary Murphy, Marcie-Jo Kresnow, David Sleet, & Richard Lowry. (1996). School-Associated Violent Deaths in the United States, 1992 to 1994. *JAMA, 275*(22), 1729–1733.
Kaufman, Phillip, Xianglei Chen, Susan P. Choy, Salley A. Ruddy, Amanda Miller, Kathryn A. Chandler, Christopher D. Chapman, Michael R. Rand, & Patsy Klaus. (1999). Indicators of School Crime and

Safety. Washington, D.C.: U.S. Departments of Education and Justice. NCES 1999-057/NCJ-178906 [Internet http://nces.ed.gov]

Kingery, Paul M., Frank A. Biafora, & Rich S. Zimmerman. (1996). Risk Factors for Violent Behaviors among Ethnically Diverse Urban Adolescents: Beyond Race/Ethnicity. *School Psychology International, 17*, 171–186.

Klockhaus, Ruth, & Brigitte Habermann-Morbey. (1986). *Psychologie des Schulvandalismus.* Göttingen: Hogrefe.

Korte, Jochen. (1993). *Faustrecht auf dem Schulhof. Über den Umgang mit aggressivem Verhalten in der Schule.* 2nd Edition. Weinheim, Basel: Beltz.

Krappmann, Lothar, & Hans Oswald. (1995). *Alltag der Schulkinder. Beobachtungen von Interaktionen und Sozialbeziehungen.* Weinheim, München: Juventa.

Krumm, Volker. (1997). Methodenkritische Analyse schulischer Gewaltforschung. In Heinz Günter Holtappels, Wilhelm Heitmeyer & Wolfgang Melzer (Eds.), *Forschung über Gewalt an Schulen* (pp. 63–80). Weinheim, München: Juventa.

Krumm, Volker, & Susanne Weiss. (2000). Ungerechte Lehrer. Zu einem Defizit in der Forschung über Gewalt an Schulen. *Psychosozial, 23*(1), pp. 57–74.

Kumpulainen, Kirsti, Eila Räsänen, Irmeli Henttonen, Fredrik Almqvist, Kaija Kresanov, Sirkka-Liisa Linna, Irma Moilanen, Jorma Piha, Kaija Puura, & Tuula Tamminen. (1998). Bullying and Psychiatric Symptoms among Elementary School-Age Children. *Child Abuse & Neglect, 23*(7), 705–717.

Laflamme, Lucie, Ewa Menckel, & Elisabet Aldenberg. (1998). Violence in the Swedish School Environment: Extent of the Problem and Its Manifestations. *Work. A Journal of Prevention, Assessment & Rehabilitation, 11*, 143–153.

Lagerspetz, Kirsti, Kaj Björkqvist, Marianne Berts, & Elisabeth King. (1982). Group Aggression among School Children in Three Schools. *Scandinavian Journal of Psychology, 23*(1), 45–52.

Lane, June R. (1991). School Caught in the Crossfire. *School Safety, Spring*, p. 31.

Lösel, Friedrich, Thomas Bliesener, & Mechthild Averbeck. (1997). Erlebens- und Verhaltensprobleme von Tätern und Opfern. In Heinz Günter Holtappels, Wilhelm Heitmeyer & Wolfgang Melzer (Eds.), *Forschung zu Gewalt an Schulen* (pp. 137–154). Weinheim, München: Juventa.

Mansel, Jürgen, & Klaus Hurrelmann. (1998). Aggressives und delinquentes Verhalten Jugendlicher im Zeitvergleich. *Kölner Zeitschrift für Soziologie und Sozialpsychologie, 50*(1), 78–109.

Mead, George H. (1968). *Geist, Identität und Gesellschaft.* Frankfurt: Suhrkamp.

Merton, Robert K. (1968). Sozialstruktur und Anomie. In Fritz Sack & René König (Eds.), *Kriminalsoziologie* (pp. 283–313). Frankfurt: Akademische Verlagsgesellschaft.

Morita, Yohji. (1997). Privatisierung in der japanischen Gesellschaft und die Struktur von Schikane an Schulen. In Gesine Foltjanty-Jost & Dieter Rössner (Eds.), *Gewalt unter Jugendlichen in Deutschland und Japan* (pp. 85–99). Ursachen und Bekämpfung. Baden-Baden: Nomos.

Morrison, Gale M., Michael J. Furlong, & Richard L. Morrison. (1997). The Safe School: Moving beyond Crime Prevention to School Empowerment. In Arnold P. Goldstein & Jane Close Conoley (Eds.), *School Violence Intervention. A Practical Handbook* (pp. 236–263). New York: Guilford Press.

Olweus, Dan. (1995). *Gewalt in der Schule. Was Lehrer und Eltern wissen sollten—und tun können.* Bern: Huber.

Olweus, Dan. (1997). Täter-Opfer-Probleme in der Schule: Erkenntnisstand und Interventionsprogramm. In Heinz Günter Holtappels, Wilhelm Heitmeyer & Wolfgang Melzer (Eds.), *Forschung über Gewalt an Schulen* (pp. 281–297). Weinheim, München: Juventa.

Olweus, Dan. (1999a). Sweden. In Peter K. Smith, Yohji Morita, Josine Junger-Tas, Dan Olweus, Richard F. Catalano & Phillip T. Slee (Eds.), *The Nature of School Bullying. A Cross-National Perspective* (pp. 7–27). London: Routledge.

Olweus, Dan. (1999b). Norway. In Peter K. Smith, Yohji Morita, Josine Junger-Tas, Dan Olweus, Richard F. Catalano & Phillip T. Slee (Eds.), *The Nature of School Bullying. A Cross-National Perspective* (pp. 28–48). London: Routledge.

Österman, Karin, Kaj Björkqvist, Kirsti Lagerspetz, Ari Kaukiainen, Ari, Simha F. Landau, Adam Fraczek, & Gian Vittorio Caprara. (1998). Cross-Cultural Evidence of Female Indirect Aggression. *Aggressive Behavior, 24*(1), 1–8.

Oswald, Hans. (1999). Jenseits der Grenzen zur Gewalt: Sanktionen und raue Spiele. In Mechthild Schäfer & Dieter Frey (Eds.), *Aggression und Gewalt unter Kindern und Jugendlichen* (pp. 179–199). Göttingen, Bern, Toronto, Seattle: Hogrefe.

Otto, Hans-Uwe, & Roland Merten (Eds.) (1993). *Rechtsradikale Gewalt im vereinigten Deutschland.* Opladen: Leske & Budrich.

Petermann, Franz, Gert Jungert, Dorothe Verbeek, & Uwe Tänzer. (1997). Verhaltenstraining mit Kindern. In Heinz Günter Holtappels, Wilhelm Heitmeyer & Wolfgang Melzer (Eds.), *Forschung über Gewalt an Schulen* (pp. 315–330). Weinheim, München: Juventa.

Popp, Ulrike. (1997). Geschlechtersozialisation und Gewalt an Schulen. In Heinz Günter Holtappels, Wilhelm Heitmeyer & Wolfgang Melzer (Eds.), *Forschung über Gewalt an Schulen* (pp. 215–232). Weinheim, München: Juventa.

Rutter, Michael, Barbara Maughan, Peter Mortimer, & Janet Ouston. (1980). *Fünfzehntausend Stunden. Schulen und ihre Wirkungen auf Kinder.* Weinheim, Basel: Beltz.

Salmivalli, Christina, Kirsti Lagerspetz, Kaj Björkqvist, Karin Österman, & Ari Kaukiainen. (1996). Bullying as a Group Process: Participant Roles and Their Relations to Social Status within the Group. *Aggressive Behavior*, 22(1), 1–15.

Salmivalli, Christina, Arja Huttunen, & Kirsti Lagerspetz. (1997). Peer Networks and Bullying in Schools. *Scandinavian Journal of Psychology*, 38(4), 305–312.

Salmivalli, Christina, Miia Lappalainen, Kirsti Lagerspetz. (1998). Stability and Change of Behavior in Connection with Bullying in Schools: A Two Year Follow Up. *Aggressive Behavior*, 24(3), 205–218.

Samples, Faith, & Larry Abers. (1998). Evaluations of School-Based Violence Prevention Programs. In Delbert S. Elliott, Beatrix A. Hamburg & Kirk R. Williams (Eds.), *Violence in American Schools* (pp. 217–252). New York: Cambridge University Press.

Schubarth, Wilfried. (1995). Gewalt an Schulen als Medienereignis. In Wilfried Schubarth & Wolfgang Melzer (Eds.), *Schule, Gewalt und Rechtsextremismus. 2nd Edition* (pp. 104–114). Opladen: Leske & Budrich.

Schubarth, Wilfried. (2000). *Gewaltprävention in Schule und Jugendhilfe.* Neuwied, Kriftel: Luchterhand.

Schubarth, Wilfried, Kerstin Darge, Manuela Mühl, & Christoph Ackermann. (1997). Im Gewaltausmaß vereint? Eine vergleichende Schülerbefragung in Sachsen und Hessen. In Heinz Günter Holtappels, Wilhelm Heitmeyer & Wolfgang Melzer (Eds.), *Forschung über Gewalt an Schulen* (pp. 101–118). Weinheim, München: Juventa.

Schubarth, Wilfried, & Christoph Ackermann. (1998). *Aggression und Gewalt. 45 Fragen zur Gewaltprävention.* Dresden: Sächsische Landeszentrale für politische Bildung.

Schwind, Hans-Dieter, Karin Roitsch, Wilfried Ahlborn, & Birgit Gielen. (1995). *Gewalt in der Schule am Beispiel von Bochum.* Mainz: Weißer-Ring-Verlag.

Smith, Peter K. (1999). England and Wales. In Peter K. Smith, Yohji Morita, Josine Junger-Tas, Dan Olweus, Richard F. Catalano & Phillip T. Slee (Eds.), *The Nature of School Bullying. A Cross-National Perspective* (pp. 68–91). London: Routledge.

Smith, Peter K., & Yohji Morita. (1999). Introduction. In Peter K. Smith, Yohji Morita, Josine Junger-Tas, Dan Olweus, Richard F. Catalano & Phillip T. Slee (Eds.), *The Nature of School Bullying. A Cross-National Perspective* (pp. 1–4). London: Routledge.

Smith, Peter K., Yohji Morita, Josine Junger-Tas, Dan Olweus, Richard F. Catalano, & Phillip T. Slee (Eds.) (1999). *The Nature of School Bullying. A Cross-National Perspective.* London: Routledge.

Der Spiegel. (2002). Das Spiel seines Lebens, 19, 118–133.

Stephens, Ronald D. (1998). "Safe School Planning." In Delbert S. Elliott, Beatrix A. Hamburg, Kirk R. Williams (Eds.), *Violence in American Schools* (pp. 253–292). New York: Cambridge University Press.

Tillmann, Klaus-Jürgen, Birgit Holler-Nowitzki, Heinz-Günter Holtappels, Ulrich Meier, Ulrich, & Ulrike Popp. (1999). *Schülergewalt als Schulproblem. Verursachende Bedingungen, Erscheinungsformen und pädagogische Handlungsperspektiven.* Weinheim, München: Juventa.

Tillmann, Klaus-Jürgen. (2000). *Sozialisationstheorien. Eine Einführung in den Zusammenhang von Gesellschaft, Institution und Subjektwerdung. 10th Edition.* Reinbek: Rowohlt.

U.S. Departments of Education and Justice. (1999). *Annual Report on School Safety.* Washington, D.C.: U.S. Departments of Education and Justice. [Internet http://nces.ed.gov]

Walker, Hill M., Geoff Colvin, & Elizabeth Ramsey. (1995). *Antisocial Behavior in School: Strategies and Best Practices.* Albany: Brooks, Cole Publishing Co.

Wieviorka, Michel, Philippe Bataille, Karine Clément, Olivier Cousin, Farhad Khosrokhavar, Séverin Labat, Eric Mace, Paola Rebughini, & Nikola Tietze. (1999). *Violence en France.* Paris: Editions du Seuil.

Willis, Paul. (1979). *Spaß am Widerstand. Gegenkultur in der Arbeiterschule.* Frankfurt: Syndikat.

CHAPTER II-5-1.3

Work-Related Violence

Vittorio di Martino

I. DEFINITIONS

The variety of behaviors which may be covered under the general rubric of violence at work is so large, the borderline with acceptable behaviors is often so vague, and the perception in different contexts and cultures of what constitutes violence is so diverse that it becomes a significant challenge to both describe and define this phenomenon.

A general definition of violence at work has yet to be agreed in the international arena. A substantial effort toward a common understanding in this area was, however, made at an Expert Meeting organized by the European Commission in Dublin in May 1995, where the following definition was proposed (Wynne et al.1997):

> incidents where persons are abused, threatened or assaulted in circumstances related to their work, involving an explicit or implicit challenge to their safety, well-being and health.

Abuse is used to indicate all behaviors which depart from reasonable conduct and involve the misuse of physical or psychological strength. Assault generally includes any attempt at physical injury or attack on a person, including actual physical harm. Threats encompass the menace of death, or the announcement of an intention to harm a person or damage their property. In real situations, these behaviors often overlap, making any attempt to categorize different forms of violence very difficult. The definition is, however, gaining increasing consensus.

It seems capable of addressing the emerging figures of violence at work, particularly psychological ones that are attracting growing attention and awareness. Not all violence is physical. In recent years, new evidence has emerged of the impact and harm caused by nonphysical violence. Such new forms of violence include bullying and mobbing.

Workplace bullying is one of the fastest growing forms of workplace violence. It constitutes offensive behavior through vindictive, cruel, malicious, or humiliating attempts to undermine an individual or groups of employees through such activities as making life difficult for those who have the potential to do the bully's job better, shouting at staff to get things done, insisting that the "bully's way is the right way," refusing to delegate because the bully feels no one else can be trusted, and punishing others by constant criticism or removing their responsibilities for being too competent.

Research carried out in the United Kingdom found that 53 percent of employees had been victims of bullying at work and that 78 percent had witnessed such behavior (Staffordshire University, 1994:2). More recent finds confirm the magnitude of the problem and show the collective nature of bullying and its persistence in time. Only a third of those bullied reported having been singled out for mistreatment while 55 percent were bullied together with several other colleagues and almost 15 percent reported that bullying was extended to the entire working group. The finds also show that bullying is a drawn out affair which for two out of three targets of bullying goes on for more than a year, and for approximately 40 percent for more than two years (Hoel & Cooper, 2000:9,10).

Ganging up or mobbing is reported as a growing problem almost everywhere. It involves ganging up on or "mobbing" a targeted employee and subjecting that person to psychological harassment. Mobbing includes constant negative remarks or criticisms, isolating a person from social contacts, and gossiping or spreading false information. In Sweden, it is estimated that mobbing is a factor in 10 to 15 percent of suicides (Leymann, 1990:122).

Attention is also growing in respect of violence which is perpetrated through repeated behavior of a type which by itself may be relatively minor but which cumulatively can become a very serious form of violence such as sexual harassment. Although a single incident can suffice, sexual harassment often consists of repeated unwelcome, unreciprocated, and imposed action which may have a devastating effect on the victim. Based on this, the inclusion of sexual harassment within the general definition of violence at work given above should be an uncontroversial matter. However, the idea that sexual harassment is just another form of violence is still often rejected, even in experts' meetings, on the basis of a pretended "different" nature of this type of behavior vis-à-vis other types of violence at work. A position, in our view, that appears absolutely unjustified.

The new profile of violence at work which emerges is one which gives equal emphasis to physical and psychological behavior, and one which gives full recognition to the significance of minor acts of violence. It is also a profile which recognizes that violence at work is not limited to the workplace. There is a risk of violence that originates in the family or during commuting and can impact severely on the workplace while, in turn, violence at work can spill over during commuting and into the family, thus activating a vicious circle extremely difficult to break.

While not covering all these situations, the definition given above, by using the term "work-related" instead of "workplace," puts violence at work in a larger perspective and one that better responds to the way many people work nowadays.

The term "workplace" is in fact fraught with problems. When official crime statistics do establish a link with occupational data and provide information about the location at which incidents of criminal violence occur, they tend to adopt a quite constrained definition of violence at work. Data may be provided about violent offenses committed in offices, commercial premises like banks, and schools or other physical settings. This construction of the workplace does not allow for mobile or geographically diverse occupational activities such as those conducted by law enforcement officials, taxi drivers or journalists, nor does it take account of occupational groups whose work takes them to people's homes, like meter readers, plumbers, and postal officials, or those who use their own homes as their workplace. The latter category of employment is becoming far more prevalent as new technologies make many traditional workplaces redundant.

Definitional issues of this type are often the grist for complex and technical legal debate about whether or not a worker is entitled to compensation for injuries arising from or during the course of employment. The intricacies of this debate do not need to be outlined here, but it is important to note the association between questions of definition, and questions of both civil and criminal legal liability and responsibility, when considering many statistics on violence at work. In the field of occupational health and safety, the recognition and expansion of the liability and responsibility for providing a violence-free workplace is now stimulating efforts in a number of jurisdictions to gather information about the incidence and prevalence of violent behaviors. The substantial gaps, which are at present commonplace, in the information on this subject are likely to be narrowed if not closed in the near future as national, regional, and international bodies all focus major attention on the issue of violence at work.

II. MAGNITUDE AND IMPACT

1. International Patterns and Trends

One of the most important and significant sources of international information about violence at work comes from the ICVS (International Crime Victim Survey), a comprehensive multinational comparative research exercise which has so far involved more than 50 countries. The third survey, undertaken 1996–97, covered more than 40 countries: 8 from Western Europe, 2 from the New World, 12 from Countries in Transition, 3 from Africa, 3 from Asia and 4 from Latin America (Alvazzi del Frate, 1998).

Due to its representative and wide geographic coverage including both developed and developing countries in various parts of the world, the ICVS can be considered one of the major international comparative criminological projects. In the ICVS, random samples of the population aged 16 years and above are interviewed about their victimization experiences. The questionnaire includes questions on 13 types of crime against the household and at the personal level. It also seeks information on opinions and attitudes about reporting to the police and police performance, patterns of crime prevention, fear of crime, and attitudes toward punishment. Therefore, the ICVS provides information on victimization experience, victimization risk, access to justice, fear of crime, and victimization by criminal justice. The ICVS questionnaire also includes reference to victimization at the workplace. Information is sought from victims of sexual incidents (women only), and from the victims of assault/threat (which is also defined as "nonsexual assault").

Despite the use of standard methodology, the ICVS revealed that the cultural messages in different contexts or in the wording of a question might elicit different answers in different languages. The interpretation of the survey results on sexual incidents may thus be problematic and should be treated with caution. In fact, for this issue more than in other parts of the survey, special attention should be paid to the terminology used. Victims were asked to provide a description of what happened, and invited to describe the incident as rape, attempted rape, indecent assault, or offensive behavior. On average, half of the incidents were defined as "offensive behavior" while 5 percent approximately were described as rapes, and 16 percent as attempted rapes; 27 percent of the victims described the incident as an indecent assault.

a) PREVALENCE OF VICTIMIZATION. As shown in Table II-5-1-3.1 that follows, victimization rates for both males and females were highest in industrialized countries and for sexual incidents. Lower victimization rates were observed not only in the regions where external employment for women is less frequent (Asia and Africa), but also in countries in transition, where low victimization rates of this type were reported throughout the region.

In general, victimization risk at the workplace is higher for women than for men, with the exception of nonsexual assault in countries in transition and Africa, which more frequently occurred to men than to women. In Western Europe, a form of "gender equality" was reached as regards male and female victims of nonsexual assault, with percentages leveled.

b) CONTEXT OF VICTIMIZATION. On average, 10 percent of all the incidents involving women victims happened at the workplace. This was particularly the case with the least serious forms of sexual harassment (offensive behavior) and nonsexual assaults. Furthermore, sexual incidents at the workplace included nearly 8 percent of the cases of rape and approximately 10 percent of attempted rapes and indecent assaults. Sexual harassment and violence against women at work thus include a substantial portion of very serious incidents. These findings suggest that the difficulties women face in obtaining access to the labor market are not limited to reduced opportunities, discrimination, and disparity in wages, but extend to sexual abuse at the workplace itself.

An overall analysis of the context of the violent victimization of men also reveals that more than 13 percent of incidents occurred at the workplace. Distribution of male victimization by place of occurrence shows that the workplace ranks before the respondent's home while women victims of nonsexual assault, even though the percentage of incidents occurring at the workplace was similar to that of male victims, were twice as frequently victims of assault in their own home.

c) AGE OF VICTIMS. Victimization at the workplace mostly affected the age categories between 25 and 49, although women victims were on average younger than men. Women victims of sexual incidents often belonged to the youngest age categories: nearly half were younger than 29, and nearly a third were between 30 and 39 years of age.

While male victims of nonsexual assaults were evenly distributed among the age groups between 25 and 49, more than 56 percent of women victims of nonsexual assault fell into the age groups from 16 to 34.

TABLE II-5-1-3.1. ICVS-Prevalence rates of victimization at the workplace, by type of accident, gender and region

Region	Assault male	Assault female	Sexual incidents female
Western Europe	2.7	3.0	5.4
New World	2.5	4.6	7.5
Countries in transition	2.0	1.4	3.0
Asia	0.4	1.0	1.3
Africa	2.3	1.9	3.7
Latin America	1.9	3.6	5.2

d) WEAPONS USED IN COMMITTING CRIMES. In comparison with crimes occurring either in the victims' home or elsewhere, weapons were least used in crimes at the workplace and mostly against male victims of nonsexual assault, a quarter of whom were exposed to a weapon during the assault.

Between 10 and 15 percent of women victims of nonsexual assault reported being threatened with a weapon at the workplace. Less than 5 percent of women victims of attempted rape and indecent assault reported such an experience.

In almost half of the cases in which a weapon was involved, a gun was used in committing nonsexual assaults against both male and female victims at the workplace. Guns were used much less frequently in incidents which occurred in locations other than the workplace.

e) REPORTING TO THE POLICE OR TO OTHER AUTHORITIES. According to the survey, nonsexual assaults which occurred at the workplace were more likely to be reported, by both male and female victims, than those which happened elsewhere. The relatively high rate of reporting to "other authorities" suggests that workplace victims often resort to the assistance of their employers, or possibly the disciplinary board of their firm, rather than to law enforcement officials.

The survey findings provide an intriguing insight into the dimension of the "dark figure," or non-reported aspects of violence at work. Overwhelmingly, this form of violence does not currently find its way in most countries into the official records of the police, employers, or other authorities. This lack of reporting may be influenced by a number of factors, some of which have already been mentioned. Thus, many employees, and in particular women, may feel constrained to remain silent about their victimization because of fear of reprisals being taken against them, including the possibility of losing their job. Unequal power relationships between employers and employees can undoubtedly influence reporting behaviors and increase the risks of exploitation.

Reporting behaviors may also be influenced by different cultural sensitivities to violence and the context in which it occurs. An enhanced awareness that sexual harassment, bullying and mobbing are completely unacceptable behaviors has resulted in higher rates of reporting of such incidents by victims. In some countries included in the ICVS, this awareness may still be low, perhaps affecting the reporting of incidents of this type to survey interviewers as well as to any other source.

Low levels of reporting violent incidents to the police or other authorities can also be explained by a lack of trust in those bodies, or a belief that there is little they could do to provide any real redress. Criminologists are already familiar with such reporting behaviors among crime victims, many of whom may also view an incident as being too trivial to warrant bringing to the attention of the police. A similar view may exist on the part of a victim of workplace violence.

2. Scale and Severity

In the years that followed the ICVS survey, better reporting both from developing and industrialized countries has progressively unveiled the dramatic importance of the problem of violence at work. Violence at work—be it physical or psychological—clearly appears as a global phenomenon, crossing borders, work settings, and occupational groups.

Table II-5-1-3.2. U.S. fatal occupational injuries by event or exposure, 1993–1998

	1993–97 average	1997 number	1998 number
Transportation incidents	2,611	2,605	2,630
Assaults and violent acts	1,241	1,111	960
Homicide	995	860	709
Contact with object and equipment	1,005	1,035	941
Falls	668	716	702
Exposure to harmful substances or environment	586	554	572
Fires and explosions	199	196	205
Other events or exposures	26	21	16

Source: Monthly Labor Review, 2000:98.

In South Africa, workplace hostilities are reported as "abnormally high." A 1998–99 Internet survey indicated that 78 percent of South Africans who took part in the survey had experienced bullying behavior at the workplace during their working life.

In the U.S., violence is a major contributor to death and injury at the workplace. It has been identified as the most important 1999 security threat to America's largest corporations, according to Fortune 1000 security executives interviewed in the annual Pinkerton survey (Pinkerton, 1999). For decades, official statistics have indicated that, after motor vehicle accidents, homicide is the second single leading cause of occupational injury death and the first cause in relation to women (Jenkins, 1996:iv). Recent data, as shown in Table II-5-1-3.2, confirm the importance and persistence in time of this trend.

Suicide has become the number two cause of death for bureaucrats in Japan with a death toll higher than that of heart diseases and second only to that of cancer. A record of 33,048 people committed suicide in Japan in 1999, with debt or job loss blamed for one in five of the deaths.

A 2000 European Union survey based on 21,500 face interviews with workers throughout the European Union indicates that in its 15 member states 2 percent (3 million) workers are subjected to physical violence from people belonging to their workplace; 4 percent (6 million) are subjected to physical violence from people outside their workplace; 2 percent (3 million) are subjected to sexual harassment; and 9 percent (13 million) are subjected to intimidation and bullying (Paoli, 2000:1). Most important, the data show the close connection between precarious work, gender, young age, and sectors at special risks. Thus, a young woman with a precarious job in a high-risk industry is likely to be many times more exposed to the risk of sexual harassment (see Fig. II-5-1-3.1) than the average worker (Paoli, 2000:2).

3. The Cost of Violence at Work

What is the cost? Violence causes immediate and often long-term disruption to interpersonal relationships, the organization of work, and the overall working environment. Cost factors will include direct costs such as those deriving from absenteeism, turnover, accidents, ill-

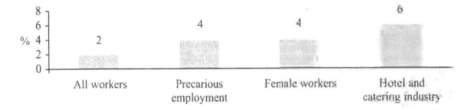

FIGURE II-5-1-3.1. Sexual harassment. *Source*: P. Paoli, 2000:2.

ness, disability, and death; and indirect costs, including diminished functionality, performance, quality, and timely production and competitiveness. Increasing attention is also given to the negative impact of violence on "intangible factors" such as company image, motivation and commitment, loyalty to the enterprise, creativity, working climate, openness to innovation, knowledge building, learning, etc. A recent Finnish study of more than 5,000 hospital staff found that those who had been bullied had 26 percent more certified sickness absence than those who were not bullied (Kivimaki, Elovainio, & Vahtera, 2000:656–660).

Previous data from the European Union had already shown a very significant correlation between health-related absences and violence at work. As shown in the following Fig. II-5-1-3.2, we can see that 35 percent of workers exposed to physical violence were absent from work over the last 12 months, as well as 34 percent of those exposed to bullying and 31 percent of workers exposed to sexual harassment, compared to an average of 23 percent among workers in general.

Also a clear and important correlation is now established in the European Union between violence and stress (Paoli, 2000:5), with the cost of stress calculated at EUR 20 billion each year (European Commission, 1999:13). In the U.S., the cost of stress has been calculated at $350 billion per year while the cost of violence alone has been calculated at $35.4 billion (Kaufer & Mattman, 1998).

Altogether, it has been estimated by a number of reliable studies that stress and violence possibly account for approximately 30 percent of the overall costs of ill health and accidents. Based on the above figures, it has been suggested that stress/violence may account for approximately 0.5–3.5 percent of GDP per year (Hoel, Sparks, & Cooper, 2001:52).

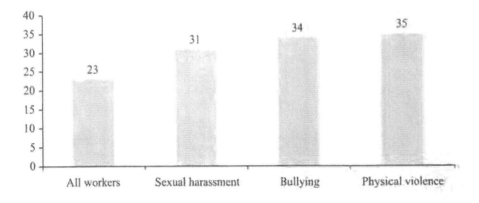

FIGURE II-5-1-3.2. Absenteeism in % over the last 12 months (1996).

The realization and quantification of the cost of violence is of the highest importance in the shaping of antiviolence strategies both in the developing and the industrialized world. The spreading of informal, precarious, and marginal situations at work increasingly moves the attention toward an economically self-sustainable response whereby the key role of programs and action that are cost-effective and naturally fit into the socioeconomic development of the enterprise is highlighted and used as enhancer for further initiatives. Combining economic and social issues in a positive-sum game results in this new type of response being quickly adopted for its own merits. Before embracing this "high road" option, it is, however, necessary to make our way through the many approaches and methodologies that are proposed to analyze and understand how violence at work is built up and operates.

III. APPROACHES AND METHODOLOGIES

1. The Reactive Approach

There is a strong and natural desire among most citizens to seek simple explanations and solutions to the violence which may be gripping their society and threatening "the way decent people live." It is often the media who provide such explanations and convey lasting impressions of the type of people responsible for "an epidemic" of violence in the workplace. Those impressions are often dominated by images of "disgruntled employees" and "angry spouses," "unhappy desperate, often psychiatrically impaired people," venting their anger on colleagues at the workplace. Those media images, of course, also spread with amazing speed around the globe and affect public and official perceptions of violence far beyond their place of origin. Is the "disgruntled worker" the "everyman" of workplace violence? News reports of violent workplace incidents often stress acts of an individual: enraged, aggrieved, irritated, or frustrated for one reason or another, either personal or professional, or under the influence of alcohol or drugs. The prevailing approach to violence is consequently often of a reactive, individual-based, type. It is tempting (or convenient) for many to regard violence as arising from a single cause, and consequently to perceive a reduction in violence as certain to arise from a single solution. For example, there are those who think that the removal of televised violence represents the answer to violent behavior. There are others who perceive more rigorous controls on firearms as the way to eliminate violence.

Much of the current literature on violence at work reflects such an approach, with the development of preemployment tests to screen out and exclude those who might be violent; of profiles to identify those who might become violent in the existing workforce; and of measures to deal with violence when it occurs. This approach is also characterized typically by an emphasis on the need for "target hardening" through the use of a range of security measures to restrict entry to and movement within the workplace (See Bush & O'Shea, 1996:283–298).

Other developments of this approach include the proliferation, in recent years, of "zero tolerance" policies at the workplace and the increasing "criminalization" of acts of violence at work. In the United Kingdom, for instance, legislation has made it a criminal offence to pursue a course of conduct which amounts to harassment of a person. Although not directed specifically at violence at work, the legislation is of sufficient breadth to cover harassment at this and many other locations (United Kingdom, 1997). In France, legislation was enacted along similar lines in 1992, although the French provision on abuse of authority and sexual matters in employment relations does make specific mention of sexual harassment in the workplace as a penal offence, punishable under both the Labor and Penal Code with imprisonment and fines (France, 1992). New legislation is under consideration that would extend these penal provisions to a wider range of situations of violence at work, notably mobbing (*harcèlement moral*).

Measures of this type may well assist—and have effectively assisted—in reducing the incidence of violence at the workplace and in the wider community. They do not, however, tackle at its roots an extremely complex and diverse problem which defies either an easy explanation or solution. A recognition and an understanding of the variety and complexity of the factors which contribute to violence must be a vital precursor of any effective violence prevention or control program. Along these lines, more articulated and comprehensive approaches have been developed.

2. The Behavioral Approach

"Workplace violence can be viewed as individual behavior, with particular psychological roots and occurring in a specific situational context. Some writers have discussed workplace violence from this perspective. Most reports of this type specifically addressing workplace violence usually have been case-studies or accounts of personal experiences in workplace violence prevention, rather than systematic research on the interaction between personality and situational causes. Nonetheless, these reports provide useful leads" (VandenBos & Bulatao, 1996:16).

Significant efforts have been devoted by those seeking to explain violence in this way to predict also when an individual might behave in an aggressive manner. There is no doubt that certain identifiable factors do increase the likelihood that certain individuals, and population groups, will behave in such a way, such as those included in the following list:

- A history of violent behavior;
- Being male;
- Being a young adult;
- Experience of difficulties in childhood, including inadequate parenting, troubled relationships within the family and low levels of school achievement;
- Problems of psychotropic substance abuse, especially problematic alcohol use;
- Severe mental illness, the symptoms of which are not being adequately identified or controlled through therapeutic regimes; and/or
- Being in situations conducive to self-directed or interpersonal violence, including having access to firearms (adapted from McDonald & Brown, 1997:2).

Whatever the list of factors chosen and their combination, the fact remains that, when seeking to predict whether aggressive behavior will occur, a distinction must be made between predicting at the level of the general population, or at that of the individual. The available evidence does permit statements to be made, with some degree of accuracy and reliability, about the heightened risk of violence at work being committed by population groups who display certain key characteristics.

The dilemma remains, however, of predicting with sufficient accuracy and reliability that a particular individual within that group may become violent. It is not possible in the current state of knowledge to predict with complete certainty that a specific person will behave in an aggressive way. Thus, there is always the possibility, if prediction techniques are applied, based on a list of key characteristics like those referred to above, that some individuals may be falsely identified as being at risk of committing acts of violence, and others of not being at risk. These so-called "false positive" and "false negative" aspects of the prediction equation mean that these techniques, if considered for use in the context of the workplace, should only be applied with extreme caution and care. Enterprises and workers alike have a vested interest in ensuring that individuals who do represent a credible threat to the safety and well-being of the workplace are denied entry, or are provided with assistance to minimize the likelihood that they will behave aggressively either toward themselves or others. There is, however, a clear potential for these predictive tools to be used in a prejudicial or discriminatory fashion, in order to exclude from the workplace undesirable persons, or even groups, who are judged to fit a loosely defined category or profile.

3. The Interpersonal Approach

A further step in enlarging the spectrum of attention and the understanding of how violence is generated is by focusing on the interrelationship between the perpetrator and the victim of violence at work. Although sabotage and work-related suicide are important forms of violence, it takes usually two or more—the perpetrator(s) and the victim(s)—to activate violence at work.

a) PERPETRATORS. The personal attributes of the perpetrator have been already been discussed under the "behavioral approach." It is also important to consider the overall nature of the relationship between the perpetrator and the workplace. This criterion has been incorporated into official guidelines in the state of California (California, 1994:11-15) where three main types of "hazardous agent" have been identified. The first type is the "criminal intruder" with no legitimate relationship to the workplace and who usually enters the workplace to commit a robbery or other criminal act. The second type is the "dissatisfied client," when the agent is either the recipient or the object of a service provided by the affected workplace or the victim, e.g., the assailant is a current or former client, patient, customer, passenger, criminal suspect, or prisoner. The third type is the "scorned employee." Usually, this involves an assault by a current or former employee, supervisor, or manager; by a current/former spouse or lover; a relative or friend; or some other person who has a dispute involving an employee of the workplace. Each of these types of hazardous agent requires a different, specific response.

b) VICTIMS. There are many attributes of a victim of workplace violence, who is in most cases likely to be an employee, which could be associated with the risk of violence. These include appearance, health, age and experience, gender, personality and temperament, attitudes and expectations.

Appearance and first impressions are important in any job, as they can set the tone of the interaction and establish the role characteristics for an encounter. In occupations involving direct contact with members of the public, for instance, the wearing of a uniform may encourage or discourage violence. Uniforms are often worn in occupations where employees are expected to act with authority or have the respect of members of the public. Uniforms also identify staff and distinguish them from the public. It is likely that in many circumstances uniforms will discourage violence, but there are situations in which the presence of uniformed staff is resented, and which can provoke abusive or violent behavior. In the United Kingdom, for example, an increasing number of cases of aggression against ambulance staff has been reported because of general public hostility toward people wearing a uniform like those of police officers. For this reason, ambulance staff are now beginning to wear green boiler suits rather than blue uniforms, to distinguish them from law enforcement officials.

The health of workers can also influence how they interact with clients and the public at large. Stress from a heavy workload, or mild forms of mental illness, may lead to misunderstandings or misleading behavior which precipitate aggressive responses. The age and experience of workers is another factor that can either increase or diminish the possibility of aggression. Previous experience of handling similar difficult situations, which is obviously associated with age, should enable workers to react more wisely than inexperienced staff.

A person's gender can influence aggressive behavior in a number of ways. Men are more likely than women to respond in an aggressive way to many workplace situations while women are also at much greater risk of certain types of victimization at work than men.

The personality and attitude of workers is also relevant in considering risks of victimization. Some staff members are often better than others in handling difficult situations—a quality which is usually associated with an individual's less tangible personality characteristics and style of behavior. The attitude of workers, and their job expectations, can also be factors influencing aggressive behaviors. For example, staff members who are working in an enterprise which is about to be shut down, or which is experiencing massive layoffs, are less likely to be tolerant in their encounters with clients. Similarly, uncertain role definitions associated with a particular job can influence how a violent or potentially violent incident is handled. Schoolteachers expect to deal with unruly children, but bus drivers may not; police officers anticipate encounters with disturbed or dangerous people, but firemen and other emergency service providers may not.

Overall, the ways in which victims react to aggressive behavior appear to be important in determining whether that aggression diminishes or escalates. It seems to be important that the victim is not seen by the aggressor to behave in some unfair or unreasonable way. Anxious or angry behavior by the victim may also trigger violence while controlled behavior may help defuse tensions.

4. The Environmental Approach

Further enlarging the area of observation, the environmental approach focuses on the fact that the interrelationship perpetrator–victim does not operate in a vacuum, but that both the perpetrator and the victim interact in macro-social as well as in micro-social environments.

Within this framework, the working environment, including its physical and organizational settings or structure and its managerial style and culture, can greatly influence the risks of violence.

The physical design features of a workplace can be a factor in either defusing or acting as a potential trigger for violence. Australian research has shown, for example, that the levels of violent and destructive behavior in or near licensed premises (pubs, clubs, bars, and like establishments) are influenced by a range of situational factors including the physical design and comfort of the premises. Overcrowded, poorly ventilated, dirty and noisy premises experience higher rates of violence than do those which exhibit good physical design features (Homel, Tomsen, & Thommeny, 1992:679–697; Homel & Clark, 1994:1–46).

The organizational setting appears to be equally if not more important in this respect. Poor organization may, for instance, lead to an excessive workload for a specific group of workers (while others may be relatively inactive), slow down their performance, create unjustified delays and queuing, develop negative attitudes among such workers, and induce aggressive behavior among the customers. The same effects may be induced by labyrinthine bureaucratic procedures, putting both employees and customers under serious stress.

In a broader context, the type of interpersonal relationship, the managerial style, the level at which responsibilities are decentralized, and the general culture of the workplace, must also be taken into consideration. A "participatory" working environment, for instance, where dialogue and communication are extensively exercised, may help defuse the risks of violence. In contrast, a "closed" authoritarian working environment where people work in isolation, with mutual suspicion and defensive attitudes toward external people, may increase the risk of violence.

Along the same lines, the decentralization of services and responsibilities at a local level may help employees to become more aware of local issues and better respond to the needs of the customers, as well as to forecast difficult situations which might degenerate into violence. This would be quite difficult to achieve within a centralized, depersonalized organization where relationships are highly formalized. A company culture based on racial tolerance, equal opportunities, and cooperation can also contribute to the establishment of a working climate where violence has little play. In contrast, if discrimination and segregation are explicitly or implicitly part of the culture of the company, this can be reflected in all behaviors and relationships, both internally and with the outside world.

The interrelationship between the external environment and the working environment also appears significant in terms of predicting violence. Although the "permeability" of the working environment to the external environment is far from automatic, it is evident, for instance, that a bank or shop located in a very dangerous area will be more likely to be subject to robberies; that bus routes will have different levels of risks of violence, depending on which part of the city they serve; and that the level of frustration and aggression of the public in an office may vary according to the level of frustration and aggression in their living environment.

Fully in line with this approach, environmental laws in Norway, Sweden, and the Netherlands highlight the importance of a working environment designed for the people working in it; the key role of work organization and job design in reducing risks; the relevance of both physical and psychological factors at work; the need to provide each worker with a meaningful occupation and with opportunities for occupational development, as well as for self-determination and occupational responsibility; and the need to ensure that workers are informed and involved in all matters concerning health and safety.

The linkage between the working environment and violence at work is becoming much more explicit in this type of legislation. Amendments to Norwegian legislation, for example, have made clear the right of the employee "not to be subject to harassment or other improper conduct" within the working environment (Norway, 1997). In 1993, the National Board of Occupational Safety and Health in Sweden issued two comprehensive and innovative ordinances covering violence and menaces in the working environment and victimization at work (Sweden, 1993). The emphasis is on a combination of prevention strategies that deal with violence in the context of environmental and organizational issues, rather than through its containment at the level of the individual. The ordinances require employers to plan and organize work in a way that seeks to prevent the occurrence of violence and victimization. They must also make it clear that violence will not be tolerated in the workplace.

5. The Situational Approach

Any prediction of the possibility of violent incidents occurring at the workplace will thus depend upon a thorough analysis of the characteristics of the working environment, the external environment, and those of the perpetrator and victim in the particular situation. Each situation is a unique mixture and thus requires a unique analysis. That is why the prediction of specific acts of violence occurring is extremely difficult. Nonetheless, it seems possible and useful to identify, in much greater detail than has previously been attempted, a number of working situations which appear to be both highly relevant to an understanding of this type of aggression, and to the development of strategies for its prevention or control (Toohey, 1993). These "situations at risk" include those associated with working alone; working with the public; working with valuables; working with people in distress; working in education; and working in conditions of special vulnerability.

a) WORKING ALONE. The number of people working alone is increasing. As automation spreads in factories and offices, often accompanied by processes of rationalization of production and reorganization of the workplace, solitary work becomes more frequent. This trend extends outside the traditional workplace into the growing practice of subcontracting, outplacement, teleworking, networking, and "new" self-employment. The push toward increased mobility and the development of interactive communication technologies also favor one-person operations. Working alone full-time is only part of the picture. A much greater number of people work alone part of the time. In a survey among public employees in Canada, for example, nearly 84 percent of respondents indicated that they often worked alone (Pizzino, 1994:15).

Solitary work does not automatically imply a higher risk of violence. It is generally understood, however, that working alone may increase the vulnerability of the workers concerned. This vulnerability level will depend on the type of situation in which the lone work is being carried out. For the lone worker, a shortcut down a backstreet may be perfectly reasonable in broad daylight, but might be asking for trouble on a dark night. Mail delivery may be a dangerous activity in a crime-infested area while being completely safe in a crime-free district.

Workers working alone in small shops, gas stations, and kiosks are often seen as "easy" targets by aggressors. In the U.S., gas station workers rank fourth among the occupations most exposed to homicide (Jenkins, 1996:5). Cleaners, maintenance or repair staff, and others who work alone outside normal hours are at special risk of suffering physical and sexual attacks. Of lone workers, taxi drivers in many places are at the greatest risk of violence. Nighttime is the highest risk driving period for taxi drivers and, as in other types of violence, customer intoxication appears to play a role in precipitating violence. A 1993 Australian study of taxi drivers revealed that 81 percent had experienced abuse, 17 percent threats, and 10 percent physical attacks (Mayhew, 1999).

b) **WORKING IN CONTACT WITH THE PUBLIC.** A wide variety of occupations and numerous working situations involve contact with the public. While in most circumstances this type of work can be generally agreeable, there are cases where exposure to the public can create a higher risk of violence.

The reasons for such violence are multiple. In very large organizations, dealing with a large number of the general public, workers are likely to meet some individuals with a history of violence, dangerous mental illness, or who are intoxicated. This "random" aggression is very difficult to predict and can lead to very serious incidents.

In other cases, violent behavior may be provoked by or result from a perceived or poor quality of service. Violence may also be triggered by dismissive and uncaring behavior by the worker providing the service, or be a more general attack on the organization itself, based on a general nonfulfillment of the wishes and expectations of the customer, which has nothing to do directly with the actual conflict at a particular moment.

c) **WORKING WITH VALUABLES AND CASH HANDLING.** Whenever valuables are, or seem to be, within "easy reach" there is a risk that crime, and increasingly violent crime, may be committed. Workers in many sectors are exposed to such a risk. At special risk are workers in shops, post offices, and financial institutions, and particularly those who handle cash.

d) **WORKING WITH PEOPLE IN DISTRESS.** Violence is so common among workers in contact with people in distress that it is often considered an inevitable part of the job. Frustration and anger arising out of illness and pain, old-age problems, psychiatric disorders, alcohol and substance abuse can affect behavior and make people verbally or physically violent. Increasing poverty and marginalization in the community in which the aggressor lives; inadequacies in the environment where care activities are performed, or in the way these are organized; insufficient training and interpersonal skills of staff providing services to this population; and a general climate of stress and insecurity at the workplace, can all contribute substantially to an increase in the level of violence.

e) **WORKING IN AN ENVIRONMENT INCREASINGLY "OPEN" TO VIOLENCE.** Working environments which traditionally have been quite immune from violence are becoming progressively affected. This worrying trend seems to reflect a general growth in community violence and unrest, and the collapse of a number of societal values. Violence in school is part of this trend. Teachers have been exposed to the risk of violence for a long time. However, the level of risk to which they are now exposed in a number of countries is most disturbing.

f) **WORKING IN CONDITIONS OF SPECIAL VULNERABILITY.** This includes the following situations:

- Increasing numbers of workers are becoming involved in precarious and occasional jobs. Such workers are the majority of the employees in a growing number of enterprises, and some are likely to become exposed to violence because of their marginal status. A recent survey in the European Union indicates that the number of "atypical workers" is increasingly approaching that of "regular" workers, with only half of the workers occupying new jobs on indefinite contracts (Merllié & Paoli, 2001:12).

- Immigrant workers and people of different ethnic origin experience a disproportionate share of violent incidents.
- Workers in export processing enterprises operating in free trade zones also experience exploitative conditions and exposure to violence.
- Workers in rural areas and miners, particularly in developing countries, experience high levels of violence.
- The most vulnerable group of all, children, are working by the millions both in industrialized and developing countries, often exposed to physical and mental abuse.

6. The Interactive Approach

Building on the previous approaches, the interactive approach develops a combined analysis of individual, social, organizational, and environmental risk factors, with particular attention being given to the situational context in which certain types of work tasks are performed. Analysis of this type first originated from a study conducted for the United Kingdom Health and Safety Executive by the London-based Tavistock Institute of Human Relations (Poyner & Warne, 1988), highlighting the importance of the interaction of a number of factors that could cause or contribute to a risk of violence at work:

The problem may lie in the assailant, in that there may be something about him which makes him strike out at the employee. The employee may be partly to blame because of incompetence or because of an unsympathetic attitude, or the way the organization works may sometimes lead to misunderstanding or frustration (Poyner & Warne, 1988:2.)

The Tavistock researchers then brought together in a framework or model the various factors they found to be relevant in explaining how an interaction between an assailant (perpetrator) and an employee (victim) produced a violent outcome in the workplace (Poyner & Warne, 1988:2–7). The model was further developed by D. Chappell and V. Di Martino (Chappell & Di Martino 2000:63) in order to incorporate the risk factors associated with the prediction of violence and the types of work task or situation recognized as having an increased vulnerability to aggressive acts. This model, shown below in a simplified version, also adds detail to the outcome or consequences of a violent interaction, linking the impact of the aggression back to both the workplace and the victim and perpetrator.

IV. THE HIGH ROAD TO ELIMINATE VIOLENCE AT WORK

There is growing awareness that in confronting violence a comprehensive approach is required. Instead of searching for a single solution good for any problem and situation, the full range of causes which generate violence should be analyzed and a variety of intervention strategies adopted. The response to workplace violence is too frequently limited and ill-defined. There is also growing awareness that violence at work is not merely an episodic, individual problem but a structural, strategic problem rooted in wider social, economic, organizational, and cultural factors. And it is increasingly recognized that violence at work is detrimental to the functionality of the workplace, and any action taken against such violence is an integral part of the organizational development of a sound enterprise.

Consequently, response is more and more directed to tackle the causes, rather than the effects of violence at work . In this respect, the importance of a preventive, systematic,

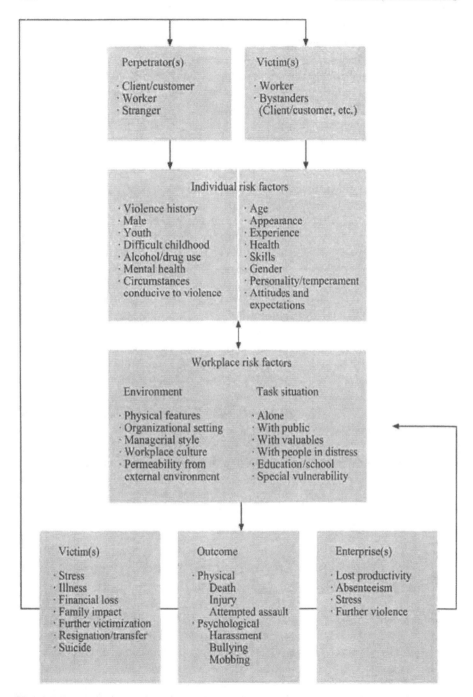

FIGURE II-5-1-3.3. **Workplace violence: an interactive model.** *Source*: New model prepared by Chappell and Di Martino, based on Poyner and Warne, 1988:7.

and targeted approach to violence at work is strongly stressed. This includes the formulation of clear antiviolence policies and programs; the issuing of support legislation and guidelines; the dissemination of information on positive examples; enhanced quality of the working environment as well as of work organization, contents of jobs, and styles of management; improved training opportunities; the involvement of all those concerned and the active engagement of workers' and employers' organizations; counseling and support of those affected by violence and the best use of these interventions to reshape preventive policies and action on a continuous basis. Much of this antiviolence response would in any case be needed to develop a healthy, competitive enterprise, thus making the "violence-conscious" manager a "smart" manager. It is increasingly clear that a "high road" response based on a combined enterprise-individual development is not only possible but necessary.

This requires refocusing the entire approach to violence from an exclusively normative one to a socioeconomic and eventually a developmental one. The traditional response to workplace violence based on the mere enforcement of regulations has in fact the disadvantage of not reaching many working situations of great and increasing relevance both in the developing and the industrialized worlds, including the micro, the informal, and the virtual workplace.

Attention has therefore increasingly focused on the socioeconomic costs of violence at work. As seen above, these are being quantified, showing the magnitude of the negative impact of violence on the efficiency and performance of the enterprise. The introduction of an economic dimension in organizing the response to violence is proving a powerful weapon in effectively addressing violence at work. However, disentangling the costs of violence from other costs is not an easy matter and the positive logic of the cost-benefits response can backfire when examples of enterprises surviving, and even making profits, in a climate of intimidation and exploitation, are shown.

A "high road" response is thus progressively emerging whereby workers' health, safety, and well-being become integral parts of enterprise growth. Here the focus is on the new "intangible assets" of the modern enterprise such as knowledge, learning, quality and, most of all, people, whose development is totally incompatible with any presence of violence at work. By directly linking health and safety issues with managerial and developmental issues, this response offers the tools for immediate, self-sustained action at the workplace to reduce and eliminate violence at work.

The "high road" approach opens the way to a natural process of proliferation of initiatives largely based on their self-sustainability. Policies should stimulate and sustain this natural process by ways of stimulation and encouragement, creation of networks, awareness-rising, which will be accompanied by the issuing of guidelines, best practice, framework and support legislation.

A virtuous circle can thus be activated that develops from inside the workplace to progressively expand in a strategic prospective independently from the mechanics of short-term influences and forced interventions. Triggering the virtuous circle is the great challenge at stake.

REFERENCES

Alvazzi del Frate, Anna. (1998). *Special Analysis for the ILO of the 1996 ICVS Data.* Rome: UNICRI.
Bush, David F., & P. Gavan O'Shea. (1996). Workplace Violence: Comparative Use of Prevention Practices and Policies. In Gary R. Vandenbos & Elisabeth Q. Bulatao (Eds.), *Violence on the job.* Washington: American Psychological Association.

California. Department of Industrial Relations (CAL/OSHA). (1994). *Guidelines for Workplace Security.* San Francisco: Division of Occupational Safety and Health, State of California.

Chappell, Duncan, & Vittorio Di Martino. (2000). *Violence at Work.* Geneva: International Labour Office.

European Commission. (1999). *Guidance on Work-Related Stress. Space of Life or Kiss of Death?* Luxembourg: European Commission.

France. (1992). *Act No. 92-1179 of November 2, 1992,* amending the Labour Code and the Code of Criminal Procedure.

Hoel, Helge, & Cary Cooper. (2000). *Destructive Conflict and Bullying at Work.* Manchester: University of Manchester Institute of Science and Technology.

Hoel, Helge, Kate Sparks, & Cary Cooper. (2001). *The Cost of Violence/Stress at Work and the Benefits of a Violence/Stress-Free Working Environment, Destructive Conflict and Bullying at Work.* Manchester: University of Manchester Institute of Science and Technology.

Homel, Ross, Stephen Tomsen, & Jenny Thommeny. (1992). Public Drinking and Violence: Not Just an Alcohol Problem. *Journal of Drug Issues,* 22, 679–697.

Homel, Ross, & Jeff Clark. (1994). The Prediction and Prevention of Violence in Pubs and Clubs. *Crime Prevention Studies,* 3, pp. 1–46.

Jenkins, E. Lynn. (1996). *Violence in the Workplace: Risk Factors and Prevention Strategies. National Institute for Occupational Safety and Health (NIOSH). Publication No. 96-100.* Washington: U.S. Government Printing Office.

Kaufer, Steve, & Jung W. Mattman. (1998). *The Cost of Workplace Violence to American Business.* Report by The Workplace Violence Research Institute. Palm Springs, CA.

Kivimaki Mika, Marko Elovainio, & Jussi Vahtera. (2000). Workplace Bullying and Sickness Absence in Hospital Staff. *Occupational and Environmental Medicine,* 57, 656–660.

Leymann, Heinz. (1990). Mobbing and Psychological Terror at Workplaces. *Violence and Victims,* 5(2), 119–126.

Mayhew Claire. (1999). Occupational Violence: A Case Study of the Taxi Industry. In Claire Mayhew & Chris L. Peterson, *Occupational Health and Safety in Australia: Industry, Public Sector and Small Business.* Sydney: Allen and Unwin.

McDonald, David, and Melanie Brown. (1997). *Indicators of Aggressive Behaviour: Report to the Minister for Health and Family Services from an Expert Working Group, Canberra, August 1996.* Research and Public Policy Series. No. 8. Griffith: Australian Institute of Criminology.

Merllié, Damien, & Pascal Paoli. (2001). *Ten Years of Working Conditions in the European Union. Working Document.* Dublin: European Foundation for the Improvement of Living and Working Conditions.

Norway. (1997). Paragraph 12, point 2 of Act No. 4, Respecting Workers' Protection and the Working Environment, dated February 4, 1977 (Norsk Lovtidend, Part I, No. 4, February 14, 1977), as amended up to Act No. 2, dated January 6, 1995, (Norsk Lovtidend, Part I, No. 12, 1987).

Paoli, Pascal. (2000). *Violence at Work in the European Union—Recent Finds.* Dublin: European Foundation for the Improvement of Living and Working Conditions.

Pinkerton. (1999). *Workplace Violence Greatest Security Threat to Corporate America: Pinkerton Survey Findings.* URL: http://members.aol.com/endwpv/pinkerton-survey.html [July 7, 1999]

Pizzino, Anthony, A. (1994). *Report on CUPE's (Canadian Union of Public Employees) National Health and Safety Survey of Aggression Against Staff.* Ottawa: Canadian Union of Public Employees.

Poyner, Barry, & Caroline Warne. (1988). *Tavistock Institute of Human Relations: Preventing violence to staff.* London: Health and Safety Executive.

Staffordshire University (1994). *Data from a 1994 survey, as cited in Hazards (Sheffield),* No. 48, Autumn 1994.

Sweden. (1993). *Statute Book of the Swedish National Board of Occupational Safety and Health.* Ordinance (AFS 1993:2) on Violence and Menaces in the Working Environment, 14 January 1993, and Ordinance (AFS 1993:17) on Victimization at Work, September 21, 1993.

Toohey, John. (1993). *Corporate Culture and the Management of Violence.* Unpublished Conference Paper Presented at the "Occupational Violence: Were You Threatened at Work today?" Seminar Series Held at the University of Queensland, Australia, Brisbane.

Vandenbos Gary R., & Elisabeth Q. Bulatao (Eds.) (1996). *Violence on the Job.* Washington: American Psychological Association.

Wynne, Richard, Nadia Clarkin, Tom Cox, & Amanda Griffiths. (1997). *Guidance on the Prevention of Violence at Work.* Brussels: European Commission.

United Kingdom. (1997). *Protection from Harassment Act, No. 40,* March 21, 1997.

CHAPTER II-5-1.4

Violence and Sport

ERIC DUNNING

I. INTRODUCTION: SPORT IN THE "CIVILIZING" OF THE WEST

During the late nineteenth and twentieth centuries, modern forms of sport spread around the globe and correlatively increased in cultural centrality and social significance. One of the chief ideologies underlying the initial stages in this process of diffusion was the idea that sport is "cathartic," i.e., that it can serve as an antidote to violence in its various forms. From about the 1970s onwards, however, such an idea fell into disrepute and the opposite idea gained ground, namely that sport is an arena where violent behavior can be learned. Let me start to unpack the development of these contradictory ideas.

It is reasonable to suppose that one of the preconditions for the development of the idea of sport as cathartic and hence for its diffusion on a worldwide scale was the fact that, during the eighteenth and nineteenth centuries, sport forms which were less violent than their predecessors had begun to develop in the West. In a word, modern sport can be said to have emerged, initially at least, as part of what Norbert Elias (1939, 2000) called a "civilizing process." Developments at the level of language as well as social structure, and personality ("habitus")[1] were involved in this connection. More particularly, the term "sport" originated in England, crucially in the eighteenth century, when it began to be used to describe a set of activities—in the first instance mainly foxhunting, horse racing, cricket, and boxing—which developed in a "civilizing" direction in conjunction with what Elias (1971) called "the parliamentarization of political conflict." More particularly, there took place in that period, according to Elias, a transformation of the "habitus" of the English ruling classes which led them simultaneously to develop relatively nonviolent party political forms of ruling and forms of physically vigorous leisure activities which were less

---

[1] The concept of habitus refers to 'second nature' or 'embodied social learning.' It is popularly associated with the work of Pierre Bourdieu but was in common use in German sociology before the Nazi period and was used by Elias in *Über den Prozess der Zivilisation* (1939).

W. Heitmeyer and J. Hagan (eds.), *International Handbook of Violence Research*, 903–920.
© 2003 Kluwer Academic Publishers. Printed in the Netherlands.

violent and warlike than those which had been popular amongst their predecessors. The relationship between these processes was correlative rather than causal. What happened, in effect, was that forms of physical pastimes began to emerge in which, ideally, the contradiction between friendship and enmity was resolved. A crucial feature of modern sport, in other words, came, ideally, to be friendly or nonhostile competition. This ideal was backed up by the ethos of "fair play." However, despite such "civilizing" developments, violence can be said to be inherent in modern sports in at least two ways.

All modern sports are inherently competitive and concerned with dividing people between "winners" and "losers." Hence taking part, whether as direct participant or spectator, can be frustrating and conducive to aggression-arousal and violence. In some sports, however,—such as boxing, hockey, rugby, soccer, and American, Australian, and Gaelic football—violence and intimidation in the form of a "play fight" between two individuals or groups are central ingredients. Such sports involve the socially acceptable, ritualized expression of violence but, just as the real battles that take place in war can involve a ritual component, so these mock battles that take place on a sports field can involve elements of, or be transformed into, "real" or non-ritual violence. This may occur when, perhaps as a result of external pressures or of striving, individually or as part of a team, for the financial and prestige rewards that are available in top-level and professional sport, people participate too seriously and stop treating sport as "play."

How and why did it come to be widely believed that sports, many of which have an element of violence at their core and which often lead to violent outcomes, can be cathartic, that they can serve as a substitute for or antidote to aggression, crime, and war? In order to address this complex issue, I shall first provide a brief examination of the history of the catharsis theory. I shall then undertake a review of the literature on sport as a learning environment for violent behavior, before concluding with an empirical and theoretical discussion of "football (soccer)[2] hooliganism" as a worldwide problem.

II. THEORETICAL APPROACHES AND EMPIRICAL RESEARCH

1. Some Conceptual and Theoretical Issues

a. SPORT AS CATHARSIS. Although it seems to have originated in the nineteenth century and continues, at least in Britain, to be popular in political circles (Gratton & Taylor, 2000), the theory of sport as cathartic seems to have been most widely adhered to during the 1950s and 1960s, i.e., in a period when, shortly after the Second World War, the so-called "Cold War" between East and West was at its height. For example, writing in 1968—a year when troops of the former USSR invaded former Czechoslovakia and it seemed that the Vietnam conflict might escalate into World War III—Philip Goodhart and Christopher Chataway described sport as a form of "war without weapons" and used that idea as the title for a book. More particularly, reversing the signs of an idea of George Orwell's from positive to negative, they reached the conclusion that:

> ... sport is an outlet for the aggression that lurks beneath the surface in every society. In describing international sport as 'war minus the shooting', Orwell was, indeed, advancing its ultimate justification (Goodhart & Chataway, 1968:158).

[2] 'Soccer' is an abbreviation of 'association.' The proper name of the game is 'Association football.'

This idea has been enshrined in the ideology of modern Olympism since the early days when Baron de Coubertin expressed the hope that, through the quadrennial Games, "the spirit of international comity may be advanced by the celebration of their peaceful contests" (quoted in Goodhart & Chataway, 1968:158). As I noted earlier, the idea probably had its origins in nineteenth century Britain, more particularly in the public schools[3] where sports, especially team sports, came to be viewed as ideal vehicles for "character training" and instilling self-controls (Dunning & Sheard, 1979; Mangan, 2000). It was the ethologist Konrad Lorenz, though, who first developed this idea *systematically* and *at length* as an *explicit scientific* theory.

The idea that underlay Lorenz's theory of sport is that forms of fighting which are "ritualized" or "ceremonial" in character have evolved within many species of nonhuman animals and fish. These fights are *intraspecific* and involve, e.g., fights of wolves against wolves, sticklebacks against sticklebacks. They are held to be exclusively male and to involve trials of strength over territory, access to receptive females, and dominance within the group. Perhaps most crucially of all, they are said to be restrained by inborn mechanisms which are held in turn to minimize physical injury, especially the occurrence of death. It was Lorenz's contention that the processes of "phylogenetic (i.e., biological) evolutionary ritualization" among "lower animals" have their "cultural" parallels among humans, and that principal among the latter is sport. The "difficult task" that had to be performed in both cases, he argued, was that of "avoiding killing without destroying the important functions performed by fighting in the interests of the species." Conceived in these terms, sport, according to Lorenz, can be defined as a "specifically human form of nonhostile combat, governed by the strictest of culturally developed rules." Because what he argued has been widely misunderstood, Lorenz's development of these ideas is worth quoting. He wrote:

> ... the main function of sport today lies in the cathartic discharge of aggressive urge; besides that, of course, it is of the greatest importance in keeping people healthy.
>
> The value of sport, however, is much greater than that of a simple outlet of aggression in its coarser and more individualistic behaviour patterns, like pummelling a punch ball. It educates man (sic!) to a conscious and responsible control of his own fighting behaviour. Few lapses of self-control are punished as immediately and severely as loss of temper during a boxing bout. More valuable still is the educational value of the restrictions imposed by the demands for fairness and chivalry which must be respected even in the face of the strongest aggression-eliciting stimuli.
>
> The most important function of sport lies in furnishing a healthy safety valve for that most indispensable and, at the same time, most dangerous form of aggression that I have described ... as collective militant enthusiasm. The Olympic Games are virtually the only occasion when the anthem of one nation can be played without arousing any hostility against another ...
>
> Sporting contests between nations are beneficial not only because they provide an outlet for the collective militant enthusiasm of nations but also because they have two other effects that counter the danger of war: they promote personal acquaintance between people of different nations or parties and they unite, in enthusiasm for a common cause, people who would otherwise have little in common ... (Lorenz, 1963:242–243).

Three aspects of Lorenz's theory have—at least partially—stood the test of time. More particularly: to the extent that it is adhered to, the demand in sport for fairness and chivalry can be said to be socially valuable; sport does promote acquaintance between members of different nations; and it does unite people with little in common "in enthusiasm for a common cause." Against this, however, there has for a long time now been a growing tendency, connected with the intensification of individual, club, and national com-

---

[3] In Britain, the term 'public school' refers to a set of fee-charging boarding schools which cater primarily for the upper and middle classes. They are public, partly in the sense that they took over their educational functions from private tutors, and partly in the sense that they operate in terms of government charters.

petition and striving for financial and prestige rewards, for gamesmanship, cheating, and violence to be used instrumentally ("rationally") at the highest levels of international and professional sport. Moreover, because sportspersons at these levels act as role models, this trend has had repercussions down the hierarchy of sporting success. Nor is sport unique in promoting international acquaintance. Trade and politics promote it, too, and so do religion and the arts, though perhaps sport scores by promoting international acquaintance at lower levels in the age and stratification hierarchies. Finally, people who have little in common can be united by an interest in almost anything, for example, stamp collecting, gardening, and cooking. Where sport appears to score in this regard is by being functionally homologous to religion and war. Perhaps that is not surprising since it seems, in part, to be an outgrowth of both.

More importantly, Lorenz's theory is based on an idealized picture of sport that fails properly to take account of the fact that sport inherently divides as well as unites and that, under certain conditions, the divisive pole takes precedence over the uniting one. For example, so intent have they become on their own side winning that the national anthems and emblems of opposing sides have come to be regularly booed by at least substantial numbers of spectators in the context of English soccer. Some English soccer fans also regularly symbolically defile the flags and other representative symbols of foreign countries even when they are these countries' guests.[4] Moreover, competitive sport, especially at the highest levels, is not always conducive to keeping people healthy. On the contrary, as Waddington (2000) has shown, the competition-induced demands made on professional sportspersons to play when they are injured frequently lead to their being disabled, sometimes seriously, at an early age. It also seems likely that ambitious amateur sportspersons not infrequently impose such demands upon themselves.

b. SPORT AS CATHARSIS. The idea of sport as a "safety valve," a vehicle for the "cathartic" discharge of aggression, received support from psychoanalysts such as Anthony Storr who found Freud's idea of a "death instinct" problematic. More particularly, Storr wrote, explicitly with reference to Lorenz's theory, that: "rivalry between nations in sport can do nothing but good" (Storr, 1968:117). However, the dominant view of the catharsis theory has been dismissive. For example, noting how the concept of catharsis originated with Aristotle,[5] American sports historian, Allen Guttmann, went on to express his doubts about

> ... use of the concept of catharsis as it relates to sports. After all, the most 'dramatic' ball game is very different from the experience that Aristotle analyses in the *Poetics*. Social psychologists have done an enormous amount of work devoted to testing the catharsis theory ... (and it all) seems to indicate that sports spectacles increase rather than decrease acts of violence ... (Guttmann, 1992:157).

Guttmann writes here as if this conclusion referred equally to sports participants and sports spectators. Arguing with direct participants or players in mind, psychologist Jeffrey Goldstein (1989) summarized the results of his own research and reading thus:

---

[4]For example, on the occasion in April 2000 when two Leeds United fans were stabbed to death in Istanbul, some Leeds fans—not, reportedly, the victims—were said to have publicly insulted Turkish women and, in public gestures that were particularly obscene, to have defiled the Turkish flag by symbolically using it as if to wipe their behinds.

[5]In our *Quest for Excitement* (1986), Norbert Elias and I use Aristotle to develop a different concept of catharsis, namely one in which sports and comparable leisure events are conceptualized as tension- and emotion-arousing.

Research with high school and college athletes finds that they are more quick to anger than non-athletes and that those who participate in combative sports, such as hockey and football, respond to frustration with a greater degree of aggression when compared to athletes in non-contact sports and non-athletes.

In fact, Goldstein contends that, far from providing a vehicle for "letting off steam," sports are, in effect, sorts of pressure cookers in which steam is allowed to build up. What seems to have happened in respect of this issue is that Lorenz's theory of catharsis has been collapsed into the interpretation of that concept proposed by American behaviorist psychologists such as Dollard, Doob, Miller, Mowrer and Sears (1939), the original proponents of the "frustration-aggression hypothesis." An example is provided by the late Mike Smith in his otherwise pathbreaking book, *Violence and Sport* (1983). In it, he summarizes one of the hypotheses of Dollard et al. and immediately goes on to add: "The ethologist Konrad Lorenz (1963) later argued, on the basis of animal observations, that watching others aggress, as when attending a violent sports contest, is cathartic" (Smith, 1983:125). In order to show how this arguably involves a misinterpretation of Lorenz, let me briefly summarize both the behaviorist version of the theory of catharsis and the behaviorist critique.

According to Dollard et al., the experience of frustration is the fundamental cause of aggressive acts. Although they did not write directly on sport as catharsis, they did suggest that performing aggressive acts in fantasy reduces aggressive desire even if the fantasy acts are directed against targets unrelated to the source of frustration. Support for this view was provided by Feshbach and Singer (1971) who claimed to have demonstrated experimentally that observing others aggress on television lowers the aggressiveness of the observers. However, reflecting the dominant view among behaviorist psychologists, Richard Goranson, a behaviorist himself, wrote that "(t)he idea of vicarious aggression catharsis seems to be false" (1980:137). More particularly, he suggested that to claim that watching sportspersons fight "drains off feelings of aggressiveness in the watcher is as illogical as arguing that watching someone eat a sumptuous meal drains off feelings of hunger, or that looking at erotic pictures drains off feelings of sexual arousal" (Goranson, 1980; cited in Smith, 1983:126). It is Goranson's contention, furthermore, that 90 percent of the research evidence on this subject "indicates that the observation of violence on television, film, or in real life, results, if anything, in *increased* feelings of hostility and aggressiveness, and aggressiveness in aggressive, sometimes violent behaviour" (Goranson, cited in Smith, *loc cit*).[6] However, contrary to the currently dominant position on this issue in the sociology of sport and related fields, this cannot be held to constitute a total refutation of Lorenz's theory. That is because Lorenz was concerned with sport as a context where, on account of its violence and the physical and psychological challenges that are involved, people can *learn* to exercise self-control and where, he maintained, lapses in that regard are immediately and severely punished. He also alluded to the "educational value" of the demands imposed in sport "for fairness and chivalry ..." even in the face of what he called "the strongest aggression-eliciting stimuli." In other words, Lorenz proposed a theory which is, in part, sociological and which implied that, because they are learned, such features of sport as the values of fairness and chivalry depend on socialization and proper teaching. They can, of course, also fall into abeyance.

In fact, there is evidence which suggests that inappropriate aggression and violence are more likely to occur in some sports than others. Rees, Howell and Miracle (1990), for

---

[6]For example, Phillips (1983) found that, in the years 1973–78, homicide rates in the USA increased by more than 12% immediately after heavyweight championship boxing matches. The greatest increase came after heavily publicized bouts.

example, have shown that, when provoked, participants in contact sports are considerably more likely to respond aggressively than participants in noncontact sports. Other research (e.g., Widmeyer & Birch, 1984) suggests that aggression may be—or may be believed to be—an effective, success-enhancing strategy when applied early in a contest, or that it may be—or, again, may be believed to be—effective as a reaction to failure. This is consistent with the old idea in British soccer that, in his/her first tackle, a defender should aim to hit an opposing player rather than the ball in order to show him/her "who's boss." The equivalent of this in the British Rugby Union is the humorous, superficially paradoxical adage about "getting one's retaliation in first." Consistently with this, coaches may demand aggressive play from the teams under their command and, interestingly, research by Rees and Miracle (1984) suggests that participants in organized sports sometimes lower their self-controls and break violence taboos because they assume that it is the referee's job to control inappropriate aggression.

Experimental research on the martial art Tae Kwon Do (Trulson, 1986) seems to provide support for Lorenz's theory. In one experiment, a group of 13–17 year old males who had been classified as delinquent were divided into three groups matched on levels of aggression and personality adjustment. The first group was given traditional instruction in Tae Kwon Do, including a training in its "philosophical" component. Especially involved in this connection was a threefold stress on: responsibility, the building-up of self-confidence, and self-esteem, and the expression of respect for others. Physical skills and meditation were included as well. Members of the second group were required to practice a more modern form of Tae Kwon Do and were taught only the fighting and self-defense elements of the "sport." By contrast, the third group were given no martial arts training at all but, instead, played basketball and (American) football. Trulson's findings run counter to what the behaviorist research would lead one to expect. More particularly, after six months the youths in the first group showed lower levels of aggression; those in the second group showed higher levels of aggression; and those in the third group showed no change. It would be interesting to see if results similar to those achieved for group one would be obtained in sports such as soccer by instructing players in the amateur code of the old Corinthians, a code which stressed "fair play" and "gentlemanly" behavior[7] and which was in that respect similar to the ethos of the Eastern martial arts.

Where the standard behaviorist studies of sport and catharsis seem, then, to go astray, is through working with an overly simple, reductionist, mechanistic, ahistorical, and insufficiently sociological/relational model of human behavior. This results in them ignoring or underplaying the element of active choice; i.e., they treat humans as if they were similar to reactive chemicals and expect catharsis to be experienced independently of (i) people's aims, beliefs, values, socialization/training, and active involvements; and (ii) the sociohistorical context. Related to this, they conceptualize sport as tension-releasing/tension-reducing rather than as tension-arousing (Elias & Dunning, 1969, 1986).[8] In addition, they fail to appreciate that one of the keys to catharsis through sport, as Lorenz saw it, has to be the consistent instruction of both players and spectators in the ethos of fair play and the need for this ethos to be kept alive if sport is to fulfill its apparently contradictory

[7]The Corinthians were an amateur soccer team formed in England in the late nineteenth century with a view to competing against the then increasingly dominant professional sides both in terms of playing achievements and gentlemanly standards of behavior. An example of the latter was provided when the penalty kick for foul play near the goal was introduced. Arguing that gentlemen did not deliberately cheat and that they (the Corinthians) did not wish to benefit from a bad law, when they were awarded penalties, the Corinthians would deliberately kick the ball wide of goal.

function of being *friendly rivalry*, i.e., nonhostile competition or conflict. Players and spectators also need consistent training from an early age in the importance of abiding by the rules, obeying match officials, valuing one's opponents because without them the enjoyable play-fight would be impossible, and above all socialization/habituation in the exercise of self-control. In fact, Lorenz seems to have regarded physically aggressive sports such as boxing as particularly valuable vehicles for teaching self-control precisely because, given their violent and aggressive component, they can provide people with the opportunity to be taught that, in order to maximize their chances of winning, it is essential to "keep cool." It is, of course, this ethos and the related pattern of socialization which have fallen into abeyance in much of modern sport, especially top-level sport where, in conjunction, e.g., with commercialization, professionalization and media-fed national rivalries, achievement-striving and an orientation towards seeking victory at all costs have been raised to the status of core values with deleterious consequences, not only for top-level sport itself, but also downwards in the hierarchy of sporting success.

This attempt at correcting a currently dominant view in the field of sports studies should not be regarded as an expression of anything other than support for the *sociological/ sociocultural* parts of Lorenz's theory. As far as humans are concerned, its psychological parts are dubious, especially the idea, which Lorenz shared with Freud, that humans have an "aggressive instinct." Elias (1988) has written a persuasive critique of this issue. The idea that humans have an innate aggressive drive which structurally resembles the sex drive, he says, is a false way of posing the problem. What we do have is an "innate potential to shift (our) whole physical apparatus to a different gear if (we) feel endangered." This is the so-called "flight–fight mechanism" through which the human body reacts to danger by "an automatic adjustment which prepares the way for intensive movement of the skeletal muscles, as in combat or flight." According to Elias, however, human "drives" such as the hunger or sex drive are released physiologically, "relatively independently of the actual situation" in which people find themselves. By contrast, the shifting of the body economy "to combat—or—flight readiness is conditioned to a far greater extent by a specific situation, whether present or remembered." Such situations can be "natural," for example being attacked by a wild animal, or social, especially conflict. However, in conscious opposition to Lorenz and others who ascribe an aggression drive to people on the model of the sexual drive, it is not, says Elias, "aggressiveness that triggers conflicts but conflicts that trigger aggressiveness."

Of course, there is a degree of rhetorical exaggeration in this. Elias would not have denied that some conflicts result from the disruptiveness of aggressive individuals or that, in some cases, the aggressiveness of disruptive individuals has psychological and perhaps even genetic roots. He also stressed the interdependence of different human drives (Elias, 1939, 2000:161). In other words, he was aware of the interconnectedness of the sex, hunger, and thirst drives and aggression, particularly if the former are frustrated. What he wanted above all to do was to counter the crude psychological reductionism involved in the notion of an "aggressive instinct." Summing up, it was Elias's contention that whether the "fight–flight mechanism" is directed into fighting or into fleeing is fundamentally a question of culture and social learning. More particularly, it is a question of the degree to which the values of the society or group into which one is born or of which one later becomes a member, e.g. through immigration, lay stress on the physically violent as opposed to the peaceful end of the continuum between extremely violent and wholly pacific means of handling tensions and con-

---

[8] With its stress on what he called 'arousal,' psychologist Albert Bandura's (1973) 'social learning' theory of aggression is similar in some respects.

flicts. There is, in fact, a growing body of evidence which suggests that, in the twentieth century, sport became one of the primary arenas where physical violence is learned, particularly by males (Messner & Sabo, 1994). In other words, there is evidence that sport became a context where the fair play ethos and associated values atrophied.

c. SPORT AS AN ARENA WHERE PHYSICAL VIOLENCE CAN BE LEARNED. The pioneering 1970s work on sport and violence of the late Michael D. Smith is revealing with respect to sport as a context where violent behavior can be learned. He shows, for example, how the parents and coaches of the youths involved in sports such as (American) football and (ice) hockey,[9] socialize them directly into (i) violent ways of playing and (ii) lack of identification and empathy with their opponents as fellow humans. A revealing example is provided by the following set of rules devised by parents for a Californian football team whose average age was eight:

> *Rules for a Successful Packer to Live By:*
> Become an all-out tackler: dig for more yards! Punish the tackler! Put fear in his eyes! Bruise his body! Break his spirit! Bust his butt! Make him pay a price for tackling you! Dig for more yards!
> Become a competitor! A competitor never quits. Be hostile. Be violent! Be mean! Be aggressive! Be physical! Remember always—loosing (sic!) is nothing! Winning is everything! (Quoted in Smith, 1983:91–92)

Bredemeier, Shields and Smith (1986) have persuasively argued that sport in the modern West emerged as a relatively autonomous moral sphere which "enjoys" a high degree of separation and distinctness from the rest of society. That is, it became a context in which forms of behavior considered deviant in the wider social world, especially forms of violent behavior, could be engaged in with relative impunity. Hughes and Coakley (1991) applied the concept of positive deviance in this connection. As they understand it, "positive deviance" involves *over*-conformity to the goals and norms of an institution such as sport. In sport, displays of *machismo*, playing with injuries and pain, and intentionally seeking to injure an opponent may, according to Hughes and Coakley, be "grounded in athletes' uncritical acceptance of and commitment to what they have been told by important people in their lives ever since they began participating in competitive programs; in a real sense, it is the result of being too committed to the goals and norms of sport" (Hughes & Coakley, 1991:311). Since values such as fair play remain, at least officially, among the goals of sport, what Hughes and Coakley mean here is too committed to the success goal, i.e., to winning. Where winning comes to be valued above all else, they suggest, athletes may use aggression to show their total commitment or, more particularly, their total commitment to winning. In other words, their "positive deviance" may turn into "negative deviance," i.e., into forms of delinquency and crime. In the words of Hughes and Coakley:

> In the case of athletes in highly visible sports, this process of developing fraternity, superiority and disdain for outsiders might also lead some of them to naively assume they are somehow beyond the law, and the people outside the athletic fraternity do not deserve their respect. This could lead to serious cases of negative deviance including, for example, assault, sexual assault, and rape (including gang rape), the destruction of property, reckless driving, and alcohol abuse (Hughes & Coakley, 1991:314).

One of the core recurrent elements in cases such as this is the conceptions of masculinity that tend to be involved. Modern sport initially developed in large part as a male preserve (Sheard & Dunning, 1973), that is, as a context where masculinity-validating behavior

---

[9] In North America, the term 'hockey' refers to the version of that game which is played on ice, whereas in Britain, 'hockey' refers to what North Americans call 'field hockey'.

tends to occur (Messner, 1987). Indeed, one might say that sport has come to rival the military and the police as an institutional setting where males are directly socialized into norms of violent and aggressive masculinity. Connected with this, there is currently occurring in the USA and Canada something of a moral panic over the incidence of sexual harassment, assault, and rape by male athletes and coaches. More particularly, a high incidence of these crimes has been reported by Bohmer and Parrot (1983); Koss and Gaines (1993); Lenskyj (1992); Melnick (1992); Moore (1991); Nelson (1991, 1994); and Toufexis (1990).[10] Statistical support in this regard was provided by Crosset et al. in 1995 in a study which found that male college student athletes, especially those in men's basketball and football, were implicated in a disproportionately high number of sexual assault cases (Crosset, Benedict, & McDonald, 1995; cited in Coakley, 1998:163).

Here are some illustrative facts and figures. A survey of 200 U.S. College police departments carried out in 1986 by the *Philadelphia Daily News* discovered that male basketball and football players were reported to the police for sexual assault about 38 percent more frequently than their male college peers (Hofman, 1986:104; Nelson, 1994:130). In 1993, researchers Mary P. Koss and John A. Gaines surveyed 530 undergraduate males about their participation in a continuum of "sexually aggressive" behaviors ranging from whistles and catcalls; unwanted touching of a woman's breasts, buttocks, or genitals; attempted or completed intercourse by the use of arguments or verbal threats; attempted or completed intercourse by plying a woman with alcohol, threatening bodily harm, and using physical force, through to a group of men forcibly overcoming a woman in order to have intercourse with her. Koss and Gaines found that (American) football and basketball players were more likely to engage in sexually aggressive behavior than their peers, including those who played other sports (Koss & Gaines, 1993; Nelson, 1994:130). A three-year survey carried out by the U.S. National Institute for Mental Health in the 1980s found that athletes took part in around one third of the 862 sexual attacks known to have taken place on college campuses in that period (Nelson, 1994:130). Finally, a survey of more than 10,000 students by the Campus Violence Center at Towson State University, Maryland, carried out in 1991 found that, although athletes/sportsmen constituted only 16 percent of the total male student population, 55 percent of all admitted acquaintance rapes were committed by sportsmen/athletes (Nelson, 1994:130).

In order to explain figures such as these, it has been plausibly suggested that sports function to sustain and consolidate traditional forms of male dominance or "patriarchy" by linking maleness with the objectification and vilification of females and positively sanctioned aggression and violence against them (Sheard & Dunning, 1973; Dunning, 1986, 1999; Bryson, 1987; Messner & Sabo, 1994). Such issues remain controversial. It has been held that sportsmen/athletes are singled out for unfair stereotyping as a result of their high visibility and, paradoxically, by the fact that they are typically expected to uphold higher standards of behavior than others (Miracle, Chick, & Loy, 1996). It also has to be admitted that there is an often unacknowledged racial or racist element sometimes involved in incidents of this kind.

So far in this chapter, I have focused mainly on the violence and aggressiveness of athletes/players, that is, of direct participants in sport. I have only touched marginally on the violence and aggressiveness of indirect participants or spectators. However, in the eyes of many people one form of sports-related violence, namely "football" or "soccer hooliganism," tends to be synonymous with sports violence *per se*. It is accordingly with a

---

[10] All cited in Coakley, 1998: 163.

discussion of this issue that I shall conclude this chapter. As will be seen, questions of masculinity tend to be a common feature as far as both spectator violence and player violence in sport are concerned. Moreover, the major forms of football hooliganism appear not to be match-related or even football-related in any direct or simple sense but, rather, related to problems in the wider social structure. Accordingly, in order to explain them, specifically sociological theories are necessary as well as psychological and social theories of the kind so far discussed in this chapter. Before discussing such theories, I shall first of all look critically at some widely held beliefs and attempt to establish some basic facts.

2. Spectator Violence: Football Hooliganism as a World Problem

a. EMPIRICAL DATA. Violence at or in conjunction with sports events can involve spectators in one of three ways: players may attack spectators, spectators may attack players and/or match officials, or spectators may fight among themselves. Probably the most frequently reported form of spectator violence in the modern world is the so-called problem of football/soccer hooliganism, a form which involves attacks on players and match officials but above all fights between spectator groups. Following the publicity given to the death of 39 Italians at the European Cup Final between Liverpool and Juventus at the Heysel Stadium, Brussels, in 1985, it came to be widely believed around the world that "soccer hooliganism," that is spectator violence at or in conjunction with Association Football matches or associated with groups which claim allegiance to soccer clubs, is a solely or mainly English or British problem. Research, however, suggests that this is not and has never been the case (see Table II-5-1-4.1).

If asked, it seems not unlikely that a majority of people, perhaps especially in Western countries, would identify Heysel as the worst directly hooligan-related football tragedy to have occurred in modern times. The data in Table II-5-1-4.2, however, suggest again that this is not the case and that football *outside* Europe has experienced a greater number of fatalities and perhaps also a greater incidence of murderous violence than is the case in Europe, the continent where people, especially in the West, consider themselves to stand at the "apex of civilization" and where, if Elias (1939, 2000) was right, a degree of "civilizing" can be demonstrated factually to have occurred since the Middle Ages.[11]

Sketchy though they are, the figures on football-related murders in Table II-5-1-4.3 point in the same direction. Italy, the European country with the highest reported incidence of football-related murders in the years 1996–1999, had five, whereas Argentina, largely as a result of the activities of the notorious *barras bravas*, had a reported incidence of 39, almost eight times as many (see also Duke & Crolley, 1996).

b. THEORETICAL APPROACHES. What explanations of football hooliganism have been proposed? In Britain, the country with the longest history of football hooliganism and

---

[11] There is a substantial amount of evidence which suggests that, with the breakdown of the Yugoslav state, a 'de-civilizing process' of considerable proportions has recently been going on in the constituent parts of that former nation-state. That is exactly what Elias's theory would lead one to expect.

For longer discussions of this in some ways controversial issue, see Elias and Dunning: Quest for Excitement (1986), Dunning et al.: The Roots of Football Hooliganism (1988), Dunning and Rojek: Sport and Leisure in the Civilizing Process (1992), Dunning et al.: The Sports Process (1993), and Dunning: Sport Matters (1999). Each of these texts responds to different misconstruals and critiques of Elias's pioneering theory of civilizing processes and brings different evidence to bear. For critiques of the Leicester work, see Armstrong and Harris (1991); Armstrong (1998); Giulianotti (1999); Hobbs and Robins (1991).

Table II-5-1-4.1. Worldwide incidence of football-related violence as reported in English newspapers, 1908–1983

Argentina	(ca.) 1936, 1965, 1968
Australia	1981
Austria	(ca.) 1965
Belgium	1974, 1981
Bermuda	1980
Brazil	1982
Canada	1927
China	1979, 1981, 1983
Columbia	1982
Egypt	1966
France	1960, 1975, 1977 (2 incidents), 1980
Gabon	1981
Germany*	1931, 1965 (2 incidents), 1971, 1978, 1979 (2 incidents), 1980, 1981 (3 incidents), 1982 (6 incidents)
Greece	1980 (2 incidents), 1982, 1983
Guatemala	1980
Holland	1974, 1982
Hungary	1908
India	1931, 1982
Ireland**	1913, 1919, 1920 (3 incidents), 1930, 1955, 1970, 1979 (3 incidents), 1981
Italy	1920, 1955, 1959, 1963 (2 incidents), 1965 (2 incidents), 1973, 1975, 1979, 1980, 1981, 1982
Jamaica	1965
Lebanon	1964
Malta	1975, 1980
Mexico	1983
New Zealand	1981
Nigeria	1983
Norway	1981
Peru	1964
Portugal	1970
Rumania	1979
Spain	1950, 1980 (2 incidents), 1981, 1982
Sweden	1946
Switzerland	1981
Turkey	1964, 1967
USSR	1960, 1982
USA	1980
Yugoslavia	1955 (2 incidents), 1982 (2 incidents)

Source: Williams et al., 1984. *Apart from the reported incident in 1931, these incidents were reported as having taken place in the former Federal Republic (West Germany). **Includes incidents reported as having taken place in both Eire and Ulster as well as incidents reported before the partition.

Table II-5-1-4.2. Selected incidents at which serious crowd violence was reported

Country	Year	Match	Number of deaths	Number of injuries
Argentina	1968	River Plate vs. Boca Juniors	74	150
Brazil	1982	San Luis vs. Fortaleza	3	25
Columbia	1982	Deportivo Cai vs. Club Argentina	22	200
Peru	1964	Peru vs. Argentina	287–328	5000
Turkey	1964	Kayseri vs. Sivas	44	600
USSR	1982	Spartak Moscow vs. Harlem	69	100

Source: Williams et al., 1984.

football hooligan research, six main approaches to the study of this issue can be distinguished: the "anthropological" approach (Armstrong & Harris, 1991; Armstrong, 1998); the "quasi-ethnographic, postmodernist" approach (Giulianotti, 1999); the Marxist approaches (Taylor, 1971, 1982; Clarke, 1978); the "ethogenic" approach (Marsh, Rossner, & Harré, 1978; Marsh, 1978); the approach in terms of "psychological reversal theory" (Kerr, 1994); and the "figurational"[12] approach of the so-called "Leicester School" (Williams, Dunning, & Murphy, 1984; Dunning, Murphy, & Williams, 1988; Murphy, Williams, & Dunning, 1990). Each of these explanations has its particular strengths. However, each has its particular weaknesses, too. Interestingly, if I am right, only the figurationalists attempt, in developing their sociological explanation, to build to any degree on the psychological theories discussed in the previous sections of this chapter. They do so, firstly, by seeking to explain how people can learn to gain pleasure from the infliction of violence; secondly, by explaining how *macho* forms of masculine habitus and behavior can be unintentionally socially produced; and thirdly, by seeking to explain how football has come to be a locus for the regular expression of *machismo*.

The anthropological work on football hooliganism of Armstrong and Harris is based on rich case studies of the behavior of hooligan fans from Sheffield, Yorkshire. It is, however, largely descriptive and ahistorical as is also the work of Giulianotti. That is, insufficient attention is paid by these authors to issues of social change, the changing character of football hooligan behavior and the perception of it as a social problem. That is not true of the work of Taylor and Clarke which is set more directly within the sociological canon of

Table II-5-1-4.3. Number of football-related murders reported in selected English newspapers, June 1996–October 1999

Country	Number
Argentina	39
England	3
Italy	5
Netherlands	1
Total	48

Source: Dunning, 2000.

---

[12] The term 'figurational' (or 'process') sociology refers to the growing body of work influenced by the empirically based theories of Norbert Elias.

replicable, testable work. Taylor and Clarke's work is also insightful regarding ways in which developments in English football have been bound up with the developing capitalist economy. However, neither of these Marxist authors appears to grasp the significance of the fact that football hooliganism principally involves conflict between working-class groups which only regularly become involved in conflict with the football authorities and the police—and less directly with other representatives of the state—as part of an attempt to fight among themselves. Nor do Taylor and Clarke consider the possibility that such intra-class conflict and fighting might be partly explicable using the psychological concept of displacement (Allport, 1954). In his early (1971) work, Taylor even romantically described football hooliganism as a "working class resistance movement." Marsh, Rossner and Harré do not make such mistakes. However, like that of Armstrong, Harris and Giulianotti, their work lacks an historical dimension with the consequence that they tend to see "aggro" or football hooligan fighting as an unchanging historical constant. Moreover, in their stress on aggro as "ritual violence"—as violence which is mainly symbolic or metonymic in the sense of involving more aggressive posturing than the consummation of aggressive acts—they fail to see that the ritualized aggression of football fans can become seriously violent as a result of the dynamics of fan-group interactions and not simply as a result of heavy-handed interference by the authorities. Finally, through his use of "reversal theory," Kerr seems to do little more than dress up in complex jargon some relatively simple sociological ideas. For example, Kerr seems to think that the football hooligans' quest for excitement and arousal through engaging in deviant, delinquent, and violent acts can be explained as a simple "reversal" from one "metamotivational state," "boredom," to another, "excitement" (Kerr, 1994:33ff). It is difficult to see what this does other than dress up in psychological language what Elias and I (1969, 1986) wrote more than twenty years before. Above all, there is no reference in what Kerr writes to what are arguably mainly at stake in football hooligan fighting, namely norms of masculinity. These figure centrally in the figurational explanation.

The figurational approach to football hooliganism does not constitute a "super theory" that explains everything. It is offered only as a beginning on which to build. Its distinctive features are that it is based on a synthesis of psychology, sociology, and history, and that it involves an exploration of the meanings of hooligan behavior to the hooligans themselves. In this last regard, analysis of a range of hooligan statements made over a period of more than 30 years revealed that, for the (mainly) young men involved, football hooligan fighting is basically about masculinity, territorial struggle, and excitement. For them, fighting is a central source of meaning, status or "reputation," and pleasurable emotional arousal. They speak of the respect among their peers that they hope their hooligan involvements will bring, and of "battle excitement," "the adrenaline racing," and of "aggro" as almost erotically arousing. Indeed, Jay Allan, a leading member of "the Aberdeen Casuals," a Scottish football hooligan "firm" in the 1980s, wrote of fighting at football as even more pleasurable than sex (Allan, 1989). American author Bill Buford, who traveled with English football hooligans in the 1980s described it in the book he wrote about them thus: "... Violence is one of the most intensely lived experiences and, for those capable of giving themselves over to it, one of the most intense pleasures ... (C)rowd violence was their drug" (Buford, 1991:201).

Table II-5-1-4.4 summarizes what is known about the occupational class of employed English football hooligans and trends in this regard between 1968 and 1987. Research on the social class of football hooligans in Scotland (Harper, 1989), Belgium (Van Limbergen, Colaers, & Walgrave, 1987), the Netherlands (Van der Brug, 1986), and Italy

Table II-5-1-4.4. Trends in the occupational class of employed English football hooligans, 1968–1998*

Occupational class	Harrington, 1968		Dunning et al., 1988		Armstrong, 1998	
	No	%	No	%	No	%
Professional	2	0.5**	—	—	3	2.1
Intermediate	—	—	8	5.7	7	4.9
Skilled non-manual	19	4.9	2	1.42	24	16.8
Skilled manual	50	12.9	34	24.1	67	46.8
Semi-skilled	112	28.8	10	7.0	14	9.8
Unskilled	206	52.9	25	17.7	28	19.6

Source: Dunning, 2000. *Figures exclude those for schoolboys, apprentices, the unemployed and those with occupations unclassifiable in terms of the Registrar General's scheme. **Professional and intermediate classified together.

(Roversi, 1994) suggests that hooligans in other countries tend to come from social backgrounds similar to those of their English counterparts.

The fact that violent spectator disorder occurs more frequently in conjunction with soccer than any other sport would thus appear to be partly a function of the social composition of its crowds. Soccer is the world's most popular team sport and, worldwide, a majority of its spectators tend to be male and to come from the lower reaches of the social scale, that is, from social backgrounds where norms tend to legitimate a higher incidence of overt aggressiveness and violence in everyday social relations than tends to be the case among the middle and upper classes.[13] More particularly, lower-class males tend to develop a violent and aggressive habitus and mode of presenting themselves to the world. This involves a complex of learned traits which seem fundamentally to derive *inter alia* from: (i) a pattern of early socialization characterized by ready resort to violence by parents and siblings; and (ii) adolescent socialization on the streets in the company of age peers, i.e., in adolescent "gangs" (Dunning, Murphy, & Williams, 1988). In these contexts, because ability and willingness to fight are criteria for membership of and prestige within the group, i.e., for the status of these males in their own and others' eyes as "men," they learn to associate adrenaline arousal in fight situations with warm, rewarding, and hence pleasurable feelings rather than with the guilt and anxiety that tend to surround the performance and witnessing of "real" (as opposed to "mimetic") violence in the wider society.

This kind of violent habitus tends to be reinforced to the extent that such males live and work in contexts characterized by high levels of gender and age-group segregation. That is because of the relative absence in such contexts of "softening" pressure from females and older men.[14] Furthermore, in most societies, groups lower down the social scale are less likely to be highly individualized and more likely readily to form intense "we-group" bonds and identifications (Elias, 1978:134–148) which involve an equally intense hostility towards "outsiders" (Elias, 1994) than is the case among the more powerful, more self-steering and usually more inhibited groups who stand above them. At a soccer match, of course, the

---

[13] Upper- and middle-class people may, of course, behave violently in private and also cause the state's monopoly of violence to be used in a variety of violent ways.

[14] In militaristic societies, females and older males often exert pressures on young men which enhance the violence of their behavior.

outsiders are the opposing team and its supporters, and, in some cases, the match officials. Soccer tends to be chosen by these groups as a context in which to fight because it, too, is about masculinity, territory, and excitement. Given a widespread pattern of travel to away-matches, the game also regularly provides a set of ready-made opponents with whom to fight. Moreover, large crowds form a context where it is possible to behave violently and in other deviant ways with a relatively good chance of escaping detection and arrest.

Having said this, it would be wrong to view soccer hooliganism as always and everywhere a function solely or mainly of social class. As a basis for further research, it is reasonable to hypothesize that the problem will be contoured and fuelled, *ceteris paribus*, by what one might call the major "fault lines" of particular countries. In England, that means class and regional inequalities and differences; in Scotland (at least in Glasgow) and Northern Ireland, religious sectarianism; in Spain, the partly language-based subnationalisms of the Catalans, Castilians and Basques; in Italy, city-based particularism and perhaps the division between North and South as expressed in the formation of the "Northern League," and in Germany, relations between the generations (Heitmeyer & Peter, 1992; Elias, 1996) and those between East and West. Religious, subnational, city-based, regional, and generation-based fault lines may draw into football hooliganism more people from higher up the social scale than tends to be the case in England. Arguably, however, a shared characteristic of all these fault lines—and, of course, each can overlap and interact with others in a variety of complex ways—is that they correspond to what Elias (1994) called "established-outsider figurations" that is, social formations involving intense "we-group" bonds ("us") and correspondingly intense antagonisms towards "outsiders" or "they-groups" ("them").

The association of hooliganism with soccer is also partly a function of the greater worldwide media exposure that the game receives. Other sports do not get as much media coverage; accordingly, such violence as accompanies them is not so publicly apparent. The media also tend to generate myths and these, too, contribute to public perceptions. For example, in the years from the late 1920s to the mid-1960s, the occurrence of soccer hooliganism in Central and South America, Continental Europe (especially the Latin countries), Scotland, Wales, and Northern Ireland was regularly reported in the English press, together with statements to the effect that such behavior "couldn't happen in England." However, unruly behavior had been rife at English soccer matches before the First World War and had never died out completely (Dunning, Murphy, & Williams, 1988:32–90).

In 1977, U.S. journalist Peter S. Greenberg wrote that: "Fear and loathing in the stands is certainly not a new phenomenon, but mass recreational violence has never been so rampant in the sports arenas of America" (Greenberg, 1977; cited in Yiannakis et al., 1979). This judgment was backed up by sociologists Harry Edwards and Van Rackages who wrote, also in 1977, that "sport-related violence flourishes today in crisis proportions ... violence has indeed increased and become more malicious—particularly over the last three years" (Edwards & Rackages, 1977; cited in Yiannakis et al., 1979). During the 1980s, however,—and something similar happened regarding soccer hooliganism in England in the 1990s—this panic over sports and spectator violence seems to have subsided. It is impossible on the basis of present knowledge to say whether the concern expressed in the United States in the 1970s was more media invention than fact. What is certain is that player and spectator violence in sport constitute a worldwide problem and that, in their various manifestations, they represent a serious and threatening breach of the socially valuable ethos of fair play. It is clear that more attention should be paid in sports education to instilling this ethos into both players and spectators.

III. CONCLUSION

In this chapter, I have discussed the sociological, psychological, and ethological/ethogenic literature on sport and violence and sought to show that modern sport emerged as part of a "civilizing process" in Norbert Elias's (1939, 2000) sense. I also looked critically at the "catharsis" theory and showed how Konrad Lorenz's ethological version of that theory contains a sociological/sociocultural dimension which the critics have ignored, namely a stress on violent sports such as boxing as useful media for teaching self-control. This is an issue deserving of further research. So is the question of whether a form of the fair play ethos could ever be devised which is compatible with modern, high-pressure, achievement-orientated, top-level, professional sports and which could help to deal with the problems of mounting violence in that context.

The increasing participation of females in sport, even in what used to be thought of as "hypermasculine" sports such as boxing and rugby, is another area crying out for systematic research. Does participation in such sports lead to a "de-civilization"/"brutalization" of the females involved? Do these and other sports constitute an environment where women as well as men learn violent ways of behaving? Or do the traditional norms of femininity, with their stress on cooperative, nurturing forms of behavior, act as a kind of functional equivalent of the fair play ethos in male sports, leading to a tempering of the violence which might otherwise occur? And what about females and spectating? Are there female equivalents of soccer hooliganism? Under what combinations of circumstances do females increase the aggressiveness of males, and under what circumstances do they decrease it? And what about issues of policing and social control? These are all questions on which it would be possible to speculate ideologically. However, what is needed if sport is to be able to fulfill its promise as a context where friendly rivalry can be enjoyed is detached, hardheaded, nonideological research.

REFERENCES

Allan, Jay. (1989). *Bloody Casuals: Diary of a Football Hooligan.* Glasgow: Famedram.
Allport, Gordon. (1954). *The Nature of Prejudice.* New York: Addison-Wesley.
Armstrong, Gary, & Rosemary Harris. (1991). Football Hooliganism: Theory and Evidence. *Sociological Review, 30*(3), 427–458.
Armstrong, Gary. (1998). *Football Hooligans: Knowing the Score.* Oxford: Berg.
Bandura, Arnold. (1973). *Aggression: A Social Learning Analysis.* Englewood Cliffs: Prentice-Hall.
Bohmer, Carol, & Andrea Parrot. (1993). *Sexual Assault on Campus: the Problems and the Solution.* Lexington: Lexington Books.
Bredemeier, Brenda, David L. Shields, & Michael D. Smith. (1986). Athletic Aggression: an Issue of Contextual Morality. *Sociology of Sport Journal, 3*(1), 15–28.
Bryson, Lois. (1987). Sport and the Maintenance of Masculine Hegemony. *Women's Studies International Forum, 10,* 349–360.
Buford, Bill. (1991). *Among the Thugs.* London: Secker and Warburg.
Clarke, John. (1978). Football and Working Class Fans: Tradition and Change. In Roger Ingham (Ed.), *Football Hooliganism: The Wider Context* (pp. 37–60). London: Inter-Action Imprint.
Coakley, Jay J. (1998). *Sport in Society: Issues and Controversies.* Boston/ New York: Irwin McGraw-Hill.
Crosset, Todd, Jeffrey R. Benedict, & Mary A. McDonald. (1995). Male Student-Athletes Reported for Sexual Assault: Survey of Campus Police Departments and Judicial Affairs. *Journal of Sport and Social Issues, 19,* 126–140.
Dollard, John, Leonhard W. Doob, Neal E. Miller, O. H. Mowrer, & Robert S. Sears. (1939). *Frustration and Aggression.* New Haven: Yale University Press.

Duke, Vic, & Liz Crolley. (1996). *Football, Nationality and the State.* London: Longman.
Dunning, Eric. (1986). Sport as a Male Preserve. In Norbert Elias & Eric Dunning, *Quest for Excitement: Sport and Leisure in the Civilizing Process* (pp. 267–283). Oxford: Blackwell.
Dunning, Eric. (1999). *Sport Matters: Sociological Studies of Sport, Violence and Civilization.* London: Routledge.
Dunning, Eric. (2000). Towards a Sociological Understanding of Football Hooliganism as a World Phenomenon. *European Journal on Criminal Policy and Research, 8,* 141–162.
Dunning, Eric, & Kenneth Sheard. (1979). *Barbarians, Gentlemen and Players: A Sociological Study of the Development of Rugby Football.* Oxford: Martin Robertson.
Dunning, Eric, Patrick Murphy, & John Williams. (1988). *The Roots of Football Hooliganism.* London: Routledge.
Dunning, Eric, & Chris Rojek. (Eds.) (1992). *Sport and Leisure in the Civilizing Process: Critique and Counter-Critique.* London: Macmillan.
Dunning, Eric, Joseph Maguire, & Robert Pearton. (Eds.) (1993). *The Sports Process.* Urbana-Champaign. Illinois: Human Kinetics.
Edwards, Harry, & Van Rackages. (1977). The Dynamics of Violence in American Sport. *Journal of Sport and Social Issues,* 7(2), 3–31.
Elias, Norbert. (1939). *Über den Prozess der Zivilisation.* 2 Vols. Basel: Haus zum Falken.
Elias, Norbert. (1971). The Genesis of Sport as a Sociological Problem. In Eric Dunning (Ed.), *The Sociology of Sport: A Selection of Readings* (pp. 88–115). London: Cass.
Elias, Norbert. (1978). *What is Sociology?* London: Hutchinson.
Elias, Norbert. (1988). Violence and Civilization: The State Monopoly of Physical Violence and its Infringement. In John Keane (Ed.), *Civil Society and the State: New European Perspectives* (pp. 177–198). London: Verso.
Elias, Norbert. (1994). *The Established and the Outsiders.* London: Sage.
Elias, Norbert. (1996). *The Germans: Studies of Power Struggles and the Development of Habitus in the Nineteenth and Twentieth Centuries.* [Trans., with a Preface, by Eric Dunning and Stephen Mennell] Oxford: Polity.
Elias, Norbert. (2000). *The Civilizing Process.* [Integrated Edition, Revised by Eric Dunning, Johan Goudsblom, and Stephen Mennell] Oxford: Blackwell.
Elias, Norbert, & Eric Dunning. (1969). The Quest for Excitement in Leisure. *Society and Leisure, 2,* 28–63.
Elias, Norbert, & Eric Dunning. (1986). *Quest for Excitement: Sport and Leisure in the Civilizing Process.* Oxford: Blackwell.
Feshbach, Seymor, & Robert D. Singer. (1971). *Television and Aggression.* San Francisco: Jossey-Bass.
Giulianotti, Richard. (1999). *Football: A Sociology of the Global Game.* Cambridge: Polity.
Goldstein, Jeffrey H. (1989). Sports Violence. In D. Stanley Eitzen (Ed.), *Sport in Contemporary Society: An Anthology. 3rd Edition* (pp. 81–87). New York: St. Martin's Press.
Goodhart, Philip, & Christopher Chataway. (1968). *War Without Weapons.* London: W. H. Allen.
Goranson, Richard E. (1980). Sports Violence and the Catharsis Hypothesis. In Peter Klavora & Kirk A. Wipper (Eds.), *Psychological and Sociological Factors in Sport* (pp. 131–138). University of Toronto: School of Physical and Health Education.
Gratton, Chris, & Philip Taylor. (2000). *Economics of Sport and Recreation.* London: E. and F.N. Spon.
Greenberg, Peter S. (1977). Wild in the Stands. *New Times,* 9(10), 25–27.
Guttmann, Allen. (1992). Chariot Races, Tournaments and the Civilizing Process. In Eric Dunning & Chris Rojek (Eds.), *Sport and Leisure in the Civilizing Process: Critique and Counter Critique* (pp. 137–160). London: Macmillan.
Harper, Colin. (1989–90). *A Study of Football Crowd Behaviour.* Lothian and Borders Police, Mimeo.
Harrington, John A. (1968). *Soccer Hooliganism.* Bristol: John Wright.
Heitmeyer, Wilhelm, & Jörg Ingo Peter. (1992). *Jugendliche Fussballfans.* Weinheim, Munich: Juventa.
Hobbs, Dick, & David Robins. (1991). The Boy Done Good: Football Violence, Changes and Continuities. *Sociological Review,* 39(3), 551–579.
Hofman, Rich. (1986). Rape and the College Athlete. *Philadelphia Daily News,* March 17; cited in Nelson, 1994.
Hughes, Robert, & Jay J. Coakley. (1991). Positive Deviance Among Athletes: The Implications of Overconformity to the Sport Ethic. *Sociology of Sport Journal, 8,* 307–325.
Kerr, John H. (1994). *Understanding Soccer Hooliganism.* Philadelphia: Open University Press.
Koss, Mary P., & John A. Gaines. (1993). The Prediction of Sexual Aggression by Alcohol Use. Athletic Participation and Fraternity Affiliation. *Journal of Interpersonal Violence, 8,* March, 94–108.
Lenskyj, Helen. (1992). Sexual Harassment: Female Athletes' Experiences and Coaches' Responsibilities. *Science Periodical on Research and Technology in Sport,* 12(6), p. B2.

Lorenz, Konrad. (1963). *On Aggression.* New York/ Harcourt: Brace and World.
Mangan, J. Anthony. (2000). *Athleticism in the Victorian and Edwardian Public School.* London: Frank Cass.
Marsh, Peter. (1978). *Aggro: The Illusion of Violence.* London: Dent.
Marsh, Peter, Elizabeth Rosser, & Rom Harré. (1978). *The Rules of Disorder.* London: Routledge and Kegan Paul.
Melnick, Merrill J. (1992). Male Athletes and Sexual Assault. *Journal of Physical Education, Recreation and Dance, 63*(5), 32–35.
Merton, Robert. (1957). *Social Theory and Social Structure.* New York: Free Press.
Messner, Michael. (1987). The Life of a Man's Seasons: Male Identity in the Life-Course of the Jock. In Michael S. Kimmel (Ed.), *Changing Men* (pp. 53–67). London: Sage.
Messner, Michael, & Don Sabo. (1994). *Sex, Violence and Power in Sports: Rethinking Masculinity.* Freedom: Crossing Press.
Miracle, Andrew, Gary Chick, & John Loy. (1996). Aggression. In David Levinson & Karen Christenson (Eds.), *Encyclopaedia of World Sport, 1*(1), 12–17.
Moore, D. L. (1991). Athletes and Rape: An Alarming Link. *USA Today,* August 27, 1c–2c.
Murphy, Patrick, John Williams, & Eric Dunning. (1990). *Football on Trial.* London: Routledge.
Nelson, Mariah B. (1991). *Are We Winning Yet? How Women Are Changing Sports and Sports Are Changing Women.* New York: Random House.
Nelson, Mariah B. (1994). *The Stronger Women Get, the More Men Love Football: Sexism and the American Culture of Sports.* New York: Harcourt Brace.
Phillips, David P. (1983). The Impact of Mass Media Violence on US Homicides. *American Sociological Review, 48,* 560–568.
Rees, C. Roger, & Andrew W. Miracle. (1984). Conflict Resolution in Games and Sport. *International Review of Sport Sociology, 19,* 145–156.
Rees, C. Roger, Frank M. Howell, & Andrew W. Miracle. (1990). Do High School Sports Build Character? A Quasi-Experiment on a National Sample. *Social Science Journal, 27,* 303–315.
Roversi, Antonio. (1994). The Birth of the 'Ultras': The Rise of Football Hooliganism in Italy. In Richard Giulianotti & John Williams (Eds.), *Game Without Frontiers: Football, Identity and Modernity* (pp. 359–380). Aldershot: Arena.
Sheard, Kenneth, & Eric Dunning. (1973). The Rugby Club as a Type of Male Preserve. *International Review of Sport Sociology, 5,* 5–24.
Smith, Michael. (1983). *Violence and Sport.* Toronto. Butterworths.
Storr, Anthony. (1968). *Human Aggression.* London: Allen Lane.
Taylor, Ian. (1971). Football Mad: A Speculative Sociology of Football Hooliganism. In Eric Dunning (Ed.), *The Sociology of Sport: A Selection of Readings* (pp. 352–377). London: Frank Cass.
Taylor, Ian. (1982). Putting the Boot into Working Class Sport: British Soccer After Bradford and Brussels. *Sociology of Sport Journal, 4,* 171–191.
Taylor, Ian. (1986). Putting the Boot into Working Class Sport: British Soccer After Bradford and Brussels. *Sociology of Sport Journal, 4,* 171–191.
Toufexis, Anastasia. (1990). Sex and the Sporting Life. *Time,* August 6, 76.
Trulson, Michael E. (1986). Martial Arts Training: A Novel 'Cure' for Juvenile Delinquency. *Human Relations, 39,* 1131–1140.
Van der Brug, Hans. (1986). *Voetbalvandalisme.* Harlem: De Vriesebosch.
Van Limbergen, Kris, C. Colaers, & Lode Walgrave. (1987). *Research on the Societal and Psycho-Sociological Background of Football Hooliganism.* Leuven: Catholic University.
Waddington, Ivan. (2000). *Sport, Health and Drugs: A Critical Sociological Perspective.* London: E. and F.N. Spon.
Widmeyer, W. Neil, & Jack S. Birch. (1984). Aggression in Professional Ice Hockey: A Strategy for Success or a Reaction to Failure? *Journal of Psychology, 117*(1), 77–84.
Williams, John, Eric Dunning, & Patrick Murphy. (1984). *Hooligans Abroad.* London: Routledge. (2nd Edition, 1989).
Yiannakis, Andrew, Tom McIntyre, Melnick Merrill, & Donald Hart. (1979). *Sport Sociology: Contemporary Themes. 2nd Edition.* Dubuque: Kendall Hunt.

PART II-5-2

VIOLENCE IN THE PUBLIC SPACE

CHAPTER II-5-2.1

Violence on the Roads

RALF KÖLBEL

I. INTRODUCTION

Traffic offenses are a mass phenomenon, and the "misbehavior of the good" is more apparent here than in any other sphere. And yet even those breaches of norms that cause accidents incur only comparatively mild state sanction, in spite of their immense social cost. Both the ubiquity of offenses committed and the tolerance displayed by criminal law derive from purely instrumental systems of traffic law, which remain devoid of any historical or traditional link to moral standards. Traffic offenses are "folk crimes" (see Ross, 1960). Only the most serious violations meet with severe legal consequences and decisive opprobrium from road users. These types of traffic offense include some of those violations of integrity that are experienced as aggression.

There are considerable blind spots when it comes to identifying aggressive behavior on the roads, however. It is certainly not always the case that there is intuitive and immediate consensus on what constitutes aggressive driving. In everyday practice on the roads, aggressive driving is that kind of driving which road users perceive and interpret as the deliberate intent to cause various damages and violate norms. Evaluation of this, however, always takes place within a concrete situation, and is dependent on the perspectives of those involved, which may diverge, converge, or shift over time (for the sphere of traffic Linneweber, 1997:21). It is possible to demonstrate this relative nature of assessment by looking at various instances of a vehicle driving up close to the vehicle in front. When a vehicle approaches a slower car in the outside lane at high speed and then brakes so late as to dangerously reduce the distance separating the two vehicles, observers often see this as aggressive behavior (see the experiment in Bösser, 1987:32ff.). From the point of view of the approaching driver, however, this is often merely a case of erroneous (belated) readjustment of speed. No influence on the driver in front was intended in these cases (see Bösser, 1987:40ff.; Rajalin, Hassel, & Summala, 1997:726f.), and the real danger of this kind of driving is often underestimated (see Wagstaff, 1992). The development of the scenario then depends on the way in which the driver in front interprets the situation. If he feels infringed upon, he might brake suddenly in annoyance; if not he will calmly leave the outside lane, and other drivers will interpret each of his maneuvers as aggressive or appropriate. Thus contextual interpretations made by road users determine whether a maneuver is seen as aggressive or merely risky driving. Road users' perspectives are situational, but they also contain relatively constant criteria for appropriate or aggressive driving (see the poll in Ellinghaus, 1986:36ff.). Because drivers' shared preconceptions are (indirectly) relevant for action, they can serve as a basis for an initial description of the subject.

This approach does not only (and not even primarily) concentrate on physical aggression, but rather on the influence that driving practices may exert on other road users. Three aspects of the phenomenon are of interest here, and although they frequently refer to differing levels of danger, they all concentrate on the question of conflict. The sphere of lower intensity can be classified as inconsiderate behavior (see also Bösser, 1987:61). Inconsiderate driving practices differ from merely uncooperative driving by reason of the hindrance and annoyance they engender. Examples of inconsiderate practice include the inappropriate use of main beam headlamps, double-parking, parking on sidewalks, veering in and out of gaps in lanes of moving traffic, line-jumping, and the tailgating described above. The second aspect is characterized by a common element of a kind of coercion specific to road traffic. By using the particular situational characteristics of the road and the dynamics of traffic flow, drivers may seriously hinder each others progress or inflict psychological distress. This can be characterized as aggressive driver behavior. It includes instances of tailgating with protracted minimum clearance and the flashing of lights, sudden braking and cutting in after overtaking, and the protracted blocking of a lane (see Novaco, 1991:282; Goldstein, 1994:27). Patterns of conflict such as these require a certain traffic flow, and they are therefore predominant on highways. Unlike inconsiderate driving, aggressive driving may often be punished by law, in Germany for example as violent intimidation (see Kaiser, 1995). Finally, the third group is defined by conflicts in which drivers insult each other verbally or with gestures and sometimes even resort to physical violence (see Novaco, 1991:301; Eisner, 1997:253ff.). Scenarios that escalate to the use of physical violence normally call for direct contact between drivers, and thus mainly occur in urban traffic.

Rather than traditional forms of physical violence, road traffic thus displays those kinds of conflict whose appearance and structure arise out of the particular traffic situation. It is necessary to find terminology and analytical methods which differentiate these kinds of conflict, but sociological definitions should thereby not lose sight of seemingly less serious infringements. A restrictive concept concentrating on physical violence risks viewing the phenomena from a purely external perspective, and thus neglecting the experience and the independent interpretations of those involved. If a concept of violence sets arbitrary limits to analysis, then these insofar as they transcend a merely differentiating use of language also have further counterproductive effects, since their reductive view of the subject will influence research results. This problem is particularly noticeable in research on road traffic. The interactive dynamics of conflict means that all three of the spheres of aggression named above can frequently be observed in one incident, and the urge to assign one kind of behavior to a particular group reveals that the borders between the groups are in fact fluid. The common element of psychological coercion makes it necessary to deal with the entire spectrum of behavior in the context of "violence on the roads," including the less concrete violations caused by inconsiderate driving.

II. THEORETICAL APPROACHES AND EMPIRICAL RESULTS

It is difficult to find a place for research on "violence on the roads" in the more general discourse on violence. On the one hand, this is due to the situational and temporary nature of aggressive driving practices, which are harder to define than more straightforward physical violence and which are clearly also less socially disturbing. But this dilemma is also and primarily due to the general state of research on violence. Criminology and sociology are the disciplines which usually deal with interpersonal aggression, and they show little interest for any aspect of road use. The same is true for aggressive driving practices. More recent, detailed descriptions of (everyday) violence ignore road traffic (e.g., Sofsky, 1996). "Studies of human aggression and violence curiously have ignored the roadway context" (Novaco, 1991:254). Psychology and traffic psychology do look into deviant driving practice, investigating motivational aspects behind driver behavior rather than perceptual-motor aspects, but to date this research has treated aggressive conflict as a peripheral issue. The state of research on road aggression is thus largely unsatisfactory. Existing research uses mainly heuristic approaches.

1.

Most research makes use of a variety of theoretical approaches to transfer general theories on the origins of violence to the sphere of road traffic. None of these investigations see a particular and independent theoretical significance in the traffic context. This problem is observed most clearly in approaches based on personality theory. Up to the middle of the 1970s, traffic psychology, for example, was determined by a paradigm based on the concept of accident liability. This stated that a large proportion of all road accidents was caused by a small group of high-risk drivers, who were liable to accidents as a consequence of shared personality traits relevant to driving behavior. The task of research would be to investigate these personality traits (overview in Whitlock, 1971:16ff.). The first large-scale examination of aggression in road traffic was a programmatic analysis in precisely this tradition (see Parry, 1968). A key assumption here is that various types of aggressive driving are an expression of the road users' various aggressive tendencies. But this approach was not developed to include an investigation of the origins of such tendencies and also fails to examine the concrete manifestations of the tendencies in aggressive driving scenarios. Parry sees his work as a first pilot study and thus does not collect data on the relevant personality traits. He merely uses the results of a written survey to postulate a connection between high personal accident liability, self-avowed aggressive attitudes to traffic and aggressive driving practice, and diverse demographic factors (younger drivers, male, lower middle class, see Parry, 1968:97ff.). Though Parry's statistical findings are flawed by the fragmentary nature of his entire study, his protocols of partly structured interviews in which some drivers both report and reflect on their aggressive driving (see Parry, 1968:21ff.) are more instructive.

It is important to note that today both sociology and traffic psychology reject the accident liability theory entirely: There is a substantial amount of research on the driver personality, and as a whole this shows that there are certainly important differences in the propensity to be involved in accidents and to commit traffic offenses (for basic information on the J curve in the distribution of different levels of conformity in driving behavior see Clarke, 1996; Morlok & Kölbel, 1998). This is not a result of stable temporal conditions, however, but of variable biographical features. On the whole, studies based on traffic psychology reveal hardly any shared personality traits among the members of high-risk groups (see Ranney, 1994; Wilde, 1994:165: "weak, inconsistent and contradictory findings galore"). Only demographic factors appear to be of consistent significance, for even when the relevant offense probability factors, which vary with individual driving skills, are taken into account (on exposure to risk see Elander, West, & French, 1993:282), young male road users are still more conspicuous than older and female ones. In addition to this, there are also indicators of a disproportionately represented small group of drivers in the sphere of risk-related offenses, a group which generally behaves in a dangerous or socially detrimental manner both on and off the road (see Jonah, 1990; OECD, 1994:27ff.). In spite of these observations, it is still the rule that "normal citizens" are involved in the large majority of all traffic offenses (on the status of research see Evans, 1991:133ff.; Elander et al., 1993; Wilde, 1994:161ff.). As individual conformity or risky behavior relating to driving practice mostly finds its expression in a consistent style of driving, then it also proves to be evident in various areas of behavior of the mass of road users. Thus investigations to date have shown that the structures of general traffic offense discussed above conform to the structures of distribution of aggressive driving (see Evans, 1991:137ff.; Hülimann & von Hebenstreit, 1996:78ff.; Rajalin et al., 1997). Apart from smaller groups who display a particular propensity for conflict, inconsiderate driving and traffic violence are typical and everyday phenomena throughout the entire driving population, within which it is only possible to identify minimal demographic variations in levels of incrimination (relevant research in Hauber, 1980; Hülimann & von Hebenstreit, 1996:92ff.; Atzwanger, 1995:39ff.; Eisner, 1997:258ff.; Barthelmess, 1998:153; confirmed by the secondary analysis in overviews of direct and indirect indicators in official documents, traffic statistics, surveys and traffic observation in Kölbel, 1997:45ff.). Classical explanations based on personality theory (alongside Parry, 1968 then finally also Macmillan, 1975) do not do justice to these statistics.

A more fruitful approach to these findings than the accident liability theory is possibly found in a number of experimental investigations, which attribute aggressive driving to environmental conditions such as heat, heavy traffic, and other disturbing occurrences in the traffic situation (Kenrick & MacFarlane, 1986; Hennessy & Wiesenthal, 1999). In numerous field experiments an assistant remained stationary with his car at traffic lights on green, or walked across the road immediately in front of an approaching car (see Turner, Layton, & Simons, 1975; Hauber, 1980; Ellison et al., 1995). In the first instance, these manipulated disturbances were designed to measure the particular value of various forms of provocation (e.g., the gender of the driver in the obstructing car). In addition, the various negative forms of reaction were described (honking the horn, gesturing, rapid driving up to the pedestrian), and these were widely distributed with the exception of frequently conspicuous young male drivers. Generally, the theoretical model underlying these investigations is not discussed, but it is the frustration-aggression hypothesis, which Novaco (1991:303ff.) first used in detail for road traffic. This view states that the road is a favorable location for processes which engender aggression, because it has a disinhibitory effect in a number of ways. High traffic density and other environmental conditions produce numerous stress factors, frustrations, and ill-feeling. This activates the readiness to respond violently to provocative stimuli. This readiness is heightened with the arousal which is connected with every use of the road, especially since this kind of reaction can be learned. Simultaneously, factors that inhibit aggression become negligible in traffic as a result of a low level of control in traffic situations (Goldstein, 1994:29f. agrees with all of this). Thus Novaco's theory at least displays a certain appreciation of the situational framework of driving practice (in more detail in II.2.). But a psychological perspective would require further detail, on differing biographical levels of tolerance of and reactions to frustration, for example, or on the differing tendency of various road incidents to engender aggression. But regardless of this shortcoming, this nonspecific approach reduces all communicative processes between road users to their ability to disturb the driving process, which thus becomes a stress factor not categorically different to the temperature inside the vehicle, for example. The conflictual nature of aggressive driving and the dynamics of these processes are lost to individual and internal human factors. This kind of approach thus also remains one-sidedly related to the individual.

An approach which sees aggressive driving as territorial behavior might better do justice to the social dimension of aggressive driving. According to decision theory models, which assume a rational cost-effect analysis (on this for behavior in traffic in general Corbett & Simon, 1992), protagonists with a claim to territory evaluate the resources of the territory against the effort required to defend it, even if this is only a symbolic and value-oriented territory, linked with notions of identity, control, or competence. Results of secret observations and experiments show that drivers about to leave their parking space delay driving off if other drivers are waiting for the space to be vacated, and especially if the waiting drivers exert pressure by honking their horn (see Ruback & Juieng, 1997). This shows that cars and traffic areas are symbolic territorial spaces. If these spaces are challenged by others, then the threat of a loss of status and control leads to defensive action which may, in some cases, also be manifested in the form of aggressive driving. This is certainly how Richman (1972) explains his observations of aggressive reactions displayed by various drivers who were subjected to checks by traffic authorities whilst they were parking. But aggressive territorial behavior on the road may just as well be explained psychologically, by the theory of reactance or as a crowding effect. If the freedom to move and to make decisions is felt to be restricted, then this causes motivational tension and may lead to various forms of defensive action (on traffic in general Schönbach, 1996). And yet this whole approach to aggression on the road remains underdeveloped. Unless it is accompanied by further analysis, it proves unconvincing. Here too, the postulate of a connection between aggression and territory remains one-dimensional. From a temporal point of view, aggressive driving is seen here as a merely momentary reaction with no history, and communicative processes in road traffic are reduced to an interest in spatial factors.

Nonetheless, the territorial approach is a major emphasis in the studies by Whitlock (1971) and Atzwanger (1995), though in the former case in an ethological context. This approach assumes that every road user possesses an innate human drive to compete for higher social status and better access to resources, and that this may release aggressive behavior if provoked. The territory represented by the automobile and the road areas to which a driver makes a claim is seen as a commodity with social status, and if this is threatened, the response will be aggression. In this view, the male of the species fulfills a role which includes higher claims to dominance, and thus also a higher propensity to aggressive driving than is the case for women drivers. And road traffic is constituted by comparatively less stringent systems of norms, and is thus a favorable sphere in which to live out aggressive behavioral strategies inherent to the human biological make-up. Whitlock attempted to support these theses empirically by asserting a statistical relationship between violent offenses and road accidents in various regions, and by seeing the cause of these two allegedly related phenomena in a biologically driven and culturally influenced "aggression mass" at work in each society (Whitlock, 1971:101; replicated by Sivak, 1983). By contrast, Atzwangers approach is methodically far subtler. He secretly observed drivers under conditions with no speed restrictions who drive up close to the vehicle in front. But his findings (a higher incrimination of middle-aged male drivers, larger vehicles, no passengers; see Atzwanger, 1995:39ff.) are too general and thus clearly show the limitations of the underlying theoretical framework. Although Atzwanger states that he wishes to consider cultural factors alongside biological structures (Atzwanger, 1995:7), he then goes on to explain conflict on the road only in terms of motivations for action based purely on status and dominance. Because his study lacks the necessary theoretical impetus, he is unable to discuss the intermediate processes between the alleged propensity and the aggressive behavior. This means that the drivers'interactive processes and subjective perceptions are reduced to an undefined trigger impulse. Nonetheless, the ethological insight that a need for self-esteem and to demonstrate status can lead to risky driving should be retained and integrated into other theoretical traditions.

2.

All the above approaches to "violence on the roads" share the view that a particular style of driving is a relatively isolated act rooted within the driver, and that the aggressive quality of this act follows from its course. None of these theories is open to sociological viewpoints. They overlook the subjective experience of those involved (see I. above), and they also ignore the dynamic, interactive origins of driver conflict. Studies on these issues do exist (II.3. below), but they cannot be properly understood unless the potential conditions and situations which permit, encourage, and facilitate aggression in traffic have first been defined (on the following see Kölbel, 1997:161ff.). One expression of the significance of the context on the road for such a situational model is the fact that all specific phenomena in traffic aggression depend in the first place on the social development and institutionalization of road traffic. Furthermore, the findings outlined above point to the particular influence of the sphere of action, since they indicate considerable heterogeneity among inconsiderate road usersnotwithstanding some groups of drivers which are more prone to conflictand also that the road users'ability to withstand stress depends on their driving skills. The significance of situational conditions is also demonstrated in the fact that the road produces its own particular forms and means of aggression. The studies of the defense of territory, crowding, and numerous stress factors on the road (II. 1. above) may point in this direction, but they are based on inconclusive and unconvincing theoretical approaches. Nonetheless they indicate one defining factor of the road traffic system, in that the human being appears to be biologically, psychologically and socially ill matched to this sphere. This thesis would not only mean that the risk of motorized mobility is fundamentally uncontrollable, but also that the road is a social arena with an unusually high potential for conflict. The characteristics of the system understood in this manner can now be defined heuristically by using concrete features of the traffic situation, and can be linked to inconsiderate driving (which then also indicates a theoretical connection to more recent criminological theories such as interactionist approaches, rational choice, routine activity approach, opportunity structure, and lifestyle model, all of which tend to place greater emphasis on the value of situational conditions):

On the road as it is experienced, drivers are at least abstractly conscious of the dangers linked to risky and inconsiderate driving. Perceived driving errors are thus easily neutralized by attribution to environmental factors. Frequently, the risks caused by a driver him or herself, and those caused by other drivers, are not recognized and are not taken into account. Thus empirical research repeatedly reveals drivers'unrealistic belief in their own competence (above all for road users whose driving is unsafe), which leads to an overestimation of the individuals ability to control danger when driving inconsiderately (see Evans, 1991:322ff.; McKenna, 1993). On the road as a communicational sphere, road users interact in fleeting, hermetic, and mass encounters, which permit only reduced means and channels of interaction. This leads to numerous misunderstandings and misinterpretations and implies a generally dehumanizing tendency (see the experimental approach to this in Ellison et al., 1995). Empathy or mutual relations are rare here, and cultural attitudes of consideration are neither practiced nor informally guaranteed. Thus the general preconditions of the road, even before conflict has arisen, are characterized by a distanced level of communication with considerable potential for conflict (on communication code and the culture of interaction see the traffic observations in Risser, 1988). On the road as a system of control, many traffic norms frequently have only a small effect on actual behavior. Low density of control leads to a low risk of being caught, and there is a social acceptance of rule violations, which are perceived to be harmless. This leads to a practice which varies according to the given situation, whereby the utility and risk of an action take priority over normative expectations and thus weaken adherence to rules (see Karstedt, 1993; Yagil, 1998; Morlok & Kölbel, 1998).

The traffic situation is also influenced by other conditions outside the realm of traffic, which bear upon this realm and thus must be seen as part of the context of action. The social environment, for example, creates the need for most instances of road use, and thus links these to a performance-related goal. Particular acts of driving are instrumentally subordinate to the fulfilling of obligations (frequently chains of obligations). The safety dimension in road traffic is thus fundamentally restricted by the performance dimension. The tendency to react aggressively to hindrances on the road rises in proportion to how binding the external obligation and reason for using the road is perceived to be (particularly clear when under time pressure, see Rajalin et al., 1997:727; Hennessy & Wiesenthal, 1999:418). In addition, social values and other general and supraindividual systems of reflection also bear on driving behavior. Our general achievement-oriented culture affirms mobility and a culture of traffic, in which the ideal driver is committed to routine ability, athleticism, and a confident mastery of risk (Näitänen & Summala, 1976:21; on the "speed ethos" see Rothe, 1993:133ff.). Guiding values such as these are reproduced in communication during or associated with road traffic. Various subjective patterns of behavior are influenced by these values and are expressed in assertive driving practice. Many drivers also experience the movement of their vehicle, and particularly their control over it in demanding road situations, as positive and a major factor in the affirmation of the self (see the subtle interviews in Schönhammer, 1991:137ff.). Thus, conspicuous driving practice is closely linked to a need for self-assertion, enhanced self-esteem, the testing of limits, and dominance over a situation. General deficiencies in self-esteem therefore lead to compensatory driving practice (see Opaschowski, 1999:51ff. and also Schlag, 1987, using the example of younger drivers). A potential for violence which originates elsewhere is transferred to the traffic system, and over time this also creates phases of an increasingly or decreasingly aggressive "traffic climate."

From an analytical point of view, road users move within a potential sphere which is constituted, as described above, by spatial conditions, stable chains of interaction, and conditions of subjective experience, which taken together create a highly conflictual environment. This general background becomes relevant for behavior as a situational structure of an opportunity for action, providing numerous potential causes of conflict and also favorable (anonymous, control-low) conditions for an aggressive way of dealing with this conflict. This increases the probability of aggression and violence (in the sense of reciprocal selection) above all for those people who are susceptible to aggression (see Kölbel, 1997:188f.; Eisner, 1997). In addition, the traffic-specific potential space is significant in the socialization of drivers. Merely to view participation in traffic as a series of situational decisions is not sufficient. Apart from certain maneuvers which are undertaken with a high degree of conscious control, the majority of driving practice is based on habitual schemes of behavior, which also determine individual potential for conflict and individually acceptable levels of risk in a given situation (see Wagenaar, 1992). Empirical studies today generally analyze these patterns of driving behavior in terms of modern attitude theory. Specific aspects of attitude can be linked to criminological theories (e.g., reduced individual acceptance of norms, increased individual wish to test limits and take risks), and these attitudes have been shown in research on psychological aspects of traffic to demonstrate stable links to reduced conformism on the road (see OECD, 1994; the representative studies in Rothengatter & Carbonell Vaya, 1997:353ff.). There are links here to the frameworks of action in traffic, which represent the backdrop to individual driver biographies and enter into a relationship of reciprocal influence with developing patterns of driving behavior. Thus situational elements, processes of socialization, and motivational aspects all interact. It has to be said that the structure of disposition and situation outlined here does not explain differences in conspicuous driving behavior. But it remains conceptually open to relevant analysis of a propensity to aggression in various groups of drivers, an analysis which may link to ego-compensation by means of offensive driving (for a similar programmatic approach see Eisner, 1997).

3.

Finally, contemporary research also offers initial studies on such defining processes within road traffic whereby objectively disturbing or dangerous driving practice is perceived to be uncooperative, inconsiderate or aggressive, and can thus set in motion considerable dynamics of conflict. In addition to the observable interactive nature of the traffic situation, there is a further indicator that the participants in traffic are themselves the prime interpreters and givers of significance in a particular situation. This is the fact that aggressive driving, unlike the majority of traffic offenses, is not officially brought into the realm of the criminal justice system, but frequently ends up there as a result of (often reciprocal) private reports to the police (see Kölbel, 1997:67). Empirical analysis is gradually addressing this phenomenon.

Whereas surveys of common reactions to provocative driving practice have been of little use to date (see Ellinghaus, 1986:68ff.; Opaschowski, 1999:114f.), much more direct data are to be found in interview records from criminal proceedings. Records of police investigations made it possible to reconstruct the typical course of reciprocally aggressive conflict on the road (see Eisner, 1997:253ff.; Barthelmess, 1998). These studies also see themselves as a test of a method, and this reflects on the theoretical approach to empirical findings. Instead of linking their findings to further (perhaps criminological) contexts, Eisner and Barthelmess attempt to generalize structures of conflict inductively on a middle level. Eisner (1997) normatively emphasizes the territorial aspect discussed above

(II.1.), according to which formal and informal rules define the various claims to road space. Aggressive incidents between road users derive from the inability to assert rightful claims, as described by Eisner for conflicts around parking spaces, pedestrian crossings, right of way, and overtaking. For an incident to lead to conflict, the driver involved has to interpret any hindrance as a deliberate action and not as a mistake on the part of the other driver. The first driver will then frequently communicate this interpretation in gesture or verbally. If the other driver responds to this and neither party breaks off the conflict, then symbolically expressed conflict can increase to physical aggression. Of course the external conditions have to facilitate the kind of contact in which gestures, words, and physical actions may be exchanged. According to Eisner, in addition to these situational conditions the degree of drivers' emotional involvement will also influence the dynamics of conflict or allow the process to be broken off.

Eisner does not discuss norms in the traffic system in view of their reduced validity (as in II.2. above). By clearly emphasizing the normative distribution of territorial claims, he rather foregrounds their role as potential causes of conflict. It would be fruitful to relate the two aspects to each other and see the distribution of territorial claims in traffic as violable due to the reduced level of influence of normative systems on behavior, and thus also as favorable to conflict. The theory of territorial distribution also remains incomplete for certain areas of conflict. In particular, aggressive driving practice outside the city (tailgating, blocking the outside lane, braking suddenly in front of another vehicle) frequently involves motivation whereby the factor of space is increased and multiplied by the factor of time, for here the conflict derives from choice of speed and ensuing hindrances (see Barthelmess, 1998:154f.). But the process structures otherwise resemble each other. Barthelmess (ibid.) describes their dynamic elements more subtly. His findings revealed the noteworthy fact that drivers react aggressively to hindering, dangerous, or restricting driving when they interpret this disturbance as a violation of their honor. If this reaction then also makes the other driver feel insulted and emotionally agitated, because he or she too feels identity questioned, and if the general conditions on the road are conducive, then this can set in motion a process of reciprocally spiraling driving, gestural, or physical aggression. Every attempt by one party to act to cancel out the violation a previous action has caused will fuel further escalation, since counteraggression implies increasing aggression to ensure that the response is appropriate. Here it is no longer significant whether the original driving was actually intended as hindrance. The only thing that counts is the attribution of motivation (I. above), which is influenced by individual styles of interpretation and thresholds of injury.

III. DESIDERATA

Present research on "violence on the roads" is too fragmentary, unsystematic, and preliminary for fundamental controversies worthy of investigation to be filtered out from the various approaches. This kind of discussion is not yet taking place. At the present, the main aim has to be to join with the general discourse on violence and then systematically to define the future goals of research. Until a general, interdisciplinary criminology of violence is developed, research will refer to more pragmatic questions linked to specific areas of investigation. The starting point for such considerations is the observation that aggression on the road develops from prior forms of action. This happens in two interlinked ways. Firstly, only reciprocal processes of interpretation and attribution of motive allow certain risky, dangerous, or uncooperative maneuvers to be seen as driving aggression—as intentional hindering and restricting and to become relevant to interaction. Secondly, the intensity of the inconsiderate behavior mostly runs through a chain of escalation before it reaches violent action, and is only seldom physically violent from the outset. This phenomenon makes it necessary to take seriously the social processes involved in traffic. Driving behavior can no longer be seen merely as the expression of particular abilities or character traits. This is a question of the kind of communicative behavior that constitutes social realities on the road. Of particular interest are the situational ways in which drivers deal with and express their perspectives on reality and their individual experience, whereby material, cultural, and personal conditions in everyday road practice attain their own specific social relevance to action and thus create longer-term stable characteristics in the traffic system (see Rothe, 1993; Morlok & Kölbel, 1998). This can be described in more detail as follows:

- Driving practice with a tendency to conflict is in no way per se linked logically to its interpretation as aggression, but this is often de facto the case. This means that research on driver personality is still relevant, particularly as different groups of drivers display various degrees of conformism on the road, irrespective of the level of control, although it has to be said that findings to date do not show any serious differences. Initially, therefore, it is necessary to investigate more closely the subjective state of mind of those road users who more readily enter into aggressive conflict. This certainly includes the need to examine approaches which assume complex, dangerous behavioral patterns in certain people both on and off the road (for example Jonah, 1990; Rajalin et al., 1997).
- Using these results, it would be possible to investigate interpretations of violence in other spheres that have been undertaken by the social sciences, and to examine their relevance for the realm of driving. Present developments indicate, however, that further analysis would have to be undertaken to document traffic situations which encourage aggression and also to describe the reciprocal effects these have on the various experiences and requirements of the entire driving population (see Eisner, 1997; Kölbel, 1997). In this context, the heuristic situational model described above (II.2.) could be supplemented by an examination of the interactionist structure within the vehicle (see Schönhammer, 1991:166ff.), or by the power and performance of the vehicles and the reciprocal effects these factors may have on opportunity for acting and drivers'perspectives.
- A further new direction in research should be undertaken. This is research on the victims of the road, which should however be undertaken without repeating the limitations of early research into victimology. It is necessary to understand the ways in which harassing and threatening driving practice works (for a general investigation of the effects of psychological coercion see Popitz, 1992:79ff.), and also what effects these practices have on the experience of the victims. Just in themselves, the effects on the victim represent important factors for research on aggressive forms of driving (on fear and nervousness see Sofsky, 1996:71ff.).
- On the other hand, the opportunity structures of road traffic can only be understood by investigating the driver perspective. On the subjective level, it is first necessary to assess the expectations and criteria for acceptable driving on the part of other road users. Then it is necessary to demonstrate which violations of expectations are not understood as minor hindrances, but rather as encroachment on

territory, insult, or aggression, and thus create a readiness for counteraggressive reactions and potential dynamics of escalation. Because it is likely that there will be intersubjective differences of sensitivity in this context, analysis of the personal level will also be fruitful here, if it takes into account the temporal variations of sensitivity, as a result of social change, for example. It is only on the basis of these investigations that the objective elements of opportunity structures (typical speeds, types of intersection, traffic lanes) can be satisfactorily understood.

Moving on to the "perpetrator": once the individual patterns of experience of conflict on the road have been clearly examined for all those involved, and after this information has been supplemented by observation of external communicative processes, research is in a position to further examine conflict structure. Research on traffic has largely ignored this interactive level to date. Wherever this integrative frame of reference is missing, it is hardly surprising that research can only provide preliminary results at best. Frequently results diverge significantly, and research offers only heuristic outlines, providing no more than a glimpse of the structural, interactive and personal conditions which link aggression on the road to the everyday violence of modern societies.

IV. APPROACHES TO PREVENTION

The prevention of accidents, delinquency, and aggression in road traffic is the responsibility of the sector that Bourdieu calls the "left hand of the state." In general this realm is intended to balance out the long-term real costs of the market and of the primacy of (economic) policy, whilst enjoying only half-hearted social support (see Bourdieu, 1998:9ff.). In traffic, this "hand" has to deal with material and cultural conditions whereby the participants themselves reproduce the structures which permanently overwhelm them. Against this backdrop, the traffic systems immense propensity to conflict necessitates social and political debates that question the ubiquity of road traffic and subordinate it to (ecological and) security and safety priorities. For the individual, to dismantle the system of risk would mean to enter into a process of self-reflection, self-control and empathetic driving, whereas the state would have to encourage discourse on these matters. This discourse (and also of course any short-term traffic safety program) has to include those initiatives discussed under the classical three "Es" (engineering, enforcement, education): Technical systems in the vehicle primarily serve to protect the driver and passengers, but they do not influence their behavior, which may even counteract technical safety gains (see Wilde, 1994). Street and road design, when incorporated appropriately into urban planning, may curb speed levels and support new regulation on speed limits, producing a homogenizing and therefore favorable effect on latent conflict and the general culture of interaction (see Linneweber, 1997:20). Traffic research gives little reason to expect that traffic law can have a direct effect on driving aggression (in particular the deterrent effects of stricter punishments for violation of legal norms), as the chances of enforcement are questionable. Moreover, there are fundamental doubts as to whether criminal law and its orientation on questions of guilt provide the right terms of reference for the environmental conditions pertaining to traffic. At the least, forms of sanction more adequate to the actual offense should be developed. It seems that pacifying effects are most likely to come from perceivably intensified (police) checks at accident and conflict hot spots (see Rothengatter, 1982). Finally, various education campaigns have also proved ineffective (see OECD, 1994). On the other hand, greater reason for optimism is provided by a new emphasis on driver training and retraining, which teach perception of danger, communicative techniques in traffic, and shifts in perspective, as well as making the driver conscious of his or her own expressive motivation when driving (see Schlag, 1987:221ff.). But especially for those groups of young drivers who display a complex propensity to conspicuous driving this certainly has to be coordinated and combined with projects for the prevention of violence outside the traffic sphere.

Translated by Tradukas

REFERENCES

Atzwanger, Klaus. (1995). *Der Steinzeitjäger im Straßenverkehr.* Dissertation Universität Wien.
Barthelmess, Wolfgang. (1998). Aggressives Verkehrsverhalten. *Zeitschrift für Verkehrssicherheit, 44*, 150–158.
Bösser, Tom. (1987). *Gefährliche und aggressive Verhaltensweisen des Fahrers bei der Regelung des Abstandes auf der Autobahn.* Köln: Verlag TÜ Rheinland.
Bourdieu, Pierre. (1998). *Contre feux.* Paris: Liber.
Clarke, Ronald V. (1996). The Distribution of Deviance and Exceeding the Speed Limit. *British Journal of Criminology, 36*, 169–181.
Corbett, Claire, & Frances, Simon. (1992). Decision to Break or Adhere to the Rules of the Road. *British Journal of Criminology, 32*, 537–549.
Eisner, Manuel. (1997). *Das Ende der zivilisierten Stadt?* Frankfurt, New York: Campus.
Elander, James, Robert West, & Davina French. (1993). Behavioral Correlates of Individual Differences in Road-Traffic Crash Risk. *Psychological Bulletin, 113*, 279–294.
Ellinghaus, Dieter. (1986). *Rücksichtslosigkeit und Partnerschaft.* Köln: Uniroyal.
Ellison, Patricia, John Govern, Herbert Petri, & Michael Figler. (1995). Anonymity and Aggressive Driving Behavior. *Journal of Social Behavior and Personality, 10*, 265–272.
Evans, Leonard. (1991). *Traffic Safety and the Driver.* New York: Van Nostrand Reinhold.
Goldstein, Arnold P. (1994). *The Ecology of Aggression.* New York, London: Plenum Press.
Hauber, Albert R. (1980). The Social Psychology of Driving Behaviour and the Traffic Environment. *International Review of Applied Psychology, 29*, 461–474.
Hennessy, Dwight A., & David L. Wiesenthal. (1999). Traffic Congestion, Driver Stress, and Driver Aggression. *Aggressive Behavior, 25*, 409–423.
Hilimann, Fred W., & Benedikt von Hebenstreit. (1996). *Typologie und Verkehr.* Züch: Huber.
Jonah, Brian. (1990). Age Differences in Risky Driving. *Health Education Research, 5*, 139–149.
Kaiser, Güther. (1995). Keine Gewalt im öffentlichen Straßnverkehr? *Gruppendynamik, 26*, 125–145.
Karstedt, Susanne. (1993). Normbindung und Sanktionsdrohung. Frankfurt: P. Lang.
Kenrick, Douglas T., & Steven W. MacFarlan. (1986). Ambient Temperature and Horn Honking. *Environment and Behavior, 18*, 179–191.
Kölbel, Ralf. (1997). *Rücksichtslosigkeit und Gewalt im Straßenverkehr.* Frankfurt: P. Lang.
Linneweber, Volker. (1997). Aggression im Straßnverkehr. *Zeitschrift für Verkehrssicherheit, 43*, 19–22.
Macmillan, John. (1975). *Deviant Drivers.* Lexington: Lexington Books.
McKenna, Frank. (1993). It Wont Happen to Me. *British Journal of Psychology, 84*, 39–50.
Morlok, Martin, & Ralf Kölbel. (1998). Stop-Schilder in der Rechtssoziologie. *Zeitschrift für Rechtssoziologie, 20*, 136–162.
Näien, Risto, & Heikki Summala. (1976). *Road-User Behavior and Traffic Accidents.* Amsterdam: North Holland Publishing Company.
Novaco, Raymond. (1991). Aggressions on Roadways. In Ronald Baenninger (Ed.), *Targets of Violence and Aggression* (pp. 253–325). Amsterdam: Elsevier Science Publisher.
OECD Road Transport Research. (1994). *Improving Road Safety by Attitude Modification.* Paris: OECD.
Opaschowski, Horst. (1999). *Umwelt, Freizeit, Mobilität.* Opladen: Leske & Budrich.
Parry, Meyer H. (1968). *Aggression on the Road.* London: Tavistock.
Popitz, Heinrich. (1992). *Phänomene der Macht.* Tübingen: Mohr.
Rajalin, Sirpa, Sven-Olof Hassel, & Heikki Summala. (1997). Close-Following on Two-Lane Highways. *Accident Analysis and Prevention, 29*, 723–729.

Ranney, Thomas A. (1994). Models of Driving Behavior. *Accident Analysis and Prevention*, 26, 733–750.
Richman, Joel. (1972). The Motor Car and the Territorial Aggression Thesis. *Sociological Review*, 20, 5–27.
Risser, Ralf. (1988). *Kommunikation und Kultur des Straßenverkehrs*. Wien: Literas Universitätsverlag.
Ross, Laurence. (1960). Traffic Law Violation: A Folk Crime. *Social Problems*, 8, 231–241.
Rothe, J. Peter. (1993). *Beyond Traffic Safety*. New Brunswick: Transaction Publishers.
Rothengatter, Talib. (1982). The Effect of Police Surveillance and Law Enforcement in Driver Behaviour. *Current Psychological Reviews*, 2, 349–358.
Rothengatter, Talib, & Enrique Carbonell Vaya (Eds.) (1997). *Traffic and Transport Psychology*. Amsterdam: Pergamon.
Ruback, Barry, & Daniel Juieng. (1997). Territorial Defense in Parking Lots. *Journal of Applied Social Psychology*, 27, 821–834.
Schlag, Bernhard. (1987). *In meinem Alter führt man an sich recht zügig. Untersuchungen zu Risikoverhalten und Risikobereitschaft junger Fahrer.* Habilitationsschrift Essen.
Schönbach, Peter. (1996). Massenunfälle bei Nebel. *Zeitschrift für Sozialpsychologie*, 27, 109–125.
Schönhammer, Rainer. (1991). *In Bewegung. Zur Psychologie der Fortbewegung*. München: Quintessenz.
Sivak, Michael. (1983). Society's Aggression Level as Predictor of Traffic Fatality Rate. *Accident Analysis and Prevention*, 14, 93–99.
Sofsky, Wolfgang. (1996). *Traktat über die Gewalt*. Frankfurt: S. Fischer.
Turner, Charles W., John F. Layton, & Lynn S. Simons. (1975). Naturalistic Studies of Aggressive Behavior. *Journal of Personality and Social Psychology*, 31, 1098–1107.
Wagenaar, Willem A. (1992). Risk Taking and Accident Causation. In Frank Yates (Ed.), *Risk-Taking Behavior* (pp. 257–281). Chichester: Wiley.
Wagstaff, Graham F. (1992). What Constitutes Reckless Driving? In Friedrich Lösel, Doris Bender & Thomas Bliesener (Eds.), *Psychology and Law* (pp. 86–94). Berlin, New York: de Gruyter.
Whitlock, Francis A. (1971). *Death on the Road*. London: Tavistock.
Wilde, Gerald J.S. (1994). *Target Risk*. Toronto: PDE Publications.
Yagil, Dana. (1998). Instrumental and Normative Motives for Compliance with Traffic Laws among Young and Older Drivers. *Accident Analysis and Prevention*, 30, 417–424.

CHAPTER II-5-2.2

Juvenile and Urban Violence

FRANÇOIS DUBET

The sociology of violence constantly encounters a variety of problems with the vagueness of the actual definition of violence. The first of these problems concerns the diversity of forms of what is referred to as 'violent' conduct: even if violence is considered as being restricted to physical assault against the person, it is unreasonable to take the view that delinquent assault, urban unrest, violent political demonstrations, street fighting between gangs, and domestic violence all form part of the same family of phenomena. In fact, the only unifying factor in violence is the moral condemnation it provokes: there is a general consensus to the effect that violence is a bad thing, and indeed, when an act of violence appears to be useful and desirable, it is often difficult to regard it as violence at all. The second academic problem arises from the fact that violence is so varied in form that there is no reason to think that it all originates from a single, consistent cause. Violence may be an uncontrolled reaction or a carefully considered act; it may be an emotional reaction or a controlled strategy, a form of group conduct or a personal symptom, a cultural obligation or a form of 'acting out.' In addition, whether a form of conduct is described as violent largely depends on cultural and social contexts, and it may be that the reason we are so sensitive to violent conduct today is that we live in a society which can find no place for it, cannot tolerate it after a long period of declining civil violence. Although there is no certainty that violence in private circumstances has increased, there is also no doubt that our tolerance of it has lessened, as in the instances of rape or conjugal violence. Finally, how should we classify economic, institutional, and social violence, which are not forms of violence in the strict sense, although many distinctive forms of violence are evidently triggered by them?

The only unifying principle of violence is that it is the breakdown of order: violence occurs when institutionalized and regulated behavior gives way to unpredictable conduct that is perceived as being antisocial. The way in which regulated behavior gives way to violence may take two contrasting forms. The first is the crisis situation, where a social system can no longer regulate or control the conduct of individuals and groups, and so breaks down. In this instance, the violence stems from the crisis and from the disintegration of social ties and systems. The second instance is the case of conflict, or more precisely the impossibility of conflict: violence breaks out when social conflicts fail to gain recognition as being legitimate and cannot be institutionalized.

I. VIOLENCE AND SOCIOLOGICAL THEORIES

I do not know whether violence is at the heart of all social existence, all religion, and the majority of myths, as Girard asserts, but it is clear that most of the major sociological paradigms have been constructed as interpretations of violence (Girard, 1972). In this sense, violence lies at the foundation of social theory, insofar as its paradigms can be regarded as answers to the following question: how can violence be reduced or neutralized to enable social life to exist? It would appear that, despite the more or less modern and sophisticated character of such theories, the intellectual scenarios applied are always the same.

1. Control and Integration

The whole of what, for simplicity's sake, could be called classical or functionalist sociology asserts that violence is central to human nature, and that it is the function of socialization and social control to eradicate this violence—these forces of destruction, this death wish. No one has propounded this theory so forcefully as Durkheim, who conceives human nature as fundamentally driven by the infinite nature of desires and tells us that anomie opens a Pandora's box to release violence, suicide, and so on. Human desires cannot be limited or controlled by man himself; society has to take that responsibility, using the weapons of education and social control. In other words, violence arises when society steps back; when moral education is no longer capable of compelling individuals to control their instincts. We may note that psychoanalysis has taken this same view by defining the structure of the personality as the confrontation between the libido and morality. The individual can escape violence only to the extent that he fully accepts a social law that suppresses direct violence and allows it to be channeled to and sublimated in cultural activities.

This very long-established idea has appeared in countless different forms in every theory of social integration and control. It dominates the theories, evolved by the Chicago School, of delinquency as a form of social disorganization; delinquency and violence occur when individuals are no longer enmeshed in the socialization and control networks of traditional communities, but have not yet passed into the control of those sectors of society that have already been modernized (Shaw and McKay, 1940; Thrasher, 1936). The theory of relative frustration evolved by Graham and Gurr is very largely based on the same type of reasoning (Graham & Gurr, 1979). Violence emerges when the divide between aspirations and the means of achieving them becomes too wide, in other words when the adjustment of standards and ends is undermined, either because a group undergoes a rapid decline or because its aspirations become higher. In every case, violence is perceived as the product of a weakness of social integration, as a *retour du refoulé* (return of the repressed), or as a decline of 'civilization.' Elias has developed a theory of modernization perceived as the eradication of violence by the very process of civilization, the replacement of external social control exercised by institutions, the internalization of rules of good behavior and courtesy, or the actual regulation of violence, for example in sports (Elias, 1973). In all these theories, violence is seen as a 'natural condition' which society neutralizes and diverts to its own ends. Society is a machine for eliminating violence because education is moral in nature, teaching the individual to control himself and to defer the gratification of his needs and drives.

Let it be clear from the outset that the strength of this paradigm derives from the fact that it is an intellectual and academic structuring of beliefs and perceptions that are or have become commonplace. We need only study press reactions or the friendly chat that accompanies violent news stories, especially those featuring young people, to see a reflection of the crisis in family life, the decline in parental authority and moral values, to hear the denunciation of the degeneracy of morals and education. Plato was advancing this type of argument over 2000 years ago, and we know that any authoritarian response to violence is based on this implied reasoning: Violence occurs when the moral socialization of the individual declines.

2. Violence and Legitimacy

If "man is a wolf to man," as Hobbes put it, social life is possible only to the extent that each individual relinquishes some of his own violence in order to submit to a stronger violence, a greater violence, the violence of the sovereign. For Hobbes, moral socialization was not enough to eradicate violence; it was also necessary for violence by the state, a legitimate violence, to confiscate and prohibit private violence. Because the state has a monopoly of legitimate violence, the cycle of private violence and vendetta can be broken. Hence, the problem of violence is less one of socialization than one of the legitimacy of authority. The unleashing of private and social violence is caused by the weakness of authority, and above all by its lack of legitimacy. The Weberian problem of legitimacy has a place in this line of analysis because it defines legitimacy as approbation of the use of force. Authority is legitimate when the power it imposes is accepted by those who are subjugated to it and see it as just. Violence arises when there is a crisis of legitimacy; when the authority of the police, the legal system, the state, and, in general terms, all controlling institutions is no longer accepted, no longer recognized as just. Tilly has shown that outbreaks of violence occur when the state is too weak to oppose them and opportunities for success become apparent (Tilly, 1975).

This analysis, like the previous one, forms part of the natural sociology of the actors. It is a commonplace, too, to explain violence among young people as being caused by the decline of authority, reduced fear of the police, and the crisis of authority. Behind most urban unrest lie errors or crimes committed by police officers, blunders that prove to young rioters and local inhabitants that the police and the justice system are devoid of legitimacy, representing nothing more than the forces of unjust repression. As a consequence, violence directed against the police, as the force of illegitimacy, itself becomes legitimate.

3. Violence and Advantage

Analyses that deal in terms of crisis and legitimacy are based on a pessimistic system of anthropology: Since man is 'by nature' violent and evil, education and authority constitute a social system capable of providing a counterweight to these forces of destruction. In this case, violence is perceived as an irrational, expressive force—an aggressive drive that can be stopped by nothing except morality and the fear of a legitimate social order. But it may also be considered that violence is not just the physical expression of an attitude: it may also be a rational form of action, one means among others of attaining certain ends.

This analysis applies to much of that delinquency whose violence appears to be only an unlawful means of obtaining certain goals (Cusson, 1989). The situation is just as if the delinquent were a businessman for whom violence is one among several possible forms of action when he operates in an illegal market, a market in which the law and mutual trust cannot control conflicts. In the case of gangs defending their territories and trying to control drug markets, violence—like cunning and corruption—is a 'normal' means of action. Similarly, political violence is not necessarily irrational: it may be a way of gaining access to the political stage, and it may also force the actors to choose sides, or it may attract media attention to a cause. As Hirschman has shown, anyone who cannot play the quiet game of integrity has little alternative but to choose between retreat and violence (Hirschman, 1972). Violent demonstrations and terrorism cannot be reduced to forms of despair, cries for help: they are also action strategies, ways in which political entrepreneurs mobilize resources.

Here again, this type of analysis does find an echo in the spontaneous sociology of the actors. Delinquency and violence are often interpreted as 'normal' means of reducing the tension experienced by certain actors between the common values of a society and the unequal resources available to individuals or groups. When a society extols the virtues of consumption and participation, say many theorists, is it surprising that the least favored and least understood groups should resort to violence? In this case, violence is not so much the consequence of a crisis of socialization as the result of clinging to the dominant standards, a form of frustrated conformism (Merton, 1965). It should be noted that this theory of violence holds that the violent actors have been oversocialized to comply with the dominant values, which explains their frustration, whereas the theories of integration hold that violence is the result of anomie.

4. Violence and Revolt

There is a whole tradition, closer to Rousseau than to Hobbes, which considers that violence is not 'natural' to man but is a response to violence experienced. Taking this view, violence may be just in that it is a response to unjust violence, to the oppression or denial of the actor. For more than a century, the more or less Marxist revolutionary myth has constantly held that some forms of violence could be legitimate as giving rise to a more just and less violent social order. The manifest violence of the oppressed is nothing but a response to violence experienced. From this standpoint, violence arises from the absence of a recognized conflict; it is the form of expression for social actors whose existence as legitimate actors is not identified or accepted; it is the way in which those actors enter institutional political life (Moore, 1978). Before their violence becomes a social movement, the "primitive rebels" are regarded as delinquents and madmen (Hobsbawm, 1965).

The history of the labor movement is that of a social actor born of violent unrest in response to violence experienced. The first strikes and the first demonstrations are riots and revolts comprising a mixture of moral protest, demands for freedom from poverty, and delinquent conduct. One man's terrorist is another man's liberator. All these forms of action are perceived not as social conflicts but as instances of deviance, social explosions created by 'dangerous classes,' and it was not until several decades had passed that the labor movement came to be seen as a political and social actor, gradually integrated into the political system (Thompson, 1966). In fact, violence occurs when conflict is impossible, when the dominated actors do not find expression as antiestablishment actors. Violence is a response to the negation of individuals denied by domination; it is seen as the only available resource in cases where the classes of social domination ignore the existence of individuals by reducing them to the faces and stigmata of domination. When the identity of the slave is entirely merged into the stigma imposed upon him by his master, he can find release only by killing his master (Fanon, 1961). The impossibility of conflict leaves no room for anything but hatred and rage, and delinquency takes on from the outset the responsibility for social revolution, while those in power endeavor to reduce revolution to the status of delinquency.

The fact that revolutionary movements have created more totalitarianism than liberty, and the further fact that revolutionary eschatologies have been replaced by forms of religious radicalism and fundamentalism, do not necessarily invalidate this analysis of certain forms of violence. Moreover, here again, spontaneous sociology willingly resorts to this type of interpretation when confronted by the need to explain the collective violence of urban unrest, the revolution of the "wretched of the earth," whose intolerable situation makes violent revolt understandable if not necessarily tolerable.

These four explanations of juvenile violence are to be found to different degrees in every analysis: urban violence among the young comes from the crisis in education, authority's lack of legitimacy, the delinquent economy, and ultimately the revolt of the young against the injustice done to them. All sociological analyses, to a greater or lesser extent, advance these four models in different combinations. How can these explanations be combined?

II. TOLERATED DEVIANCE AND SOCIAL CONTROL

Violence particularly favors the theme of 'always something new,' something unheard-of, the exceptional nature of violence, especially among the young, which never fails to surprise one generation after another. For as far back as our historical memory extends, contemporary witnesses and chroniclers have never ceased to complain about violence among the young (Chesnais, 1981). In fact, adolescence has always been perceived as a 'dangerous' stage of life, imbued with the risk of excesses of all kinds—social, political, sexual, etc. There is nothing very new about that, except that highly integrated societies—'communities'—have found a special way of responding to these types of violence: *tolerated deviance*.

It is as if traditional societies had been able to construct times and places where youth could violate the rules without this deviance posing a serious threat to the social order. To a large extent, this violence has been ritualized and tolerated through festivals, carnivals, and rites of passage. Sometimes, Shorter tells us, these forms of tolerated deviance have been especially violent; it was not unusual for patronal feasts and carnivals to leave a few bodies in their wake (Shorter, 1975). Within highly integrated societies, confident in their standards and capable of exercising tight social control, there were places and times at which those standards could be blithely violated. Within the most integrated and conservative societies, such excesses or outbreaks of juvenile violence are tolerated. We need only think of the episodes of violence in the colleges of England, the medieval universities, or the German universities of the nineteenth century. Again, we have instances of tolerated violence in barracks life, craft guilds, and village fetes.

Not only were such cases of violence regarded as 'safety valves' but they were encouraged, as a way of putting the virility and courage of young men to the test. Basically, traditional societies, better integrated than our own, were able to come to terms with a paradox. On the one hand, they condemned deviance, but on the other, they encouraged the young to put the law to the test by violating standards. This kind of violence contributed to the social integration of the actors. In the villages of France, a brawl after the village dance was all part of the tradition, and the villagers shut their eyes to it with a certain pride in the courage of 'their' young people, those who fought to defend the honor of the village. This kind of juvenile violence has long formed part of popular culture, as with the brawling among football club supporters in working-class England (Pearson, 1983). In this connection, it is worth noting the ambivalent attitude of American culture to juvenile gangs. The gangs are condemned for their violence and their excesses, but at the same time, they are tolerated and their standing is enhanced because they put the courage and solidarity of the young to the test. Adults condemn the violence of the young, their ordeal-style games, yet there are few conversations during which those same adults can refrain from boasting of their own juvenile violence: they call upon young people, *simultaneously*, to fight and not to fight (Dubet, 1987). In fact, much of the violence of the young derives from social integration and, from that angle, the most integrated societies are not the least violent.

This concept of violence seems under threat today from the decline of traditional societies, communities, and their processes of social control. Violence associated with 'mechanical solidarity' cannot survive the breakdown of the community. That is not necessarily to say that such violence has become more extreme and more dangerous, but that it has moved beyond the old controlling systems. When the individualistic, 'hygienistic,' and 'civilized' self-controlled cultural models of the middle classes become broader, all these forms of violence are literally no longer understood (Elias & Dunning, 1986). The teachers of the middle classes no longer understand the traditional violence of their pupils; they can no longer 'read' it as tolerated deviance but perceive it as outbreaks of savagery and barbarism. There is nothing new about violence among football supporters, especially in Britain, but it can no longer claim to be an aspect of sport, now that sport has become a mass event, a televised spectacle whose function is to stage moderate passions and which relies upon a predetermined script (Dunning et al., 1989). In a society where the middle classes have universalized their standards, surviving instances of tolerated violence will be interpreted as 'blind' violence. If such violence seems particularly violent, it is partly because the communities that determined its framework are in no position to exert the social control that formerly kept it within acceptable limits. Tolerated deviance requires a high degree of cultural and social connivance, dense social networks, and many forms of intervention on many levels. What was possible in villages and working-class communities is no longer possible in big cities dominated by large blocks of flats or residential suburbs. In such places, families hardly know each other. At all events, they do not know each other sufficiently well to establish a diffuse kind of social control, a spontaneous system of regulation. Once they are outside their own families, children and adolescents no longer belong to anyone. No one has authority to intervene in their games when they get out of hand. Informal social control has been replaced by the professional control of the social workers, teachers, police, concierges, and is always poorly adapted to the conduct of the young. It takes the form of excessive reaction to behavior that is not serious, or lack of action when the behavior has become serious. Very often, the only form it takes in the inner cities is an aggressive confrontation between young people and the police. Lawbreaking in many forms occurs: damage to public property, graffiti, offensive language, provocation, etc. The controlling authorities take action too late. The result is a climate of violence and insecurity linked to minor delinquency—delinquency that is too minor to be prosecuted but is nevertheless delinquency for the local residents, who experience a sense of impotence and inevitability.

Traditional social control is giving way to processes of *social disorganization* (Shaw & McKay, 1940). The policy of settling people in large suburban estates, the effects of the economic crisis, and the ascendancy of the mass culture have destroyed popular cultures. They are no long capable of providing areas of tolerated deviance, shared by all the inhabitants. Not only is deviance among young people increasing, but it seems to be uncontrollable and to involve younger and younger children (Roché, 1996). Even though our societies extol childhood and youth, they are no longer able to provide children and young people with acceptable spaces of their own. Where it was once possible for the young to have an independent life of their own, controlled by the community, we now have policies and institutions responsible for supervising the young. Leisure activities and games are more and more organized, yet this public activity is unable to provide effective compensation for the defects of social disorganization arising from the destruction of the traditional popular culture.

The bottom line is that the modern city, because it is the scene of the migratory process and because it breaks down the traditional links of solidarity, gives rise to an 'anomic' form of juvenile violence. More specifically, the modern city weakens diffuse social control and the tolerated expression of violence among the young. Not only are young people, perhaps, more violent but, more importantly, that violence is less contained.

III. FROM CRISIS TO CONFLICT, UNREST AND RAGE

In the 1960s, the black ghettos of major American cities experienced outbreaks of racial unrest in which groups of young people were both perpetrators and victims (Feagin & Hahn, 1973). This collective violence is generally a response to violence and police provocation, and it combines elements of delinquency and political protest. European societies have not been spared such forms of juvenile violence. During the summer of 1981, a few months after France had elected a socialist President of the Republic, there was a series of outbreaks of unrest in the suburbs of Lyons. This marked the start of a period of unrest that occurred over and over again in various urban districts until it became commonplace. France experienced urban outbreaks comparable to those seen in Great Britain and the United States, although their seriousness and level of violence were not comparable with the American unrest. It goes without saying that this kind of violence no longer has anything to do with the model of tolerated deviance or the crisis of social control; it is an 'infrapolitical' violence, closer to the wildcat strike than to juvenile play. By 'infrapolitical' we mean that this violence has overtones of social criticism, the rejection of domination and exclusion, but that it is not associated with any political agenda, debate, or organization. It lies between delinquency and organized political action; between deviance and social movement.

The scenario for this unrest is always the same. It begins with an incident involving the police. They are accused of brutality, of having protected an aggressor or killer of young people, of being guilty of racist acts or language, etc. As a result, the young people burn a few cars, damage a few social facilities, attack the local shopping center. They destroy the district in which they themselves live, committing acts of vandalism and delinquency. They fight the police who are trying to restore order. Very frequently, the riots take place in the presence of TV cameras and microphones, which record events as if they were theatrical performances. What is the meaning of these images? What is the meaning of this language used by the young to give vent to their hatred?[1]

There is an essential expressive aspect of unrest. It is the theatrical expression of the *rage* of the young people in deprived areas. What does this rage mean, and what form does it take? The notion of a protest against injustice is not a sufficient explanation; after all, there are plenty of other kinds of injustice that do not give rise to this kind of violence. In Europe, urban unrest, the return to the 'emotions' of the nineteenth century, are mainly explicable in terms of the decline of class-consciousness and militant labor organizations. For many years, working-class consciousness provided a focus for the anger of the exploited and gave them a purpose and an organization (Dubet, 1987). That working-class consciousness was first and foremost a cognitive framework. It made it possible to interpret society, to explain to the actors the reasons for their misfortune, and to point the finger at those responsible: the governing classes, by whatever name. Also, working-class consciousness was based on a sense of pride: through that agency, the dominated and the exploited could perceive themselves as essential elements of society, groups who were indispensable for the production of wealth and value. Finally, working-class consciousness was able to create a sense of solidarity and to result in forms of organized collective action. In a word, it was able to transform anger into revolt, and revolt into organized action.

In the deprived suburbs, this class-consciousness is absent or greatly weakened. The number of 'workers' is declining. Working-class utopias, whether communist or socialist, hardly exist. The majority of young people are excluded from regular employment and have no sense of being industrially exploited; they cannot see that they hold any place in society. In such cases, rage seems an essential aspect of their experience; it is anger without object, without principle, without objective. It becomes a hatred directed at the adversaries within reach: The various powers closest to the actors, including those that trace their origin to the labor movement itself, and especially directed against the police as a symbol of an unjust, racist, and unacceptable social order. Their rage is directed against everyone, but most of all against themselves and against their own environment. Thus, it destroys the district and the social facilities created for the young. In many cases, indeed, the better equipped the district the more powerful the rage, because social policies enable some people to escape, while all the remainder are 'buried' in their exclusion. Everything is turned around, and the 'allies' of the young, those who can help them but who seem impotent or dishonest, themselves become a target for this rage.

We need to understand that rage is all the stronger because it is based on a paradoxical aspect of social exclusion in the most modern societies. The suburban young are not 'marginalized;' they are not trapped in minority cultures or cultures of poverty. Many of them are immigrants or the children of immigrants; and most of them have very strongly assimilated the essence of the current standards and values of their host society (Tribalat, 1995). The 'subculture' of the suburban young is not exotic, marginal, or traditional, but takes the form of a kind of adaptation to the constraints of relative poverty and economic exclusion. Young people participate fully in the cultural models of the mass society dominated by the middle classes; rap culture is not an 'ethnic' culture, but one that mingles the expression of rage by the excluded young and the most caricaturistic emblems of mass consumption with the display of 'designer labels' on clothing; these young people are both socially marginalized and culturally overintegrated. They have spent long periods in

---

[1]Mathieu Kazowitz's film *La haine* tells the story of a group of suburban young people carried away by this rage; it scored a great success in France.

full-time education, despite their failures; there are various social services to take care of them; they are consumers of fashions and youth cultures. Thus, the sense of social exclusion is all the keener the more the actors are culturally assimilated. This tension, analyzed by Merton, between the ascendancy of a mass culture and the mechanisms of social exclusion gives rise to various types of deviant conduct (Cohen, 1955; Cloward & Ohlin, 1960; Merton, 1965). Some withdraw into a subculture of marginalization; the neighborhood protects them, they are no longer involved in the game. Others opt for a deviant conformism and seek a strategy of integration within delinquency. But all share the same rage, the same purposeless anger which is all the stronger as the gap widens between symbolic and cultural assimilation, on the one hand, and social exclusion, on the other. The racism and contempt directed against the suburban young play an essential role in this mechanism. They constantly reactivate the contradiction between a society that exalts egalitarian and democratic models and a social exclusion emphasized by racism, unemployment, academic failure, disdain, and so on.

This tension is not only social and structural; it becomes an 'intrapsychical' component. Violence then becomes an 'esthetic,' a projection of oneself, an aspect of 'personality.' At the same time, as it is the expression of the destruction of a social subject, it is a form of resistance by the individual who feels constantly under threat because he cannot manage to conform to his own image of himself. Provocation, offensive language, the unpredictable nature of attitudes, the obsession with 'face' and 'honor' dominate the social behavior of these young people. Each individual defends his honor and 'face' as the last bastions of personality, when there is no longer any secure social footing to provide a foundation for personal autonomy. Violence, however, cannot succeed in constructing a collective identity because it contributes to the permanent self-destruction of the social existence of the suburbs. Violence is a short-circuited social movement, expressing both the claim to be a recognized individual and the destruction of that individual within violence itself.

This is a recent phenomenon which explains the violence directed by young people against the social services, against activity and leisure centers, and against the various training structures and forms of assistance for job seekers. These young people have the sense of being invited to participate in and become part of society, although these various institutions have no real capacity to accomplish that task. Social facilities symbolize both the desire to integrate and the inability to do so. Sometimes young people may even have the feeling that social workers are 'profiting' from their situation to develop their own activities without offering them any opportunity for real integration. So it is unsurprising that urban unrest very often breaks out in the districts best provided with social services and social workers.

Unrest is not only expressive. It also has an instrumental aspect, insofar as it constructs a balance of power in the districts that favors the young. Various social services, educational and training personnel, and organizers of leisure and cultural activities take charge of the housing projects with a view to helping the young. These activities and policies are broadly positive, preventing the more extreme excesses and the creation of ghettos. At the same time, however, these policies emphasize the paradoxes of exclusion, because they do not result in the social integration desired by the young, because they do not provide jobs, and because they form part of a 'colonial' relationship. A great many institutional actors, most of whom do not live locally, are employed to take charge of the 'sensitive' neighborhoods; they distribute aid and support in accordance with a professional 'handicap system' (a grid from which personal and social handicaps can be read), which reduces the actors to the mere sum of their problems and difficulties. In these cases, unrest is tantamount to a 'wildcat strike' because it enables the local young to conduct a dialogue with the public services and local politicians. Outbreaks of unrest do not occur in the poorest, most run-down districts. Their end product is a kind of acknowledgment and negotiation designed to achieve the opening of a facility, changes in the police, or various other concessions. Leaders come to the fore, the struggle becomes part of the official record, an appeal to public opinion becomes possible, and elected representatives are all the more likely to yield because the unrest gives a very negative image of their community. Unrest and violence take the form of resources of collective action that are more or less controlled by the young; they are the last resort for those who cannot go on strike and who carry no electoral weight. They are all the more effective now that young people have learned to exploit the media, the existence of television significantly restricting opportunities for large-scale recourse to violent repression.

These forms of violence are rooted in a strong sense of social domination. Many districts feel abandoned and forsaken on the outskirts of the cities, preventing their inhabitants from achieving the full and complete social life to which they aspire. The symbols of this marginalization, especially public transport, then become targets for a juvenile violence that fluctuates between horseplay and social protest. Young people protest against second-class status and stigma, but ultimately contribute to the production of the stigma. Violence may be seen, paradoxically, as an aspiration to integration and participation. Nor should we pass over the fact that young people from immigrant backgrounds encounter a racialization of social relations which finds daily expression in their search for accommodation, job seeking, relations with the police, and such routine aspects of social life as access to leisure facilities. In fact, urban violence is not—as it is too often claimed to be—the product of a phenomenon of immigration, but of the formation of minorities. The vast majority of young people in the suburbs are no longer immigrants, or never were. Through the effect of the mass culture and the influence of school they participate fully in the common culture and share the same aspirations as the others, so that they are no longer immigrants. Yet, at the same time, these young people encounter more or less direct expressions of segregation and racism. The desire for unachievable integration turns to violence when these young people find that "society does not want them" (Wieviorka et al., 1999).

IV. BETWEEN TERRITORIES AND DELINQUENCY

Rage may be regarded as a pure form of violence that may find expression in various directions. Those directions often become confusingly mingled, but they can still be identified.

a) The first is a form of appropriation of the urban district as an autonomous enclave. Despite the deterioration of the suburban projects and despite the stigma attaching to them, young people very often have a positive relationship with their home district. It is the arena of their social life, their loves, and their friendships. They have all known each other from childhood; they were all educated there. For those young people who come from an immigrant background or from one of the various minorities and who no more belong to their parents' society of origin than they do to global society, which appears not to want them, their home district is their real place of belonging, the location of their shared roots and identities. Stigmatized and rejected by their environment, they also see the district as a protective, familiar space, a territory that has to be defended.

According to the models of the Chicago School, this results in the formation of gangs of young people who see themselves as the best defenders of their district (Thrasher,

1936). Often, these gangs can have an ethnic dimension, black or Arab, but in essence they are the expression of local solidarity among the young. They provide an integration and an affective security which neither family nor job is now capable of supplying. The gangs are not necessarily delinquent and violent, but they can only exist within a logic where territories have to be defended, often against other organized bands. The gang asserts itself and survives in a form of more or less open warfare with other gangs, an interplay of provocation, attack, and defense. We in Europe are unfamiliar with 'gang warfare' on a scale comparable to what happens in the United States, but the same territorial logics apply. There are certain symbolic locations—open spaces, stands at sports grounds—that have to be defended, as do the girls who 'belong' to the district. ... The gang sometimes resorts to violence because it becomes embroiled in an exchange of challenges and provocations. When the gang moves outside the district, it also has to display its strength and courage, in other words its violence: it refuses to pay fares on public transport, challenges other travelers, indulges in provocation. ... It sets the scene for potential violence.

b) The district is also a more or less protected territory, a place of solidarity and secrecy, fertile soil for delinquent activity. From this angle, it offers many more or less deviant resources. In many cases, it shelters a drug trade and a variety of networks in which many people are more or less intensively involved. The disorganized zone is protected from police intervention, and local residents shut their eyes because they fear reprisals and also because they profit from the proceeds of unlawful activities. Stolen property is sold, dirty money is laundered. These delinquent activities are rarely violent, and in any case, they call for a discreet form of violence so as not to run the risk of rejection by the local people and intervention by the police.

Violence, like cunning and dexterity, is a resource of delinquency. Its purpose is to ensure silence, the complicity of witnesses, and the 'consent' of victims. It plays an important part in the neighborhoods by increasing the sense of insecurity, because the local people feel they are not protected by public institutions or the police. It turns the district in upon itself and locks it into a spiral of deterioration, because it is in the interests of the delinquents to cut the district off from its surroundings and make it a protected territory—a 'ghetto.'

Organized delinquency and youth gangs seem to be antonyms, like instrumentalism and expressivity. But it is very clear, too, that these two logics are constantly mingled, and that many actors participate in both at once. However, not all the members of the gangs are delinquent, and not all delinquents belong to gangs.

V. SOCIAL VIOLENCE AND POLITICAL VIOLENCE

Can social violence be converted to political action? The question arises every time France experiences a wave of terrorism, and the story of Khaled Kelkal, the young man from the Lyons suburbs who became a bomber and was killed by the French police in 1995, illustrates this type of deviant career, which resembles that of certain leaders of the Black Panthers. This young Arab, the product of a suburban housing estate, gradually drifted into delinquency and then, after spending time in prison during which he came into contact with Islamic militants, turned to political violence and terrorism. Can this story, which is all the clearer because Khaled Kelkal gave his own account of it, be regarded as a typical one?

The life story of Khaled Kelkal is exemplary in more than one respect (Loch, 2000).

First, it is the story of a man who was a well-behaved child and adolescent, completed a conventional school education, and then failed to find a steady job. It is also the story of a youth from the suburbs who was involved in the local unrest and revolt following the murder of a young man that was blamed on a police officer. Finally, it is the story of a young man embarking on a career of delinquency with a series of attacks. The story of Khaled Kelkal is also typical in terms of his discovery of his culture, origins, and ethnicity. He tells how, being neither French nor Algerian, he identified and asserted himself as a Muslim, not so much as a return to his roots as in a form of protest against racism and segregation. This self-identification was initially an expression of his rejection of domination and disdain. His career resembles those of the leaders of the American black radical movement, Malcolm X for example. Self-identification is first a rejection of racism, a reversal of the stigma: since you don't accept me when I want to be like you, I will conform to the stereotype you reject and be proud of it. In different ways, Hegel, Sartre, and Fanon have provided good explanations of this phenomenon of stigma conversion. No doubt the same process will recur in many suburban young from immigrant backgrounds: an identity that is perceived as a cause for shame is reversed to become a proud awareness of being black or Muslim, and these young people are certainly influenced by the black American model.

However, an active move to political violence requires something else: it involves a political input from outside the actual experience of the young. In this case, it was the political violence of the Algerian fundamentalists. In other cases, we have seen the beginnings of an alliance between the young subproletariat of Italy and the terrorist students in the mid-1970s, under the auspices of "Comrade P 38" (Wieviorka, 1988). But this was an encounter between two independent phenomena: one purely social, the other purely political; one a product of the suburbs, the other of the radical lower middle class. This encounter gave rise to political violence. It can be admitted, though, that the violence of the suburban young contains the seeds of political violence.

The same argument can be advanced in connection with young skinheads. Their situation is not very different. They are often members of the young white proletariat, every bit as excluded and disoriented as the young immigrants. They cannot lean either on a working-class community or on class-consciousness. Their substitute for an analysis of the social representation of their situation is a racist representation of the world. The struggle of the working and middle classes is replaced by the race struggle and the defense of the nation. These young people form racist gangs, go on 'immigrant hunts,' and confront the immigrants' rap with racist, 'white' rock. They go looking for trouble and aggression. However, their contact with political violence is confined to their encounters with far-right groups and ideologists who can give this social hatred a sense of purpose. The story of the young skinhead stewards of the French National Front who murdered a Moroccan worker during a party demonstration parallels that of Khaled Kelkal. They are an acute and extreme manifestation of the shift of a section of the working class toward the tenets of the far right. They form an important section of the 'hard-line' members of various football supporters' clubs who transform matches into racist demonstrations.

In the cases just mentioned, we can see a fundamental process of change in industrial society. That society has long seen itself as being organized around class relationships. Social conflicts were initially labor conflicts, and the political parties identified themselves as representatives of class interests. This type of social representation and organization does not assume that industrial society was more just or more harmonious than what we have today. But it did supply a framework for collective action and for identities.

The violence of the urban young, whether French or immigrant by origin, takes us outside this framework. Relationships of inclusion and exclusion replace relationships of exploitation, and, within a dominant mass culture, new cultural and social identities form that sometimes invoke ethnic and racist views of the social relationships.

VI. VIOLENCE IN SCHOOLS

The analysis of school violence that has grown up over the past few years highlights the diversity of meanings of juvenile violence and the meaning of the major sociological paradigms of the analysis of violence. France has been familiar with school violence for some years now (Dubet, 1994). There have been more and more incidents in secondary and high schools, mainly but not exclusively in deprived areas. The new situation is not solely concerned with the escalation of violence but also with the propensity of the teaching staff to denounce it, bring it to public attention, and report it to the authorities. This violence receives much attention in the media, all the more so because schools have long been seen as places protected from the various social 'diseases.'

In 1993, the following incidents of violence were recorded (Debarbieux, 1996): one pupil murdered, 771 complaints of assaults and injuries among pupils, 983 charges of extortion, 244 of indecency. In the same year, one teacher was murdered by a pupil and 210 complaints of physical violence against teachers were filed, while there were 770 cases of deliberate damage to facilities and 3,694 cases of straightforward theft. For years, violence in schools has increased constantly, both in terms of complaints by teachers and pupils to the legal authorities and in their depiction of school life. Safety has become the main concern (Debarbieux, 1999). The figures are significant and show that violence in schools is a genuine phenomenon. At the same time, though, they have to be seen in the context of the size of the population group concerned: nearly 10 million pupils and several hundred thousand teachers. School, then, is not a dangerous place, even if this new violence gives cause for concern, all the more so in that the number of incidents appears to be increasing and the tendency to report them to the authorities is also becoming stronger.[2] Rather than straightforward and readily identifiable incidents of violence, the pattern is of a growing climate of violence in schools, with teachers calling for disciplinary action and specific training, and many acts that are not strictly speaking violent being interpreted as forms of diffuse violence: absenteeism, rowdiness in class, illegal activities, etc. These forms of violence are very different in nature, and the logical principles we have identified recur in them.

The spreading of education to the masses has been the major phenomenon of the last twenty years. A great many pupils go on to secondary education. Although the traditional school was based on a mechanism for the early separation of the academic public from the social public, a very large number of establishments have to deal with heterogeneous school populations, populations whose expectations and cultural models are not necessarily in line with those of the institution itself. The teaching staff can no longer rely upon automatic, implicit cooperation, and perceive many pupils as "outsiders" (Dubet & Martuccelli, 1996). Mass education has given rise to severe deregulation of relations between staff and pupils, in which the 'motivation' of pupils has become a central problem. To this phenom-

---

[2] These figures have to be regarded as indicators more than as a reflection of violence; as with any delinquency statistics, there are problems with the way they are arrived at and with the number of unreported cases.

enon must be added two others. The first relates to the intake of adolescents and young people into schools, since all pupils now spend a long period in school and the new student bodies identify with a youth culture far removed from the academic world. The second phenomenon concerns the intrusion of social problems into schools: when long-term, full-time education was the preserve of a few privileged pupils, schools were relatively well screened from social problems, domestic crises, racism, unemployment, and juvenile violence. Today, schools have to cope with these problems directly.

The first aspect of violence in schools is a direct consequence of the deregulation of the system. The social and cultural gap between staff and pupils has widened in many establishments. The 'colonial' aspects of the staff–student relationship have become more marked. The areas of 'tolerated deviance' have dwindled between middle-class teachers and pupils from the lower classes whose behavior is interpreted as symptomatic of social disease. It is true that many pupils are not prepared to abide by the ground rules. Tranquillity and silence can no longer be taken for granted, attention to lessons is no longer automatic, and teachers have to commit themselves actively to developing a relationship that no longer establishes itself. The traditional mischief has been replaced by agitation and noise; the lifestyle of the young invades the schools and most teachers see this behavior as violent. It is not so much violence in the strict sense as conduct that is perceived as violent because it disrupts school life.

The second aspect of violence in schools is not strictly characteristic of school life: it originates from the importation of delinquent, violent behavior into schools. The life of the district invades the school, bringing with it its aspects of theft, offensive language, assault, and provocation between groups of young people. Schools in the working-class districts are directly confronted with the forms of behavior endemic in those districts. Here again, schools are destabilized by behavior, which demands a return to traditional discipline, prompts thoughts of cooperation with the police and justice authorities, and, especially, encourages teachers to change their role. Violent children are also, in most cases, themselves the victims of violence and ill-treatment, they come from poor and broken homes, and their teachers can no longer disregard the children that their pupils are.

The third aspect of violence is the most significant from a sociological standpoint, because it is not a form of social violence invading the school but an anti-school violence, the expression of a conflict between the pupils and their school. Pupils are aggressive toward teachers, threaten them, destroy school equipment, etc. Looked at closely, this violence displays the characteristics of rage. The pupils who indulge in it do so in the wake of an incident which is perceived as a challenge: either the pupil accepts the judgments of the teachers, in which case he loses face and self-esteem, or he reacts aggressively and reverses the stigma against the school. Anti-school violence is a way of refusing to come to terms with a judgment by the school that is unacceptable to the person concerned. The democratic school pushes the paradox of integration and exclusion to its extreme. All children, who are equal in principle, are called upon to work and succeed. Those who fail to do so can only, in the long run, blame it upon their own shortcomings: lack of intellectual ability, lack of zeal and industry, lack of virtue, etc. School both integrates and rejects; it requires the individual to see himself as responsible for his own progress and, therefore, for his own failure. It is this need to see oneself as the author of one's own existence that is the courage of the individualist ethos of democratic societies. Confronted by this obligation, pupils who fail have a choice of two solutions only: 'exit' or 'voice,' retreat or protest. But as organized and civil protest is hardly possible for a person who is responsible for his own misfortune, only violence remains.

Thus, violence within school cannot be reduced to the social violence that enters it from outside. There are also forms of violence directed against the school itself, with attacks on staff, damage to premises, and aggression against the school as such. These forms of violence are, in fact, responses to the perceived violence of the school itself. That violence does not lie within the burden of discipline, or even within the cultural and social divide that separates teachers from their pupils. Its roots are in a more complex, more internalized phenomenon, whose structure recurs in other fields. Mass education calls upon all pupils to become involved in an extended period of education and mobilizes substantial resources to ensure their success. However, from the beginning of high school, many pupils find that it gradually relegates them toward careers and courses that are far distant from the hopes of success that mass education had created in them. They feel, then, that they are both drawn into the school and rejected by it because of their poor performance. In this case, either they cease to cooperate and withdraw from school life, or they develop forms of anti-school violence as a way of saving face and dignity by relying on the youth culture 'against' the school culture.

The violent behavior of young people in urban society fluctuates between a number of different models and calls for various types of explanation. To a large extent, it is the product of modern life itself and of the continuous weakening of community ties and of the social control that the group exerts over young people. The consequences of these 'anomic' aspects of modern life are many and paradoxical. As youth continues to become longer and longer, the areas of 'tolerated deviance' become narrower, and the violence of the young no longer contributes to the legitimate culture of the working class, but has become an intolerable disease. But this inadequate integration generates independent practices of integration, the best known and most spectacular of which are those of the gangs of young people who re-create social ties where the community is no longer adequate to do so. However, the youth community is a powerful vector of violence because it depends on 'warlike' relations with other youth gangs and the police, territorial control, and a weak capability for collective regulation. 'Tribal' wars among the young integrate young people with their environment through ties of violence.

In addition to this expressive form of violence, the more instrumental aspects of violence in the networks formed within the delinquent economy must also be considered. Violence is not just a form of community expression but a rational resource of action when illegal economic activity involves replacing the law with violence. However, unlike the warlike violence of the gangs, the violence of the delinquent economy is controlled and targeted, restrained, and for this reason is often better tolerated by the population of the cities.

With unrest and revolt among young people in the working-class districts, the ghettos in the United States, and the suburban housing projects in Europe, there is no doubt that the paradigms of crisis and rational action are no longer adequate. No doubt this violence is both expressive and instrumental, but it is above all an embryonic form of social movement, a protest against what is regarded as intolerable injustice and inequality. This violence results from the contradiction into which the young people from these districts are cast: they are socially excluded but culturally integrated. Their situation is all the more intolerable in that it cannot be interpreted politically as a conflict. It is more a manifestation of rage than a revolt against the 'system.'

Finally, all these forms of violence pose a problem of legitimacy, as is demonstrated by the case of the school violence referred to in this contribution. When traditional forms of legitimacy are insufficient to justify order, not only do young people cease to believe in institutions, but they perceive them as mere tools of oppression and marginalization. School, justice, and above all the police then cease to be regarded as legitimate institutions and become the machinery of violence, in view of which the violence of the young seems to them legitimate by default.

Translated by Richard Sharp

REFERENCES

Chesnais, Jean-Claude. (1981). *Histoire de la violence en Occident de 1800 à nos jours*. Paris: R. Laffont.
Cloward, Richard A., & Lloyd E. Ohlin. (1960). *Delinquency and Opportunity. A Theory of Delinquent Gangs*. New York: The Free Press.
Cohen, Albert. (1955). *Delinquent Boys. The Culture of the Gang: A Theory of Delinquent Gangs*. New York: The Free Press.
Cusson, Maurice. (1989). *Croissance et décroissance du crime*. Paris: Presses Universitaires de France.
Debarbieux, Eric. (1996). *La violence en milieu scolaire*. Paris: ESF.
Debarbieux, Eric. (1999). *La violence en milieu scolaire. Le désordre des choses*. Paris: ESF.
Dubet, François. (1987). *La galère. Jeunes en survie*. Paris: Fayard.
Dubet, François. (1994). Les mutations du système scolaire et les violences à l'école. *Les cahiers de la sécurité intérieure*, 15, 11–26.
Dubet, François, & Danilo Martuccelli. (1996). *A l'école. Sociologie de l'expérience scolaire*. Paris: Ed du Seuil.
Dunning, Eric, Patrick Murphy, & John Williams. (1989). *The Roots of Football Hooliganism: an Historical and Sociological Study*. London: Routledge and Kegan Paul.
Elias, Norbert. (1973). *La civilisation des mœurs*. Paris: Calmann-Lévy. [German: Elias, Norbert. (1939). *Über den Prozeß der Zivilisation*. 2 Vols. Basel: Haus zum Falken.]
Elias, Norbert, & Eric Dunning. (1986). *Quest for Excitement: Sport and Leisure in the Civilizing Process*. Oxford: Blackwell.
Fanon, Frantz. (1961). *Les damnés de la terre*. Paris: Maspéro.
Feagin, Joe R., & Harlan Hahn. (1973). *Ghetto Revolts: The Politics of Violence in American Cities*. New York: MacMillan.
Girard, René. (1972). *La violence et le sacré*. Paris: B. Grasset.
Graham, Hugh Davis, & Ted Gurr (Eds.) (1979). *Violence in America*. London, Beverly Hills: Sage Publication.
Hirschman, Albert O. (1972). *Exit, Voice and Loyalty: Responses to Decline in Firms, Organizations, and States*. Cambridge: Harvard University Press.
Hobsbawm, Eric J. (1965). *Primitive Rebels: Studies in Archaic Forms of Social Movement in the 19th and 20th Centuries*. New York, London: Norton.
Loch, Dietmar. (2000). *Jugendliche magrebinischer Herkunft zwischen Stadtpolitik und Lebenswelt. Eine Fallstudie in der französischen Vorstadt Vaulx-en-Velin*. Opladen: Leske & Budrich.
Merton, Robert K. (1965). *Social Theory and Social Structure*. New York: The Free Press.
Moore, Barrington. (1978). *Injustice: The Social Bases of Obedience and Revolt*. London: MacMillan Press.
Pearson, Geoffrey. (1983). *Hooligan: An History of Respectable Fears*. London: MacMillan.
Roché, Sebastian. (1996). *La société incivile: Qu'est-ce-que l'insécurité?* Paris: Ed du Seuil.
Shaw, Clifford R., & Henry D. McKay. (1940). *Juvenile Delinquency in Urban Areas*. Chicago: University of Chicago Press.
Shorter, Edward. (1975). *The Making of the Modern Family*. New York: Basic Books.
Thompson, Edward P. (1966). *The Making of the English Working Class*. New York: Vintage Books.
Thrasher, Frederik. (1936). *The Gang: A Study of 1,313 Gangs in Chicago*. Chicago: University of Chicago Press.
Tilly, Charles, Louise Tilly, & Richard Tilly. (1975). *The Rebellious Century: 1830–1930*. London: Dent.
Tribalat, Michèle. (1995). *Faire France: une grande enquête sur les immigrés et leurs enfants*. Paris: La Découverte.
Wieviorka, Michel. (1988). *Société et terrorisme*. Paris: Fayard.
Wieviorka, Michel, Philippe Bataille, Karin Clément, Oliver Cousin, Farhad Khosrokhavar, Séverine Labat, Éric Macé, Paola Rebughini, & Nikola Tietze. (1999). *Violence en France*. Paris: Seuil.

PART II-6

VIOLENCE DISCOURSES: IDEOLOGIES AND JUSTIFICATIONS

PART II-6-1

DISCOURSES AND IDEOLOGIES

CHAPTER II-6-1.1

Political Cultural Studies and Violence

THOMAS MEYER

I. INTRODUCTION

1. The Issue of Violence in Political Cultural Studies

Since the very inception of political science the central focus has been on the question of a binding societal order and thus on the conditions and prerequisites for its formation and maintenance. The issue of *legitimate physical violence* has thus always been at the center of political theory and research. *Max Weber's* widely accepted definition of the state as the holder of the monopoly on *legitimate violence* on its own territory underlines the basic fact that violence, meaning direct physical coercion, has never really been seen as a fundamentally problematic issue in politics and thus also in political science and political cultural studies. Rather, with rare exceptions provided by the anarchist tradition, *legitimate violence*, first and foremost that of the state, figures throughout the history of political thought as a prerequisite and guarantee of good political order. However, in both political praxis and political research there was some dispute as to which conditions were necessary to legitimize the exercise of the state monopoly of violence, and when they are met. From the tyrannicide debates in the ancient world up to the resistance and revolution theories of the early modern age, there have thus always been arguments in political theory for the view that violence against the representatives of constitutional state power can be legitimate if they have violated the recognized conditions for legitimacy. Precursors of political cultural studies from Aristotle to Montesquieu and Tocqueville speculated on the basis of historical experience and comparative observations as to whether putative "national character" and its respective political institutions make particular peoples more inclined to resolve conflicts peacefully or to habitually resort to violence.

In political cultural studies, an empirical social science with hermeneutic methodology, this is one of the central questions. Political cultural studies examines the shared collective mentalities, attitudes, deep-seated values, manners of communication, types of action, and world views which really shape and direct the behavior of members of groups in the sphere of political action. The very notion of *political culture*, the accompanying analytical concept and the first—but nevertheless fundamental—research results were introduced to political science in 1963. The pioneering study by the American researchers Gabriel Almond and Sidney Verba "The Civic Culture" (Almond & Verba, 1963) is now legendary and is considered to have been the *birth* of studies in political culture. It was an attempt to use the methods of empirical attitudinal research in a five-nation comparative study to ascertain which political cultural features predominate in societies with stable democratic traditions (United States and Great Britain) and which are to be found in societies with precarious democratic traditions (Italy, Germany, and Mexico). The actual object of the research bore no direct relationship to violence. The aim was to ascertain which long-term political orientations are to be found in different societies and how they contribute to the maintenance of a system based on democracy and the rule of law and thus to the rejection of illegitimate violence in state actions. The research concept of "political culture" seeks empirically founded answers to the questions of:

a) the connection between individual behavioral dispositions and the real political actions of large groups;
b) the role of stable, long-term action orientations of social groups that can neither be reduced to inflexible quantities (such as national character) nor are just a mere reaction to the given constellations at the time;
c) the interrelationship between societies' concrete historical experiences of crisis and the ways in which they are assimilated politically.

The comprehensive and varied research conducted subsequent to Almond and Verba's study has generally justified the hopes that political science placed in the new field of research into political culture. Research into political violence primarily examines the preconditions of violence used by oppositional forces, and the key questions for political cultural research are therefore:

a) Which orientations and mentalities handed down in discrete groups encourage advocacy of violence, propensity to violence, and use of violence in contexts of political action?
b) Which factors contribute to the development and handing down of the orientations which encourage violence?

In view of the clear relevance of these questions for political science and politics, it is surprising that they have largely been neglected or have played merely a marginal role in large-scale political cultural studies projects. Looking at the exemplary case of right-wing extremism, Armin Pfahl-Traughber (1994:66ff.) rightly pointed out that whereas the essential task of political cultural studies must be to show the key *connection* between individual or collective *dispositions to action* and real, performed *acts of political violence*, research to date has failed to address precisely this desideratum, or has not done so satisfactorily. Political culture which encourages violence plays a double causal role in the development and triggering of the propensity to violence, as shown by the example of right-wing extremism. It leads to the learning of the corresponding political attitudes in the process of socialization and, as a cultural opportunity structure, it provides the justifications and environment which determine individuals' behavior in the given action situation (Winkler, 1996:41). Nevertheless the question of political violence in the collective mentalities of political cultures has only very rarely been raised directly in research, and where this has been done, it has often only been as an aside in specialized fields such as research on right-wing extremism, xenophobia, fundamentalism, and the autonomist movement. The main contribution of the discipline itself stems from its own research approach and the input of a number of allied disciplines. It consists in the basic insight that, as a rule, in each particular political culture, conducive mentalities must join with other necessary motivational factors before the active groups *acquire* adequate motivation for the overt use of violence. Apart from the limited areas mentioned, the discipline's contribution to the issue up to now must therefore be pieced together, partly from the results of indirect research, and partly from more marginal findings.

2. Defining Political Culture and Violence

The following will consider the question as to the contribution made by *political cultural studies* to explaining *violence* in the framework of *democratic* polities. Political culture here refers to the totality of cognitive, evaluative, and emotional orientations of social groups toward established political structures. The classic study by Gabriel Almond and Sidney Verba (1963), with which research in this discipline began, did not directly address the issue of violence and the propensity to violence as a model of collective orientation—the focus here was rather on the basic structures of stable democracy. The same is also true of subsequent important studies in the discipline looking at other regions, issues, or the history of individual countries (Pye & Verba, 1965; Greiffenhagen & Greiffenhagen, 1979; Almond & Verba, 1980; Reichel, 1981, 1984; Berg-Schlosser & Rytlewski, 1993; Niedermayer & von Beyme, 1994).

Nonetheless these classic studies and the following main trends in political cultural analysis are able indirectly to offer some interesting insights into political violence, particularly into the nature and development of the basic orientations which lead to *nonviolent* political action.

A study of violence in the scope of political cultural studies first requires that the notion of violence be clarified and a definition laid down. Three different semantic variants of the notion of violence can be identified:

- The broad notion of "structural violence" coined by Johan Galtung states that the very refusal of the gratification of desires whenever gratification is possible should be considered a form of violence (Galtung, 1993:52). Although Galtung supports his extremely broad concept of violence by introducing the notion of "cultural violence", which could possibly connect up with political culture, his concept of violence would appear too broad for it to play a role in political cultural studies. When almost everything is violence, then ultimately almost nothing is violence.
- The narrow concept of *legitimate state violence* has always been one of the implicit prerequisites informing political cultural studies. Those features of a political culture which guarantee that social groups still adhere to the norms and rules of democracy in times of crisis are logically those which are underdeveloped in those political cultures which encourage violence. In this respect the notion of democracy central to political culture is indirectly of considerable importance for the question of the political cultural basis of political violence.

- In their comparative international study "Political Action", Max Kaase and Samuel H. Barnes adopted a narrower definition of violence which included a specifically political dimension: "Political violence can be defined as the use of physical force against objects or persons for political reasons." In order to make the notion applicable for empirical research on forms of political participation they add: "Almost all forms of direct political action, including many conventional ones, are, at least potentially, prone to violence" (Barnes & Kaase, 1979:44).

This more narrow definition of violence as illegitimate, physically coercive, and injurious force intruding on the integrity of persons, and also force aimed at destroying property for the attainment of political goals or for political motives is relevant when dealing with the question of the role of political culture in encouraging and using violence in contexts of political action, and this definition is taken as the basis here. The authors postulate a close relationship between forms of direct political action and the propensity to use physical violence for political ends—but it remains a different and fundamentally unresolved question, in which cases and to what extent this relationship actually exists.

II. EMPIRICAL RESULTS AND THEORETICAL APPROACHES

1. Concepts

The aim of political cultural studies when applied to the problem of political violence is to analyze and explain the *relatively stable collective mentalities and cultural dispositions which function as opportunity structures for the political actualization of violence potentials.* This aim does not extend to explaining the individual and collective dispositions to violence assumed to be present in each given case. There is a broad agreement within all the disciplines involved in explaining political violence that this can only be researched adequately by adopting interdisciplinary approaches. There is no dispute in political cultural studies as to the double pivotal role of political culture in the process of constituting political violence, and the related disciplines have correspondingly high expectations of political cultural studies. Social psychology examines the structures, experiences, and processes which typically lead to individual dispositions to violence, but it cannot explain under which specific conditions and in which particular way these can then be translated into collective acts of political violence. Sociology diagnoses the conditions of social and sociocultural life such as loss of orientation, alienation, frustration, or deprivation, and looks at how they encourage collective dispositions to violence, but it is unable to explain the conditions under which these phenomena abruptly transform into specific varieties of violent political action. The action analysis in political science examines either the real actions of collective actors using violence, such as autonomist and right-wing extremist groups, or the political constellations which encourage violence and the legitimizing ideologies invoked to justify it. However, action analysis cannot make the decisive link from here to the individual motives behind participation in these organizations, actions and ideologies. *Political cultural studies* examines the social plane where the microlevel of individual action dispositions intersects with the macrolevels of social developments and the political actions of collective actors. It looks at the long-term, habitual action orientations of collective actors, and thus the socialization processes to which members of the respective group are subjected, with the result that the political orientations handed down can become an *unquestioned opportunity structure* for those individuals. However, the notion of socialization should not be so restricted as to become deterministic. Even the primary socialization of children and adolescents is a process rich in contradictions, and the given political culture is only one formative factor alongside individual experiences and problems, albeit a very significant one in each particular social milieu. In the course of their secondary socialization, adults are then increasingly able to influence the factors which are of importance for the shaping of their mentality.

Karl Rohe (1994:1ff.) introduced the important distinction between *political socioculture* and *culture of political interpretation*. This distinction is an effective analytical tool for understanding the complex links between experiences, cultural habits, and situation-related theoretical models of interpretation. Every individual or collective disposition to protest and use violence must go through a *process of politicization* before it can be manifested in concrete forms of political action (Barnes & Kaase, 1979:46). In this politicization process, the mentalities existing in the respective reference groups play a crucial role, as do the concrete situational interpretations and options for action which follow. In this respect, the ideological interpretations which are available in the given situations appertain to the political culture of violence in the same way as the expressions of art and culture which help shape violence-oriented attitudes and activate violence potentials. It is the interpretative culture which ultimately lends currency and plausibility to the practical, effective socioculture in everyday life. It helps link handed-down mentalities with most recent social and political developments. This is particularly true because the political culture of a group always encompasses the totality of its attitudes, involving not only the cognitive, but also the evaluative and affective aspects. Songs, images, rituals, lyrics, and music have thus often contributed significantly to the emotional cohesion of political cultures, as is shown by the history of the European workers' movement. The same is true, in a different way, in the case of the contemporary xenophobic subculture.

2. Classic Empirical Results: Preconditions for Avoiding Political Violence

The issue of political cultures of violence is always posed at *two levels*, one for the respective social groups at an overall, national level, and the other for subnational groups sharing the same basic political orientations. This understanding of political violence and the role which political culture plays in its actualization and social evaluation is well illustrated by an interesting reference made by Almond and Powell to a feature of politics in Peru. The authors explain that for a long time it was an accepted element of political culture in Peru for the political elites to be put under pressure by threats of mass violence or the direct use of violence. This was so as to force them to deal with the demands of groups which had no other means of influencing the central decision-making bodies of their country's political system. At the same time such use of violence or the threat of violence was not perceived as a threat to the political system as a whole, but rather established itself as a regular and generally accepted way for disadvantaged groups to gain access to the political decision-making process. According to these findings, under certain circumstances the political culture of Peru permitted a level of political violence as a legitimate form of political action which was in direct contradiction to the normative legal requirements of the constitutional, institutional system (Almond & Powell, 1966:81ff.). This can be seen as a classic example of a political culture justifying illegitimate violence.

This example pinpoints the crucial role of political culture in actualizing dispositions to political violence. On the one hand, it is a key component of the *political opportunity structures* (Tarrow, 1991; della Porta, 1995) which lead to the real actualization of individual and collective dispositions to political violence, and in this respect it is one of the codeterminant causes of violence. It also acts as an interpretative and evaluative framework for the way in which the institutional/legal elements of the political opportunity structures (elections, parliaments, parties, governments, courts) can attain significance for politically active groups. If, as in the Peruvian case, there is a widespread political-cultural orientation which considers that the existing institutions and the forms of participation they provide for allow little possibility of decisions acceptable for all of society, and if the violent intervention of the excluded groups is also habitually perceived as legitimate by the majority of the population, a political culture of this kind in effect invites the groups concerned to use violence as a "normal" form of political action. Its effect is motivating in two ways—especially if we are dealing with a political culture on a national scale and not just that of a smaller, specific social group—since as a rule it leads the state and its agencies to react to the violent groups in an erratic fashion.

Political cultural studies has not produced any systematic studies on national phenomena such as the Peruvian example, but there are a number of more specific findings, as well as indirect contributions by the classic studies. These have essentially concentrated on the question as to which collective orientations correspond to citizens' preparedness to respect the democratic state's monopoly of violence and in their own actions to place their trust exclusively in nonviolent means, such as supporting democratic organizations and relying on collective initiative of their own. The study by Almond and Verba (1963) presented clear findings on this. In political cultures which had developed a pronounced degree of *social trust* and *belief in the reliability of the political institutions*, such as the United States and Great Britain, it was evident that a vast majority of citizens embodied the attitudes, orientations, propensities to action, and patterns of activity which enabled democratic stability even in times of crisis. Political cultures such as Germany and Italy, where *social trust* was poorly developed or there were even predominant orientations of *mistrust, suspicion* or *alienation* among citizens and toward the authorities, were those in which citizens' relationship to democracy was remote and their attitude passive and reserved. In the participatory political cultures, the majority of citizens had a positive conception of their role as citizens—they willingly participated in the decision-making processes and were interested in the results of the political process. In passive political cultures, by way of contrast, in the main citizens showed interest only in the results of state action and did not demand an active role for themselves.

As the example of the United States has shown, the basic orientation of *social trust* led citizens molded by it to come together whenever necessary with their fellow citizens in their respective social environments in order to agree to and carry out joint political action. They do this whenever their interests call for it. They expect that *communication with others* is possible and that on this basis it will be possible to act conjointly to achieve common interests or goals oriented toward the common good within the framework of the given political institutions. The experiences which citizens acquire in this process then confirm and reinforce their basic orientation. In political cultures of this kind, the basic interpersonal and democratic common ground of the whole population is rated more highly than the divisions between competing party allegiances or other political differences. At the time of the study, it was seen as largely unproblematic in the United States and Great Britain for members of one family to belong to and vote for different parties, but for the vast majority of citizens in the problematic political cultures such as Italy and Germany this was unimaginable. Here there was a predominant all-or-nothing tendency which generally extended the agreement present in the small group to all further public issues; political differences were then considered grounds or justification for irreconcilability in all other social and interpersonal matters. Basic social trust obviously fosters the willingness to deal with conflicts in a nonviolent fashion in the scope of democratic forms of participation. This is likely to result in a culture of cooperative conflict resolution, which in turn strengthens social trust. Social alienation, on the other hand, leads to a mistrust of consensual ways of resolving conflicts. It nurtures a culture of conflict resolution which is either authoritarian or prone to violence, and this in turn strengthens social alienation.

These basic findings have been confirmed again and again by subsequent empirical studies on political culture. A political culture which unconditionally recognizes the monopoly of violence of the democratic constitutional state, which therefore accepts the nonviolence of the citizenry, is characterized by an *interrelationship between basic social trust in the ability to communicate with other people, independent of political differences, and the habitual limitation of political conflicts.* It consists in an emotionally founded balance, reinforced in daily life, between basic agreement and limited nonagreement on particular issues, whereby the basic agreement in elementary social and interpersonal matters predominates. William A. Gamson (1968:50ff.) has shown that four discrete but interrelated dimensions of trust are of relevance for the comparison of political cultures:

- trust in the political authorities,
- trust in the political institutions,
- trust in the public philosophy, and
- trust in the political community.

Political alienation increases to the degree that trust in these dimensions decreases, and there is a greater likelihood of a disposition to violent protest.

Basic orientations of this kind are not abstract convictions of faith but elements of a living political culture. They are long-term, deep-rooted attitudes interwoven at the emotional, evaluative, and cognitive levels, and are embedded in the everyday life of a social environment. The plausibility of these attitudes and the ties between them are re-experienced there every day afresh through contact with the other members of the reference group manifesting the same attitudes. Like all culture they are part of a collective everyday praxis. And like political culture as a whole, at the same time they are fused with the totality of the social culture and the lifestyle of the groups that share them. The particular role of political culture as an independent factor molding people's behavior consists precisely in the fact that it helps structure the way each generation experiences the world inherited from its forebears, i.e., each generation assimilates its own experiences in the light of the orientations that have been passed down. Political culture is regenerated through everyday praxis at the individual's *places of social interaction*: in the family, at school, at work, in social contacts, in the neighborhood, and in the peer groups in the streets and squares. In today's media societies, this also occurs with ever increasing intensity through the mass media.

The development of a political culture is a highly complex process. New experiences intermingle with handed-down orientations and are interpreted through this prism in many different and often contradictory ways. Each area of human experience makes its own specific contribution to the reproduction of political culture. Almond and Verba pointed out in their pioneering study that a nonviolent and democratic political culture based on trust can only arise where it is supported by functioning democratic institutions, which prevents conflicts in the political arena from developing into irreconcilable contradictions. At around the same time, Seymour M. Lipset (1963:64ff.) published the results of his international comparison and historical overview of the stability of democracies and the causes of political extremism. Without explicitly using the term political culture, Lipset emphasized the particular importance of the relationship between the *legitimization* and the *achievements* of democratic institutions and systems for the development of democratic political culture. Although intimate, this relationship is in practice always unstable—even democratic institutions can engender a degree of political alienation if in the long term they are unable to produce the results affected groups expect of them, and this in turn can lead to the development of a violent orientation.

Statistical analysis in the five-nation study by Barnes and Kaase (1979) showed that in all countries the propensity to *political action with an open orientation toward violence* was so low that it did not merit being recorded separately on the scale of protests. On the other hand, there was quite substantial propensity to other forms of political protest (e.g., 15 percent for traffic blockades on a five-nation average) which all the studies' authors diagnose as somewhat related to a propensity to violence. There were considerable differences from country to country. By far the greatest propensity to political protest was in the Netherlands, followed at a considerable distance by the United States, Great Britain and the Federal Republic of Germany, while in Austria the inclination toward political protest of any kind was rare (Barnes & Kaase, 1979:72ff.). G. Bingham Powell summarized political science's empirical research on the causes of political violence and added research findings of his own. Since a certain number of individuals with a propensity to violence for personal reasons will be found in all societies and political systems, Bingham Powell considers that two main factors are relevant for explaining the use of real collective violence for political ends in democracies: firstly, what kind of government actions lead to substantial collective disappointments and secondly, in what political situations does the strategic resource of violence hold promise of political success? When political counterelites bargain on the strategic resource of violence, when this bargain seems to promise success, and when they are able to integrate their followers through plausible interpretations of events, political violence can always be expected to ensue. As the historical statistics on violence in democracies show, this is most successful—and most dangerous—in ethnically and religiously fragmented societies when ethnic or religious conflict interpretations are employed.

According to this theory, which is partially supported by statistics, the actualization of political violence potentials is always possible when speculation by the given elite makes strategies of political violence seem preferable to strategies of exerting democratic pressure, and where the ethnic or religious conflict interpretations on offer connect up with the experiences and motivations of large groups and facilitate their integration into these strategies. Whereas democratic political strategy is based on the promise that participation and responsiveness will lead to nonviolent conflict resolution, the theory that violence is a superior strategic resource for attaining one's political goals results from a lack of faith in democratic premises. At the same time the goals can be diverse: "From a strategic point of view organized political violence has three very general objectives: to change the bargaining rules of the democratic game, to undermine the support enjoyed by the regime or its major parties, or to intimidate the opposition while mobilizing support" (Powell, 1982:158). Empirical evaluation of acts of political violence resulting in fatalities leads to the conclusion that ethnic and religious legitimization strategies in ethnically and religiously fragmented societies are most effective in terminating the democratic pact and achieving violence-oriented mobilization. This is obviously because they are supported by strong cultural dispositions. The practice and results of violent actions against foreigners in the Federal Republic of Germany in the 1990s, especially in areas on the territory of the former GDR, suggest that they are nourished by a mixture of political-cultural legitimization models and success-oriented speculation. Those who commit violence have in fact been increasingly successful in keeping foreigners away from the regions under their control and in effect have induced a section of the political system to respect de facto their activity and their goals.

3. Analyzing Collective Acts of Violence

Descriptive and investigative work in the recent past has focused in particular on three groups of political-cultural mentalities relevant to various European and non-European societies. These are mentalities which act as *opportunity structures* in the activation of the kind of violence potential under discussion. Despite considerable differences in terms of content, they can all equally be described as orientations of *political extremism* because they show certain key similarities in the way they legitimize violence in opposition to the monopoly of violence held by the democratic constitutional state. Firstly, there is religiously defined *political fundamentalism* in all contemporary cultures; secondly, there are the *autonomist movements* drawing on left-wing extremist ideology; and thirdly, there are *xenophobic, ethnically based* mentalities drawing on extreme right-wing ideology. All three mentalities play a significant role both at the level of the *political socioculture* and of the *political interpretative culture*. In some societies and cultures, fundamentalism and xenophobia even have attained a position of prominence.

a. FUNDAMENTALISM. The comparative study by the *American Society of Arts and Sciences* included virtually every cultural sphere and established the existence of fundamentalist mentalities and political movements in all cultures and societies in the world (Marty & Appleby, 1996). Among other things, fundamentalism is a comprehensive sociopolitical culture which encompasses the totality of the given group. Although there are many gradations in fundamentalist cultures which depend on the social and political environment, their partial or comprehensive basic structure which helps cause political violence is similar in all cultures and societies. This basic structure consists in an orientation which lays claim to absolute religious-political or ideological-political *certainty*, and which thus cannot recognize any legitimate differences in opinion on questions of religious truth, lifestyle, ethics, or ultimately even of social coexistence and political order. The absolute rules and regulations of both the religious and the superficially nonreligious varieties of fundamentalist culture are accompanied by their promise of salvation, which on the one hand makes any deviation appear as an absolute danger to the whole collective, and on the other hand calls for tutelage over renegades which can also be achieved with force as required (Meyer, 2001). Anyone who does not share the fundamentalist views is considered not to belong to the respective community, to be of lesser value and to have lesser rights, to be a threat to the fundamentalist community's existence and its certainty of salvation, and to be a pariah endangering the vital interests of the community. A feature of almost all varieties of fundamentalism is that on the one hand they accept violence as a self-evident means of self-assertion toward the supposed threat from outside, and that on the other hand they see it as their duty to play the role of savior for those outside the fundamentalist community—their integration into the community through violent means is seen as being in their own interest. In fundamentalist-oriented communities this two-dimensional justification of violence—for self-protection and as a means of conversion—is considered part of the religion's or ideology's everyday praxis. Fundamentalism exists in subgroups of different sizes in all the societies examined—it can be a socioculture of real everyday life and also an interpretative culture of religious, ethnic, or political elites (Marty & Appleby, 1996). Research has shown that when cultural identity crises coincide with crises of social status and economic crises, fundamentalism can become a dominant factor in the political culture of a society within a very short space of time.

A study of fundamentalism in the Federal Republic of Germany by Heitmeyer, Müller and Schröder has revealed that almost one third of young ethnic Turks aged between fifteen and twenty-one manifested fundamentalist attitudes and were firmly rooted in corresponding milieus and social environments (Heitmeyer, Müller, & Schröder, 1997). The study also again corroborated the connection between fundamentalist mentalities, social milieus and the propensity to violence. Another feature of religious-political fundamentalism is that it uses its (religious) convictions more or less directly as a theory to legitimize the establishment of the political community and the political action of its supporters, thus forming a highly effective opportunity structure for the activation of political violence potentials. Over and above the religious justification of violence which involves the promise of redemption, in its everyday social contexts fundamentalism provides meaning, security, protection, and identity, so that violence and the exclusion of the others are experienced as logical components of a way of life that offers security.

b. XENOPHOBIC VIOLENCE. The sociocultural structures of *xenophobic extremism* are similar to those of fundamentalism, although they are based on different cognitive content. There is the same predominant mechanism of the exclusion of others from one's community, which in this case is constructed as an *ethnic identity*. Those who belong to the ethnic community are considered members of a kind of community of law who are to be protected, but only as long as they share the orientations of the right-wing extremists or ethnofundamentalists. Foreigners or renegades from the ingroup, on the other hand, are seen as a threat to the fundamental identity of the community. Here too a self-justification ritual of self-preservation can be observed. This ritual can be cultural, social, economic, or existential and makes the use of violence appear a normal form of political action.

As a rule the sociocultural milieus of right-wing extremism or ethnofundamentalism consist in a network of spatially compact communities as well as forms of interaction affecting the whole of society. In this case, too, the sociocultures of everyday life are often interlinked with intellectual or party-political cultures of interpretation. The examples of Nazism and neo-Nazi extremism in Germany today show that social integration in such milieus is aided significantly by a highly elaborate aesthetic-cultural lifestyle with its own songs, rituals, celebrations, and literature. It is not uncommon for emotionalizing events of this kind, such as the rhythms and lyrics of songs used in the milieu, to form the immediate starting point for outbursts of xenophobic violence. The sociocultural milieus of these extremist groups offer firm orientations, stabilizing world views bestowing meaning, as well as models of action and rituals in which violence plays a central role. Violence becomes the central element of the lifestyle, the ritual that determines the group hierarchy, entertainment for the group members, and is at the same time a strategic resource toward the goal of an "ethnically cleansed national community" (Wagner, 1998:53). The world views, lifestyles and forms of action produced in this way become firm, habitual behaviors—the "natural" view on things, as it were.

In the Federal Republic of Germany and a range of other European countries, there is a connection between right-wing extremists with an orientation toward violence and established racist mentalities present in the political culture of *mainstream society*. In the member countries of the European Union between 30 and 50 percent of the population admit to being "very" or "quite" racist (Eurobarometer Opinion Poll, 1997). The part-culture of violent right-wing extremists is thus shaped by the elitist claim that their habitual use of violence is in the interests of the whole people and that they are simply putting into practice—sometimes at great personal sacrifice—what large majorities think and wish, but dare not risk.

c. AUTONOMIST MOVEMENTS. The *autonomist movements*, by way of contrast, are socially isolated in all European countries and can at best count on small milieus of supporters. The mentality structures of their part-culture are similar to those of fundamentalism and right-wing extremism in one crucial respect, although their world view claims to represent the opposite. Taking elements borrowed from Marxist and Maoist ideological tradition as their starting point, they interpret the conditions of their social environment, to which their milieu has formed in opposition, as a structural attack on the vital interests of the vast majority of the population through ongoing imperialist exploitation and structural violence. Only the destruction of the prevailing system and the struggle against its representatives can bring about conditions that would take account of the real interests of humanity. In view of their great goal, they believe that the use of violence to combat the dominant structures is always justified, and is in fact a fundamental duty. The small cultural milieus of the autonomists sustain themselves on borrowed cultural elements and fragments of theory from the European workers' movement, which developed an exceedingly effective and diverse counterculture in the last third of the nineteenth century, though in the Western democracies this was overwhelmingly characterized by a democratic orientation. The autonomist counterculture takes the rituals, world views, myths, literature, and art from this cultural tradition and combines them to form a syndrome with a clear orientation toward violence. Reference to the great theoretical traditions of "scientific socialism" plays a crucial role in vindicating this orientation.

4. Theories and Structural Features of Violence-Oriented Political Culture

a. POLITICAL CULTURE AND THE DISPOSITION TO VIOLENCE: DEPRIVATION AND DISINTEGRATION THEORIES. A particularly controversial issue in political science, especially in the field of research into forms of political participation and action, concerns the question as to which constellations of motivations play the decisive role when looking at groups with a propensity to violence, and which can be considered to lead to actual politically oriented violence. For instance, there have been heated debates in connection with ambitious empirical studies, in particular on the degree to which various types, forms, and extents of *collective deprivation*—disappointment of expected gratification of one's needs and values—contribute to the development of a propensity to violence. For a long time the predominant opinion was that dynamics in the gratification of collective expectations whereby a previously high standard gives way to a much lower one is particularly conducive to violence. By way of contrast, the "potential for political violence" index of Grofman and Muller (1973:514ff.) was based on the theory that dynamics whereby the gratification of social needs in a group initially falls and then rises significantly contributes most to the development of a propensity to political violence. Barnes's and Kaase's five-nation study confirmed and further differentiated this conclusion, using the scale of inclination to protest as its basis. According to this study, an inclination to protest with potential for violence is most likely to arise with groups which first experience a drop in the gratification of their expectations and then a distinct rise. In any case this correlation is significantly more pronounced than with groups which experience a rise and then a fall. At the same time differences emerged between the individual countries under investigation. In the Netherlands, Great Britain, and the United States, people with a constant level of gratification of their expectations showed the least inclination to protest, whereas in Germany and Austria this was surprisingly the case precisely for those with a falling level of gratification of their expectations (Barnes & Kaase, 1979:396ff.). It should be mentioned that these results are relative *statistical* differences, and all the groups compared in the studies showed some degree of willingness to protest. The results of this research thus do not answer the question as to which factors ultimately make the key contribution to actualizing the ascertained inclination toward protest, nor the question as to what extent the protest motivation and the political-cultural and other political *opportunity structures* are involved in the different cases where dispositions abruptly transform into real acts of political violence. It remains beyond dispute that experiences of deprivation are among the causal factors which lead to the emergence of dispositions toward political violence. This research has not yet been able to answer the questions concerning the character and relative importance of these further joint causes of the actualization of violence potentials of this kind, nor concerning their interactions with political culture.

In his research into the causes and forms of youth violence, Wilhelm Heitmeyer comes to the conclusion that it is chiefly *disintegrative processes* which arise in the course of social modernization that make people inclined to commit acts of violence (Heitmeyer, 1987, 1994:11ff.). The "losers of modernization", according to this theory, fall into a double trap which they feel they can only break out of through the use of violence. On the one hand, they perceive the social change caused by individualization, pluralization, and increased mobility in the process of social modernization as causing insecurity, impotence, isolation, and the loss of ties and trust. On the other hand, access to functional systems such as work and education becomes uncertain, and participation in public life, i.e., in political and other matters, is increasingly perceived as meaningless, at least in terms of the traditional forms of political participation. The objective problems of access, of political participation being perceived as meaningless, and the crisis of belonging are all based mainly on the relevant subjective experiences and fears of a decline in recognition (see Anhut & Heitmeyer, 2000). If in this situation social and political elites proceed to put ideologies of human inequality on the political agenda—ideologies which can be used to legitimize acts of violence—and if violence is also learned in early socialization, key preconditions are fulfilled in particular for extreme right-wing orientations. These finally take shape when groups are in a position to offer new opportunities of integration and thus to provide young people (for example) with a stable identity, which involves violence and the degrading of foreigners.

Pfahl-Traughber (1994:60ff.) and others have raised two main objections to this theory. Firstly, that it is not completely in keeping with empirical findings of other studies, according to which socially integrated young people are often more prone to use violence than the less integrated, and girls are always less prone to use violence than boys. A second objection is that the disintegration theory may be able to contribute to explaining the propensity to violence at a general level, but it cannot explain why the persons in question then resort to specifically *political* violence and why they find their way to "extreme rightwing" groups or others with a propensity to violence. Although these objections are justified per se, they are far from suitable for refuting the disintegration theory. However, they are useful in showing the limits of the theory's applicability and ability to explain the problem. Heitmeyer himself did not claim that the theory was capable of anything more than naming one significant causal factor, and could be considered an adequate explanation of concrete forms of political violence. His later investigations of fundamentalism and right-wing extremism are devoted precisely to the analysis of specific *conducive mentalities* in political part-cultures as opportunity structures for the abrupt shift from a personal disposition to violence to the actual use of political violence. Moreover, his concept of denied access refers not only to external features of participation but also and in particular to experienced or denied recognition.

b. COMMON FEATURES OF VIOLENT SUBGROUPS. Despite their divergent claims in matters of substance, all three political part-cultures outlined above reveal key structural similarities. They hand down world views with claims to absolute certainty, they define the others who cannot or do not wish to belong to their group as enemies of the salvation which their own world view promises. The very existence of the "enemies" and their actions is portrayed as an acute threat to fundamental, vital interests of the ingroup. This *definitional inversion* turns the violent groups themselves into victims of aggression, making their own violence, as it were, merely counterviolence in self-defense. In their core milieus they combine shared lifestyles with ritualized acts of violence. The "intellectual" interpretative culture which supplies them with elements of ideology, world views, and definitions of enemies, represents a *bridge to corresponding characteristics of the general political culture of their society*, albeit to differing degrees. For autonomist culture this is true in just a few countries and to a limited extent, but for religious-political fundamentalism and xenophobic extremism it holds true in many societies and to a considerable extent.

In all cases the political-cultural effect of the handed-down mentalities consists in making the corresponding orientations appear a habitual, self-evident truth, giving a convincing interpretation of the individual's experiences, giving his or her acts legitimacy, purpose and meaning, and securing the person's membership in the relevant reference group.

In the media societies of the present day, the mass media and their manner of reporting also play a significant role in the reproduction of violence-oriented political part-cultures. New communications technologies such as the internet and mobile phones contribute significantly to both the cohesion of the milieu and to the preparation and organization of their violent actions.

If we see German history in the last one hundred and fifty years as a large-scale experiment in political culture, because society had to cope with frequently changing political systems from one extreme to the other, then the abrupt integration of East German society into West Germany's developed democracy can also be seen as a similar large-scale experiment. There is much to suggest that the conflict-shy, harmonistic, and purportedly also largely homogeneous political culture, which the political system of the GDR worked toward at all levels, has ramifications even now after the state's collapse. For example, the few foreigners who lived in the GDR were never recognized as citizens of equal status. Public articulation and settlement of political conflicts was taboo. On the one hand, the political culture prescribed by the GDR regime inevitably had the paradoxical effect of increasing people's distance from the political system, which ultimately led to its demise. On the other hand, the old political culture's prescribed internal harmony and pressure toward homogeneity obviously still have an effect in the new democratic system too, as reflected in the brutal violence of young people against foreigners, often with the tacit approval of broad sections of the surrounding society. An increasing loss of trust and distance from the political institutions can be observed (Tacke, 1999:28-35). Furthermore, this experience shows that the xenophobic attitudes of a very large section of mainstream society in many European countries and the way in which these directly encourage the violent actions of the relatively small extremist groups, should definitely be seen as complementary facets of the political culture of violence (see Ohlemacher, 1993).

III. CONCLUSIONS

Although there is consensus that political cultural studies makes a significant contribution to explaining the political actualization of violence potentials, there is a lack of comprehensive empirical studies on this issue. In particular there are still no studies—including comparative international work—which methodically examine the political cultures which significantly encourage the actualization of political violence potentials both at the level of mentalities and at the level of real action and symbolic forms and rituals. This research would also involve detailed examination of the interrelationship between xenophobic orientations in mainstream society and the propensity to violence of the groups which carry out the violence.

Although the current state of political cultural studies into the prerequisites for stable democracy and important individual aspects is far from satisfactory, the research conducted to date does allow a preliminary resume on political culture and violence:

- A political culture's mentalities and modes of behavior are opportunity structures which are significant causal factors in the political actualization of individual and collective dispositions to violence.
- Religious-political fundamentalism, the autonomist movement, and xenophobic extremism are at present the most significant cultural models of orientation worldwide which habituate and legitimize political violence.
- The structures of political culture which legitimize violence closely resemble each other in key functional respects despite the important differences in content. A clearly defined homogeneous identity—be it ethnic, religious, or ideological— is attributed to the ingroup. Absolute value is attached to the preservation and active development of this identity for the group itself or even for the whole of humanity (salvation, survival, emancipation), and this value is seen as being under acute threat from the outgroup defined as the enemy. The very existence of the enemy or their actions is perceived as an acute threat to the absolute values of the ingroup. Consequently the ingroup considers its own violence a kind of self-defense against the elemental external threat.
- Through the habitual exercise of violence this world view can become the real praxis of an everyday culture, as is the case in the hardcore milieus of the violence-oriented cultures. But at the same time it can also take effect as a passive

legitimizing sociocultural environment whose members share the decisive patterns of exclusion and humiliation of the "others", but for various reasons do not currently wish to draw the practical conclusions and resort to violence themselves. This pattern of relationships involving a soft version of the orientation which is based on exclusion and its hard version in habitually violent core milieus can frequently be observed in religious-political fundamentalism and the culture of xenophobia, but very rarely in the political part-culture of the autonomists.
- Political culture takes effect as a habitual orientation of social collectives. It is dependent on social structures in which values and behaviors are handed down, and which the individual becomes part of in a way that is taken for granted, though in particular situations conscious personal decisions may be involved. When the communication structures and worlds of experience in which the orientations are handed down and individuals interact are more close-knit, the more stable and unchallenged they become.

The individual's political culture, often perceived as "natural" and without alternative, offers him or her the elementary gratification of recognition, belonging, and orientation, which to a considerable extent makes the person resistant to pressure, punishment, and processes of learning.

Translated by Tradukas

REFERENCES

Almond, Gabriel A., & Sidney Verba. (1963). *The Civic Culture. Political Attitudes and Democracy in Five Nations.* Princeton: Princeton University Press.
Almond, Gabriel A., & Sidney Verba. (Eds.) (1980). *The Civic Culture Revisited.* Boston: Little, Brown Company.
Almond, Gabriel A., & G. Bingham Powell. (1966). *Comparative Politics. A Development Approach.* Boston: Little, Brown Company.
Anhut, Reimund, & Wilhelm Heitmeyer. (2000). Desintegration, Konflikt und Ethnisierung. Eine Problemanalyse und theoretische Rahmenkonzeption. In Wilhelm Heitmeyer & Reimund Anhut (Eds.), *Bedrohte Stadtgesellschaft. Soziale Desintegrationsprozesse und ethnisch-kulturelle Konfliktkonstellationen* (pp. 17–75). Weinheim, München: Juventa.
Barnes, Samuel H., & Max Kaase. (1979). *Political Action. Mass Participation in Five Western Democracies.* Beverly Hills, London: Sage.
Berg-Schlosser, Dirk, & Ralf Rytlewski. (Eds.) (1993). *Political Culture in Germany.* Basingstoke: Macmillan.
Della Porta, Donatella. (1995). *Social Movements, Political Violence, and the State. A Comparative Analysis of Italy and Germany.* New York: Cambridge University Press.
Eurobarometer Opinion Poll No. 47.1. (1997). *Racism and Xenophobia in Europe.* Luxemburg: European Commission.
Galtung, Johan. (1993). Kulturelle Gewalt: Zur direkten und strukturellen Gewalt tritt die kulturelle Gewalt. In Hans-Peter Nolting & Hans-Georg Wehling (Eds.), *Aggression und Gewalt* (pp. 52–73). Stuttgart: Kohlhammer.
Gamson, William A. (1968). *Power and Discontent.* Homewood: Dorsey Press.
Greiffenhagen, Martin, & Sylvia Greiffenhagen. (1979). *Ein schwieriges Vaterland. Zur politischen Kultur Deutschlands.* München: List.
Grofman, Bernard N., & Edward N. Muller. (1973). The Strange Case of Relative Gratification and Potential for Political Violence: The V-Curve Hypothesis. *American Political Science Review, 67,* 2, 514–538.
Heitmeyer, Wilhelm. (1987). *Rechtsextremistische Orientierungen bei Jugendlichen. Empirische Ergebnisse und Erklärungsmuster einer Untersuchung zur politischen Sozialisation.* Weinheim, München: Juventa.

Heitmeyer, Wilhelm. (Ed.) (1994). *Das Gewalt-Dilemma. Gesellschaftliche Reaktionen auf fremdenfeindliche Gewalt und Rechtsextremismus.* Frankfurt a. M.: Suhrkamp.
Heitmeyer, Wilhelm, Joachim Müller, & Helmut Schröder. (1997). *Verlockender Fundamentalismus. Türkische Jugendliche in Deutschland.* Frankfurt a. M.: Suhrkamp.
Lipset, Seymour M. (1963). *Political Man. The Social Basis of Politics.* Garden City: Doubleday & Company.
Marty, Martin E., & Scott A. Appleby. (1996). *Herausforderung Fundamentalismus. Radikale Christen, Moslems und Juden im Kampf gegen die Moderne.* Frankfurt a. M., New York: Campus.
Meyer, Thomas. (2001). *Identity-Mania: Fundamentalism and the Politicization of Cultural Differences.* London: Zed Books.
Niedermayer, Oskar, & Klaus von Beyme. (Eds.) (1994). *Politische Kultur in Ost- und Westdeutschland.* Berlin: Akademie-Verlag.
Ohlemacher, Thomas. (1993). *Bevölkerungsmeinung und Gewalt gegen Ausländer im wiedervereinigten Deutschland. Empirische Ergebnisse zu einem unklaren Verhältnis.* Berlin: Wissenschaftszentrum Berlin für Sozialforschung.
Pfahl-Traughber, Armin. (1994). Ursachen des gegenwärtigen Rechtsextremismus. Politik- und sozialwissenschaftliche Ansätze. In Der Bundesminister des Inneren (Eds.), *Extremismus und Gewalt. Vol. III* (pp. 51–80). Bonn: Bundesminister für Inneres.
Powell, G. Bingham. (1982). *Contemporary Democracies. Participation, Stability, and Violence.* Cambridge: Harvard University Press.
Pye, Lucian W., & Sidney Verba. (Eds.) (1965). *Political Culture and Political Development.* Princeton: Princeton University Press.
Reichel, Peter. (1981). *Politische Kultur der Bundesrepublik.* Opladen: Leske & Budrich.
Reichel, Peter. (Ed.) (1984). *Politische Kultur in Westeuropa. Bürger und Staaten in der Europäischen Gemeinschaft.* Frankfurt a. M., New York: Campus.
Rohe, Karl. (1994). Politische Kultur: Zum Verständnis eines theoretischen Konzepts. In Oskar Niedermayer & Klaus von Beyme (Eds.), *Politische Kultur in Ost- und Westdeutschland* (pp. 1–22). Berlin: Akademie-Verlag.
Tacke, Walter. (1999). Vertrauen in Institutionen. *Umfrage & Analyseheft, 11/12,* 28–35.
Tarrow, Sidney. (1991). Kollektives Handeln und politische Gelegenheitsstrukturen in Mobilisierungswellen. Theoretische Perspektiven. *Kölner Zeitschrift für Soziologie und Sozialpsychologie, 43,* 4, 647–670.
Wagner, Bernd. (1998). *Rechtsextremismus und kulturelle Subversion in den neuen Ländern. Studie.* Berlin: Zentrum Demokratische Kultur.
Winkler, Jürgen R. (1996). Bausteine einer allgemeinen Theorie des Rechtsextremismus. Zur Stellung und Integration von Persönlichkeits- und Umweltfaktoren. In Jürgen W. Falter, Hans-Gerd Jaschke & Jürgen R. Winkler (Eds.), *Rechtsextremismus. Ergebnisse und Perspektiven der Forschung* (pp. 25–48). Politische Vierteljahresschrift, Sonderheft 27/1996.

CHAPTER II-6-1.2

The Role of Elites in Legitimizing Violence

HERFRIED MÜNKLER AND MARCUS LLANQUE

I. TYPES OF ELITES AND FORMS OF LEGITIMATION

Niklas Luhmann called for the social sciences to be more courageous in recognizing and investigating the significant role of physical violence in social developments (Luhmann, 1983:110f.). This courage does indeed seem to be required, as there is a plethora of moral reservations toward any kind of recognition of the social function of violence. The mere description of positive effects of physical violence invites the charge of indirect or tacit legitimation of violence. Luhmann sees the evolutive quality of physical violence in the fact that it is universally applicable and easy to organize. Unlike Georges Sorel, who emphasized the significance of violence in the struggle for political power, Luhmann has no intention of entering into the debate on legitimation: he sees Sorel's theory as a partisan appeal rather than a theoretical description. For Luhmann the long process of evolution culminates in the state monopoly of violence, whereby the hierarchy of the political system of a society replaces physical violence (Luhmann, 1985:539f.). This hierarchy channels opportunities of conflict, it discourages actors lower down the ladder, and thus it extends the immune system of society, which reacts to the problem of a lack of flexibility and innovation at an early stage and thus significantly reduces the potential for "ultima ratio" decisions ranging from the use of physical violence to emigration (on this see Hirschman, 1970). Nonetheless, the formation of hierarchies is unable to neutralize certain legal paradoxes. Whenever legal regulations are intended to punish types of behavior which cannot be (completely) rationalized, Luhmann argues, it is no coincidence that this leads to physical violence in the form of self-defense and states of emergency—the borderline cases of legal norms (Luhmann, 1993:285).

The highly abstract way of looking at violence advocated by Luhmann is a step toward a productive treatment of the phenomenon, but it does not deal with the *political problem* of the legitimations which have accompanied the creation of monopolies of violence. Has the development of the state monopoly of violence in the modern age really rendered the question of physical violence in the political sphere obsolete? It has to be noted that the advent of the state monopoly of legitimate political violence has created a remarkable asymmetry, whereby the use of non-state violence requires a far greater degree of justification than the state use of violence (Neidhardt, 1986:135f.). Civilization theory legitimizes the state monopoly of violence because it leads to a clear reduction in interhuman violence. But the state monopoly of violence has not only absorbed and concentrated existing social violence, it has also meant that unprecedented new means of violence have been developed and used. This is most evident in the state's ability to wage war (Münkler, 1987:135–144). In recent decades research in the social sciences has developed a particular sensitivity for subtle forms of political violence, noting for example an admittedly objectified, but ultimately physical use of violence in the institutions of discipline and punishment, which does not take place between individuals but asymmetrically through institutions (Foucault, 1979). This problem, however, had already been recognized and interpreted by Max Weber, the one theorist who is most identified with the notion of the state monopoly of violence. Weber saw the costs and ethical challenges associated with the objectification and depersonalization of violence from a religious perspective as the "mimicry of brutality" (Weber, 1976:361).

Norbert Elias's civilization theory approach based on Max Weber initially intended no more than a description of the parallel institutionalization of the state monopoly of violence and the development of far-reaching individual self-disciplining (Elias, 1969). Elias nonetheless registered the continuing requirement of a justification of violence. Weber's thesis on monopolization is summarized by Elias: "The form of cohabitation based on the state and the accompanying pacification are both themselves the product of violence. The antagonism of civilization and violence, which may seem to be absolute at first sight, in fact transpires on closer inspection to be relative. The hidden truth amounts to the difference between those people who threaten or attack others with weapons or pure physical force in the name of the state and under protection of the law, and those people who do the same without the permission of the state and the protection of the law" (Elias, 1989a:227f.). In a lecture in the Frankfurt trade unions building in 1932, when the threat of the National Socialist reign of terror was imminent, Elias considered the use of counterviolence for the defense of the constitutional order (Elias, 1989b:290). Did the Weimar Republic fail as a result of too little or too much violence? Speaking to students in 1932, Hermann Heller, an expert on constitutional law, justified his appeal to the students to defend the constitution with force if necessary by referring to the spirit of the constitution. How can this kind of self-empowerment be justified? Can the use of physical force ever be legitimate, and what is the nature of the link between the legitimation and those who legitimize?

This question first relates to the competence of the *interpreting elites* when it comes to providing definitions, and secondly to the control of the means of violence by the *functional elites*. Elites are seldom actors using direct physical violence. *Interpreting elites* exert power through institutions and actors whose self-image they form, whose voluntary willingness to obey they know how to direct, and whose aims they significantly influence. The most important resource behind the power of elites to control physical violence is thus their authority to interpret, and this sets in with a definition, in this case of the nature of violence itself. The political theory approach to defining violence shows that it is precisely here that the borders between a scholarly attempt to clarify terms and an elitist intervention in the discourse which authorizes action can become confused. One reason for this is that political theory's cyclical endeavors to define violence as precisely as possible are closely linked to the practical relevance of the issue. The problem starts with the conceptual delimitation of a core area of "physical violence." The moral condemnation which goes hand in hand with "violence" in most discourses and the resulting delegitimation of political action supported by violence lead to competing definitions as to how broad or how narrow the concept of violence should be. Thus we can observe "definition maneuvers" (Neidhardt) at both the political level and at the level of competing interpreting elites in the academic disciplines. Legal definitions and analyses of violence in the social sciences, for example, are notoriously divergent. There are debates on *nonviolent resistance, violence which is not directed against persons but against property* (allegedly justified), and even on *counterviolence* against subtle means of state repression seen to be quasi-violent. The opposing side sharply distinguishes between state violence which is, by definition, justified, and illegitimate "private" means of violence, and demands that the democratic state does not passively refrain from using the means of force it has at its disposal (Merten, 1975). In the German supreme court ruling, which led to the "intellectualization" of the concept of violence in connection with crimes of coercion (Läpple ruling by the German Federal Court of Justice), extension of police activity was held to be legitimate on the basis of existing laws. Admittedly, such "definition maneuvers" cannot always simply be disqualified as the transparent strategic operations of the elites and their vested interests. Rather they themselves are influenced by cultural transformations, which as a feature of the above-mentioned "intellectualization" of the definition of violence find their expression in both legal practice and the thinking of the social protest movements (Neidhardt, 1986:127f.). The extension of the definition of violence undertaken within the latter, in the form of the theory of "structural violence" (Galtung, 1975:9–31) was intended to raise awareness of the violence embedded in the institutions of the social and political system. In the long term, however, this strategy of definition has in fact compromised the idea of nonviolent resistance by extending and "intellectualizing" the definition of violence (Kleger, 1993:208).

It is possible to distinguish two forms of legitimation of physical violence by the interpreting elites. On the one hand, violent acts which were not initiated by the elites themselves can be justified by referring to the causal factors: revolt, rebellion as a result of famine, uprisings, and revolutions with their accompanying use of physical violence are attributed to misery and repression. The actors' use of violence is thereby seen in a context of justification which amounts to an apology for "personal violence," or, failing this, at least appeals for some sympathy. Physical violence can also be justified prospectively, amounting to a call to arms which appeals to legitimate reasons. This second case is the politically more interesting. The difference here can be demonstrated by means of two examples of legitimation of violence from the modem liberal nation-state. At the end of the nineteenth century, Ernest Renan was concerned with the retrospective justification of the violent creation of the modern nation-state. He wished to point out the danger to the state that would ensue if historical research were to disclose the history of its violent beginnings, and thus to delegitimize it: "Forgetting ... plays a significant role in the emergence of a nation, and therefore the progress of historical scholarship often represents a danger to the nation. Historical research results in the disclosure of the violent events which took place in the early days of all political forms of organization, even those with the most benevolent consequences. The unification of northern and southern France was the result of nearly a century of extermination and terror" (Renan, 1995:45). Renan's position was that of a member of the interpreting elite of a nation which had entered a period of crisis after defeat in the war with Germany and the violent repression of the Paris Commune, and which wished to use the idea of the present-day nation to justify the violent means of the past, which were reprehensible in ethical and religious terms, without once mentioning a possible future use of violence. Renan's famous definition of the nation, which directly follows on from his appeal to constructive forgetfulness, is that the nation is a daily plebiscite in which every individual affirms his national affiliation. From antiquity to the present day, political theorists have often recommended forgetting the violence each side has suffered at the hands of the other, in particular in cases of civil war, as an effective means of putting an end to violence (Meier, 1995). The memory of past violence can be the cause of future violence, irrespective of whether it is the politicians or the historians who uphold it. This is not only true of civil war, but also of war between states (see Völkel, 1993:63ff.).

The problem is seen quite differently by Max Weber, in his legitimation of the use of violence by the bourgeois democracies. The nineteenth-century political theory of liberalism assumed the existence of a powerful state, which had to be brought under political and legal control. The political logic of the creation and the preservation of the state through internal and external violence was never central to liberalist political theory. Weber, though, connected the liberal bourgeoisie's theoretical claim to authority with the question as to whether it would be able to use the state means of violence responsibly after it had taken possession of them, in particular in the legal gray zone of a violent defense of the constitution. All kinds of political system, whether they are democratic, socialist, or autocratic, have to be prepared for coups, acts of sabotage, and "similar sterile eruptions," and they have to resist them with military law if necessary. "But: the proud traditions of politically mature nations who know no cowardice have always been proven by the fact that they were able to keep their nerve and their cool heads; they may have used violence to repress violence, but they subsequently attempted to resolve the issues behind the outbreak of conflict rationally, and above all to restore the *guarantees of free liberal order* immediately, and they never once allowed such events to distract from the principles of their political decision-making" (Weber, 1988:405, Weber's emphasis). The politically interesting issue requiring particular legitimation thus concerns not so much the creation of the monopoly of violence, but rather its maintenance and use in times of political crisis.

II. HISTORICALLY INFLUENTIAL VERSIONS OF THE LEGITIMATION OF VIOLENCE BY THE ELITES

1. Elitist Conceptions of Violence in the Foundation and Maintenance of the State

With his appeal to overlook the subject of violence in the formation of states and genesis of nations, Renan completely upturned the view held by Niccolò Machiavelli, the founder of modern political thought. Machiavelli saw physical violence as the *indispensable precondition* to the foundation of a state, exemplified by the mythical tales of the fratricides Cain and Romulus. Machiavelli believed that it was dangerous to ignore the violent origins of political systems, because this would mislead the functional political elites about the challenges they had to face. This argument represented a provocative view of a problem that had been seen as a fault of secular statehood throughout political thought since Aurelius Augustine, and was used by Augustine as an argument against the sacralization of the Roman Empire by political neopaganism in the late fourth century. The fault lay in the genetic foundation of statehood through fratricide in the cases of Cain and Abel and Romulus and Remus. "The first founder of the earthly state," Augustine wrote that Cain "was thus a fratricide, for, overcome by envy, he killed his brother, who was a citizen of the eternal state and a stranger on this earth. Thus it is no surprise that a long time later when the city was founded, which was to become the head of the earthly state of which we speak and was to rule over so many peoples, this act resembled that first example ... For here too the same shameful deed occurred, as one of the city's poets said: 'Scarcely had they been built, the walls were dripping with the brother's blood'" (Augustinus, 1977:bk 20, ch 5= II, 218f.). Augustine here attributed the de facto monopolization of violence by the political system to the vanity and lust for glory of the state's founding fathers, and thus argued that politics would notoriously fail to achieve its own aim of justice. Subsequent medieval political thought in Europe, up to the rediscovery of Aristotle's *Politics*, attributed the origin of power and statehood to man's fall from God and saw the state as the punishment for sin (Stürner, 1987:103ff.). The use of violence by the functional and power elites was therefore directly linked to a theological worldview: the violence of the powerful was legitimized to the extent that it could claim to limit the effects of human sin.

Martin Luther further developed this idea in his doctrine of the two realms and two governments, making it particularly fruitful for German Protestant political thought by taking up Augustine's ideas and writing of a division between those men who belong to the realm of God and those who belong to the earthly realm. Those within the realm of God had no need of secular government, "no secular sword or law. And if every man were a righteous Christian, that is, a righteous believer, then there would be neither need nor use for princes, kings, lords, swords, or laws" (Luther, 1982a:43). But, Luther argued, the world was not only peopled by Christians, and Christians made up only the small part of the world and would remain so until the end of the world. Here Luther differed strongly from those he called "fanatics," who lived under the notion that the realm of Christ should be erected in this world, whereupon every form of violence would disappear as foretold in the visions of the prophets, and there would be no need for any kind of repressive means of power. For Luther this idea was a ploy of the devil, which is why he often attacked these ambitions vehemently, especially in his writings on the Peasants' War (Luther, 1982b). It is the propensity for violence caused by man's sinful condition that makes the permanent threat of violence necessary for the secular authorities. But Luther took his argument a step further and justified secular authority and the responsibilities and offices pertaining to it as expressly instituted by God. For this reason it is every Christian's duty to be prepared to enter into the service of the secular authority, and if necessary even to use violence against those who, without the threat of violence from the authorities, wish to cause suffering and pain to their fellow men. Luther appeals to every pious Christian: "There is the other part, that you are bound to serve the sword and to foster it with whatever means you can, be this with your body, your goods, your honor, or your soul" (Luther, 1982a:50). This faced Luther with the pressing question arising from the fifth commandment ("Thou shalt not kill"), whether "soldiers can also be blessed"? He answered this with a firm yes: the transgressions of God's commandments carried out in the service of authority and the fulfillment of the duties of office were to be attributed not to the man, but to the office and the profession and thus to God himself who had created these (Luther, 1982c:174f.). Service in the name of secular authority, including the use of violence, is the fulfillment of God's will. A more comprehensive justification of the use of violence by the elites of power is hard to imagine, and the Lutheran doctrine of authority has frequently been sharply criticized on this point. It is important not to forget, however, that Luther defined clear norms for the duties of secular authority and that his doctrine does not approve any use of violence which goes beyond these.

On the question of a legitimate use of violence Luther's most significant opponent within the Reformation camp was Thomas Müntzer, and here as with many other issues, the difference lies in Müntzer's active eschatological views, his inversion of the realms of secular events and salvation. Müntzer understood secular authority to be the interim bearer of the authority of God and he thus warned the princes that their power would be taken from them and given to the people if they disobeyed God's commandments. This meant that the violence of the elites is only legitimate when it is used in accordance with God's commandments and intentions, and the authority to decide this lay—in modern terms—not in the hands of the functional elites, but with the interpreting elites. Once Müntzer had concluded that the ruling elites were resisting God's intentions, he saw himself in the position of the prophets Jeremiah and Elias, and he appealed to the people to violently overthrow the princes, so as to free the way for God's works in the world. His aim was not to justify any kind of popular rule, rather he saw the people as an instrument of God, like the princes before them, who now should be overthrown because they had failed in this role. In his letter of April 26/27, 1525, to the people of Allstedt, signed "Thomas Müntzer, a servant of the Lord against the heathens," he writes: "To work, to work, as long as the fire is hot. Do not let your sword grow cold, do not let it go lame! Forge your weapons on Nimrod's anvils, cast their tower down to the earth! ... To work, to work, as long as the sun shines! God is leading you, follow, follow!" (Müntzer, 1990:214). Müntzer saw the people as an elite called upon to use force, whenever and insofar as this would enact the will of God on earth. Müntzer represents the outstanding figure of eschatological prophecy in the history of political ideas, legitimizing violence from the perspective of salvation. This phenomenon can be seen in many early modern revolutionary movements (Cohn, 1957), had some influence on the revolutionary labor movement (Hölscher, 1989), was clearly influential in the "political religions" of the twentieth century (Voegelin, 1996; Maier, 1996/97), and has most recently informed a number of fundamentalist movements.

Machiavelli, a contemporary of Luther and Müntzer, had a completely different view of the legitimation of violence. To justify the violent basis to the monopoly of power held by the founding fathers' of the state, and the audacious fratricide with which it all began, Machiavelli does not appeal to the offices and professions instituted by God or to the eschatological and apocalyptic role of violence in God's intentions on earth. For Machiavelli the single decisive factor is success. His view thus amounts to the self-legitimation of violence as a result of its positive effects: "An intelligent thinker will never reprobate a man because of an exceptional deed which he has done in order to found a kingdom or to establish a free state. The deed may speak against him, but his success excuses it. And if the success is as good as in the case of Romulus, then it will excuse him forever" (Machiavelli, 1966: bk 1, ch 9:36). It is this justification of acts of violence carried out by the political elites on the basis of the outcome of the violence that have made Machiavelli's ideas so controversial in the history of political thought. Again and again, Machiavelli's thoughts and advice have figured in the question as to the dividing line between the legitimate and illegitimate use of violence by political elites. The basic tenet of Max Weber's famous lecture, "The Profession and Vocation of Politics" (Weber, 1985), is a late attempt to integrate both Luther's ethos of office and profession and Machiavelli's cold power rationale and his passionate devotion to political aims. The political elites' use of violence can now only be justified in terms of an ethics of responsibility, and not in terms of an ethics of conviction.

2. Social-Revolutionary Legitimations of Violence

The French Revolution was not the instigator of the concept of revolution in political theory, for this concept had been previously inscribed for the notion of the reformation of states, beneficial regeneration, and the violent attributes involved (Griewank, 1973:189). It was the French Revolution, nonetheless, that introduced the adjective "revolutionary" into the terminology of political concepts. An idea which had previously been understood as a description of processual changes to constitutional systems now acquired a progressive, dynamic, and also legitimizing meaning. The latter involved justification in terms of a theory of history, in that the violent determination of the political process was seen to lead either to a return to better conditions that had prevailed in the past, or to anticipate a future social order. At the same time acts or events that were deemed to contradict future expectations and wishes were considered counterrevolutionary, thus justifying their suppression through force. It now became possible not only to explain violent changes in political structures using a secular argumentation, but also to understand violence as an accelerator into the future. Parallels and links between eschatological and social-revolutionary arguments also became increasingly apparent. The direct consequences of violence still remained regrettable, but the prospect of creating a political system based entirely on rational principles made it possible to legitimize violence both retrospectively and prospectively. Ideas that had remained clearly distinct from one another for Luther, Müntzer, and Machiavelli were now interlinked, and what had previously remained in the domain of religious conceptions of salvation now figured within a secular and political formulation of goals (Löwith, 1953).

When Marx described violence as the midwife of the new society, which arises within the old (Marx, 1972:779), he deciphered it as a social and political force to be understood in terms of the process and its results, notwithstanding any direct harmful consequences. Marx thus introduced a further explanation for the historical role of violence, and furthermore he advanced a new strategy of legitimation, since the metaphor of midwifery or birth combines both a historical-philosophical and an epistemological approach. The new society is not seen as something alien to the existing society which, like a conqueror, approaches from beyond and overthrows and destroys the old order through violence. The new society rather develops out of the old, violently, and in a revolutionary outburst, and the conditions of production are broken like chains. Here an idea was created which was to be paradigmatic for an entire movement of social-revolutionary legitimation of violence, especially as Marx also rejected any form of—in his view—shortsighted purely political and military theory of revolution, as exemplified by Blanqui (Blanqui, 1968). Socialism along Marxist lines adhered firmly to the primacy of political economy and social theory as the crux to any legitimation of political violence. This is why Marx himself clearly approved of the destruction of prebourgeois conditions through the violence of bourgeois society—the destruction of the feudal idyll and also of premodern social structures by European colonialism. All of these were justified in social historical terms. "It was the British intruder who broke up the Indian handloom and destroyed the spinning wheel," he noted in 1853 (Marx, 1975:130). He gave a detailed description of the disastrous consequences of the destruction of traditional forms of living and working in India, and then concluded: "The question is: can mankind fulfill its destiny without a fundamental revolution in the social state of Asia. If not, whatever may have been the crimes of England, she was the unconscious tool of history in bringing about that revolution" (Marx, 1975:133).

A key question, however, was which form of violence the proletarian revolution was to adopt, if its successful outcome should lead to the demise of the repressive bourgeois state, and thus put an end to the dominance of man by man? Was it not the case that the progress of civilization and the advent of the true age of humanitarian society after the removal of conditions of alienation would coincide with and ultimately be recognizable by a minimization of the use of violence? Karl Kautsky, the leading theoretician of German social democracy, and Lenin, the intellectual leader of the Bolshevik revolution, both based their ideas on the Marxist analysis, according to which violent relations were inherent within bourgeois society in the characteristic institution of private property and in the social medium of capital, and that the effects of these violent relations were comparable to the physical violence exerted through political means. In 1917, when the Bolsheviks both overran the weak bourgeois leadership that itself had only recently gained power, and also soon after brought the other socialist movements in Russia under their minority control, this led to vehement criticism from prominent Marxist theoreticians ranging from Rosa Luxemburg to Karl Kautsky (Schissler, 1976; Schöler, 1990). The issue was not whether bourgeois society was based on violence, for the catastrophe of World War I had convincingly proven the violence of this form of society for all socialists. The problem was rather which means should and may be used to overcome this form of society. The conflict centered in the main on the question whether Marx's vision of proletarian dictatorship intended nothing other than democratic forms of government using the most peaceable means possible to implement the political will of the majority of the population, as Engels had put it pointedly in his later works, or whether the early expectations of violent revolutions were now again relevant, thus making proletarian revolution primarily a matter of a politically organized use of violence. This conflict was not so much a theoretical discussion about the correct interpretation of Marx's works, but rather a dispute over the monopoly of interpretation of the political self-image of the European labor movement (Lösche, 1967:250–258). It was a conflict which found its main expression in the German labor movement, within which both differences of political opinion and conflicts between various interpreting and functional elites played a role. There was continuous disagreement on the line to be taken between the reformists involved in practical politics and the ideologues who adhered to revolutionary aspirations.

Lenin was quick to criticize the dominant discourse of legitimation in socialist theory. He saw its point of reference as merely bourgeois ideology, which was to be shamed by being held up to the mirror of its own normative assumptions. In contrast, according to Lenin, socialist intellectuals should educate the working class and provoke the masses to outrage and political action through propaganda and agitation. To plan these activities, a new type of party should organize the class struggle. This idea was not only directed against the "apolitical" theoreticians, but also against terrorists in Russia, who had their own separate tradition in the struggle against czarism. Lenin thought that purely theoretical intellectuals, Marxist "economists," and the "terrorists" all shared a common misunderstanding of Marxist theory, and thus falsely interpreted the prevailing society and failed in political terms: they believed in the spontaneity of the masses, a view which Lenin saw as a bourgeois perspective on the working classes. Political organization of the working class by professional revolutionaries was therefore intended to change the form of the class struggle and also in particular to repress uncontrolled terrorist violence, and it was also intended to bring the intelligentsia closer to the masses and their needs and language. Violence was thus not to be seen as a political principle, but as a political means to be used purely tactically. The practice of repression of socialist dissenters in Russia, the civil war, and the accompanying acts of violence which were legitimized through an interpretative monopoly in terms of the interests of the working class all led to Kautsky's vehement criticism—he saw violence against czarism as necessary and justified, but disagreed with the foundation and protection of the new state through violence (Kautsky, 1990:7–88). Kautsky interpreted Marx's work on the Paris Commune, which Lenin had used to justify his politics, as a sign that proletarian rule would have to be proven by the fact that it did not wish to employ the same violent means that the old regime had used. But for Lenin the destruction of the bourgeois claim to ascendancy was inconceivable without dismantling its apparatus of power through violence. Because, however, proletarian violence used force only to destroy every state based on the class system, the nature of its violence was different, and it could not be judged using the same criteria that applied to the violent preservation of the bourgeois system (Lenin, 1990:117). Lenin saw any failure to comprehend this as a fault inherent to the self-image of the political and theoretical elite, and not as question of the interpretation of Marx. For Lenin the crucial question was whether the elite should lead the workers as a political avant-garde, or merely accompany them in the style of bourgeois critics. At the same time Lenin adhered to the idea of violence as a *tactical means* of revolution and rejected the communist rebellion in Germany in the early 1920s as the "infantile disorder of 'left-wing' communism."

Leon Trotsky, the mind behind the Red Army, was far more open than Lenin when it came to legitimations of violence. With undisguised frankness he treated all forms of violence as justified revolutionary means when used appropriately. Trotsky compared war and revolution (see Papcke, 1973:331–389 on the "transformation of revolution into war") and drew numerous parallels. As in wars, the aim of revolutions is to break down the will of the enemy, and the most important means of class struggle is violence (Trotzki, 1990:53f.). Thus Trotsky sees terror as essentially tied up with revolution; taking hostages is also a legitimate means, and the destruction of enemies is the best way of protecting the lives of allies. Trotsky rejects the use of more moderate means of repression in favor of the immediate execution of prisoners, as the former lack sufficient deterrence. By equating politics with war and universalizing violence as a characteristic political medium (an idea which is also found in Max Weber's lecture "The Profession and Vocation of Politics"), Trotsky treated violence as a means that should be evaluated from an exclusively *political* viewpoint. Anywhere, however, where the pertaining political conditions meant that the negative "bourgeois" connotations of violence were still relevant, as was the case for Georg Lukács's ultra-Leninist stance, revolutionary violence still required a particular legitimation. In this case it is the thesis of the fetishization of peaceable legal systems and barbaric means of violence which is seen as the bourgeois intellectual's internal inhibition before an appropriate approach to the question of revolutionary violence (Lukács, 1979:247). It is only the "fetish" of legal order that conceives of nonviolence, whereas in reality the law and violence are no more than different forms of violence—law is *latent* and political violence is *acute* violence. In this way violence is justified as an element of legitimate tactics (252), whereby revolutionary violence is not indiscriminate but rather the will of the proletariat become conscious (258). This view already shows signs of the self-image of revolutionary intellectuals tending to subjugate personal opinion to the party line and to see a willingness to use violence as essential to the development of class consciousness. This became a standard feature for communist intellectuals when it came to justifying Stalinism, and the rejection of this view was seen as characteristic of disloyalty.

3. National And National-Revolutionary Legitimations of Violence

Carl Schmitt's attempt to discard the ballast of moral reservations against violent forms of political self-assertion, as in "The Concept of the Political," reads like a response to Georg Lukács's social-revolutionary legitimation of violence. Like Lukács, Schmitt wishes to overcome the liberal stigmatization of violence. But Schmitt differs from Lukács in that he claims that the sign of a politically self-assured people is the ability to distinguish between friend and foe, with the result that a definition of politics includes and even requires the possibility of using violence against both internal and external enemies (Schmitt, 1963a). According to Schmitt, it is homogeneous national democracy in particular that has to be prepared to remove heterogeneous elements, and thus also to expel or even destroy them. Whereas Max Weber called on the bourgeoisie to protect legal order through the use of controlled violence, Schmitt raises this exceptional case to the level of an existentially significant condition which bestows dignity on the normal conditions of a legal system. Here social-emancipatory and national-emancipatory legitimations of violence compete with one another.

The mental approach taken by many German intellectuals and writers to the outbreak of war in August 1914 can be seen as national-emancipatory: as a liberation of a world dominated by the older generations, as an escape from bourgeois existence based on business and earning a living, and finally as the scope for great idealist aspirations. Georg Simmel, for example, celebrated the war as the liberator toward a state of existential essence, which overcame the alienation of bourgeois society, and Max Scheler saw the nation on the way to its true identity (see Lübbe, 1974:217–225; Flasch, 2000:103–223). This initial outbreak of enthusiasm for war and violence lasted several months and was by no means only a German phenomenon, although it certainly was most intensive there. What remained after the defeat of 1918 was that introverted experience of violence gained in the adventure of war and the camaraderie of the trenches, on which the nationalist right drew to develop its models of political and social order (in the idea of "Volksgemeinschaft," or "national community," for example; see Verhey, 2000), in whose realization the use of violence against internal enemies was never in doubt. Ernst Jünger provided a pointed summary of these ideas: "Just as the war is not a part of life, but the expression of life in its full violence, so this life is in itself fundamentally warlike" (Jünger, 1934:88). Thus it is not surprising that during the climax of the terrorist activities of the "Red Army Faction" comparisons were made between the self-image of the RAF and of the nationalist right in the Weimar Republic—analogies to the terrorists' self-image were clearly identified in Jünger's work "The Battle as an Inner Experience." Around this period Carl Schmitt isolated his concept of the political, which lay in the ability of violent self-assertion, entirely from any questions as to political structures or systems. He now believed the "partisan" to be the final and also most modern type of political individual. The partisan is not legitimized by a legal system to which he belongs, and not protected by international law; instead he proves the caliber of his political will to self-assertion by risking his own life (Schmitt, 1963b; Llanque, 1990). On the other hand, a national-revolutionary legitimation of violence has drawn on or occasionally combined with a social-revolutionary legitimation, as was particularly the case in the period of decolonization in Southeast Asia and sub-Saharan Africa after World War II, and also most recently in the strongly anti-imperialist strains within Islamic fundamentalism: in the struggle against the United States, the Soviet Union, and now Russia.

4. Social-Emancipatory Legitimations of Violence

The *social-revolutionary* legitimation of violence refuses to reject the use of violent means to achieve its revolutionary goals as a matter of principle, and rather tended to equate the violent conditions of the pertaining system with the violent means of its own revolutionary transformation, seeing the differences only in the respective legitimations of violence. These consisted either in the liberation from oppression, or the preventive or counterrevolutionary maintenance of violent conditions. The *social-emancipatory* legitimation of violence, on the other hand, concentrates less on the envisaged result, but rather hopes that violence itself will bring about a fundamental change in human attitudes and behavior. Georges Sorel, for example, distinguishes between power and violence, arguing that a state of peace which maintains oppression can be more brutal than open class struggle and the willingness to use political violence. Thus the violence of the open class struggle, in contrast to a covert struggle for power, represents the liberation of civilization from true barbarism (Sorel, 1969:106f.). This idea is based on the assertion that in a power struggle the will to power of the victor is cloaked by legal arrangements and the losing party is ultimately destroyed as a conspirator, whereas violence is a means which increases political vitality to attain liberty. Power requires authority and automatic obedience, whereas violence does not wish to ape bourgeois power, but rather to liberate the worker (208ff.). This theory, on which twentieth-century ideologies of violence frequently drew, is certainly not without its contradictions. In fact it is only really comprehensible in the context of the struggle for interpretative authority on matters relating to the revolutionary labor movement. Sorel's arguments are directed against the self-legitimation of intellectual workers' leaders who used their theoretical knowledge as a means of asserting their claim to authority, but whose ultimate aim was merely a new ruling elite rather than workers' liberation. Sorel places himself in the anarchist tradition, which sees the motor of self-liberation coming "from below," in spontaneous action by the working masses. Apparently civilized appeals to the workers to keep the peace, on the other hand, merely lead to the barbaric effects of further oppression. Socioeconomic or political theory is rejected as the basis of legitimation, to be replaced by the political-revolutionary myth of a potential which already exists within the working masses, and which cannot be organized intellectually. Sorel illustrated these ideas using the myth of the general strike, which cannot be evaluated according to the violent forms its takes or along party-political lines, but only by assessing the extent to which the oppressed working masses develop their own consciousness during the strike and then create authentic forms of organization.

This view of violence as a medium of self-liberation is even more clear in the works of Frantz Fanon, who, as a member of the functional elite of colonized Algeria, deals with the difficult issue of liberation not only from the political and economic dominance of the colonial masters, but also their mental and cognitive dominance. The latter is more effective in restricting the will to liberation, for example in the form of the humanist culture of the proscription of violence. So as to evade this kind of cultural restraint, Fanon takes recourse to precisely those elements of the indigenous culture which are seen to be barbaric from the European perspective. Through detailed criticism of the master-slave chapter in Hegel's *Phenomenology of the Spirit*, and the interpretation of this by Alexandre Kojéve (Paris, 1947), Fanon appeals to the active use of violence as both a means of *political* liberation and also the medium of self-therapy for the colonized to lose their sense of inferiority toward the colonial master (Fanon, 1980:137ff.). Fanon replaces Hegel's choice of work as a means of liberation with violence (see Münkler, 1981:437–468). "For the colonizer this violence is absolute praxis. Thus the warrior sees himself as a worker: to work is to work toward the death of the colonial master ... Colonized man liberates himself in and through violence. This praxis enlightens the actor, because it reveals the means and the end" (Fanon, 1966:65f.).

What Fanon sees as the culture of the colonial masters, which has been forced on the colony, Herbert Marcuse, probably the most influential thinker behind the students' movement, sees as capitalist consumer culture. It is necessary to first liberate yourself from this before the struggle for true freedom can begin. Consumer culture, Marcuse argues, has led to the vast majority of the population losing their sense of political freedom, which is the reason why the students, and also the socially marginalized, have now become the avant-garde of the revolutionary movement. In the struggle against the self-inflicted loss of self-determination by the majority of the population, ethical appeals to nonviolence should be treated with circumspection: "There is a difference in the historical functions of revolutionary and reactionary violence, the violence of the oppressed and the violence of the oppressors. In ethical terms, both of these forms of violence are inhuman and evil—but since when has history been made in ethical terms?" (Marcuse, 1966:114).

Hannah Arendt observed the increasing acceptance of violence amongst left-wing intellectuals with some concern, seeing a climax in the writings of Fanon and Jean-Paul Sartre's approval of them, and the consequences of this in the students' movement. For Arendt, the self-authorization of a violent challenge to the political order is based on an unclear distinction between power and violence. In contrast to the semantically similar distinction in Georges Sorel, Arendt sees power constituted by the actions of citizens and in an opposition to violence which is unbridgeable in theories of legitimation, since violence is based on a relationship between means and ends (Arendt, 1969:145 and 150). Violence cannot become power, which is the reason why a revolutionary movement which defines itself through the medium of violence will inevitably arrive at the point where it has to declare violence to be permanent. The distinction between power and violence also means that there are two different legitimations. Power is its own means and is thus preferable to violence within the terms of Arendt's Aristotelian definition, since violence can only be a means to an end. Power does not require any justification, since any political system which removes physical violence from its realm of influence is a peaceful system and thus self-justifying. Violence, on the other hand, cannot be legitimized, but rather only justified in terms of the ends it pursues. The closer means and end are to each other, then the more plausible the justification becomes—this is most evident in cases of self-defense. Politics should be concerned to establish free institutions, and thus Arendt discounts violence as a political tool, even if violence is legitimized by the interpreting elites. Arendt removes violence from the political realm, although the political system is still able to resist the violent expression of a will for change by taking recourse to the idea of self-defense.

Arendt's theory admittedly loses the idea of the liberation through revolutionary violence, which, after World War II, Albert Camus did not wish to relinquish so lightly. Having become acquainted with the emancipatory potential of violence in the resistance to the National Socialist occupation of France, Camus retained the idea that in certain situations violence was ethically acceptable. He tried to protect social-revolutionary aspirations from the logic of the violent means, to which the revolutionaries' own legitimations of violence had regularly succumbed. Once the goals have been achieved, the same violence which was used for the purpose of liberation tends to establish itself as a permanent system of violence which betrays its original justification. "Complete nonviolence justifies slavery and its violence negatively; systematic violence destroys the living community positively ..." (Camus, 1969:236). This is why Camus suggests a distinction between rebellion and revolution. Rebellion relinquishes the systematic use of violence and thus has to accept the dilemma that it may not be able to consolidate the results of the revolution. By renouncing systematic violence, however, the rebel gains the legitimation for his momentary and always temporary use of violence. "If the goal is absolute, i.e., viewed historically: if it is believed in with all certainty, then it is possible to go so far as to sacrifice everyone else ... Does the end justify the means? Possibly. But who will justify the end? To this question, which historical thought leaves open, the rebellion answers: the means" (237).

III. CONCLUSION

Interpreting elites are best able to legitimize politically motivated violence when they link violence with the question of the political system, its establishment, and its consolidation. The more comprehensively they manage to present violence as the starting point of or the accompaniment to a large-scale process of political chains of events or historical developments, the more they become independent of the ethical requirement to justify concrete violence against individuals. Disinterest in the victims, however, leads to the long-term delegitimation of the interpreting elites, for they get caught up in the circle of self-justification, as is the case for most terrorist groups. The legitimation of violence becomes self-referential for those who apply violence, violence becomes a means of self-assertion, and the alleged elite becomes an elite through the practice of violence.

Translated by Tradukas

REFERENCES

Arendt, Hannah. (1969). On Violence. In Hannah Arendt, *Crises of the Republic* (pp. 103–198). New York, London: Harvest.
Augustinus, Aurelius. (1977). *Vom Gottesstaat (De civitate Dei)*. Zürich: Artemis.
Blanqui, Auguste. (1968). *Instruktionen für den Aufstand. Aufsätze, Reden, Aufrufe* [Ed. von Frank Deppe]. Frankfurt a. M., Wien: Europäische Verlagsanstalt.
Camus, Albert. (1969). *Der Mensch in der Revolte*. Reinbek bei Hamburg: Rowohlt [1953].
Cohn, Norman. (1957). *The Pursuit of the Millennium*. Fairlawn: Essential books.
Elias, Norbert. (1969). *Über den Prozeß der Zivilisation. Soziogenetische und psychogenetische Untersuchungen*. 2 Vols. Bern: Francke.
Elias, Norbert. (1989a). Zivilisation und Gewalt. Über das Staatsmonopol der körperlichen Gewalt und seine Durchbrechungen. In Norbert Elias, *Studien über die Deutschen. Machtkämpfe und Habitusentwicklung im 19. und 20. Jahrhundert* (pp. 223–270) [Ed. von Michael Schröter]. Frankfurt a. M.: Suhrkamp.
Elias, Norbert. (1989b). Die Zersetzung des staatlichen Gewaltmonopols in der Weimarer Republik. In Norbert Elias, *Studien über die Deutschen. Machtkämpfe und Habitusentwicklung im 19. und 20. Jahrhundert* (pp. 282–294) [Ed. von Michael Schröter]. Frankfurt a. M.: Suhrkamp.
Fanon, Frantz. (1966). *Die Verdammten dieser Erde*. Reinbek bei Hamburg: Rowohlt [1961].

Fanon, Frantz. (1980). *Schwarze Haut, weiße Masken*. Frankfurt a. M.: Syndikat.
Flasch, Kurt. (2000). *Die geistige Mobilmachung. Die deutschen Intellektuellen und der Erste Weltkrieg*. Berlin: Alexander Fest Verlag.
Foucault, Michel. (1979). *Discipline and Punish*. New York: Vintage.
Galtung, Johan. (1975). *Strukturelle Gewalt. Beiträge zur Friedens- und Konfliktforschung*. Reinbek bei Hamburg: Rowohlt.
Griewank, Karl. (1973). *Der neuzeitliche Revolutionsbegriff. Entstehung und Geschichte*. Frankfurt a. M.: Suhrkamp.
Hirschman, Albert. (1970). *Exit, Voice, and Loyality: Responses to the Decline in Firms, Organizations and States*. Cambridge: Harvard University Press.
Hölscher, Lucian. (1989). *Weltgericht oder Revolution. Protestantische und sozialistische Zukunftsvorstellungen im deutschen Kaiserreich*. Stuttgart: Klett-Cotta.
Jünger, Ernst. (1934). *Blätter und Steine*. Hamburg: Hanseatischer Verlag.
Kautsky, Karl. (1990). *Diktatur des Proletariats* [Ed. von Hans-Jürgen Mende]. Berlin: Dietz Verlag [1918].
Kleger, Heinz. (1993). *Der neue Ungehorsam. Widerstände und politische Verpflichtung in einer lernfähigen Demokratie*. Frankfurt a. M., New York: Campus.
Kojéve, Alexandre. (1947). *Introduction à la lecture de Hegel*. Paris: Gallimard.
Lenin, Wladimir Ilitsch. (1990). *Die proletarische Revolution und der Renegat Kautsky* (pp. 89–175) [Ed. von Hans-Jürgen Mende]. Berlin: Dietz Verlag [1918].
Llanque, Marcus. (1990). Ein Träger des Politischen nach dem Ende der Staatlichkeit. Der Partisan in Carl Schmitts politischer Theorie. In Herfried Münkler (Ed.), *Der Partisan. Theorie, Strategie, Gestalt* (pp. 81–95). Opladen: Westdeutscher Verlag.
Lösche, Peter. (1967). *Der Bolschewismus im Urteil der deutschen Sozialdemokraten 1903 bis 1920*. Berlin: Colloquium.
Löwith, Karl. (1953). *Weltgeschichte und Heilsgeschehen. Die theologischen Voraussetzungen der Geschichtsphilosophie*. Stuttgart: Kohlhammer.
Lübbe, Hermann. (1974). *Politische Philosophie in Deutschland*. München: Deutscher Taschenbuchverlag.
Luhmann, Niklas. (1983). *Rechtssoziologie*. 3rd Edition. Opladen: Westdeutscher Verlag.
Luhmann, Niklas. (1985). *Soziale Systeme. Grundriß einer allgemeinen Theorie*. 2nd Edition. Frankfurt a. M.: Suhrkamp.
Luhmann, Niklas. (1993). *Das Recht der Gesellschaft*. Frankfurt a. M.: Suhrkamp.
Lukács, Georg. (1979). *Geschichte und Klassenbewußtsein. Studien über marxistische Dialektik*. Darmstadt, Neuwied: Luchterhand [1923].
Luther, Martin. (1982a). Von weltlicher Obrigkeit, wieweit man ihr Gehorsam schuldig sei. In Martin Luther, *Ausgewählte Schriften. Vol. 4* (pp. 36–84). Frankfurt a. M.: Insel Verlag [1523].
Luther, Martin. (1982b). Wider die räuberischen und mörderischen Rotten der andern Bauern. In Martin Luther, *Ausgewählte Schriften. Vol. 4* (pp. 132–139). Frankfurt a. M.: Insel Verlag [1525].
Luther, Martin. (1982c). Ob Kriegsleute auch in seligem Stande sein können. In Martin Luther, *Ausgewählte Schriften. Vol. 4* (pp. 172–222). Frankfurt a. M.: Insel Verlag [1526].
Machiavelli, Niccolò. (1966). *Discorsi. Gedanken über Politik und Staatsführung* [Ed. von Rudolf Zorn]. Stuttgart: Kröner.
Maier, Hans. (Ed.) (1996/97). *Totalitarismus und Politische Religionen. Konzepte des Diktaturvergleichs*. 2 Vols. Paderborn: Schöningh.
Marcuse, Herbert. (1966). Repressive Toleranz. In Robert Paul Wolff, Barrington Moose & Herbert Marcuse, *Kritik der reinen Toleranz* (pp. 91–128). Frankfurt a. M.: Suhrkamp.
Marx, Karl. (1972). *Das Kapital. Kritik der politischen Ökonomie. Erster Band. Marx-Engels Werke. Vol. 23*. Berlin (East): Dietz Verlag.
Marx, Karl. (1975). Die britische Herrschaft in Indien. In *Marx-Engels Werke. Vol. 9* (pp. 127–133). Berlin (East): Dietz Verlag.
Meier, Christian. (1995). Erinnern—Vordrängen—Vergessen. Zum öffentlichen Umgang mit schlimmer Vergangenheit in Geschichte und Gegenwart. In *Berichte und Abhandlungen der Berlin-Brandenburgischen Akademie der Wissenschaften. Vol. 3* (pp. 59–99). Berlin: Akademie Verlag.
Merten, Dieter. (1975). *Rechtsstaat und Gewaltmonopol*. Tübingen: Mohr.
Münkler, Herfried. (1981). Perspektiven der Befreiung. Die Philosophie der Gewalt in der Revolutionstheorie Fanons. *Kölner Zeitschrift für Soziologie und Sozialpsychologie, 33*, 437–468.
Münkler, Herfried. (1987). Staat, Krieg und Frieden. Die verwechselte Wechselbeziehung. *Friedensanalysen 21: Kriegsursachen* (pp. 135–144). Edition Suhrkamp, Frankfurt a. M.: Suhrkamp.

Müntzer, Thomas. (1990). *Schriften, Liturgische Texte, Briefe* [Eds. von Rudolf Bentzinger & Siegfried Hoyer]. Berlin: Union Verlag.
Neidhardt, Friedhelm. (1986). Gewalt. Soziale Bedeutungen und sozialwissenschaftliche Bestimmungen des Begriffs. In Bundeskriminalamt (Eds.), *Was ist Gewalt? Auseinandersetzungen mit einem Begriff*. Vol. 1 (pp. 109–147). Wiesbaden: Bundeskriminalamt.
Papcke, Sven. (1973). *Progressive Gewalt. Studien zum sozialen Widerstandsrecht*. Frankfurt a. M.: S. Fischer.
Renan, Ernest. (1995). *Was ist eine Nation? Und andere politische Schriften*. Wien, Bozen: Folio Verlag.
Schissler, Jakob. (1976). *Gewalt und gesellschaftliche Entwicklung. Die Kontroverse über die Gewalt zwischen Sozialdemokraten und Bolschewisten*. Meisenheim: Hain.
Schmitt, Carl. (1963a). *Der Begriff des Politischen* [Text von 1932 mit einem Vorwort und drei Corollarien]. Berlin: Duncker und Humblot.
Schmitt, Carl. (1963b). *Theorie des Partisanen. Zwischenbemerkungen zum Begriff des Politischen*. Berlin: Duncker und Humblot.
Schöler, Uli. (1990). 'Despotischer Sozialismus' oder 'Staatssklaverei'? *Die theoretische Verarbeitung der sowjetrussischen Entwicklung in der Sozialdemokratie Deutschlands und Österreichs (1917–29)*. 2 Vols. Münster: Lit.
Sorel, Georges. (1969). *Über die Gewalt*. Frankfurt a. M.: Suhrkamp.
Stürner, Wolfgang. (1987). *Peccatum und Potestas. Der Sündenfall und die Entstehung der herrscherlichen Gewalt im mittelalterlichen Staatsdenken*. Sigmaringen: Thorbecke.
Trotzki, Leo. (1990). *Terrorismus und Kommunismus: Anti-Kautsky* (pp. 7–174) [Ed. von Hans-Jürgen Mende]. Berlin: Dietz Verlag [1927].
Verhey, Jeffrey. (2000). *The Spirit of 1914. Militarism., Myth, and Mobilization in Germany*. Cambridge: Cambridge University Press.
Voegelin, Eric. (1996). *Die Politischen Religionen* [Ed. von Peter J. Opitz]. München: Wilhelm Fink.
Völkel, Markus. (1993). Geschichte als Vergeltung. Zur Grundlegung des Revanchegedankens in der deutsch-französischen Historikerdiskussion von 1870/71. *Historische Zeitschrift*, 257(1), 63–108.
Weber, Max. (1976). *Wirtschaft und Gesellschaft. Grundriß der verstehenden Soziologie*. 5th Edition. Tübingen: Mohr-Siebeck.
Weber, Max. (1985). Politik als Beruf. In Max Weber, *Gesammelte Politische Schriften*. 5th Edition (pp. 505–560). Tübingen: Mohr-Siebeck [1919].
Weber, Max. (1988). Parlament und Regierung im neugeordneten Deutschland. In Max Weber, *Gesammelte politische Schriften*. 5th Edition (pp. 306–443) [Ed. von Johann Winckelmann]. Tübingen: Mohr (Paul Siebeck) [1918].

CHAPTER II-6-1.3

Violence in Contemporary Analytic Philosophy

Keith Burgess-Jackson

> *violence* The exercise of physical force so as to inflict injury on, or cause damage to, persons or property; action or conduct characterized by this; treatment or usage tending to cause bodily injury or forcibly interfering with personal freedom. (*Oxford English Dictionary*, 2nd ed.:221)

I. INTRODUCTION

The philosopher, qua philosopher, has neither evaluative nor factual expertise. What he or she can contribute to the discussion of public affairs is something different, but no less important: clarification. This is not to say that philosophers never argue or theorize, much less that when they *do* argue or theorize, they are (or must be) evaluatively neutral. It is to say that when philosophers engage in these activities, they are acting in a nonphilosophical capacity. This should come as no surprise, for each of us is many things, including citizen, moral agent, and (for lack of a better term) valuer.

A given essay by a philosopher, whether on violence, famine relief, the moral status of nonhuman animals, capital punishment, or some other topic, may have—and the good ones do have—both philosophical and nonphilosophical dimensions. It may even be divided, explicitly, into philosophical and nonphilosophical sections, the better to keep the dimensions distinct. It is important to keep this fact in mind, for, as I said, the philosopher's expertise is limited. One does not wish to defer to an authority that does not in fact exist (even if the philosopher in question asserts or implies that it exists, which is regrettable but not uncommon).

What needs to be clarified? The most important objects of clarification are concepts, which are, to put it crudely (but usefully), categories of thought. Our concepts, whether of ordinary life or of specialized practices (e.g., law) or disciplines (e.g., biology), are inter-

---

W. Heitmeyer and J. Hagan (eds.), *International Handbook of Violence Research*, 989–1004.
© 2003 Kluwer Academic Publishers. Printed in the Netherlands.

related, just as points on a map are interrelated. To understand or analyze a concept is to situate it in a scheme, to see how it relates to (is similar to, different from, included in, excluded from) other concepts. It is to locate the concept in logical space. The concept of a bachelor, for example, is related in a particular way both to the concept of a male and to the concept of marriage. To say that someone *has* a concept of a bachelor means that he or she grasps these relations and is able and disposed to deploy them in conversation (including that special mode of conversation known as argument).

Alas, concepts can be confused, and not just by those, such as children, who are intellectually immature. This would be the case if someone thought that a particular person, X, were both a bachelor and married (i.e., a married bachelor). It is the responsibility of the philosopher, as such, to identify and eliminate these confusions. What the philosopher would say in such a case is that, logically (conceptually) speaking, X cannot *be* both a bachelor and married. The concepts exclude each other, as it were, which is to say that neither category is contained in the other (put differently, no object is in both categories). Compare the concepts of being a bachelor and being a male. The latter category contains, but is not exhausted by, the former. Being a bachelor entails being a male, but being a male does not entail being a bachelor. Other pairs of concepts, such as male and parent, are only contingently related. It is logically possible for someone to be both a male and a parent, just as it is logically possible for an act to be both a shooting and a killing, although either state can obtain without the other obtaining.

Since concepts are abstract (as opposed to concrete), there must be a means by which to gain access to them. This means is—and there is reason to think it *must* be—language. To understand the concepts that structure and inform our thinking (either ordinary or technical), the philosopher attends to what is said (orally or in writing). Words (linguistic entities) *express*, *represent*, or *symbolize* concepts (logical entities), just as numerals express, represent, or symbolize numbers and names express, represent, or symbolize people. This does not, as might be suspected, conflate philosophy and linguistics. To quote Alan White, "What makes the philosopher different from the linguist is his interest in *what* we say rather than in *how* we say it, in our *use* of words rather than in our use of *words*" (White, 1975:110; italics in original).

II. OVERVIEW OF RESEARCH

> There are concepts which are essentially contested, concepts the proper use of which inevitably involves endless disputes about their proper uses on the part of their users. (Gallie, 1955–56:169)

It should be clear from what has been said thus far that the philosopher's interest in violence differs from that of the moralist, on the one hand, and the scientist, on the other. The philosopher, as such, is interested in the *concept* of violence, not in *violence*; in what it is for a thing to *be* violent, not in which persons, acts, or states of affairs *are* violent; in the *class* of violent things, not in the *things* that belong to that class (White, 1975:104). The philosopher, strictly so-called, is engaged in a second-order inquiry—an inquiry into the logic of violence. The philosopher asks how (the concept of) violence differs from, and how is it similar to, (the concepts of) force, power, aggression, coercion, compulsion, persuasion, injury, domination, threat, terrorism, torture, harm, illegality, immorality (including injustice), punishment, oppression, and brutality.

Those who seek to understand the causes and consequences of violence (viz., scientists) are engaged, by contrast, in a first-order inquiry. Both types of inquirer seek understanding, but their understanding is of different objects. In the case of the scientist, the object being scrutinized is the world (or some segment of it); in the case of the philosopher, the object being scrutinized is a particular representation of the world (or some segment of it). Moralists, in contrast to both scientists and philosophers, seek to *change* the world. Their aim is practical, not theoretical or conceptual. If changing the world requires understanding it, as seems plausible, then moralists are dependent, ultimately, on both philosophers and scientists, for philosophers map the conceptual world (the world of ideas) and scientists describe (theorize about) the actual world (the world of things). It follows that if one's aim is to prevent or channel violence, then one must understand its nature and causes.

These reflections suggest that there can be—and indeed there are—two types of *theory* of violence. A first-order or scientific theory seeks to understand the causes and consequences of violence, either for its own sake or for the sake of various practical ends (such as prevention or mitigation). This inquiry presupposes (makes use of) the concept of violence. A second-order or philosophical theory, in contrast, seeks to understand the concept of violence. Philosophers *study*, rather than *use*, the concept. Put differently, whereas scientists theorize about violence, philosophers theorize about the concept of violence. It is important that these activities (and the associated disciplines) be kept distinct; otherwise, confusion will result.

Among the conceptual issues discussed by philosophers are the following. First, there is the metaphysical or ontological question of what sort of thing violence is (see MacCallum, 1993 [1970]:236; Lawrence, 1970:34). How should we understand (classify) it? Is it an event? If so, is it concrete or abstract, a particular or a universal? Is it a process? If so, how is it individuated (marked off, distinguished) from other processes or events, and is there any logical limit on its duration? Is it, rather than being a process, the *result* of a process? If so, from which process does it result? Is violence a state of affairs? Is it a type of action (a species of event)? However, we conceive of violence—as event, process, state of affairs, or action—is it a matter of degree? For instance, does it make sense to say, of two actions, that one is more violent than the other, or that an action is "extremely," "moderately," or "somewhat" violent? Some philosophers (e.g., Betz, 1977:345) believe that it does make sense to conceive of violence as a matter of degree. They say that killing or torturing a person, for example, is *more violent* than punching him or her (see Garver, 1981:228; Van de Vate, 1969:6–7; Machan, 1990). Here, as elsewhere, the way in which we speak (or write) provides the best evidence of the nature of the concept.

A second conceptual issue, or rather, cluster of issues, concerns the nature of the agent or perpetrator of violence. Who or what can act violently (i.e., perpetrate an act of violence)? Must it be a natural person? Can a group or collectivity do violence, and, if so, how is that to be understood? (See, e.g., Lawrence, 1970:36, who maintains that "Violent acts can be performed by individuals or by groups." See also Gert (1969):627), who speaks of collective violence.) Can a nonhuman animal, such as a tiger or a snake, act violently or commit an act of violence? Can a disembodied being, such as God or an angel, do violence? Van de Vate (1969:31) says that only a human person can do violence.

A related issue concerns the nature of the patient or victim of violence. Who or what can be acted upon in a violent way? A nonhuman animal? (For an affirmative answer to this question, see Betz, 1977:348; Harris, 1980:20.) A plant? A mere object? Does the violence done to persons act upon them qua persons or qua objects (since all persons—theism notwithstanding—are embodied)? In other words, is it *through* their bodies? (See Van de Vate, 1969:28; cf. MacCallum, 1993 [1970]:251; Wade, 1971:373; Betz, 1977:345.) There is also an important issue involving the relation of agent and patient. Can one do violence to or use violence against oneself? Gert (1969:617) says "Yes," citing suicide. This does not mean that all suicides are *in fact* acts of violence, only that logically speaking they can be. MacCallum (1993 [1970]:241) and Betz (1977:349) express doubt about this possibility, since it implies a bifurcation or dichotomization of the self into two elements or aspects. This, they say, is conceptually problematic.

Suppose we conceive of violence as a type of action rather than as a process or state of affairs. We may wonder about the mental state of the actor. Is violence necessarily intentional? That is to say, can one accidentally do violence? (Lawrence (1970:37) answers "Yes" to this question; Miller (1971:16) answers "No.") Can violence be unknowing? Done by mistake? Can it be negligent? Reckless? There is also the question of motivation. Must the perpetrator of an act of violence have a particular motive or purpose, such as malevolence? (Miller (1971:23) says "No": "As far as I can tell, violence may be committed for what we would call 'no reason'; for itself; or as a means to some end—to secure wealth, fame, or revenge." Misra (1975:387–388) concurs.) Is it possible, logically, to do violence out of benevolence? Must violence, to be violence, be intended to be recognized as such by the patient or victim? Van de Vate (1969:28) answers "Yes" to this question. This latter issue, incidentally, raises the question of the *meaning* of violence. Is violence a speech act? If so, what is its locutionary, illocutionary, and perlocutionary meaning or force (see Austin, 1975 [1962]:103)? What, in other words, does it say; what does it do; and what effect does it have on the recipient?

Probably the most widely discussed conceptual issues surrounding violence concern its evaluative and normative status. Is violence, like pain, intrinsically bad (i.e., bad in and of itself, independently of its consequences and other extrinsic factors)? If so, how bad is it, and why? What, *precisely*, makes violence bad? Suppose, as some philosophers (e.g., Holmes, 1989) have argued, that violence is intrinsically bad. Does it follow that it is always wrong to act violently (if conceived as an action or instrument) or bring violence about (if conceived as a state of affairs)? This question is ambiguous, so, to avoid confusion and misunderstanding, one must disentangle its various meanings. (For a failure to do so, see Lawrence, 1970:44; but cf. ibid., p. 47 n. 35.) The question could mean either "Is violence presumptively wrong?" or "Is violence always wrong, all things considered?"

Let us consider the second meaning first. Someone might maintain that violence is by definition a wrongful act, which would entail that it is always wrong, all things considered. Is this a coherent and plausible position? Miller (1971) answers "No." His reasoning is as follows: "If violence were wrong by definition, then the pacifist position that violence is evil would be a tautology, and thus true, if only trivially. However, the pacifist claim that violence is evil is not at all clearly true, but is rather a complex moral judgment" (Miller, 1971:23). Conversely, a person who says of a particular act that it is both an act of violence and morally permissible (i.e., not wrong) is contradicting him- or herself. Defining "violence" as wrongful—that is, viewing wrongfulness as an essential property of the concept of violence—precludes discussion of the acceptability of violence, when in fact it is an open and important question whether a particular act of violence is wrong.

The work of Joseph Betz, while in many respects illuminating, illustrates this problem. Betz (1977:348) conceives of violence as the use of physical force on a person to defeat his or her rights or ends. According to Betz, it is for this reason that "All good men oppose the violent use of force" (1977:346; note the redundancy). But Betz's conception of violence requires him to say that when a police officer shoots a robber who has just shot a victim, only the robber does violence. The officer has used *force*, Betz says, but not all force is violence. As Betz explains, "The power of the pistol is exemplified in both cases, but the robber uses it to violate a right and so is humanly violent, whereas the policeman uses it to vindicate a right and so is not similarly violent" (1977:347).

What makes this conception odd—and in my opinion implausible—is that it prevents us from describing an act as an act of violence unless and until we determine whether someone's rights or ends have been defeated. And yet, most of us would describe the police officer's action (as well as the robber's action) as an act of violence, since it is an exercise of physical force to inflict injury on, or cause damage to, a person. (Whatever else we want to say about robbers, they are persons.) We would quickly add, however, that the violence is, or may be, *justified*. Indeed, the criminal justice system as a whole works by means of coercion backed by force. The state says, in effect, "If you engage in any of the following activities, you will be apprehended (violently, if necessary) and punished." It is a large question of political philosophy whether state coercion backed by violence is justified, and, if so, under what conditions. (See, e.g., Nozick, 1974; Simmons, 1979; Feinberg, 1984.) My point is that most of us, most of the time, believe that violence (as well as the threat thereof) *can* be justified. On Betz's analysis, these acts, being vindications of rights, would not count as violence. Betz would appear to have the normative cart before the conceptual horse.

We are considering the question whether it is always wrong to use, or bring about, violence. The question, as I said, is ambiguous. In its second meaning, which we have been examining, the question is whether violence is always wrong, all things considered. Let us turn to the first meaning: "Is violence presumptively wrong?" An action can be presumptively wrong but not wrong, all things considered. (In philosophical terms, it can be prima facie but not ultima facie wrong.) If violence is only presumptively wrong (because, e.g., it is intrinsically bad), then in principle (although perhaps not in practice) it can be justified (see Honderich, 1973:197). The normative question would then be: "What sorts of consideration can justify it (i.e., rebut the presumption against it)?" Many philosophers (and others) have sought to answer this question (see, e.g., Audi, 1971). Note that this way of conceiving of violence, unlike that just discussed, does not lead to redundancy or self-contradiction. To say that an act is an act of violence, in this way of thinking, is not to foreclose inquiry into its wrongfulness; it is to shift the burden to those who maintain that it is *not* wrong, all things considered (see Holmes, 1989).

In addition to the justifiedness or moral permissibility of violent conduct, there is a question of the prudence of engaging in it. Suppose a particular act of violence is justified (by whatever standard you think appropriate); does it follow that the act is the best means or tactic, given one's long-term aims and values, and given that there is a nonzero—maybe a high—probability that it will alienate or provoke otherwise sympathetic observers who approve of one's ends but reject violent means? Singer (1990 [1975]:xi–xiii) argues that violence—understood as physical harm to persons—does not serve the purposes of the animal-liberation movement, of which he is a prominent and influential member. "The strength of the case for Animal Liberation," he writes, "is its ethical commitment; we occupy the high moral ground and to abandon it [by using violent means or tactics] is to play into the hands of those who oppose us" (Singer, 1990 [1975]:xiii; cf. Rawls, 1999 [1969]:186, who makes a similar point concerning nonviolent civil disobedience).

A further question, one that presupposes wrongfulness (i.e., lack of justification), concerns responsibility for acts of violence. What, if anything, excuses them? Accident? Inadvertence? Insanity? Compulsion? Immaturity? Intoxication? Duress? Mistake of fact? Ignorance of circumstances? Hypnosis? Brainwashing? (see Feinberg, 1984:108). Note that the philosopher, as such, is incompetent to determine what justifies or excuses violence.

The most he or she can do, while acting as a philosopher, is to state the considerations that are *relevant* to these determinations, leaving it to moralists and others to make the case. (See MacCallum, 1993 [1970]:253–254; cf. Lawrence, 1970:48; Audi, 1971; and Honderich, 1973:208, who take positions on the justification of violence, thereby acting in a nonphilosophical capacity.)

Other conceptual questions concerning violence are the following:

(1) Can there be nonphysical (e.g., psychological) violence? Does it make sense to say that X did violence to Y's psyche (e.g., to Y's self-esteem)? If so, can a given act do both physical *and* nonphysical violence? (See Lawrence, 1970:35; Miller, 1971:41; Ranly, 1972:419, 421; and Coady, 1986 [1985]:15.)

(2) Can one consent to violence (i.e., can one waive one's putative right not to be subjected to violence or treated violently)? Gert (1969:627) defines "violence" in such a way that the answer to this question is "Yes." As we shall see, he defines "violence" as an unwanted violation of a moral rule, which implies that if the violation in question is wanted, then it is not violence. An alternative view would hold that a particular violation *can* be both wanted (indeed, consented to) and violent.

(3) Can an omission be violent? That is, must violence be an action? Suppose I allow a person to drown in a situation in which I could have prevented the death. Leave aside the question of responsibility (causal, legal, or moral). Does it make sense to say that the death was *violent*? If so, then violence is far more pervasive than most of us think it is. (Wade (1971:372) believes that violence requires action, since "Nonaction destroys nothing; only action against can infringe on another." Miller (1971:20) concurs. But see Harris, 1974, who argues that there are "negative actions" as well as positive actions and that both types can inflict injury or suffering upon others.) What the drowning case shows is that one's conception of violence reverberates throughout one's belief system. Conceiving of violence in one way rather than another makes certain beliefs necessary (logically speaking) and others impossible. The philosopher's job, as indicated in Part I, is to map these logical connections as faithfully as a cartographer maps physical terrain.

III. RESULTS AND CONTROVERSIES

> In disputes over which features are constitutive of the concept of violence both political and philosophical motives play a part, and it may be that there is no final answer, no definitive analysis. (Harris, 1974:219)

Now that we have a clear(er) understanding of what it is that philosophers do, and why, let us ask what they have had to say, and *are* saying, about the concept of violence. How, to be precise, have philosophers answered some of the questions set out in Part II? Which disagreements or controversies loom largest within the discipline? Where, conversely, is there the most disciplinary and professional agreement, and what might account for this confluence of opinion?

The first distinctively philosophical essay on the topic of violence appeared in 1968—in, ironically, a nonphilosophical publication. Newton Garver, a professor of philosophy at The State University of New York at Buffalo, identified violence not as force (although he said that it can *involve* force) but as a violation of a person, conceived as a locus of rights (including the right to property), autonomy, and dignity (Garver, 1968:819). The violator, Garver said, can be either a natural person or an institution, and the violation can be either overt or covert (as he put it, "quiet").

These distinctions cut across one another, creating four jointly exhaustive and mutually exclusive categories. Category 1, overt personal violence, includes such things as murder, battery, and forcible rape (which do physical harm); category 2, covert personal violence, includes intimidation, coercion, and threat (which do psychological harm); category 3, overt institutional violence, includes warfare, riots, and corporal punishment; and category 4, covert institutional violence, includes slavery, colonial oppression, and "ghettoization."

While crude in some respects (as befits a pioneering effort), Garver's short essay and accompanying typology inaugurated the project of mapping the logical space surrounding the concept of violence. The next few years—which, not coincidentally, were a time of social ferment, strife, and questioning of traditional values in the United States—saw a burst of philosophical activity. Garver's essay, like all pathbreaking works, fell in for criticism, some of it, it must be admitted, harsh (which is not to say unfair). Betz, for example, took Garver to task for conceiving of violence too broadly:

> If violence is violating a person or a person's rights, then every social wrong is a violent one, every crime against another a violent crime, every sin against one's neighbor an act of violence. If violence is whatever violates another, embezzling, locking one out of his house, insulting, and gossiping are all violent acts. (Betz, 1977:341; see also Coady, 1986 [1985]:4)

Betz's technique, familiar to analytic philosophers but probably not to others, is known as refutation by counterexample. It works as follows: Someone (in this case Garver) offers an analysis of a concept. The critic points out either that the analysis includes too much (Betz's criticism here) or that it excludes too much. In other words, it is off the mark. The analytic objective is to state the necessary and sufficient conditions for application of the term that expresses the concept. Whether this is always, often, or even sometimes possible is a matter of controversy among philosophers (see, e.g., Gallie, 1955–56). It may be, for example, that the concept of violence, like that of game, is a "family-resemblance" concept. The idea, which derives from the work of Ludwig Wittgenstein, is that there is no feature that all games (or, one might say, all acts of violence) share, but that we can nonetheless recognize games (or acts of violence) as such by virtue of a "network of resemblances" (Blackburn, 1994:136).

To the uninitiated, this may appear as so much wordplay (in the vernacular, "just semantics"), but it is not (see Lee, 1996:68). We are dealing with ideas, not words; with the categories in which we think, not the labels for those categories. Few people doubt the practical or theoretical importance of ideas (or the usefulness of avoiding confusion), even if they believe that the labels we use are conventional or arbitrary. As Betz points out, Garver's conception of violence makes the expression "nonviolent social wrong" self-contradictory, since every wrong, to Garver, is *by definition* an act of violence. Unless we are prepared to abandon this expression—or rather, the associated category in our thinking—we should resist Garver's analysis.

Another problem, Betz says, is that, on Garver's understanding of violence, "The distinction between violent and nonviolent civil disobedience and resistance evaporates" (Betz, 1977:341). It does so because trespassing (to cite one common form of disobedience to law) is a violation of property rights, hence, on Garver's analysis, an act of violence. So the expression "nonviolent civil disobedience," which strikes most of us as both coherent and useful (see, e.g., Rawls, 1999 [1969]), turns out to be self-contradictory, like "married bachelor." Something has gone awry. Any analysis that has counterintuitive results must be defective in some way, even if we cannot identify (or agree upon) the defect.

Betz goes on to find fault specifically with Garver's second category, viz., covert personal violence. According to Betz (1977:342), "There is no psychological or covert violence, (...) except by analogy and extension, simply because all violence is necessarily and by conventional definition overt or physical." The reasoning for this view is interesting. Betz begins by highlighting "the condemnatory powers of the concept" of violence and the role that that concept plays in our individual and collective thinking. To label an act "violent," he writes, is to condemn it, and not just to condemn it (which is itself revealing) but to condemn is strongly or vociferously (see also Coady, 1986 [1985]:17). Not all wrongs are egregious wrongs, after all, so we need terms in our language to pick out those that are especially condemnable (contemptible, outrageous). "Violence," Betz says, performs this essential function. By conceiving of violence as a (mere) violation of a person, as Garver does, we weaken the concept, thus undermining its efficacy as a condemnatory tool.

The remedy for this defect is to limit application of the term "violence" to those acts that are particularly egregious or despicable (even if they are ultimately—all things considered—justifiable). These, Betz says, are acts that do physical harm (i.e., harm to bodies, not just to minds). In his view, "Violence is adequately defined as *physical force* defeating ends and rights" (Betz, 1977:343; emphasis added). Garver's mistake, Betz concludes, is that he "so spiritualizes violence that it becomes unrecognizable" (ibid.). "Doing 'psychological violence' to a person would be something like pushing his soul down the steps: there is a category mistake involved (...)" (ibid., 345). (Note that Betz is both criticizing Garver and offering his own analysis of violence. Philosophers who do conceptual analysis—and not all of them do—hope thereby to refine our concepts. It is a collective or communal activity, requiring both philosophical skill and competence in and attention to language. The process of refutation by counterexample, in particular, is supposed to move us progressively closer to a full, accurate, and illuminating understanding of each concept to which we apply it.)

At least one prominent philosopher, Robert Paul Wolff, has challenged the very coherence of the concept of violence, calling it "inherently confused." "Strictly speaking," Wolff writes, "violence is the illegitimate or unauthorized use of force to effect decisions against the will or desire of others" (1969:606). But this definition, he says, leads to incoherence. Here is Wolff's reasoning:

1. "[E]very man has a fundamental duty to be autonomous" (607).
2. "The autonomous man is of necessity an anarchist" (608).

Therefore,

3. "[P]hilosophical anarchism is true" (607) (from 1 and 2).

Therefore,

4. "[T]here is no such thing as legitimate political authority" (607) (from 3).

Therefore,

5. "[I]t is impossible to distinguish between legitimate and illegitimate uses of force" (607) (from 4).

6. "[T]he concept of political violence depends upon the concept of *de jure*, or legitimate authority" (607; italics in original).

Therefore,

7. "The concept of violence is inherently confused" (602) (from 5 and 6).

Wolff's concern in this essay is political violence, not violence generally, so the most that he has shown is that the concept of *political* violence is inherently confused. This is an important limitation on his argument, since not all violence—maybe only a small fraction of it—is political violence (see, e.g., Honderich, 1973:195, 197).

But let us ignore this point for the sake of argument. Has Wolff established even the lesser claim that the concept of *political* violence is inherently confused? According to Wolff, the incoherence of the concept of (political) violence manifests itself in the following way: Suppose someone asks, "When is it permissible to resort to violence in politics?" If violence is the unjustified use of force, the answer is "Never" (by definition). On the other hand, if violence is the illegitimate use of force, the answer is "Always," since, in Wolff's view, "there is no such thing as legitimate authority" (608). So the question is trivial; violence is either never justified or always justified, in each case by definition. Wolff thinks that this shows the incoherence of the concept.

A critic might respond as follows: What Wolff has shown is not (as he thinks) that the concept of (political) violence is incoherent, but that one or more of his assumptions is false (or, if that manner of speaking offends, unacceptable). In other words, it is more likely that his conclusion is false than that all of his premises are true. (This maneuver is called "the G. E. Moore shift"; see Rowe, 1979:339.) Therefore, instead of inferring that the question is trivial from the assumption that violence is unjustified/illegitimate force, as Wolff does, we should infer that violence is *not* unjustified/illegitimate force from the assumption that the question is *not* trivial. How many of us have wondered, in a reflective moment, whether it is permissible to resort to violence in politics—and, if so, in what circumstances? I suspect the answer is, "Most of us." Thus, we have no reason to accept Wolff's pessimistic and skeptical conclusion. The concept of (political) violence may be incoherent, but Wolff has not established that it is. (This illustrates a logical point: that an invalid—i.e., non-truth-preserving—argument can have a true conclusion.)

(I should point out, for the benefit of nonphilosophical readers, that Wolff's essay has generated a great deal of philosophical commentary, most of it critical, much of it acerb, and some of it, regrettably, mocking. See, e.g., Coady, 1986 [1985]:13 (pointing out the "strange consequences of Wolff's position"); Konrad, 1974:40 (asserting that "Wolff's discussion of violence is of no value in helping to shed light on the social problems connected with violence, nor is it of any help for the moral philosopher in his task of clarifying questions about practical judgment"); and Flanagan, 1972:271 (claiming that "Wolff's fundamental theses are demonstrably untenable").

Let us turn to those philosophers who, unlike Wolff, believe that the concept of violence is coherent. Here, in chronological order, are some of the many definitions of "violence" that have been propounded by philosophers:

> [V]iolence in human affairs amounts to violating persons. (Garver, 1968:819)
>
> In the select meaning, then, an act of violence (a violent act, a case of acting violently) is a two-person, face-to-face interaction, where the agent wrongfully and intentionally violates the body of the patient. (Van de Vate, 1969:8)

> Strictly speaking, violence is the illegitimate or unauthorized use of force to effect decisions against the will or desire of others. (Wolff, 1969:606)

> [Violence is] an intentional violation of any of the first five rules [viz., don't kill; don't cause pain; don't disable; don't deprive of freedom or opportunity; don't deprive of pleasure] toward someone who has no rational desire to have the rule violated with regard to himself. (Gert, 1969:617)

> To say that violence has occurred is to say that there is a fairly sudden, fairly radical change, effected by external forces, which results in injury, damage, or destruction (to the integrity of the thing). (MacCallum, 1993 [1970]:255)

> "Violence" shall be defined to mean: the entire class of actions which result, or are intended to result, in serious injury to life or its material conditions. Serious injury must include the ideas of biological damage, severe physical restraints or property destruction and psychological impairment. (Lawrence, 1970:35)

> An act of violence is any act taken by A that (1) involves great force, (2) is in itself capable of injuring, damaging, or destroying, and (3) is done with the intent of injuring, damaging, or destroying B (a being), or O (an inanimate object), (...) where the damage or destruction of an object by A is only an act of violence when it was not done with the intention of doing something of value for the object's owner. (Miller, 1971:25–26)

> Violence is the physical attack upon, or the vigorous physical abuse of, or vigorous physical struggle against, a person or animal; or the highly vigorous psychological abuse of, or the sharp, caustic psychological attack upon, a person or animal; or the highly vigorous, or incendiary, or malicious and vigorous, destruction or damaging of property or potential property. (Audi, 1971:59–60)

> An act of violence (...) is a use of considerable or destroying force against people or things, a use of force that offends against a norm. (Honderich, 1973:197)

> Violence is adequately defined as physical force defeating ends and rights. (Betz, 1977:343)

> An act of violence occurs when injury or suffering is inflicted upon a person or persons by an agent who knows (or ought reasonably to have known), that his actions would result in the harm in question. (Harris, 1980:19)

Some of these definitions purport to be lexical in nature, which is to say that they are (mere) reports of how the word "violence" is used (see Robinson, 1950:35). As such, they are either true or false. Other definitions are avowedly precising or theoretical in nature, which is to say that they deviate from ordinary usage to some extent in order to emphasize certain salient features of the objects encompassed by the term (see Coady, 1986 [1985]:3).

Precising or theoretical definitions are a curious mix of report and recommendation. Qua report, they are either true or false. Qua recommendation, they are (only) more or less useful. If they deviate too much from ordinary usage, they become stipulative (see Robinson, 1950:59–92) or persuasive (see below). If they deviate too little from ordinary usage, they lose their theoretical usefulness. The trick, which turns out to be surprisingly difficult to pull off, is to isolate those features of the conventional definition of the term that shed the most practical and theoretical light on the underlying phenomena. (For a discussion of the various types of definition, together with their criteria of evaluation, see Robinson, 1950; Copi & Burgess-Jackson, 1996:137–144.)

Having stated some of the definitions of "violence" and examined a few of the philosophical controversies surrounding the concept, let me sketch what I believe is the correct analysis, or at least an analysis that seems to me to be on the right track. I claim no originality for the general approach. Let us begin by distinguishing two features of concepts, or, to put it linguistically rather than conceptually, two types of meaning. A word (or other symbol) has either evaluative meaning or descriptive meaning (or both). To say that a word has evaluative meaning is to say that it is used to evaluate: either to commend (give a favorable evaluation of) or to condemn (give an unfavorable or adverse evaluation of). To say that a word has descriptive meaning, as the adjective implies, is to say that it is used to describe (i.e., convey information about).

It is important to note that a given word, such as "good," can have both types of meaning, as Hare (1952:111–126) pointed out nearly half a century ago. To say of object X that it is a *good* X is to do two things: to describe X and to commend X. The information conveyed depends on the shared standards of goodness in X-type objects. For example, if someone tells me that a pot contains "good coffee," I understand the expression to mean that the coffee is hot, full-bodied, and fresh, since these are the prevailing or conventional criteria of goodness in coffee—and I, a longtime coffee drinker, am acquainted with them. (In other words, I know my coffee.)

But compare: If someone tells me that a particular plumbing tool is good, I may have no idea what its features are, since I do not know the criteria of goodness in tools of that sort. (In other words, I do not know my plumbing tools.) I do know, however, that the tool is being *commended*. I know this because I am a competent speaker of the language. I know—I have learned—that the word "good" is the most general term of commendation in the English language. The word "bad," conversely, is the most general term of condemnation. It appears that children learn the evaluative meanings of these terms long before they learn the criteria of goodness and badness of the various objects to which they are applied. Why this is so, is not, of course, a philosophical issue, but it does have philosophical implications, since it bears on the learnability and comprehensibility of terms as well as on the acquirability of concepts.

Some words, such as "good," are such that their evaluative meanings are primary and their descriptive meanings secondary. Other words, such as "tidy" and "industrious," are such that their descriptive meanings are primary and their evaluative meanings secondary. The word "violence" and its cognates, I submit, fall into this latter category. To say of an act that it is violent is both to describe and to condemn it (see Betz, 1977:341, 344). The information conveyed by the word (i.e., its descriptive meaning) includes (although it may not be limited to) the following: that physical force is being exercised by someone and that injury or damage (harm) is being done to person or property. (Strictly speaking, property cannot be harmed, since harm is a setback to interest (see Feinberg, 1984), and inanimate objects have no interests; but persons can and do have interests in property, which means that *their* interests in those objects can be set back.) If someone tells me that act X is violent, I know at least that it is an act of physical force that does injury—assuming that the word is being used literally rather than sarcastically, ironically, or figuratively. (I cannot discuss the topic here, despite its inherent interest, but it seems to me that locutions such as "She did violence to the language" are metaphorical rather than literal; they are extensions rather than central applications of the term. This is not to say that there is anything illegitimate or disreputable about such usages, because there is not.)

The unfavorable (adverse) evaluation of the term "violent" (or its cognates) does not, of course, foreclose discussion or debate about whether the act is wrong, all things considered. What it does—indeed, *all* it does—is create a presumption against the act, the presumption being founded on its intrinsic badness. How strong the presumption is depends on how bad violence is. Perhaps a given act of violence is necessary in order to avert or prevent a greater evil, such as nuclear catastrophe or genocide; in such a case we might say that the violence is, all things (including its intrinsic badness) considered, justified (morally permissible). By the same token, it is not always wrong (impermissible) to be untidy or unindustrious. There may be good reasons (an adequate justification) for having a dirty house or for not working hard.

Robert Holmes, who has written widely and persuasively on the topic of violence, captures the complex descriptive and evaluative nature of the term "violence" in the following passage, which is worth quoting at length:

> We can now say that primary violence [i.e., force used against persons or animals, as opposed to force used against mere objects] is an evaluative notion by virtue of the centrality to its analysis of the notion of harm. (...) To determine that someone has been harmed requires making an evaluative judgment. But this does not make primary violence wrong by definition, if by that we mean actually or absolutely wrong. . . . It is important to distinguish between evaluative concepts in our judgments of the goodness or badness of things and normative concepts used to judge that conduct as right, wrong, or obligatory. Violence in its central uses is of the first type. (Holmes, 1989:37)

Holmes goes on to say that, "if violence is not wrong by definition, it is nonetheless prima facie wrong, or wrong all other things being equal, just by virtue of the fact that it is prima facie wrong to harm people" (Holmes, 1989:37).

One virtue of Holmes's analysis—and there are several—is that it explains how two people can disagree about whether a particular act is an act of violence (see, e.g., Betz, 1977:344). To injure or damage a thing is to adversely affect its integrity, to interfere with its normal functioning. If my interlocutor believes that the thing in question *has* no integrity (i.e., is not integrated or functional), then he or she will be disinclined to describe the act as an act of violence, and will disagree with me if I so describe it. An example might be chopping wood for a fireplace. Since the tree from which the wood came is dead (having been felled some time past), the wood has no integrity. (In Holmes's terminology, it cannot be harmed.) The interlocutor may also disagree with my assessment (implied in my use of the word "violence") that the effect in question is *adverse*. In this case, too, he or she will be disinclined to describe the act as an act of violence. An example of this might be using a wrecking ball to demolish an uninhabitable and unsafe structure.

A second virtue of the Holmesian analysis is that it explains why people feel compelled to excuse or justify acts of violence (their own or others'). They feel this way because they appreciate the evaluative meaning of the term. Just as those who keep dirty houses are inclined to say, "I'm untidy, but . . . ," those who defend the use of violence tend to say such things as, "It's violent (an act of violence), but (...)." The condemnatory force of the word creates a presumption, as it were, against acts that exemplify it. For consider: One does not excuse or justify that which is good, right, just, fair, or acceptable. Only bad, wrong, unjust, unfair, or unacceptable things need to be excused or justified.

A third virtue of the analysis is that it illuminates the technique known as "persuasive definition" (see Stevenson, 1938; Robinson, 1950:168–170). To persuasively define a word (or other symbol) is to exploit its evaluative meaning in order to expand or contract the range of objects to which it applies. Take "rape," for example (see Burgess-Jackson, 1995). This English word, as every competent speaker of the language knows, has powerful negative evaluative (and emotive) meaning. Someone may apply the term to acts that are not rape, strictly speaking, in order to attach opprobrium to those acts (and, by extension, to their perpetrators). For example, I may say that "rape" means unwanted sexual intercourse. The negativity of the word rubs off, if you will, on the objects (in this case, the actions, or, by extension, the persons) to which it is applied. Unwanted sexual intercourse *becomes*, through this process, a very bad thing.

The problem with persuasive definitions is that they can be, and often are, used as propaganda devices. The person doing the defining is more interested in changing attitudes (in this case, toward unwanted sexual intercourse) than in accurately stating the descriptive meaning of the term. Richard Robinson describes the dilemma posed by this type of definition:

> The habit of evaluating things is presumably ineradicable from human nature, and certainly desirable. The habit of trying to get other persons to share our own valuations is equally ineradicable and equally legitimate. What is hard to decide is whether persuasive definition is a desirable way of trying to change people's opinions. The argument against it is that it involves error and perhaps also deceit. The only persons who are influenced by a persuasive definition, it may be said, are those who do not realize its true nature, but take it to be what every real definition professes to be, a description of the objective nature of things. A persuasive definition, it may be urged, is at best a mistake and at worst a lie, because it consists in getting someone to alter his valuations under the false impression that he is not altering his valuations but correcting his knowledge of the facts. (Robinson, 1950:169-170)

There may be legitimate uses of persuasive definition; I cannot address the issue here. (For a discussion, see Robinson, 1950:170; Coady, 1986 [1985]:8; Burgess-Jackson, 1995.)

Let us apply this analysis of persuasive definition to the word "violence." Since the word has unfavorable (adverse, negative) evaluative meaning (that much is uncontroversial, even among philosophers; see, e.g., Miller, 1971:24; Prior, 1972:83), one might surreptitiously apply it to acts or states that are not, strictly speaking, violent, in hopes of changing attitudes toward those acts or states. A good example of this, one of many that I could cite, is Garver's citation of "ghettoization" as a case of violence. Garver's objective in doing so is transparent; he wishes to condemn ghettoization. Perhaps it deserves to be condemned. But not everything bad or condemnable is a case of violence (see Betz, 1977:342). One can condemn something for being unjust, for being unfair, for being coercive, for being manipulative, for being degrading, for being exploitative, or for being indecent—not all of which are, or need be, cases of violence. This suggests an ulterior (and perhaps unsavory) motive on the part of the definer. Honderich puts the point well:

> We are given definitions [of "violence"] issuing from political intention and required for simple *tu quoque* argument. Such definitions enable the man who sets a bomb to reply to those who condemn him that they, too, engage in violence, perhaps the "violence" which others of us might describe as unfairness, victimization or degradation. (Honderich, 1973:196)

It would serve the causes of clarity and precision, not to mention honesty and good faith, to condemn something as violent only if it satisfies, or plausibly satisfies, the descriptive meaning of the term "violent." Admittedly, the descriptive meaning of this term is vague (see Audi, 1971:64), but not infinitely or intractably so. That the meaning of a term is not perfectly clear does not entail that it is perfectly unclear. To reason in such a fashion is fallacious. Arguably, ghettoization fails even this minimal test, since it does not (or rather: does not *necessarily*) involve physical force.

IV. CONCLUSION

> When one looks into the literature on the subject, he discovers soon that philosophers in our tradition have been laggard. Unfortunately they have written little about violence as such. (Gray, 1970:2)

The concept of violence came to the attention of professional philosophers in the late 1960s and early 1970s (see Konrad, 1974:37; Lee, 1996:67). There were, of course, forerunners (see, e.g., Dewey, 1939 [1916] and Somerville, 1952), but, lacking a community of like-minded scholars with whom to discuss their work, as well as the literary organs by which to disseminate it, they had little influence. A great deal was written about the concept of violence in the 1970s. We might call this the "golden age" of philosophical work on the concept. A sociologist or historian might say that this is because the 1960s and 1970s were periods of social upheaval. There was concern, in the United States at least, about the use of violence as a means to protect and promote civil rights for African-Americans. There was also concern about the legitimacy and scope of collective violence such as that deployed in riots and warfare. (The war in Southeast Asia was raging.) As more and more people thought about, advocated, and embraced nonviolent means of resistance to what were viewed as unjust laws, its opposite, violence, demanded attention and analysis. To commit oneself to nonviolence is, eo ipso, to repudiate and eschew violence.

More recently, the concept of violence has been discussed in connection with so-called crimes of violence against women, the paradigmatic examples of this being rape and battery (see, e.g., French, Teays, & Purdy, 1998). In 1994, the United States Congress enacted, and President Clinton signed into law, the Violence Against Women Act, which is designed, among other things, to hold perpetrators of domestic violence and sexual assault (including assault on one's wife) civilly responsible for their actions. This, it is hoped, will contribute to the widely shared goal of deterring these acts of violence, most of which are already prohibited and punished by the criminal law. There is also growing concern in contemporary societies that members of various disfavored, despised, or disadvantaged classes, such as homosexuals, Semites, resident aliens, religious cult members, and abortion providers, are being victimized at ever-increasing rates by acts of violence.

I would be remiss if I did not mention guns. Firearm deaths and injuries, both deliberate and accidental, are at all-time highs in the United States, which is viewed by many people around the world as a particularly violent place. This leads naturally to attempts to understand the etiology, correlates, and consequences of gun (and other forms of) violence, which, in turn, leads to the philosophical question of what violence *is*, and how it differs from such things as force, coercion, aggression, and injustice. (For an attempt to disentangle the concepts of force, coercion, and violence in the context of rape, see Burgess-Jackson, 1999.) After all, one can hardly study or regulate a phenomenon if one lacks a clear idea of its nature. This is why historians of violence (the good ones, anyway) are so careful to define their terms; how one defines "violence" determines how much violence one finds (see, e.g., Burgess-Jackson, 1983:57–58).

My objective in this essay has been modest: to describe, analyze, and evaluate some of the philosophical work that has been done on the concept of violence during the past three decades. There is no reason to think that philosophers have reached a consensus on the matter, or, indeed, that a consensus is forthcoming. Nor, in my opinion, is this cause for alarm. There is no consensus among philosophers about the nature of causation, either, but this has hardly stopped ordinary people or scientists from making or relying upon causal ascriptions. Each generation must rethink and reanalyze its fundamental concepts (as well as grapple with its social problems, whatever they may be). Unless and until violence is eliminated from human affairs—a state that, honesty compels one to admit, may never obtain—there will be a need for a category of violence in our thinking. This category, or concept, or idea, like all others of a social nature, requires careful, painstaking analysis, a task that, for better or worse, falls to the philosopher.

REFERENCES

Audi, Robert. (1971). On the Meaning and Justification of Violence. In Jerome A. Shaffer (Ed.), *Violence: Award-Winning Essays in the Council for Philosophical Studies Competition* (pp. 45–99). New York: David McKay Company.
Austin, John L. (1975). *How to Do Things with Words*. 2nd Edition. Cambridge: Harvard University Press. [1st Edition published in 1962.]
Betz, Joseph. (1977). Violence: Garver's Definition and a Deweyan Correction. *Ethics: An International Journal of Social, Political, and Legal Philosophy*, 87(4), 339–351.
Blackburn, Simon. (1994). *The Oxford Dictionary of Philosophy*. Oxford: Oxford University Press.
Burgess-Jackson, Keith. (1983). Violence on the Michigan Frontier: The Incidence of Sporadic Assault in Michigan Territory, 1817–1830. *Detroit in Perspective: A Journal of Regional History*, 7(1), 46–74.
Burgess-Jackson, Keith. (1995). Rape and Persuasive Definition. *Canadian Journal of Philosophy*, 25(3), 415–454.
Burgess-Jackson, Keith. (1999). A Theory of Rape. In Keith Burgess-Jackson (Ed.), *A Most Detestable Crime: New Philosophical Essays on Rape* (pp. 92–117). New York: Oxford University Press.
Coady, C. A. J. (1986). The Idea of Violence. *Journal of Applied Philosophy*, 3(1), 3–19. [First published in *Philosophical Papers*, 14(1), 1–19, 1985.]
Copi, Irving M., & Keith Burgess-Jackson. (1996). *Informal Logic*. 3rd Edition. Upper Saddle River: Prentice Hall. [First published in: *Philosophical Papers*, 14(1), 1–19, 1985]
Dewey, John. (1939). Force, Violence and Law. In Joseph Ratner (Ed.), *Intelligence in the Modern World: John Dewey's Philosophy* (pp. 486–498). New York: Modern Library. [Essay first published (in two parts) in 1916.]
Feinberg, Joel. (1984). *Harm to Others. Vol. 1 of The Moral Limits of the Criminal Law*. New York: Oxford University Press.
Flanagan, Patrick. (1972). Wolff on Violence. *Australasian Journal of Philosophy*, 50(3), 271–278.
French, Stanley G., Wanda Teays, & Laura M. Purdy. (Eds.) (1998). *Violence Against Women: Philosophical Perspectives*. Ithaca, London: Cornell University Press.
Gallie, Walter Bryce. (1955–1956). Essentially Contested Concepts. *Proceedings of the Aristotelian Society*, n.s., 56, 167–198.
Garver, Newton. (1981). What Violence Is. In Arthur K. Bierman, & James A. Gould (Eds.), *Philosophy for a New Generation*. 4th Edition (pp. 217–228). New York: Macmillan Publishing Company. [Revised version of essay first published in *The Nation*, 206(26), 819–822, 1968.]
Gert, Bernard. (1969). Justifying Violence. *The Journal of Philosophy*, 66(19), 616–628.
Gray, J. Glenn. (1970). Understanding Violence Philosophically. In J. Glenn Gray, *On Understanding Violence Philosophically and Other Essays* (pp. 1–33). New York, Evanston, London: Harper and Row.
Hare, Richard M. (1952). *The Language of Morals*. Oxford: Clarendon Press.
Harris, John. (1974). The Marxist Conception of Violence. *Philosophy and Public Affairs*, 3, 192–220.
Harris, John. (1980). *Violence and Responsibility*. London, Boston, Henley: Routledge and Kegan Paul.
Holmes, Robert L. (1989). *On War and Morality*. Princeton: Princeton University Press.
Honderich, Ted. (1973). Democratic Violence. *Philosophy and Public Affairs*, 2(2), 190–214.
Konrad, A. Richard. (1974). Violence and the Philosopher. *The Journal of Value Inquiry*, 8, 37–45.
Lawrence, John. (1970). Violence. *Social Theory and Practice: An International and Interdisciplinary Journal of Social Philosophy*, 1(2), 31–49.
Lee, Steven. (1996). Poverty and Violence. *Social Theory and Practice: An International and Interdisciplinary Journal of Social Philosophy*, 22(1), 67–82.
MacCallum, Gerald C., Jr. (1993). What Is Wrong with Violence? In Gerald C. MacCallum, Marcus G. Singer & Rex Martin (Eds.), *Legislative Intent and Other Essays on Law, Politics, and Morality* (pp. 235–256). Madison: The University of Wisconsin Press. [Essay first read at a conference in 1970.]
MacCallum, Gerald C., Jr. (1993). Violence and Appeals to Conscience. In Gerald C. MacCallum, Marcus G. Singer & Rex Martin (Eds.), *Legislative Intent and Other Essays on Law, Politics, and Morality* (pp. 178–202). Madison: The University of Wisconsin Press. [Essay first read at a conference in 1974.]
Machan, Tibor R. (1990). Exploring Extreme Violence (Torture). *Journal of Social Philosophy*, 21(1), 92–97.
Miller, Ronald B. (1971). Violence, Force and Coercion. In Jerome A. Shaffer (Ed.), *Violence: Award-Winning Essays in the Council for Philosophical Studies Competition* (pp. 9–44). New York: David McKay Company.
Misra, Ramashanker. (1975). On Violence. *Indian Philosophical Quarterly*, 2, 383–393.

Nozick, Robert. (1974). *Anarchy, State, and Utopia*. New York: Basic Books.
Prior, Andrew. (1972). Is the Concept of Violence Coherent? *Philosophical Papers*, *1*, 82–88.
Ranly, Ernest W. (1972). Defining Violence. *Thought: A Review of Culture and Idea*, *47*, 415–427.
Rawls, John. (1999). The Justification of Civil Disobedience. In Samuel Freeman (Ed.), *Collected Papers* (pp. 176–189). Cambridge: Harvard University Press. [Essay first published in 1969.]
Robinson, Richard. (1950). *Definition*. Oxford: Clarendon Press.
Rowe, William L. (1979). The Problem of Evil and Some Varieties of Atheism. *American Philosophical Quarterly*, *16*(4), 335–341.
Simmons, A. John. (1979). *Moral Principles and Political Obligations*. Princeton: Princeton University Press.
Singer, Peter. (1990). *Animal Liberation*. *2nd Edition*. New York: The New York Review of Books. [1st edition published in 1975.]
Somerville, John. (1952). A Key Problem of Current Political Philosophy: The Issue of Force and Violence. *Philosophy of Science*, *19*, 156–165.
Stevenson, Charles Leslie. (1938). Persuasive Definitions. *Mind: A Quarterly Review of Psychology and Philosophy*, n.s., *47*(187), 331–350.
Van de Vate, Dwight, Jr. (1969). Violence and Persons. *The Philosophy Forum: A Quarterly Journal*, *7*, 1–31.
Wade, Francis C. (1971). On Violence. *The Journal of Philosophy*, *68*, 369–377.
White, Alan R. (1975). Conceptual Analysis. In Charles J. Bontempo & S. Jack Odell (Eds.), *The Owl of Minerva: Philosophers on Philosophy* (pp. 103–117). New York: McGraw-Hill Book Company.
Wolff, Robert Paul. (1969). On Violence. *The Journal of Philosophy*, *66*(19), 601–616.

CHAPTER II-6-1.4

Sacrifice and Holy War: A Study of Religion and Violence

VOLKHARD KRECH

I. THE SIGNIFICANCE OF VIOLENCE IN COMPARATIVE RELIGIOUS STUDIES

Religions are a part of the cultural interpretation of primary experience and as such are intimately bound up with the elementary conditions and driving forces of human life. Depending on their orientation, religions can channel, sublimate, or arouse both vital and destructive forces. Religions deal with the forces of nature and attempt to interpret them; they are also able both to avert and to unleash psychological driving forces and conflicts of interest in society. Religions are able to do this because they are symbolic systems behind the binding ways through which people understand themselves and the world. They are prone to generate conflict when they are "an aggregate state of a given culture ... arming itself to go to its limits" (Assmann, 1992:157). If religions are concerned with "the whole" and strive for ultimate values and binding ways of understanding themselves and the world, then particular conditions—be they economic, political, or broadly cultural and thus not necessarily inherent to the given religion—can often mean that representatives and adherents of these religions develop a certain fanaticism. However, whether or not their commitment is expressed violently depends on numerous variables both inherent and exterior to the actual religion. The history of religions has not been able to establish a *definite* correlation—be it positive or negative—between religion and violence. Religion can give violence content and an object, but it is not its original source. Nor is there sufficient evidence for the opposite correlation. Violence can be unleashed without religion, of course, and can also be averted without taking recourse to religion. However, what needs to be explained is the observation that religious convictions are particularly well suited to incite violence and to make it erupt.

W. Heitmeyer and J. Hagan (eds.), *International Handbook of Violence Research*, 1005–1021.
© 2003 Kluwer Academic Publishers. Printed in the Netherlands.

Irrespective of a possible systematic correlation, it is a historical fact that all religions have made reference to violence in one way or another: be it that they develop ritual or other religiously inspired or legitimized practices for regulating or freely exercising violence, or alternatively for averting it; or be it that they refer to violence affirmatively or reflect upon it critically within a system of myths or dogmas.

In the history of religions there have been two types of action in which violence has played an outstanding role: sacrifice and war.[1] This can be dealt with at two levels. When violent acts reveal a connection with religion—in whatever form—interpretations always refer back to traditions. Being a culturological discipline, research into religion must first adopt a *historical* approach. This is particularly the case with a responsible, scholarly use of the terms "sacrifice" and "holy war." The task is then to *systematically* explain the relationship between violence and religion. Toward this end, research into religion seeks to benefit from the insights of other disciplines in the social sciences and culturology, such as ethnology, sociology, psychology, and behavioral research, and is itself involved in the elaboration of transdisciplinary cultural theories.

II. VIOLENCE IN THE HISTORY OF RELIGIONS

1. Human Sacrifice

Throughout history religions have made use of numerous different sacrificial practices. These are among the most elementary of religious rituals and were possibly the origin of all religions (see Heinsohn, 1997). A fundamental distinction must be made between blood sacrifice and bloodless sacrifice. Gifts of cereals and other material offerings, as well as sublimation and spiritualization through prayer, are by nature nonviolent. Blood sacrifice, by the most general definition, can be seen as a ritual act in which animals or humans are killed as an offering to a deity. Participants in religious rituals generally categorize their victims as an offering (see Gladigow, 1984:21). According to this definition the term "human sacrifice" in comparative religion denotes "killing which is not seen as illegal ... in the scope of the ritual offerings which (a) are generally accepted within the given rel[igion] and culture, and (b) are used in a similar way for the killing of other living beings" (Cancik-Lindemaier, 1999:1253). In the history of religions animal sacrifice is much more widespread than human sacrifice. In animal sacrifice violence is done to the surrounding sentient environment. The question of a historical relationship between human and animal sacrifice, if indeed there is one, cannot be answered conclusively.

A *motif* frequently encountered in the history of religions is that of people in extreme affliction and other crisis situations performing a ritual act to sacrifice their most valuable possession—human life. The *sources* on human sacrifice, however, are far from adequate. A cautious and critical approach to the sources often raises doubts as to the historical authenticity of pictorial representations and written accounts. Archaeological finds are even rarer, and in practice their interpretation is equally difficult (see Rind,

---

[1] Mention should also be made of ritual killings, cannibalism, head-hunting, mutilation such as clitoridectomy, violent exorcism, inquisitional practices, pogroms and violence at processions, frenzied, ecstatic or orgiastic states in which unbridled violence is exercised, violence against oneself (such as ascetic self-denial and suicide), and martyrdom. Furthermore, religion exerts an influence on sublimated forms of violence (e.g., practices which repress drives or establish and maintain discipline. Due to limitations of space the editors have requested that I limit myself here to human sacrifice rituals and the issue of war.

1998:14ff.). Even in the case of established findings that pose no difficulties in interpretation, questions still remain unresolved—how frequently was human sacrifice practiced, what cultural status was attached to it, who participated in it, and what was its social function? Due to the lack of unambiguous sources the issue of "human sacrifice" is frequently ideologized (see Grottanelli, 1999)—be it through contesting the phenomenon (see Arens, 1979), be it through overdramatizing it (see Davies, 1981).

Modern archeology has come to the conclusion that evidence of human sacrifice in prehistory is rather scarce and that the material poses difficulties in interpretation (see Rind, 1998). On the other hand, there are occasional proven examples of human sacrifice in the early advanced civilizations, but with just a few exceptions there is no historical evidence to support the common assumption that ritual practices of human sacrifice were widespread in the ancient Near East. Most recent research has come to the conclusion that there was very little human sacrifice of adults or of children among the Phoenicians and in their colonies (see Moscati, 1987, 1994). In terms of the ancient Near East there are essentially only epigraphic findings of human sacrifice, in particular for the Hittites (see Kümmel, 1967), for the early dynasty of Ur (see Collon, 1987), for the Phoenician/Punic area, and for Syria/Palestine. These epigraphic findings are confirmed by archaeological studies of the so-called Royal Cemetery of Ur (see Woolley, 1982) and the Punic colonies of the western Mediterranean (documented in Seebass, 1997:205ff.). The rite of the Israelites expressly prohibited human sacrifice. But Thomas Römer (1999) considers that the criticism in the Hebrew Bible proves that human sacrifice was indeed practiced in biblical times in Israel and Judah and took the form of *herem* (war sacrifice), sacrifice of the firstborn child, and the so-called offering to Moloch.

Evidence of funerary sacrifice in the first Egyptian dynasty has been found in Abydos and Saqqara (see Griffiths, 1982). The ceremonial killing of enemies in the course of a ritual was one of the religious practices of ancient Egypt. In contrast to the concepts of sacrifice in the Near East, Israel, and Greece, sacrifice in ancient Egypt symbolized "the exercise of legitimate political violence, i.e., the persecution, punishment and extermination of the enemies of the pharaoh" (Assmann, 1995:73f.).

In classical myths, histories, and literature there is often mention of the Greek gods demanding human sacrifice. The frequent recurrence of this topos is the product of a certain "sensationalism." But hard archeological evidence is comparatively rare, and the lack of excavatory documentation from the first half of the twentieth century makes thorough assessment virtually impossible (see Rind, 1998:80, and the list of grave sites in Hughes, 1991). Human sacrifice is mentioned in mythical literature, for example, in connection with the main festival of Arcadia celebrated in honor of Zeus in the mountains of Lykaion (see Plato, Resp. 565d, and Theophrastus, Porph. De Abst. 2.27), and also in the cult of Dionysus among the Agrionians in Orchomenus (see Plutarch, Q.Gr.299ef).

In the Vedic religion there are two known variants of the ritual killing of human victims (see Malamoud, 1999). The religions collectively referred to as Hinduism, as well as Buddhism and Jainism, did not practice human sacrifice.

In China, too, the transition from the Neolithic to advanced civilization was characterized not only by bronze metallurgy, the advent of writing, and the use of the chariot, but also by human sacrifice (see Chang, 1963:136). However, the only provable instances of human sacrifice there were connected with funerary practices.

In terms of human sacrifice among the Celts there are, for example, reports in Caesar's "De bello Gallico" and Tacitus's "Germania." Whereas Rind (1998:149) is of the opinion that the archaeological findings leave no doubt as to the existence of human sacrificial practices among the Celts, Marco-Simón (1999) argues that Celtic ritual killings cannot with certainty be considered human sacrifice.

In the case of the southern Germanic tribes and Vikings there are even fewer reliable sources. The history of the religion of the southern Germanic tribes is virtually unknown, and our only detailed knowledge about the Vikings derives from literary sources written after Christianization. The relevant archaeological findings are difficult to interpret and it cannot be determined conclusively whether we are dealing with victims of sacrifice or of execution, or whether the people were buried after dying a natural death (see Rind, 1998:162ff.;169ff.).

Human sacrifice was an element of Mayan culture from its earliest period (see Helfrich, 1973; esp. 176ff.). Numerous iconographic artifacts are backed up by archaeological evidence. This shows that although human sacrifice was a firm element of the Mayan cult, it was offered relatively rarely and always required a special occasion. Some sacrificial rituals have proved to be specific old forms of ritual killing taken over from ancient agrarian cults. In their original conception these were not acts of sacrifice but the cult's ritual reenactment of the mythical killing of a primeval deity using a human likeness. The ethnologist Peter Hassler (1992) endorses this interpretation. After conducting a detailed analysis of the sources considered to be evidence of human sacrifice among the Mesoamerican peoples, Hassler concludes that there is no proof of an institutionalized cultic practice of human sacrifice or ritual killings among the Aztecs, Mayas, or other peoples of Mesoamerica. Rather, the ritual killing conventionally interpreted as human sacrifice "should be seen as the symbolic or theatrical reenactment of myths ... in the context of cultic mystery plays" (Hassler, 1992:247). From this perspective the sources which had been considered reliable actually convey only a distorted image of the Aztec cult. The descriptions and analyses are "projections by European authors" and are "based on misunderstandings, preconceived ideas, or even deliberate misinformation" (Hassler, 1992:247, 249).

2. Wars and Other Violent Conflicts in the History of Religions

Religions can constitute a significant cause of conflicts and wars without necessarily coinciding with other motives, such as the welfare of the people, national defense, economic interests, the interests of the state, or national identity. The religious factor is, however, still accompanied by a whole range of political, economic, and other interests. Therefore, as a rule, the historical relationship between war (and other violent conflicts) and religion cannot be viewed in isolation.

The most intimate connection between war and religion—at least in semantic terms—is the term "holy war."[2] The use of the term "holy" in conjunction with war has precursors in the anti-Napoleonic wars of liberation of the early nineteenth century (documented in Colpe, 1994:15ff.). It underwent a renaissance in World War I parallel to the aestheticizing semantics of sacrifice and fallen heroes. The foundations for describing Islamic wars of liberation as "holy war" (a translation of ǧihād) were laid in political and scholarly consciousness under the influence of World War I (see Colpe, 1994:19). The use of the term received renewed impetus during and subsequent to the Iranian Revolution of 1979. The

---

[2]The following account owes much to the excellent essay by Carsten Colpe (1994) and the article by Hans Süssmuth (1971).

SACRIFICE AND HOLY WAR

term was also in frequent use during both Gulf Wars (1980/88 and 1990/91). It is hard to say why the term "holy war" enjoys such great popularity. Possibly the language of the belligerents or those who prepare for war has exercised an influence, and as such it is right to be skeptical about the idea that any archaic sense of religion provides the basis for this modern justification of war (see Colpe, 1994:45). The question is therefore which historical facts—both in warfare and in the ideologies legitimizing and inciting violence—can meaningfully be termed "holy war," and what other relationships between religion and war can be found throughout the history of religions.

In undifferentiated societies and those with little stratification it is difficult to neatly separate religion from violent collective conflicts or from other political and economic activities. Attempts at reconstructing the relations in the ancient world on the basis of "archaic societies" extant today are fraught with methodological questions as to whether groups, clans, tribes or peoples waged holy wars; these difficulties are similar to those encountered in the reconstruction of prehistoric sacrificial practices. It can only be asserted that warlike acts had ceremonial character if religious history assumes a state of "pansacrality," i.e., that there was a unified ritual/religious culture, out of which other sections of society then developed. But even if one accepts this premise, the acts of war were no holier than legal, economic, or other practices (see Colpe, 1994:37).

In ancient China war was considered ubiquitous. But there was no concept of holy war (see Colpe, 1994:39f.). Rather, conceptions of war were embedded in cosmological theories and speculations about social order and the community. According to these views, an act was to be judged not by its motive but by the category of its result and as a consequence of a particular constellation (see Trauzettel, 1995).

It is not possible to speak of holy war in the Babylonian and Assyrian empires either. Although there is evidence of ritual and religious/ideological elements, this does not mean that military practice therefore amounted to "holy wars," since it is inseparable from "secular" warfare (see Weippert, 1972).

In ancient Egypt there was the conception of a "strong state," to complement a negative anthropology of greed and to protect the weak from the strong. The state's task was also to hold out foreigners or—from the New Kingdom onwards—to subjugate them (see Assmann, 1995). Rulership was seen in divine/cosmic terms—the creator-deity and sun god himself bore the deadly insignia of kingship, and the task of the pharaoh was to implement the *Ma'at*, the legal system—but the idea of a holy war was unknown. Rather, war was regarded as a necessary evil (see Assmann, 1995:82).

In the religions collectively referred to as Hinduism, the idea of nonviolence (*ahiṃsā*) developed in parts of the Mahābhārata (see Schreiner, 1979). Buddhism then systematically developed the idea of *ahiṃsā*. However, wars were still waged in the name of Buddhism, or were at least legitimized through Buddhist ideology (see Schmithausen, 1996). An early example of this is seen in the policies of the Mauryan emperor Aśoka in the third century B.C. On this basis the Buddhist canon developed the ideal of the world ruler (*cakravartin*) who conquers the whole world with an army, albeit without battle or bloodshed. Thereafter he is to rule justly and without resorting to violence. Wars of conquest were legitimized however, by arguing that the nonviolence of the Buddhist cakravartin applied only to the utopian phase of world rule. Despite the religious motivation or ideological legitimization we are not dealing here with wars of religion, since in most cases the enemy was also Buddhist. Violence is even sanctioned in Mahāyāna and Vajrayāna Buddhism, e.g., when it is necessary to defend the "true" Buddhist doctrine (see the detailed treatment in Schmithausen, 1996:75ff.).

In the influential study by Gerhard von Rad (1965), the term "holy war" was applied to acts of war by the ancient Israelites. Subsequent studies showed, however, that the theory of holy war in ancient Israel is not tenable (see Weippert, 1972; Stolz, 1972). On the one hand no form of warfare has been found there that differed from "secular" wars (see Weippert, 1972:490). On the other hand, the Sabbath, particular festivals, places and objects can all be holy, $q^e dæš$, but there is no passage in the Hebrew bible where war, $milḥāmā$, bears this attribute. The reason seems to be that the Israelites believed they were God's chosen people, and therefore Israel was not fighting for YHWH, but YHWH for Israel.

It was different with the Jewish uprising in the second century B.C. against the Seleucid king Antiochus IV Epiphanes who demanded the dissolution of the Jewish cult and pursued the hellenization of Jerusalem (see Kippenberg, 1995:111ff.). The Maccabees followed Phinehas's example (see Numbers 25:7ff.) and "strove for the Law and stood up for the bond with YHWH" (see 1 Macc. 2:24ff.). The idea of a messianic, apocalyptic war developed from their exemplary interpretation of the Phinehas legend and inspired both the first Jewish-Roman war (66–74 A.D.) and the second Jewish insurrection (132–135 A.D.). The idea of a final war (Armageddon) in ancient Judaism and early Christianity (see Böcher, 1994) was to have a strong influence on American Protestantism (see Tuveson, 1968), extending up to the U.S. war rhetoric of the twentieth century.

Unlike the other advanced cultures of the ancient world, ancient Greece had a term for holy war (*hiëros pólemos*). The Amphictyonic League, a ritualistically oriented political alliance, had its centers at the shrines of Demeter at Anthela and Apollo at Delphi. From the sixth to fourth century B.C. it carried out warlike acts against communities that had contravened sacral law. There is evidence of the term *hiëros pólemos* being used for such actions (documented in Colpe, 1994:55, note 54). However, this does not constitute any particular form of ancient warfare, and its validity is limited to the three historical instances of warlike acts carried out by the Amphictyonic League.

There were also forms of religious warfare and war ideology in ancient Rome (see Rüpke, 1990, 1994). When preparations were being made for a war, supplicatory prayer days were occasionally set. Sacrifices were made, and the offerings were examined by haruspices, Etrurian soothsayers. The "fetialis," experts in international law, were also an important factor in the political and religious legitimization of wars. Religion was not used to sanctify war in ancient Rome. "But it gave war a form which made it an ideal medium for competing for prestige within the Roman ruling class" (Rüpke, 1994:78).

The warfare of the Aztec empire between the late fourteenth century and the Spanish conquests of 1521 is regarded as an example of religiously motivated aggression. In research on ethnology and the history of religions the procuring of prisoners to be sacrificed at the great festivals is seen as an important motive, albeit not the actual purpose of war (Rüpke, 1993:458). However, recent critical insights into the sources on the Aztec practice of human sacrifice (see above) cast considerable doubt on the alleged connection between Aztec warfare and religious motivations and legitimization.

Despite Christianity's message of peace, in its history wars have been justified and even sanctified (see the overview by Kretschmar, 1995 and Maron, 1996). The motif of messianic war was known to early Christianity from the Revelation of St. John (Rev. 19:11–21), but it was rejected as a concrete guide to action. After the conversion of Constantine, the Council of Arles (314 A.D.) gave Christian legitimization to military service, but killing an enemy in battle was still considered a moral stain which had to be atoned for (see Erdmann, 1935:14). Following Cicero and others, the Latin Father of the Church, Aurelius Augustine (354–430 A.D.), then developed the theory of *bellum iustum*, which had already been touched on by Origenes. The first religious interpretation of a war to diverge from the concept of *bellum iustum* came with the Persian wars under Emperor Herakleios (622–630 A.D.). In the Carolingian period the stage was set for the development of missionary warfare—Charlemagne's campaigns of conquest involved converting the vanquished to Christianity. Otto the Great subsequently made the "mission to the Slavs" a driving force behind his military expansion to the east—at least in ideological terms (see Kretschmar, 1995:305).

The decisive change in the church's attitude to war did not come, however, until after the end of the millennium. The crusades in the Christian west in the period between the eleventh and the thirteenth centuries were clearly holy wars (see Erdmann, 1935; Cowdrey, 1976; Schwinges, 1996). The Christian holy war was "a war on behalf of the papal church which in turn saw itself as the representative of God. Participation in a war of this kind, whose instigator was ultimately God himself, was considered a positive, commendable, and redeeming act" (Schwinges, 1996:102). There are several reasons for referring to the crusades as holy wars: "the popes' theocratic understanding of the state; the blessing of the knights, who turned an already holy pilgrimage into an armed crusade; the blessing of the flags under which they marched to liberate the grave of Christ; the difference to other wars of the Middle Ages" (Colpe, 1994:56). Release from sin and penance is an additional criterion (see Schwinges, 1996:107ff.). Thomas Aquinas took up Augustine's ideas and further developed the doctrine of *bellum iustum*. In his view a just war had to fulfill three conditions: 1. the authority of the ruler (*auctoritas principis*); 2. a just cause (*causa iusta*); 3. the clear intention (*intentio recta*) of those who were going to war. Opposition came from Francis of Assisi who spoke out for an exclusively peaceful mission. Members of the Franciscan order were strictly forbidden to bear arms.

Research on the history of religions sometimes argues that the idea of the crusades was carried on in the religious wars and wars against the Turks of the fifteenth, sixteenth and seventeenth centuries. However, this view is untenable (see Colpe, 1994:69). The denominational and religious wars in Europe in the early modern age were an element of the structural and functional interrelatedness of religion and politics, of church and state, as they still existed in the transition from the Middle Ages to the early modern age. The formation of denominational churches as bureaucratic organizations and the internal emerging of states were two particular interrelated factors in the wars of religion (see Schilling, 1996).

The current popularity of the term "holy war" is connected in particular to warlike conflicts in the Muslim world. "Holy war" is a rendering of the Arabic word *ǧihād*. However, modern Islamic theologians reject this translation (see Peters, 1979:118), a view that is now shared by Western scholars of Islam (on the Western discussion see Murphy, 1976). Albrecht Noth (1996:112) identifies three separate connotations of the expression in the Koran in the context of "using of armed for *ǧihād* means the activity of the individual Muslim; it lends that person's physical struggle a religious dimension by becoming the focus of a general spiritual attitude; and it emphasizes the individual believer's praiseworthiness.

In the eighth century, Islamic legal specialists, theologians, and philosophers began dealing with the issue of *ǧihād* more intensively and giving it within the Sharia a legal form. Classical Islamic international law sees the entire world as divided into two parts, on the one hand the "abode of Islam" (*dār al-islām*)—those regions under Islamic rule—and on the other hand the countries not controlled by Muslims, the "abode of war" (*dār al-ḥarb*). The goal of wars of expansion was not to destroy the enemy, but to allow the unfettered practice of Islam in the conquered territory. The war against non-Muslims conducted by armies of professional soldiers and slaves "had little or nothing to do with religious enthusiasm—it followed the postulates of political necessity and opportunity" (Noth, 1996:117). However, the de facto cessation of the duty to perform ğihād increased the generally recognized praiseworthiness of voluntary ğihād, of ğihād as a token of the faith and devoutness of the muğāhidūn ("those who perform ğihād") or ġuzāt ("those who, like the Muslims at the time of the Prophet, carry out attacks against infidels") (see Noth, 1996:118f.).

Because participation in a military expedition could be motivated exclusively by the prospects of acquiring material wealth, the criterion of niya—pious intention—was introduced. Ğihād thus reverted more strongly to an act of individual piety. The emphasis shifted from the "holy war" of the Umma to the "holy struggle" of each individual Muslim (see Rotter, 1979:262). According to this shift in meaning, the individual Muslim can fulfill his obligation to do ğihād in four different ways—with the heart, the tongue, the hands, and the sword. The greatest form of ğihād is not the one done by the sword, but by the heart (ğihād an-nfs), i.e., the struggle against (evil inclinations in) oneself (see Rotter, 1979:262f.) However, this shift did not prevent numerous Islamic war ideologists from propagating ğihād as armed struggle as the highest duty of every Muslim (see examples in Rotter, 1979:263ff.).

When religions play a role in wars and other violent conflicts of the present day they are associated with nationalist and/or ethnic interests (see Appleby, 2000:58ff.). In the twentieth century there were no purely religious wars, waged solely for the sake of a religion. Whereas up until the nineteenth century religion was the sole acceptable justification for campaigns of terror (see Rapaport, 1984:659), modern terrorism has to date been primarily political in its motivations. More recently there appears to have been a revival of terrorist activities conducted for religious reasons, legitimized by theological doctrines and thus referred to in research as "sacred" or "holy terror." According to Bruce Hoffman (1995:272), roughly 20 percent of the approximately fifty known terrorist groups show a religious component in their motivation. Examples are the Islamist groups in Algeria and the Southeast Asian region (Indonesia, Malaysia, the Philippines), in the Near East (e.g., Hezbollah and Hamas; see Kippenberg, 1999), the Muslim Brothers and the Takfir groups in Egypt (see Ramadan, 1993), Gush Emunim in Israel (see Aran, 1991), militant Christian groups in the United States such as the Aryan Nations and their Church of Jesus Christ (see Hoffman, 1995:275ff.), and also the Christian Identity movement (see Juergensmeyer, 1998). National liberation theologies often play an important role, particularly among Islamist groups (see Pottenger, 1989). However, religious terrorist groups often have more in common with other radical groups than with their respective official and traditional theologies (see Kennedy, 1999:17).

Of the 268 ethnic minorities politically active in the 1990s, 105 can be identified as religious. In twenty-eight of these 105 ethnic conflicts religion played no role at all. In sixty-five further cases religion was a subordinate factor. Only in twelve cases was religion a factor of equal or greater importance than the other factors involved in the conflict. These were the Hindus in Bangladesh, the Hui Muslims in China, the Muslims in India (see van der Veer, 1994; Kakar, 1997), the Arabic Muslims in Myanmar, the Ahmadis and the Hindus in Pakistan, the Coptic Christians in Egypt, the Bahais and Christians in Iran, the Shiites in Iraq and Saudi-Arabia, and also the animists and Christians in Sudan (see Fox, 1997, 1998:56 and note 41).

Religion plays a role in civil wars or civil-war-like situations in a number of countries. These include Northern Ireland, where conflicts between Catholics and Protestants are based on the assumption made by the Catholics that they are discriminated against and disadvantaged in terms of opportunities for social participation (see Kelley & McAllister, 1984). Other examples are Afghanistan (see Grevemeyer, 1985), and more recently also other Central Asian countries (see Freedman, 1996); Sudan (see Warburg, 1996); Nigeria (see Aguwa, 1997); and the war in Bosnia.

It is debatable whether and to what extent religious factors played a role in the war in Bosnia. Most studies emphasize economic, nationalist, and ethnic factors (see Calic, 1998), and the notion of "ethnic cleansing" dominated in public opinion. However, these views cannot explain why there were ethnic conflicts in spite of the fact that Serbs, Bosnian Muslims, and Croats all trace their origins back to the same tribes. Michael A. Sells tries to provide an answer to this question: "The violence in Bosnia was a religious genocide in several senses: the people destroyed were chosen on the basis of their religious identity, those carrying out the killings acted with the blessing and support of Christian church leaders; the violence was grounded in a religious mythology that characterized the targeted people as race traitors and the extermination of them as a sacred act, and the perpetrators of the violence were protected by a policy designed by the policy makers of a Western world that is culturally dominated by Christianity" (Sells, 1996:144). This assessment may also be one-sided in the way it attributes the primary role in the Bosnian war to the religious factor. But at any rate it shows that religion became an instrument which served to oversimplify the conflict, identify the conflicting parties, and incite violence.

III. THE THEORY OF THE RELATIONSHIP BETWEEN VIOLENCE AND RELIGION IN THE SCOPE OF ANTHROPOLOGICAL AND CULTUROLOGICAL APPROACHES

1. Theories of Sacrifice

Since the development of comparative religion in the second half of the nineteenth century, attempts have been made to discover the origins of sacrifice. Five types of theory have had an impact on the understanding of sacrifice (see Colpe, 1992): 1) a *sociological* approach dealing with contributing, repossession and sharing (William Robertson Smith, Emile Durkheim, Marcel Mauss); 2) a *psychoanalytical* approach looking at collective murder, the death wish and sublimation (Sigmund Freud); 3) an approach based on *cultural anthropology* and dealing with the hunt (Karl Meuli); 4) an *ethological* approach looking at aggression (Konrad Lorenz, Irenäus Eibl-Eibesfeldt); Walter Burkert modified cultural anthropology by combining it with ethological theory; and 5) a *culturological ethological* approach dealing with the ritual restriction of mimetic violence (René Girard). I will restrict myself below to the latter three approaches.

The approach of the Hellenist Karl Meuli is based on cultural anthropology. He is convinced that "the Olympic sacrifice was nothing but ritual slaughter" (1975:948) which has its closest analogies in the slaughter and sacrificial rites of Inner Asian nomadic peoples. This rite, in turn, goes back to the hunting rites of Arctic hunter cultures (see Meuli, 1975:948ff.). Meuli considers that hunting developed into a ritual because a feeling of guilt arises whenever a living creature is killed. The ritual then takes on the function of repentance and atonement. This need is based on fear for future life in view of the fact of death.

Walter Burkert takes up Meuli's genealogy and extends it, adding biological insights from behavioral research and elements of psychoanalysis. His theory begins with the conviction that "all social orders and forms of rule in human society are based on institutionalized violence" (Burkert, 1972:8). Religion is no exception to this, he says. On the contrary: "In the very midst of religion there lurks the bloody and fascinating threat of violence" (Burkert, 1972:8). The core experience of the "sacred," according to Burkert's definition, is blood sacrifice. "Homo religiosus acts and becomes aware of his own self as homo necans" (Burkert, 1972:9). Following on from Meuli, Burkert also asserts that there is a continuity from Paleolithic hunter culture through to the rite of sacrifice. However, Burkert does not restrict the genealogy to the Olympic food sacrifice, but extends it to all sacrificial practices. He also draws on ethological and psychoanalytical theories about an innate human aggressive impulse and thus sees sacrifice theory in anthropological terms. Burkert assumes there is intraspecific human aggression which was externalized in the hunt and then ritualized in the form of sacrificial practices. By diverting aggression away from the human subjects, the sacrificial ritual then takes on the function of building and upholding the community. Here the rule applies that "the closer the commitment is to be, the more brutal the rites become" (1972:47). With the advent of crop farming, ritual killings were partially transformed into bloodless sacrificial practices, but "the counterbalance to terrifying reality"—animal sacrifice and occasionally even human sacrifice—was still required time and time again (1972:56).

Today sacrificial practices no longer exist, at least not in the industrialized societies. The question is therefore whether other (ritual) practices today take on the function of community-building and overcoming social crises. Is there a need for a functional equivalent of sacrificial rituals? And if so, what form does it take? René Girard's theory can be seen as an answer to these questions. It is based on the assumption that the human individual has an inherent mimetic instinct. Mimetic desire for the same objects (possessive mimesis) gives rise to rivalry, which in turn leads to violence. An essential feature of mimetic violence is that it is repressed and goes unrecognized. At the same time it represents the center of religion (see Girard, 1983:25)—initially as rituals, then also in the form of myths. The relationship between mimetic violence and rituals is paradoxical, says Girard—the ritual turns against antimimetic prohibitions and at the same time has the function of creating and maintaining (or reestablishing) solidarity. What makes religion violent is the assumption that ritual violence can be used to conserve or reestablish peace.

In modern society the ritual is replaced by the scapegoat phenomenon, a spontaneous psychological mechanism. Girard defines the scapegoat phenomenon as "substitute sacrifice" (see 1983:44) and sees it as unconscious collective violence practiced by a majority against a minority (see 1988). He sees parallels between the genuine sacrificial ritual and the scapegoat mechanism in that both processes involve a double transfer. On the one hand, the aggression prevailing in the community is transferred to the victim, and thus made responsible for the crisis. On the other hand, this transferal reestablishes solidarity in the community, which is also attributed to the victim. Due to this double transferal, the sacrifice acquires an infinite and abundant significance.

Seeing the sacrificial ritual and the scapegoat phenomenon in parallel doubtlessly offers the heuristic advantage of being able to explain the scapegoat mechanism and the ways in which is works. The two phenomena are similar, on the one hand, in functional terms. On the other hand, they are different because in scapegoating the active participants must be unaware of the mechanism's function of overcoming a crisis through performing a violent act and thereby reestablishing the inner peace, as Girard repeatedly emphasizes.

Otherwise the scapegoat mechanism would lose its effect. Scapegoating is therefore not an *intentional "offering"* made by the active participants, as is the case with the sacrificial rituals described above. For this reason the terminology appertaining to sacrifice is not relevant to acts of violence such as the scapegoat mechanism. The terminological extension of the notion of sacrifice from a rite to a metaphor occurred at an early stage in Christian theology, with the consequence that religion glossed over moral issues—from acts of renunciation to acts of killing—instead of making them the subject of ethical reflection (see Cancik-Lindemaier, 1991).

Finally, brief reference should be made to Georges Bataille (1997), who also sees a systematic relationship between the sacred and violence: the sacred, which represented the common basis for sacrifice, festivals, and war, is violent by nature because it aims for the fusion of that which is separate, the destruction of the tangible individuation necessary in the profane world.

2. War and Religion

a. The Sanctification and Holiness of War and Warriors. The overview of the history of religions given above shows that the sanctification of war has only been attested in a small number of cases. These cases are based, among other things, on the psychological constitution of the person calling to war, which is characterized by what Carsten Colpe calls "ascetic self-renunciation." A war can be said to be holy if it is "compensation for spiritual self-belittlement. In this way a pious person can transmute his or her humility in order to appeal to the judging God. This appeal to God's power is made so as to obtain God's favor, even to enforce it. If the war for which preparations are being made is then claimed to be God's war, such humility can lead directly to theocratic presumptions" (Colpe, 1994:63). Colpe gives two historical examples of this state of mind: Bernhard of Clairvaux and Ruhollah Khomeini (see Colpe, 1994:63ff.). Bruce Hoffman (1995) analyzes the heightened propensity to violence connected with this state of mind by looking at the example of religiously motivated terrorists. They are inclined toward heightened violent activity in particular because they regard violence as a "holy act." As a result of referring to a transcendental dimension, they do not feel ethically responsible for their actions, rather they are acting "on behalf of" and "in the name of" the divine. A related fact is that, in contrast to purely politically motivated terrorists, they show no consideration for public opinion, but act exclusively according to their convictions. Thirdly, religiously motivated terrorists are in total opposition to the political system, which they seek not to change but to replace. They do not employ violence as an instrument with which to achieve the greatest benefit for the greatest number of people, but rather work toward their aims with merely themselves and their fellow believers in mind. In this way the use of violence against enemies can become an end in itself.

The sociological function of these attitudes is to produce a (self-)charismatization and (self-)stigmatization of the leader and activists, mobilizing militants and creating clearcut boundaries between "friend" and "enemy." The ideology of the war hero is also based on this mechanism. The soldier is screened out as an individual and is glorified for his service to a "holy cause"—the nation, the honor of a collective or individual, or whatever. Although Georges Bataille's theory of religion is not free of ideological interpretations of violence, he exposes the attitude of the war hero as the "most blatant attempt" to inject divine order into the category of the individual via initial negation of the individual: "In order to be indifferent to what one overrates [sc. one's own individuality], and to praise oneself for having thought oneself worthless, one needs not only strength but equally a good dose of naivety—and stupidity" (Bataille, 1997:51).

The attribute "holy" refers to a specifically religious connotation which goes beyond the violent struggle for economic, political, and cultural resources. A war qualified as "holy" merges with "the morphological and functional order of phenomena and actions which are indisputably or at least primarily religious: its killing merges with the practice of sacrifice, its emotional commitment with the probably archaic relationship of the manifestations of Eros and Thanatos, its strategy with ritual struggle, and its inevitability with periodic repetition" (Colpe, 1994:32).

Colpe sees the use of the dramatic expression "holy war," particularly in cultural discourse in the present and recent past, as evidence for the theory that "where no one believes in God or gods any more, the sacred does not disappear but attaches itself all the more readily to given conditions, an act of attribution which previously could only be performed or withdrawn by God or the gods. War is the most extreme of these conditions. Therefore both affirmative and negative talk of war inherently contains the suggestion that war is something obligatory and normative, and perhaps it is here that the sacred finds its contemporary expression" (Colpe, 1994:46f.). In the same sense Roger Caillois describes the process of internalizing the sacred as an element in the process of secularization in the modern age: "When the sacred is oriented more toward conscience than toward any objective manifestation of itself, and when the inner self has priority over outer ceremony, every external criterion is unsatisfactory. Under these conditions it is only logical that the word 'holy' is used beyond the original sphere of religion as an expression for the highest value a person can fully subscribe to ... It seems that an object, cause, or living being can become holy simply through being elevated to the supreme purpose, and by people then devoting themselves to it, i.e., dedicating their time and energy, interests and ambitions, and if necessary sacrificing their life" (Caillois, 1988:174, 176f.). It is thus understandable that particular values and their defense—in extreme cases by military means—can be referred to as "holy." The "moral justification" of wars, as occurs under secular conditions (for example the reference to human rights in justifying military intervention by NATO forces in the Kosovo conflict), can be seen from the point of view of comparative religion as the functional equivalent of the sanctification of war. "The (moral) purpose *justifies* the (martial) means" is a stock phrase which demonstrates the historical link between war and its religious justification. However, the decisive difference in analyzing this continuity is in whether it is reflected upon in the context of a critique of ideology—and perhaps also of religion—or whether it retains its affirmative function in theoretical reflection. This difference is particularly relevant to the question of the cultural and genealogical link between sacrifice and war.

b. WAR AS A CONTINUATION OF SACRIFICE BY OTHER MEANS?

When dealing with the violent act of legitimized killing, which is not the same as murder, human sacrifice and warlike acts initially culminate at the phenomenological level. Where both complex phenomena are examined theoretically with reference to biological/anthropological and cultural/genealogical assumptions, some theories claim there is a systematic link. "With their progress in consciousness," Walter Burkert proposes, advanced civilizations demand more than just theatrical sacrifice ritual—they call "for absolute earnest—for real, executed killings" (1972:57f.). The highest expression of state violence is thus the execution of a criminal, which, as a public festival, corresponds to a sacrificial ritual (cf. 1972:58). The "more serious form" of redirecting aggression away from oneself "and integrating large groups of men in collective fighting frenzy" is war (1972:58). Burkert argues that there is a cultural/genealogical continuity between sacrificial practices and wars and supports his theory by referring to the full "symbolic" interchangeability of the hunt, sacrifice, and war, and to the way in which war in antiquity was accompanied by sacrificial rituals (cf. 1972:59; 79).

The theory of war as a "collective sacrificial ritual" is put forward most forcedly by Caillois (1988). Bataille considers the notion of sacrifice and Caillois's theory of war derived from it to be "a banal extension of the word's meaning" (Bataille, 1997:170). Caillois's interpretation "fails to grasp the notion of the *sacred* as well as the notion of war; above all he fails to register the insights of people in the modern world ... Without the sacred, people would not be able to capture the totality and the richness of existing, they would be incomplete; but as soon as the *sacred* assumes the form of war it threatens them with complete annihilation" (Bataille, 1997:177f.). Even if we ignore the possibility that modern military technology could completely destroy the basis of all life, the extension of the term sacrifice to include acts of war still begs the question: if dead soldiers and civilians are a "sacrifice" by a belligerent, e.g., a nation, then who are they actually a sacrifice to? When the ideologists of war speak of "necessary *sacrifices*" which a nation needs to make, the semantics can be analyzed from the perspective of comparative religion as a sacralization of the nation and other political values. The sacrifice semantics of "political religions" serves to create a demure attitude among the combatants and the civilian population affected by the war, to stylize death (at least that of the soldiers) as being voluntary and in the service of a "higher" cause—the warring nation—and to present war as "the unavoidable hand of fate." Sacrifice semantics of this kind are a fact within the history of religions but should not be included in comparative religion's terminology. Otherwise the object language will no longer be the subject of the analysis but will become confused with the scholarly metalanguage, and *nolens volens* one becomes an ideological tool of "political religions," as is the case with Caillois.

IV. RESUME AND CONCLUSIONS

Religious models of interpretation can be among the cultural factors which determine whether violence is considered legitimate or reprehensible, legal or criminal. This overview from the perspective of comparative religion has given examples of violent practices and pointed out under what conditions and in what forms they can be religious acts or acts motivated and legitimized by religion. It is clear that acts of violence can stem directly from religious discourses establishing or interpreting traditions. Ritual acts of violence and those which are religiously motivated thus cannot be separated from myths, holy texts, religious dogmas, and doctrines.

The theoretical overview raised the question of the genealogical and systematic relationship between religion and violence. There are two core questions here: Firstly, is there a direct cultural historical connection between religion and human aggression and violence, which would mean that interhuman violence always assumes a sacral character even where it is no longer explicitly religiously legitimized and no longer follows any pattern of religious rituals? The theories of Girard, Burkert, Caillois and Bataille answer this question in the affirmative, albeit with different intentions, emphases and arguments (on the anthropological and cultural/genealogical assumptions see Gladigow, 1986:150–165). And secondly, does a religious conviction which lays claim to unconditional and exclusive validity inevitably lead—at least in its dominant form—to intolerance and violent missionary zeal and thus to hostility toward democracy and pluralism? This position is put forward by Ernest Gellner (1994) and Samuel Huntington (1996) with reference to current examples of combined cultural and religious conflict, concentrating in particular on Islamism. However, this approach does not always make sufficient distinction between religious positions, nationalism, and ethnicity or communalism.

It is possible to examine religions without making anthropological and cultural/genealogical assumptions, and to note the *intrinsic* link between religion and violence, as has been done by Heinrich von Stietencron (1979:328ff.). On the one hand, particular forms of violence have a cathartic, reinvigorating, exalting, and at times even redemptive function within religions. The act of sacrifice is based on the idea of the purification and exaltation of the victim of sacrifice, e.g., via its deification, or of the occasion of sacrifice, e.g., in order to sanctify a place (building sacrifice) or the person who has died (suttee, etc.). A religion's system of punishment and penance is also based on the purification and exaltation of the person who suffers violence. In the religion's conception of itself the act of violence is seen as a means for the victim's salvation.

The second intrinsic function of the use of violence in religions consists in warding off forces which could jeopardize salvation. Already the ritual praxis of visualizing mythical violence serves to restore the order which has been endangered or destroyed by evil powers. If the evil is manifested in particular people then they are subjected to persecution (extermination of magicians and witches, seducers, heretics, heathens and infidels). Ultimately, the struggle against evil can also lead to invasions and the subjugation of foreign cultures. In this case religion is not (or is no longer) a private concern in its unobtrusive modern form, i.e., an individual choice of faith (see Kippenberg, 1999). Whenever religion is involved in the escalation of violence, it is always only one factor among many. However, due to the intrinsic reasons mentioned, religion does seem particularly well suited to fuel aggression and increase the propensity to violence, particularly as a result of the "symbolic surplus value" which religions add to "profane" motivations and goals through "sanctifying" them.

If one goes beyond the functions of violence within religion and assumes the anthropological and social ubiquity (or even necessity, and thus indelibility) of violence, then religion is one cultural form among others for dealing with violence—for channeling, sublimating, or inciting it. When based on the assumption of innate human aggression, theories of sacrifice and the anthropological and social function of war (and other violent conflicts) conducted or legitimized with religious means "prove to be all the more well-founded, the clearer it is made that peace-making is foreign to human nature. But they go too far when they also incorporate the origins of religion and the sacred" (Colpe, 1992: 881). Religion has the potential to trigger mechanisms of violence and contribute to their intensification. But dealing with the relationship between religion and violence must not lead us to ignore the intrinsic value of religions. One of the origins of religion, and also its cultural and social location, is in peaceful existence, for example in nonutilitarian playfulness and the creative imagination—far from the realm of escalating violence. Religion is not only an instrument of political power, but it also shows no less markedly that the world is more than just the sum of its technically exploitable parts.

Translated by Tradukas

REFERENCES

Aguwa, Jude C. (1997). Religious Conflict in Nigeria. Impact on Nation Building. *Dialectical Anthropology*, 22, 335–351.
Appleby, R. Scott. (2000). *The Ambivalence of the Scared: Religion, Violence, and Reconciliation*. London: Rowman & Littlefield Publishers.
Arens, William. (1979). *The Man-Eating Myth*. New York: Oxford University Press.
Aran, Gideon. (1991). Jewish Zionist Fundamentalism. The Bloc of the Faithful in Israel (Gush Emunim). In Martin S. Marty & R. Scott Appleby (Eds.), *Fundamentalisms Observed* (pp. 265–344). Chicago, London: The University of Chicago Press.
Assmann, Jan. (1992). *Das kulturelle Gedächtnis. Schrift, Erinnerung und politische Identität in frühen Hochkulturen*. München: Beck.
Assmann, Jan. (1995). Ägypten und die Legitimierung des Tötens. Ideologische Grundlagen politischer Gewalt im alten Ägypten. In Heinrich von Stietencron & Jörg Rüpke (Eds.), *Töten im Krieg* (pp. 57–85). Freiburg i.Br., München: Alber.
Bataille, Georges. (1997). *Theorie der Religion*. München: Matthes & Seitz.
Böcher, Otto. (1994). Der Krieg der Endzeit im antiken Judentum und im Neuen Testament. In Hans Wißmann (Ed.), *Krieg und Religion* (pp. 45–54). Würzburg: Königshausen & Neumann.
Burkert, Walter. (1972). *Homo necans. Interpretationen altgriechischer Opferriten und Mythen*. Berlin, New York: de Gruyter.
Cancik-Lindemaier, Hildegard. (1991). Opfersprache. Religionswissenschaftliche und religionsgeschichtliche Bemerkungen. In Gudrun Kohn-Waechter (Ed.), *Schrift der Flammen. Opfermythen und Weiblichkeitsentwürfe im 20. Jahrhundert* (pp. 38–56). Berlin: Orlanda Frauenverlag.
Cancik-Lindemaier, Hildegard. (1999). Menschenopfer. In Hubert Cancik & Helmuth Schneider (Eds.), *Der Neue Pauly. Enzyklopädie der Antike, Vol. 7* (pp. 1253–1255). Stuttgart, Weimar: Metzler.
Chang, Kwang-Chih. (1963). *The Archeology of Ancient China*. New Haven, London: Yale University Press.
Caillois, Roger. (1988). *Der Mensch und das Heilige*. München, Wien: Hanser.
Calic, Marie-Janine. (1998). Religion und Nationalismus im jugoslawischen Krieg. In Heiner Bielefeldt & Wilhelm Heitmeyer (Eds.), *Politisierte Religion. Ursachen und Erscheinungsformen des modernen Fundamentalismus* (pp. 337–359). Frankfurt: Suhrkamp.
Collon, Dominique. (1987). *First Impressions. Cylinder Seals in the Ancient Near East*. Chicago: University of Chicago Press.
Colpe, Carsten. (1992). Opfer, 1. Religionsgeschichtlich. In Erwin Fahlbusch, Jan M. Lochman, John Mbiti, Jaroslav Pelikan & Lukas Vischer (Eds.), *Evangelisches Kirchenlexikon, Bd. 3: L-R. 3. Aufl* (pp. 877–881). Göttingen: Vandenhoeck & Ruprecht.
Colpe, Carsten. (1994). *Der 'Heilige Krieg'. Benennung und Wirklichkeit, Begründung und Widerstreit*. Bodenheim: Athenäum, Hain, Hanstein.
Cowdrey, H. E. John. (1976). The Genesis of the Crusades. The Springs of Western Ideas of Holy War. In Thomas P. Murphy (Ed.), *The Holy War* (pp. 9–32). Columbus, Ohio: Ohio State University Press.
Davies, Nigel. (1981). *Opfertod und Menschenopfer. Glaube, Liebe und Verzweiflung in der Geschichte der Menschheit*. Düsseldorf: Econ.
Erdmann, Carl. (1935). *Die Entstehung des Kreuzzugsgedankens*. Stuttgart: Kohlhammer.
Fox, Jonathan. (1997). The Salience of Religious Issues in Ethnic Conflicts. A Large-N Study. *Nationalism and Ethnic Politics*, 3, 1–19.
Fox, Jonathan. (1998). The Effects of Religion on Domestic Conflicts. *Terrorism and Political Violence*, 10, 43–63.
Freedman, Robert O. (1996). Radical Islam and the Struggle for Influence in Central Asia. *Terrorism and Political Violence*, 8, 216–238.
Gellner, Ernest. (1994). *Conditions of Liberty. Civil Society and its Rivals*. London: Hamish Hamilton.
Girard, René. (1983). *Das Ende der Gewalt. Analyse des Menschheitsverhängnisses*. Freiburg i.Br.: Herder.
Girard, René. (1987). *Das Heilige und die Gewalt*. Zürich: Benzinger.
Girard, René. (1988). *Ausstoßung und Verfolgung. Eine historische Theorie des Sündenbocks*. Frankfurt: Fischer.
Gladigow, Burkhard. (1984). Die Teilung des Opfers. Zur Interpretation von Opfern in vor- und frühgeschichtlichen Epochen. *Frühmittelalterliche Studien*, 18, 19–43.
Gladigow, Burkhard. (1986). Homo publice necans. Kulturelle Bedingungen des Tötens. *Saeculum*, 37, 150–165.
Grevemeyer, Jan-Heeren. (1985). Religion, Ethnizität und Nationalismus im afghanischen Widerstand. *Leviathan*, 13, 115–128.

Griffiths, John G. (1982). Menschenopfer. In Wolfgang Helck (Ed.), *Lexikon der Ägyptologie, Bd. IV* (p. 64). Wiesbaden: Harrassowitz.
Grottanelli, Cristiano. (1999). Ideologie del sacrificio umano: Roma e Cartagine. *Archiv für Religionsgeschichte, 1*, 41-59.
Hamerton-Kelly, Robert G. (Ed.) (1987). *Violent Origins. Walter Burkert, René Girard & Jonathan Z. Smith on Ritual Killing and Cultural Formation*. Stanford: Stanford University Press.
Hassler, Peter. (1992). *Menschenopfer bei den Azteken? Eine quellen- und ideologiekritische Studie*. Bern: Lang.
Heinsohn, Gunnar. (1997). *Die Erschaffung der Götter. Das Opfer als Ursprung der Religion*. Reinbek bei Hamburg: Rowohlt.
Helfrich, Klaus. (1973). *Menschopfer und Tötungsrituale im Kult der Maya*. Berlin: Mann.
Herrmann, Peter. (Ed.) (1996). *Glaubenskriege in Vergangenheit und Gegenwart*. Göttingen: Vandenhoeck & Ruprecht.
Hoffman, Bruce. (1995). 'Holy Terror' The Implications of Terrorism Motivated by a Religious Imperative. *Studies in Conflict and Terrorism, 18*, 271-284.
Hughes, Dennis D. (1991). *Human Sacrifice in Ancient Greece*. London, New York: Routledge.
Huntington, Samuel P. (1996). *The Clash of Civilizations and the Remaking of World Order*. New York: Simon & Schuster.
Juergensmeyer, Mark. (1998). Christian Violence in America. *The Annals of the American Academy of Political and Social Science, 558*, 88-100.
Kakar, Sudhir. (1997). *Die Gewalt der Frommen. Zur Psychologie religiöser und ethnischer Konflikte*. München: Beck.
Kelley, Jonathan, & Ian McAllister. (1984). The Genesis of Conflict. Religion and Status Attainment in Ulster, 1968. *Sociology, 18*, 171-190.
Kennedy, Robert. (1999). Is One Person's Terrorist Another's Freedom Fighter? Western and Islamic Approaches to 'Just War' Compared. *Terrorism and Political Violence, 11*, 1-21.
Kippenberg, Hans G. (1995). 'Pflugscharen zu Schwertern.' Krieg und Erlösung in der vorderasiatischen Religionsgeschichte. In Heinrich von Stietencron & Jörg Rüpke (Eds.), *Töten im Krieg* (pp. 99-123). Freiburg i.Br., München: Alber.
Kippenberg, Hans G. (1999). Kriminelle Religion. Religionswissenschaftliche Betrachtungen zu Vorgängen in Jugoslawien und im Libanon. *Zeitschrift für Religionswissenschaft, 7*, 95-110.
Kretschmar, Georg. (1995). Der Heilige Krieg in christlicher Sicht. In Heinrich von Stietencron & Jörg Rüpke (Eds.), *Töten im Krieg* (pp. 297-316). Freiburg i.Br., München: Alber.
Kümmel, Hans Martin. (1967). *Ersatzrituale für den hethitischen König*. Wiesbaden: Harrassowitz.
Malamoud, Charles. (1999). Modèle et réplique. Remarques sur le paradigme du sacrifice humain dans l'Inde védique. *Archiv für Religionsgeschichte, 1*, 27-40.
Marco-Simón, Francisco. (1999). Sacrificios humanos en la Céltica antigua: entre el estereotipo literario y la evidencia interna. *Archiv für Religionsgeschichte, 1*, 1-15.
Maron, Gottfried. (1996). Frieden und Krieg. Ein Blick in die Theologie- und Kirchengeschichte. In Peter Herrmann (Ed.), *Glaubenskriege in Vergangenheit und Gegenwart* (pp. 17-35). Göttingen: Vandenhoeck & Ruprecht.
Meuli, Karl. (1975). Griechische Opferbräuche. In Karl Meuli, *Gesammelte Schriften, Zweiter Band* (pp. 907-1012) (Ed. Thomas v. Gelzer). Basel, Stuttgart: Schwabe.
Moscati, Sabatino. (1987). *Il sacrificio dei fanciulli*. Rom: Accad. Naz. Dei Lincei.
Moscati, Sabatino. (1994). *Il sacrificio dei bambini*. Rom: Accad. Naz. Dei Lincei.
Murphy, Thomas P. (Ed.) (1976). *The Holy War*. Columbus, Ohio: Ohio State University Press.
Noth, Albrecht. (1996). Glaubenskriege des Islam im Mittelalter. In Peter Herrmann (Ed.), *Glaubenskriege in Vergangenheit und Gegenwart* (pp. 109-122). Göttingen: Vandenhoeck & Ruprecht.
Peters, Rudolph. (1979). *Islam and Colonialism. The Doctrine of Jihad in Modern History*. The Hague, Paris, New York: Mouton.
Pottenger, John R. (1989). Liberation Theology. Its Methodological Foundation for Violence. In David C. Rapaport & Yonah Alexander (Eds.), *The Morality of Terrorism. Religious and Secular Justifications* (pp. 99-123). New York: Columbia University Press.
Rad, Gerhard von. (1965). *Der heilige Krieg im alten Israel. 4th Edition*. Göttingen: Vandenhoeck & Ruprecht.
Ramadan, Abdel Azim. (1993). Fundamentalist Influence in Egypt. The Strategies of the Muslim Brothers and the Takfir Groups. In Martin E. Marty & R. Scott Appleby (Eds.), *Fundamentalisms and the State* (pp. 152-183). Chicago: The University of Chicago Press.

Rapaport, David C. (1984). Fear and Trembling. Terrorism in Three Religious Traditions. *American Political Science Review, 78,* 658–677.

Rind, Michael M. (1998). *Menschenopfer. Vom Kult der Grausamkeit. 2nd Edition.* Regensburg: Universitäts-Verlag.

Römer, Thomas. (1999). Le sacrifice humain en Juda et Israël au premier millénaire avant notre ère. *Archiv für Religionsgeschichte, 1,* 17–26.

Rotter, Gernot. (1979). Dschihad. Krieg im Namen. In Heinrich von Stietencron (Ed.), *Angst und Gewalt. Ihre Präsenz und ihre Bewältigung in den Religionen* (pp. 252–267). Düsseldorf: Patmos.

Rüpke, Jörg. (1990). *Domi militiae: Die religiöse Konstruktion des Krieges in Rom.* Stuttgart: Steiner.

Rüpke, Jörg. (1993). Krieg. In Hubert Cancik, Burkhard Gladigow & Karl-Heinz Kohl (Eds.), *Handbuch religionswissenschaftlicher Grundbegriffe, Vol. III* (pp. 452–460). Stuttgart: Kohlhammer.

Rüpke, Jörg. (1994). Die religiöse Konstruktion des Krieges in Rom. In Hans Wißmann (Ed.), *Krieg und Religion* (pp. 55–78). Würzburg: Königshausen & Neumann.

Schilling, Heinz. (1996). Die konfessionellen Glaubenskriege und die Formierung des frühmodernen Europa. In Peter Herrmann (Ed.), *Glaubenskriege in Vergangenheit und Gegenwart* (pp. 123–137). Göttingen: Vandenhoeck & Ruprecht.

Schmithausen, Lambert. (1996). Buddhismus und Glaubenskriege. In Peter Herrmann (Ed.), *Glaubenskriege in Vergangenheit und Gegenwart* (pp. 63–92). Göttingen: Vandenhoeck & Ruprecht.

Schreiner, Peter. (1979). Gewaltlosigkeit und Tötungsverbot im Hinduismus. In Heinrich von Stietencron (Ed.), *Angst und Gewalt. Ihre Präsenz und ihre Bewältigung in den Religionen* (pp. 287–308). Düsseldorf: Patmos.

Schwinges, Rainer C. (1996). Kreuzzug als Heiliger Krieg. In Peter Herrmann (Ed.), *Glaubenskriege in Vergangenheit und Gegenwart* (pp. 93–108). Göttingen: Vandenhoeck & Ruprecht.

Seebass, Horst. (1997). *Genesis II/2: Vätergeschichte I.* (11, 27–22, 24). Neukirchen-Vluyn: Neukirchener.

Sells, Michael A. (1996). *The Bridge Betrayed: Religion and Genocide in Bosnia.* Berkeley: University of California Press.

Stietencron, Heinrich von. (Ed.) (1979). *Angst und Gewalt. Ihre Präsenz und ihre Bewältigung in den Religionen.* Düsseldorf: Patmos.

Stietencron, Heinrich von, & Jörg Rüpke. (Ed.) (1995). *Töten im Krieg.* Freiburg i.Br., München: Alber.

Stolz, Fritz. (1972). *Jahwes und Israels Kriege.* Zürich: Theologischer Verlag.

Süssmuth, Hans. (1971). 'Heiliger Krieg'—Barriere des Friedens. *Saeculum, 22,* 387–401.

Trauzettel, Rolf. (1995). Fürstenmord im China des Altertums. In Heinrich von Stietencron & Jörg Rüpke (Eds.), *Töten im Krieg* (pp. 125–145). Freiburg i.Br., München: Alber.

Tuveson, Ernest Lee. (1968). *Redeemer Nation. The Idea of America's Millennial Role.* Chicago, London: The University of Chicago Press.

Veer, Peter van der. (1994). *Religious Nationalism. Hindus and Muslims in India.* Berkeley, Los Angeles: University of California Press.

Warburg, Gabriel R. (1996). The Sudan under Islamist Rule. *Terrorism and Political Violence, 8,* 25–42.

Weippert, Manfred. (1972). 'Heiliger Krieg' in Israel und in Assyrien. Kritische Anmerkungen zu Gerhard von Rads Konzept des 'Heiligen Krieges im alten Israel'. *Zeitschrift für Alttestamentliche Wissenschaft, 84,* 460–493.

Wißmann, Hans. (Ed.) (1994). *Krieg und Religion.* Würzburg: Königshausen & Neumann.

Woolley, Charles L. (1982). *Ur 'of the Chaldees'. The Final Account: Excavations at Ur.* Revised and updated by Peter R. S. Moorey. London: Herbert Press.

CHAPTER II-6-1.5

Violence and the Glorification of Violence in the Literature of the Twentieth Century

JÜRGEN NIERAAD

I. INTRODUCTION

The historical period between the outbreak of World War I and the collapse of socialism, including the bloody subsequent wars in the Balkans and in Eastern Europe, brought an estimated 187 million violent deaths, and "was without doubt the most murderous century of which we have record, both by the scale, frequency and length of the warfare which filled it, barely ceasing for a moment in the 1920s, but also by the unparalleled scale of the human catastrophes it produced, from the greatest famines in history to systematic genocide" (Hobsbawm, 1994:13). Twentieth-century literature has reacted to the violence of its age and in so doing it has both developed new forms and techniques and also taken recourse to traditional patterns of representation. Real-world violence, from its massive physical reality to its most hidden symbolic manifestations, has always been dealt with in literature and has evolved its own specific genres and forms of representation, which remain relevant to the present day. In particular drama has developed its own forms of violence, from the Greek myths centered around murder to medieval dramas of martyrdom and the Baroque "Haupt- und Staatsaktion" (sensationalist and gory theater of people in high places) to the modern theater of cruelty (see on this Redmond, 1991; Gould, 1991). In addition there is war narrative from every period, and the mass murder and Holocaust literature of our own time.

W. Heitmeyer and J. Hagan (eds.), *International Handbook of Violence Research*, 1023–1039.
© 2003 Kluwer Academic Publishers. Printed in the Netherlands.

II. IMAGES AND CONCEPTS OF VIOLENCE AS A SUBJECT IN AESTHETICS AND LITERARY THEORY

Whilst images of violence are thus a firm element of literary practice, for a long time their significance was neglected by aesthetics and literary theory, and it is only in more recent years that a thorough theoretical interest in the issue has developed. There are reasons for this. Isolation, destruction, mutilation, torture, screams, blood, secretions, death—violence enters the stage in an ugly and irrational guise, and thus violence and the ugly in general enjoy a precarious position within literary theory and in the philosophical and aesthetic metadiscourse which precedes it. Since the onset of the modern theoretical discourse in the seventeenth century, both art and literature have been linked to the idea of beauty and remained within the parameters of a Western philosophy of the beautiful and good, which was first expounded by Plato (see Politeia: books 2, 3, and 10), whose views remained long authoritative. According to this theory, the beauty of the art form is linked to categories such as proportion, harmony, a quasi-natural "purposiveness without a purpose" (Kant), and the organic relationship between the part and the whole. The beauty of the work's contents lies in the presentation of a rounded fictional world, principally modeled according to the demands of reason, a world which is understood as a likeness of creation or as a counterdesign to an inferior or evil reality. In this context the discourse on the requirements for the acceptable representation of violence in literature concentrated on the idea of the sacrifice: the demise of the suffering hero proves to be a manifestation of the higher order of the gods, God, or a moral law. The body marked by violence is a sublime witness to a transcendental reality, and thus at the same time confirms the social order which is sustained by this other reality. René Girard (1972) ascribed an originally cathartic and later culturally sublimated function to such sacrifices. According to Girard's thesis (for a critical view see Mack, 1987), the process of civilization is accompanied by the development of increasingly covert forms of the renewal of the sacrificial act, the transformation of impure into pure violence with the capacity for symbolic value. Tragedy is one of the most important forms of the transformation of violence into symbol, and it is an institution whose sublimating function in Western society can hardly be overestimated. The origin of tragedy in the violent orgies of sacrificial ritual can be seen in the Aristotelian theory of tragedy with its central concept of catharsis—the "pleasure" derived from the cleansing and purging of passions. When Georges Bataille writes in his essay on Genet that the imaginative transgression of the law not to kill restores the "sacral act" to poetry, he is referring to this "evil" origin of tragedy.

With the loss of transcendence—a metaphysical or social confidence in salvation, a belief in the teleology of the historical process or in art as the location of reconciliation—the link between the aesthetic and the moral becomes increasingly tenuous. More recent aesthetics and literary theory deal with the question of the valence and the function of literary images of violence in connection with the irritating fact that the horrific can be pleasurable and also with the general problem of the artistic treatment of the ugly. Dubos, Burke, and Diderot prepared the ground for the recognition of the ugly as an independent aesthetic value (see Zelle, 1987; Dieckmann, 1968). In his essay on the study of Greek poetry (1795), Friedrich Schlegel does recognize the ugly as a central category of modern literature, but he refuses to accord it the status of an ontological entity. As a result he sees the theory of the ugly merely as an "aesthetic interim" to be overcome by the reconstitution of beauty (see Oesterle, 1985). Karl Rosenkranz, the author of an early aesthetics expressly devoted to the ugly, also unquestioningly states: "The beautiful is the positive condition of its [the ugly, J. N] existence. . . . The beautiful is thus, like the good, an absolute, and the ugly, like evil, is only relative" (1973:8). This view, most recently stated in Hans Georg Gadamer's provocatively study "Die Aktualität des Schönen" (1977) (The Relevance of the Beautiful, 1986), also pervades the first extensive publication on the subject, the 1968 volume on poetics and hermeneutics entitled "Die nicht mehr schönen Künste. Grenzphänomene des Ästhetischen" ("The no Longer Fine Arts. Borderline Cases of the Aesthetic"). Expressly raising the question of the acceptability of the ugly in art and literature implies an unquestioning value of beauty. Since the 1980s a growing interest in a literature of evil, violence, and the horrific has produced a number of investigations which either call for or sketch out an aesthetic of the horrific (Bohrer, 1978), which examine approaches to an aesthetics of the ugly since the late eighteenth century (Funk, 1983; Zelle, 1987), or look at the history of the horrific in literature and literary theory (Nieraad, 1994), or catalogue gruesome, repulsive, and ugly phenomena in the literary texts and epochs themselves (Wertheimer, 1986). There is a small number of overviews on the subject of images of violence in twentieth-century literature (see Fowlie, 1967; Fraser, 1974; Howlett & Mengham, 1994), and a large number of investigations of the subject relating to specific areas such as futurism, the theatre of cruelty, Holocaust literature, and the literature of the world wars. A question which has been of particular interest since the 1960s is that of possible negative effects of images of violence in the media (see Larsen, 1968 vs. Barker & Petley, 1997). Instead of addressing questions of rhetoric and the art of violence, Armstrong and Tennenhouse (1989) look at the aspect of a violence of art and rhetoric, i.e., of writing "as a form of violence in its own right." Here it is a question of the violence which is produced by the representation itself—a form of violence which is underpinned by various concepts of social order, as for example in Charlotte Bronte's "Jane Eyre."

III. IMAGES AND CONCEPTS OF VIOLENCE IN MODERN LITERATURE

1. The Status of Violence in the Process of Civilization (Eighteenth–Twentieth Centuries)

One central driving force in the process of civilization involves the transformation of violent relations into contractual relations, to deal with conflict as far as possible by nonviolent means and generally to shape the individual so that violence in social relations is principally a nonviable option. This process of the pacification of society (see Elias, 1989:225ff.) evolves over centuries and is accompanied by the establishment of the state monopoly of violence, and thus by the view of violence legitimized by the "appearance of power, or external power" (Hegel, 1957:715). In this context it is common to distinguish between two forms of violence, as shown by dichotomies such as "legal–illegal," "controlled–uncontrolled," "predictable–unexpected," "public–private," or "useful–harmful." One form of violence is connoted with positive values, in contrast to the second which is censured as a deviation. In the first case, however, violence is still seen as an ultima ratio with a purely instrumental function, and as a measure to be avoided wherever possible. The excessive use of violence indicates the breakdown of the legal power itself: "Power and violence are opposites; when the one rules absolutely, the other is absent" (Arendt, 1970:56). The principally negative evaluation of violence is determined by the dominant nineteenth-century view that violence is fundamentally irrational and will be progressively brought under control in the course of the historical process and then finally overcome: "The fact is that the nineteenth century draws its optimistic and confident perspective precisely from its own realistic-activistic currents of thought. Its great secular faiths—historicism, positivism, Marxism, evolutionism—find inspiration, in various ways, in the idea of progress ... and in its pacifying capability, and they come to the final conclusion that violence will be overcome" (Cotta, 1985:21). This kind of uncomplicated condemnation of violence is also still common in the conservative world view of the first half of the twentieth century, as shown for example in the following statement by W. H. Auden: "Every educated middle-class man (or woman) really knows to be true ... that violence is always and unequivocally bad. No personal experience, no scientific knowledge, gives any other verdict than what you can selfforgetfully love, you can cure" (quoted from Fraser, 1974:140f.).

An opposing positive evaluation of violence in the aesthetic and real world contexts was also already visible in the nineteenth century, and this further developed into the twentieth century. Modernist literature began with the early French avant-garde (Baudelaire, Rimbaud, Mallarmé, Lautréamont), one of whose programmatic declarations entailed liberating images of violence from every aspect of moralist didactism. The semiotic instinctual subject (see Kristeva, 1974) acts out that which is repressed by the cultural symbolic order—the horrific, the violent, and the "evil"—without censorship in his or her fantasies of violence. The authentic evil is liberated, not merely as a negation of the good or a transgressive act which ultimately only confirms the existing order, but as the active, demonic, and "beautiful" energy inherent to a passion which casts off all forms of restriction and does so with a destructive power that attracts admiration and horror (see Lautréamont, "Les chants de Maldoror," 1869). In the draft of "Préface des Fleurs," Baudelaire says that the most difficult task of art is to extract beauty from evil ("d'extraire la beauté du Mal," Baudelaire, 1975:181), and he says it is "the wondrous privilege" of art to make the horrific beautiful through aesthetic expression (see Friedrich, 1977:40). Thus he still confirms the guiding function of beauty for literature and art, but the provocation lies in the fact that he relates this principle to the traditional opposite of beauty, evil and the horrific. The historical avant-garde of the twentieth century followed on from here. The independent value of violence directed against the world of legal order assumes a key position in Nietzsche as a consequence of his concept of nihilism (see Goodman, 1996): "To speak of right and wrong per se has no meaning; clearly, injury, rape, exploitation, destruction cannot be 'wrong' per se, since life and its basic functions are essentially based on injury, rape, and exploitation and cannot be even conceived of without this character" (Nietzsche, 1969:817). In the first third of the twentieth century, the European avant-garde on both the political right and left advocated the concept of a cathartic, purifying form of violence, which was connected with life philosophy and drew heavily on Nietzsche. This violence was expressed in fantasies of destruction, of shock, and of sudden awakening. The majority of intellectuals thus welcomed the outbreak of World War I. Any condemnation of violence is seen to represent a bourgeois world view and a life-negating rationalism: "There are so many legal precautions against violence, and our upbringing is directed towards so weakening our tendencies towards violence, that we are instinctively inclined to think that any act of violence is a manifestation of a return to barbarism" (Sorel, 1969:213). The idea of a therapeutic form of violence was taken up by fascism and the Nazis. A revival of the humanist tradition after 1945, as a reaction to the millions of war dead and victims of the Nazis, meant that violence was denied any value and its representation deemed unacceptable: "One of the well-known peculiarities of modern civilized opinion is its refusal to acknowledge the value of violence ... We train ourselves to be shocked or bored by cultural images of violence, and our very concept of heroism tends to be a passive one ... And in the criticism of popular culture ... the presence of images of violence is often assumed to be in itself a sufficient ground for condemnation" (Warshow, 1954, quoted from Fraser, 1974:3). In the 1960s the student revolutions led to violence again being connoted positively, as it was seen as a living and unmasking force directed against the system. Here writers such as Georges Sorel, Vilfredo Pareto, Frantz Fanon, and Walter Benjamin were influential. Hannah Arendt investigated the situation at the time in her book "On Violence" (1970) and noted: "Not many authors of rank glorified violence for violence's sake; but these few—Sorel, Pareto, Fanon—were motivated by a much deeper hatred of bourgeois society and were led to a much more radical break with its moral standards than the conventional Left ... To tear the mask of hypocrisy from the face of the enemy, to unmask him and the devious machinations and manipulations that permit him to rule without using violent means, that is, to provoke action even at the risk of annihilation so that the truth may come out—these are still among the strongest motives in today's violence on the campuses and in the streets" (Arendt, 1970:65f.). Here violence has its independent value as that which eludes the particular order and thus questions its legitimacy, as "something that cannot be recycled into something useful, handled with available tools ... If order-making means coercing things into regularity, 'violence' stands for irregular coercion, such as saps the regularity here and now, that regularity which is synonymical with order" (Bauman, 1991:XXX).

2. Positions in Twentieth-Century Literary Images of Violence: Critique of and Apologia for Violence

In line with the basic opposition between negatively and positively connoted violence prevalent since the nineteenth century, literary representations of violence in the twentieth century have adopted two characteristic positions: critical and censuring presentations of violence or apologies for violence. For the former, violence is a fundamental expression of an inhuman realm and of that which threatens the individual, both as victim *and* perpetrator, in his very humanity, whereas the latter bestows violence with its own vital or artistic value as a manifestation of life or as an aesthetic happening. As indicated above, the experience of the Holocaust was a watershed. An apology for violence was practiced more or less without qualms in the philosophy, literature, and art of the first half of the century in the context of vitalism (then used ideologically by fascism), and in the context of the aesthetics of the "destructive character" (Benjamin). After 1945 there was a moral censure on apologies for violence, which began to relax in the late 1960s. At the same time, the critical representation of violence in art and literature has increasingly developed new concepts for an artistic approach to the issue and its specific moral implications. Alongside these characteristic new forms, there remain, on the one hand, the broad mass of literature which makes use of traditional genres, and continues to employ violence episodically or thematically in an unproblematic and reader-friendly manner within the context of fictional constructs of meaning and narrative conventions, and on the other hand, there is a market-oriented literature which glorifies violence, employing images of violence for the satisfaction of sadomasochistic needs and fantasies of omnipotence. There are therefore four basic types of literary representation of violence in the twentieth century:

a. Rationalist critical representation of violence from the point of view of a literature committed to moral values;
b. Trivializing representation of violence within traditional constructs of meaning;
c. Representation of violence as a value in itself from a radical-aesthetic or vitalistic perspective;
d. Market-oriented exploitation of images of violence with the aim of satisfying culturally censured needs.

With their critical or provocative approach, types a and c have the potential to develop new literary techniques and also to question traditional concepts of literature. Therefore they can take on board avant-garde forms. In contrast, types b and d are oriented toward reader expectations and literary conventions. Nonetheless the oppositions a and b, and c and d, are not always easy to uphold entirely in practice. The following overview will concentrate on types a and c, as here the problem of literary images of violence finds its most striking expression.

IV. CRITICAL REPRESENTATIONS OF VIOLENCE IN TWENTIETH-CENTURY LITERATURE

1. Critical Representations of Violence in War Literature

Critical representation of violence before the Holocaust remains within the tradition of seeing history as a process of civilization and pacification and tends to see violence as a separate territory which is fundamentally alien and hostile to human nature. Violence appears as a more or less anonymous power which strives to destroy the individual and his value system. The experience of this kind of violence, as exemplified in World War I, is normally depicted from the point of view of the victim, and uses narrative conventions which promote identification (see Fussell, 1975). Mass-audience antiwar literature by authors such as Arnold Zweig (Der Streit um den Sergeanten Grischa, 1927; The Case of Sergeant Grischa, 1927), Ludwig Renn (Krieg, 1928; War, 1929), and Erich Maria Remarque (Im Westen nichts Neues, 1929; All Quiet on the Western Front, 1929), adheres to this pattern (see Müller, 1986). Better-known English antiwar poetry, such as the World War I poetry by Wilfred Owen, Siegfried Sassoon, and others, makes use of generally traditional forms to express the experience of violence. A deep abhorrence and utter condemnation of violence is conveyed in an artistically controlled manner (see the rather apologetic overview in Silkin, 1972; a more circumspect view in Featherstone, 1995; and the critique in Stephen, 1996). The same can be said for literary approaches to World War II, as in Theodor Plievier (Stalingrad, 1945; Stalingrad, 1948), or Gert Ledig (Vergeltung, 1956 [Reprisal]). For American literature on the two world wars, and on the Korean and Vietnam wars, Jones (1976) sees one trend of the war narrative as a novel of character development ("Bildungsroman"): "Typically, the hero brings to his war experience a set of apparently coherent and complete moral precepts, which finally prove inadequate. The subsequent process of revision and rationalization is often the true center of the book" (1976:4). Works such as James Jones's "From Here to Eternity," Anton Myrer's "The Big War," Joseph Heller's "Catch-22," and Norman Mailer's "Why Are We in Vietnam?" must be seen in the light of earlier works of the genre, such as Stephen Crane's "The Red Badge of Courage," John Dos Passos's "Three Soldiers," and Hemingway's "A Farewell to Arms."

Alongside the late poems of Khlebnikov, it is the texts of Isaac Babel which give expression to the horrors of the Russian civil war of 1918–1921, in depictions of violent acts, torture, hunger, and death, all of which open the gates of hell (see Howlett, 1994). Pablo Neruda reacted to the Spanish Civil War with his collection of poems "Spain in the Heart" (1936/37), evoking a poetic world, which, notwithstanding its involvement with the horrific realities of war, proclaims the restoration of a natural order in the tradition of the bucolic idyll. In contrast, Cesar Vallejo's cycle of poems "España aparta de mí este cáliz" (1937) (Spain Take this Cup From Me) is a more exact and convincing expression of the sufferings and death of the individual (see Sinclair, 1994).

As a contrast to the above, new means of representation were used experimentally in expressionist antiwar texts (see Minden, 1994; Bridgwater, 1985), and by authors such as Otto Nebel (Zuginsfeld, 1919 [Field Campaign]), Karl Kraus (Die letzten Tage der Menschheit, 1919; The Last Days of Mankind), Edlef Köppen (Heeresbericht, 1930 [Military Dispatch]), Alexander Kluge (Schlachtbeschreibung, 1964; The Battle, 1967), and Alfred Andersch (Winterspelt 1974; Winterspelt, 1978). Using new literary techniques such as episodic narrative, montage, and documentary forms, and by disregarding temporal and psychological continuity, these works reacted to the fact that since World War I contemporary conflict between states no longer displays any simply narratable experiential reality, but has rather made "true experience" impossible, as Adorno wrote (1976:63). Modern warfare has developed its own mechanics, which no longer involve the decisive battle ending in simple victory and defeat in the classical sense. In the matériel battle, with tanks, heavy bombing, and walls of fire, warfare has become a scenario to which the individual feels helplessly exposed as to a force of nature, and which he can no longer relate to any meaningful context of experience: "Was it not noticeable at the end of the war that men returned from the battlefield grown silent—richer, but poorer in communicable experience ... A generation that had gone to school in horse-drawn streetcars now stood in the open air, amid a landscape in which nothing was the same except the clouds and, at its center, in a force field of destructive torrents and explosions, the tiny, fragile human body" (Benjamin, 1992:439). Alexandar Hermon also works with advanced literary techniques in his depiction of the postcommunist Yugoslav era of war and violence (The Question of Bruno, 2000).

The vast majority of texts on World War I written in the "patriotic spirit," as well as all affirmative war literature of the century, follows traditional nineteenth-century patterns of narrative and imagery, and continues with the pathos and the rhetoric of the patriotic concept of the victim deriving from late pietism (see Kaiser, 1973). Here there is no clear distinction to the pure glorification of violence. Violent scenarios are presented in words and images, making liberal use of the aesthetic tradition of the horrific and the sublime, and of techniques of exaggeration and contrast, without there being any moral framework, except that of an uncritical and subliminal ideology of national glory and individual sacrifice.

2. Literary Approaches to the Holocaust

The Holocaust—industrial mass murder at the center of civilization—is generally interpreted as the collapse of all the securities of civilization offered by the Western idea of humanity, and the extreme negation of the modern identity of the individual (see Diner, 1988). It has become evident that creativity and destructiveness are inseparable aspects of modernity: As rationalization and technical perfection increase, so does the efficiency of potential socially-generated inhumanity (Bauman, 1992:23). After 1945, art and literature were faced with the question of whether to represent the mass murder of the Jews, which had been legalized by the state and organized with bureaucratic and technical means: "It is barbaric to write a poem after Auschwitz, and that is why it has become impossible to write poetry today" (Adorno, 1955:31). This much-cited verdict against representation from Adorno's 1951 essay "Kulturkritik und Gesellschaft" (Cultural Criticism and Society) marks the beginning of the debate on the question of how—and whether—to represent the Holocaust, and it has figured in this debate ever since (see Laermann, 1993; and also Steiner, 1974). By explicitly withdrawing this verdict in his "Negative Dialectics" (see Adorno, 1966:353), Adorno then accepted that literature can address "Auschwitz," and indeed must do so on behalf of the right of the victims not to be forgotten. The question then is centered on the means of representation, and thus on a reversal of the usual point of view. The question as to how literature may present the Holocaust with the available techniques then becomes the question as to the consequences of the Holocaust for literature and art and their traditional forms of expression (see Young, 1988; Friedländer, 1992; Köppen, 1993; Friedman, 1993; Hartman, 1994; LaCapra, 1994; Berg, 1996; Langer, 1999; Taterka, 1999). Mistrusting traditional literary forms, Brecht also voiced early doubts as to the literary representability of events in Auschwitz, in the Warsaw Ghetto, or in Buchenwald (see Brecht, 1967:313). Here Brecht identifies exactly what Adorno critically calls the "aesthetic principle of stylization:" traditional forms of artistic representation which aim for internal unity and closure, and a statement or a "meaning." The terror engendered by horrific violence has forced a critique of traditional means of representation, bringing forth aesthetic innovations and radical forms. Autobiography, documentary literature, and fiction are the classical genres used to address the Holocaust, and it is evident that this subject breaches the parameters and conventions of these genres.

As far as autobiographical Holocaust literature is concerned, the early postwar years saw a preponderance of eye-witness accounts with no further literary pretensions (G. Spieß, Drei Jahre Theresienstadt, 1945 [Three Years in Theresienstadt]; A. Hochhäuser, Unter dem gelben Stern, 1948 [Under the Yellow Star]; E. de Martini, Vier Millionen Tote klagen an, 1948 [Four Million Dead Accuse]; Zenon Rosanski, Hats Off, 1948). In contrast, narratives by survivors written after a certain time has passed (see Primo Levi, Se Questo è un Uomo, 1947 [If This is a Man]; T. Borowski, Kamienny [wiat, 1959 [World of Stone]) display a category of autobiographical writing which is characterized by the work of memory, whereby the dimensions of the past and the present, of the writing and remembering subject, and the remembered past subject blend together. A mistrust of the images of memory is prevalent, comfortable distinctions such as that between victims and perpetrators are relativized, and the narrative text itself is replete with reflection and commentary. In later autobiographical Holocaust narratives (see Jorge Semprun, Le grand voyage, 1963 [The Long Voyage, 1964], and L'écriture ou la vie, 1994 [Literature or Life, 1997]; Cordelia Edvardson, Braent barn soeker sig till elden, 1984 [Burned Child Seeks the Fire, 1997], Art Spiegelman, Maus. A Survivor's Tale, 1986; Ruth Klüger, weiter leben, 1992, [continue living]), this tendency is predominant and the conventions of the genre—the closed, chronological, and meaningful construct of a life—are thrown open by the consideration of the dialectics of memory and forgetting. Furthermore, autobiography can take on the form of fiction, with the reference to the experiences of the author still recognizable, and thus making claims to authenticity (see Edgar Hilsenrath, Nacht, 1964 [Night, 1966]; Imre Kertész, Sorstalansag, 1975 [Fateless, 1992]; Ida Fink, Podroz, 1990 [The Journey, 1992]; Liana Millu, Smoke Over Birkenau, 1991). The reverse case, fiction in the form of autobiography, is not uncommon in literary tradition, but it seems to be unacceptable for a treatment of the Holocaust, as is shown by the case of the Swiss author Wilkomirski/Doesseker, who enjoyed initial success when presenting himself as a survivor and a victim, with vivid depictions of excessive acts of violence (see Binjamin Wilkomirski, Bruchstücke, 1995 [Fragments, 1996]). Beyond the scandal of deliberate deception, or perhaps overidentification with the victims as a result of a guilty conscience, this case also pointed to a mechanism of reception which takes place either openly or covertly in autobiographical Holocaust literature. The narrative of the victim excludes the reader as belonging to the perpetrators and sets in motion a mechanism of guilty conscience, a wish for symbolic reparation, and the self-avowed duty of remembrance, all of which makes it impossible or extremely difficult for the reader to gain aesthetic distance to the text, to criticize, or to doubt the historical credibility of the narrative.

For a long time, documentary Shoah literature (see Anatoly Kuznetsov, Babi Jar, 1967 [Babi Yar, 1970]; Rolf Hochhuth, Der Stellvertreter, 1963 [The Deputy, 1964]; Peter Weiss, Die Ermittlung, 1965 [The Investigation, 1966]) derived its impetus from the desire to counter the perpetually appealing and conciliatory illusion of fiction through the "authenticity" of the historical truth of the genocide as revealed in documents. More recent theories on historical narrative (see White, 1978) and on the culture of remembrance (see Assmann & Harth, 1991) have shown, however, that "facts," even in documents, only exist as already interpreted facts. Literary montage of documents always has its interpretation written into it, as the reproduction of "facts" from a particular perspective in the documents and also in the selection and contextualization of the documents themselves. A number of works have used documents in this way, without including any unreflected claims to authenticity (see M. Franke, Mordverläufe, 1993 [Processes of Murder]; H. Bäcker, Nachschrift, 1986, 1998 [Postscript]; H. Krall, Legoland, 1989 [Legoland]).

In early fictional Holocaust literature there was a predominance of plain narrative working with the usual conventions of representation (for example Jean-François Steiner, Tréblinka. La révolte d'un camp d'extermination, 1966 [Treblinka, 1967], see the critique in Ezrahi, 1980:25ff.), but in the innovative works of this genre, the closure of a fictional version of the world with its hero and symbolism is countered by grotesque and provocative elements which challenge established discourse (Yoram Kaniuk, Adam ben-kelev [Adam Resurrected, 1969]; George Tabori, The Cannibals, 1968; Edgar Hilsenrath, Der Nazi und der Friseur, 1977 [The Nazi and the Barber, 1971]). A further strategy occurs when the traditional forms are undermined by a documentary gesture with an ironically cited claim to reality (see Alexander Kluge, Lebensläufe, 1964 [Biographies] ; W. G. Sebald, Die Ausgewanderten, 1992 [The Emigrants, 1996]). Alternatively the narrative text enfolds in the postmodern manner, with commentary, poetological reflection, chronological distortions and omissions, as well as the coexistence of various genres (see David Grossman, See Under Love, 1986).

Holocaust literature divides into two basic complementary narratives, the (German) perpetrator narrative and the (Jewish) victim narrative. The different perspectives of perpetrators and victims regarding the events—and the accompanying differences in imagery of violence—can be roughly characterized as follows. On the one hand, there is a sense of alienation from guilt and responsibility, caused by the bureaucratic division of labor which made mass murder possible, and on the other hand, there is the existential experience of life-threatening violence and suffering. Further differences are the functional versus the intentional explanation of mass murder, a tendency to universalize or particularize the events, relativization versus emphasis of the distinction between victims and perpetrators, and distance versus identification (see Diner, 1998). One study of the perpetrator narrative has convincingly revealed and investigated its blind spots (Schlant, 1999; on Holocaust literature written in German see also Bier, 1979; Cernyak-Spatz, 1985; Gilman & Zipes, 1997).

3. The Theory of a Critical Representation of Violence

Fraser (1974) has investigated the most important aspects of a critical representation of violence in terms of reception theory and psychology. In particular he refers to 1960s American art and literature, a period which saw an increase in images of violence and a shift in the attitude of intellectuals toward violence. Fraser begins by discounting those typified genres and representations which leave the viewer or reader cold, such as the frequent constellation of a monster pitted against heroic innocence. The Paris Grand Guignol theatre certainly belongs to this genre; from 1897 to 1962 it presented true-to-life cruelty to an audience entertained by fearsome events. "Aided by trick lighting, fearsome props and make-up, the Guignolers (went) happily, if homicidally, about their business of gouging out one another's eyes, cooking villains in vats of sulphuric acid, hurling vitriol and cutting throats, all to the accompaniment of hysterical laughter and hideous shrieks," reads a report from Life magazine on April 28, 1947 (quoted from Callahan, 1991:165; see also Emeljanow, 1991). Fraser refers to depictions of violence in works such as "Oedipus Rex," "MacBeth," "King Lear," Goya's "Los Caprichos," Picasso's "Guernica," Solzhenitsyn's "One Day in the Life of Ivan Denisovich," Resnais' "Night and Fog," Roussell's "L'univers concentrationaire" (The Concentration Camp Universe), Franjus's "La tête contre les murs," (Head Against the Wall), Kafka's "In the Penal Colony," Koestler's "Darkness at Noon" or Céline's "Death on the Installment Plan." In these works violent acts have the function of "windows," "and it is in relation to what one sees through them—bourgeois awfulness, or the horrors of war, or intensities of ecstasy or dread, and so on that the deepest challenges and confrontations occur. If one is made to feel more or less deeply uncomfortable, it is because one is being confronted with facts that one hadn't known, or hadn't thought carefully enough about, or is still reluctant to feel intensively enough about" (1974:47). Criticizing the intellectualization of violence as an instrument of rebellion against society common at the time of the students' revolts, and also criticizing the reduction of violence to an antirational mode of shoring up identity, Fraser sees the precondition for truly shocking presentations of violence "in the simple fact that one believes that such violences could actually happen" (1974:50). The fundamental principle is identification—"penetration into and empathy with other consciousnesses in action" (1974:53)—with victims *and* perpetrators. One of the major factors causing empathy is the depiction of the broader life story or context and of the physicality of the victim, thus showing his vulnerability. Holocaust research in recent years (Browning, Goldhagen, research on local history) in particular has shown that mass murder was by no means organized and carried out by a small group of criminals, but rather that large numbers of "ordinary people" took part both directly and indirectly. This means that any depiction which sets the perpetrator apart as a monster, sadist, or sexual abuser, is unacceptable, as it provides the reader with a comfortable distance without questioning his moral security and identity. Thus Fraser also calls for the option of empathy with the perpetrator and his world of ideas which motivate and justify violence: "The more ordered and channelled the energies making for violence are, the more significant the violences themselves are likely to be, and the more enlightening the entailed empathy" (1974:92). The depiction should not offer the reader any position, or system, which neutralizes violence through the act of bestowing greater meaning. "In contrast, the truly shocking and cruel in art, I suggest, occurs when the artist's gaze has been turned as firmly and in a sense disinterestedly as possible on concrete human behaviour" (1974:116).

Céline used this method of the registering gaze with radical and shocking effect in "Journey to the End of the Night:" "What is missing from all Céline's fiction is a set of beliefs that will allow ethical distinctions to become a living force for the individual" (Tilby, 1994:102). In Fraser's enlightenment model of representations of violence, successful artistic treatment of violence, like real experience of violence itself, is at "the cutting edge of ideas and ideologies." It has the purpose "to reaffirm or reassess one's own values and to acknowledge the necessity of having as strong and clearly articulated a value-system, as sharply defined a self, as much alertness to others, and as firm a will as possible" (157; see a similar point in Jones, 1976, chap. 2). Fraser's approach adheres to a "realistic" theory of human nature which includes violence, such as has been developed by Markovic (1974).

V. LITERARY APOLOGIES FOR VIOLENCE

1. Literary Apologies for Violence in the Avant-garde and (Pre-)Fascism

Conceptions of violence as emancipatory, or life-affirming, or as a fascinating phenomenon with aesthetic value which has been repressed by bourgeois culture, all belong to the central strategies of the European political, artistic, and intellectual avant-garde, and in the case of a great number of the protagonists involved, these concepts are linked to the fascist cult of violence (Heidegger, Céline, Pound, Hamsun, D'Annunzio, Yeats, Maurras, Marinetti, Gentile, Pirandello, Drieu de la Rochelle, Marcel Jouhandeau, Wyndham Lewis, Cocteau, Ernst Jünger, Gottfried Benn). Ze'ev Sternhell (1983, 1992) argues that European fascism first articulated itself as a cultural phenomenon, as a nonconformist, avant-garde, revolutionary movement against the project of the Enlightenment, and a movement which was an integrating force in European culture at the beginning of the twentieth century. By investigating the relations between Italian and French futurism and the later fascist programs, Sternhell shows how the nineteenth-century traditions of European irrationalism and nationalism, on the one hand, and political and artistic dissident movements (syndicalism in the school of Georges Sorel and futurism), on the other hand, came together with the common objectives of destroying liberal bourgeois society, its culture, and its political structures. With his theory of the cultural fascism of the avant-garde movements, Sternhell raised an issue that had long been taboo, and he contradicted views which saw the futurists merely as a picturesque concomitant to fascism (E. Nolte), or as eccentrics court jesters (G. L. Mosse), or merely as an erratic movement of "to and fro and fro and to" (P. Demetz).

"4. We affirm that the world's magnificence has been enriched by a new beauty: the beauty of speed. A racing car whose hood is adorned with great pipes, like serpents of explosive breath—a roaring car that seems to ride on grapeshot is more beautiful than the Victory of Samothrace. 9. We will glorify war—the world's only hygiene—militarism, patriotism, the destructive gesture of freedom-bringers, beautiful ideas worth dying for, and scorn for woman. 10. We will destroy the museums, libraries, academies of every kind, will fight moralism, feminism, every opportunistic or utilitarian cowardice." These are the best-known paragraphs from Marinetti's "Manifesto of Futurism," published on February 20, 1909, in "Figaro." Here the central aspects of the avant-garde rhetoric of violence are to be found in nuce, as they were later varied and intensified in artistic and political contexts. Marinetti links the glorification of violent technology, of war, of destruction, and of the break with tradition in a particularly unambiguous manner with Italianità, a nationalist form of patriotism. Two significant elements of this are the emphasis on the hygienic aspect of violence and a dissociation from the female, with the accompanying heightening of the male.

In more recent research these elements have led to the thesis that avant-garde and fascist apologies of violence are the expression of the male fear of bodily contact with the other, and of contamination by the other: "The literature of Italian Futurism and anti-Semitic Nazism are linked in a discourse of anxiety about the regulation of bodily boundaries and the need for a distinct or purified identity" (Howlett & Mengham, 1994:1). Klaus Theweleit (1987) interprets protofascist glorification of violence in the diaries, memoirs, and fictional texts of the Free Corps movement in the light of the Frankfurt School thesis of the Oedipal internalization of authority as a specifically male fantasy, which is directed against the female and its threat to male integrity. Elizabeth Wright (1994) sees images of violence in the early plays of Brecht in this light as a reaction to the fear of bodily disintegration. David Forgacs (1994) came to the following conclusion in his investigation of the rhetorics of violence in Italian fascism: "The body of the state administration is bloated with bureaucracy, infested with parasites which must be cut out ... modern society is sick and appropriate forms of political intervention—by state, the party, the movement—can make it well. Such forms will be made clean, in operations carried out with sterile instruments: the scalpel, the drip and the needle, the cauterising iron. These are the commonplaces of a medicalising rhetoric of violence which will be found also in Nazism" (7). From here Forgacs sees a direct line to futurism and its apology for violence as a therapy for an imagined body, the body of the nation. "War is imagined as regulating the health of the nation and global body by cleansing and purifying" (1994:12). For futurists such as Marinetti (see his prose poem "Bataille, Poids et Odeur," 1912 [Battle Weight + Smell]), however, or nationalists such as Giovanni Papini (see Let Us Love the War, 1914), violence is imagined and celebrated as an aesthetic event, and the real violent course of war is made unreal: "Papini talks about blood, but the blood is, like Marinetti's sanitising 'shower,' a 'bath,' a 'watering' of the earth, a cleansing, a fertilizing, a regeneration. In other words it is symbolic blood, endowed with magical, thaumaturgical functions. He talks about slitting throats, slashing bellies, ripping out guts, tearing and crunching, but in a way that dematerialises the acts by foregrounding the sound of the words (reinforced in the Italian by alliteration: 'si sgozza e si sbuzza, si sbudella e si sbrana; si spezza e si sfracassa')" (1994:13). Works by the Russian futurists Vladimir Mayakovsky and Velimir Khlebnikov should also be seen in this context, as they celebrated war as the realization of their ideas, as a mythical event, and as the liberation of the word, but also voiced critical standpoints (see Hodgson, 1994). One of the best-known representatives of an avant-garde aesthetics of violence, and of the glorification of war and struggle, is Ernst Jünger. His 1922 war diaries, "In Stahlgewittern. Aus dem Tagebuch eines Stoßtruppführers" (The Storm of Steel: From the Diary of a German Stormtroop Officer on the Western Front, 1933), were republished in their fourth and final version in 1935, and this edition reached 150,000 by the end of the war. Here as in other Jünger texts a heightened sense of life "at the abyss" is celebrated, "the confluence of the nameless crowd, ... its pulsating, its rhythm, its tension, which is then released into the higher trajectory of the individual emerging to be thrown at the light. The heroes shine forth, the lonely soldiers from the hordes of warriors and the gray armies, the soloist steps out from the ballet in a finer array, and the voice of the great singers is heard in the concert of the chorus" (Jünger, 1988:257; on Jünger's aesthetics of violence see Kaempfer, 1981; Arnold, 1990; Midgley, 1994; a more general approach in Eksteins, 1989). The Spanish author Valle-Inclan also provides an aestheticizing depiction of the front in his report "Midnight: Sidereal Vision of a Moment of War" of 1917 (see Sinclair, 1994).

As a continuation of futurism, Antonin Artaud's theater of cruelty proclaims the independent value of cruelty as a metaphor of life, consciousness, meaning, and vitality. In the first manifesto of 1932 Artaud writes: "The theatre will never find itself again ... except by furnishing the spectator with the truthful precipitate of dreams, in which his taste for crime, his erotic obsessions, his savagery, his chimeras, his utopian sense of life and matter, even his cannibalism, pours out, on a level not counterfeit and illusory, but interior" (1958:92) In his prose piece "Heliogabale" (1934) Artaud writes: "And poetry, which reinstates order, first renews the disorder, that disorder with its fiery aspects; it allows aspects to collide with each other, and to be drawn back to one single point: fire, gesture, blood, scream" (quoted from Wertheimer, 1986:329).

Without considering the affinities between Sorel's revolutionary syndicalism and Italian fascism—Sorel's "Réflexions sur la violence" was published in 1906 in Italy and deeply impressed Mussolini—Forgacs emphasizes the imaginary and symbolic character of Sorel's concept of violence. Real acts of violence are less important than imagined violence, the myth of violence, which has an organizing effect on the proletariat as the subject of violence, because it constitutes class consciousness. In his investigation of the relationship between Sorel's theory of syndicalism and Wyndham Lewis's view of the role of the avant-garde in bourgeois society, Mengham (1994) concludes that Lewis's activities and theories affirming the social and political function of violence are directly derived from Sorel: "... the parallel that can be drawn between the ethics of Sorel and the principles or programme of Vorticism is less striking than the way in which the history of Lewis's actual involvements in a whole succession of separatist movements reflects a Sorelian insistence on the necessity for a permanent adversarial stance" (38; on Lewis see also Jameson, 1979).

2. Literary Apologies of Violence in the 1960s

In the 1960s violence began again to enjoy theoretical justifications, linked to the historical avant-garde and within the context of the students' revolutions (see Arendt, 1970). Due to his biography and his violent texts (The Thief's Journal, Notre-Dame des Fleurs), Jean Genet became a central cult figure. Jean-Paul Sartre had devoted a long essay to Genet (Saint Genet, Actor and Martyr, 1952), and Georges Bataille had considered Genet in his theory of violence: "Never again should we forget that the meaning of the word 'saint' is 'sacred,' and that the sacred designates the forbidden, that which is violent, dangerous, and that with which the only contact is destruction: it is Evil. ... Genet's sainthood is the most profound, because it introduces Evil, the 'sacred,' that which is forbidden on earth" (Bataille, 1975: 212f.). Literary treatments of violence began to flood the market. Looking at war literature, Jones (1976) notes: "... novels of sex and violence are near the center of contemporary American literature of the late 1950s and 1960s. Running throughout the works ... is the broad vigorous stream of Romantic protest against the machine age, opposed to the very concept of 'progress'" (14). Works such as Irwin Shaw's "The Young

Lions," Glenn Sire's "The Deathmaker," and John Hersey's "The War Lover" show: "Combat may provide avenues for the sublimated dissipation of sexual energies, or it may be a direct sexual release, suggesting an occasional equivalency between the intensity of sexual experience and combat action" (115f.). Geoffrey O'Brien (1997) has examined the subject of sex and violence in American paperback literature and compiled an informative list of "hardboiled American lurid paperbacks" for the period 1929 to 1960. In the 1980s new English drama began to attract attention with its excessive depictions of violence. Jimmy Boyle's "The Hero of the Underworld" (1998) became a cult book, which, like the life of the author, is reminiscent of Genet. Its images of violence derive from the milieus of the psychiatric prison ward and the slaughterhouse, and are loaded with the experiences of the author, but finally they are neutralized by the hero's decision for the good.

VI. SUMMARY

This article begins with the treatment of the subject of violence in aesthetics and literary theory, and then looks at debates on the position of violence in modern civilization, showing that a critique and an apology for violence are the two main tendencies in the literary treatment of violence in the twentieth century. Without doubt, the decisive experiences of violence in this period were the two world wars and the Holocaust. Thus it is to be expected that a critical representation of violence will deal in particular with these two areas of experience. It has been observed that the unprecedented nature of modern military technology and the unique phenomenon of bureaucratic, industrial mass murder both led to experimentation with new techniques and means of expression in literary treatments. The apologies for violence of the avant-garde prior to World War I, and between the world wars, also took their material from the experience of war, and more generally from the development of modern technology and its products. The idea of cathartic violence linked to the metaphor of surgical hygiene and dissociation from the other, the female, links aspects of this artistic and literary avant-garde with fascism. The censure of apologies for violence after the experience of the Holocaust began to relax in the 1960s. In the context of the "students' revolution," violence enjoyed renewed theoretical justification and corresponding literary treatment.

Translated by Tradukas

REFERENCES

Adorno, Theodor W. (1955). *Prismen. Kulturkritik und Gesellschaft*. Frankfurt a. M.: Suhrkamp.
Adorno, Theodor W. (1966). *Negative Dialektik*. Frankfurt a. M.: Suhrkamp.
Adorno, Theodor W. (1976). *Minima Moralia*. Frankfurt a. M.: Suhrkamp.
Arendt, Hannah. (1970). *On Violence*. London: Allan Lane.
Armstrong, Nancy, & Leonard Tennenhouse. (Eds.) (1989). *The Violence of Representation*. London, New York: Routledge.
Arnold, Heinz Ludwig. (Ed.) (1990). *Text und Kritik 105/106, Ernst Jünger*. München: Edition Text und Kritik.
Assmann, Aleida, & Dietrich Harth. (Eds.) (1991). *Mnemosyne. Formen und Funktionen der kulturellen Erinnerung*. Frankfurt a. M.: Suhrkamp.
Barker, Martin, & Julian Petley. (Eds.) (1997). *Ill Effects. The Media/Violence Debate*. London, New York: Routledge.
Bataille, Georges. (1975). *La littérature et le mal*. Paris: Gallimard.

Baudelaire, Charles. (1975). *Oeuvres Completes*. Paris: Gallimard.
Bauman, Zygmunt. (1991). *Modernity and Ambivalence*. Ithaca: Cornell University Press.
Bauman, Zygmunt. (1992). *Dialektik der Ordnung. Die Moderne und der Holocaust*. Hamburg: Europäische Verlagsanstalt.
Benjamin, Walter. (1977). *Gesammelte Schriften, Vol. 2.* (Ed. Rolf Tiedemann & Hermann Schweppenhäuser.) Frankfurt a. M.: Suhrkamp.
Berg, Nicolas. (Ed.) (1996). *Shoah—Formen der Erinnerung*. München: Fink.
Bier, Jean-Paul. (1979). *Auschwitz et les nouvelles littératures allemandes*. Bruxelles: Édition de l'université de Bruxelles.
Bohrer, Karl-Heinz. (1978). *Die Ästhetik des Schreckens. Die pessimistische Romantik und Ernst Jüngers Frühwerk*. München: Hanser.
Brecht, Bertolt. (1967). *Gesammelte Werke. Vol. 20. Schriften zu Politik und Gesellschaft*. Frankfurt a. M.: Suhrkamp.
Bridgwater, Patrick. (1985). *The German Poets of the First World War*. London, Sydney; Croom Helm.
Callahan, John M. (1991). The Ultimate in Theatre Violence. In James Redmond (Ed.), *Violence in Drama* (pp. 165–175). Cambridge: Cambridge University Press.
Cernyak-Spatz, Susan E. (1985). *German Holocaust Literature*. New York: Peter Lang.
Cotta, Sergir. (1985). *Why Violence? A Philosophical Interpretation*. Gainesville: Florida University Press.
Dieckmann, Herbert. (1968). Das Abscheuliche und das Schreckliche in der Kunsttheorie des 18. Jahrhunderts. In Hans Robert Jauß (Ed.), *Die nicht mehr schönen Künste* (pp. 271–317). München: Fink.
Diner, Dan. (Ed.) (1988). *Zivilisationsbruch. Denken nach Auschwitz*. Frankfurt a. M.: Suhrkamp.
Diner, Dan. (1998). Der Holocaust im Geschichtsnarrativ. In Stefan Braese (Ed.), *In der Sprache der Täter* (pp. 13–30). Opladen: Westdeutscher Verlag.
Eksteins, Modris. (1989). *Rites of Spring. The Great War and the Birth of the Modern Age*. Boston: Moughton Mifflin.
Elias, Norbert. (1989). *Studien über die Deutschen. Machtkämpfe und Habitusentwicklung im 19. und 20. Jahrhundert*. Frankfurt a. M.: Suhrkamp.
Emeljanow, Viktor. (1991). Grand Guignol and the Orchestration of Violence. In James Redmond (Ed.), *Violence in Drama* (pp. 151–163). Cambridge: Cambridge University Press.
Ezrahi, Sidra D. (1980). *By Words Alone. The Holocaust in Literature*. Chicago: University of Chicago Press.
Featherstone, Simon. (1995). *War Poetry*. London, New York: Routledge.
Forgacs, David. (1994). Fascism, Violence and Modernity. In Jana Howlett & Rod Mengham (Eds.), *The Violent Muse. Violence and the Artistic Imagination in Europe, 1910–1939* (pp. 5–21). Manchester: Manchester University Press.
Fowlie, Wallace. (1967). *Climate of Violence. The French Literary Tradition from Baudelaire to the Present*. New York, London: Macmillan.
Fraser, John. (1974). *Violence in the Arts*. Cambridge: Cambridge University Press.
Friedländer, Saul. (Ed.) (1992). *Probing the Limits of Representation. Nazism and the 'Final Solution'*. Cambridge: Harvard University Press.
Friedman, Saul S. (Ed.) (1993). *Holocaust Literature: A Handbook of Critical, Historical, and Literary Writings*. Westport: Greenwood Press.
Friedrich, Hugo. (1977). *Die Struktur der modernen Lyrik*. Reinbek bei Hamburg: Rowohlt.
Funk, Holger. (1983). *Ästhetik des Häßlichen. Beiträge zum Verständnis negativer Ausdrucksformen im 19. Jahrhundert*. Berlin: Agora-Verlag.
Fussell, Paul. (1975). *The Great War and Modern Memory*. Oxford: Oxford University Press.
Gilman, Sander, & Jack Zipes. (Eds.) (1997). *Yale Companion to Jewish Writing and Thought in German Culture 1096–1996*. New Haven: Yale University Press.
Girard, René. (1972). *Le sacré et la violence*. Paris: Grasset.
Goodman, Steve. (1996). Nihilism and the Philosophy of Violence. In Colin Sumner (Ed.), *Violence, Culture and Censure* (pp. 159–188). London: Taylor and Francis.
Gould, Thomas. (1991). The Uses of Violence in Drama. In James Redmond (Ed.), *Violence in Drama* (pp. 1–13). Cambridge: Cambridge University Press.
Hartman, Geoffrey. (Ed.) (1994). *Holocaust Remembrance: The Shape of Memory*. Oxford: Blackwell.
Hegel, Georg Friedrich. (1957). *Werke*. (Ed. Hermann Glockner.) Stuttgart: Fromans.
Hobsbawm, Eric. (1994). *Age of Extremes. The Short Twentieth Century 1914–1991*. London: M. Joseph.
Hodgson, Katharine. (1994). Myth-Making in Russian War Poetry. In Jana Howlett & Rod Mengham (Eds.), *The Violent Muse. Violence and the Artistic Imagination in Europe, 1910–1939* (pp. 65–76). Manchester: Manchester University Press.

Howlett, Jana. (1994). Death, War, Revolution: the Literature of the Russian Civil War. In Jana Howlett & Rod Mengham (Eds.), *The Violent Muse. Violence and the Artistic Imagination in Europe, 1910–1939* (pp. 88–99). Manchester: Manchester University Press.
Howlett, Jana, & Rod Mengham. (Eds.) (1994). *The Violent Muse. Violence and the Artistic Imagination in Europe, 1910–1939*. Manchester: Manchester University Press.
Jameson, Frederic. (1979). *Fables of Aggression: Wyndham Lewis, the Modernist as Fascist*. Berkeley, Los Angeles, London: University of California Press.
Jones, Peter G. (1976). *War and the Novelist. Appraising the American War Novel*. Columbia: University of Missouri Press.
Jünger, Ernst. (1988). *Strahlungen II*. München: Deutscher Taschenbuchverlag.
Kaempfer, Wolfgang. (1981). *Ernst Jünger*. Stuttgart: Metzler.
Kaiser, Gerhard. (1973). *Pietismus und Patriotismus im literarischen Deutschland*. Frankfurt a. M.: Athenäum.
Köppen, Manuel. (Ed.) (1993). *Kunst und Literatur nach Auschwitz*. Berlin: Erich Schmidt.
Kristeva, Julia. (1974). *La révolution du Langage Poétique*. Paris: Éditions du Seuil.
LaCapra, Dominick. (1994). *Representing the Holocaust: History, Theory, Trauma*. Ithaca: Cornell University Press.
Laermann, Klaus. (1993). 'Nach Auschwitz ein Gedicht zu schreiben, ist barbarisch.' Überlegungen zu einem Darstellungsverbot. In Manuel Köppen (Ed.), *Kunst und Literatur nach Auschwitz* (pp. 11–15). Berlin: Erich Schmidt.
Langer, Lawrence L. (1999). *Preempting the Holocaust*. Newhaven: Yale University Press.
Larsen, Otto N. (Ed.) (1968). *Violence and the Mass Media*. New York: Harper and Row.
Mack, Burton. (Ed.) (1987). *Violent Origins*. Stanford: University Press.
Markovic, Mihailo. (1974). Violence and Human Self-Realization. In Philip Wiener & John Fischer (Eds.), *Violence and Aggression in the History of Ideas* (pp. 234–252). New Brunswick: Rutgers University Press.
Mengham, Rod. (1994). From Georges Sorel to Blast. In Jana Howlett & Rod Mengham (Eds.), *The Violent Muse. Violence and the Artistic Imagination in Europe, 1910–1939* (pp. 33–44). Manchester: Manchester University Press.
Midgley, David. (1994). The Ecstasy of Battle: Some German Perspectives on Warfare between Modernism and Reaction. In Jana Howlett & Rod Mengham (Eds.), *The Violent Muse. Violence and the Artistic Imagination in Europe, 1910–1939* (pp. 113–123). Manchester: Manchester University Press.
Minden, Michael. (1994). Expressionism and the First World War. In Jana Howlett & Rod Mengham (Eds.), *The Violent Muse. Violence and the Artistic Imagination in Europe, 1910–1939* (pp. 45–55). Manchester: Manchester University Press.
Müller, Hans-Harald (1986): *Der Krieg und der Schriftsteller: Der Kriegsroman der Weimarer Republik*. Stuttgart: Metzler.
Nieraad, Jürgen. (1994). *Die Spur der Gewalt. Zur Geschichte des Schrecklichen in der Literatur und ihrer Theorie*. Lüneburg: von Klampen.
Nietzsche, Friedrich. (1969). *Werke II*. München: Hanser.
O'Brien, Geoffrey. (1997). *Hardboiled American Lurid Paperbacks and the Masters of Noir*. New York: Da Capo.
Oesterle, Günter. (1985). Friedrich Schlegels Entwürfe einer Theorie des ästhetisch Häßlichen. In Helmut Schanze (Ed.), *F. Schlegel und die Kunsttheorie seiner Zeit* (pp. 397–451). Darmstadt: Wissenschaftliche Buchgesellschaft.
Redmond, James. (Ed.) (1991). *Violence in Drama*. Cambridge: Cambridge University Press.
Rosenkranz, Karl. (1973). *Ästhetik des Häßlichen*. Darmstadt: Wissenschaftliche Buchgesellschaft. [1853, Reprint]
Schlant, Ernestine. (1999). *The Language of Silence. West German Literature and the Holocaust*. New York, London: Routledge.
Silkin, Jon. (1972). *Out of Battle. The Poetry of the Great War*. London: Oxford University Press.
Sinclair, Alison. (1994). Disasters of War: Image and Experience in Spain. In Jana Howlett & Rod Mengham (Eds.), *The Violent Muse. Violence and the Artistic Imagination in Europe, 1910–1939* (pp. 77–86). Manchester: Manchester University Press.
Sorel, Georges. (1969). *Über die Gewalt*. Frankfurt a. M.: Suhrkamp [first published in France 1906].
Steiner, George. (1974). *Language and Silence*. New York: Atheneum.
Stephen, Martin. (1996). *The Price of Pity. Poetry, History and Myth in the Great War*. London: Led Cooper.
Sternhell, Ze'ev. (1983). *Ni droite, ni gauche. L'idéologie fasciste en France*. Paris: Éditions du Seuil.

Sternhell, Ze'ev, Mario Sznajder, & Maia Ashéri. (1992). *Naissance de l'idéologie fasciste*. Tel Aviv (Hebrew): Am Oved.
Taterka, Thomas. (1999). *Dante Deutsch. Studien zur Lagerliteratur*. Berlin: Erich Schmidt.
Theweleit, Klaus. (1987). *Male Fantasies, I: Women, Floods, Bodies, History*. Cambridge: Manchester University Press.
Tilby, Michael. (1994). The Imaginary Violence of Louis-Ferdinand Céline. In Jana Howlett & Rod Mengham (Eds.), *The Violent Muse. Violence and the Artistic Imagination in Europe, 1910–1939* (pp. 100–112). Manchester: Manchester University Press.
Wertheimer, Jürgen. (Ed.) (1986). *Ästhetik der Gewalt. Ihre Darstellung in Literatur und Kunst*. Frankfurt a. M.: Suhrkamp.
White, Hayden V. (1978). *Tropics of Discourse. Essays in Cultural Criticism*. Baltimore, London: Johns Hopkins University Press.
Wright, Elizabeth. (1994). Dismembering the Body Politic: Brecht's Early Plays. In Jana Howlett & Rod Mengham (Eds.), *The Violent Muse. Violence and the Artistic Imagination in Europe, 1910–1939* (pp. 22–32). Manchester: Manchester University Press.
Young, James E. (1988). *Writing and Rewriting the Holocaust. Narrative and the Consequences of Interpretation*. Bloomington: Indiana University Press.
Zelle, Carsten. (1987). *Angenehmes Grauen. Literaturhistorische Beiträge zur Ästhetik des Schrecklichen im 18. Jahrhundert*. Hamburg: F. Meiner.

PART II-6-2

JUSTIFICATION STRATEGIES

CHAPTER II-6-2.1

The State Monopoly of Force

DIETER GRIMM

I. THE CONCEPT OF *GEWALT* IN PUBLIC LAW

The notion of "monopoly of force" refers to the German *"Gewaltmonopol." Gewalt* comprises meanings of violence, power, force, authority, etc., and is a central notion of public law. The realm of public law, like its counterpart private law, is determined by its object. While the object of private law is the relationships between private individuals, the object of public law is public power or state power. It regulates the establishment and exercise of that power, including, in particular, the relationship between the state and individuals as well as private associations (for more detail see Grimm, 1988). *Gewalt* in this sense invariably means legal authority in the sense of the Latin *potestas*, the right to exercise control over others. This was the original meaning of the word *Gewalt* in German, whereas *Gewalt* in the sense of *violentia*, violence, did not come to the fore until later (Fenske, 1979:942f.; Faber, 1982:830). Today, however, if not otherwise qualified, the notion of *Gewalt* is associated more with the (private) use of force. By comparison, lawful *Gewalt* is associated with public authority, state authority, sovereign power, etc.

The Preamble of the Basic Law for the Federal Republic of Germany, for example, gives constituent power to the German people. Article 20 of the Basic Law, which contains the guiding principles of the polity, continues on from here and states: "All state authority is derived from the people. It shall be exercised by the people through elections and other votes and through specific legislative, executive, and judicial bodies." These functions express state authority; they, too, are referred to in German as *"Gewalten,"* just as the institutions that carry them out. State authority is thus exercised not only by the people themselves but also by various institutions. This does not necessarily involve the actual use of violence or force. Rather, the notions of state authority, sovereign power, and public authority denote the basic relationship between the state and its citizens. The state exercises authority over them. It is entitled to determine their behavior without necessarily having to employ force.

This is reflected in the notion of the "general relationship of power," which means that the state is entitled to give orders to individuals who are obliged to comply. These orders may be general ones in the form of laws, or they may be more specific ones in the form of decrees, commands, verdicts, etc. (The "special relationship of power," on the other hand, denotes a more intensive subordination of individuals to government authority, for instance in the case of soldiers, prison inmates, or students at public educational institutions.) This basic relationship (the "general relationship of power") is part and parcel of the state—it exists independent of the type of state or constitution. It usually determines the purpose for which the state may exercise its power, the parameters within which it may do so, the means which it is allowed to use, and possibly how individuals can defend themselves against public authority. The latter is of great significance for the tolerability of the relationship of power. However, the basic distribution of command and compliance remains unaffected by the particular form of this relationship.

Public authority, however, is not given to the state as an end in itself, but rather in the interest of the public weal. It is from this that the public authority draws its legitimacy, and in turn state authority, under normal circumstances, does not have to use force in order to ensure compliance. At the same time, the state comes under a constant pressure of legitimization. Since state authority is not an end in itself but has its purpose beyond itself, namely in the common weal that requires definition, it must prove its entitlement to rule. On the level of political meaning, such justifications are generated through theories or ideologies. They are made credible, above all, by the state exercising its power in a legal and consistent way, i.e., within a legal framework. This is true for any kind of polity, irrespective of what the laws are actually about, and irrespective of whether or not a given state can be considered a constitutional state based on the rule of law.

In contrast, with few exceptions, there is no justification for private (physical) violence. Private violence becomes wrapped up in public force. State authority suppresses the private use of violence, usually making use of the severest means at its disposal—that of criminal law. The illegal use of private violence is met with harsh negative legal consequences, such as fines, dismissal from work, preventive detention, the breaking up of demonstrations, etc. Of course, this shows that the notions of illegal private violence and legal public authority are far from separate. If bad comes to worse, public authorities resort to violent means to enforce the public interest against private interests. Violence is used to prevent violence (Luhmann, 2000:192). However, insofar as the state itself resorts to the use of force in order to carry out its tasks, for example by arresting or deporting someone, or by confiscating somebody's property, one speaks not of violence, but of *coercion*.

It is an essential characteristic of public authority to claim the *exclusive* right to the use of force in order to fulfill its primary function. That function is to safeguard internal and external security and to foster the public interest. However, moving toward that goal does not entail full elimination of private violence. That would exceed the ability of any public authority. It can aim to control the possession of weapons, but it cannot take away individuals' natural strength nor all the everyday objects that can be used as weapons in particular situations. This area is thus made the subject of law (Luhmann, 2000:192ff.). The state alone has the *right* to use violence, while individuals or social groups essentially only have it if it has been bestowed on them by the state. The established name for this is the state *monopoly of force*.

The state and the monopoly of force are inseparably connected. Max Weber's widely accepted definition, which has also entered into the field of jurisprudence, defines as a state a human community "which, within a particular territory, (successfully) claims the monopoly of legitimate physical violence for itself" (Weber, 1972:822, see also 29ff.; Anter, 1995). Referring to the "*state* monopoly of force" is thus pleonastic. Where there is no monopoly of force, there is no state, but either a different form of polity or anarchy. As soon as a polity monopolizes the use of force it turns into a state. The monopoly of force therefore is not an attribute of political rule per se, but of a particular form, namely the state. Like the state, it emerged in continental Europe in the modern age and since then has been universally established and has survived as the predominant form of rule, despite frequently being pronounced dead.

II. THE EMERGENCE OF THE MONOPOLY OF FORCE

The entitlement to use force belongs to every sort of polity, whatever else its rule may be based on. What is new is only the aspect of *monopoly* (Weber, 1972:516). Before its emergence, rulers had a series of individual prerogatives, which included the authority to use force. These prerogatives were spread among various bodies and individuals that exercised them in their own right (often as an annex to other rights which today are classed as "private" rights, such as the right to ownership of land or the *patria potestas*) and were usually linked not to a territory but to a particular person. Various prerogatives were thus able to exist side by side on a given territory; they did not necessarily conflict with each other because they concerned different people and different objects. The sovereign princes, too, only held a limited number of individual prerogatives, although these were often numerous and far-reaching. It was precisely due to the large number and the centrality of their prerogatives that they were able to become a crystallization point for the monopoly of force.

It was not the case that naked violence prevailed between the various rulers and ruling groups, but rather everyone was entitled to see to their rights, if need be by force of arms. Inversely, everyone was equally entitled to use violence in self-defense. In particular the feud, which from a modern perspective is often seen as being tantamount to war, was not just a power struggle but a legal dispute. It was conducted with violent means, and for want of a central law-enforcement authority it could not have been carried out any other way (Brunner, 1965:1ff.). While there were rules for the use of violence, these were not backed up by any enforcement mechanism. Under these circumstances, what decided the dispute was the readiness to deploy violence effectively. The legal dispute, therefore, ultimately led to the "right of the strongest" and initiated, more often than not, a long chain of violence and counterviolence. Still, the repeated attempts to enforce a ban on feuds meant a breach with existing rights, given the legal status of the feud.

The emergence of the monopoly of force is not an event, but a process, and it is hard to specify when exactly the change occurred in any particular territory. The denominational civil wars that flared up as a result of the religious divisions of the sixteenth century served as the decisive catalyst. It seemed they could only be settled by disempowering the many independent wielders of authority and by concentrating the scattered prerogatives in the hands of the princes. The tremendous increase of violence in society could only be overcome by disempowering all those with a share in the ruling structures and by concentrating power in one hand. This was first recognized and developed into a theory by the French "Politiques" (Schnur, 1962; Quaritsch, 1970; Kriele, 1975). It was then put into practice, first in France and soon afterwards in other parts of continental Europe. In England, where the religious cleavages did not lead to civil war and there was thus no necessity of uniting the various prerogatives into one comprehensive public authority, this development did not occur until much later (Elias, 1982:142ff.; Willoweit, 1986; Grimm, 1986, 1987).

This new concentration of power found its expression in the notion of sovereignty. Sovereignty means two things. Internally, it denotes the highest legal authority. Bodin defined it as the ruler's authority to determine the law for everyone without himself being legally bound. Externally, sovereignty meant legally independent authority. Sovereignty was initially bound to the person of the prince. After the princes had been deposed or been integrated into a systemic ruling structure not dependent on personal rule, sovereignty passed on to the state. Therefore, sovereignty and the monopoly of force are connected but not identical. Sovereignty is the quintessence of all prerogatives condensed into one uniform public authority, the exercise of which is determined by the holders themselves. Physical violence is the state's legitimate means of enforcing its claim to power (Jellinek, 1966:435ff, especially 454ff.).

However, the monopoly of force does not mean that the subjects are stripped of all rights. There is a difference between the state's monopoly of force and its right to make use of it. While the monopoly of force takes the right to use violence from private individuals and gives it to the state, the state is not authorized to use it as it sees fit. Conceptually, the monopoly of force merely implies that individuals relinquish the right to enforce their legal claims and interests by way of violence. It can coexist with various degrees of freedom and rights vis-à-vis the state. Given the experience of civil war, of course, it was widely considered that internal peace could not be restored by simply renouncing violence. All other rights, so it seemed, had to be relinquished, too, for the sake of the one supreme good: the security of life and of property. This led to the emergence of the absolutist state. The absolutist state, however, was by no means a necessary consequence of the monopoly of force, but rather a historically contingent development.

Despite its name, the monopoly of force has rarely been a monopoly in the full sense of the word. The absolutist state never succeeded in bringing together and controlling all the scattered prerogatives and rights to use force. Above all, peasants were still long to remain subject to the sovereignty of the lords of the manors. Other associations, differing from country to country, were also able to preserve their authority to use force. In many cases, the state's claim did not go beyond maintaining that this authority had been granted by it or at least derived from it. The state was rarely able to reclaim this authority or even regulate it. In this respect, the monopoly of force was perfected only when the absolutist, princely state was overcome and replaced by the modern institutional state. It dissolved or privatized all intermediate authorities and stripped them of their right to use force.

III. THE MONOPOLY OF FORCE IN LEGAL SHACKLES

The emergence of the monopoly of force strengthened the power of its holders, thus bringing forth the danger of its abuse. Justification and limitation were required. The theoretical justifications for sovereignty and the emergence of the monopoly of force were thus soon followed by social contract theories. They proceeded from the assumption that there had been a situation with no organized system of government. While that situation was no legal vacuum, it had no organized mechanism to ensure compliance with the law. Everyone had the right to realize his or her legal claims; success, however, depended on their strength. The problem with this initial situation was the profound uncertainty of rights. The criteria for the legitimization and limitation of the monopoly of force thus needed to be derived from the conditions under which sensible people would be prepared to give up their natural freedom and right to enforce their own rights, and submit to the rule of the state.

Most social contract theories emphasize the idea of fair exchange. Natural freedom includes the right to use force to achieve one's personal interests, and relinquishing this right is justified only if the state, in return, guarantees the safety of life and personal integrity and the security of property. If this relationship is disturbed, the use of force is illegitimate. The right to use violence reverts to private individuals, at least to the extent that they are entitled to resist illegitimate state authority and to use self-defense against aggressors (Kaufmann, 1972; Kersting, 1974). As civil wars increasingly became a thing of the past, the assumption that natural freedom had to be completely relinquished in the interests of security also faded. Instead, it was replaced by the idea of a partial relinquishment allowing for a limitation of state power. Such limitation was two-fold: human rights on the one hand, and separation of powers on the other.

These possibilities, which theoreticians had proposed earlier, were later made legally binding and enshrined in the constitution. The constitution, in turn, codified the monopoly of force by spelling out the conditions under which the state was entitled to use force (Merten, 1975; Pernthaler, 1986:116ff.). According to these rules, every coercive measure must have a legal basis. That basis cannot be determined by the authority with the means of force at its disposal. Rather, it must be supplied by a body representing the people and deliberating the subject in public procedure. However, this body is not entirely free to create the legal basis as it sees fit. It is bound to respect the fundamental rights guaranteed in the constitution. Particular means of force, such as the death penalty or torture, may be completely banned, while others may be used only under particular circumstances or for particular purposes. It is above all the principle of proportionality that has been developed for the authorities' use of force. That principle has emerged with regard to police action and is now also used to determine whether legislation and other governmental acts conform to the values and principles of the constitution. It involves a three-step process of reasoning: the means used must be appropriate to the achievement of the legitimate end, the means used must have the least restrictive effect on a constitutional value, and the burden on the right must not be excessive relative to the benefits secured by the state's objective.

In this light, fundamental rights have the effect of barring any potential challenge to social differentiation. They ensure the operation of the various functional systems of society in an environment relatively free of violence and can thus enact their own criteria of rationality to their best advantage in each case (Luhmann, 2000:56ff.). This "de-differentiation" took effect with the emergence of the monopoly of force and well before its integration into legal bounds. Political, economic, religious and cultural conflicts could no longer be borne out with violent means. Rather, those affected by violations of the law were dependent on the state warding off the danger or enforcing the law. Constitutions supplemented this development by seeing to it that state power could no longer be used to exploit the various societal functional systems for political or other purposes and in the process diminish their social efficiency.

The constitution, however, has no effect whatsoever on the monopoly of force. Rather, it was the concentration of force in one hand that made possible the emergence of instruments designed to limit power (Grimm, 1994:37ff.). Constitutional provisions presuppose the monopoly of force and merely attempt to tame its use. Particularly, separation of powers does not indicate a return to the situation that existed before the rise of the modern state—that of scattered prerogatives. The power *of* the state must be distinguished from power *within* the state (Jellinek, 1966:457). State authority is not affected at all by the separation of powers because the various authorities only have a limited share in it. However, they do not possess that share in their own right, but merely as authority derived from the more comprehensive monopoly. Thus, the monopoly of force is characteristic not just of the authoritarian or totalitarian state, but also of the constitutional state. They differ only on the issue of what purposes the state may use force for, and under what conditions.

Also, the problem of the right to resist state authority is defused by a constitution. In a constitutional state individuals have legal means at their disposal to defend themselves against the state. The most modern instrument is judicial review which, after its beginnings in the early nineteenth century in America, has gained universal acceptance in the second half of the twentieth century. These possibilities to defend oneself against the state, which are granted by the law, have rendered moot the right to take violent resistance measures against the state. That right has turned into some sort of back-up right in case the legal means of defense against state authority fail (see Article 20 Section 4 of the Basic Law). Civil disobedience is a lesser offshoot of the right to resist, and is characterized by limited infringements of rules. It is no challenge to the monopoly of force but only seeks to denounce particular forms of violence as illegitimate. Even revolutions claim the right to use force, though usually not so as to abolish the monopoly of force, but rather to put it in different hands or to change the conditions of its use, i.e., the constitution (Matz, 1975; Laker, 1986; Pernthaler, 1986).

IV. THE MONOPOLY OF FORCE AND ITS SCOPE

Since the monopoly of force is claimed by the state, it is limited to the territory of that state. No state is justified in taking action on the territory of another sovereign state without its consent. This ban is part of the general rules of public international law. However, the monopoly of force is not limited to a state's citizens. It is not personal sovereignty, but rather territorial sovereignty and thus extends to all persons within the territory of the state. The distinction between nationals and nonnationals, of course, frequently determines the extent of rights and duties (as a rule of thumb, nationals have more of each, for example the right to vote, but also the duty of compulsory military service), but it does not determine subordination to state authority as such. The only exception is the immunity granted to diplomatic missions and foreign heads of state and government by public international law.

The state monopoly of force also allows for the continued existence of areas of private legal violence. The most important case is parental authority, which is restricted, through family law only, in the best interest of the child. Another example is the relationship between the state monopoly of force and the state's duty to protect its citizens from violence. The individual is allowed to act in self-defense or in an emergency, or to react to law-breakers or threats from others' property if the state is unable to grant protection in time (see, for instance, §§ 227ff., 561, 859ff., 904 German Civil Code; §§ 32ff. German Penal Code). These limited entitlements of the individual to use force in the form of violence prevent the act from being considered unlawful, or are advanced as excuses. In contrast, resistance against the rightful exercise of state authority is punished without exception.

There is heated debate about whether these pockets of permissible private use of force may be claimed in their own right and have only been recognized by the state, or whether they are derived rights, granted to individuals by the state. We need not decide this question here. The monopoly of force does not depend on the state acting through its organs whenever coercion is used. Rather, the requirements of the monopoly of force are satisfied if the state has the right to lay down the conditions under which the use of force by individuals is admissible and if it has the ability to monitor whether the conditions are observed. It is sufficient that the state has the power to determine the legal limits of the use of force by third parties (Kriele, 1975:84ff.). However, this authority can hardly be realized without the state disposing of an adequate potential of force of its own.

The state's monopoly of force does not require that it continually make use of its right to use physical violence. While physical violence is a means of state control, it is far from being the only one. Force is a scarce resource and would soon be exhausted if all state acts had to be enforced by force. A state has to rely on acceptance. Acceptance reduces the necessity to use force. To be sure, acceptance of the state can be increased through threats of force, but only to a very limited extent. Still, no state enjoys such a level of legitimacy that it can renounce the use of force entirely. Violence can ultimately be suppressed with violence only. This paradox can be mollified by integrating the use of force into a legal framework, but it cannot be done away with entirely.

Of course, the fact that private acts of violence still occur does not call the monopoly of force into question. This is not a monopoly of physical force per se, but of *legitimate* physical force. It distinguishes between lawful and unlawful violence, and the use of violence by the state is allowed so that private violence can be suppressed or sanctioned (Luhmann, 2000:192ff.). Nevertheless, there is a connection between the scale of private violence and the state monopoly of force. The monopoly of force needs to be *successfully* claimed by the state. This is to say that the state uses its coercive apparatus against private violence in general (and is not to say it has to be successful every single time). It is only nonaction or chronic failure that jeopardizes the monopoly of force. The reason for collapsing state authority can often be found in the fact that the state has failed to uphold the monopoly of force.

V. PRIVATIZATION OF SOVEREIGN POWER

It is a particularly relevant question whether and to what extent the state may leave the legal use of force that goes beyond parental authority and emergency measures to private parties (see Gramm, 2001). The last years have witnessed an ongoing tendency toward privatization of state tasks. This tendency has various roots. Most significantly, the state is overburdened with tasks while its coffers are empty. In this light, privatization promises an easing of the burden of (recurring) expenditure on the one hand, and (one-off) revenue through the selling of service systems on the other hand. Another reason for the popularity of privatization is the advance of neoliberal ideas in various academic disciplines and areas of society. The promise is that the state may withdraw from directly providing services without these disappearing or declining in quality. On the contrary, what is expected is that services will be provided more effectively and cheaply under private enterprise, with the result that the state can restrict itself to setting the framework and steering the context.

The monopoly of force is adversely affected by this development only when those public institutions that typically perform their tasks by using physical force are transformed into private organizations. These include the army, the police, jails, and other closed institutions. Germany, up to this point, has seen little of such transformation. There are plans, however, to reinforce the police with private auxiliary staff and to run prisons through private parties. That would not be unprecedented. Private security services have long been a familiar sight, and a range of coercive institutions, for example in psychiatry, are also run by non-state actors today.

In terms of the use of force, private security services are of course limited to such acts as a person under attack or in danger would be allowed to perform in self-defense, in an emergency, or in a self-help situation. As we have seen, such rights of self-defense etc. do little to challenge the state monopoly of force; the monopoly would equally suffer very little if the enforcement of such rights was transferred to privately run security staff. In other cases things are more complicated. Admission to a closed institution, for example, requires a state decision, but the use of force goes far beyond fending off an immediate danger. However, here too the state's monopoly of force does not demand that physical force is used only by the state itself, e.g., by its civil servants. The monopoly of force is also maintained when the private holders of authority use force on behalf of the state, under conditions set by the state, and under its supervision. There is no reason why this arrangement should per se be impossible for prisons or police tasks.

While outsourcing the authority to use force does not necessarily dispense with the monopoly of force, it would indeed jeopardize that monopoly if certain limits were exceeded. Effective control of the private use of violence on behalf of the state can only be ensured if the state retains means of force superior to those of the private organizations. Privatization of police and armed forces therefore is different from that of prison staffs. Should the state give away direct control of police and armed forces, and thus to a certain extent privatize its power of command, it would no longer be in a position to effectively monitor its private holders and, if need be, force them back to their rightful place. No political system can survive in the long run if the right to exercise control over physical force is located primarily outside the state (Luhmann, 1981a:82; Luhmann, 1981b:171).

Armed and uniformed private armies such as those once maintained by political parties therefore represent a threat to the monopoly of force. Even if the authorization to use force is as tightly restricted as that of private security services, for example, such private armies in effect constitute a potential threat by hindering the state in enforcing its authority. Things are different if the state loses control of its own armed forces, for instance if they do no longer follow state orders but rather their own nonauthorized leaders. This is invariably the result of a loss of legitimacy, and ends up in a coup where the right to exercise control over the coercive apparatus is entrusted to new forces.

VI. VIOLENCE BETWEEN STATES

The state monopoly of force is territorially limited, as is the state that claims it. Every state has the monopoly of force within the boundaries of its own territory, and thus the monopoly has effect only with regard to the relationship between the state and the inhabitants of that territory. There is no coercive force beyond the state. Rather, with the emergence of the monopoly of force, the rights of armed conflict—hitherto scattered—were transferred to the state and have not yet been taken from it. Every polity that has been constituted and can assert itself is entitled to maintain armed forces and use them if necessary. What follows is that the use of force between states, unlike that among citizens, is not prohibited in principle. Since between states, no form of centralized law enforcement has emerged yet, war as a means of law enforcement is not illegal as such.

Whether or not a state decides to enter into armed conflict with another state is a matter of its internal disposition and objectives. The principle of sovereignty guarantees every state legal independence. This does not exclude the possibility of other states exerting pressure and making threats. Due to the fact that power, among states, is far from equally distributed, it is only natural that a state's preferences and decisions will be considerably influenced and, sometimes, even determined by the reaction of other states. However, state sovereignty prevents foreign states from interfering in its internal disposition and objectives unless they have specific authorization to do so, for example owing to a state's capitulation following a war. Such subjugation does not necessarily rob the state concerned of its statehood, but it loses its full sovereignty.

However, every state can restrict itself in terms of the right to wage war. Self-restraint does not infringe on state sovereignty, i.e., the right to form their own political will legally independent from other states. Self-restraint can consist in unilateral renunciation of the use of military means in international conflicts. Germany, for example, in Article 26 of the Basic Law, is unilaterally committed not to wage wars of aggression (but not wars in general). Furthermore, states may conclude bilateral or multilateral treaties committing themselves to abstain from force in relation with each other. A state can even voluntarily transfer the decision of whether or not to use armed forces to another state or to a supranational institution without relinquishing its sovereignty. Sovereignty does not mean the absence of legal commitments.

If states wage war, they are bound by legal rules, just as there once were binding rules for the feud. Public international law calls that body of norms ius in bello. However, unlike in national law, there is no international body competent or authorized to enforce these rules. For the longest time, public international law had to bemoan any consented sanction mechanism beyond self-defense and the reaction of other states. Every state needed to take the protection and realization of its rights into its own hands—a situation comparable to the feud, and international law, like the feud, ultimately led to the "right of the strongest." On the level of enforceability, international law was thus unable to protect and safeguard states' rights. International dispute settlement mechanisms were not established until the late nineteenth and early twentieth century, and a state can only initiate legal action against another state before an international tribunal if both states have agreed beforehand to subject themselves to that tribunal's jurisdiction.

Sovereignty also means that no state has the right to dictate any other state its internal behavior. In international law the principle of noninterference in the internal affairs of other states is considered to flow from state sovereignty. A state's influence on foreign territory is therefore limited to the diplomatic protection of its citizens. As a consequence, a state's internal use of the monopoly of force does not give other states a right to intervene. This holds true even if the use of force is in stark contradiction with the principles other states consider right or even compelling. On the other hand, they are, of course, free to react, for example by imposing an embargo in order to exert indirect pressure. Interference was considered a cause for war; therefore, the principle of noninterference was long considered a precondition for peace. In this respect, signs of change have begun to emerge only recently.

VII. MOVES TOWARD BREAKING UP THE MONOPOLY OF FORCE

As far as states' relationship to violence is concerned, remarkable changes have occurred in recent international law in two different respects. The first concerns the legality of the use of force. In the United Nations Charter the Member States have agreed to "refrain in their international relations from the threat or use of force against the territorial integrity or political independence of any state" (Article 2 Section 4). This does not affect the right to self-defense and the establishment of security alliances. The Charter commitment does not only apply to relations among Member States. Rather, it stipulates that generally, Member States have to abstain from the use of force in international relations for attaining the purposes mentioned. Hence, the Charter introduced to international politics a radically new notion: a general prohibition of the unilateral resort to force by states. Meanwhile, the Charter provision has gained recognition as ius cogens—a norm thought to be so fundamental that it invalidates rules consented to by states in treaties or custom.

Force in the sense of Article 2 Section 4 of the UN Charter is armed force. There have been attempts at extending the notion of force to include political or economic pressure; they have been rejected though. Moreover, the prohibition of violence is limited to states' external relations. It does not apply to internal conflicts, which a state can resolve using whatever means it sees fit. Consequently, states have to refrain from interfering in other states' internal conflicts, even if these conflicts are being carried out with violence. The UN General Assembly's Friendly Relations Declaration of 1970 not only bans the organization of subversive activities in other states, or the support of such activities, but also expressly bans intervention in conflicts such as civil war.

A second change affects precisely the principle of nonintervention. Exceptions to this principle are increasingly becoming accepted in the context of humanitarian actions conducted with military means. Human rights are gaining precedence over the classical principles of nonintervention in internal affairs of other states (Steiner & Alston, 2000). One example is intervention by United Nations forces which is permissible on the basis of the 1948 UN Genocide Convention. Increasingly, humanitarian intervention seems like the justifiable use of force for the purpose of protecting the inhabitants of another state from treatment so arbitrary and persistently abusive as to exceed the limits within which the sovereign is presumed to act with reason and justice. Naturally, however, the right of the sovereign state to act without interference within its own territory is of such importance that states have been cautious in admitting the pleas of humanity as a justification for armed action against another state. Many details are hotly disputed: the compatibility of such actions with the Charter of the United Nations, the question of the universality of human rights and their interpretation (the conflict increasingly shifts to such "contested universals"), the threshold of the abuses which justifies intervention, procedural preconditions, etc.

Finally, an international criminal law with its concurrent jurisdiction is in the process of emerging (Meron, 1998; Cassese, 1998; Fordham Symposium). It reaches beyond the traditional subjects of international law—states and international organizations—and seizes individual suspects regardless of whether they acted as representatives of a state or on the orders of a state's government. International criminal law pierces the veil of immunity otherwise protecting to heads of state or senior representatives of state. Criminal responsibility is also independent of the cooperation of the state of which the accused is a citizen. We can observe the emergence of rights to put perpetrators of this kind on trial in international courts with or without the consent of the state of which they are citizens. Here, things are in flux, too. However, it is safe to assume that this development is irreversible.

In its external dimensions the state monopoly of force is thus relativized. One can imagine cases in which international law will allow for a foreign power to take coercive action on the territory of another state against that state's will. However, this development is not accompanied by the emergence of a supranational monopoly of force. To be sure, it is usually supranational institutions, such as the United Nations, that take the decision to intervene. They do not, however, have a coercive apparatus of their own yet which would be able to put such missions into practice. Rather, they have to "borrow" means of armed force from states. That, of course, is impossible without the consent of the state to which the request is put. The state then decides the matter according to the procedure stipulated by its constitution.

VIII. THE SPECIAL CASE OF THE EUROPEAN UNION

The European Union occupies a special place among the world's supranational organizations because its Member States have ceded it a large number of their sovereign rights, including an increasing number of legislative powers, which the EU exercises with direct effect in the Member States. Unlike other obligations under international law, the legal acts of the EU do not need to be transformed into national law. On the contrary, Community law has direct effect and trumps national law. National bodies must not apply conflicting national legislation. All state agencies, including national courts, have to observe the supremacy of Community law. Therefore, the EU can do without enforcement of Community law through special EC institutions, but it does need a court to mediate in conflicts between the Community and its Member States.

The EU thus has the authority to exercise public power with direct effect in its Member States and for their citizens. This is unprecedented on the international plane. Nonetheless, the EU is not yet a state in itself. The public power it possesses is not *state* power. Up to this point, it has been possible to use these two terms synonymously. Now they are drifting apart. The EU lacks the quality of a state because it does not determine its own basis, namely primary Community law, by itself and in its own right. Rather, this is done by the Member States through international treaties concluded during intergovernmental conferences. It is this classical international law basis that is the framework for secondary Community law legislated by Community institutions. Its legal basis is thus heteronomous and determined by other bodies than Community institutions themselves. It is precisely in this regard that the Union differs from a state with its concomitant principle of self-determination (Grimm, 1995).

The move toward institutional integration in the EU has also stopped short of dealing conclusively with the monopoly of force. While the EU, through its legislation, is able to lay down conditions for the Member States' use of their monopoly of force—conditions which the states must follow—it depends on the coercive apparatus of the Member States to enforce EC legislation. It cannot control the Member States directly in this regard. Although the Member States are legally bound to take all necessary steps, all the Union can do in case of Member States' noncompliance is take legal action before the European Court of Justice in Luxembourg. Unlike in federal states, the Union cannot institute a coercive apparatus of its own which would force a state to take action or which would become active in its place.

This is also the case for institutions such as the European Police Office (Europol) which was set up to promote cooperation in police matters. In contrast to the elaborate apparatus of institutional and procedural integration in the European Community, which is the first pillar of the EU, the other two pillars—Common Foreign and Security Policy and Police and Judicial Cooperation in Criminal Matters—involve intergovernmental cooperation along customary international law lines. Europol is an EU-wide system for the exchange of intelligence. But it is not a police force with the right to directly apply coercive measure against EU citizens or residents of the Member States. However, the third pillar on Justice and Home Affairs (JHA) was in need of reform. Arguments ranged from improving the institutional provisions under JHA as it stood to absorbing the third pillar entirely into the Community pillar. What emerged in the Amsterdam Treaty was somewhere between these two, with parts of what was JHA being incorporated into a new EC title, and the remaining parts being expanded and subjected to a wide range of institutional controls.

As far as the ultima ratio of physical violence is concerned, the monopoly of force thus remains with the Member States of the Union. Unlike in federal states, the monopoly is not divided between the individual states and the central state, with particular fields allocated to particular institutions. It is true, many decisions in the EU are now made by the community of states rather than by the individual state; it is equally true that the "communitization," i.e., the scope of elaborate and far-reaching procedural and institutional integration, has extended to broad policy areas hitherto considered as *domaines réservées* of the nation-state, and that this undoubtedly makes the EU the world's most advanced supranational organization. However, the Union still needs to rely on the power structure of the Member States to enforce its legal acts. It does not have the possibility, as the United Nations has in certain limited and exceptional cases, to entrust the coercive apparatus of one member state with actions in another state.

IX. THE MONOPOLY OF FORCE IN THE CONTEXT OF GLOBALIZATION

In the context of our topic, the numerous phenomena comprised in the catchword of globalization have one particular effect: There is a clear disjuncture between the formal authority of the state and the spatial reach of contemporary systems of production, distribution, and exchange which often function to limit the competence and effectiveness of national political authorities. Consequently, there is a widening gulf between economic behavior and political regulation. Global actors are increasingly withdrawing their actions from the scope of national legal systems and national law-enforcement agencies, thus devaluing national and even supranational law such as that of the EU.

But even the actions of global players need a legal framework, which cannot be provided by national legislatures. On the one hand, the gap is filled by international organizations such as the World Trade Organization (WTO), and on the other hand global players create their own laws the basis of which is not a state order or binding international agreements but private contracts relying on voluntary commitment instead of state sanctions. Multinational corporations agree on rules for cooperation that exempt them from all national jurisdictions and substantive national law. In the case of conflict they have recourse to arbitration independent of national laws. Here the norms of transnational commercial law are applied, though these are not yet fully elaborated and are often developed as cases come up (Teubner, 1997, 2000:240).

The reaction of states has been partly to create transnational law in those areas in which an international legal system is still dependent on them. One of the most important reasons for this dependence is, of course, the continuing state monopoly of force, which to date has not been amended in the slightest, let alone replaced, by a global or at least regional monopoly of force. Here we are dealing above all with national security law, a field that manifests a particular proximity to the monopoly of force. States can assert their law-making superiority in the international struggle against organized crime more readily than in the field of commercial law.

To date, the consequences of this development for the monopoly of force have been of a more indirect nature. Change has occurred, however, in the legal conditions under which the monopoly of force may be exercised. The legal basis that justifies the use of coercion in the case of cross-border incidents is increasingly not unilaterally created by individual states, but by international organizations, or by a majority of states which negotiate matters and settle them by way of international treaties. The state is involved in this, but no longer bears sole responsibility. It "lends" its force to law legislated by others, not by itself. However, since we are dealing with enforced implementation, to date the state has been indispensable.

It is in keeping with the logic of this development that the authorization to use force has also been pluralized. But in view of the needs of the global economy it is unlikely that this development will revert us back to the premodern fragmentation of scattered rights to use force. Max Weber already pointed to the connection between the expansion of power and the monopolization of force (Weber, 1972:519). In the future there will probably no longer be numerous, territorially demarcated monopolies. Rather, as in federal states, the authority to use force in order to enforce the law will be shared by state monopolies and supranational institutions, with the latter either controlling parts of the state coercive apparatus or building a coercive apparatus of their own. The *monopoly* of force, a historically contingent phenomenon and not per definitionem part of a polity, would then disappear. This would not affect public authority per se, however; it would pass on to a different aggregate state.

Translated by Tradukas and Ulrich Haltern

REFERENCES

Anter, Andreas. (1995). *Max Webers Theorie des modernen Staates*. Berlin: Duncker und Humblot.

Brunner, Otto. (1965). *Land und Herrschaft. 5th edition*. Wien: Brunner.

Cassese, Antonio. (1998). On the Current Trends Towards Criminal Prosecution and Punishment of Breaches of International Humanitarian Law. *European Journal of International Law*, 9, 2.

Elias, Norbert. (1982). *Über den Prozeß der Zivilisation. Vol. II. 8th edition*. Frankfurt a. M.: Suhrkamp.

Faber, Karl-Georg. (1982). Macht, Gewalt I. In Otto Brunner, Werner Conze & Reinhart Koselleck (Eds.), *Geschichtliche Grundbegriffe, Vol. III* (pp. 817–820). Stuttgart: Klett Cotta.

Fenske, Hans. (1979). Gewaltenteilung. In Otto Brunner, Werner Conze & Reinhart Koselleck (Eds.), *Geschichtliche Grundbegriffe, Vol. II* (pp. 923–958). Stuttgart: Klett Cotta.

Gramm, Christof. (2001). *Privatisierung und notwendige Staatsaufgaben*. Berlin: Duncker und Humblot.

Grimm, Dieter. (1986). The Modern State. In Franz-Xaver Kaufmann, Giandomenico Majone & Vincent Ostrom (Eds.), *Guidance, Control and Evaluation in the Public Sector* (pp. 89–109). Berlin, New York: de Gruyter. [German: Grimm, Dieter. (1987). *Recht und Staat der bürgerlichen Gesellschaft* (pp. 53–137). Frankfurt a. M.: Suhrkamp.]

Grimm, Dieter. (1988). Öffentliches Recht. *Staatslexikon. Bd. IV. 7th edition* (pp. 119–124).

Grimm, Dieter. (1994). Entstehungs- und Wirkungsbedingungen des modernen Konstitutionalismus. In Dieter Grimm, *Die Zukunft der Verfassung, 2nd edition* (pp. 31–66). Frankfurt a. M.: Suhrkamp.

Grimm, Dieter. (1995). *Braucht Europa eine Verfassung?* München: Carl-Friedrich-von-Siemens-Stiftung. [English: Peter Gowan, & Perry Anderson. (Eds.) (1997). *The Question of Europe* (pp. 239–258). London, New York: Verso.]

Jellinek, Georg. (1966). *Allgemeine Staatslehre. Reprint of the 3rd Edition*. Bad Homburg v. d. Höhe: Gehlen.

Kaufmann, Arthur (Ed.) (1972). *Widerstandsrecht*. Darmstadt: Wissenschaftliche Buchgesellschaft.

Kersting, Wolfgang. (1994). *Die politische Philosophie des Gesellschaftsvertrages.* Darmstadt: Wissenschaftliche Buchgesellschaft.
Kriele, Martin. (1975). *Einführung in die Staatslehre.* Reinbek bei Hamburg: Rowohlt.
Laker, Thomas. (1986). *Ziviler Ungehorsam.* Baden-Baden: Nomos-Verlagsgesellschaft.
Luhmann, Niklas. (1972). *Rechtssoziologie.* Reinbek bei Hamburg: Rowohlt.
Luhmann, Niklas. (1981a). *Politische Theorie im Wohlfahrtsstaat.* München: Olzog.
Luhmann, Niklas. (1981b). Rechtszwang und politische Gewalt. In Niklas Luhmann, *Ausdifferenzierung des Rechts* (pp. 154–172). Frankfurt a. M.: Suhrkamp.
Luhmann, Niklas. (2000). *Die Politik der Gesellschaft.* Frankfurt a. M.: Suhrkamp.
Matz, Ulrich. (1975). *Politik und Gewalt.* Freiburg: Alber.
Meron, Theodor. (1998). *War Crimes Law Comes of Age.* Oxford: Oxford Press.
Merten, Detlef. (1975). *Rechtsstaat und Gewaltmonopol.* Tübingen: Mohr.
Quaritsch, Helmut. (1970). *Staat und Souveränität.* Frankfurt a. M.: Athenaeum Verlag.
Pernthaler, Peter. (1986). *Allgemeine Staatslehre und Verfassungslehre.* Wien et al.: Springer.
Schnur, Roman. (1962). *Die französischen Juristen im konfessionellen Bürgerkrieg des 16. Jahrhunderts. Ein Beitrag zur Entstehungsgeschichte des modernen Staates.* Berlin: Duncker und Humblot.
Steiner, Henry J., & Philip Alston. (2000). *International Human Rights in Context. 2nd edition.* Oxford: Oxford University Press.
Symposium. (1999). Genocide, War Crimes, and Crimes against Humanity. *Fordham International Law Journal, 23,* 275.
Teubner, Gunther. (2000). Des Königs viele Leiber. In Hauke Brunkhorst, & Matthias Kettner (Eds.), *Globalisierung und Demokratie* (pp. 240–273). Frankfurt a. M.: Suhrkamp.
Teubner, Gunther. (1997). *Global Law without a State.* Aldershot et al.: Dartmouth.
Weber, Max. (1972). *Wirtschaft und Gesellschaft. 5th edition.* Tübingen: Mohr.
Willoweit, Dietmar. (1986). Die Herausbildung des staatlichen Gewaltmonopols im Entstehungsprozeß des modernen Staates. In Albrecht Randelzhofer & Werner Süß (Eds.), *Konsens und Konflikt* (pp. 313–323). Berlin, New York: de Gruyter.

CHAPTER II-6-2.2

The Monopoly of Legitimate Violence and Criminal Policy

ALBRECHT FUNK

I. INTRODUCTION: VIOLENCE AND THE STATE

The modern state emerged in centuries of bitter fights, in which competing power holders were brought down and robbed of their capacities to use violence as a political means of exerting power. "In the past" Max Weber stated succinctly, "the most diverse kinds of associations—beginning with the clan—have regarded physical violence as a quite normal instrument. Nowadays, by contrast, we have to say that the state is that human community which (successfully) lays claim to the monopoly of legitimate physical violence within a certain territory, this 'territory' being another of the defining characteristics of the state. For the specific feature of the present is that the right to use physical violence is attributed to any and all other associations or individuals only to the extent that the state for its part permits this to happen. The state is held to be the source of the 'right' to use violence" (Weber, 1994:310f.).

In the past, states have taken on many different functions. The diversity did not diminish in the era of globalization. Modern states do not differ from their predecessors in the specific set of tasks they pursue, but in their institutional structure. On this point at least, the majority of scholars who currently debate the future of the nation-state follow Weber's thought, in particular the "new institutionalisms" in social science, economics and history. This is true even though many authors do not accept Weber's defining criteria of the modern state.[1] For Weber the modern state is the one and only rule of man over man—Herrschaft—that has the capacity for maintaining social order regardless of the

---

[1] Giddens, 1987:20, Mann, 1993:54, and Tilly, 1985:171 depart from Weber by eliminating the concept of legitimacy (Thomson, 1994:7). For the new institutionalism debate, see Evans, Rueschemeyer & Skopol, 1985; North, 1990; Peters, 1999.

W. Heitmeyer and J. Hagan (eds.), *International Handbook of Violence Research*, 1057–1077.
© 2003 Kluwer Academic Publishers. Printed in the Netherlands.

specific content. Weber defines the modern state not by specific functions, as Hobbes or Locke do, but by its specific instrument—the monopoly of legitimate physical violence. The monopoly is the indispensable prerequisite for the capacity of any form of government to enforce binding decisions in a given territory (Weber, 1994:309–311, 1978:54–56).

From a Weberian point of view, however, it is not the superiority of the state's coercive powers and its capacities to force resisting subjects into submission that constitutes and defines the monopoly of the modern state. In order to speak of a successful monopolization of violence the state has to embody a power "super terram" (Hobbes) that is entitled to assert its authority by force.

The state has to be able to count on the subordination of those citizens and aliens who are subjected to its rule in a given territory. A use of violence—the sheer force of arms—may compel compliance. In order to establish enduring subordination, the authority to enforce rules by force needs credible 'inner justification' (Weber, 1994:311). This holds true for any form of rule of man over man. It is only the modern state, however, which succeeds in establishing an exclusive and universally binding "spatial system of authority and subordination and to maintain it permanently by its monopoly of legitimate violence" (Rokkan & Urwin, 1983:21; Tilly, 1975). This spatial system of authority is based on the specific instrument of the state—its monopoly of violence—and the superiority of the legal/bureaucratic rule to any form of private efforts to enforce social order.

The superiority and efficacy of the bureaucratic state supplies only a necessary, not a sufficient justification of the monopoly. "In using the notion of violence," Luhmann argues, "state theory refers to the system of society" (2000:195). Without some degree of societal acceptance, any effort to institutionalize a state monopoly of physical violence is doomed to fail. Consequently, governments and their agents have to justify the use of force—its purposes as well as the specific ways they try to compel compliance. In democratic states these justifications amount to the assumption that it is exclusively a 'government by law' not by man that finds expression in and subsequently legitimizes the authority of the state. Citizens are willing to accept coercive measures by the police and the criminal justice system as long as they become convinced that the use of force—in order to enforce the law, to maintain public order or to implement binding decisions—is governed by the rule of law (Weber, 1994:311–313; Lassman, 2000:88).

In order to claim a monopoly of legitimate physical violence, states are not required to reserve the legitimate use of force for a central apparatus. All modern states do in fact delegate the authority to use legitimate force to a wide range of state and societal institutions. Furthermore, the state's claim to a monopoly of legitimate violence does not apply to all possible ways actors can exert power, whether by psychological pressure, intimidation or material constraints. The claim is restricted to direct physical coercion, to acts which "aim at the physical vulnerability of persons" (von Trotha, 1995:131, FN. 3). And finally the state's claim to a monopoly does not imply that the coercive institutions successfully eradicate all violent acts in a society, either by individuals or by groups. Violence remains the most ubiquitous resource on which every social actor can depend. In societies in which the state successfully exerts a monopoly of physical violence, however, such individual acts of violence become the extreme opposite of "legitimate force;" they become illegitimate and therefore "criminal violence" (Luhmann, 2000:195).

As a synonym for the Leviathan, the term "monopoly of violence" is widely used in social science and jurisprudence. Social historians, too, attach significance to the "extraction-coercion cycles and the successive monopolization of violence in the formation of the European nation-states" (Finer, 1975:96; cf. Reinhard, 1999:306–369). The rising territorial states emerged from victories over external enemies and the subjugation of competing power holders (Tilly, 1985:169; 1990). From a historic point of view, the dictum which Weber borrows from Trotsky is plausible: the dictum that every state is founded on force (Weber, 1994:310). But crucial questions remain open: To what extent are modern states today still based on violence? Which role does this public force play in modern societies? To what extent can the state monopoly of violence lay claim to legitimacy in highly differentiated modern societies?

II. THE FUTURE OF THE STATE AS AN AUTHORITATIVE RULE MAKER AND COERCIVE POWER

1. Theoretical Approaches

In democratic societies the authority of governments to enforce binding rules does not rely on superior coercive powers but on the assumption that these rules result from deliberate decisions of free representatives of the people. The Leviathan loses his frightening character because he is restricted, civilized, and made accountable to the citizens. In the process of civilization, Norbert Elias argues, the monopoly of violence is more and more hidden in the backdrops of everyday life (Elias, 1982). The democratic process reduces the coercive character of the state further—realist as well as normative theorists of democracy equally assume—even if the coercive quality of the state does not vanish altogether (Dahl, 1989:50). The chances of governments to make and shape politics and consequently to exert power result from the capabilities of political actors to mobilize diverse political interests and to bind them into coherent political programs and policies.

However, there is no getting away from the fact that even democratic governments need "some organized physical force" (Mann, 1993:55). Coercive power remains necessary for a nonviolent resolution of societal conflicts and for the capacities of state institutions to make binding decisions. Without the chance to resort to force, it would be difficult for governments to implement policies in cases where powerful political groups or individual citizens put up resistance to particular rules and regulations. And in relation to other states, the capacity to assert national interests over the claims of external powers in bi-, multi- or supranational negotiations still relies to a large degree on the military power of the states involved.

Since governments possess unique power resources and capacities to realize policy goals, political sociologists frequently demand that the state be brought back into the analysis of politics as an autonomous actor (last Evans, Rueschemeyer, & Skocpol, 1985). The current discussion of globalization meets this demand, however, there has been a clear shift of emphasis. The debate does not any more revolve around the question of to what extent modern states manage to gain autonomy. What is at stake is the concept of the modern state itself, its capacity to define and enforce binding social order. And many scholars in this globalization debate definitely assume that the nation-states are loosing their capacity to control the boundaries of their political decisions and legal norms (van Creveld, 1999; Giddens, 1990; Strange, 1996).

Externally, the growing interdependence of states and the increasing chances transnational actors have to evade national laws and regulations diminish the capacities of governments to enforce their territorial rule (Krasner, 1999). Consequently in almost all policy areas, national governments are increasingly forced to cooperate, while their chances of asserting national interests through power politics decreases (Zürn, 1998). This holds true even for classic national security policy. In their efforts to address increasing external risks—for instance of epidemics, global warming, mass migration, terrorism or "transnational organized crime"—governments can no longer rely on military force and deterrence (Katzenstein, 1996:10; Buzan, Waever, & de Wilde, 1998).

Internally, the increasing transnational reach of crucial societal actors—managers, investors, lobbyists or activists in social movements—reduces the capabilities of nation-states even further to decide autonomously and to enforce hierarchical decisions uniformly throughout their territory (Scharpf, 1997:206–208; Reinicke, 1998:66). Since governments cannot anticipate all the consequences of decisions they make autonomously, in more and more policy areas they are dependent on the cooperation of those who will be affected by their rules. The hierarchical bureaucratic state seems to devolve into a web of horizontal policy networks in which high officials, experts, and representative of interest groups negotiate and make compromises (Héritier, 1993). In complex policy fields like monetary policies or the definition of technical standards and norms, the authority to establish binding decisions are delegated to regulatory bodies (Majone, 1996). The classic bureaucratic state turns into a negotiating state. Instead of looking for ways to implement top down decisions, governments are in search of governance in complex multilevel, private/public arrangements.

Public administration theory, policy science, political economy, and state theory, to name only a few, differ in the analytic conceptualization of the modern nation-state. However, the starting point remains the same: the assumption that the nation-states which emerged in the eighteenth and the nineteenth century have undergone a fundamental change.[2] The only point at issue is whether the ongoing transformation alters the nature of the modern state itself. The loss of boundary controls which governments experience indicate for many economists and political scientists that the modern nation-state, based on the monopoly of violence (and its conjunct law and tax monopoly), is disintegrating (Ohmae, 1990; Bauman, 1998; van Creveld, 1999). In his detailed history of the modern state and its monopoly of violence, the historian Reinhard sums up this position pointedly: "The modern state ... does not exist any more ... the unity of territory, people and sovereignty, which once was painfully extracted from the *ancien régime* no longer applies" (Reinhard, 1999:535).

Critics of this sweeping renunciation of the state do not question the fact that its organization and policy reach are subject to fundamental changes. They cast doubt on the assumption that the challenges which stem from globalization will affect all nation-states in the same way by limiting their capacities to make deliberate political choices. Empirical studies reveal that national governments of highly industrialized countries at least still have the capacity to act on their own account and still have many policy options at their disposal (Garrett, 1988; Wade, 1996:60–88). On a theoretical level, critics argue that globalization may result in increasing heterogeneity and segmentation of the social order in Western societies. Social differentiation, however, does not automatically erode the authority of the modern, hierarchical state and its monopoly of violence as long as the state possesses the capacity to guarantee social order—as heterogeneous as this order may be.

---

[2]In international politics: Krasner, 1999 and Reinicke, 1998. As early as 1990, Ohmae announced the end of nation-state. For a pointed critique of such sweeping globalization statements see Berger & Dore, 1996; for the debate in political science Held et al., 1999 and Narr & Schubert, 1994; for sociology see Giddens, 1990 and Bauman, 1998; in the context of European integration see Scharpf, 1999.

In its capacity as an authority which makes final binding decisions and has the legitimacy to enforce them, the state cannot be replaced by other institutions. This holds true for the international system as well as for the members of societies whose capacities to act transnationally require that they belong to a state as identifiable citizens (Narr & Schubert, 1994:159; Schachter, 1997:22). From this point of view, the metaphor of the vanishing state is analytically misleading. What we have to deal with is "a changing distribution of violence, in which the state has to share its authority to rule with other institutions" (Breuer, 1998:298).

The conceptual dismissal of the state, at least in the way Weber defined it, conceals this redistribution of coercive force. The metaphor of decline or retreat does not tell us anything about the ways in which the state and its monopoly of legitimate physical violence will be transformed. Consequently, the following discussion is not directed by the empirically futile question of whether the state's monopoly of violence will disintegrate and the modern state vanish. Instead, we will inquire into the consequences which the institutional changes we observe currently have on the distribution of public and private force in the current nation-states, in particular in the Western democracies. In order to pinpoint the transformation of organized physical force and the authority of the modern state, we focus in the following sections on three topics that are at the center of the current debate:[3]

1. The first topic concerns the construction of the world in international law and politics as a community of nations, built exclusively on states. At issue is whether the successive dissemination of states around the globe in the twentieth century finally results—after the break down of the Soviet bloc—in worldwide democratization; a process which will reduce the risk of further use of threat and violence between states and strengthen civil societies and their power. The many cases in which states fail to monopolize physical violence, however, point to the opposite: the limits of the principle of organizing political power in liberal-democratic states, like those which emerged in the West in the last several centuries. "Failed states" challenge the faith in progress, which pins its hope on modernization and democratization. They disturb, too, the hope that a further democratization of the world community will limit or even reduce those external security risks which the highly industrialized Western states are increasingly exposed to in a liberalized international political economy.

2. In contrast to the states in the Third World that in fact do fall apart, a dissolution of organized physical force in North America or Western Europe is out of the question. These states can still rely on powerful military and police forces. Many observers, however, claim that an increasing loss of territorial control in even the most powerful nation-states makes it impossible for them to respond effectively to external security threats like terrorist attacks, transnational organized crime, and illegal immigration.

3. In Western democracies, political scientists, legal scholars, and criminologists detect that in addition the "relatively unified institutional structure of the state monopoly of legitimate physical violence" is breaking up (von Trotha, 1995:156). This disintegration calls into question the legitimacy of a coercive force which relies on its impartiality and its strict adherence to the rule of law. A criminal

---

[3]The current debate on the changing role of the nation-state in the international system stimulated also renewed research interest in the genesis of the modern state and the historical development of the international system. Since this research does not add crucial points to my argument, I will not here review this strand of literature. See for this debate Spruyt, 1994; Thomson, 1994; Finer, 1997; Ertmann, 1997.

policy based on equal rights and protection gives way to selective forms of policing and networks of private/public governance.

2. The State in Question: Topics of Discussion

2.1. SUCCESS OR FAILURE OF THE WESTERN MODEL OF THE MODERN STATE? Emerging from Western Europe, territorial states spread over the globe. The number of recognized states under international law claiming a specific territory in which the government has exclusive authority over its citizens increased from 50 in 1945 to 187 today. States are still the irreplaceable corner stone of the international world order in spite of the challenge global movements of capital, goods, and persons may pose to their authority. (World Bank, 1997:20). Without states no accountable parties exist in the international sphere which can commit themselves to legally binding agreements and have the power to enforce them. In cases where governments lose this authority, there are no social groups left which can claim to represent the general interest of the citizenry. Such territories lack even an accountable addressee for international sanctions, which explains why the United States as well as the EU member states prefer the stability of dictatorial regimes to the violent competition of warlords.

International law regards 'failed states,' states which still exist as a legal entity but lack a functioning government, as an anomaly in an international order constituted of a community of states (Schachter, 1997:18). A look into newspapers, however, shows that failed states are in fact not a rare occurrence. From Africa (Sierra Leone, Congo) to Oceania (Papua New Guinea, Solomon or Fiji Islands), news turns up of states in which persons and groups with a rightful claim to government can neither exercise authority over the territory nor rely on a monopoly of physical violence.

In extreme cases, such as Somalia or in parts of the former Yugoslavia, the institutions that constitute and hold together the central state collapse totally. Governments which are at least to a certain degree accountable to international pressure dissolve in violent clashes between tribal chiefs, warlords and guerrilla fractions which exploit the power vacuum for their own interests (Jean & Rufin, 1996). What characterizes many parts of Africa, Asia, and Oceania more frequently, however, are states in which the authority of the government does not go beyond the capital or small parts of its territory. To the extent the executive tries to implement policies and enforce the law in areas which are not under the control of the government, its representatives need to engage in negotiations and deals with local power holders, landowners and tribal chiefs. In many Central and Latin American states finally, the states have established considerable coercive forces. The governments, however, did not succeed in subordinating them under civil authority. The military and the police "privatized" the monopoly of physical violence, often pursuing their own interests and security policies with brutal force and terror as para-state institutions (von Trotha, 1995:144).

In the context of this article, we do not need to explore how to conceptualize the "types of violent order" which result from the breakdown of the monopoly of legitimate coercion.[4] What is of interest here is the question of whether these "violent orders" indicate a general crisis of the modern Western state, as Reinhard and others argue (1999:509).

---

[4] The legal anthropologist von Trotha defines three distinct "forms of order" that differ from the classic state order: the neodespotic order which is characteristic of rural peasant cultures of Africa, the para-state order in Latin America, and a post-acephalous constitutional order. Trotha distinguishes these forms from the constitutional order of the welfare states with its monopoly of legitimate violence (von Trotha, 1995:135).

Or does the opposite apply: that these failed states are only an artifact of the globalization of a state system, which was limited to the Western hemisphere until 1945? The spread of nation-states all over the globe after World War II inevitably increased the risks of failure and at the same time restricted the possibilities for other states to intervene or to invade and occupy such territories (Krasner, 1999:218f.).

For many scholars, failed states are only a transitional phenomenon in an ongoing modernization process in which globalization will result in an increasingly peaceful international order. They pin their hopes on two interconnected assumptions. First, many political economists assume that no state can avoid further integration into the international economy without risking destruction (Ohmae, 1990). Since intervention in markets and arbitrary acts toward citizens or foreign investors will result in capital flight and economic stagnation, all governments are under some constraint to commit to binding rules, to make themselves accountable, and to refrain from an arbitrary use of force (World Bank, 1997:157ff.).

Secondly, putting their hopes on the civilizing effects of capitalism which Adam Smith and Comte described, optimistic observers of globalization conclude that the necessity for accountable government in the long run makes room for the active participation of the citizens. In a liberal market regime citizens will claim their rights and force the further democratization of authoritarian regimes. Of course, backlashes in this process are inevitable, waves of democratization, which Huntington detected in human history after the end of the communist regimes in the 1990s, are followed by the rise of new dictatorial regimes. However, the last, third wave of democratization after the breakdown of the Eastern bloc makes democratic government the most popular and dominant model in the world, Huntington and other scholars argue (Held et al., 1999:46; Huntington, 1991). According to counts of Potter et al., the share of authoritarian regimes in the world drastically decreased from 68.7% in 1997 to 26.2% in 1995 (Potter et al., 1997:9).

Critics have good reasons to question the classification of many states as democratic regimes. In sum, however, there is no doubt that more states than ever in history are committed to free elections and some form of rule of law. Using this criteria as a benchmark, "democratization" is undoubtedly a social fact. But it does not tell us a lot about the social fabric and politics in these states. The classification is a reaction to the existence of totalitarian regimes that emerged in the last decades and were ruled by dictators and authoritarian rulers who secured their regime with brutal force and extensive social control, like in Libya or North Korea. States which are able to organize elections but incapable of establishing an effective government do not fit into the dichotomous view of "democratic states" versus "totalitarian regimes" in the Cold War era.

Of course, from a historic point of view failing governments in internationally recognized/established states are nothing new. Decolonization after 1945 resulted quite often in the collapse of newly established states in Africa or Asia. But in the bipolar international order before 1989, failed states remained a marginal transitional phenomenon. This holds true even if one takes into account that both superpowers devoted all their energies to expanding their zones of influence by financing liberation and guerrilla movements from Angola to Zimbabwe. At the same time, the superpowers tried to prevent regimes from collapsing by every means—material support or, if necessary, even by direct military intervention. On the international level, the Soviet Union and the United States tried to avoid through bilateral consultations and agreements that regional conflicts expand and pose a security risk for the two blocs (Rufin, 1991).

Today this pacifying effect of the bloc constellation has worn off. And it is not any more in the strategic interest of the West or Russia to help crumbling states with costly support measures, at least in those cases where no important economic interests are at stake. Regional conflicts deteriorate without outside intervention (Kaldor, 1999; Buzan et al., 1998:61). In many cases, the lines become blurred between politically motivated civil wars and an economy of extortion, where local warlords use violence to enrich themselves and cover their actions scantily with ideological and political propaganda. They are rarely impeded by foreign powers. Relying on arsenals of weapons that any affluent buyer can obtain easily in the international market, local cliques are able to defend their claims and zones of exploitation. On a higher level, the ubiquitous means of warfare make it possible for warlords and ethnic groups to start plundering raids and ultimately loot the state itself (Jean & Rufin, 1996). Power holders in those 'states' are, UN Secretary-General Kofi Annan complained while looking at Sierra Leone, "national leaders who are so insular whose vision is so narrow, that in their concern about their own power and survival, the interest of their people don't count" (Crossette, 2000:6). After the downfall of the Soviet Union, Jean Jacques Rufin, one of the founders of "Médecins Sans Frontières," concluded that the new world order will not be one in which states in the third world stabilize and democratize further but one which will be wrecked by violent conflicts, collapsing states, and disintegration (Rufin, 1991).

However, the growing concern over failed states does not indicate that the modern state itself is in decline even if one endorses Rufin's dire forecast. His argument only points to the complexities of the process of state building. It took Europe several centuries before its competing territorial rulers succeeded in establishing states which successfully claimed sovereignty and a monopoly of legitimate violence. And it took even longer, in fact until after World War II, before the Western European states succeeded in establishing solid democratic governments.

2.2. Loss of Territorial Control—Decline of the Nation-State?

Without doubt, compared to the "zones of turmoil" in many parts of Africa or Asia, the Western states are still an "oasis of peace" (Singer & Wildavsky, 1996). However, the industrialized, democratic West cannot dissociate from the rest of the world, all the more so at a time when their governments push for a further liberalization of the international economy. The industrial nation-states preserve their legal sovereignty at the same time as their governments can less effectively seal off their territories from external risks. The capacities of even the most powerful governments to decide unilaterally are diminishing and even more so their chances of implementing policies and enforcing rules uniformly (Zürn, 1995:1998).

For obvious reasons, the loss of territorial control affects in particular those institutions dealing with risks that governments perceive and define as a threat to their "national security." The capacities of modern states to ensure territorial rule by the show of military power and extensive border controls have always been extremely limited. In an era, however, in which international traffic becomes more global and liberalized at the same time, these control efforts become even less effective and more limited. In contrast to the last century, today the highly industrialized states are directly and domestically exposed to the consequences of regional conflicts, ecological catastrophes, and failing states elsewhere, in the form of refugee movements and illegal immigration, of transnational crime, terrorism, and the rapid spread of epidemics.[5]

---

[5] Report of the Commission on the Advancement of Federal Law Enforcement, 2000:71–86; Zürn, 1998. A comprehensive list of possible threats can be found for instance in the "National security strategy for a new century" of the U.S. government (A national security strategy, 1999).

Inside the nation-states the liberalization of cross border movement and communication opens up new opportunities for those social actors who have the required material and cultural resources to escape controls and the enforcement of national laws. Tax and crime havens as well as the virtual world of the internet offer transnational actors abundant chances to exploit the limited reach of national controls for their own purposes—drug dealing, money laundering, illegal arms trade or "cyber attacks" on computer systems (Friman & Andreas, 1999).

It is hard to miss the limits of territorial controls today. In the debate on globalization many observers conclude that nation-states have lost or deliberately abandoned their capacity to control the boundaries of their policies and subsequently of their territories (Strange, 1996; van Creveld, 1999). These arguments find support in the alarming news from security experts who complain about the complete failure of national law enforcement and security agencies when they have to deal with global crime (Newman, 1999:223ff.).

The vulnerability of the highly industrialized states which experts of the police/military complex claim, is not sufficient evidence, however, that the nation-states have lost their capacities to define and enforce a particular legal and social order. It would be wrong to dismiss the many threat scenarios simply as exaggerated or unreal. But it is still very much a question whether international terrorism and transnational organized crime amount to an existential threat to the modern state.[6] The fact that the United States or the European Union define these phenomena as a serious threat to national security results in active responses by their governments: they intensify international cooperation, approve additional financial resources and establish new national security agencies (Report, 2000; Reinicke, 1998; Zürn, 1998). In this perspective the intense debate about the threats of globalization to national security indicates not a decline of the nation-state but its vitality.

On the one hand, these new policies aim at more efficient means of transnational control and a new framework for "nation security," in which the traditional focus on military deterrence is shifted toward the many risks for the complex social fabric posed by terrorists, drug traffickers or hackers who attack the "critical infrastructure" of the economy and society (A National Security Strategy for a New Century, 1999; Buzan et al., 1998). On the other hand, governments expand the capacities of nation-states to overcome their strict territorial limits by new forms of informational and operational cooperation (Bigo, 1996; Ward, 2000:285–312).

The institutional structures and policies governments choose in pursuing this goal differ considerably. The United States firmly insists on its sovereignty. Therefore the federal government tries to expand the reach of its national agencies by bi- and multilateral agreements which do not infringe on their autonomy. A crucial element of this strategy is the deployment of hundreds of "liaison officers" in other countries (Nadelman, 1993).[7] By comparison, in Western Europe the majority of member states decided to establish a common border control regime (Schengen), in which the members try to enhance the reach and efficacy of national security agencies by a joint run information system and uniform standards for the control of their external borders (Bigo, 1996; Kapteyn, 1996:71–91).

---

[6] The alarming description of apparently new security threats should not be accepted at face value. They reflect the vested interests of the military and of national agencies (like the DEA, FBI, NSA) which compete with one another for scarce resources in a border area between external and internal security (Buzan et al., 1998:24).

[7] However, any expansive interpretation of national security powers faces the opposition of the senate as well as of the supreme court, which tend to rule in favor of the states, see Report of the Commission on the Advancement of Federal Law Enforcement, 2000:87.

The American efforts to strengthen bilateral cooperation of law enforcement agencies contrast sharply with the decision of European nation-states. Both, however, have the same goal—to expand the reach and efficacy of national security agencies. This holds true even for those cases where cooperation—as in the case of the EU—results in a loss of decision-making autonomy for the member states and in their discretion to set different national norms. To conclude from the increasing significance of international cooperation that the nation-state is in decline is fallacious (Reinicke, 1998:228ff.; Zürn, 1995, 1998).

There is no general answer to the question of whether the new forms of intergovernmental or supranational cooperation can compensate the nation-states for the loss of territorial control they experience. The question needs to be answered specifically, case by case (Anderson et al., 1995; Reinicke, 1998). It is obvious, however, that the growing importance of information exchange, operational cooperation, and the shift of decision-making into international arenas is beyond the control of the national legislature and courts. What the internationalization of law enforcement puts at risk is not the sovereignty of the nation-states but the accountability of the executives and a coercive force that gains legitimacy through the comprehensive legislative and juridical control of the executive (Scheuerman, 1999:3).

2.3. FRAGMENTATION OF PUBLIC ORDER? No state can redeem its promise in full that it will protect life, liberty, and property of its citizens. This holds true even in those countries like France or Germany, where governments historically claimed an exclusive security mandate and the executives maintained law and order with centralized police forces. The protection of the citizen remained a by-product of policing the society in order to protect state security, by centralized forces like the gendarmerie, state police, or the military. Thus citizens had to rely on self-help, on renting private security guards, and the purchase of security commodities not only in states like the United States, where the federal government gained very limited national security competencies after the Civil War, but too in continental Europe with its absolutist state tradition.[8]

Institutions which enable citizens to enhance their own private security are not a new phenomena but develop over centuries. They reflect private security interests, which are not met by the public institutions established to enforce law and order in the society. Rooted in the conviction that individuals have a primordial right to self-help, the institutions based on this conviction do not in principle conflict with a concept of public security defined by a democratically elected legislator and enforced by communal and state agencies. The empirical fact that the private security sector is on the rise in the United States as well as in Europe does not equate to a loss of public security—like in a zero sum game—or the erosion of the state's monopoly of legitimate physical violence (Forst, 2000:61f.).

Public and private security complemented and supported each other historically (Forst, 1999:4–20). However, the demand of citizens for general and accountable institutions through which equal rights can be protected resulted in the primacy of public security in all Western countries during the nineteenth century. This primacy stems first from the fact

---

[8] The U.S. criminal justice system is shaped to a large degree by the communities, the idea of "popular justice" and the tradition of vigilantism. In contrast to continental European states, it is consequently highly decentralized and its reach far more limited (Walker, 1980). "The central functions of policing—preserving domestic peace and order, preventing and responding to crimes—have always been conducted first, foremost, and predominantly by private means" (Forst, 1999:19).

that professional police forces and law enforcement agencies were superior to the arbitrary enforcement of narrow security interests by local and private agents. Secondly, the primacy is the consequence of the overriding interest of a liberal citizenry in subjecting every infringements on the liberties and the property of the individual to the rule of law.[9]

With the definition of strict legal norms for the use of coercive force by state authorities and exclusive competencies for security institutions in many areas which were made accountable to the judiciary, the pursuit of private security interests by violent force inevitably fell into a legal twilight. The legislature and the courts did not deprive the citizens of far reaching rights to secure their lives and their property—the right to self-defense, vigilantism, and even the right to deploy private security forces in strikes. However, legally these rights became inferior instruments: primordial forms of self-help which can be chosen only if those agencies in charge of public security are not at hand or fail to respond.[10]

Today the primacy of public security needs further qualification. In the legal and political debate scholars on both sides of the Atlantic state that the authority of governments to define and enforce public security shifts to a multitude of semipublic and private, local and intergovernmental organizations and networks. This shift turns public security into a patchwork of security tasks that are delivered either as public good, commercial commodities, or as the organized self-help of citizens (Forst, 2000:34ff.; Sack et al., 1995). Security is not any longer the outflow of the government's authority to define a coherent public realm of security for its citizens but the outcome of complex security regimes "in which governance is accomplished through the operation of 'loosely coupled' networks of institutions" (Shearing, 1995:77).

Making inroads from neoliberalist politics into the security debate, privatization became one of the most popular terms to depict the change. However, privatization does not really capture the shift from hierarchical rule-making and enforcement to diffuse forms of private/public governance, which Shearing describes. Without any doubt, in some sectors private companies or citizens take over functions that had been fulfilled by government agencies. But privatization does not result in a general retreat of the state from areas where interests of national security, public order, and law enforcement are at stake. Nor does privatization in general reduce the efficacy of law enforcement and public policing. On the contrary, public security institutions enhance their control capacities considerably by cooperating with security corporations or community activists (for a summary of the debate, see Forst & Manning, 1999). For this reason the idea of a privatization of public security is misleading. What is up for discussion is to what extent the emerging diffuse, cooperative network structures will restrict or even dissolve the state's ultimate authority. Will the authority to guarantee the recognition of legally defined social orders dissolve in complex governance structures in which public security results from the interaction of interdependent but autonomous actors pursuing their partial security tasks and interests? The existing empirical evidence varies and does not provide definite answers. What emerges from the vast legal and social science literature are four topics that seem to indicate the rise of new governance structures in criminal justice, and affecting too the monopoly of legitimate violence.

---

[9] "The government shall not deprive any person of life, liberty, or property without due process of law; nor deny to any person within its jurisdiction the equal protection of the laws." For the impact of the rule of law on policing in the United States see Monkkonen, 1981, for the Rechtsstaat in Germany see Funk, 1985.

[10] See for the continental European tradition, Keller, 1982. The statement has to be modified for the United States with its strong natural right and popular justice tradition (Walker, 1980).

a. The superior authority to maintain "public order" in a uniform way for all its citizens that the traditional hierarchical states claims is challenged first by the increasing economic and social differentiation of postindustrial societies (Shearing, 1995:75; Heitmeyer, 1997:44ff.). Which norms need to be policed as part of the general public order cannot any more be established exclusively in general legal terms but need specific contextual interpretations. In highly segregated agglomerations, top down strategies of policing are doomed to fail and elicit mistrust or even resistance by social movements, minorities, or powerful interest groups. The complex social fabric of modern societies require flexible forms of policing and law enforcement. Effective policing in complex societies requires horizontal cooperation and efforts to incorporate bottom up strategies of policing into the traditionally hierarchical/bureaucratic organization of police and security agencies (Greene, 2000:322; Manning, 1999:49; Skogan & Harnett, 1997).

b. Hierarchical bureaucratic strategies of policing and law enforcement fall short in all those cases where rapid technological and economic changes produce new societal risks. The executive and its security agencies do not have the knowledge and the scientific competencies needed for a proper assessment of security risks in areas like the security of computer systems, trade in hazardous waste, or international banking. They are not capable of autonomously defining effective rules and regulations which national security or public safety requires; nor do these agencies have the instruments to enforce these rules (Willke, 1992:290ff.).

Since hierarchical decision-making in such areas is highly ineffective and efforts to implement decisions by force doomed to fail, federal and state governments in the United States as well as in Europe had in the nineteenth century already transferred many competencies to specialized regulatory authorities. They started to define specific safety standards in many areas, from construction to food handling to transportation and drugs. The police, on the other hand, were stripped of most regulatory powers which fell to them in the tumultuous period of urbanization and industrialization (Bittner, 1970:18ff.; Funk, 1985:230ff.).

In spite of the continuous transfer of powers to specialized regulatory bodies, governments still claimed the superior authority to define security risks and enforce security norms and standards wherever necessary. Today, however, policy makers and scholars question the authority of the hierarchically organized state itself. Computer crime, international money laundering, attacks on the communication infrastructure, or illicit use of modern biotechnology, all these cases (like many others) exceed by far the technical expertise, the capacities to asses the risks, and the capacities of hierarchical decision-making bodies to anticipate the interests at stake.[11] Efforts to regulate complex social relations by highly centralized hierarchically organized decision-making bodies are doomed to fail.

The inherent limits of the hierarchical/bureaucratic decision-making process in the last decades have given rise to political demands which ask for total deregulation. Others do not endorse a general transfer of decision-making to the wisdom of markets but argue for specialized regulatory authorities and informal policy networks in which state agents, experts, delegates of affected interest groups negotiate on binding regulations and possible control strategies.[12]

[11] From different theoretical point of views Scharpf, 1991; Willke, 1992; Guéhenno, 1990; Strange, 1996; Breuer, 1998:272ff.; Luhmann, 2000.

[12] In general Scharpf, 1997:195ff.; Zürn, 1998, for regulatory politics see Majone, 1996, for the private/public cooperation aiming at international regulatory regimes, in respect to money laundering; Reinicke, 1998:135–172.

c. A move from a comprehensive public security policy to a mixed private/public management of security risks can be observed too in the patchwork of public policing. The surveillance of private and semiprivate areas, from malls to universities, is left almost entirely to private security firms. Even military barracks, police headquarters, or airports are increasingly patrolled by private companies which also take over the checks of visitors and passengers. Some communities in the United States have even tried to transfer police patrols to private companies, which promise to deliver cheaper and more efficient services. In the United States as well as in many Western European societies it is safe to assume that more people are employed in the private security sector than in public police forces (Beste, 1998:180ff.; Forst, 1999:14ff.; Sack et al., 1995). At the same time, citizens make greater efforts to secure their property and safety. The growth rates for all sorts of security commodities are in the double digits while at the same time citizens are increasingly willing to invest their time in 'neighborhood watches,' 'citizen patrols,' or 'vigilance committees' (Beste, 1998; Greene, 2000:323f.; Skogan & Harnett, 1997). Taken together, these new forms of private policing foster a new concept of security in all Western societies in which "the police no longer monopolize public safety" (Forst, 1999:15).

d. The failure of pretentious government programs of crime prevention finally gave rise to political demands that argued for a shift from cause-oriented programs toward cost-efficient policies. The dream of preventive policies of social control and an enlightened administration of criminal justice evaporated in the United States as well as in Europe. The hope for social policies to prevent crimes and supplement repressive crime-fighting strategies came up against hard financial and political limits—in spite of the fact that Johnson in the United States declared war not on only crime but also on poverty. Crime rates soared, and in many American cities law enforcement agencies and police pulled out of violent, predominantly black neighborhoods altogether (Hagan, 1995:31; Walker, 1980:235). It just confirmed the views of conservatives and neoliberals first in the United States and subsequently in Europe who were critical of far-reaching government programs which aimed at the roots of existing social ills. What is necessary, J. Q. Wilson argued 1975 in his "Thinking about Crime," is a law enforcement policy which develops and selects effective strategies of policing, sentencing, and incarceration and undertakes a realistic cost benefit analysis of crime control measures—from crime reducing police patrol patterns to selective incarceration.

Static criminal justice policies which enforce existing laws dissolve into proactive crime control policies. They target risks high on the political agenda and try to reduce them through "zero tolerance policing" (Greene, 2000:316ff.). Risk-oriented criminal law, diversification, actuarian justice or communitarian criminal justice are different concepts which all aim at a criminal justice system in which a hierarchical, state-oriented juridical system and a rigid universal enforcement of norms give way to a more informal, flexible, victim and citizen-oriented criminal justice (Braithwaite, 1989, Ludwig-Mayerhofer, 1998, Karp & Clear, 2000). The lines between the enforcement of law and deliberate security policy choices become blurred.

However, law and politics will not simply merge, whatever the impact these ideas may have on the criminal proceedings in the United States or European countries. As long as processing and sentencing in the criminal justice system can be achieved successfully only under the condition that all parts of the criminal justice system comply to strictly legally defined rules of criminal proceedings, the invasion of means/ends programs into the criminal justice system comes up against limiting factors. From a system theory perspective, Luhmann insists on the distinct operational logic of the juridical system, which gives legitimacy to a democratic state founded on the rule of law (Luhmann, 2000:391). Efforts to make the legal system less formal and state-bounded run the risk of undermining the basic legitimacy of the judiciary as an autonomous institution, separated from politics, directed by principles of justice, and oriented toward the administration of the rule of law (Scheuerman, 1994:199ff.; Naucke, 2000:414ff.).

Since criminal policies cannot be separated from the idea of an impartial administration of justice, there are even more limits to any attempt to privatize criminal investigation and prosecution. For this reason successful attempts to privatize or informalize criminal justice take place primarily in those parts of the criminal justice system which precede the court-controlled criminal proceeding—in the police and the prosecuting attorney's office on the one hand, in the prison system on the other hand (see below).

It is impossible to assess the extent to which the ubiquitous rhetoric of a new political economy of security and a risk-oriented crime policy penetrate the existing law enforcement system. The many claims about a new quality of the state, based on adjectives like 'prevention,' 'risk,' 'security' lack the necessary empirical foundation. Existing case studies prove the heavy weight of the traditional criminal justice system, its hierarchical structures, the professional ideologies of police officers, prosecutors and judges, and prevailing bureaucratic control strategies.[13] There is, however, a far-reaching consensus in the criminological and legal literature that the new thinking about criminal justice affects the criminal justice system in two respects:

a. Modern police forces emerged in the nineteenth century as institutions which claimed autonomy from politics. The legitimacy of the administration of law and order is based on the assumption that its agents do not make political choices but simply enforce the rule of law. From a legal point of view, policing refers to the way professional officers select effective means for enforcing existing, legally defined norms. In reality, however, proactive policing and crime fighting strategies are much more than simple instruments of law enforcement. They become crucial playgrounds of politics in all Western societies. Promises of better policing and more effective law enforcement become the cornerstone of political strategies, which try to mobilize majorities by addressing existing fears of crime and appealing to security interests of important constituencies.[14]

There is an abundance of models traded in an increasingly international marketplace of policing ideas. To mention only three influential concepts: The most popular one is "community policing," in the United States as well as in Western Europe. The concept argues for a direct feedback between the security interests of citizens in a particular neighborhoods and the police (Greene, 2000:301ff.). The concept of "zero tolerance" toward crime and disturbances of public order, marketed first by the Major and the former police chief of New York, relies on early intervention, "heavy policing," and the identification of crime spots (Kelling & Coles, 1996:108ff.). Methods of "Total Quality Management" attempt to optimize law enforcement by combining specific policing strategies with methods which reduce the fear of crime and eliminate multiple offenders (Moore & Trojanowicz, 1988).

---

[13] See for the discussion on policing Manning, 1999:49–126.

[14] Policing becomes a crucial part of the symbolic use of law and order politics. This politicization of policing is different from the traditional use of the police by corrupt municipal administrations in the 1920s and 1930s (Monkkonen, 1981; Walker, 1980). The politics of policing focuses on the deliberate choice of particular public security policies which help to mobilize political majorities. See Funk, 1991:367–388.

The concrete strategies which governments, mayors, and police chiefs use, deviate considerably from the ideal model (Manning, 1999:72). In whatever way local officeholders and law enforcement agencies construct their specific concept, however, they have two elements in common: First, their understanding of the police as an institution which gains legitimacy by orienting policing toward the security needs of the majority of citizens. Second, their search for flexible policing methods which promise better results—for the security agencies and the political actors who struggle to demonstrate their political capacities to act decisively.

b. Classic nineteenth-century criminal law tried to strike a balance between demands for punishment and efforts to secure the liberty of all subjects (Naucke, 2000:56). Today, criminal policies in the United States as well as in Western European countries are increasingly dominated by a utilitarian approach to punishment (Lyons & Scheingold, 2000:112). Strategies of selective incarceration try to identify the violent, risk-prone multiple offenders and put them behind bars. To what extent popular policies like the "three strikes and you're out" movement in the United States reduced violent crime effectively in the 1990s is a matter of dispute. Empirically sound answers are hard to get (Lynch & Sabol, 2000:31ff.). What we do know for certain, however, is the discriminatory effect of this policy which finds expression in the disproportionately high incarceration rates of African-Americans (and to a lesser degree Hispanics see Hagan, 1995:32; Tonry & Petersilia, 1999).[15]

III. CONCLUSION: A PREMATURE FAREWELL TO THE NATION-STATE

Without any doubt, all the signs are that the nation-state is undergoing fundamental institutional changes. And more and more scholars of different disciplines infer from the changes they observe in nation-states and their monopoly institutions that "the modern state abandons the commanding heights which it reaches between 1945 and 1975 ..." For this reason Creveld concludes that "some of its most characteristic institutions are likely to decline. Among them are, naturally enough, ... the justice system ...; the prison system ...; the armed forces ...; the police ..." (van Creveld, 1999:417).

The state which manages to control its territory effectively, which offers personal, and to some degree even social security, marks a very late stage of development of Western democratic societies. Whether the empirically observed changes of this post-World War II welfare state we know amounts to a decline or the end of the modern state depends entirely on the general state model and conceptual features one uses as a point of reference. The crucial question is whether these empirical changes undermine/demolish the modern state itself, as a general form of Herrschaft, of rule of man over man. If one bases the answer to this question on Weber's ideal type of the state, defined by its monopoly of legitimate physical violence, the critical point is clear. The idea of the modern state becomes fuzzy

---

[15] The prison population in the United States quadrupled in the last twenty years (Lynch & Sabol, 2000:9ff.) The rising costs of the rapidly expanding prison system result in efforts to rely on private companies which promise to built and run prisons at lower costs. The efforts to privatize prisons succeed in fact only in those sectors, where surveillance of prisoners does not require high security standards. Only 90,000 of 1.7 Million prisoners in Federal, state prisons and county jails are confined in privately run prisons (Schlosser, 1998:64). This does not indicate a sweeping move toward privatization; the current development may be better labeled as a trend toward a new public/private "prison-industrial complex" (Schlosser, 1998).

when state institutions loose their exclusive territorial competence and their legitimacy as guarantor of social order. In such a case the state would be the territorially-bounded institution in a society which is organized locally, regionally, nationally, and globally. Under such circumstances states would not be more than organizations specialized in the production of public goods in networks of public and private actors (Willke, 1992). The state would go out of existence as a hierarchical institution that has the legitimacy to make final decisions, binding for every subject of its territorial rule, and that has the power to enforce these decisions with its monopoly of legitimate violence.

There are no signs of such a dissolution from a Weberian point of view. The promise of security remains an essential for the legitimacy of the modern state. And since security is in principle an indivisible public good, attempts to privatize parts of it are extremely limited even in those areas where privatization does not come up against hard constitutional barriers. Even the minimal state of neoliberal or libertarian thinking remains a strong security state that guarantees a social order necessary for the functioning of free markets and the rights and liberties of individual citizens (Nozick, 1974; North, 1990).

Governance in decentralized, horizontal policy networks and complex multilevel governance systems still refers to governments which have the capacity and legitimacy to make and enforce binding decisions. Without such an authority the willingness of political and social actors to compromise would be slim and the everyday life of citizens would fall under the permanent threat of violence. Even in the "negotiation state," deliberations still take place in the shadow of the Leviathan (Scharpf, 1991:624).

The objections of institutionalist economists and political scientists who follow Weber do not invalidate empirical findings that indicate changes in the institutional structure of the modern state. The limitations which governments have to face in their policy choices and their efforts to enforce binding decisions are real and substantial. Diminished capacities of boundary control and an increasing significance of the private security market forces governments in all Western countries to take back ambitious claims to a comprehensive regulation and control of law and order (Shearing, 1995:70–95). Crime policies and policing are made to fit in with the majority's security interests or those of powerful political actors.

Selective enforcement strategies and proactive policing methods consequently become the cornerstone of the government's crime and security policy. They gain legitimacy through two claims: the concrete outcomes of crime policies (reducing crime by zero tolerance strategies, for instance) and an effective allocation of resources (by proactive crime control, problem-oriented policing, risk assessments, etc.). Output-oriented legitimization of proactive crime and security policies displaces the traditional idea of law enforcement by accountable police forces and agencies.[16] This shift in the legitimization of law enforcement does not only result in internal changes in the law enforcement system and its control and strategies. It also has considerable social and political effects.

Socially, the new crime policies accept an increasing imbalance of security risks, in which those segments of the population already disadvantaged suffer further losses. On the political level, the security interests of these groups are at risk of being marginalized.

---

[16] The accountability of the state's monopoly of violence and its subordination under the rule of law, however, are more than procedural rules which contribute to the input-oriented legitimacy of the criminal justice system. The procedural rules reflect the normative concept of a society in which even felons are not stripped of their human and civil rights and excluded from being part of the society (Nauke, 2000:414–418). Scharpf discusses the difference between input and output-orientated legitimization in greater detail, Scharpf, 1997:7ff.

At the same time, most citizens in poor neighborhoods with high crime rates do not have the material resources at their disposal that would enable them to buy private security like many middle and upper class people (Manning, 1999:49–126).

Legally, the new policies make accountability of policing increasingly difficult. This holds true first of all for the private security agencies. But it is also increasingly true for public agencies which operate domestically as well as transnationally in a legally not well-defined private/public network of governance (Scheuerman, 1999:3ff.; Reinicke, 1998:226).

Politically, the new security governance through private/public networks undermines the basic legitimization of the modern state that guarantees personal and private security in a way that respects the equal rights of every citizen, even those of offenders. Policies which focus exclusively on effective strategies of crime reduction lose credibility from those ethnic or social groups who have to pay the often implied costs—heavy policing, racial profiling, and disproportionate rates of incarceration, for instance. As a result such policies often divide communities further politically and socially and make alienated individuals or groups even more inclined to resort to violence.[17]

The social, legal, and political impact of the relocation of governance into private/public networks can be observed in all Western countries. However, the shift in crime policies does not uniformly affect the constitutional and institutional structure of the state and the capacities of governments to enforce political decisions by coercion.

Differences in the constitutional and institutional structures of Western democracies matter. The understandings of law and order diverge, even between and in Western societies (Lyons & Scheingold, 2000:117ff.). This holds true even more for the limits citizens want to impose on the privatization of security. Societies differ considerably in their tolerance of illegitimate violence and in their perceptions of where violence challenges the monopoly of legitimate violence. In the everyday life of all Western societies, violence has been pushed into the background; however, it is still more prevalent in the United States than in France or then in Japan (Walker, 1980).

The many farewells to the modern state avoid the critical question of where its capacities to make binding decisions and enforce them in fact falter. From a theoretical point of view, the state is hard to replace in this capacity by private or supranational organizations—as elaborate and important as multilevel governance structures may be. "The resilience of the state system for the past three centuries signifies more than the strength of governing elite. The critical fact is that states alone have provided the structures of authority needed to cope with the incessant claims of competing societal groups and to provide public justice essential to social order and responsibility" (Schachter, 1997:22).

The metaphor of the declining state is based on an ahistorical and schematic concept of the modern state. It blocks the view of some crucial questions: In what ways does an immanent redistribution of violence take place in societies and how does this process affect the authority of governments and their coercive forces? Where precisely do the new forms of "policing as governance" erode the authority of state institutions to make and enforce binding decisions? Those questions require additional empirical research. So far we do not even know whether the state has reached the beginning of its end, and as long as that is the case, we had better search for its impact than for its miraculous decline.

---

[17] In those cases where law enforcement is perceived as arbitrary and brutal by the general public, the proponents of such law and order politics lose support even in those sectors of the community or society which profits from such policies (for get-tough policies of punishment in the United States see Lyons & Scheingold, 2000:125ff.). From the citizen's point of view, security always has a double meaning: security by the state's coercive forces as well as security from its arbitrary use.

REFERENCES

A National Security Strategy for a New Century. (1999). Washington, DC: White House, Press Release, December 1999.

Anderson, Malcom, Monica den Boer, Peter Cullen, Charles Raab, & Neil Walker. (1995). *Policing the European Union.* Oxford: Claredon Press.

Bauman, Zygmunt. (1998). *Globalization. The Human Consequences.* New York: Columbia University Press.

Berger, Suzanne, & Ronald Dore. (Eds.) (1996). *National Diversity and Global Capitalism.* Ithaca, New York: Cornell University Press.

Beste, Hubert. (1998). Policing the Poor: Profitorientierte Sicherheitsdienste als neue Kontrollunternehmer. In Christoph Gusy (Ed.), *Privatisierung von Staatsaufgaben: Kriterien—Grenzen—Folgen* (pp. 180–214). Baden-Baden: Nomos.

Bigo, Didier. (1996). *Polices en réseaux. L'expérience européenne.* Paris: Presses de Sciences Po.

Bittner, Egon. (1970). *The Functions of the Police in Modern Society.* Washington, DC: National Institute of Mental Health.

Boyer, Robert. (1996). The Convergence Hypothesis Revisited: Globalization but still the Century of Nations? In Suzanne Berger & Roland Dore (Eds.), *National Diversity and Global Capitalism* (pp. 29–59). Ithaca, London: Cornell University Press.

Braithwaite, John. (1989). *Crime, Shame and Reintegration.* New York, London: Cambridge University Press.

Breuer, Stefan. (1998). *Der Staat. Entstehung, Typen, Organisationsstadien.* Reinbek b. Hamburg: Rowohlt.

Buzan, Barr, Ole Waever, & Jaap de Wilde. (1998). *Security. A New Framework for Analysis.* Boulder, London: Lynne Rienner.

Creveld, Martin van. (1999). *The Rise and Decline of the State.* Cambridge, New York, Melbourne: Cambridge University Press.

Crossette, Barbara. (2000). UN Chief Faults Reluctance of US to Help in Africa. *New York Times,* May 13, A1 & 6.

Dahl, Robert A. (1989). *Democracy and Its Critics.* New Haven, London: Yale University Press.

Elias, Norbert. (1982). *The Civilization Process.* 2 Vol. New York: Phantheon.

Ertman, Thomas. (1997). *Birth of Leviathan. Building States and Regimes in Medieval and Early Modern Europe.* New York, London: Cambridge University Press.

Evans, Peter B., Dietrich Rueschemeyer, & Theda Skocpol. (1985). *Bringing the State Back In.* Cambridge, New York: Cambridge University Press.

Finer, Samuel E. (1975). State and Nation-Building in Europe: The Role of the Military. In Charles Tilly (Ed.), *The Formation of the Nation State in Europe* (pp. 84–163). Princeton: Princeton University Press.

Finer, Samuel E. (1997). *The History of Governments from the Earliest Times. Vol. III: Empires, Monarchies, and the Modern States.* New York, Oxford: Oxford University Press.

Forst, Brian. (1999). Policing with Legitimacy, Equity, and Efficiency. In Brian Forst & Peter K. Manning (Eds.), *The Privatization of Policing* (pp. 1–48). Washington, DC: Georgetown University Press.

Forst, Brian. (2000). *The Privatization and Civilization of Policing, U.S. Department of Justice, National Institute of Justice. Boundary Changes in Criminal Justice Organization, Criminal Justice 2000. Vol. 2* (pp. 19–79). Washington, DC: National Institute of Justice.

Forst, Brian, & Peter K. Manning. (1999). *The Privatization of Policing.* Washington, DC: Georgetown University Press.

Friman, Richard H., & Peter Andreas. (Eds.) (1999). *The Illicit Global Economy and State Power.* Lanham, Boulder, New York, Oxford: Rowman and Littlefield Publishers.

Funk, Albrecht. (1985). *Polizei und Rechtsstaat.* Frankfurt: Campus.

Funk, Albrecht. (1991). Innere Sicherheit: Symbolische Politik und exekutive Praxis. In Bernhard Blanke & Helmut Wollmann (Eds.), *Die 'alte' Bundesrepublik. Leviathan Sonderheft 12* (pp. 367–388). Opladen: Westdeutscher Verlag.

Garrett, Geoffrey. (1998). *Partisan Politics in the Global Economy.* Cambridge: Cambridge University Press

Giddens, Anthony. (1987). *The Nation-State and Violence.* Berkley, Los Angeles: University of California Press.

Giddens, Anthony. (1990). *The Consequences of Modernity.* Berkeley, Los Angeles: University of California Press.

Greene, Jack R. (2000). *Community Policing in America: Changing the Nature, Structure, and Function of the Police. U.S. Department of Justice, National Institute of Justice. Policies, Processes, and Decisions of the Criminal Justice System, Criminal Justice 2000. Vol. 3* (pp. 299–370). Washington, DC: National Institute of Justice.

Guéhenno, Jean M. (1993). *La fin de la démocratie*. Paris: Flammarion.
Hagan, John. (1995). Rethinking Crime Theory and Policy: The New Sociology of Crime and Disrepute. In Hugh D. Barlow (Ed.), *Crime and Public Policy* (pp. 29–42). Putting Theory to Work. Boulder: Westview Press.
Heitmeyer, Wilhelm. (1997). Gibt es eine Radikalisierung des Integrationsproblems? In Wilhelm Heitmeyer (Ed.), *Was hält die Gesellschaft zusammen? Bundesrepublik Deutschland: Auf dem Weg von der Konsens- zur Konfliktgesellschaft*. Vol. 2 (pp. 23–65). Frankfurt: Suhrkamp.
Held, David, Anthony Mc Grew, David Goldblatt, & Jonathan Perraton. (1999). *Global Transformations. Politics, Economics and Culture*. Stanford: Stanford University Press.
Héritier, Adrienne. (Ed.) (1993). *Policy-Analyse. Kritik und Neubestimmung*. Opladen: Westdeutscher Verlag.
Huntington, Samuel P. (1991). *The Third Wave: Democratization in the Late Twentieth Century*. Norman: University of Oklahoma Press.
Jean, François, & Jean-Christophe Rufin. (Eds.) (1996). *Economie de guerres civiles*. Paris: Edition Pluriel, Hachette.
Kaldor, Mary. (1999). *New and Old Wars. Organized Violence in a Global Era*. Stanford: Stanford University Press.
Kapteyn, Paul. (1996). *The Stateless Market. The European Dilemma of Integration and Civilization*. London, New York: Routledge.
Karp, David R., & Todd R. Clear. (2000). *Community Justice: A Conceptual Framework*. U.S. Department of Justice, National Institute of Justice: Boundary Changes in Criminal Justice Organization, Criminal Justice 2000. Vol. 2 (pp. 323–368). Washington, DC: National Institute of Justice.
Katzenstein, Peter. (Ed.) (1996). *The Culture of National Security. Norms and Identity in World Politics*. New York: Columbia University Press.
Keller, Rainer. (1982). *Strafrechtlicher Gewaltbegriff und Staatsgewalt*. Berlin: Duncker und Humblot.
Kelling, George L., & Catherine M. Coles. (1996). *Fixing Broken Windows*. New York, London, Toronto: The Free Press.
Krasner, Stephen D. (1999). *Sovereignty. Organized Hypocrisy*. Princeton: Princeton University Press.
Lassman, Peter. (2000). The Rule of Man Over Man: Politics, Power and Legitimation. In Stephen Turner (Ed.), *The Cambridge Companion to Weber* (pp. 83–98). Cambridge: Cambridge University Press.
Ludwig-Mayerhofer, Wolfgang. (1998). *Das Strafrecht und seine administrative Rationalisierung. Kritik der informalen Justiz*. Frankfurt: Campus.
Luhmann, Niklas. (2000). *Die Politik der Gesellschaft*. Frankfurt a. M.: Suhrkamp.
Lynch, James P., & William J. Sabol. (2000). *Prison Use and Social Control*. U.S. Department of Justice, National Institute of Justice. Policies, Processes, and Decisions of the Criminal Justice System, Criminal Justice 2000, Vol. 3 (pp. 7–44). Washington, DC: National Institute of Justice.
Lyons, Williams, & Stuart Scheingold. (2000). *The Politics of Crime and Punishment*. U.S. Department of Justice, National Institute of Justice. The Nature of Crime: Continuity and Change. Criminal Justice 2000. Vol. 1 (pp. 103–149). Washington, DC: National Institute of Justice.
Majone, Giandomenico. (Ed.) (1996). *Regulating Europe*. London: Routledge.
Mann, Michael. (1993). *The Sources of Social Power. Vol. II. The Rise of Classes and Nation-States 1760–1914*. New York, London: Cambridge University Press.
Manning, Peter K. (1999). A Dramaturgical Perspective. In Brian Forst & Peter K. Manning (Eds.), *The Privatization of Policing* (pp. 49–126). Washington, DC: Georgetown University Press.
Monkkonen, Eric H. (1981). *Police in Urban America*. New York, London: Cambridge University Press.
Moore, Mark H., & Robert C. Trojanowicz. (1988). *Corporate Strategies for Policing, Perspectives on Policing*. Washington, DC: U.S. Department of Justice, Office of Justice, National Institute of Justice.
Nadelman, Ethan A. (1993). *Cops across Borders: The Internationalization of U.S. Criminal Law Enforcement*. Pittsburgh: Pennsylvania State University Press.
Narr, Wolf-Dieter, & Alex Schubert. (1994). *Weltökonomie. Die Misere der Politik*. Frankfurt a. M.: Suhrkamp.
Naucke, Wolfgang. (2000). *Über die Zerbrechlichkeit des rechtsstaatlichen Strafrechts*. Baden-Baden: Nomos.
Newman, Graeme. (Ed.) (1999). *Global Report on Crime and Justice*. (Published for the United Nations Office for Drug Control and Crime Prevention.) New York, Oxford: Oxford University Press.
North, Douglass C. (1990). *Institutions, Institutional Change and Economic Performance*. New York, London: Cambridge University Press.
Nozick, Robert. (1974). *Anarchy, State, and Utopia*. New York: Basic Books.
Ohmae, Kenichi. (1990). *The Borderless World*. New York: Harper Collins Publishers.
Peters, Guy. (1999). *Institutional Theory in Political Science. The 'New Institutionalism'*. London, New York: Pinter.

Potter, David, David Goldblatt, Margaret Kiloh, & Paul Lewis. (1997). *Democratization. Democracy—From Classic Times to the Present 2*. Cambridge: Polity Press.

Reinhard, Wolfgang. (1999). *Geschichte der Staatsgewalt. Eine vergleichende Verfassungsgeschichte Europas von den Anfängen bis zur Gegenwart*. München: Beck.

Reinicke, Wolfgang H. (1998). *Global Public Policy. Governing without Government*. Washington, DC: Brookings Institution Press.

Report of the Commission on the Advancement of Federal Law Enforcement. (2000). *Law Enforcement in a New Century and a Changing World*. Washington, DC: Government Printing Office.

Rokkan, Stein, & Derek Urwin. (1983). *Economy, Territory, Identity, Politics of West European Peripheries*. London, Beverley Hills, New Delhi: Sage.

Rufin, Jean-Christophe. (1991). *L'empire et les nouveaux barbares*. Paris: Lattès.

Sack, Fritz, Michael Voss, Detlev Frehsee, Albrecht Funk, & Herbert Reinke. (Eds.) (1995). *Privatisierung staatlicher Kontrolle: Befunde, Konzepte, Tendenzen*. Baden-Baden: Nomos.

Schachter, Oscar. (1997). The Decline of the Nation-State and Its Implications for International Law. *Columbia Journal of Transnational Law*, 37(1/2), 7–23.

Scharpf, Fritz. (1991). Die Handlungsfähigkeit des Staates am Ende des zwanzigsten Jahrhunderts. *Politische Vierteljahresschrift*, 32(4), 621–634.

Scharpf, Fritz. (1997). *Games Real Actors Play: Actor-Centered Institutionalism in Policy Research*. Boulder: Westview Press.

Scharpf, Fritz. (1999). *Governing in Europe: Effective or Democratic?* New York, Oxford: Oxford University Press.

Scheuerman, William. (1994). *Between Norm and the Exception. The Frankfurt School and the Rule of Law*. Cambridge, London: The MIT Press.

Scheuerman, William. (1999). Economic Globalization and the Rule of Law. *Constellations*, 6(1), 3–25.

Schlosser, Eric. (1998). The Prison-Industrial Complex. *The Atlantic Monthly*, Dec. 1998, 51–77.

Shearing, Clifford. (1995). Reinventing Policing: Policing as Governance. In Fritz Sack, Michael Voss, Detlev Frehsee, Albrecht Funk & Herbert Reinke (Eds.), *Privatisierung staatlicher Kontrolle: Befunde, Konzepte, Tendenzen* (pp. 70–87). Baden-Baden: Nomos.

Singer, Max, & Aaron Wildavsky. (1996). *The Real World Order: Zones of Peace/Zones of Turmoil*. New York: Chatham House.

Skogan, Wesley G., & Susan M. Harnett. (1997). *Community Policing, Chicago Style*. New York, Oxford: Oxford University Press.

Spruyt, Hedrik. (1994). *The Sovereign State and Its Competitors*. Princeton: Princeton University Press.

Strange, Susan. (1996). *The Retreat of the State: The Diffusion of Power in the World Economy*. Cambridge: Cambridge University Press.

Thomson, Janice E. (1994). *Mercenaries, Pirates and Sovereigns. State Building and Extraterritorial Violence in Early Modern Europe*. Princeton NJ: Princeton University Press.

Tilly, Charles. (Ed.) (1975). *The Formation of National States in Western Europe*. Princeton: Princeton University Press.

Tilly, Charles. (1985). War Making and State Making as Organized Crime. In Peter B. Evans, Dietrich Rueschemeyer & Theda Skocpol (Eds.), *Bringing the State Back In* (pp. 169–191). Cambridge, New York: Cambridge University Press.

Tilly, Charles. (1990). *Coercion, Capital and European States. A.D. 990–1990*. Cambridge: Basil Blackwell.

Tonry, Michael, & Joan Petersilia. (Eds.) (1999). *Prisons. Crime and Justice: An Annual Review of Research. Vol. 26*. Chicago: University of Chicago Press.

Trotha, Trutz von. (1995). Ordnungsformen der Gewalt oder Aussichten auf das Ende des staatlichen Gewaltmonopols. In Brigitta Nedelmann (Ed.), *Politische Institutionen im Wandel. Sonderheit der KZfSS, Band 35* (pp. 129–166). Opladen: Westdeutscher Verlag.

Trotha, Trutz von. (Eds.) (1997). *Soziologie der Gewalt. Sonderheft der KZFSS, Band 37*. Opladen: Westdeutscher Verlag.

Wade, Robert. (1996). Globalization and Its Limits: Reports of the Death of the National Economy Are Greatly Exaggerated. In Suzanne Berger & Roland Dore (Eds.), *National Diversity and Global Capitalism* (pp. 60–88). Ithaca, London: Cornell University Press.

Walker, Samuel. (1980). *Popular Justice. A History of American Criminal Justice*. New York, Oxford: Oxford University Press.

Ward, Richard H. (2000). The Internationalization of Criminal Justice. Boundary Changes in Criminal Justice Organization, *Criminal Justice 2000, Vol. 3* (pp. 267–321). Washington, DC: National Institute of Justice.

Weber, Max. (1978). *Economy and Society: An Outline of Interpretative Sociology* (Ed. Guenther Roth & Claus Wittich). Berkeley, Los Angeles: University of California Press.

Weber, Max. (1994). *Political Writings* (Ed. Peter Lassman & Ronald Speirs). Cambridge, New York: Cambridge University Press.

Willke, Helmut. (1992). *Ironie des Staates*. Frankfurt a. M.: Suhrkamp.

Wilson, James Q. (1975). *Thinking About Crime*. New York: Basic Books.

World Bank. (1997). *World Development Report 1997. The State in a Changing World*. Oxford, New York: Oxford University Press.

Zürn, Michael. (1995). The Challenge of Globalization and Individualization: A View from Europe. In Hans-Henrik Holms & Georg Sørensen (Eds.), *Whose World Order? Uneven Globalization and the End of the Cold War* (pp. 137–163). Boulder: Westview Press.

Zürn, Michael. (1998). *Regieren jenseits des Nationalstaates*. Frankfurt a. M.: Suhrkamp.

CHAPTER II-6-2.3

Freedom to Demonstrate and the Use of Force

Criminal Law as a Threat to Basic Political Rights

OTTO BACKES AND PETER REICHENBACH

INTRODUCTION

In theory, the exercise of the right of freedom of assembly for demonstrations is something we like to celebrate as an expression of living democracy—an indispensable functional element of any parliamentary democracy offering few rights of participation through referendum. In the everyday world of politics and criminal justice, however, this view does not always prevail. Occasionally, it gives way to the concern that freedom to demonstrate, like other freedoms, may be abused: the argument is that anyone who assembles with others and, with no great effort to put forward a logical case, endeavors by physical presence alone to draw attention to public abuses and to enforce political changes is emotional, easily led astray by demagoguery, and therefore—at least potentially—a threat to public order and the state's duty to keep the peace. If the demonstrators' protest *in favor* of different political decisions or different political views can successfully be portrayed as an attack *against* the existing political order, which has to be protected, then there is a great temptation to brand political dissenters as potentially violent criminals and treat them accordingly. Recourse to the criminal law, as a way of disciplining political opponents, is widespread and ever topical, even though the position of the battle lines may vary.

Over the last thirty years, the controversy over the criminal nature of political demonstrations has dominated the public and academic debate in the Federal Republic of Germany. Meanwhile, the broadening of the concept of violence in criminal legislation to protect private legal rights, such as the protection of life and limb in road traffic or in the area of sexual self-determination, has met with no significant public response (with the exception of the recent criminalization of marital rape). This chapter traces this trend and illustrates it with examples of court decisions, most of them handed down in connection with political demonstrations. The course of events shows that the criminal law definition of violence in Germany is increasingly being shaped by constitutional law. As a result, strict limits are being imposed on the possibility of punishing the exercise of political civil rights by applying the criminal law.

I. THE PROBLEM

A civilized society cannot permit its citizens to resolve their disputes by the use of force. If it did, the inevitable consequence would be the domination of the weak by the strong. Apart from cases of self-defense, therefore, the state prohibits the use of force by its citizens. Anyone who nevertheless indulges in the use of force must be prepared to be punished by the state—meeting force with force, if necessary. Punishment, therefore, is a necessary response by the state to the contravention of legislation by which the state endeavors to regulate and ensure the nonviolent and peaceful coexistence of its citizens.

But if the state holds a monopoly on the legitimate use of coercion, it is impossible to rule out the danger that the state, too, with no one to control it, may employ force for the disproportionate limitation of its citizens' liberties. Force wielded by the state is still force, and no less detrimental to a civilized society than individual force if it is used exclusively, or primarily, as a way of exercising power rather than safeguarding the law as the foundation of society. "If not *controlled by the constitution*, the state monopoly on force runs the risk of leading to dictatorship and totalitarianism. But *without the state monopoly on coercion*, the constitution ... *cannot perform its function of keeping the peace* in the interests of all" (Schwind et al., 1990:249). What does that really mean?

A man who clubs another to the ground and robs him is indisputably using force. But is it not equally an act of force to hold a doped pad of cotton wool under the victim's nose and then quietly take his money when he is unconscious? What about a driver who compels another to concede the outside lane by tailgating him for miles at a distance of two meters and a speed of 100 MPH? What about people who sit down together in the road to block the movement of traffic as a protest against fare increases, the stationing of weapons, or the closure of factories? Are these not also more subtle, more modern, or technical forms of force? And, if so, would it not be logical to categorize public tirades of hatred against those who think differently or look different as "verbal violence"? Ultimately, why should the law not punish "structural violence" inflicted on "people who are so affected that their somatic and intellectual self-realization is less than their potential self-realization" (Galtung, 1975:52)?

This chapter deals with the question of *what criteria* are to be applied in deciding whether a form of conduct is classified as violence under the criminal law; inseparably associated with this question, and indeed preliminary to it, is the question of *who decides* on these criteria; who holds the power of definition? The answer to that question derives from the legal framework within which the criminal law is embedded.

II. THE LEGAL FRAMEWORK

All state authority is derived from the people (Section 20(2), first sentence, GG[1]). The people cannot simply wield that state authority as it sees fit, however, but is restricted to the forms prescribed by the constitution: The state authority shall be exercised by the people (only) through elections and other votes and (otherwise) through specific legislative, executive, and judicial bodies (Section 20(2), second sentence, GG). Ultimately, then, the state authority derived from and wielded by the people is exercised only by the institutions of state empowered to do so by the *Grundgesetz*. Their powers and the control of those powers (separation of powers) are laid down in the constitution: The legislature is bound by the constitutional order, the executive and the judiciary by law and justice (Section 20(3) GG). The constitution is thus the foundation of all three state authorities; it is the basic law, against which legislation and justice—including criminal legislation—must be measured.

If the state wishes to react to massive violations or disruptions of the life of society, such as may be created by violent confrontations between its citizens, then it can of course—exercising its monopoly on coercion—criminalize such forms of violent behavior. In doing so, however, it must observe the constitutional law dictates of the *Grundgesetz*. These prescribe that an act may be punished by the state only if it was defined by a law as a criminal offense before the act was committed, in other words if the criminal offense was already "laid down by law" (Section 103(2) GG). This requirement that criminal legislation must define the nature of offenses is intended to perform two functions. First, it should enable the citizen to refer to criminal legislation to discover the forms of conduct from which he must refrain unless he is prepared to commit a criminal offense. Of course, it is more than doubtful whether criminal legislation can really achieve this objective and give the citizen a clear idea of what is prohibited and what is permitted in a given case. Secondly, criminal legislation is intended to draw a clear dividing line between the two powers of legislation and judiciary. Judges may punish only those offenses that the legislator has "defined" as such by statute law. If the citizen's conduct is not covered by any criminal legislation, then the judge must not punish him, even if he—and the great majority of the population—may regard the conduct in question as thoroughly deserving of punishment: no law, no punishment. Whether conduct that is deserving of punishment but not recognized as such by the law is to be punished in future, is a question of legal policy, to be decided upon by parliament alone, whose members—unlike judges—must answer to the people through the electoral process. The law makes strict provision, with no ifs or buts, to prohibit any arbitrary anticipation of this parliamentary decision by the courts.

And yet there are more than thirty provisions of the *Strafgesetzbuch*[2] in which the legislator has penalized forms of conduct in which the perpetrator uses force or acts of violence in the commission of an offense: treason with violence, violence against officials in the execution of their duties, forcible coercion, forcible rape, etc. Has the legislator adequately "defined" what constitutes "violence" or "force" here? Can the citizen, or at least the judge, determine, from the use of the word "force" or "violence" in the designation of the facts constituting the offense, which forms of conduct the legislator intended to criminalize and which he did not? Anyone answering that question in the affirmative would certainly have to be able to resolve the examples given above—a virtually impossible

---

[1] GG = *Grundgesetz* (Basic Law) for the Federal Republic of Germany of May 23, 1949, as last amended by the Amending Act of July 16, 1998.
[2] German Penal Code (StGB) of May 15, 1871 in the version published on November 13, 1998.

task. But anyone answering it in the negative would either have to conclude that the criminal legislation in question is collectively unconstitutional or to find a way of interpreting the courts' duty to uphold the law—an indispensable prerequisite of the rule of law—in a way that would allow the courts, in determining the existence of violence, also to resort to the objective criteria associated with the word. It is inevitable that the judge will indeed have to resort to the objective content of features of the law, which then will ultimately allow him a limited freedom of interpretation in determining what the legislator subjectively intended the legislation to mean. For it is impossible for the legislator, when drafting criminal legislation, to describe in detail the many specific acts regarded as criminal; in view of the diversity of human existence, he is compelled to use abstract and general terms in criminal legislation which, although they name and identify the essence of the criminal act, are often imprecise in marginal areas. They thus require interpretation by the judge in each individual case to determine whether or not they still cover a particular form of behavior. This ceases to be a matter of interpretation, however, if the judge goes beyond the substance of a statutory criminal law provision, extends the definition of criminality to cases that are merely "similar" in meriting punishment, and so strays across the boundaries of his office in appropriating to himself the legislator's right of definition. However clear the theoretical dividing line may be between *admissible interpretation* and *inadmissible analogy*, it is nevertheless difficult to draw that distinction in practice, even if it is recognized that the possible meaning of the wording of a feature of the law marks the outermost boundary of admissible judicial interpretation.

The historical development of the criminal law concept of violence clearly shows the extent to which case law has to walk a perilous tightrope between interpretation and analogy.

III. THE CRIMINAL LAW CONCEPT OF VIOLENCE BETWEEN INTERPRETATION AND ANALOGY (SECTION 103(2) GG)

1. The Evolution of Jurisdiction on the Concept of Violence—the Example of Criminal Coercion (Section 240 StGB)

Criminal coercion is committed by a person who unlawfully compels another, by force or the threat of serious harm, to commit, tolerate, or refrain from any act. This form of violence undoubtedly exists if the perpetrator uses *substantial physical force* to overcome actual or expected resistance. The classic example of this is attacking a victim with a club in order to compel him to commit an act. (As the criminal law protects the freedom to form and act upon an intent, the definition of force has to include the subjective element of intention—that the perpetrator intends to break the will of the victim by the use of force. For example, a driver who parks his car across the entrance to a property with a view to blocking ingress or egress is using force, though he would not be if he merely parked his car across the entrance accidentally.

This classical definition of violence as the physical deployment of force to produce a physical effect on a person was later broadened in two stages.

It is indisputable that a physical influence can be exerted on a person to break his will, even without the use of force by the perpetrator, if the latter makes use of technical means producing an equivalent effect. Thus, the *Bundesgerichtshof* [German Federal Court of Justice] decided that violence was used if the perpetrator deprived the victim of his power of resistance by administering a narcotic to him "without the use of force" (*BGHSt* [*BGH Decisions in Criminal Cases*] 1, 141—the "Chloraethyl [Ethyl chloride]" case). In the statement of grounds, the court noted that it was immaterial, for the purposes of determining logically whether violence had been used, whether the perpetrator overcame physical resistance by physical strength alone—to a greater or lesser extent—or also made use of other natural forces, such as physical, chemical, or other effects. Similar considerations also prompted those decisions in which the locking of the victim in a room or the firing of warning shots was regarded as violence although the perpetrators had used "no significant force." In all cases, the courts found that the effects had been perceived not just as mental compulsion but as directly *physical compulsion.*

This shift in focus from the physical use of force by the perpetrator to compulsion perceived as physical by the victim prepared the way for the next stage of the broadening of the concept of violence. "Effects of physical compulsion," it was argued, could be achieved not only by physical domination but also *by mental influences* on the victim. Whether a streetcar driver was physically prevented from proceeding by the building of barricades or mentally influenced by a sit-in on the rails, the effect was the same. For a presumption of force, ultimately, it was generally sufficient for there to be an effect of compulsion that impaired the victim's freedom to form or act upon an intent, as the BGH found in the Laepple case of 1969.

BGHSt[3] 23, 46 ("Laepple" decision)

Protesting against fare increases on public transport, Laepple, a student, had sat down on the support of a streetcar rail and so prevented the driver from proceeding. The court saw this conduct as forcible coercion, since mental compulsion was exercised. The coercive effect upon the victim lay in the fact that the protester, albeit with minimal physical force, was triggering a process determined by mental factors. The decisive point, said the court, was how much weight attached to the compulsion exercised: if a person sat down in front of a streetcar, that constituted irresistible coercion of the driver, since he would be guilty of unlawful killing if he failed to stop.

In 1986, the *Bundesverfassungsgericht* [Federal Constitutional Court—BVerfG] had the opportunity to comment on the constitutional law aspects of this far-reaching BGH precedent. The occasion for this was provided by the sentences passed on participants in sit-ins protesting outside a German army special weapons store against the storage of short-range nuclear missiles.

BVerfGE[4] 73, 206 (the first "Sitzblockaden [Sit-in]" decision)

The Constitutional Court found that the case law of the BGH, to the effect that the concept of violence was no longer significantly determined by the requirements of physical use of force by the perpetrator or physical effect on the person of the victim, was compatible with the constitution. However, this was not the unanimous view of the court. Only four of the judges, whose opinion carried the judgment, expressed the view that the broadening of the

---

[3] *BGHSt* = *Decisions of the BGH in Criminal Cases* (volume, page).
[4] *BVerfGE* = Decisions of the BVerfG (volume, page).

concept of violence established by this precedent did not exceed the limits of admissible interpretation. The boundary drawn by the literal meaning of the words was observed, at least, if the irresistible coercive effect on the victim involved the use of a degree of physical force, albeit slight, by the perpetrator, as was the case with the formation of a human barrier by people sitting down to block access. The four judges who voted against the court's decision, however, regarded the broadening of the concept of violence as the drawing of a prohibited analogy. Among other criticisms, they observed that case law had never interpreted the completely passive—and hence by definition nonviolent—behavior of sit-down strikers as violence, and so had not treated mental compulsion by peaceful sit-ins as a case of coercion by acts of physical force. It was evident, they said, that the boundaries of admissible interpretation had been crossed, not only by reason of this "conceptual confusion" but on another ground as well. If any compulsion restricting people's freedom to form and act upon an intent were in itself sufficient for the courts to regard it as an act of violence, then the legislator could have refrained from criminalizing only the coercive effect upon freedom of decision exerted "by violence or the threat of serious harm." But if he had regarded it as necessary, for the purposes of defining criminality, to lay down a restricted number of identified means of coercion, then the requirement of definition contained in Section 103(2) GG would have required him to abide by that decision, even if the application of the law were to leave loopholes. In any case, it could not be a matter for the courts to close such loopholes by "intellectualizing" or "voiding" the literal wording of the definition of the offense. In such a case, punishment would be based not on the legislator's ruling, conceived before the event, but on the judge's subsequent perception that the offense was deserving of punishment.

Nine years later, the BVerfG again had to decide whether it was constitutional to penalize sitters-in for coercion.

BVerfGE 92, 1 (second "Sitzblockaden" decision)

In contrast to the first "Sitzblockaden" decision, the BVerfG now accepted that the broadening interpretation of the concept of violence in Section 240 StGB in connection with sit-ins was a contravention of the constitutional requirement of definition. In essence, five judges adopted the arguments of their colleagues who had failed to support the first "Sitzblockaden" decision. They objected that, as a consequence of the broadening of the concept of violence, it was no longer possible to predict with sufficient certainty which physical acts that mentally prevented others from acting upon their intent were to be prohibited and which were not. The different treatment of sit-in protests against nuclear rearmament, on the one hand, and those protesting against factory shutdowns, increased charges, cuts in subsidies, or traffic plans, on the other, confirmed this. If the BGH was trying to reintroduce restrictions on its own broadening of the concept of violence by attaching significance to the "weight" of the mental influence, the burden of that intended limitation was being imposed on a concept far vaguer even than that of violence. It was therefore not sufficient for a presumption of "force" for a person to be physically occupying a position that another person wanted to occupy or pass through if the latter was mentally inhibited by the presence of the former from acting upon his intent. Three judges dissented, however, taking the view that the sitters-in had been fully able to perceive the risk of being punished for their actions, and that the blocking of a thoroughfare with the intention of preventing the vehicle occupants from proceeding further was a form of physical, not merely mental, influence on the freedom of decision of those in the vehicle.

The criminal courts have sometimes had difficulty in applying, in cases brought before them, the limitation of the concept of violence imposed upon them by the BverfG in the second "Sitzblockaden" decision. This is particularly apparent from the next decision considered.

BGHSt 41, 182 ("Autobahn-Sperrung [highway blockade]")

Kurds wishing to draw attention to the political treatment they were receiving in Turkey had obstructed approaching vehicles on a highway, thus forcing them and the cars behind them to stop.

Anyone who felt free to interpret decision *BVerfGE* 92, 1 as meaning that there could be no punishment for coercion if someone, by his mere physical presence, inhibited another person from taking the place he occupied was confronted by the BGH with a completely different interpretation. As far as the obstruction of drivers was concerned, said the court, a distinction had to be made. Those drivers who had been the first to reach the group of people blocking the carriageway, and could possibly have broken through, might have stopped because of "a purely mental coercive effect." That mental coercive effect could not, therefore, be classified as use of force by the blockaders. The drivers that followed, however, had been prevented from continuing their journey not only mentally but also *physically* by the vehicles that had already stopped; they could not have proceeded, even if the mental compulsion had made no impression on them. The physical blocking effect produced by the first vehicles to stop upon those that followed must therefore be classified as the use of force by the blockaders. Amelung (1996:231) has rightly described this piece of sophistry as a case of "barely disguised disobedience" of the BVerfG by a division of the BGH.

The opinions expressed in the *literature* are just as inconsistent as those of the courts (cf., by way of example, with additional references in each case: Eser (1997) on Sections 234ff, paragraphs 6ff; Kühl (1999), Section 240, paragraphs 19ff; Weber (2000), Section 9, paragraphs 55ff; Amelung (1995)). Where authorities call for the courts to classify as force any harmful act which, in prospect, constitutes the threat of serious harm, they are completely abandoning the physical aspect of compulsion, although *BVerfGE* 92, 1 says that this is a specifically necessary element of force. By contrast, those who recognize only physical compulsion as a harmful act are hardly progressing beyond the—not uncontested—jurisdiction of the BVerfG.

2. Authors' Opinion

The debate regarding the concept of violence, and the extent of what constitutes coercion, is more than a reflection of substantial disagreement in jurisdiction and literature. It also gives the impression that the actual reason for the dispute has not really been identified or addressed. As long as the argument over the concept of violence related to situations which—as, for example, in the case where the victim was overcome by ethyl chloride, or in the case of high-speed tailgating to force a driver to vacate the outside lane—exerted a coercive effect on the victim, in the form of an imminent threat of harm, virtually no one was concerned at the fact that the element of physicality had increasingly been abandoned, as far as both perpetrator and victim were concerned. The freedom of the individual to form and act upon an intent, free of constraints, legitimized the punishment of individuals endeavoring to enforce their own interests in a socially unacceptable manner. This tacit consensus regarding the justified dematerialization of the concept of violence broke down, however, when criminal law was required to evaluate situations that were structurally different from those decided previously. The sit-in protests against fare increases, rearmament, and the building of nuclear power plants were not exclusively or primarily a reflection of individual concerns, but rather drew attention to the interests of particular groups or a broad section of the public; those responsible were not trying to force (nor could they have forced) those whom they were obstructing to act in such a way as to comply with their interests; their aim, rather, was to draw attention to a problem that called for public debate by—literally—demonstrative behavior.

Even so, there is no doubt that the concept of violence, as interpreted by case law prior to the decision in *BVerfGE* 92, 1, did extend sufficiently far to include sit-ins. But when the BVerfG holds that it was impossible for the sitters-in to predict whether their conduct was criminal or not, that may be correct if we assume that people actually do refer to the *Strafgesetzbuch* to establish whether or not their acts are criminal. Such an assumption, however, is unrealistic in the extreme. In real life, media reporting alone would have left the demonstrators in no doubt that the courts would punish sit-ins as coercion. Whether or not it was constitutional to treat sit-ins as criminal was a question that the BVerfG had answered sometimes in the affirmative and sometimes in the negative, with variable majorities, depending simply on which judges made up the court. The issue had been examined in the context of the dividing line between admissible interpretation and inadmissible analogy, and the findings of the BVerfG therefore did nothing either to clarify or to calm the debate. Because, even if one agreed with *BVerfGE* 92, 1 that it was unconstitutional to apply Section 240 StGB to sit-ins, because they did not involve "violence" within the meaning of that provision, there was nothing to prevent the legislator's amending the wording of Section 240 StGB so that it did include sit-ins. Thus, the commission on violence appointed by the federal government also proposed that violence, within the meaning of Section 240 StGB, be restricted to physical violence (in line with *BVerfGE* 92, 1) and that a new means of coercion—"comparably severe mental compulsion"—be added to the specified elements of the offense. Although this change would have clarified the terminology, it would not have dispelled existing fundamental doubts as to whether the legislator had any right at all to penalize the new forms of public protest represented by the sit-ins.

To suggest that sit-ins should be penalized as coercion only if they are also regarded as "reprehensible"—in other words, the objectives pursued are morally undesirable or antisocial—necessarily results in a substantive assessment by the judge (which is to be rejected) of the (long-term) aims pursued by the demonstrators, and a decision by the judge as to whether the blockade is a form of admissible demonstration or inadmissible exploitation of the blockaded. If that interpretation were to be accepted, it would ultimately mean that whether or not an act was criminal was decided not by the law but by the political views of the judge.

The problems which the sitters-in hope to bring to the attention of the public are *political* problems, a desirable subject of discussion and (new) regulation in the public interest. They must therefore be discussed and resolved in the political arena. But anyone who seeks to classify sit-ins designed to draw public attention to these matters simply as violence, reprehensibility, and wrongdoing is thus criminalizing from the outset what may be a politically necessary confrontation. It is dubious whether the (overly) hasty application of the criminal law to political issues is legitimate under the *Grundgesetz*.

First, according to the system established by the *Grundgesetz*, political disputes are a matter for parliaments. The people, as the repository of the authority of the state, participates in such debates by determining the composition of parliaments through elections. In addition, every citizen also has the option of becoming politically involved in parties and associations (Sections 21 and 9 GG) and enjoys freedom of expression and assembly (Sections 5 and 8 GG) to enable him to express his political views. Critics of the BVerfG's decisions on the criminal nature of sit-ins have therefore rightly pointed out that this problem should have been resolved by the constitutional court in the context of the basic right of freedom of assembly, particularly since that basic right would have to be respected by the legislator, too, as a boundary drawn by constitutional law and setting a clear limit on possible attempts at criminalization.

It is true that the state's monopoly of coercion gives it a duty, as already pointed out above, to keep the peace in society by protecting its citizens against violence and against interference with their freedom or property. Not only that, but a modern state is also expected to safeguard its citizens against nuclear threat, traffic noise, atmospheric ozone, the exploitation of commercial monopolies, and many other perils. Basic rights are also regarded as protected privileges; by exercising them, the citizen can ensure that the state actually does keep the peace.

This, however, presupposes that sociopolitical differences can be aired and that basic political rights (Sections 5 and 8 GG) can be exercised. The forum for public debate which the state is required to guarantee would be worthless if the state alone also had the power to dictate the content of such discussions or to prohibit certain subjects. The duty of the state is to provide a forum for its citizens where they can articulate and discuss their concerns and fears—such as problems of rearmament, destruction of the environment, or xenophobia. These fears originate in the social or public sphere and must be dealt with in equally social or public debate, irrespective of whether the state itself regards their concerns as justified.

The interaction between the state monopoly on coercion and the basic rights thus produces two contrasting effects. On the one hand, the state's function as keeper of the peace and protector of basic rights obliges it to ensure that *private disagreements* are kept entirely free from violence of any kind. On the other hand, however, because of the defensive function of the basic rights, the state is also required to allow the freest possible discussion in the *public arena* and not to be overly hasty in stigmatizing it as the use of violence and prohibiting it through criminal legislation. Of course, the state must also ensure that the basic right of freedom of assembly does not become *carte blanche* for those who are prone to violence.

The critical question, then, is where the boundary should be drawn between the criminal and noncriminal exercise of the basic right of freedom of assembly in the course of public debate.

IV. THE CRIMINAL LAW CONCEPT OF VIOLENCE IN THE LIGHT OF BASIC POLITICAL RIGHTS (SECTIONS 5 AND 8 GG)

1. The Restrictive Interpretation of the Concept of Violence in Political Matters

Even though it may be surprising that Germany's highest courts decided the cases referred to above (in III,1) without recourse to Sections 5 and 8 GG, in other cases both the BVerfG and the BGH have emphasized the significance of these basic rights and made allowance for their influence on criminal legislation that restricts them. These cases concerned large-scale demonstrations that turned violent. The decisions quoted below by the BGH ("Startbahn-West [west runway]") and the BVerfG ("Brokdorf") show different ways in which, in the context of public debate on political matters, the rigid criminal law interpretation of violence, fixated on the use of physical force and physical/mental coercion, can be loosened so that the basic political rights guaranteed by constitutional law are not strangulated but, rather, can be efficiently exercised.

BGHSt 32, 165 ("Startbahn-West")

A number of action groups were formed to oppose by "active and nonviolent resistance" the addition of an extra runway to Frankfurt airport. At a public assembly, the accused, as one of the representatives of an action group, called upon the *Land* government to accept a political solution in the form of immediate permission to petition for a referendum and the immediate declaration of a moratorium on the runway project, including the suspension of all work on clearing the site. He then called upon those attending this public meeting to pay a visit to the airport the following day: the demonstration must be nonviolent, he said, but the airport must be shut down for several hours. Several thousand opponents of the new runway responded to this call: for over nine hours, the airport was almost completely closed, not only to aircraft but also to other incoming and outgoing traffic. Although all airline passengers were able to reach the airport on foot, in some cases being jostled in the process, the protesters against the runway had also built barricades, which they defended with the use of clubs and stones against the police presence deployed to clear them. In some cases, the barricades were set on fire. At times, all four lanes of the freeways around Frankfurt were closed, and federal highways were also blocked. The accused, when calling for this kind of action, had expected a significant proportion of the violence that later took place.

The charges against the accused were: coercion of constitutional bodies (Section 105 StGB), breach of the peace (Section 125 StGB), and coercion of passers-by and airport personnel (Section 240 StGB). All these provisions call for the existence of force or violence.

Under Section 105 StGB, it is a criminal offense forcibly to coerce the government of a *Land* not to exercise its powers or to exercise them in a particular manner. The demands made by the accused for the granting of a moratorium and a suspension of building work were designed to procure such acts by the *Land* government. However, the BGH was unable to interpret the excesses that actually took place as "forcible" within the meaning of Section 105 StGB. The reasons the court gave are informative.

First, the court points out that a judgment as to whether a specific act is forcible, within the meaning of a specific criminal law definition, cannot simply be based on the fact that the act in question is measured against an "abstract construction of the concept of force;" the act must, rather, be judged in the context of its intentions, as they appear from the circumstances of the act, and in the context of the relationship between the act and those whom it is intended to affect or influence. The decision also states the reason why higher standards are applied to the proof of the requisite force than in other cases: constitutional bodies are at the very center of political life and are exposed to the currents, forces, and counterforces that dictate political life; the many different instruments of power employed by the conflicting groups in the political debate have—at least indirectly—an effect on them. If this debate were to be judged by reference to a low threshold of violence, such as is inherent in the basic circumstances of coercion, it would mean carrying the political struggle into the courts. "In that case, ultimately, the difficult and essentially *political question* of the conditions under which political activism becomes reprehensible *would be laid on the shoulders of the courts*" (emphasis added). In order to avoid this, public disturbances should be regarded as the use of force within the meaning of Section 105 StGB only if the pressure exerted reached such a degree that a responsible government might feel compelled to capitulate to the perpetrators' demands in order to avert serious harm to the common good or to individual citizens. The activities connected with the west runway lacked any such "legislatively identifiable" element of compulsion. The *Land* government had been able to stand up to the threat "in calm confidence."

For the reason already noted, the court clearly rejected the obvious assumption that, if the force used in the case under consideration fell short of the threshold of Section 105 StGB, it was nevertheless quite sufficient to constitute forcible coercion under Section 240 StGB and hence to be penalized under that section; the legislator, said the court, had not wanted to place the burden of decision in difficult and ultimately *political issues upon the courts—and that applied to Section 240 StGB as well.*

By contrast, the BGH upheld the accused's conviction for breach of the peace (Section 125 StGB). Under that provision, it is a criminal act in itself to participate in *acts* of violence against persons or things which are committed by a crowd of people who have joined forces in a manner endangering public safety; there is no requirement here, as there is in Section 105 StGB (coercion of constitutional organs), that the coercion should produce any more extensive result. At the same time, the court also regarded this conduct as coercion under Section 240 StGB, as there had been deliberate interference with the rights of the airline passengers and airport personnel. When the accused cited his basic rights under Sections 5 and 8 GG to avert a judgment under Sections 125 and 240 StGB, the BGH rejected this on the correct ground that the accused had not incited attendance at a peaceful assembly, protected by the *Grundgesetz*, nor had he been inciting a mere blockade, whether seated or standing (which would have attracted no punishment). He had, rather, encouraged a large-scale action that did not follow a peaceful course and resulted in the building of barricades and resistance to the forces of order deployed to remove them—acts that the accused had tacitly condoned. However, the court expressly pointed out that the incitement to a peaceful demonstration, although its course had led to predictable excesses that could have been averted by appropriate precautions, could not have been punished as a breach of the peace.

This problem, merely hinted at by the BGH on this occasion, of whether, and if so to what extent, predictable acts of violence in the course of demonstrations can be attributed to their organizers, with the consequence that the event can be prohibited, was addressed in detail by the BVerfG in the "Brokdorf" decision. The guidelines laid down there are also to be observed when deciding on the criminal liability of the organizers for breach of the peace and coercion.

BVerfGE 69, 315 ("Brokdorf")

The BVerfG was required to decide whether Section 8 GG had been contravened by the prohibiting of demonstrations planned against the building of the Brokdorf nuclear power plant.

Section 8 GG guarantees the right of "peaceful and unarmed" assembly and states that this right may be restricted by law in the case of "outdoor" assemblies; meaning that, where assemblies come into contact with the outside world, they need to be regulated under organizational and procedural law, partly to create the conditions in which they are to be held and partly to provide adequate safeguards for the conflicting interests of others. The legislator, whose function it is to supply the specific regulation required, must take as his starting point the basic decision in favor of freedom of assembly enshrined in constitutional law, and may only restrict the exercise of that right in order to protect other interests of equal importance and in strict compliance with the principle of proportionality. In line with this duty, the *Versammlungsgesetz* [Assembly Act] requires advance notice of outdoor assemblies (which, of course, does not permit the automatic prohibition or breaking-up of "spontaneous demonstrations" arising on the spur of the moment simply because they contravene the notification requirement); the Act also provides for the imposing of conditions, and only then for the assembly to be prohibited or broken up. The latter measures are permitted only as a last resort in the event of a "direct" threat to public safety and order. The existence of such a threat may not be assumed on the basis of mere suspicion or presumption—there must be "identifiable circumstances." What specific requirements have to be satisfied by this prediction of threat cannot be laid down in isolation from the specific circumstances, but depends on the extent to which—in large-scale demonstrations, for example—the organizers are willing to cooperate on the preparations, and whether trouble is expected only from third parties or a small minority.

The BVerfG, referring to relevant reports of previous experience, identifies the following cooperative measures to create trust: That both sides refrain from provocation and incitement to aggression; that the organizers encourage the participants to behave peacefully and to isolate anyone responsible for violence; that the authorities display measured restraint—establishing police-free areas if necessary—and avoid disproportionate reaction; and, in particular, that contact is established early to enable the two sides to get to know one another, exchange information, and if possible cooperate on a basis of trust, which makes it easier to deal with unforeseen conflict situations as well (p. 355). The more the organizers, "when giving notice of a large-scale demonstration, are prepared to take unilateral steps to create trust or even to cooperate in a manner favorable to demonstration, the higher the threshold becomes for official intervention because of the threat to public security and order" (p. 357).

The recommendations put forward here by the BVerfG for consideration by the organizers of large-scale demonstrations and their participants, and by the government authorities, in the context of the application of the *Versammlungsgesetz*, also have an effect on the question of whether excesses by individuals or a minority justify the prohibition or breaking-up of the demonstration, and if so under what conditions; these recommendations also have an effect on the organizers' liability for such excesses under the criminal law.

- If the organizer and his followers intend acts of violence, or at least condone such acts by others, as the BGH held had occurred in the "Startbahn-West" case, the demonstration is a nonpeaceful one and not covered at all by Section 8 GG, so that prohibiting it or breaking it up cannot violate this basic right at all; in such cases, a criminal conviction for breach of the peace and coercion is justified.
- If, conversely, the organizer and his followers conduct themselves peacefully and if trouble emanates only from outsiders (counterdemonstrators or disruptive

groups), the action of the authorities must be directed primarily against these troublemakers, and the organizers are not liable under criminal law for the conduct of these third parties.
- If there is no reason to expect that the demonstration as a whole will turn to violence or riot, or that the organizer or his followers intend or condone such a development or regard it as furthering the aims of their demonstration, the protection of freedom of assembly must be retained even if excesses are committed by individual other demonstrators or a minority. It has rightly been pointed out that it would not be just if the nonpeaceful conduct of individuals were to result in the forfeiture of the protection of basic rights for the whole event rather than merely for the perpetrators. Otherwise, the latter would have the power to "convert" demonstrations; that would mean, in practice, that any large-scale demonstration could be prohibited, since it is virtually always possible to "identify" nonpeaceful intent on the part of some participants. In this case as well, then, the conduct of the nonpeaceful participants cannot, in principle, be charged against the organizer under the criminal law.
- If a demonstration results in a public nuisance which—in the words of the BverfG—"arises as a necessary consequence of the mass exercise of the basic right and cannot be avoided without disadvantage to the purpose of the event, third parties will in general have to tolerate (this)" (p. 353). Since it is generally possible to make arrangements to ensure that the streets can be used simultaneously by demonstrators and moving traffic, it follows that there is no question of any prohibition or, consequently, any criminal liability here.

2. Authors' Opinion

The decisions in "Brokdorf" and "Startbahn-West" move away from the concept of violence defined by "abstract construction." In disputes over political issues, violence refers not to the acute manifestation of the use of physical force, nor even to all acts of violence occurring in connection with it, but is interpreted more with reference to the purpose of legislation and to the specific circumstances that immediately preceded the acute manifestation and were intended to prevent it. The reason for the change of perspective (regulative as opposed to descriptive concept of violence; concrete as opposed to abstract view) is that this is the only way both to guarantee the freedom of assembly protected by the *Grundgesetz* and to ensure that equally important interests of others can be adequately protected. Literature and judiciary repeatedly describe the stabilizing function of freedom of assembly for the representative system: it is said to allow dissatisfaction, displeasure, and criticism to be publicly expressed and worked off and to act as a necessary condition of a political early warning system that highlights the potential for trouble, makes lack of integration apparent, and so also enables the course of official policy to be corrected (*BVerfGE* 69, 315, 347). Little would remain of this function if the mass exercise of this basic right by many people were immediately and always to be perceived as a deliberate campaign of violence, intended to restrict others' freedom of movement and action, even though the organizers have behaved cooperatively in the run-up to the demonstration and acts of violence are committed only by third parties or small minorities; the exercising of the basic right of freedom of assembly would automatically be converted to a criminal activity, and constitutional law thus frustrated by criminal law.

The broadening of the criminal law concept of violence to allow for the principles of constitutional law in disputes on political issues has considerable advantages over the previous debate. Hitherto, that debate has mainly focused on the question of whether the long-term political aims of the demonstrators—peace, human rights, environmental protection, etc.—in favor of which they are publicly demonstrating, mean, in themselves, that the sit-ins cannot be reprehensible even though they technically constitute violence, or whether these aims should only be considered in the context of determining the penalty; in both cases, the criminal court judge is involved in this decision and the liability to or extent of the penalty depends on his political attitude to the long-term aims pursued by the demonstrators. But in that case, legal decisions cease to be calculable because of these political implications.

On the other hand, neither the constitution nor the *Versammlungsgesetz* that gives specific form to Section 8 GG envisages any control by the authorities over the substantive form of assemblies; neither the constitution nor the *Versammlungsgesetz* concern themselves with anything more than the organizational conditions for the holding of the assembly. All that the authorities can ask of organizers and participants is that they refrain from nonpeaceful behavior and minimize adverse effects on the interests of third parties. Consequently, demonstrations by both Left and Right—irrespective of the (long-term) aims propagated—are admissible so long as it is ensured, or can be ensured by appropriate arrangements, that the event will run its course peacefully. If, however, specific indications become apparent in the run-up to a demonstration, such as certain types of incitement to participate circulated on the Internet, that suggest the direct commission of acts of violence, and those responsible for arranging the assembly give no clear signals distancing themselves from groups sympathizing with the aims of the assembly with a view to preventing their expected acts of violence, the holding of the event must be prohibited (as recently stated by the BVerfG in *Neue Juristische Wochenschrift*, 2000, p. 3051, in connection with an outdoor rally planned by the NPD [German National Democratic Party] in Göttingen). These standards for the planning and organization of events so as to protect basic rights must also be observed under criminal law. Provided that events are not prohibited or broken up and that there is no violation of the conditions laid down to prevent acts of violence, there is no reason for criminal law to prohibit what the constitution and administrative law permit.

The fears occasionally expressed (Otto, Krey, & Kühl, 1994:897) that allowing sit-ins creates a risk that the political debate may become more radical and may open the floodgates to serious breaches of the peace can be wholly disregarded if priority is given to the *Versammlungsgesetz* and the possibility of flexible imposition of restrictions that it provides. Thus, in the decision of July 14, 2000, mentioned previously, the BVerfG rightly pointed out that, in the case of an NPD rally, appropriate measures could be taken to prevent, for example, the use of drums and fanfares or the carrying of banners, so as to rule out any threats to public safety and order that might arise specifically from such activities; similarly, measures could be imposed requiring the deployment of ambulances or fire service personnel at demonstrations.

The tendency apparent in the "Startbahn-West" and "Brokdorf" decisions not to impose upon the criminal courts the burden of dealing with demonstrations on "political issues" cannot, of course, provide a definitive indication of what "political issues" are. While there is no doubt that, for example, demonstrations in favor of peace or human rights are ("altruistic") political themes, the closure of a large factory resulting in the loss of jobs may be a "call to the barricades," not only for those whose livelihoods are jeopardized but also for the general population wishing to express solidarity with them. In an open democracy, which thrives on the conflict of opinions, it is therefore possible in principle for "private" issues to become political and hence the subject of a public difference of opinion (such as the continued existence of a nursery school or the closing of a residential street to through traffic). The argument here is that if the constitution and the *Versammlungsgesetz* refrain from substantive judgments on outdoor events, it is logical that the authorization of demonstrations must not be made conditional on a list of issues that has been limited in advance. The concern that a collective expression of opinion manifested by sit-ins may immediately encourage those with different views to join in and stage sit-ins of their own, representing a serious threat to the general peace, is unjustified; not only can the flexible strategy of restrictions imposed by the authorities mentioned earlier prevent events taking a nonpeaceful course, but the organizers and participants will themselves have to take into account the fact that it is only by peaceful conduct that they will be able to promote their aims effectively among the public; violent confrontations, as the BVerfG rightly observes, will always ultimately be subject to the authority of the state and, at the same time, cast a shadow over the aims they pursue.

There is therefore no reason to classify any sit-in, especially if its timing and location have been limited by rules laid down by the governmental authorities, as nonpeaceful and therefore criminal.

V. CRIMINAL LEGISLATION AGAINST THE VERBAL PREPARATION AND DEPICTION OF VIOLENCE—ON THE MARGINS OF BASIC POLITICAL RIGHTS (SECTIONS 5 AND 8 GG)

The legislator has adopted a considerable body of criminal legislation to counteract the creation of a political climate that might in various ways be propitious to acts of violence. Most of the provisions concerned involve the intention of the state to nip right-wing violence in the bud at an early stage.

For example, the offense of *incitement to violence against segments of the population* (Section 130 StGB) is committed by any person who disturbs the public peace in that he

1. incites hatred against segments of the population or calls for violent or arbitrary measures against them; or
2. assaults the human dignity of others by insulting, maliciously maligning, or defaming segments of the population.

However praiseworthy the legislator's intent here may be, to prevent, by means of this provision, even the creation of a hostile atmosphere in society, closer inspection shows it to be a problematical exercise. If the BGH (*BGHSt* 32, 310, 313) does not regard the slogans "Jews out!," "Foreigners out!," and "Turks out!" as being in themselves an incitement to others to take particular measures against the groups named, but takes the view that the association of the slogan "Jews out!" with a swastika obviously does constitute such an incitement to violence and arbitrary measures, in view of the historical background of the National Socialist persecution of the Jews, then it becomes hard to understand how the swastika, as the symbol of violent and arbitrary authority, ceases to be in the nature of an incitement when it is used in connection with the slogan "Foreigners out!" or "Turks out!" There can be little doubt in the public mind that the combination of such slogans and the swastika means something more than, and different from, "Yanks go home!"

In criminal jurisprudence (cf., for example, Kühl (1999), Section 130, paragraph 8a), the legitimacy of Section 130(3) StGB is sometimes also called into question. This section criminalizes what has become known as "Holocaust denial" (disputing the use of gas chambers for mass murder at Auschwitz and elsewhere). Here again, it is not difficult to follow the legislator's political aim of countering public statements which, by playing down the violent and arbitrary rule of National Socialism, poison the political climate and so disturb the peace; at the same time, however, it is legally problematical, from the standpoint of freedom of opinion, to treat as a criminal offense the mere denial of a historical fact without any intention to create agitation by doing so (cf. also *BGHSt* 40, 97ff).

As in the case of the propagation of Holocaust denial, so too in connection with Section 130(1) 1 StGB the legislator has refrained from imposing the restriction that the incriminated statements—over and above their capability of disturbing the peace—must also constitute an assault on the human dignity of others. This extension of criminal legislation, associated with the abandonment of the requirement of an affront to human dignity, creates the risk that political debates vehemently conducted in public may be subject to control under the criminal law and that the criminal law may be used as a means to enforce political correctness. In particular, the legislator is not insignificantly restricting the public forum for political debate and demonstration created and defended by the case law of the BVerfG. This can be demonstrated by reference to the slogan "Soldiers are murderers" that caused great controversy a few years ago. The BVerfG (*BVerfGE* 93, 266) considered that the critical aspect when drawing the boundary between the criminal and noncriminal use of this expression was whether its primary purpose was the defamation and denigration of the soldier or a dispute on a matter of public interest, such as the purpose of killing soldiers and civilians during wartime. If the statement was made only in order to accuse a soldier of particularly reprehensible individual conduct, and to defame him in public for defects of character, basic rights provided no protection whatsoever for this defamation, since only the individual was affected and only one person's dignity affronted. If, however, the expression was uttered in order to articulate a fundamental attitude to the destruction of human life in war, even if that expression was overemphatic, exaggerated, or even abusive, then it became necessary to consider, by conducting an examination that precisely ascertains the specific circumstances of the case, whether the expression of opinion might nevertheless be entitled to take precedence over the protection of the soldier's honor. The drawing of this boundary is also significant in connection with the criminal nature of incitement to violence against segments of the population: the slogan "Soldiers are murderers" is not criminal provided that the person uttering it is expressing an opinion—albeit an emphatic one—on a political matter and is not additionally expressing the view that the solider concerned is therefore a person with fewer rights. But if—as in the case of Section 130(1)(1) StGB—the requirement of an additional assault on a person's human dignity is waived and it is considered sufficient for criminality that others are incited by provocative slogans to hatred in the sense of hostility against, for example, soldiers, it becomes more than problematical whether this provision is constitutional in the light of Section 5 GG as interpreted by the BVerfG (cf. Rudolphi (1998), Section 130, paragraph 7; Weber (2000), Section 44, paragraphs 44ff).

Similar reservations regarding threats to freedom of opinion, art, and political debate also exist regarding *Section 130a StGB (Incitement to criminal acts)*, which is in any case largely superfluous and virtually meaningless in the light of Section 111 StGB (Public incitement to criminal acts) (Rudolphi (1998), Section 130a, paragraph 2).

VI. SUMMARY

The apparent obviousness and conceptual concision of "violence" as a phenomenon that is detrimental to a civil society and must therefore be prevented by the resources of the criminal law are lost to the extent that

1. specific forms of violence over and above acts of violence are included and
2. are penalized in association with the exercise of democratic rights such as freedom of assembly and opinion.

Political freedoms granted here by constitutional law with one hand may not be taken away again by criminal law with the other. There is nevertheless a great temptation for the legislator, in order to show the flag against brutalizing and aggressive trends in society, to lapse into a placatory and symbolic penal actionism which often far oversteps the boundaries of the criminal law's protection of legitimate interests, strictly tied to the principle of definition, and can be brought under control only by a restrictive interpretation of criminal legislation geared to the constitutional guarantee of basic political rights.

EXTRACTS FROM THE *GRUNDGESETZ*

Section 5 (Freedom of expression)

1. Every person shall have the right freely to express and disseminate his opinions in speech, writing, and pictures and to inform himself without hindrance from generally accessible sources. Freedom of the press and freedom of reporting by means of broadcasts and films shall be guaranteed. There shall be no censorship.
2. These rights shall find their limits in the provisions of general laws, in provisions for the protection of young persons, and in the right to personal honor.
3. Art and scholarship, research, and teaching shall be free. The freedom of teaching shall not release any person from allegiance to the constitution.

Section 8 (Freedom of assembly)

1. All Germans shall have the right to assemble peacefully and unarmed without prior notification or permission.
2. In the case of outdoor assemblies, this right may be restricted by or pursuant to a law.

Section 20 (Federal constitution; right to resist)

1. The Federal Republic of Germany is a democratic and social federal state.
2. All state authority is derived from the people. It shall be exercised by the people through elections and other votes and through specific legislative, executive, and judicial bodies.
3. The legislature shall be bound by the constitutional order, the executive, and the judiciary by law and justice.
4. All Germans shall have the right to resist any person seeking to abolish this constitutional order, if no other remedy is available.

Section 103 (Basic rights before the Criminal Law)

1. In the courts every person shall be entitled to a hearing in accordance with law.
2. An act may be punished only if it was defined by a law as a criminal offense before the act was committed.
3. No person may be punished for the same act more than once under the general criminal laws.

Translated by Richard Sharp

REFERENCES

Amelung, Knut. (1995). Sitzblockaden, Gewalt und Kraftentfaltung. *Neue Juristische Wochenschrift*, 2584–2591.
Amelung, Knut. (1996). Anmerkung zu BGHSt 41, 182ff. *Neue Zeitschrift für Strafrecht*, 230–231.
Eser, Albin. (1997). In Adolf Schönke & Horst Schröder (Eds.), *Kommentar zum Strafgesetzbuch. 25th Edition*. München: Beck.
Galtung, Johan. (1975). Gewalt, Frieden und Friedensforschung. In Dieter Senghaas (Ed.), *Kritische Friedensforschung* (pp. 55–104). Frankfurt a. M.: Suhrkamp.
Kühl, Kristian. (1999). In Karl Lackner & Kristian Kühl (Eds.), *Kommentar zum Strafgesetzbuch. 23th Edition*. München: Beck.
Otto, Harro, Volker Krey, & Kristian Kühl (Eds.) (1994). Verhinderung und Bekämpfung von Gewalt aus Sicht der Strafrechtswissenschaft, Gutachten der Unterkommission VII. In Hans-Dieter Schwind, Jürgen Baumann, et al. (Eds.), *Ursachen, Prävention und Kontrolle von Gewalt. Analysen und Vorschläge der Unabhängigen Regierungskommission zur Verhinderung und Bekämpfung von Gewalt (Gewaltkommission). Vol. II: Erstgutachten der Unterkommissionen. 2nd Edition* (pp. 857–954). Berlin: Duncker und Humblot.
Rudolphi, Hans-Joachim. (1998). In Hans-Joachim Rudolphi, Eckhardt Horn & Hans-Ludwig Günther (Eds.), *Strafgesetzbuch, Systematischer Kommentar. 6th Edition, 50th Consignment*. Neuwied, Kriftel, Berlin: Luchterhand.
Schwind, Hans-Dieter, Jürgen Baumann, Ursula Schneider, & Manfred Winter. (1990). Kurzfassung des Endgutachtens der Unabhängigen Regierungskommission zur Verhinderung und Bekämpfung von Gewalt. In Hans-Dieter Schwind, Jürgen Baumann, et al. (Eds.), *Ursachen, Prävention und Kontrolle von Gewalt. Analysen und Vorschläge der Unabhängigen Regierungskommission zur Verhinderung und Bekämpfung von Gewalt (Gewaltkommission). Vol. I: Endgutachten und Zwischengutachten der Arbeitsgruppen* (pp. 238–285). Berlin: Duncker und Humblot.
Weber, Ulrich. (2000). In Gunther Arzt & Ulrich Weber, *Strafrecht, Besonderer Teil*. Bielefeld: Gieseking.

CHAPTER II-6-2.4

The Right to Resist

HEINER BIELEFELDT

I. A HISTORICAL OUTLINE

The question of the legitimacy of resistance—including violent resistance—against established authority is as old as political and social thought itself (cf. Bauer, 1965). Not only does it permeate the history of "Western" political thought, but it can also be found in other cultural contexts, such as ancient Chinese literature and the oral traditions of sub-Saharan Africa (cf. Kühnhardt, 1987:237ff and 261ff, respectively). Ever since the dawn of research, representatives of different disciplines have expressed opinions on the right and duty to resist: first came theologians, philosophers, and lawyers, later to be joined by historians, political scientists, sociologists, and ethnologists. The literature on the right to resist, written over three millennia by representatives of different disciplines and transcending all cultural frontiers, has therefore long since become so extensive as to defy any survey.

Thoughts on resistance can be found in a source as old as the *Hebrew Bible*, which recounts numerous conflicts between political and religious leaders. Thus, the prophet Samuel, in the name of God, announces the deposition of Saul, the first king of Israel: "For thou hast rejected the word of the Lord, and the Lord hath rejected thee from being king over Israel" (1 Samuel 15:26). In quite different, conceptual and discursive terms, the proponents of the *sophist enlightenment* of the fifth century BC in Greece questioned the basis of the legitimacy of the political order (cf. Stüttler, [1965], 1972:19ff). By comparing and contrasting nature (*physis*) and law (*nomos*) or convention (*thesis*), they demonstrate that political dominion is conditional and hence open to criticism, reform, and, if appropriate, resistance.[1] "He who steals a right is a villain," wrote the Chinese philosopher Mong Dsi in about 300 B.C., so emphasizing the ties that bind political dominion to the law; if those ties are broken, the monarch forfeits the right to obedience (quoted in Bauer, 1965:18).

---

[1] Cf., for example, *Antiphon the Sophist*: "... for the [edicts of the] laws are imposed artificially, but those of nature are compulsory; and the edicts of the laws have been agreed upon and have not developed, but those of nature have developed and not been agreed upon" (quoted in Diels & Kranz, 1964: 346f).

W. Heitmeyer and J. Hagan (eds.), *International Handbook of Violence Research*, 1097–1111.
© 2003 Kluwer Academic Publishers. Printed in the Netherlands.

Influenced by religious expectations of apocalypse, the *early Christian Church* initially refrained from promulgating or applying any politico-religious concept of justice. In the event of conflict between governmental authority and religious duty, the Church argued in favor of *passive resistance*, in other words the refusal of obedience—if necessary, resulting in martyrdom (cf. Spörl, [1956], 1972:91f). This situation was altered by the "Constantinian change," as a result of which the Church became the main source of political power in Europe for well over a thousand years. In the *medieval* perception of the law, the politico-legal system as a whole was subject to the standards of Christian ethics and Christian truth. From that standpoint, both the Church and the temporal "great and good" inferred a right of active and, if necessary, *violent[2] resistance* to an unjust or heretical ruler (cf. Kern, [1914], 1962). Manegold von Lautenbach, a partisan of the Pope in the investiture controversy of the eleventh century, went so far as to compare an unjust king with a swineherd who, if he forgets his duties, can be dismissed and violently expelled (cf. Spörl, [1956], 1972:95f).

The question of the legitimacy of resistance—and its extreme manifestation, tyrannicide—was the subject of many treatises in the *scholastic philosophy* of the High and Late Middle Ages, such as those by John of Salisbury, Thomas Aquinas, and Marsilius of Padua (cf. Meinhold, [1959], 1972:253ff). The position adopted by Thomas Aquinas was typical: although revolt in itself was sinful, resistance against a tyrant was not rebellion as such but a struggle against unjust dominion—dominion that itself amounted to a rebellion against the law.[3] Resistance to an unjust government, in the medieval perception, was not merely a right but a duty. In the vernacular of the *Sachsenspiegel* (about1230), this idea is expressed as follows: "And a man must even resist his king and judge if he does wrong, and even help to fight him by any means, even if he is his kinsman or liege lord. And in so doing he does not breach his duty of loyalty" (quoted in Weinkauff, [1956], 1972:395).

The development of the *nation-state of early modern times* was accompanied by a tendency to codify legal norms. Building on beginnings under the corporate state of the late Middle Ages—England's Magna Carta of 1215 being one obvious example (cf. Bertram, 1970:19)—this resulted in a more precise definition of the group of persons who, in the marginal case, had the power and duty to practice resistance (cf. Wolzendorff, [1916], 1968:23ff). This effort at *codification* received an additional stimulus from the *Reformation*, because Luther's distinction between "spiritual" and "worldly rule"[4]—more sharply emphasized than in the past—resulted in a secularization, and in its wake a further positivization, of politico-legal standards and also of the right to resist (cf. Heckel, [1954], 1972:125). In the face of attempts to repress or even deny the right to resist, made by various theoreticians of *absolutism* in the early modern era, such as Bodin and Hobbes, both Calvinist and Catholic writers defended the legitimacy of resistance against unjust

---

[2] Cf. Bertram, 1970: 25: "Resistance consisted in all cases, even where nothing was expressly stated, in armed resistance."

[3] Cf. Thomas Aquinas (1963), *Summa theologiae* II/2, Q. 42, Article 2(3): "*regimen tyrannicum non est iustum: quia non ordinatur ad bonum commune .... Et ideo perturbatio huius regiminis non habet rationem seditionis .... Magis autem tyrannus seditiosus est* ["... tyrannical government is unjust because it is directed not to the common good ... and therefore the overthrow of this government does not have the character of sedition ... rather, it is the tyrant that is seditious"].

[4] Cf. Luther, [1523], 1982:46: "Therefore one must carefully distinguish between the two kingdoms and allow both to remain: one that creates goodness and the other that outwardly provides peace and a defense against evil works."

governments. The best-known of these *"monarchomachs"* were Hotoman, Beza, Buchanan, Fickler, and Mariana (cf. Wolzendorff, [1916], 1968:95ff).

In England, the disputes regarding the rights of throne and parliament in the seventeenth century resulted in civil wars, culminating in the execution of King Charles I and the subsequent republican dictatorship of Cromwell (cf. Schröder, 1986).

At the end of these constitutional struggles in Britain, *John Locke* laid the foundations of the theory of constitutionalism in his *Two Treatises of Government* (1690), in which he once again emphasized the right to resist an unjust ruler—a right that he expressly recognized as belonging to the people as a whole and thus, in a sense, democratized: "The people shall be judge" (Locke, [1690], 1977:353). In the case of a struggle against tyrannical rule, Locke believed that even the risk of civil war was acceptable in certain circumstances: "Force between either persons, who have no known superior on earth, or which permits no appeal to a judge on earth, being properly a state of war, wherein the appeal lies only to Heaven" (Locke, [1690], 1977:354).

It was during the great *democratic revolutions* of the late eighteenth century that the right to resist was first proclaimed as a universal *human right*. In Article 3, following on from the remarks about the purposes of the state, the Virginia Bill of Rights of 1776 states: "Whenever any government shall be found inadequate or contrary to these purposes, a majority of the community hath an indubitable, unalienable, and indefeasible right to reform, alter or abolish it, in such manner as shall be judged most conducive to the public weal" (quoted in Heidelmeyer, 1982:57). Article 2 of the French Revolutionary Declaration of Rights of Man and Citizen (1789) puts it even more concisely: "The aim of all political association is the preservation of the natural and imprescriptible rights of man. These rights are liberty, property, security, and resistance to oppression" (quoted in Heidelmeyer, 1982:69).

The philosophy of *Kant* had a lasting effect on the theory of the right to resist, especially in areas under German law. Although Kant was unambiguously committed to the principles of the French Revolution, he rejected any right to resist a legally constituted state (however provisional and even "autocratic" its structure might be) for reasons of legal logic, as being "in the highest degree unjust" (Kant, [1795], 1973:164). Instead, he called for a permanent reform within the existing legal framework. Influenced by Kant, and also by an awareness of successive advances in the field of legal institutions, the liberal *legal positivism* of the nineteenth and early twentieth centuries largely came around to the view that the right to resist had been replaced by the protection against the arbitrary exercise of power provided by the rule of law and had thus become superfluous (cf. Bertram, 1970:38f). Characteristic of this trend was Wolzendorff's historico-philosophical study that declared the theory of the right to resist to be definitively obsolete: "With the spread of the constitutionally based rule of law, therefore, the theory of resistance had become sociologically defunct. Its legal and moral premise had been satisfied; its logical justification for existence had ceased to exist" (Wolzendorff, [1916], 1968:534). The typically German "legality fetishism" (Mommsen, 2000:18) and the fundamental rejection of a right to resist that had become widespread in many sectors of the population were ultimately to prove a critical obstacle to political resistance against National Socialism.

A fundamental *change* took place in Germany *after World War II*. The impact of the National Socialist dictatorship, systematically organized genocide, and other crimes against humanity had not only lastingly shaken the expectation of steady progress guaranteed within the process of civilization but also prompted renewed recognition of the right to resist. This movement away from legal positivism, leading to the *renaissance of the right to resist*, is encapsulated in the much-quoted "Radbruch's formula." In an effort to strike a balance between the edicts of legal certainty and of justice, the former Social Democratic justice minister under the Weimar Republic wrote "that positive law, secured by constitution and by force, takes precedence even if it is substantively unjust and inexpedient, unless the contradiction of positive law reaches such an intolerable level that the law, as an 'unjust law,' has to yield place to justice" (Radbruch, [1946], 1999:216). Irrespective of the "renaissance" of the right to resist in postwar Germany, however, it is striking that the courts, when hearing restitution cases, were at first extraordinarily restrictive in the legal acknowledgment of acts of resistance (cf. Scheidle, 1969:38ff). This reflects the one-sided reception of the history of resistance to National Socialism, which long remained fixated primarily on the national conservative resistance—the "resistance 'from the high command'" (Mommsen, 2000:21), while largely disregarding other campaigns and forms of active political resistance (for an overview, cf. Steinbach & Tuchel, 1994), or even going so far as to cast doubt on their motives.[5]

The right to resist was formally enshrined in some of the new German *Land constitutions* that came into being after World War II. Thus, Article 147 of the Hessian constitution of 1946: "It is the right and duty of every citizen to resist the unconstitutional exercise of violence by the public authority." And Article 23(3) of the Berlin constitution of 1950 reads: "If the basic rights laid down in the constitution are clearly being violated, every citizen has the right to resist" (both quoted in Klug, 1984:11). The right to resist was not incorporated into the *Grundgesetz* (Basic Law or constitution) of the Federal Republic of Germany until 1968, in the course of the debate on emergency legislation. By way of a complement, as it were, to the democratic emergency of an antidemocratic *coup d'état*, Article 20(4) of the *Grundgesetz* reads: "All Germans shall have the right to resist any person attempting to abolish this constitutional order, if no other remedy is available."

Constitutional endorsement of the right to resist—with explicit sanctioning of the use of violence!—can also be found in the 1976 constitution of the *Republic of Portugal*, where Article 21 reads: "Every citizen shall have the right to resist any order that violates his rights, freedoms, and guarantees, and to use force to defend himself against any attack on such rights if it is impossible for him to turn to the authorities." The 1958 constitution of the *French Republic* contains in its preamble a reference to the French Revolutionary Declaration of the Rights of Man and Citizens of 1789, including a reference to its recognition of the right to resist in Article 2.

Leaving aside such guarantees offered by positive law, there is reason to assume that the right to resist is *generally acknowledged* today. Denial of that right as a matter of principle, which was in any case fairly unusual in past history as a whole (the most prominent examples are Hobbes's absolutism and Kant's rejection of the right as a matter of legal logic), is virtually nowhere to be found in the current literature. Even those in political and academic circles who warn against thoughtless and inflationary recourse to the right to resist (cf., for example, Kröger, 1971) do not challenge the existence of that right.

An issue that is still controversial today, however, is whether legitimate resistance can be possible also in a democracy under the rule of law. This question arises primarily in connection with "civil disobedience," which is conceived by its most prominent advocates

---

[5] A more recent example of casting doubt on the moral motives for political resistance outside the conservative military or intellectual elite is the controversy regarding the failed assassination attempt by the joiner and watchmaker Johann Georg Elser. On this point, cf. the article by Lothar Fritze, the reader's letter from Alfons Söllner, and the article by Peter Steinbach and Johannes Tuchel, *Frankfurter Rundschau*, November 8, 17, and 18, 1999, respectively.

as a nonviolent form of organized political resistance. The definition and significance of nonviolence have been major factors in political and legal controversies that still endure today (cf. section III below).

II. SYSTEMATIC THOUGHTS ON THE RIGHT TO RESIST

1. A Definition of the Right to Resist

Like other key political terms, so too the word "resistance" is used very broadly and quite often confusedly in common parlance. The spectrum of activities popularly identified as resistance ranges from arson through hunger strikes to peaceful torchlight processions; it encompasses public incitements to consumer boycotts along with conspiracy to commit sabotage; it includes terrorist attacks along with the collection of signatures to petition against a refuse incinerator. But systematic consideration of the right to resist makes sense only if the concept of resistance is more narrowly defined and delimited from other phenomena (such as political criticism, opposition, refusal to obey, self-defense and assistance in an emergency). In the remarks that follow, therefore, "resistance" should be understood as meaning a *genuinely political act whose purpose is the elimination of grievous political injustice (alleged or actual) and which resorts to means other than existing lawful political or legal options.*

If resistance is understood as a genuinely political act, this implies a *primary thrust directed against the state* as the critical reference point of political power (cf. Scheidle, 1969:17). This may be the resistor's own state, or an occupying foreign power; furthermore, supranational and international organizations such as the European Union or the World Trade Organization (WTO) are also possible targets for resistance activity. The idea that resistance is directed against the state must be understood *in the broadest sense* here. Resistance need not in all cases be targeted against the direct agents or institutions of government violence; it may also aim at "intermediary" bodies (such as political parties and associations) that are associated with the authority of the state, or against social and economic interests (such as the "military industrial complex" or the nuclear industry) that are perceived as important parameters influencing unjust activity by governments (cf. Scheidle, 1969:22).

2. Delimitation from Other Phenomena

a. DISSENT AND RESISTANCE. In a liberal democracy, criticism and opposition are not merely permitted; the right to public dissent is one of the cornerstones of democratic legitimacy. "Freedom of the pen," wrote Kant, is "the sole palladium of the rights of the people" (Kant, [1793], 1973:102), because open criticism is the only way of ensuring that the holders of political offices exercise their power as representatives of the people and in the service of the common good. The function of political dissent as a contributory factor to liberal democracy is apparent in the fact that freedom to express an opinion openly is recognized and specially protected as a basic right in democratic constitutional systems— as, for example, in the First Amendment (1791) to the American Constitution or Article 5 of the German *Grundgesetz* of 1949 (cf. Schwartländer & Willoweit, 1986). In a much-quoted dictum of the German Federal Constitutional Court, freedom of opinion is "to some extent the basis of *all* freedom" (German Federal Constitutional Court Judgments (BVerfGE) 7 [1958]:198–230, here: 208). The exercising of this constitutionally guaranteed fundamental human right cannot, therefore, be classified as resistance. Similar considerations also apply to collective forms of protest, such as demonstrations, which for many people represent, *de facto*, the only available way of expressing critical opinions in public. The German Federal Constitutional Court made it clear in its "Brokdorf" judgment of May 14, 1985 that the nonviolent exercise of freedom of public assembly (guaranteed in Article 8 of the *Grundgesetz* for the Federal Republic of Germany) takes precedence even over the governmental authority's justified interest in order. Public assemblies, according to the Court, quoting the constitutional lawyer Konrad Hesse, "contain a fragment of original, unfettered, direct democracy, which has the capability of safeguarding political activity against the danger of the stagnation of administrative routine" (BVerfGE 69 [1985]:315–372, here: 347).

In a free democracy, a clear distinction is drawn between dissent and resistance. By contrast, it has been a specific feature of authoritarian regimes, both past and present, that they do not know—or at least do not respect—this distinction. Under the totalitarian rule of National Socialism, as we know, the telling of a political joke could lead to savage reprisals. The distribution of critical leaflets cost several members of the "White Rose" group their lives (cf. Steinbach & Tuchel, 1994:235ff).

b. RESISTANCE AND "DISOBEDIENCE". Blatant refusal to comply with a statutory imposition by the state—such as payment of taxes—oversteps the boundaries of lawful behavior. It thus meets one essential criterion of the definition of resistance. However, it should be borne in mind that not every act of disobedience against the state can be categorized as resistance. Under the definition given earlier, disobedience becomes resistance only if it is to be understood as a genuinely *political act* whose aim is to change existing political structures or remedy an injustice (cf. Arendt, [1970], 1989:122). Parents who refuse on religious grounds to allow their children to receive compulsory education (in biology, for example) are admittedly setting themselves at odds with Germany's legal system, but such an act could not be interpreted as resistance unless, for example, it was accompanied by a "political" call for the general abolition or modification of that education. Provided the parents confine themselves to attempting to secure an exemption for their own children in order to avoid conflict with their religious convictions, their action cannot be construed as genuine resistance.

c. RESISTANCE AND SELF-DEFENSE/ASSISTANCE IN AN EMERGENCY. Situations of self-defense or assistance against unwarranted attack can involve representatives of the government authority as well as private individuals. As in the case of disobedience, however, so too in this case, it must be emphasized that it is only a link with political demands that qualifies such actions as resistance in the narrower sense. One example of this would be public action to provide urgent assistance for refugees threatened with deportation, as happens in Germany, for example, under the "sanctuary" rule.

3. Justification of the Right to Resist

Reference to the *right* to resist implies that political resistance must be legitimate under certain conditions. This requires special justification. If we assume that resistance goes beyond the statutory political and legal options of a struggle for justice and so acquires an aspect of *unlawfulness*, it is clear that the legislative basis for the right to resist can only be looked for in positive law itself. The tendencies to "positivize" the right to resist, which can be traced back to the High Middle Ages, are therefore not in fact aimed at constitutionalizing this right in the true sense. They are more concerned with the formal strengthening of the right to resist, whose existence is already postulated, and defining more precisely the conditions under which it can be exercised—for example, defining those who are entitled to exercise it. Article 20(4) of the *Grundgesetz* of the Federal Republic of Germany also has a merely declaratory rather than constitutional effect (cf. Bertram, 1970:11).[6]

Since the legislative justification for the right to resist cannot be derived directly from positive law, all that remains is recourse to *superpositive* law. One example of this is offered by *religious concepts of law*, which may take very different substantive forms. The appeal to divine justice is to be found not only in Old Testament prophets or the medieval investiture controversy: occasional echoes are also to be found in John Locke's liberal theory of the state. Primacy of divine over human justice permeates the agendas of Islamic resistance movements that have set themselves the objective of "crushing the kingdom of human despotism on earth and bringing the kingdom of the divine Sharia to the world of men" (Sayyid Qutb, quoted in Meier, 1994:202). But religious motives also played a critical part in justifying Martin Luther King's campaigns of nonviolent civil disobedience. In his letter from Birmingham city jail in Alabama (King, [1963], 1991), he emphasizes: "A just law is a man-made code that squares with the moral law or the law of God" (King, 1980:62f). Quite apart from the question of whether, and if so in what circumstances, the religious justification for acts of resistance also extends to acts of violence, a direct appeal to divine justice in a pluralistic society may clash with the principles of democratic discourse, possibly giving rise to crises and breakdowns of communication.[7]

A distinction must be made (though an association is often postulated) between the religious justification and the *natural law justification* of the right to resist. The tradition of natural law, which influenced more than two millennia of Western legal thinking from the stoic philosophers of antiquity through scholasticism to the present day (cf. Welzel, 1962), includes positive legislation based on the yardstick of a higher law grounded in the nature of mankind (or in the nature of a particular case), to which it may have to give way in case of conflict. Substantive notions of what can be demanded in the name of the natural law, however, are hardly less varied than those to be found in the religious normative concepts of a divine law.

A somewhat different emphasis again attaches to *human rights justifications* of the right to resist. Admittedly, human rights are also open to interpretation as far as their substance is concerned. Even so, they exhibit a higher degree of substantive certainty than the ideas of natural law. Another point is that human rights, although their claimed sphere extends beyond positive law (cf. Bielefeldt, 1998), have now increasingly been recognized by both national and international positive law—in the constitutions of states and in conventions under international law. The enshrinement of human rights as basic rights in constitutions opens up the possibility that the right to resist will fasten on the distinction

---

[6] Otherwise there would be justification for the criticism that this kind of "legalized resistance" (Isensee, 1969) amounts to a "caricature" of the right to resist (Kaufmann, 1972:XI).

[7] That is not to say that any appeal to divine justice or religious principles must become a trial of strength for democratic discourse. The problem, rather, is a particular *modus*, specifically the modus of the *directness and exclusiveness* of religious argument. Cf., on this point, Bielefeldt & Heitmeyer, 1998:14f.

between "higher" constitutional provisions and "simple" provisions of law, and so move closer to a form of subsidiary constitutional jurisdiction, which may come into play where the procedures offered by the rule of law fail.[8] At the same time, this provides opportunities for a discursive justification of acts of resistance with a view to principles of human rights and democracy that attract a universal consensus, as is, for example, demanded and practiced in the context of civil disobedience (cf. below, section III).

4. Conditions for Exercising the Right to Resist

The recognition of the right to resist has always gone hand in hand with efforts to limit the conditions for its legitimate exercise, so that recourse to resistance does not result in a general erosion of obedience to the law, possibly leading on to anarchy and civil war. Not every injustice can justify resistance. Radbruch's celebrated formula, "that positive law, secured by constitution and force, takes precedence even if it is substantively unjust and inexpedient," and that it is only in the borderline case, when injustice reaches an "intolerable level," that the positive legal system forfeits its entitlement to obedience (Radbruch, [1946], 1999:216), can serve as a paradigm for the difficult attempt to find a balance between obedience to the law in the interests of legal certainty, on the one hand, and the possibly inevitable resistance against a fundamentally unjust politico-legal system, on the other.

There is a large degree of unanimity that resistance can only be legitimate as a last resort. Scheidle combines with this limitation, as further criteria for legitimate resistance, the principles of subsidiarity, proportionality, necessity, and prospect of success. All these criteria, he says, can be inferred from the overriding principle of the prohibition of excess (cf. Scheidle, 1969:30ff). Despite these restrictions (typical of the debate as a whole), extensive scope remains for political discretion: this is as indisputable as the fact that resistors act within a politico-legal "gray area" and so submit themselves and others to a high level of risk.

5. Resistance and Violence

The use of violence is *not a defining feature* of political resistance (cf. Kaufmann, 1972:XIII). The vital boundary, the crossing of which constitutes resistance, runs not between nonviolence and violence but between legality and illegality. Despite all the problems associated with the concept of violence (on this, cf. Neidhardt, 1986:114ff), it is also possible to list undeniably nonviolent forms of what is nevertheless unlawful oppositional activity (the politically motivated tax strike is just one example), which therefore fall within the definition of resistance. The use of violence, is thus a more extreme form of resistance, legitimation of which therefore requires particularly critical scrutiny (with reference to the criteria already listed: last resort, necessity, appropriateness, and proportionality).

Violence in the context of political resistance arises from various motives, in various constellations, and with varying degrees of intention, and, not least, with various objectives. It may, for example, be directed both *against individuals* and *against objects*. There are cases where violence is used *as a direct instrument*, but there are also cases where it is

---

[8] This is precisely the function of Article 20(4) of the *Grundgesetz* of the Federal Republic of Germany.

used as a *means of dramatizing* the campaign of resistance. The use of violence may serve to *eliminate a specific ill* but also to *overthrow the entire political system*. Finally, a distinction also has to be made between the planned use of violence and acts of violence that arise in an unplanned way ("spontaneously") from political resistance (for all the above, cf. Bell, 1973:63).

The "classic" case of the directly instrumental use of violence against a person is "tyrannicide"—in contemporary language, a deliberate attempt to murder a dictator and, by disposing of him through violence, at the same time to eliminate the political injustice that is the target of the struggle. The analogous form of the use of violence against material objects—sabotage—is directed against means of asserting authority (such as arms stores or propaganda institutions) whose destruction will, it is hoped, eliminate or at least weaken political oppression. In contrast to such directly instrumental use of violence, its "theatrical" use (which again may be directed either against persons or against objects) serves to attract public attention, especially media attention, to the acts of resistance, without any prospect of the direct abolition of the unjust regime (or the means by which it exercises power). But while the "theatrical" use of violence, too, represents a form of consciously instrumental activity, there have also been cases of spontaneous outbreaks of violence as the unintended consequences of resistance activity—one example being the massive protests that broke out against the Shah of Persia, resulting in the Iranian revolution of 1978–79. But even where violence is used instrumentally, and thus limited from the outset, the danger still exists of *unintentional escalations of violence*—ranging, in the extreme case, up to open civil war (cf. the contribution by Waldman in this volume).

A special case of the "theatrical" use of violence in the context of political resistance is *violence against oneself*. Examples here include hunger strikes as a form of protest, which, at least in more extreme cases, must be interpreted as violence against one's own person or—particularly drastically—public self-immolations, such as those used by Buddhist monks to protest against the Vietnam War (cf. Ebert, 1981:184ff). Civil disobedience, too, may include an aspect of (indirect) self-inflicted violence, if the resistors deliberately run the risk of violent action by the state and use it to dramatize their protest publicly.

III. CIVIL DISOBEDIENCE UNDER THE DEMOCRATIC RULE OF LAW

1. Defining Civil Disobedience

While the right to resist a dictatorship finds virtually unanimous recognition today, it is still disputed whether acts of political resistance can be legitimate in a democratic state under the rule of law (cf. Meyer, Miller, & Strasser, 1984). This question arises especially in respect of campaigns of civil disobedience, which took place on a large scale in all Western democracies from the 1960s through the 1980s, with protests against racial discrimination, the Vietnam War, the stationing of new nuclear weapons, and the expansion of the nuclear industry. Even if it seems almost certain at present that these protest movements have long passed their apogee, the question of the legitimacy of civil disobedience remains a problem of practical politics.

In the extensive literature on the subject, there are constant references to what have now become the three "classic" models: Henry David Thoreau, Mahatma Gandhi, and

Martin Luther King. In the case of Thoreau, to whom we owe the term "civil disobedience" (cf. Thoreau, [1849], 1991), it is nevertheless contentious whether his refusal to pay taxes can be construed as a genuinely political act, since Thoreau did not associate that refusal with public campaigns and, indeed, initially did not even make it public. For Hannah Arendt, Thoreau's action is therefore a model case of refusal to cooperate for reasons of conscience, with no actual political agenda (cf. Arendt, [1979], 1989:125).[9] As far as Gandhi is concerned, it can be said that his acts were directed against British colonialism, in other words against a state which, although seeing itself as liberal and democratic on its home soil, played the part of a colonial power in India. It is therefore questionable whether, and if so to what extent, Gandhi's variant of civil disobedience can also be relevant and legitimate within a democratic state under the rule of law.[10] Of the three repeatedly cited models, then, this essentially leaves Martin Luther King, whose nonviolent resistance was undoubtedly politically motivated, its purpose being the public and widespread mobilization of democratic support within his own country.

It is therefore probably no matter of chance that the academic debate on civil disobedience has been largely dominated by the American experience. Those liberal theoreticians such as Hugo Adam Bedau or John Rawls, who seek to provide a critical justification, base their arguments principally on four features of civil disobedience: the *deliberate breaking of rules*, the *public nature* of the acts in question, their strict *nonviolence*, and finally the willingness to *accept the penalty* by which the breach of the rules may be sanctioned (cf. Bedau, [1970], 1991:51; Rawls, 1971:363ff) The last two points, however, as we will see, are not undisputed among the adherents of civil disobedience.

3. Violation of the Principle of Democracy?

The activists and proponents of civil disobedience have often been accused of jeopardizing the principle of democracy. Behind the publicly staged—and therefore particularly provocative—contravention of democratically established legislation, runs the argument, lies the presumption of an elitist minority which, motivated by its allegedly clearer insight, overrules the democratic majority (Scholz, 1983). This argument has to be taken seriously, because there are certainly some factions that view the democratic rule of law as a mere façade and for that reason, from the outset, disregard the need to justify their lawbreaking in democratic terms.[11] This contempt for democratic equality is evident, for example, in the case of Christian Bay, when he asserts the existence of a qualitative difference between the rights of decision of the "concerned" and the "intelligent," on the one hand, and the "indifferent" and the "foolish," on the other.[12]

A very different line of argument, however, is adopted by those theoreticians who try to justify the possibility of civil disobedience on the ground of an—expressly acknowl-

---

[9] In fact, Thoreau admits: "However, the government does not concern me much, and I shall bestow the fewest possible thoughts on it" ([1849], 1991:46).

[10] Blume (1987:301) emphasizes that Gandhi himself believed in the universal applicability of this strategy and the possibility of transferring it to Western society.

[11] Cf., for example, Bay & Walker, 1975:25 f: "... the most elementary requirement of political education, thus conceived, is liberation from the prevailing pluralist democratic myth ..."

[12] Cf. Bay, [1967], 1971:82: "'One man, one vote' means equal weight for the concerned vote and the indifferent vote; for the intelligent and the foolish vote; for the vote in defense of elemental dignities of life and the vote in pursuit of added privileges for groups already favored."

edged—democratic rule of law. First, they refer to the *public nature* of protest, citing it as evidence that the resistors aim to communicate with the majority among the population and gain their support for their own political ends. Civil disobedience, according to Bedau, appeals to the *generally recognized principles of justice* in a democracy and is thus to be understood as "part of civic life" (Bedau, 1991:7). In order to take account of the democratic principle of equality, Rawls additionally demands that those who claim the right to civil disobedience on the basis of their own convictions of justice and interests, must, in a hypothetical universalization of their political principles, allow the same level of disobedience to other groups in support of their own specific interests.[13] The practical consequence of this (admittedly vague) stipulation is a restriction of disobedience to rare, exception cases, because the hypothetical universalization of the entitlement to disobey to include analogous situations would otherwise be incompatible with the maintenance of the democratic constitutional order.

4. Erosion of the Rule of Law?

The critical inquiry into the compatibility of civil disobedience with democratic equality is often associated with the fear that deliberate, politically motivated lawbreaking must result in the erosion of the consciousness of law and hence, ultimately, a threat to the rule of law (cf. Püttmann, 1994:60ff). It is obvious that this concern, too, must be taken seriously. For this reason, the critical defenders of the possibility of civil disobedience warn against the unthinking exercise of that right and demand that the available legal options be exhausted first. Civil disobedience, according to Rawls, can be legitimate only in cases of grievous injustice, and even then only as a "last resort" (Rawls, 1971:373). Habermas also cautions against the inflationary resort to civil disobedience: "the lawbreaker must scrupulously consider whether the choice of spectacular means is really appropriate to the situation and not merely the product of an elitist turn of mind or narcissistic impulse—presumption, in other words" (Habermas, 1983:42).

It is also frequently urged that lawbreakers must follow the examples of Thoreau, Gandhi, and King in accepting the penalties laid down by administrative and criminal law (cf. Hook, [1967], 1971:59). The *willingness to accept punishment meted out by the state* is seen by Greenawalt, ([1987], 1991:187) as evidence of serious political conviction and, at the same time, willingness to be reconciled both with the legal system, in general, and with political opponents, in particular. It is precisely this demand for acceptance of punishment that has now been rejected by some adherents of civil disobedience because such moral heroics are unworldly and therefore unpolitical (Arendt, [1970], 1989:122).

5. The Question of Violence

As far as what are now the "classic" models of civil disobedience campaigns are concerned, the nonviolence of their actions cannot be seriously doubted. This is true even if the concept of violence is interpreted in the broadest possible sense. Gandhi, for example, tried to rule out for himself and his followers not only physical attacks on people and

---

[13] Cf. Rawls, 1971:373: "If a certain minority is justified in engaging in civil disobedience, then any other minority in relevantly similar circumstances is likewise justified."

property but also negative speeches and even aggressive thought.[14] He wanted his opponents to be able to rely completely on the nonviolent nature of the protest and be able to feel completely safe even in the presence of the protestors (cf. Gandhi, 1961:56). Strict nonviolence is therefore seen by many adherents as an indispensable part of the definition of civil disobedience (cf., for example, Bedau, [1970], 1991:51; Rawls, 1971:364).

Nonetheless, the question of violence represents a particularly contentious aspect of civil disobedience from the political standpoint. First, there are undoubtedly adherents of civil disobedience who endorse nonviolence merely on the basis of pragmatic considerations and not reasons of principle, or even make a specific effort to keep the option of violence open. Second, the concept of violence—and the same applies to the concept of nonviolence—is open to interpretation in different ways, narrow and broad. In view of the tendency to broaden the concept of violence, noticeable in recent decades, the boundaries between nonviolence and violence have become blurred—with the consequence that inhibitions that serve to damp down escalation may disappear.

Even among those proponents of civil disobedience who argue in favor of nonviolence in general, there is a considerable number of authors whose arguments are not based on principle, but are rather pragmatic and strategic. Thus, for example, although Cohen, Bay, and Zinn regard nonviolence as a desirable objective, they specifically do *not* regard it as a defining feature of civil disobedience (cf. Cohen, 1971:24f; Bay, [1967], 1971:79; Zinn, 1968). For Bay and Walker, the question of the use of violence ultimately comes down to a problem of calculating the cost and the prospects of success (cf. Bay & Walker, 1975:18).

Morreal ([1976], 1991) takes this an important step further, positively justifying the possibility of using violence in a context of civil disobedience. In doing so, he adopts an extremely broad concept of violence, in which the differences of category between state repression and general social injustice, or even between mental violence and physical violence, become blurred. Morreal therefore poses the rhetorical question of why the one special form of physical violence should be excluded from campaigns of civil disobedience: "To say that only *physical* violence is to be ruled out in civil disobedience seems an arbitrary stipulation" (*ibid.*:134f).

The vague broadening of the concept of violence, as is to be found in Morreal among others, results in a situation where violence becomes a virtually ubiquitous phenomenon and, ultimately, an inevitable component of any political activity. The logical conclusion of this, however, is that an idea of "counterviolence" emerges which is no less diffuse than the ubiquitous violence diagnosed by social critics. But if, simply because of conceptual vagueness, it is uncertain where the boundary between nonviolence and violence lies, then the risk of escalation of (physical!) violence undoubtedly increases since no clearly identifiable "inhibition levels" remain (cf. Neidhardt, 1986:126).

Such a broadly conceived and therefore problematical interpretation of violence has meanwhile become apparent, not only in the rhetoric of social resistance movements but, complementarily, also in certain court judgments dealing with relevant cases. Thus, German courts have repeatedly regarded sit-ins outside barrack gates as "coercion" (within the meaning of Section 240 of the German Civil Code (StGB)) and punished them accordingly, even when these sit-ins have only been short-term and, to that extent, more or less symbolic actions. In the Federal Constitutional Court, this question twice resulted in "stale-

---

[14] Cf. Gandhi, 1961:56: "Satyagraha excludes the use of violence in any shape or form, whether in thought, speech or deed."

mate" decisions during the 1980s—with the effect that the appeal against the classification and punishment of these activities as coercion was denied (cf. BVerfGE 73, 206–261 and BVerfGE 76, 211–219). Critics of the relevant court decisions saw them as representing a tendency to "intellectualize" the concept of violence (cf. Schulte, 1983:37). This, they say, is dubious under the rule of law insofar as it undermines the principle of certainty as to what constitutes a criminal offense, which is fundamental to a liberal criminal law, and opens many doors to the politically motivated criminalization of protest (*ibid.*), unintentionally strengthening precisely those groups responsible for inciting indiscriminate "counterviolence" against repression by state and society. The tendency to broaden the concept of violence was, however, expressly rejected in a Federal Constitutional Court decision of January 1995 (BVerfGE 92, 1–20), reminding the courts of the need to apply stricter criteria when classifying protest as coercion (on this point, cf. also the article by Backes and Reichenbach in this volume).

Translated by Richard Short

REFERENCES

Arendt, Hannah. (1989). Ziviler Ungehorsam. In Hannah Arendt, *Zur Zeit. Politische Essays* (pp. 119–159) [Ed. Marie Luise Knott]. München: Deutscher Taschenbuchverlag [Original, 1970].

Bauer, Fritz. (compilation) (1965). *Widerstand gegen die Staatsgewalt. Dokumente der Jahrtausende*. Frankfurt a. M.: Fischer.

Bay, Christian. (1971). Civil Disobedience: Prerequisite for Democracy in Mass Society. In Jeffrie G. Murphy (Ed.), *Civil Disobedience and Violence*. Belmont: Wadsworth Publishing Co. (pp. 73–92) [Original, 1967].

Bay, Christian, & Charles C. Walker. (1975). *Civil Disobedience. Theory and Practice*. Montréal: Black Rose Books.

Bedau, Hugo Adam. (1991). Introduction. In Hugo Adam Bedau (Ed.), *Civil Disobedience in Focus* (pp. 1–12). London: Routledge.

Bedau, Hugo Adam. (1991). Civil Disobedience and Personal Responsibility for Injustice. In Hugo Adam Bedau (Ed.), *Civil Disobedience in Focus* (pp. 49–67). London: Routledge [Original, 1970].

Bell, David V. J. (1973). *Resistance and Revolution*. Boston: Mifflin.

Bertram, Karl Friedrich. (1970). *Das Widerstandsrecht des Grundgesetzes*. Berlin: Duncker und Humblot.

Bielefeldt, Heiner. (1998). *Philosophie der Menschenrechte*. Darmstadt: Wissenschaftliche Buchgesellschaft.

Bielefeldt, Heiner, & Wilhelm Heitmeyer. (1998). Einleitung: Politisierte Religion in der Moderne. In Heiner Bielefeldt & Wilhelm Heitmeyer (Eds.), *Politisierte Religion. Ursachen und Erscheinungsformen des modernen Fundamentalismus* (pp. 11–33). Frankfurt a. M.: Suhrkamp.

Blume, Michael. (1987). *Satyagraha. Wahrheit und Gewaltfreiheit, Yoga und Widerstand bei M. K. Gandhi*. Gladenbach: Hinder und Deelmann.

Cohen, Carl. (1971). *Civil Disobedience: Conscience, Tactics, and the Law*. New York: Columbia University Press.

Diels, Hermann, & Walter Kranz. (1964). *Die Fragmente der Vorsokratiker. Griechisch und Deutsch. Vol. 2. 11th Edition*. Zürich, Berlin: Weidmannsche Verlagsbuchhandlung.

Ebert, Thomas. (1981). *Gewaltfreier Aufstand. Alternative zum Bürgerkrieg, 4th Edition*. Waldkirch: Waldkirchener Verlagsgesellschaft.

Gandhi, Mohandas K. (1961). *Non-Violent Resistance*. New York: Schocken Books.

Greenawalt, Kent. (1991). Justifying Nonviolent Disobedience. In: Hugo Adam Bedau (Ed.), *Civil Disobedience in Focus* (pp. 170–188). London: Routledge [Original, 1987].

Habermas, Jürgen. (1983). Ziviler Ungehorsam—Testfall für den demokratischen Rechtsstaat. Wider den autoritären Legalismus in der Bundesrepublik. In Peter Glotz (Ed.), *Ziviler Ungehorsam im Rechtsstaat* (pp. 29–53). Frankfurt a. M.: Suhrkamp.

Heckel, Johannes. (1972). Widerstand gegen die Obrigkeit? Pflicht und Recht zum Widerstand bei Martin Luther. In Arthur Kaufmann (Ed.), *Widerstandsrecht*. Darmstadt: Wissenschaftliche Buchgesellschaft (pp. 114–134) [Original, 1954].

Heidelmeyer, Wolfgang. (Ed.) (1982). *Die Menschenrechte. Erklärungen, Verfassungsartikel, Internationale Abkommen*. 3rd Edition. Paderborn: Schöningh.
Hook, Sidney. (1971). Social Protest and Civil Disobedience. In Jeffrie G. Murphy (Ed.), *Civil Disobedience and Violence* (pp. 53–63). Belmont: Wadsworth Publishing [Original, 1967].
Isensee, Josef. (1969). *Das legalisierte Widerstandsrecht. Eine staatsrechtliche Analyse des Art. 20 Abs. 4 Grundgesetz*. Berlin: Duncker und Humblot.
Kant, Immanuel. (1973). Über den Gemeinspruch: Das mag in der Theorie richtig sein, taugt aber nicht für die Praxis. In Immanuel Kant, *Kleinere Schriften zur Geschichtsphilosophie, Ethik und Politik* (pp. 67–113) [Ed. Karl Vorländer]. Hamburg: Meiner [Original, 1793].
Kant, Immanuel. (1973). Zum ewigen Frieden. In Immanuel Kant, *Kleinere Schriften zur Geschichtsphilosophie, Ethik und Politik* (pp. 115–169) [Ed. Karl Vorländer]. Hamburg: Meiner [Original, 1795].
Kaufmann, Arthur. (1972). Einleitung. In Arthur Kaufmann (Ed.), *Widerstandsrecht* (pp. IX–XIV). Darmstadt: Wissenschaftliche Buchgesellschaft.
Kern, Fritz. (1962). *Gottesgnadentum und Widerstandsrecht im frühen Mittelalter. Zur Entstehungsgeschichte der Monarchie*. Reprint, 3rd Edition. Darmstadt: Wissenschaftliche Buchgesellschaft [Original, 1914].
King, Martin Luther, Jr. (1980). *Schöpferischer Widerstand. Reden—Aufsätze—Predigten* [Ed. Heinrich W. Grosse]. Gütersloh: Gerd Mohn.
King, Martin Luther, Jr. (1976). *Das Testament der Hoffnung. Letzte Reden, Aufsätze und Predigten* 2nd edition [Ed. Heinrich W. Grosse]. Gütersloh: Gerd Mohn.
King, Martin Luther, Jr. (1991). Letter from Birmingham City Jail. In Hugo Adam Bedau (Ed.), *Civil Disobedience in Focus* (pp. 68–84). London: Routledge [Original, 1963].
Klug, Ulrich. (1984). Das Widerstandsrecht als allgemeines Menschenrecht. In Werner Hill (Ed.), *Widerstandsrecht und Staatsgewalt. Recht im Streit mit dem Gesetz* (pp. 11–23). Gütersloh: Gerd Mohn.
Kröger, Klaus. (1971). *Widerstandsrecht und demokratische Verfassung. Recht und Staat, Heft 399*. Tübingen: Mohr-Siebeck.
Kühnhardt, Ludger. (1987). *Die Universalität der Menschenrechte. Studie zur ideengeschichtlichen Bestimmung eines politischen Schlüsselbegriffs*. München: Olzog.
Locke, John. (1977). *Zwei Abhandlungen über die Regierung* [Ed. Walter Euchner]. Frankfurt a. M.: Suhrkamp [Original, 1690].
Luther, Martin. (1982). Von weltlicher Obrigkeit, wie weit man ihr Gehorsam schuldig sei. In Martin Luther, *Ausgewählte Schriften. Vol. 4.: Christsein und Weltliches Regiment* (pp. 36–84) [Ed. Karin Bornkamm & Gerhard Ebeling]. Frankfurt a. M.: Insel [Original, 1523].
Meier, Andreas. (Ed.) (1994). *Der Politische Auftrag des Islam. Programme und Kritik zwischen Fundamentalismus und Reformen. Originalstimmen aus der islamischen Welt*. Wuppertal: Peter Hammer.
Meinhold, Peter. (1972). Revolution im Namen Christi. Ein Beitrag zur Frage von Kirche und Widerstand. In Arthur Kaufmann (Ed.), *Widerstandsrecht*. Darmstadt: Wissenschaftliche Buchgesellschaft (pp. 235–279) [Original, 1959].
Meyer, Thomas, Susanne Miller, & Johano Strasser. (Eds.) (1984). *Widerstandsrecht in der Demokratie. Pro und Contra*. Köln: L'80 Verlagsgesellschaft.
Mommsen, Hans. (2000). *Alternative zu Hitler. Studien zur Geschichte des deutschen Widerstandes*. München: C. H. Beck.
Morreal, John. (1991). The Justifiability of Violent Civil Disobedience. In Hugo Adam Bedau (Ed.), *Civil Disobedience in Focus* (pp. 130–143). London: Routledge [Original, 1976].
Neidhardt, Friedhelm. (1986). Gewalt—soziale Bedeutungen und sozialwissenschaftliche Bestimmungen des Begriffs. In Bundeskriminalamt (Eds.), *Was ist Gewalt? Auseinandersetzungen mit einem Begriff. Vol. 1* (pp. 109–147). Wiesbaden: Bundeskriminalamt.
Püttmann, Andreas. (1994). *Ziviler Ungehorsam und christliche Bürgerloyalität. Konfession und Staatsgesinnung in der Demokratie des Grundgesetzes*. Paderborn: Schöningh.
Radbruch, Gustav. (1999). Gesetzliches Unrecht und übergesetzliches Recht. In Gustav Radbruch, *Rechtsphilosophie. Studienausgabe* [Ed. Ralf Dreier & Stanley L. Paulson] (pp. 211–219). Heidelberg: C. F. Müller [Original, 1946].
Rawls, John. (1971). *A Theory of Justice*. Oxford: Oxford University Press.
Scheidle, Günter. (1969). *Das Widerstandsrecht. Entwickelt anhand der höchstrichterlichen Rechtsprechung in der Bundesrepublik Deutschland*. Berlin: Duncker und Humblot.
Scholz, Rupert. (1983). Rechtsfrieden im Rechtsstaat. Verfassungsrechtliche Grundlagen, aktuelle Gefahren und rechtspolitische Folgerungen. In *Neue Juristische Wochenschrift*, 705–712).
Schröder, Hans Christoph. (1986). *Die Revolutionen Englands im 17. Jahrhundert*. Frankfurt a. M.: Suhrkamp.

Schulte, Hans. (1983). Gewaltloser Widerstand—ziviler Ungehorsam. Strafrechtliche Aspekte. In Gustav-Heinemann-Initiative (Eds.), *Recht zum Widerstand* (pp. 34–43). Stuttgart: Radius.

Schwartländer, Johannes, & Dietmar Willoweit. (Eds.) (1986). *Meinungsfreiheit—Grundgedanken und Geschichte in Europa und USA*. Kehl, Straßburg: N. P. Engel.

Spörl, Johannes. (1972). Gedanken um Widerstandsrecht und Tyrannenmord im Mittelalter. In: Arthur Kaufmann (Ed.), *Widerstandsrecht. Darmstadt: Wissenschaftliche Buchgesellschaft* (pp. 87–113) [Original, 1956].

Steinbach, Peter, & Johannes Tuchel. (Eds.) (1994). *Widerstand in Deutschland 1933–1945. Ein historisches Lesebuch*. München: C.H. Beck.

Stüttler, Anton. (1972). Das Widerstandsrecht und seine Rechtfertigungsversuche im Altertum und im frühen Christentum. In Arthur Kaufmann (Ed.), *Widerstandsrecht. Darmstadt: Wissenschaftliche Buchgesellschaft* (pp. 1–58) [Original, 1965].

Thomas von Aquin. (1963). *Summa theologiae*. Salamanca: Biblioteca de Autores Christianos.

Thoreau, Henry David. (1991). Civil Disobedience. In Hugo Adam Bedau (Ed.), *Civil Disobedience in Focus* (pp. 28–48). London: Routledge [Original, 1849].

Weinkauff, Hermann. (1972). Über das Widerstandsrecht. In Arthur Kaufmann (Ed.), Widerstandsrecht. Darmstadt: Wissenschaftliche Buchgesellschaft (pp. 392–415) [Original, 1956].

Welzel, Hans. (1962). *Naturrecht und materiale Gerechtigkeit. 4th, extended Edition*. Göttingen: Vandenhoeck & Ruprecht.

Wolzendorff, Kurt. (1968). *Staatsrecht und Naturrecht in der Lehre vom Widerstandsrecht des Volkes. Zugleich ein Beitrag zur Entwicklungsgeschichte des modernen Staatsgedankens*. Reprint. Aalen: Scientia Verlag [Original 2nd Edition, 1916].

Zinn, Howard. (1968). *Democracy and Disobedience: Nine Fallacies on Law and Order*. New York: Vintage Books.

CHAPTER II-6-2.5

Individual Violence Justification Strategies

SIEGFRIED LAMNEK

I. ON THE DEFINITION OF VIOLENCE

Any attempt to define individual violence justification strategies must first decide what it is that is being justified, and thus which concept of violence to apply. This is particularly important for empirical research, where the consequences are considerable. A broad definition of violence will lead to a notable increase in the extent of violence and violence will be overestimated. Public debate on violence, whether in the mass media, in research, in the political arena, or in discussion of police tactics, is heterogeneous, and sometimes runs the risk of turning the concept of violence into an "elastic definition" (Neidhardt, 1997). Some approaches, on the other hand, prefer to reduce the concept of violence to actual physical violence (Rammstedt, 1989; von Trotha, 1997). This is seen to make data easier to handle in research, and further arguments for the approach concern the qualitative special status of physical coercion, its lack of preconditions, and the universal applicability of the concept (Willems et al., 1993:92). A too narrow definition of violence, however, which is limited only to forms of physical violence, can mean that acts which are experienced as violence within particular social contexts are not taken into account. Violence is underrecorded and the object of research limited (Popp, 1997:218).

Violent actions can be ordered according to various criteria, including the violent subject, his or her motivation, the kind of violent effect, the legal definition, the question of intention, or of legitimacy. In the following, violence is viewed as a completed action which is personal, individual, direct, expressive or instrumental, predominantly physical, illegal, and also illegitimate (or even legitimate), and intentional. Thus this includes more everyday and less serious violent acts, such as beatings among school children, as well as serious forms of violent crime. For two reasons the following will refer to violence and violent crime in general, but will focus on youth violence and crime. First, less serious violence in police statistics is predominantly youth violence, which is seen as a social problem requiring interpretation and containment. Secondly, in the course of their socialization, the perpetrators learn both to view violence as a subjectively legitimate act, and also to justify their violent acts to themselves and others. For an investigation of the personal, direct use of violence, therefore, the phase of youth and adolescence is highly significant, even if serious (criminal) violent acts are more likely to be committed by older people, who can of course take recourse to analogous strategies of justification.

II. TERMINOLOGICAL DISTINCTIONS BETWEEN MOTIVE AND JUSTIFICATION

If violent acts are social acts, then they are motivationally determined, which means that the act stems from a motive and intends to achieve a situation which is not given in the present. The meaning of the act is then the act which is planned in advance, and the objective which should be achieved through the process of action (Schütz, 1981:78ff.). The intentionality involved in objective-orientation is significant in both the legal and the everyday contexts. Acts are frequently judged on the basis of their motives, and even illegal acts can be legitimized and justified in this way.

A "motive" signifies the meaningful context which produces a "meaningful reason to act" in the opinion of the actor or the observer (Weber, 1980:5). Schütz criticizes this approach as being too imprecise. Just to look at the meaning intended by the actor is to ignore the dimension of time—the meaning of an experience constitutes itself precisely in the "internal consciousness of time" (Schütz, 1981:54). In order better to distinguish motives, Schütz divides them into "in order to" and "because" motives (Schütz, 1981:115). In an in "order-to-motive," the actor plans his action with a view to the future, and the objective that he wishes to achieve through concrete action. A robbery is undertaken in order to get money. If the actor is forced to take part in the robbery by group pressure, then the motive is a "because-motive."

This distinction is particularly significant for justification strategies. Plans, or motives for action, precede the concrete act. After the act the "real" motive is used as an argument justifying it. This retrospective justification is not a far-fetched, legitimizing argument which contradicts reality. Instead it stems from the "reciprocity of the motives," and is analogous to argumentation in legal criminal proceedings (Smaus, 1998:137). Thus, when questioned about the reasons for his act, the violent offender may perhaps refer to the "real" preceding "because-motive." Congruence between motive and ex post facto explanations has an inherently justifying character, for example by referring to social conditions. Irrespective of whether third parties accept that the perpetrator's justification of his act in terms of the identity of motive and explanation of the act is "true" or not, the motives of violent offenders must therefore be taken into account by the social sciences.

In addition, "violent offenders" also give ex post facto explanations which sometimes have nothing at all in common with the real motives for action. The explanations may go well beyond the motives, but may also partially encompass them, or they may represent "freely invented" strategies of exculpation. In other words, justification is understood in the following as explanations of the act which do not correspond to the "truth," but which in some way are intended to deny the actor's own responsibility or to relativize guilt. "Ex post facto justification" means that the perpetrator remembers the violent act which has already been committed, and he reflects on it and reinterprets it for the present situation, redefining motives in the process. This structure corresponds to Schütz's "because-motive." Only from an objectifying perspective can it be said that this kind of explanation involves a reduced level of truth. Subjectively, from the point of view of the perpetrator, his testimony may really represent the truth. Thus, redefinitions can be performed retrospectively, and then may also be believed. Therefore only analytical distinctions can be made between the definition of justification and constructs such as motive and attitudes.

Justifications possess an internal and an external aspect. The internal aspect concerns the ways in which the perpetrator justifies his action to himself so as to avoid self-reproach (Sykes & Matza, 1968 [1957]). The external aspect refers to the fact that the addressees of the ex post facto justification are third parties such as the police, the courts, and also peer groups (for example friends, cliques, the gang). When the violent offender comes before the prosecuting institutions, he experiences this external aspect as an unpleasant situation with considerable consequences.

To summarize: ("because-") motives which may precede violent acts are potential justifications of the acts. Congruence between the "real" motive and its explanation by the actor can make the act (partially) explicable and comprehensible, and make it seem justified. It is necessary to draw analytical distinctions between these explanations and justifications in the more narrow sense. The latter represent ex post facto strategies which attempt to legitimize violent acts for oneself or others, and to allow the act or the perpetrator to appear in a more favorable light. Justifications for violent actions are often (analytically) external to the actual motive for and origin of the action. Their structure corresponds to the "because-motive," but they are rather forms of stigma management in Goffman's sense of the word (Goffman, 1991). The individual is discredited insofar as the violent act has become public knowledge. In order to limit the damage to his social identity, the perpetrator then provides ready-made interpretations of his act. He thereby wishes to control and limit the spectrum of possible explanations, attempting either to avoid stigmatization entirely or at least to control its direction and extent.

III. MOTIVES FOR ACTION AS A JUSTIFICATION OF VIOLENCE

Violent offenders may draw on the (actual) motives for action for an ex post facto justification of their action. Motivations can vary greatly from case to case, but it is possible to analyze certain specific motives which regularly occur in reality (Esser & Dominikowski, 1997). These may be approximately divided into "in-order-to" and "because"-motives. Some common "in-order-to"-motives are:

1. Violence is used instrumentally as a means to an end. The use of violence serves to achieve some personal advantage or aim (including political aims). Violence may be used in (serious) cases of robbery in order to gain money which can be used to buy goods (or in order to steal the goods themselves) intended to increase respect and status within the peer group (Lamnek & Schwenk, 1995).
2. Violence can be used as a means of communication. Violence is especially used as a means of communication by young people who have experienced violence as the expression of the prohibitions, demands, needs, and wishes of their parents

or other adult carers in the process of socialization. The motivation for the use of violence here stems from the most strongly internalized or perhaps even the only possible way of communicating. Here violence is used as a means of resolving a conflict or of stating a case.

3. In its expressive form violence is used as a form of pleasure. This is particularly the case for violence among youth or post-adolescent groups, such as hooligans, and also extreme right-wing groups. Individual perpetrators may also use violence in this way (violent or intensive perpetrators) (Böttger, 1998:192). The "kick," or the "shot of adrenalin" is the result of the violent act, but it can also be used as a means of justification. The "fun" motive can become a normative orientation when the action is enjoyable because it makes other people afraid, through provocative behavior or when the use of violence is threatened (Stüwe, 1993).

4. Violence serves to create and stabilize identity, both within the group (clique, gang) and also externally. Gangs in particular frequently use violence as a principle of group organization. (Collective) violent action proves a sense of belonging, reinforces the structures of solidarity within the group, and serves to distinguish the group from others (Klein, 1995). The reference system within a group also means that the use of violence contributes to the creation of identity. A direct, socially effective sense of self-affirmation, achievement, and significance is experienced through successful defense against attacks, or a demonstration of strength, especially by young males from socially deprived backgrounds.

"Because-motives" give violent actions a normative orientation which justifies the use of violence for the perpetrators. Some of these patterns can also be found in ex post facto justifications (see section IV).

A frequent motive for violence named by individuals and groups is defense or self-defense. Violence is seen here as counterviolence, as a reaction to provocation or attacks by an "enemy." Counterviolence is defined by the role of the perpetrator as a victim, and is no more than a reaction to a challenge. This pattern is particularly significant in the context of (youth) groups (cliques, gangs) who are prepared to use violence. (Counterviolence by individuals is more likely to be a result of experience of violence in the parental home or in a partnership; after a period of toleration, the individual hits back.)

Violent action can also be the channel for frustration and the experience of failure in everyday life. In the case of extreme right-wing youths, violence frequently has the function of crisis management. A lack of orientation and a sense of frustration are the motivating factors which lead to the choice of a victim who corresponds to a collective idea. The victims are then defined as foreigners or youths from other political camps (Willems et al., 1993).

Without seeing violent phenomena in a bivariate or even monocausal way, one variable is particularly significant (and perhaps even dominant) in all research on the subject. This is the question of gender. Isolated, contrary findings which show that girls are also violent (for example Messerschmidt, 1997:30; Laidler & Hunt, 1997; Miller, 1998:47) do not contradict the general trend. A further, no less significant variable in the context of the use of violence is the group situation. An investigation of the common ground between individual and group motivated violence shows that especially violence which can be theoretically substantiated and empirically proven is a predominantly male phenomenon. As a consequence of the consistent and clear difference in patterns of aggression between men and women across cultures, Euler argues that data on violence should always be "differentiated according to gender" (Euler, 1997:194). This does not mean that "maleness" is understood as a monolithic concept (Jefferson, 1994), nor that this is a monocausal explanation. The feature of "gender (group affiliation)" only becomes significant in the context of sociostructural and inequality factors, such as social background, formal education, prestige or power status, the housing situation, and the nature of integration into the labor market. Notwithstanding phenomenological differences in the individual violently active groups, Findeisen and Kersten (1999) see the gender and the age of the group members, and also the territorial claims which the group derives from "local identification" (Müller, 1999:87), as the common ground in all groups. The territorial claim, which may also be virtual, leads to the necessity of defending the selected locations, be they a quarter in a town, a street, a soccer stadium, or a youth club.

Defending your own territory, or standing up for your honor or the honor of a female group member (Müller & Burschel, 1997; Cohen & Vandello, 1998; Toprak, 2000), and defending these with a demonstration of maleness, is seen as being particularly masculine, and thus becomes a normative requirement. Young males take on the role of the "warrior" or "weekend mercenary" and stake out their heroism, masculinity, and honor (Findeisen & Kersten, 1999). They actively seek confrontation to prove their bravery in the fight.

In political groups the motivation for violence is also not entirely politically driven. In the case of right-wing extremists the extreme right-wing political motivation is only one (not even necessarily predominant) possibility. Some violent acts are motivated by pleasure, just as in the case of hooligans. Young people look for a kind of entertainment and for action when they use violence, and their acts are thus beyond any political ideology. This is probably also the case for left-wing "autonomists" (groups in Germany which have frequently engaged in active violence). Punks are also politically motivated, through their opposition to right-wing groups with whom they often brawl. Those who behave violently are aggressive toward larger groups, such as right-wing extremists, and also toward the social order and the police. Their violent action can be rationally planned or may be a reaction to a subjective perception of provocation (Böttger, 1998).

Youth violence, therefore, to a large extent involves the experience of a male gender role model (doing gender) specific to the status of the group, in which strength, force, honor, and other similar values (Miller, 1998:38) are traditionally associated with masculinity. The young men believe that they are expected to show these values (at least within their group), and also that the other sex demands them as a proof of "suitability for marriage." In addition these values are seen to be necessary in terms of the general male social role stereotype. Youth violence ultimately aims at and is often motivated by the need to comply with a gender role stereotype, in order to gain recognition and respect.

This phenomenon also shows that violence can be based on "because-motives." The violent acts assume a normative orientation through their link to status-group-specific notions of masculinity, and thus the violent acts are legitimized as a means of conforming to and achieving the dictated goals. The motive "explains" the act and allows it to appear to be acceptable and justified, at least from the point of view of the perpetrator.

IV. JUSTIFICATION STRATEGIES FOR VIOLENCE

Convicted criminals frequently evaluate their own delinquency in terms which are not entirely positive. Instead of "indignation" or "martyrdom" they articulate a sense of guilt and shame. They also paradoxically accept the demands to conformity made by the dominant social order, although they have contravened the official norms. This observation led Sykes and Matza (1968 [1957]) to undertake a theoretical investigation of the phenomenon. Their fundamental conclusion, the neutralization thesis, stems from a critical appraisal and expansion of the theory of subcultures (Cohen & Short, 1968, [1958]), and also of the theory of differential association (Sutherland, 1968, [1956]). The subcultural aspect is only marginal, however, and their approach should rather be understood as the application of theories of cognitive dissonance.

The subculture theory argues that delinquent behavior has its origins in an orientation toward the partially deviant norms and values of the subculture. Sometimes the individual who follows subcultural norms does not see his deviant behavior—when measured against the standards of the mainstream culture—as illegal or morally wrong. But the fact that something akin to a guilty conscience can be observed does seem to indicate at least a partial effect of the dominant social norms.

Because a delinquent subculture is not a counterculture (Yinger, 1960), the member of a subculture is faced with a conflict. On the one hand, he at least partially accepts social norms, but on the other hand, he has to act according to the subcultural norms. If he tends toward the dominant social norms, then he violates the subculture, and if he tends toward the subcultural norms, he violates society. Because direct social contacts mean that the subculture normally has greater presence than the more distant mainstream culture, the individual is more likely to conform to the subcultural values. He then has to deal with the resulting conflict. The strategy used to solve this dilemma involves the individuals developing justifications for their behavior. The very flexibility of the normative system makes excuses possible. Some of these, such as self-defense or being a minor, are recognized by the legal system, while others—dealt with below—are only accepted by the delinquents themselves (Lamnek, 1999:213).

The content and the structure of deviance and justification are complementary, and thus the first thing to note is that techniques of neutralization, like deviant and violent behavior, can be learnt. Specific forms of reinforcement are necessary for violence as an option for action to be learnt or upheld, but this also depends on there being certain cognitive justification processes which can be called upon to give the act an individually legitimized meaning, and to make it seem subjectively "excused." Techniques of justification are rationalizations, retrospective, and partially unconscious justifications in the psychoanalytical sense (Lamnek, 1999:214). Justifications thus form links between the acts. They exculpate the actor from the previous act and (psychosocially) open up the possibility of the coming act. In this way they can become "because-motives." "This may involve, for example, the establishment of a self-reinforcement system for delinquent activities (as with a sense of pride in criminal skills): and the development of a denial or distortion of perceptions or the effects on the victim ('he's a mug anyway' or 'he's covered by insurance' or 'he deserved it') in order to justify the criminal acts and to reduce guilt and distress regarding the victims of offences" (Rutter & Giller, 1984:252).

There are differences in the ways in which deviant behavior is learnt and the relevant justification strategies are internalized, and these are generally influenced by the specific subcultures. The probability that justification strategies will occur increases with the extent to which the social contacts of young people (in the main) are restricted to their peer-group relations (Kühnel, 1999:178). The justifications, which are mediated through interaction, can limit the effectiveness of mechanisms of social control. Neutralization techniques make it possible to recognize the valid normative system whilst at the same time violating the norms. The perpetrator's cognitive dissonance is reduced, he becomes immune to reproach, be this self-reproach or originating from third parties. Sykes and Matza describe five types of justification strategy or neutralization technique, all of which follow the pattern of the "because-motives."

1. When rejecting responsibility the actor argues that his action was caused by external forces beyond his control. The violent act is in no way presented as unintentional, or as a product of chance, but the responsibility for it is transferred to conditions which are beyond the realm of the actor. If the intention behind the violent act was personal enrichment, for example, then the act can be justified by disadvantage through poverty or unemployment, which the individual himself has not caused. The deviant behavior may also be attributed to unloving and/or violent parents (Böttger, 1999, 1998). A lack of opportunities for employment and leisure-time activities for young people is also often mentioned by the actors in an (ex post facto) justification for the use of violence: "Boredom! ... That's why we did all that shit!" (Böttger, 1999:57), or "I had a blackout" (Stiels-Glenn, 1997:253). In general the perpetrator feels he is the victim of unpleasant circumstances (Weidner, 1997:58; the "billiards" concept).

2. Denying the injustice: the actor accepts the illegality of his action, but he is able to justify it morally by pointing out that no great damage has been done or no one was directly harmed. In cases of fare dodging (not a violent act, of course), it is often argued that no one was harmed because the train or bus was running anyway. In cases of physical violence the perpetrator may argue that the extent of the victim's injuries has been exaggerated, or that he had control over his use of violence. "I was standing right next to him, and five or ten seconds more would have been enough to give him the final kick, but I didn't do it. I didn't do it because I didn't want to do it. I didn't want this man to die, and now the law tells me that was an antisocial act" (Weidner, 1992:188). "You've got to see it this way, what I do prevents violence. I never hit anyone twice, I take care of that in advance" (Weidner, 1992:198). This kind of neutralization technique attempts to at least minimize the damage or the injustice.

3. Rejection of the victim: guilt is transferred from the actor to the victim. The violent act is seen as a necessary reaction and thus legitimized. "He really asked for that, he simply didn't want to understand that that was my seat" (Burschyk, Sames, & Weidner, 1997:85). In this context it is important not to forget that the roles of perpetrator and victim are generally not fixed. Alongside "only perpetrators" and "only victims" there is also a group of "perpetrators/victims" (Rostampour & Melzer, 1997), which has been shown to be significantly involved in serious violence and violent crime (Pfeiffer & Wetzels, 1999). A further category of victim rejection involves assignation of identity based on "special" features which form the basis for character description or moral judgment. These features stigmatize the victim for the perpetrator and thus allow the use of violence to appear justified. The features may be tangible or visible personal matters such as color or physical disabilities (Weidner, 1997; Willems et al., 1993), but they may also be alleged or supposed features: "Something about him made me think he was gay" (Weidner, 1997:46). RAF (Red Army Fraction) terrorists, for example, used the term "pigs" for the police (pigs are commonly slaughtered). After a black man had been beaten to death, a skinhead made a public statement on German television, and said that he felt no sympathy because this person was "not human." The

victim is frequently also rejected by being represented as a wrongdoer. An example of this is the case of racist youths who act as a result of a hardened political conviction. They perceive foreigners as a threat and develop a sense of their own disadvantage out of this. The foreigners are made responsible for deficits in the youth's own lives (Baacke, 1993:87). The perpetrators see their violent action as a revenge reaction or as their own initiative, caused by a loss of trust in politics (Willems et al., 1993).

4. Condemning those who condemn: here the attention is transferred from the perpetrators' own behavior to the controlling or sanctioning institutions. The legitimacy or credibility of the institutions is cast into doubt and criticized, and thus their right to impose sanctions on the violent criminals is questioned. This technique of neutralization makes it possible to dispute the legitimacy of the controlling and sanctioning state institutions (police, legal system, youth welfare department, etc.), and of parents. In the late 1970s and early 1980s, conflicts over Germany's nuclear power and defense policies were not resolved by politics and the legal system, and this caused members of left-wing protest groups to enter into a "career from the thug to the warrior" (Eckert, 1999:164). In the 1990s this career pattern was repeated among racist right-wing extremist youths.

5. When recourse is taken to higher authorities this entails a conflict of norms. The actor appeals to "higher" values, which neutralized other, less important values in the concrete situation (Sykes & Matza, 1968, [1957]: 360ff.). In the South of the United States there is a general rule: "In the South, insults have very serious meanings, and they must occasionally be answered with violence" (Cohen & Vandello, 1998:568). It is not only the insult which "requires" the appropriate reaction, but the consequence of not reacting to the insult also seems to lead to violent action and make it appear justified: "All knew that the failure to respond to insult marked them as less than real men, branded them, in the most telling epithets of the time, as 'cowards' and 'liars'" (Cohen & Vandello, 1998:569). Turkish youths in Germany, for example, value the "honor of the family" (the mother, the sister) more highly than nonviolence. "If anyone so much as touches my wife's hair, then I'll kill him," a young man said on television. A violent offender said: "I had to help the little one, perhaps I should not have been so rough" (Burschyk et al., 1997:84). In addition it is often necessary to act violently so as not to seem a sissy and also to prove maleness (Collison, 1996). Youths often state that they did not act in their own interest, but on behalf of their friends. This assistance to friends takes priority over nonviolence (Toprak, 2000). Youths from extremist right-wing groups frequently refer to their strong links to the group and justify their actions as the result of group dynamics (Willems et al., 1993). Violent acts such as beatings, mugging, and also murder and manslaughter are often seen by the members of a group as actions on behalf of the group (Böttger, 1998). This kind of explanation can be extended. Extremist right-wing youths, for example, have stated in interviews that they were only doing or acting out what the "general" public would like to do itself. This is an attempt to externalize guilt and exculpate the individual.

Notwithstanding all the advantages of the concept of Sykes and Matza, it still remains limited as an interpretative model. It leaves open the question as to which techniques are used in which concrete situations. The varying intensity of the internalization of whole social values and norms is largely neglected, as is the question as to the relationship between intensity of the neutralization techniques and the probability of delinquent behavior. The grounds for justification presented by Sykes and Matza are by nature individual, in that they involve either the justification of violent behavior in advance, or the retrospective compensation of potential feelings of guilt, the reduction of cognitive dissonances, and finally of course the reduction of possible negative sanctions.

Justification strategies are not only significant for the individual (intrapersonal), but also between individuals (interpersonal), as they constitute the social identity of the actor. The actor justifies a certain act within his group of friends and also in the context of court proceedings. His standpoint with regard to the norm is always under scrutiny. He is in a position to use this standpoint as a means of negotiation, as ultimately only he is able truthfully to define his relationship to the norm. This means that the actor has certain means at his disposal which may alleviate the sanctioning consequences of the obvious violation of the rules. This makes it necessary for him to show clearly that—in spite of the violation of the rules—he does not question the norm fundamentally, as is in fact already apparent because the violent act (normally) takes place covertly and/or is then kept secret. "Through ritual action the individual has to show that his lack of respect with regard to the norm was only a pretence. In reality he approves of the rules. With these same means he can naturally also hide his illegitimate intent!" (Smaus, 1998:142). Because sanctions are to be expected, and also because a cognitive dissonance has to be reduced, other kinds of protective mechanism can play a role in the retrospective justification. The individual may claim that the action never took place, or that he was not the perpetrator.

Alongside these very basic and very banal "defense strategies" there are further justifications, whereby the act, the responsibility, and also the consequences are seen and conceded, but only retrospectively. At the time of the act the situation and above all its interpretation were clearly different. "Corrective" measures to avoid assignation of deviant identity such as explanations, apologies, or requests and pleas, are more significant in everyday contexts than they are before the courts, of course, for in the courts a far broader typing prevails, as a result of generalizing suppositions.

Explanations make a claim to alleviating circumstances. Reasons such as a high intake of alcohol (Matt, 1999:267; Stiels-Glenn, 1997:253), or the fact that the actor is a minor, for example, mean that the actor cannot be made fully responsible for his violent action. Thus the actor may deny his guilt and/or claim that his personality was altered at the time of the act, and in this way distance himself from it. These explanations are an attempt on the part of the actor to avoid the impression that the immoral act really derives from his immoral character. Guilt is denied in order to avoid a deviant identity. "'Acting bad' and 'being bad' are not the same" (Miller, 1998:39).

One form of apology which is highly significant in criminal proceedings (the settlement between the perpetrator and the victim) may be used as a justification strategy. This strategy recognizes the norm, distances itself from the act (the offense), implies an admission of guilt, and is also a gesture toward the victim and/or the sanctioning authority offered in the hope of clemency or understanding. Apologies lead to the division of the delinquent into one individual who committed the deviant act and thereby became guilty, and the other individual who accuses himself by accepting the norm and distancing himself from the violent act.

Requests or pleas, on the other hand, are attempts to make the person (potentially) affected by the act tolerate the deviant behavior (Goffman, 1974:163ff.). If this happens prior to the act, then the actor bears only "limited" guilt because the victim agreed to the act.

If the requests or pleas follow the act (for example, a request not to press charges in the case of offenses such as bodily harm, which are prosecuted only on the petition of the injured party), then the aim is to avoid any negative sanction by using justifications or apologies.

Scott and Lyman (1970) begin with the thesis that only that actor who cannot give his action a positive interpretation will be deemed to be "deviant." In this context he can make use of apologies, justifications, or "accounts." In the case of an apology the actor admits on the one hand that he has behaved wrongly and he basically accepts the condemnation of his action as "deviant." But he diminishes his guilt by emphasizing his reduced responsibility for his action and he also wishes to reduce the reprehensibility of the action. The argument is that the act was a "coincidence" or an "accident," that the consequences were not intended (a mistaken relationship between means and aims), that the action occurred on impulse, or that the actor is being scapegoated by the persecuting institutions.

In contrast to this, the actor who justifies his act for an audience assumes the responsibility for it, but does not accept that the act was deviant or wrong. The mechanisms largely correspond to the neutralization strategies described by Sykes and Matza (1968 [1957]). They entail denying the wrongdoing, denying that there was a victim, condemning the condemning authorities, and appealing to the like-minded. In addition the actor may appeal to his own sad fate, justifying himself as a victim or asking for sympathy and pity, or he may appeal to a fateful, self-fulfilling prophecy. Here the actor justifies himself in a way which is functionally analogous to the rejection of responsibility described by Sykes and Matza (1968 [1957]), claiming that not he, but conditions which he could not avoid were responsible. Justifications which appeal to the phenomenon of the fellow traveler work in a similar way: "Everyone does this, and yet only I am being punished for it." The perpetrators are convinced that "violence is normal, as violence has become the norm in their social orientation and is no longer seen as an extreme in human interaction. They have internalized this text and they act" (Hopf, 2000:170) and justify their actions accordingly. Subcultural justification is also relevant here, as it appeals to the like-minded, and is a form of justification which is frequently observed in the political sphere, and also in cliques and gangs (Smaus, 1998:145). The truth is that everyone would like to do it, and yet only the perpetrator had the courage.

Another justification strategy which attempts to deny the violent act or at least any wrongdoing before the investigating authorities entails a different definition of violence. (This relates back to the thoughts on definition at the beginning of this paper!) A youth may speak of "giving someone a scratch," but in fact have almost killed someone (Weidner, 1997:175). These strategies of belittlement also include the creation of myth or legend, and they attempt to redefine the wrongdoing. "One perpetrator complained that he had been given an eight and a half year sentence just for one kick. What he did not say was that this kick broke the victim's breastbone and that the victim died" (Weidner no date:46). A man renowned for his use of a knife spread the myth that he had "put" a superior opponent "out of action" in a fair fight. In reality he stabbed the victim from behind in the back as he was withdrawing (Weidner, 1997:170). "A youth brags about a robbery to the rest of his clique. The perpetrator is fairly small and the victim was large. In prison everyone admires the perpetrator for his achievement, as do all the members of his clique. But the perpetrator neglected to tell us one small detail. The victim had both arms amputated, and so it was easy to pull a plastic bag over his head from behind and then to rob him" (Geretshauser, Lenfert, & Weidner, 1993:35). The dual function of myth creation consists of both bragging to enhance male status and also belittling the offense before the potential sanctioning authorities.

Justification strategies may also be politically motivated, as an analysis from South Africa shows: "The ideological violence of apartheid was thus this creation of a language of social representations which justified the differential treatment of people according to their political group assignment: black, coloured, Indian and White, Zulu and Xhosa. That language is not dead but lives on as the linguistic precursor of direct physical violence" (Dawes & Finchilescu, 1996:53). The linguistic option for the classification of victims can on its own provide the justification for violent acts. The "ideology of supremacy" (Connell, 1995) gives the (male) violent criminal his "authorization" (Gilgun & McLeod, 1999:167).

A further justification relevant to the question of definition claims that the violent act was a perfectly normal and everyday type of behavior. "A schoolboy justified the 'normality' of his act by appealing to his experience of violence where he lived. Another boy appealed to the experience of violence in his family, and a third boy said that he had already been threatened with weapons several times in his father's store" (Hopf, 2000:169). On the one hand this is clearly to be seen as neutralization strategy, but it also points to the existence of group-specific and milieu-specific realities and definitions of normality. Particularly in the case of violence-prone youths with a strong attachment to a certain area, violence is seen as the "last authentic form of life ... These milieus require patterns of behavior involving a rejection of whatever is female and of homosexual tendencies, a striving after success, power, and the exercise of power, a repression of the emotions, and high-risk behavior" (Matt, 1999:262; Lamnek & Schwenk, 1995:121). Factors of inequality, such as a low social status due to social background, the experience of violence in socialization within the family, negative educational careers resulting in poor opportunities on the labor market (which can lead to the reinforcement of delinquent cliques), living in a deprived area (satellite towns with a high concentration of problem families or problem social groups) (Eckert, 1999) all influence attitudes toward violence and above all make violent cliques attractive for young males. Expectations of behavior within these cliques or gangs encourage the use of violence and also provide group-typical patterns of justification.

A further strategy for the individual legitimization of deviant behavior is the "disclaimer," as proposed by Hewitt and Stokes (1975) (see also Smaus, 1998:146). This can also be an excuse which precedes the action. These disclaimers represent an attempt to prevent dissonances between personal identity and assignations of identity by third parties in advance, and to reduce and ultimately to balance these out. The origin of the act is transferred to other circumstances. The following disclaimers are mentioned:

"Hedging": the actor attempts to justify himself by means of his inability, in order to leave his identity unaffected: "I'm no expert, of course, but ..." (Hewitt & Stokes, 1975:4). "Credentialing": the actor attempts to prevent himself from being accused of bad intentions: "I'm not prejudiced—some of my best friends are Jews, but ..." (Hewitt & Stokes, 1975:4). By means of the "sin license" the actual violation of the norm is seen to conform to the intended meaning of the norm or to higher priority norms. The deviation is (re)interpreted according to a hierarchical system of norms: "What I'm going to do is contrary to the letter of the law but not its spirit" (Hewitt & Stokes, 1975:5). By means of "cognitive disclaimers" the actor wishes to present himself as being reasonable and thoughtful, because he believes that his environment might view him as being without any sense of reality and perceive his act as being meaningless. "This may seem strange to you ..." (Hewitt & Stokes, 1975:5). The "appeal for the suspension of judgment" is intended to prevent the partner in interaction from judging the act (too) quickly and becoming impatient and angry: "Under such circumstances, individuals appeal to their fellows to suspend judgment until the full meaning of the act can be made known ... 'Hear me out before you explode ...'" (Hewitt & Stokes, 1975:6).

The above overview shows that justification strategies can neither be integrated into a unified theoretical concept, nor can their variety be reduced to a single dimension. The lowest common denominator is that strategies for the justification of violence are (by definition) presented ex post facto and are intended as exculpation. Furthermore it is possible to note (relatively consistent) specific concepts of maleness and links to social and culturally specific groups both in terms of the use of violence and in terms of its justification.

V. WHY ARE JUSTIFICATIONS OF VIOLENCE A SUBJECT WORTHY OF STUDY (IN THE FUTURE)?

Strategies for the justification of violence were dealt with as long as three decades ago (Sykes & Matza, 1968 [1957]), but subsequently the subject was somewhat neglected as investigations of violent situations and explanations for violence became predominant. Yet an analysis of the justification strategies used by violent offenders would be useful for two areas of study. These are an understanding of the process of violence or of the violent act itself, and prevention and intervention. Violence is a form of social action and therefore "contains meaning" (Heitmeyer et al., 1992, 1995); it is learned—not least in the family (Honig, 1990:351)—and also legitimized a priori or ex post facto. The necessity of looking more closely at violent action also entails a closer investigation of the justification or legitimization strategies for violence.

In this context changes to the macrostructural framework should not be ignored. It was renewed modernization (with the consequences of individualization and [value] pluralism), the development toward erosion of the state monopoly of violence (Bauman, 2000), and the increasing variety of youth (part-)cultures (Baacke, 1993; Ferchhoff & Neubauer, 1997) that caused the strong normative association of young people with (deviant) groups. In particular young people react to the difficulties and excess demands of individualization (Heitmeyer et al., 1995) with "regressive" strategies, with violence, and its justification strategies.

Youth violence and the corresponding justification strategies are closely interlinked. Notwithstanding the great heterogeneity of the motives and justifications for violence, the relevant attribution of meaning is determined by the (part-)culture. All the various violence-prone and justifying attitudes, be these in the drugs scene, among hooligans, skinheads, young Bosnians, Turks, or ethnic German immigrants from Russia, all share one variously influential cultural aspect—the production of maleness (typical to the part-culture). The use of violence and of its justifications is based on a concept of hegemonic maleness. Norms specific to maleness are also practiced in the justification of violence, be these the defense of male honor or the protection of the family and in particular its female members, as required by the male role (Böttger, 1997; Strobl, 1996). It is simply "male" to defend oneself against "attacks," and this norm provides the arguments for justification.

Because violent crime is primarily a group offense, the groups provide the corresponding justification strategies. In particular when the groups deviate considerably from established norms, the strong links which young people experience in these groups become problematic (Heitmeyer & Möller, 1995). "Subcultures of violence" may arise (Wolfgang & Ferracuti, 1967). Forms of hegemonic maleness typical of subcultures and/or part-cultures very often appeal to valid whole social value systems and then redefine these in a specific manner. Taking recourse to mainly abstract and thus often unclear values makes it possible to interpret and instrumentalize these according to the actor's utilitarian standpoints. This is particular evident in the case of violent acts deriving from the "Robin Hood mentality." The "man" sees himself as a "good" man fighting for justice, no matter whose justice that is (Böttger & Silkenbeumer, 2001). The (fictional) stereotype of justice popularized by the mass media, for example the character of "Dirty Harry," the "hard, but fair" policeman presents images which provide especially young people with the justifications for their acts.

Finally it should be noted that research to date has paid too little concentrated attention to violence justification strategies. Findings in research are ultimately products of "serendipity" (Merton, 1964:103), and can be found sporadically and by chance in asides, rather than as the object of explicit analysis. Scholarship has the urgent task of extending and adding to the work done in the "classical" studies by Sykes and Matza, and further empirical research appears essential.

Translated by Tradukas

REFERENCES

Baacke, Dieter. (1993). *Jugend und Jugendkulturen. Darstellung und Deutung*, 2nd Edition. Weinheim, München: Juventa.

Bauman, Zygmunt. (2000). Alte und neue Gewalt. *Journal für Konflikt- und Gewaltforschung, 2*, 28–42.

Böttger, Andreas. (1997). 'Und dann ging so 'ne Rauferei los....' Eine qualitative Studie zu Gewalt an Schulen. In Heinz-Günter Holtappels, Wilhelm Heitmeyer, Wolfgang Melzer & Klaus-Jürgen Tillmann (Eds.), *Forschung über Gewalt an Schulen* (pp. 155–168). Weinheim, München: Juventa.

Böttger, Andreas. (1998). *Gewalt und Biographie: Eine qualitative Analyse rekonstruierter Lebensgeschichten von 100 Jugendlichen*. Baden-Baden: Nomos.

Böttger, Andreas. (1999). 'Die ganze Schule hatte Angst gehabt...' Ergebnisse eines qualitativen Forschungsprojekts zu gewalttätigen Jugendlichen. In Landesstelle Jugendschutz Niedersachsen & Andreas Böttger (Eds.), *Jugendgewalt—und kein Ende? Hintergründe—Perspektiven—Gegenstrategien* (pp. 47–66). Hannover: Landesstelle Jugendschutz Niedersachsen.

Böttger, Andreas, & Mirja Silkenbeumer. (2001). Gewalt in Schulen. Eine kulturvergleichende Untersuchung in China und Deutschland. In Andreas Böttger, Jiazhen Liang & Mirja Silkenbeumer (Eds.), *Früher war ich nicht so ...! Biographien gewalttätiger Jugendlicher in China* (pp. 204–222). Baden-Baden: Nomos.

Burschyk, Leo, Karl-Heinz Sames, & Jens Weidner. (1997). Das Anti-Aggressivitäts-Training. In Jens Weidner, Rainer Kilb & Dieter Kreft (Eds.), *Gewalt im Griff* (pp. 74–90). Weinheim, Basel: Beltz.

Cohen, Albert K., & James F. Short. (1968). Zur Erforschung delinquenter Subkulturen. In Fritz Sack & René König (Eds.), *Soziologie der Jugendkriminalität* (pp. 372–394). Köln, Oplalen: Westdeutscher Verlag. [Original: Cohen, Albert K., & James F. Short. (1958). Research in Delinquent Subcultures. *The Journal of Social Issues, 14*, 20–37.]

Cohen, Dov, & Joe Vandello. (1998). Meanings of Violence. *The Journal of Legal Studies, 27*(2), 567–584.

Collison, Mike. (1996). In Search of the High Life. Drugs, Crime, Masculinities and Consumption. *British Journal of Criminology, 36*(3), 428–444.

Connell, Robert W. (1995). *Masculinities*. Berkley: University of California Press.

Dawes, Andrew, & Gillian Finchilescu. (1996). Fear and Loathing at the Southern Tip: Violence and Teenagers in South Africa. *Development, 1*, 53–57

Eckert, Roland. (1999). Gewalt unter Jugendlichen. Die Problemlage. In Heiner Timmermann & Eva Wessela (Eds.), *Jugendforschung in Deutschland. Eine Zwischenbilanz* (pp. 161–172). Opladen: Leske & Budrich.

Esser, Johannes, & Thomas Dominikowski. (1997). *Die Lust an der Gewalttätigkeit bei Jugendlichen. Krisenprofile—Ursachen—Handlungsorientierungen für die Jugendarbeit*, 3rd Edition. Frankfurt: Institut für Sozialarbeit und Sozialpädagogik.

Euler, Harald. (1997). Geschlechtsspezifische Unterschiede und die nicht erzählte Geschichte in der Gewaltforschung. In Heinz-Günter Holtappels, Wilhelm Heitmeyer, Wolfgang Melzer & Klaus-Jürgen Tillmann (Eds.), *Forschung über Gewalt an Schulen* (pp. 191–206). Weinheim, München: Juventa.

Ferchhoff, Wilfried, & Georg Neubauer. (1997). *Patchwork-Jugend. Eine Einführung in postmoderne Sichtweisen*. Opladen: Leske & Budrich.

Findeisen, Hans V., & Joachim Kersten. (1999). *Der Kick und die Ehre. Vom Sinn jugendlicher Gewalt*. München: Kunstmann.

Geretshauser, Monika, Thomas Lenfert, & Jens Weidner. (1993). Konfrontiert rechtsorientierte Gewalttäter mit den Opferfolgen. *DVJJ-Journal, 1*, 33–36.

Gilgun, Jane F., & Laura McLeod. (1999). Gendering Violence. *Studies in Symbolic Interaction, 22*, 167–193.

Goffman, Erving. (1974). *Das Individuum im öffentlichen Austausch: Mikrostudien zur öffentlichen Ordnung*. Frankfurt: Suhrkamp.

Goffman, Erving. (1991). *Stigma: über Techniken der Bewältigung beschädigter Identität*. Frankfurt a. M.: Suhrkamp.

Heitmeyer, Wilhelm, Heike Buhse, Joachim Liebe-Freund, Kurt Möller, Joachim Müller, Helmut Ritz, Gertrud Siller, & Johannes Vossen. (1992). *Die Bielefelder Rechtsextremismus-Studie*. Weinheim, München: Juventa.

Heitmeyer, Wilhelm, Birgit Collmann, Jutta Conrads, Ingo Matuschek, Dietmar Kraul, Wolfgang Kühnel, Renate Möller, & Matthias Ulbrich-Herrmann. (1995). *Gewalt. Schattenseiten der Individualisierung bei Jugendlichen aus unterschiedlichen Milieus*. Weinheim, München: Juventa.

Heitmeyer, Wilhelm, & Renate Möller. (1995). Gewalt in jugendkulturellen Szenen. In Wilfried Ferchhoff, Uwe Sander & Ralf Vollbrecht (Eds.), *Jugendkulturen—Faszination und Ambivalenz. Einblicke in jugendliche Lebenswelten* (pp. 203–216). Weinheim, München: Juventa.

Hewitt, John P., & Randall Stokes. (1975). Disclaimers. *American Sociological Review, 40*(1), 1–11.

Honig, Michael-Sebastian. (1990). Gewalt in der Familie. In Schwind, Hans-Dieter, Jürgen Baumann et al. (Eds.), *Ursachen, Prävention und Kontrolle von Gewalt. Analysen und Vorschläge der Unabhängigen Regierungskommission zur Verhinderung und Bekämpfung von Gewalt. (Gewaltkommission), Bd. III* (pp. 343–361). Berlin: Duncker & Humblot.

Hopf, Werner. (2000). Gewalt an Schulen: Prävention, Intervention und soziales Lernen—Teil I. *SchulVerwaltung BY, 5*, 169–175.

Jefferson, Tony. (1994). Theorizing Masculine Subjectivity. In Tim Newburn & Elizabeth A. Stanko (Eds.), *Just Boys Doing Business?* (pp. 10–31). London: Routledge.

Klein, Malcolm W. (1995). *The American Street Gang: Its Nature, Prevalence and Control*. New York: Oxford University Press.

Kühnel, Wolfgang. (1999). Soziale Beziehungen, Gruppenprozesse und delinquentes Verhalten beim Statusübergang von der Schule in die Ausbildung. In Heiner Timmermann & Eva Wessela (Eds.), *Jugendforschung in Deutschland. Eine Zwischenbilanz* (pp. 173–192). Opladen: Leske & Budrich.

Laidler, Karen A. Joe, & Geoffrey Hunt. (1997). Violence and Social Organisation in Female Gangs. *Social Justice, 4*, 148–169.

Lamnek, Siegfried, & Otto Schwenk. (1995). *Die Marienplatz-Rapper. Zur Soziologie einer Großstadt-Gang*. Pfaffenweiler: Centaurus.

Lamnek, Siegfried. (1999). *Theorien abweichenden Verhaltens, 7th Edition*. München: Fink.

Matt, Eduard. (1999). Jugend, Männlichkeit und Delinquenz. Junge Männer zwischen Männlichkeitsritualen und Autonomiebestrebungen. *Zeitschrift für Soziologie der Erziehung und Sozialisation, 19*(3), 259–276.

Merton, Robert K. (1964). *Social Theory and Social Structure*. London: Collier-MacMillan.

Messerschmidt, James. (1997). Von der Analyse der Männerherrschaft zur Forschung über Geschlechterverhältnisse: Unterschiede und Vielfalt bei der Bewerkstelligung von Geschlecht am Beispiel der 'Mädchen in der Gang'. In Joachim Kersten & Heinz Steinert (Eds.), *Starke Typen. Iron Mike, Dirty Harry, Crocodile Dundee und der Alltag von Männlichkeit* (pp. 13–36). Baden-Baden: Nomos.

Miller, Jody. (1998). Up it Up: Gender and the Accomplishment of Street Robbery. *Criminology, 36*(1), 37–66.

Müller, Jan, & Maria Loreto Burschel. (1997). *Junge Männer und Gewalt—eine qualitative Untersuchung*. Diplomarbeit. München.

Müller, Joachim. (1999). Sozialräumliche Aspekte von Gewalt mit ethnisch-kulturellem Hintergrund. *Journal für Konflikt- und Gewaltforschung, 1*, 84–96.

Neidhardt, Friedhelm. (1997). Gewalt, Gewaltdiskussion, Gewaltforschung. *Bielefelder Universitätsgespräche und Vorträge, 7*, 19–28.

Pfeiffer, Christian, & Peter Wetzels. (1999). *Zur Struktur und Entwicklung der Jugendgewalt in Deutschland*. http://www.unics.uni-hannover.de/~n5x5link/jugendgew.html.

Popp, Ulrike. (1997). Geschlechtersozialisation und Gewalt an Schulen. In Heinz-Günter Holtappels, Wilhelm Heitmeyer, Wolfgang Melzer & Klaus-Jürgen Tillmann (Eds.), *Forschung über Gewalt an Schulen* (pp. 207–223). Weinheim, München: Juventa.

Rammstedt, Otthein. (1989). Wider ein individuum-orientiertes Gewaltverständnis. In Wilhelm Heitmeyer, Kurt Möller & Heinz Sünker (Eds.), *Jugend—Staat—Gewalt* (pp. 47–56). Weinheim, München: Juventa.

Rostampour, Parviz, & Wolfgang Melzer. (1997). Täter-Opfer-Typologien im schulischen Gewaltkontext. Forschungsergebnisse unter Verwendung von Cluster-Analyse und multinominal logistischer Regression. In Heinz-Günter Holtappels, Wilhelm Heitmeyer, Wolfgang Melzer & Klaus-Jürgen Tillmann (Eds.), *Forschung über Gewalt an Schulen* (pp. 169–189). Weinheim/ München: Juventa.

Rutter, Michael, & Henri Giller. (1984). *Juvenile Delinquency.* New York: Penguin.

Schütz, Alfred. (1981). *Der sinnhafte Aufbau der sozialen Welt, 2nd Edition.* Frankfurt a. M.: Suhrkamp.

Scott, Marvin B., & Stanford M. Lyman. (1970). Accounts, Deviance and Social Order. In Jack D. Douglas (Ed.), *Deviance and Respectability. The Social Construction of Moral Meanings* (pp. 89–119). New York: Basic Books.

Smaus, Gerlinda. (1998). *Das Strafrecht und die gesellschaftliche Differenzierung.* Baden-Baden: Nomos.

Stiels-Glenn, Michael. (1997). Das Anti-Gewalt-Training in der Jugendgerichts- und Bewährungshilfe. In Jens Weidner, Rainer Kilb & Dieter Kreft (Eds.), *Gewalt im Griff* (pp. 238–261). Weinheim, Basel: Beltz.

Strobl, Rainer. (1996). 'Fremd-Verstehen'? Zur Interpretation von Interviews mit türkischen Männern und Frauen. In Rainer Strobl & Andreas Böttger (Eds.), *Wahre Geschichten? Zur Theorie und Praxis qualitativer Interviews* (pp. 131–158). Baden-Baden: Nomos.

Stüwe, Gerd. (1993). Gewalt als Jugendphänomen? Ergebnisse von zwei Jugendarbeitsstudien in Frankfurt/ Main. *Theorie und Praxis der sozialen Arbeit, 44*(1), 11–18.

Sutherland, Edwin H. (1968). Die Theorie der differenziellen Kontakte. In Fritz Sack & René König (Eds.), *Kriminalsoziologie* (pp. 395–399). Frankfurt: Akademische Verlagsgesellschaft. [Original: Sutherland, Edwin H. (1956). A Statement of the Theory. In Albert K. Cohen, Alfred Lindesmith & Karl Schuessler (Eds.), *The Sutherland Papers.* Bloomington: Indiana University Press.]

Sykes, Gresham M., & David Matza. (1968). Techniken der Neutralisierung: Eine Theorie der Delinquenz. In Fritz Sack & René König (Eds.), *Kriminalsoziologie* (pp. 360–371). Frankfurt: Akademische Verlagsgesellschaft. [Original: Sykes, Gresham M., & David Matza. (1957). Techniques of Neutralization: A Theory of Delinquency. *American Sociological Review, 22,* 664–670.]

Toprak, Ahmed. (2000). Ehre, Männlichkeit und Freundschaft. Auslöser für Gewaltbereitschaft Jugendlicher und Heranwachsender türkischer Herkunft in München. *DVJJ-Journal, 2,* 174–176.

Trotha, Trutz von. (Ed.) (1997). *Soziologie der Gewalt. Sonderheft 37 der Kölner Zeitschrift für Soziologie und Sozialpsychologie.* Opladen: Westdeutscher Verlag.

Weber, Max. (1980). *Wirtschaft und Gesellschaft, 5th Edition.* Tübingen: J.C.B. Mohr.

Weidner, Jens. (1992). Gewaltbereite Jugendliche trainieren Friedfertigkeit. *Loccumer Protokolle, 53,* 185–196.

Weidner, Jens. (1997). *Anti-Aggressivitäts-Training für Gewalttäter, 4th Edition.* Bonn/Bad-Godesberg: Forum-Verlag.

Weidner, Jens. (no date). Anti-Aggressivitäts-Training für Gewalttäter. *Mitt. LJA, 110,* 44.

Willems, Helmut, Roland Eckert, Stefanie Würtz, & Linda Steinmetz. (1993). *Fremdenfeindliche Gewalt. Einstellungen, Täter, Konflikteskalation.* Opladen: Leske & Budrich.

Wolfgang, Marvin E., & Franco Ferracuti. (1967). *The Subculture of Violence. Toward an Integrated Theory in Criminology.* London: Travistock Publications.

Yinger, John M. (1960). Contraculture and Subculture. *American Sociological Review, 25,* 625–635.

PART II-7

PROCESSES AND DYNAMICS: ESCALATION AND DE-ESCALATION

CHAPTER II-7.1

Fear of Violent Crime

KLAUS BOERS

I. INTRODUCTION

Fear of crime means fear of violence and sex offences. It is a phenomenon that receives a great deal of attention in international criminological and crime policy debate. The first time it came to be considered a problem and a subject of study was in the United States in the 1960s (see Boers, 1991:15–39; Ferraro, 1995:1–5). The American example is also particularly apt for depicting the domestic political discussions dominating public awareness in the 1960s and 1970s in Western Europe as well. These had a major impact on the emerging interest in this topic at that time. As a result, the history of the fear of crime is also, above all, a history of politics (Lee, 1999).

1. The History of the Fear of Crime

As the number of violent crimes registered by the police increased rapidly from the mid-1960s onward, "crime" became—alongside race riots and the movement to end the war in Vietnam—the central domestic policy problem. In 1968, Richard Nixon won the presidential election on a law-and-order ticket. His predecessor, Lyndon B. Johnson, had set up the Katzenbach Commission, which addressed the crime problem in a way that was to guide government policy in the following years (President's Commission, 1967; Arzt, 1976). At the same time, the most consequential change to official crime policy in the 1970s and 1980s involved a new focus on the victims of crime: the shift from resocializing offenders to protecting victims that also led to the reintroduction of harsher offender punishment, attaining its contemporary peak in the zero-tolerance strategies of the 1990s (Ortner et al., 1998; Hopkins Burke, 1998; see, for a very uncritical analysis, Silverman, 1999).

The increasing interest in the victims of crime certainly also marks the birth of research on the fear of crime. Alongside increases in violent crime, growing public concern

W. Heitmeyer and J. Hagan (eds.), *International Handbook of Violence Research*, 1131–1149.
© 2003 Kluwer Academic Publishers. Printed in the Netherlands.

was one of the most important issues for the Katzenbach Commission. The victim studies carried out in the Commission's name—the first of their kind—along with the Eight-City Surveys (Hindelang et al., 1978) conducted at the beginning of the 1970s in preparation for the current National Crime Victimization Survey, were also particularly concerned with the relation between becoming a victim and fear of crime. In the 1980s and 1990s, there were numerous local, but only few national surveys in the United States (Fattah, 1993; Ferraro, 1995:27–28, 33–34). In Great Britain, fear of crime has been surveyed regularly since 1982 as part of the British Crime Survey run by the Home Office (Maxfield, 1987; Hough, 1995). This soon became a (purportedly objective) basis for crime policy, not only in the "administrative criminology" of the Home Office but also—triggering some irritation and annoyance—among previously critical and now "new-realist" criminologists (Jones et al., 1986; see, for a critique, Sparks, 1992).

Fear of crime received little attention in German criminology before the political upheavals in the German Democratic Republic in November 1989 (Boers, 1991:33–39). Since then, research interest has increased notably. Alongside the pressing problems with political and economic reform as well as the social security system, a serious increase in crime and fear of crime was anticipated in the new German states. Several crime surveys were carried out at brief intervals in which fear of crime as a subjective reaction to criminality became a fixed feature (Kury et al., 1992; Kury, 1997; Wetzels et al., 1995; Boers & Kurz, 1997).

Round about the mid-1970s, it became apparent that crime rates were not dropping despite a range of measures, particularly in the policing domain (improved equipment, centralizing structural reforms). This led to an increasing concentration on reducing the subjective consequences of crime: by the late 1980s and the early 1990s at the latest, fear of crime had become recognized as an autonomous issue in nearly all crime policy programs, and even one that is just as significant as crime itself. Community crime prevention and, somewhat later, community policing came to be central concepts of American and European crime policy (see Skogan, 1990; Dölling & Feltes, 1993; Becker et al., 1996).[1]

2. What Is Fear of Crime?

A variety of phenomena are understood as "fear of crime" in both the public and academic debates. It is only one of many attitudes toward crime. One useful distinction to make seems to be between social and personal attitudes toward crime (Louis-Guérin, 1984:627). A person may call for harsher punishment or may judge the "growth in crime" to be a serious problem for the "government and society" when rank-ordering lists of various social problems, as frequently practiced in public opinion polls (social attitude toward crime), for example. However, this same person will not necessarily also feel personally unsafe or threatened. Fear of crime is an emotional reaction to crime risks that are perceived as a personal threat. As such, it is a personal attitude. It contains further cognitive components, including the important issue of personal risk assessment ("How likely is it that you will become the victim of a crime: *not at all, somewhat, rather, very likely*") as well as behavioral reactions such as avoiding parks, dark streets, public transport, or certain groups of persons. Although these personal attitudes toward crime intercorrelate, they are not identical (Ferraro, 1995:27–33). In the past, fear of

---

[1] For full or selected bibliographies, see Hale, 1996; Ditton & Farrall, 2000.

crime was measured as the feeling of insecurity experienced "being out alone in one's neighborhood after dark" (the standard item).[2] However, because this item does not describe offenses or risk situations in more detail, it taps an unspecific feeling of threat in relation to crime-relevant risks (general fear of crime) that may also involve diffuse fears of "darkness" or "being alone." Nonetheless, "crime" as such exists only as a (crime-policy) meta-phenomenon. In real life, there are only concrete behaviors. Therefore, criminologically, one has to distinguish between particular offenses, and certainly between violent and sex offenses, and burglary (specific fear of crime). *"Being out alone in your neighborhood after dark, how much do you worry about being threatened or verbally abused, beaten up, robbed or mugged, murdered, sexually molested, assaulted, raped, or having someone break into your home?"* (not at all, somewhat, rather, very much worried). Admittedly, the use of such a choice of offenses, which has become common practice in recent studies (Maxfield, 1984:5; Warr, 1987:33; Ferraro & LaGrange, 1987:79–82; Ferraro, 1995:34–37; Wetzels et al., 1995:191; Boers & Kurz, 1997:196–204), reproduces a rather classic image of crime that is oriented toward street crime and focuses on the impairment of the individual's physical and psychological integrity. Hence, "fear of crime" essentially concerns fear of violence, sex offenses, and burglary. Other forms of offense should then correspond less with fear or anxiety but more with "concern" (white-collar crime) or "annoyance" (theft) (see, for a discussion of the operationalization problems, Farrall et al., 1997).

Finally, behavioral reactions to crime threats are generally assessed as follows: as avoidance behavior regarding certain forms of transport and certain locations (streets, squares, parks) and groups (young persons and foreigners), as active behavior to protect one's own person (carrying tear gas, sticks, or other weapons), and as measures to protect one's own household (see, for an overview, Ferraro, 1995:21–33).

II. THEORETICAL APPROACHES AND EMPIRICAL RESULTS

1. Prevalence and Development of Fear of Crime

On a national level, the secular growth in fear of crime in the United States and West Germany can be plotted over a longer time only in terms of the mostly dichotomous standard item used in public opinion polls (e.g., General Social Survey, Institut für Demoskopie, ALLBUS; see Fig. II-7-1.1). Because of the poor discriminatory power of these instruments as well as the insufficient number of waves in general, it is only possible to depict trends, and these have to be interpreted with caution.

These trends indicate two peaks and troughs in the general fear of crime since the mid-1960s, and these seem to take a very similar course in both West Germany and the United States. The main peaks are in the 1970s and again in the first half of the 1990s. Fear of crime dropped most strongly up to the middle/end of the 1980s and at the end of the 1990s. The two nations do not seem to exhibit very large differences over time in the degree of fear (this is also the case for other West European countries such as Great Brit-

---

[2] Either as a dichotomous item with two response alternatives (e.g., *afraid* vs. *not afraid*) as used in many opinion polls, or with four response alternatives as commonly used in criminological surveys (*very safe, rather safe, somewhat unsafe, very unsafe*).

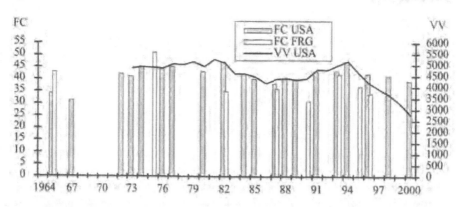

FIGURE II-7-1.1. **General fear of crime (FC) in the United States (USA) and West Germany (FRG) 1965–2000 plus victims of violence per 100,000 population (VV) in the United States 1973–2000.** Percentage of "afraid to go out at night in one's own residential area" (dichotomous item) or (in West Germany since 1993) "somewhat" and "very unsafe." *Sources*: Boers, 1991:8; Bureau of Justice Statistics, 1998: 8; 2001: Table 3.2 (National Crime Victimization Survey), Table 2.41 (General Social Survey); van Dijk & Toornvliet, 1996:3 (Eurobarometer 1996); own data.

ain, see Mirrlees-Black & Allen, 1998:4), despite the major differences in their social systems and the much higher (violent) crime rate registered by the police in the United States. However, American victimization rates for violent offenses differ hardly at all from European ones (Bureau of Justice Statistics, 2001: Table 3.2; Boers, 1994:125–127; 1996: 319; Mirrlees-Black & Allen, 1998:iii, vi), though this may well be due to the well-known deficits in police crime statistics.

However, the limited validity of the dichotomous standard item does not permit even approximately reliable statements on the extent[3] of the fear of crime or on specific fears, and, finally, also on whether the degree of a parallel between the American rates of fear and violent victimization development (Fig. II-7-1.1)[4] can justify assuming that the growth of fear of crime relates to crime trends. Such a statement would already be questionable in methodological terms because of the risk of an ecological fallacy when comparing aggregated data.

More reliable statements on time trends should therefore be based on at least multistage measurement instruments of the specific fear of crime. Time series for the fear of violent offenses can be plotted only for England and Wales since 1984 at two-year intervals (Mirrlees-Black & Allen, 1998:4) and for Germany since 1992 (i.e., since reunification).

These reveal that in western Germany between 1992 and 2000, rates of the various forms of specific fear of crime remained quite stable (see Fig. II-7-1.2).[5] In eastern Ger-

---

[3] This can be seen already when comparing the dichotomous and the four-level response scale: Whereas throughout the United States in 1998, 41 percent said they were *fearful* on the dichotomous scale, in the 12-City Survey (including Chicago, Los Angeles, and New York), only 7 percent of the residents of big cities reported feeling *very fearful* in their own residential area (35 percent said they were *somewhat fearful*; Smith et al., 1999:18).
[4] Victimization data comparable to the National Crime Victimization Survey are not gathered in Germany.
[5] Table 2 was compiled by the author from data collected by the GfK Nuremberg (Association for Consumer and Market Research) for the R+V Insurance Company (approximately 1,000 respondents from eastern Germany and 2,000 from the West). I wish to thank the R+V Insurance Company for kindly allowing me to use their data. The representative examples are only fear of robbery as the street crime triggering the strongest fear and fear of burglary. The subjective impact of burglary is similar to that of a severe act of violence because of the encroachment into the private sphere.

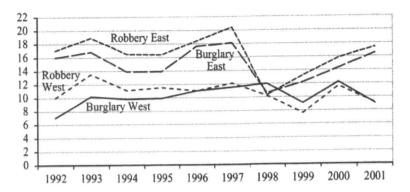

FIGURE II-7-1.2. Trends in fear of crime (robbery and burglary) in eastern and western Germany 1992–2001. Percentage of *very anxious* (value on a 7-point scale).[6] *Source:* R+V-Versicherungen.

many, however, the social transition process—even at the end of the 1990s—seems to be reflected in on-and-off movements of the fear of crime. Nonetheless, these were marked by a strong decrease between 1997 and 1998: in this period the proportion of *very anxious* respondents dropped by 50 percent (from 20 percent to 10 percent) and reached the moderate West German fear level. This declining basic trend is also found in (all) other published German surveys as well as in the British Crime Survey (Boers, 2001:13; Reuband, 1999:16, based on a panel study in eastern Germany; Mirrlees-Black & Allen, 1998:4).

The increase in fear of crime in Germany at the beginning of the 1990s was related predominantly to the *social transition in eastern Germany*. It would seem that the population of eastern Germany was confronted with completely new forms of crime after reunification, and the fear of crime increased markedly following the political and social change—sometimes attaining levels twice as high as those in the West. Although crime increased rapidly (according to victim surveys) after the fall of the Berlin Wall, it did not rise beyond the West German level (Boers, 1996:318–328). Hence, major increases in fear of crime depend less on absolute crime levels but more strongly on a rapid increase in (violent) crime. Together with becoming aware of previously unfamiliar phenomena of serious crime, this was apparently perceived as a *qualitative* change in personal safety. In *western Germany*—based on the sole measurements of the general fear of crime performed up to then—the feeling of insecurity dropped strongly between 1984 and 1989, but had regained the level observed in the mid-1980s by the mid-1990s (see Fig. II-7-1.1).

However, the effects of radical social change could not just be seen in an increase in fear of crime in eastern Germany. It is notable that this did not follow the same trend across all sizes of community. In western Germany and Western societies, the feeling of insecurity is always (much) higher in *big cities* compared with small towns and rural districts. However, trends in the fear of crime in eastern Germany reveal notable peaks and troughs as a function of community size that seem to follow a *retardation effect*: whereas fear of crime was initially (up to 1991) highest in the East German metropolitan areas

---

[6] This 7-point rating scale actually labeled only the values *not anxious at all* (1) and *very anxious* (7). To ensure a reliable demarcation of the group of fearful respondents, the usual presentation of means with such scales was dropped in favor of depicting trends in the extreme score (7). We assume that the value (7), but not (any longer) the value (6), can be compared unequivocally with the category *very worried* on a 4-point scale. If both extreme scores (6 and 7) are aggregated, the current retrograde trend starts one year earlier.

(East Berlin, Leipzig, and Dresden), it declined there until 1993, while simultaneously attaining its highest level in medium-sized cities (100,000–500,000 inhabitants). Between 1993 and 1995, it declined here as well, but now increased most strongly in towns with 50,000–100,000 inhabitants. During these years, fear rates were also very high compared with other nations (e.g., 25–31 percent who were very worried about being robbed;[7] see Table II-7-1.1).

This unusual trend in the new German states could be interpreted as indicating that initial shock over the new crime situation had already given way to self-regulative adaptation processes. Against the background of the "mental autodynamics" of the social transition process, this trend soon reversed to a degree that—as far as can be seen—has never been achieved through community prevention measures. In any case, fear of crime in big cities does not affect all city districts in general, but particularly those socially destabilized communities that are found more frequently in larger urban areas (see, also, the section on the social control perspective below).

In all studies to date, *women* have expressed the greatest fear of crime (Fig. II-7-1.3). Generally, this is attributed to their greater physical vulnerability, and, against the background of traditional female role socialization, their greater mental vulnerability as well (Skogan & Maxfield, 1981:69–78; Killias, 1990; Killias & Clevici, 2000).[9] As far as their mental vulnerability is concerned, the decisive element is probably that it is based strongly on the risk of very stressful and humiliating victimization through male sexual violence. Because rape is an asymmetrical act of violence directed almost exclusively toward women (and children), and fear of rape is accompanied by self-imposed restrictions to freedom of movement, to occupational and social life, as well as to individual development, patriarchal gender roles may be perpetuated through self-regulation (Stanko, 1997; Gordon & Riger, 1989). Moreover, it is only through the communicative medium of fear that rape acquires its significant social function: the assertion of male control. Nonetheless, the claim that fear of rape is significant enough to overshadow all other forms of fear of crime in women, and fearful women are, for example, unable to discriminate between a robbery and a rape (the "shadow effect," Ferraro, 1995:86–100; Warr, 1984:698–700; 1985:245–247), is certainly not true in such a generalized form.

TABLE II-7-1.1. Fear of robbery and city size in western and eastern Germany: Percentage of "very worried"[8]

		> 500,000	100–500,000	50–100,000	20–50,000	< 20,000
1991	East	25	18	18	9	13
1993	East	18	26	23	17	13
	West	16	9	18	8	6
1995	East	17	20	31	13	8
	West	16	9	10	3	5

[7] This trend contained all violence and sex offenses, but was most conspicuous for robbery and rape.
[8] When no other sources are cited, empirical findings come from a cooperation project between criminologists in eastern and western Germany who carried out crime and victim surveys based on representative samples in 1991 (East: $n = 2,011$), 1993 (East: $n = 2,212$, West: $n = 2,034$), and 1995 (East: $n = 1,095$, West: $n = 2,114$). Response rates varied between 67 percent and 72 percent (see, for detailed information, Boers et al., 1997).
[9] See, on the relation between masculinity and (suppressed) fear, Goodey (1997).

FEAR OF VIOLENT CRIME

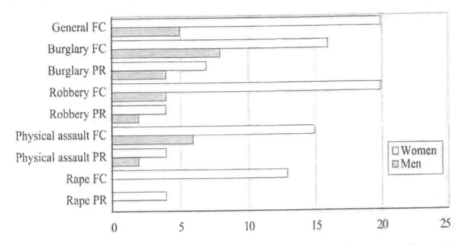

FIGURE II-7-1.3. Fear of crime (FC), personal risk assessment (PR), and gender in large cities (>100,000 residents) in western Germany in 1995 (n = 681). Percentage of *very worried* or *very likely*.

Any empirical study of this assumption would require an analysis of panel data (which would, however, have to be gathered at a very early stage). Cross-sectional analyses of women have shown, on the one hand, that both the estimation of risk as well as the fear of robbery, physical injury, or burglary are no lower (and, in part, even higher) than the fear of rape (see Fig. II-7-1.3). On the other hand, when *age* is also taken into account, the assumption of a shadow effect proves to be justified in *young* women: they express—in line with their actual risk of victimization and their assessment of it—the strongest fear of both sexual and violent offenses (Ferraro, 1995; Warr, 1984), although their fear of sex offenses is greater than that of violent offenses (see Fig. II-7-1.4).

At the latest, it is such observations that make it necessary to reassess the concept of a basic *age and gender distribution* in fear of crime that originated in the 1960s and 1970s and remains widespread even today. The traditional assumption was that older persons and, above all, older women have the strongest fear. However, because fear of crime is inversely proportional to the risk of victimization (young men are the most frequent victims of crime), a *fear of crime paradox* was proposed. This presupposes that the fears of older persons and women were irrational, and that fear of crime might pose a greater problem for the aged than crime itself, as if the aged were, so to speak, prisoners of their own fear (see Boers, 1991:57–84; Ferraro, 1995:67–69). However, the existence of such a paradox depended decisively on which measurement instrument was applied: it was observed continuously with the standard question (general fear of crime) in the early years when this was the only instrument used. When various offense types were discriminated (specific fear of crime), results showed that it was predominantly young women who were afraid—quite realistically—of being raped, whereas relations appeared to be curvilinear for a variety of violent offenses:[10] it is both the younger and the older who are most insecure here. Only older men—from about the age of 60–65 years onward—express, in contrast to their experiences of victimization, a somewhat higher fear of violent offenses than younger and middle-aged men (Fig. II-7-1.4; see

---

[10] These relations were found not only for robbery but also—though somewhat weaker—for fear of physical assault or burglary.

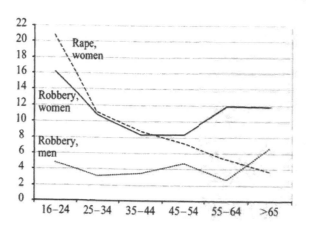

FIGURE II-7-1.4. Fear of robbery and rape, given for gender and age in western Germany, 1995 (n = 2,114). Percentage of *very worried*.

Warr, 1984:687–694; Yin, 1985:55–61; Ferraro, 1995:67–83; Greve et al., 1996:31–66; Greve, 1998; Wetzels et al., 1995:228–233, 261–268; Kury, 1997:247–255; Mirrlees-Black & Allen, 1998:3). Thus, it is no longer really possible to talk of a "fear of crime paradox." Looking at the formulation of the standard question, the stimuli "alone," "outside," and "in the dark" seem to have a stronger impact on the aged than crime itself—naturally, always against the background of their greater vulnerability. These examples also reveal the significance of the type and quality of the assessment instrument in producing an adequate description and interpretation of the phenomenon.

2. Empirical Findings and Theoretical Approaches

The ideas developed to explain fear of crime take three basic perspectives that reflect levels of analysis in the social sciences: the so-called *victimization perspective* on the personal level, the *social problem perspective* on the societal macrolevel, and the *social control perspective* on the societal mesolevel of the neighborhood (see, for a detailed discussion, Boers, 1991:45–182). Up to now, none of these three approaches have enjoyed any decisive empirical confirmation, although the social control perspective has gained the most support. Nonetheless, the explanatory approaches raised in these perspectives continue to play a major role in the public debate, probably because of the implications each has for crime policy.

a. THE VICTIMIZATION PERSPECTIVE. Since the 1960s and 1970s, the victimization perspective has been based, above all, on well-known studies carried out for the government (see Biderman et al., 1967; Hindelang et al., 1978; Kury et al., 1992:223–229). It assumes that fear of crime is triggered predominantly through severe personal experiences of both violent and sexual victimization. Proposals for prevention are predominantly individual measures designed to reduce opportunities for victimization (avoiding risky locations, security systems in the home).

However, not only bivariate but also, in particular, the methodologically decisive multivariate relations on the level of individual comparisons have revealed that even victims of violent offenses are only slightly more distressed—if at all—than nonvictims. Sociodemographic variables, above all, gender, have proved continuously to have the strongest explanatory power (Hindelang et al., 1978:193; Arnold, 1991:118–119; Schwarzenegger, 1991:711; LaGrange et al., 1992:323–326). At most, women who have been sexually molested or assaulted respond somewhat more fearfully to these crimes (Boers, 1995a:22–31).[11] This basic finding can be anticipated already on the basis of distribution theory: the proportion of those with more intensive experiences of being a victim is much smaller than the proportion of those who fear crime. Things are basically no different for the more frequent form of indirect victimization (knowing victims among one's circle of family and friends). Victimizations particularly have an indirect impact on fear of crime through the *personal risk assessment*. First, moderate relations have been ascertained repeatedly between personal risk assessment and victimization experience (Tyler, 1980:21; Maxfield, 1987:20–21; Ferraro, 1995:51, 59), particularly also in the way that victims of a certain offense assert that they are more likely to become a victim of this certain offense (specific risk assessment; Boers, 1991:261, 269–274). Second, interaction effects can be observed between risk assessment and victimization experience (Boers, 1995a:27–30). Therefore, merely discriminating between cognitive and affective attitudes as well as between types of victimization reveals that risks are generally perceived in a way that reflects experience adequately. However, their processing may be accompanied by strong or only weak fear depending on how personal coping skills are judged. In this sense, one can speak of "differential victimization effects," which also implies that there is little sense in interpreting the relation between victimization experiences and attitudes toward crime with categories such as "rational" or "irrational" (Garofalo, 1981:856–857; Boers, 1991:109–111; Ferraro, 1995).

Finally, in contradiction to a frequently held belief, victims also scarcely differ from nonvictims in their demands for punishment, and express an open interest in restitution, even when regarding their own victimization (Sessar, 1992:164–200; Pfeiffer, 1993:74–78; Hough & Roberts, 1998:41–42). Furthermore, in line with the difference between personal and social attitudes toward crime, fearful persons' attitudes are hardly any more punitive (Boers & Sessar, 1991:139–143). In all, it can be seen that the "victim" does not provide a very suitable justification for a policy of harsher punishment.

b. The Social Problem Perspective (Impact of the Media, Transmission of Social Fears). Such inconsistencies have led to frequent attempts to explain fear of crime by positing that the existential and political uncertainties that emerge particularly in periods of social change and crisis are transferred to crime as a sort of meta-symbol for social problems (the *social problem perspective*). Sometimes, the mass media, with their sensation-oriented reporting and notorious distortions of violent crime, are assigned a major influence here (Lamnek, 1990:165; Liska & Baccaglini, 1990:367). Indeed, from a political perspective, law-and-order campaigns or moral panics in the mass media may well provide a welcome distraction from unresolved economic and social problems (Cohen & Young, 1973; Hall et al., 1978; Fishman, 1978; Smaus, 1985:10; Sessar, 1997; see, for a discussion oriented toward the "postmodern" city, Taylor, 1997).

---

[11] Bilsky et al. (1995), Bilsky and Wetzels (1997), e.g., obtained generally stronger victimization effects—particularly when domestic violence was also taken into account. Skogan (1987) also found a stronger impact in a two-wave panel study. However, these stronger correlations were also due to the use of a multiplicative index as the dependent variable that consisted of fear of crime *and* the cognitive attitudes of personal risk assessment or concern about crime (theoretically and methodologically unconvincing in this area: Kury, 1997:240–247).

On the theoretical level, such assumptions can be countered by pointing out that the images of crime constructed in political and mass media contexts (which are, above all, relevant for their self-reproduction) have no direct relevance for the psychological regulation of external risk perceptions (which follow other structural guidelines). This corresponds with a standard outcome of research on the impact of the mass media revealing that they have at best an agenda-setting and reinforcement function, but not a causal one (Schenk, 1987; Merten, 1994).

Furthermore, empirical findings on *crime reporting* have long shown that the impact of the mass media is, at best, differential (Tyler & Cook, 1984). This means that a positive relation between mass media consumption and fear of crime is to be anticipated less for the mostly sensation-oriented reports on nonlocal events but, at best, when the personal, social, or spatial situation of the reader is affected ("local media"). Nonlocal reports on violence have even revealed fear-reducing relations in the sense of cognitive downward comparisons ("things are even worse elsewhere," see Heath, 1984:267–271; Liska & Baccaglini, 1990:366–367; for an experimental study, Winkel & Vrij, 1990:258–262; for an overview, Boers, 1991:164–175). If such a differentiation is not made, effects can cancel each other out and manifest as a zero correlation (Skogan & Maxfield, 1981:176–179). As a methodological result, combined content and effect analyses are necessary. However, instead of "local" reports, one should talk about recipient-oriented ones. For example, in an eastern German study, researchers found stronger effects of television investigation programs whose crime reenactment scenarios seem to capture the everyday situation of the viewers more directly. Regarding the causal direction, this panel study managed to reveal for the first time that television viewing seemed to precede fear of crime and was not a consequence of stronger fear (Reuband, 1998:136–139, 142, 149). Finally, multivariate analyses have confirmed that the generally only weak relations, as in victim experiences, are predominantly indirect and mediated by personal risk judgment (Reuband, 1998:144–148; Baker et al., 1983:328; O'Keefe & Mendelsohn, 1984:21).

Regardless of what form the effect of crime reporting takes on individual personal attitudes, the mass media nonetheless play a significant role in the public discourse on crime. Information that the media treats as a marketable commodity is conceived by politicians, administrations, the police, or the general public as a factual indication of a need for political and administrative action along with corresponding programs. Such programs, in turn, then have a mass media value in the next round of discussions under such headings as "What are our politicians doing to fight the crime wave?" (Scheerer, 1978 called this the "political-journalistic circle of reinforcement"). This is also in line with the observation that mass media reports have a stronger impact on social rather than personal attitudes toward crime (Tyler, 1980:21; Doob & Macdonald, 1979:178–179; Killias, 1989:194, 226).

Regarding the supposed *projection of social fears onto fear of crime*, the initial observation in eastern German society during its transition (in which such processes could be anticipated much more strongly than under "normal" conditions, Sessar, 1997), was that concern over developments in the social, economic, and political spheres was much stronger than the fear of crime related to one's own person and residential area. Moreover, factor analyses also showed that there was generally a clear discrimination between crime problems and other social problems. Thus, respondents who were concerned about issues such as unemployment, asylum seekers, losing their accommodation, or the restitution demands of West German property owners were not necessarily also worried about violence or sex offenses. Admittedly, multivariate analyses confirm an indirect (but no main) effect here as well, which, in this case, is mediated by social disorganization: social concern strengthened the fear of violence or sex offenses to a moderate extent in those who perceived their residential area as problematic (Boers & Kurz, 1997:217–219). Finally, there was no notable relation between fear of crime and a general anxiety syndrome (Boers, 1991:283, 295). Once again, it is the degree of theoretical and methodological differentiation that is crucial.

c. THE SOCIAL CONTROL PERSPECTIVE (DISORGANIZATION OF THE NEIGHBORHOOD). Changes to the social structure of a neighborhood, particularly in times of rapid social transformation, may play a crucial role in reinforcing the perception of being personally at risk of becoming a victim and the growth of personal insecurity. Such processes are the focus of the *social control perspective*. Drawing on Shaw and McKay (1942), who examined the collapse and reorganization of communities in Chicago during the waves of migration in the 1930s, the causes of fear of crime are thought to lie in social disorganization processes within communities and residential districts as well as in the accompanying loss of informal social controls (Lewis & Salem, 1986; see Skogan, 1990; Boers, 1991:113–122; Stangl, 1996). Crime policy has proposed various models of community crime prevention for strengthening the informal structures of control in local communities ranging from community social work to "community policing" (see below). These have become increasingly popular since German reunification. This approach has been joined by forms of a repressive regulating policy since the broken-windows hypothesis of Wilson and Kelling (1982) and the resulting order-maintenance tactics of the New York police (Ortner et al., 1998; see Hopkins Burke, 1998).

Criminological studies assess "social disorganization" from the perspective of the perceptions of local residents. Following these studies, the degree of social disorganization depends on how far residents perceive certain signs of social disorganization (or incivility) in their residential area as a problem (originally, Hunter, 1978; Skogan & Maxfield, 1981:91–98; Hope & Hough, 1988). A discrimination is made between physical and personal signs of social disorganization. Both play quite a significant role in British, German, and American cities. For example, approximately two fifths of the residents of British inner cities (1998), and of West German (1995) and American big cities (1998) reported that dirt and trash, graffiti, or vandalism were a rather major problem, and almost one quarter of residents thought that empty buildings were a similar problem (physical signs). Two fifths also complained about young persons hanging out or being loud, drug users, and drunks; however, at 60 percent, the biggest problem (though only assessed in Germany) was reported to be rowdy automobile drivers (personal signs). In eastern Germany, scores were even higher (although throughout Germany, they were lower in 1995 than in 1994). That the perception of incivilities is just as widespread in German as in American or British inner cities seems to have less to do with the condition of the residential area (which is, on average, better) than with a lower tolerance of problems. In Germany, however, the problem perception did not only address physical or personal incivilities but also the lack of social and cultural facilities (Boers & Kurz, 1997:214; Mirrlees-Black & Allen, 1998:2; Smith et al., 1999:21–23).

The signs of social disorganization thus move through a gray zone of behaviors ranging from nondeviance to slight deviance. What they have in common is the ability to symbolize a general state of normlessness, a loss of social organization and control in the daily life of a neighborhood. The perception of personal incivilities could, moreover, also be interpreted as a subjective potential for the social exclusion of such population groups. Combined with analyses of attitudes toward crime, signs of social disorganization may contribute to clarifying whether fear of crime and personal risk assessment judgment refer almost exclusively to crime phenomena or whether they also relate to phenomena that are perceived as a structural, social, and cultural change of one's neighborhood.

Multivariate analyses have shown that fear of crime and, above all, personal risk assessment correlate most strongly with the perception of incivility. This permits the conclusion that the social control perspective possesses more explanatory power than the other two perspectives (Boers & Kurz, 1997:211–218; Skogan & Maxfield, 1981:123; see, for a less marked approach, Hough, 1995:28; for risk judgment alone, Ferraro, 1995:62–63). The following analyses of a more comprehensive interactive model nonetheless show that this relationship is not linear or causal.

d. THE INTERACTIVE MODEL. To summarize, it is almost impossible to analyze such a complex phenomenon as the subjective reaction to criminal events in the population by using the traditional explanatory approaches presented above. Their main deficit is a monocausal restriction to only one area of explanation in each case (either the personal microlevel or the social meso- or macrolevel). A more precise understanding can be obtained only with a holistic perspective: That which can be perceived only subjectively as a risk of victimization or as the emotion of fear on the personal level emerges as a result of threatening events as well as their communication on the community level and is shaped by the political-journalistic crime discourse on the societal macrolevel. However, relations between and within these three analytical levels should not be viewed in causal terms. This is because cause-effect models are not very appropriate for the complex, indeed, interactive relations whose total structural and processual context characterizes the phenomenon of fear of crime (see, also, Schwarzenegger, 1992:23; Ferraro, 1995:7–19; for a model based on facet theory, Bilsky, 1996:369; for a model based on a social psychology, Farrall et al., 2000; for fear in women, Gordon & Riger, 1989:119). The interactive model of attitudes toward crime depicted in Fig. II-7-1.5 therefore tries to view the communicational and interactional processes within and between these three levels as system-environment relations in the mental and social systems involved (see, for more detail, Boers & Kurz, 1997:188–196).

The first important feature of this model is the above-mentioned discrimination between personal and social attitudes toward crime. By referring to attitude research in social psychology, *personal attitudes toward crime* can be differentiated further into cognitive (personal risk assessment), emotional (fear of crime), and conative (avoidance behavior) components. However, this differentiation reveals nothing about how such attitudes arise, change, and so forth internally, that is, within mental systems. Ideas from coping theory (Lazarus & Averill, 1972) could be of assistance here. These would relate anxiety or fear to two cognitive appraisal processes: First, the appraisal of a certain situation in the environment as being threatening (primary appraisal); and, second, the appraisal of the personal capabilities of coping with such a threatening situation (secondary appraisal). The outcome of these evaluation processes is either a feeling of fear accompanied by flight or avoidance reactions, a feeling of helplessness accompanied by anxiety, or, finally, an annoyance or concern corresponding with active protective and defensive measures (coping). Hence, one can also view these ideas as a model of the internal regulation of external threats through mental systems.

FEAR OF VIOLENT CRIME

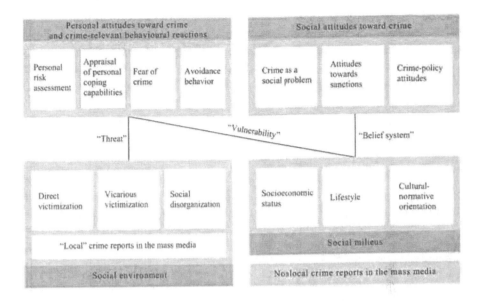

FIGURE II-7-1.5. Interactive model of attitudes toward crime.

Personal risk assessment can be viewed as an adequate operationalization of primary appraisal directed toward external threat situations. Because particularly serious threats are relatively infrequent events, it generally functions anticipatively, in other words, without any reference to a current threat. It is based essentially on earlier personal experiences as well as, in particular, the communicated environmental experiences of others. As a result, it can be anticipated that the communications and interactions on this topic in the closer social environment (becoming a victim, indirect experience of victimization, perceived social disorganization, consumption of recipient-oriented crime reports) relate more strongly to personal risk assessment than to the fear of crime. The term "threat" indicates that this is the decisive information for the emergence of attitudes toward crime that can be obtained from the social environment.

The secondary appraisal of *personal coping capabilities* should not be confounded with the attitudes toward crime, but denotes the internal regulation process.[12] Up to now, this has been operationalized only inadequately. As a rule, researchers try to assess coping capabilities indirectly in terms of personal or social vulnerability through variables such as gender, age, level of education, and social class. However, "vulnerability" has always been conceived as being more than the social or biological characteristics represented by sociodemographic variables. The aim here is to tap part of what is described as "social role" or "lifestyle." It therefore seems meaningful to study this within the framework of the social milieu concept that has become the focus of recent research on social structures. This concept assumes that the social structure of modern societies cannot just be differentiated *vertically* in terms of economic and social status (as in traditional approaches) but also *horizontally* in terms of (internal) cultural-normative orientations and (expressive) lifestyles. Therefore, the *social milieu* should be understood as the specific web of vertical and horizontal factors in social space (Hradil, 1992; see Bourdieu, 1987; Beck, 1986).

---

[12] In Warr (1987:30–32), this is called the "sensitivity to risk" influenced by the severity of offense.

Because different social conditions, lifestyles, and normative orientations distinguish separate social milieus in this way, they correspond in different ways to the two kinds of attitudes toward crime. To pick out two particularly relevant areas, it can be assumed, for example, that personal coping capabilities will be rated lower in social milieus marked by a higher degree of social, psychological, or physical vulnerability, and that this will be accompanied by the expression of a stronger fear of crime and—also in the sense of a feedback effect—a higher estimated personal risk of victimization. Second, it can be assumed that the components of one's belief system (political, religious, philosophical) represented in cultural-normative orientations will be reflected in corresponding social attitudes toward crime (e.g., "restitutive" vs. "punitive"). Up to now, it has been possible to test this model only with different data sets (Boers & Kurz, 1997;2001), none of which contained all the variables. Lifestyle has still not been assessed in any study on fear of crime. Nonetheless, the first studies carried out with multiple correspondence analyses (HOMALS, see Gifi, 1990) indicate the existence of completely different fear milieus in eastern and western Germany. It has also been found that taking social milieus into account breaks down the previous importance of gender and age, making them appear less significant.

Whereas, for example, in eastern Germany, it was older women with conventional value orientations, lower to intermediate levels of education and income, as well as good social contacts who were most strongly afraid of violent crime ("disappointed reunification optimists"), in western Germany, it tended to be socially and economically marginalized, younger, and predominantly female adults with hardly any social contacts and difficulties in developing any normative orientation at all. As anticipated, the strongest fear was accompanied by the highest risk assessment and the most frequent avoidance behavior. The "fearless" group, in contrast, consisted of adventure-, consumer-, and peer group-oriented ("hedonistic") young women and men, though in western Germany, also of middle-aged men from the highly educated bourgeoisie with liberal-conservative attitudes (that has yet to form as such in eastern Germany). Moreover, it is worth noting the milieu contexts in which experiences and perceptions of the environment were significant: whereas direct victimization experiences corresponded only with an above-average perception of disorganized neighborhoods and the highest fear categories mediated by the risk judgment, the highest levels of social disorganization were also reported by the fearless "hedonists" and the "bourgeois milieu." This can no longer be interpreted with linear models. However, it becomes conceivable against the background of the (admittedly different) coping resources of these milieus: the social disorganization of the neighborhood may be part of one person's lifestyle and perceptions, whereas, for other persons, it may be a conspicuous sign that is registered pointedly because of a bourgeois distinction, though obviously not perceived as a personal threat but rather as an *annoyance* in one's social environment.[13]

One indication from the findings of such milieu analyses is the importance of a differentiated approach to integrating the immediate social construction context. It is also absolutely essential to pay more attention to the local life context, as has been carried out already in some qualitative socio-spatial studies producing basically similar results (Walklate, 1998; Karazman-Morawetz and Hanak in Hammerschick et al., 1996; see, also, Legnaro, 1998).[14]

---

[13] See, for further analyses with the hypothetical assessment of coping capabilities, Boers & Kurz, 2001; within a concept of vulnerability, Killias & Clerici, 2000.

[14] Recent qualitative studies on the age or gender relation also appear to be promising (Tulloch, 2000; Holst, 2001)

III. FEAR OF CRIME AND COMMUNITY PREVENTION

Whether fear of crime can be reduced in any notable way through crime prevention measures has to be judged rather reservedly at the present time. The "retardation effect" sketched above, which characterizes trends in fear of crime in the new German states, already points to the importance of self-regulative processes (which is even larger particularly in times of social change). The decreasing trends in the 1990s may well also relate to this. Following previous findings on the evaluation of community crime prevention or community policing programs in the United States and Great Britain, these decreases could hardly be achieved with such programs. Although, as a rule, these programs managed to improve relations between the police or neighborhood organizations and citizens, they finally achieved hardly any change in fear rates or crime rates. Whereas the fear of crime dropped slightly in several of the quasi-experimentally studied neighborhoods after the programs were implemented (but not in relation to the influential repressive police order-maintenance strategies advocated by Wilson & Kelling, 1982:19), in others, it even increased. A certain "class bias" in positive effects should also be noted: Some projects were accepted positively particularly in middle-class districts, which generally do not have above-average crime or problem loads. Acceptance was particularly high when these bordered directly on to "problem" districts, and there was a fear of negative consequences for the social structure and property values in their own residential area (Rosenbaum, 1988, 1994; Hope & Shaw, 1988; Skogan, 1990; Bennett, 1991; Boers, 1991, 1995b:97–138; Becker et al., 1996; Skogan & Hartnett, 1997:207–209).[15]

For such reasons, there is a need for skepticism toward some trends in current crime policy, regarding not only the cost-utility effects on state resources of increasing police presence on the streets but also the constitutional and social imponderables of *de facto* or *de juro* extension of police controls as part of a "fear-reducing" community work (see Frehsee, 1998). Naturally, there can be no objections to community policing when carried out within the framework of a community social prevention whose problem analyses, counseling, and practical activities are performed by all those involved in the "social factory" of a community (and also always affected by it). Here, the police have an important problem mediation function that simultaneously "keeps their area of competence within predictable and controllable bounds" (Kerner, 1994:174, translated).

IV. DESIDERATA

In the debates on crime policy in European nations, comparisons with trends in fear of crime in other European nations and the United States in particular continue to play an important role. For such comparisons to be methodologically sound, future studies should use standardized *instruments to assess* specific fear of crime. In addition, it would also be generally desirable to use continuous qualitative examinations to improve the reliability and validity of fear items, particularly in terms of their reference to offenses, times of day, and locations.

---

[15] The widespread video surveillance of public places (CCTV) in Great Britain has also failed to show a convincing impact on crime or fear of crime rates up to now. Most British state budget resources for crime prevention are now spent on CCTV (see, for further evidence, Coleman & Norris, 2000:146–175; Ditton, 2000).

In order to finally free ourselves from the sweeping causal explanations of the 1970s and 1980s based solely on demographic standard features and experiences of victimization, disorder, or the mass media, analyses of fear of crime must draw on the *horizontally structured construction context* of their respondents, using milieu and socio-spatial data. This is the only way in which context-appropriate and therefore potentially successful proposals for prevention will become possible. Initial "qualitative analyses of quantitative data" as well as qualitative comparative studies of urban districts appear promising in this light. Nonetheless, it will be necessary to ensure that the generally promising recourse to risk, modernization, and system theories, which merits further development, empirically deepens the level of terminological and conceptional differentiation achieved so far and does not lose its way in vague observations and statements on "insecurity generalizations in the risk society," the dependence on "local construction contexts," and the like.

Translated by Jonathan Harrow

REFERENCES

Arnold, Harald. (1991). Fear of Crime and Its Relationship to Directly and Indirectly Experienced Victimization. In Klaus Sessar & Hans-Jürgen Kerner (Eds.), *Developments in Crime and Crime Control Research* (pp. 87–125). New York: Springer.

Arzt, Gunther. (1976). *Der Ruf nach Recht und Ordnung*. Tübingen: Mohr.

Baker, Mary Holland, Barbara C. Nienstedt, Ronald S. Everett, & Richard McCleary. (1983). The Impact of a Crime Wave. *Law and Society Review, 17*, 319–335.

Beck, Ulrich. (1986). *Risikogesellschaft*. Frankfurt a. M.: Suhrkamp.

Becker, Monika, Klaus Boers, & Peter Kurz. (1996). Kriminalitätsfurcht und Prävention im sozialen Nahbereich. In Edwin Kube, Hans Schneider & Jürgen Stock (Eds.), *Kommunale Kriminalprävention in Theorie und Praxis* (pp. 79–110). Lübeck: Schmidt-Römhild.

Bennett, Trevor. (1991). The Effectiveness of a Police-initiated Fear-reducing Strategy. *British Journal of Criminology, 31*(1), 1–14.

Biderman, Albert D., Luise A. Johnson, Jenny McIntyre, & Adrianne W. Weir. (1967). *Report on a Pilot Study in the District of Columbia*. Washington: Government Printing Office.

Bilsky, Wolfgang. (1996). Die Bedeutung von Furcht vor Kriminalität in Ost und West. *Monatsschrift für Kriminologie und Strafrechtsreform, 79*(5), 357–371.

Bilsky, Wolfgang, Peter Wetzels, Eberhard Mecklenburg, & Christian Pfeiffer. (1995). Subjektive Wahrnehmung von Kriminalität und Opfererfahrung. In Günther Kaiser & Jörg-Martin Jehle (Eds.), *Kriminologische Opferforschung. Band II* (pp. 73–106). Heidelberg: Kriminalistik-Verlag.

Bilsky, Wolfgang, & Peter Wetzels. (1997). On the Relationship between Criminal Victimization and Fear of Crime. *Psychology, Crime and Law, 3*, 309–318.

Boers, Klaus. (1991). *Kriminalitätsfurcht*. Pfaffenweiler: Centaurus.

Boers, Klaus. (1994). Crime, Fear of Crime and Social Transition in Germany. *European Journal on Criminal Policy and Research, 2*(4), 124–136.

Boers, Klaus. (1995a). Kriminalitätseinstellungen und Opfererfahrungen. In Günther Kaiser & Jörg-Martin Jehle (Eds.), *Kriminologische Opferforschung. Teilband 2: Verbrechensfurcht und Opferwerdung* (pp. 3–36). Heidelberg: Kriminalistik-Verlag.

Boers, Klaus. (1995b). Ravensburg ist nicht Washington. *Neue Kriminalpolitik, 7*(1), 16–21.

Boers, Klaus. (1996). Sozialer Umbruch und Kriminalität in Deutschland. *Monatsschrift für Kriminologie, 79*(5), 314–337.

Boers, Klaus. (2001). Kriminalprävention und Kriminalpolitik mit der Kriminalitätsfurcht. *Neue Kriminalpolitik, 13*(2), 10–15.

Boers, Klaus, Günther Gutsche, & Klaus Sessar. (Eds.) (1997). *Sozialer Umbruch und Kriminalität in Deutschland*. Opladen: Westdeutscher Verlag.

Boers, Klaus, & Peter Kurz. (1997). Kriminalitätseinstellungen, soziale Milieus und sozialer Umbruch. In Klaus Boers, Günther Gutsche & Klaus Sessar (Eds.), *Sozialer Umbruch und Kriminalität in Deutschland* (pp. 187–253). Opladen: Westdeutscher Verlag.

Boers, Klaus, & Peter Kurz. (2001). Kriminalitätsfurcht ohne Ende? In Günter Albrecht & Otto Backes (Eds.), *Gewaltkriminalität zwischen Mythos und Realität* (pp. 123–144). Frankfurt a. M.: Suhrkamp.

Boers, Klaus, & Klaus Sessar. (1991). Do People Really Want Punishment? In Klaus Sessar & Hans-Jürgen Kerner (Eds.), *Developments in Crime and Crime Control Research* (pp. 126–149). New York, Berlin: Springer.

Bourdieu, Pierre. (1987). *Die feinen Unterschiede.* Frankfurt a. M.: Suhrkamp.

Bureau of Justice Statistics. (1998). *Displaying Violent Crime Trends Using Estimates from the National Crime Victimization Survey.* Washington: U.S. Department of Justice.

Bureau of Justice Statistics (2001). *Sourcebook of Criminal Justice Statistics 2000.* Washington: U.S. Department of Justice.

Cohen, Stanley, & Jock Young. (Eds.) (1973). *The Manufacture of News.* London: Constable.

Coleman, Clive, & Clive Norris. (2000). *Introducing Criminology.* Devon: Willian.

Dijk, van Jan J., & Leo G. Toornvliet. (1996). *Ein Eurobarometer für öffentliche Sicherheit.* Leiden: Institut für Kriminologie.

Ditton, Jason. (2000). Crime and the City. Public Attitudes towards Open-Street CCTV in Glasgow. *British Journal of Criminology, 40*(4), 692–709.

Ditton, Jason, & Stephen Farrall. (Eds.) (2000). *The Fear of Crime.* Aldershot: Dartmouth.

Dölling, Dieter, & Thomas Feltes. (1993). *Community Policing.* Holzkirchen: Felix.

Doob, Anthony N., & Glenn E. Macdonald. (1979). Television Viewing and Fear of Victimization. *Journal of Personality and Social Psychology, 37*(2), 170–179.

Farrall, Stephen, Jon Bannister, Jason Ditton, & Elizabeth Gilchrist. (1997). Questioning the Measurement of the 'Fear of Crime'. *British Journal of Criminology, 37*(4), 658–679.

Farrall, Stephen, Jon Bannister, Jason Ditton, & Elizabeth Gilchrist. (2000). Social Psychology and the Fear of Crime. *British Journal of Criminology, 40*(4), 399–413.

Fattah, Ezzat A. (1993). Research on Fear of Crime. In Wolfgang Bilsky, Christian Pfeiffer, & Peter Wetzels (Eds.), *Fear of Crime and Criminal Victimisation* (pp. 45–70). Stuttgart: Enke.

Ferraro, Kenneth F. (1995). *Fear of Crime.* New York: SUNY Press.

Ferraro, Kenneth F., & Randy LaGrange. (1987). The Measurement of Fear of Crime. *Sociological Inquiry, 57*(1), 70–101.

Fishman, Mark. (1978). Crime Waves as Ideology. *Social Problems, 25,* 531–543.

Frehsee, Detlev. (1998). Politische Funktionen Kommunaler Kriminalprävention. In Hans-Jörg Albrecht, Frieder Dünkel, Hans-Jürgen Kerner, Josef Kürzinger, Heinz Schöch, Klaus Sessar & Bernhard Villmow, *Internationale Perspektiven in Kriminologie und Strafrecht. Festschrift für Günther Kaiser. 1. Halbband* (pp. 739–763). Berlin: Duncker und Humblot.

Garofalo, James. (1981). The Fear of Crime: Causes and Consequences. *Journal of Criminal Law and Criminology, 72*(2), 839–857.

Gifi, Albert. (1990). *Nonlinear Multivariate Analysis.* Chichester: Wiley.

Goodey, Jo. (1997). Boys Don't Cry. Masculinities, Fear of Crime and Fearlessness. *British Journal of Criminology, 37*(3), 401–418.

Gordon, Margaret T., & Stephanie Riger. (1989). *The Female Fear.* New York: The Free Press.

Greve, Werner. (1998). Fear of Crime among the Elderly. *International Review of Victimology, 5,* 277–309.

Greve, Werner, Daniela Hosser, & Peter Wetzels. (1996). *Bedrohung durch Kriminalität im Alter.* Baden-Baden: Nomos.

Hale, Chris. (1996). Fear of Crime: A Review of the Literature. *International Review of Victimology, 4,* 79–150.

Hall, Stuart, Chas Critcher, Tony Jefferson, John Clarke, & Brian Roberts. (1978). *Policing the Crisis.* London: Macmillan Press.

Hammerschick, Walter, Inge Karazman-Morawetz, & Wolfgang Stangl. (Eds.) (1996). *Die sichere Stadt.* Baden-Baden: Nomos.

Heath, Linda. (1984). Impact of Newspaper Crime Reports on Fear of Crime. *Journal of Personality and Social Psychology, 47*(2), 263–276.

Hindelang, Michael J., Michael R. Gottfredson, & James Garofalo. (1978). *Victims of Personal Crime.* Cambridge: Ballinger.

Holst, Bettina. (2001). Kriminalitätsfurcht von Frauen. Normal oder hysterisch? *Neue Kriminalpolitik, 13*(1), 10–15.

Hope, Tim, & Michael Hough. (1988). Area, Crime and Incivilities. In Tim Hope & Michael Shaw (Eds.), *Communities and Crime Reduction* (pp. 30–47). London: Home Office.

Hope, Tim, & Michael Shaw. (1988). Community Approaches to Reducing Crime. In Tim Hope & Michael Shaw (Eds.), *Communities and Crime Reduction* (pp. 1–28). London: Home Office.

Hopkins Burke, Roger. (Ed.) (1998). *Zero Tolerance Policing*. Leicester: Perpetuity Press.

Hough, Michael. (1995). *Anxiety about Crime*. London: Home Office.

Hough, Michael, & Julian Roberts. (1998). *Attitudes to Punishment*. London: Home Office.

Hradil, Stefan. (1992). Alte Begriffe und neue Strukturen. In Stefan Hradil (Ed.), *Zwischen Bewußtsein und Sein* (pp. 15–56). Opladen: Leske & Budrich.

Hunter, Albert. (1978). *Symbols of Incivility*. Evanston: Northwestern University.

Jones, Trevor, Brian MacLean, & Jock Young. (1986). *The Islington Survey*. Aldershot: Gower.

Kerner, Hans-Jürgen. (1994). Kriminalprävention. *Kriminalistik, 48*(3), 171–178.

Killias, Martin. (1989). *Les Suisse face au crime*. Grüsch: Rüegger.

Killias, Martin. (1990). Vulnerability. *Violence and Victims, 5*(2), 97–108.

Killias, Martin, & Christian Clerici. (2000). Different Measures of Vulnerability in Their Relation to Different Dimensions of Fear of Crime. *British Journal of Criminology, 40*(4), 437–450.

Kury, Helmut. (1997). Kriminalitätsbelastung, Sicherheitsgefühl der Bürger und Kommunale Kriminalprävention. In Helmut Kury (Ed.), *Konzepte Kommunaler Kriminalprävention* (pp. 218–295). Freiburg: iuscrim.

Kury, Helmut, Uwe Dörmann, Harald Richter, & Michael Würger. (1992). *Opfererfahrungen und Meinungen zur inneren Sicherheit in Deutschland*. Wiesbaden: Bundeskriminalamt.

LaGrange, Randy L., Kenneth F. Ferraro, & Michael Supancic. (1992). Perceived Risk and Fear of Crime. *Journal of Research in Crime and Delinquency, 29*(3), 311–334.

Lamnek, Siegfried. (1990). Kriminalitätsberichterstattung in den Massenmedien als Problem. *Monatsschrift für Kriminologie und Strafrechtsreform, 73*(3), 163–176.

Lazarus, Richard S., & James R. Averill. (1972). Emotions and Cognition. In Charles D. Spielberger (Ed.), *Anxiety, Vol. 2* (pp. 242–283). New York, London: Academic Press.

Lee, Murray. (1999). The Fear of Crime and Self-governance. *The Australian and New Zealand Journal of Criminology, 32*(3), 227–246.

Legnaro, Aldo. (1998). Die Stadt, der Müll und das Fremde. *Kriminologisches Journal, 30*(4), 262–283.

Lewis, Dan A., & Greta Salem. (1986). *Fear of Crime: Incivility and the Production of a Social Problem*. New Brunswick, Oxford: Transaction.

Liska, Allen E., & William Baccaglini. (1990). Feeling Safe by Comparison: Crime in the Newspapers. *Social Problems, 37*(3), 360–374.

Louis-Guérin, Christiane. (1984). Les réactions sociales au crime: peur et punitivité. *Revue Française de Sociologie, 25*, 623–635.

Maxfield, Michael, G. (1984). *Fear of Crime in England and Wales*. London: Home Office.

Maxfield, Michael, G. (1987). *Explaining Fear of Crime*. London: Home Office.

Merten, Klaus. (1994). Wirkungen von Kommunikation. In Klaus Merten, Siegfried J. Schmidt & Siegfried Weischenberg (Eds.), *Die Wirklichkeit der Medien* (pp. 291–328). Opladen: Westdeutscher Verlag.

Mirrlees-Black, Catriona, & Jonathan Allen. (1998). *Concern about Crime*. London: Home Office.

O'Keefe, Garrett J., & Harold Mendelsohn. (1984). *Taking a Bite Out of Crime*. Washington, DC: Government Printing Office.

Ortner, Helmut, Arno Pilgram, & Heinz Steinert. (1998). *Die Null-Lösung. New Yorker 'Zero-Tolerance'-Politik— das Ende der urbanen Toleranz?* Baden-Baden: Nomos.

Pfeiffer, Christian. (1993). Opferperspektiven. In Peter-Alexis Albrecht, Alexander P. F. Ehlers, Franziska Lamott, Christian Pfeiffer, Hans-Dieter Schwind & Michael Walter (Eds.), *Festschrift für Horst Schüler-Springorum* (pp. 53–79). Köln, Berlin, Bonn, München: Heymanns.

President's Commission on Law Enforcement and Administration of Justice. (1967). *The Challenge of Crime in a Free Society*. Washington, DC: Government Printing Office.

Reuband, Karl-Heinz. (1998). Kriminalität in den Medien. *Soziale Probleme, 9*(1/2), 125–153.

Reuband, Karl-Heinz. (1999). Kriminalitätsfurcht. *Neue Kriminalpolitik, 11*(2), 15–20.

Rosenbaum, Dennis P. (1988). Community Crime Prevention. *Justice Quarterly, 5*, 323–395.

Rosenbaum, Dennis P. (1994). *The Challenge of Community Policing*. Thousand Oaks: Sage.

Scheerer, Sebastian. (1978). Der politisch-publizistische Verstärkerkreislauf. *Kriminologisches Journal, 10*, 223–227.

Schenk, Michael. (1987). *Medienwirkungsforschung*. Tübingen: Mohr.

Schwarzenegger, Christian. (1991). Christian Public Attitudes to Crime. In Günther Kaiser, Helmut Kury & Hans-Jörg Albrecht, *Victims and Criminal Justice* (pp. 681–730). Freiburg: Max-Planck-Institut.

Schwarzenegger, Christian. (1992). *Die Einstellungen der Bevölkerung zur Kriminalität und Verbrechenskontrolle.* Freiburg: Max-Planck-Institut.

Sessar, Klaus. (1992). *Wiedergutmachen oder Strafen?* Pfaffenweiler: Centaurus.

Sessar, Klaus. (1997). Die Angst des Bürgers vor Verbrechen. In Helmut Janssen & Friedhelm Peters (Eds.), *Kriminologie für soziale Arbeit* (pp. 118–138). Münster: Votum.

Shaw, Clifford R., & Henry D. McKay. (1942). *Juvenile Delinquency and Urban Areas.* Chicago: University of Chicago Press.

Silverman, Eli B. (1999). *NYPD Battles Crime.* Boston: Northeastern University Press.

Skogan, Wesley G. (1987). The Impact of Victimization on Fear. *Crime and Delinquency, 33*(1), 135–154.

Skogan, Wesley G. (1990). *Disorder and Decline.* New York: Free Press.

Skogan, Wesley G., & Susan M. Hartnett. (1997). *Community Policing Chicago Style.* New York, Oxford: Oxford University Press.

Skogan, Wesley G., & Michael G. Maxfield. (1981). *Coping with Crime.* Beverly Hills, London: Sage.

Smaus, Gerlinda. (1985). *Das Strafrecht und die Kriminalität in der Alltagssprache der deutschen Bevölkerung.* Opladen: Westdeutscher Verlag.

Smith, Steven K., Greg W. Steadman, Todd D. Minton, & Med Townsend. (1999). *Criminal Victimization and Perceptions of Community Safety in 12 Cities 1998.* Washington, DC: Bureau of Justice Statistics.

Sparks, Richard. (1992). Reason and Unreason in 'Left Realism'. In Roger Matthews & Jock Young (Eds.), *Issues in Realist Criminology* (pp. 119–135). London, Newbury Park, New Delhi: Sage.

Stangl, Wolfgang. (1996). Wien—Sichere Stadt. *Kriminologisches Journal, 28*(1), 48–68.

Stanko, Elisabeth. (1997). Safety Talk: Conceptualising Women's Risk Assessment as a 'Technology of the Soul'. *Theoretical Criminology, 1*(4), 479–499.

Taylor, Ian. (1997). Crime, Anxiety, and Locality. *Theoretical Criminology, 1*(1), 53–76.

Tulloch, Marian. (2000). The Meaning of Age Differences in the Fear of Crime. *British Journal of Criminology, 40*(4), 451–467.

Tyler, Tom R. (1980). Impact of Directly and Indirectly Experienced Events. *Journal of Personality and Social Psychology, 39*(1), 13–28.

Tyler, Tom R., & Fay L. Cook. (1984). The Mass Media and Judgments of Risk. *Journal of Personality and Social Psychology, 47*(4), 693–708.

Walklate, Sandra. (1998). Excavating the Fear of Crime: Fear, Anxiety or Trust? *Theoretical Criminology, 2*(4), 403–418.

Warr, Mark. (1984). Fear of Victimization: Why Are Women and the Elderly More Afraid? *Social Science Quarterly, 65,* 681–702.

Warr, Mark. (1985). Fear of Rape among Urban Women. *Social Problems, 65,* 238–250.

Warr, Mark. (1987). Fear of Victimization and Sensitivity to Risk. *Journal of Quantitative Criminology, 3*(1), 29–46.

Wetzels, Peter, Werner Greve, Eberhard Mecklenburg, Wolfgang Bilsky, & Christian Pfeiffer. (Eds.) (1995). *Kriminalität im Leben älterer Menschen.* Stuttgart: Kohlhammer.

Wilson, James Q., & George L. Kelling. (1982). Broken Windows. *Atlantic Monthly, 3,* 29–38.

Winkel, Frans Willem, & Aldert Vrij. (1990). Fear of Crime and Mass Media Crime Reports. *International Review of Victimology, 1,* 251–265.

Yin, Peter. (1985). *Victimization and the Aged.* Springfield: C.C. Thomas.

CHAPTER II-7.2

Public Opinion and Violence

HANS MATHIAS KEPPLINGER

I. INTRODUCTION: ON THE CONCEPT OF PUBLIC OPINION

"Public opinion" is usually equated with results from representative surveys (Childs, 1965). This also applies to perceptions of the frequency of violence, anxieties about acts of violence, and opinions about their prevention. There are several arguments, however, that speak against equating findings from representative surveys with public opinion. First, respondents do not express their views publicly, but in a dialogue conducted face-to-face or by telephone. Whether they would repeat these views in public, for instance in an open-plan office or at a school party, is a moot question. Second, the opinion of the majority of the population has to be distinguished from the publicly predominant public opinion (Noelle-Neumann, 1989). One indicator of this is the population's perception of the majority opinion. Another is the presence of opinions in day-to-day mass media reporting. For these reasons, the results of representative surveys constitute aggregated private opinions whose public relevance is not known. It thus normally remains unclear whether respondents would, for example, admit to their fear of violent crime in public, whether they would publicly demand preventive measures because of their fear, and whether they would be prepared to bring pressure to bear in this way on political decision makers. This applies to the opponents of stricter gun control in the United States, for example, who tend to be more vociferous in public than those in favor (Adams, 1996), an aspect that may have contributed significantly to their political success. In spite of these problems, the concept of "public opinion" will be used here in the way outlined and criticized above, the sole reason being that nearly all the relevant data consist of findings from public opinion polls which reflect majority and minority opinions.

In the interpretation of surveys on the subject of violence, several aspects need to be considered. First, individual surveys provide only "snapshots" of perceptions and opinions of violence. Both the latter are often influenced, however, by current events or their media coverage. Second, questions relating to specific issues, such as the fear of being robbed, for example, do not produce any reliable findings on general dispositions (fear of crime). By analogy, this is also true of attitudes. Third, general questions asked about opinions on terrorist attacks, for example, tend to produce results that are different from results obtained by specific questions about opinions on a concrete terrorist attack. Fourth, the majority of the population may differ in their assessment of events from a minority living in the social environment of violent criminals. They are few, but important individuals. Fifth, perceptions and opinions of the population are often inconsistent. The likelihood of this increases with respondents' decreasing educational levels. For this reason, one can expect contradictory replies from respondents with low educational standards. Sixth, small differences in the way questions are formulated may lead to substantial differences in results. In turn, these results reveal that opinions are not deep-rooted and firmly established, but depend on numerous influencing factors (Noelle-Neumann & Petersen, 1996; Flanagan, 1996).

II. THEORETICAL APPROACHES AND EMPIRICAL RESULTS

1. Empirical Results on the Concept of Violence

The term "violence" can be defined or measured. In the first case, theoretical considerations determine what the term will signify. In the second case, an empirical investigation is undertaken to establish how it is understood by the population or a part thereof. The basis of the present paper is the population's perception of the term. Consequently, the focus will be on what the population considers to be violence. One answer to this is provided by a comparative survey conducted in twelve European countries (Kaase & Neidhardt, 1990:43). In these countries violence was rated as similarly negative along an "evaluation dimension". It was considered "unnecessary," "bad," "ugly," and "dangerous." By contrast, judgments made along the "power dimension" were less unambiguous. Violence was considered neither "strong" nor "weak," "exciting" or "boring," but was thought to be "ineffective" by most. Some notable national differences were observed, though. In southern countries (France, Italy, Spain, Greece), violence was associated with power more often than in northern countries (Great Britain, The Netherlands, Denmark). At the same time, it was considered ineffective more often in southern than in northern countries. This paradoxical finding could be attributed to culture-specific aspects of Mediterranean countries (machismo). In these countries violence may be viewed as a successful way of social positioning rather than an effective means of instrumental action.

The associations discussed above are applicable to all kinds of violence, albeit not to "left" and "right" positions. Presumably, they refer implicitly to politically motivated violence. They could thus be interpreted as the "ideological dimension" of violence. In nearly all countries, violence was associated with the political right rather than the political left. Again, obvious differences were observed between southern and northern countries. Especially in Greece, Spain, France, and Italy, violence was associated with the right. In Ireland it was associated mostly with the left. These particularities could be related to those countries' recent political past. Taken together, the findings suggest that perceptions of the power and political source of violence, in particular, stem from different cultural and political backgrounds. The (negative) evaluation of violence in Europe, on the other hand, seems to be a largely universal cultural phenomenon.

The abstract notion of violence needs to be distinguished from the concrete judgment of an act as violent. In this respect, there are clear differences between men and women as well as between young and old people (Früh, 1995), as experiments with the presentation of real and fictional violence on television have shown. Women are quicker than men to view specific acts as violent, as are older persons compared to younger ones. These differences relate to the verbal and visual presentation of violence, of real and fictional violence, and of limited and great brutality. The educational background of viewers had no influence on the perception of activities shown as violent or nonviolent. This seems to indicate that women and old people will, more quickly than men and young people, consider particular acts as violent—regardless of other factors. Two explanations are conceivable: The groups concerned may have different concepts of violence, classifying as different those acts they perceive as similar. Or, though espousing the same concepts of violence, they may perceive the indicators of violence with greater or lesser sensitivity. Which of the two explanations is correct has to remain open at this point. The stable differences between young and old or men and women suggest that in the analysis of public opinion on the question of violence, men and women should be considered separately. But this very rarely happens. In contrast to sociodemographic factors, individual dispositions such as anxiety (trait anxiety) or aggressiveness (trait aggression) have no independent influence on the perception of violence; but there are individual differences in the degree of emotional response to violence. Respondents experience varying levels of excitement, aggressiveness, fear, and pity (Sander, 1997).

There is a close connection between the assessment of media contents as violent and the fear of various types of crime (cf. below). Thus, individuals who think that media coverage of violent crime is too frequent are more afraid of housebreaking than individuals who think that the coverage of violence is insufficient (Haghighi & Sorensen, 1996). It is unclear whether fear is a cause of judgments about the media or whether the media themselves are a cause of fear. The findings of studies in this field should therefore be distinguished from analyses of media effects. Such analyses should take into account media contents and media reception as potential causes. The perception of media contents is only one, albeit an important intervening variable.

2. Empirical Findings on the Specifics of Politically and Nonpolitically Motivated Violence

Nonpolitically motivated violence does not challenge the validity of social norms: generally, criminals do not want to change accepted norms; for their own individual reasons, they simply ignore them. By contrast, politically motivated violence is aimed at changing social norms: violent demonstrators, terrorists, and guerilla fighters usually want to change accepted norms. They attack them for supraindividual motives. Both types of violence may become the subject of political conflicts—for example, over the lawfulness of the use of force by the police against criminals, or over the legitimacy of violence used by terrorists against the police. Neither political conflicts over the lawfulness of the use of force by the police, nor the behavior of the police themselves actually challenge the validity of social norms. Both are aimed at upholding valid norms. Violence as a *means* in a political conflict must therefore be distinguished from violence as a *subject* of political conflict.

The violence of criminals and the use of force on the part of the police against criminals are not normally part of a conflict over the validity of social norms. An overwhelming majority of people can be said generally to approve of existing norms and their defense. Unlawful violence is always perceived by that majority as illegitimate violence, lawful violence nearly always as legitimate violence. The majority tends to identify with the police more than it does with criminals, and it approves of the use of force by the police rather than of the violence of criminals. Where this is no longer the case, there is a greater likelihood that nonpolitically motivated violence will turn into politically motivated violence. In 1989 in Western Europe, an overwhelming majority of the population rejected illegal, politically motivated violence on principle (Kaase & Neidhardt, 1990; Schulz, 1997). The differences between countries were relatively small; figures varied between 85 percent (France) and 93 percent (Germany, Spain). At the same time, considerable differences were observed in the rejection of the use of coercive measures by the state against politically motivated violence. In northern countries (Germany, Netherlands, Great Britain), the use of force by the state was clearly rejected less often than in southern countries (France, Spain, Italy). In Spain, with an ongoing violent political conflict, the rate of rejection was quite high (31 percent), whereas in the Netherlands, where no such conflict existed, it was quite low (4 percent). This apparent paradox may be explained by the fact that part of the Spanish population rejected illegal violence, while more or less approving of the objectives of violent criminals.

Surveys conducted in the social environment of politically motivated criminals—including their potential reference individuals—produce a different picture than that obtained by representative population surveys. In the United States, at the end of the 1960s, more than half the population living in ghettos did not think taking part in violent racial unrest was "essentially bad." Half of them sympathized with the perpetrators. About 30 percent to 50 percent thought the riots served a purpose (Caplan, 1970). During the same period, 2 percent to 6 percent of the total German population approved of the use of violence directed against material objects, or property, for political motives. In the social environment of violent criminals (well-educated youths under twenty-nine years of age), the percentage was 18 percent to 22 percent, depending on the type of crime (Kepplinger, 1981). Even in nonpolitical subcultures certain ritualized forms of violence are judged in a positive light. They are considered as a means to further the social integration of individuals and to strengthen group identity (Inhetveen, 1997).

3. Media Coverage of Real Violence

The press, broadcasting, and television report on real acts of violence with different degrees of intensity. Data on the type of violent acts covered are provided by an analysis of reports published by three German quality dailies (*Frankfurter Allgemeine Zeitung, Süddeutsche Zeitung, Die Welt*) from 1951 to 1995 (Kepplinger, 2000). Based on a sample of all reports, 5,364 articles on crimes committed in Germany were analyzed. There was a clear emphasis in the reports on crimes of violence, which were the subject of 45 percent of all reports on criminal offenses, although they accounted for only a fraction of the total number of criminal offenses. Within this category, reports on murder cases dominated, accounting for 17 percent of all reports. There was a marked difference between reports on violent crimes and reports on politically motivated crimes (22 percent) and property offenses (21 percent), which appear very rarely (politically motivated offenses) or very frequently (property offenses) in the criminal statistics. Reports on defamations (2 percent) were quite rare, in line with their insignificant role in criminal statistics. The remainder of the reports dealt with a variety of other criminal offenses (10 percent), which were subjected to a differentiating analysis, but can be placed within various categories of offenses, depending on the perspective taken.

In the analysis of long-term changes in crime reporting, two distinct questions should be raised. First, has crime reporting increased or decreased? Second, what is the cause of this development—a change in crime frequency or a change in selection criteria? This requires a comparison of crime frequency and the frequency of media reports. The percentage of undetected crimes—that is, the number of cases remaining unknown—can be neglected here since the media can report only on what is known. This qualification does not apply to the analysis of temporary waves in crime reporting because this kind of massive coverage can raise the public's readiness to report crime, thus reducing the number of undetected crimes. This aspect—and not only the phenomenon of copycat crimes prompted by media reports—may also cause a development in which the frequency of offenses corresponds to the frequency of reports. In these circumstances, the frequency of reports is not only a consequence, but also a cause of the frequency of offenses found (Kepplinger & Habermeier, 1995).

For reasons related to the cost of research, long-term trend analyses are practicable only on the basis of samples of the frequency of offenses and their coverage. This results in a conflict of goals which can only be solved pragmatically. First, to ensure an adequate empirical base for quantitative analyses, criminal offenses have to be relatively frequent. This applies to less serious offenses more than it does to serious ones. Consequently, for the sake of a sound data base, comparisons should refer to less serious crimes. Second, for the same reason, the probability of the media reporting on a criminal offense should be relatively high. This applies to serious offenses rather than less serious ones. As a result, for the sake of a sound data base, comparisons should refer to serious crimes. From 1951–53 to 1993–95, the number of reports on criminal offenses published in the three newspapers mentioned more than doubled. Overall, this reflects the actual increase in criminal offenses—as shown in a differentiated analysis of reports on individual cases (Kepplinger, 2000).

One cause for the substantial increase in reports on criminal offenses in some media in the 1980s in Germany, the United States, and other countries was a change in the media landscape, especially the emergence of private television stations. At the same time, this intensified competition between the public television stations and other media. Probably for this reason, the proportion of television reports on violent acts rose from an average of 21 percent to 26 percent in the period 1988 to 1991. Even allowing for differences in reporting styles, this trend was nevertheless observed in all the stations surveyed up to that time (ARD, ZDF, RTL, SAT.1). In the following three years, the average total share of these reports increased again from 26 percent to 38 percent, although the proportion of coverage of violent acts had not increased in the established television stations. The reason for this increase was that further stations (PRO 7, RTL2, VOX, n-tv) had been established and had entered the statistics, and that their programs contained a high proportion of reports on violent acts (Bruns & Marcinowski, 1997:194–196). Apart from competition, there are other cultural factors affecting the coverage of real violence. News magazines in Germany and Austria, for instance, report on xenophobic offenses much more extensively than comparable media in France and England, in spite of the fact that in France a significantly greater number of people are self-confessed racists, and a far greater number of xenophobically motivated offenses occur in England (Esser, 2000).

The accepted standards of news selection, which tend to change relatively slowly over the years, may be affected for a short time by "key events" ("Schlüsselereignisse", Kepplinger & Habermeier, 1995). Such events are "spectacular occurrences which are widely reported, or spectacular reports on more or less everyday events." Reports on key events arouse the public's interest in a specific type of event, raise the alertness of journalists to such events, and intensify their sense of competition as well as co-orientation. This in turn means that editorial decisions are increasingly influenced by the decisions made by other publications and editors. A result of this multiple feedback is a change in selection criteria and thus a growing probability of reports appearing on a specific type of event. Thus, after a key event, the media report extensively on occurrences they would not otherwise have covered, or would have done so only in passing (focusing). When not enough similar events take place, the media make other events look similar by emphasizing superficial commononalities (assimilation). They also fall back on similar events in the past, presenting them as precursors of current events (re-thematization).

In 1976 in the United States, for example, a wave of reports on violent crimes against old people was prompted by such mutually reinforcing effects, although the actual number of such crimes had not increased according to the criminal statistics (Fishman, 1978). The waves of reports on specific types of crimes mentioned above can probably be explained in a similar way. In these cases, it can be assumed that the occurrence of key events subsequently led to a change in the criteria of news selection rather than in the frequency of the types of events reported. Some special cases have to be considered separately from this general pattern, namely when reporting triggers copycat crimes. Examples of this have been documented with particular regard to politically motivated acts of violence (Weimann & Winn, 1993; Brosius & Esser, 1995). It is true that an increase in reports actually reflects a growing number of similar acts, but this is, at least in part, a result of previous reporting. In all these cases, however, reporting waves tend to fade away after a while because interest in the subject subsides and news selection again adheres to previous long-standing criteria.

4. Perceptions of the Frequency of Violent Acts

From the population's point of view, violence is a risk to which they themselves or others are exposed. In general, people are capable of fairly realistic judgment about the relative frequency of events to which they might fall victim. They think that most deaths are caused by frequent rather than rare causes. The rank order of perceived causes of death thus corresponds largely to the rank order of actual causes of death. Nevertheless, most people make the mistake of a general error of judgment: they underestimate the frequency of frequent causes of death and overestimate the frequency of rare causes of death (Lichtenstein et al., 1978). One reason for this error is that the mass media tend to report on rare rather than frequent causes of death (Combs & Slovic, 1979). These general findings may also apply to perceptions of the frequency of violence, though no specific studies have been done on this aspect. Such studies might look at different types of violence, for example involving or not involving a weapon, and different settings of violence, for example the family and the public sphere.

The relative majority of the population in (West) Germany and the United States believe that crime rates have increased (Kury et al., 1992:269; Flanagan, 1996:10). This belief is largely independent of the gender and age of respondents, but is clearly related to the size of their place of residence. Respondents living in towns with more than 10,000 inhabitants believe much more strongly that the number of crimes has increased than respondents living in towns with less than 10,000 inhabitants. Judgments made by the population about their immediate environment ("Nahbild": microscopic view, based on personal experience) frequently differ from those about the nation as a whole ("Fernbild": media-based or telescopic view). In the United States, during the period 1972 to 1992, an average of merely 48.4 percent of the population thought that the number of crimes in their region had increased, though no clear trend was observed that confirmed this. These judgments remained largely constant, despite some fluctuations. But in the period 1989 to 1993, an average of 86.0 percent was convinced that the number of crimes in the United States had increased (Warr, 1995). These and similar discrepancies are usually the result of media coverage. Presumably, in forming their judgment on the development of criminality, small-town inhabitants tend to be guided by what happens in their immediate environment, whereas city dwellers primarily rely on media reports which give the impression that criminality is increasing, thereby presenting a distorted picture of reality (Potter et al., 1997).

According to the views of most Germans, the following five types of crimes had increased in 1996: child abuse (88 percent), housebreaking (69 percent), rape (67 percent), vandalism (61 percent), and kidnapping (61 percent). Comparatively few of those questioned were of the opinion, though, that the number of bank raids (47 percent), robberies (44 percent), murder (38 percent), and terrorist acts (19 percent) had risen (Noelle-Neumann & Köcher, 1997:763). The widespread belief that child abuse had increased was probably a result of spectacular media reports on particular cases of child abuse in Belgium and Germany. Indeed, a large part of the population was aware of this fact. Thus, in 1997 only a minority (40 percent) was convinced that "child abuse has increased in recent years," while a majority (51 percent) felt that today there was "merely greater coverage of it" (Noelle-Neumann & Köcher, 1997:776). These doubts regarding an actual increase in cases of child abuse, however, which were mostly expressed by men, did not prevent a majority of them from believing that the number of cases had increased. This may be attributable to the fact that the suggestive power of spectacular reports on particular cases may be stronger than any knowledge of statistics, which present a different picture (Gibson & Zillmann, 1994).

5. Fear of Crime

The fear of crime can be operationalized and measured in different ways. One standard of measurement is the rational assessment of the probability of falling victim to a (violent) crime (crime risk). Another is the emotional fear of falling victim to a (violent) crime (crime fear). Different models of questionnaires tend to produce different results, which are therefore not comparable (Haghighi & Sorensen, 1996). One major reason for this is that fear depends not only on the probability of victimization, but also on the individual perception of potential injury. Thus, men from the lower and upper classes who, in a particular situation, are exposed to the same risk of, for example, becoming embroiled in a brawl, may experience a different kind of fear because in the lower classes individually practiced violence is more acceptable as a way of settling conflicts.

The assessment of individual risk and individual fear has to be distinguished from the risk assessment and fear of the population in general. Again, an individual's assessment of his or her own situation (microscopic view) depends primarily on personal experience and observations, while assessments of society (telescopic view) are based on media coverage. Unlike reports on pleasant events, those on disquieting events cause a situation in which the probability of risks of all kinds (being mugged, being struck by lightning, becoming impotent) is generally assessed as being higher. This effect occurs even when there is no similarity between the event reported and the risk to be assessed. The cause of these general effects is the actual atmosphere generated by the media: depending on positive or negative moods, risks are assessed as lower or higher (Johnson & Tversky, 1983). This leads one to conclude that representative risk assessments always reflect the predominant mood in a particular country.

The perceptions of *individual risks* were surveyed in Germany in 1990 (Kury et al., 1992:252–265). Respondents were asked about the probability of falling victim to a violent crime within the coming twelve months. West Germans considered it "highly probable" or "probable" that they "would be verbally abused" (24.0 percent), 12.6 percent thought they would be "mugged or robbed in the street," 11.9 percent thought that their "apartment would be broken into," 5.6 percent thought they would be "beaten up," 4.7 percent of women thought they would be "raped." Respondents who had become the victim of a crime within the previous five years assessed all these risks as markedly higher. But there were considerable differences between victims of crimes who had had direct contact with the perpetrators (contact offenses) and those victims where this had not been the case (noncontact offenses). Victims of contact offenses (robbery, sexual harassment, etc.) considered the risks much higher than did those of noncontact offenses (theft, damage to cars and other items). Regarding the risk of "being verbally abused," differences in assessment were particularly wide (73.6 percent vs. 48.2 percent). This suggests that direct contact with perpetrators increased the fear of public discrimination. Contact and noncontact offenses partly differ in terms of the seriousness of the crime. Whether the differences mentioned can be attributed to contact with the perpetrator or the seriousness of the offense remains a moot point. Further investigation would also have to examine whether victims assess as especially high the risks of those types of offenses that were committed against them.

Individual fear constitutes a complex psychological problem which has several causes and manifests itself in various ways. Causes include persistent dispositions (traits) as well as a momentary excitement or mood. In these circumstances, the formulations of questions to be asked may have a considerable impact on results. In spite of this, there are considerable variations between models of questionnaires used in this field. Thus, answers to the question of how "secure" or "insecure" a person feels, and whether certain places should be avoided after dark (Kury et al., 1992:223–251) are hardly comparable with answers to the question "How afraid are you?" (Warr, 1995). Similarly, answers to these three questions can be assumed to differ from answers to the question "Do you worry frequently ..." (Haghighi & Sorensen, 1996). Nevertheless, there is a stable connection between the fears thus measured and the gender of respondents: women are generally more afraid of (violent) crime than men.

In the United States there is widespread fear of empty apartments being broken into ("your home being burglarized while no one is at home," 45.4 percent). Similarly widespread is the fear of the respondent or a family member of falling victim to a sexual crime ("yourself or someone in your family getting sexually assaulted," 38.4 percent). On the other hand, comparatively few respondents are afraid that they might fall victim to a murder attempt ("getting murdered," 18.6 percent). These and a number of other results cannot be explained by the actual number of the corresponding offenses, nor the risk of their occurring. In the United States the ratio between property offenses and violent crime is about 10:1. If risk alone determined fear, the fear of housebreaking compared to that of falling victim to a murder attempt would need to be felt by ten times the number of people. In actual fact, though, the ratio is 2:1 rather than 10:1. As to sexual crime, the ratio is nearly 1:1 (Haghighi & Sorensen, 1996). Two causes may explain the discrepancy between risks and fears: The first is an overestimation of infrequent risks and an underestimation of frequent ones, as discussed above. The second is subjective experience and the extent of the perceived injury. Thus, the fact that Americans of Spanish-Mexican descent (Hispanics) are twice as afraid of sexual offenses as other respondents (Haghighi & Sorensen, 1996) could be partly explained by cultural factors. It is possible that Roman Catholics consider sexual assault as an especially serious violation of their freedom from moral and bodily harm.

6. Opinions on Sanctions

It is highly probable that the population's opinions about types of sanctions depend, among other things, on their perceptions of the causes of offenses committed and of the objectives of sanctions, which are themselves socioculturally and psychologically conditioned. In case of politically motivated violence (cf. above), the individual's position in a conflict plays an important role. An example of the role of psychological factors are the individually varying perceptions of the causes of a criminal offense (causal attributions). Causes may be seen to be located within the perpetrator or in his or her context for action. In the first case, the perpetrator seems to be the sole cause and is consequently held fully responsible for the offense he or she committed. In the second case, the circumstances at least appear to be a concurrent cause of the offense ("extenuating circumstances"), and the perpetrator will be held only partly responsible. Different versions of attribution theory (Meyer & Schmalt, 1984) make numerous references to conditions in which observers localize the causes of violent crime in the perpetrator or the circumstances. In representative analyses of the population's opinions on sanctions, however, such approaches do not play a significant role. Rather than focusing on the causes of individual opinions, which include the predominant tenor of the media (cf. above), these analyses focus on the distribution of opinions for and against sanctions in the population.

One example of the relevance of causal attributions for attitudes to sanctions is provided by views on capital punishment in the United States. Whites support the death penalty much more than blacks (77 percent vs. 40 percent). Some factors suggest that the different views of whites and blacks are the result of different perceptions of the causes of offenses (personal vs. social) (Longmire, 1996). The perceptions of the causes, though, hardly explain the extremely different development of opinions on capital punishment in the United States and Germany, for example. In the United States, the proportion of those in favor increased from ca. 45 percent to ca. 75 percent from the mid-1960s to the mid-1990s (Longmire, 1996), whereas in Germany, the proportion of those in favor decreased from ca. 50 percent to ca. 35 percent in the same period. Excluding East Germany, the last figure was only 30 percent (Noelle-Neumann and Köcher, 1997:767). Quasi experiments have shown that opinions on capital punishment may be influenced in the short term by relevant information (Longmire, 1996). This suggests that public communication—especially the presumably different nature of media reports on capital punishment—may be a cause of this contrary development.

III. THEORIES OF THE INFLUENCE OF MEDIA COVERAGE ON THE OPINIONS OF THE POPULATION

The relation between the perceptions of the population and mass media presentation can be approached from two angles: that of the population and that of the media. Concerning the population, the relevant question is: what are the causes underlying the population's perceptions of the type and frequency of violence and their opinions about the admissibility and necessity of combating violence? To answer this, several sources have to be distinguished: persistent personality traits and attitudes, personal experiences, conversations with friends and acquaintances, as well as mass media reports. Conversations and reports that discredit or dehumanize individuals, groups or peoples are liable to increase approval of violence and readiness to engage in it even when no violence has been mentioned or shown (Kelmann, 1973). This may be caused by an assertion that a group enjoys advantages it is not entitled to, violates generally accepted moral standards, or is biologically, aesthetically or culturally inferior. An example of this is the stigmatization of Mexicans in the 1940s by the Los Angeles press, which prompted riots against Mexican immigrants (Turner & Surace, 1956/57). Concerning the media, the relevant question is: what are the effects of the presentation of violence on the perceptions and opinions of the population? A distinction has to be made here between types of violence—real violence (e.g., in television news programs) and fictional violence (e.g., in Westerns). Moreover, two types of presentations have to be distinguished—realistic presentations (e.g., in crime films) and unrealistic presentations (e.g., in animated cartoon films). Realistic presentations of real violence have stronger effects than unrealistic presentations of fictional violence (Unold, 1989). Theoretically, though, even unrealistic presentations of fictional violence may influence the perceptions and opinions of the population. By analogy, the above arguments apply to the relation between the presentation and reception of related topics. More or less dramatic reports on murders may thus theoretically influence opinions on capital punishment without actually mentioning this.

1. The complex interrelations between violent content in the mass media and the perceptions of the population have so far been only partially investigated. The most comprehensive approach is the *cultivation thesis* (Gerbner & Gross, 1976; Gerbner et al., 1986). Gerbner and his colleagues start on the assumption that in the United States, television has become the most significant factor in the enculturation process. According to Gerbner, the presentation of reality by television shapes the population's perceptions of reality, with the contents of informational programs and entertainment becoming inseparably intermingled in the population's perceptions. As a result, these perceptions can no longer be attributed to particular reports or genres (news, films, etc). According to Gerbner, the more frequently people watch presentations of crime or crime control on television, the greater their fear of falling victim to a crime, and the more prone they become to overestimate the number of persons engaged in crime control. These hypotheses have been corroborated by Gerbner's own research as well as similar investigations by other authors (Combs & Slovic, 1979; Groebel, 1982). Gerbner's theoretical assumption about the effects of television—his undifferentiating treatment of all forms of presentation of violence—has been criticized (Hawkins & Pingree, 1981), as have his analytical methods—different definitions of control groups in various studies and a neglect of exogenous variables operating "be-

hind" the interrelations he identifies (Hughes, 1980; Hirsch, 1980). But the impact of the presentation of violence on television on perceptions and crime fear has also been corroborated by experiments (Kunczik, 1994:122-134).

2. The *agenda-setting thesis* is based on the assumption that the mass media have little influence on the strength and direction of attitudes, but a considerable influence on perceptions of the urgency of problems (McCombs & Shaw, 1972). In contrast to the cultivation approach, this thesis addresses the presentation and reception of particular themes over certain periods of time. Such themes might refer to the number of violent crimes, for example, or the need for crime control. Theoretically, the influence of media reports manifests itself in the ranking of problems at particular times as well as in the rise and fall in problem awareness over time. In the United States, a wave of press reports on "Crime and Law" in the early 1960s had no impact on the concerns of the population. At the end of the 1960s, however, a close relation was observed (Funkhouser, 1973). In Germany in 1986, the emergence of television reports on "public safety" did nothing to change problem awareness. But there was a delayed effect in that the change in problem awareness on the part of the population was in turn reflected in TV reporting (Kepplinger et al., 1989:141, 149). In 1998, again in Germany, TV reports on ten issues—"criminality" among them—had a significant influence on the importance these issues assumed for society. But reports had no influence on the importance of the issues for the respondents themselves. The media influenced the "telescopic view" ("Fernbild") albeit not the "microscopic view" ("Nahbild") of the population (Kepplinger, 1999). The differences between the telescopic view and the microscopic view in the perceptions of the development of crime frequency (cf. above) can be assumed to have similar causes.

3. The *theory of the spiral of silence* ("Schweigespirale") explains the development of the public debate on highly charged issues. It is based on the assumption that people are afraid of social isolation and therefore carefully take note of opinions expressed on such issues by relying on two sources: conversations with people they know and media reports. These themes probably include opinions about the punishment of rape and murder, for instance. Where people perceive their opinions as minority opinions, they tend to keep silent about them in public, according to the theory of the spiral of silence. This diminishes public visibility of their opinions, while at the same time increasing the pressure generated by the actual or apparent majority opinion. If the media are largely unanimous in reporting opinions that contradict the actual majority opinion of the population, however, a dual climate of opinion is created. As a result, many people mistake the tenor of media reports for the opinion of the majority, initially suppressing their own opinion and eventually adopting the apparent majority opinion (Noelle-Neumann, 1984, 1989). If one starts from the hypothesis—which can probably be empirically verified—that the German media present capital punishment almost unanimously in a negative light, while the media in the United States present a more heterogeneous picture, the different opinions on capital punishment can, at least in part, be explained by the theory of the spiral of silence. This theory may also help to explain the development of opinions on the violent crime committed by minorities and the individual or societal causes of violent acts. Studies on these questions are still outstanding, though.

4. The *theory of instrumental actualization* undertakes to explain the influence of reports on value-laden events on generalizing opinions. The assumption here is that some media report extensively on value-laden events which accentuate their editorial line, and that recipients who are repeatedly exposed to such reports tend to infer from them seemingly cogent conclusions which go beyond the events actually reported (Kepplinger et al., 1991a). One relevant example is the presentation of acts of violence committed in Nicaragua and El Salvador in the 1980s. Newspapers that supported U.S. policies in Central America reported extensively on violent acts that made these policies look justified. Conversely, newspapers taking the opposite view presented the same events with reversed premises (Kepplinger, 1992). Thus, media coverage influenced opinions about U.S. Central American policy, regardless of existing attitudes (Kepplinger et al., 1991b). Similarly, it can be assumed that spectacular reports on murders, for example, may give rise to seemingly cogent demands for more severe sanctions against murderers.

IV. DESIDERATA

Published and public opinion exert a largely neglected influence on the victims of violence and the course of criminal proceedings. Evidence of the influence of public opinion in the widest sense on the course of spectacular criminal proceedings is provided by an in-depth survey of 125 judges, public prosecutors, and defense counsels who have been involved in such proceedings (Gerhardt, 1990). All the defense counsels questioned considered the influence of the media as ranging from "not insignificant" to "substantial," attributing considerable importance to the yellow press, in particular. Several judges and prosecutors made similar statements, not ruling out an influence on the demand for and fixing of the penalty. Nor has much research been done into how victims of violence are presented in everyday media reports. Quantitative analyses of media coverage of violent crimes in Germany have shown that in a great number of reports victims are presented in a way that makes them identifiable. Thus, about 23 percent of crime-related articles in newspapers and periodicals reveal the victim's full name (Ionescu, 1998:67; Kury & Baumann, 1998:197). Nearly a third (29 percent) of reports published in radio and television magazines and other illustrated papers show photographs of the victims (Kury & Baumann, 1998:197). Not much research has been done, either, on the influence of media coverage about violent acts on the victims of violence and their immediate social environment. Evidence of this influence is provided by a survey of 264 victims of violent crimes. More than four fifths (83 percent) reported that their friends were aware of the reports on their case. Half stated that colleagues at work knew the reports. Nearly half (45 percent) of those who were asked about the reports felt uncomfortable about this. This could be a reason why, according to the views of many victims, media reports hampered the victim's coming to terms with what happened (Kunczik & Bleh, 1995:91f). A reason for these experiences is that a major proportion of press reports on criminal offenses include photographs, details of occupation, information about addresses, making it easy for people to identify victims in general, and particularly for those sharing the victims' social environment (Ionescu, 1998; Kury & Baumann, 1998).

The great majority of studies of the effects of the presentation of crime investigate the influence of a positive or negative, verbal or visual, dramatizing or muted presentation of the perpetrators. In this connection, the effect of the presentation of the victims of violence on the viewers of television news programs, for example, has so far been neglected. Both in Westerns and action movies as well as in the realm of political propaganda, the violence employed by "good" violent actors is usually justified by previously showing the victims of the "bad" violent actors. The more intensively the suffering of the victims is presented, the more justified the "counterviolence" of the "good" violent actors appears. The significance of this victim-centered rhetoric is also reflected in current reports on violent clashes between the police and demonstrators. The presentation of perpetrators or victims of violence is more effective than any judgmental comment on their behavior. For example, the presentation of the police as victims of violence polarizes the views of their supporters among the viewers: they perceive the police as particularly positive, but view the demonstrators as particularly negative (Kepplinger & Gießelmann, 1993). This suggests that in current reporting an exaggerated presentation of the victims of violence justifies the use of "counterviolence", thus possibly contributing to an escalation of violent conflicts. Obviously, an empirically underpinned theory of victim-centered rhetoric will be required to examine this problem.

The most acute research gap probably concerns the unexplained relation between information about violent acts and related events (criminal prosecution, criminal proceedings etc.), on the one hand, and the emotional reactions of readers, listeners and viewers of media reports triggered by this information, on the other. A basis (for such an explanation) is provided by *appraisal theories*. They assume that emotional responses occur intuitively and spontaneously on the basis of cognitive assessments and in turn guide the interpretation of new information. Thus, injury caused without any higher motives on the part of those responsible provokes anger. This is further reinforced, among other things, by the perception that the actors involved could have very well foreseen the consequences of their action in advance. For example, if a piece of information is missing from newspaper articles, it is "suitably" filled in by readers (Brosius, 1995:214–238). Stimulated by emotions and guided by the available information, they insinuate, for example, that those who caused the injury could have foreseen the consequences of their action (Nerb, Spada & Wahl, 1998). It can thus be assumed that dramatic reports of brutal acts of violence cause strong emotions—an aspect that may lead, inter alia, to a situation in which particularly vicious motives are attributed to the perpetrators, even when no relevant details have been reported. Such reciprocal action between information and emotions may also explain the connections between the frequency of xenophobic crimes and xenophobic opinions (Ohlemacher, 1993).

Translated by Adelheid E. Baker

REFERENCES

Adams, Kenneth. (1996). Guns and Gun Control. In Timothy J. Flanagan & Dennis R. Longmire (Eds.), *Americans View Crime and Justice* (pp. 109–124). Thousand Oaks, London, New Delhi: Sage.

Brosius, Hans-Bernd. (1995). *Alltagsrationalität in der Nachrichtenrezeption. Ein Modell zur Wahrnehmung und Verarbeitung von Nachrichteninhalten.* Opladen: Westdeutscher Verlag.

Brosius, Hans-Bernd, & Frank Esser. (1995). *Eskalation durch Berichterstattung? Massenmedien und fremdenfeindliche Gewalt.* Opladen, Wiesbaden: Westdeutscher Verlag.

Bruns, Thomas, & Frank Marcinowski. (1997). *Politische Informationssendungen im Fernsehen. Eine Längsschnittstudie zur Veränderung der Politikvermittlung in Nachrichten und politischen Informationssendungen.* Opladen, Wiesbaden: Westdeutscher Verlag.

Caplan, Nathan. (1970). The New Ghetto Man: A Review of Recent Empirical Studies. *Journal of Social Issues*, 26, 59–73.

Childs, Harwood L. (1965). *Public Opinion: Nature, Formation, and Role*. Princeton: Van Nostrand.

Combs, Barbara, & Paul Slovic. (1979). Newspaper Coverage of Causes of Death. *Journalism Quarterly*, 56, 837–849.

Esser, Frank. (2000). Massenmedien und Fremdenfeindlichkeit im Ländervergleich. Eine Analyse internationaler Nachrichtenmagazine. In Heribert Schatz, Christina Holtz-Bacha & Jörg-Uwe Nieland (Eds.), *Migranten und Medien. Neue Herausforderungen an die Integrationsfunktion von Presse und Rundfunk* (pp. 82–105). Opladen: Westdeutscher Verlag.

Fishman, Mark. (1978). Crime Waves as Ideology. *Social Problems*, 25, 531–543.

Flanagan, Timothy J. (1996). Public Opinion on Crime and Justice. History, Development, and Trends. In Timothy J. Flanagan & Dennis R. Longmire (Eds.), *Americans View Crime and Justice* (pp. 1–15). Thousand Oaks, London, New Delhi: Sage.

Früh, Werner. (1995). Die Rezeption von Fernsehgewalt. Eine empirische Studie zum wahrgenommenen Gewaltpotential des Fernsehprogrammangebots durch verschiedene Zielgruppen. *Media Perspektiven*, 4, 172–185.

Funkhouser, G. Ray. (1973). The Issues of the Sixties: An Exploratory Study in the Dynamics of Public Opinion. *Public Opinion Quarterly*, 37, 62–75.

Gerbner, George, & Larry Gross. (1976). Living with Television. The Violence Profile. *Journal of Communication*, 26, 173–199.

Gerbner, George, Larry Gross, Michael Morgan, & Nancy Signorielli. (1986). Living with Television: The Dynamics of the Cultivation Process. In Jennings Bryant & Dolf Zillmann (Eds.), *Perspectives on Media Effects* (pp. 17–40). Hillsdale, London: Lawrence Erlbaum.

Gerhardt, Rudolf. (1990). Der Einfluß der Medien auf das Strafverfahren aus medialer Sicht. In Dietrich Oehler, Friedrich A. Jahn, Rudolf Gerhardt, Manfred Burgstaller & Winfried Hassemer (Eds.), *Der Einfluß der Medien auf das Strafverfahren* (pp. 19–45). München: C.H. Beck.

Gibson, Rhonda, & Dolf Zillmann. (1994). Exaggerated versus Representative Exemplification in News Reports: Perception of Issues and Personal Consequences. *Communication Research*, 21, 603–624.

Groebel, Joe. (1982). Macht das Fernsehen die Umwelt bedrohlich? Strukturelle Aspekte und Ergebnisse einer Längsschnittstudie zu Fernsehwirkungen. *Publizistik*, 29, 152–165.

Haghighi, Bahram, & Jon Sorensen. (1996). America's Fear of Crime. In Timothy J. Flanagan & Dennis R. Longmire (Eds.), *Americans View Crime and Justice* (pp. 16–30). Thousand Oaks, London, New Delhi: Sage.

Hawkins, Robert P., & Suzanne Pingree. (1981). Using Television to Construct Social Reality. *Journal of Broadcasting*, 25, 347–364.

Hirsch, Paul M. (1980). The 'Scary World' of the Nonviewer and Other Anomalies. A Reanalysis of Gerbner et al.'s Findings on Cultivation Analysis—Part I. *Communication Research*, 7, 403–456.

Hughes, Michael. (1980). The Fruits of Cultivation Analysis: A Reexamination of Some Effects of Television Watching. *Public Opinion Quarterly*, 44, 285–302.

Inhetveen, Katharina. (1997). Gesellige Gewalt. Ritual, Spiel und Vergemeinschaftung bei Hardcore-Konzerten. In Trutz von Trotha (Ed.), *Soziologie der Gewalt* (pp. 235–260). Opladen, Wiesbaden: Westdeutscher Verlag.

Ionescu, Andra. (1998). Kriminalberichterstattung in der Tagespresse—Ergebnisse einer Auswertung deutscher Zeitungsartikel. In Dieter Dölling, Karl-Heinz Grössel & Stanislaw Waltoš (Eds.), *Kriminalberichterstattung in der Tagespresse. Rechtliche und kriminologische Probleme* (pp. 45–85). Heidelberg: Kriminalistik Verlag.

Johnson, Eric J., & Amos Tversky. (1983). Affect, Generalization, and the Perception of Risk. *Journal of Personality and Social Psychology*, 45, 20–31.

Kaase, Max, & Friedhelm Neidhardt. (1990). Politische Gewalt und Repression. Ergebnisse von Bevölkerungsumfragen. In Hans-Dieter Schwind, Jürgen Baumann et al. (Eds.), *Ursachen, Prävention und Kontrolle von Gewalt. Analysen und Vorschläge der Unabhängigen Regierungskommission zur Verhinderung und Bekämpfung von Gewalt (Gewaltkommission). Vol. IV: Bevölkerungsumfragen* (pp. 1–288). Berlin: Duncker & Humblot.

Kelman, Herbert C. (1973). Violence without Moral Restraint: Reflections on the Dehumanization of Victims and Victimizers. *Journal of Social Issues*, 29, 25–61.

Kepplinger, Hans Mathias. (1981). Gesellschaftliche Bedingungen kollektiver Gewalt. *Kölner Zeitschrift für Soziologie und Sozialpsychologie*, 33, 469–503.

Kepplinger, Hans Mathias. (1992). Put in the Spotlight—Instrumental Actualization of Actors, Events, and Aspects in the Coverage on Nicaragua. In Stanley Rothman (Ed.), *The Mass Media in Liberal Democratic Societies* (pp. 201–219). New York: Paragon House.

Kepplinger, Hans Mathias. (1999). Vom Kompetenz- zum Machtverlust. In Elisabeth Noelle-Neumann, Hans Mathias Kepplinger & Wolfgang Donsbach Kampa (Eds.), *Meinungsklima und Medienwirkung im Bundestagswahlkampf 1998* (pp. 215–236). Freiburg: Alber.

Kepplinger, Hans Mathias. (2000). Die Entwicklung der Kriminalitätsberichterstattung. In Bundesjustizministerium (Eds.), *Kriminalität in den Medien* (pp. 58–77). Köln: Eigenverlag.

Kepplinger, Hans Mathias, Klaus Gotto, Hans-Bernd Brosius, & Dietmar Haak. (1989). *Der Einfluß der Fernsehnachrichten auf die politische Meinungsbildung*. Freiburg: Alber.

Kepplinger, Hans Mathias, Hans-Bernd Brosius, & Joachim Friedrich Staab. (1991a). Instrumental Actualization: A Theory of Mediated Conflicts. *European Journal of Communication, 6*, 263–290.

Kepplinger, Hans Mathias, Hans-Bernd Brosius, & Joachim Friedrich Staab. (1991b). Opinion Formation in Mediated Conflicts and Crises: A Theory of Congnitive-Affective Media Effects. *International Journal of Public Opinion Research, 3*, 132–156.

Kepplinger, Hans Mathias, & Thea Gießelmann. (1993). Die Wirkung von Gewaltdarstellungen in der aktuellen Fernsehberichterstattung. *Medienpsychologie, 5*, 160–189.

Kepplinger, Hans Mathias, & Johanna Habermeier. (1995). The Impact of Key Events on the Presentation of Reality. *European Journal of Communication, 10*, 371–390.

Kunczik, Michael. (1994). *Gewalt und Medien*. Köln, Weimar, Wien: Böhlau.

Kunczik, Michael, & Wolfgang Bleh. (1995). *Kriminalitätsopfer in der Zeitungsberichterstattung. Folgen der Berichterstattung aus der Perspektive der Opfer*. Mainz: Weißer Ring Verlagsgesellschaft.

Kury, Helmut, Uwe Dörmann, Harald Richter, & Michael Würger. (1992). *Opfererfahrungen und Meinungen zur inneren Sicherheit in Deutschland. Ein empirischer Vergleich von Viktimisierungen, Anzeigeverhalten und Sicherheitseinschätzung in Ost und West vor der Vereinigung*. Wiesbaden: BKA.

Kury, Helmut, & Ulrich Baumann. (1998). Das Opfer der Straftat in der deutschen Medienberichterstattung. In Dieter Dölling, Karl-Heinz Gössel and Stanislaw Waltoś (Eds.), *Kriminalberichterstattung in der Tagespresse. Rechtliche und kriminologische Probleme* (pp. 159–196). Heidelberg: Kriminalistik Verlag.

Lichtenstein, Sarah, Paul Slovic, Baruch Fischhoff, Mark Layman, & Barbara Combs. (1978). Judged Frequency of Lethal Events. *Journal of Experimental Psychology: Human Learning and Memory, 4*, 551–578.

Longmire, Dennis R. (1996). Americans' Attitudes about the Ultimate Weapon. Capital Punishment. In Timothy J. Flanagan & Dennis R. Longmire (Eds.), *Americans View Crime and Justice* (pp. 93–108). Thousand Oaks, London, New Delhi: Sage.

McCombs, Maxwell E., & Donald L. Shaw. (1972). The Agenda-Setting Function of Mass Media. *Public Opinion Quarterly, 38*, 176–187.

Meyer, Wulff-Uwe, & Heinz-Dieter Schmalt. (1984). Die Attributionstheorie. In Dieter Frey & Martin Irle (Eds.), *Theorien der Sozialpsychologie* (pp. 98–136). Bern, Stuttgart, Toronto: Huber.

Nerb, Josef, Hans Spada, & Stefan Wahl. (1998). Kognition und Emotion bei der Bewertung von Umweltschadensfällen: Modellierung und Empirie. *Zeitschrift für Experimentelle Psychologie, 45*, 251–269.

Noelle-Neumann, Elisabeth. (1984). *The Spiral of Silence. Public Opinion—Our Social Skin*. Chicago: The University of Chicago Press.

Noelle-Neumann, Elisabeth. (1989). *Öffentliche Meinung. Die Entdeckung der Schweigespirale* [First Published, 1980]. Frankfurt, Berlin: Ullstein.

Noelle-Neumann, Elisabeth, & Thomas Petersen. (1996). *Alle, nicht jeder. Einführung in die Methoden der Demoskopie*. München: dtv.

Noelle-Neumann, Elisabeth, & Renate Köcher. (Eds.) (1997). *Allensbacher Jahrbuch der Demoskopie 1993–1997*. München, Allensbach am Bodensee: K.G. Saur.

Ohlemacher, Thomas. (1993). *Bevölkerungsmeinung und Gewalt gegen Ausländer im wiedervereinten Deutschland. Empirische Anmerkungen zu einem unklaren Verhältnis*. Discussion Paper FS III 93–104. Wissenschaftszentrum Berlin für Sozialforschung.

Potter, W. James, Ron Warren, Misha Vaughan, Kevin Howley, Art Land, & Jeremy Hagemeyer. (1997). Antisocial Acts in Reality Programming on Television. *Journal of Broadcasting & Electronic Media, 41*, 69–75.

Sander, Ingo. (1997). How Violent Is TV Violence? An Empirical Investigation of Factors Influencing Viewers' Perceptions of TV Violence. *European Journal of Communication, 12*, 43–98.

Schulz, Wolfram. (1997). Die Akzeptanz und Beurteilung von Gewalt als Mittel politischer Auseinandersetzung im europäischen Vergleich. In Mike Friedrichsen & Gerhard Vowe (Eds.), *Gewaltdarstellungen in den Medien. Theorien, Fakten und Analysen* (pp. 43–68). Opladen, Wiesbaden: Westdeutscher Verlag.

Turner, Ralph H., & Samuel J. Surace. (1956/57). Zoot-Suiters and Mexicans: Symbols in Crowd Behavior. *American Journal of Sociology, 62,* 14–20.

Unold, Michaela. (1989). *Die Wirkung von Gewaltdarstellungen: Der relative Einfluß des Ereignisses—real vs. fiktional—bzw. der Darstellungsformen—künstlich vs. natürlich—auf die Rezipienten.* Mainz: Johannes Gutenberg-Universität (unveröffentlichte Magisterarbeit).

Warr, Mark. (1995). The Polls—Poll Trends. Public Opinion on Crime and Punishment. *Public Opinion Quarterly, 59,* 296–310.

Weimann, Gabriel, & Conrad Winn. (1993). *The Theater of Terror. Mass Media and International Terrorism.* White Plains: Longman.

CHAPTER II-7.3

Groups, Gangs and Violence

WOLFGANG KÜHNEL

I. INTRODUCTION

The significance of the group for violent behavior has been studied in various social scientific disciplines using a range of different theoretical and methodological approaches. Criminology is one of the disciplines which has dealt with the context of groups and violence very comprehensively. Pioneering work has been produced by the Chicago School (Park, 1984; Shaw & McKay, 1969), which has delivered decisive stimuli for the sociology of deviant behavior. The representatives of the Chicago School place the phenomena of group violence in a larger context. They take account of aspects of migration, social and ethnic inequality, as well as urban development, and investigate the effects of the (marginal) social and spatial situation of different social groups, in particular of immigrants, on (violent) crime. In the United States most of the representatives of what has come to be called gang research are in this tradition (Curry, Ball, & Fox, 1994; Huff, 1990; Klein, 1995; Short, 1997; Thornberry & Burch, 1997). This is also an important point of reference for studies conducted in France (Dubet & Lapeyronnie, 1992; Loch, 1998; Wacquant, 1994), Britain (Hobbs, 1997), Germany (Bohnsack et al., 1995; Eckert, Reis, & Wetzstein, 1999; Kühnel & Matuschek, 1995; Lamnek & Schwenk, 1995; Ohder, 1992; Tertilt, 1996; von Trotha, 1993) and Switzerland (Eisner, 1997). However, none of these studies fully elaborate the definition of the group. Depending on the researcher's point of view this can extend from (delinquent and nondelinquent) gangs, conflict gangs (Decker, 1996), wilding groups (Cummings, 1993), near-groups (Yablonski, 1966), unsupervised groups (Short, 1997:81), and peer groups to subcultures or subcultural trends. The lowest common denominator in understanding groups is that they are microsocial structures determined by the collectivity of behavior and experience. Groups are social systems of personal relationships in which individuals can express their feelings and interests (Neidhardt, 1983:14). One distinctive feature of groups is their introversion. The consequences of group activity can more readily be attributed to personal features than to structures, and group processes

---

W. Heitmeyer and J. Hagan (eds.), *International Handbook of Violence Research*, 1167–1180.
© 2003 Kluwer Academic Publishers. Printed in the Netherlands.

are to a large extent directed by feelings. Trust between members is an important precondition for the existence of the group. But feelings and trust are at the same time highly fragile media susceptible to change—trust can be disappointed and the consequences of actions become less predictable. For this reason group relationships are also very unpredictable and at the same time are under a certain pressure to develop structures. Some degree of dependability in behavioral expectations is required in order for interactions to take place.

Forming new group structures involves making distinctions. Group members dissociate themselves from the surrounding world, particularly from other groups, and create a we-feeling. Problematic life-situations can reduce perception of the world outside and relations to it and increase the internal homogeneity of the group. Furthermore, if groups are also confronted with limited action alternatives and are perceived by the surrounding world as deviant, this can reinforce the process of dissociation (see Eckert and Willems in this volume).

Status and changes in status are also perceived in microsocial relationships. Group members thrive on comparing themselves with others and derive identity from this (Tajfel, 1981). If discrepancies in status or changes in status are experienced as deprivation, this can be a cause of conflict, or can cause existing conflicts to escalate. The studies by Willems (1997) showed that conflicts develop independent dynamics of contingent events (Willems, 1997:478–484). Conflicts originate with the differential perception of conflict situations and attribution of causes. Conflict situations are characterized by mistrust and the lack of communication between the parties to the conflict. The opponent is assumed to have particular (negative) intentions, and this is made the basis of one's own interpretation and actions—a kind of "self-fulfilling prophecy" that in turn triggers reactions from the opponent. Groups produce their own values and norms. If group members consider the group's goals achievable but increasingly experience failures in the course of the conflict, this gives rise to deprivations which can either inflame the cycle of conflict or lead to resignation.

Groups act in a social context. External influences in the form of disorganization and stigmatization can lead a group to increase its organizational efforts. This phenomenon has long been a subject of criminological studies (Shaw & McKay, 1969), and it leads to new approaches to the relationship between social organization and disorganization in the community (Sampson & Groves, 1989).

In criminology, groups or gangs are described as "interstitial groups" (Trasher, 1927:38). These occur only in a particular age-group or part icular urban areas, and their existence is temporary. However, groups can also become stabile, endure even for generations, and develop into organizations with a firm division of labor, power structure, and economic function. The transformation of groups into organizations or even businesses, or the exchange between groups and organizations, is to be found above all in the sphere of organized crime. This is very well documented with regard to American society (Blok & Chamblis, 1981). The connection between corrupt politicians, organized criminals, and criminal groups has always played a major role in local politics in the United States (Sánchez-Jankowski, 1991:206–210; Whyte, 1964:249–251). Daniel Bell (1953) pointed out that the pioneers of American capitalism had no university degree to their names. They built up their businesses in the shadow of speculation, corruption, and violence (Bell, 1953:152). Similar developments are currently taking place in Russia and other Eastern European states. Organized crime functions as the midwife of a new society.

The transformation of groups into organizations can also be found within the social movements. This can involve actors from the new social movements but also from left-wing and right-wing extremist movements. In such cases it is interesting to note to what extent local groups can be mobilized for protest actions and in addition be integrated into organizational structures (McAdam, McCarthy, & Zald, 1988; Neidhardt & Rucht, 1993). A precondition for the development of a social movement is the perception of conflicts or deprivations (the gap between expectations and the opportunities of meeting them). In order to mobilize people for particular goals, a common consciousness is required, an ideology which polarizes. Violence can play a significant part in this. Groups at the microsocial level do not only have to come together on the basis of common ideas. They also have to work out to what extent their goals can be achieved. The chances of winning and the cost burdens incurred are a question of the "political opportunity structure" (Kriesi, 1991; Tarrow, 1983). How do the institutions of social control such as political parties and the media react to the groups? To what extent do they have a stabilizing or destabilizing effect? Conflicts between political actors can have the effect of mobilizing groups. The fact that right-wing extremist groups in Germany were able to operate very successfully in the public sphere in the early 1990s was intimately linked to conflicts between the established political parties over the issue of immigration and asylum (Koopmanns, 1995; Kühnel, 1998).

The conditions under which group mobilization occurs and the groups' chances of success depend also on the given cultural patterns. The cultural context is an important condition for the symbolic integration of the group and the formulation of common goals. Sometimes social movements even develop lifestyles of their own which go on to influence society as a whole. Cultural patterns mean that groups lay down what is allowed in the group and what not, who is an ally, who an outsider or even an enemy. Culture in groups creates the rules for dissociation and helps build group identity.

II. THEORIES OF THE DEVELOPMENT OF VIOLENT GROUPS

Most explanations of the development of violent groups do not focus exclusively on group structures and relationships, but also embrace environmental factors at various levels (local community, society, culture). The best known approaches are those based on the sociology of culture and theories of social disorganization and social control. Following the introduction of the biographical perspective into criminology, in the 1990s explanations of integration in violent groups developed on the basis of life-course theory.

1. Approaches Based on Cultural Theory

The question as to the influence of culture on deviant behavior played a role in the studies of the Chicago School as early as the 1920s and 1930s. Continued immigration and its consequences for urban development gave rise to an interest in the conflicts that arose between social groups of different ethnic background. This led to ideas on a theory of cultural conflict (Sellin, 1938). However, studies of cultures or subcultures of deviant behavior did not gain acceptance in North American sociology until the 1950s and 1960s (Arnold, 1970; Becker, 1973; Cohen, 1955; Gordon, 1970; Miller, 1970; Wolfgang & Ferracuti, 1970; Yablonski, 1966; Yinger, 1970).

Subcultures are normative and cultural systems which deviate from the culture of mainstream society. While part-cultures do not differ from the values and norms of society in every respect, they are different in significant ways. The development of subcultures is explained by the process of social differentiation. Partial systems with specific functions and cultural patterns of their own develop due to specialization and the social division of labor. The diversity of cultures in complex societies relativizes conflicts between different part-cultures and definitions of deviation.

Subcultures and microsocial groups are different social phenomena. Subcultures encompass partial systems of society and set a broad frame of reference for the acceptance of deviating norms and values. Groups, on the other hand, are based on direct personal relationships. Subcultures obviously have an influence on groups or contribute to the formation of groups, as can be said, for example, of drug subcultures or the cultures of ethnic minorities. Inversely, small groups can mobilize social and symbolic resources and develop into a subculture. Sometimes subcultures and groups are even considered to be the same. This is understandable when groups which spread expectations of deviant behavior via the media and pass these on to individuals and small groups, for example, are taken as reference groups.

In the 1960s the approaches concentrated mainly on explaining drug subcultures or violence-oriented subcultures. Subculture approaches became somewhat popular due to the increase in violent crime and the spread of gangs in large American cities. In this context Wolfgang and Ferracuti (1970) developed their concept of subcultures of violence. In violent subcultures aggression is of great significance for lifestyle and social relationships. Violent behavior in groups is due to violence having become a firm behavioral norm. In particular social situations there is the expectation to act in a violent way, and here violent behavior is a norm supported through encouragement. Inversely, there are negative sanctions against nonviolence.

Criminology informed by the sociology of culture is a particularly precise and subtle approach. Even in the golden age of subculture research there were different ideas about the significance of subcultures for the development of violence. For Cohen (1955), and also Cloward and Ohlin (1966), delinquent subcultures are collective reactions by male lower-class youths to inadequate opportunities for social advancement and inadequate chances to participate in the dominant culture. Miller (1970) sees nothing negative in the deviant and violent behavior of lower-class youth groups. They are an expression of an independent lower-class culture. When youth gangs violate middle-class norms, this is not their intention but rather just the consequence of observing lower-class norms.

In the meantime cultural criminology has become even more precise and discriminating (Ferrell and Sanders, 1995). For example, culturological approaches are used to study right-wing extremist subcultures (Hamm, 1993), the link between the media and violent crime, subcultural lifestyles (Cohen, 1974/75; Hall & Jefferson, 1976; Sanders, 1994), the social construction of (violent) criminality by the institutions of social control, and the scandals and temptations caused by violence (Goode & Ben-Yehuda, 1996; Katz, 1988).

2. Social Disorganization and Social Control

The theory of social disorganization was developed in the 1920s and 1930s at the University of Chicago. Shaw and McKay (1969) explain the development of delinquent behaviors as the consequence of urban growth and industrialization's dissolution of social relationships and social control. Industrialization leads to a demand for unskilled labor which migrates from rural areas to the cities. Urbanization is connected with an increasing specialization and division of labor and contributes to the emergence of group-specific cultural norms, possibly also to conflicts. Immigrant groups are under great pressure to conform to the new conditions, and this leads to difficulties in orientation. Under such circumstances it is difficult to enter into and maintain stable social relations, and when social control decreases, social disorganization and the likelihood of deviant (violent) behavior increase. More recent approaches have expanded on the social-disorganization theory (Bursik & Grasmick, 1995; Eisner, 1997; Sampson & Groves, 1989), and the anomie theory has been taken up again (Agnew, 1996; Albrecht, 1999; Bohle et al., 1997; Messner & Rosenfeld, 1996). Sampson and Groves (1989) relate the notion of disorganization to the level of the city district. They define disorganization as a community's inability to realize social control and uphold the common values of the local population (Sampson & Groves, 1989:777). Social disorganization and social organizations are seen as opposite poles of a continuum along which social control in a community is realized. Three dimensions need to be distinguished: firstly, the inability of a community to control youths' peer-group activities; secondly, the strength of local friendship networks; and thirdly, the lack of participation in formal and voluntary organizations (Sampson & Groves, 1989:778–779). Bursik and Grasmick (1995) have pointed out that it is not only control at the level of interpersonal relationships that plays an important part, but also control through the church, school and economic institutions, as well as through political institutions and the police. The likelihood of gang activities is high when interpersonal contacts are very strong and public and institutional control is very limited.

3. Life-Course Perspective

The role of groups in violent behavior is also a question for developmental psychology or life-course-oriented criminology. This approach examines the interplay between life spheres (family, school and peer group) in the course of young people's development. Violent reactions by youths in their peer group can be the result of limited family ties, emotional rejection, inconsistent and/or excessively strict parenting, and experiences of failure at school (Farrington, 1996; Lösel, 1995). However, there is no proof of a linear relationship between inadequate social control by the family, problematic parental behavior, poor performance at school, and becoming involved in antisocial groups. The introduction of the life-course perspective led to a change in thinking in the explanation of criminal developments (Sampson & Laub, 1995, Schumann, Prein, & Seus, 1999). The life-course approach calls for a multidimensional way of proceeding and also includes transitions and trajectories in its explanations (Schumann et al., 1999:301). For example, the transition from school to vocational training and then from training to the world of employment are fundamental turning points. Trajectories refer to social contexts (the peer group) or institutions (vocational training or college, government welfare institutions, law enforcement agencies) which influence a person's path in life. These institutions act as agencies of social control. They sanction (violent) behavior which violates social norms, and thus stigmatize it. Sanctions restrict a person's opportunities in life (Paternoster & Iovanni, 1996) and can lead to reinforcement of an already delinquent career. The introduction of the life-course dimension in criminology opens up a new perspective by taking into account the interplay of various social factors in a person's life and inquiring into social predispositions for joining violent groups.

III. EMPIRICAL CONSIDERATIONS

1. Regional Distribution of Violent Groups and Gangs

Violent groups or gangs are more common in big cities or suburban areas than in small towns or rural communities (Klein, 1995:31; National Youth Gang Center, 1997). In the United States, gang activities are reported most frequently from California, Washington and Oregon.

The prevalence of gang activities especially in the social problem areas of big cities is not only related to the high population density. Rather, it is social conditions such as low economic status, ethnic heterogeneity, high mobility, and incomplete families that contribute to the high level of social disorganization and the limited social control in such communities. Eisner (1997) has arrived at similar results for Switzerland, Eckert et al. (1999) for Germany, and Dubet and Lapeyronnie (1992) for France.

2. Groups and Gangs in the Community

A low intensity of neighborhood relations, inadequate social control by parents, little control of the activities of youth groups, and inadequate integration into conventional institutions, especially school, are given as decisive factors for the development of gangs at the local level (Fagan, 1990:207; Sampson and Groves, 1989; Short, 1996:61–67). Other studies point to the connection between declining social status, unemployment, and gang activities in areas which are hit by the structural change of old industries and subsequently on the downturn (Hagedorn & Macon, 1988:138–139). Vigil (1990) concluded on the basis of field studies that there is a stable cycle of poverty and poor prospects of social advancement in city districts which are home to mainly Mexican minorities. Here marginalization is institutionalized (Vigil, 1990:123). People in this situation experience what Vigil termed "multiple marginality" (Vigil & Chong Yun, 1990:147).

However, groups or gangs are not necessarily alienated from their local neighborhoods. The study by Sánchez-Jankowski (1991) showed that there are a wide variety of relationships of gangs to the local community. These can frequently be close, and sometimes even work relationships are established (Sánchez-Jankowski, 1991:179). A close relationship between a community and gangs is documented for members of the Chinese minority in New York, for example (Chin, 1990:137). Their gang activities are controlled by powerful (criminal) organizations in the community (Chin, 1990:137).

3. The Ethnicity of Groups and Gangs

Residential mobility, ethnic heterogeneity and low socioeconomic status are factors which tend to foster (violent) crime, as Shaw and McKay (1969) observed. A range of other studies emphasize the connection between ethnic segregation, poverty, and the development of a new underclass (Huff, 1990:31). In Europe similar findings have been reported from the Netherlands (Junger & Polder, 1992), Switzerland (Eisner, 1997), Sweden (Westin, 1998) and Germany (Steffen, 1999).

Gangs are attractive for youths with limited social prospects and for whom ethnic identity is of particular significance (Chin, 1990; Vigil, 1990; Vigil & Chong Yun, 1990). Sampson and Wilson (1995) point out that there is no linear correlation between ethnic segregation, unemployment, economic deprivation and (violent) crime. They state that a combination of urban poverty, disturbed family relations, and cultural isolation among colored people in particular city districts leads to forms of cumulative disadvantage (Sampson & Wilson, 1995:40–52). The majority of youths in criminal gangs in the United States are of Afro-American and Hispanic descent (Curry et al., 1994; Klein, 1995; Miller, 1982) and live mainly in the big cities (National Youth Gang Center, 1997). Gang violence is generally directed against people or groups perceived as outsiders, and the definition of outsider is based chiefly on ethnic features (Curry & Spergel, 1992). Violent conflicts between gangs are mainly interethnic (Sanders, 1994:51).

4. Prevalence of Gangs and Groups

It is hard to estimate how many young people are actively involved in gangs, and also to confirm the reported increase in the number of violent gangs. The difficulty in assessing the prevalence and the development of gangs is due, on the one hand, to the diversity of definitions as to what constitutes a gang, and on the other hand, to the survey methods employed. According to Klein (1995:91–98) the number of U.S. cities which reported gang activities rose between 1961 and 1992. This assessment is based on statements by police officers. In the National Youth Gang Survey conducted in 1995 (National Youth Gang Center, 1997) 5,000 law enforcement agencies were questioned. At this point in time it was estimated that there were around 850,000 active members in approximately 31,000 gangs (U.S. Department of Justice, 1999). Huff (1998) estimates that the number of gangs is much smaller and gives a figure of 16,000. Results gained through longitudinal studies, such as those conducted since the late 1980s in selected areas (Rochester, New York, Denver, Colorado, and Pittsburgh), are much more meaningful than such estimates. The Rochester Youth Development Study and the Denver study examined the prevalence of gang membership and the relationship of gang members to violence. In both studies there were problems with the sample group because the respondents were mainly youths from areas with a high level of criminality, and also ethnic minorities were overrepresented (Short, 1996:33–34).

Judging by the results of the Rochester Youth Development Study, the prevalence rate for 12 to 15-year-old youths was 20 percent. Gang members accounted for 86 percent of serious crime, 69 percent of acts of violence and 70 percent of drug dealing. 55 percent of the gang members questioned belonged to a gang for one year. The proportion of those in the gang for four years dropped to 7 percent (Thornberry & Burch, 1997). In the Denver study the prevalence rate is lower than in the Rochester study. 7 percent of the young people aged twelve to eighteen reported that they were members of gangs (Esbensen & Huizinga, 1993:569). The fact that the two studies resulted in different prevalence rates has to do with the survey method employed. The Rochester study uses a relatively broad definition of gang membership.

For most young people being in a gang is a temporary phase in their lives. According to the results of the Denver study 67 percent of the young people questioned were members of a gang for one year, 24 percent for two years, 6 percent for three years, and 3 percent for four years (Esbensen & Huizinga, 1993:575).

5. Groups, Gangs, and (Violent) Crime

There is ample evidence to show that the level of criminal activity is higher among gang members than non-gang-members (Curry & Decker, 1998; Klein, 1995; Short, 1996). The probability of committing serious offenses as well as possessing and using weapons is also greater in gangs (Huff, 1998). In big cities and suburban counties a high level of gang-member involvement has been ascertained for grievous bodily harm, car theft, and robbery. Rural areas show a higher proportion of break-ins by gangs. The proportion of larcenies committed by gang members is high in all regions but is proportionally highest in suburban and rural counties (National Youth Gang Center, 1997).

The Youth Gang Survey also shows that around half of gang members are involved in drug dealing. Nevertheless, the connection between violence and drug-related crime by gangs has been greatly overestimated. Klein (1995:120) criticizes studies which assume a close connection between gangs, drugs and violence. Violence obviously plays an important role in criminal organizations—syndicates—which control the drug trade (Sánchez-Jankowski, 1991).

The assumption that gangs operate mainly using serious acts of violence is also incorrect. There are very few cases where violence has become a firm behavioral norm in groups. Situational conflicts between different groups or gangs are more common (Klein, 1995:68).

6. Personality Features of Groups and Gang Members

Risk factors for the inclusion in violent groups can be identified not only at macrosocial and microsocial levels, but also at the individual level (Short, 1997:40–41). The inability to regulate one's behavior and an inadequate level of integration into significant institutions are relevant from the point of view of control theory (Gottfredson & Hirschi, 1996). Poor social control results from limited social attachment to one's family and to institutions demanding conformity. Deficits in social control can lead to problematic developments and life decisions—behavior such as playing hooky, dropping out of school, etc., limits a person's opportunities and makes it all the more likely that they will join an antisocial group (Lösel, 1995).

However, there is no causal relationship between negative influences in the various areas of socialization and antisocial behavior. Individuals deal with such difficulties in widely varying ways. In his study of thirty-seven gangs in Boston, New York and Los Angeles, Sánchez-Jankowski (1991) analyzed a model of behavior of gang members which he defines as "defiant individualism." Gang members tend to be intensively competitive, which is expressed in particular in physical aggression. They are decidedly mistrustful of others. They develop self-confidence in a relatively isolated social environment and acquire a social Darwinist world view expressing their survival instinct (Sánchez-Jankowski, 1991:24–27). Short (1996) considers these ways of dealing with problems a form of coming to terms with fear. He sees the high degree of self-centered and defiant behavior in gangs as functional and rational because gang members have to deal with the risks brought by life in a violent environment.

IV. METHODS

There are different methods and approaches in the study of gangs and related group processes. Field studies are very common. These are informed by ethnographic methods and the standards of qualitative social research with grounded theory as their primary research framework. This involves studying gangs in a particular county or city (Chin, 1990; Moore, 1991; Padilla, 1993; Sanders, 1994; Vigil & Chong Yun, 1990). There are also comparative studies of gangs in different counties (Sánchez-Jankowski, 1991). Hagedorn (1990) argues in favor of conducting new field studies because the structural change of cities has also changed the world of gangs. In his view, studies based on the statistics of the law enforcement agencies or the testimonies of the police are hardly able to comprehend the reality of gangs (Hagedorn, 1990:241–245). Gang members are difficult to reach through opinion polls. With this goal in mind, "softer" methods are needed to allow frank responses. Another inadequacy of many studies is that they do not explicitly state their methodological principles: the process of data collection is thus hard to comprehend; gangs' or gang members' contrasting behaviors, orientations and actions are not compared; no search is made for evidence which might contradict the study's findings.

In addition to qualitative studies, surveys have also become an established method in gang research. One type of study uses data based on statements by law enforcement agencies, schools authorities, county councilors, and welfare agencies (Curry et al., 1994; Klein, 1995; National Youth Gang Center, 1997; Spergel & Curry, 1990). The studies of the gang problem in the United States published since 1975 by the National Institute of Justice (NIJ) are representative of this method.

In another type of sampling procedure, a multistage selection is made on the basis of the chain-referral method, allowing different groups to be questioned and then compared (Fagan, 1990). These methods allow not only "normal" high school graduates to enter the sample, but also respondents of ethnic minorities and school dropouts, i.e., those groups for which the likelihood of gang membership is comparatively high.

Many young people belong to a group or gang only for a certain time. However, a small proportion remain in the gang. Also in their case one has to rely on stated views about the course of their gang career. Longitudinal studies are necessary in order to study the influence of different socialization factors in the course of a person's life. The Rochster Youth Development Study (Thornberry et al., 1993) and the Denver study (Esbensen & Huizinga, 1993) show a significant turn in gang research. The advent of life-course research in criminology will enable complex statements, e.g., on the dynamics of delinquency and gang membership, or on the influence of multiple individual, micro and macrostructural factors. A combination of qualitative and quantitative methods can be useful here.

V. STRATEGIES IN DEALING WITH GANGS AND GROUP VIOLENCE

Ever since there have been violent groups there have also been ideas for dealing with gangs. Gang management programs have a strong tradition in the United States. Klein (1995) distinguishes three strategies. The first consists in mobilizing resources and organizations at the level of the county or city district (Klein, 1995:138–141). Projects at the level of the city district involve a mix of social intervention and improving the opportunities for young people in the community. The best-known project of this kind is the Chicago Area Project, which was initiated by the research of Clifford Shaw. The project aimed to develop interpersonal relationships in the neighborhood and strengthen social control through institutions such as school, police, and local government. Social workers and municipal government staff were given the task of mobilizing resources for youth work in the city district. At the same time school, education and leisure facilities for young people were improved. Meetings were organized to discuss goals in improving conditions for youth and in reducing criminality. On this basis similar programs were introduced in Boston, New York, and Philadelphia. The Mobilization for Youth (MFY) experiment became well-known. This project was introduced into New York's East Side in the early 1960s and was oriented toward Cloward and Ohlin's (1966) theory of differential opportunities. The project has been criticized for its indeterminate evaluation.

"Gang reform programs" are another strategy. These aim to change the social relationships in the groups and develop young people's prosocial motives. They are essentially social intervention projects realized through either clubs or street outreach programs. Activities more closely related to clubs offer leisure and sport facilities. In the outreach work social workers establish contact with the young people in the street and offer advice. One of the best known gang reform projects was the Roxbury Project. It was introduced in the late 1950s in cities where gang activities were particularly frequent. Walter Miller also became involved in this project with his research in an inner-city area of Boston. According to Klein (1995:144), however, the results of the project were discouraging. In gang-related projects the difficulty lies in breaking down the group bonds and at the same time achieving a shift toward the development of prosocial goals.

A further strategy is the use of repression-oriented programs (Klein, 1995:151, Spergel & Curry, 1990:297). These aim to deter and are realized through proactive police activity, arrests, and other measures. Repression-oriented programs seem to be the most widespread form, followed by social intervention strategies, strategies to change the institutional and political mechanisms in the organizations, and finally city-district activities and the improvement of neighborhood relations. This was the conclusion reached by Spergel and Curry (1990) on the basis of a study conducted in 1988. They studied different institutions' strategies and assessed their effectiveness in dealing with the gang problem. They too found that strategies of social intervention, repression and organizational change are not considered particularly effective in dealing with the gang problem. Spergel and Curry (1990) interpreted the results of their study to the effect that committing more resources for police intervention and social programs would not be any more effective in the longer term. On the contrary, mobilizing the city district and devoting more resources to education and reform of the education system and job market is considered the most effective and cost-efficient way of alleviating the gang problem (Spergel & Curry, 1990:309).

Translated by Tradukas

REFERENCES

Agnew, Robert. (1996). Foundation for a General Strain Theory of Crime and Delinquency. In Peter Cordella & Larry Siedel (Eds.), *Readings in Contemporary Criminological Theory* (pp. 149–170). Boston: Northeastern University Press.

Albrecht, Günter. (1999). Sozialer Wandel und Kriminalität. In Hans-Jörg Albrecht & Helmut Kury (Eds.), *Kriminalität, Strafrechtsreform und Strafvollzug in Zeiten des sozialen Umbruchs. Beiträge zum Zweiten deutsch-chinesischen Kolloquium* (pp. 1–56). Max-Planck-Institut für ausländisches und internationales Strafrecht: Freiburg i.Br.

Arnold, David O. (1970). A Process Model of Subcultures. In David O. Arnold (Ed.), *The Sociology of Subcultures* (pp. 112–117). Berkeley: The Glendessary Press.

Becker, Howard S. (1973). *Outsiders. Studies in Sociology of Deviance*. New York: The Free Press.

Bell, Daniel. (1953). Crime as an American Way of Life. *The Antioch Review, 13*, 131–54.

Blok, Anton, & William J. Chambliss. (1981). *Organizing Crime*. New York: Elsevier.

Bohle, Hans Hartwig, Wilhelm Heitmeyer, Wolfgang Kühnel, & Uwe Sander. (1997). Anomie in der modernen Gesellschaft: Bestandsaufnahme und Kritik eines klassischen Ansatzes soziologischer Analyse. In Wilhelm Heitmeyer (Ed.), *Was treibt die Gesellschaft auseinander?* (pp. 29–65). Frankfurt a. M.: Suhrkamp.

Bohnsack, Ralf, Peter Loos, Burkhard Schäffer, Klaus Städtler, & Bodo Wild. (1995). *Die Suche nach Gemeinsamkeit und die Gewalt der Gruppe. Hooligans, Musikgruppen und andere Jugendcliquen*. Opladen: Leske und Budrich.

Bursik, Robert J., & Harold G. Grasmick. (1995). Neighborhood-Based Networks and the Control of Crime and Delinquency. In Hugh D. Barlow (Ed.), *Crime and Public Policy: Putting Theory to Work* (pp. 107–130). Boulder: Westview.

Chin, Ko-Lin. (1990). Chinese Gangs and Extortion. In Ronald C. Huff (Ed.), *Gangs in America* (pp. 129–145). Newbury Park: Sage.

Cloward, Richard A., & Lloyd E. Ohlin. (1966). *Delinquency and Opportunity. A Theory of Delinquent Gangs*. New York: The Free Press.

Cohen, Albert K. (1955). *Delinquent Boys*. Glencoe: The Free Press.

Cohen, Stanley. (1974/1975). Breaking out, Smashing up and the Social Context of Aspiration. *Working Papers in Cultural Studies, 5–7/8*, 37–63.

Cummings, Scott. (1993). Anatomy of a Wilding Gang. In Scott Cumming & Daniel J. Monti (Eds.), *Gangs: The Origins and Impact of Contemporary Youth Gangs in the United States* (pp. 194–211). Albany: SUNY Press.

Curry, David, Richard A. Ball, & Robert Fox. (1994). *Gang Crime and Law Enforcement Recordkeeping. Research in Brief*. Washington: U.S. Department of Justice, National Institute of Justice, URL: http://www.ncjrs.org/txtfiles/gcrime.tyt

Curry, David G., & Irving A. Spergel. (1992). Gang Involvement and Delinquency among Hispanic and African-American Adolescent Males. *Journal of Research in Crime and Delinquency, 29*, 273–292.

Curry, David G., & Scott H. Decker. (1998). *Confronting Gangs: Crime and Community*. Los Angeles: Roxbury.

Decker, Scott H. (1996). Collective an Normative Features of Gang Violence. *Justice Quarterly, 13*, 243–264.

Dubet, Francois, & Didier Lapeyronnie. (1992). *Les quartier d'Exil*. Paris: Edition Seuil.

Eckert, Roland, Christa Reis, & Thomas A. Wetzstein. (1999). *Ich will halt anders sein wie die anderen—Gruppengrenzen, Gewalt und Kreativität*. Opladen: Leske und Budrich.

Eisner, Manuel. (1997). *Das Ende der zivilisierten Stadt? Die Auswirkungen von Modernisierung und urbaner Krise auf Gewaltdelinquenz*. Frankfurt a. M./New York: Campus.

Esbensen, Finn-Aage, & David Huizinga. (1993). Gangs, Drugs, and Delinquency in a Survey of Urban Youth. *Criminology, 32*, 565–589.

Fagan, Jeffrey. (1990). Social Processes of Delinquency and Drug Use among Urban Gangs. In Ronald C. Huff (Ed.), *Gangs in America* (pp. 183–219). Newbury Park: Sage.

Farrington, David. (1996). The Explanation and Prevention of Youthful Offending. In Peter Cordella & Larry Siegel (Eds.), *Readings in Contemporary Criminological Theory* (pp. 257–272). Boston: Northeastern University Press.

Ferrell, Jeff, & Clinton R. Sanders. (1995). *Cultural Criminology*. Boston: Northeastern University Press.

Goode, Erich, & Nachman Ben-Yehuda. (1996). *Moral Panics. The Social Construction of Deviance*. Oxford/Cambridge: Blackwell.

Gordon, Milton M. (1970). The Concept of Sub-Culture and its Application. In David O. Arnold (Ed.), *The Sociology of Subcultures* (pp. 31–36). Berkeley: The Glendessary Press.

Gottfredson, Michael, & Travis Hirschi. (1996). The Nature of Criminality: Low Self-Control. In Peter Cordella & Larry Siegel (Eds.), *Readings in Contemporary Criminological Theory* (pp. 194–208). Boston: Northeastern University Press.

Hagedorn, John M. (1990). Back in the Field Again: Gang Research in the Nineties. In Ronald C. Huff (Ed.), *Gangs in America* (pp. 240–259). Newbury Park: Sage.

Hagedorn, John M., & Perry Macon. (1988). *People and Folks: Gangs, Crime, and the Underclass in a Rustbelt City.* Chicago: Lake View Press.

Hall, Stuart, & Tony Jefferson. (Eds.) (1976). *Resistance through Rituals.* London: Hutchinson.

Hamm, Mark S. (1993). *American Skinheads. The Criminology and Control of Hate Crime.* Westport: Praeger.

Hobbs, Dick. (1997). Criminal Collaboration: Youth Gangs, Subcultures, Professional Criminals, and Organized Crime. In Mike Maguire, Rod Morgan & Robert Reiner (Eds.), *The Oxford Handbook of Criminology* (pp. 801–840). Oxford: Clarendon Press.

Huff, Ronald C. (Ed.) (1990). *Gangs in America.* Newbury Park: Sage.

Huff, Ronald C. (1998). *Comparing the Criminal Behavior of Youth Gangs and At-Risk Youth. Research in Brief.* Washington: U.S. Department of Justice, National Institute of Justice, URL: http://www.ncjrs.org/txtfiles/172852.txt.

Junger, Marianne, & Wim Polder. (1992). Some Explanations of Crime among Four Ethnic Groups in the Netherlands. *Journal of Quantitative Criminology*, 8(1), 51–78.

Katz, Jack. (1988). *Seductions of Crime. Moral and Sensual Attractions in Doing Evil.* New York: Basic Books.

Klein, Malcom W. (1995). *The American Street Gang. Its Nature, Prevalence, and Control.* New York/Oxford: Oxford University Press.

Koopmanns, Ruud. (1995). *A Burning Question: Explaining the Rise of Racist and Extreme Right Violence in Western Europe.* Science Centre Berlin, Research Unit: The Public and Social Movements, Discussion Paper FS III, 95–101.

Kriesi, Hanspeter. (1991). *The Political Opportunity Structure of New Social Movements: Its Impact on Their Mobilization.* Science Centre Berlin, Research Unit: The Public and Social Movements, Discussion Paper FS III, 91–103.

Kühnel, Wolfgang, & Ingo Matuschek. (1995). *Gruppenprozesse und Devianz. Risiken jugendlicher Lebensbewältigung in großstädtischen Monostrukturen.* Weinheim/München: Juventa.

Kühnel, Wolfgang. (1998). Hitler's Grandchildren? The Reemergence of a Right-Wing Social Movement in Germany. In Jeffrey Kaplan & Tore Bjørgo (Eds.), *Nation and Race. The Developing Euro-American Racist Subculture* (pp. 148–174). Boston: Northeastern University Press.

Lamnek, Siegfried, & Otto Schwenk. (1995). *Die Marienplatz-Rapper. Zur Soziologie einer Großstadt-Gang.* Pfaffenweiler: Centaurus.

Loch, Dietmar. (1998). *Jugendliche maghrebinischer Herkunft zwischen Stadtpolitik und Lebenswelt.* Ph. D. Universität Giessen.

Lösel, Friedrich. (1995). Entwicklung und Ursachen der Gewalt in unserer Gesellschaft. *Gruppendynamik*, 26(1), 5–22.

McAdam, Doug, John D. McCarthy, & Mayer N. Zald. (1988). Social Movements. In Neil J. Smelser (Ed.), *The Handbook of Sociology* (pp. 695–737). Newbury Park/London: Sage.

Messner, Steven F., & Richard Rosenfeld. (1996). An Institutional-Anomie Theory of the Social Distribution of Crime. In Peter Cordella & Larry Siegel (Eds.), *Readings in Contemporary Criminological Theory* (pp. 143–148). Boston: Northeastern University Press.

Miller, Walter B. (1970). Lower Class Culture as a Generating Milieu of Gang Delinquency. In David O. Arnold (Ed.), *The Sociology of Subcultures* (pp. 54–63). Berkeley: The Glendessary Press.

Miller, Walter B. (1982). *Crime by Youth Gangs and Groups in the United States.* Washington: U.S. Department of Justice, Office of Justice Programs, Office of Juvenile Justice and Delinquency Prevention.

Moore, Joan W. (1991). *Going Down to the Barrio.* Philadelphia: Temple University Press.

National Youth Gang Center. (1997). *1995 National Youth Gang Survey.* Washington: U.S. Department of Justice, Office of Juvenile Justice and Delinquency Prevention, URL: http://ojjdp.ncjrs.org/pubs/96natyouthgangsrvy/state.html

Neidhardt, Friedhelm. (1983). Themen und Thesen zur Gruppensoziologie. In Friedhelm Neidhardt (Ed.), *Gruppensoziologie. Perspektiven und Materialien* (pp. 12–34). Opladen: Westdeutscher Verlag.

Neidhardt, Friedhelm, & Dieter Rucht. (1993). Auf dem Weg in die Bewegungsgesellschaft? Über die Stabilisierbarkeit sozialer Bewegungen. *Soziale Welt*, 44, 305–326.

Ohder, Claudius. (1992). *Gewalt durch Gruppen Jugendlicher. Eine empirische Untersuchung am Beispiel Berlins.* Berlin: Hitit Verlag.

Padilla, Felix M. (1993). *The Gang as an American Enterprise.* New Brunswick: Rutgers University Press.

Park, Robert E. (1984). Community Organization and Juvenile Delinquency. In Robert E. Park, Ernest W. Burgess & Roderick D. McKenzie (Eds.), *The City* (pp. 99–112). Chicago/London: The University of Chicago Press [1st published in 1925].

Paternoster, Raymond, & Leann Iovanni. (1996). The Labeling Perspective and Delinquency: An Elaboration of the Theory and an Assessment of the Evidence. In Peter Cordella & Larry Siegel (Eds.), *Readings in Contemporary Criminological Theory* (pp. 171-188). Boston: Northeastern University Press.

Sampson, Robert J., & Byron W. Groves. (1989). Community Structure and Crime: Testing Social-Disorganization Theory. *American Journal of Sociology, 94*, 774-802.

Sampson, Robert J., & John H. Laub. (1995). *Crime in the Making. Pathways and Turning Points through Life.* Cambridge: Harvard University Press.

Sampson, Robert J., & William Julius Wilson. (1995). Toward a Theory of Race, Crime, and Urban Inequality. In John Hagan & Ruth D. Peterson (Eds.), *Crime and Inequality* (pp. 37-54). Stanford: Stanford University Press.

Sánchez-Jankowski, Martin. (1991). *Islands in the Street. Gangs and American Urban Society.* Berkeley: University of California Press.

Sanders, William B. (1994). *Gangbangs and Drive-Bys. Grounded Culture and Juvenile Gang Violence.* New York: Aldin de Gruyter.

Schumann, Karl F., Gerald Prein, & Lydia Seus. (1999). Lebenslauf und Delinquenz in der Jugendphase. *DVJJ-Journal, 165*(3), 300-316.

Sellin, Thorsten. (1938). *Cultural Conflict and Crime. A Report of the Subcommittee on Delinquency of the Committee on Personality and Culture. Social Research Council, Bulletin 41.* New York: Social Research Council.

Shaw, Clifford R., & Henry D. McKay. (1969). *Juvenile Delinquency and Urban Areas. A Study of Rates of Delinquency in Relation to Differential Characteristics of Local Communities in American Cities.* Chicago/London: The University of Chicago Press.

Short, James F. (1996). *Gangs and Adolescent Violence.* Boulder: Center for the Study and Prevention of Violence, University of Colorado.

Short, James F. (1997). *Poverty, Ethnicity, and Violent Crime.* Colorado: Westview Press.

Spergel, Irving, & David G. Curry. (1990). Strategies and Perceived Agency Effectiveness in Dealing with the Youth-Gang Problem. In Ronald C. Huff (Ed.), *Gangs in America* (pp. 288-309). Newbury Park: Sage.

Steffen, Wiebke. (1999). Aktuelle Probleme der Jugendkriminalität. In Bundeskriminalamt (Eds.), *Neue Sicherheitsstrategien gegen das Verbrechen* (pp. 91-124). Wiesbaden: Bundeskriminalamt Wiesbaden.

Tajfel, Henri. (1981). *Human Groups and Social Categories. Studies in Social Psychology.* Cambridge: Cambridge University Press.

Tarrow, Sidney. (1983). *Struggling to Reform: Social Movement and Policy Change during Cycles of Protest. Occasional Paper No. 15.* Cornell University.

Tertilt, Hermann. (1996). *Turkish Power Boys. Ethnographie einer Jugendbande.* Frankfurt a. M.: Suhrkamp.

Thornberry, Terence P., Marvin D. Krohn, Alan J. Lizotte, & Deborah Chard-Wierschem. (1993). The Role of Juvenile Gangs in Facilitating Delinquent Behavior. *Journal of Research in Crime and Delinquency, 30*(1), 55-87.

Thornberry, Terence P., & James H. Burch. (1997). *Gang Members and Delinquent Behavior, Research in Brief.* Washington: U.S. Department of Justice, National Institute of Justice, URL: http://www.ncjrs.org/txtfiles/165154.txt.

Trasher, Frederic M. (1927). *The Gang. A Study of 1.313 Gangs in Chicago.* Chicago: The University of Chicago Press.

Trotha, Trutz von. (1993). Kultur, Subkultur, Kulturkonflikt. In Günther Kaiser, Hans-Jürgen Kerner, Fritz Sack & Hartmut Schellhoss (Eds.), *Kleines kriminologisches Wörterbuch* (pp. 338-345). Heidelberg: C.F. Müller Juristischer Verlag.

U.S. Department of Justice. (1999). *National Youth Gang Survey.* URL: http://ojjdp.ncjrs.org/pubs/96natyouthgangsrvy/state.html.

Vigil, James Diego. (1990). Cholos and Gangs: Cultural Change and Street Youth in Los Angeles. In Ronald D. Huff (Ed.), *Gangs in America* (pp. 116-128). Newbury Park: Sage.

Vigil, James Diego, & Steve Chong Yun. (1990). Vietnamese Youth Gangs in Southern California. In Ronald D. Huff (Ed.), *Gangs in America* (pp. 146-162). Newbury Park: Sage.

Wacquant, Loic J. D. (1994). Le gang comme prédateur collectif. *Actes des la Recherche en Sciences Sociales, 101-102*, 88-100.

Westin, Charles. (1998). On Migration and Criminal Offense. In Vorstand des Instituts für Migrationsforschung und Interkulturelle Studien (IMIS) (Eds.), *IMIS-Beiträge, 8* (pp. 7-29). Osnabrück: Universität Osnabrück.

Willems, Helmut. (1997). *Jugendunruhen und Protestbewegungen. Eine Studie zur Dynamik innergesellschaftlicher Konflikte in vier europäischen Ländern.* Opladen: Leske und Budrich.

Whyte, William F. (1964). *Street Corner Society. The Social Structure of an Italian Slum*. Chicago/London: The University of Chicago Press [1st published in 1943].

Wolfgang, Marvin E., & Franco Ferracuti. (1970). Subculture of Violence: An Integrated Conceptualization. In David O. Arnold (Ed.), *The Sociology of Subcultures* (pp. 135–149). Berkeley: The Glendessary Press.

Yablonski, Lewis. (1966). *The Violent Gang*. Baltimore: Penguin Books [1st published in 1962].

Yinger, Milton J. (1970). Contraculture and Subculture. In David O. Arnold (Ed.), *The Sociology of Subcultures* (pp. 121–134). Berkeley: The Glendessary Press.

CHAPTER II-7.4

Escalation and De-Escalation of Social Conflicts: The Road to Violence

ROLAND ECKERT AND HELMUT WILLEMS

1. INTRODUCTION: DESCRIPTION OF THE PHENOMENON AND DEFINITIONS

Conflict escalation—in the sense of an intensifying, difficult-to-control, hostile aggravation of forms of interaction—is as ubiquitous as conflict itself. From the process of increasing emotionalization in interpersonal disputes to the brutalization of relations between groups or states to the point where violence, terrorism, and war are involved: wherever conflicts arise there is a risk of escalation.

To date there has been little investigation of the many causes of this tendency to escalation, which is inherent to conflict. As we know from our everyday experience, our behavior in conflicts is generally quite different from our normal behavior, not least because our capability to deal with conflict is often poorly developed. In conflicts, we tend to look for the causes of conflict in our "adversary," especially when we are under pressure to justify ourselves. Such causal attributions, however, have consequences. In fact, they assume not only that the other started the argument, the conflict, or even the use of unfair means up to and including violence, but also that the other has particular motives for their actions. With our response or countermove, we then react not only to the other's actions but also to the motives we attribute to the other without necessarily being able to know them. We are familiar with such escalation mechanisms from everyday situations in kindergarten, the family, school, work, politics, and sport, and they have also been described for public disputes—for conflicts between social, political, and ethnic groups, as well as conflicts between states (cf. Pruitt & Rubin, 1986).

Here, willingness to commit violence and use of violence in conflicts are treated—in the first place—not as personality traits or motives of one or both parties to the conflict, nor as a simple product of structural conditions. Rather, they are seen as specific features of conflict situations in which either a) escalative patterns of behavior appear to provide a rational, effective, and auspicious problem-solving option, or b) use of violence is felt to be acceptable and without risk due to changed legitimations, ideologies, and structures of opportunity, or c) emotions like anger, hate, and thirst for vengeance take control of behavior and mask rational strategies, or d) the "fundamentalization" of the conflict serves to attract solidarity and support.

For a long time, despite its enormous importance for the development, outcome, and cost of conflicts, escalation was not an independent field of basic sociological research (cf. Giegel, 1998; Bonacker, 1996). The various theories of social conflict have concentrated primarily on the question of why such conflicts arise in society, what are the associated general social conditions for conflicts to arise, and which specific constellations of interests and conflict actors characterize a society. They have, however, paid little attention to the question of what the preconditions are for the various forms of conflict development and, in particular, what causes conflicts to escalate to the point where violence is applied. Escalation was treated either as an aspect of rational conflict strategies (cf. Schelling, 1960), or—in particular as a result of the early approaches of mass psychology—as an expression of the irrationality of collective action (cf. LeBon, 1938). Specific research into escalation has only developed in the past thirty years, with the most important stimuli coming from people looking for alternative forms of conflict resolution from a very practical point of view (Deutsch, 1976; Fisher, 1972; Doob, 1970; Kelman, 1965; Rubin & Brown, 1975; Eckert & Willems, 1992; Merkel, 1995). In the following, we will first examine the classical sociological conflict theories with respect to their contribution to the understanding of conflict escalation, before discussing a number of theoretical approaches that provide important contributions specifically concerning the explanation of conflict escalation.

We normally speak of conflict when clashes of interests between individuals, groups, social classes, etc. (latent conflicts) have turned into actual disputes and open struggle (manifest conflicts) (cf. Coser, 1960). Of course, conflicts are not simply preordained by objective structural clashes of interests (capital vs. labor), but are themselves the result of the intersubjective definition of interests, values, identities, and their limits. People fight not only over 'material' interests, for example life chances, but also over ideals. For thousands of years people have let themselves become seized by ideas, attempting to promote or prevent their dissemination. Whether people are fighting over food, land, honor, or belief, the consequences for them are often the same. In contrast to simple competition or latent conflict of interests, participants in manifest social conflicts have to inflict a defeat on the opponent by using the appropriate resources, realize their own goals even if this is at the opponent's expense, defend themselves, or force a compromise. The mere existence of a conflict does not mean that social relations between the parties are completely unregulated; on the contrary, conflict relations are usually structured and normed according to the normative and institutional conditions of a society (cf. Roberts, 1984; Simmel, 1958, [1923]). At the same time, conflicts, especially those that are not institutionally regulated in a society, have an inherent tendency to escalate, which can lead to neutralization, injury, or even destruction of one or more of the parties to the conflict.

By escalation we mean the intentional or unintentional intensification of a conflict with regard to the extent and the means used (cf. Olson, 1968; Pruitt & Rubin, 1986). As such, it represents an often self-amplifying process of action-reaction spirals, whose outcome is difficult to forecast or control. "Escalations are processes of circular interaction where all participants push one another toward growing divergence" (Neidhardt, 1989:25). Escalating conflicts lead the involved parties to adopt changing strategies and forms of action, and take up new issues and demands. They often lead to the growth and restructuring of the parties, generating new reasons and pretexts for applying additional means (additional mobilization of resources), thus usually leading to an expansion and fundamentalization of the content of the conflict. In particular, intensification of disputes to the point where physical violence is used should be regarded as characteristic for conflict escalation.

2. CLASSICAL CONFLICT THEORIES AND THE NEGLECT OF THE QUESTION OF ESCALATION

Conflict theory models were developed in a deliberate distinction to other social models based more strongly on assumptions of consensus and equilibrium (cf. Parsons, 1964). They emphasize the central importance of conflict for social development and transformation, but also the integrative function of conflict for society or sections of society.

Alongside Marx and Engels, the main proponents of social conflict theories are Simmel and—building on his work—Coser and Dahrendorf.

2.1. Sociostructural Conflict Analysis (Marx; Dahrendorf)

The Marxist theoretical tradition sees the cause of social conflict above all in the antagonism between the productive forces in society (capital and labor) and the resulting formation of classes (Marx & Engels, 1983, [1848]). The central conflict in society is the economic conflict of interests between major social groups (classes) as distinguished by their differing ownership of the means of production. Although the formation of classes (class-in-itself, class-for-itself) and the development of class struggle take a central place in the Marxist theory of class conflict, the important questions of the organization, strategy, and escalation of conflicts (up to successful revolution) and their respective historical and social conditions are not dealt with in detail, but answered schematically. "The charge against Marx or the Marxists... is...that such questions of detail are excluded or avoided through aprioristic answers," rather than investigated empirically (Bühl, 1976:22). The most prominent attempt to develop a general, empirical conflict theory for modern societies based on Marxist class theory originates from Dahrendorf (1969). Like Marx, Dahrendorf also assumes the "postulate of the societal imminence of the conflict" (Bonacker, 1996:65) and clearly states that conflicts are unavoidable in any society and are therefore universal. Unlike Marx, however, Dahrendorf sees social conflicts as arising not automatically from antagonistic structures—diverging class interests—but rather conditioned by the ubiquity of power and the social necessity to set norms and enforce binding decisions (where interests diverge). Instead of class conflicts leading to power, (necessary) power leads to class conflict as a medium of social transformation. Dahrendorf thus expands and updates a decisive point in Marxist class theory by speaking of a social ubiquity of social transformation and social conflict. However, his interest in the processual nature and momentum of social conflicts does not result in a theory of conflict development or of the escalation of conflicts, even though he does point out that social institutionalization of conflicts is a central precondition for conflicts to be beneficial to social development.

2.2. Functionalistic Conflict Theories (Simmel; Coser)

The significance of Georg Simmel (1992, [1923]) for the development of a conflict theory perspective in sociology is a matter of controversy to this day (cf. Bonacker, 1996). His influence, however, is still of great importance, especially in the work of Coser (1972). The name of Simmel stands above all for a conflict theory perspective where conflicts are described and understood as a form of socialization. Starting from the idea that interpersonal behavior is characterized by both associative and dissociative motives and tendencies, Simmel demonstrates the socializing forms that conflictive interactions can take: they are constitutive for the development and unification of social groups (as a form of unification of interests), they promote developments within the group (homogenization), and they also act as catalysts for conflicts within the group.

Simmel's conflict theory (Simmel, 1992, [1923]) was later revived and developed by Coser, in particular, as part of a functionalist perspective. Drawing on Simmel, Coser emphasizes the principally socializing function of social conflict. At the same time, however, he examines the conditions under which conflicts are functional or dysfunctional for a society. According to Coser, social conflicts are only dysfunctional when they are "unreal" conflicts (where the conflict is "displaced" from its actual subject), when society provides no institutional forms of conflict expression; or when the various social conflicts merge to form one conflict of identity, whereby the disruptive aspects of social conflicts no longer neutralize one another (cf. Simmel, 1992). Thus, according to Coser, the flexibility of social structures is absolutely decisive for the effects of social conflict on society. Coser sees open, pluralistic societies as normally characterized by a large number of conflicts that are, however, reduced in intensity ("cross-cutting conflicts") by citizens' multiple affiliations to various interest groups and identities (e.g., social class, race, religion, origin, ethnic group, etc.). However, escalation of conflicts often causes such multiple loyalties ("secondary contradictions" in the Marxist terminology) to be repressed deliberately, or, as a consequence of experience in conflict, conflict-related identities become salient. Although Coser's conflict analysis emphasizes not only questions of social functionality but also specific intra-group and inter-group effects (homogenization and conflict, conflict and the search for allies, conflict and groups), thus identifying important factors of conflict expression and potential conflict escalation; the subject of "escalation" itself has no meaning for him.

2.3. The Civilization Process and Its Limitations (Elias)

The prime importance of social structures (especially institutions) for the social effect of conflict is also thematized in Elias's civilization theory. His premise is that competition and struggle between different ruling organizations lead to the formation of ever larger units. To the extent that these are able to implement a monopoly on the use of physical violence, a wide range of legal, vocational, and social sanctions makes it increasingly risky for a person to express aggression in the form of violence (cf. Elias, 1969, 2:312–341). This leads to increasing control of the emotions, expressed as self-control. Admittedly, criticism of this part of Elias's theory has grown louder since the crimes of the twentieth century demonstrated how quickly such mechanisms of self-control can be set aside in conflict situations. Even in societies generally regarded as civilized, conditions exist that in the eyes of many call into question the meaningfulness of self-control and affect control. People live in social groups and milieus where each can develop their own definition of conflict and of legitimate and illegitimate violence. These intersubjectively mediated definitions delineate what triggers aggression and also what is defined relatively unaggressively as an object on which violence must be exerted. Von Trotha (1974) demonstrated this in his work on conditions of socialization in slums. In slums that form in modern cities due to migration and/or exclusion cycles in the labor market, and where neighborhood and police control has little effect, youth gangs resort to particularistic patterns of conflict expression and develop their own rules of fair and unfair combat. In this way, communities based on social space, ethnicity, religion, or ideology can define for their members "legitimate" reasons for violence and identify "legitimate" victims.

3. THEORETICAL APPROACHES TO CONFLICT ESCALATION

The discussion so far has clearly shown that classical conflict theories in the social sciences have barely commented on the question of escalation. In the following, we will outline some more recent approaches from social science and social psychology and examine their relevance for explaining conflict escalation and dynamics.

3.1. Sociobiological Findings

Escalation means that the respective stake is increased in order to achieve a goal against an adversary. Violence is a resource in conflict, which can—depending on the circumstances—be costly not only for the party on the receiving end, but normally also for the party exercising it. Mechanisms that have been well researched in animals are involved here (cf. Wilson, 1980). Archer and Huntingford (1994) point to struggles for sexual partners, territory, and rank, where processes of increasing and decreasing the level of violence can be found. Violent conflicts between rivals start, for example, when the relative fighting strength is unclear, they escalate until one animal "gives up," recognizing that it has little chance of winning. Corresponding behavior can certainly be interpreted in economic terms and formalized in a game theory strategy where risks and win chances are calculated (cf. Archer & Huntingford, 1994). Something very similar applies to ranking struggles among school students, for example, where relative strength and combat readiness are tested verbally and physically, and in warlike tribes where a man's status depends on the number of men he has killed (cf. Chagnon, 1988). According to Chagnon, status that is generated through readiness to combat has to be defended by fighting, should a serious rival appear. Violence only recedes when one side is clearly superior: the threat is credible.

However, when rivals know their respective strength and combat readiness and have nothing to test out, an escalation must have other causes. Raising the stakes in conflict is not always rational (i.e., instrumental in the sense of expected enforcement of one's own goals). In conflicts, emotions such as fear, hate, anger, and thirst for vengeance can develop their own logic that suppresses any strategic calculation and contributes to escalation (cf. Mummendey, 1984). That such impulsive aggression in humans is found particularly under conditions of reduced cognitive capacity, for example due to consumption of alcohol or group dynamic processes, clearly demonstrates that theories of rational choice fail here. In evolutionary biological terms, one can, of course, speculate that "rage" was probably once a precondition for a successful "berserker." Violent youth cliques also demonstrate that such states are not merely suffered, but can also be actively sought and generated (cf. Eckert et al., 2000). Psychophysical states also have a momentum of their own and often have an intrinsic value, which can also influence profit-oriented calculations and restrict the rationality of action in conflict.

3.2. Escalation as a Rational Strategy

Constructions based on rational choice and game theory have proven particularly useful for analyzing international conflicts, where a certain degree of rationality can be ascribed to the actors. These theories assume that even escalative and violent action in conflicts can be explained as the result of utilitarian calculations and decisions. Both the value-expectation approaches (Muller, 1979; Opp, 1984) and the game theory variants (Berkowitz, 1965; Rapoport, 1960; Schelling, 1960; cf. also Axelrod, 1984) understand the use of violence in conflicts as a result of individual benefit maximization strategies (with consideration to restrictions and prospects of success). However, the number of actors and the number of marginal conditions of the fight must by necessity be restricted if they are to be included in the calculation. The additional factor that not the *actual*, but the *suspected* strength of the opponent determines the calculated outcome—meaning that bluff and deception also increase the number of possible outcomes—makes it difficult to calculate returns even where the fundamental logic of the conflict is apparent (cf. Bueno de Mesquita & Morrow, 1997). This limits the suitability of play theory concepts for modeling real processes because there are often nonlinear relationships between linked variables in these processes, causing them to proceed chaotically.

Although there are difficulties associated with game theory modeling, the character of escalation is nonetheless potentially rational. Escalative intensification of conflicts can certainly make sense in the context of a rational strategy for securing direct, for example material interests (in property, territorial rule, or state power). More indirect purposes can also be the object of strategically calculated escalations. Precisely because it is subject to a strong taboo, violence is always at the center of media attention. Where violence does not merely "occur," but is justified, for example as a protest, it always draws attention to the justification. In this way, violence sets the themes of public discourse, and the media's role in escalating conflicts gains in importance (see Brosius & Esser, 1996).

According to Hardin (1995), the rationality postulate also applies to the escalation of ethnic conflicts, which are often interpreted as outbreaks of irrational hatred. Hardin's basic proposition is that conflicts between ethnic communities are not irrational, primordial, or moral, but guided by individual interests and in that sense rational, even if their outcome is often associated with negative consequences for the participating groups and their members. According to Hardin, people are linked with their groups of origin by an "epistemological advantage," because their familiarity means that time- and energy-consuming processes of learning and adaptation can be dispensed with. On this basis, particularistic norms of belonging can develop, which are at the same time norms for excluding others. With these norms, cooperation can be generated, and the antinomies of collective action, as described by Olson (1968), can be overcome because collectively created and individually realizable benefits can be expected. Thus, according to Hardin, particularistic norms are stronger than universalistic ones: universalistic norms are only strengthened by self-interest where they are self-evident in direct application or functional for self-protection.

3.3. Structural Tensions, Deprivation, and Mobilization

For a long time, the social sciences concentrated on the search for "objective" causes of violence in the sense of "structural" tensions. Cultural or economic disadvantage, social disintegration, and conflicts over norms and values were normally assumed to be objective conditions for violent conflict (cf. Smelser, 1972; Heitmeyer, 1993). The results of macrosociological and international comparative research (cf. Zimmermann, 1980) are, however, not unambiguous. Plainly it is not objective conditions as such, but collective interpretations that determine the worldview on which people base their strategies. In each case, the appearance of a promising opportunity for action must additionally be presumed before the outbreak and escalation of social conflict (on the importance of structures of opportunity, see Tarrow, 1991; Willems, 1996), or at least the idea that the difficult situation is both unjust (on ideas of justice, see Moore, 1987) and open to change (on the stabilization of collective protest and social movements, see Neidhardt & Rucht, 1993). The sociopsychological theory of "relative deprivation" (cf. Davies, 1969; Runciman, 1972; Gurr, 1970) has served relatively well to explain protest and rebellion. Dissatisfaction, protest, and violence escalate where social and economic expectations diverge from perceived chances of realization. Here, comparisons with relevant reference groups are decisive (Willems & Eckert, 1995). In political processes, individual deprivation is less important than "fraternal relative deprivation" (Runciman, 1972), where the perceived disadvantage and preferential treatment of whole social groups leads to a feeling of injustice. Here the appearance of mobilizing actors and the presence of pertinent political ideologies play a central role. In particular McCarthy and Zald (1973) and Tilly (1978) have pointed to the importance of mobilization processes. Political entrepreneurs can mobilize ideas of disadvantage and injustice, direct existing dissatisfaction into readiness for action, and recruit and organize existing resources accordingly. In this connection Zald and McCarthy even speak of "social movement industries" (Zald & McCarthy, 1997). The perception of relative deprivation can thus be the result of such mobilization processes rather than their cause (cf. also Willems, 1997), because the corresponding evaluation criteria and "frames" (McAdam, 1997) are not present in the participants' consciousness until they are established there by the actors.

This approach has also proved useful for analysis of ethnopolitical conflicts. Here, however, it is apparent that violent disputes result not so much from perceived inequality as such than from changes in the position of groups in a social hierarchy, the "incorporation transformation" (cf. Hanf, 1990:35–45), through which the comparative assets are changed.

3.4. Interactionistic Approaches

Symbolic interactionism rejects the idea that the mere existence of objective circumstances (conflicting interests, structural inequality) is enough to generate conflict and influence its progression, assuming instead that the perception and collective interpretation of these circumstances plays a crucial role (in particular Blumer, 1969; Turner & Kilian, 1972). However, according to the interactionists, the development of these collective definition processes is almost impossible to predict and control. The definition processes are influenced by spontaneous and often diffuse communication processes within the groups and by the interaction process between the conflicting parties themselves. A cycle of action, communication, and interpretation arises, which can of itself lead to unpredictable results.

This sequence applies to the generation and development of political protest and social conflict up to the use of violence (cf. Willems, 1997). Dramatic events that contribute to activating attention and interest and also trigger escalation spirals may lead to new plausible collective interpretations and normative revisions, and a new motivation for action (cf. Turner & Kilian, 1972); but these new interpretations arise above all through interaction processes between protest groups and other social groups or public opinion, politics, and the police (Willems, 1988a, b). For the understanding of politically motivated violence, this means that willingness to use violence and violent action can be attributed neither solely to individual disposition nor to a simple reaction to structural conditions. More important in many cases is the logic of specific situations where violence can either be selected rationally as a problem-solving option (cf. Gamson, 1975), or where people with a predisposition to stimulation by fighting, danger, and violence receive their particular opportunity. Especially in unregulated political conflicts, situations often arise where violent action is not just acceptable to the participants (due to past normative revisions) and associated with only limited risk (through the existing structures of opportunity), but actually appears promising and effective (through changes in the plausibility assumptions). The reaction of state control actors plays an important role here: escalation processes can be initiated both by overreaction and by underreaction (cf. Neidhardt, 1989). Of course, violence that is learned in such situations can then be generalized as an attitude and willingness to act, and take effect independently of the situation.

3.5. Social Psychological Mechanisms

From the outset, social psychological works on the formation and modification of perceptions and attitudes between groups (cf. Likert, 1932; Katz, 1960), and also on the development of stereotypes and prejudices (Allport & Postman, 1946), were characterized by strong interest in the significance of corresponding social psychological factors for describing and explaining the relations and conflicts between social groups.

Like symbolic interactionism, social psychological approaches assume that an analysis of conflict activity and interactions must account for the importance of subjective perceptions, restricted cognition, and individual attitudes and values. "How parties perceive and interpret each other's actions will be a prime determinant of how they will respond and thereby of how conflict interaction will unfold" (Fisher, 1990:7). Deutsch (1976), in particular, in his phenomenological conflict analysis, emphasized that conflict parties acted according to their perceptions and interpretations, and that conflict activity is particularly strongly oriented on the expectations regarding the opponent's actions. Social psychological conflict analyses have often stressed how, for example, individual cognitions, attitudes and emotions, and their modification in conflict can influence the behavior of the group, and how conversely factors such as group-dynamic developments during a conflict (e.g., increasing pressure for consensus and conformity in the face of concrete confrontation) in turn influence individual perceptions (cf. also Eckert & Willems, 1986; Willems, 1988a, 1997). The social psychological analysis of the interaction between the individual level and the social level has made a particularly significant contribution to the understanding of the escalative dynamic of conflict. Some of the mechanisms found here also apply very generally to interaction in conflict. When we argue or fight, we often see the cause of the quarrel ('who started it?') in the behavior of the adversary and tend to emphasize this when making justifications to third parties. Watzlawick, Beavin and Jackson (1969) describe this as punctuation of event sequences, about which the opposing sides of the conflict will be unable to agree. Instead, the opposing sides will have different ideas about where the confrontation started and how the actions relate to one another as cause or effect. Normally they become involved in a strategic metaconflict over the history of their conflict. While neutral observers tend to speak of conflict spirals, whose origins and role distribution cannot be clearly defined, the participants in a conflict normally work with an aggressor-defender model (cf. Pruitt & Rubin, 1986), which always assigns cause and blame to the other party.

Escalation in these conflict spirals is also fueled by the distinction conflict parties make between apparent behavior and the feelings and intentions claimed to be behind this behavior. The actions of the conflict opponent are interpreted as the expression of particular aims, and the reaction always relates to these imputed motives and aims. In conflict situations, which are characterized by mistrust and often by deficient communication, these attribution processes often develop their own self-amplifying dynamic: insecurity, fear, lack of information, stereotyped prejudices about the opponent, and even simple caution push the process of attribution of goals toward assuming the worst (for the significance of the "worst-case scenario," cf. Booth, 1979). Conflict action is planned according to these assumptions (which are treated as real) and can even trigger the expected reaction by the opponent in the sense of a "self-fulfilling prophecy" (Merton, 1957). Here the dimensions of the misunderstandings and problems of understanding and communication that are produced and processed cyclically in conflict action start to become apparent.

Furthermore, conflicts always generate situations with great pressure to act. This automatically reduces the time available for reflection and interpretation of experience and for planning one's own action. The actions of the conflict participants thus often have the character of spontaneous reactions to events that have just occurred, or even to events that are merely expected (Blumer, 1969; Turner & Kilian, 1972). Thus, unregulated conflict situations are relatively open, unstructured fields of action that only find their respective definition in the interaction of the conflict parties. For that reason, they initially generate insecurity and with it an increased demand for regulation and orientation on the part of the actors. For these reasons, it is highly probable that individual participants and leadership personalities will be able to have a structuring and exemplary influence. Because their charisma grows out of an exceptional situation, they often have little interest in normalization, or believe that the emphatic nature of the conflict marks the new age into which they are predestined to lead.

The complexity of the situation, the failure of familiar orientation models, and the opponent's incalculable threat (to life, health, self-image, own interests, etc.) also contribute to generating feelings of powerlessness, insecurity, fear, and anger, which can sometimes significantly influence cognition and action during conflicts (cf. Jervis, 1976; White, 1965; cf. also Euler & Mandel, 1983). Fear initially raises alertness and cognitive sensibility, thus increasing willingness to learn. At the same time, however, fear always causes physical stress and the associated aversive reactions, i.e., it forces fast elimination of the state of fear. At the cognitive level, this leads to a reduction of the learning horizon and to a de-differentiation of learned content. Contrast-intensifying and one-sided, selective information is preferred, as provided in particular in the corresponding ideologies and dehumanizing images of the enemy, (cf. Heitmeyer, 1987; Willems, 1993). Finally, the violence practiced and suffered also has to be dealt with and legitimized through a supraindividual, if possible historical meaning (Eckert, 1976; Mummendey, 1984).

However, escalation-promoting emotions relate not only to the conflict opponent. They also accompany the experience of the subject's own group. Euphoric feelings of group solidarity, competence in action, and power and superiority can be experienced in conflict. Solidarity frequently becomes the ruling norm (Gould, 1999). It ensures coherence and conformity within the group, but prohibits any tolerance of deviations. During the conflict, the fighters do not, however, normally perceive this bonding to the group and its norms as a normative requirement, experiencing it instead as feelings of trust, security, shelter, unity, and solidarity (cf. Willems, 1988b et al.), and interpreting this as the inception of a new community, a new nation, or a new human.

Regardless of the specific feelings involved, the strong emotional stimulation in conflict situations increases the memorability of learning experiences, which therefore often retain their effect beyond the concrete situation and increase the resistance to reception of additional contradictory information (on avoidance of dissonance, cf. Festinger, 1968). This often means that people remain in or join groups that back up the new cognition by confirming its reality. This can lead to extreme isolation of the individual groups, or to their splitting and differentiating into separate subgroups. So, what is learnt in conflicts is determined by both the conflict experience with the opponent and by experience within the own group. In both cases, learning in conflict is decisively influenced and characterized by concrete situations where emotions are triggered directly.

Once violence has been introduced as a means of enforcement in conflicts, it begins to take on a life of its own, both with respect to its original "causes" and to specific objectives. Violence legitimizes counterviolence, threat legitimizes counterthreat, in the end leading violence to become a routine form of interaction that ceases to pose any particular problems of legitimation.

This phenomenon, which can be observed in families and among young people, gains an additional dimension when organizations specifically for exercising violence arise within a society: squads, militias, security services, "private armies." Like all organizations, they develop their own interest in continuing to exist. This reason alone is enough to make escalation a rational strategy. At the same time the boundaries between political use of violence (which may be legally controlled) and commercial use of violence (cf. Waldmann, 1990) become unclear. This applies to "freedom fighters" and terrorists, and often also to government soldiers. Markets for violence are created and can then be used by other interested parties (cf. Elwert, 1997).

3.6. Escalation Models

Social conflicts in their various manifestations cannot be described as static phenomena, but are instead characterized in particular by the way they develop—there is general agreement in research on this. The question, however, of whether there are typical development and escalation processes that always recur in various conflicts is still debated. Attempts to create a comprehensive model of conflict escalation have to date largely dealt with military conflicts between states. Here it was Hermann Kahn (1965), in particular, who developed a (forty-four-stage) model for international conflicts, which was designed as a diagnostic framework. This escalation model is little suited to our purposes, because Kahn's differentiation of individual stages of escalation results primarily from the availability of weapons and technologies in military conflicts. Furthermore, Kahn concentrates exclusively on the instrumental escalations, meaning those actions by which parties deliberately intensify the conflict to the point where violence is used. Here, however, we also have to describe those mechanisms and factors that are responsible for unwanted, unintentional, and difficult-to-control escalation of conflicts. Glasl summarized this cataclysmic understanding of conflict in his core statement: "As soon as the escalation process has been started by one or both sides, it develops an internal dynamic that drives it ever forward and leads to increased tension. This means that conflict escalation is a pathological event that can only partially be controlled for better or worse" (Glasl, 1980:192).

For the past thirty years, conflict research has concentrated on investigating such mechanisms. The work of Richardson (1960), Rapoport (1972), Fisher (1972), and others examines such mechanisms of non-intentional conflict escalation more closely. Feelings of hostility and mistrust, as well as the manner of reciprocal perception and interpretation are identified as relevant factors of unwanted escalation processes. For conflicts within societies, however, there have so far been few attempts to systematize escalation mechanisms and combine them in a model (cf. Kriesberg, 1982; Oberschall, 1973). The investigation of collective protest and new social movements tended to focus on attempts to identify generally valid processes of progression and development phases (Rammstedt, 1978), or to identify the factors required for progress and stabilization (Schneider, 1987; Sack, 1984; Neidhardt & Rucht, 1993, Willems, 1994). The escalation processes themselves were rarely the subject of systematic investigation.

Glasl (1980) attempted to develop such a model of escalation in conflicts within organizations. Unlike many other authors, Glasl imagines the escalation process not as an ascending ladder, but as a descending movement. In this way, he describes that escalation "leads with a certain compelling force into regions" where "the capacity to correct, brake, and control" is significantly impaired (Glasl, 1980:235). Glasl assumes that each new level of escalation also restricts the options for action of the conflict parties. He thus sees the escalation process as a process of successive closings of existing alternatives for action and the opening of new (albeit specifically restricted) ones. On the individual level, this restriction of alternatives for action corresponds to a cognitive and moral regression. "The conflict parties thus allow themselves to be guided by habits of thought, feelings, and moods, as well as motives and aims that do not correspond to the degree of their actual maturity, but are throwbacks to "simple" phases of the maturing process that have already been experienced and "overcome" (Glasl, 1980:236). The three main phases of escalation can be described as follows: In main phase 1, the conflict parties are aware of the existence of tension and conflicts of interest, but are still attempting to find a proper solution by means of communication. The behavior of the conflict parties is oriented more strongly toward cooperation than one-sided enforcement of interests. In main phase 2, tension is generated not just by the objective problem, but also by the manner of interaction and the relationship between the conflict parties. The issues at stake in the conflict expand, and at the same time the reciprocal perceptions change to the point where stereotypes and foe images develop. Now, mistrust and lack of respect between the conflict parties prevent direct communication. Cooperation-based strategies are abandoned, and the parties are primarily interested in enforcing their own interests, even against the other party. Nonetheless, moral and ethical considerations still restrict the choice of means. In phase 3, the actual problem recedes completely into the background, and its place is taken by the problematic relationship between the two now-hostile conflict parties. The prime goal of each party is not to enforce its original interests, but to destroy or damage the other party, which is now said to completely lack dignity. "The greater the willingness to accept one's own demise rather than change course and possibly give the enemy a chance of winning, the greater the probability of blind ideas of vengeance becoming fixated on damaging the opposing side. In the end, further intensification of the conflict can end with fanatic self-destruction" (Glasl, 1980:237). Glasl describes the transitions between the main phases as regression thresholds, where perceptions, attitudes, and types of behavior are transformed, as is the self-understanding of the parties. He identifies various basic mechanisms of escalation, which drastically reduce the conflict parties' capacity to control the events and direct them in any direction other than escalation: "Whatever the parties do in the framework of these mechanisms to gain control of the situation, they simply maneuver themselves deeper into the conflict each time" (Glasl, 1980:200). Brockner and Rubin (1985) pertinently characterized this phenomenon as "entrapment in escalating conflicts."

Of course Glasl's phase model, which is formulated through to the most extreme form of escalation, must not be misunderstood as an inescapable life cycle for every escalation. Radicalization of actions up to the use of violence is not always preceded by a constructive trustworthy appeal, as Brand (1982) pointed out in view of the manifold youth protests and regional movements in Europe. Furthermore, conflicts do not always escalate to the stage where reciprocal destruction comes to the fore even at the risk of self-destruction. Because escalations are very costly and risky, even for those who drive them forward, there are always also (not only moral) inhibitions and calculations, which may be able to act to limit the conflict. Because Glasl concentrates on escalation-promoting factors and mechanisms, the result is necessarily an image of escalation that stresses the driving and uncontrollable dynamic rather than a process in stages where other outcomes are possible at each stage.

4. ON THE WAY TO TAMING VIOLENCE?

4.1. Conflict Regulation as a Task of Social Construction

The problem and importance of social order (Elster, 1989; Hobbes, 1996, [1651]) relates to the conflictual nature of human coexistence per se. Conflicts are both necessary and unavoidable for the development and survival of societies. However, even major conflicts do not necessarily lead to violence. Rather, it depends on whether peaceful as well as warlike options are available for regulating conflict. In this context, the level of violence in a society is decisively influenced by the relationship between the extent of conflicts occurring and the capacity of the available instruments of conflict regulation. From the perspective of evolutionary theory, the history of democracy and the legal system can be understood as a repeatedly undertaken attempt to improve the conflict-regulation competence of the society in question—always in competition with the increasing efficiency of violence and the increase in the number of conflict-laden decision-making problems. All the historical and ethnological evidence suggests that nonviolent conflict solutions require more preconditions and are therefore less probable. Primary responsibility for these solutions is held by the political organization of a society, which of course stands in a reciprocal relationship with the religious values and ethical educational models of that society.

Which factors are effective in conflict regulation? For small social groups and societies, where the degree of mutual interdependence is very high, there are many opportunities for formal and informal sanctions (Malinowski, 1976; Olson, 1968). In internal conflicts, the group as a whole, in particular, has many options for ensuring conformity, forcing conflict parties to compromise, or excluding deviating individuals (Roberts, 1984:68). Where mutual interdependence is low (Koch, 1974:110), and especially in "external" conflicts, people protect themselves using the second option—revenge and threat of revenge. This applies in particular in societies where there is no central agency of rule that can claim religious or political authority to administer and enforce justice. Accordingly, for example, blood vengeance survived longest in those parts of Europe—Scotland, Corsica, Albania, etc.—where state rule was weak. The honor (Luhmann, 1972:150) of the tribe, defended by the "man," is part of such a system of deterrence. The reason for this behavior is not a lack of "civilization" in these societies (similar patterns are also inherent to every military doctrine of deterrence, and were found, e.g., in the East–West conflict). Instead, there is—speaking in terms of game theory—a structural situation where as long as his opponents possess the option of attack, each actor has to be credibly armed. In ongoing conflicts, the interest in credibility forces the actor to follow a strategy of at least limited escalation (Leng, 1994). Precisely this armament, however, "tempts" the actor to exploit an opportune moment to carry out a first or preventive strike and collect accordingly large gains (Otterbein, 1970:942). The consequences of such a situation for all actors are instability and high security costs that do not, however, exclude existential risks.

In societies with little or no legal system, alternatives to the system of deterrence are offered only by mediators, who can formulate compromises in cases of conflict and propose solutions, and thus restrict the use of self-redress (vengeance and threat of vengeance) (Koch, 1974:107). In some societies, local and supralocal (especially religious) agencies can exert significant pressure on participants to reach a settlement between perpetrator and victim. Contemporary international politics also shares this aim. With its Kuwait resolutions, the United Nations reproduced the legal practice of the ancient Icelandic Althingi that was established a thousand years ago. When mediation attempts fail, the guilty party can be ostracized, and nobody assists him, but the victim must enforce his right with the help of his friends (whereby Kuwait had an easier position in the Gulf War than Bosnia in the ethnopolitical wars in former Yugoslavia).

The bigger the group, the less likely it is able to oblige opponents to follow rules and even less to limit violence. It follows that an actor who accepts such restrictions and thus meets the interests of others without this behavior being reciprocated is likely to suffer disadvantages from this strategy and sooner or later to feel like a "dupe." Thus, in supralocal networked societies "The need for decisions on sanctions provides one of the most active driving forces behind the institutionalization of power structures" (Popitz, 1980:53). Through a process that is normally extremely violent, a ruler or the state can establish a monopoly on jurisdiction and use of physical violence (Hobbes, 1996, [1651]). For the subjects or citizens, this produces a "disarmament advantage" (Buchanan, 1975:58; Vanberg, 1978:655). They no longer have to look after themselves through deterrence. The problem of violence does not vanish, however, but is transposed to the level of the ruler or the state, because monopolization of violence is not necessarily control or reduction thereof. Quite the contrary: during the formation of states, the process of legitimization of physical violence is accompanied by excessive violence. Once a state has monopolized violence, it can then become an actor of intensified violence. Violence also becomes modernized in terms of weapons technology, social organization, and ideological justification. The twentieth century has more than demonstrated the potential for state-organized collective crimes.

4.2. Conflict Limitation through Democracy and Rule of Law?

Alternatives to violent conflict can only be strengthened to the degree that state violence itself is subjected to rules, and to the extent that state violence is restricted to guaranteeing decision-making processes that in themselves occur nonviolently. So in a constitutional democratic state—in theory—social conflicts are resolved in state-controlled processes. This applies to conflicts over the aims of society as a whole (through votes, elections, and parliamentary decisions), to group conflicts (e.g., in collective wage bargaining), and to individual conflicts (in contracts and court rulings). The monopolization of legitimate use of violence is the precondition for democracy and the rule of law, because even in the democratic process and the legal system, consequential decisions can only be made if officials, and if necessary the police, guarantee that the decisions will be implemented. Admittedly, this is precisely the point where a problem arises that has never been satisfactorily solved. Only a state ruled by law that is willing to open up legal procedures even against itself and its office holders can fully enforce the renunciation of "private justice." The state monopolization of violence itself requires legitimation, and precisely this legitimation depends not only on the security of the citizens in their dealings with one another, but also on state activity, in particular violent activity, being controllable and subject to jurisdiction. This poses the question as to how to exert control over the state institutions of constitutional democracy. Only legal and police control that also applies to itself (reflexive control) can completely replace vengeance and threat of vengeance as a security strategy. This however, is a point where legal democracies still have major problems.

The contribution of democracy and the rule of law is that they directly influence the strategic situation of conflicting actors. In comparison to other, nondemocratic societies, modern democracies therefore demonstrate a relatively low level of internal violence because political and legal approaches are available and violent solutions are subject to sanctions. This is primarily due to the combination of democracy and the rule of law, on the one hand (as systems that demonstrate ways to deal with conflicting interests), and the state monopoly of legitimate physical violence, on the other (that punishes self-redress). Thus, alternatives to violent enforcement of interests are demonstrated, and the potential "returns" of private violence are minimized. Whether the institutions of law and democracy succeed in limiting violence certainly depends on other factors such as democratic participation, social justice, existence of a culture of dealing with conflict, etc. This was clearly pointed out by Senghaas (1994:26) in his model of a civilizatory hexagon. The constitutional democratic state can only develop its peace-securing and violence-limiting effects if, on the one hand, it actually allows the important conflicts in the society to be expressed, while, on the other, restricting their form through regulated procedures. In other words, if it develops a culture of conflict.

4.3. Mediation and De-Escalation

Relatively little research has been carried out on de-escalation (cf. Pruitt & Rubin, 1984; Eckert & Willems, 1992). Mediation and arbitration are both de-escalating conflict-resolution techniques that try to manage without legal rulings or majority decisions. Often, however, they function only where there is a latent threat of a court ruling, majority decision or even a military conflict, where the opponents do not believe (or no longer believe) that they can win. The goal of mediation and arbitration in such cases is to offer solutions in advance, and avoid escalation processes and dogmatization of positions. In some cases, the stalemate situation has to be generated in the first place. Not every stalemate situation, however, leads to de-escalation. Partisan fighting and civil wars can continue for a very long time on a "low flame" (as low-intensity war), if the parties are independent of one another through external support or their own resources. Often military elites have developed (warlords), who live off the war and therefore have no interest in peace. Finally, the "loss of face" that can be associated with abandoning the struggle is also a reason to prolong the fighting. The past victims of the struggle can also make giving up more difficult, because to give up would be to "betray" the "martyrs" to the cause.

In the final effect, confidence-building measures have to be used in a de-escalation phase to reverse all the learning processes that took place during escalation. As game theory models have shown (Axelrod, 1984), cooperation has to be built up through individual steps, each of which can initially be reversed. Even if this can theoretically be initiated by the conflict parties on their own, as demonstrated by the end of the East–West conflict, it is more likely if the process is accompanied by third parties who are less subject to mistrust. Because the channels of communication between the opponents are often unusable, and there is normally absolutely no trust between them, and negotiations are viewed internally as betrayal on both sides, mediation by a third party is generally the only chance to make communication possible, to discover shared interests, and to initiate confidence-building measures. Here, however, the question arises as to who has any interest at all in acting as mediator or arbitrator. Only if there are third parties who feel threatened by the war and its consequences, will they take on the protracted business of arbitration. This is especially important where there are no means of state power to enforce a peace, as is the case in many international conflicts. At the international level, we are still at the pre-state stage of conflict handling, equivalent to the medieval stage (like in Iceland 1000 years ago). What is now needed here is that the United Nations and alliances of states set up and develop a legal framework and instruments of sanction from the embargo through to armed intervention, in other words, successively initiate state regulation models.

If there is a shared interest, mediation can counteract emotional excesses and cognitive narrow-mindedness and influence the definition of which "game" the players are actually playing. Whether a compromise can be found, often depends on the participants' definition of what it is "actually" about, and on ideas about whether the conflict includes win–win strategies and corresponding solutions. Correction of rigid perceptions and production of shared understandings of reality are normally preconditions for agreement.

Admittedly, not all conflicts can be resolved through compromise and reciprocal concessions. Hirschman points this out in his distinction between divisible and indivisible conflicts, and at the same time emphasizes that indivisible conflicts have "recently gained in weight even in the older democracies and especially in the United States" (Hirschman, 1994:301) Even if one can doubt the descriptive value of this distinction, it makes clear that in conflicts there can always be mutually exclusive claims, where even the question of generalization of interests will not produce a decision capable of consensus. Dubiel emphasized this with the distinction between a strategic dimension and an identity dimension of conflicts (Dubiel, 1997:443). In the eyes of the participants, the loved person, the Holy Land, the temple, or the mosque are often available to only one of the competitors. Even a social order can hardly be theocratic and democratic at the same time. It could, however, be that the territorial exclusivity that states have enforced for several centuries will disintegrate in the process of global integration. Whether ethnic affiliation is understood as an exclusive categorization certainly also depends on the form in which it is debated. To the extent that competent experts and lay people are available to apply arbitration to cases of conflict, corresponding experience and expertise in conflict handling could be spread throughout society, and a higher degree of sensitivity for the conditions and methods of peaceful coexistence could be developed. Accepting other perspectives can prevent all-or-nothing games being suspected where it is about graduated advantages; prevent zero-sum games being imputed where both partners could win; prevent lack of trust and cooperation leading both opponents to lose—this can come into action against all the negative consequences of rational individual behavior, as has been described for the example of the "prisoner's dilemma" (cf. Olson, 1968; Schelling, 1960; Axelrod, 1984).

4.4. Conflict Culture and Education

People have the option not only of fighting, but also of understanding, compromise, and reconciliation. The cognitive basis for this is the theoretical possibility of thinking oneself in other's perspective, the opponent's perspective, and to accept its fundamental legitimacy. This capacity to accept perspectives allows the development of a common understanding between people and is a precondition for culture, understanding, and interaction. This makes it one of the basic preconditions for humans to be civilized beings. At the same time, it is formed and trained in social interaction. This means that socialization and education can promote it to varying degrees. Accepting perspectives is, on its own, certainly not automatically the basis for peace—it can equally well promote war. Every strategic move, and even more every deception, depends for its success on taking consideration of the opponent's perspective and plans. Nonetheless, accepting perspectives is also a precondition for peaceful regulation of conflict. Here it at least allows agreement on the object and dimensions of the dispute, and also makes it easier to assess whether there might be common ground or mutual advantages. In connection with the universalistic values that arose as human rights after the religious wars of modern Europe and are now spreading around the world, it can make it easier to respect the other and their right to their own nonviolent life.

Translated by Tradukas

REFERENCES

McAdam, Dough. (Ed.) (1997). *Social Movements: Readings on Their Emergence, Mobilization and Dynamics*. Los Angeles: Roxbury Publ. Co.
Allport, Gordon W. (1958). *The Nature of Prejudice*. Cambridge: Addison-Wesley.
Archer, John, & Felicitas Huntingford. (1994). Game Theory and Escalation of Animal Fights. In Michael Potegal & John F. Knutson (Eds.), *The Dynamics of Aggression. Biological and Social Processes in Dyads and Groups* (pp. 3–31). Hillsdale: Erlbaum.
Axelrod, Robert. (1984). *The Evolution of Cooperation*. New York: Basic Books.
Booth, Ken. (1979). *Strategy and Ethnocentrism*. London: Croom Helm.

Berkowitz, Morton. (1965). Game Theory and Human Conflict. In Elton. B. MacNeil (Ed.), *The Nature of Human Conflict* (pp. 195–226). Englewood Cliffs: Prentice Hall.

Blumer, Herbert. (1969). Social Unrest and Collective Protest. In Norman Denzin (Ed.), *Studies in Symbolic Interaction, Vol. 1* (pp. 1–54). Greenwich: Jai Press.

Bonacker, Thorsten. (1996). *Konflikttheorien. Eine sozialwissenschaftliche Einführung. Mit Quellen.* Opladen: Leske & Budrich.

Brand, Karl-Werner. (1982). *Neue soziale Bewegungen. Entstehung, Funktion und Perspektive neuer Protestpotentiale.* Opladen: Westdeutscher Verlag.

Brockner, Joel, & Jeffrey Z. Rubin. (1985). *Entrapment in Escalating Conflicts. A Social Psychological Analysis.* New York, Berlin, Heidelberg, Tokyo: Springer Verlag.

Brosius, Hans-Bernd, & Frank Esser. (1995). *Eskalation durch Berichterstattung? Massenmedien und fremdenfeindliche Gewalt.* Opladen: Westdeutscher Verlag.

Buchanan, James. (1975). *The Limits of Liberty: Between Anarchy and Leviathan.* Chicago: Phoenix Books.

Bühl, Walter L. (1976). *Theorien sozialer Konflikte.* Darmstadt: Verlag Wissenschaftliche Buchgesellschaft.

Bueno de Mesquita, Bruce, & James Morrow. (1997). Capabilities, Perception and Escalation. *American Political Science Review, 91*, 1.

Chagnon, Napoleon A. (1988). Life Histories, Blood Revenge and Warfare in a Tribal Population. *Science, 239*, 985–992.

Coser, Lewis A. (1972). *Theorie sozialer Konflikte.* Neuwied, Berlin: Luchterhand. [English original (1968) *The Functions of Social Conflicts.* London: Routledge and Kegan Paul.]

Dahrendorf, Ralf. (1969). Zu einer Theorie des sozialen Konflikts. In Wolfgang Zapf (Ed.), *Theorien des sozialen Wandels* (pp. 108–123). Köln et al.: Kiepenheuer und Witsch.

Davies, James C. (1969). The J-Curve of Rising and Declining Satisfactions as a Cause of some Great Revolutions and a Contained Rebellion. In Hugh D. Graham & Ted R. Gurr (Eds.), *The History of Violence in America. Vol. 4.* New York et al.: Praeger.

Deutsch, Morton. (1976). *Konfliktregelung—Konstruktive und destruktive Prozesse.* München et al.: Reinhardt.

Doob, Leonard W. (Ed.) (1970). *Resolving Conflict in Africa: The Fermeda Workshop.* New Haven: Yale University Press.

Dubiel, Helmut. (1997). Unversöhnlichkeit und Demokratie. In Wilhelm Heitmeyer (Ed.), *Was hält die Gesellschaft zusammen?* (pp. 425–444). Frankfurt a. M.: Suhrkamp Verlag.

Eckert, Roland. (1976). Terrorismus als Karriere. In Heiner Geißler (Ed.), *Wege in die Gewalt* (pp. 109–132). München, Wien: Olzog-Verlag.

Eckert, Roland, & Helmut Willems. (1986). Youth Protest in Western Europe: Four Case Studies. In Louis Kriesberg, Kurt Lang & G.E. Lang (Eds.), *Research in Social Movement, Conflicts and Change* (pp. 127–154). Greenwich et al.: Jai Press, 9.

Eckert, Roland, & Helmut Willems. (1992). *Konfliktintervention—Perspektivenübernahme in gesellschaftlichen Auseinandersetzungen.* Opladen: Leske & Budrich.

Eckert, Roland, Thomas Wetzstein, & Christa Reis. (2000). *Ich will halt anders sein wie die anderen.* Opladen: Leske & Budrich.

Elwert, Georg. (1997). Gewaltmärkte. Beobachtungen zur Zweckrationalität der Gewalt. In Trutz von Trotha (Ed.), *Soziologie der Gewalt. Sonderheft der Kölner Zeitschrift für Soziologie und Sozialpsychologie* (pp. 86–101). Opladen et al.: Westdeutscher Verlag.

Elster, Jon. (1989). *The Cement of Society: A Study of Social Order.* Cambridge et al.: Cambridge University Press.

Elias, Norbert. (1969). *Über den Prozess der Zivilisation.* Bern, München: Francke.

Euler, Harald A., & Heinz Mandel. (Eds.) (1983). *Emotionspsychologie. Ein Handbuch in Schlüsselbegriffen.* München, Wien, Baltimore: Urban und Schwarzenberg.

Festinger, Leon. (1968). *A Theory of Cognitive Dissonance.* Stanford: Stanford University Press.

Fisher, Ronald J. (1972). Third Party Consultation: A Method for the Study and Resolution of Conflict. *Journal of Conflict Resolution, 16*, 67–94.

Fisher, Ronald J. (1990). *The Social Psychology of Intergroup and International Conflict Resolution.* New York et al.: Springer Verlag.

Gamson, William A. (1975). *Strategy of Social Protest.* Homewood: Dorsley Press.

Giegel, Hans Joachim. (Ed.) (1998). *Konflikt in modernen Gesellschaften.* Frankfurt a. M.: Suhrkamp.

Gould, Roger V. (1999). Collective Violence and Group Solidarity: Evidence from a Feuding Society. *American Sociological Review, 64*, 356–380.

Gurr, Ted R. (1970). *Why Men Rebel?* Princeton: Princeton University Press.

Glasl, Friedrich. (1990). *Konfliktmanagement—ein Handbuch für Führungskräfte und Berater.* Bern, Stuttgart: Haupt Verlag.
Hardin, Russell. (1995). *One for All: Logic of Group Conflicts.* Princeton: Princeton University Press.
Hanf, Theodor. (1990). *Koexistenz im Krieg. Staatszerfall und Entstehen einer Nation im Libanon.* Baden-Baden: Nomos-Verlagsgesellschaft.
Heitmeyer, Wilhelm. (1987). *Rechtsextremistische Orientierungen bei Jugendlichen.* Weinheim, München: Juventa Verlag.
Heitmeyer, Wilhelm. (1993). Gesellschaftliche Desintegrationsprozesse als Ursachen von fremdenfeindlicher Gewalt und politischer Paralysierung. *Aus Politik und Zeitgeschichte, 2–3,* 3–13.
Hirschman, Albert O. (1994). *Wieviel Gemeinsinn braucht die liberale Gesellschaft?* (pp. 293–304). Leviathan, Opladen et al.: Westdeutscher Verlag.
Hobbes, Thomas. (1996). *Leviathan.* Hamburg: Reimer [1st published 1651].
Jervis, Robert. (1976). *Perception and Misperception in International Relations.* Princeton: Princeton University Press.
Kahn, Hermann. (1965). *On Escalation, Metaphors and Scenarios.* New York: Academic Press.
Katz, Daniel. (1960). The Functional Approach for the Study of Attitudes. *Public Opinion Quarterly, 24,* 163–178.
Kelman, Herbert C. (Ed.) (1965). *International Behavior.* New York: Holt, Rinehart and Winston.
Koch, Klaus-Friedrich. (1974). *War and Peace in Jalemo. The Management of Conflict in Highland New Guinea.* Cambridge: Harvard University Press.
Kriesberg, Louis. (1982). *Social Conflicts.* Englewood Cliffs: Prentice Hall.
LeBon, Gustave. (1938). *Psychologie der Massen.* Stuttgart: Kroener.
Leng, Russel J. (1994). Interstate Crisis Escalation and War. In Michael Potegal & John F. Knutson (Eds.), *The Dynamics of Aggression* (pp. 307–332). Hillsdale: Erlbaum.
Likert, Rensis. (1932). A Technique for the Measurement of Attitudes. *Archives of Psychology, 140.*
Luhmann, Niklas. (1972). *Rechtssoziologie.* Reinbek: Rowohlt Verlag.
Malinowski, Bronislaw. (1976). *Crime and Custom in Savage Societies.* Totowa: Littlefield, Adams and Co.
Marx, Karl, & Friedrich Engels. (1983). *Manifest der kommunistischen Partei.* Berlin: Dietz [1st published, 1848].
MacCarthy, John D., & Mayer N. Zald. (1973). *The Trends of Social Movements in America: Professionalization and Resource Mobilization.* Morristown: General Learning Press.
Merkel, Christine M. (1995). *Zivile Konflikttransformation. Gutachten im Auftrag der Evangelischen Akademie Loccum.* Rehburg, Loccum.
Merton, Robert K. (1957). *Social Theory and Social Structure.* New York: Glencoe.
Moore, Barrington. (1987). *Ungerechtigkeit. Die sozialen Ursachen von Unterordnung und Widerstand.* Frankfurt a. M.: Suhrkamp. [English original (1978) *Injustice. The Social Bases of Obedience and Revolt.* London: Macmillan.]
Mummendey, Amelie. (Ed.) (1984). *Social Psychology of Aggression.* Berlin et al.: Springer Verlag.
Muller, Edward. (1979). *Aggressive Political Participation.* Princeton: Princeton University Press.
Neidhardt, Friedrich. (1989). Gewalt und Gegengewalt: Steigt die Bereitschaft zu Gewaltaktionen mit zunehmender staatlicher Kontrolle und Repression? In Wilhelm Heitmeyer, Kurt Möller & Heinz Sünker (Eds.), *Jugend—Staat—Gewalt. Politische Sozialisation von Jugendlichen, Jugendpolitik und politische Bildung* (pp. 233–243). Weinheim, München: Juventa.
Neidhardt, Friedhelm, & Dieter Rucht. (1993). Auf dem Weg in die Mobilisierungsgesellschaft? Über die Stabilisierbarkeit sozialer Bewegungen. *Soziale Welt, 3,* 305–326.
Oberschall, Anthony. (1973). *Social Conflict and Social Movements.* Englewood Cliffs: Prentice Hall.
Olson, Mancur. (1968). *Die Logik des kollektiven Handelns.* Tübingen: Mohr. [English original (1965) *The Logic of Collective Action: Public Goods and the Theory of Groups.* Cambridge: Harvard University Press.]
Opp, Klaus Dieter. (1984). *Soziale Probleme und Protestverhalten.* Opladen: Leske & Budrich.
Otterbein, Keith F. (1970). *The Evolution of War: A Cross-Cultural Study.* New Haven: HRAF Press.
Potegal, Michael, & John F. Knutson. (1994). *The Dynamics of Aggression.* Hillsdale: Erlbaum.
Parsons, Talcott. (1964). *Beiträge zur soziologischen Theorie.* Neuwied, Berlin: Luchterhand. [English original (1964) *Essays in Sociological Theory.* New York: The Free Press.]
Pruitt, Dean G. (1981). *Negotiation Behavior.* New York: Academic Press.
Pruitt, Dean G., & Jeffrey Z. Rubin. (1986). *Social Conflict: Escalation, Stalemate and Settlement.* New York. Random House: Academic Press.
Popitz, Heinrich. (1980). *Die normative Konstruktion von Gesellschaft.* Tübingen: Mohr.
Rammstedt, Otthein. (1978). *Soziale Bewegung.* Frankfurt a. M.: Suhrkamp.

Rapoport, Anatol. (1960). *Fights, Games and Debates.* Ann Arbor: University of Michigan Press.
Rapoport, Anatol. (1972). Kataklysmische und strategische Konfliktmodelle. In Walter L. Bühl (Ed.), *Konflikt und Konfliktstrategie* (pp. 264–286). München: Nymphenburger Verlagshandlung.
Richardson, Lewis F. (1960). *Arms and Insecurity.* Pittsburgh: Boxwood Press.
Roberts, Simon. (1984). *Ordnung und Konflikt.* Stuttgart: Klett-Cotta.
Rubin, Jeffrey Z., & Bert R. Brown. (1975). *The Social Psychology of Bargaining and Negotiation.* New York, San Francisco, London: Academic Press.
Runciman, Walter G. (1972). *Relative Deprivation and Social Justice.* London: Routledge & Keagan Paul.
Sack, Fritz. (1984). Staat, Gesellschaft und politische Gewalt: Zur Pathologie politischer Konflikte. In Fritz Sack & Heinz Steinert, *Protest und Reaktion* (pp. 17–103). Opladen: Westdeutscher Verlag.
Schneider, Norbert. (1987). *Ewig ist nur die Veränderung. Entwurf eines analytischen Konzepts sozialer Bewegungen.* Frankfurt a. M.: Suhrkamp.
Schelling, Thomas C. (1960). *The Strategy of Conflict.* Cambridge: Harvard University Press.
Senghaas, Dieter. (1994). *Wohin driftet die Welt?* Frankfurt a. M.: Suhrkamp.
Simmel, Georg. (1992). [1923]. *Der Streit. Soziologie. Untersuchungen über die Formen der Vergesellschaftung. Collected Works, Vol. 11* (pp. 302–333). Frankfurt a. M.: Suhrkamp.
Smelser, Neil J. (1972). *Theorie des kollektiven Verhaltens.* Köln: Kiepenheuer und Witsch.
Tarrow, Sidney. (1991). Kollektives Handeln und politische Gelegenheitsstruktur in Mobilisierungswellen. Theoretische Perspektiven. *Kölner Zeitschrift für Soziologie und Sozialpsychologie,* 4, 647–670.
Trotha, Trutz von. (1974). *Jugendliche Bandendelinquenz: Über Vergesellschaftungsbedingungen von Jugendlichen in Elendsvierteln der Großstädte.* Stuttgart: Enke Verlag.
Tilly, Charles. (1978). *From Mobilization to Revolution.* Reading: Addison-Wesley.
Turner, Ralph, & Lewis M. Kilian. (1972). *Collective Behavior.* Englewood Cliffs: Prentice Hall.
Vanberg, Victor. (1978). Kollektive Güter und kollektives Handeln. *Kölner Zeitschrift für Soziologie und Sozialpsychologie,* 4(30), 655–672.
Waldmann, Peter. (1990). *Militanter Nationalismus im Baskenland.* Frankfurt a. M.: Verwuert Verlag.
Watzlawick, Paul, Janet Beavin, & Don Jackson. (1969). *Menschliche Kommunikation. Formen, Störungen, Paradoxien.* Bern, Stuttgart, Wien: Huber Verlag.
White, Ralph K. (1965). Images in the Context of International Conflicts. In Herbert C. Kelman (Ed.), *International Behavior* (pp. 238–276). New York: Holt, Rinehart and Winston.
Willems, Helmut. (1988a). Polizei, Protest und Eskalation: Die Bedeutung der Konflikterfahrungen junger Polizeibeamter. *Neue Soziale Bewegungen,* 2, 11–20.
Willems, Helmut. (1988b). *Demonstranten und Polizisten. Motive, Erfahrungen, Eskalationsbedingungen.* München: DJI Verlag.
Willems, Helmut. (1989). Jugendprotest, die Eskalation der Gewalt und die Rolle des Staates. In Wilhelm Heitmeyer, Kurt Möller & Heinz Sünker (Eds.), *Jugend—Staat—Gewalt* (pp. 219–232). Weinheim, München: Juventa Verlag.
Willems, Helmut (1993): *Fremdenfeindliche Gewalt: Einstellungen, Täter, Konflikteskalation.* Opladen: Leske & Budrich.
Willems, Helmut. (1994). Kollektive Gewalt gegen Fremde: Historische Episode oder Genese einer sozialen Bewegung von Rechts? In Werner Bergmann & Rainer Erb (Eds.), *Neonazismus und rechte Subkultur* (pp. 209–226). Berlin. Metropolverlag.
Willems, Helmut. (1995). Right-Wing Extremism, Racism or Youth Violence. How Can We Explain the Collective Acts of Violence Against Foreigners in Germany. *New Community, Special Issue 4,* 22–45.
Willems, Helmut. (1996). Mobilisierungseffekte und Eskalationsprozesse. Berliner Debatte. *Zeitschrift für sozialwissenschaftlichen Diskurs. Initial,* 1, 34–42.
Willems, Helmut. (1997). *Jugendunruhen und Protestbewegungen. Eine Studie zur Dynamik innergesellschaftlicher Konflikte in vier europäischen Ländern.* Opladen: Leske & Budrich.
Willems, Helmut, & Roland Eckert. (1995). Wandlungen politisch motivierter Gewalt in der Bundesrepublik. Gruppendynamik. *Zeitschrift für angewandte Sozialpsychologie,* 1, 89–123.
Wilson, Edward O. (1980). *Biologie als Schicksal.* Frankfurt a. M. et al.: Ullstein.
Zald, Mayer N., & John D. McCarthy. (1997). Social Movement Industries. In Louis Kriesberg (Ed.), *Research in Social Movements, Conflict and Change. Vol. 3.* Greenwich: Jai Press.
Zimmermann, Ekkart. (1980). Macro-Comparative Research on Political Protest. In Ted R. Gurr (Ed.), *Handbook of Political Conflict. Theory and Research* (pp. 331–360). New York et al.: The Free Press.

PART III

THEORETICAL AND METHODOLOGICAL ISSUES IN RESEARCH ON VIOLENCE

CHAPTER III.1

Potentials and Limits of Qualitative Methods for Research on Violence

ANDREAS BÖTTGER AND RAINER STROBL

I. INTRODUCTION

The decision on whether to apply qualitative rather than quantitative methods in research on violence depends to a large extent on three aspects associated with the specific research goal in each project:

First, qualitative methods are applied in situations in which little is known about the lives and cultural backgrounds of those being studied.

Second, they are applied particularly when the goal is to analyze complex structures of meaning or action, or results are expected to show such patterns. An example is research on the motives and causes of violence: The first thing that has to be remembered here is that purely causal or even monocausal relations can hardly ever be assumed in the explanatory models of the social sciences. Hence, examining the causes of a specific act of violence will generally bring to light a bundle of reasons, social conditions, motives, causes, and the like. These, in turn, will also interact with each other. Because the majority of individual factors in such a pattern of effects and actions as well as the interactions between them cannot be anticipated and standardized on all levels before starting to collect data, the best way to plot them empirically is to apply qualitative methods.

Finally, a qualitative approach is chosen when the empirical goal is to access violence and its backgrounds in a way designed to understand subjective experience; in other words, when the concern is to plot the perpetrators' subjective contexts of meaning behind violent acts from a phenomenological or constructivist perspective. Such a goal can be achieved only with qualitative methods of social research.

II. REFERENCE LEVELS IN QUALITATIVE RESEARCH ON VIOLENCE

One major criterion for discriminating between individual approaches in research on violence (and in social research in general), which, to some extent, runs counter to the above-mentioned classification of various reasons for a qualitative approach, is the *reference level of empirical knowledge in the social sciences*. This can differ for individual projects. Generally speaking, three levels can be distinguished: first, the "*objective" course of events or circumstances in a society*; second, the *subjective perceptions of such events or circumstances* by those individuals who are involved or observing; and, third, the *memories of formerly experienced events or formerly observed circumstances* that are recollected at a later time, for example in a research interview (see Böttger, 1999).

But—and this is a general comment—positivism's continued claim that an "objective" reality can be perceived and explained without distortions is abandoned by the form of critical rationalism that provides the most frequent basis for quantitative empiricism in the theory of science (see Popper, 1971). This is because every perception is subject to interpretations and filterings. In general, this "objective level" of social reality (labeled the *course level* in the following) no longer plays any role in qualitative social research. However, although this level remains ultimately inaccessible, the explanatory power of scientific findings can be examined critically by, for example, applying various, also nonverbal, methods of data collection (such as observations)—ideally each applied by several researchers. For qualitative research on violence, an example of when this can become decisive is when the aim is to assess the impact of "objectively" verifiable social conditions on violent acts and their motives.

Nonetheless, traditional qualitative empirical research focuses predominantly on the verbally conveyed *social world from the perspective of the actors*, that is, the persons being studied (see, e.g., Kade, 1983:67). This means the level on which social reality is experienced directly (labeled the *experience level* in the following) as well as the level of actual self-display in the research situation in which memories of earlier experience are confounded with interpretations, exclusions, and, at this stage, also subsequent amendments (labeled the *actualization level*). Strictly speaking, the levels of experience and actualization cannot be separated completely in research, because the experience level deals mostly with "momentary snapshots" that then immediately become part of memory, thus always shifting the process of studying them to the actualization level.

But respondents' earlier experience of biographical events can also serve as a goal of qualitative empirical research. The qualitative data collection process can try to reconstruct earlier subjective experience as precisely as possible since, notwithstanding later processes of interpretation, this can still largely be seen as part of an individual's reservoir of knowledge. For example, the experience level becomes the object of qualitative research on violence when the goal is to identify which motives and other subjective conditions were effective before or during the perpetration of earlier violent acts. The *actualization level*, in contrast, is relevant when the aim is to illuminate an individual's current self-concept at the time of the survey, including the retrospectively actualized biography belonging to this self-concept. Research on violence pursues such an approach when, for example, the goal is to assess the subjective experiences of violent persons from their own perspective at a certain point in time. This perspective may cover the subjective interpretation of their own socialization just as much as current problems, wishes, or dreams.

III. METHODS OF DATA COLLECTION

In North America, the methods of *ethnography* represent the most prominent tradition in qualitative research on violence (see, e.g., Thrasher, 1963, [1927]; Whyte, 1981, [1943]), and have also been the methods applied most frequently in recent decades (see, e.g., McCall, 1978; Ferrell & Hamm, 1998).

As a rule, ethnographic studies are characterized by a varied and flexible use of several individual techniques (see McCall, 1978; Jessor, Colby, & Shweder, 1996). The focus is always on "participant observation" in which the researcher adopts an active role as an investigator in the field over a long period of time, which may well extend to years. Participant observation is supplemented by unstructured interviews, focus groups, and/or content analysis techniques for examining contemporary and cultural documents or texts composed by persons in the field. The consequences of applying such a variety of methods are considered to be a particularly problematic aspect of ethnographic approaches to the phenomenon of violence (as well as to other social phenomena): it is almost impossible to subject all potential combinations to standardized rules of application and analysis. However, it is precisely this many-sided access to the field (in the sense of a triangulation of methods) that makes it possible to anticipate more "valid" results (this will be addressed below). Sometimes, the risk of losing the scientist's "external perspective" is also considered problematic. When work in the field continues over several years, scientists may unconsciously adopt the dominant norms and values of the field. Nonetheless, pointing out this "threat" also reveals a principal strength of the ethnographic approach: It is precisely this danger of a loss of distance that makes "going native" also amount to the greatest possible direct contact with the social phenomenon under study and the actors involved (see Flick, 1995:161). A good example of this is the close friendship between Whyte and one of his "corner boys" (see Whyte, 1981, [1943]:361ff). Nonetheless, researchers who take an ethnographic approach to violence may also be confronted with a dilemma: Under some circumstances, their role in the field may compel them to also become involved in illegal violence, creating not only legal but also ethical problems (see Lyng, 1998).

Compared with North America, European research on violence tends toward a more widespread use of interview procedures. Biographical approaches frequently apply the *narrative interview* method introduced about 25 years ago by Fritz Schütze (1976). He considered the goal of his procedure to be to "lure out" so-called "impromptu narratives" that should initially be allowed to flow without being interrupted by the interviewer (follow-up questions are asked during a later phase). The assumption is that precisely stories of this kind convey the subjective interpretation of biographical events in the form in which they occurred at the time the events were experienced. In other words, they are directed toward the "experience level" in the sense of the concepts developed above. Rausch (1999) has applied this method to violent racist youth. Nonetheless, it should be noted that the advantage of eliciting intrinsically closed narratives has to be weighed against the disadvantage of not always being able to systematically gather additional information relevant for the interpretation.

The *problem-centered interview* developed by Witzel (see 1982, 1996) is used to assess qualitative data—or texts—which may refer equally to either the current life world of the respondents or their interpretations of prior biographical events made at the time of the interview. Unlike the narrative interview, this form of data collection is shaped by dialogue and supported by a guideline. The use of a guideline and the interviewer's opportunities to intervene during the interview permit a more rigorous orientation toward previously formulated hypotheses or research questions. Further direct questioning on relevant narrative contents or on passages that threaten to drift away from the given topic is also possible. This may prove particularly helpful in research on delinquency and violence when an investigator is trying to access a topic that is taboo in many contexts (see, e.g., Dietz et al., 1997). At the same time, the problem-centered interview reduces the time and effort needed to collect and analyze the data—the price being admittedly a loss of the respondent's subjective biographical coherence that would have been gained through "impromptu narratives" requiring neither guidelines nor interposed questions.

Finally, the *reconstructive interview* (see Böttger, 1996, 1999) attempts to approach the earlier experience level of biographical events as closely as possible through a methodologically controlled dialogue. It is based on the realization that interviewers need a higher level of intervention in order to prevent respondents from excluding relevant information or adding fictional contents when addressing topics such as violence in which their strong emotional involvement cannot be ruled out.[1] In the dialogue of the reconstructive interview, likewise based on a guideline, the interviewer is, in some ways, the expert for the reconstruction process; the respondent, the expert for the reconstructed contents. The method exploits the rhetorical techniques of the problem-centered interview as well as the qualitative focus group procedure. If the situation permits, the discourse can even be guided by careful, well-intended provocations (by both the interviewer and the respondent). A good example is an interviewer's intervention when a 15-year-old respondent boasted that he was already in contact with the Mafia. The interviewer replied that he had heard that you can't "get in" the Mafia before the age of 18 (Böttger, 1998:108). Although this obliged the respondent to admit that he was not really in contact with the Mafia, he was still willing to carry on with the interview.

This data collection technique, drawing in many ways on everyday communication, has also been applied successfully to the study of youth violence in China, a culture that differs strongly from Western industrial societies (see Böttger & Liang, 1998; Liang, Silkenbeumer, & Böttger, 2001). This suggests that it may well be a promising technique for cross-cultural research on violence.

Alongside these various interview techniques, it is also worth noting the *focus group procedure* (which is, once again, particularly popular in German-language qualitative research on violence). Generally, such a focus group begins with a "basic incentive" for the topic (e.g., viewing a film or reading a newspaper article). Depending on the design, the group leader may then also introduce further incentives or participate in the content of the discussion in other ways (see, e.g., Nießen, 1977).

One advantage of focus groups over interview techniques is the opportunity to collect data on opinions, attitudes, and norms in everyday groups that are relevant for their members' collective (but also individual) action motives and action concepts. This is of interest to qualitative research on violence when, for example, assessing the behavior of violent groups, "cliques," or "gangs" (see Bohnsack et al., 1995). Although focus groups can be assembled specially for the data collection, such groups can then no longer be used to collect data on real-life group norms and processes.

The qualitative *analysis of documents*, frequently discussed under the heading of qualitative content analysis, is used to study texts that have not been produced specifically

---

[1] This experience may also explain why the "impromptu narratives" of the narrative interview—regardless of how interesting they are for qualitative research as a whole—have to be positioned predominantly on the actualization level because of their *current construction* of stories.

for research purposes but are documents of (institutional) everyday life. In research on violence, these are particularly court records (see Willems et al., 1993) but also newspaper reports or texts composed by the actors themselves, such as diaries. However, content or text analysis techniques are applied not only to documents that already exist in everyday life, but also in the qualitative analysis of written essays to research questions or autobiographies (in biographical research) as well as in the analysis of qualitative interviews (guided by dialogue or narrative).

IV. METHODS OF DATA ANALYSIS

There are very few published guidelines on the special methods of data analysis in *ethnographic studies*. This is mainly because of the widespread practices of using various techniques simultaneously. The analysis strategies developed in each case are not just oriented toward the analysis methods developed for these individual techniques, but also try to take account of the special project-specific constellation of data collection techniques that may well vary greatly due to the long and complex structure of field work. This imposes limits on the generalization of the specific analysis procedure. When, nonetheless, rules on analyzing ethnographic research are proposed, they focus mostly on the method of participant observation so favored in ethnography, although hardly ever applied in isolation (see Atkinson & Hammersley, 1994). The general way of analyzing ethnographic data—as with most other qualitative data collected in research on violence—takes the form of a text analysis. In participant observation, it is common practice to write up "field protocols" of the observed phenomena after single phases of exploration (see, e.g., Aster, Merkens, & Repp, 1989). In principle, the field protocol text can be analyzed—depending on how detailed it is and its structure—with a range of different content analysis procedures. To some extent, these procedures are also suitable for analyzing transcripts of qualitative interviews (which are frequently also included in ethnographic research) as well as transcripts or protocols of focus groups.[2]

One of the most detailed—and hence also most time-consuming—methods in this context is the *objective hermeneutics* approach (see Oevermann et al., 1979; Oevermann, Allert, & Konau, 1980). Its epistemological assumption is that, in the socialization process, the "objective" structures of meaning to be found in society manifest themselves in the single individual and all his or her utterances and actions, and that this is a process that does not require the individual's intention or awareness. In line with such a theoretical basis, "objective hermeneutics" does not aim to depict an individual's "subjective meaning," but, rather, to identify and plot the latent "objective meaning structures" in recorded interactions, observation protocols, or interview transcripts. This is achieved by discussing as many different ways as possible of "reading" a text passage in the research team. The discourse among researchers is the sole basis for choosing one reading as an interpretation of the text sequence. Rausch's (1999) study mentioned above is an example of this type of approach in qualitative research on violence.

For analyzing the transcripts of qualitative interviews, there are a number of approaches that resemble one another very much (see, for overviews, e.g., Heinze, Klusemann,

---

[2]There is not enough space to discuss all the different forms of qualitative content analysis. Interested readers are referred to the detailed accounts in, e.g., Mayring (1983, 1996). The following presents only a few single approaches for illustrative purposes.

& Soeffner, 1980; Lamnek, 1993). Schütze's (1983:286ff) approach has been developed specially for transcripts of *narrative interviews*. It contains six steps:

1. Formal analysis of a text's narrative passages.
2. Description of the structure and content of these passages.
3. Analytical abstraction of the results of both steps.
4. Analysis of the argumentative text passages.
5. Contrastive comparison of all cases.
6. Construction of a theoretical model.

With their concept of *social-scientific paraphrasing*, Heinze and Klusemann (1980) also present a procedure that was conceived initially for narrative interviews, but can be extended to an analysis of dialogically guided interviews and even documents (see Böttger, 1992:106ff; 1998:104ff). This method also aims at "structures and patterns of meaning" underlying the text, but not only on the level of the "subjective conceptions of reality constituting the meaning of the interaction," but also on the level of the "objective conditions of social relations that shape them."

The analytical procedure in social-scientific paraphrasing is divided into three steps that should each integrate the contextual knowledge of both the interviewee (insofar as this can be deduced from the text) and the interpreter (see Heinze & Klusemann, 1980:120f):

1. Reconstruction of the subjective interpretations and definitions of the text producer into which, under intersubjective controls, the everyday theories and scientific assumptions of the interpreter flow.
2. Systematization and assessment of the structures obtained into a hierarchic pattern.
3. Formulation of "core statements" as the "quintessence and action-guiding reference points of everyday theories and definitions of situations" of the text producer. These statements should describe the underlying patterns as an interpretation text.

The entire interpretation should be carried out on the basis of continuous access to two subprocedures: The first draws on theories obtained inductively from the statements and interpretations of the text; the second uses scientific theories applied to this text from the outside (see Heinze & Klusemann, 1980:108).

As ascertained already in Schütze's (1983) model sketched above, any final interpretation of the gathered material has to be preceded by a systematic comparison of all analyzed cases when the identified patterns (e.g., possible trends in violent activity) are to be uncovered in their individual details. This is not a quantifying of the material in a statistical sense (which qualitative research neither aspires to nor can achieve), but a confirmation of the similarities and differences between the cases analyzed in the sample. A systematic and contrastive case comparison can lead to the *formulation of types* with the goal of empirically plotting various possible types of status or course in the phenomena (of violence) studied (see, e.g., Gerhardt, 1991). A large number of different models of such type development can be found (see, for a current overview, Kluge, 1999). To identify the individual types of status or course, most of them advise not only a "minimal case comparison" to disclose the differences within the cases of one type class, but also a "maximum case comparison" to provide a systematic assessment of the differences between cases from various type classes.

V. GROUNDED THEORY

Grounded theory is currently one of the most elaborated qualitative research strategies and is applied widely in research on violence. It is used for the systematic development of an empirically founded theory of limited range that will provide an adequate description of a research field. However, it is not always necessary to pursue the main goal of grounded theory. For example, Lempert (1996) limited her study to developing empirically sound categories describing how women cope with violent partners or husbands. Such categories can provide extremely valuable starting points for further research. In contrast, Roberts' (1999) study of the relation between exposure to family violence during childhood and later drug abuse provides an example for a textbook implementation of grounded theory.

The logic underlying the theoretical sampling procedure recommended by Glaser and Strauss (1977, [1967]:45ff), Strauss and Corbin (1990:176ff), and Strauss (1991:70f) differs fundamentally from traditional approaches. It is not based on any sample plan fixed before the study. Instead, decisions on which cases should be integrated next are based on the theory that evolves during the data analysis. Hence, sampling can be determined by either a search for large differences or large similarities. Minimal contrasting increases the probability of finding similar data on a certain category. Because a feature will also have to emerge in similar cases if it is theoretically relevant, this can exclude the random properties of categories. Moreover, minimal contrasting helps to search for the conditions underlying a category's emergence. Maximal contrasting, on the other hand, increases the probability of gathering variations to a certain category. During maximal contrasting, similarities between very different cases point to important general features of a category and to central conditions for its emergence. Differences, in contrast, may lead to the detection of further features of the category (see, also, Kelle, 1997:298).

Data analysis in grounded theory is interwoven closely with data collection. The method of continuous comparison applied already in the data collection is the core of the analysis procedure. Three fundamental steps can be distinguished: open coding, axial coding, and selective coding. Strauss and Corbin (1990:61ff) conceive open coding as a fine-grade analysis: A text is analyzed precisely word for word, and each phenomenon that seems to be significant is assigned a conceptual label. When labeling phenomena, the researcher can invent new terms, use terms from the text, or refer to scientific terms. What is important is that the codes formed should not simply paraphrase the text but already represent abstractions leading toward a theory. The next step is to study relations between several categories. Strauss and Corbin (1990:96ff) call this "axial coding" because the categories are arranged along the "axis" of a very general theoretical model. The final step is "selective coding": this procedure arranges the categories around an empirically saturated central category (see Strauss & Corbin, 1990:116ff; Strauss, 1991:106ff). The outcome is a theoretical model of limited range addressing the typical activity of typical actors in the field under study.

VI. PROBLEMS OF QUALITY ASSURANCE

During the initial peak in qualitative research on violence, linked inseparably with the early research work of the Chicago School, issues of quality assurance or reflections on one's own methodological approach were often of only secondary interest. For example, methodological issues are not discussed at all in Thrasher's (1963, [1927]) famous study

"The Gang." Nor does the reader learn anything about prior assumptions or how data were gathered exactly. Kelle (1997:33ff) considers one explanation for this lack of interest in methodological issues to be the epistemological realism of leading representatives of the Chicago School. It is interesting to see that Park, the most influential representative of "naturalistic social research," did not relate the definition of the situation by the actor emphasized by Thomas (1965) to the sociological observer, whom he apparently considered to be capable of grasping social facts objectively through direct observation (see Hammersley, 1989:74f). This empiricist attitude continues to impact on the qualitative research tradition to this day in the form of a one-sided demand for the greatest possible openness accompanied by a neglect of any explication of theoretical prior assumptions (see, e.g., Glaser & Strauss, 1977, [1967]:37; Lamnek, 1988:22f).

However, the advantages of a theoretically driven approach to qualitative research on violence can be seen in studies on right-wing extremism and violence like those of Hopf et al. (1995) or Heitmeyer et al. (1992). Nonetheless, the demand for the greatest possible openness finds its echo in some representatives of a "genuine sociology of violence" (see, e.g., von Trotha, 1997:20ff). They consider the production of a context-rich descriptive text in the sense of a "thick description" (Geertz, 1983) the only appropriate method for analyzing phenomena of violence (see Neumann, 1995:67; for a critical approach, Nedelmann, 1997:68). Under this precondition—as in the former representatives of the Chicago School—an ethnographic approach would seem to be the preferable method. Researchers who have worked in violent contexts nonetheless caution against overestimating the value of this approach. Koehler and Heyer (1998) consider it to be almost impossible for a participant observer to retain the necessary scientific distance when describing an extremely violent situation. The problems of subjectivity and of the restricted testing of validity, inherent to all ethnography, multiply in violent situations:

"Put pointedly, diaries are not kept during a blood bath; one either survives or dies with the other persons involved. And after the blood bath, one is just as much engaged as all the others in exercises of meaningfulness, healing processes, or strategies of suppression" (Koehler & Heyer, 1998:16).

Koehler and Heyer's warning implies a need to refer to the "classic quality criteria" of validity, generalizability, reliability, and objectivity. Whether and in what form these quality criteria can be applied to qualitative research is, nonetheless, still a controversial topic in the discourse on the standards of qualitative research. For example, Lincoln and Guba's (1985:290ff) influential monograph contrasts the above-mentioned criteria with alternative quality criteria. These are presented in Table III-1.1.

Lincoln and Guba's (1985:294f) critique is directed particularly toward the correspondence theory concept of truth in conventional research. They prefer the epistemological assumption of multiple constructed realities, leading them to reject the unequivocal concept of truth in conventional research. Nonetheless, their proposal for establishing *credibility* through a longer presence in the field, continued observation, triangulation, analysis of counterevidence, examination of the results by impartial scientists, and communicative validation by the respondents only makes sense if reality is assumed to be constructed nonrandomly (see Hammersley, 1992:45). Lincoln and Guba (1985:316) conceive of *transferability* as an alternative to the traditional way of ensuring the generalizability of findings through representative random selection. What they consider decisive in this context is a description of the research context that is dense enough to enable the reader to decide whether findings are applicable in other contexts with which he or she is familiar. *Dependability* and *confirmability* are the alternatives to reliability and objectivity. Lincoln and

TABLE III-1.1. Lincoln and Guba's translation of the classic validity criteria

Aspects of trustworthiness of research outcomes

Conventional research	Naturalistic research
Problem: Truth of the outcome Concept: Internal validity	Credibility
Problem: Applicability/Generalizability Concept: External validity	Transferability
Problem: Consistency Concept: Reliability	Dependability
Problem: Neutrality Concept: Objectivity	Confirmability

Guba (1985:317ff) consider that the best way to achieve them is through a quality management similar to the way companies in industry are controlled through auditing. The outcome of such an audit would then be a report on the dependability (including the suitability of the research decisions, the completeness of the data analysis, the search for counterevidence, potential impact of temporal and financial restrictions on the findings), and the confirmability of the findings (including the aspect if findings are justified by the data, the plausibility of conclusions, suitability of the category system, consideration of counterevidence). Lincoln and Guba (1985:327) go on to suggest that keeping a research diary is the general means of ensuring whether a study is trustworthy. Kirk and Miller (1986:52f) also recommend field researchers to jot down their personal experiences, thoughts, and feelings and disclose these to readers so that they can trace how certain decisions and interpretations have emerged. A good example of such openness is appendix A of Whyte's (1981, [1943]) famous study on "Street Corner Society." Particularly when researchers are confronted with extreme forms of violence either in interviews or face to face, such information will often be indispensable in assessing their findings.

But it would be wrong to rashly dismiss the applicability of the classic quality criteria to qualitative research on violence. However, a simple transfer of validation strategies from the quantitative to the qualitative research tradition is bound to fail (see Kepper, 1996:200ff). Nonetheless, it would seem worth returning to the epistemological core of the traditional validity criteria, while ensuring that their operational design takes account of the specific approach and the specific problems of qualitative research on violence (see LeCompte & Goetz, 1982:32f).

"Objectivity" is certainly the most misleading of the criteria presented in Table 1. In quantitative research, the operational design of this criterion in terms of the greatest possible independence of data collection, analysis, and interpretation from the person of the researcher suggests the positivist notion of an observer-independent world that can be depicted adequately through scientific methods. Such a notion of observation, which leaves out the specific expectations, that is, the subjective perspective of the observer, is untenable from an epistemological point of view (see Popper, 1974:373f). Seen in this light, the controversy between conventional and new sociological research on violence with its strong emphasis on qualitative methods (see von Trotha, 1997; Koehler & Heyer, 1998:14ff) proves to be primarily a question of choice of perspective that may well determine the type of outcome but not its quality. Interestingly, the qualitative research tradition, which is only too eager to criticize the neglect of subjectivity, is often not that far away from an underlying "presumption of an objective world" (Merleau-Ponty, 1966:23f). Ultimately, the demand to exclude one's own perspective and one's own prior knowledge in favor of the broadest possible openness and personal involvement in the subjectivity of the respondents and the social world they construct also aims toward an objectivity that is independent of investigators, but is now sought after in the respondents (see Strobl, 1998b:92; Hammersley, 1992:43ff). Nonetheless, rejecting this observer-independent "objective" ability to gain knowledge of the world does not mean—as is often claimed—disputing the existence of an external world that can be used to judge the appropriateness and the "functioning" of a scientific construction (see Luhmann, 1990:41). If the epistemological insight that each item of knowledge is bound to the perspective from which it is seen is taken seriously, then the core of the criterion of objectivity can only be that a researcher who takes a similar research perspective and a similar attitude toward research should obtain similar findings. The questions thus lead to a consideration of not only the aspect of reliability but also that of validity.

The epistemological core of the reliability criterion addresses the consistency of research findings. This can be interpreted, first, in the sense of a synchronous agreement between various measurements or observations of the same phenomenon; second, as a diachronic consistency of the findings, in other words, as the ability to reproduce them over the course of time. This is why Kirk and Miller (1986:41) talk about synchronous and diachronic reliability. One proposal by Lincoln and Guba (1985), when discussing their dependability criterion in the sense of synchronous reliability, suggests dividing a group of researchers and then comparing findings in each subgroup—in analogy to the "split-half" procedure common to quantitative research. However, the contextual conditions in ethnographic field research on violence often differ so greatly as to make findings incomparable. It is easier to test the consistency of findings in pure interview studies than in ethnographic studies. For this purpose, one can apply, for example, the procedure of minimizing the differences described above. However, within the framework of the qualitative research process, the lack of consistency between observations of the same phenomena can also be an important incentive to seek new categories or to improve existing ones. This is why, finally, only inconsistencies that cannot be resolved should be evaluated as indicating a lack of reliability.

Ensuring diachronic reliability in the sense of an ability to reproduce observations at a later time would seem to be an almost impossible endeavor in the light of biographical and historical processes of change. This is one of the reasons, along with paying insufficient attention to contextual conditions, why the results of the few qualitative replication studies so far are rather discouraging (see Seale, 1999:142ff). Panel studies, in contrast, in which the same persons are studied across several waves of data collection, permit not only the collection of comprehensive data over a longer biographical sequence, but also a comparison of the interpretations of past events obtained at different times. This is not only useful for validating the data, but also permits an understanding of later individual approaches to specific life phases (e.g., ones marked by violence) in which their subjective significance may have been modified and their content frequently also have been reinterpreted, for example, by adapting it to fit current life concepts (e.g., after having "dropped out" successfully from a violent scene, group, or culture; see Dietz et al., 1997; Böttger, 2000). However, when performing, for example, a longitudinal study of violent youth, it is almost impossible to assume that findings in the second wave will be the same as those in the first. Rather, differences will have to be anticipated as a result of biographical development (see Heitmeyer et al., 1992:57ff; Dietz et al., 1997).

Compared with the reliability discourse, the validity issue has received far more attention in qualitative research. This may be because there can be no doubt that the validity of its findings is one of the strengths of this method. For example, Kirk and Miller (1986:30f) assign an "in-built validity" to ethnographic field studies. One reason for this is the difficulty that respondents would have in maintaining conscious deceits and distorted presentations over a longer research period. However, it is also due to the researcher's need to survive in the field and, therefore, to abandon untenable presumptions.[3] In ethnographic research on violence, this may well mean survival in literal terms. Schwandner-Sievers (1998) describes how the survival of strangers in north Albanian mountain villages may depend on a valid interpretation of the system of honor and protection. This example shows that the decisive point in the validity criterion is for findings and interpretations to *prove* themselves. This point still retains its significance even when the assumption of an observer-independent ability to gain knowledge of the world has been abandoned. However, not all qualitative procedures can benefit equally from this "in-built validity." Moreover, it is not powerful enough to guarantee a valid analysis and interpretation of the data. Therefore, various procedures have been developed to secure internal validity in qualitative research.

Qualitative interview procedures initially have to ensure clarity over the aspect of the reference level of the knowledge as discussed at the beginning of this chapter. The neutralization techniques, conscious deceits, or constructions guided by specific interests that are discussed as threats to validity in research on violence (see Eckert, Reis, & Wetzstein, 2000:29f) are not a problem as long as one wants to study exactly this way of subjectively interpreting violence (using, e.g., narrative interviews). Nonetheless, such data become problematic when the goal is to reconstruct grievous experiences or acts of violence at the time of their occurrence. This calls for techniques like the "reconstructive interview" (see, e.g., Böttger, 1996). However, at times, the goal of gaining more valid findings on the level of past experience by breaking down suppressions and neutralizations may well come into conflict with research ethics.

Problems with research ethics may also be one of the reasons why qualitative research on violence hardly ever uses the strategy of subjecting outcomes of analysis to a communicative validation through respondents. In general, one major problem with this procedure is that a respondent's disagreement is insufficient for deducing a validity problem. A respondent may also disagree because he or she considers the findings to be unpleasant or inconceivable (see Terhart, 1981:772ff). One procedure that is also used frequently in qualitative research on violence (e.g., by Heitmeyer et al., 1992; Möller, 2000), is discursive validation within the research team. Here, different investigators propose and discuss different "ways of reading" the data (as in "objective hermeneutics") until one way is confirmed through debate. The problem with this procedure is that such discussions may be very tiresome and inconclusive when theoretical perspectives differ or are even incompatible.

A further validation procedure applied in qualitative research on violence is the triangulation of different methods (see Denzin, 1970). Usually, various qualitative methods are combined, such as participant observation and problem-centered interviews. However, combinations of quantitative and qualitative procedures can also be found (see, e.g., Willems et al., 1993). Critics of the triangulation concept nonetheless point out that each

---

[3] Cicourel's (1996) concept of ecological validity takes the same direction.

method defines the object in its own specific way so that, although a combination of methods may increase the "depth" and "breadth" of findings, it cannot raise their validity (see Flick, 1991:432; Kelle & Erzberger, 1999:514ff; Fielding & Fielding, 1986:33). Alongside the triangulation of methods, Denzin (1970) has proposed investigator triangulation (to prevent subjective distortions in the data collection process), theory triangulation, and data triangulation. Analysis by different investigators leads to the same advantages and disadvantages as those in discursive validation. Theory triangulation, in contrast, is fraught with similar problems as the triangulation of methods. If one source of data (e.g., court records) is used to validate another (e.g., interviews), a lack of agreement will raise the principal question of which of the two sources actually is more valid. Nonetheless, background information from records can be very useful for clarifying contents that seemed doubtful during an interview (see Böttger, 1998:107). A further important validation strategy is the systematic search for counterevidence when testing interpretative hypotheses. In this context, the opportunities provided by modern computer-assisted text processing can be viewed as an important advance in securing the validity of outcomes of analysis (see Prein, 1996:95ff).

In qualitative research, the generalizability of findings seems to be more critical than their internal validity. Cook and Campbell (1979:70ff) have called this external validity. In this context, the demand for samples with a minimum of bias is an important issue. However, in quantitative research this issue has been reduced to drawing representative random samples. When analyzing serious violent offenses or the experiences of victims, random samples would generally have to be so large that even a quantitative approach would soon run up against the limitations of research economics. Qualitative procedures become practically impossible with such large sample sizes. However, it is often overlooked in this context that representative samples (in a statistical sense) are only necessary when one is interested in quantitative distributions in the population studied, but are not needed when constructing and testing theoretical explanations and theories. The theoretical sampling procedure described above provides the qualitative research tradition with a tried and tested procedure for compiling samples for this purpose. In this connection, it is important for the sample to contain representatives of all theoretically significant combinations of features in sufficient numbers. However, this is often problematic in qualitative research on violence. Target groups with persons who use violence are not always ready to report their experiences or even their biographies to researchers. Furthermore, their victims are also frequently unwilling to talk about what is in many ways a taboo topic. Therefore, particularly in qualitative studies that have to deal very intensively with biographical details in relation to any phenomena of violence, there is a general need for comprehensive and intensive preparations in order to make potential respondents more willing to cooperate (see, e.g., Böttger, 1998; Strobl, 1998a; Rausch, 1999).

VII. DESIDERATA

The further development of qualitative research on violence—or qualitative social research in general—requires, first of all, a loosening of the methodological poles of theory development and theory testing in order to meet practical needs. This chapter has shown that qualitative empirical research always manages both: It is guided continuously by implicit or explicit theoretical prior assumptions, and it simultaneously develops these further through new empirical knowledge (see, also, Böttger, 2001). It is only when both inseparably linked aspects are taken specifically into account in the design and implementation of qualitative research on violence that their potential for providing knowledge will be exploited suitably. The opportunity for qualitative research on violence—as for qualitative research in general—lies in the potentials of a systematic further development of a "balance between openness and being guided by theory" (Strobl & Böttger, 1996).

Moreover, the "paradigmatic dispute" whether purely qualitative or purely quantitative research (on violence) is the ideal for empirical work should give way to the idea of coordinating both approaches to address concrete research issues. If the goal of empirically plotting an unknowable, because observer-independent, "objective" social reality ("course level") is abandoned and the role of theory in empirical research (on violence) is basically grasped as involving not only its (further) development but also its testing, the barriers between qualitative and quantitative empirical approaches will also disappear from the perspective of both a theory of science and epistemology. In fact, the possibilities of coordinating both approaches open up a host of opportunities for innovative methodological project designs (see, e.g., Kluge & Kelle, 2001).

When looking at international trends in qualitative research on violence, it is particularly conspicuous that ethnographic studies are a rarity in central Europe. One reason may be the difficulty in developing standards in the sense of a set of rules that can be applied directly in practice. On the other hand, the comparatively high validity of ethnographic data should also encourage European researchers to consider these methods when studying phenomena of violence in society.

The further development of qualitative research on violence in both practical and methodological terms particularly calls for systematically performed and evaluated tests of the individual techniques. It is not just ethnography that lacks a systematized, practically manageable knowledge of methods. There is also very little confirmed practical knowledge on special techniques for qualitative interviews, focus groups, and so forth. Particularly in sensitive research fields like violence, there is a need for a systematic study of methods, for example, on how to guide qualitative interviews through dialogue.

There is also need for a broader discussion in the social sciences on the ethical constraints of qualitative research on violence. This applies not only to the individual "respondent" for whom an intensive qualitative (e.g., biographical) procedure is frequently a decisive event, but also to the problem of potential circulation of qualitative data (e.g., to an archive). This cannot comply with the guarantee of anonymity that is particularly indispensable in research on violence. The large amount of information quickly can lead to the identification of individual persons despite the application of traditional anonymity procedures (erasure or alteration of personal names, dates, and locations).

Translated by Jonathan Harrow

REFERENCES

Aster, Reiner, Hans Merkens, & Michael Repp. (Eds.) (1989). *Teilnehmende Beobachtung. Werkstattberichte und methodologische Reflexionen.* Frankfurt: Campus.

Atkinson, Paul, & Martyn Hammersley. (1994). Ethnography and Participant Observation. In Norman K. Denzin & Yvonna S. Lincoln (Eds.), *Handbook of Qualitative Research* (pp. 248–261). London: Sage.

Bohnsack, Ralf, Peter Loos, Burkhard Schäffer, Klaus Städtler, & Bodo Wild. (1995). *Die Suche nach Gemeinsamkeit und die Gewalt der Gruppe: Hooligans, Musikgruppen und andere Jugendcliquen.* Opladen: Leske & Budrich.

Böttger, Andreas. (1992). *Die Biographie des Beschuldigten im Schwurgerichtsverfahren.* Frankfurt: Haag und Heerchen.
Böttger, Andreas. (1996). 'Hervorlocken' oder Aushandeln? Zu Methodologie und Methode des 'rekonstruktiven Interviews' in der Sozialforschung. In Rainer Strobl & Andreas Böttger (Eds.), *Wahre Geschichten? Zu Theorie und Praxis qualitativer Interviews* (pp. 131–158). Baden-Baden: Nomos.
Böttger, Andreas. (1998). *Gewalt und Biographie. Eine qualitative Analyse rekonstruierter Lebensgeschichten von 100 Jugendlichen.* Baden-Baden: Nomos.
Böttger, Andreas. (1999). Das rekonstruktive Interview. In Dietmar Bolscho & Gerd Michelsen (Eds.), *Methoden in der Umweltbildungsforschung* (pp. 63–78). Opladen: Leske & Budrich.
Böttger, Andreas. (2000). Devianz als Episode. Wege des 'Ausstiegs' aus kriminalisierbarem Handeln. In Walter R. Heinz (Ed.), *Übergänge. Individualisierung, Flexibilisierung und Institutionalisierung des Lebensverlaufs. Beiheft Nr. 3 der Zeitschrift für Soziologie der Erziehung und Sozialisation* (pp. 77–90). Weinheim: Juventa.
Böttger, Andreas. (2001). Die Weiterentwicklung von Theorien auf der empirischen Grundlage 'rekonstruktiver Interviews.' In Claudia Finkbeiner & Gerhard W. Schnaitmann (Eds.), *Lehren und Lernen im Kontext empirischer Forschung und Fachdidaktik* (pp. 289–310). Donauwörth: Ludwig Auer.
Böttger, Andreas, & Jiazhen Liang. (1998). Rekonstruktion im Dialog. Zur Durchführung 'rekonstruktiver Interviews' mit gewalttätigen Jugendlichen in Deutschland und in China. In Jo Reichertz (Ed.), *Die Wirklichkeit des Rechts: rechts- und sozialwissenschaftliche Studien* (pp. 54–67). Opladen: Westdeutscher Verlag.
Cicourel, Aaron V. (1996). Ecological Validity and 'White Room Effects.' *Pragmatics and Cognition, 4,* 221–264.
Cook, Thomas D., & Donald T. Campbell. (1979). *Quasi-Experimentation: Design and Analysis Issues for Field Settings.* Chicago: Rand McNally.
Denzin, Norman K. (1970). *The Research Act. A Theoretical Introduction to Sociological Methods.* Chicago: Aldine.
Dietz, Gerhard-Uhland, Eduard Matt, Karl F. Schumann, & Lydia Seus. (1997). *Lehre tut viel ... Berufsbildung, Lebensplanung und Delinquenz bei Arbeiterjugendlichen.* Münster: Votum.
Eckert, Roland, Christa Reis, & Thomas Wetzstein. (2000). *Ich will halt anders sein wie die anderen! Abgrenzung, Gewalt und Kreativität bei Gruppen Jugendlicher.* Opladen: Leske & Budrich.
Ferrell, Jeff, & Mark S. Hamm. (Eds.) (1998). *Ethnography at the Edge. Crime, Deviance and Field Research.* Boston: Northeastern University Press.
Fielding, Nigel G., & Jane L. Fielding. (1986). *Linking Data.* London: Sage.
Flick, Uwe. (1991). Triangulation. In Uwe Flick, Ernst von Kardorff, Heiner Keupp, Lutz Rosenstiel & Stephan Wolff (Eds.), *Handbuch Qualitative Sozialforschung: Grundlagen, Konzepte, Methoden und Anwendungen* (pp. 432–434). München: Beltz/PVU.
Flick, Uwe. (1995). *Qualitative Sozialforschung. Theorie, Methoden, Anwendung in Psychologie und Sozialwissenschaften.* Reinbek bei Hamburg: Rowohlt.
Geertz, Clifford. (1983). *Dichte Beschreibung. Beiträge zum Verstehen kultureller Systeme.* Frankfurt a. M.: Suhrkamp.
Gerhardt, Uta. (1991). Typenbildung. In Uwe Flick, Ernst von Kardorff, Heiner Keupp, Lutz Rosenstiel & Stephan Wolff (Eds.), *Handbuch Qualitative Sozialforschung: Grundlagen, Konzepte, Methoden und Anwendungen* (pp. 435–439). München: Beltz/PVU.
Glaser, Barney G., & Anselm L. Strauss. (1977). *The Discovery of Grounded Theory, 8th Edition.* Chicago: Aldine.
Hammersley, Martyn. (1989). *The Dilemma of Qualitative Method.* London: Routledge.
Hammersley, Martyn. (1992). *What's Wrong with Ethnography? Methodological Explorations.* London: Routledge.
Heinze, Thomas, & Hans W. Klusemann. (1980). Versuch einer sozialwissenschaftlichen Paraphrasierung am Beispiel des Ausschnittes einer Bildungsgeschichte. In Thomas Heinze, Hans W. Klusemann & Hans-Georg Soeffner (Eds.), *Interpretationen einer Bildungsgeschichte. Überlegungen zur sozialwissenschaftlichen Hermeneutik* (pp. 97–152). Bensheim: päd-extra.
Heinze, Thomas, Hans W. Klusemann, & Hans-Georg Soeffner. (Eds.) (1980). *Interpretationen einer Bildungsgeschichte. Überlegungen zur sozialwissenschaftlichen Hermeneutik.* Bensheim: päd-extra.
Heitmeyer, Wilhelm, Heike Buhse, Joachim Liebe-Freund, Kurt Möller, Joachim Müller, Helmut Ritz, Gertrud Siller, & Johannes Vossen. (1992). *Die Bielefelder Rechtsextremismus-Studie. Erste Langzeituntersuchung zur politischen Sozialisation männlicher Jugendlicher.* Weinheim: Juventa.
Hopf, Christel, Peter Rieker, Martina Sanden-Marcus, & Christiane Schmidt. (1995). *Familie und Rechts-*

extremismus. Familiale Sozialisation und rechtsextreme Orientierungen junger Männer. Weinheim: Juventa.

Jessor, Richard, Anne Colby, & Richard A. Shweder. (Eds.) (1996). *Ethnography and Human Development: Context and Meaning in Social Inquiry.* Chicago: University of Chicago Press.

Kade, Sylvia. (1983). *Methoden des Fremdverstehens: ein Zugang zu Theorie und Praxis des Fremdverstehens.* Bad Heilbrunn: Klinkhardt.

Kelle, Udo. (1997). *Empirisch begründete Theoriebildung. Zur Logik und Methodologie interpretativer Sozialforschung, 2nd Edition.* Weinheim: Deutscher Studien Verlag.

Kelle, Udo, & Christian Erzberger. (1999). Integration qualitativer und quantitativer Methoden. *Kölner Zeitschrift für Soziologie und Sozialpsychologie, 51,* 509–531.

Kepper, Gaby. (1996). *Qualitative Marktforschung: Methoden, Einsatzmöglichkeiten und Beurteilungskriterien.* 2nd Edition. Wiesbaden: DUV.

Kirk, Jerome, & Marc L. Miller. (1986). *Reliability and Validity in Qualitative Research.* London: Sage.

Kluge, Susann. (1999). *Empirisch begründete Typenbildung.* Opladen: Leske & Budrich.

Kluge, Susann, & Udo Kelle. (Eds.) (2001). *Methodeninnovation in der Lebenslaufforschung. Integration qualitativer und quantitativer Verfahren in der Lebenslauf- und Biographieforschung.* Weinheim: Juventa.

Koehler, Jan, & Sonja Heyer. (1998). Einleitung. Soziologisches Sprechen und empirisches Erfassen—Explaining Violence. In Jan Koehler & Sonja Heyer (Eds.), *Anthropologie der Gewalt: Chancen und Grenzen der sozialwissenschaftlichen Forschung* (pp. 9–26). Berlin: VWF.

Lamnek, Siegfried. (1988). *Theorien abweichenden Verhaltens. Eine Einführung für Soziologen, Psychologen, Pädagogen, Juristen, Politologen, Kommunikationswissenschaftler und Sozialarbeiter.* München: Fink.

Lamnek, Siegfried. (1993). *Qualitative Sozialforschung, 2 Vol.* Weinheim: Beltz/PVU.

LeCompte, Margaret D., & Judith Preissle Goetz. (1982). Problems of Reliability and Validity in Ethnographic Research. *Review of Educational Research, 52*(1), 31–60.

Lempert, Lora Bex. (1996). Women's Strategies for Survival: Developing Agency in Abusive Relationships. *Journal of Family Violence, 11,* 269–289.

Liang, Jiazhen, Mirja Silkenbeumer, & Andreas Böttger. (2001). *Früher war ich nicht so. Biographien gewalttätiger Jugendlicher in China.* Baden-Baden: Nomos.

Lincoln, Yvonna S., & Egon G. Guba. (1985). *Naturalistic Inquiry.* London: Sage.

Luhmann, Niklas. (1990). Das Erkenntnisprogramm des Konstruktivismus und die unbekannt bleibende Realität. In Niklas Luhmann (Ed.), *Soziologische Aufklärung, Vol. 5* (pp. 31–58). Opladen: Westdeutscher Verlag.

Lyng, Stephen. (1998). Dangerous Methods. Risk Taking and the Research Process. In Jeff Ferrell & Mark S. Hamm (Eds.), *Ethnography at the Edge. Crime, Deviance and Field Research* (pp. 221–251). Boston: Northeastern University Press.

Mayring, Philipp. (1983). *Qualitative Inhaltsanalyse. Grundlagen und Techniken.* Weinheim: Beltz.

Mayring, Philipp. (1996). *Einführung in die qualitative Sozialforschung.* Weinheim: Beltz/PVU.

McCall, George J. (1978). *Observing the Law. Field Methods in the Study of Crime and the Criminal Justice System.* New York: The Free Press.

Merleau-Ponty, Maurice. (1966). *Phänomenologie der Wahrnehmung.* Berlin: de Gruyter.

Möller, Kurt. (2000). *Rechte Kids. Eine Langzeitstudie über Auf- und Abbau rechtsextremistischer Orientierungen bei 13- bis 15 jährigen.* Weinheim: Juventa.

Nedelmann, Birgitta. (1997). Gewaltsoziologie am Scheideweg. In Trutz von Trotha (Ed.), *Soziologie der Gewalt. Sonderheft Nr. 37 der Kölner Zeitschrift für Soziologie und Sozialpsychologie* (pp. 59–85). Opladen: Westdeutscher Verlag.

Neumann, Michael. (1995). Schwierigkeiten der Soziologie mit der Gewaltanalyse. Einige Bemerkungen zum Beitrag Birgitta Nedelmanns. *Mittelweg 36*(5), 65–68.

Nießen, Manfred. (1977). *Gruppendiskussion: interpretative Methodologie, Methodenbegründung, Anwendung.* München: Fink.

Oevermann, Ulrich, Tilman Allert, Elisabeth Konau, & Jürgen Krambeck. (1979). Die Methodologie einer 'objektiven Hermeneutik' und ihre allgemeine forschungslogische Bedeutung in den Sozialwissenschaften. In Hans-Georg Soeffner (Ed.), *Interpretative Verfahren in den Sozial- und Textwissenschaften* (pp. 352–434). Stuttgart: Metzler.

Oevermann, Ulrich, Tilman Allert, Elisabeth Konau. (1980). Zur Logik der Interpretation von Interviewtexten. In Thomas Heinze, Hans W. Klusemann & Hans-Georg Soeffner (Eds.), *Interpretationen einer Bildungsgeschichte. Überlegungen zur sozialwissenschaftlichen Hermeneutik* (pp. 15–69). Bensheim: päd.-extra.

Popper, Karl R. (1971). *Logik der Forschung.* Tübingen: Mohr.

Popper, Karl R. (1974). *Objektive Erkenntnis. Ein evolutionärer Entwurf*, 2nd Edition. Hamburg: Hoffmann und Campe.
Prein, Gerald. (1996). Interpretative Methodologie und Computer. In Rainer Strobl & Andreas Böttger (Eds.), *Wahre Geschichten? Zu Theorie und Praxis qualitativer Interviews* (pp. 93–110). Baden-Baden: Nomos.
Rausch, Thomas. (1999). *Zwischen Selbstverwirklichungsstreben und Rassismus. Soziale Deutungsmuster ostdeutscher Jugendlicher.* Opladen: Leske & Budrich.
Roberts, Carol A. (1999). Drug Use among Inner-City African American Women: The Process of Managing Loss. *Qualitative Health Research*, 9, 620–638.
Schütze, Fritz. (1976). Zur Hervorlockung und Analyse von Erzählungen thematisch relevanter Geschichten im Rahmen soziologischer Feldforschung—dargestellt an einem Projekt zur Erforschung von kommunalen Machtstrukturen. In Arbeitsgruppe Bielefelder Soziologen, *Kommunikative Sozialforschung: Alltagswissen und Alltagshandeln, Gemeindemachtforschung, Polizei, politische Erwachsenenbildung* (pp. 159–260). München: Fink.
Schütze, Fritz. (1983). Biographieforschung und narratives Interview. *Neue Praxis*, 13(3), 283–293.
Schwandner-Sievers, Stephanie. (1998). Wer besitzt die 'Lizenz zum Töten' in Albanien? oder: Fragen zu Gruppensolidarität und Gewaltlegitimation in einer 'anderen Modernisierung.' In Jan Koehler & Sonja Heyer (Eds.), *Anthropologie der Gewalt. Chancen und Grenzen der sozialwissenschaftlichen Forschung* (pp. 71–88). Berlin: VWF.
Seale, Clive. (1999). *The Quality of Qualitative Research*. London: Sage.
Strauss, Anselm L. (1991). *Grundlagen qualitativer Sozialforschung*. München: Fink.
Strauss, Anselm L., & Juliet Corbin. (1990). *Basics of Qualitative Research*. London: Sage.
Strobl, Rainer. (1998a). *Soziale Folgen der Opfererfahrungen ethnischer Minderheiten*. Baden-Baden: Nomos.
Strobl, Rainer. (1998b). Zur Bedeutung theoretischer Vorannahmen bei der Durchführung qualitativer Interviews mit türkischen Opfern. In Jo Reichertz (Ed.), *Die Wirklichkeit des Rechts: rechts- und sozialwissenschaftliche Studien* (pp. 87–100). Opladen: Westdeutscher Verlag.
Strobl, Rainer, & Andreas Böttger. (Eds.) (1996). *Wahre Geschichten? Zu Theorie und Praxis qualitativer Interviews*. Baden-Baden: Nomos.
Terhart, Ewald. (1981). Intuition—Interpretation—Argumentation. *Zeitschrift für Pädagogik*, 27, 769–793.
Thomas, William Isaac. (1965). *Person und Sozialverhalten*. Neuwied: Luchterhand.
Thrasher, Frederic M. (1963) [1927]. *The Gang. A Study of 1.313 Gangs in Chicago*. Abridged and with a New Introduction by James F. Short. Chicago: The University of Chicago Press.
Trotha, Trutz von. (1997). Zur Soziologie der Gewalt. In Trutz von Trotha (Ed.), *Soziologie der Gewalt. Sonderheft Nr. 37 der Kölner Zeitschrift für Soziologie und Sozialpsychologie* (pp. 9–56). Opladen: Westdeutscher Verlag.
Whyte, William Foote. (1981) [1943]. *Street Corner Society*, 3rd revised and expanded Edition. Chicago: The University of Chicago Press.
Willems, Helmut, Roland Eckert, Stefanie Würtz, & Linda Steinmetz. (1993). *Fremdenfeindliche Gewalt. Einstellungen, Täter, Konflikteskalation.* Opladen: Leske & Budrich.
Witzel, Andreas. (1982). *Verfahren der qualitativen Sozialforschung*. Frankfurt a. M., New York: Campus.
Witzel, Andreas. (1996). Auswertung problemzentrierter Interviews. Grundlagen und Erfahrungen. In Rainer Strobl & Andreas Böttger (Eds.), *Wahre Geschichten? Zu Theorie und Praxis qualitativer Interviews* (pp. 49–76). Baden-Baden: Nomos.

CHAPTER III.2

Strategies and Problems in Quantitative Research on Aggression and Violence

RAINER DOLLASE AND MATTHIAS ULBRICH-HERRMANN

I. INTRODUCTION

In gathering, analyzing, and interpreting its data, quantitative research on violence and aggression draws on the well-known range of techniques in empirical social research—techniques that are extraordinarily well documented (Bortz & Döring, 1995; Erdfelder et al., 1996; Feger, 1996; Friedrichs, 1985; Koolwijk & Wieken-Mayser, 1975ff; Lewis-Beck, 1993). As a result, many of the problems in this specific field are typical to all quantitative empirical social research.

Nonetheless, the comprehensive corpus of research on aggression and violence, estimated in sociology and psychology data banks at more than 30,000 publications, reveals numerous specific assessment instruments (e.g., violence questionnaires, aggressiveness tests). Theoretically, this is no surprise, because each research question requires its own specifically tailored quantitative assessment method.

Apart from presenting such special assessment instruments, two questions need to be clarified: (1) Given that the methods in both empirical social research and research on aggression and violence are largely identical, what potential function remains for a handbook article on quantitative methods? (2) Which systematic features distinguish quantitative research on aggression and violence from research on other areas of behavior?

II. METHODS OF RESEARCH ON AGGRESSION AND VIOLENCE: A SPECIAL DOMAIN?

1. Functions of Secondary Literature on Methods

The first thing to do is to describe the functions of the existing secondary literature on methodological issues, particularly in research on aggression and violence (Albrecht, 1999; Krumm, 1997; Krumm & Baumann, 1996; Schwind, 1997; Tedeschi & Quigley, 1998). Some authors aim to provide a short overview for nonexperts or persons starting training (e.g., Schwind, 1996); others, a well-founded criticism of dominant operationalizations in, for example, experimental aggression research (e.g., Tedeschi & Quigley, 1998). Further concerns are to provide encouragement and critique, or to document recent options for overcoming difficulties in assessing "problematic behavior," which can include violence and aggression just as much as, for example, drug use (e.g., Albrecht, 1999). Finally, one can also find specific criticism of the methods applied in German research on violence and aggression from 1990–1996 (Krumm, 1997). In summary, the secondary literature on methods in research on aggression and violence aims to set standards and norms, to make suggestions, to elucidate the breadth of possible operationalizations and methods of analysis, to identify errors, and also, in particular, to express critique.

Critique of current research practice addresses not only the assessment and analysis of quantitative data but also, for example, misleading titles, unsatisfactory theoretical reflection on central concepts, the completely inadequate coverage of the state of research (which is hardly surprising in light of the enormous number of studies), and the neglect of theory (Krumm, 1997). One of Krumm's methodological criticisms addresses "one-sided" assessment procedures, namely, questionable operationalizations that are not matched to the different perspectives on acts of violence and aggression taken by the offender, the victim, and the observer. Further deficits are a failure to control for the serial position effects of items, a lack of different response alternatives for the same topic, different and noncomparable response formats, unreliable informants (e.g., teachers asked to say something about increasing aggressiveness among students), a lack of pretests, unfamiliarity with the classic quality criteria (objectivity, reliability, and validity), but also weaknesses in reporting research (e.g., questionnaires and questions are not documented in full, or missing values are not assessed despite the availability of a special SPSS program). Furthermore, comparative studies are infrequent, and, finally, there are one-sided reports presenting unacceptable interpretations of correlation coefficients as proof of causality. The questionable use of the terms "predictor" and "risk factor" can be found when only correlative studies have been performed, and one-sided, in part, insufficiently reflected criteria are used to judge which findings are to be labeled "dramatically high" or "low," without recourse to reliable and precisely defined standards. The tacit agreement to accept correlational statements in the form of correlation coefficients, path analyses, or regression analyses as proof of a one-sided causal direction is very widespread and is mostly excused by claiming that it is suggested by "theoretical considerations." It has long been known that a number of even mutually exclusive causal models can be "confirmed" through a significant fit in a path analysis (Stelzl, 1982).

Only parts of this critique are specific to research on aggression and violence. Most points apply to a wide range of quantitative empirical work. Nonetheless, the extent of this critique is a good indication that research on aggression and violence is considered to have a strong social relevance, justifying the need to take far greater care to ensure precise and transparent methods than those practiced in far less relevant domains such as adolescent fashions. The explosive social nature of the research topic provokes a harsher methodological and theoretical critique.

2. Systematic Characteristics Particular to Quantitative Research on Aggression and Violence

Characteristics particular to quantitative research on aggression and violence can be sought in the following domains: (a) The social relevance of aggression and violence; (b) the frequency and prevalence of real violence and aggression; (c) perspectives for its reconstruction; (d) its subjective antecedents and concomitants; (e) the specific repertoire of quantitative methods for assessment, analysis, and interpretation; and (f) problems with data protection.

a. AGGRESSION AND VIOLENCE ARE TABOO IN MANY AREAS OF THIS SOCIETY. This can be illustrated by violence within the family (violence toward spouses, abuse, violence toward children) or by other aggressive and violent behaviors that are against the law. Methodologically speaking, their formal and informal relevance leads to the risk of distorted responses in, for example, surveys. The formal and informal norms generate problems in the form of response bias (e.g., social desirability or the acquiescence tendency) in questionnaires (Mummendey, 1995), simulation (drastic descriptions, exaggerations), and dissimulation (playing down or denial of facts). Other problems include the assessment of unregistered cases. These particular problems are to be found not only in surveys of individuals but also in analyses of police crime statistics, insurance company accident statistics, and the like, whose data scarcely meet theoretically adequate operationalization standards. As a result, there is a particularly strong risk that data on violence and aggression from official statistics will give a distorted picture of reality.

b. FREQUENCY AND PREVALENCE OF REAL VIOLENCE AND AGGRESSION. Violent acts are rare events to be found with only a low if not the lowest frequency in the framework of random samples. Reliable estimates indicate that to obtain results on the group of potential offenders with a statistical power of *alpha* = .05, it is necessary to survey approximately 100,000 persons for physical injuries and even 400,000 persons for robbery (Albrecht, 1999). Together with the above-mentioned response bias and tendencies toward simulation and dissimulation, this often results in unclear and methodologically hardly surmountable errors, that is, an over- or underestimation of the real frequency and prevalence of aggression and violence. Hence, prevalence rates can be approximated only with a relatively high degree of uncertainty.

c. PERSPECTIVES FOR THE RECONSTRUCTION OF REAL VIOLENCE AND AGGRESSION. As some studies (Schwind, 1996; Schwind, Roitsch, & Gielen, 1997) have shown, reports on the frequency of real violence and aggression vary quite considerably as a function of whether they are given from the offender, victim, or observer perspective. This is because each perspective tries to give a different definition of violence or aggression. Offenders, for example, do not rate their own behavior as aggression but as self-defense. Even laboratory research indicates dissent over definitions and operationalizations. Frequently, a behavior is assumed to be an expression of aggression or violence, although participants themselves would not describe it as such. One analysis (Tedeschi & Quigley, 1998) has shown that behavior in the experimental laboratory that is defined from the observer perspective of the scientist as aggressiveness may even be understood as prosocial by the laboratory participants.

d. Subjective Antecedents and Concomitants of Real Violence and Aggression. Research on aggression and violence in the social sciences and psychology does not just address real violence and real aggression. It also examines its antecedents and concomitants, such as propensity toward violence, approval of violence, aggressive tendencies, aggressive feelings, or aggression-prone risk situations throughout socialization. It does not only study offenders who have been caught—which is more a topic of criminological research—but also the "soft" areas of verbal aggressions, insults, exclusion from in-groups, mobbing, bullying, and the like (Schäfer & Frey, 1999; Schäfer, 1997). Because the antecedents and concomitants of real violence and aggression are linked inseparably to theories on the origins of violence, the methods of assessment and analysis have to be extended to cover the problems of general attitude measurement as well as the explanation of the significance of attitudes for behavior. A further risk is that conclusions on the causality of aggression and violence will be drawn from concomitant phenomena that covary with them. In conclusion, the formulation of causal relationships requires a theoretical categorization that does not just claim but confirms which factors determine the effects.

e. Quantitative Assessment Instruments. There are numerous specific assessment instruments within the research field, for example, violence questionnaires, experimental paradigms, psychological tests, and registration forms for offenders that have been tried out and tested in line with the classic validity criteria. Nonetheless, their dissemination is impeded by their dependence on theories and specific research questions: everybody who wants to study something new (also) requires new operationalizations. Research findings would be more comparable if researchers were to use standardized and frequently applied instruments. The test procedures and scales documented in the German database PSYNDEX PLUS also include numerous German-language instruments for assessing aggressiveness and violent behavior (developed since 1945). A compilation of international procedures for assessing violence in juveniles can be obtained through SOCIOFILE or is documented in specific reports (e.g., Minogue, Kingery, & Murphy, 1999). Another potential source is the information system (ZIS) run by the Center for Survey Research and Methodology (ZUMA, Mannheim), a database of German-language assessment instruments for the social sciences.

f. Data Protection Problems. When researchers ask about "problematic" behaviors such as drug use, aggressiveness, or the use of violence, or when they wish to access criminal records and official documents, they are confronted with data protection regulations that vary in severity from nation to nation. A study of violence and aggression in German schools in the state of North Rhine-Westphalia, for example, requires the voluntary permission of the school director, the teachers, the parents, and, finally, the children and adolescents themselves. This sometimes imposes theoretically problematic restrictions on access to samples that have to be accepted as a pragmatic handicap to the power of statements.

A further serious problem in Germany is that scientists, unlike physicians and priests, have no privilege to refuse to give evidence. This means that they may be obliged to hand over data on, for example, criminal offenses to the criminal prosecution authority in extreme cases. Although techniques for rendering participation anonymous are an aid here, they have to be supplemented with time-consuming cryptographic codings in true panel studies to make data comparable across different waves of measurement without it becoming possible to work out each respondent's identity.

The particular problems listed here are not exclusive to quantitative research on aggression and violence, but, with the exception of the last point, also apply to quantitative research on "problem" behaviors (Albrecht, 1999), such as drug use, sexual practices, family relationships, sociometric structures, mental disorders, and the like. This chapter can only illustrate particular characteristics for the example of research on aggression and violence, thereby mentioning techniques that have also been applied successfully in other domains of problem behavior.

The aims of a methodological overview of systematic characteristics particular to research on aggression and violence are therefore to discuss certain areas relevant to the specific field, such as, for example, specific instruments for measuring aggression and violence, and also to illustrate methodological problems that emerge quite generally in the assessment of "problem" behaviors through specific examples from research on aggression and violence.

III. DEFINING THE CONTENTS OF RESEARCH AND QUANTIFICATION STRATEGIES

1. Facet Design

The methodological commonplace that determines the underlying theory, the definition of terms, and the operationalization of measurements of violence or aggression should require no further explanation. Nonetheless, it is a common research practice to take merely vague definitions of concepts in a topical discussion context and to subsume them into a scale in an ad hoc manner along with a collection of similarly sounding questions or statements. It is then claimed that the items tap the construct. Roskam (1996:20) has criticized this approach: "It is rare to find a way of ensuring that the measured variable actually corresponds to the intended concept." Therefore, along with other authors (e.g., Borg, 1995, 1996), he has proposed defining the contents of research in terms of a "facet design." A facet is an observable category or an aspect of a behavior process, in other words, a situation-person reaction.

Facet design is a technique for defining an area of behavior that mediates precisely and in detail between the concepts and the observable behavior. In general terms, an area of behavior can be defined as follows: One data unit in the area of behavior is a reaction x by a person P in relation to a stimulus or a situation S that is recorded by an observer in terms of the facets X_1, X_2, and so forth (Roskam, 1996). Facets must be objective, empirical categories. They have to contain all relevant, observable aspects of the area of behavior; they must be exhaustive; and they need to be logically dependent on each other (Roskam, 1996:15).

When applied consistently, the facet design procedure (which has a long history, see Borg, 1996), overcomes numerous errors in research on aggression and violence:

1. The meticulous definition of an area of behavior prevents empirical research from focusing exclusively on verbal concepts as psychological realities rather than on the psychological environment of the concept and the reaction. The failure to link "mobbing" and "bullying" and related concepts to the long-known outsider problem (Prose, 1974), or for research on violence in the 1990s to address the prior studies carried out under the label of "aggression" is due to past and present laxity in the definition of terms and the failure to apply facets in operationalizations. The motive for using "new" terms that are actually highly identical to old ones is probably the need for academic success. Faceting, however, permits a specific and precise localization of one's own research.

2. Integrating the operationalization into the hypothesis or theory also strengthens the relationship between the hypothesis and its operational test. Frequently, an empirically obtained relation can also be interpreted in other ways because the relationship between the hypothesis and the method for testing it is too arbitrary. Harmless operationalizations of the concept of violence (such as "Have you ever insulted other students?") soon encourage misleading findings indicating, for example, that the level of violence is high or has increased. Integrating the operationalization as such into the theoretical prediction frequently prevents overreaching theoretical statements when the results are delivered. It is not "violence in general" that has increased, but that "the group of persons x marked 'yes' more frequently when answering an item tapping recall on 'Have you ever insulted other students?'" A "theory on the structure of the data" is a rarity in research on violence. Therefore, one should avoid the practice of trying to manage without a theory to mediate the relation between concept and items as well as their ranking. In what he calls a "cookbook" approach, Borg (1995) recommends starting with the items, sorting them, then explaining the ties between the sorted items, and then testing the facets empirically (can the a priori sorting also be found in the data?), before finally revising the definition system. Borg (1995:31) states: "Items play a central role in facet theory . . . [and] it [facet theory] defines the construct by defining the set of all items that measure it."

When faceting the contents of research, it is advisable not only to integrate the research background by collecting and analyzing all prior studies as well as taking account of findings on constructs with related verbal labels, but also to gather different perspectives. Various studies have used graphs to illustrate the individual everyday theories on aggressiveness and violence (Langfeldt & Langfeldt-Nagel, 1990). These can be used to show how one can link one's own construct to the everyday theories and thereby also facet them. Another option is to gather different perspectives on one and the same violent event at schools, for example, those of teachers, parents, janitors, students, and so forth. Schwind et al. (1997) presented their operationalizations to all respondents and then asked which of the given items they would label as violence and which not.

However, checking with respondents in this way cannot replace a theoretical faceting designed to ensure construct validity. Construct validity (MacCorquodale & Meehl, 1948) examines (possibly also empirically) whether the new construct measures that which other constructs with the same name measure, or whether it results in similar empirical networks. It also needs to be distinguished clearly from the "empirical validity" of the indicators, constructs, or variables that are present in an operationalization as a substantial correlation with a criterion variable. The researcher has to decide which of these two validities should stand in the foreground.

2. Conceiving the Contents of Research on the Basis of a Theory of Action or a Theory of Variables

One fundamental differentiation when planning any study of aggression or violence should be whether one uses the data gathered in the sense of a theory of variables, which mostly assumes a multifactorial model (i.e., many different dimensions, factors, or variables determine the final behavior), or whether one follows a theory of action. In an *action theory*, the interactions and events that lead, for example, to a certain violent act are plotted with care, and the researcher tries to ascertain regularities in the course of behavior. The proximity to qualitative procedures is clearly evident here. However, an action theory approach can also be linked to quantification. This is often found in experimental research on aggression and violence (Milgram, 1982). A *theory based on variables* tries to predict the violent activity from the interplay of different quantitative dimensions in such a way that the covariation with the variable "performance of the act" is as high as possible (an example's propensity toward violence as a function of age, gender, social status, external locus of control, etc.).

In an aggression study based on action theory, an analysis of videotapes in preschool groups could be used to show that winners of object conflicts (dispute over a toy) possess different behavior strategies compared with losers (winners are more skilled than losers in threatening and protesting as well in fighting the other person rather than in fighting for the object). Quantification consists in having to identify strategies that occur particularly frequently.

A study using a theory based on variables might present a correlation table as the final outcome in which the variables of social isolation, support, control, and aggressive severity, need for stimulation, and conscientiousness are plotted in relation to "propensity toward violence" (Mansel, 1995; Rojek, 1995).

Quantification strategies differ in the two types of study. On the basis of action theory, the concern is to plot the dominant patterns of behavior out of many different patterns through quantification and, if possible, to identify the most frequent (modal) strategies in two groups (winners and losers). In theories based on variables, the concern is generally with dimensional, quantifiable (latent) variables and their interplay in the dimensionally measured genesis of violence and aggressiveness. The preferred strategies of statistical analysis are then multiple regression analyses, path analyses, canonic correlation analyses, and other procedures based on the general linear model.

3. Tried and Tested Constructs and Operationalizations

The use of certain conceptions of the contents of research is not completely arbitrary for functional reasons. Certain forms of aggression are already so well studied or categorized through factor analysis as to confirm not only their factorial independence but even a different genesis and motivation. For example, a contemporary textbook on aggression (Nolting, 2000) uses the available literature to differentiate between "angry aggression," "instrumental aggression," and "spontaneous aggression." Another distinction is between aggressions with aggressive and nonaggressive motivation. Angry aggression includes expressions of ill humor and retaliatory aggressions. Expressions of ill humor are reactive and impulsive. Although they have an aggressive impact, they are not aggression in the stricter sense. Retaliatory aggressions are reactive, aggressive, and intrinsically motivated.

They are borne by resentment, hate, and similar feelings; deliberate infliction of pain brings inner satisfaction; self-esteem and justice are reattained. Instrumental aggressions include defensive and acquisitive aggressions. Defensive aggressions are reactive, not aggressively but extrinsically motivated, serve to fend off injury, and aim to protect. Nonetheless, they are often linked to strong emotions ranging from fear to anger. Acquisitive aggressions are active, not aggressively motivated, and extrinsic; their goal is assertion, winning, gaining attention and recognition; and they may well be performed unemotionally. Spontaneous aggression (or belligerence and sadism) is aggressive and intrinsically motivated. It serves to inflict pain and probably conveys emotional satisfaction through self-enhancement and self-stimulation (Nolting, 2000:120, Figure 11). Aggression and violence overlap, but only more severe forms of aggression should be labeled as violence. Relational aggression (Werner, Bigbee, & Crick, 1999) is defined as injuring the relationship to peers or injuring feelings of belonging and being accepted.

Depending on how closely one orients oneself toward these examples of tried and tested concepts of aggression or violence, one's own work will exhibit stronger or weaker ties with the prior state of research. In general, the freedom to form one's own and even more complex objects of research, which do not have to refer to the history of research on a phenomenon, represents a completely legitimate approach that may well be very productive. On the other hand, one has to take care to avoid reification, and one should not believe that every word to be found in a dictionary or that can be put together to produce a meaning in one language is also a new phenomenon. Just because concepts such as spontaneous, current, structural aggression, self-aggression, instrumental retaliatory aggression, relational aggression, approval of violence, propensity toward violence, aggressiveness, violence as a personality trait, and so forth have the character of constructs does not mean that they can also always be distinguished from each other empirically. They may well appear in mixed forms: analytical separability does not necessarily imply empirical separability as well.

Nowadays, propensity toward violence or aggressiveness as a personality trait (Wild & Noack, 1999) have not only been categorized as dimensions within the framework of personality tests (e.g., through the "Big Five" in the NEO Personality Inventory: extraversion, introversion, conscientiousness, agreeableness, and openness to experience), but also standardized internationally within the framework of the ICD 10 Classification of Mental and Behavioral Disorders (WHO, 1999). ICD 10 stipulates diagnostic criteria to determine, for example, emotionally unstable personality disorder (Category F 60.3) or personality (disorder) aggressiveness. First, the general criteria for personality disorder must be present (Category A, F60), and then at least three of the following traits or behaviors, one of which must be (2): "(1) marked tendency to act unexpectedly and without consideration of the consequences; (2) marked tendency to quarrelsome behavior and conflicts with others, especially when impulsive acts are thwarted or criticized; (3) liability to outbursts of anger or violence with inability to control the resulting behavioral explosions; (4) difficulty in maintaining course of an act that offers no immediate reward; (5) unstable and capricious mood" (WHO, 1999:229). International standardizations of concepts also include aggressive personality characteristics under the rubric "dissocial personality disorder" when social bonds are lacking. Detailed German-language discussions and evaluations of the standardization system as well as overviews on diagnosing aggressiveness can be found in Krampen (2001) or Petermann and Petermann (2000).

Although standardized operationalizations and concepts promote the networking of research, critique is still necessary and unavoidable. Criticism of experimental laboratory methods of research on aggression has addressed the relation between the concept (aggression or violence) and its corresponding experimental operationalization. The participants' motives for aggressive behavior—wanting to exert influence, to reestablish justice, or to display a specific identity—can scarcely be assessed with the experimental paradigms applied. These paradigms include (a) the "teacher–student paradigm," (b) the "assessment of essays," (c) the "competitively oriented reaction-time game" in which the loser receives a certain number of electric shocks from the winner, and (d) the "bobo-doll modeling" game (Tedeschi & Quigley, 1998). Bobo is a plastic doll maltreated by an adult in model learning experiments, and the frequency with which children imitate the adult's aggressive act is taken as an indicator of their aggressiveness. However, all four measures could also actualize other motives.

Initially, each operationalization of a concept is only a claim that it can be used to assess aggressiveness (see above). Tedeschi and Quigley (1998) have shown that it is necessary to tap motives for aggressive behavior (the need to exert influence, the motive of reestablishing justice, and the attempt to display a specific identity) before aggressiveness can be measured satisfactorily. This focuses operationalizations on the issue of the social motives underlying the use of aggressive acts to, for example, coerce others. It points to the more general problem of the meaningful application of research and the associated interaction between theory, state of knowledge, and methodological implementation as items within the framework of a new study.

IV. ASSESSMENT PROCEDURES AND RELATED PROBLEMS

At the present time, research on aggression and violence seems to be dominated by questionnaire studies. It is probably cost-benefit considerations that lead to the selection of this easy-to-apply methodological instrument. The quality of a questionnaire depends not only on how carefully the operationalizations are selected and integrated into the context of the theoretical and empirical argumentation but also on whether the breadth of item concepts and known or new measures to counteract response bias, simulations, and dissimulations are applied. It is also necessary to consider alternative methods and compare these with the questionnaire.

1. Rarely Applied or New Procedures

Some areas within questionnaire methods are chosen less frequently in research on aggression and violence. These include surveys paying stronger attention to the different perspectives of victim, offender, and observer; and, second, an old instrument that also proved its worth in earlier research on aggression and violence: sociometric status and structure in groups (Moreno, 1934; Dollase, 1996). The latter can use "relational" sociometry to assess and reciprocally validate not only victim and offender perspectives but also those of observers. For example, there are always persons who say that "X threatened me." Sociometry can be used to check whether X admits this as well ("I threatened Y") or whether others have also perceived this ("Who threatened whom?"). Furthermore, peers can be examined with the peer estimation technique (Owens & MacMullin, 1995) to assess, for example, the prevalence rate for aggressiveness and violence among fellow students.

Questionnaires occasionally include comprehensive violence and aggression scenarios understood as hypothetical descriptions of cases, processes, or stories that participants then have to judge. Scenarios make sense because they may help to phrase the research question in more concrete terms, avoid misunderstandings, or fend off criticism of the questionnaire by respondents ("You can't always say whether it's one or the other; you have to give me a specific example"). However, scenarios can also be used to influence answers, because they represent a major part of the questionnaire context, and we know that this can influence responding just as much as individual questions and the ways in which these are formulated (Kennedy & Forde, 1996; Otten, Mummendey, & Wenzel, 1995). The "exposure to violence interview" (Kindlon et al., 1996; Schäfer, 1997) has demonstrated that a videotaped confrontation with a violent or aggressive scenario can lead to marked changes in the respondents' answers. Such studies indicate the importance of the context of a questionnaire assessment or the immediately preceding experiences and stimuli—even when these are only the conditions set by the study. If the potential impact of the questionnaire context is known, this (in many cases, actually undesired) effect can also be exploited in experimental questionnaire design. One and the same questionnaire could be introduced with a story eliciting sympathy for the offender in a first version versus the victim in a second. This would permit an empirical study of the consequences of "inducing sympathy."

There is comprehensive methodological literature on the unwanted consequences of a survey and the assessment context (Mummendey, 1995). It shows, for example, that the sequence of questions in a questionnaire and the assessment situation (whether a survey is performed by telephone or in writing, is unstructured or structured) can exert a marked influence on response frequencies. Recent studies (in the framework of terror management theory) have also shown that even individual items may trigger negative or positive mood by, for example, bringing to mind ruminations on one's own death, and influence subsequent questionnaire and real-life behavior (Ochsmann & Mathy, 1993). When estimating prevalence rates, one should at least introduce systematic variation of both the sequence of questions and the context of the questionnaire.

Items describing hypothetical situations ("If somebody were to annoy me, I would defend myself"), are not unusual in aggression and violence questionnaires. In other fields of empirical social science, such as traffic research in which questionnaire data can be validated against actual road traffic, simulation surveys have been further elaborated. These techniques would be very suitable for research on aggression and violence. In the "stated preference" response mode, respondents report which alternatives (e.g., action alternatives) they prefer. In "stated tolerance," they report under which circumstances they could imagine resorting personally to various behavior alternatives (including, e.g., the use of violence). In the "stated adaptation" mode, they are asked "What would you do if the following restrictions were to be imposed on your behavior?" This is followed by a detailed scenario of different restrictions such as not being able to respond immediately to aggressive behavior. In the "stated prospect" mode, respondents are asked under which conditions a person would change his or her aggressive behavior and how he or she would cope with this (Bradley & Hensher, 1992).

Such examples show that the breadth of potential refinements to surveys in research on aggression and violence is far from exhausted. This is even more true for further effective but time-consuming procedures such as observation procedures, physiological measurements, nonreactive measurement procedures, or "unobtrusive measures." These are applied just as infrequently as various reactive scaling methods (multidimensional scaling, ranking procedures) or also subtests from well-known personality tests such as the Freiburg Personality Inventory (FPI), the NEO Personality Inventory (NEO-FFI), the Rosenzweig Picture-Frustration Test (PFT), the Thematic Apperception Test (TAT), or the Hidden Patterns Test (HPI) that all contain aggression subscales. Both the PFT and the TAT are projective test procedures: picture materials showing ambiguous social situations are presented to respondents, and the predominance of aggressive problems or the way of reacting to frustration (impunitive, intropunitive, extrapunitive) are assessed.

2. Process-Generated Data

When working with process-generated data, one is often dependent on data sources that could not have been planned or constructed in the research context. These then frequently contain systematic biases in both the data and sample recruitment that may well clash with the research question. This is the case in all studies using crime statistics gathered by the police (Albrecht, 1998; Böttger, 1997; Mansel, 1995; Sanders, 1994; Wright, Rossi, & Daly, 1983). For violence in the family, one may depend either on clinical data, perhaps from unstructured interviews in shelters for battered women, police statistics (the Uniform Crime Reports, UCR, in the United States, or reports from government commissions in other countries), or, once again, survey data that are problematic because of the low base rate for criminal and violent incidents.

This points to the urgent need for methodological options to compensate for these problems. Both the "snowball system" and the above-mentioned peer estimation technique provide ways of working with nonrepresentative samples (Albrecht, 1999). These two techniques are able to compensate for the high selectivity of process-generated samples. Generally, all methods for recruiting samples are exposed to some kinds of filtering error. Regardless of whether a gatekeeper is applied to access the samples, or whether victims of acts of violence are recruited through advertising, in each case, it is necessary to give specific consideration to sampling bias and selectivity. Experimental and quasi-experimental research generally requires a cover story whose nondisclosure has been criticized repeatedly since the days of the Milgram (1982) experiments, and this also contributes to sample selectivity. In general, as Kiefl and Lamnek (1986:53, translated) put it: "Official crime statistics, offender surveys, studies of undetected crime, and victim surveys each reveal specific advantages and shortcomings, so that none of these methods will completely uncover all of the victimization that has occurred." The general recommendation is to search for different and varied paths (the so-called multimethod approach). For each research issue, it is precisely a combination of different procedures that promises more sound knowledge (Kiefl & Lamnek, 1986:53). Telephone or Internet surveys, for example, can be used as an up-to-date form for an additional victim survey (Baurmann et al., 1991), although these are themselves subject to new sources of error. Directories of land-line telephone numbers reveal increasingly large gaps due to the trend toward (prepaid) cellular phones, and Internet surveys cannot be recommended without reservation because of sampling theory problems.

3. Avoiding Response Bias, Simulation, and Dissimulation

The susceptibility of many aggression and violence questionnaires to response bias, in other words, false statements, distortions, and misrepresentations, led to the development of a number of new assessment procedures in the 1990s (Albrecht, 1999; Bierhoff, 1996). These procedures should minimize these problems by making the respondent feel that nobody can decode their answers. One of the most well-known is the "randomized response technique" in which the respondent has to draw one card out of a set containing 100. Eighty of the 100 cards ask "How high is your monthly income?" 10 ask "Add $500 to your monthly income," and the final 10 ask how much the monthly income is after deducting $500. Because the researcher does not know which card the respondent has drawn, he or she cannot assign the response to the individual. However, the actual level of monthly income can be worked out for the sample as a whole on the basis of the distribution of the cards in the pile. While level of income is used here as an example of problematic self-disclosure, the procedure could also be adapted for research on aggression and violence.

There are a number of variants of the randomized response technique (see Albrecht, 1999:791). For example, an urn could hold eight red balls and two white ones. The red balls contain the item "I get involved in aggressive confrontations on a regular basis: Yes/No"; the white, the item "I was born in November: Yes/No." Using the known probability of being born in November, the percentage involved regularly in aggressive actions can be estimated for a sample (but not for the individuals, see Himmelfarb & Edgell, 1980). Furthermore, asking respondents to lie or tell the truth or to add or subtract a constant number to a frequency (such as the weekly frequency of violent acts) can be used to construct a prevalence rate for the sample mean on the basis of probability considerations. Preliminary studies with such procedures have tended to show higher prevalence rates for drug use and other problem behaviors. Nominative techniques can be used to ask "How far have your friends or relatives been involved in violent conflicts?" Such techniques can be used to overcome response inhibitions by recruiting a "shadow sample" that is not surveyed itself. Another method for providing anonymity to respondents—and thus avoiding response bias—is microaggregation (see Albrecht, 1999): some questionnaires are passed on to a subpopulation that provides the researcher with only the mean score.

In an anonymous written survey (i.e., not face-to-face questioning) in which several respondents complete questionnaires individually (e.g., in a school class), respondents' fears of disclosure can be alleviated by subsequently placing questionnaires in a closed envelope and sealing it directly in front of them. Bierhoff (1996) reports a more recent assessment procedure that measures reaction times (RTs) to paired associations (Fazio & Williams, 1986; Gaertner & McLaughlin, 1983). When studying ethnic stereotypes, RTs to paired associations such as "black and lazy" or "white and hard-working" can be used to measure the degree of negative stereotyping. RTs to real prejudices are faster. This procedure could also be applied to assess violence and propensity toward or approval of violence. Advances are also being made in the assessment of ambivalent feelings (see Bierhoff, 1996), by, for example, transforming bipolar scales into unipolar ones and computing an ambivalence index as a variable. These are ways of reducing bias by responding seriously to the criticism that choosing the points in the middle of a bipolar scale may indicate not just neutrality but also ambivalence.

V. ANALYZING AND INTERPRETING DATA: ASPECTS PARTICULAR TO RESEARCH ON AGGRESSION AND VIOLENCE

Hypothesis testing in quantitative empirical social research generally concludes with a confirmation of significant findings, that is, with the acceptance of the zero hypothesis or the alternative hypothesis. It is well known that this follows more or less conventionalized confidence intervals or *alpha* levels (mostly five percent). Explorative data analyses require an *alpha* adjustment. When a number of significance tests are performed without testing a specific hypothesis, it is necessary to lower *alpha*—reducing the final number of significant findings. This is because when a large number of significance tests are performed, five percent of the tested differences may be significant by chance (Bortz & Döring, 1995).

Although significance is frequently enough to make a difference scientifically meaningful, it does not provide an estimate of its practical relevance. It is a well-known fact that smaller and smaller differences can become significant as sample sizes increase. This has led to the introduction of a number of measures of practical significance or coefficients of effect size (Rosenthal & DiMatteo, 2001) that often confirm how disappointingly small the size of effects may be. The question is then how to decide when an effect size can be described as "large" or "small." A correlation of .20 would explain approximately four percent variance—is this effect large or small? Correlations of .20 or less, in other words, explained proportions of variance of up to four percent, are thoroughly relevant in the light of the realistic expectations regarding the explanation of effects in the social sciences (Ditton, 1990). If, for example, one translates a *phi* coefficient of .20 into percentage differences in the column percentages of a four-field table (two conditions, two genders), a 20 percent difference could already be tied to this coefficient size, in other words, a major effect. It all depends on how it is presented.

As in clinical research, instead of adjusting *alpha*, in other words, tightening the significance level, one could also think about relaxing it. The same applies when evaluating effect sizes. If the concern is to reduce a behavior that is highly undesirable for society, even weak effects should be taken seriously and used as a basis for policy measures. An increase in *alpha* error would be more acceptable than an increase in *beta* error. However, one has to be aware that there are major conventionalist and pragmatic objections within the scientific community to relaxing significance levels and judging lower effect sizes more leniently. Here as well, it is advisable to compute different measures of effect size and to compare the resulting coefficients with those from other studies. Or—when testing significance—to report the exact probability. Then readers can make up their own minds.

It is not just significance, relevance, and effect sizes that are desirable to determine reference norms for evaluating empirical differences but also, and above all, time change studies (through replications using the same locations and methods, comparisons based on matching similar tests, and research designs based on sequence analyses; see Dollase, 1986). These make it possible to compare current with earlier phenomena. A comparison of findings with empirically gathered ideal and real norms is also worthwhile—although this requires prior assessments of ideas on what is normality; for example, what is the normal frequency of aggressive conflicts.

Yet another path can be taken to provide empirical norms for evaluating the differences in findings. This requires an exchange or an overlapping of items between different studies, or, when planning a study, with previous studies. Then, one can compare one's own findings with those of other researchers (Schwind, 1996). This, in turn, highlights the need to document one's own study in a replicable way in the final research report. Particularly studies that provide the reader only with LISREL graphs or factor scores (or only z-score transformations) can no longer be replicated in later decades, because the original data and items are generally no longer available. One should recall the old virtue of writing up the study report in sufficient detail to permit full and identical replication. Researchers who report no raw data, no original statements, but only *beta* coefficients, make it impossible for future generations to replicate the study. Their research findings will have no permanent value.

Translating quantitative results or evaluating numbers in theoretical and practical contexts calls for an orientation toward the potential addressee. It is well known that the relation between attitude and behavior is always very low. In other words, it is always necessary to question the validity of questionnaire studies in relation to real behavior (Fishbein & Ajzen, 1975). Means obtained from one sample or subsample cannot be transferred to the single case, just as, vice versa, data from individual cases cannot be generalized without further ado. It also seems as if nobody remembers Cournot's or Condorcet's paradox. Back in the nineteenth century, this already showed that an average triangle based on several right-angled triangles is no longer a right-angled triangle but has lost one essential characteristic—its right-angledness (Guilbaud, 1966). It is just as inadmissible to misinterpret what are only means (e.g., obtained from extreme right-wing violent offenders in a certain data set) in an individualistic way, perhaps according to the motto: "The typical right-wing extremist is . . . ." Hummel (1972) has compiled a list of further false conclusions for empirical social research that also require greater consideration in research on aggression and violence (group, individual, cross-level, contextual, selective, and universalistic false conclusions).

Just as frequently, one can find a hermeneutic approach to the questionnaire text when interpreting questionnaire findings such as the percentage agreement with a statement. In other words, an attempt is made to deduce the attitudes of the respondent beyond what is intended by the derivation of the operationalization by interpreting the text of the statement with which the respondent has agreed. As shown above, such errors can be avoided through an early faceting of the contents of research and an appropriate operationalization.

VI. DESIDERATA AND SUMMARY

It is almost impossible to perform quantitative research on aggression and violence that will comply with all the methodological recommendations. Pragmatic compromises are necessary in the dimensions of time, breadth, quality criteria, thoroughness, complexity, effect sizes, and causal explanation. On the other hand, the variety of methodological quality is high: one can find everything from listing a number of percentages taken from a sample that is too small and highly selective, up to longitudinal field studies; from offender surveys to experiments. Hence, improvements are possible, because they have already been made. An orientation toward "best practice" is the recommended way to optimize one's own research.

The broad variance in available research work reveals what main directions this optimization has to take.

1. Cooperation with Qualitative Research

First, operationalizations can be improved. Facet theory reveals ways in which more emphasis can again be placed on the item. This strategy also implies that more attention should be paid to the findings of qualitative research on aggression and violence. This is the only field that is very close to subjective constructions or—when observing real aggression and violence—phenomenal, perspectivist aspects. It is precisely through forging stronger contacts with the reality of aggression and violence constructed from the subjective or the observer perspective that quantitative research on aggression and violence will become more professional.

2. Optimizing the Strengths of Quantitative Research

When sweeping doubts as to whether there is any sense in carrying out quantitative research on aggression and violence are raised (as has been the case; see von Trotha, 1997; Nedelmann, 1997), it becomes necessary to clarify whether such a criticism does itself not become almost meaningless by losing sight of the specific quantitative contribution. This contribution is certainly not to provide full descriptions of acts of violence. Qualitative approaches are clearly more appropriate for this. However, only quantitative research can answer theoretical and epidemiological questions on the extent, the quantitative trends, the generalizability of findings, the nomothetic trends, and potential factors that covary with phenomena of violence. In addition, it should not be forgotten that only quantitative research can take precautions regarding the transparency of replication, of reliability, and validity. It has already been pointed out that one cannot deduce a causal relation from a covariation alone. This is a field in which quantitative research on violence has made great contributions to our knowledge, as is easily confirmed by inspecting the papers collected in this handbook. Nonetheless, it is still necessary to minimize or overcome the methodological and measurement problems addressed in this chapter.

Good research on aggression and violence is characterized by a clear construction of operational definitions. It pays attention to the contents of its research by, for example, focusing on construct validity just as much as on empirical validity to guarantee that the spectrum of forms of aggression and violence is in line with the existing empirical clusterings of the field, and ensuring empirical validity by gathering different opinions about which operationalizations apply to which higher-level concept (aggressiveness, violence, propensity toward violence, etc.).

Depicting an empirical relative through a numerical one is and remains a challenge for quantitative research on aggression and violence. The problems of conceptual fuzziness presented in the main part of this chapter, and the resulting problems with the operationalization and measurement of phenomena of violence should continue to have the highest priority. Although the wide range of quantitative empirical studies on aggression and violence is almost too broad to grasp, it still seems as if there has been hardly any progress in the assessment of phenomena going beyond physical violence and extending to mental and even structural violence. Particularly in this field, we are still far from a standardization of measurement instruments that would enable us to compare findings across different studies.

3. Dealing with Phenomenal Fuzziness

It is often the case that high methodological standards and demands for extremely restrictive quality criteria are confronted with a fuzziness due to the phenomena in actual research practice. From such a perspective, a large number of quantitative measurements may seem unreliable or even invalid. On the other hand, one can find the practice of reducing quality criteria to such an extent that analyses face the threat of generating arbitrary findings—something that cannot lead to any serious testing of scientific hypotheses. Here, it is necessary to propose a more pragmatic orientation that not only emphasizes the goal of optimizing the specific measurement instruments, but also tolerates an inherent fuzziness that is not uncommon for social phenomena. Here as well, one should not develop all one's measurement instruments oneself, but draw on the recognized and reliable instruments accessible in test archives. A pragmatic approach to the judgment of statistical validity criteria or test scores requires an experience-based judgment on whether the distortions in the measurement or the analysis are negligible in relation to the strength of the true measurement score. The sum of measurement errors and their consequences are the reason why the general structures of the phenomenal domain are confirmed repeatedly in research on aggression and violence, whereas the fine-scale structures, in contrast, remain hidden or, at least, evade statistical proof. This is augmented by the variety of factors influencing aggressive and violent behavior as well as their situation-specific changes in meaning.

4. Interdisciplinary Networking

In all, a further interdisciplinary networking of research on aggression and violence seems to be needed because, on the one hand, violent types of behavior relate to economic and social contexts, and, on the other hand, (social) psychologically significant aspects of the individual can take on a major moderating function. In all cases, it is advisable to integrate sociological and psychological approaches to research on aggression and violence and to take an interdisciplinary approach so that not only the different professional perspectives can complement each other but also, perhaps, an effective use of the wide range of available methods can be ensured.

5. Longitudinal Studies

Regardless of whether individual biographies of violence should be gathered with qualitative methods, or the extent and developmental paths of violent types of behavior should be studied within the framework of population surveys, there is still a need for a greater number of longitudinal studies, particularly in Europe. Ideally, these should have designs permitting international comparisons.

6. Meta-Analyses

The pragmatic limitations of quantitative research on aggression and violence imposed by cost-benefit considerations or external restrictions to their potential design lead to a renewed interest in meta-analyses. That which cannot be attained in one single study has to be performed with many. Summarizing the results of many studies and analyzing them critically does not only reveal methodological deficits but also sound findings, contradictions, and options for further research (Rosenthal & DiMatteo, 2001). A good example for the knowledge gained from a meta-analysis is the integration of approximately 200 studies on the hypothesis that prejudice can be broken down through intergroup contact (Pettigrew & Tropp, 2000).

7. Experimental Research

As always, and here as well, there is a need for an increase in experimental studies on aggression and violence that evade a simple classification into either qualitative or quantitative research through their use of indicators from both paths. This is because only experimental studies have the capacity to deliver a (greater) certainty about causal conclusions. Experimental elements could also be integrated into questionnaire studies, for example, by constructing different questionnaire contexts (scenarios) for one and the same question and distributing these randomly among participants.

The results of research on aggression and violence possess a high practical relevance because both phenomena are so dysfunctional for modern societies. They function as guidelines for policymaking and public discussion and for the daily activities of those working in education and administration. This calls for particular care in scientific reporting to the mass media and policymakers. Successful reporting can be achieved only through a methodologically critical judgment of scientific findings and their appropriate translation into everyday language.

Translated by Jonathan Harrow

REFERENCES

Albrecht, Günther. (1999). Methodische Probleme der Erforschung sozialer Probleme. In Günther Albrecht, Axel Groenemeyer & Friedrich W. Stallberg (Eds.), *Handbuch Soziale Probleme* (pp. 768–882). Opladen: Westdeutscher Verlag.

Albrecht, Hans Joachim. (1998). Jugend und Gewalt. *Monatsschrift für Kriminologie und Strafrechtsreform, 81*(6), 381–398.

Baurmann, Michael C., Dieter Hermann, Hans Udo Stoerzer, & Franz Streng. (1991). Telefonische Befragung von Kriminalitätsopfern. Ein neuer Weg ins Dunkelfeld? *Monatsschrift für Kriminologie und Strafrechtsreform, 74*(3), 159–173.

Bierhoff, Hans Werner. (1996). Neuere Erhebungsmethoden. In Edgar Erdfelder, Rainer Mausfeld, Thorsten Meiser & Georg Rudinger (Eds.), *Handbuch Quantitative Methoden* (pp. 59–70). Weinheim: PVU.

Borg, Ingwer. (1995). Zur Rolle von Items in der Facettentheorie. *ZUMA Nachrichten, 36*, 24–34.

Borg, Ingwer. (1996). Facettentheorie. In Edgar Erdfelder, Rainer Mausfeld, Thorsten Meiser & Georg Rudinger (Eds.), *Handbuch Quantitative Methoden* (pp. 231–240). Weinheim: PVU.

Bortz, Jürgen, & Nicola Döring. (1995). *Forschungsmethoden und Evaluation.* Berlin: Springer.

Böttger, Andreas. (1997). *Gewalttaten von Jugendlichen in Deutschland (Forschungsberichte 62).* Hannover: Kriminologisches Forschungsinstitut Niedersachsen.

Bradley, Mark A., & David A. Hensher. (1992). Workshop Summary: Stated Preference Surveys. In Elizabeth S. Ampt, Allen J. Richardson & Arnim H. Meyburg (Eds.), *Selected Readings in Transport Survey Methodology.* Melbourne: Eucalyptus.

Ditton, Hartmut. (1990). Anmerkungen zum praktischen Umgang mit Anteilen erklärter Varianz. *Empirische Pädagogik, 4,* 289–309.

Dollase, Rainer. (1986). Sind Kinder heute anders als früher? Probleme und Ergebnisse von Zeitwandelstudien. *Bildung und Erziehung, 39*(2), 133–147.
Dollase, Rainer. (1996). Wege zur Überwindung der Asozialität. In Vorwort zu Moreno, Jacob L. *Grundlagen der Soziometrie*. Opladen: Leske & Budrich.
Erdfelder, Edgar, Rainer Mausfeld, Thorsten Meiser, & Georg Rudinger. (Eds.) (1996). *Handbuch quantitative Methoden*. Weinheim: PVU.
Fazio, Russel. H., & Christopher J. Williams. (1986). Attitude Accessibility as a Moderator of the Attitude Perception and Attitude-behavior Relations. An Investigation of the 1984 President Elections. *Journal of Personality and Social Psychology, 51*, 505–514.
Feger, Hubert. (1996). Methoden der Sozialpsychologie. In Edgar Erdfelder, Rainer Mausfeld, Thorsten Meiser & Georg Rudinger (Eds.), *Handbuch Quantitative Methoden* (pp. 529–538). Weinheim: PVU.
Fishbein, Martin, & Icek Ajzen. (1975). *Belief, Attitude, Intention and Behavior. An Introduction to Theory and Research*. Reading: Addison-Wesley.
Friedrichs, Jürgen. (1985). *Methoden empirischer Sozialforschung*. Opladen: Westdeutscher Verlag.
Gaertner, Samuel, & John P. McLaughlin. (1983). Racial Stereotypes: Associations and Ascription of Positive and Negative Characteristics. *Social Psychology Quarterly, 46*, 23–30.
Guilbaud, Georges Théodule. (1966). Theories of the General Interest, and the Logical Problem of Aggregation. In Paul Felix Lazarsfeld & Neil W. Henry (Eds.), *Readings in Mathematical Social Science* (pp. 262–308). Cambridge: MIT Press.
Himmelfarb, Samuel, & Stephen E. Edgell. (1980). Additive Constants Model. A Randomized Response Technique for Eliminating Evasiveness to Quantitative Response Questions. *Psychological Bulletin, 87*, 525–530.
Hummel, Hans-Juergen. (1972). *Probleme der Mehrebenenanalyse*. Stuttgart: Teubner.
Kennedy, Lawrence W., & Darryl Forde. (1996). Pathways to Aggression. A Factorial Survey of Routine Conflict. *Journal of Quantitative Criminology, 12*(4), 417–438.
Kiefl, Walter, & Siegfried Lamnek. (1986). *Soziologie des Opfers. Theorie, Methoden und Empirie*. München: Fink.
Kindlon, Daniel J., Brian D. Wright, Stephen. W. Raudenbush, & Felton Earls. (1996). The Measurement of Children's Exposure to Violence. A Rasch Analysis. *International Journal of Methods in Psychiatric Research, 6*(4), 187–194.
Koolwijk, Jürgen van, & Maria Wieken-Mayser. (Eds.) (1975ff.) *Techniken der empirischen Sozialforschung*. München: Oldenbourg.
Krampen, Günter. (2001). Differenzialdiagnostik sowie allgemeine und differenzielle Psychotherapie pathologischer Aggressivität. *Report Psychologie, 26*(9), 540–558.
Krumm, Volker. (1997). Methodenkritische Analyse schulischer Gewaltforschung. In Heinz Günther Holtappels, Wilhelm Heitmeyer, Wolfgang Melzer & Klaus Jürgen Tillmann (Eds.), *Forschung über Gewalt an Schulen* (pp. 63–79). Weinheim, München.
Krumm, Volker, & Birgit Baumann. (1996). Was über Gewalt in der Schule geschrieben wird. In Evelin Witruk & Gisela Friedrich (Eds.), *Pädagogische Psychologie im Streit um ein neues Selbstverständnis* (pp. 570–576). Landau: Verlag empirische Pädagogik.
Langfeldt, Hans-Peter, & Maria Langfeldt-Nagel. (1990). Rekonstruktion und Validierung prototypischer Alltagstheorien aggressiven Verhaltens. *Sprache und Kognition, 9*(1), 12–25.
Lewis-Beck, Michael S. (Eds.) (1993). *International Handbooks of Quantitative Applications in the Social Sciences*. London: Sage.
MacCorquodale, Kenneth, & Paul Everett Meehl. (1948). On a Distinction Between Hypothetical Constructs and Intervening Variables. *Psychological Review, 55*, 95–107.
Mansel, Jürgen. (1995). Quantitative Entwicklung von Gewalthandlungen Jugendlicher und ihrer offiziellen Registrierung. *Zeitschrift für Sozialisationsforschung und Erziehungssoziologie, 15*(2), 101–121.
Milgram, Stanley. (1982). *Das Milgram Experiment*. Reinbek: Rowohlt.
Minogue, Nicholas, Paul Kingery, & Lisa Murphy. (1999). *Approaches to Assessing Violence Among Youth (Report)*. Rosslyn: The Hamilton Fish National Institute on School and Community Violence.
Moreno, Jacob L. (1934). *Who Shall Survive?* Washington: Nervous and Mental Disease Publishing.
Mummendey, Hans Dieter. (1995). *Die Fragebogenmethode*. Göttingen et al.: Hogrefe.
Nedelmann, Birgitta. (1997). Gewaltsoziologie am Scheideweg. Die Auseinandersetzungen in der gegenwärtigen und Wege der künftigen Gewaltforschung. In Trutz von Trotha (Ed.), *Soziologie der Gewalt. Sonderheft 37 der Kölner Zeitschrift für Soziologie und Sozialpsychologie* (pp. 59–85). Opladen: Westdeutscher Verlag.

Nolting, Hans-Peter. (2000). *Lernfall Aggression, 20th ed.* Reinbek: Rowohlt.
Ochsmann, Randolph, & Marcel Mathy. (1993). Depreciating of and Distancing from Foreigners. Effects of Mortality Salience. *Beiträge zur Sozialpsychologie, 4*, 1–38.
Otten, Sabine, Amélie Mummendey, & Michael Wenzel. (1995). Evaluation of Aggressive Interactions in Interpersonal and Intergroup Contexts. *Aggressive Behavior, 21*, 205–224.
Owens, Louis Dean, & Colin E. MacMullin. (1995). Gender Differences in Aggression in Children and Adolescents in South Australian Schools. *International Journal of Adolescence and Youth, 6*(1–2), 21–35.
Petermann, Franz, & Ulrike Petermann. (2000). *Aggressionsdiagnostik.* Göttingen: Hogrefe.
Pettigrew, Thomas F., & Linda R. Tropp. (2000). Does Intergroup Contact Reduce Prejudice? Recent Meta-analytic Findings. In Stuart Oskamp (Ed.), *Reducing Prejudice and Discrimination. Social Psychological Perspectives* (pp. 93–114). Mahwah: Erlbaum.
Prose, Friedemann. (1974). Abgelehnte und Unbeachtete. Zur Differenzierung von Außenseitern in Gruppen. *Zeitschrift für Sozialpsychologie, 5*(1), 30–47.
Rojek, Marian. (1995). Der Beitrag der psychologischen Erziehungsstil- und Persönlichkeitsforschung zur Analyse der Gewalt an Schulen. In Walter Funk (Ed.), *Nürnberger Schüler Studie 1994. Gewalt an Schulen* (pp. 101–130). Regensburg: Roderer.
Rosenthal, Robert, & Massimo R. DiMatteo. (2001). Meta-Analysis. Recent Developments in Quantitative Methods for Literature Reviews. *Annual Review of Psychology, 52*, 59–82.
Roskam, Edward Elias. (1996). Beobachtung und Daten. In Edgar Erdfelder, Rainer Mausfeld, Thorsten Meiser & Georg Rudinger (Eds.), *Handbuch quantitative Methoden* (pp. 3–22). Weinheim: PVU.
Sanders, William B. (1994). *Gangbangs and Drive-Bys. Grounded Culture and Juvenile Gang Violence.* New York: DeGruyter.
Schäfer, Mechthild, & Dieter Frey. (1999). *Aggression und Gewalt unter Kindern und Jugendlichen.* Göttingen: Hogrefe.
Schäfer, Mechthild. (1997). *Aggression unter Schülern (Bullying). Spezifische Einflüsse bei der Erfassung (1997/10).* München: Max Planck Institut für Psychologische Forschung.
Schwind, Hans-Dieter. (1996). *Kriminologie.* Heidelberg: Kriminalistik Verlag.
Schwind, Hans-Dieter, Karin Roitsch, & Birgit Gielen. (1997). Gewalt in der Schule aus der Perspektive unterschiedlicher Gruppen. In Heinz Günther Holtappels, Wilhelm Heitmeyer, Wolfgang Melzer & Klaus Jürgen Tillmann (Eds.), *Forschung über Gewalt an Schulen. Erscheinungsformen und Ursachen, Konzepte und Prävention* (pp. 81–100). Weinheim: Juventa.
Stelzl, Ingeborg. (1982). *Fehler und Fallen der Statistik.* Bern: Huber.
Tedeschi, James T., & Brain M. Quigley. (1998). Frühere und zukünftige Methoden der Aggressionsforschung. In Hans Werner Bierhoff & Ulrich Wagner (Eds.), *Aggression und Gewalt. Phänomene, Ursachen und Interventionen* (pp. 88–106). Stuttgart: Kohlhammer.
Trotha, Trutz von. (Ed.) (1997). *Soziologie der Gewalt. Sonderheft 37 der Kölner Zeitschrift für Soziologie und Sozialpsychologie.* Opladen: Westdeutscher Verlag.
Werner, Nicole, Maureen A. Bigbee, & Nicki R. Crick. (1999). Aggression und Viktimisierung in Schulen. Chancengleichheit für aggressive Mädchen. In Mechthild Schäfer & Dieter Frey (Eds.), *Aggression und Gewalt unter Kindern und Jugendlichen* (pp. 153–178). Göttingen: Hogrefe.
WHO. (Ed.) (1999). *Pocket Guide to the ICD-10 Classification of Mental and Behavioural Disorders.* Edinburgh: Churchill Livingstone.
Wild, Elke, & Paul Noack. (1999). Stabilität und Wandel in den Einstellungen von Jugendlichen und Eltern zur Gewalt. In Mechthild Schäfer & Dieter Frey (Eds.), *Aggression und Gewalt unter Kindern und Jugendlichen* (pp. 135–152). Göttingen: Hogrefe.
Wright, James D., Peter H. Rossi, & Kathleen Daly. (1983). *Under the Gun. Weapons, Crime and Violence in America.* Hawthorne: Aldine Publishing.

PART IV

Subject Index

abuse, 29, 68, 100, 101, 105, 106, 108, 111, 113, 114, 116, 117, 173–179, 184–187, 190, 194, 195, 198, 201, 203, 204, 215, 222, 324, 325, 344, 349, 459, 463, 466, 475, 476, 491, 499, 503, 504, 508, 529, 533, 534, 544, 569, 590, 598, 605, 606, 616, 626, 632, 642, 654, 674, 676, 716, 720–735, 741–745, 755, 759, 769, 770, 777, 782, 783, 795, 802, 811, 814, 818–823, 827–832, 837–845, 847, 848, 850–862, 864, 869, 875, 877, 883, 885, 888, 893, 897–899, 910, 998, 1032, 1046, 1052, 1079, 1133, 1157, 1158, 1209, 1221

adolescence, 71, 81, 112, 184, 409, 433, 491, 497, 499, 500, 504, 505, 507–509, 528, 536, 537, 547, 548, 550, 551, 554, 555, 558, 560–565, 599, 601, 605, 607, 612, 613, 630, 634, 635, 641–643, 645, 648–651, 653, 654, 656, 718, 720, 722, 724–727, 732–734, 782, 817, 819, 822, 825, 826, 828–832, 852, 858, 866, 868, 870, 871, 876, 882, 883, 916, 941, 942, 948, 950, 961, 1114, 1116, 1177, 1179, 1221, 1223, 1237

adrenalin, 279, 915, 916, 1116

aggression research, 460, 463, 465, 467, 468, 469, 474, 477, 506, 544, 545, 556, 592, 1219–1225, 1227, 1228, 1230–1235

aggression, 14, 17–19, 29, 36, 53, 72, 73, 76, 77, 89, 102, 105, 111, 115, 116, 174, 180, 182, 184, 198, 249, 270, 288, 289, 324, 326, 355, 361, 363, 365, 379, 386, 409, 432, 433, 459–465, 467–489, 491–493, 495–509, 512, 515, 516, 520, 521, 524–528, 532, 536–541, 543–565, 570, 572, 584–586, 589, 590, 592–594, 598–607, 615, 619–621, 625, 629, 635, 642, 646, 648–650, 656, 716, 725, 726, 737, 738, 748, 753, 754, 758, 762, 763, 786, 790, 791, 794, 818, 820, 822–824, 826, 830, 832, 838, 843, 844, 847, 848, 856, 858, 860–862, 864–866, 872, 874, 875, 878, 881–884, 895–899, 902, 904–911, 915, 918–920, 923–928, 930–935, 948, 951, 969, 971, 990, 1002, 1010, 1013, 1014, 1017, 1018, 1038, 1051, 1090, 1116, 1153, 1170, 1174, 1184–1186, 1196, 1198, 1219–1237

aggressiveness, 19, 111, 437, 461, 444, 472, 473, 475, 479, 481, 487, 506, 544, 545, 563, 590, 592–594, 599–601, 603, 605, 635, 636, 682, 778, 907, 909, 911, 916, 918, 1153, 1219, 1220, 1222, 1224–1227, 1233

aggressor, 477, 478, 489, 501, 502, 509, 519, 525, 547, 551, 553, 560, 790, 821, 867, 895, 897, 898, 943, 1047, 1189

alcohol, 52, 112, 174, 178, 179, 181, 182, 198, 217, 405, 414, 421, 460, 468, 472, 473, 475–478, 482, 489, 491, 492, 499, 527, 570, 583, 586, 598, 605, 632, 648, 666, 674, 676, 690, 694, 741, 743, 753, 761, 768, 773, 776, 782, 819, 841, 854, 869, 892, 893, 898, 900, 902, 910, 911, 919, 1121, 1185

alienation, 24, 90, 93, 328, 546, 618, 649, 827, 960, 962–964, 980, 982, 1031

ambiguity, 500, 682–684, 687, 710, 711

ambivalence, 6, 7, 248, 249, 253, 327, 332, 334, 339, 829, 1019, 1037, 1230

anarchy, 193, 376, 379, 443, 957, 983, 996, 1004, 1045, 1075, 1104, 1197

anomie, 53, 69, 70, 76, 85, 173, 360, 375, 386, 408, 419, 432, 563, 614–616, 620, 622, 628, 637, 641, 643, 644, 647, 650–652, 703, 715, 760, 763, 864, 866–868, 883, 938, 940, 943, 951, 1171, 1177, 1178

anthropology, 7, 23, 58, 83, 95, 124, 187, 193, 194, 250, 258, 259, 261–272, 277, 278, 280, 281, 285–290, 295, 302, 323, 336, 411, 449, 585, 702, 738, 741, 744, 783, 793, 795, 914, 939, 1009, 1013, 1014, 1016, 1018, 1019, 1062, 1217, 1218

anti-semitism, 140, 150, 151, 154, 157, 159, 331, 335, 366, 406, 427, 780, 788, 793

assimilation, 134, 249, 572, 823, 945, 1156

asylum seeker, *see* refugee

attachment, 27, 36, 70, 78, 96, 109, 131, 278, 327, 329, 508, 571, 615, 616, 628, 633, 635, 636, 638, 649, 653, 656, 687, 705, 716, 722, 726, 728, 820, 825–827, 829–831, 856, 859, 861, 879, 916, 917, 938, 951, 1010, 1123, 1174, 1176, 1190, 1226

1239

SUBJECT INDEX

attitudes to violence, 75, 147, 160, 190, 371, 378, 409, 412, 413, 415, 418, 426, 429–431, 451, 472, 477, 501, 612, 613, 729, 747, 772, 777, 780, 782, 796, 813, 814, 854, 858, 887, 925, 961, 1032, 1094, 1123

attribution, 8, 266, 354, 355, 357, 460, 468, 469, 471, 473, 475–477, 481, 482, 496, 498, 500, 505, 531, 553, 573, 626, 637, 639, 821, 824, 830, 866, 929, 931, 1016, 1124, 1159, 1165, 1168, 1181, 1189

Auschwitz, 140, 147, 154, 155, 162, 163, 166–168, 201, 797, 1030, 1037, 1038, 1094

authoritarianism, 252, 330, 333, 334, 390, 408

autonomous identity, 358

autonomy, 54, 126, 128, 147, 201, 227–234, 241, 243, 281, 297, 304, 358, 371, 374, 376, 378, 379, 389, 443, 444, 508, 583, 619, 633, 634, 683, 726, 740, 945, 995, 959, 960, 965, 967–971, 1059, 1065, 1066, 1070, 1117

awareness, 17, 18, 97, 99, 108, 131, 183, 190, 209, 221, 231, 259, 281, 401, 427, 489, 520, 525, 612, 672, 720, 726, 727, 731, 734, 781, 786, 813, 814, 819, 528, 885, 889, 899, 901, 944, 948, 975, 982, 983, 1008, 1016, 1032, 1035, 1099, 1107, 1114, 1131, 1161, 1169, 1187, 1207

basic right, 31, 131, 222, 512, 1043, 1047, 1048, 1051, 1079, 1081, 1087–1096, 1100, 1101, 1103

behavioral research, *see* ethology

behaviorism, 907, 908

bias, 70, 92, 135,195, 216, 219, 325, 333, 355, 428, 452, 459, 460, 468, 469, 471, 473, 475, 477, 496, 498, 500, 503, 547, 551, 574, 592, 723, 767, 773, 775, 780, 781, 791, 796, 801, 802, 804, 805, 809, 810, 814, 815, 821, 824, 830, 840, 849, 862, 1145, 1214, 1221, 1227, 1229, 1230

blockade, 4, 34, 369, 832, 964, 1083, 1083–1086, 1087, 1089, 1092, 1093, 1096, 1108

boigraphy, 102, 106, 112, 114, 117, 148, 163, 165, 167, 316, 387, 434, 504, 505, 507, 508, 543, 550, 552, 554, 562, 563, 601, 607, 620, 631, 634, 646, 647, 650, 651, 653, 654, 656, 693, 696, 730, 734, 765, 798, 799, 878, 920, 926, 927, 930, 1030, 1031, 1035, 1125, 1169, 1169, 1175, 1204–1207, 1212–1218, 1234

brain, 570, 573, 590, 603, 604, 727, 734, 754, 759, 819, 820, 822, 823, 831, 993

brutality, 14, 136, 180, 181, 193, 209, 215, 217, 224, 257, 296, 297, 346, 364, 390, 391, 404, 413, 430, 438, 531, 690, 795, 827, 918, 944, 974, 990, 1095, 1153, 1181

bullying, 181, 467, 509, 600, 729, 798, 827, 864, 869, 872–874, 876, 879–883, 885, 889–891, 900, 902, 1222, 1224, 1237

capitalism, 5, 53, 59, 68, 84, 105, 123, 125, 127–129, 139, 249, 250, 272, 282, 298, 324, 332, 333, 345, 370, 374, 376, 379, 380, 384, 390, 449, 556, 561, 562, 564, 619, 652, 684–687, 695, 697, 698, 703, 704, 708, 713, 768, 867, 915, 980, 984, 989, 1062, 1063, 1074, 1076, 1159–1161, 1165, 1168, 1182, 1183

catharsis, 460–462, 475, 476, 485–488, 491, 492, 520, 521, 904, 906–908, 918, 919, 1024

Catholicism, 128, 129, 198

child abuse, *see* abuse

child maltreatment, *see* maltreatment

childhood, 106, 113, 186, 408, 495, 497–501, 503–509, 540, 543, 544, 547–551, 554, 555, 560–565, 569, 599–601, 606, 607, 613, 632–635, 645, 646, 648, 649, 655, 722, 725–728, 734, 814, 818, 822, 823, 829–832, 861, 866,, 82, 893, 900, 943, 946, 1209

Christianity, 134, 145, 146, 157, 158, 164,204, 325–328, 330–332, 334, 335, 337, 346, 379, 406, 428, 434, 797, 977, 986, 989, 1008–1013, 1015, 1020, 1098, 1106, 1111, 1149

church, 75, 128, 129, 157, 160–162, 166, 167, 256, 257, 296, 323, 330, 331, 333, 335, 336, 338, 341, 3, , 405–407, 450, 812, 1010–1013, 1098

cities, 11, 42, 43, 48, 55, 57, 58, 68, 72, 77, 79, 81–96, 121–123, 125–129, 132, 136, 137, 155, 218, 281, 290, 296, 302, 315, 318, 328, 336–340, 343, 346, 347, 349, 354, 373, 377, 394, 416, 425, 428, 443–445, 448, 478, 532, 535, 559, 561, 562, 564, 565, 575, 577, 588, 619, 621, 623, 625, 645, 648, 666, 668, 669, 673, 675–677, 681, 697, 698, 703, 708, 716, 719, 731, 761, 808, 870, 874, 896, 917, 931, 942, 943, 946, 951, 952, 972, 977, 1068, 1069, 1074, 1075, 1103, 1110, 1117, 1123, 1132, 1134–1136, 1140, 1147, 1149, 1156, 1157, 1134–1137, 1142, 1149, 1170–1179, 1185, 1198, 1218

civil society, 317, 375, 405, 411, 417, 432, 688, 776, 919, 1019, 1061, 1095

civil war, 11, 17, 30, 32, 121, 230, 233, 234, 245, 256, 257, 259, 260, 274, 275, 279, 285, 290–308, 316, 353, 354, 359, 391, 399, 445–447, 513, 621, 976, 981, 1012, 1029, 1038, 1045–1047, 1052, 1066, 1099, 1104, 1105, 1195

civilization, 7, 11, 14, 20, 33–35, 37, 41, 51–55, 57, 58, 137, 140, 223, 262, 325, 336, 371, 492, 587, 640, 704, 714, 912, 918, 919, 938, 974, 980, 983, 1007, 1016 1020, 1024, 1025, 1028, 1029, 1036, 1059, 1074, 1075, 1099, 1184, 1193,

civilization theory, 51–53, 55, 704, 974, 1184

class struggle, 123, 247, 980, 981, 983, 1183

coercion, 14, 17–20, 23, 24, 29, 32, 41, 59, 98–100, 110, 112, 130, 189, 207, 208, 210–212, 216, 221, 231, 234, 317, 324, 330, 333, 344, 386, 400, 425, 459, 466, 472, 563, 583, 694, 742, 838, 844, 924, 932, 957, 975, 990, 993, 995, 1002, 1003, 1027, 1044, 1049, 1055, 1058, 1059, 1062, 1073, 1076, 1080–1090, 1108, 1109, 1113

coercive force, 17, 24, 31, 34, 35, 54, 194, 195, 196, 205, 207, 212, 233, 237, 324, 341, 342, 439, 445, 465–468, 477, 496, 503, 509, 557, 581, 583, 687,

SUBJECT INDEX

695, 701, 716, 742, 743, 747, 748, 822, 844, 960, 1001, 1047, 1049, 1050, 1052–1055, 1058, 1059, 1061, 1062, 1066, 1067, 1073, 1083–1085, 1154

cognition, 36, 106, 107, 184, 186, 192, 193, 197, 202, 273, 276, 300, 360, 392, 441, 449, 459, 462, 463, 468, 469, 472–474, 481, 482, 492, 495–497, 503, 508, 521–523, 526, 528, 531, 532, 547, 553, 558, 570, 578, 586, 592, 600, 632, 634, 637, 646, 658, 726, 731, 734, 747, 751, 755, 763–765, 775, 778, 786, 729–731, 822, 824, 944, 959, 961, 963, 966, 983, 1118, 1121, 1123, 1132, 1139, 1140, 1143, 1148, 1163, 1185, 1188–1191, 1195–1197, 1216

communication, 2, 5, 83, 84, 123, 155, 231, 256, 257, 262, 266, 268, 279, 309, 311, 318, 320, 327, 355, 361, 362, 364, 405, 414, 436, 438, 444, 476, 478, 499, 521–523, 527, 530, 533, 536–539, 612, 613, 706, 723, 726, 814, 832, 866, 879, 896, 897, 929, 958, 962, 969, 971, 1065, 1068, 1103, 1115, 1142, 1143, 1159, 1164, 1165, 1168, 1187, 1189, 1191, 1195, 1206

communism, 6, 10, 153, 154, 193, 198, 230, 232, 234, 238, 314, 318, 327, 338, 342, 343, 346, 376, 427, 434, 454, 944, 981, 982, 1029, 1063

community, 26, 29, 57, 71, 73, 75–78, 80, 82, 85–89, 91–95, 102, 115–117, 124, 125, 128, 129, 132, 134, 135, 137, 153, 155, 156, 161, 162, 180, 185, 195, 208, 213, 218, 220, 223, 224, 228, 232, 248, 250, 251, 257, 258, 265, 276, 280, 287, 296, 298, 299, 302, 303, 305, 318, 327, 337–345, 347, 348, 352, 361, 383, 389, 391, 404, 416, 423, 425, 431–433, 453, 538, 541, 543, 547, 550, 556, 558–560, 562–564, 577, 603, 622, 624, 628, 638, 639, 641–643, 645, 649, 653, 656, 666, 668–670, 672, 673, 676, 680, 682, 686, 687, 689, 691–693, 710, 712, 723–725, 728–735, 737, 748, 749, 763, 768, 771, 773, 775, 788–791, 793, 796, 804, 808, 811, 813–815, 821, 829–831, 848, 851, 852, 857, 858, 869, 871, 877, 880, 893, 898, 938, 941–943, 946, 948, 951, 963, 965–967, 982, 985, 1002, 1009, 1010, 1014, 1044, 1053, 1054, 1057, 1061, 1062, 1066, 1067, 1069, 1070, 1073–1076, 1099, 1132, 1135, 1136, 1144, 1142, 1145–1149, 1168, 1169, 1171, 1172, 1176–1179, 1185, 1186, 1190, 1199, 1231, 1236

comradeship, 173, 174, 181, 183, 392, 393, 406, 697, 948, 982

conditioning, 152, 320, 359, 462, 523, 819

conflict dynamics, 297, 376, 440, 451, 924, 930, 931, 1188

conflict prevention, 242, 243, 275, 294, 301, 303, 334, 360, 370, 520, 1193

conflict research, 245, 372, 1191

conflict resolution, 18, 19, 52, 75, 244, 252, 279, 281–284, 307, 319, 363, 365, 377, 381, 445, 499, 505, 520, 524, 687, 724, 813, 879, 920, 963, 964, 1182, 1184, 1185, 1197

conflict theory, 94, 264, 272, 357, 381, 409, 410, 417, 420, 425, 432, 1183, 1184, 1195, 1199

conformity, 27, 70, 82, 129, 150, 200, 228, 252, 392, 523, 623, 627–629, 631, 635, 637, 670, 776, 867, 910, 920, 925, 926, 930, 932, 940, 945, 1033, 1117, 1174, 1188, 1190, 1193

constitutional law, 32, 974, 1080, 1081, 1083, 1087, 1088, 1090–1092, 1095, 1102

constructivism, 229, 230, 266, 1203

consumption, 52, 182, 243, 274, 468, 437, 517–520, 523–528, 530, 531, 534, 535, 614, 632, 684, 706, 741, 871, 876, 940, 944, 1125, 1140, 1144, 1185

control mechanisms, 222, 385, 623, 628

control theory, 70, 82, 549, 563, 564, 615, 616, 624, 627–630, 632, 635, 641, 646, 648, 649, 651, 654, 859, 1161, 1174

controlling authorities, 356, 359, 360, 362, 405, 867, 939, 942

coping, 5, 106, 107, 201, 210, 562, 616, 636, 643, 650, 733, 810, 818, 820, 823, 825, 826, 855, 1139, 1143–1145, 1149

coping strategies, 32, 140, 149, 300, 410, 638, 868, 942, 1162, 1174

corporal punishment, 52, 117, 189–191, 463, 477, 497, 498, 621, 624, 654, 729, 730, 733, 742, 842, 861, 882, 995

corruption, 173, 195, 198, 223, 233, 283, 299, 680, 684, 686, 696, 699, 940, 1070, 1168

crime, 13, 14, 29, 31–33, 39–44, 47, 51–58, 68–82, 85–96, 98, 109–111, 114, 116, 117, 122, 126, 136, 143, 145, 148–150, 157, 159, 161, 173, 179, 184, 190, 192–194, 197, 202, 205, 211, 213, 216, 219, 222, 223, 281, 314, 316, 324, 326, 329, 333, 336, 339–341, 345–247, 349, 363, 365, 379, 404, 407, 409, 414, 420, 422, 424, 425, 427, 428, 434, 435, 447, 459, 476–478, 479, 491–493, 504, 515, 518, 519, 529, 530, 532, 562–564, 575, 585–588, 594–598, 601–607, 611–633, 635, 636, 638–646, 648–656, 658, 666–668, 671–677, 679–699, 701–706, 709–716, 719, 721, 725, 739–741, 749–751, 769–774, 776, 778, 780–783, 785, 786, 790–792, 794–796, 798, 799, 801–815, 817, 839, 840, 844, 845, 847, 858, 859, 862, 865, 870, 871, 874, 882, 883, 886, 887, 889, 897, 898, 902, 904, 910, 911, 923, 935, 939, 952, 975, 980, 995, 1002, 1003, 1035, 1055, 1056, 1060, 1061, 1064–1066, 1068–1077, 1099, 1113, 1114, 1124, 1125, 1131–1168, 1170, 1173, 1174, 1176–1179, 1184, 1193, 1198, 1217, 1221, 1229, 1237

crime control, 87, 211, 219, 222, 698, 715, 1069, 1072, 1146, 1147, 1160, 1161

crime policy, 57, 919, 1057, 1070, 1070–1072, 1131, 1132, 1139, 1141, 1143, 1147

crime reporting behavior, 42, 625, 670, 810, 889

criminal law, 4, 33, 43, 50, 57, 58, 70, 80, 89, 94–96, 183, 192, 194, 202, 204, 205, 211–213, 223, 224, 378, 477, 512, 587, 601, 607, 611, 631, 641, 644, 649, 652, 668, 673, 674, 676, 677, 683, 687, 688, 691, 695, 697, 699, 702, 711, 713, 715, 716, 737, criminal law (*cont.*), 740, 746, 749, 750, 771, 779–781, 783, 787, 798, 804, 811, 813, 815, 839, 857, 874, 887, 893, 923, 930, 933, 993, 1048, 1058, 1002, 1003, 1044, 1052, 1066, 1067, 1069, 1070–1076, 1079, 1080–1082, 1086–1088, 1090–1092, 1094–1096, 1107, 1109, 1147–1149, 1217

criminal liability, 1089, 1091

criminology, 9, 56, 58, 69, 80, 82, 90, 94, 95, 101, 112, 115, 149, 185, 204, 223, 224, 354, 408, 409, 434, 475, 477, 487, 526, 562–564, 574, 576, 586–588, 605, 607, 612, 641–656, 676, 677, 697, 698, 701–705, 708, 710–712, 714–716, 748–752, 770, 782, 783, 858, 887, 889, 902, 925, 958, 930, 931, 934, 1061, 1070, 1125–1127, 1131–1133, 1136, 1141, 1147–1150, 1167–1171, 1175–1179, 1222, 1236

critical theory, 105

cults, 310, 346, 385, 428, 450, 621, 799, 1002, 1007, 1008, 1010, 1033, 1035, 1036

cultural identity, 132, 134, 336, 366, 966

cultural studies, 9, 333, 714, 957–963, 970, 1006, 1013, 1169, 1170, 1177

culturalism, 290, 360, 361, 617

damage to property, 14, 29, 33, 34, 369, 376, 383, 384, 421, 512, 863, 869

data source, 7, 42–50, 55, 70–72, 79, 85–88, 90–92, 98, 102, 103, 106–113, 116, 150, 175, 176, 183, 192, 199, 216, 217, 219, 222–224, 228, 234–239, 241, 295, 298, 303, 320, 329, 358, 374, 389, 417, 420, 421, 423, 424, 427, 428, 430, 480, 481, 484, 514, 517, 518, 524, 549, 551, 552, 557, 559, 561–563, 575, 582, 587, 606, 612, 615, 634, 635, 640, 653, 654, 663, 665, 666, 669, 672, 675, 680, 690, 691, 693, 694, 702, 705, 706, 709, 711, 712, 715, 721, 723, 728–731, 739, 740, 750, 759, 769, 770, 779, 791, 793–795, 804, 805, 807–810, 812, 823, 829, 839–847, 849–852, 859, 869, 870, 874, 878, 886, 890, 891, 901, 902, 912, 925, 930, 1113, 1116, 1134, 1137, 1144, 1146, 1151, 1154, 1155, 1155, 1203–1207, 1209–1216, 1219–1221, 1223–1225, 1228, 1229, 1231, 1232

death penalty, 24, 129, 191, 285, 324, 33, 708, 768, 802, 989, 1047, 1159–1161, 1165

death squads, 341–344, 399, 773, 782, 802

de-escalation, 9, 10, 239, 241, 253, 258–260, 287, 289, 290, 362, 404, 414, 670, 1129, 1181, 1194, 1195

defense, 8, 23, 28, 124, 174, 213, 249, 265, 266, 275, 297, 315, 331, 337, 344, 345, 352, 354, 370, 389, 411, 437, 444, 450, 584, 619–621, 648, 669, 672, 677, 696, 740, 741, 751, 761, 778, 803, 847, 853, 854, 870, 908, 928, 935, 947, 969, 970, 973, 974, 976, 984, 1008, 1016, 1045, 1047, 1048, 1050–1052, 1067, 1080, 1098, 1101, 1102, 1106, 1116, 1118, 1120, 1121, 1124, 1154, 1162, 1221

definition of violence, 4, 13–15, 17–22, 24, 26–28, 30, 33–35, 37, 38, 83, 100, 111, 267, 324, 369, 383, 400, 512, 516, 600, 740, 838, 864, 885, 886, 924, 937, 942, 959, 960, 975, 990–992, 994–997, 1001–1004, 1035, 1079, 1080, 1082–1087, 1091, 1092, 1104, 1107–1109, 1113, 1122, 1152, 1221, 1224

dehumanization, 28, 150, 198, 199, 201, 202, 256, 257, 276, 392, 401, 414, 415, 776, 929, 1160, 1164, 1189

delinquency, 30, 69–71, 76, 80–82, 88, 94–96, 223, 463, 476, 497, 503, 507, 508, 526, 527, 539, 543, 549, 550, 558, 561–565, 595, 601, 604, 606, 613, 615, 616, 620, 622–624, 627–633, 635, 641–656, 714, 721, 734, 735, 777, 778, 783, 881, 910, 920, 933, 938, 940, 941, 943, 945–949, 952, 1117, 1127, 1148, 1149, 1175–1179, 1206

democracy, 7, 31, 34, 84, 95, 133, 168, 169, 183, 204, 217, 223, 228, 232, 237, 238, 241–243, 252, 253, 257, 259, 310, 312, 314, 316–318, 320, 321, 344, 370, 375, 380, 381, 385, 389, 391, 396–398, 428, 435, 440, 441, 553, 691, 714, 958, 959, 962, 964, 967, 969–972, 976, 980, 982, 1018, 1059, 1061, 1073, 1074, 1076, 1079, 1093, 1100–1102, 1104, 1107, 1109, 1111, 1192, 1194, 1195

demography, 95, 108, 146, 148, 249, 254, 300, 301, 346, 377, 574, 577, 582, 618, 651, 694, 702, 705, 708, 710, 712, 715, 723, 727, 738, 742, 786, 849, 850, 925, 926, 1139, 1144, 1146, 1153

demonstration, 31, 34, 122, 155, 182, 214, 219, 223, 234, 235, 339, 341, 343, 344, 351, 363, 374–376, 380, 381, 384, 389, 397, 400, 401, 403, 404, 415, 416, 439, 529, 937, 940, 948, 1044, 1079, 1097, 1080, 1086, 1088–1094, 1102, 1116, 1117

deportation, 155, 157, 158, 160, 162, 165, 190, 1102

depression, 174, 184, 274, 461, 523, 550, 557, 560–562, 724–726, 733, 743, 753–755, 758, 759, 762, 764, 765, 810, 819, 826, 852, 853

deprivation, 23, 69, 72, 73, 75, 86, 87, 92, 95, 96, 189, 190, 195, 220, 265, 295, 355, 356, 358, 363, 366, 371–373, 377, 381, 386, 387, 408–410, 419, 420, 426, 431, 481, 487, 617, 618, 621, 628, 640, 641, 645, 654, 704_706, 710, 741, 818, 859, 872, 960, 967, 968, 1168, 1169, 1173, 1187, 1199

desensitization, 28, 35, 198, 343, 471, 490, 528, 774, 777, 778, 828

deterrence, 31, 82, 159, 171, 196, 220, 275, 501, 520, 532, 583, 614, 630–633, 641, 642, 645, 649, 651–656, 667, 672, 677, 695, 713, 748, 750, 751, 780, 797, 813, 814, 933, 981, 1002, 1060, 1065, 1193

developing countries, 69, 195, 200, 252, 292, 349, 715, 887, 889, 892, 899, 901

developmental psychology, 460, 504, 507–509, 537, 556, 561–565, 607, 649, 733, 872, 1171

deviance, 81, 95, 96, 107, 117, 198, 218, 219, 223, 224, 259, 337, 339–348, 357, 477, 603, 616, 620, 626, 633, 635, 641, 642, 646, 648, 650, 651, 653–656, 698, 775778, 780–783, 860, 864, 867, 910, 919, 934, 940–943, 950, 951, 1118, 1127, 1142, 1177, 1216, 1217

SUBJECT INDEX

direct violence, 21, 24, 31, 32, 84, 86, 87, 198, 314, 483, 543–561, 563–565, 600, 624, 780, 883, 911, 938, 959, 973, 1105

disability, 173, 674, 722, 743, 769, 772, 829, 857, 891, 1119

discipline, 3, 9, 11, 33, 38, 41, 52–54, 116, 117, 127, 131, 135, 136, 145, 146, 150, 172, 173, 177–180, 182, 183, 185–187, 190, 191, 193, 194, 196, 200–202, 212, 262, 272, 288, 293, 294, 304, 305, 323, 324, 327, 333, 335, 370, 371, 402, 430, 463, 468, 477, 497, 498, 500, 523, 535, 572, 588, 607, 655, 686, 688, 691, 729, 730, 733, 738, 743, 744, 748, 822, 832, 860, 864, 573–875, 889, 925, 931, 949–951, 959, 960, 974, 975, 986, 989, 991, 995, 1003, 1006, 1049, 1071, 1079, 1167, 1234

discrimination, 13, 25, 84, 85, 90–92, 95, 145, 160, 189, 218, 230, 231, 234–237, 239, 241–243, 255, 299, 347, 354, 369, 431, 438, 517, 523, 619, 715, 728, 797, 801, 811, 863, 888, 896, 1105, 1141–1143, 1158, 1237

disintegration, 5, 8, 55, 278, 297, 300, 313, 355, 410, 419, 424, 425, 431, 432, 636–639, 796, 867, 868, 967, 969, 1034, 1062, 1064, 1187

disobedience, 34, 197, 234, 369–371, 376, 465, 468, 993, 995, 996, 1004, 1048, 1085, 100, 1102–1111

disorganization, 75–77, 82, 564, 617, 623–625, 627, 637, 643–645, 652, 653, 656, 703, 824, 825, 938, 943, 1141–1145, 1168–1172, 1179

displacement, 18, 23, 157, 166, 233, 259, 264, 265, 329, 352, 461, 462, 525, 649, 673, 747, 915, 979, 1201, 1213

distribution of power, 6, 21, 34, 97, 125, 130, 147, 254, 256, 297, 299, 304, 305, 309, 312, 314, 316, 342, 352–354, 357–359, 474, 625, 695, 803, 889, 945, 978, 1046, 1117

dominance, 10, 27, 105–107, 109, 172, 230, 254, 277, 283, 409, 417, 454, 490, 553, 591, 604, 629, 634, 695, 715, 802, 877, 905, 911, 927–929, 980, 983, 1031, 1229

drugs, 75–77, 81, 82, 88, 90, 112, 174, 178, 181, 182, 198, 217, 274, 277, 279, 292, 302, 333, 339, 343, 379, 491, 603, 605, 614, 616, 633, 636, 643, 645, 648, 668, 670, 673, 676, 677, 685, 691, 692, 695–699, 743, 753, 768, 769, 775, 776, 783, 813, 815, 819, 864, 869, 871, 876, 892, 900, 902, 915, 920, 940, 947, 1065, 1068, 1075, 1124, 1125, 1142, 1170, 1173, 1174, 1177, 1209, 1218, 1220, 1222, 1223, 1230

ecology, 70, 82, 370, 375, 381, 585, 587, 612, 645, 733, 859, 872, 934

education, 4, 14, 51, 54, 87, 108, 126, 143, 155, 177, 183, 198, 203, 277, 278, 334, 386, 390, 413, 418, 466, 508, 512, 534, 535, 537, 555, 565, 603, 620, 621, 624, 636, 669, 671, 720, 722, 724, 745, 747, 748, 751, 763–765, 781, 813, 815, 827, 841, 842, 855, 861, 865, 867, 870, 872, 873, 875, 876, 878, 880, 883, 884, 897, 900, 905, 907, 917, 919, 920, 933, 934, 938, 939, 941, 945, 948–951, 968, 1044, 1102, 1106, 1117, 1123, 1144, 1152, 1153, 1176, 1192, 1196, 1217, 1235

educational science, 747, 873

elite, 21, 67, 68, 122, 126, 127, 136, 148, 151, 152, 163, 173, 179, 180, 214, 229, 254, 259, 265, 268, 276, 290, 300, 316, 339, 342, 344, 373, 384, 388, 390, 395, 396, 403, 405, 407, 408, 411–414, 445–447, 961, 964, 966, 968, 973–981, 983–985, 987, 1007, 1073, 1100, 1195

emergency, 31, 104, 158, 202, 211, 213, 217, 236, 667, 719, 738, 743, 839, 895, 973, 1048–1050, 1100–1102

emotion, 149, 466, 469, 474, 477, 479, 485, 487–489, 491–493, 538, 727, 778, 820, 831, 1142, 1165–1195, 1197–1199

employment, 53, 69, 75, 77–82, 92, 100, 105, 109, 124, 125, 146, 147, 150, 151, 155, 156, 165, 174, 177, 178, 214, 269, 272, 274, 277, 278, 309, 339, 342, 345, 362, 364, 370, 413, 418, 442, 466, 561, 563, 574, 617–621, 635, 643, 649, 650, 668, 670, 671, 685–688, 690, 691, 694, 696, 704, 706, 710, 715, 721, 723, 742–744, 751, 760, 765, 788, 793, 796, 811, 851, 867, 876, 887, 888, 890–893, 897, 940, 944, 945, 948, 950, 978, 980, 983, 1031, 1117, 1119, 1123, 1141, 1168, 1170–1173, 1182, 1183, 1185

enemy image, 362, 431, 531, 792, 1189, 1191

enmity, 264, 401, 402, 408, 411, 422, 426, 431, 904

environmental factors, 507, 558, 590–596, 600, 601, 603–606, 728, 851, 854, 868, 929, 1169

equality, 25, 34, 103, 124, 126, 133, 251, 329, 359, 381, 384, 556, 638, 639, 715, 789, 856, 888, 1106, 1107

escalation, 4, 9–11, 21, 31, 32, 49, 68, 126, 196, 233, 239, 241, 244, 248, 253–256, 258–260, 269, 270, 272, 276, 287, 289, 290, 294, 297, 300–302, 306, 333, 345, 360–362, 365, 366, 370, 376–379, 384, 388–391, 396, 397, 404, 407, 408, 411, 412, 414, 415, 417, 427, 428, 431, 432, 449, 466, 467, 474, 496, 500, 501, 503, 506, 508, 529, 532, 533, 575, 577, 584, 653, 654, 657, 668–670, 745, 799, 808, 812, 822, 825, 869, 879, 895, 904, 924, 931–933, 949, 1018, 1105, 1108, 1129, 1163, 1168, 1181

eschatology, 337, 941, 978, 979

ethics, 104, 127, 179, 190, 195, 200, 214, 221–223, 279, 288, 303, 324, 336, 337, 390, 517, 679, 681, 695, 768, 778, 919, 965, 974, 976, 979, 984, 985, 993, 1003, 1015, 1033, 1035, 1098, 1191, 1192, 1205, 1213, 1215

ethnic group, 84, 92, 134, 135, 139, 142, 227, 228, 235, 244, 245, 248–251, 254–257, 259, 265, 266, 277, 286, 297, 299, 302, 307, 351, 353, 354, 357–359, 361, 362, 416, 553, 618, 622, 624, 639, 667, 709, 789, 872, 1064, 1178, 1181, 1184

ethnic identity, 229, 230, 233, 238, 250, 256, 258, 265, 289, 966 ethnic minorities, 93, 94, 134, 217, 218, 251, 254, 295, 299, 353, 356, 418, 430, 631, 786, 789, 790, 795, 796, 798, 1012, 1170, 1173, 1175

ethnicity, 10, 83, 85, 86, 90–96, 173, 228, 229, 231, 238, 243–245, 254, 255, 258–260, 265, 266, 290, 304, 328, 357, 364, 365, 565, 617, 618, 625, 626, 633, 642, 652, 654, 723, 738, 790, 806, 850, 851, 872, 877, 883, 948, 1018, 1172, 1179, 1185

ethnocentrism, 264, 364, 366, 413, 427, 429, 1196

ethnocide, 248–250, 255, 259

ethnography, 85, 88, 89, 105, 264, 269, 272, 288–290, 441, 448, 558, 578, 587, 655, 693, 697, 741, 914, 1175, 1179, 1205, 1210, 1212, 1213, 1215–1217

ethology, 524, 537, 585–588, 860, 905, 907, 918, 927, 928, 1013, 1014

ethos, 126, 173, 178, 221, 253, 381, 691, 904, 908–910, 917, 918, 929, 950, 979

evolution, 7, 9, 14, 17, 30, 31, 36–39, 41, 52, 67, 68, 84, 93, 122, 123, 130–135, 193, 194, 221, 245, 258, 289, 292, 294, 296, 302, 307, 308, 310, 312, 316, 318–320, 325, 326, 328, 331, 333, 335, 336, 338, 341, 353, 355, 359, 362, 365, 366, 370, 371, 374, 377, 381, 382, 385, 387–392, 395, 396, 398, 403, 406–428, 429, 440, 441, 443–445, 453, 454, 459, 499, 569–575, 577, 579, 585–588, 607, 680, 687, 696, 699, 703, 710, 738, 744, 748, 752, 768, 856, 858, 861, 905, 940, 941, 957, 973, 975, 978–986, 1008, 1026, 1027, 1033, 1035, 1036, 1038, 1048, 1082, 1089, 1100, 1105, 1109–1111, 1183, 1185, 1192, 1196–1199, 1218

expressive violence, 4, 21, 33, 413, 855, 939, 951, 1113, 1116

family, 14, 29, 50, 51, 59, 67, 70, 75, 80, 82, 86, 89, 91, 97, 101, 102, 105, 107, 110, 113, 114, 117, 122, 124, 126, 127, 129–131, 133, 135, 136, 150, 154, 162, 172, 175–178, 181–186, 196, 229, 248, 266, 283, 296, 344, 371, 384, 392, 394, 396, 397, 412, 445, 463, 476, 497, 500, 505–509, 527, 534, 535, 543–565, 586, 588–594, 598, 601–603, 605–607, 613, 617, 618, 621–625, 629, 636, 638–640, 645, 648–651, 653, 655, 656, 671, 681, 686, 692, 695, 696, 698, 705, 715, 720–726, 728, 730–733, 735, 742, 744, 745, 749–752, 761, 765, 783, 803, 818, 821, 827–832, 837–843, 847–862, 867, 868, 871, 872, 876–879, 886, 893, 900, 902, 937, 939, 942, 947, 952, 962, 963, 995, 1048, 1120, 1123, 1124, 1139, 1156, 1158, 1171–1173, 1174, 1181, 1190, 1209, 1217, 1221, 1223, 1229

family structure, 82, 105, 508, 555, 556, 558, 561, 617, 618, 621, 623, 629, 648, 651, 705, 854, 856, 858

fanaticism, 315, 319, 330, 780, 1005

fans, 420, 529, 530, 647, 906, 914, 915, 918, 919

fascist, 123, 144, 282, 310, 376, 385, 389–391, 401, 403, 410, 1026, 1027, 1033–1039

fear/anxiety, 5, 6, 8, 20, 23, 80, 96, 109, 113, 128, 134, 157, 160, 174, 181, 230, 244, 255, 256, 259, 267, 269, 270, 272, 273, 275, 279, 287, 300, 302, 309, 315, 319, 341, 363, 378, 396, 401, 411, 413, 416–420, 447, 463, 470, 471, 473, 481, 482, 489–491, 502, 520, 523–525, 528, 530, 531, 536, 543, 544, 658, 668, 671, 676, 682, 689, 722, 725–727, 743, 759, 767, 775, 782, 783, 786, 790, 796, 810, 811, 824, 829, 849, 853, 866, 887, 889, 895, 910, 916, 917, 932, 939, 947, 1013, 1021, 1034, 1070, 1107, 1125, 1131–1153, 1157–1161, 1164, 1175, 1185, 1189, 1226

fear of crime, 782, 783, 887, 1070, 1131–1150, 1152, 1157, 1164

feminism, 97–108, 113–117, 133, 335, 371, 482, 549, 562, 565, 588, 612, 644, 646, 654, 744, 747, 748, 751, 752, 838, 844, 856, 861, 862, 1033

feudalism, 90, 208, 213, 216, 269, 276, 516, 589, 657–659, 663, 665–668, 672, 674–677, 716, 720, 721, 755, 761, 812, 869–871, 874, 880, 892, 893, 1002

firearms, see guns

forms of aggression, 465, 481, 501, 506, 507, 544–546, 548–550, 555, 557, 559–561, 604, 1225, 1226, 1233

framing, 4, 255, 360, 373, 382, 390, 409, 687

freedom, 6, 14, 16, 19, 22, 23, 107, 128, 131, 133, 222, 274, 310, 317, 334, 337, 369, 384, 389, 391, 400, 418, 429, 435, 468, 512, 799, 811, 838, 870, 920, 927, 940, 941, 983, 984, 989, 998, 1019, 1020, 1033, 1046, 1047, 1066, 1067, 1071, 1072, 1079, 1080, 1082–1085, 1087, 1090, 1091, 1094, 1095, 1099–1102, 1137, 1159, 1190, 1197, 1226

freedom of speech, 512, 811, 1094, 1095, 1101, 1102

French Revolution, 17, 98, 130–135, 441, 453, 979, 1099, 1100

frustration, 70, 72, 73, 76, 77, 180, 201, 341, 347, 360, 386, 387, 460–462, 469, 474, 475, 477–482, 487, 491–493, 618, 619, 621, 622, 630, 632, 637, 671, 673, 704, 762, 787, 788, 824, 855, 871, 896–899, 907, 918, 926, 927, 938, 940, 960, 1116, 1229

frustration-aggression hypothesis, 460–462, 474, 477, 480, 481, 491–493, 907, 926

functionalism, 144, 147, 148, 151, 248, 263, 288, 372, 385–387, 938, 1184

fundamentalism, 310, 314, 315, 326–328, 330, 334, 336, 395, 647, 941, 948, 959, 965–967, 969–972, 978, 983, 1019, 1020, 1109, 1110

gang violence, 30, 93, 332, 405, 450, 624, 656, 686, 690, 719, 792, 796, 817, 824, 874, 876, 937, 940, 947, 951, 1116, 1167, 1168, 1172–1175, 1177, 1179, 1180, 1237

gangs, 30, 81, 82, 90, 92, 93, 95, 96, 122, 292, 332, 333, 337, 343, 363, 405, 413–415, 438, 439, 450, 504, 529, 619, 620, 622, 624, 643–645, 649, 654–656, 666, 669, 670, 673, 677, 685–687, 690, 696, 699, 719, 769, 787, 788, 791, 792, 796, 817, 824, 871, 874, 876, 910, 916, 937, 940, 942, 946–948, 951, 952, 1115, 1116, 1122, 1123, 1126, 1167–1180, 1185, 1206, 1210, 1218, 1237

SUBJECT INDEX

gender, 29, 38, 43, 45, 49, 56–58, 97–99, 101–103, 105–108, 110, 112–116, 124, 127, 152, 163, 175, 278, 325, 334, 413, 506–508, 528, 543–545, 548–554, 558–565, 573, 579, 586, 593, 594, 595, 602, 612, 613, 616, 620, 622, 625, 627, 629, 630, 633, 641–647, 649–652, 654, 656, 710, 711, 723, 735, 739, 743, 744, 751, 752, 802, 805, 817, 852, 858, 861, 862, 869, 870, 873–875, 877, 888, 890, 894, 895, 900, 916, 926, 1116, 1117, 1126, 1137–1139, 1144, 1145, 1156, 1158, 1225, 1237

generation, 11, 76, 89, 102, 125, 145, 149, 173, 178, 187, 199, 204, 249, 270, 281, 324, 326, 387, 392, 446, 482, 564, 578, 629, 659, 680, 730, 852, 854, 863, 917, 941, 963, 982, 1002, 1003, 1029, 1034, 1168, 1188, 1232

genetics, 277, 278, 375, 377, 381, 446, 462, 495, 571, 572, 578, 580–582, 585, 586, 589–607, 635, 786, 856, 905, 909, 977

genocide, 10, 34, 79, 134, 139–142, 145, 148, 151, 157, 160, 161, 163, 164, 166–168, 191, 205, 239, 240, 243, 244, 247, 252, 254, 257–259, 269, 280, 287, 288, 291, 325, 329, 333, 336, 337, 353, 354, 366, 437, 439, 445–447, 453, 611, 773, 783, 789, 999, 1013, 1023, 1031, 1052, 1056, 1099

government, 5, 8, 16, 25, 30–32, 68, 69, 72, 79, 111, 130–134, 143, 147, 158–160, 187, 191, 199, 200, 203, 204, 223, 227, 228, 232–234, 236, 237, 241–243, 251, 253, 254, 256, 277, 284, 289, 291, 292, 295, 297, 299, 300, 302, 304, 310, 311, 313, 314, 316, 317, 320, 334, 339–349, 351–354, 357, 363, 375, 390, 401, 414, 415, 418, 419, 424, 427–430, 432, 438–440, 443–445, 449, 477, 511, 532, 533, 574, 586, 672, 674, 676, 680, 683, 684, 687–693, 696, 698, 705, 710–713, 721, 724, 728, 729, 764, 768, 772, 773, 780, 781, 783, 787, 789, 792, 793, 803, 805, 808, 813–815, 861, 869, 870, 876, 881, 902, 905, 962, 964, 977, 980, 1044, 1046–1048, 1052, 1053, 1058–1060, 1062–1069, 1071–1074, 1076, 1086, 1088–1090, 1093, 1098, 1099, 1101, 1102, 1106, 1131, 1132, 1139, 1147, 1149, 1171, 1176, 1190, 1229

gray area, 4, 31, 424, 430, 513, 863, 1104

group conflict, 258–260, 279, 287, 289, 290, 359, 362, 459, 640, 1194, 1198

group identity, 5, 229, 231, 232, 235, 237, 324, 328, 329, 332, 359, 1154, 1169

group membership, 10, 27, 92, 153, 250, 254, 256, 257, 264, 266, 278, 285, 333, 334, 353, 362, 370, 504, 613, 619, 622, 637, 645, 773, 812, 872, 916, 969, 1116, 1117, 1173, 1175, 1184

group perpetrators, 401

group process, 28, 88, 90, 150, 181, 196, 202, 245, 248, 249, 252, 329, 357–359, 361, 362, 390, 392, 408, 432, 459, 477, 501, 505, 506, 512, 611, 625, 654, 796, 803, 824, 884, 966, 969, 970, 1114, 1167, 1175, 1190, 1206, 1222

group victims, 401, 405, 422, 424

group violence, 27, 92, 205, 353, 402, 404, 405, 409, 426, 680, 1167, 1175

guerrilla, 10, 181, 205, 233, 234, 292, 302, 304, 310, 346, 391, 398, 446, 1062, 1063,

guilt, 2, 28, 34, 151, 157, 179, 181, 329, 362, 479, 483, 488–493, 524, 532, 631, 754, 774, 778, 872, 916, 934, 943, 1013, 1031, 1083

gun violence, 658, 666, 670, 672, 673, 676, 677, 764, 846

guns, 38, 90, 95, 114–117, 141, 156, 161–168, 179, 186, 217, 221, 233, 241, 251, 288–290, 307, 311, 315, 318, 319, 323, 329, 330, 340, 349, 366, 367, 381, 382, 396, 398, 421, 433–436, 446, 464, 470, 474, 479, 487, 507, 512, 526, 537–540, 553, 558–561, 563, 589, 646, 832, 843, 846, 849, 870, 881, 882, 884, 889, 903, 935, 987, 1002, 1019–1012, 1038, 1051, 1055, 1056, 1096, 1111, 1123, 1126, 1146, 1151, 1163–1165, 1178, 1179, 1197–1199, 1216, 1217, 1235, 1237

handgun, 657–659, 662, 663, 665–671, 674–677, 722, 729, 870

handicap, 619, 768–772, 852, 853, 856, 857, 861, 945, 1223

harmful behavior, 5, 6, 12, 18, 19, 21–23, 25, 27, 30, 34, 42, 70–107, 150, 173, 197, 248, 249, 265, 267, 278, 290, 309, 334, 365, 369, 376, 378, 383, 384, 421, 432, 438, 439, 443–445, 449, 452, 453, 459, 463–468, 472, 473, 476, 479, 483, 485, 488–491, 508, 512, 514, 515, 517, 519, 528, 540, 544–546, 553, 554, 564, 615, 619, 623, 626, 658, 672, 682, 698, 709, 725, 728, 740, 743, 753, 755, 778, 794, 795, 797, 817, 838, 841, 848, 849, 854, 863, 864, 866, 869, 875, 885, 911, 923, 929, 942, 943, 948, 949, 951, 969, 970, 977, 989, 990, 993, 995, 996, 998–1000, 1003, 1024, 1025, 1082, 1084, 1085, 1089, 1115, 1119, 1122, 1158, 1159, 1174, 1191, 1224

hate crimes, 324, 426

health, 80, 100, 105, 107, 112, 116, 117, 125, 129, 163, 176, 186, 205, 213, 223, 470, 476, 477, 485, 486, 537, 544, 556, 561–565, 569, 577, 580, 586, 607, 616, 636, 642, 645, 671, 675, 706, 719, 721, 724, 730–734, 737, 739, 743, 746, 748, 749, 751, 769, 771, 782, 819, 832, 840–842, 859–862, 881, 882, 885, 887, 891, 894–896, 899–902, 905, 906, 911, 919, 920, 934, 1034, 1074, 1190, 1218

hegemony, 99, 116, 127, 918, 1124

holocaust, 36, 37, 139–151, 157, 158, 160, 162–169, 186, 248, 252, 335, 366, 399, 403, 408, 788, 797, 801, 1023, 1025, 1027–1032, 1036–1039, 1094

holy war, 325, 335, 429, 1005, 1006, 1008–1012, 1016, 1019–1021, 1030

homelessness, 68, 339, 422, 646, 734, 738, 769

homicide, 4, 18, 20, 21, 36, 41–59, 68–70, 72, 81, 82, 86, 87, 91, 95, 96, 136, 140, 141, 150, 196, 281, 291, 363, 420, 421, 459, 460, 472, 476, 478, 490,

homicide (*cont.*), 539, 540, 544, 573–580, 583–588, 617, 618, 621, 632, 646, 648–652, 654, 658–660, 662–669, 671, 673, 676, 679, 689, 696, 699, 704–716, 720, 739, 741, 749, 751–755, 761, 762, 764, 765, 772, 776, 778, 782, 783, 809, 838–841, 844, 847, 850, 859, 862, 890, 897, 907, 920, 977, 998, 1024, 1120
homosexuality, 110, 116, 332, 335–337, 341, 344, 374, 563, 618, 646, 722, 769, 775, 776, 780, 782, 783, 786, 788, 801–815, 822, 830, 838, 849, 858, 860, 1002, 1123, 1119
honor, 16, 49, 51–54, 58, 77, 126, 127, 150, 165, 173, 249, 271–275, 277, 281, 283, 296, 302, 337, 450, 474, 477, 517, 532, 573, 587, 621, 630, 681, 684, 692, 695, 831, 942, 945, 978, 1007, 1015, 1094, 1095, 1117, 1120, 1124, 1182, 1193, 1213
hooligan, 30, 214, 362, 416, 426, 459, 529, 620, 643, 904, 911, 912, 914–920, 952, 1116, 1117, 1124, 1177, 1215
hostility, 72, 129, 182, 238, 269, 291–293, 297, 299, 303–306, 311, 355, 357–359, 365, 378, 427, 434, 460, 462, 468, 469, 475, 477, 483–486, 488, 489, 493, 533, 600, 690, 725, 727, 758, 765, 773, 793, 890, 895, 905, 907, 916, 1018, 1094, 1191
human rights, 6, 131, 173, 186, 190–192, 194, 195, 198, 200, 202–205, 216, 218, 219, 222–224, 237, 239, 241, 259, 260, 293, 317, 341, 342, 344, 347–349, 375, 447, 453, 709, 773, 782, 802, 815, 1016, 1047, 1052, 1056, 1067, 1092, 1099, 1102–1104, 1196
humanism, 199, 265, 288, 838, 983, 1026
humiliation, 25, 29, 113, 173, 181, 249, 289, 363, 470, 483, 634, 824, 828, 863, 864, 866, 971
hunger, 359, 369, 519, 531, 580, 907, 909, 975, 989, 1029, 1101, 1105

identity, 5, 54, 58, 84, 89, 90, 96, 131, 132, 134, 186, 196, 198, 228–233, 235, 237, 238, 244, 245, 247–250, 256, 258, 265, 266, 277, 282, 287–290, 297, 304, 314, 324, 327, 329–331, 333, 336, 338, 358, 361, 364, 366, 370, 373, 374, 384, 387, 388, 390–394, 406, 408, 409, 415, 416, 421, 428, 432, 435, 436, 442, 447, 465–467, 474, 626, 637–639, 642, 645, 646, 681, 690, 692, 697, 714, 726, 795, 797, 798, 803, 815, 865, 866, 881–883, 920, 927, 931, 941, 945, 946, 948, 949, 966, 968, 970, 972, 982, 1008, 1012, 1013, 1019, 1029, 1032, 1034, 1075, 1114–1116, 1119, 1121, 1123, 1126, 1154, 1169, 1173, 1182, 1184, 1195, 1223, 1227
ideology, 9, 10, 17, 24, 25, 28, 30, 33, 34, 140, 148, 149, 156, 161–163, 165, 166, 180, 193, 194, 196–198, 202, 203, 205, 210, 250, 258, 263, 269, 274, 283, 293, 294, 302, 310, 319, 326, 327, 331–335, 337, 342, 354, 356, 359, 362, 371, 375, 376, 389–394, 397–405, 408, 411–414, 416, 420, 421, 424, 427, 429–435, 454, 517, 531, 683, 684, 686, 688, 696, 738, 785, 786, 788, 791–793, 798, 807, 808, 817, 903, 905, 918, 948, 960, 961, 965–970, 980, 983, 1007, 1009–1012, 1015–1017, 1019, 1020, 1027, 1029, 1033, 1044, 1064, 1070, 1117, 1123, 1147, 1152, 1164, 1169, 1182, 1185, 1187, 1189, 1193
immigration, 90–92, 94–96, 162, 347, 358, 359, 409, 425, 427, 760, 787, 789–791, 793, 909, 946, 1061, 1064, 1169
imperialism, 195, 376, 391, 572, 967, 983
imprisonment, 91, 92, 106, 190–192, 194, 195, 201–204, 324, 438, 607, 647, 668, 802, 893, 1044, 1069, 1071, 1073
incest, 29, 725, 794
incitement, 352, 424–426, 518, 1089, 1090, 1092–1094, 1101
individualism, 53, 123, 377, 622, 649, 684, 704, 705, 709, 714, 716, 1174
individualization, 55, 622, 634, 636, 637, 640, 866–868, 882, 968, 1077, 1124
inequality, 24, 68, 69, 72–79, 81, 82, 86, 88, 94, 96, 99, 106, 117, 124, 230, 241, 243, 299, 311, 347, 386, 401, 402, 404, 408, 409, 411, 414, 424, 427, 432, 544, 550, 553, 554, 562, 575, 576, 585–588, 616, 617, 620, 621, 636, 643, 644, 650, 653, 655, 704–708, 710, 713–716, 782, 786, 852, 854, 861, 869, 877, 917, 951, 968, 1117, 1123, 1167, 1179, 1187
infanticide, 10, 14, 51, 173, 343, 349, 521, 530, 578–580, 585, 587, 658, 719, 720, 730, 761, 768, 828, 6, 860, 948
initiation, 174, 267, 290, 324, 333, 343, 360, 384, 449, 623, 642, 941
insecurity, 245, 308, 418, 432, 898, 943, 947, 968, 1133, 1135, 1141, 1146, 1189, 1199
instinct, 14, 23, 53, 196, 262, 460, 480, 485, 753, 798, 906, 909, 938, 1014, 1026, 1174
insurgency, *see* rebellion
insurrection, *see* rebellion
intelligence, 180, 193, 194, 342, 466, 504, 531, 571, 699, 815, 825, 1003, 1054
intensity of violence, 8, 11, 14, 20, 108, 111, 233, 250, 256, 280, 293, 295, 323–325, 328, 332, 333, 376, 377, 406, 462, 464, 472, 519, 932, 1154
interactionism, 465–468, 470, 478, 549, 562, 625–628, 636, 642, 645, 650, 651, 656, 748, 866, 928, 932, 1187, 1188
international law, 32, 171, 172, 191, 203, 205, 982, 1010, 1011, 1048, 1051–1053, 1055, 1056, 1061, 1072, 1076, 1103
international laws of war, 32, 179, 181, 184, 1063
intervention, 24, 30, 36, 80, 81, 85, 98, 103, 104, 107, 114–116, 128, 130, 135, 148, 158, 171, 211, 245, 283, 293, 303, 308, 317, 360, 376, 432, 451, 506–509, 544, 559, 602, 628, 642, 646, 647, 650, 654, 673, 695, 712, 713, 724, 727–734, 737, 738, 745–750, 763, 764, 787, 792, 793, 796, 797, 815, 817, 823, 831, 832, 838, 839, 852, 855, 858, 869, 882, 883, 889, 901, 942, 947, 962, 975, 1016, 1034,

SUBJECT INDEX

1052, 1063, 1064, 1070, 1090, 1124, 1126, 1176, 1195, 1197, 1206, 1237
intimate relationship, 476, 624, 656, 737–744, 747, 748, 837, 839, 844, 849, 853
Islam, 193, 311, 315, 325, 327, 330, 334–336, 791, 947, 983, 1008, 1011, 1012, 1018–1021, 1103, 1110
isolation, 31, 77, 86, 87, 89, 93, 96, 112, 178, 182, 378, 394, 397, 403, 418, 569, 617, 640, 679, 695, 722–726, 851, 896, 968, 1008, 1024, 1090, 1161, 1173, 1190, 1207, 1225

judiciary, 15, 16, 42–44, 50, 70, 85, 89, 92, 95, 96, 107, 131, 193, 194, 205, 215, 216, 223, 224, 332, 342, 345, 347, 349, 380, 595, 596, 611, 631, 645, 667, 668, 671, 673, 675, 677, 693–695, 711, 735, 740, 747, 750, 751, 778, 780, 783, 787, 804, 811, 813–815, 828, 839, 844, 846, 847, 858–860, 862, 879, 883, 930, 939, 981–993, 1009, 1054, 1058, 1066, 1067, 1069–1072, 1074, 1075, 1081, 1091, 1095, 1098, 1102, 1104, 1107, 1118, 1120, 1147, 1171, 1173, 1175, 1177–1179, 1192–1194, 1217
justification, 9, 10, 20–22, 25, 28, 29, 32, 34, 107, 126, 134, 142, 148, 211, 250, 262, 263, 265, 267, 288, 289, 320, 326, 337, 342, 344, 377, 386, 401, 405, 411–415, 418, 424, 432, 437, 469, 470, 471, 528, 529, 536, 684, 774, 775, 778, 791, 796, 857, 904, 958, 963, 966, 973–976, 978–985, 993, 994, 1000, 1003, 1004, 1009, 1012, 1016, 1020, 1035, 1036, 1044, 1046, 1052, 1058, 1075, 1099, 1102–1104, 1106, 1113–1125, 1127, 1140, 1182, 1188, 1190, 1193, 1194, 1218
justification of violence, 21, 22, 25, 29, 34, 134, 262, 263, 267, 326, 337, 386, 401, 413, 418, 424, 437, 471, 684, 778, 796, 857, 966, 973–976, 978–985, 993, 994, 1003, 1104, 1044, 1113–1119, 1121–1125, 1127, 1186, 1193, 1194
juvenile crime, 44, 57, 70, 81, 82, 96, 508, 558, 564, 595, 601, 604, 616, 624, 627, 628, 631–633, 646, 648, 649, 651, 653, 675, 677, 881, 920, 952, 1127, 1149, 1178, 1179

labeling, 33, 344, 409, 414, 453, 613, 625–627, 642, 646, 647, 649, 650, 653, 691, 728, 779, 780, 849, 866, 867, 878, 1179, 1209
labor movement, 342, 370, 686, 940, 944, 978, 980, 983
law, 4, 6, 9, 15, 16, 18, 19, 28, 31–33, 42–44, 50, 53, 57, 58, 70, 75, 79, 80, 82, 83, 85, 89, 90, 92–97, 99, 100, 102, 122, 127–134, 143, 149, 171–173, 177, 179, 181, 183, 184, 186, 191–195, 198, 200, 202–205, 209, 211–216, 218, 219, 222–224, 229, 232, 237, 239, 241–243, 248, 251, 259, 260, 266, 281, 283–285, 293, 297, 309, 312, 317–319, 328, 332, 340–349, 352, 355, 356, 360, 370, 371, 375, 376, 378, 381, 384, 396, 400, 401, 405, 428, 429, 441, 447, 448, 453, 465–467, 470, 475–477, 482, 512, 517, 518, 530, 535, 559, 561, 563, 564, 578,
586–588, 595, 596, 601, 603, 607, 611, 618, 627, 631, 638, 639, 641, 643–645, 649, 652–654, 656, 659, 667, 668, 671–673, 675–677, 680, 683, 684, 687, 688, 690–697, 699, 702, 709, 711, 713–716, 721, 727, 729, 731, 732, 734, 735, 737, 740, 741, 746–751, 764, 776, 767, 771, 773, 778–783, 787, 788, 797, 798, 802–804, 808, 811, 813–815, 828, 831, 839, 840, 844, 846, 847, 857–863, 874, 876, 882–884, 886, 887, 889, 895, 908, 910, 923, 924, 926, 927, 930, 933, 935, 938–940, 942, 950–952, 958, 965, 966, 974–977, 981, 982, 989, 992, 993, 995, 996, 998, 1002, 1003, 1009–1012, 1016, 1024, 1043–1056, 1058, 1060–1076, 1079–1100, 1102–1107, 1109–1111, 1118–1120, 1123, 1125, 1126, 1131, 1134, 1140, 1146–1149, 1161, 1163–1165, 1171, 1173, 1175, 1177–1179, 1187, 1192–1194, 1196, 1198, 1217, 1221, 1226, 1227
learning, 14, 126, 198, 204, 380–382, 408, 409, 411–413, 432, 448, 460, 462, 463, 470, 474, 476, 480, 495–500, 503–506, 508, 509, 514, 521–523, 526, 528, 531, 532, 536, 571, 589, 612–614, 624, 627, 629, 633, 636, 641, 642, 645, 654–656, 725, 820, 827–829, 854, 857, 879, 891, 901, 903, 904, 909, 918, 958, 971, 1165, 1186, 1189, 1195, 1198, 1227
learning theory, 408, 409, 460, 462, 463, 470, 495–497, 503, 526, 531, 532, 613, 614, 624, 627, 629, 633, 636, 641, 642, 656, 854, 879, 909
left-wing extremism, 376, 965
legitimation, *see* justification
liberalism, 158, 198, 976
lifestyle, 52, 54, 67, 78, 96, 128, 278, 356, 505, 619, 621, 623, 637, 646, 649, 651, 653, 698, 753, 768, 769, 772, 774–776, 777, 791, 872, 928, 950, 963, 965–967, 969, 1143–1145, 1169, 1170
living environment, 878, 896
longitudinal study, 35, 81, 94, 470, 504, 505, 524, 549, 555, 559–563, 565, 601, 626, 628, 633, 634, 641, 650, 653, 655, 706, 707, 734, 830, 831, 840, 851, 877, 878, 1173, 1175, 1212, 1232, 1234
lower class, 70, 136, 619, 654, 916, 950, 1157, 1170, 1178
loyalties, 83, 84, 131, 182, 196, 251, 288, 299, 394, 426, 774, 791, 891, 952, 982, 1098, 1184
lynch law, 282, 332, 335, 340, 353, 354, 357, 358, 363, 366, 481, 493, 642, 646–648, 655, 709, 715, 722, 734, 798, 1071, 1075

machismo, 178, 217, 910, 914, 1152
mafia, 33, 284, 682–684, 687, 692, 695–699, 1206
maltreatment, 29, 186, 463, 624, 643, 720, 721, 723, 724, 727, 728, 730, 733–735, 751, 822, 829–831, 839–844, 847, 850, 856–859, 861
manslaughter, *see* homicide
marginalization, 24, 79, 93, 145, 265, 266, 277, 278, 286, 364, 372, 378, 397, 404, 417, 419, 426, 713, 769, 774, 777, 781, 791, 802, 864, 878, 898, 944–946, 951, 984, 1072, 1144, 1172

Marxism, 75, 81, 105, 198, 302, 304, 325, 326, 384, 391, 409, 410, 698, 914, 915, 940, 967, 979, 980, 986, 1003, 1026, 1183, 1184
mass media, 8, 13, 18, 25, 34, 83, 92, 197, 198, 217, 237, 255, 311, 319, 320, 339, 343, 362, 380, 404, 405, 408, 411, 412, 414–417, 436, 459, 468, 470, 475, 477, 487, 511–541, 589, 613, 671, 694, 706, 722, 727, 737, 793, 802, 869–872, 874, 876, 892, 909, 917, 918, 920, 940, 946, 949, 963, 969, 1025, 1036, 1038, 1086, 1105, 1113, 1125, 1140, 1141, 1143, 1144, 1146, 1149–1166, 1168–1170, 1186, 1235
mass murder, 142, 155, 157, 159, 179, 239, 250, 352, 783, 1023, 1029–1032, 1036, 1094
massacre, 140, 141, 147, 148, 161, 168, 190, 236, 247, 248, 250, 254–256, 269, 275, 291, 346, 352–354, 365, 366, 390, 447, 671, 789, 871, 872, 875, 881
media effects research, 520, 524, 525, 1153, 1164, 1165
media reporting, 92, 405, 411, 414, 529, 532, 694, 870, 1086, 1141, 1151, 1155–1157, 1159–1163
mediation, 208, 243, 244, 255, 260, 284, 324, 334, 397, 460, 484, 530, 630, 686, 747, 880, 882, 1146, 1193–1195
methodology, 56, 90, 91, 94, 95, 101, 109, 111, 112, 116, 117, 125, 135, 141, 143, 167, 190, 192, 194, 195, 200, 215, 218, 219, 275, 286, 329, 347, 353, 354, 363, 366, 375–377, 413, 414, 416, 418, 420, 422, 426, 430, 431, 433, 525, 532, 547, 549, 551, 612, 616, 617, 624, 626, 643, 655, 691, 693, 698, 702, 703, 709–712, 714, 716, 737, 741, 747, 751, 759, 769, 779, 786, 788–791, 793, 794, 807, 808, 841, 862, 878, 887, 892, 899, 944, 946, 948, 949, 958, 1009, 1021, 1060, 1134, 1139–1141, 1146, 1167, 1175, 1179, 1185, 1206, 1209, 1210, 1214–1218, 1220, –1223, 1227–1229, 1232–1235
migration, 82–84, 90–92, 94–96, 125, 134, 162, 302, 347, 358, 359, 363, 409, 425, 427, 562, 621–624, 655, 760, 787, 789–791, 793, 909, 946, 973, 1031, 1060, 1064, 1124, 1141, 1160, 1164, 1167, 1169, 1171, 1179, 1185
milieu, 37, 100, 112, 253, 283, 285, 345, 363, 409, 434, 613, 617, 628, 636, 638, 647, 651, 684, 687, 692, 745, 798, 826, 882, 952, 961, 966, 967, 969–971, 1036, 1123, 1126, 1143–1147, 1178, 1185
militarism, 126, 214, 224, 349, 376, 987, 1033
military, 24, 38, 126, 127, 130–133, 136, 149, 157, 165, 171–187, 190, 193, 194, 198, 199, 203, 209, 214, 217, 219, 221, 231, 236, 241, 253, 265, 268, 279, 297, 298, 301, 305, 315, 317, 326, 341–343, 346, 353, 355, 375, 376, 392, 394, 395, 438–440, 443–446, 533, 621, 635, 683, 727, 911, 976, 979, 1009–1012, 1016, 1017, 1029, 1036, 1048, 1051, 1052, 1059–1066, 1069, 1074, 1100, 1101, 1191, 1193–1195
militia, 129, 231, 254, 256, 292, 297, 311, 332, 334, 340, 342, 346, 347, 349, 406, 407, 412, 414, 426, 428, 433, 434, 436, 659, 773, 1021, 1190

mobbing, 877, 885, 886, 889, 893, 900, 902, 1222, 1224
mobility, 72, 75, 81, 88, 311, 414, 623, 624, 636, 689, 723–725, 742, 743, 897, 928, 929, 968, 1172
mobilization, 127, 128, 130, 131, 133, 135, 203, 216, 236, 245, 249, 253, 254, 258, 265, 275, 277, 282, 292, 311–314, 316, 317, 341–343, 345, 355, 356, 358, 362, 371–373, 377, 379, 381, 382, 385, 387–389, 393, 394, 398, 403, 409, 410, 412, 414–417, 427, 429, 435, 441, 443, 444, 584, 789, 965, 987, 1106, 1169, 1176, 1178, 1183, 1187, 1196, 1198, 1199
modern age, 5–7, 14, 16, 35, 41, 42, 47, 48, 53–58, 83, 84, 94, 141, 199, 229, 247, 250–253, 296, 311, 327, 351, 372, 386, 391, 399, 408, 410, 419, 424, 425, 427, 624, 636–638, 703, 708, 710, 714, 716, 793, 860, 866, 867, 938, 957, 968, 974, 1011, 1016, 1037, 1045, 1061, 1063, 1124, 1146, 1193
monopoly of violence, 5, 13, 24, 29–32, 51, 126, 203, 207, 209, 213, 221, 223, 255, 274, 284, 285, 299, 317, 325, 359, 640, 682–685, 690, 695, 739, 916, 919, 939, 957, 962, 963, 965, 973, 974, 976, 978, 1025, 1043–1055, 1057–1067, 1071–1073, 1080, 1081, 1087, 1124, 1184, 1193, 1194
morality, 8, 79, 106, 187, 197, 201, 221, 224, 310, 320, 448, 679, 918, 938, 939, 1003, 1020
motives for violence, 4, 21, 22, 27, 98, 147, 151, 257, 263, 273, 275, 277, 283, 284, 302, 465–467, 574, 781, 791, 795, 992, 994, 1027, 1114–1119, 1124, 1153, 1154, 1163, 1182, 1203, 1204
murder, *see* homicide

national identity, 134, 230, 258, 421, 435, 1008
national minorities, 228, 229, 231, 233, 234, 237, 427
National Socialism, 140–146, 148, 150, 152, 157, 159, 160, 163, 166, 354, 403, 406, 410, 517, 788, 974, 984, 1093, 1094, 1099, 1100, 1102
nationalism, 53, 84, 94, 132, 134, 135, 158, 228, 229, 232, 234, 237, 239, 242–245, 248, 251, 252, 257–260, 290, 297, 301, 306, 310, 323, 325, 326, 328, 329, 336, 337, 344, 362, 364–367, 401, 427, 433, 441, 443, 531, 788, 792, 797, 917, 982, 1012, 1013, 1018, 1019–1021, 1033, 1034, 1199
nation-state, 32, 37, 51, 247, 250–254, 257–259, 294, 399, 683, 702, 704, 710, 713, 912, 975, 1054, 1057–1066, 1071, 1074–1076, 1098
neglect, 9, 18, 29, 53, 160, 176, 177, 185–187, 190, 235, 262, 294, 325, 351, 364, 372, 438, 452, 459, 463, 474, 476, 486, 500, 556, 574, 589, 626, 627, 654, 720–723, 727, 728, 731–735, 770, 779, 818, 819, 821, 824, 826, 827, 829, 831, 832, 838, 840–842, 844, 848–850, 853, 856, 859, 860, 862, 883, 924, 958, 1024, 1121, 1122, 1124, 1155, 1162, 1163, 1183, 1210, 1212, 1220
neighborhood, 67, 70, 71, 75–78, 81, 82, 86–90, 93, 95, 96, 214, 339, 341, 349, 403, 438, 444, 448, 505, 544, 553, 558–563, 565, 575, 577, 588, 625, 643, 645, 651–653, 669, 673, 703, 719, 721, 722,

SUBJECT INDEX 1249

724, 729, 733, 806, 807, 821, 857, 868, 871, 872, 879, 945, 947, 963, 1069, 1070, 1073, 1133, 1139, 1141, 1145, 1172, 1176, 1177, 1185
neo-nazi, 376, 381, 389, 390, 401, 403, 406, 407, 416, 422, 428, 436, 790, 793, 797, 808, 966, 1199
nonviolence, 5, 19, 34, 35, 330–332, 334–336, 376, 379, 397, 963, 981, 984, 985, 1002, 1009, 1101, 1104, 1106–1108, 1120, 1170

obedience, 18, 24, 34, 129, 156, 178, 182, 197, 198, 202, 204, 205, 234, 299, 369–371, 376, 386, 467, 468, 477, 824, 865, 952, 983, 1097, 1098, 1104, 1198
offense, 14, 18, 29, 34, 42, 43, 44, 46–51, 54, 70, 71, 73, 91, 102, 104, 173, 179, 212, 421, 424, 425, 427, 512, 517, 527, 532, 590, 603, 612, 614, 615, 617, 618, 622, 623, 626, 630–634, 643, 649, 655, 657, 703, 705, 705, 709, 711, 728, 773, 776, 790, 796, 806, 809, 813, 863, 867, 874, 880, 886, 892, 893, 923, 925–927, 930, 933, 1081, 1084, 1086, 1088, 1093, 1094, 1096, 1109, 1118, 1121, 1122, 1124, 1131, 1133, 1134, 1136–1139, 1141, 1144, 1146, 1154, 1155, 1158, 1159, 1162, 1174, 1179, 1214, 1223
opportunity structure, 409, 411, 412, 414, 616–618, 622, 632, 792, 928, 932, 933, 958, 960–962, 965, 966, 968–970, 998, 1169, 1178, 1182, 1187, 1188
organized crime, 14, 33, 39, 314, 316, 622, 679–699, 769, 817, 1055, 1060, 1061, 1065, 1076, 1168, 1178,
organized violence, 137, 227, 234, 262, 264, 279, 284, 307, 357, 384, 393, 1075

parenting, 14, 497, 499, 505, 506–508, 549, 555–557, 560, 563, 580, 590, 624, 635, 723, 729–731, 820, 876, 893, 1026, 1171
parents, 107, 129, 173, 178, 213, 214, 276, 341, 412, 463, 468, 496–500, 503, 505, 506, 535, 536, 549, 556, 557, 562, 579, 587, 589, 590, 592, 593, 595, 596, 598, 599, 603, 604, 606, 614, 616, 620, 624, 627–629, 631, 632, 635, 636, 656, 719, 721–726, 728–731, 733, 758, 761, 813, 821, 826, 843, 844, 848–852, 854, 856, 857, 860–862, 865, 866, 870–873, 879, 880, 910, 916, 946, 1102, 1115, 1119, 1120, 1172, 1222, 1224
parliamentarianism, 181, 210, 283, 348, 371, 375, 379, 380, 401, 903, 962, 1079, 1081, 1087, 1099, 1194
pathology, 8, 14, 29, 67, 76, 77, 79, 186, 249, 348, 385–387, 408, 488, 507, 509, 544, 564, 569, 571, 573, 583, 584, 587, 604, 606, 607, 650, 725, 726, 733, 734, 779, 820, 824, 829, 831, 854, 858, 1191, 1199, 1236
patriarchy, 99, 102, 105, 114, 175, 335, 376, 573, 629, 630, 646, 749, 802, 803, 849, 854, 856, 911, 1137
patriotism, 131, 132, 152, 320, 428, 430, 447, 1029, 1033, 1034, 1038
peace, 5, 11, 19, 37, 38, 117, 128, 135, 135, 159, 171, 179, 181–183, 185, 187, 198, 214, 215, 221, 223, 233, 237, 242–245, 250, 258, 260, 263, 264, 271, 275, 276, 279, 280, 283, 286, 288, 290, 293, 296–298, 303–307, 312, 318, 319, 325, 331, 333–338, 348, 349, 355, 365, 366, 370, 375, 376, 378, 380, 384, 418, 447, 870, 983, 984, 1010, 1014, 1018, 1046, 1051, 1064, 1066, 1076, 1079, 1080, 1087–1090, 1092–1094, 1098, 1194–1196, 1198
peer groups, 29, 150, 392, 412, 495, 501–503, 505–508, 525, 528, 547, 613, 645, 826, 827, 829, 865, 868, 873, 876–878, 963, 1115, 1118, 1144, 1167, 1171
peoples, 14, 90–92, 123, 132, 154, 194, 198, 227–235, 237–245, 251, 258, 2059, 288, 290, 328, 332, 674, 957, 977, 1008, 1009, 1013, 1160
permissiveness, 312, 470, 497, 499, 526, 659, 672
personality, 51, 53, 68, 96, 178, 180, 184, 185, 199, 283, 313, 369, 432, 462, 468, 474–477, 492, 493, 507–509, 524, 525, 527, 536, 537, 560, 561, 563, 587, 592–594, 598, 600, 601, 605, 607, 632–634, 637, 644, 646, 647, 671, 682, 703, 726, 738, 741, 744, 745, 748, 758, 764, 822, 824, 831, 853, 854, 857, 866, 868, 871, 893–895, 900, 903, 908, 925, 926, 932, 934, 935, 938, 945, 1121, 1147–1149, 1160, 1164, 1174, 1179, 1182, 1226, 1229, 1236
phenomenology, 13, 20, 22, 27, 268, 520, 770, 984, 1017, 1117, 1188, 1203
physical violence, 16, 17, 22, 23, 25, 29, 31, 68, 99, 100, 102, 106, 108–111, 117, 175, 179, 186, 213, 217, 220, 278, 324, 343, 351, 512, 518, 559, 583, 611, 682, 684, 742, 838, 843, 844, 846, 848, 849, 856, 861, 873, 874, 876, 877, 885, 890, 891, 910, 919, 924, 925, 949, 957, 960, 973–976, 980, 984, 994, 1044–1046, 1049, 1054, 1057, 1058, 1061, 1062, 1066, 1071, 1086, 1108, 1113, 1119, 1123, 1183, 1184, 1193, 1194, 1234
pluralism, 313, 401, 403, 1018, 1103, 1106, 1124, 1184
pogrom, 30, 152, 248, 250, 252, 254, 256–258, 351–367, 406, 409, 453, 790, 791, 798, 1006
police, 5, 14, 24, 31, 34, 43, 44, 50, 89, 111, 122, 126, 129, 131, 132, 135, 136, 148–151, 158, 163, 175, 176, 179, 180, 190, 191, 193, 194, 198, 199, 200, 203, 204, 207–224, 232, 236, 316, 318, 340–349, 352, 353, 355, 356, 362, 376–381, 384, 389–392, 394, 396, 401, 405, 414, 416, 420–424, 430, 433, 442, 448, 451, 452, 492, 529, 531, 532, 565, 574, 593, 594, 611, 625, 634, 649, 666, 668, 670, 671, 673, 675, 682, 683, 685, 686, 688, 690, 691, 693–695, 713, 715, 721, 729, 731, 738, 745, 746, 750, 751, 761, 767, 771, 773, 776, 777, 782, 788–791, 793, 794, 796–798, 804–811, 813, 815, 839, 840, 867, 875, 879, 880, 887, 889, 895, 911, 915, 918, 919, 930, 933, 935, 939, 942–944, 946–948, 950–952, 975, 992, 993, 1047, 1049, 1050, 1053, 1054, 1058, 1061, 1062, 1065–1076, 1074, 1074, 1088, 1090, 1113–1115, 1117, 1119, 1120, 1131, 1132, 1134, 1141, 1145–1149, 1153, 1154, 1163, 1171, 1173, 1176, 1185, 1188, 1194, 1221, 1229

policy of annihilation, 125, 148, 154, 155, 160
political elite, 67, 300, 316, 396, 961, 966, 968, 976, 978, 979
political power, 23, 30, 78, 263, 294, 304, 326, 327, 330, 357, 359, 407, 413, 659, 973, 1018, 1061, 1098, 1101
polity, 37, 128, 130, 131, 310, 312, 314, 336, 348, 443, 574, 959, 1043–1045, 1050, 1055
populism, 343, 344, 401, 403, 418–420, 426, 430, 432, 433, 435, 436, 691
pornography, 460, 468, 470–472, 517, 527, 537, 685, 876
post-traumatic stress disorder (PTSD), 68, 184–187, 202, 726, 727, 731, 734, 818, 819, 823, 824, 829–832, 852
poverty, 24, 67–83, 85, 86, 89, 93, 95, 96, 264, 267, 347, 409, 428, 487, 561, 563, 564, 575, 587, 617, 619, 621, 625, 648, 652–654, 669, 704, 721, 723, 724, 728, 741, 808, 815, 817, 850, 870–872, 898, 941, 944, 1003, 1069, 1119, 1172, 1173, 1179
power, 6–8, 10, 14–19, 21, 23–25, 30–32, 34, 38, 42, 51–53, 58, 68, 76, 78, 90, 97, 99, 100, 104–106, 109, 115, 116, 121–132, 134, 135, 146, 147, 159, 161, 165, 180, 182, 185, 191, 197, 198, 200, 207, 213, 214, 217, 221–223, 229, 231, 249, 251, 253, 254, 256, 257, 259, 260, 263, 266, 271–279, 281, 283–287, 290, 292, 294, 297, 299–301, 304, 305, 309, 312, 314, 316, 318, 326, 327, 330, 331, 335, 337, 342, 344, 345, 349, 352–354, 357–361, 363, 365, 366, 370, 374–376, 382, 384, 388, 400, 401, 403–407, 409, 411, 413–421, 426, 431, 432, 437, 441, 445–448, 450, 454, 465, 473, 474, 489–492, 508, 511, 533, 544, 549, 553, 563, 564, 573, 583, 589, 593, 615, 616, 625, 629, 630, 632, 633, 639, 646, 648, 654, 655, 659, 676, 680–687, 690, 694–697, 704, 714, 742–744, 750–752, 780, 788, 793, 803, 808, 826, 827, 855, 858, 862, 873, 877, 889, 919, 920, 932, 939, 941, 945, 957, 971, 973, 974, 977–981, 983, 984, 990, 1015, 1018, 1025, 1026, 1028, 1043–1051, 1053–1055, 1057–1062, 1064, 1072, 1074–1076, 1080, 1083, 1086–1089, 1091, 1098, 1099, 1101, 1105, 1106, 1117, 1120, 1123, 1133, 1139, 1142, 1152, 1157, 1168, 1179, 1183, 1186, 1190, 1193, 1195, 1204, 1221, 1223
prejudice, 32, 90, 134, 141, 157, 180, 210, 218, 223, 230, 237, 354, 358, 360, 364–366, 413, 432, 449, 459, 483, 489, 570, 773, 780, 781, 786, 790, 791, 794, 796, 801, 802, 809, 810, 813, 814, 918, 1123, 1188, 1189, 1196, 1226, 1230, 1235, 1237
presentation of violence, 93, 326, 459, 464, 472, 489, 512, 513, 515, 517– 521, 523–527, 529, 534, 535, 613, 853, 1024, 1027, 1028, 1029, 1031, 1032, 1036, 1093, 1153, 1160, 1161
prevention, 35, 38, 79, 80, 96, 107, 183, 191, 192, 202, 203, 222, 239, 242–245, 275, 294, 300, 301, 303, 306, 316–318, 333, 334, 347, 349, 360, 365, 370, 377–380, 382, 396, 414, 445, 446, 488, 497, 514,

520, 534, 544, 559, 605, 631, 633, 645, 650, 652, 673, 677, 689, 694, 696, 697, 702, 713, 716, 721, 730–732, 734, 735, 750, 751, 763, 765, 780–782, 789–792, 796, 798, 813–815, 817, 828, 830, 832, 858, 860, 869, 878–884, 887, 893, 897, 899, 901, 902, 933–935, 945, 946, 983, 991, 1044, 1066, 1069, 1070, 1075, 1084, 1092, 1124, 1132, 1136, 1139, 1141, 1145, 1146, 1149, 1151, 1177–1179, 1193
prison, 68, 79, 80, 92, 125, 126, 136, 145, 150, 154, 158, 160, 162, 166, 179–182, 184–186, 189–193, 195, 198, 199, 201–205, 213, 256, 343, 345, 356, 391, 395, 468, 668, 699, 758, 767, 769, 772, 798, 825, 829, 894, 947, 981, 1010, 1036, 1044, 1049, 1050, 1070, 1071, 1075, 1076, 1103, 1110, 1122, 1138, 1196
prognosis, 4, 271, 279, 283, 286, 377, 430, 486, 561, 564, 587, 641, 705, 710, 712, 760, 894, 896, 897, 899, 902, 1064, 1090, 1183, 1224
property crime, 14, 29, 33, 34, 78, 81, 87, 88, 92, 121, 324, 329, 353, 369, 376, 383, 384, 421, 512, 545, 575, 596–599, 604, 615, 623, 633, 654, 657, 703, 742, 863, 864, 869, 885, 910, 942, 947, 960, 975, 989, 998, 999, 1154, 1159
prosecution, 42, 50, 102, 143, 145, 146, 203, 219, 222, 256, 374, 746, 747, 750, 813, 1055, 1070, 1163, 1223
protest, 30, 31, 34, 53, 59, 121, 122, 128, 129, 133, 135, 152, 154, 157, 158, 160, 161, 168, 200, 214, 219, 223, 233–236, 238, 241, 247, 254, 295, 298–300, 312, 319, 320, 326, 328, 334, 336, 353, 355, 356, 359, 363, 367, 369, 370, 373–382, 384, 385, 387–393, 396–398, 417, 454, 480, 529, 653, 768, 940, 943–946, 948, 950, 951, 961, 963, 9*64, 968, 975, 977, 986, 1010, 1013, 1035, 1079, 1080, 1083, 1084, 1086, 1088, 1102, 1105, 1107–1110, 1120, 1169, 1179, 1186–1188, 1191, 1192, 1197–1199, 1225
Protestantism, 53, 128, 1010
psychoanalysis, 105, 260, 329, 475, 520, 523, 753, 758, 829–832, 866, 881, 906, 938, 1013, 1014, 1118
psychological violence, 23, 25, 113, 844, 994, 996
psychopath, 180, 186, 386, 489, 493, 507, 509, 544, 564, 587, 604, 606, 607, 650, 725, 726, 733, 734, 774, 779, 820, 824, 829, 831, 853, 858
psychotherapy, 101, 104, 109, 112, 205, 763, 832, 861, 1236
public opinion, 13, 21, 157, 165, 217, 222, 247, 316, 317, 347, 377, 381, 417, 433, 474, 475, 484, 488, 502, 512, 532, 533, 536, 628, 729, 873, 946, 967, 1013, 1015, 1026, 1093, 1132, 1133, 1151–1153, 1161–1166, 1188, 1198
public security, 1066, 1067, 1069, 1070, 1090, 1263, 1272
punishment, 5, 14, 43, 52, 82, 95, 117, 121, 129, 136, 150, 189–195, 198, 200, 284, 291, 324, 333, 343, 356, 362, 460, 463, 465, 474, 477, 497, 498, 502,

SUBJECT INDEX 1251

506, 516, 518, 519, 526, 532, 563, 585, 621, 624, 630, 631, 642, 649, 654, 656, 658, 688, 696, 708, 714, 729, 730, 733, 742, 762, 767, 775, 779, 780, 782, 791, 802, 813, 826, 842, 861, 867, 882, 887, 933, 971, 974, 977, 989, 990, 995, 1007, 1018, 1055, 1071, 1073, 1075, 1080–1086, 1089, 1107, 1109, 1122, 1131, 1132, 1140, 1147, 1148, 1159–1161, 1165, 1166

qualitative research, 10, 110, 113, 116, 215, 316, 547, 558, 560, 702, 751, 779, 793, 847, 878, 1145, 1146, 1175, 1203–1218, 1225, 1233–1235
quality of life, 187, 577, 658, 747, 762
quantitative research, 10, 43, 45, 85, 107, 108, 110, 116, 215, 219, 316, 389, 561, 702, 705, 709, 710, 751, 752, 769, 779, 793, 862, 878, 1146, 1155, 1162, 1175, 1203, 1204, 1211–1215, 1217, 1219–1233, 1225, 1231–1237

racial unrest, 7, 37, 72, 73, 76–79, 82, 83, 85–92, 94, 96, 134, 135, 140, 142, 146, 152, 154, 158, 168, 183, 185, 186, 192, 193, 223, 224, 230, 249, 251, 264, 273, 282, 288, 295, 296, 302, 318, 329, 331, 332, 338, 339, 353, 354, 357, 359, 361, 363–367, 427, 428, 430–433, 425, 436, 445, 453, 492, 531, 538, 539, 562, 565, 585, 601, 614, 616, 642, 644, 651, 653, 667, 669, 670, 672, 673, 675, 676, 693–695, 738, 765, 780, 786, 789, 792, 798, 802, 806, 807, 810, 827, 829, 850, 851, 859, 865, 872, 878, 883, 919, 920, 944, 948, 1002, 1013, 1034, 1080, 1103, 1131, 1160, 1166, 1178, 1179, 1184, 1211
racism, 1, 25, 72, 76–79, 82–90, 92, 94–96, 131, 135, 139, 141, 145–147, 180, 194, 214, 218, 223, 232, 245, 248, 249, 258–260, 298, 315, 333, 334, 352, 353, 357, 358, 365, 366, 400, 401, 406, 416, 418, 420–424, 426, 427, 429, 433–436, 438, 517, 538, 546, 644, 648, 649, 651, 655, 705, 708, 728, 738, 765, 780, 781, 785–799, 801, 802, 806, 807, 810, 811, 815, 827, 829, 850, 851, 859, 865, 872, 878, 883, 896, 911, 919, 920, 943–946, 948–950, 967, 971, 1002, 1013, 1073, 1080, 1103, 1105, 1120, 1131, 1154, 1156, 1160, 1166, 1178, 1179, 1184, 1199, 1205, 1211, 1236
radicalization, 131, 148, 253–255, 313, 314, 317, 373, 381, 389, 390, 393–397, 403, 415, 426, 429, 1192
rage, 174, 181, 184, 268, 306, 335, 354, 362, 373, 375, 377, 448, 460, 462, 464, 466, 469, 470, 474, 475, 477, 479, 481–489, 491–493, 545, 546, 553, 584, 600, 657, 681, 704, 725–727, 743, 753, 754, 758, 762, 796, 810, 819, 824–826, 828, 879, 892, 898, 907, 941, 943–946, 950, 951, 1163, 1182, 1185, 1189, 1226
rape, 4, 14, 29, 42, 44, 68, 70, 86–88, 96, 98–102, 104–107, 109–113, 115–117, 129, 173, 174, 179, 181, 182, 186, 195, 247, 249, 250, 257, 259, 263, 296, 324, 329, 333, 439, 447, 472, 493, 544, 597, 621, 626, 649, 657, 741, 751, 774, 783, 786, 794,
809, 817, 838, 844–847, 856, 859, 861, 869, 887–889, 910, 911, 919, 920, 937, 995, 1000, 1002, 1003, 1026, 1080, 1081, 1133, 1136–1136, 1150, 1157, 1158, 1161
rational choice theory, 248, 364, 371, 426, 612, 614, 618, 630, 633, 636, 641, 642, 644, 645, 652, 653, 928, 1185, 1186
rebellion, 24, 30, 39, 127, 128, 131, 133, 147, 153–155, 162, 164, 185, 190, 191, 199, 202, 205, 232–244, 262, 288, 291, 294, 297, 299, 310, 326, 334, 341, 342, 344, 349, 353, 370, 371, 375, 377, 381, 382, 387, 398, 442–444, 446–448, 451, 452, 425, 614, 615, 940, 941, 944, 948, 951, 952, 975, 981, 985, 1010, 1032, 1098, 1187, 1197, 1198
recognition, 6, 8, 34, 35, 99, 103, 104, 112, 180, 199, 200, 228, 257, 265, 266, 281, 408–411, 413, 416, 431, 432, 449, 453, 488, 536, 560, 619, 627, 638, 639, 748, 787, 858, 866, 875, 876, 886, 887, 893, 938, 968, 969, 971, 973, 1024, 1052, 1067, 1099, 1100, 1104, 1105, 1117, 1226
refugee, 91, 93, 158, 190, 194, 199, 243, 244, 259, 265, 300–302, 342, 349, 362, 414, 415, 417, 420, 424, 425, 433, 446, 529, 532, 788, 1141, 1064, 1102
regime, 30, 32, 91, 94, 137, 139–143, 147, 148, 153, 159, 161, 162, 190, 192, 193, 196, 197, 200, 201, 203, 238, 241, 242, 253, 276, 290, 297, 301, 310, 312, 314, 316–318, 320, 331, 346, 383, 388, 396, 403, 439–441, 444–446, 690, 768, 773, 775, 790, 893, 964, 970, 981, 1062, 1063, 1065, 1068, 1074, 1098, 1102, 1105, 1110
rehabilitation, 194, 195, 201, 203, 204, 750, 883
relative deprivation, 69, 72, 295, 355, 356, 358, 366, 371, 372, 377, 381, 386, 387, 409, 420, 426, 431, 487, 628, 654, 706, 1187, 1199
religion, 25, 59, 127, 167, 258, 259, 265, 266, 292, 304, 323–328, 357, 366, 714, 737, 738, 741, 760, 797, 798, 805, 806, 906, 938, 966, 978, 986, 987, 1005–1021, 1109, 1184, 1185
religious community, 128, 250, 327, 345, 731
religious minorities, 198, 428, 780, 785, 787, 789, 790, 792, 795
religious violence, 250, 319, 326, 328–332, 336, 337
religious war, 328, 329, 337, 1010–1012, 1196
repression, 10, 14, 19, 31, 32, 36, 37, 53, 130, 136, 190, 200, 228, 231, 235–237, 241, 242, 255, 258, 297, 302, 312, 313, 320, 326, 339, 344, 349, 373, 377, 379, 381, 382, 386, 390, 391, 393, 394, 396, 439, 443–447, 448, 780, 811, 880, 889, 939, 946, 947, 975, 981, 1028, 1102, 1108, 1109, 1123, 1164, 1176, 1198
republic, 131, 143, 193, 213, 294, 296, 342, 375, 392, 427, 443, 444, 453, 512, 913, 943, 964–967, 974, 982, 985, 1043, 1079, 1081, 1095, 1100, 1102–1104, 1132
resistance, 16, 18, 21, 25, 34, 100, 128, 131, 144, 151–157, 162, 163, 166–168, 180, 202, 211, 233, 234, 265, 268, 293, 321, 328, 335, 337, 338, 383, 391,

resistance (cont.), 406, 438–444, 448, 449, 451, 452, 454, 499, 677, 771, 780, 795, 797, 808, 857, 871, 915, 945, 957, 971, 975, 984, 995, 1002, 1048, 1059, 1068, 1082, 1083, 1088, 1089, 1097–1106, 1108, 1109, 1178, 1190
resource mobilization, 133, 311, 313, 314, 316, 356, 358, 371–373, 382, 385, 387–389, 393, 394, 398, 409, 1183, 1198
revolt, *see* rebellion
revolution, 14, 17, 30, 31, 36–39, 67, 68, 84, 93, 122, 123, 130–135, 193, 194, 245, 292, 294, 296, 302, 307, 308, 310, 318–320, 325, 326, 328, 331, 333, 335, 336, 338, 341, 353, 359, 362, 365, 366, 370, 374, 377, 379, 381, 382, 385, 387, 391, 392, 398, 406, 429, 440, 441, 443–445, 453, 454, 459, 680, 940, 941, 975, 978–986, 1008, 1027, 1033, 1035, 1036, 1038, 1048, 1099, 1100, 1105, 1109–1111, 1183, 1197, 1199
right to resist, 28, 1048, 1095, 1097, 1105
right-wing extremism, 11, 84, 268, 399–431, 433–436, 532, 619, 620, 638–640, 785–788, 790–796, 801, 874, 958–960, 965–967, 969, 970, 971, 1087, 1117, 1120, 1155, 1163, 1169, 1170, 1199, 1210, 1232
right-wing populism, 401, 418–420, 426, 430, 432
riots, 11, 22, 126, 127, 131, 132, 152, 190, 191, 215, 219, 234, 248, 255–259, 287, 291, 294, 295, 320, 324, 329, 351–357, 359, 361–367, 384, 385, 416, 417, 428, 430, 447, 452, 453, 459, 789, 797, 919, 939, 940, 943, 995, 1002, 1007, 1029, 1033, 1034, 1038, 1091, 1131, 1154, 1160
risk factor, 117, 178, 185, 186, 433, 500, 544, 555, 557, 558, 560, 562, 574, 586, 590, 647, 650, 721, 724, 741, 771, 772, 781, 821, 822, 829, 849, 850, 852, 853, 859, 861, 865, 868, 871, 873, 875, 877, 878, 881, 883, 899, 900, 902, 1174, 1220
risk of maltreatment, 150, 291, 722–725, 728, 730–733, 819, 850–855, 858, 859, 861, 897
ritual, 21, 23, 25, 26, 37–39, 52, 58, 100, 121, 122, 124–127, 129, 136, 182, 256, 262, 263, 266, 267, 270, 275, 281, 323, 324, 326, 328, 329, 332, 333, 360, 361, 366, 367, 374, 375, 413, 414, 429, 439–442, 445, 449, 450, 452–454, 476, 614, 651, 904, 905, 915, 946, 961, 966, 967, 969, 970, 996, 1006–1011, 1013–1018, 1020, 1024, 1098, 1121, 1126, 1154, 1164, 1178
rivalry, 124, 248, 231, 326, 439, 442, 450, 588, 648, 906, 909, 918, 1014
road traffic, 924–930, 932–934, 1080, 1228
rule of law, 317, 319, 352, 684, 958, 1044, 1058, 1061, 1063, 1067, 1070, 1072, 1076, 1082, 1099, 1100, 1104–1107, 1109, 1194

sadomasochism, 21, 26, 37, 39, 1027
school violence, 863, 866, 869, 870, 872–883, 949–951
school, 14, 34, 53, 68, 69, 71, 75, 80, 89, 105, 108, 131, 144, 146, 147, 182, 193, 210, 270, 287, 290, 295, 303, 323, 341, 382, 385, 389, 412, 449, 468, 477, 491, 498, 499, 501, 503, 505–509, 517, 519, 524, 526, 534–537, 547–554, 558, 559, 562, 578, 589, 593, 595, 603, 619, 620, 628, 635, 653, 669–671, 676, 684, 693, 719–722, 725, 727, 729, 732, 734, 738, 764, 782, 813–815, 821, 824, 826, 827, 831, 841, 863–884, 886, 893, 895, 898, 900, 905, 907, 914, 916, 919, 920, 938, 946–951, 963, 1029, 1033, 1034, 1076, 1093, 1113, 1123, 1151, 1167, 1169, 1171, 1172, 1174–1176, 1181, 1185, 1209, 1210, 1222, 1224, 1225, 1230, 1236, 1237
secret police, 149, 155, 167, 168, 191, 194, 200, 204, 318, 346
secret services, 24, 158, 342–344, 391, 533
sects, 228, 330, 332, 337, 371, 386, 917
security, 24, 31, 93, 109, 111, 149, 171, 177, 191, 193, 200, 202, 203, 207, 208, 213, 214, 222, 224, 231, 232, 238, 241, 242, 244, 255, 257, 259, 297, 300, 302, 305, 306, 308, 313, 317, 318, 342, 347, 360, 377, 418, 420, 432, 445, 466, 499, 500, 530, 617, 659, 685, 691, 696, 697, 699, 707, 788, 820, 867, 868, 871, 880, 890, 892, 898, 902, 933, 943, 947, 966, 968, 1029, 1032, 1044, 1046, 1047, 1049, 1050, 1052–1054, 1060–1075, 1090, 1099, 1132, 1133, 1135, 1139, 1141, 1189, 1190, 1193, 1194, 1199
security measures, 93, 530, 880, 892
security police, 149, 207, 317, 420, 1065, 1066–1068, 1071, 1073
security policy, 313, 1053, 1060, 1062, 1069, 1070, 1072
security services, 24, 207, 317, 1049, 1050, 1065, 1066, 1068, 1071, 1073, 1190
segregation, 76–80, 82–96, 201, 214, 287, 324, 333, 358, 378, 554, 617, 624, 647, 772, 896, 916, 948, 1068, 1173
self-confidence, 908, 1174
self-control, 51, 53, 56, 177, 356, 487, 491, 576, 632, 633, 641, 644, 646, 649, 652, 656, 703, 824, 905, 907–909, 918, 933, 942, 1177, 1184
self-defense 28, 213, 265, 275, 344, 345, 389, 437, 444, 669, 672, 677, 740, 741, 751, 761, 847, 870, 908, 969, 973, 984, 1045, 1047, 1048, 1050–1052, 1067, 1080, 1101, 1102, 1118, 1221
self-determination, 99, 134, 135, 231–233, 258, 865, 896, 1053, 1080
self-esteem, 107, 178, 180, 483–485, 492, 493, 546, 558, 571, 626–628, 636, 637, 639, 648, 653, 654, 724–726, 733, 755, 803, 866, 872, 873, 908, 928, 929, 950, 994, 1226
separatism, 227–239, 241–243, 245, 253, 432, 433, 435, 436, 1035
serotonin, 603, 604, 754, 755, 759, 763
sexism, 25, 472, 780, 803, 815, 920
sexual abuse, 29, 106, 175–177, 463, 720–722, 725, 726, 728, 732, 733, 821, 823, 830–832, 841, 843, 844, 850, 857–861, 888, 1032

SUBJECT INDEX

sexual minorities, 11, 77, 80, 91–95, 134, 135, 137, 139, 147, 150, 152, 154, 156, 157, 198, 217, 218, 224, 227–229, 231–239, 241–244, 251, 252, 254, 258, 295, 299, 302, 304, 310, 327, 331, 342, 352–354, 356, 357, 359, 362, 363, 365, 370, 378, 409, 413, 415, 418, 420, 421, 427, 428, 430, 436, 443, 445, 447, 454, 490, 508, 518, 529, 618, 631, 667, 676, 767, 774, 775, 780, 785–799, 803, 850, 944, 946, 980, 1012, 1014, 1068, 1090, 1091, 1106, 1107, 1152, 1157, 1161, 1170, 1172, 1173, 1175

sexual offense, 29, 99–102, 105–107, 109–111, 113, 115, 116, 174, 175, 182–185, 187, 475, 527, 740–743, 751, 802, 815, 817, 847, 863, 869, 886, 888–891, 893, 897, 911, 919, 1137, 1158, 1159

sexuality, 97, 102, 105, 114, 182, 204, 337, 477, 547, 617, 654, 737, 740, 748, 776, 802, 803, 807, 831, 856, 909, 1185

shame, 53, 203, 273, 289, 299, 483–485, 489, 491, 493, 628, 631, 643, 774, 811, 825, 828, 849, 862, 948, 977, 980, 1074, 1118

sit-ins, 4, 34, 369, 1083, 1084, 1086, 1087, 1092, 1093, 1108

skin color, 250, 789, 810, 1119

skinheads, 339, 344, 363, 406, 407, 412–414, 416, 420, 423, 427, 428, 434, 436, 529, 620, 651, 791, 792, 797, 808, 948, 1119, 1124, 1178

slavery, 68, 79, 122, 179, 262, 263, 265, 268, 332, 438, 449, 621, 760, 802, 941, 984, 985, 995, 1012

social anthropology, 261–263, 266, 268, 270–272, 277, 278, 280, 281, 285, 286, 302

social behavior, 23, 473, 475–477, 496, 537, 539, 548, 564, 565, 635, 642, 879, 934, 945

social change, 17, 49, 55, 57, 77, 84, 114, 173, 185, 272, 285, 287, 349, 370, 372, 410, 425, 453, 623, 624, 638, 650, 697, 703, 705, 749, 780, 782, 858, 914, 933, 968, 1135, 1140, 1145

social class, 56, 69, 71, 73, 74, 81, 82, 93, 94, 364, 607, 615, 618, 619, 626, 643, 655, 734, 740, 770, 915, 917, 1144, 1182, 1184

social control, 18, 52, 57, 58, 70, 75, 82, 87–89, 309, 355, 357, 360, 365–367, 385, 465, 467, 616, 621, 625–629, 631, 632, 635, 636, 639, 641–645, 647–652, 655, 670, 778, 885, 859, 865, 918, 938, 941–943, 951, 1063, 1069, 1075, 1118, 1136, 1139, 1141, 1142, 1169–1172, 1174, 1176,

social identity, 89, 96, 361, 364, 384, 408, 432, 803, 815, 949, 1115, 1121

social integration, 5, 8, 81, 113, 153, 202, 244, 251, 260, 290, 329, 361, 367, 374, 386, 405, 409, 410, 413, 416, 419, 432, 436, 482, 503, 552, 572, 613, 616, 621, 624, 625, 628, 629, 638, 639, 646, 647, 650, 708, 710, 760, 763, 765, 780, 781, 825, 826, 858, 938–940, 942, 945–947, 950, 951, 964, 966, 968, 969, 972, 1047, 1053, 1054, 1060, 1063, 1075, 1091, 1117, 1154, 1169, 1172, 1174, 1196, 1217, 1235

social movement, 20, 98, 244, 312, 318, 351, 359, 360, 362–364, 369–375, 377, 379, 381, 382, 384, 385, 387–393, 396–398, 435, 440, 441, 453, 798, 940, 943, 945, 951, 952, 971, 1060, 1068, 1169, 1178, 1179, 1187, 1191, 1196–1199

social psychology, 106, 178, 185, 205, 295, 301, 316, 360, 364, 408, 411, 432, 459, 460, 463, 467, 468, 471, 474–478, 492, 493, 507–509, 536–539, 560–565, 586, 587, 607, 627, 641, 646–648, 656, 815, 854, 856, 858, 906, 934, 935, 960, 1142–1144, 1147–1149, 1164, 1179, 1185, 1188, 1197–1199, 1234, 1236, 1237

social space, 51, 122, 287, 400, 413, 416, 417, 650, 1144, 1185

social system, 261, 270, 271, 277, 278, 385, 619, 638, 692, 703, 855, 937, 940, 1134, 1143, 1167

socialism, 140–146, 148, 150, 152, 157, 159, 160, 163, 166, 250, 354, 379, 384, 399, 403, 406, 410, 517, 788, 943, 944, 967, 974, 976, 979–981, 984, 1023, 1093, 1094, 1099, 1100, 1102

socialization theory, 105, 408, 432, 868

socialization, 90, 105, 182, 184, 276, 362, 377, 392, 394, 405, 408–412, 430, 432, 506, 508, 509, 524, 525, 528, 531, 544, 552, 553, 557, 563, 589, 590, 592, 612, 614, 616, 621–624, 628, 629, 632, 640, 669, 729, 778, 865, 867, 868, 882, 907–909, 916, 930, 938–940, 958, 960, 961, 968, 1114, 1116, 1123, 1137, 1174, 1175, 1184, 1185, 1196, 1204, 1207, 1222

soldier, 126, 130, 131, 153, 157, 162, 163, 172–175, 177–183, 185, 186, 269, 385, 343, 345, 397, 446, 452, 533, 977, 1012, 1015, 1017, 1028, 1035, 1044, 1094, 1190

sport violence, 26, 449, 450, 904, 907–912, 917–919, 938

sports, 13, 26, 439, 440, 449, 450, 529, 904–912, 917–920, 938, 947

state authority, 15, 16, 34, 285, 292, 299, 376, 395, 531, 1043, 1044, 1047–1049, 1054, 1058, 1081, 1087, 1093, 1095, 1101

states, 3–7, 9–11, 14–17, 20, 23, 24, 27–31, 34, 37–39, 43, 44, 48–55, 57–59, 72, 76, 79, 85, 86, 90–95, 98–104, 107, 110–113, 121–137, 139–145, 147, 151, 152, 158–161, 164, 171, 173–176, 182, 186, 190–196, 199–205, 207, 209, 212–217, 219, 221, 223, 224, 227–239, 241–245m 247, 249–251, 257–260, 290–297, 299–302, 305–307, 310–321, 323, 325, 326, 328, 330–332, 334, 336, 337, 340–346, 348, 349, 352–354, 356, 358–360, 362–365, 370–373, 375–384, 386, 389–392, 394, 395, 397–399, 401, 406, 407, 409, 411, 413, 415–418, 422–424, 426–430, 444–447, 453, 460, 470, 473, 475–477, 479–491, 501, 514, 515, 521, 524, 527, 531, 533, 535, 548, 571, 572, 575, 576, 578, 583, 584, 587, 593–595, 613, 615, 618, 619, 621, 623, 625, 629, 634, 636, 640, 643, 646, 650, 653, 654, 657–659, 668, 669, 671–676, 680–685, 688, 691, 695, 697, 702, 704, 709, 710, 712–716, 719–722, status (cont.), 726, 728–731, 734, 740, 741, 745, 752, 758, 759, 761, 762, 768, 769, 772, 782, 783, 787, 788, 793, 795, 799, 801–805, 808, 809, 811–815, 817–820, 824, 825, 839, 840, 842–844, 859–863, 868–872, 874–877, 879–882, 890, 893, 894, 902, 911, 912, 915–917, 919, 923, 925, 926, 928, 932, 933, 939, 943, 947, 951, 952, 957–959, 962–965, 968–971, 973–983, 986, 990–995, 998, 110, 1002, 1004–1006, 1008, 1009, 1011, 1012, 1015, 1016, 1019, 1020, 1024–1026, 1029, 1030, 1034, 1035, 1043–1055, 1057–1077, 1079–1081, 1083, 1087, 1088, 1090, 1092–1095, 1098, 1099, 1101–1103, 1105–1109, 1119, 1120, 1124, 1127, 1131–1134, 1136, 1142, 1145, 1146, 1151, 1154–1162, 1167, 1168, 1172, 1173, 1175, 1177–1179, 1181, 1183, 1186, 1188–1191, 1193–1196, 1198, 1208, 1220, 1222–1224, 1226–1230, 1232, 1235

status, 43, 51, 67, 68, 70, 71, 78, 79, 83, 85, 87–90, 92, 128, 130, 131, 166, 177, 178, 186, 198, 228, 229, 233, 235, 239, 254, 270, 271, 273, 276, 282, 290, 300, 335, 357, 359, 360, 374, 399, 413, 414, 419, 427, 430–432, 463, 470, 490, 500, 508, 509, 522, 523, 546, 555, 556, 560, 563, 574, 575, 577, 583, 593, 603, 618, 619, 629, 638, 639, 646, 647, 649, 653, 669, 682, 687, 710, 723, 730, 760, 774–777, 786, 791, 796, 802, 853, 866, 869, 884, 898, 909, 915, 916, 926–928, 941, 946, 966, 970, 989, 992, 1007, 1020, 1024, 1025, 1045, 1113, 1115, 1117, 1122, 1123, 1126, 1143, 1144, 1168, 1172, 1185, 1208, 1225, 1227

stereotype, 92, 101, 114, 255, 257, 262, 265, 324, 330, 333, 459, 473, 528, 780, 781, 911, 948, 1117, 1125, 1188, 1189, 1191, 1230, 1236

stigma, 30, 90, 259, 277, 304, 397, 404, 529, 626, 628, 645, 671, 687, 774–776, 778–781, 788, 803, 879, 882, 941, 946, 948, 950, 982, 1015, 1087, 1115, 1119, 1126, 1160, 1168, 1171

strain theory, 72, 76, 89, 94, 614, 616, 620, 624, 630, 634, 636, 641–643, 648, 652, 1176

street children, 343, 773, 783

stress theory, 616, 634, 636, 835

stress, 5, 67, 68, 125, 126, 154, 178, 183–187, 195, 196, 201, 202, 205, 210–212, 215, 219, 222, 255, 276, 279, 312, 352, 360, 362, 385–387, 391, 392, 412, 473, 476, 477, 481, 484, 487–491, 544, 556, 560–564, 616, 620, 634, 636, 643, 648, 650, 683, 684, 688, 689, 704, 705, 722–728, 731–734, 738, 743, 755, 762, 810, 815, 818–823, 826, 829–832, 841, 851, 852, 854, 855, 857, 860, 861, 871, 891, 892, 895–898, 900–902, 908, 909, 915, 918, 924, 926–928, 934, 1118, 1137, 1139, 1188, 1189, 1192

structural violence, 4, 18, 23–26, 34, 106, 123, 267, 272, 369, 512, 959, 967, 1080, 1233

subcultural theory, 88, 89, 91, 409, 432, 613, 618, 620, 622, 623, 1118

subculture, 26, 68–70, 76, 77, 81, 82, 84, 88, 89, 91, 92, 95, 96, 285, 312, 314, 363, 374, 376, 394, 406, 408–411, 413–415, 432, 433, 435, 436, 529, 531, 573, 613, 618–623, 628, 641, 644–647, 650–653, 656, 762, 774, 776, 778, 798, 944, 945, 961, 1118, 1122, 1124, 1125, 1127, 1154, 1167, 1169, 1170, 1177, 1178, 1180

suicide, 36, 42, 56, 81, 155, 173, 288, 314, 362, 363, 471, 636, 665–667, 671, 715, 716, 720, 721, 726, 743, 753–765, 819, 852, 870, 871, 886, 890, 894, 900, 938, 992, 1006

survey, 8, 35, 44, 70, 71, 86, 91, 95, 96, 107, 108, 110–117, 144, 152, 162, 174, 187, 191, 211, 216, 217, 224, 228, 231, 233, 241, 245, 282, 343, 377, 401, 415, 418, 419, 432, 436, 473, 489, 523, 525, 530, 547, 549, 555, 559, 562, 565, 615, 645, 672, 673, 676, 677, 705, 706, 709, 711, 714, 716, 735, 739–742, 748, 750, 751, 769, 770, 772, 777, 783, 790, 794, 799, 810, 822, 830, 839–852, 858–862, 869, 870, 874, 877, 887, 889, 890, 897, 898, 902, 911, 918, 925, 926, 930, 1097, 1132–1136, 1147, 1148, 1151, 1152, 1154, 1155, 1158, 1162, 1173–1175, 1177–1179, 1204, 1221, 1222, 1227–1230, 1232, 1234–1236

systems theory, 84, 704, 859

teachers, 34, 131, 213, 214, 463, 467, 506, 535, 547, 548, 550–552, 589, 590, 593, 600, 616, 671, 731, 813, 820, 821, 824, 827, 863, 865, 867, 869, 870, 872, 874, 875, 877–880, 895, 898, 942, 949–951, 1220, 1222, 1227

television, 139, 215, 255, 275, 362, 459, 460, 470, 471, 475–477, 513–519, 524–528, 535–541, 570, 907, 919, 946, 1119, 1120, 1140, 1147, 1153–1155, 1160–1165

terror, 11, 14, 24, 29–32, 34, 39, 106, 125, 131, 134, 137, 150, 151, 181, 190, 191, 193, 194, 198, 199, 204, 205, 233, 234, 247, 252–255, 257, 259, 268, 309–321, 325, 333, 335–337, 342, 344, 347, 354, 357, 362, 370, 371, 374, 377, 379, 384, 386, 392, 397, 398, 400, 406, 407, 412–415, 427, 429, 430, 433–436, 439, 459, 490, 518, 532, 536, 653, 697, 698, 783, 797–799, 902, 940, 947, 948, 952, 974, 976, 980–982, 985, 987, 990, 1012, 1015, 1019–1021, 1030, 1060–1062, 1064, 1065, 1101, 1119, 1152, 1153, 1157, 1166, 1181, 1190, 1197, 1228

tolerance, 53, 96, 99, 156, 180, 208, 276, 305, 313, 326, 331, 336, 346, 347, 378, 380, 525, 537, 605, 632, 780, 781, 813, 814, 817, 824, 892, 896, 923, 927, 937, 1018, 1069, 1070, 1072, 1073, 1131, 1142, 1148, 1149, 1190, 1228

torture, 14, 23, 25, 32, 52, 106, 128, 173, 179, 181, 189–205, 236, 267, 324, 344, 345, 369, 511, 512, 802, 990, 1003, 1024, 1029, 1047

totalitarianism, 6, 38, 144, 173, 193, 310, 312, 318, 401, 688, 768, 941, 1048, 1063, 1080, 1102

trauma, 5, 10, 23, 68, 103, 106, 107, 114–116, 142, 183–187, 201, 202, 204, 205, 231, 400, 486, 528,

SUBJECT INDEX

590, 726, 733, 734, 743, 790, 795, 810, 814, 817–832, 852, 866

underclass, 25, 69, 71, 74, 76, 77, 80–82, 86, 91, 95, 96, 125, 565, 588, 615, 619, 628, 1172, 1178
unemployment, 75, 82, 277, 364, 418, 561, 563, 617–619, 621, 643, 649, 650, 706, 715, 723, 743, 760, 765, 793, 851, 867, 945, 950, 1119, 1141, 1172, 1173
United Nations (UN), 135, 141, 179, 181, 182, 185, 186, 189–191, 204, 242, 245, 260, 699, 706, 711, 732, 1051, 1052, 1054, 1064, 1074, 1075, 1193, 1195
uprising, *see* rebellion
utilitarian, 76, 148, 191, 342, 363, 364, 619, 630, 632, 1018, 1033, 1071, 1125, 1186
Utopia, 5, 7, 287, 358, 944, 1004, 1009, 1035, 1076

vandalism, 29, 36, 333, 401, 442, 505, 512, 790, 807, 864, 869, 873, 875, 881, 883, 920, 943, 1142, 1157
victim, 4, 5, 8–10, 21–23, 25, 27–30, 32, 33, 35, 43–45, 49, 50, 56, 68, 79, 82, 85, 86, 89, 91, 95, 99, 104, 109–117, 122, 141, 145–148, 150–152, 157, 162, 164, 166, 172–175, 178, 182, 184, 186, 189, 190, 195–199, 201–205, 216, 235, 247, 250, 252, 256–258, 267, 268, 270, 271, 275, 291, 296, 314, 331, 344, 345, 348, 352, 353, 363, 378, 390, 400, 405, 411, 414, 420, 422, 424, 433, 447, 460, 464–466, 470–472, 477, 479, 489–491, 500–503, 507–509, 516, 519, 521, 525, 527, 530–532, 537, 545–547, 552, 560–564, 578, 579, 582, 583, 588, 619, 623, 646, 649, 651, 653, 658, 667, 668, 671, 672, 687, 690, 692, 704, 705, 709–711, 714, 719–725, 737–742, 744–748, 750–752, 760, 761, 767–783, 785–791, 783–798, 801–815, 817, 821–823, 829–833, 837–840, 842–844, 852–854, 857–860, 862, 864, 869–874, 877, 880, 882, 886–889, 894–897, 899, 900, 902, 906, 932, 943, 947, 950, 969, 985, 991, 992, 1001, 1002, 1006–1008, 1014, 1018, 1026–1032, 1069, 1080, 1082–1085, 1116, 1118–1123, 1131, 1132, 1134–1150, 1156–1160, 1162–1164, 1185, 1193, 1195, 1214, 1220, 1221, 1227–1229
victimization, 68, 82, 85, 86, 89, 91, 95, 113, 14, 164, 173, 186, 197, 198, 201, 216, 314, 433, 500–502, 505, 507, 508, 530, 552, 560–564, 582, 646, 651, 667, 672, 704, 705, 709–711, 719–728, 730–734, 740, 742, 746, 767–769, 781–783, 789, 790, 794, 797, 809–811, 814, 823, 829, 840, 842–844, 846, 847, 852, 853, 858, 882, 887, 888, 895–897, 900, 902, 1001, 1132, 1134, 1137–1140, 1142–1147, 1149, 1150, 1157, 1229
victimization rate, 44, 86, 91, 709, 720, 728, 730, 739, 740, 772, 777, 843, 887, 888, 895, 1134
victimization risk, 772, 775, 776, 727, 852, 887, 888, 895, 1138, 1142, 1144
victimology, 258, 750, 770, 782, 783, 788, 789, 795, 830, 859, 932, 1148, 1150
victims help, 30, 104, 106, 108, 114, 181, 205, 727, 745, 769, 778, 781, 839, 1193
vigilantism, 309, 339–349, 354, 357, 517, 585, 727, 734, 773, 782, 1066, 1067, 1069
violence prevention, 4, 5, 14, 35, 38, 79, 80, 96, 107, 126, 127, 183, 190–192, 202, 222, 239, 245, 265, 267, 268, 275, 323, 324, 334, 345, 347, 349, 355, 373, 377–380, 382, 396, 414, 487, 514, 520, 534, 559, 605, 631, 689, 694, 696, 702, 713, 716, 730–732, 750, 780–782, 796, 813–815, 817, 825, 828–830, 858, 861, 865, 866, 869, 872–881, 884, 893, 897, 890, 901, 902, 934, 945, 983, 991, 993, 1044, 1048, 1092, 1095, 1119, 1124, 1151, 1179
violence research, 3, 4, 8–11, 79, 114, 115, 117, 253, 264, 277, 285, 286, 295, 459, 514, 626, 701, 709, 749, 771, 779, 781, 848, 858, 859, 862, 902, 940, 959, 991, 1035
violent conflict, 5, 7, 10, 11, 14, 17–19, 21, 22, 27, 32, 34, 38, 51, 52, 54, 55, 57, 68, 70, 75, 84, 85, 90, 91, 94, 100, 101, 106, 110, 113, 122, 126, 149, 159, 171, 172, 183, 186, 194, 196, 214, 221, 227, 228, 232, 239, 241–245, 247–253, 256–261, 264–266, 268–277, 279–304, 306–308, 311, 312, 315–317, 319, 325, 327–330, 334, 335, 337, 349, 351, 353, 355–359, 361–363, 365, 366, 371, 372, 375–378, 380, 381, 383–394, 396–398, 400, 404, 408–410, 415, 420, 421, 425, 432, 435, 440, 445–448, 451, 454, 459, 466, 469, 473–475, 477, 478, 482, 483, 488, 496–500, 502, 505, 506, 509, 516, 518–520, 524, 527, 529, 531, 547–549, 552, 553, 557, 558, 565, 573, 575, 578, 579, 581, 583, 586–588, 604, 619, 622, 624, 638, 640, 642, 646, 648, 657, 668, 685, 687, 692, 693, 696, 708, 713, 723, 724, 730, 738, 739, 742, 744, 747, 751, 755, 783, 787, 795, 813, 818, 819, 824, 832, 840, 843, 846, 847, 853, 858, 864, 865, 877–879, 898, 902–904, 909, 915, 920, 924–933, 938, 940, 941, 943, 948, 950, 951, 963, 964, 969, 970, 973, 976, 980, 1005, 1008, 1009, 1011–1013, 1016, 1018–1020, 1025, 1029, 1045, 1047, 1050–1054, 1059, 1063, 1064, 1066, 1088, 1090, 1093, 1097, 1098, 1102, 1103, 1116, 1118, 1120, 1153–1155, 1157, 1159, 1163, 1165, 1167–1171, 1173, 1174, 1179, 1181–1199, 1213, 1226, 1230, 1231, 1236
violent crime, 14, 44, 48, 50, 51, 55, 57, 58, 68, 71–73, 78, 81, 82, 85, 87, 88, 90, 91, 94–96, 104, 407, 459, 466, 504, 537, 584, 587, 590, 594, 597–599, 601–604, 611–618, 620–626, 628, 629, 631, 632, 635, 636, 638–640, 642, 643, 645, 651, 652, 654, 655, 657, 672, 673, 675, 677, 684, 692, 701–705, 709, 712, 713, 715, 719, 725, 748, 755, 777, 792, 796, 801, 809, 824, 845, 853, 886, 898, 927, 995, 1071, 1079, 1113–1115, 1119, 1120, 1123, 1124, 1131, 1134, 1135, 1137–1140, 1144, 1147, 1151–1154, 1156–1159, 1161, 1162, 1167, 1170, 1172–1174, 1179, 1214, 1232
violent offender, 33, 584, 645, 755, 792, 824, 853, 1114, 1115, 1120, 1124, 1232

violent ritual, 21, 23, 25, 26, 58, 122, 124, 136, 256, 263, 281, 323, 324, 326, 328, 329, 332, 333, 414, 429, 439–442, 449–454, 904, 905, 915, 941, 966, 969, 996, 1013, 1014, 1017, 1018, 1154

vulnerability, 23, 296, 311, 312, 386, 443, 452, 455, 672, 768, 771, 775–777, 779, 781, 797, 810, 528, 852, 861, 897–900, 1032, 1058, 1065, 1137, 1138, 1143–1145, 1148

war, 10, 11, 14, 16–18, 20, 24, 29–32, 37–39, 55, 79–81, 84, 91, 106, 121–131, 133, 134, 137, 142–145, 147–154, 161, 164–166, 168, 171, 173, 174, 178, 179, 181–187, 194, 198, 199, 204, 205, 210, 214, 221, 227, 230, 231, 233, 234, 237–245, 247, 249, 251, 256–260, 262, 263, 267, 270, 271, 274–277, 279–285, 287–308, 310, 311, 314, 316, 320, 324–326, 328–333, 335–338, 342, 344, 345, 347, 349, 353, 354, 359, 371, 374, 376, 385, 391, 398, 399, 406, 415, 428, 429, 434, 438–440, 442–447, 449, 478, 492, 513, 517–519, 529, 531, 533, 583, 585, 587, 613, 621, 643, 650, 658, 665, 668, 687–690, 692, 695, 697, 698, 733, 763, 764, 768, 780, 790, 793, 797, 831, 874, 903–906, 917, 919, 947, 951, 976, 977, 980–984, 995, 1002, 1003, 1005–1021, 1023, 1025, 1026, 1028–1030, 1032–1038, 1044–1047, 1050–1052, 1056, 1062–1064, 1066, 1069, 1071, 1075–1077, 1094, 1099, 1100, 1104, 1105, 1120, 1131, 1181, 1185, 1192, 1193, 1195–1198

warlord, 274, 275, 284, 292, 302, 303, 1062, 1064, 1195

woman, 100, 103, 105, 108, 109, 111, 116, 117, 133, 185, 513, 575, 580, 582, 585, 596, 602, 629, 654, 739, 741, 743, 745, 749, 750, 824, 839, 853, 862, 890, 911, 1026, 1033

women as victims, 14, 29, 49, 50, 98, 99, 101, 102, 104, 106, 108, 112, 113, 114–117, 740, 741, 744–746, 846–848, 850, 887–889, 895, 906

women's shelter, 98, 100, 103–106, 108, 109, 111, 114, 116, 581, 745, 746, 749, 839, 1229

working class, 74, 313, 391, 559, 620, 686, 915, 918, 920, 942, 948, 950–952, 980, 981

working climate, 891, 896

workplace, 76–82, 86, 87, 89, 92, 96, 100, 101, 116, 174, 197, 276, 279, 293, 347, 442, 466, 468, 505, 558, 562, 570, 598, 625, 653, 655, 670, 690, 802, 806–808, 824, 829, 855, 861, 867, 882, 885–902, 908, 928, 944–948, 963, 994, 1092, 1162, 1176

world war, 14, 32, 55, 79, 84, 91, 133, 134, 142, 144, 149, 165, 166, 179, 181, 184, 251, 293, 294, 311, 342, 354, 385, 445, 643, 650, 658, 764, 780, 904, 917, 980, 983, 984, 1008, 1023, 1025, 1026, 1028, 1029, 1036–1038, 1063, 1064, 1071, 1099, 1100

xenophobia, 11, 85, 268, 400, 409, 412, 414, 418–421, 424–426, 431, 433, 436, 532, 620, 639, 640, 785–788, 790–796, 801, 874, 959, 961, 965, 966, 969–971, 1155, 1163

youth, 44, 70, 81, 82, 88, 90–93, 95, 96, 149, 153, 154, 164, 219, 278, 279, 289, 323, 337, 339, 346, 349, 363, 374–376, 379, 380, 393, 405, 406, 413, 414, 434, 474, 493, 497, 499, 504, 505, 507, 508, 531, 535, 537, 543, 544, 546, 547, 549, 550, 551, 555, 558, 559, 561–565, 599, 601, 613, 619, 620, 622, 624, 628, 630, 634, 635, 640, 644–649, 651, 652, 656–659, 662, 663, 665, 666, 668, 670, 673, 675–677, 719–721, 727, 729, 733–735, 787, 788, 791, 792, 796, 806, 808, 813, 815, 824, 826, 828, 830–832, 840, 842, 861, 866–868, 870, 880–882, 900, 941, 943, 945, 947, 948, 950, 951, 968, 1114, 1116, 1117, 1120, 1122, 1124, 1170, 1172–1179, 1185, 1186, 1192, 1197, 1199, 1205, 1206, 1213, 1236, 1237

youth culture, 90, 406, 531, 945, 950, 951

youth gangs, 92, 93, 95, 96, 332, 337, 405, 414, 620, 624, 645, 673, 677, 719, 788, 791, 796, 947, 951, 1170, 1172–1175, 1177–1179, 1185

youth violence, 379, 555, 562, 645, 647, 652, 657–659, 668, 676, 719, 720, 729, 735, 828, 830, 867, 881, 882, 968, 1114, 1117, 1124, 1199, 1206

PART V

Name Index

Abbink, Jon 261, 263, 277, 278
Adler, Freda 614, 705
Adorno, Theodor W. 180, 408, 1019, 1030
Agnew, Robert 89, 616, 620, 623, 628, 629, 634, 636, 1171
Aho, James A. 333, 792
Ainsztein, Reuben 144, 153, 154, 156
Akers, Ronald L. 613, 614, 632, 636
Akins, Scott 83, 87
Alarid, Leanne F. 613, 629
Albrecht, Günter 14, 33, 407, 409, 431, 611, 612, 615–618, 623, 625–628, 636, 637
Allport, Gordon W. 915, 1188
Almond, Gabriel A. 958, 959, 961, 963
Alpert, Geoffrey P. 217, 218
Altemeyer, Bob 333, 408
Aly, Götz 146, 148
Anhut, Reimund 410, 420, 638, 640, 968
Appadurai, Arjun 248, 250
Appleby, R. Scott 326–334, 965, 966, 1012
Arad, Yitzhak 144, 154
Archer, Dane 705, 706, 708
Archer, John 583, 584, 1185
Arendt, Hanna 18, 152, 156, 199, 310, 437, 448, 984, 1025, 1027, 1035, 1102, 1106, 1107
Arlacchi, Pino 681, 682, 684, 687, 692, 713
Armer, J. Michael 83, 84
Armstrong, Gary 912, 914, 915
Aron, Raymond 221, 309, 387
Aronson, I. Michael 354, 362
Artzt, Heinz 181, 182
Assmann, Jan 1005, 1007, 1009
Athens, Lonnie 626, 742
Atzwanger, Klaus 926–928
Audi, Robert 993, 994, 998, 1001
Averill, James R. 469, 470, 482
Axelrod, Robert 1886, 1195, 1196

Baacke, Dieter 1120, 1124
Bachman, Ronet 111, 472, 740, 840, 846, 847

Backes, Otto 14, 1079, 1109
Baker, Laura A. 589, 590, 595, 596, 600, 602
Bandura, Albert 408, 409, 460–463, 470, 495, 496, 503, 521, 526, 531, 613, 918
Banfield, Edward 67, 76, 77
Bankier, David 147, 157
Banton, Michael 215, 217
Barnes, Samuel H. 960, 961, 964, 968
Barnes, Tony 692, 695
Barth, Frederik 264, 265
Barthelmess, Wolfgang 926, 930, 931
Bartusch, Dawn J. 89, 90, 627
Basu, Amrita 354, 364
Bataille, Georges 1015–1017, 1024, 1034, 1035
Bates, John E. 498, 590
Bauer, Yehuda 139–41, 155, 156, 159, 1095, 1097
Bauman, Zygmunt 35, 253, 679, 693, 790, 1027, 1030, 1060, 1124
Baumeister, Roy F. 470, 479, 483–491
Baurmann, Michael C. 103, 770, 1129
Bay, Christian 1106, 1108
Bayley, David 207, 215, 216
Bear, George G. 544, 546, 548, 549, 551
Beck, Aaron T. 755, 763
Beck, Ulrich 636, 867, 1144
Becker, Howard S. 626, 1169
Becker, Monika 1132, 1145
Bedau, Hugo A. 1106–1108
Bell, Carl C. 719, 725, 727, 822
Bellair, Paul E. 78, 79, 88, 625
Benard, Cheryl 109, 110
Bender, Doris 612, 634
Benjamin, Walter 1027, 1029
Benney, Mark 691, 695
Benz, Wolfgang 145, 354
Berger, Ronald J. 703, 705
Bergmann, Werner 248, 256, 351, 358, 359, 374, 407
Berk, Richard A. 626, 632, 739, 746, 747
Berkowitz, Leonard 460, 461, 463, 464, 469, 471, 481, 482, 520, 525, 549

1257

Bernard, Thomas J. 69, 616, 620
Berrill, Kevin T. 332, 771, 809, 811
Bertram, Karl Friedrich 1098, 1099, 1103
Betz, Hans-Georg 403, 420, 421, 426
Betz, Joseph 991–993, 995, 996, 998–1001
Beyme, Klaus von 403, 959
Bielefeldt, Heiner 1097, 1103
Bierhoff, Hans Werner 19, 1230
Bigbee, Maureen A. 545, 560, 1126
Bilsky, Wolfgang 635, 1139, 1142
Birn, Ruth Bettina 148, 151, 163
Bittner, Egon 207, 209–215, 217, 218, 220, 1068
Bjørgo, Tore 84, 314, 403, 406, 412, 416, 424, 785, 788, 791–793, 796
Black, Donald 360, 631
Blau, Judith R. 69, 71, 72, 76, 85, 575, 621, 713
Blau, Peter M. 69, 71, 72, 76, 85, 575, 621, 713
Block, Alan A. 684–690, 692, 693, 695
Blok, Anton 682, 683, 1168
Blumer, Herbert 357, 1187, 1189
Blumstein, Alfred 657, 666, 669
Boers, Klaus 1131–1136, 1138–1145
Bograd, Michele 101, 102, 107
Bohle, Hans Hartwig 614, 615, 637
Bohman, Michael 595, 598
Bohner, Gerd 105, 107, 112
Bohnsack, Ralf 620, 1167, 1206
Bohstedt, John 362, 364
Boldizar, Janet P. 496, 497
Bollig, Michael 261, 278, 280
Bonacker, Thorsten 18, 1182, 1183, 1184
Borg, Ingwer 1223, 1224
Bortz, Jürgen 1219, 1231
Bösser, Tom 923, 924
Böttger, Andreas 878, 1117, 1119, 1120, 1124, 1125, 1203, 1204, 1206, 1208, 1212–1215
Bourdieu, Pierre 25, 249, 272, 273, 903, 933, 1144
Bowker, Lee H. 104, 113, 745
Bowlby, John 499, 820
Bowling, Benjamin 403, 422, 787, 789, 790, 795
Boyle, Michael H. 555, 556
Bradshaw, Catherine P. 719
Braithwaite, John 68, 70, 628, 634, 708, 1069
Brand, Karl-Werner 373, 1192
Brandstetter, Anna-Maria 269, 275
Brass, Paul R. 229, 254–256, 352, 354, 355, 362, 364, 452
Breitman, Richard 148, 158, 159
Brener, Nancy B. 869, 872
Breuer, Stefan 17, 52, 1061, 1068
Brezina, Timothy 616, 624
Brodeur, Jean-Paul 207, 221
Bronfenbrenner, Urie 722, 732, 868
Brooks-Gunn, Jeanne 558–560
Brosius, Hans-Bernd 414, 415, 515, 520, 523, 526, 529, 532, 1156, 1163, 1186
Broszat, Martin 143, 144, 148

Browne, Angela 725, 726, 730, 741–743, 852
Brownfield, David 71, 612, 615
Browning Christopher R. 28, 140, 145, 150, 151, 179, 180, 182, 490, 1032
Brubaker, Rogers 84, 94, 247, 248, 253, 351, 353, 363
Brückner, Margrit 104, 105
Brusten, Manfred 867, 873
Brysk, Alison 232, 233
Buchanan, James M. 685, 1099, 1193
Buchmayer, Susan 578, 580
Burch, James H. 1167, 1173
Burgess, Robert L. 613, 856
Burgess-Jackson, Keith 989, 998, 1000–1102
Burghartz, Susanna 51, 54
Burkert, Walter 1013, 1014, 1017
Bursik, Robert J. 75, 624, 1171
Burt, Jo-Marie 345, 346
Burton, Velmer S., Jr. 613, 629
Bushman, Brad J. 472, 473, 479, 482, 484–486, 488
Buss, Arnold H. 460–463, 544–546

Cadoret, Remi J. 595, 596, 599
Caillois, Roger 1016, 1017
Cain, Colleen A. 595–597, 599
Cairns, Robert B. 546, 551, 554, 555
Caldero, Michael A. 214, 222
Calic, Marie-Janine 249, 1013
Callaghan-Chaffee, Martha E. 175, 178
Campbell, Donald T. 357, 1214
Campbell, Jacquelyn C. 86, 92, 98, 99, 741, 743, 746
Cancik-Lindemaier, Hildegard 1006, 1015
Cantor, David 44, 618
Cantor, Joanne 523, 524, 531
Capeci, Jerry 679, 693
Card, Noel A. 495, 501–503
Carey, Gregory 592, 594, 595, 597, 598, 604
Carlsson, Yngve 788, 796
Carment, David 237, 242
Caspi, Avshalom 544, 634
Cassese, Antonio 192, 318, 1052
Catalano, Richard F. 628, 629, 869, 879
Catanzaro, Raimondo 682, 683
Cernkovich, Stephen A. 615, 629
Chagnon, Napoleon A. 263, 583, 584, 1185
Chambliss, William J. 684, 686, 687, 693
Charlton, Michael 520, 526
Chen, Danny J. H 704, 710
Chesnais, Jean-Claude 35, 42, 49, 55, 941
Chesney-Lind, Meda 550, 612
Chevigny, Paul 136, 217
Chin, Ko-Lin 1172, 1173, 1175
Chong Yun, Steve 1172, 1173, 1175
Cicchetti, Dante 722, 727, 820, 822
Clarke, John 914, 915, 1148
Clarke, Ronald V. 632, 764, 926
Clausewitz, Carl von 121, 171, 221
Clinard, Marshall B. 614, 615, 624

NAME INDEX

Cloninger, C. Robert 594–598, 601, 602
Cloward, Richard A. 70, 80, 622, 945, 1170, 1176
Clutton-Brock, Timothy H. 575, 584
Coady, C. A. J. 994–998, 1001
Coakley, Jay J. 910, 911
Cockburn, J. S. 43, 50
Cohen, Albert K. 461, 619, 620, 945, 1117, 1169, 1170
Cohen, Dov 474, 572, 583, 1120
Cohen, Lawrence E. 575, 583, 621, 623, 777
Cohen, Stanley 772, 1140, 1170
Coie, John D. 497, 500, 504, 506, 544, 545, 549, 550, 555–557
Coleman, James S. 387, 556
Collmer, Candace W. 851, 852
Colpe, Carsten 1008–1011, 1013, 1015, 1016, 1018
Combs, Barbara 1156, 1160, 1161
Comstock, Gary David 332, 801, 802, 809, 812
Comstock, George A. 527, 528
Comte, Auguste 122, 1063
Connor, Walker 229, 264
Cook, Philip J. 617, 658
Cook, Thomas D. 470, 1214
Cooper, Cary 886, 891
Cooper, Harris M. 472, 473, 482
Cork, Daniel 666, 669
Coser, Lewis A. 264, 359, 1182–1184
Coulton, Claudia J. 723, 724
Crank, John P. 214, 217, 222
Crelinsten, Ronald D. 189, 194, 197, 198, 200, 309, 317
Crenshaw, Martha 310–313, 317
Cressey, Donald R. 687–689, 691
Creveld, Martin van 32, 291, 298, 1059, 1060, 1065, 1071
Crick, Nicki R. 496, 506, 545–553, 555, 557, 559, 560, 1226
Crowe, Raymond R. 595–597, 599
Crutchfield, Robert D. 67, 69, 75, 78, 79
Cullen, Francis T. 613, 629, 633, 701
Curry, David 1167, 1173–1176
Curtis, Lynn A. 89, 847

Dadrian, Vahakn N. 249, 254
Dahrendorf, Ralf 271, 1183
Daly, Kathleen 601, 612, 1229
Daly, Martin 569, 573–584, 690, 711, 749–741, 744, 847, 856
Danieli, Yael 199, 201
David, Steven R. 294, 298–300, 303, 304
Davies, James C. 358, 1187
Dawidowicz, Lucy S. 144, 790
Dees, Morris 346, 406, 429, 808
DeKeseredy, Walter S. 110, 111
della Porta, Donatella 219, 312–314, 371, 372, 377, 380, 383, 384, 389, 391–395, 397,962
Denton, Nancy A. 76, 77, 80
Deschenes, Elisabeth Piper 613, 630

Devine, John 869–872, 880
Di Martino, Vittorio 885, 899
Dietz, Gerhard-Uhland 1206, 1212, 1213
Dijk, van Jan J. 709, 710, 1134
DiMatteo, Massimo R. 1231, 1235
Diner, Dan 1029, 1032
Ditton, Jason 1132, 1145
Dobash, Emerson R. 737
Dobash, Rebecca E. 99, 101, 102, 110, 574, 737–747, 847, 856
Dobash, Russell P. 99, 101, 102, 110, 574, 737–747, 839, 847, 856
Dodge, Kenneth A. 468, 496–498, 500, 502–506, 544, 545, 549, 550, 555–557, 590, 821, 822, 824
Dollard, John 460, 480, 481, 485, 907
Dollase, Rainer 1219, 1227, 1231
Donselaar, Jaap van 403, 420, 422, 423, 794
Doob, Anthony N. 90, 461, 480, 555, 1141
Doob, Leonard W. 461, 480, 907, 1182
Doorn, Jacques van 179, 181
Döring, Nicola 1219, 1231
Dower, John W. 179, 490
Dubet, François 416, 957, 942, 944, 949, 1167, 1172
Dubrow, Nancy F. 80, 822
Ducey, Charles P. 823, 837
Dülmen, Richard van 53, 54
Dunning, Eric 26, 903, 905, 908, 910–912, 914, 916, 917, 942
Durkheim, Emile 5, 49, 53, 54, 69, 75, 325, 326, 385, 637, 701, 705, 760, 763, 867, 938, 1013
Dutton, Donald G. 747, 823, 824
Dutton, Mary Ann 743, 744
Dwork, Debórah 147, 152

Eckenrode, John 722, 726
Eckert, Julia 253, 277, 282
Eckert, Roland 414, 415, 540, 619, 640, 1120, 1123, 1167, 1168, 1172, 1181, 1182, 1186–1189, 1194, 1213
Eckstein, Harry 295, 296, 372, 386
Edleson, Jeffrey L. 104, 744, 747
Egan, Susan K. 496, 501
Egeland, Byron 724, 851, 853
Eidheim, Frøydis 788, 793
Eisikovits, Zvi C. 104, 747
Eisner, Manuel 35, 41, 45, 49, 53, 55, 612, 617, 618, 640, 703, 924, 926, 930–932, 1167, 1171, 1172
Elias, Norbert 17, 26, 34, 35, 51–54, 106, 207, 210, 682, 703, 903, 906, 908, 909, 912, 914–918, 938, 942, 974, 978, 1025, 1046, 1059, 1184
Eliass, Peter 199, 201
Ellinghaus, Dieter 924, 930
Elliott, Delbert 544, 613, 625, 635
Ellison, Patricia 926, 929
Elster, Jon 576, 1192
Elwert, Georg 249, 255, 256, 261, 263, 266, 269, 270, 272, 272, 274, 280, 302, 1190

Engel, Ulf 298, 300
Engels, Friedrich 980, 1183
Enquist, Magnus 575, 578, 580, 584
Enzensberger, Hans Magnus 292, 296
Eron, Leonard D. 498, 515, 524
Erzberger, Christian 415, 1214
Esbensen, Finn-A. 613, 625, 630, 1173, 1175
Eschwege, Helmut 153, 155
Esser, Hartmut 249, 255
Etzioni, Amitai 36, 838
Euler, Harald 874, 1116, 1189
Evans, Leonard 926, 929
Evans, Peter B. 84, 94, 1057, 1059
Evans-Pritchard, Edward 263, 264

Faber, Karl-Georg 15, 16, 1043
Fagan, Jeffrey 741, 746, 747, 1172, 1175
Fajnzylber, Pablo 706, 712, 713
Falcone, Giovanni 680–682, 685, 686, 692
Fanon, Frantz 941, 948, 973, 984, 1027
Farrall, Stephen 1121, 1133, 1143
Farrington, David P. 556, 634, 879, 1171
Fattah, Ezzat A. 767, 770, 772, 774, 775, 777, 778, 780, 1132
Feder, Sid 687–689
Feinberg, Joel 993, 999
Felson, Marcus 623, 777
Felson, Richard B. 464, 465, 467, 469, 470, 474, 626, 701
Fend, Helmut 412, 865
Ferraro, Kenneth F. 1131–1133, 1137–1139, 1142
Feshbach, Norma D. 545, 550
Feshbach, Seymor 520, 907
Fetscher, Iring 313, 391
Feuchtwang, Stephan 256, 261, 272, 280
Finer, Samuel E. 1058, 1061
Finkelhor, David 107, 733, 734, 737–739, 742, 755, 852, 855, 859, 860, 869
Finnegan, Regina A. 499, 503
Fisher, Ronald A. 591, 182, 1188, 1191
Fishman, Mark 1140, 1154
Flanagan, Timothy J. 1152, 1156
Flick, Uwe 1205, 1214
Flitcraft, Anne 105, 112, 743
Forst, Brian 1066, 1067, 1069
Foster, Holly 90, 543, 549, 556, 557, 559
Foucault, Michel 33, 135, 192, 193, 200, 974
Freud, Sigmund 325, 326, 331, 360, 471, 480, 485, 571, 753, 866, 906, 909, 1013
Friedländer, Saul 140, 1012
Fromm, Erich 19, 102
Früh, Werner 512, 514, 1153
Funk, Albrecht 207, 1057, 1067
Funk, Walter 874, 876, 1068, 1070

Gabrielli, William F., Jr. 595, 596, 598, 599
Galen, Britt Rachelle 546, 547, 553, 558

Gallie, Walter Bryce 990, 995
Galtung, Johan 18, 24, 25, 106, 267, 959, 975, 1080
Gambetta, Diego 680, 684–686, 690
Gamson, William A. 377, 390, 963, 1188
Gandhi, Mohandas K. 334, 1106, 1108
Gantzel, Klaus Jürgen 292, 295
Garbarino, James 80, 556, 719, 720, 723–725, 729, 732, 822, 856–857
Garner, Joel H. 213, 216, 746
Garofalo, James 215, 216, 623, 766, 1139
Gartin, Patrick R. 623, 632
Gartner, Rosemary 574, 618, 704–708, 710–712
Garver, Newton 991, 994–997, 1001
Gastil, Raymond 68, 621
Geen, Russell G. 461–463, 482, 486, 525
Geertz, Clifford 229, 323, 1210
Gelles, Richard J. 102, 110, 175, 723, 837, 839, 840, 842, 844, 846–849, 851, 855
Gellner, Ernest 229, 230, 247, 1018
Gerbner, George 515, 526, 530, 1160
Gert, Bernard 991, 992, 994, 998
Geyer, Michael 18, 32
Ghodsian-Carpey, Jilla 600
Giddens, Anthony 30, 251, 680, 681, 694, 1059, 1060
Giesselmann, Thea 513, 531
Gil, David G. 463, 852
Gilbert, Neil 721, 728
Giller, Henri 545, 1118
Gilligan, Carol 106, 547
Gillis, A. R. 93, 626, 629
Giordano, Peggy C. 613, 615, 624
Girard, René 31, 302, 326, 332, 938, 1013, 1014, 1017, 1024
Giulianotti, Richard 912, 914, 915
Gladigow, Burkhard 1006, 1018
Glaser, Barney G. 1209, 1210
Glasl, Friedrich 1191, 1192
Gluckman, Max 262, 264, 272
Godenzi, Alberto 29, 104, 113
Godson, Roy 680, 681
Goffman, Erving 182, 373, 467, 866, 1115, 1121
Goldhagen, Daniel J. 28, 147
Goldstein, Arnold P. 869, 924, 927
Goldstein, Jeffrey H. 906, 907
Gondolf, Edward W. 104, 747
Goode, William J. 97, 578, 778
Gordon, Milton M. 1137, 1169
Gordon, Thomas P. 879, 972
Gosztonyi, Kristóf 272, 279
Gottesman, Irving I. 594–599, 602
Gottfredson, Denise C. 872, 879
Gottfredson, Michael R. 467, 576, 632, 633, 701, 776, 1174
Gove, Walter R. 75, 626
Graham, Hugh D. 369, 383, 938
Grasmick, Harold G. 75, 624, 630, 632, 1171
Green, Laura R. 546, 549, 553

NAME INDEX

Greenfeld, Lawrence A. 90, 216
Grimm, Dieter 1043, 1046, 1053, 1047
Groebel, Jo 513–516, 518, 519, 527, 1160
Gross, Larry 515, 530, 1160
Grotpeter, Jennifer K. 506, 545, 546, 548, 550, 551, 553, 555, 557, 559, 560
Groves, Byron W. 67, 75, 625, 705, 731, 732, 1168, 1171
Grumke, Thomas 406, 415, 416, 428, 429
Gruner, Wolf 146, 147, 155
Guba, Egon G. 1210–1212
Gurr, Ted R. 41, 42, 49, 55, 67, 227, 228, 231, 233, 235, 236, 238, 239, 247, 252, 254, 265, 295, 315, 356, 358, 369, 377, 383, 386, 395, 409, 938, 1187
Gutman, Yisrael 145, 154–156

Haas, Harald 179, 181
Habermas, Jürgen 24, 25, 1107
Habermeier, Johanna 1155, 1156
Haferkamp, Hans 619, 709
Hagan, John 3, 71, 88, 90, 408, 409, 544, 550, 556, 616, 620, 621, 626, 629, 630, 680, 1069, 1071
Hagemann-White, Carol 97, 99, 100, 105, 108, 110, 111, 113
Haghighi, Bahram 1153, 1157–1159
Hale, Chris 790, 1132
Hamburg, Margaret A. 871, 872, 879
Hamm, Mark S. 406, 409, 412, 413, 747, 801, 802, 1170, 1205
Hammersley, Martyn 1207, 1210, 1212
Hampton, Robert L. 723, 849
Hanagan, Michael 121
Hanetseder, Christa 104, 106
Hanewinkel, Reiner 874, 880
Hanf, Theodor 301, 303, 351, 365, 1187
Hanmer, Jalna 99, 101, 105, 112
Hannerz, Ulf 89, 437, 448
Harff, Barbara 239, 254
Hargreaves, David H. 865, 866
Harnett, Susan M. 1068, 1069
Harney, Patricia A. 101, 111
Harris, John 991, 994, 998
Harris, Mark A. 89, 617
Harris, Rosemary 912, 914, 915
Harry, Joseph 631, 776
Harten, Hans Christian 100, 105
Hartnagel, Timothy F. 575, 620, 708
Hawkins, Gordon 688, 709
Hawkins, J. David 629, 631, 634, 879
Hay, Dale 545, 549, 550, 556
Hearold, Susan 470, 528, 535
Heath, Linda 526, 1140
Heatherton, Todd F. 483, 487, 488
Hechter, Michael 229, 230, 295
Hegel, Georg Friedrich 948, 954, 1025
Heiland, Hans-Günther 617, 703, 710
Heim, Susanne 146, 148

Heimer, Karen 469, 470, 544, 550
Heitmann, Helmut 406, 413
Heitmeyer, Wilhelm 3, 35, 55, 403, 404, 409, 410, 412, 416, 417, 420, 557, 620, 634, 636–640, 786, 788, 791, 792, 966, 968, 869, 1068, 1103, 1124, 1187, 1189, 1210, 1213
Helbling, Jürg 263, 272
Held, David 1060, 1063
Helfferich, Cornelia 103, 104, 109
Helvarg, David 342, 346
Hendrix, William J. 179, 181
Hennessy, Dwight A. 926, 929
Henry, Andrew F. 762, 763
Hepworth, Joseph T. 480, 618
Herbert, Ulrich 145, 147, 149
Herder, Johann Gottfried 123, 132
Herek, Gregory M. 332, 771, 803, 809–811
Herman, Judith L. 104–106, 819
Hernandez, Jeanne T. 722, 724, 726, 727
Herrenkohl, Todd I. 555, 629
Herrnstein, Richard J. 466, 576
Hester, Marianne 101, 105
Heyer, Sonja 1210, 1211
Heynen, Susanne 104, 106
Hicks, David 462, 463, 526
Hilberg, Raul 27, 142, 152, 156, 790
Hindelang, Micheal J. 68, 71, 601, 776, 1132, 1139
Hirschi, Travis 68, 70, 71, 467, 487, 576, 613, 616, 628, 629, 632, 633, 635, 701, 1174
Hirschman, Albert O. 940, 973, 1195
Hobbes, Thomas 53, 939, 940, 1058, 1098, 1100, 1192, 1193
Hobbs, Dick 679–681, 685, 688, 690, 912, 1167
Hobsbawm, Eric 269, 399, 940, 1023
Hockenos, Paul 403, 406, 427
Hodges, Ernest V. E. 495, 499, 501, 502, 503
Hoel, Helge 886, 891
Hofer, Hanns von 43, 44, 49
Hoff, Lee Ann 102, 106, 743, 745
Hoffman, Bruce 293, 299
Hoffman, Martin L. 463, 488
Holmes, Robert L. 992, 993, 1000
Holsti, Kalevi J. 293, 299
Holtappels, Heinz Günter 865, 867, 873
Honderich, Ted 993, 994, 997, 998, 1001
Honig, Michael-Sebastian 103, 105, 1124
Hope, Tim 1144, 1145
Hopf, Christel 408, 412, 1210
Hopf, Werner 524, 1122, 1123
Hopkins Burke, Roger 1131, 1141
Horowitz, Donald 229, 230, 254, 255, 353
Hotaling, Gerald T. 175, 840, 844, 853
Hough, Michael 1132, 1140, 1142
Hovland, Carl I. 480, 618
Howard, Gregory J. 709, 711
Howe, Carl-Werner 615, 616, 623
Howlett, Jana 1025, 1029, 1034

Hrdy, Sarah B. 578–580, 856
Huang, W. S. Wilson 705, 709
Huesmann, L. Rowell 471, 498, 515, 517, 527
Huggins, Martha K. 193, 343, 346, 773
Huizinga, David 70, 613, 625, 1173, 1175
Huntington, Samuel P. 199, 328, 1018, 1063
Hurrelmann, Klaus 616, 867, 873, 875
Hutchings, Barry 595, 596, 598, 599
Huttunen, Arja 501, 873

Imbusch, Peter 13, 14, 18, 400
Inhetveen, Katharina 26, 1154
Irving, David 144, 403
Isaacs, Jenny 495, 501–503
Itzin, Catherine 105, 112

Jäckel, Eberhard 140, 141, 144, 148
Jacobs, Bruce A. 620, 693
Jacobs, David 575, 620, 693
Jacobs, James B. 693, 694, 795, 802
Jacobvitz, Deborah 724, 851
Jäger, Herbert 27, 149, 150, 151, 314
Jang, Sung J. 628, 629
Janssen, Wilhelm 292, 296
Jean, François 1062, 1064
Jefferson, Tony 214, 221, 1117
Jellinek, Georg 1046, 1048
Jenkins, E. Lynn 890, 897
Jenkins, Esther J. 719, 725, 727, 822
Jenkins, J. Craig 351, 370
Jentleson, Bruce W. 237, 243
Jervis, Robert 297, 1189
Joas, Hans 14, 32
Johnson, Eric A. 42, 44, 50, 55, 1158
Johnson, Holly 110, 111, 740, 742, 777
Jonah, Brian 926, 932
Jones, Jayme W. 101, 111
Jones, Peter G. 1028, 1033, 1035
Jones, Trevor 208, 1132
Jongman, Albert J. 192, 294, 311
Juergensmeyer, Mark 314, 326, 238, 332–334, 1012
Jünger, Ernst 982, 1033–1035
Junger, Marianne 795, 1172

Kaase, Max 13, 960, 961, 964, 968, 1152, 1154
Kakar, Sudhir 329, 354, 362
Kaldor, Mary 135, 292
Kant, Immanuel 1024, 1099–1101
Kantor, Glenda 840, 846
Kaplan, Howard B. 626–628, 630
Kaplan, Jeffrey 416, 428, 429, 792
Karstedt, Susanne 622, 626, 640, 705, 709, 929
Katz, Jack 481, 491, 681, 689, 692, 695, 1170
Kaufman, Phillip 865, 869, 870
Kaufmann, Arthur 1047, 1103, 1104
Kautsky, Karl 980, 981
Kavemann, Barbara 103, 105, 113

Keen, David 292, 302
Kelle, Udo 1209, 1210, 1214, 1215
Kelling, George 208, 1070
Kelly, Liz 101, 102, 105, 112
Kelly, Robert J. 679, 680, 776
Kelman, Herbert 196, 198, 276, 1182
Kende, Istvan 32, 291
Kepplinger, Hans Mathias 513, 531, 1151, 1154–1156, 1161–1163
Kerner, Hans-Jürgen 529, 695, 1146
Kernic, Franz 179–182
Kernis, Michael H. 484, 485
Kerr, John H. 914, 915
Kershaw, Ian 146, 157
Kersten, Joachim 105, 612, 1117
Kick, Edward L. 705, 708
Kilian, Lewis M. 1187–1189
Killias, Martin 709, 1137, 1141, 1145
King, Charles 297, 304
King, Martin Luther, Jr. 334, 448, 1103, 1106, 1107
Kippenberg, Hans G. 1010, 1012, 1018
Kirk, Jerome 1211–1213
Klandermans, Bert 371, 372, 390
Klein, Malcolm W. 612, 626, 623, 1116, 1167, 1172–1176
Klein, Paul 171
Kleiter, Ekkehard F. 521, 525
Klewin, Gabriele 863
Klier, John D. 351, 352, 354, 790
Klusemann, Hans W. 1207, 1208
Knaack, Reimer 874, 880
Köcher, Renate 1157, 1159
Koehler, Jan 273, 282, 1210, 1211
Kokko, Katja 542, 635
Kölbel, Ralf 921, 926, 928–930, 932
Konrad, A. Richard 997, 1001
Koopmans, Ruud 374, 403, 414, 424, 426, 793
Koss, Mary P. 100–102, 107, 111, 911
Kostelny, Kathleen 724, 725, 822
Kowalewski, David 339, 343, 345, 346
Krahé, Barbara 100, 112
Krahn, Harvey 575, 708
Krasner, Stephen D. 1059, 1060, 1063
Krausnick, Helmut 145, 179
Krech, Volkhard 1005
Kretschmann, Ulrike 106, 109
Krüger, Udo Michael 512–514, 516, 519
Krumm, Volker 863, 868, 877, 878, 1220
Kruttschnitt, Candace 526, 556
Kühl, Kristian 1085, 1092, 1094
Kühnel, Wolfgang 14, 403, 614, 640, 792, 1118, 1167, 1169
Kulka, Erich 154, 157
Kulka, Otto D. 154, 157
Kümmel, Gerhard 171, 172, 1007
Kunczik, Michael 527, 533, 1161, 1162
Kürti, László 403, 427

NAME INDEX

Kurtz, Lester R. 29, 333
Kury, Helmut 1132, 1138, 1139, 1156, 1158, 1162
Kushner, Tony 158, 159, 354
Kwiet, Konrad 153, 155

Labrousse, Alain 680, 691
LaFree, Gary D. 626, 703, 705, 707, 708
Lagerspetz, Kirsti 501, 545–549, 552–555, 873
LaGrange, Randy L. 628, 633, 1133, 1139
Laitin, David D. 84, 94, 229, 231, 248, 253, 351, 353, 363
Lamnek, Siegfried 524, 527, 614, 620, 625, 874, 875, 1113, 1115, 1118, 1123, 1140, 1167, 1208, 1210, 1229
Langan, Patrick A. 216, 746
Lapeyronnie, Didier 1167, 1172
Laub, John H. 534, 544, 549, 555, 556, 560, 617, 634, 635, 1171
Lauritsen, Janet L. 93, 89, 623
Lawrence, John 14, 991, 992, 994, 998
Lazarus, Richard S. 616, 1143
LeBon, Gustave 386, 1182
Lee, Rensselaer W. 680, 691
Lee, Steven 995, 1001
Leimar, Olof 575, 584
Lemarchand, René 249, 254, 256
Lenin, Wladimir Ilitsch 134, 980, 981
Lester, David 753, 754, 758–760, 762–764
Leventhal, Tama 558–560
Levin, Jack 414, 428, 792, 795, 801, 804, 806–808, 811, 812
Levinson, David 741, 818, 850
Lévi-Strauss, Claude 272, 360
Lewy, Guenter 141, 160, 331, 333
Licklider, Roy 296, 297, 304
Lifton, Robert J. 194, 315, 330
Linneweber, Volker 468, 923, 933
Lipman, Ellen L. 555, 556
Liska, Allen E. 79, 88, 630, 631, 640
Little, Todd 544, 546, 548, 550, 551
Littleton, C. Scott 329, 671
Liu, Xiaoru 628, 630
Lizotte, Alan J. 613, 621
Llanque, Marcus 973, 982
Lloyd, Cathie 787, 794
Locke, John 1058, 1099, 1103
Loeber, Rolf 463, 544, 545, 549, 555, 556, 634
Loftin, Colin 72, 621
Longerich, Peter 139, 147, 148, 151, 248, 399, 634
Lööw, Heléne 406, 412, 414
Lorenz, Konrad 262, 905–909, 918, 1013
Loseke, Donileen R. 102, 105
Lösel, Friedrich 527, 529, 612, 623, 874, 1171, 1174
Luedtke, Jens 874, 875
Luhmann, Niklas 24, 25, 273, 281, 283, 285, 973, 974, 1044, 1047, 1049, 1050, 1058, 1068, 1070, 1193, 1212
Lukács, Georg 981, 982

Lukesch, Helmut 412, 511, 514, 517, 520, 524–526, 530, 531, 535, 613
Lustiger, Arno 153, 154
Luther, Martin 334, 448, 977–979, 1098
Lyman, Stanford M. 250, 1122
Lyons-Ruth, Karlen 499, 500, 820

Maas, Peter 687, 692, 693
MacCallum, Gerald C., Jr. 991, 992, 994, 996
Machalek, Richard 575, 583
Machiavelli, Niccolò 976, 978, 979
MacKinnon, Catherine A. 101, 472
MacKinnon-Lewis, Carol 498, 500
MacMillan, Ross 556, 560
MacNamara, Donal E. J. 769, 776
Majone, Giandomenico 1060, 1068
Makepeace, James M. 840, 844
Males, Mike A. 589, 590, 601
Malkki, Liisa H. 249, 250, 255
Manning, Peter K. 215, 1067, 1068, 1070, 1071, 1073
Mansel, Jürgen 616, 875, 1225, 1229
Marrus, Michael 145, 153, 155
Marsh, Peter 914, 915
Martinez, Ramiero, Jr. 71, 72
Marty, Martin E. 330, 965, 966
Marx, Gary 221, 353, 356, 357, 360, 371
Marx, Karl 5, 68, 123, 283, 325, 331, 979–981
Massey, Douglas S. 76, 77, 80, 87–89, 93
Massey, James L. 618, 628
Matsueda, Ross L. 613, 620, 627, 629
Matt, Eduard 630, 1121, 1123
Matthies, Volker 18, 300, 303
Matza, David 527, 628, 777–779, 1115, 1118–1122, 1124, 1125
Maxfield, Michael G. 1132, 113, 1137, 1139–1142
Maxim, Paul S. 618, 632
Maxwell, Christopher D. 216, 746
McAdam, Doug 372–374, 389, 409, 440, 1169, 1187
McCall, Patricia L. 617, 621
McCarthy, Bill 550, 620
McCarthy, John D. 371, 372, 393, 1169, 1187
McCord, Joan 463, 502, 544, 590
McDevitt, Jack 786, 792, 795, 801, 804, 806–808, 811, 812
McFarlane, Alexander C. 823, 827
McKay, Henry D. 70, 75, 938, 943, 1141, 1167, 1168, 1170, 1172
McPhail, Clark 353, 362–364
McPherson, J. Miller 553, 554
Mead, George H. 196, 866
Mednick, Sarnoff A. 594–596, 598, 599, 602
Mehler, Andreas 298, 300
Menaghan, Elizabeth G. 543, 560
Menard, Scott 613, 618
Mengham, Rod 1025, 1034, 1035
Menninger, Karl 753, 754
Mentzel, Thomas 412, 414

Merkens, Hans 408, 1207
Merkl, Peter H. 314, 412, 424
Merten, Roland 788, 874
Merton, Robert K. 70, 72, 76, 220, 543, 614–616, 622, 867, 940, 945, 1125, 1189
Messerschmidt, James W. 612, 1116
Messner, Michael 910, 911
Messner, Steven F. 69, 71, 72, 86, 88, 615, 621, 625, 631, 701, 704–708, 710, 713, 1171
Meuli, Karl 1013, 1014
Meyer, Thomas 957, 965, 1105
Milgram, Stanley 180, 181, 196, 467, 1125, 1229
Minkenberg, Michael 374, 403, 409, 429
Miracle, Andrew W. 907, 908, 911
Mirowsky, John 558, 634
Mirrlees-Black, Catriona 111, 740, 794, 1134, 1135, 1138, 1142
Moffitt, Terrie E. 504, 505, 507, 601, 634, 741
Moldea, Dan E. 685, 686
Möller, Kurt 409, 412, 413, 1124, 1213
Mommsen, Hans 144, 148, 1099, 1100
Monahan, John 184, 583
Monjardet, Dominique 207, 210, 211, 221
Monkkonen, Eric H. 42–44, 55, 1067, 1070
Moore, Barrington 31, 332, 333, 940, 1187
Moore, Will H. 235, 236
Morenoff, Jeffrey D. 83, 89, 625
Morita, Yohji 868, 872
Morlok, Martin 926, 929, 932
Muchembled, Robert 42, 43, 53, 54
Muehlenhard, Charlene L. 100, 101, 111
Mühlmann, Wilhelm E. 263, 265
Mullender, Audrey 745, 746
Muller, Edward N. 968, 1186
Müller, Joachim 412, 619, 639, 791, 966, 1028, 1117
Mummendey, Amélie 468, 626, 1185, 1189, 1221, 1228
Münkler, Herfried 265, 292, 973, 974, 984
Murphy, Patrick 914, 916, 917
Murray, Charles 67, 76, 77, 79, 70
Mustain, Gene 679, 693

Nagin, Daniel S. 505, 551, 556, 631–633, 672
Narr, Wolf-Dieter 14, 30, 1060, 1061
Naucke, Wolfgang 1070, 1071
Neapolitan, Jerome L. 703–705, 709, 711
Nedelmann, Birgitta 22, 614, 1210, 1233
Neff, James 685, 686
Neidhardt, Friedhelm 13, 15, 23, 34, 369, 374, 376, 392, 410, 415, 974, 975, 1104, 1108, 1113, 1152, 1154, 1167, 1169, 1183, 1187, 1188, 1191
Neubert, Dieter 255, 256, 261, 269, 272, 275, 280
Neuman, W. Lawrence 703, 705
Newberger, Eli H. 849, 852
Newman, Graeme R. 705, 709, 711, 1065
Newton, Phyllis J. 632, 746
Nieraad, Jürgen 1023, 1025
Nisbett, Richard E. 474, 572, 583

Nitz, Kathrine 594, 600
North, Douglass C. 1057, 1072
Novaco, Raymond W. 924–927
Nozick, Robert 993, 1072

Ofer, Dalia 152, 156
Ohbuchi, Ken-ichi 466, 467
Ohlemacher, Thomas 970, 1163
Ohlin, Lloyd E. 70, 80, 622, 945, 1170, 1176
Ohmae, Kenichi 1060, 1063
Olk, Thomas 634, 867
Olson William J. 680, 681, 1182, 1187, 1192, 1196
Olweus, Dan 467, 501, 504, 507, 872, 873, 877, 879, 880
Olzak, Susan 353, 358
Opp, Karl-Dieter 612, 1186
Ortmann, Rüdiger 616, 637
Ortner, Helmut 1131, 1141
Ortoleva, Giuseppe 389, 392
Orywal, Erwin 261, 269, 271, 280
Osgood, D. Wayne 613, 623, 625
Osofsky, Joy D. 719, 725, 730, 731, 848
Österberg, Eva 42, 43, 45, 49, 52
Österman, Karin 872, 873
Oswald, Hans 827, 878
Otto, Hans-Uwe 788, 874
Owens, Laurence 545, 547, 560

Pagelow, Mildred 108, 745, 839, 856
Pahl, Jon 323, 332
Pampel, Fred C. 618, 708
Paoli, Pascal 890, 891, 898
Papatola, Kathleen 851, 724
Paquette, Julie A. 546, 560
Parke, Ross D. 549, 851, 852
Pate, Anthony M. 549, 851, 852
Paternoster, Raymond 616, 626, 631–633, 1171
Patterson, Gerald R. 496–498, 500, 501, 503, 506
Paymar, Michael 742, 747
Pearson, John 681, 685, 692, 694
Pence, Ellen 742, 747
Pepler, Debra J. 544, 547, 557
Perrineau, Pascal 403, 419
Perry Louise C. 496, 497, 500–503
Perry, Barbara 403, 404, 409, 412, 414, 424, 427, 428
Perry, Bruce D. 819, 822
Perry, David G. 496, 497, 500–503
Peter, Jörg Ingo 620, 917
Peters, Edward 192–194, 197, 201, 331
Peterson, Ruth D. 67, 75, 78–90, 617
Pfahl-Traughber, Armin 403, 958, 968
Pfeiffer, Christian 112, 612, 613, 622, 1119, 1140
Pileggi, Nicholas 689, 690, 692
Pillemer, Karl 848, 853
Pitsch, A. 227
Plomin, Robert 591, 592, 594, 600, 601
Pohl, Dieter 146, 151

NAME INDEX

Polk, Kenneth 574, 741
Popitz, Heinrich 17, 20, 23, 25, 100, 248, 932
Popp, Ulrike 878, 1113
Popper, Karl R. 1204, 1211
Posen, Barry R. 232, 255
Potter, Gary W. 686, 688
Potter, Kimberly 795, 802
Poulin, Francois 502, 545
Powell, G. Bingham 961, 964
Powers, Jane L. 722, 723
Poznanski, Renée 153, 155
Pruitt, Dean G. 1181, 1182, 1189, 1194
Ptacek, James 742, 746, 747
Pulkkinen, Lea 544, 635
Putnam, Frank, W. 819, 822, 823, 827
Pye, Lucian W. 199, 959

Quanty, Michael B. 461, 486
Quigley, Brain M. 1220, 1222, 1227

Radbruch, Gustav 100, 1104
Raines, Adrian, J. 820, 824
Rajalin, Sirpa 923, 926, 929, 932
Rammstedt, Othein 1113, 1191
Ramsey, Elizabeth 501, 871
Rankin, Joseph. H. 623, 626
Rapoport, Anatol 1186, 1191
Rauchfleisch, Udo 14, 30
Rausch, Thomas 1205, 1207, 1214
Rawlings, Edna 520, 525
Rawls, John 993, 996, 1106–1108
Ray, Glen E. 502, 553
Reemtsma, Katrin 427, 791
Reichenbach, Peter 1079
Reinares, Fernando 299, 309–314, 317, 318
Reiner, Robert 211, 215, 218
Reinhard, Wolfgang 1058, 1060, 1062
Reis, Christa 1167, 1213
Reiss, Albert J., Jr. 702, 775
Reiter, Herbert 219, 380, 397
Rejali, Darius M. 193, 199, 200
Remschmidt, Helmut 519, 520, 534
Renan, Ernest 975, 976
Renzetti, Claire M. 110, 849
Retzinger, Suzanne M. 484, 628
Reuband, Karl-Heinz 1135, 1140
Reuter, Peter 679, 685–688, 692, 693
Rieseberg, Angela 523, 525
Riger, Stephanie 1137, 1143
Rind, Michael M. 1006–1008
Risman, Barbara J. 549, 552, 553
Robey, Ames 853, 854
Robinson, Richard 998, 1000, 1001
Rodley, Nigel S. 189–192, 194, 195
Roeder, Philip G. 229, 230, 238
Rogger, Hans 351, 354
Rose, Amanda J. 547, 557, 559, 560

Rösel, Jakob 255, 256, 353, 354, 358, 363
Rosenbaum, H. Jon 339, 346
Rosenfeld, Richard 83, 88, 615, 704, 707, 713, 1171
Rosenthal, Robert 1231, 1235
Rosenwald, Richard 853, 854
Ross, Catherine E. 558, 625, 634
Rothe, J. Peter 929, 932
Rothengatter, Talib 930, 933
Rousseau, Jean-Jacques 123, 940
Rousseaux, Xavier 42, 43, 45, 49, 53
Rowe, David C. 511, 594, 595, 600, 601
Ruback, R. Barry 701, 711, 712, 927
Rubin, Jeffrey Z. 1181, 1182, 1189, 1192, 1194
Rucht, Dieter 369–371, 373–375, 379, 384, 1169, 1187, 1191
Rueschemeyer, Dietrich 1057, 1059
Rufin, Jean-Christophe 302, 1062–1064
Ruggiero, Vincenzo 679, 682, 694
Rule, James R. 363, 372, 395
Runtz, Marsha 818, 823
Russell, Diana E. 741, 847
Rutter, Michael 543, 545, 549, 553, 555, 556, 591, 694, 722, 726, 865, 1118
Rys, Gail S. 544, 546, 548, 459, 551, 560

Sabo, Don 910, 911
Sacco, Vincent F. 111, 742, 760, 777
Sack, Fritz 625, 626, 1067, 1069, 1191
Saft, Elizabeth W. 723–726, 728, 729
Salmivalli, Christina 501, 502, 873
Saltzman, Linda E. 631, 740, 840, 846
Sampson, Robert J. 67, 75, 77, 88–90, 543, 544, 549, 555, 556, 560, 617, 621, 623, 625, 634, 635, 710, 1168, 1171–1173
Sánchez-Jankowski 1168, 1172, 1174, 1175
Saunders, Daniel G. 742, 747, 847
Schachter, Oscar 1061, 1062, 1073
Schäfer, Mechthild 1222, 1228
Scharpf, Fritz 1060, 1068, 1072
Scheidle, Günter 1100–1102, 1104
Schelling, Thomas C. 685, 1182, 1186, 1196
Scherrer, Christian P. 247, 297
Schetter, Conrad 247, 250, 255
Scheuerman, William 1066, 1070, 1073
Scheungrab, Michael 511, 517, 526, 527
Schilling, Heinz 250, 1011
Schlag, Bernhard 929, 934
Schlee, Günther 261, 264, 270, 281
Schmid, Alex P. 191, 192, 197, 199, 200, 309, 311, 317
Schneider, Barry H. 545, 546, 548, 551, 560
Schneider, Hans Joachim 207, 524
Schönhammer, Rainer 929, 932
Schorsch, Eberhard 102, 105, 113
Schröder, Helmut 639, 966
Schröttle, Monika 104, 106
Schubarth, Wilfried 874, 879, 880

Schulz, Gerhard 292, 296
Schüssler, Martin 43, 45, 49, 50
Schuster, Peter 44, 51, 53, 54
Schütze, Fritz 1205, 1208
Schwandner-Sievers, Stephanie 263, 273, 1213
Schwartz, Martin D. 110, 740
Schwarzenegger, Christian 1139, 1142
Schwenk, Otto 620, 1115, 1123, 1167
Schwind, Hans-Dieter 380, 874, 1080, 1220, 1221, 1224, 1232
Scott, James C. 220, 441, 442
Sears, Robert R. 480, 618, 907
Sederberg, Peter 339, 346
Sedighdeilami, Farrokh 544, 547, 557
Segev, Tom 161, 181
Seifert, Ruth 175, 182, 249
Selg, Herbert 512, 520, 527
Sells, Michael A. 328, 329, 1013
Senghaas, Dieter 19, 250, 1194
Sessar, Klaus 1140, 1141
Shainess, Natalie 853, 854
Sharpe, James A. 42, 43, 49, 50, 52
Shaw, Clifford R. 70, 75, 1141, 1167, 1168, 1170, 1172, 1176
Shaw, Donald L 70, 75, 1161
Sheard, Kenneth 905, 910, 911
Shearing, Clifford 1067, 1068, 1072
Shelley, Louise I. 703, 710
Sherman, Lawrence W. 623, 626, 631, 746
Short, James F., Jr. 83, 85, 92, 612, 619, 625, 702, 762, 763, 1118, 1167, 1172–1174
Sickmund, Melissa 719–725, 730
Sigvardsson, Soeren 595, 602
Silkenbeumer, Mirja 1125, 1206
Silverman, Robert A. 623, 633, 722
Simmel, Georg 296, 982, 1182–1184
Sinclair, Alison 1029, 1035
Singh, Lisa S. 580, 581
Skinner, Katherine M. 174, 175
Skogan, Wesley G. 1068, 1069, 1132, 1137, 1139–1142, 1145
Slovic, Paul 1156, 1160
Smaus, Gerlinda 1114, 1121–1123, 1140
Smelser, Neil J. 355, 356, 360, 385, 386, 1187
Snell, John 853, 854
Snow, David A. 373, 390
Snyder, Howard N. 719–723, 725, 730
Snyder, Jack 242, 243, 252
Soeffner, Hans-Georg 36, 41, 1208
Solomon, Richard L. 490, 1062
Somberg, Daniel R. 468, 821, 822
Sorel, Georges 973, 983, 984, 1026, 1027, 1033, 1035
Sorensen, Jon 1153, 1157–1159
Spergel, Irving 1173, 1175, 1176
Spierenburg, Pieter 42–45, 49–52, 55
Spitzer, Steven 69, 768
Sprinzak, Ehud 312, 313, 330, 409, 415, 786, 792

Stafford, Mark C. 613, 623
Staley, Sam 67, 75, 76
Stanko, Elisabeth 101, 1137
Steffensmeier, Darrell J. 72, 78, 618, 622
Steinbach, Peter 1100, 1102
Steiner, George 140, 1030
Steinmetz, Suzanne K. 102, 840, 842, 846–849, 851, 853, 855
Stiels-Glenn, Michael 1119, 1121
Stillwell, Arlene M. 483, 488
Stohl, Michael 310, 311, 314
Stokes, Randall 1123, 1124
Stone, Lawrence 43, 44, 51, 53
Stöss, Richard 402, 409
Strange, Susan 1059, 1065, 1068
Straus, Murray A. 102, 107, 110, 175, 471, 739, 744, 839, 840, 842, 846–849, 851, 852, 855
Strauss, Anselm L. 1209, 1210
Streeck-Fischer, Annette 817, 821–823, 827
Strobl, Rainer 1124, 1203, 1212, 1214, 1215
Sugarman, David B. 844, 853
Summala, Heikki 923, 929
Sutherland, Edwin H. 70, 76, 612, 613, 1118
Sutker, Patricia B. 179, 184
Swan, L. Alex 352, 353, 357
Sykes, Gresham M. 527, 628, 690, 777–779, 1115, 1118–1122, 1124, 1125

Tambiah, Stanley 255, 256, 329, 330
Tang, Catherine S. 721, 730
Tangney, June P. 483, 488, 489
Tarrow, Sidney 312, 372, 374, 384, 388, 389, 409, 437, 440, 962, 1169, 1187
Taylor, Ian 904, 914, 915, 1140
Taylor, Stuart P. 472, 473
Tedeschi, James T. 459, 461, 464, 465, 467–470, 474, 613, 701, 1220, 1222, 1227
Teeple, Gary 704, 713
Teicher, Martin H. 822, 827
Temrin, Hans 578, 579
Tertilt, Herrmann 620, 1167
Thoennes, Nancy 110, 740, 840, 846
Thomas von Aquin 332, 1011, 1098
Thome, Helmut 53–55, 618, 640
Thompson, Tony 691, 692
Thomson, Janice E. 1057, 1061
Thoreau, Henry David 1105–1107
Thornberry, Terence P. 613, 628, 727, 1167, 1173, 1175
Thrasher, Frederic M. 92, 938, 946, 1205, 1209
Tillmann, Klaus-Jürgen 863, 865, 867, 874–876, 878, 879
Tilly, Charles 30, 31, 52, 121, 373, 383, 385, 388, 409, 437, 440, 442, 451, 1057–1059, 1187
Tishkov, Valery 231, 265, 281, 283
Tittle, Charles R. 68, 70, 73, 83, 615, 630, 633, 634
Tjaden, Patricia 110, 840, 846
Tobler, Hans Werner 32, 399

NAME INDEX

Toch, Hans H. 466, 468, 490, 742
Tolman, Richard M. 742, 744, 747
Tomada, Giovanna 545, 546, 548, 551, 560
Tonry, Michael H. 85, 91, 92, 94, 1071
Toprak, Ahmed 1117, 1120
Tornay, Serge 274, 281
Tremblay, Richard E. 505, 544, 545, 547, 549, 551, 555–557, 559
Trickett, Penelope K. 822, 823
Trotha, Trutz von 20, 248, 280, 354, 1058, 1061, 1062, 1113, 1167, 1185, 1210, 1211, 1233
Truscott, Susan 175, 176, 178
Tuchel, Johannes 1100, 1102
Turkus, Burton B. 687–689
Turner, Ralph H. 1160, 1187–1189

Uggen, Christopher 79, 80, 629
Ulbrich-Herrmann, Matthias 1219
Underwood, Marion K. 546, 547, 553, 558, 560

Van de Vate, Dwight, Jr. 991, 992, 997
van den Berghe, Pierre 229, 254
van der Kolk, Bessel A. 201, 817, 819, 820, 822, 823, 827
Van der Veer, Peter 351, 361, 1012
van Kampen, Norbert 626, 628
Vanberg, Victor 630, 1193
Vandello, Joe 11, 1117, 1120
Verba, Sidney 958, 959, 962, 963
Vigil, James D. 1172, 1173, 1175
Virdee, Satnam 790, 794
Virtanen, Timo 420, 421, 423
von Beyme, Klaus 403, 959

Wade, Francis C. 991, 994
Wadsworth, Tim 67, 78
Wagner, Bernd 406, 967
Wait, Tracey 175, 176, 178
Waldmann, Peter 24, 30–32, 249, 253, 255, 257, 270, 274, 275, 293–296, 299–305, 311, 313, 314, 351, 392, 399, 1105, 1190
Walker, Charles C. 1106, 1108
Walker, Samantha 546, 548, 549
Walker, Samuel 1066, 1067, 1069, 1070, 1073
Walklate, Sandra 612, 1145
Walter, Barbara F. 242, 243, 296, 297, 300, 304, 305
Walters, Richard H. 461, 463, 526
Wang, Lu-In 802, 812, 813
Warr, Mark 613, 623, 635, 1133, 1137, 1138, 1144, 1157, 1158
Warshow, Robert 679, 1027
Wasileski, Maryann 175, 178
Weber, Max 5, 17, 18, 31, 52, 53, 207, 209, 212, 213, 220, 248, 274, 285, 299, 325, 326, 331, 957, 974, 976, 978, 981, 982, 1044, 1045, 1055, 1057–1059, 1061, 1071, 1072, 1085, 1114
Weidner, Jens 1119, 1122

Weimann, Gabriel 532, 1156
Weinberg, Leonard 311, 313, 403, 406, 416, 428, 429, 792
Weingart, Gail 863
Weis, Joseph G. 68, 71, 840
Weis, Kurt 529, 774
Weiß, Rudolf H. 517, 524, 525, 529, 531
Weiss, Susanne 863, 878
Wells, L. Edward 623, 626, 628
Werner, Nicole E. 506, 560
Wertheimer, Jürgen 1025, 1035
Wessinger, Catherine 328, 332
Westley, William 215, 217
Wetzels, Peter 112, 412, 818, 1132, 1133, 1138, 1139
Wetzstein, Thomas A. 26, 1167, 1213
White, Helene R. 616, 628
White, Robert W. 314, 386, 391, 392
Whitlock, Francis A. 925, 927, 928
Widom, Cathy S. 463, 727, 840, 851
Wiesenthal, David L. 926, 929
Wieviorka, Michel 219, 312, 392, 406, 410, 416, 426, 863, 868, 946, 948
Wilde, Gerald J.S. 926, 933
Wilkinson, Paul 311, 312, 317, 383, 386
Willems, Helmut 362, 409, 412–416, 420, 619, 640, 788, 791, 792, 1113, 1116, 1119, 1120, 1168, 1181, 1182, 1187–1189, 1191, 1194, 1207, 1213
Williams, Christopher 773, 1230
Williams, George C. 573, 583
Williams, John 913, 914, 916, 917
Williams, Kirk 69, 71–74, 631, 852
Williamson, Jennifer 428, 786, 801
Willke, Helmut 1068, 1072
Willms, J. Douglas 545, 559
Willoweit, Dietmar 1046, 1101
Wilson, Barbara J. 514, 515
Wilson, James Q. 208, 466, 1069, 1141, 1145
Wilson, Margo 569, 573–584, 680, 739–741, 744, 747, 847, 848, 856
Wilson, Melvin N. 726–730
Wilson, Susan K. 110, 848
Wilson, William J. 67, 69, 71, 74–78, 80, 86–89, 558, 580, 617, 1173
Wimmer, Andreas 247, 248, 250, 253, 266, 354
Winslow, Donna 179, 181, 182
Winterhoff-Spurk, Peter 529, 530
Wiseman, Karen A. 580, 581
Witte, Rob 421, 424, 787, 789
Wolfe, David A. 110, 747, 821, 848
Wolfe, Jessica 174, 175
Wolff, Robert Paul 996–998
Wolfgang, Marvin E. 612, 620, 690, 760, 1124, 1169, 1170
Wolzendorff, Kurt 1098, 1099
Wright, Jack C. 502, 582

Yablonski, Lewis 1167, 1169

Ylikangas, Heikki 43, 45
Yllo, Kersti 742, 844, 847, 856
Young, Frank 264, 267

Zald, Mayer N. 372, 387, 393, 1169, 1187
Zartman, William 237, 304, 305
Zeichner, Amos 473, 583

Zelle, Carsten 1024, 1025
Zillmann, Dolf 464, 469, 472, 1157
Zimbardo, Philip 180, 198
Zimmermann, Ekkart 31, 295, 872, 1187
Zitelmann, Thomas 277, 281
Zürn, Michael 1060, 1064–1066, 1068
Zwerman, Gilda 391, 395

PART VI

The Authors

I. THE FRAMEWORK OF THE HANDBOOK

1. Violence: The Difficulties of a Systematic International Review

Wilhelm Heitmeyer (Dr. Phil.) is Professor of Socialization and Director of the Institute for Interdisciplinary Research on Conflict and Violence at Bielefeld University. His research interests concentrate on violence, right-wing extremism, and ethnic-cultural conflicts. His publications include *Rechtsextremistische Orientierungen bei Jugendlichen* [Right-Wing Extremism Among Young People] (1987); *Gewalt* [Violence] (with colleagues) (1995); *Bedrohte Stadtgesellschaften* [Urban Societies Under Threat] (co-edited with Reimund Anhut) (2000).

John Hagan is John D. MacArthur Professor of Sociology and Law (Northwestern University) and Senior Research Fellow (American Bar Foundation). His principal research and teaching interests encompass crime, law and the life course. His books: *Mean Streets: Youth Crime and Homelessness* (with Bill McCarthy) (1997); Northern Passage: American Vietnam War Resisters in Canada (2001); Youth Violence and the End of Adolescence (with Holly Foster, American Sociological Review) (2001).

2. The Concept of Violence

Peter Imbusch (Dr. phil.) is *Privatdozent* at the Institute of Sociology at Philipps University in Marburg and Research Associate at the Institute for Interdisciplinary Research on Conflict and Violence at Bielefeld University. His principal teaching and research areas are in political sociology, sociological theory, conflict and violence, and social structures. Recent books: *Macht und Herrschaft* [Power and Rule] (ed.) (1998); *Friedens- und Konfliktforschung* [Peace and Conflict Studies] (co-edited with Ralf Zoll) (1999); *Zivilisation und Gewalt* [Civilization and Violence] (2002).

3. **The Long-term Development of Violence: Empirical Findings and Theoretical Approaches to Interpretation**

Manuel Eisner (Dr. phil.) is Reader in Sociological Criminology and deputy director of the Institute of Criminology at the University of Cambridge. His work focuses on the fields of social transformation and criminality, research into youth delinquency, environmental sociology, and cultural sociology. Recent publications include *Das Ende der zivilisierten Stadt? Die Auswirkungen von Individualisierung und urbaner Krise auf Gewaltdelinquenz* [The End of the Civilized City? The Effects of Individualization and Urban Crisis on Violent Delinquency] (1997); *Violent Crime in the Urban Community: A Comparison of Stockholm and Basel* (with Per-Olof Wikström, European Journal of Criminal Policy and Research, 1999); *Modernization, Self-Control and Lethal Violence—The Long-Term Dynamics of European Homicide Rates in Theoretical Perspective* (British Journal of Criminology, 2001).

II. RESEARCH ON VIOLENCE: AN INTERDISCIPLINARY APPROACH WITH A FOCUS ON SOCIAL SCIENCES

1. Societal Structures and Institutions: Social Conditions and State Agents

1.1 Social Structures and Inequalities

1.1.1 Poverty and Violence

Robert D. Crutchfield (Ph.D., Vanderbilt University) is Professor of Sociology and Department Chair at the University of Washington in Seattle. He is a past Vice-president of the American Society of Criminology and is currently on the Council of the American Sociological Association's Crime, Law and Deviance Section. His publications include *Labor Stratification and Violent Crime* (Social Forces, 1989) and *Ethnicity, Labor Markets and Crime* (1995). He co-authored many articles, e.g., *Racial and Ethnic Disparities in Imprisonment* (Government Report, 1986); *Work and Crime: The Effects of Labor Stratification* (Social Forces, 1997); *A Tale of Three Cities: Labor Markets and Homicide* (Sociological Focus, 1999).

Tim Wadsworth (M.A., University of Washington) is a Ph.D. Candidate in the Sociology Department at the University of Washington and a National Institute of Justice Dissertation Fellow. His current work focuses on the relationship between work and criminal behavior at both the individual and community levels. He published *Labor Markets, Delinquency and Social Control Theory: An Empirical Assessment of the Mediating Process* (2000) in Social Forces, as well as several public policy reports addressing issues of juvenile justice in Washington State.

1.1.2 Ethnic Segregation and Violence

James F. Short Jr. is Professor Emeritus of Sociology and Senior Research Associate of the Social and Economic Sciences Research Center at Washington State University. He was Director of Research (with Marvin Wolfgang) of the National Commission on the

Causes and Prevention of Violence (1968-1969), a member of the National Academy of Science, National Research Council Committee on Law and Justice, and that committee's Panel on the Understanding and Control of Violent Behavior. He served as editor of the American Sociological Review and as President of the American Sociological Association, the Pacific Sociological Society, and the American Society of Criminology. His latest book is *Poverty, Ethnicity, and Violent Crime* (1997).

1.1.3 A Comparative Examination of Gender-Perspectives on Violence

Carol Hagemann-White (Dr. phil.) is professor of educational theory and feminist studies at the University of Osnabrück. Her focal research areas are gender-based violence: intervention, prevention, and social change; women and health; socialization and the construction of gender; women, power and the politics of equality. Besides empirical research she is involved in building European research networks in these areas. Important publications are: *Socialization: feminine-masculine?* (1984); *Strategies against Violence in Gender Relations* (1992), *Male Violence and Control: Building a Comparative European Perspective* (in: Duncan and Pfau-Effinger: Gender, Economy and Culture in the EU, 2000); and *Comprehensive Report on the Health of Women in Germany* (with other authors) (2001).

1.2 Violence in and by State Institutions

1.2.1 Violence and the Rise of the State

Michael Hanagan (Ph.D., University of Michigan) is Senior Lecturer at the New School University in New York City. He is currently collaborating on a world history textbook and on a comparative study of the welfare state in England, France, and the United States. His publications include two books on labor history and numerous articles on world history, globalization, and violent social movements. He has co-edited several books, most recently *Expanding Rights, Reconfiguring States* (1999) with Charles Tilly and *Challenging Authority: The Historical Study of Contentious Politics* (1998) with Leslie Moch and Wayne Te Brake. He is a senior editor of *International Labor and Working-Class History*.

1.2.2 Holocaust

Peter Longerich (Dr. phil.) is a professor at Royal Holloway College, University of London. His main research interest are the Weimar Republic, National Socialism and Holocaust. Selected publications: *Politik der Vernichtung. Eine Gesamtdarstellung der nationalsozialistischen Judenverfolgung* [Policies of Extermination: An Overall Description of National Socialist Persecution of the Jews] (1998); *Der ungeschriebene Befehl. Hitler und der Weg zur "Endlösung"* [The Unwritten Order: Hitler and the Road to the "Final Solution"] (2001);. He co-edited the German edition of *Enzyklopädie des Holocaust* [Encyclopedia of the Holocaust] (3 volumes) with Eberhard Jäckel and Julius Schoeps.

1.2.3 Violence Within the Military

Gerhard Kümmel (Dr. phil.) is Research Associate at the German Armed Forces Institute for Social Research (SOWI). His current research projects include violent behavior of the youth and integration of women in the Bundeswehr. He has published books and articles on issues of international relations, European integration and security policy. One of the most important publications is *Transnationale Wirtschaftskooperation und der Nationalstaat. Deutsch-amerikanische Unternehmensbeziehungen in den 30er Jahren* [Trans-national Economic Cooperation and the Nation-State. German-American Corporate Relations in the 1930s.] (1996), *Zwischen Differenz und Gleichheit. Die Öffnung der Bundeswehr für Frauen* [Between Difference and Equality—The Opening of the Bundeswehr for Women] (2000, co-authored), *Warum nicht?—Die ambivalente Sicht männlicher Soldaten auf die weitere Öffnung der Bundeswehr für Frauen* [Why not?— The Ambivalent Attitudes of Male Soldiers toward the Integration of Women into the Bundeswehr] (2001, co-authored) He co-edited *European Security* (1997), *Military Sociology* (2000) and edited *The Challenging Continuity of Change and the Military* (2001).

Paul Klein (Dr. rer. soc.) is Acting Scientific Director at the German Armed Forces Institute for Social Research (SOWI) and Lecturer at the Bundeswehr University in Munich. His current research topics include military multinationalism and the force structure of the Bundeswehr. He has published numerous books and articles on military-sociological topics. His books include *Militär und Gesellschaft* [Armed Forces and Society] (co-edited with Ekkehard Lippert) (1979); *Deutsch-französische Verteidigungskooperation—Das Beispiel der Deutsch-Französischen Brigade* [German-French Defense-Cooperation—The Example of the German-French Brigade] (1990); *Mitbestimmung in den Streitkräften* [Co-Determination within the Armed Forces] (1991). He co-edited *Eine einzigartige Zusammenarbeit—Das Deutsch-Niederländische Korps* [A Unique Cooperation—The German-Dutch Corps] (1996).

1.2.4 Violence in Prisons/Torture

Ronald D. Crelinsten is Professor of Criminology at the University of Ottawa. His research interests include the media, policy-making and human rights, the relationship between insurgent and state violence, and problems of security and global governance in the post-Cold War era. He is editing a volume, with Iffet Özkut, on the consequences of torture for perpetrators, victims, and society-at-large.

1.2.5 Violence and the Police

Jean-Paul Brodeur (Ph.D., University of Paris) is a professeur titulaire at the Centre International de Criminologie Comparée (CICC) of the Université de Montréal. He was director of the CICC for eight years and the director of research of the Canadian Sentencing Commission. He is now the French editor of the Canadian Journal of Criminology and member of The Royal Society of Canada. He is the author of several books and articles on the various state coercive organizations. His three latest books are *Violence and Racial Prejudice in the Context of Peacekeeping* (1997), *How to Recognize Good Policing* (1998) and *Democracy, Law and Security: International Security Systems in Contemporary Europe (2002)* (Ed. together with Peter Gill and Dennis Töllborg).

2. Groups and Collectivities: Political and Ideological Violence

2.1 Ethnopolitical Conflict and Separatist Violence

Ted Robert Gurr (Ph.D.) is Distinguished University Professor at the University of Maryland, College Park, and is founding director of the Minorities at Risk project. In 1993–1994 Professor Gurr was president of the International Studies Association and in 1996–1997 he held the Swedish government's Olof Palme Visiting Professorship at the University of Uppsala. From 1994 to 2000 he was senior consultant to the U.S. government's State Failure Task Force. He has written or edited twenty books and monographs including *Why Men Rebel* (1970), *Peoples versus States: Minorities at Risk in the New Century* (2000) and, most recently, *Peace and Conflict 2001: A Global Survey of Armed Conflicts, Self-Determination Movements, and Democracy* (2001), with Monty G. Marshall and Deepa Khosla.

Anne Pitsch (Ph.D., University of Maryland) is the Conflict Management Coordinator for the University of Maryland-National University of Rwanda Partnership funded by USAID. She is also conducting individual and joint research on gacaca, the community-based system of justice that will adjudicate 120,000 genocide suspects in Rwanda, the return of the Rwandan diaspora, and a comparative analysis of autonomy agreements applied in different conflict situations. Prior to joining the Partnership, she was the Minorities at Risk Project Coordinator for four years.

2.2 Ethnic Violence

Andreas Wimmer (Dr.) is professor for comparative and historical sociology at the University of California Los Angeles. His current research interests relate to migration and intercultural relations, ethnic conflicts and nationalism, and cultural theory. Book publications include *Ethnologie im Widerstreit* [Ethnology in Contention] (Ed.) (1991); *Die komplexe Gesellschaft* [The Complex Society] (1995); *Transformationen* [Transformations] (1995); *Integration—Transformation* [Integration—Transformation] (Ed.) (1996); *Nation and National Identity* (Ed.) (1999); *Nationalist Exclusion and Ethnic Conflicts* (2002).

Conrad Schetter (Dr. phil.) is Research Associate at the Center for Development Research at Bonn University. His publications focus on ethnicity, ethnic conflicts, war economy and political transformation in Afghanistan, and nomadism in Iran. *Afghanistan in Geschichte und Gegenwart* [Afghanistan Past and Present] (Ed.) (1999); *Afghanistan—A Country without State?* (Ed.) (2002).

2.3 The Socio-Anthropological Interpretation of Violence

Georg Elwert (Dr.) is Professor of Social Anthropology at the Institute of Ethnology at the Free University in Berlin. His research interests focus on anthropological studies, and ethnicity and conflict. Publications include *Nationalismus und Ethnizität* [Nationalism and Ethnicity] (1989); *Switching of We-Group Identities* (1997); *Markets of Violence* (1999).

2.4 Civil War

Peter Waldmann (Dr. jur.) is Professor of Sociology at Augsburg University. His research concentrates on dictatorships and state violence, resistance, guerrilla movements and terrorism, ethnic minorities and conflicts, and civil wars, their consequences and possibilities for regulation. Important publications are *Der Peronismus 1943–1955* [Peronism, 1943–1955] (1974); *Ethnischer Radikalismus, Ursachen und Folgen gewaltsamer Minderheitenkonflikte* [Ethnic Radicalism, Causes and Effects of Violent Minority Conflicts] (1989); *Terrorismus, Provokation der Macht* [Terrorism, Provoking Power] (1998); *Der anomische Staat. Über Recht, öffentliche Sicherheit und Alltag in Lateinamerika* [The Anomic State: On Law, Public Security, and Everyday Life in Latin America] (2002).

2.5 Terrorism

Fernando Reinares is Professor of Political Science, as well as Academic Director of the degree and research program in security sciences, at King Juan Carlos University in Madrid. Member of the Standing Committee for Social Sciences, European Science Foundation. His most recent books on political violence and security policy include *Terrorismo y Antiterrorismo* [Terrorism and Antiterrorism] (1998); *Sociedades en Guerra Civil. Conflictos Violentos de Europa y América Latina* [Societies in Civil War. Violent Conflicts of Europe and Latin America] (1999); *European Democracies against Terrorism. Governmental Policies and Intergovernmental Cooperation* (2000), and *Patriotas de la Muerte. Quiénes han militado en ETA y por qué* [Patriots of Death. Who Joined ETA and Why] (2001). He also serves as Contributing Editor of the international academic journal *Studies in Conflict and Terrorism*.

2.6 Violence from Religious Groups

Jon Pahl (Ph.D., The University of Chicago) is Associate Professor of American Religious History at The Lutheran Theological Seminary at Philadelphia. He is member of the Colloquium Violence and Religion and is completing a manuscript entitled *Violence and the Scared in America*. He is the author *of Paradox Lost: Free Will and Political Liberty in American Culture, 1630–1760* (1992); *Hopes and Dreams of All: The International Walther League and Lutheran Youth in American Culture, 1893–1993* (1993); *Youth Ministry in Modern America: 1930–Present* (2000).

2.7 Vigilantism

David Kowalewski (Ph.D., University of Kansas) is Professor of Comparative and International Politics at Alfred University. He has been a Fulbright Scholar in the Philippines and Kenya. His works on political violence have appeared in Journal of Conflict Resolution, Social Science Quarterly, Journal of Politics, and elsewhere. He is recently the author of *Global Establishment* (1997) and *Deep Power: The Political Ecology of Wilderness and Civilization* (2000).

2.8 Pogroms

Werner Bergmann (Dr. phil.) is a professor at the Center for Anti-Semitism Research at the Technical University in Berlin. His research focuses on the sociology and history of anti-Semitism and related fields such as xenophobia, right-wing extremism, and the theory of collective behavior, in particular social movements and collective violence. Recent publications are *Antisemitismus in öffentlichen Konflikten* [Anti-Semitism in Public Conflicts] (1997), (co-author with Rainer Erb); *Anti-Semitism in Germany. The Post-Nazi Epoch since 1945* (1997); *Geschichte des Antisemitismus* [The History of Anti-Semitism] (2002). In company with Christhard Hoffmann and Helmut Walser Smith he is the editor of *Exclusionary Violence. Anti-Semitic Riots in Modern German History, 1819–1938* (2002).

2.9 Violence and New Social Movements

Dieter Rucht (Dr. rer. pol.) is Professor of Sociology at the Social Science Research Center Berlin (WZB). His research focuses on political sociology, participation, social movements and social conflict, and protest. Publications include *Modernisierung und neue soziale Bewegungen* [Modernization and New Social Movements] (1994); *Social Movements in a Globalizing World* (co-editor with Donatella della Porta and Hanspeter Kriesi) (1999); *Jugendkulturen, Politik und Protest. Vom Widerstand zum Kommerz?* [Youth Cultures, Politics, and Protest: From Resistance to Commercialization?] (co-editor with Roland Roth, 2000); *Transnationaler politischer Protest im historischen Längsschnitt.* [Transnational Political Protest: A Historical Longitudinal Section] (2001).

2.10 Violence and the New Left

Donatella della Porta (Ph.D.) is full professor of Political Science and Director of the Department of Political Science and Sociology at the University of Florence. She has carried out research on social movements and political violence in Italy, France, Germany, Spain, and the United States, and directed a cross-national research project on the control of mass demonstrations in Europe. Among her publications are: *Policing Protest* (1998) (with Herbert Reiter); *La politica locale* [Local Politics] (1999); *Social Movements: An Introduction* (1999) (with Mario Diani); *Social Movement in a Globalizing World* (1999) (with Hanspeter Kriesi and Dieter Rucht); *Identità, riconoscimento e scambio* [Identity, Recognition and Exchange] (Ed.) (2000); *Introduzione alla scienza politica* [Introduction to Political Science] (2001); *Scienza politica* [Political Science] (2001) (with Maurizio Cotta and Leonardo Morlino); *I partiti politici* [Political Parties] (2001);.

2.11 Right-Wing Extremist Violence

Wilhelm Heitmeyer (see under Framework of the Handbook)

2.12 Large-Scale Violence as Contentious Politics

Charles Tilly, after holding teaching and research appointments at Delaware, Princeton, Harvard, MIT, Toronto, Michigan, and the New School for Social Research, he now teaches social sciences at Columbia University. Among his recent books are *Roads from Past to Future* (1997); *Work Under Capitalism* (1998) (with Chris Tilly), *Durable Inequality* (1998) and (with Doug McAdam and Sidney Tarrow) *Dynamics of Contention* (2001). He has recently completed *Stories, Identities, and Political Change* (2002) and *Collective Violence* (2003). He is currently writing *Contention and Democracy in Europe, 1650–2000*.

3. Violent Individuals: Perpetrators and Motives

3.1 *Processes of Learning and Socialization*

3.1.1 *The Social Psychology of Aggression and Violence*

James T. Tedeschi (Ph.D.) († 2001) was Professor for Social Psychology at the University of Albany, State University of New York. His work centered on power, influence and self-presentation. He published about 200 papers. Most relevant for the topic of the handbook are *Violence, Aggression, and Coercive Actions* (with Richard B. Felson) (1994) and *Social Psychology of Violence* (2000).

3.1.2 *Emotions and Aggressiveness*

Roy F. Baumeister (Ph.D., Princeton University) holds the E.B. Smith Professorship in the Liberal Arts at Case Western Reserve University. His research interests include self and identity, self-control, self-esteem, aggression and violence, sexuality, meaning, emotion, and human nature. He has nearly 250 scientific publications, including the books *Escaping the Self* (1991); *Losing Control: How and Why People Fail at Self-Regulations* (1994); *Evil: Inside Human Violence and Cruelty* (1997) and *The Social Dimension of Sex* (2001) as well as many articles in the scientific journals in psychology.

Brad J. Bushman (Ph.D., University of Missouri) is Associate Professor at Iowa State University. His research interests are causes and consequences of aggression, violent media, social influence, experimental personality and meta-analysis. Some of the most important publications are: *Threatened egotism, narcissism, self-esteem, and direct and displaced aggression: Does self-love or self-hate lead to violence?* (co-author) (1998); *Catharsis, aggression, and persuasive influence: Self-fulfilling or self-defeating prophecies?* (co-author) (1999); *Is it time to pull the plug on the hostile versus instrumental aggression dichotomy?* (co-author) (2001); *Media violence and the American public: Scientific facts versus media misinformation.* (co-author) (2001).

3.1.3 *Learning of Aggression in the Home and the Peer Group*

Ernest V. E. Hodges (Ph.D., Florida Atlantic University) is an Assistant Professor of Psychology at St. John's University. His recent publications have focused predominantly on aggression and victimization among children and adolescents. He has also published recent articles involving attachment relationships, parenting practices, children's friendships, and academic achievement. His current research interests focus on how aggression and victimization by peers may lead to weapon carrying in schools.

Noel A. Card (B.A./B.S., Michigan State University) is an advanced doctoral student in clinical psychology at St. John's University. His research interests include aggression and victimization, attachment relationships, and enemy relationships among children and adolescents. His recent presentations have focused on the interpersonal dynamics of aggression among school children and relationships between victimization and the characteristics of children's enemies.

Jenny Isaacs (B.A., State University of New York, New Paltz) is an advanced doctoral student in clinical child psychology at St. John's University. Her research interests include aggression, victimization, and weapon carrying in schools. Her recent presentation have focused on the social-cognitions involved in children's decisions to carry weapons in school, as well as the social and personal factors that lead to these cognitions and the enactment of weapon carrying behavior.

3.1.4 Violence and the Media

Helmut Lukesch (Dr.) is Professor of Psychology at Regensburg University. His research interests are grouped primarily around the media and its influence. Important publications include *Wenn Gewalt zur Unterhaltung wird...* [When Violence Becomes Entertainment ...] (1994); *Medien und ihre Wirkungen* [Media and Their Influence] (1997); *Medienkonsum und Medienwirkungen* [Media Consumption and Media Influence] (2001).

3.1.5 Patterns and Explanations of Direct Physical and Indirect Non-Physical Aggression in Childhood

Holly Foster (Ph.D., University of Toronto) is a Postdoctoral Fellow (National Consortium on Violence Research, Carnegie Mellon University, Pittsburgh). Her research interest include social contexts of youth violence. Her dissertation is entitled *Neighbourhood and Family Effects on Childhood Gendered Aggression* (2001) Publications (with John Hagan) are: *Making Criminal and Corporate American Less Violent: Public Norms and Structural Reforms* (2000) and *Youth Violence and the End of Adolescence* (American Sociological Review, 2001).

John Hagan (see under Framework of the Handbook)

3.2 Evolutionary and Social Biological Approaches

3.2.1 Evolutionary Psychology of Lethal Interpersonal Violence

Martin Daly (Ph.D., University of Toronto) is Professor of Psychology and Biology at McMaster University in Canada. His main areas of research are the behavioral ecology of desert rodents, human social cognition, and interpersonal violence. A former J.S. Guggenheim Fellow and past president of the *Human Behavior & Evolution Society*, he is the co-author (with Margo Wilson) of *Sex, Evolution & Behavior* (2nd ed., 1983); *Homicide* (1988) and *The Truth about Cinderella* (1998), and is presently co-editor-in-chief of the journals *Behaviour* and *Evolution & Human Behaviour*.

Margo Wilson (Ph.D., University of London) is Professor of Psychology at McMaster University in Canada. Her current research focuses on risk-taking and risk evaluation, marital conflict, and lethal and nonlethal violence. She is the co-author (with Martin Daly) of *Sex, Evolution & Behavior* (2nd ed., 1983); *Homicide* (1988) and *The Truth about Cinderella* (1998), and is co-editor-in-chief of the journal *Evolution & Human Behaviour*.

3.2.2 The Nature–Nurture Problem in Violence

Laura Baker (Ph.D., University of Colorado) is Associate Professor of Psychology at the University of Southern California. Of general interest are the development, refinement, and application of quantitative genetic models in the study of individual intellectual domains. Of particular interest are multivariate behavioral genetic models of juvenile delinquency, human aggression, and criminal behavior. She published *Agression: Definition and Measurement* (1999); *Biological Theories of Violence* (1999); *Psychological Theories of Human Aggression* (1999).

3.3 Violent Individuals

3.3.1 Sociological Approaches to Individual Violence and their Empirical Evaluation

Günter Albrecht (Dr. phil.) is a professor at the Faculty of Sociology at Bielefeld University and a member of the committee of the Institute for Interdisciplinary Research on Conflict and Violence. His work focuses on sociology of deviant behavior, especially criminology and psychiatric sociology, sociology of poverty, sociology of migration, and medical sociology. Publications include *Diversion and Informal Social Control* (co-editor) (1995); *Handbuch Soziale Probleme* [Handbook of Social Problems] (co-editor) (1999); *Gewaltkriminalität zwischen Mythos und Realität* [Violent Criminality between Myth and Reality] (co-editor, 2001).

3.3.2 Youth Violence and Guns

Alfred Blumstein is the Erik Jonsson University Professor of Urban Systems and Operations Research. He also directs the National Consortium on Violence Research (NCOVR). His research over the past twenty years has covered many aspects of criminal-justice phenomena and policy, including crime measurement, criminal careers, sentencing, deterrence and incapacitation, prison populations, demographic trends, juvenile violence, and drug-enforcement policy. The most important publications are: *Report of the National Academy of Sciences Panel on Research on Criminal Careers*; *Deterrence and Incapacitation: Estimating the Effects of Criminal Sanctions on Crime Rates* (co-author) (1978); *Criminal Careers and "Career Criminals"* (co-author) (1986); *Youth Violence, Guns, and the Illicit-Drug Industry* (1995); *The Crime Drop in America* (with Joel Wallmann) (2000).

3.3.3 Organized Crime and Violence

Dick Hobbs is Professor of Sociology at the University of Durham UK. He has published widely on policing, detective work, ethnography, working class entrepreneurship, professional and organized crime and various aspects of deviant cultures. The most important publications are: *Doing the Business* (Oxford, 1989); *Bad Business* (Oxford, 1995) and (with Simon Winlow, Stuart Lister and Philip Hadfield) *Night Moves* (Oxford 2002), a study of violence and the night-time economy. He is currently working with Geoffrey Pearson on a study of drug markets.

3.3.4 Understanding Cross-National Variation in Criminal Violence

Steven F. Messner (Ph.D., Princeton University) is Professor of Sociology and Chair at the University at Albany, State University of New York. His research has focused on the relationship between social organization and crime, with a particular emphasis on criminal homicide. He has also studied the spatial patterning of violent crime, crime and delinquency in China, and the situational dynamics of violence. In addition to his extensive publications in professional journals, he is co-author of *Crime and the American Dream* (1997); *Perspectives on Crime and Deviance* (1999); *Criminology: An Introduction Using Explorit* (2000, 4th ed.) and co-editor of *Theoretical Integration in the Study of Deviance and Crime* (1989) and *Crime and Social Control in a Changing China* (2001).

4. Victims of Violence: Individuals and Groups

4.1 Violence against Children

James Garbarino (Ph.D., Cornell University) is the Elizabeth Lee Vincent Professor of Human Development at Cornell University and co-director of the Family Life Development Center. He formerly served as president of the Erikson Institute for Advanced Study in Child Development in Chicago, IL. He has authored seventeen books including *What Children Can Tell Us* (1989); *Children in Danger: Coping with the Consequences of Community Violence* (1992); *How We Can Save Them, Raising Children in a Socially Toxic Environment* (1995) and *Lost Boys: Why Our Sons Turn Violent* (1999).

Catherine P. Bradshaw (M.Ed., University of Georgia) is a doctoral Student in the Department of Human Development at Cornell University and a Research Assistant for the Family Life Development Center. She has several years of clinical experience working with high-risk children and families referred for services by the juvenile court. Her current research focuses on the development of aggressive and violent behavior in children and adolescents. She is the co-author of *Multi-Observer Assessment of Problem Behavior in Adjudicated Youths: Patterns of Discrepancies* (2001) (with Brian Glaser, Georgia Calhoun, Jeff Bates and Robert Socherman); *Mitigating the Effects of Gun Violence on Children and Youth* (2002) (with James Garbarino and J. Vorrasi) and *Psychological Maltreatment* (2002) (with Joseph Vorrasi and Ellen deLara).

4.2 Violence in Intimate Relationships

Rebecca Emerson Dobash is Professor of Social Research and **Russell P. Dobash** is Professor of Criminology in the Department of Applied Social Science at the University of Manchester. They have co-authored several books, numerous government reports, and scores of scientific articles in journals and anthologies. Their books include *Violence against*

Wives (1979); *The Imprisonment of Women* (1986); *Woman Viewing Violence* (1992); *Gender and Crime* (1995); *Rethinking Violence against Women* (1998) and *Changing Violence Men* (2000).

4.3 Suicide

David Lester has Ph.D. degrees from Brandeis University (United States) in psychology and from Cambridge University (United Kingdom) in social and political science. He is a former President of the International Association for Suicide Prevention and Professor of Psychology at the Richard Stockton College of New Jersey, Pomona, NJ. His research interests are concentrated on suicide. Important publications are: *Why people kill themselves* (2000); *By their own hand: Suicides of the rich and famous* (2000); *Suicide prevention: Resources for the millennium* (ed.) (2001).

4.4 Violence against the Socially Expendable

Ezzat A. Fattah (Ph.D.) is Professor (emeritus) of Criminology at Simon Fraser University in Vancouver. His work centers on victimology. He is the author/co-author, editor/co-editor of fifteen books and over a hundred and twenty book chapters and scholarly papers published in learned journals in ten languages. Among his recent publications are: *Understanding Criminal Victimization* (1991); *The Interchangeable Roles of Victim and Victimizer* (1994); *Criminology: Past, Present and Future (1997);Toward a Victim Policy Aimed at Healing not Suffering* (1997); *Victimology: Past, Present and Future* (2000).

4.5 Violence against Ethnic and Religious Minorities

Tore Bjørgo (Dr.) is a senior research fellow and social anthropologist at the Norwegian Institute of International Affairs in Oslo. His main fields of research are racist and right-wing violence, delinquent youth gangs, and political extremism and terrorism. His most recent books are *Racist and Right-Wing Violence in Scandinavia: Patterns, Perpetrators, and Response* (1997) and *Violence, Racism and Youth Gangs: Prevention and Intervention* (1999). He has also (co)authored books on political communications, and terrorism (in Norwegian), and has (co)edited the volumes *Racist Violence in Europe* (1993); *Terror from the Extreme Right (1995)* and *Nation and Race: The Developing Euro-American Racist Subculture* (1998).

4.6 Hate Crimes Directed at Gay, Lesbian, Bisexual and Transgendered Victims

Jack McDevitt is the Associate Dean for Graduate Studies and Research, Director of the Center for Criminal Justice Policy Research and an Assistant Professor in Northeastern University's College of Criminal Justice. His past research in the area of criminal justice has involved such issues as arbitrariness in the administration of the death penalty, and the role of mandatory sentence in gun control policy. He authored the first study of hate-motivated violence which became the basis of *Hate Crimes: The Rising Tide of Bigotry and Bloodshed* (1993) co-authored with Jack Levin. He also authored *The 1990 Hate Crime Resource Book for the FBI* and published *Victimology: A Study of Crimes Victims and Their Roles* (2002).

Jennifer Williamson serves as Deputy Director of Strategic Planning and Resource Development for Boston Police Commissioner Paul F. Evans. In this position she is responsible for fostering innovation in policing through strategic planning, resource development, program and partnership creation, intergovernmental relations, policy development, and documentation of "best practices."

4.7 Trauma and Violence in Children and Adolescents: A Developmental Perspective

Bessel A. van der Kolk (M.D., University of Chicago) is Professor of Psychiatry at Boston University, School of Medicine. His works centers on trauma and extreme stress. He published more then one hundred articles. His books includes: *PTSD: Psychological and Biological Sequelae* (Ed.) (1984); *Psychological Trauma* (1987); *Traumatic Stress: the effect of overwhelming experience on mind, body and society* (with Alexander McFarlane and Lars Weisaeth, Ed.) (1996).

Annette Streeck-Fischer (Dr. med.) a senior physician in the Department of Clinical Psychotherapy for Children and Young People at Tiefenbrunn Teaching Hospital, Göttingen. Since 1980 lecturer at the medical faculty of Göttingen University, co-editor of the journal "Praxis der Kinderpsychologie, Kinderpsychiatrie" [Practical Child Psychology, Child Psychiatry]. Publications on adolescence, right-wing extremism, violence, trauma, maltreatment, abuse.

5. Social Opportunity Structures: Institutions and Social Spaces

5.1 Violence in Social Institutions

5.1.1 Violence in the Family

Richard J. Gelles holds the Jeanne and Raymond Welsh Chair of Child Welfare and Family Violence in the School of Social Work at the University of Pennsylvania. He is the Director of the Center for the Study of Youth Policy and Co-Director of the Center for Children's Policy, Practice, and Research. His book *The Violent Home* was the first systematic empirical investigation of family violence and continues to be highly influential. He is the author or co-author of twenty-three books and more than one hundred articles and chapters on family violence. His latest books are: *The Book of David: How Preserving Families Can Cost Children's Lives* (1996) and *Intimate Violence in Families*, 3rd Edition (1997).

5.1.2 Violence in School

Gabriele Klewin holds a degree in education and was Research Associate in the "Gender Socialization and Violence in Schools" project at Bielefeld University from 1998 to 2000. Her research focuses on women's and gender studies, and violence in schools.

Klaus-Jürgen Tillmann (Dr. paed.) is Professor of School Education Theory at Bielefeld University and Academic Director of the Laborschule. His work concentrates on empirical school and socialization research, school and teaching theory, and reform developments in the secondary school system. His most important publications include *Sozialpädagogik in der Schule* [Social Paedagogics in Schools] (1976); *Sozialisationstheorien—eine Einführung* [Socialization Theories—An Introduction] (12th ed., 2002); *Was ist eine gute Schule?* [What is a Good School?] (1989); *Schülergewalt als Schulproblem* [Student Violence as a School Problem] (co-author with Günter Holtappels et al.) (1999).

Gail Weingart holds a degree in psychology and is a teacher. She studied in Berlin, Harvard, and Bielefeld and has many years of teaching experience in schools in the United States and Germany. Currently she is Research Associate at the Research Institute Laborschule at Bielefeld University, and also carries out school evaluation.

5.1.3 Work-Related Violence

Vittorio Di Martino is an international consultant specialized in health and safety at work, enterprise development and organizational well-being. He has been responsible for the programs on stress and violence at work at the European Foundation for the Improvement of Working and Living Conditions, Dublin, from 1980 to 1988 and at the International Labour Organisation, Geneva, from 1988 to 2001. He is Visiting Fellow in Employment Policies at the University of Bath and Senior Research Fellow at UMIST in Manchester, UK. His recent publications include *Work Organisation and Ergonomics,* ILO, Geneva, 1998; *Violence at Work,* ILO, Geneva, 1st ed., 1998, 2nd ed. 2000; *The High Road to Teleworking,* ILO, Geneva, 2001; *SOLVE Package—Managing Emerging Health Problems at Work—Stress, Violence, Tobacco, Alcohol, Drugs, HIV/AIDS*—ILO, 2002; *National Guidelines for the Prevention of Stress and Violence at the Workplace,* Malaysian Government, 2002.

5.1.4 Violence and Sport

Eric Dunning (Ph.D.) is currently Emeritus Professor of Sociology at the University of Leicester where he remains an Associate Lecturer. His sociological interests are in sociological theory, violence, race, class and gender, and "civilizing" and "decivilizing" processes. Some of his publications are: *Sport and Leisure in the Civilizing Process* (with Norbert Elias) (1986); *Roots of Football Hooliganism* (with John Williams and Patrick Murphy) (1988); *Sport Matters: Sociological Studies of Sport, Violence and Civilization* (1999).

5.2 Violence in the Public Space

5.2.1 Violence on the Roads

Ralf Kölbel (Dr. iur.) is Research Associate at the Friedrich Schiller University in Jena. His work focuses on legal sociology and traffic criminology, criminal law and criminal procedure. His publications include *Rücksichtslosigkeit und Gewalt im Straßenverkehr* [Recklessness and Violence on the Roads] (1997) and several articles in the scientific journals in law and legal sociology.

5.2.2 Juvenile and Urban Violence

François Dubet is Professor of Sociology at Bordeaux University and Director of Studies at the Ecole des Hautes Etudes en Sciences Sociales (EHESS/CNRS) in Paris. His research focuses on youth violence, social movements, and sociological theory. His publications include *A l'école* [At School] (with Danilo Martuccelli) (1996); *Dans quelle société vivons-nous?* [What Society Are We Living In?] (with Danilo Martuccelli) (1998); *Pourquoi changer l'école?* [Why Change School?] (1999); *L'hypocrisie scolaire. Pour un collège enfin démocratique* (with Marie Duru-Bellat) [Scholarly Hypocrisy: For a Secondary School that Is at Last Democratic] (2000); *Les inégalités multipliées* [Multiple Inequalities] (2001).

6. Violence Discourses: Ideologies and Justifications

6.1 Discourses and Ideologies

6.1.1 Political Cultural Studies and Violence

Thomas Meyer (Dr. phil.) is Professor of Politics at Dortmund University, Academic Director of the Friedrich Ebert Foundation's Academy of Political Education, and Deputy Chairman of the German Social Democratic Party's Basic Values Commission. His work focuses on political aesthetics, political communication, culture and politics, and socialism and social democracy. His publications include *Was bleibt vom Sozialismus?* [What is Left of Socialism?] (1991); *Alltagsästhetik und politische Kultur* [Everyday Aesthetics and Political Culture] (co-author with Berthold Flaig and Jörg Ueltzhöffer) (1993); *Identitätswahn. Die Politisierung des kulturellen Unterschieds* [Identity Obsession: The Politicization of Cultural Differences] (1997); *Die Inszenierung des Politischen* [The Staging of the Political] (2000); *Soziale Demokratie und Globalisierung* [Social Democracy and Globalization] (2001) and *Media Democracy* (2002).

6.1.2 The Role of Elites in Legitimizing Violence

Herfried Münkler (Dr. phil.) is Professor of Politics at the Department of Political Theory at the Humboldt University in Berlin. Since December 1992 he has been a member of the Berlin-Brandenburg Academy of Sciences. His publications include *Machiavelli. Die Begründung des politischen Denkens der Neuzeit aus der Krise der Republik Florenz* [Machiavelli: The Origins of Modern Political Thought in the Crisis of the Florence Republic] (1982); *Pipers Handbuch der politischen Ideen* [Piper's Handbook of Political Ideas] (co-edited with Iring Fetscher, 5 vols) (1985–1993); *Gewalt und Ordnung. Das Bild des Krieges im politischen Denken* [Violence and Order: The Image of War in Political Thought] (1992); *Hobbes* [Hobbes] (1992).

Marcus Llanque (Dr. rer. soc.) is Research Associate at the Humboldt University in Berlin, Institute for Social Sciences. His research focuses on the history of political ideas, republicanism, the Weimar Republic, and theory of democracy. His publications include *Demokratisches Denken im Krieg. Die deutsche Debatte im Ersten Weltkrieg* [Democratic Thought During War: The German Debate During World War One] (2000); *Massendemokratie zwischen Kaiserreich und westlicher Demokratie* [Mass Democracy Between the Kaiser's Reich and Western Democracy] (2000); *Verfassungsgebung als Ort politischer Kreativität* [Constitution-Writing as an Act of Political Creativity] (2001).

6.1.3 Violence in Contemporary Analytic Philosophy

Keith Burgess-Jackson (J.D, Ph.D., University of Arizona) is Associate Professor of Philosophy at The University of Texas at Arlington. He is the author of *Rape: A Philosophical Investigation* (1996); co-author (with Irving M. Copi) of *Informal Logic* (1996); editor of (and a multiple contributor to) *A Most Detestable Crime: New Philosophical Essays on Rape* (1999).

6.1.4 Sacrifice and Holy War: A Study of Religion and Violence

Volkhard Krech (Dr. rer. soc.) is fellow for Sociology at the Protestant Institute for Interdisciplinary Research in Heidelberg. His research focuses on empirical and theoretical sociology of religion, the history of the study of religion, and cultural sociology. His most important publications include *Georg Simmels Religionstheorie* [Georg Simmel's Theory of Religion] (1998); *Religionssoziologie* [Sociology of Religion] (1999); *Kunst und Religion im 20. Jahrhundert* [Art and Religion in the Twentieth Century] (co-edited with Richard Faber) (2001); *Wissenschaft und Religion. Studien zur Geschichte der Religionsforschung in Deutschland 1871 bis 1933* [Science and Religion: Studies on the History of the Study of Religion in Germany from 1871 to 1933] (2002).

6.1.5 Violence and the Glorification of Violence in Twentieth-Century Literature

Jürgen Nieraad (Dr. phil.) is Lecturer for German literature in the Department of German Language and Literature at the Hebrew University in Jerusalem. He has published on modern German literature, the Jewish-German Holocaust discourse, literary theory, and aesthetics, for example *Standpunktbewusstsein und Weltzusammenhang* [Standpoint Awareness and World Context] (1970); *Die Spur der Gewalt. Zur Geschichte des Schrecklichen in der Literatur und ihrer Theorie* [Trail of Violence: On the History of the Horrific in Literature and Literary Theory] (1994).

6.2 Justification Strategies

6.2.1 The State Monopoly of Force

Dieter Grimm (Dr. iur.) was a justice at the Federal Constitutional Court, and is Professor of Public Law at the Humboldt University in Berlin and Rector of the Institute for Advanced Study in Berlin. His work focuses on constitutional law, constitutional history, constitutional adjudication, and comparative politics. His most important publications include *Recht und Staat der bürgerlichen Gesellschaft* [Law and State in Bourgeois Society] (1987); *Staatsaufgaben* [State Tasks] (Ed.) (1994); *Die Verfassung und die Politik. Einsprüche in Störfällen* [Constitution and Politics: Objections in Problem Cases] (2001); *Die Zukunft der Verfassung* [The Future of the Constitution] (3rd ed. 2002).

6.2.2 The Monopoly of Legitimate Violence and Criminal Policy

Albrecht Funk (Dr. habil) is co-founder of the Institute for Civil Rights and Public Security at the Free University in Berlin and Research Associate at the EU Center at the University of Pittsburgh. His research focuses on the creation and transformation of the police and criminal justice systems in Europe and the United States, and the Europeanization of judicial and domestic policy. His most important publications are *Polizei und Rechtsstaat* [Police and the Constitutional State] (1985); *Die Polizei der Bundesrepublik* [Police in the Federal Republic of Germany] (co-author) (1985); *Polices d'Europe* [European Police Systems] (co-author) (1992).

6.2.3 Freedom to Demonstrate and the Use of Force: Criminal Law as a Threat to Basic Political Rights

Otto Backes (Dr. jur.) has been Professor of Criminal Law, Law of Criminal Procedure, and Legal Sociology at Bielefeld University since 1983. Co-founder of the Institute for Interdisciplinary Research on Conflict and Violence. His publications include *Strafrechtswissenschaft als Sozialwissenschaft* [Criminal Law Studies as Social Science] (1976); the volumes in the series *Verdeckte Gewalt* [Hidden Violence] (co-editor) (1990); *Gewaltkriminalität zwischen Mythos und Realität* [Violent Crime Between Myth and Reality] (2001); and he is co-author of several proposed alternatives to the Criminal Code, including *Politisches Strafrecht* [Political Criminal Law] (1968); *Umweltstrafrecht* [Environmental Criminal Law] (1971).

Peter Reichenbach, Assistant Judge, Research Associate in the Department of Criminal Law and Law of Criminal Procedure at Bielefeld University. Publications include *Ist die medizinisch-embryopathische Indikation bei dem Schwangerschaftsabbruch nach § 218a II StGB verfassungswidrig?* [Is the Medical Embryopathic Indication for Abortions Following Paragraph 218a II of the Criminal Code Unconstitutional?] (2000); *Der Anspruch behinderter Schülerinnen und Schüler auf Unterricht in der Regelschule* [The Rights of Disabled Students to Teaching in Normal Schools] (2001); *Irrungen, Wirrungen: Einige Anmerkungen zur Interpretation des § 177 Abs. 1 Nr. 3 StGB aus verfassungsrechtlicher Perspektive* [Aberrations and Confusion: Some Comments on Paragraph 177, Art. 1, Item 3 of the Criminal Code from the Constitutional Perspective] (2002).

6.2.4 The Right to Resist

Heiner Bielefeldt (Dr. phil.) is a lecturer at Bielefeld University, member of the Institute for Interdisciplinary Research on Conflict and Violence, and *Privatdozent* for Philosophy at Bremen University. Among other things, his work focuses on questions relating to the justification of human rights, legal rights of religious minorities (e.g., Muslim groups in Germany), social contract theories, and the philosophy of the Enlightenment. He has written and edited or co-edited ten books, including *Neuzeitliches Freiheitsrecht und politische Gerechtigkeit* [The Liberty and Political Justice] (1994); *Philosophie der Menschenrechte* [The Philosophy of Human Rights] (1998); *Kants Symbolik* [Symbolic Representation in Kant's Practical Philosophy] (German 2001, English 2002).

6.2.5 Individual Violence Justification Strategies

Siegfried Lamnek (Dr.) is Professor of Sociology at Eichstätt University. His work focuses on methodology and methods of social sciences, sociology of deviant behavior and social problems, sociology as profession, and violence in schools. His publications include *Der Sozialstaat zwischen "Markt" und "Hedonismus"?* [Welfare State between "Market" and "Hedonism"] (co-editor) (1999); *Zeit und kommunikative Rechtskultur in Europa. Verfassung, Medien, Biotechnologie und Datenschutz* [Time and Communicative Legal Culture in Europe: Constitution, Media, Biotechnology and Data Protection] (co-editor) (2000); *Theorien abweichenden Verhaltens, Leistungsmissbrauch, Steuerhinterziehung und ihre (Hinter-)Gründe* [Theories of Deviant Behavior, Abuse of Benefits, and Tax Evasion, and Their (Back)Grounds] (co-author) (2000).

7. Processes and Dynamics: Escalation and De-Escalation

7.1 Fear of Violent Crime

Klaus Boers (Dr. jur.) is Professor of Criminology and Juvenile Penal Law, Director of the Institute of Penal Sciences at the Westfälische Wilhelms-University in Münster and co-editor of the Neue Kriminalpolitik. His research focuses on attitudes to crime, victim and self-reported delinquency surveys, social transition and modernization processes, crime development and social control in the life course, and economic crime. His most important publications include *Kriminalitätsfurcht* [Fear of Crime] (1991); *Sozialer Umbruch und Kriminalität in Deutschland* [Social Transition and Crime in Germany] (Co-editor and author) (1997); *Wirtschaftskriminologie* [Economic Criminology] (2001); *Kriminalität und Kausalität* [Crime and Causality] (2002).

7.2 Public Opinion and Violence

Hans Mathias Kepplinger (Dr. phil.) is Professor of Communications at the Johannes Gutenberg-Universität Mainz, Germany. He served as director of the Institute for Journalism, Dean of the Faculty of Social Sciences. He is corresponding editor of the *European Journal of Communication*, and member of the advisory board of *Political Communication Research* and *Journal of Communication*. His recent books are *Die Demontage der Politik in der Informationsgesellschaft [The Dismantling of Politics in Information Society]* (2nd edition, 2000) and Die Kunst der Skandalierung und die Illusion der Wahrheit [The Art of Creating a Scandal and the Illusion of Truth, 2001].

7.3 Groups, Gangs and Violence

Wolfgang Kühnel (Dr. phil.) is Professor of Criminology at the University of Applied Sciences for Administration and Legal Affairs Berlin. His work focuses on juvenile crime, sociology of migration, group sociology, and research on the extreme right and violence. His latest book (co-authored with Rainer Strobl) is *Dazugehörig und ausgegrenzt. Analysen zu Integrationschancen junger Aussiedler* [Belonging and Excluded: Analyses on Integration Chances of Young Ethnic German Immigrants] (2000) and he is co-editor (with Günter Albrecht and Otto Backes) of *Gewaltkriminalität zwischen Mythos und Realität* [Violent Crime between Myth and Reality] (2001).

7.4 Escalation and De-Escalation of Social Conflicts: The Road to Violence

Roland Eckert (Dr. phil.) is Professor of Sociology at Trier University. His research focuses on youth and politics, new media, violence, and conflict and conflict resolution. His publications include *Wiederkehr des "Volksgeistes"? Ethnizität, Konflikt und politische Bewältigung.* [The Return of the "National Spirit"? Ethnicity, Conflict and Political Management] (Ed.) (1998); *Neue Quellen des Rechtsextremismus* [New Sources of Right-Wing Extremism] (1999 *"Ich will halt anders sein wie die anderen"—Abgrenzung, Gewalt und Kreativität bei Gruppen Jugendlicher* ["I Just Want to be Different from the Others": Exclusion, Violence, and Creativity in Groups of Young People] (co-author with Christa Reis/Thomas Wetzstein) (2000).

Helmut Willems (Dr. phil.) is Privatdozent for Sociology at the University of Trier, a committee member of the Social Science Research and Training Working Group at Trier University and a freelance project developer and consultant. His research focuses on youth sociology, violence and criminality, political sociology, democracy theory, protest and social movements, xenophobia and research into right-wing extremism, and evaluation research. His books include *Konfliktintervention: Perspektivenübernahmen in gesellschaftlichen Auseinandersetzungen* [Conflict Intervention: Adopting Perspectives in Social Conflicts] (1992); *Fremdenfeindliche Gewalt: Einstellungen, Täter, Konflikteskalationen* [Xenophobic Violence: Attitudes, Perpetrators, Conflict Escalations] (1993); *Jugendunruhen und Protestbewegungen: Eine Studie zur Dynamik innergesellschaftlicher Konflikte in vier europäischen Ländern* [Youth Unrest and Protest Movements: A Study of the Dynamics of Conflicts within Society in Four European Countries] (1997).

III. THEORETICAL AND METHODOLOGICAL ISSUES IN RESEARCH ON VIOLENCE

1. Potentials and Limits of Qualitative Methods for Research on Violence

Andreas Böttger (Dr. phil.) is member of the board and project leader at the arpos Institute e.V. in Hannover and Associate Professor in the Department of Education at Hannover University. His work focuses on youth sociology, criminology, socialization theory, research into biography, violence and right-wing extremism, euthanasia and care for the dying, and methods of empirical research. His publications include *Die Biographie des Beschuldigten im Schwurgerichtsverfahren* [The Biography of the Accused in Jury Trials] (1992); *Gewalt und Biographie* [Violence and Biography] (1998); *"Früher war ich nicht so..." Biographien gewalttätiger Jugendlicher in China* ["I Used to Be Different..." Biographies of Violent Adolescents in China] (co-author with Jiazhen Liang und Mirja Silkenbeumer) (2001).

Rainer Strobl (Dr. phil.) is Research Associate at the Institute for Interdisciplinary Research on Conflict and Violence at Bielefeld University. He is also a member of the managing board of the arpos Institute e.V. in Hanover. His work focuses on migration sociology, victimology, research into right-wing extremism and methods of empirical research. He is the author of *Soziale Folgen der Opfererfahrungen türkischer Minderheiten* [Social Consequences of the Victimization of Ethnic Minorities] (1998); *Dazugehörig und ausgegrenzt:*

Analysen zu Integrationschancen junger Aussiedler [Belonging and Excluded: Analyses on Young Ethnic German Immigrants' Chances of Integration] (co-authored by Wolfgang Kühnel) (2000); *Wahre Geschichten? Zur Theorie und Praxis qualitativer Interviews* [True Stories? On Theory and Practice of Qualitative Interviews] (co-edited by Andreas Böttger) (1996).

2. Strategies and Problems in Quantitative Research on Aggression and Violence

Rainer Dollase (Dr. phil.) is Professor of Psychology at Bielefeld University and Deputy Director of the Institute for Interdisciplinary Research on Conflict and Violence. His research focuses on studies on intercultural integration in school classes, change-over-time studies, risk constellations in everyday police work, and empirical studies on xenophobia and violence in schools. His publications include *Soziometrische Techniken* [Sociometric Techniques] (1976); *Entwicklung und Erziehung* [Development and Education] (1985); *Demoskopie im Konzertsaal* [Demoscopics in the Concert Hall] (1986 with Michael Rüsenberg, Hans J. Stollenwerk); *Politische Psychologie der Fremdenfeindlichkeit* [The Political Psychology of Xenophobia] (co-edited with Thomas Kliche, Helmut Moser) (1999); *Temporale Muster* [Temporal Patterns] (co-edited with Kurt Hammerich, Walter Tokarski) (2000).

Matthias Ulbrich-Herrmann (Dr. phil.) is a sociologist and a member of the Scientific Services at the University of Applied Sciences of Public Administration of North Rhine-Westphalia. He is also a member of the Institute for Interdisciplinary Research on Conflict and Violence at Bielefeld University. His research relates to youth violence, social inequality, interethnic conflict, and research methods in social science. His publications include *Lebensstile Jugendlicher und Gewalt* [Youth Lifestyles and Violence] (1998). He is also co-author of *Gewalt: Schattenseiten der Individualisierung bei Jugendlichen aus unterschiedlichen Milieus* [Violence: Drawbacks of Individualization in Young People from Different Milieus] (1995) and co-editor of *Zukunftsperspektiven Jugendlicher* [Future Perspectives for Young People] (2001).